and educational

Fün ^Places to go With Kids ^and adults

in Southern California

"My own book of Susan's <u>Fun Places to go With Kids</u> is only kept together by tape. My friends and relatives are constantly asking to borrow what I think is the best tour book in Southern California. Not only does it provide a complete guide to all that Southern California has to offer, but also provides her personal views, which are invaluable when planning time with the family."
Donna Baker

Producer
Parenting Rollercoaster and Cul-de-Sac Chronicles

"I have to tell you. I've raved and raved about my new book to everyone who would listen. I am a 'bargain hunting' (OK, cheap) Mom of 3, (one income, private school). I pride myself on finding "fun places" (<cough> that is cheap fun and educational places, LOL!), but was AMAZED by your book. I have lived in So. Cal for 30 years and never heard of half the places mentioned in your book! . . . My book will also be passed on to Grandma who thinks it sounds perfect for her senior club!"
Corby Wagner

Mom of three kids

"It's 10:30am and I've already had five telephone calls from leaders thanking me for inviting you to the meeting last night, praising your fun-filled presentation, pleasant personality, great ideas, . . . Believe me, Susan, I have never looked so good. It's just not that easy to impress *or* entertain the "been there, done that" woman in Irvine. . . . You may be sure that you have substantially improved the quality of Girl Scout field trips in Irvine so I feel confident that I can offer you the appreciation of the 1600 girls affected."
Mary Pearlman

Membership Development Director
Girl Scouts, Orange County

"First of all, I absolutely love your book. Your recommendations have all been wonderfully accurate and it's saved me SO much hassle! . . . Thank you for contributing to the sanity of numerous CA moms!!"
Angie Smith

Mother of twins

"Over 20 copies of <u>Fun and Educational Places to go With Kids</u> are continually checked out in the Orange County Public Library System; we can't keep them on the shelves! Children's librarians feel confident referring parents to this title. It's perfect for planning local inexpensive family outings."
Elke Faraci

Senior Administrative Librarian
Orange County Public Library System

"Susan Peterson's book <u>Fun and Educational Places to go with Kids</u> has been a great addition to our children's bookstore. Its extensive collection of family outings makes it a great resource for our customers. It is well organized, making it easy to find wonderful local outings to fit everyone's taste and budget. It has been a big seller, and we recommend it highly."
Ane & David Miller

Through a Child's Eyes (bookstore)
Downey

Fün ^and educational^ Places to go With Kids ^and adults^

in Southern California

A comprehensive guide to Los Angeles, Orange, Riverside, San Bernardino, San Diego, and Ventura counties, plus Big Bear and Palm Springs

By Susan Peterson

Fun Places Publishing, California
www.funplaces.com

Published by Fun Places Publishing
P.O. Box 376
Lakewood, California 90714-0376
(562) 867-5223
susan@funplaces.com
www.funplaces.com

ISBN 0-9646737-4-6

Printed in the United States of America

Fifth Edition - April, 2001
Fourth Edition - October, 1998
Third Edition - May, 1997
Second Edition - May, 1996
First Edition - May, 1995

ACKNOWLEDGMENTS

A book is _never_ put together alone! I especially want to thank:

My husband, Lance, who is also my best friend and partner. Your computer skills, commitment, love, and support have turned my ideas into a book and have constantly encouraged my heart. Thank you, honey - you are God's greatest gift to me;

My three boys (who are the only kids I know that sometimes ask, "Can we please stay home?") - Thank you for being so much fun to travel with!: Kellan (age 13), whose brilliant mind conceived the title - you are a delightful and trustworthy young man, and a genuine pleasure to talk with. Bryce (age 11), whose artistic ability is displayed on the cover - you make me laugh when I try so hard to be serious! I love your servant's heart and thought-provoking questions. Terrell (age 9), who is the last jewel in my crown - your hugs are a great source of encouragement. Your sensitivity and compassion to others is an asset to be treasured;

My parents, sisters, in-laws, and best friend, Renee, who listened to my ~~whining~~, I mean sharing, and blessed me with consistent support, encouragement and love;

My treasured friend, Jewelene Pate, who, along with daughter Sarah, were our travel buddies, even though we weren't always sure where we were going! Thank you for being so easy going, for listening to me, and for your steadfast and faithful friendship;

My wonderful editors, without whom this book would be rife with ~~eros! erors!~~ oops, errors! How humbling it is to pour your heart and time into writing a book, hand it to someone else, and get it back with lots of red marks! (Reminds me of school.) Some of my favorite comments include, "I have no idea what you mean" and "Did you make this word up?" Thank you all for taking time out of your busy schedules to read, edit, and redirect my writing efforts: Pauline Hirabayashi, Mary Kettles, Cathy Martinez, Gayle Karon, and Linda Clark;

My cauliflowered-eared friends, who helped me call and verify facts: Pat Raymer (and no, there really isn't any company picnic!), Jewelene Pate (see Treasured Friend reference above), my mom, Char Cornelius, Elaine Strang, and Eileen, Aaron, and Becky Williams (a family affair!); and

All of the people associated with places mentioned in this book that were so willing to talk with me, send me information, and enable my family to come and visit - thank you, THANK YOU, **THANK YOU!!!**

TABLE OF CONTENTS

INTRODUCTION and LEGEND EXPLANATION

In this world there are specifically fun places to go with kids, and there are places we go and bring our kids, anyhow. I think going shopping is great, but when my boys were younger, and I would look at clothes, they thought it was fun to climb in the clothing racks and maybe even pull off a ticket or two to bring home as "prizes." This was not a fun family outing. I've tried to do the weeding for you so that anywhere you choose to go in this guidebook, whether it's an all-day outing or just for an hour, would be an enjoyable time for you and your child. Some places are obvious choices; some are places you might have simply forgotten about; some are hidden treasures; and some are new attractions.

The book is set up by category. Under each category, counties are listed alphabetically; and under each county, attractions are listed alphabetically. The names of places in all capital letters used in a description (e.g. DISNEYLAND), are attractions listed separately elsewhere in the book. Tips: Look for discount coupons for main attractions in hotel lobbies and visitors centers. Also, if you belong to AAA, ask if admission to the attraction you're visiting is discounted for members.

Each attraction has a set of directions in parenthesis. The "TG" at the end of the directions is *The Thomas Guide* map page and grid reference number.

Next to most of the places described are symbols, meant to be at-a-glance guidelines. The **sun** indicates the average amount of time needed to see this attraction. You might decide you need more or less time - this is just a guideline. The **dollar signs and exclamation mark** are price guidelines. They incorporate *the entrance cost for one adult, a 10-year-old child, and the parking fee* (if there is one). If you have more than one child, or one who gets in for free, your cost will vary. "**Ages**" stands for recommended ages. It is meant to be an aid to help you decide if an attraction is appropriate and/or meaningful for your child. Some of the age restrictions, however, are designated by the place you are visiting. The **birthday cake** symbol represents an attraction that is a good place to 1) have a birthday party (the place may or may not have a separate party room), or 2) incorporate with a birthday party.

☀ = 15 minutes to 1 hour	!	= FREE!
☀ = 1½ hours to half a day	!/$	= FREE, but bring spending money.
☼ = all day	$	= 1¢ - $5
⛹ = good for birthday parties	$$	= $5.01 - $10
	$$$	= $10.01 - $20
	$$$$	= $20.01 - $40
	$$$$$	= over $40

NEVER LEAVE HOME WITHOUT THESE ESSENTIALS

1. **SNACKS**: Always carry snacks and a water bottle with you and/or in the car. Listening to a child whine because he is hungry or thirsty can drive any sane parent over the edge. (And kids will not stop this endearing behavior until they actually get their food or drink!)

2. **MAP**: I would be lost without it! Invest in a street-finder map such as *The Thomas Guide* or *Rand McNally Streetfinder*.

3. **TISSUES AND/OR WIPES**: For obvious reasons.

4. **QUARTERS**: A few quarters tucked away in a container in the car can come in handy for phone calls, those snacks I told you to pack but you forgot, metered parking, or arcade games.

5. **TOYS/BOOKS/GAMES**: Keeping little fingers busy helps keep little hands out of trouble. (Check out Educational Toys, Books, and Games under the IDEAS/RESOURCES section.)

6. **TAPES**: Audio tapes can get kids singing instead of fussing. (And if kids cry really loud, just turn up the volume of the tape even louder!) We've found story tapes to be a real blessing, too. (See Audio Tapes under the IDEAS/RESOURCES section.)

7. **FIRST AID KIT**: Fill it with the essentials including band aids, ointment, tweezers, adhesive tape, scissors, an ice pack, Benedryl®, disposable gloves, and Tylenol™ (both children's and adults').

8. **ROADSIDE EMERGENCY KIT**: This kit should contain jumper cables (know how to use them!), flares, a flashlight, batteries, extra drinking water, tools, matches, screwdrivers, wrenches, etc.

9. **JACKET**: Pack a light jacket or sweater for the unexpected change in weather or change of plans. Throw in a change of clothes, too, for little ones who don't always make it to the bathroom in time. (This last tip could save your outing from being cut short.)

10. **BLANKET**: We use ours mainly for picnics, but it doubles as an "I'm cold" helper, and is handy for other emergencies.

11. **FANNY PACK**: Even if your kids are still in the diaper/stroller stage, a fanny pack is great for storing snacks and water bottles, and keeping your hands free to either help your children or grab them before they dart away.

12. **SUNSCREEN**: With our weather, we almost always need it.

13. **CAMERA AND FILM**: Capture those precious moments in a snap!

14. **GROCERY BAG**: It holds trash, excuse me, I mean treasures, that kids collect such as rocks, sticks, and creepy crawly things. The bag helps keep your car clean and makes it easier to throw everything away once you get home!

15. **A SENSE OF HUMOR!**

MISCELLANEOUS TIDBITS

OTHER HELPFUL ITEMS TO BRING:
1. **Cell phone**
2. **Walkie talkies** - Instead of just hoping that you'll actually meet up with your spouse, friends, or kids at the appointed place and time, communicate! Most walkie talkies have a two-mile radius.
3. **Video camera**
4. **Tape recorder** - Carry a hand-size tape recorder and press "record" anytime. This is a great way to document trips (remember to state the date and location) and interview kids, as well as get genuine reactions and impromptu stories, songs, and arguments.

MATCHING ARTICLES OF CLOTHING: Dress your kids in the same shirt (no, I don't mean one big shirt), or at least shirts of the same color (orange, yellow, and red are bright choices) when you go on an outing. I thought this would look silly, but while we do get stares and comments, I can find my kids at just a glance. If kids balk at wearing the same-colored shirt, invest in solid color baseball caps. Not only can you spot your children quickly, but hats help shade their faces from the sun.

SAFETY PRECAUTIONS (just a few to get you started):
1. Dress kids in brightly colored or easily identifiable shoes. If someone should try to snatch your child, shoes are the hardest thing to change.
2. Carry your child's picture for easy identification purposes.
3. Instruct your child where to meet or who to talk to in case you get separated from each other.

EXPECTATIONS:
1. Be aware - Simply because you have a fun outing planned, whether it's going to the "happiest place on earth" or just an hour of play, please don't expect your child to necessarily enjoy every moment of it. Know and expect that your child will probably fuss about something, or seemingly nothing. Beware of the fun-stealers - tiredness and hunger. Visit places before or after nap time, and always bring food, even if you just ate.
2. Be prepared - Call ahead and make sure the place you want to visit is open, especially if there is something that you particularly want to see; check off your list of essentials; set realistic expectations for all participants; be flexible; and go for it!
3. Family mottos - We no longer promise our kids that we'll take them on an outing. A promise, as any parent knows, cannot be broken; it is an absolute. A plan, however, can be altered depending on weather, circumstance, and/or attitude! One of our family mottos is, "It's a plan, not a promise." Another one is, "Oh well." Feel free to use either or both as the situation warrants.

SOME IDEAS TO EXTEND THE MEMORIES
OF YOUR OUTING

1. **PHOTO ALBUMS** - Buy your child an inexpensive 35mm camera (even a disposable one) and let him document the fun you have together. Keep ticket stubs and brochures. Have your older child keep a journal of his travels; where he went, when, and what he liked best. (See information on ordering the FUN PLACES SCRAPBOOK / JOURNAL at the back of this book.) Give younger children duplicate pictures (or ones that aren't going in the family album) so each child can put together his/her own album. Use craft scissors with patterned blades for creative cutting. Have kids use acid-free construction paper and stickers for decorations. Coming up with captions can be lots of fun - and funny! Spending this time together is a great way to extend a trip and continue making special memories. Note: Photo albums with magnetic pages will discolor your pictures eventually, but ones that use acid-free paper will not. See Photo Albums under the IDEAS/RESOURCES section.

2. **COLLECTIONS** - Collect key chains, refrigerator magnets, mugs, pencils, decks of cards, or something else inexpensive from each place you go, and display them.
   A. Patches - I collect patches and sew them on a quilt, for each child. Using a twin-size, colored flannel sheet and thin batting, I folded the sheet in half with the batting in between, and "quilted" it. (i.e. sewed the edges together and a few semi-straight lines, both vertically and horizontally.) I sew, or iron, on the patches as we get them. My kids love their "travel blankets."
   B. Postcards - Ask your younger children, "What's the most fun thing you remember about this place?" and jot down the answers on the back of this inexpensive memory-keeper. Make older kids write out the answers themselves. Be sure you date the postcard, too. Keep all the postcards in a small, three-ring binder. Another option: If you're going away on a trip, bring stamps and mail the postcards home. Kids love to receive mail.

3. **EDUCATION** - Spend some time doing a little (or a lot) of research about a particular place (or time period) before you visit. It will make your outing more meaningful and make a lasting impression upon your child. Think of your field trip as curriculum supplement! Call the attraction to get a brochure on it or use an encyclopedia to look up pertinent information, or do some on-line research. Other educational activities to enhance your outing include:
   A. Read stories - If you're going apple picking, for instance, read stories that have something to do with apples such as Johnny Appleseed, William Tell, Snow White, Adam and Eve, Sir Isaac Newton, and specifically, *The Giving Tree* by Shel Silverstein or *Ten Apples on Top* by Theo LeSieg.

B. Theme books - There are thematic study books for almost every subject written. Teacher Created Materials, Inc., P.O. Box 1040, Huntington Beach, CA 92647, has over fifty thematic unit study books available. Each book includes lessons and projects that incorporate math, arts and crafts, history, science, language arts, and cooking, into a study about one particular subject. (i.e. weather, birds, the human body, holidays, and more.)

C. Spelling words - Give your child a spelling list pertaining to the attraction you are visiting.

D. Maps - Have older children use a map to track your way to and from your outing - this is an invaluable skill, especially if they learn to do it correctly!

E. Flash cards - Take pictures of the places you go. Put the picture on a piece of construction paper and write the facts about the attraction on the back. "Laminate" it with contact paper. Use the cards as flash cards. Tip: If you're not a picture taker, buy postcards instead.

F. Bingo / Memory Game - Get duplicate pictures made of the places you go. Make bingo boards and cards or play the Memory game, where all the cards are turned over and have to be matched up. When the kids get a match, they have to tell you at least one fact about the place.

G. Use my FUN PLACES SCRAPBOOK / JOURNAL. (See information on ordering the FUN PLACES SCRAPBOOK / JOURNAL at the back of this book.)

4. **LISTEN TO YOUR AUDIO TAPE** - Nothing refreshes your memory about a trip like playing back on-the-road commentary. (See Miscellaneous Tidbits.)

These are just a few ideas - I'm sure you'll come up with many of your own!

5. **YOUR IDEAS -**

ROAD GAMES

"Are we almost there yet?" and "I'm bored!" (along with "I have to go to the bathroom!") are common cries from children (and adults) who are traveling. Tapes, books, toys, and snacks all help to keep kids entertained, as do car games. Here are just a few of our favorites with brief explanations on how to play:

<u>FOR THE YOUNGER SET</u>:
MISSING LETTER ABC SONG - Sing the ABC song, leaving out a letter. See if your child can figure out what letter is missing. Now let your child sing (or say) the alphabet, leaving out a letter. Suggest correct (and incorrect) letters and see if your child agrees with you on what letter is missing. (Tip: Know your alphabet!)

MISSING NUMBER GAME - Count up to a certain number and stop. See if your child can figure out what number comes next. Now let your child do the counting. See if he/she agrees with what you say the next number should be.

COLOR CAR GAME - Look out the window for just red cars (or just blue or just green, etc.). Each time your child sees a red car, he/she can shout "red!" (or "blue!" or "green!", etc.) Count together the number of cars of a particular color you see on your trip. Your child can eagerly share at night, "Daddy, we had a fifteen-red-car day!" A variation of this game is to count a particular type of car; VW Bug is the popular choice for our family.

ABC WORD GAME - A is for apple; B is for bear; etc. Encourage your child to figure out words that start with each letter of the alphabet.

<u>FOR OLDER CHILDREN</u>:
ALPHABET SIGN GAME - Each person, or team, looks for a word outside the car (i.e. billboards, freeway signs, bumper stickers, etc.) that begins with each letter of the alphabet. When the words are found, the person, or team, shouts it out. The words must be found in alphabetical order, starting with the letter A. Since words beginning with a Q, X, or Z are hard to find (unless you're near a Quality Inn, X-Ray machine, or a Zoo), players may find these particular letters used <u>in</u> any word. A word on a sign, billboard, etc., can only be used once, by one player or team member. Other players must find their word in another sign, billboard, etc. The first one to get through the alphabet wins! Warning #1: Try to verify that the word has been seen by more than just the player who shouted it out, or learn to trust each other. Warning #2: From personal experience: If the driver is competitive and wants to play, make sure he/she keeps his/her eyes on the road!

ALPHABET WORD GAME - This is a variation on the above game. Instead of finding words that begin with each letter of the alphabet, each player must look outside the car and describe his surroundings using letters of the alphabet, in alphabetical order. This game can be played fast and gets creative, depending on the quick-thinking skills of the people playing. Example: Someone who is on the letter D might look at the land and see dirt; a person looking for an S might say soil; someone else who is on the letter G might say ground. All are correct.

Players may use the same point of reference as long as the exact same word is not used. Whoever gets through the alphabet first wins.

GHOST - (Or whatever title you choose.) The object of this game is to add one letter per turn and be in the process of spelling a word, without actually spelling out a word. Players take turns adding letters until someone either spells a word, or can't think of another letter to add without spelling a word. A player may try to bluff and add a letter that doesn't seem like it spells a word. If he gets challenged by someone asking what he is spelling, he must come up with a legitimate word. If he doesn't, he loses the round. (If he does have a word, however, then the challenger loses that round.) Whoever spells a word or can't think of a letter to add, gets a G. The second time he loses a round, he gets an H, etc. Whoever earns G-H-O-S-T (i.e. loses 5 rounds) is eliminated from the game. Example: Player 1 says the letter "B." Player 2 adds the letter "E." (Words must be at least 3 letters long to count as a word.) Player 3 says "T." Player 3 gets a G, or whatever letter-round he is on. He loses the round even if his intent was to spell the word "better" because "bet" is a word.

WORD SCRAMBLE - Make sure players have a piece of paper and a writing implement. Using a word on a sign or billboard, or using the name of the place you are visiting, see how many other words players can make. To spice up the game, and add stress, set a time limit. Whoever has the most words wins. A variation is that letters are worth points: 2 letter words are worth 2 points, 3 letter words are worth 5 points, 4 letter words are worth 8 points, etc. The player with the most points wins. (Although a player may have fewer words, he/she could win the game by being long-worded.) Note: This game can be played for only a brief period of time by players who are prone to motion sickness.

FOR ALL AGES:
BINGO - This is the only game that you have to prepare for ahead of time. Make up bingo-type cards for each child. Cards for younger children can have pictures of things kids would typically see on their drive (although this depends on where you are traveling, of course): a blue car, McDonalds, a cow, a pine tree, etc. Cards for older children can have pictures, signs, license plates, and/or words that they would typically see on their drive: exit, stop, a traffic light, curvy road ahead, etc. Use magazines, newspapers, etc., and glue the pictures and words onto posterboard, one card per child. Tip: Have your kids help you prepare the cards as it's a fun project. Use raisins (or M&M's) as markers and when your child has bingo (or has seen a certain number of objects on his card), he can eat his reward. For those parents who intend to use the bingo boards more than once, "laminate" them with contact paper. Put small pieces of velcro on a part of each picture or sign on the card and make (non-edible) markers that have the other part of velcro on them. (This will keep markers from sliding off the cards during sudden turns!) Keep the cards and markers together in a plastic baggy in the car.

20 QUESTIONS - This time-honored game has many variations. (Our version is usually called 40 Questions.) The basic rules are for one player to think of a well-known person, or at least someone well-known to your children, and for other players to ask questions about the person to try to find out his/her identity. Only yes or no answers can be given. Whoever figures out the mystery person, in 20 questions or less, wins. Tip: Encourage players to ask general questions first to narrow down the field. (Inevitably, my youngest one's first question was, "Is it George Washington?") Teach them to ask, for instance: "Is it a man?"; "Is he alive?"; "Is he real?"; "Is he a cartoon?"; "Is he on T.V.?"; "Is he an historical figure?"; "Is it someone I know personally?" You get the picture. For a variation of the game, think of an object instead of a person. (Tip: Tell the others players first, though, about the switch in subject matter.)

3 THINGS IN COMMON - This is a great thinking game that is easily adaptable for kids of all ages. One person names 3 words (or things) that have something in common. Everyone else takes turns guessing what that something is. Examples for younger children: 1) sky, ocean, grandpa's eyes (or whomever). Answer: Things that are blue. 2) stop sign, fire truck, Santa's suit. Answer: Things that are red. Examples for older kids and adults: 1) house, butter, horse. Answer: Things that have the word fly at the end of them. 2) chain, missing, sausage. Answer: Things that can end with the word link. 3) tiger, nurse, sand. Answer: Kinds of sharks. My favorite example is the one my middle child came up with: 4) lion, Jesus, Budweiser. Answer: They are all kings! (Who says kids aren't affected by commercials?)

I'M GOING ON A PICNIC. . . - This game tests a player's abilities to remember things and remember them in order. Player 1 starts with the words, "I'm going on a picnic" and then adds a one word item that he will bring. The next player starts with the same phrase, repeats player 1's item, and then adds another item, and so on. Play continues until one of the players can't remember the list of things, in order, to bring on a picnic. Example: Player 1 says, "I'm going on a picnic and I am going to bring a ball." Player 2 says, "I'm going on a picnic and I'm going to bring a ball and a kite." Variations of the game include adding items in alphabetical order or adding items beginning with the same letter.

PLEASE be aware that although the facts recorded in this book are accurate and current as of March, 2001:

• HOURS CHANGE!
• EXHIBITS ROTATE!
• ADMISSION COSTS ARE RAISED WITHOUT FANFARE!
• PLACES CLOSE, EITHER TEMPORARILY OR PERMANENTLY!

To avoid any unexpected (and unpleasant) surprises:

Always, ALWAYS, *ALWAYS*
CALL BEFORE YOU VISIT AN ATTRACTION!!!

AMUSEMENT PARKS

Webster's definition of amusement is: "To cause to laugh or smile; entertainment; a pleasant diversion." So, from roller coasters to water slides - have fun!

Tips: If you *really* enjoy a particular amusement park, look into getting season passes. Also, many parks offer discounts on admission after 3pm or 4pm. The best days to visit an amusement park are usually Mondays or Tuesdays, when the crowds are less prevalent.

PACIFIC PARK

(310) 260-8744 / www.pacpark.com   *$$$*

At the western end of Colorado Boulevard, on Santa Monica Pier, Santa Monica

(Exit Santa Monica Fwy [10] N. on 4th St., L. on Colorado Blvd. It dead-ends at the pier. There is limited parking on the pier. From Colorado Blvd., other parking is available by turning L. on Oceanside, R. on Seaside, R. on Appian Way. [TG-671 E3])

The major kid-attraction on the Santa Monica pier is Pacific Park. It has twelve family rides, including six kiddie rides. The rides include a fifty-five-foot Ferris wheel, an historic carousel (with horses, camels, and lions), bumper boats, a seven-passenger bench that zooms riders up in the air, and a ship that swings back and forth like a pendulum. A three-minute, motion simulator ride features one of two action films. A rock climbing wall is also available. See SANTA MONICA PIER, under the Piers and Seaports section, for details about the pier.

Hours: All rides and games are up and running in the summer Sun. - Thurs., 11am - 11pm; Fri. - Sat., 10am - midnight. Open during the school year Fri., 6pm - midnight; Sat., 11am - midnight; Sun., 11am - 9pm. All the games and only one ride are open during the school year Mon. - Thurs., noon - 6pm.

Admission: Rides and activities cost between $2 - $6 each. An all-day rides wristband is $15.95 for 42" and taller; $8.95 for 41" and under. All day parking prices range between $3 - $7.

Ages: 2 years and up.

RAGING WATERS

(909) 802-2200 / www.ragingwaters.com   *$$$$$*

111 Raging Waters Drive, San Dimas

(Exit San Bernardino Fwy [10] N. on the 210 Fwy, or follow the Orange Fwy [57] where it turns into the 210 Fwy; exit at Raging Waters Dr. [TG-600 B4])

What a cool place to be on a hot day! Raging Waters is out*rage*ous with its fifty acres of chutes, white-water rapids, slides, drops, enclosed tubes (which make these slides dark and scary), a wave pool, lagoons, and sandy beaches. The rides run the gamut from a peaceful river raft ride in only three feet of water, to the ultimate in daredevil, such as plunging headfirst on High Extreme, a 600-foot ride off a 100-foot tower, or free falling off the Wedge where a feeling of near-zero gravity is terrifyingly fun. Ride high, well, three-feet high, on waves that roll out into the Wave Cove

The younger set reigns at Kids Kingdom as they splash around in this water area designed just for them. It has a big water play structure to climb on that shoots out water, plus tyke-size water slides, and a tire swing. The Little Dipper Lagoon is also for youngsters with its wading pools, shooting fountains, and waterfalls. Elementary-school-aged kids have their own, separate, fantastic, activity pool with slides, a ropes course, and Splash Island. The Island is a five-story treehouse with slides, water cannons, cargo nets, swinging bridges, and a huge bucket on top that spills over gallons of water. Holy smoke! Volcano Fantasia is a smoking volcano with several slides oozing down its sides into hip-deep water and more water activities.

Life vests are available at no extra charge. Inner tubes are available at no charge for some of the rides, but you must wait in long lines to get them. On busy days, I recommend renting a tube ($5). A picnic area is available just outside the main entrance gate. Outside food is not allowed inside, but there are many food outlets throughout the park. Hot tip: Wear water shoes, or sandals, because the walkways get very hot.

Hours: Open mid-April through May, and Labor Day through October, on weekends only 10am - 6pm. Open Memorial Day through June, Mon. - Fri., 10am - 6pm; Sat. - Sun., 10am - 7pm. Open July through August, Mon. - Fri., 10am - 9pm; Sat. - Sun., 10am - 9pm. Call first as hours fluctuate.

Admission: $24.99 for 48" and taller; $14.99 for seniors and kids 47" and under; children 2 and under are free. After 4pm, prices are $14.99 for 48" and taller; $9.99 for seniors and kids 47" and under. Purchase season passes by May and save $! Parking is $6.

Ages: 1½ years and up.

SIX FLAGS HURRICANE HARBOR

(661) 255-4111 / www.sixflags.com $$$$$

Magic Mountain Parkway, Valencia

(Exit Golden State Fwy [5] W. on Magic Mountain Pkwy. It's right next to Magic Mountain. [TG-4550 A1])

Pirates and lost tropical islands are the themes creatively integrated throughout every attraction in this twenty-two-acre water park. Older kids enjoy the swashbuckling thrill of the vertical drops, enclosed tube rides, and a combination of the two in the tallest enclosed speed slide this side of the Mississippi. The wave pool is a hit for those practicing surfing techniques. The five-person raft ride is fun without being too scary, and the lazy, looping river ride in only three feet of water is great for everyone in the family.

Relax in lounge chairs while your younger children play in a shallow pool with mini-slides, cement aquatic creatures, and a wonderful water play structure. The next harbor over is ideal for elementary-school-aged mateys to get wet and play on board the "floating" pirate ship. An adult activity pool is great for swimming, plus it has a net for water volleyball and, of course, it also has several slides. Sand volleyball is available, too.

Tube rentals run between $6 and $8, although tubes are included in some of the rides. Food is available to purchase inside the Harbor as outside food is not allowed in. Hot tip: Wear water shoes, or sandals, as the walkways get very hot. Note: The Harbor shares the same parking lot as Magic Mountain.

Hours: Open May and September on weekends only 10am - 6pm. Open June through Labor Day daily 10am - 7pm.

Admission: $19.99 for 48" and taller; $12.99 for seniors and kids 47" and under; children 2 and under are free. Parking is $7. Combo tickets for Hurricane Harbor and Magic Mountain are available.

Ages: 1½ years and up.

SIX FLAGS MAGIC MOUNTAIN   ☼
(661) 255-4111 / www.sixflags.com   *$$$$$*
Magic Mountain Parkway, Valencia   ♨
(Exit Golden State Fwy [5] W. on Magic Mountain Pkwy. [TG-4550 A1])

Thrill seekers and/or roller-coaster fanatics consider action-packed Magic Mountain the most daring place to go. The roller coasters range from the classic, wooden Colossus, to some of the world's tallest and fastest coasters - Superman and Goliath (a 255 foot drop!) - to the vertical drops, loops, and speed spirals (while standing!) of the intense Riddler's Revenge. This theme park boasts of being the extreme park with DejaVu, a suspended coaster ride that plummets riders down a hill and, with a boomerang-style turn, back up. Riders are going forward and backward, so they don't know if they are coming or going! X, yet another coaster ride, spins vehicles independently of one another while going along the tracks. My stomach and I just like to watch these rides and not actually participate. Magic Mountain has over forty-three rides and attractions, geared mostly for kids 8 years and older.

Other highlights here include the Log Ride and Jet Stream (both wet rides), bumper cars, and a visit to Pirate's Cove, where a fifteen-foot-tall volcano erupts. The Sky Tower is a "must-do" for all ages because it affords a 360-degree view of the park and the surrounding area. Bugs Bunny World is ideal for the younger crowd (2 to 8 year olds). Looney Tunes characters are often here for hugs and pictures. The rides include a pint-size free fall, train ride, bigfoot truck ride, balloon ride, roller coasters (of course), and Tweety's Escape, which is a ride in an oversized bird cage. Another high-ranking attraction in this section is the Looney Tunes Lodge, a two-story funhouse. Visitors in here use cannons and other creative gadgets to shoot, drop, or otherwise send hundreds of foam balls hurling through the air at one another. A petting zoo and a fountain area where Looney Tunes statues spew out water complete this world.

Magic Mountain has entertainment such as live music and spectacular special events in the 3,200-seat theater; stunt shows, such as the Batman and Robin Live Action special effects show; water shows; periodic wildlife presentations; and interactive shows for younger kids such as Bugs Bunny in Rabbit Hood. Catch the nighttime extravaganza in the summer as Looney Tunes characters and DC Comic Book superheros participate in a parade through the park that ends with a fireworks show.

Cyclone Bay is toward the back of the park, where specialty shops are the specialty. Bayshore Candy is an especially sweet stop as kids can watch fudge, caramel apples, and all sorts of mouth-watering delights being made before their very eyes. If it's real food that you're hankering for, try Mooseburger Lodge. In a forest-like setting, the waiters and waitresses sometimes sing, a moose talks, and the dessert, chocolate "moose," is served in an edible chocolate shell.

Wear walking shoes because although there are lots of grassy, shady areas to rest, Magic Mountain is spacious and hilly. Tip: Visit this Mountain on a Monday or Tuesday, if possible, as it is normally less crowded then. Note: If you want wet, summertime fun check out SIX FLAGS HURRICANE HARBOR, right next door to Magic Mountain.

Hours: Open April through October daily 10am - 6pm. Call for extended summer hours. Open the rest of the year weekends and holidays only 10am - 6pm.

Admission: $40.99 for 48" and taller; $20.50 for seniors and kids 47" and under; children 2 and under are free. Certain discounts available through AAA. Parking is $7. Combo tickets for Magic Mountain and Hurricane Harbor are available.

Ages: 1½ years and up.

UNIVERSAL STUDIOS HOLLYWOOD   ☼

(818) 508-9600 / www.universalstudios.com $$$$$

Universal Center Drive, Universal City

(Going NW on Hollywood Fwy [101], exit NE on Universal Center Dr. Going SE on 101, exit R. on Lankershim. At the end of the off ramp, turn L. on Cahuenga Blvd., L. on Universal Center Dr. [TG-563 C6])

This huge, unique, Hollywood-themed amusement park is really one of the world's biggest and busiest motion picture and television studios. Personal advice is to go on the forty-five-minute, guided tram tour first, as lines get long later on. Each tram is outfitted with a monitor that shows film clips and how various sets and sound stages have been used in productions over the years. The tour takes you behind the scenes and through several of Hollywood's original and most famous backlots. You'll learn about the shows currently being filmed at Universal and see sound stages and lots of props. Along the way, some of the elaborate special effects that you'll encounter are: a confrontation with King Kong; the shark from *Jaws*; Earthquake - The Big One, where buildings collapse and a run-away big-rig crashes within inches of you, followed by fire and a flood coming toward you; and more disasters, such as the collapsing bridge and the flash flood. Some of it can get a bit overwhelming for younger kids.

Want to go Back to the Future? Be prepared in this ride for an intense, jolting, simulated experience through the Ice Ages, into the mouth of a Tyrannosaurus Rex, and forward to the year 2015. Down on the lower lot at Universal, kids can fly on a bike with E.T. and visit his planet. Although a little darker in tone, this ride is best described as Disneyland's "it's a small world" meets a world of E.T.s. If you are at least 46" tall, enter through the gates of Jurassic Park to river raft through the primordial forest. It starts off as a peaceful ride, but it ends up as a very wet, terrifying, face-to-face encounter with bellowing dinosaurs! Follow this ride with Backdraft, where you literally feel the heat of the hottest attraction here. (You'll dry off from the Jurassic waters.) This sound stage becomes a fiery furnace, ablaze with ruptured fuel lines and melting metal. In the sound stage show of Cinemagic, you can watch or sometimes participate in some of the special effects created for big and small screens. Lovers of Lucy can visit the heart-shaped facility and "walk through" her career, with the aid of photos, videos, costumes, and other memorabilia. Splash Zone is a kids play ground with both a wet area (obviously) where rocket ships spray water and fountains shoot up from the ground, and a dry area where kids can run, jump, slide, and just play. Tip: Bring a change of clothes.

As Universal Studios is synonymous with quality productions, the live shows here are entertaining and highlighted with special effects. Some of the current shows include Animal Actors Show, which employs lot of humor with a variety of well-trained animals and the Wild, Wild, Wild West Stunt Show, which is a funny western farce employing great stunts. (Get there early to watch the Charlie Chaplin character interact with the crowd.) Waterworld is the "coolest" production here with explosive stunts and special effects that blow you out of the water. Terminator 2: 3-D mostly follows the storyline of the *Terminator 2* movie. This version is very intense, often violent, action-packed, and a combination of a 3-D action movie projected onto a huge screen with live actors that pop in and out of the scenery. The changing Nickelodeon stage currently features a spectacular special effects, interactive musical/magic show starring the *Rugrats* characters. Some of Universal's shows are seasonal, and/or performed on weekends and holidays only.

Get an early start for your adventure at Universal Studios, and don't forget to bring your camera for some wonderful photo opportunities.

If you're interested in "edutainment," ask about the Universal Studios Hollywood Course of Study Program. Fourth through twelfth grade students are introduced to a variety of subjects on a field trip here, including dinosaurs, sound effects, and careers in advertising and entertainment. Other programs include assemblies at Universal for seventh through twelfth graders, where speakers and live performances address important issues facing today's youth. Kids can then spend the remainder of the day at Universal Studios. Call (800) 959-9688 for more information on these programs.

Check out the adjacent UNIVERSAL CITYWALK, listed under the Potpourri section, for unusual shopping and dining experiences.

Hours: Open the majority of the year daily 9am - 7pm. During the peak summer season, it's open daily 8am - 10pm. Call to find out the hours for the day of your visit. Tours in Spanish are available Sat. and Sun. Closed Thanksgiving and Christmas.

Admission: $43 for adults; $37 for seniors; $32 for ages 3 - 11; children 2 and under are free. Certain discounts available through AAA. Parking is $7. Annual passes are a good deal - deluxe passes (no black out dates) are $72 for adults; $67 for seniors; $52 for kids. Other annual passes (good for 330 days of the year) are $52 for adults; $47 for seniors; $42 for ages 3 - 11. The Hollywood CityPass, $49.75 for adults and $38 for ages 3 - 11, is good for one-time admission to American Cinematheque's Egyptian Theatre in Hollywood, AUTRY MUSEUM OF WESTERN HERITAGE, HOLLYWOOD ENTERTAINMENT MUSEUM, MUSEUM OF TELEVISION AND RADIO, MUSEUM OF TOLERANCE, PETERSEN AUTOMOTIVE MUSEUM, REAGAN PRESIDENTIAL LIBRARY AND MUSEUM, and UNIVERSAL STUDIOS within a 30 day period. (All of the entries mentioned, except for the theater, are listed separately.) Call (888) 330-5008 / www.citypass.com for more information.

Ages: 3 years and up.

ADVENTURE CITY

(714) 827-7469 / www.adventure-city.com

10120 S. Beach Boulevard, Anaheim

(Exit Artesia Fwy [91] S. on Beach Blvd. It's 2 miles S. of Knott's Berry Farm on the L. in the Hobby City complex. [TG-797 J1])

☼
$$$$

My family travels a lot and one of our favorite cities to visit is Adventure City. This clean, two-acre little theme park, located in the HOBBY CITY complex (look under the Potpourri section), is perfect for younger children. The colorful city scene facades throughout resemble storybook illustrations. The twelve or so rides, designed to accommodate parents, too, include a wonderful train ride around the "city," a few roller coasters, an airplane ride, and a bus with wheels that goes 'round and 'round. Kids can have a really hot time dressing up in full fireman apparel before (or after) they "drive" around on the 9-1-1 vehicle ride.

Adventure City also offers do-it-yourself face painting, a few video and arcade games, plus terrific interactive, educational puppet shows at the theater. After the show, kids are allowed to try their hand at puppeteering. Classes in puppeteering are also available. Thomas the Tank play area has a huge wooden train set that encourages toddlers' imaginations to go full steam ahead. A small petting zoo has goats, sheep, chickens, bunnies, and a llama. Mount Adventure is a rock climbing wall just the right size for kids (and adults) to scale. It's twenty-five-feet high and cost $3 per person to climb.

The food is good and reasonably priced. Note: You may not bring your own food inside, but there is a small picnic area just outside the gates. Come and spend a delightful day in this city!

Hours:　Open in the summer Mon. - Thurs., 10am - 5pm; Fri., 10am - 8pm; Sat., 11am - 9pm; Sun., 11am - 8pm. Open the rest of the year Fri., 10am - 5pm; Sat. - Sun., 11am - 7pm. Call for holiday hours.

Admission:　$11.95 for ages 1 and up; $8.95 for seniors; children under 12 months are free. Certain discounts are available through AAA.

Ages:　1 - 10 years.

CALIFORNIA ADVENTURE

(714) 781-4565 - recorded information; (714) 781-4560 - operator / www.disneyland.com

1313 Harbor Boulevard, Anaheim

(Going S. on Santa Ana Fwy [5], exit R. on Disney Way. Going N. on the 5, exit L. on Disneyland Dr. Follow the signs. Trams go from the parking lots to California Adventure. [TG-798 H2])

☼
$$$$$

This is Disney's version of California, which is sometimes realistic, and always entertaining. The California Adventure is one-third the size of Disneyland, which is directly across the way, with twenty-two rides and attractions. Enter through 11.5 feet high letters that spell out "CALIFORNIA", under a large scale replica of the Golden Gate Bridge, and to the central plaza, which features a landmark fifty-foot "Sun" made of gold titanium. The park is divided into three major sections.

To the left of the entrance is **Hollywood Pictures Backlot**, which describes exactly what it looks like. The main road looks like a real street with a huge backdrop of blue sky and a few white clouds at the end. Famous Hollywood movie facades line the streets. The ten-minute Muppet Vision 3D show is great for Muppet fans. Watch out for objects that come flying "out of the screen". The Muppet preshow, shown on several large screens in a dressing room with lots of costumes and props, is equally entertaining. The Superstar Limo ride is similar to Roger Rabbits ride in Disney's Toontown. Stars (i.e. guests) sit in limos and are driven through Beverly Hills, kind of, as signs and cartoonish characters pop out along the way. The Hyperion Theater, which seats 2,000, presents professional musicals and shows. The Disney Animation building is a main attraction. It offers two different shows and three small rooms with interactive exhibits. The shows, *Drawn to Animation* and the *Art of Animation*, use animated figures on the screen that interact with live Disney staff to show the creative process of animation - from inception to evolution to the final product. A small adjacent "museum" shows this process via sketches and sculpture of several famous Disney characters. In the Sorcerer's Workshop, which is decorated in a dark dungeon-style tone, draw your own Zoetrope (i.e. an early animation strip); enter the Beast's Library, which looks like a set from *Beauty and the Beast*, to match up your personality traits with a Disney character by having your picture taken and pressing buttons on a "magic" book; and, relive (as well as rewrite) Disney scenes in Ursula's Grotto by replacing the real voices with your speaking or singing voice, matched to an on-screen scene. One of the most interesting restaurants in this area is ABC Soap Opera Bistro, where each room is decorated just like a scene from ABC's soap operas. The waiters and waitresses are dressed up like the television characters and occasionally act out scenes.

Behind and to the right of the sun in the plaza is **Golden State.** To the immediate right is the highly touted, and rightly so, Soarin' Over California ride. A plane has crash landed and guests walk through its nearby hanger, whose walls are lined with airplane photos. Sit in a chair, feet dangling over the edge, in front of a giant screen. The film's camera angles immerse you in the aerial shots of California imagery; sweeping over San Francisco, seemingly dipping your feet into the Pacific Ocean, barely avoiding treetops - watch riders lift their feet! - while literally smelling the orange blossoms and pine trees, and swooping down on a golf course in Palm Springs. You will get wet on Grizzly River Run, an eight-passenger raft ride that goes down mountain sides, through caverns, and down a river onto a spouting geyser. Notice the huge rock formation of the ride - it's carved in the shape of a bear. The Redwood Creek Challenge Trail is an outdoor play area made to look like it's in a Redwood forest. Kids can let off steam by running around, scaling a short rock climbing wall, going up fire towers, down slides, and across cargo nets, zip lines, and swaying bridges. The twenty-two-minute film, *Golden Dreams*, is narrated by Whoopie Goldberg, who plays Queen Califa, the essence of the state of California. It shows and tells the history of California through present day via various immigrant's eyes, ending on an up note about the California dream. The farming section of this area features plots of California-based crops, plus farm equipment. *It's Tough to be a Bug* 3-D animation show is not for those with arachnophobia. The entrance line winds through a re-creation of an ant farm, until you get to the theater, which is in an underground anthill, albeit people-sized. The show features bugs of all kinds, such as termites, huge tarantulas that seemingly come out of the screen, stinkbugs (with an olfactory emission), an angry hoard of hornets that buzz loudly in a blackened room as a "stinger" pokes through the back of your chair. Also, experience the sensation of bugs crawling over you. O.K. - it wasn't my favorite attraction! Walk through an on-site tortilla factory and a sourdough bread factory, which is a great spot for lunch as salad or soup comes in a freshly-made bread bowl. Watch a seven-minute film on the making of wine at Wine Terrace. Wine sampling is available for adults.

On to **Paradise Pier**, which is like a boardwalk carnival, filled with old-fashioned rides and carnival-type games. The "E-ticket" ride here is California Screamin', a colossus roller coaster that earns its name with steep hills, high speed drops, and a loop-de-loop around a huge Mickey Mouse face. The giant Ferris wheel is another heart-stopper. Cages, which seat up to eight people, swing independently of each other, so passengers go around and around, and around and around! Other rides here include a swing ride, inside a large orange; a carousel; the Jumpin' Jellyfish parachute ride; old-fashioned-looking spinning rockets; a smaller roller coaster; and the Mailboomer, which catapults riders up in two seconds, and brings them down bungee style. Younger children enjoy a small ship that's really a play area. They can climb on deck, hang-ten on a stationary surfboard, turn the ship's wheels, and squirt each other with fireboat hoses.

Eureka, the Spirit of California, is a multi-cultural parade with participants in colorful costumes, plus live drummers, other music, skate and bike performers on-board floats, larger-than-life puppets, and street performers.

There is a lot of "eye candy" at the park. Buildings, like Dinosaur Jack's Sunglass Shack is in the shape of an enormous, friendly-looking dinosaur wearing shades. Play-on-word store names, such as Sam Andreas Shakes and Pop-arazzi Popcorn (in the Hollywood section) are scattered throughout. This is not your parent's Disneyland; it's a new Adventure, definitely geared for older kids and adults. Note: There are traditionally fewer crowds here on Mondays and Tuesdays. See DISNEYLAND, in this section, which is just across the walkway from California Adventure, and DOWNTOWN DISNEY, a huge walkway between the two Disneys that offers unique shopping and dining experiences. Look this up under the Potpourri section.

Hours: Open daily in the summer 8am - 1am. Open the rest of the year Mon. - Thurs., 9:30am - 6pm; Fri. - Sat., 9am - midnight; Sun., 10am - 10pm. Hours fluctuate, so call before you visit.

Admission: $43 for adults; $41 for seniors; $33 for ages 3 - 11; children 2 and under are free. Parking costs $7. Ask about 2 or 3 day passes. Several times throughout the year Southern California residents are offered a substantial discount on admission.

Ages: 6 years and up.

DISNEYLAND

(714) 781-4565 - recorded information; (714) 781-4560 - operator /
www.disneyland.com
1313 Harbor Boulevard, Anaheim
(Going S. on Santa Ana Fwy [5], exit R. on Disney Way. Going N. on the 5, exit L. on Disneyland
Dr. Follow the signs. Trams go from the parking lot to Disneyland. [TG-798 H1])

The world-famous "happiest place on earth" amusement park has so many
things to do, see, and ride on, that entire books are written about it. The
following description is just a brief overview. Note that Disney has a "Fastpass"
system, which means that computer-assigned boarding passes (dispensed from
ticket machines in front of the most popular attractions) reserve a designated
time for you to be in line and board the ride.

The park is "divided" into different sections and each section favors a
particular theme. The following attractions are just *some* of the highlights in
these various areas. **Fantasyland** is located mostly inside the castle "walls."
Rides include Mr. Toad's Wild Ride, Alice in Wonderland (where the ride
vehicle is shaped liked a caterpillar), a carousel, and more. This area is definitely
geared for the younger set, although some of the images on the rides may be
scary for them. Storybook Land is a boat ride through canals lined with
miniature buildings that are from Disney's classic tales. Fantasyland also
features Matterhorn Bobsled (a roller coaster), and "it's a small world," where a
slow moving boat takes you past animated children from all over the world
dressed in their culture's attire and singing the theme song in their native
language. (If you didn't know the song at the beginning of the ride, you will
never forget it afterward.) **Mickey's Toontown** is put together at crazy,
cartoonish angles. Meet Mickey and Minnie in "person" at each of their houses
and get your picture taken with him/her. Kids enjoy Goofy's Bounce House, the
scaled down roller coaster ride, simply sitting in cars that look like they are
straight out of a cartoon, as well as just running all around this toddler-friendly
"town." Roger Rabbit is the most popular ride here as riders sit in a car that they
can actually spin around. **Frontierland** features Big Thunder Mountain Railroad
(a roller coaster), Mark Twain River boat (which looks authentic), and Tom
Sawyer's Island. On the island, kids can climb on (fake) rocks, go through secret
passages in the rocks, and play at the frontier fort. **New Orleans Square** boasts
Pirates of the Caribbean. Yo ho, yo ho, with its catchy music and cannons
"blasting" under a nighttime setting, it's a pirate's life for me. The Haunted
Mansion is a ride through, well, a haunted mansion, that showcases various
ghosts. **Critter Country** has an un*bear*ably funny show starring singing country
bears. Splash Mountain, a wet roller coaster ride, is also here. **Adventureland**
has the thrilling (and jolting) Indiana Jones Adventure roller coaster ride. You'll
encounter snakes, skeletons, a huge boulder rolling toward your jeep, and other
dangers. Height restrictions apply as younger children will most likely be
frightened by the content. **Tomorrowland**, with its sixty-four-foot mobile of
gold, spinning planets, at the entrance ushers in a new era. Zoom through the
darkness of outer space in Space Mountain, one of the fastest roller coaster rides
at Disneyland. Bump along through Star Tours, a motion simulator ride. *Honey,
I Shrunk the Audience* is an exciting 3-D movie experience where objects

seemingly come out at you from the screen. Warning: If you do not like mice, keep your feet off the floor. Bring a bathing suit (or change of clothing) in the summertime if you want to get wet running through the huge fountain in Tomorrowland. The water shoots up in some sort of pattern, but my kids usually just got wet, pretty much on purpose, I think. Be entertained by film tributes to past and future technology while waiting in line for Rocket Rods, a ride in a speeding, futuristic car. We could have stayed inside the Innoventions building all day. This showcase rotates as it features educational and entertaining computer and video games on the first floor. I can only liken the second level to a terrific, hands-on, science "museum" that features technology and games of the future. Play virtual reality games, listen to the rhythm of human heart beats, and use a ultrasound machine on a model pregnant woman to see how the baby is forming inside her.

The daily (and nightly) themed parades and shows are truly memorable. They are usually based on Disney's latest animated films. *Fantasmic* is usually shown daily in the summer, and on the weekends only the rest of the year. This twenty-five-minute show, presented near Tom Sawyer's Island, centers around Mickey Mouse's imagination battling evil forces. Fountains of water create a misty "screen" for film images from *The Sorcerer's Apprentice*, *Dumbo*, and others. Lighted boats cruise by with costumed characters on board acting out scenes from Disney movies. Fire flashes on the water, fireworks explode, and the finale is played with a thunderous symphony of music. Weekend evenings throughout most of the year and every night during the summer (at 9:30pm) comes Believe, a choreographed fireworks extravaganza accompanied by a mesmerizing soundtrack. You have to see it to Believe it! Call for a complete list of show information and times.

Main Street, U.S.A. is perfect for all your mini (and Mickey) shopping needs. Your child's favorite Disney characters are strolling all around the park, so keep your eyes open and your camera ready. Quite a few of the characters are gathered at Town Square when Disneyland opens in the morning. Come spend at least a day at the "Magic Kingdom." Note: There are traditionally fewer crowds here on Mondays and Tuesdays. See CALIFORNIA ADVENTURE, in this section, which is another Disney theme park adjacent to Disneyland, and DOWNTOWN DISNEY, a huge walkway between the two Disneys offering unique shopping and dining experiences. Look this up under the Potpourri section.

Hours: Open daily in the summer 8am - 1am. Open the rest of the year Mon. - Thurs., 9:30am - 6pm; Fri. - Sat., 9am - midnight; Sun., 10am - 10pm. Hours fluctuate, so call before you visit.

Admission: $43 for adults; $41 for seniors; $33 for ages 3 - 11; children 2 and under are free. Parking costs $7. Ask about 2 or 3 day passes. Several times throughout the year Southern California residents are offered a substantial discount on admission.

Ages: All

KNOTT'S BERRY FARM   ☼

(714) 220-5200 / www.knotts.com   *$$$$$*
8039 Beach Boulevard, Buena Park
(Exit Artesia Fwy [91] S. on Beach Blvd. [TG-767 H3])
    The atmosphere of the Old West is re-created throughout most of
California's original theme park. The Old West Ghost Town has a humorous
Wild West Stunt Show, an old-fashioned Stagecoach ride, train rides, lots of
stores with a Western motif, and usually some cowboys hanging around. Catch a
professionally acted play at the Bird Cage Theater. A huge, relatively long,
wooden-trestle roller coaster named Ghost Rider is an absolute thrill ride. (Part
of the time I was lifted out of my seat!) Indian Trails has tepees to go in, Indian
crafts to see, and terrific shows featuring Native American dancers. The hoop
dance is our favorite.

    Fiesta Village's rides and shops have a Mexican theme. Enter Jaguar, a
roller coaster, through a Mayan-styled pyramid temple and experience ancient
wonders (and a fun ride!). Take a free fall as you drop steeply at faster than 50
miles per hour in the appropriately named Supreme Scream. Go down Perilous
Plunge at your own peril as it's the tallest water rides in the world (at least for
now). One of the most popular rides at Knott's is Kingdom of the Dinosaurs
(guess why?), though it's a bit dark and scary for younger kids. Beware - the
Roaring Rapids raft ride **will** get you wet. There are roller coasters, bumper cars,
and many other amusement park rides and attractions at Knott's.

    Kids 2 to 7 years old can spend almost the whole day in Camp Snoopy. This
"camp" has kiddie rides, ball pits, a petting zoo, pony rides, a large Snoopy
bounce, a funhouse, and several rides geared just for young Peanut's fans.

    There are also "hidden" parts to Knott's Berry Farm. For instance, in front
of Roaring Rapids is a small, but terrific, Ranger Station. Inside, kids can see
and hold a variety of insects and arachnids such as a giant millipede and a
hissing cockroach. They can also pet a snake and touch animal pelts. The Edison
Room in Camp Snoopy is a great first exposure to the science of how things
work, utilizing magnets, generators, and more. A lot can be learned about the
Old West and Native American life styles by talking to some of the costumed
employees, visiting the old-fashioned schoolroom, and using some of the stores
as mini-museums. There are many terrific educational tours available through
Knott's education department. Learn about our early American heritage, pan for
gold, see a blacksmith at work, explore Indian Trails with an Indian guide, learn
about energy in motion, go on a natural history adventure, and much more!
Knott's even provides educational assemblies that come to your school. Call
(714) 220-5244 for information on field trips.

    In addition to Knott's Berry Farm's rides and attractions, there are twenty-
six shops; delicious restaurants, including the famous Mrs. Knott's Chicken
Dinner Restaurant; the Good Time Theater, where major entertainers, including
Snoopy, perform; a full-size reproduction of INDEPENDENCE HALL (look
under the Potpourri section for a description of the hall); and a water park called
SOAK CITY U.S.A. (Buena Park). Look under this section for details. Note:
Mondays and Tuesdays are the best days to come here as it's usually less
crowded then.

Hours: Open in the summer, Sun. - Thurs., 9am - 11pm; Fri. - Sat., 9am - midnight. Open the rest of the year Mon. - Fri., 10am - 6pm; Sat., 10am - 10pm; Sun., 10am - 7pm. Hours may vary. Closed Christmas.

Admission: $40 for adults; $30 for seniors and ages 3 - 11; children 2 and under are free. Certain discounts available through AAA. Parking is $7. Knott's offers numerous special admission deals throughout the year, including some for California residents and some for admissions after 4pm.

Ages: All

KNOTT'S SOAK CITY U.S.A. (Buena Park) ☼

(714) 827-1776 / www.soakcityusa.com *$$$$$*
8039 Beach Boulevard, Buena Park
(Exit Artesia Fwy [91] S. on Beach Blvd. It's across the street from Knott's Berry Farm. [TG-767 H3])

Hang ten at this thirteen-acre water park with a 1950's, early 1960's, Southern California beach cities theme. Longboards and surf woodies dot the landscape and surf music plays in the background. The numerous intense rides and attractions include six high-speed slides - lie on your back and let 'er rip; tube rides that range from a little thrilling to hair raising; a relaxing tube ride that circles around a portion of the park in two-and-a-half feet of water; Tidal Wave Bay, where a series of waves roll out into a good-sized "bay" every few minutes; a racing slide (six people side by side) that utilizes mats; and two activity areas for kids. The Beach "House" is four stories of hands-on water fun with squirt guns, slides, and a huge bucket that periodically unloads hundreds of gallons of water to deluge everyone below. For younger children, the colorful Gremmie (surfer lingo for "young surfer wanna be") Lagoon is a pint-sized playground with gadgets to squirt, sprinkle, and soak fellow playmates. Climb aboard a submarine in the middle of the lagoon which is covered by an octopus with slides for tentacles. A few grassy areas and plenty of lounge chairs round out this way cool water park. Full-service food and snack stations abound, of course. Tip: Bring a picnic lunch to enjoy on the grounds of INDEPENDENCE HALL (see the Museums section), located just outside the gates. Hot tip: Wear water shoes, or sandals, as the walkways get very hot.

Hours: Open the end of May through the end of June daily 10am - 6pm. Open July 1 through Labor Day daily 10am - 8pm; weekends in September, noon - 8pm.

Admission: $21 for adults; $14.95 for ages 3 - 11; children 2 and under are free. After 3pm, admission is $13.95 for adults; $11.95 for ages 3 - 11. Parking is $7 per car.

Ages: 1 ½ years and up.

WILD RIVERS WATERPARK ☼

(949) 768-WILD (9453) / www.wildrivers.com *$$$$$*
8770 Irvine Center Drive, Irvine
(Exit San Diego Fwy [405] S. on Irvine Center Dr. [TG-891 A3])

This park's all wet with twenty acres of over forty water rides and attractions! The mild to wild rides include a relaxing river raft ride, wave pools (one has "real-size" waves), completely enclosed slides (i.e. dark and scary), and vertical drops. My boys also enjoyed shooting the rapids, and the opportunity to go belly-sliding down Surf Hill.

Younger kids have their own terrific water play area at Pygmy Pond. It has a climbing structure that shoots out water, a gorilla swing, just-their-size slides, and kiddie tube rides. Tunnel Town offers both wet and dry fun with twisting and turning tunnels to crawl through.

Two pools just for swimming are also here. One pool is three-and-a-half-feet deep, while the other is a bit deeper and has a water basketball area. All of this, and plenty of sun-bathing opportunities, makes Wild Rivers a fantastic beach alternative.

Picnic areas are available outside the park, as no outside food may be brought in. Locker rentals are between $4 to $7, depending on the size. Additional tube rentals are available. Hot tip: Wear water shoes, or sandals, as the cement walkways get very hot.

Hours: Open May through mid-June and mid-September through the beginning of October on weekends only 11am - 5pm. Open mid-June through mid-September daily 10am - 8pm.

Admission: $24 for adults; $18 for ages 3 - 9; children 2 and under and seniors are free. Parking is $5. After 4pm, admission is only $12 for ages 3 and up. Ask about Monday Carloads, offered June through Labor Day, when admission is $40 for up to eight people after 4pm; each additional person is $5.

Ages: 1½ years and up.

CASTLE PARK   ☼

(909) 785-3000 / www.castlepark.com $$$

3500 Polk Street, Riverside   ♨

(Exit Riverside Fwy [91] N. on La Sierra Ave., R. on Diana St., L. on Polk St. It's between the Galleria at Tyler and La Sierra Ave., and visible from the freeway. [TG-744 F1])

Castle Park has a lot of action packed into its twenty-five acres. The compactness of the park makes it easy to walk all around. It has four scenic and challenging eighteen-hole miniature golf courses, complete with waterfalls, a miniature Big Ben, Dutch windmill, and western fort; a three-level arcade with over 400 video games and games of skill, plus a redemption center; and over thirty rides and attractions! The rides include the log ride (which will get you wet), a huge carousel, roller coasters, the sea dragon ride, a Ferris wheel, two train rides, and more. There are plenty of "big kids" rides, as well as delightful kiddie rides. The atmosphere here reminds me of Coney Island in that the flashy rides are interspersed with carnival-type games. Special events and package deals are on going at Castle Park, so call for a schedule and more information.

The massive BIG TOP FOOD 'N' FUN RESTAURANT looks like a circus Big Top, and serves pizza and other food. Look under the Edible Adventures section for more details.

Hours: Miniature golf and the arcade area are open Sun. - Thurs.,10am - 11pm; Fri. - Sat., 10am - midnight. The ride park is open Fri., 5pm - 10pm; Sat., 10am - 10pm; Sun., 10am - 8pm. During the summer and on holidays the entire park is open daily, starting at 10am. Big Top Restaurant is open the same hours as the ride park.

Admission: There is no general admission fee. Miniature golf is $5.99 for 48" and taller; $4.99 for 47" and under. Each ride takes between 3 to 5 tickets and tickets are 75¢ each, or purchase an unlimited rides wristband for $14.99 for 48" and taller; $12.99 for 47" and under. Parking is $5.

Ages: All

PHARAOH'S LOST KINGDOM   ☼
(909) 335- PARK (7275) / www.pharaohslostkingdom.com $$$$
1101 N. California Street, Redlands   ⛟
(Exit San Bernardino Fwy [10] N. on California St. It's the first pyramid off the fwy. [TG-607 F6])

"Mummies" (and daddies) looking for a place to keep kids royally entertained have found their answer at Pharaoh's Lost Kingdom. Enter through the giant Sphinx. Inside is a massive number of arcade, video, and virtual reality games. The Kid's Clubhouse is a large, soft play area with ball pits, slides, tubes, and obstacle courses for ages 2 to 8. On the upper level, take your best shot in Laser Tag. With over 5,000 square feet of darkness, mazes, obstacle courses, and opponents just waiting to zap you, the twelve-minute game is action-packed. And all this is only the tip of the pyramid!

Outside, the Race Car Complex offers three different tracks - kiddie, Grand Prix, and a banked Indy speed track; some height and age restrictions apply. Bumper boats are another great family attraction. Travel to ancient and exotic lands via the four, nine-hole miniature golf courses. The holes don't have a lot of challenging obstacles, but they are intriguingly embellished. For an adrenaline rush, dare to try Sky Coaster, a harnessed "ride" that lets you fly and swing from over 100-feet high for $15; height and age restrictions apply. The sixteen amusement rides, geared for young kids and older kids (i.e. adults), include a Ferris wheel, carousel, Tilt-A-Whirl, bumper cars, mini motorboats, a Screaming Mummy roller coaster, and more.

We found a lot of fun at the Lost Kingdom water park. Climb up the central tower to go down the six slides that range from enclosed body slides with a sheer drop, to open tube rides that hurl riders down. (The Wrath of Ra is aptly named.) Enjoy a blissful raft ride in three feet of water on the Endless River, a large circular river encompassing the water park. Body or board surf with the wave machine at Riptide. Younger children have their own wading pool with a big water play structure and slides. Another activity pool, for elementary-school-aged kids, has a few short slides, a water volleyball area, and a challenging ropes course over hard foam mummies and tiles. A beach and a sand volleyball court are also here. King Tut never had it so good! Note that there are two full-service snack bars here and that no outside food is allowed in.

Self-guided and docent-guided school and group tours are offered that can be tailored to a specific age group or interest. Topics can include pyramids, hieroglyphics, science (dealing with gravity and roller coasters), and more. Call for more information and prices.

Hours: Open Sun. - Thurs., 10am - 10pm; Fri. - Sat., 10am - midnight. The amusement rides usually open in the early afternoon. The water park is open April through October daily 10am - 8pm. Call for its "off season" hours.

Admission: Unlimited miniature golf is $6 per person. Bumper boats are $4 per person per ride. Laser tag is $5 a game. Kid's Clubhouse is $3 per child; adults are free. Race cars rides range from $3 - $5 per ride, depending on the type of car and track. Amusement rides cost between $1 to $4 per ride. Children under two years are not permitted on the rides. An unlimited use pass for amusement rides cost $10.95 for ages 11 and up; $8.95 for ages 3 - 10. An unlimited use pass for all the rides and activities, excluding the water park and arcade games, is $19.99 for ages 11 and up; $13.99 for ages 2 - 10. Admission to the water park is $19.99 for ages 11 and up; $13.99 for ages 2 - 10; children 1 and under are free. Unlimited amusement rides, attractions, and usage of the water park is $24.99 for ages 11 and up; $18.99 for ages 2 - 10. Season passes are a great deal at $39.99 per person for all (dry and wet) activities. Parking is $4.

Ages: 1 ½ years and up.

KNOTT'S SOAK CITY U.S.A. (Chula Vista)   ☼
(619) 661-7373 / www.soakcityusa.com   *$$$$$*
2052 Entertainment Circle, Chula Vista
(From San Diego Fwy [5] exit E. on Main St., which turns into Otay Valley Rd. From Jacob Dekema Fwy [805], exit E. on Otay Valley Rd./Auto Park Dr. From Otay Valley, turn R. on Entertainment Circle. [TG-1331 A6])

Welcome to Southern California circa 1950! San Diego's liquid gold attraction is colorful, beach-themed, fun, and most important, very wet. The park is spread over thirty-three acres with a large, centrally located grassy area. The kids come here in hordes to plunge down the sixteen water slides lined up side by side: six inner-tube slides, six body slides, and four speed slides.

Rip the curl in the wave pool, where waves can reach up to three-and-a-half-feet high. Don't wipe out! This huge pool can hold hundreds of swimmers and surfer "wannabes" at one time. A four-story, interactive kid's water play structure has water cannons to shoot, cargo nets to crawl and climb on, and a floating lily-pad bridge across the pool. Going across on the "lily pads" is more challenging than it looks. A large toddler play area has mini slides, splash pools with waterfalls, and a climbing structure in shallow waters. Sunset River is a restful inner tube ride inviting you to float along a continuous river that encircles a good portion of the park. Take your Big Kahuna, Gidget, and rest of the family for an exciting raft adventure down the Coronado Express slide.

Knott's Soak City also features a softball field, sand volleyball courts, a game arcade area, lockers, and showers. If you get hungry, choose from three, full-service eateries, or snack from one of the "stands" scattered throughout the park. No outside food is allowed inside the park. So splish splash, forget about your bath, and come and put your swimming suits on. Hot tip: Wear water shoes, or sandals, as the cement pathways can get hot.

Hours: Open mid-May to the end of May on weekends only 10am - 6pm. Open the month of June daily 10am - 6pm. Open July through Labor Day daily 10am - 8pm. Open weekends in September noon - 8pm.

Admission: $21 for adults; $14.95 for ages 3 - 11; children 2 and under are free. After 3pm, admission is $13.95 for adults; $11.95 for ages 3 - 11. Parking is $5.

Ages: 1 ½ years and up.

LEGOLAND CALIFORNIA ☼
(760) 438-LEGO (5346) / www.legolandca.com $$$$$
1 Lego Drive, Carlsbad
(Exit San Diego Fwy [5] E. on Cannon Rd., R. on Lego Dr. It's next to the flower fields. [TG-1126 J2])

Lego mania reaches an all-time high at the 128-acre Legoland California which features family rides, shows, interactive attractions, areas to build and play with Legos™, and restaurants. (There are two other Legolands, one in Denmark and one in England.) Over thirty *million* Legos create the models used in and around this unique amusement park (and you will get tired of reading the word "Lego" by the end of this entry). The following are some highlights of the six main attraction areas:

The Ridge is situated in the center of the park and helps orient guests. Sit in outward-facing seats and pull yourself up a thirty-foot tower, then experience a controlled "free fall" down. At the base of a tower is a walk-through maze. For another perspective, pedal the Sky Cycle around an elevated circular track.
Village Green has a boat ride through an enchanted forest, past animated classic fairy tale characters and settings. Take a short ride in a Lego jeep through a "jungle" that has ninety animated animals made of Legos. At the Waterworks area turn a handle and aim water spray at objects and pretend animals to bring them to "life." Younger children can happily while away the day at the Duplo playground. It has a maze to crawl through, a train ride, an ambulance and police motorcycle to "drive," and lots more. A magic show and puppet theater round out this area. **Fun Town** offers two driving schools, one for young kids, one for younger kids - no adults allowed. Drive Lego-looking electric cars (not on a track!), complete with a stop signs, traffic lights, turns, and traffic jams. (There is a reason kids this young do not have licenses.) Other attractions in this area include piloting a kid-size helicopter up and down via a joystick; maneuvering a bumper boat around buoys (and other boats); seeing inhabitants of the rain forest, ancient Egypt (look out for the mummy), and the Arctic (Legos and their builders really are amazing); watching a stage show; touring a small-scale Lego factory to see how the bricks are made and packaged; and eating an ice cream at the Cool Cafe where a Lego Robot Band performs. The medieval-themed **Castle Hill** has a roller coaster that takes all-age riders through a castle and into a cave

past a fire-breathing dragon. Kids (only) can also mount a "horse" and take part in a simulated joust. Everyone can have adventures at a multi-level playground that has rope ladders, cargo nets, and slides; pan for "gold" to be exchanged for a Lego medallion; and take a nature walk past models of native animals. **Miniland** re-creates five areas of the U.S. constructed in 1:20 scale. Each area has fourteen to thirty-three animations and some interactivity: *New England Harbor* has farmlands, a traditional harbor and a shipyard, and underwater divers exploring a sunken ship; *Washington, D.C.* is impressive with its Lincoln Memorial, Washington Monument, White House, a presidential motorcade, baseball games, and more capital activities; *New York City* showcases the Manhattan and Brooklyn bridges, Central Park (i.e. joggers, the zoo, etc.), Times Square complete with police cars with lights and sirens, and the Statue of Liberty; *California Coast* combines beaches and mansions in Beverly Hills with cable cars and Ghiradelli Square; and *New Orleans* offers paddle steamers on the river front, plantation houses, Mardi Gras, and the sound of jazz. The mostly hands-on **Imagination Zone** offers both free-play opportunities and structured workshops and contests for all ages. Inspiration is all around, such as a twelve-foot submarine, a Technic T-Rex, and a fifteen-foot Einstein. A learning center here also features computers with Lego software for Mindstorms robots. Tip: If you're interested in taking a class sign up early in the day. The Imagination Zone theater shows a ten-minute movie in which you help choose the outcome via control devices - very cool. Another picturesque part of Legoland is a large lake, where families can take a cruise and see - what else - more Lego animals and characters!!

Hours:	Open most of the year daily 10am - 5pm. Open in the summertime 10am - 9pm.
Admission:	$38 for adults; $32 for seniors and ages 3 - 16; children 2 and under are free. Certain discounts available through AAA. Parking is $7. Two-day passes, to be used within a 5-day period, are $46 for adults; $40 for seniors and ages 3 - 16.
Ages:	Most of the rides and shows are geared for ages 2 - 11, but you are never too old to play with Legos.

THE WAVE

(760) 940-WAVE (9283) / www.wave-waterpark.com
161 Recreation Drive, Vista
(Exit 78 Fwy N. on Vista Village Dr., R. on Recreation Dr. [TG-1087 H6])

　　Catch a wave at The Wave on the Flow Rider wave machine. Swoosh on down the four water slides here - two are enclosed, and two are convertible-style (no tops). Some height restrictions apply. Slip 'n slide down the fifth slide, which is short, slopes gently, and ends into Crazy River, a large ring of water that encircles the slide and lounge area. For those 48" and under, there is also a small, children's water play area with climbing apparatus that has water spouting out and a few slides. The large rectangular pool, usually used for lessons and the swim team, is open to the public during Wave hours. There are a limited number of picnic tables here, as well as a few grassy areas for picnicking or sunbathing. You may bring in your own lounge chairs. Lockers, double inner tubes, and shade pavilions are all available for a small fee. Use of single inner tubes and body boards are included in your admission price. Outside food is not allowed in, but there is a full-service snack bar here that sells food at very reasonable prices. Have big time fun at this small water park!

Hours: Open the end of May through the beginning of June, and the month of September, on weekends and holidays 11am - 5pm. Open the beginning of June through Labor Day daily 10:30am - 5:30pm.

Admission: $9.95 for 42" and taller; $6.95 for 41" and under; children 2 and under are free. Spectators pay the full admission price, but if their wristbands are dry when they leave, they receive a $7 refund.

Ages: 1½ years and up.

ARTS AND CRAFTS

Children have creative urges and need a place to express themselves. Since art classes are offered in a dizzying array and fluctuating times and prices, most of the places listed here are paint-it-yourself ceramic stores, along with a variety of other places, that assist your young artists in developing their talents - move over Monet! Note: Museums are also great resources for arts and crafts workshops.

Bryce

COLOR ME MINE

(877) COLOR ME (265-6763) - for a listing of all locations. Beverly
Hills - (310) 247-1226; Brea - (714) 671-2808; Carmel Mountain Ranch
- (858) 487-5432; Costa Mesa - (949) 515-8612; Encino - (818) 784-
0400; Fashion Valley - (619) 220-8989; Huntington Beach - (714) 960-
3834; Long Beach - (562) 433-4177; Los Angeles - (323) 465-1680;
Mission Viejo - (949) 367-9757; San Diego - (619) 220-8989; Santa
Monica - (310) 393-0069; Studio City - (818) 762-4434; Torrance -
(310) 325-9968; Tustin - (714) 505-3975; Valencia - (661) 284-2927;
and Westlake Village - (818) 707-6903. / www.colormemine.com

Do your kids have an artistic flair? Or think they do? Color Me Mine is a
delightful, cozy, paint-your-own ceramic store. Kids can express themselves by
first choosing their own ceramic piece, and then their own palette. White
dinosaurs, dolphins, mugs, plates, and more will be transformed into vibrant
works of art that will be treasured forever, or at least a while. My boys were so
intent on their artistry that the hours just flew by. Warning: This recreational
activity can become quite addicting! Pieces are glazed and fired, then ready to be
picked up in a day or two. Each store has a computer that has 25,000 drawings to
be printed out and traced.

Some stores also offer wood works and iron works. Note: The Encino and
San Diego stores offer glass works and mosaics.

Hours: Most stores are open Sun. - Thurs., 11am - 10pm; Fri. - Sat.,
11am - 11pm.

Admission: Prices for mugs and vases start at $6. Most stores also charge $6
an hour per painter, plus a fee (usually $3) for glazing.

Ages: 4 years and up.

KID'S ART

(818) 248-2483 - the main number for all the centers.
*Kid's Art is located in the cities of Clairmont, Glendora, La Canada,
Northridge, Pasadena, Tarzana, and Valencia.*

This small, wonderful classroom is a great setting for teaching kids realistic
fine art skills using mediums such as drawing, painting, charcoal, pastel, and
water color. Subject matter covered includes still life, landscape, animals,
cartooning, and more. Each class has one instructor per eight students, so there is
plenty of individualized instruction. The room has an intimate feel with kid-size
easels, and kid-level shelves all around that hold stuffed animals, vases with
flowers, and other objects to inspire your young artist. Week-long summer
workshops are also offered in clay, animation, and more.

Hours: Classes are given after school Tues. - Fri., 3:30pm - 4:30pm, and
on Sat.

Admission: Classes vary in cost. A one-hour class, once a week for four
weeks, costs $64. There is also a $25 first-time registration fee,
plus a drawing course material fee of $10.

Ages: 5 years and up.

BARNSDALL ART PARK / JUNIOR ART CENTER
(213) 485-4474   !/$$$
4814 Hollywood Boulevard, Los Angeles
(Exit Hollywood Fwy [101] E. on Hollywood Blvd., up a driveway to the park and center. [TG-594 A4])

This art park/center is comprised of four facilities: 1) The Jr. Art Center with on-going classes for ages 3 to 17 that range from film making and animation to drawing and pottery; 2) Barnsdall Art Center which offers classes for adults; 3) L.A. Municipal Art Gallery, (213) 485-4581, that has year round exhibitions for adults; and 4) two small children's galleries that feature rotating exhibits, such as art work produced by kids, or by illustrators of children's books.

Another key element is Sunday Open Sunday (yes, this is the real name of it), which is offered thirty-five Sundays a year at various art sites and locations throughout the Los Angeles area. These free, two-hour workshops produce an eclectic array of collages, paintings, cardboard houses, jewelry, masks, and other works of art.

The art park also has the famed Hollyhock House designed by Frank Lloyd Wright. Unlike most house tours, the emphasis is almost entirely on the architecture, not on the few furnishings inside the house.

Hours: Call for class and event information.
Admission: Free to the small galleries and Sunday Open Sunday. Class fees range from $18 - $36.
Ages: 3 years and up.

CERAMIC ART SPACE
(888) CERAMIX / (818) 752-9767 / www.ceramicartspace.com $$$
12532 Riverside Drive, Hollywood
(Going W. on Ventura Fwy [101], exit N. on Laurel Canyon, L. on Riverside Dr. Going E. on 101, exit N. on Coldwater Canyon, R. on Riverside Dr. [TG-562 F3])

This older ceramic store is one of our favorite places to paint ceramic and plastercraft pieces because of the selection and the price. (i.e. The place is packed with inventory and there is no hourly fee.) Choose from ornaments, plates, mugs, banks, figurines, and lots more. Sit at a table and use the paints, brushes, smocks, etc. for your take-home masterpiece. Products range from clay, greenware, bisque, and plaster to kiln supplies, glazes, ceramic pens, and ceramic crayons. Note: The store sells prepackaged kits so kids can take an item home. It also sells paints, brushes, and everything else needed to complete their project. Buy a kit for a friend, too and share the messy fun!

Hours: Open Tues. - Sun., 10:30am - 5pm.
Admission: Items range from $3 up to $90. There is no hourly fee.
Ages: 4 years and up.

CLAY BISQUE
(310) 316-5669 / www.claybisque.ohgolly.com/sys-home.asp $$$$
1704 S. Catalina Avenue, Redondo Beach

(Exit Harbor Fwy [110] W. on Pacific Coast Hwy., L. on Ave I (second L. after Palos Verdes Blvd.), L. on Catalina. [TG-792 J1])

This airy, paint-it-yourself ceramic art studio is located on a main shopping strip, not far from the beach. The small intimate setting, coupled with brightly colored walls and high and low tables (for kids) adds up to a friendly atmosphere. The selection of ceramic items ranges from cups, plates, and picture frames to knick knacks, tiles, vases, and everything in between. Included in the per-hour price are unlimited paints, glaze, brushes, sponges, stencils, and assistance. After glazing, your piece will be ready in about three days for pick up.

Hours: Open Mon. - Wed., 10am - 7pm; Thurs. - Sat., 10am - 9pm; Sun., noon - 5pm.

Admission: The price of your item plus $5.50 per hour for adults, pro-rated every 15 minutes after the first hour; $4 per hour for children 10 and under. Ask about special rates on certain dates and hours. Metered street parking is available.

Ages: 4 years and up.

CLAY CLUB

(310) 202-0888 / www.clayclub.com
10522 Pico Boulevard, Los Angeles
(Exit Santa Monica Fwy [10] N. on Overland, R. on Pico. [TG-632 D5])

Figurines, frames, mugs, and vases are just some of the items to choose from in painting your own ceramic masterpiece. Be prepared to spend some time here - it takes kids (and adults) time to choose what they want to paint and then to actually paint it. But what a fun time to share together!

Hours: Open Mon. - Fri., 11am - 6pm; Sat., noon - 6pm.

Admission: The cost of the item, plus a flat fee of $7 for adults; $5 for ages 12 and under.

Ages: 4 years and up.

KAR-LAN'S KRAFTS

(661) 251-7924
17743 Sierra Highway, Canyon Country
(Exit Golden State Fwy [5] N. on Antelope Valley Fwy [14], N. on Via Princessa, R. on Sierra Hwy. [TG-4552 A1])

Kids kan kultivate their kreativity at Kar-Lan's Krafts. Both plastercraft and ceramics are available to paint and glaze at this roomy and well-lit krafts store. Please note that plastercraft items are more fragile than ceramic pieces, but they are also less expensive. This is a wonderful way to spend an hour or so together!

Hours: Open Tues., 10am - 5:30pm; Wed. - Thurs., 10:30am - 9pm; Fri. - Sat., 11am - 5pm.

Admission: Prices start at $2 for a piece of unfinished art, plus $5 a day for paint and brushes. Firing costs extra, depending on the size of the piece.

Ages: 4 years and up.

OUR WAY CERAMIC
(562) 690-7306
2351 W. Whittier Boulevard, La Habra
(Exit Riverside Fwy [91] N. on Beach Blvd., which dead-ends on Whittier after about 5 miles. Go L. and into the second driveway. [TG-708 B4])

Is there a special gift-giving holiday coming up? This is the place to create that one-of-a-kind present. Choose a ready-to-paint ceramic piece, created on the premises, and enjoy the artistic endeavors that flow out of your paint brush, or just look around at finished products for inspiration. A definite plus to this ceramic place - there is no hourly painting fee! The cost of the item includes paints, brushes, and other necessary materials. This store also carries raw clay and other crafting supplies.

Hours: Open Mon., Wed., Fri., 10am - 5pm; Tues. and Thurs., 10am - 9pm; Sat., 10am - 3pm.
Admission: The cost of your item.
Ages: 4 years and up.

SANTA MONICA MUDD
(310) 315-9155 / www.smmudd.com
2918 Santa Monica Boulevard, Suite 2, Santa Monica
(Exit San Diego Fwy [405] W. on Santa Monica Blvd. [TG-631 H6])

Make mirror frames, masks, sculptures, mugs, plates, and more out of clay, then paint it, and have it fired. Walk ins are welcome, but taking a series of classes, based on a once-a-week, four-week program is highly recommended as most projects take more than just a day to create and finish. Fees include materials, including paints, plus instruction and the usage of the pottery wheel, if desired. After-school programs are available.

Hours: Kid's classes are offered Mon, Tues., and Thurs., 3:30pm - 4:45pm and Mon. - Tues., 5pm - 6:15pm. Call for hours and for a schedule of classes.
Admission: $30 per class.
Ages: Children must be at least 8 years old.

SWIRLRAMICS
(562) 425-3553 / www.esitemakers.com/swirlramics/swirlramics.html
4154 Norse Way, Long Beach
(Exit Artesia Fwy [91] S. on Lakewood Blvd., L. on Norse Way. [TG-766 A6])

Swirls, twirls, stripes, or dots - at Swirlramics you can paint your own ceramic piece any way you want. Although the store is intimate (i.e. small), the prices are reasonable and the selection is terrific. We perused dragon cups, sunflower picture frames, car banks, a wide variety of figurines, bowls, and lots more. If your time (and/or money) is tight, a shelf contains small ceramic items that can be purchased and painted relatively quickly for only $5, inclusive. Tip: Ask about monthly specials or sale items.

Need direction on decorating your item? Stencils and carbon paper are some of the available artistic aids. Because there is a flat rate charged to paint - brushes, a colorful array of paints, and glazing are included in the price - you can stay for hours and not feel rushed!

Hours: Open Tues - Thurs., 12:30pm - 8pm, Fri., noon - 9pm; Sat., 11am -9pm.

Admission: The price of the item plus $8 per painter. Ask about weekday specials.

Ages: 4 years and up.

A PERSONAL TOUCH

(714) 693-8777

5655 E. La Palma Avenue, Suite 125, Anaheim

(Exit Riverside Fwy [91] N. on Imperial Hwy, L. on La Palma Ave. [TG-770 E1])

$$$$

Come to this inviting store to make a keepsake designed with a personal touch. There are several ceramic pieces to choose from such as animal figurines, plates, trinket boxes, sports balls (e.g. baseballs, footballs, etc.), mugs, and oven tiles for hand or footprints. Paints, brushes, and studio time are all included in the hourly fee. Having trouble deciding on how to paint your item? Look around at the finished products for ideas. Kids love expressing themselves in the creative fashion that A Personal Touch encourages, and it is so much better than watching TV!

Hours: Open Mon., 3pm - 6pm; Tues., noon - 6pm; Wed., 4pm - 9pm; Thurs. - Sat., 11am - 9pm; Sun., noon - 5pm. Open longer hours in the summer.

Admission: The price of your ceramic item, plus a flat fee of $7 for adults; $4 for children 12 and under. Glazing and firing cost between $2 to $5, depending on the size of the piece.

Ages: 4 years and up.

ARTMAKER

(562) 596-8896

12371 Seal Beach Boulevard, Seal Beach

(Exit San Diego Fwy [405] N. on Seal Beach Blvd. It's in Rossmoor Shopping Center. [TG-796 J5])

$$

Are your kids crafty? I mean that question in the artistic sense. Whether your answer is "yes" or "no," they will thoroughly enjoy their visit to the Artmaker. Each arts and crafts session features a special project or two, with only general instructions given so that imaginations have free reign. Recycled and everyday materials such as newspaper, egg cartons, glitter, glue, ribbons, buttons, paints, and milk jugs, become party hats, bird feeders, banners, and other fun products. A snack is provided for your starving artists, and a bubble machine is turned on to entertain those who are done early. (Did you know that if you wet your hands, you can catch and hold a bubble?)

The Artmaker is decorated with children's creations, lending inspiration to your artists. Parents, you can assist your younger kids, or just relax as staff is on hand to help out. As an added bonus, when your child is done crafting, you can just leave without having to clean up the inevitable mess! The Artmaker has become a favorite place for my kids to come and create. Tip: This is a great place for a birthday party!

Hours: Classes are offered at varying times throughout the week, including mornings for Mommy/Daddy and Me, after school for older children, and every Sat. for drop-ins from 1pm - 2pm. Call for a schedule, and for adult class information, too.

Admission: One-hour classes are $8 per artist. Other classes start at $10 per artist.

Ages: 2 years and up, depending on the class.

CLAYNATION ☼
(949) 673-5969 $$$$
2919 E. Coast Highway, Corona Del Mar
(Take the San Diego Fwy [405] or the Costa Mesa Fwy [55] to the Corona Del Mar Fwy [73], which turns into MacArthur Blvd. Exit MacArthur Blvd. S. on E. Coast Hwy. [TG-919 F2])

Bowls, mugs, figurines, jewelry boxes, and frames are just a few of the ceramic pieces available to paint here. Pick out an item, and with paints and stencils galore to use, let your creative side take over, or at least have fun making something you can take home. This is a great indoor activity for kids (and adults) who will treasure what they've made.

Hours: Open Mon., 3pm - 9pm; Wed - Sat., noon - 7pm; Sun., noon - 6pm. Closed Tues.

Admission: Items cost between $2 - $40, plus $8 per hour per painter. The clock doesn't start ticking until you actually start painting. Glazing and firing cost between $1 - $5, depending on the size of your item.

Ages: 4 years and up.

IRVINE FINE ART CENTER ☼
(949) 724-6880 !/$$
14321 Yale Avenue, Irvine
(Exit Santa Ana Fwy [5] S. on Culver, L. on Walnut, L. on Yale. It's in HERITAGE PARK. [TG-860 G2])

Irvine Fine Art Center is host to various monthly exhibits of art work and photography by students, and/or by local artists. The Center also offers special programs and holds numerous art classes such as watercolor, drawing, calligraphy, and cartooning. Two of the on-going classes are listed below:

The **Children's Open Studio** is an after-school, drop-in program for elementary-aged kids. This semi-structured class provides a great opportunity for kids to be creative using a variety of materials such as clay, papier-mache, paints, and more. It is also a wonderful environment for making new friends. Supervision, materials, and fun are all provided.

The **Teen Open Studio** is an open-ended ceramics class for high schoolers. An instructor is available for assistance. All materials are provided. (Also look up HERITAGE PARK [Irvine], under the Great Outdoors section, for an adjacent attraction.)

Hours: Tour the Center, Mon. - Thurs., 9am - 9pm; Fri., 9am - 5pm; Sat., 9am - 3pm; Sun., 1pm - 5pm. Children's Studio is offered Mon. - Fri., 3pm - 5:30pm. Teen Studio is offered Tues. and Thurs., 4pm - 6pm. (Days are subject to change.)

Admission: The Center is free. Children's Studio is $9 per child, per visit, or purchase a multiple-day pass and save money. Teen Studio is $5 per visit.

Ages: 6 - 11 years for Children's Open Studio; 13 - 18 years for Teen Open Studio.

CALIFORNIA CERAMIC
(909) 784-0670
5686 Mission Boulevard, Riverside
(Exit Pomona Fwy [60] S. on Rubidoux Blvd., R. on Mission [TG-685 D2])

This small studio offers a colorful array of ceramic and greenware pieces, and a variety of ways to enjoy painting them. Come in for a two-hour "workshop" (i.e. pick a piece and paint it), sign up for a specialty class, or make this a regular stop during the month for a special price. Note: Birthday parties are a great deal - $10 per person, minimum ten people, which includes an item from a selected group of pieces, plus all the paints, brushes, and other supplies needed.

Hours: Open Mon. - Fri., 9am - 5pm; Sat., 10am - 5pm.

Admission: The workshop price is the price of an item, which also includes the paints, brushes, and glaze.

Ages: 4 years and up.

CLAY & MORE
(909) 600-8474
25100 Hancock Avenue #106, Murrieta
(From Temecula Fwy [15], exit N.E. on Murrieta Hot Springs Rd., L. on Hancock. From Escondido Fwy [215], exit W. on Los Alamos Rd., L. on Hancock. It's near Chuck E. Cheese. [TG-928 D4])

Choices, choices. Customers may paint their ceramic piece, using a myriad of colors, and/or actually make their own clay product, such as wind chimes or a pot, and then paint and glaze it. Clay & More offers clay and mosaic-making classes for both kids and adults. The studio fee covers paints, brushes, materials, and time spent here.

Hours: Open Tues. - Thurs., 11am - 8pm; Fri. - Sat., 11am - 9pm; Sun., 11am - 5pm. Closed Mon.

Admission: Price of the item or class, plus a $6 studio fee for adults; $5 for ages 11 and under.

Ages: 4 years and up.

KIDS PAINT PALACE
(909) 699-4941
27540 Ynez Road, Suite J11, Temecula
(Exit Temecula Valley Fwy [15] E. on Rancho California Rd., just past Ynez Rd. It's located near Target. [TG-958 H6])

As the title suggests, this place is for kids. Parents may paint if they promise to behave themselves. Try your hand at painting your own plaster or ceramic work of art at the seven or so tables set up with supplies. The palace is stocked with a wide variety of items to choose from and all the paints, brushes, and even paint aprons are provided. This store/workshop offers two advantages over other places that offer similar services: You pay only one price, so there are no additional per hour charges, and you can take your finished product home as soon as you're finished as an acrylic spray is used, not a fire and glaze method.

Hours: Open Mon. - Sat., 10:30am - 6pm.

Admission: Prices generally range from $5 - $15 per item. There is no hourly charge.

Ages: 2 years and up.

PAINTED EARTH

(909) 676-2447

27493 Ynez Road, Temecula

(Exit Temecula Valley Fwy [15] E. on Rancho California Rd., L. on Ynez Rd. [TG-958 H6])

Paint your own ceramic masterpiece at Painted Earth. Choose from decorative figurines to microwavable plates and mugs. All the paints, brushes, and glazes are included in the studio fee, so feel free to express yourself and enjoy a lasting, hand-crafted treasure.

Hours: Open Mon., Tues., Thurs., 11am - 8pm; Wed., 11am - 8pm; Fri. - Sat., 11am - 10pm; Sun., 11am - 6pm.

Admission: The price of the item - for example $4 for figurines, $10 a bowl or coffee mug, or $12 a dish - and a $6 all-day studio fee.

Ages: 4 years and up.

BAUBLES ETC.

(619) 448-2422 / sandiego.citysearch.com/E/V/SANCA/0007/84/65/

1363 N. Cuyamaca, El Cajon

(Exit San Vincente Fwy [67] W. on Fletcher Pkwy / Broadway, R. on N. Cuyamaca. [TG-1251 D3])

This small, storefront ceramic studio has a good selection of ceramic, greenware, and bisque. Besides the normal fun of painting your own ceramic piece, children's classes are offered that include firing and casting demos. Come here to make something more special than just a bauble.

Hours: Open Mon. - Fri., 10am - 5pm (Tues. until 6pm); Sat., 9am - 2pm

Admission: The price of the item, plus $5 studio time for the first hour, $2.50 for each hour after that. Studio time prices include paints, brushes, stencils, and other materials.

Ages: 4 years and up.

CERAMICAFE (Del Mar)

(858) 259-9958

12921 El Camino Real, Del Mar

(Exit San Diego Fwy [5] E. on Del Mar Heights, R. on El Camino Real and into Del Mar Heights Town Center. Ceramicafe is toward the N. end. [TG-1188 A6])

This well-lit, paint-your-own ceramics store has a great array of objects to choose from. We painted dragon figurines, deep mugs, a vase, and a heart-shaped tile. (We were busy!) I used the stencils and stamps, while my boys free-formed it. All the artistic aids, paints, and brushes are included in the price. Finished masterpieces are ready for pick up in about three days. Ceramicafe also offers after-school activities where kids can learn painting techniques, creating with clay, mosaics, and more.

Hours: Open daily 10am -10pm.
Admission: There is no per-hour studio fee. Mugs range from $15 - $18, bud vases are $15, 4 x 4 tiles are 4 for $20, etc.
Ages: 4 years and up.

CERAMICAFE (La Mesa)
(619) 466-4800
5500 Grossmont Center Drive, La Mesa
(Exit 8 Fwy N. on Jackson Dr., R. on Fletcher Pkwy, R. on Grossmont Center Dr. It's in a shopping center. [TG-1271 A1])
See CERAMICAFE (Del Mar), for details.

CLAY 'N LATTE
Chula Vista - (619) 482-4458; Encinitas - (760) 633-2254;
La Mesa - (619) 462-8719; San Deigo - (858) 487-9293
Chula Vista - 945 Otay Lakes Rd.; Encinitas - 162 S. Rancho Santa Fe Rd.; La Mesa - 5636 Lake Murray Blvd.; San Diego - 10175 Rancho Carmel Dr.

A ceramic piece, some paint, and a little latte from a machine (at least at some of the locations!) goes a long way in making a ceramic masterpiece to take home. Choose from a wide selection of items, such as plates, bowls, flower pots, goblets, salt and pepper shakers, animal figurines, and more. Kids will have a field day picking out colors and thinking of ways to design their chosen piece. Warning: This recreational activity can become habit forming! Paints, paintbrushes, and stencils are all provided - you simply provide the artistic creativity (and the money).

Hours: Most stores are open Mon. - Fri., 10am - 9pm; Sat., noon - 9pm; (Sat. 9am - noon for adults only); Sun., 1pm - 5pm.
Admission: Price of item, plus an $8 studio fee for adults, $6 for children 11 and under. Ask about specials.
Ages: 4 years and up

CAROUSEL CERAMICS
(818) 879-8292
31149 Via Colinas, Suite 604, Thousand Oaks
(Exit Ventura Fwy [101] N. on Lindero, L. on Via Colinas. It's in an industrial park, on a corner curve, next to Grason's art supply store. [TG-557 E4])
This workshop studio stocks the largest quantity of bisque, greenware, and plaster pieces I've ever seen. Two rooms are fully stocked with statues, figurines, picture frames, bowls, mugs, vases, dinner sets, and more. Long tables are completely set up for you to design and paint your piece. There are many finished samples at the studio that lend inspiration. Carousel, however, is not

your typical paint-a-piece-in-one-session place. It is primarily a teaching studio where instructors give formal classes for groups or individuals. Just a few of the several classes offered throughout the year include acrylic painting on glass and painting wisteria or dogwood flowers on greenware. One-on-one tutoring is available for brush strokes, handmade flowers, airbrushing, drybrushing, glazing, and more. With such a variety of items to choose from, and all of this assistance being offered, even I could produce a work of art here! Come create a special gift, or make coming here a hobby and start your own heirloom collection.

Hours: Open Mon., Thurs., Fri., and Sat., 9am - 6pm; Tues., 10am - 9pm. (Closed Wed. and Sun.)

Admission: The cost of your piece, plus the brushes, paints, and other supplies you purchase. The owner will work out a price for those who want to use the store's supplies. Or, pay a yearly fee of $25 and paint without any hourly fee.

Ages: 5 years and up.

PAINT PALS CLUBHOUSE

(805) 581-4676

1716 Erringer Road, #106, Simi Valley

(Exit Simi Valley - San Fernando Valley Fwy [118] S. on Erringer Rd. It's on the N.E. corner of Heywood St. and Erringer. [TG-498 A3])

Clubhouses weren't this much fun when I was a kid! The colorfully decorated Paint Pals Clubhouse offers paint-your-own bisque, and a whole lot more. One section has shelves of items to paint, plus long tables and all the paint, brushes, smocks, and other materials needed. Popular items include sunflowers, pigs, jars with ceramic lids, magnets, and picture frames. Creating a masterpiece is a terrific activity. But, while moms (this one, anyway) sometimes take longer to do a project than kids do, there are plenty of other things here to keep the younger set busy. Karaoke is a popular option, and whether or not children can actually sing on key seems to be irrelevant. Next to the stage are costumes for dressing up. Toward the back of the store, and through a short tunnel of mirrors, is a small black light maze that my boys enjoyed going through. Kids can also play with soft foam blocks, make "pictures" in a shadow room, try to solve metal shape puzzles, and blow giant bubbles.

Hours: Open during the school year Tues. - Thurs. and Sun.,10am - 6pm; Fri. - Sat., 10am - 8pm. Closed Mon., except holiday Mon. Open in the summer on Mon., 10am - 6pm, in addition to its other days and hours.

Admission: $1 per child (toddlers, too) entrance fee; free to adults. Items cost from $2.50 on up, which includes use of the paints and other supplies. Karaoke is 50¢ for one song; $1 for 3 songs.

Ages: 3 years and up.

BEACHES

Beaches are a "shore" bet for a day of fun in the sun. Along with sand and water play, in-line skating, and/or biking, some beaches have playgrounds, picnic tables, and waveless waters that make them particularly younger-kid friendly. This section includes just a few suggestions of where to go beaching.

Tip: If you and your family are Orange County beach bunnies, consider purchasing a parking pass for $50. The pass price is $30 for seniors. An annual pass for the beach, all Orange County Regional Parks, and a Wilderness pass is $75 per car, $60 for seniors. For more information, call the South Coastal Operations at (949) 661-7013 / www.oc.ca.gov/hbp.

CABRILLO BEACH   ☼
(310) 548-2645 / www.sanpedro.com $$
3720 Stephen M White Drive, San Pedro
(Take Harbor Fwy [110] to the end, L. on Gaffey St., L. on 9ᵗʰ St., R. on Pacific Ave., almost to the
end, L. on 36ᵗʰ St., which turns into Stephen M White Dr. [TG-854 C2])
    This sometimes windy beach has a gated entrance, wonderful sandy
stretches, a playground, rock jetties to climb out on, and several fire rings. The
water quality is not always the best, however. Ask about the seasonal grunion
runs. A paved, wheelchair-accessible trail runs from the parking lot to the
aquarium, across the beach, and to the water's edge at the tidepools. See
CABRILLO MARINE AQUARIUM, under the Zoos and Animals section, as
this terrific museum is adjacent to the beach (and it's free!).
    Hours: Open daily sunrise to 10:30pm
    Admission: $6.50 per vehicle in the summer; the rest of the year, Mon. - Fri.,
            $4.50; Sat.- Sun., $5.50. Very little street parking is available.
    Ages: All

COLORADO LAGOON   ☼
(562) 570-3215 / www.ci.long-beach.ca.us   !
E. Colorado Street & E. Appian Way, Long Beach
(Exit San Diego Fwy [405] S. on Bellflower Blvd., R. on Colorado Blvd. As the road forks, keep
along the lagoon on Appian Wy. [TG-796 B7])
    This half-mile stretch of lagoon water is fed through a large pipe from the
ocean. The water quality is tested daily and usually deemed good, except after
rain. Kids can swim the length of the lagoon or a much shorter distance across it,
from shore to shore. They can also jump off a wooden dock that spans across the
water. Just beyond the sandy beach area is a grassy area. A playground,
featuring a large plastic boat, is shaded by a canopy. A few scattered picnic
tables, shade trees, and barbecue pits make this an ideal location for a picnic.
    Although the lagoon has residential quarters and a fairly busy street on one
side of it and a golf course on the other, we found it to be a relatively quiet place
to spend the day. Lifeguards are on duty daily mid-June through mid-September.
See the Calendar Section, under June, for information on the Colorado Lagoon
Model Boat Shop for a first-rate, boat-building opportunity.
    Hours: Open daily sunrise to sunset.
    Admission: Free
    Ages: All

LEO CARRILLO STATE BEACH   ☼
(805) 986-8591 - state beach; (818) 880-0350 - camping info; (800) 444- $
7275 - camping reservations. / parks.ca.gov
36000 Pacific Coast Highway, Malibu
(Exit Ventura Fwy [101] S. on Westlake Blvd. [Hwy 23], which turns into Mulholland Hwy., which
turns into Decker Rd. Go to the end, and turn R. on Pacific Coast Hwy. [TG-626 B6])
    Leo Carrillo combines the best of everything that's enjoyable about the
beach - a beautiful, sandy beach; good swimming and surfing; sea caves to
carefully explore; tidepools; a playground; lifeguards; and nature trails. Camping

near the beach (campsites are a five minute walk from the beach) makes this one of our favorite campgrounds. Each campsite has a fire pit and picnic table. Pack a sweater!

Hours: Open daily 7am - dusk.
Admission: $3 per vehicle for day use. Camping is $12 a night; there are no hook-ups. Each campsite can have up to 8 people and 2 vehicles.
Ages: All

MARINA BEACH or "MOTHER'S BEACH"

(562) 570-3215 / www.ci.long-beach.ca.us
5839 Appian Way, Long Beach
(Take San Gabriel River Fwy [605] to Garden Grove Fwy [22] W., exit on Studebaker and eventually head S., R. on Westminster, R. on Appian Way, which is just over a bridge. It's across from the Long Beach Marina. [TG-826 D2])

This beach is aptly nicknamed because it is a mother/child hang out. There are waveless waters in this lagoon-type setting, lifeguards, a nice grassy playground, and barbecues. Single and double kayak rentals are available daily during the summer, and weekends only the rest of the year.

Hours: Open daily sunrise to 10:30pm.
Admission: Bring either lots of quarters for parking - 25¢ for each half hour - or get here early to park on the street for free. Kayak rentals are $5 an hour for a single; $15 an hour for a double.
Ages: All

MOTHER'S BEACH

(310) 306-3344 / beaches.co.la.ca.us
4142 Via Marina/Washington, Marina Del Rey
(Exit the San Diego Fwy [405] W. on Washington, L. on Via Marina. It's in back of the Cheesecake Factory. [TG-671 J7])

This tiny patch of waveless water where younger children can swim is adjacent to a large marina. A half circle of sand has play equipment, such as a big play boat, several swings, a tire swing, and slides. There are numerous picnic tables set up under a covered area right on the beach, near volleyball nets. It's pleasant scenery. Tip: A visit to the adjoining Cheesecake Factory makes it an extra fun (and tasty) excursion.

Hours: Open daily sunrise to sunset.
Admission: Free. Parking is about $3.
Ages: Toddler to 8 years old.

ROYAL PALMS STATE BEACH

www.sanpedro.com
Western Avenue and Paseo Del Mar, San Pedro
(Take Harbor Fwy [110] to the end, continue S. on Gaffey St., R. on 25th St., L. on Western to the end. [TG-853 G1])

Park on the top of the bluff or drive down to the "beach". I put this word in quotes because there is precious little sand here, as the shoreline is composed of tons of rocks. Numerous tidepools are just beyond the parking lots, so you'll have a great day of exploring and searching for small marine organisms. My boys, of course, also loved climbing out on the rocks and the jetty. Note: A lifeguard is on duty here, too. Tip: Come during low tide. We've also come during high tide, though, and watched the waves slam into the rocks, and shoot high into the sky. Bring your camera!

One side of the beach has a cement patio with picnic tables (and restrooms) under the palm trees (hence the name of the park) that are snug up against the cliffs - very picturesque.

Hours: Open daily sunrise to sunset.
Admission: Free, although a toll booth is located here, too.
Ages: 4 years and up.

SEASIDE LAGOON

(310) 318-0681 / www.redondo.org
200 Portofino Way, Redondo Beach
(Exit San Diego Fwy [405] S. on Western, R. on 190th St., which turns into Anita St., which then turns into Herondo St., L. on Harbor Dr. It's on the S.W. Corner of Harbor Dr. and Portofino Way. Park in the lot on Harbor Blvd. [TG-762 H4])

Have a swimmingly good time at the gated, Seaside Lagoon. This large saltwater lagoon, next to an ocean inlet and rock jetties, is heated by a nearby steam generating plant, so the average water temperature is seventy-five degrees. Warm waveless waters, plus a lifeguard, make it an ideal swimming spot for little ones. A large water fountain sprays out water in the shallow end of the lagoon and there are a few slides in the deeper end. There is also a beach area, grass areas that ring the sand, playgrounds with a big plastic pirate ship and swings, barbecues, picnic tables, and volleyball courts. Tip: Bring your own beach chair. An easily accessible snack bar is sponsored by Ruby's and several other restaurants are in the immediate vicinity.

Hours: Open daily Memorial Day through Labor Day 10am - 5:45pm.
             Open in September on weekends only 10am - 5:45pm.
Admission: $3.50 for adults; $2.50 for ages 2 - 17; children under 2 are free.
             Parking is $2 an hour, although the first 20 minutes are free. If
             you eat at Ruby's you receive the first 2 hours of parking free
             with a validation.
Ages: All

VENICE BEACH

www.laparks.org
1800 Ocean Front Walk, between Washington Boulevard and Rose Avenue,
Venice
(Exit San Diego Fwy [405] W. on Venice Blvd. Park at the end of Venice or Washington Blvds., or in lots along Speedway. [TG-671 G6])

I think Southern California's reputation of being offbeat, quirky, funky, etc., comes directly from Venice Beach. This area actually has a three-mile stretch of beach, but visitors come here mainly to gawk at and mingle with the eclectic Venice population of street performers including jugglers (one juggler specializes in chain saws), musicians, artists, magicians, mimes, and fortune tellers, as well as people sporting unusual haircuts and colors, numerous tattoos, bikini-clad women (and men), skaters, and more - self expression reigns. Two hot spots here are Muscle Beach, where weight lifters of all levels pump iron, and the International Chess Park. This park, south of Santa Monica pier and north of Venice pier, has rows of picnic tables where players run the gamut of older, scruffy-looking men to teens in street clothing. Watch and learn strategies as players compete in traditional play or speed chess. Venice Beach also has a bike path, playground, basketball courts, handball courts, shuffleboard, souvenir shops, a boardwalk, and restaurants.

Hours: Open daily sunrise to sunset.
Admission: Free, although parking may cost.
Ages: All

ZUMA BEACH

beaches.co.la.ca.us
30050 Pacific Coast Highway, Malibu
(Exit the Ventura Fwy [101] S. on Kanan Rd., which turns in to Kanan Dume Rd. Take this to the end and turn R on P.C.H. [TG-667 C3])

This is one of the busiest and biggest beaches in Southern California. Besides the miles of sand, good swimming, lifeguard stations, and ample parking, these ocean waters are often home to schools of dolphins that ride the waves.

Hours: Open daily sunrise to sunset.
Admission: $5 per vehicle.
Ages: All

ALISO BEACH

(949) 661-7013 / www.ocparks.com
31131 Pacific Coast Highway, Laguna Beach
(Exit San Diego Fwy [5] S. on Laguna Fwy, which turns into Laguna Cyn., L. on Pacific Coast Highway. Or, exit San Diego Fwy [5], S. on Crown Valley Pkwy., R. on P.C.H. [TG-951 B7])

This beautiful, cove-like beach has a small playground, plus barbecues, and picnic tables.

Hours: Open daily 7am - 10pm.
Admission: Metered parking is 75¢ an hour (or a parking pass).
Ages: All

BOLSA CHICA STATE BEACH

(714) 846-3460 / parks.ca.gov
Pacific Coast Highway, Huntington Beach
(Exit Garden Grove Fwy [22] S. on Bolsa Chica Rd., R. on Warner Ave., L. on Pacific Coast Highway. Going N. on San Diego Fwy [405], exit E. on Warner Ave., L. on P.C.H. [TG-857 C3])

There are six miles of beach here that are ideal for families because of the picnic areas (campfires are allowed), outdoor showers, five snack bars, and beach rentals. Year-round camping in self-contained vehicles is allowed, but there are no hook ups. No tent camping is permitted.

Hours: Open daily 6am - 9pm.

Admission: $3 per vehicle. Camping is $18 a night.
Ages: All

CORONA DEL MAR STATE BEACH and TIDEPOOL ☼ TOURS

(949) 644-3044 / parks.ca.gov

On Poppy Avenue and Ocean Avenue, Corona Del Mar

(Take the San Diego Fwy [405] or the Costa Mesa Fwy [55] to the Corona Del Mar Fwy [73], which turns into MacArthur Blvd., S. on E. Coast Highway, R. on Poppy Ave. [TG-919 E3])

Come for a few hours of some of the best tidepool exploration in Southern California, then spend the rest of the day playing at the adjacent beach. Tidepools are a rich natural resource and a fascinating way for kids to learn about marine life. You are welcome to investigate the tidepools on your own, or sign up for a guided tour. After giving a short lecture, tour guides are helpful in pointing out interesting animal and plant life.

Just a short drive away, off Ocean Boulevard, is the big beach of Corona Del Mar. Besides sand and water, Big Corona provides fire rings, picnic tables, volleyball courts, and a snack bar.

Hours: Open daily sunrise to sunset. Tidepool tours are given by reservations only.
Admission: $3 per vehicle for day use. Tours are $25 per group, up to thirty people, which includes parking fees.
Ages: 3 years and up.

CRYSTAL COVE STATE PARK BEACH

(949) 494-3539 / parks.ca.gov

E. Coast Highway, between Laguna Beach and Newport Beach, Laguna Beach

See CRYSTAL COVE STATE PARK, under the Great Outdoors section, for details.

DANA COVE PARK, "BABY BEACH", and TIDEPOOLS ☼

www.danapoint.org

Dana Point Harbor Drive, Dana Point

(Exit San Diego Fwy [5] N. on Pacific Coast Highway, L. on Street of the Green Lantern, L. on Cove Rd. It's at the intersection of Cove Rd. and Dana Point Harbor Dr. [TG-971 G7])

The protected harbor of "Baby Beach" (called so because of its waveless waters) offers picnic tables on the bluffs, plus barbecues, free parking, showers, and lifeguards. A good tidepool area is just around the "corner". See DANA POINT HARBOR under the Piers and Seaports section for more details about the surrounding area.

Hours: Open daily sunrise to sunset.
Admission: Free
Ages: All

DOHENY STATE BEACH PARK   ☼

(949) 496-6172 / www.dohenystatebeach.org $

25300 Dana Point Harbor Drive, Dana Point

(Exit San Diego Fwy [5] N. on Pacific Coast Highway, L. on Doheny State Beach Pkwy. [TG-972 A6])

Doheny State Beach Park is big and absolutely gorgeous. The park is divided into three parts. The northern area, also accessible by metered parking off Puerto Place, is for day use. It is five acres of grassy, landscaped picnic area, with barbecue grills and fire rings along the beach. The rocky area is ideal for tidepool exploration during low tide. Since DANA POINT HARBOR (see the Piers and Seaports section) is right next door, this is also a perfect spot to watch the boats sail in and out.

The central section, south of the San Juan Creek, is a campground with 121 sites. Farther south is another day use area with fire rings, beach volleyball, and showers. Throughout the entire stretch of the park there are sandy beaches and beckoning ocean waves!

A small Interpretative Center is to your left as you go through the entrance gates. It contains a simulated tidepool (not a touch tank), with sea stars and leopard sharks. The mural-covered wall has wood shells that pose questions such as, "Do all sharks kill?" Lift the shell tab for the answer. There are also a few tanks of fish, plus taxidermied animals, fossils, and skeletons of a fox, raptor, and whale.

Hours: The park is open daily 6am - 8pm. Summer hours are daily 6am - 10pm. The Interpretative Center is open daily 10am - 4pm.

Admission: $3 per vehicle for day use. Admission to the Interpretative Center is free. Camping prices are $12 a night.

Ages: All

MAIN BEACH / HEISLER PARK   ☼

(949) 497-0716 $

Cliff Drive & Myrtle Street, Laguna Beach

(Exit San Diego Fwy [5] S. on Laguna Canyon Rd. [133], to the end. Turn R. on P.C.H. [1] for Main Beach. Heisler Park is just N. of the beach. [TG-950 F3/G3])

I mention this park and beach together because they are on either side of Highway 133. Both are incredibly popular (i.e. crowded) and noted for their unparalleled views of the ocean. The water is clear, and the horizon seems to go on forever.

Some activities available at Heisler Park are lawn bowling, shuffleboard, and biking or skating on the paved paths. Main Beach offers a grass play area along with basketball courts, volleyball courts, and a small playground. This is a terrific place for beaching it and for swimming. Good luck finding a parking spot, though!

Hours: Both are open daily sunrise to sunset.

Admission: Free. Most parking is metered.

Ages: All

NEWPORT DUNES RESORT MARINA   ☼
(949) 729-3863 / www.newportdunes.com   *$$*

1131 Backbay Drive, Newport Beach   ⛺

(Take Newport Fwy [55] S.W. to the end, which turns into Newport Blvd., L. on W. Coast Hwy., L. on Jamboree Rd., L. on Backbay Dr. Or, from Corona Del Mar Fwy [73], exit S.W. on Jamboree Rd., R. on Backbay Dr. before E. Coast Hwy. [TG-889 D6])

Toddlers to teens will enjoy the enclosed acres of clean beach here, along with a waveless lagoon and a myriad of boating activities. There is a large fiberglass, stationary whale, nicknamed Moe B. Dunes, in the water for kids to swim out to, and one on the beach. The playground equipment includes a pirate ship to climb aboard - ahoy mateys!

Remember the joys of collecting seashells? Newport Dunes is one of the rare beaches around that still has shells. Note: Shellmaker Island and UPPER NEWPORT BAY ECOLOGICAL RESERVE (look under the Great Outdoors section) are adjacent to the resort marina.

If you forget to bring food, have no fear of a growling tummy as a grocery store and cafe are inside the gates, just around the corner from the beach. Two outdoor showers are also available. RESORT WATER SPORTS (see the Transportation section) rentals is located in the park for your kayaking, pedalboat, and windsurfing needs.

Overnight camping is available here and there are plenty of RV hook-ups. Free-standing (i.e. no stakes) tent camping is allowed, too. The surroundings are pretty; activities for campers, such as crafts, ice cream socials, and special movie showings are offered; and the Dunes has a swimming pool, indoor showers, and laundry facilities. What more could you want out of life? This local resort is my kind of "roughing it" vacation!

      Hours: Open daily 8am - 10pm.
Admission: $7 per vehicle for day use. Camping prices start at $32 a night, depending on location and camping equipment.
       Ages: All

SEAL BEACH   ☼
www.ci.seal-beach.ca.us   *!/$*

Main Street, Seal Beach   ⛺

(Exit San Diego Fwy [405] S. on Seal Beach Blvd., R. on Pacific Coast Highway, L. on Main St. [TG-826 E4])

This beach has lifeguards, a pier, great swimming, and a playground. My kids love to gather the crabs crawling along the pier wall and put them in buckets. (We let them go before we go home.) Take a walk on the pier as the coastline view is terrific. No license is required for fishing off the pier and bait is available to purchase. There is also a RUBY'S diner (see the Edible Adventures section) at the end of the pier. Directly across the street from the beach is Main Street, which is lined with unique shops and restaurants.

      Hours: Open daily sunrise to sunset.
Admission: Park along the street or in a nearby lot for free for a few hours, or pay a $5 entrance fee for the day at the parking lot at the beach.
       Ages: All

CORONADO MUNICIPAL BEACH ☼
www.coronadovisitors.com
Ocean Boulevard, Coronado
(Exit San Diego Fwy [5] onto the Coronado Bridge. Continue straight off the bridge as the street turns into 4ᵗʰ St., L. on Orange Ave., R. on Isabella Ave., straight onto Ocean Blvd. [TG-1288 G7])

This beach offers a long stretch of sand, plus a lifeguard station, volleyball courts, a few sand dunes, and a view of Navy vessels who use this waterway. If you walk toward the south, you'll end up in front of the famous Hotel Del Coronado.

Hours: Open daily sunrise to sunset.
Admission: Free
Ages: All

LA JOLLA COVE ☼
www.sandiegocity.org
Coast Boulevard, La Jolla
(Exit San Diego Fwy [5] W. on La Jolla Village Dr., L. on Torrey Pines Rd., R. on Prospect Pl., R. Cave St., stay L. for Coast Blvd. It's just north of Coast Walk Shopping Center. [TG-1227 F6])

In this beautiful seaside city is a wonderful cove, which is a favorite spot for exploring tidepools, and watching or participating in some great surfing, snorkeling, scuba diving, and swimming. The cove is located near the SEAL ROCK MARINE MAMMAL RESERVE, listed under the Zoos and Animals section. Just down the way, past the green lawns, is the La Jolla Underwater Park, which is a haven for divers and snorkelers.

Hours: Open daily.
Admission: Free
Ages: All

LA JOLLA SHORES BEACH ☼ $
www.sandiegocity.org
La Vereda, La Jolla
(Exit San Diego Fwy [5] W. on La Jolla Village Dr., L. on Torrey Pines Rd., R. on Calle De La Plata, L. on Avenida De La Playa, R. on La Vereda. [TG-1227 H4])

This beach comes fully loaded for a full day of fun! The nearly two-mile stretch of beach offers year-round lifeguard service, rest rooms, showers (a parent's essential), and a few playgrounds for the kids, complete with swing sets and climbing apparatus. Enjoy your time at the beach, and maybe even incorporate a drive around picturesque La Jolla with a visit here.

Hours: Open daily
Admission: Free - good luck with parking!
Ages: All

MISSION BAY PARK
www.sandiegocity.org
2581 Quivira Court, San Diego

See MISSION BAY PARK under the Great Outdoors Section for details.

TIDE BEACH PARK   ☼

www.ci.solana-beach.ca.us   !

302 Solana Vista Drive, Solana Beach

(From San Diego Fwy [5], exit W. on Lomas Santa Fe, R. on N. Coast Hwy [101], L. on Solana Vista Dr. to the end. Street park where ever possible. It's right next to Cardiff State Beach. [TG-1167 E6])

This is a beach for tidepool explorers and rock collectors. The beach is accessible by stairs and is part of cliff overhangs that create small caves or nooks and crannies along the shoreline. Don't hang out here during high tide! The tidepools are not the best I've seen for observing marine life, but they are fun nonetheless. We did see lots and lots of limpets, plus muscles, sea anemones, and some small crabs.

Just north of the tidepools is Cardiff State Beach, which we promptly nicknamed "Rocky Beach". There isn't a lot of uncovered sand towards the southern end of the beach, but there are literally tons of multi-colored, round, smooth rocks here. Bathrooms are available and lifeguards are on duty here, too.

> **Hours:** Open daily.
> **Admission:** Free
> **Ages:** 2 years and up.

EDIBLE ADVENTURES

To market, or a restaurant,
  or maybe high tea,
We'll go together,
  my child and me;
Or maybe we'll stop
  for an ice-cream cone,
Or go apple picking,
  and then head for home.

BENIHANA OF TOKYO

Anaheim - (714) 774-4940; Beverly Hills - (323) 655-7311; City of
Industry - (626) 912-8784; Encino - (818) 788-7121; Marina Del Rey -
(310) 821-0888; Newport Beach - (949) 955-0822; Ontario - (909) 483-
0937; San Diego - (619) 298-4666; Torrance - (310) 316-7777 /
www.benihana.com

$$$$

Enjoy the "show" and the food at Benihana. With their choreographed
cooking, the chefs prepare the food on a grill right in front of you, hibachi-style.
Knives flash as the food is chopped up seemingly in mid-air, as well as on the
frying table, with lightning speed - this is the show part. (Don't try this at home.)
Although my kids are not normally prone to trying new foods, they readily taste
new entrees here because the food is fixed in such an intriguing way!

The atmosphere is unique and the food, which ranges from chicken to
seafood to steak and fresh vegetables, is delicious. Sushi is also available. The
communal tables seat up to ten people. Adult lunch prices range from $7.50 to
$14; dinners, from $15 to $30. Kids' meals range from $6 to $7.50 for a choice
of chicken, steak, or shrimp. Their meals also come with soup or salad, shrimp
appetizer, rice, and ice cream. Several Benihana locations have a koi pond and a
traditional Japanese arched bridge as part of their outside decor.

Hours: Most locations are open daily for lunch, 11:30am - 2pm; for
dinner, 5pm - 10:30pm.

Ages: 5 years and up.

BULLWINKLE'S RESTAURANT

Fountain Valley (ironically, though, there are no fountain shows at this
location) - (714) 841-6469; Upland - (909) 946-9555; Vista - (760) 945-
9474

$$$

*Fountain Valley - 16922 Magnolia Avenue; Upland - 1560 W. 7th Street;
Vista - 1525 W. Vista Way*

Fa*moose* Bullwinkle's Restaurants are adjacent to FAMILY FUN
CENTERS (see the Family Pay and Play section) in the city's listed above.
Eating here is always a highlight for my kids. The woodsy-themed, family-
oriented restaurants serve great food at delicious prices. Menu selections include
pizza ($10.45 for a medium-size), ribs ($7.45, and it comes with a biscuit), a
sixteen-piece chicken meal ($20.95, and it comes with eight biscuits), salads,
and more. Kids' meals average $3.29 for a choice of chicken nuggets, a hot dog,
ribs(!), or a hamburger. Each meal comes with fries, a drink, and ice cream.
Most of the restaurants feature Rocky and Bullwinkle cartoons on the T.V.
monitors and/or they have a small stage where the electronic figures of Rocky
and Bullwinkle come out and tell jokes. Children enjoy the water show, too,
where fountain waters "dance" to music and change colors via spotlights. Come
here to eat, and then play at the Family Fun Centers, because your kids won't let
you go home without doing so. Food and fun - what more could you want?!

Hours: Open Mon. - Thurs., 11am - 9pm; Fri., 11:30am - 11pm; Sat.,
10am - 11pm; Sun., 11am - 9pm.

Ages: All

CARNEY'S

Studio City - (818) 761-8300; West Hollywood - (323) 654-8300 / $$
www.carneytrain.com

Studio City - 12601 Ventura Blvd.; West Hollywood - 8351 Sunset Blvd

Railroad the kids and take them to Carney's for a bite to eat on board passenger train cars. The West Hollywood location has a 1920's Union Pacific dining car and the Studio City location has two 1940's train cars and a caboose. Grab a burger ($3.95); hot dog ($1.65); chicken breast filet sandwich ($3.60); beef or chicken soft taco ($1.75 each) or tuna melt ($3.60).

Hours: Open daily 11am. Closing times vary from 10pm - 2am.
Admission: Prices listed above.
Ages: All

CHUCK E. CHEESE

Check your yellow pages for a local listing. / www.chuckecheese.com $$$

These popular indoor eateries and play lands for young kids offer token-taking kiddie rides and video and arcade games, as well as the all-important prize redemption centers. Many facilities also have play areas with tubes, slides, and ball pits. Chuck E. Cheese, the costumed rat mascot, is usually walking around giving hugs and high fives. An electronic version of Chuck E. performs several stage shows throughout the day.

Every child's favorite food is served here - pizza! A large cheese pizza is $13.99; a jr. drink is $1.29; and a one-time visit to the salad bar is $3.49. All purchases come with a few tokens, but kids always want more. Bring in their report cards (especially if they have good grades!) to redeem for extra tokens and check out the website for on-line coupons. Note: This place is often noisy at peak lunch and dinner times, especially on weekends when crowds descend.

Hours: Usually open Sun. - Thurs., 10am - 10pm; Fri. - Sat., 10am - 11pm. Call for a particular location's hours.
Admission: Free admission, but count on spending money on pizza and tokens.
Ages: 2 - 11 years.

CLAIM JUMPER

(800) 949-4538 / www.claimjumper.com $$$

Come jump claim at this restaurant if you've got a hankerin' for good food, or if your kids are studying about the Gold Rush. Each location's lobby and restaurant artifacts are genuine, reflecting California's golden heritage. The tastefully rustic decor includes stone fireplaces, authentic log chairs, colorful Tiffany lamps, pick axes, buffalo heads, and lanterns.

Strike it rich with any menu item - the food is delicious and reasonably priced, and the portions are large. The selections include barbeque ribs (with their signature sauce), rotisserie chicken, hamburgers, Porterhouse steak, lobster tail, fresh fish, a large choice of salads, and pizza prepared in a wood-fired oven.

(Kids love to watch the "pizza guy" tossing the dough.) Little Jumpers can order macaroni and cheese, mini burgers, chicken tenderloins, pizza, mini corn dogs, or ribs for $4.95. *Try* to save room for dessert. I recommend sharing the mud pie or a slice of motherlode cake, which is six scrumptious layers of chocolate cake. This place is a gold mine!

Ages: All

FARMER'S MARKETS

(213) 244-9190 - Southland Farmer's Market Association /
www.cafarmersmarkets.org.

Many cities host a weekly farmer's market. These markets usually consist of open-air (outside) booths set up for customers to purchase fresh produce, bakery goods, meats, and more - taste the difference! Freshly-cut flowers are often available, too. Indulge yourself and let your kids pick out a "new" foods to try. We think the food and ambiance of a market is much more enticing than a grocery store. Please call your local city hall or chamber of commerce to see if there is a farmer's market near you. Here are just a few of the cities that I know of that host a market: Beverly Hills, Burbank, Calabasas, Coronado, Costa Mesa, Culver City, Encino, Gardena, Julian, Long Beach, Los Angeles, Malibu, Mission Valley, Monrovia, Montrose, Northridge, Ocean Beach, Oceanside (with llama rides!), Ojai, Oxnard, Pacific Beach, Palm Springs, Pasadena, Pomona, Redondo Beach, Riverside, San Dimas, Santa Monica, Studio City, Temecula, Tustin, Ventura, Vista, Westwood, and Woodland Hills.

GAMEWORKS

Irvine - (949) 727-1422; Ontario - (909) 987-4263; Orange - (714) 939-9690 /
www.gameworks.com
Irvine - 31 Fortune Drive at the Irvine Spectrum Center; Ontario - 4541 Mills Circle at Ontario Mills Mall; Orange - 20 The City Drive at The Block of Orange.

See GAMEWORKS under the Family Pay and Play section for details.

HARD ROCK CAFE

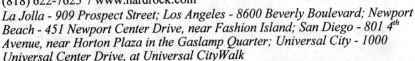

La Jolla - (858) 456-7625; Los Angeles - (310) 276-7605; Newport Beach - (949) 640-8844; San Diego - (619) 615-7625; Universal City - (818) 622-7625 / www.hardrock.com
La Jolla - 909 Prospect Street; Los Angeles - 8600 Beverly Boulevard; Newport Beach - 451 Newport Center Drive, near Fashion Island; San Diego - 801 4th Avenue, near Horton Plaza in the Gaslamp Quarter; Universal City - 1000 Universal Center Drive, at Universal CityWalk

This has become the "in" place to eat and hang out if you are a rock 'n roll fan. Each Cafe has its own unique memorabilia displayed in glass cases on the walls, but the essence of all the cafes - paying tribute to music industry legends and the hot artists of today, and promoting an environmentally aware motto, "Save the Planet" - is the same. Hard Rock Cafe is part restaurant and part museum, so before or after your meal, take a walk around to see your favorite musician's guitar, record album, or stage costume on exhibit. And, oh yes, rock music is constantly played. Souvenir T-shirts and glasses bearing the Cafe's logo and location (as they are restaurants throughout the world) have become collectible items among Hard Rock Cafe enthusiasts.

The Cafe at UNIVERSAL CITYWALK (look under the Potpourri section), for instance, has a gigantic electric guitar out front. Inside are numerous guitars (one is covered with snake skin), a few saxophones, a cool-looking car spinning on a pedestal, a gleaming motorcycle, gold records, autographed items, and an outfit worn by Elton John.

Menu items include Chinese chicken salad ($7.99), burgers (average $7), barbeque ribs ($12.99), fajitas ($10.99), T-bone steaks ($15.99), and sandwiches (average $7.50). Personal dessert favorites include chocolate chip cookie pie ($3.99) and Heath Bar rain forest nut crunch sundae ($4.99). Kids' meals are $5.99 each for macaroni and cheese, a burger, a hotdog, chicken tenders, or a grilled cheese sandwich. Meals also come with applesauce, fries, and a beverage in a souvenir cup.

Hours: Open Sun. - Thurs., 11:30am - 11pm; Fri. - Sat., 11:30am - 12am.
Admission: Certain discounts are available through AAA.
Ages: 5 years and up.

JOE'S CRAB SHACK

$$$

Long Beach - (562) 594-6551; Newport Beach - (949) 650-1818;
Redondo Beach - (310) 406-1999; San Diego - (619) 260-1111 /
www.joescrabshack.com
Long Beach - 6550 Marina Drive; Newport Beach - 2607 W. Coast Highway;
Redondo Beach - 230 Portofino Way; San Diego - 7610 Hazard Center Drive,
#703

If you're in a *crab*by mood, this is the restaurant for you! At the Newport Beach restaurant the outside has a collage of large, marine-related items such as a life-size carved wooden captain, a whale's tail, a surfboard, fishing nets, and a wooden alligator.

Inside, a lot of stuff fills the walls and ceiling. From the corrugated tin roof hangs plastic seagulls, netting, crab and lobster decorations, animals made out of shells, surfer clothing, and small boats - you get the picture. The wall is completely covered with photographs of everyday people, some holding fish, some not. At almost any of the wooden tables, the waterfront view of the harbor is terrific. The servers must have fun because they sometimes dance on the table and break out into song.

Most of the meals are large enough to be shared; even the kid's meals are more than adequate. Crab is the featured specialty, but other foods are available. My oldest son fell in love with the crab cake sandwiches ($6.99). Other entrees include top sirloin ($11.99), coconut shrimp ($9.99), one pound of snow crab ($15.99), lobster tail ($16.99), appetizer of fried calamari with marinara ($3.99), and a delicious salad with fried chicken strips ($6.99). Kids' meals, for children 12 and under, are $3.99 for a choice of chicken fingers, hot dog, burger, popcorn shrimp, pizza, or fish and chips. Drinks are extra.

Hours: Open Sun. - Mon., 11am - 9pm; Tues. - Thurs., 11am - 10pm;
Fri. - Sat., 11am - 11pm
Admission: Prices are listed above.
Ages: All

JOHNNY REB'S SOUTHERN SMOKEHOUSE ☼

Bellflower - (562) 866-6455; Long Beach - (562) 423-7327; $$$
Orange - (714) 633-3369   ♨
Bellflower - 16639 Bellflower Boulevard; Long Beach - 4663 Long Beach
Boulevard; Orange - 2940 E. Chapman Avenue

This roadhouse restaurant serves up southern hospitality, as well as good ol'
southern cookin'. Walk past the bales of hay and cow bells into the main room
with its wood beam ceilings, wooden tables and benches, and rustic ambiance.
Large U.S. (and a few other) flags hang from the ceiling. The walls and counter
tops are decorated with straw hats, old wash basins, musical instruments, license
plates, old-fashioned kitchen gadgets and tools, and pictures of farms framed by
shutters. Bluegrass music plays in the background.

The immediate attraction for kids (and adults) is the bowl of peanuts on
each table because peanut shells are to be thrown on the floor! (My floor looks
like this too, sometimes. The only difference is that kids are allowed to do it
here.) I have to mention that even the bathrooms fit into the Ma and Pa Kettle
theme because they look like (nice) outhouses, and barnyard noises are piped in.

Our waiter, who wore a long johns shirt, served our beverages in canning
jars. Breakfast items include grits ($1.69), omelettes (average $6.50), pancakes
(average $4.25), and country ham and eggs ($7.99). Meals come with all the
fixin's. The children's menu offers an egg and toast, french toast, pancakes, or
bacon and egg biscuit, for $1.95 each. The lunch menu is the same as the
following dinner menu, only the portions are smaller, so prices are lower. Going
along with the southern attitude toward food - anything tastes better when fried -
choices include fried green tomatoes, okra, fried sweet potatoes, hushpuppies
(i.e. fried cornbread), catfish, and chicken fried steak. Y'all may also select ribs,
hamburger, blackened T-bone steak, stuffed Cajun sausage sandwich, chicken
salad, and more. Dinner prices range from $7 to $15. The homemade desserts are
delicious, especially the peach cobbler. Personal advice - don't even think about
dieting, at least for the meal you eat here. The kids' menu offers chicken, catfish,
or beef ribs from $3.50 to $5.50. Beverages are extra. "Put some south in your
mouth" and grab some grub at Johnny Reb's! Note: The Long Beach location is
the smallest one. The Orange County location is large, the wall hangin's are
more orderly than the mish mash decor of the other locations, and it has a tin
roof porch for outside seating.

Hours: Open Sun. - Thurs., 7am - 9pm; Fri. - Sat., 7am - 10pm.
Ages: 2 years and up.

THE OLD SPAGHETTI FACTORY

Duarte - (626) 358-2115; Fullerton - (714) 526-6801; Hollywood - (323) $$$
469-7149; Newport Beach - (949) 675-8654; Rancho Cucamonga - (909)
980-3585; Riverside - (909) 784-4417; and San Diego - (619) 233-4323
/ www.osf.com

These elegant "factories" have posh, velvet seats in a variety of colors. The overhead fabric lamps are from a more genteel era. The old world antiques and the dark, rich furniture exudes a quiet, classy atmosphere. Yet, the restaurants are also very kid friendly. Old Spaghetti Factories usually have a train or trolley car to eat in - this is a highlight. The franchised restaurants differ only in regional decor. For instance, the one in Riverside, being in a citrus city, has orange crate labels on the walls.

The food is fine fare, such as spaghetti (what a surprise!), with a wonderful variety of sauces to choose from, and pastas such as lasagna, tortellini, and ravioli. Prices range from $3.50 to $8.95. Kids' meals cost between $3.35 to $4.35 for a choice of pasta and a choice of sauces (with or without meat), plus a salad, beverage, and dessert.

Hours: Open Mon. - Fri., 11:30am - 2pm and 5pm - 10pm; Fri., noon - 3pm and 5pm - 10:30pm; Sat. - Sun., 11:30am - 10pm.

Ages: 4 years and up.

OLIVIA'S DOLL HOUSE and TEA ROOM

Newhall - (661) 222-7331; Thousand Oaks - (805) 381-1553; West $$$$$
Hollywood - (310) 273-6631
Newhall - 22700 Lyons Avenue; Thousand Oaks - 1321 E. Thousand Oaks Boulevard, #110; West Hollywood - 8804 Rosewood Avenue

These small, Victorian-style house-like buildings are beautifully decorated with flowers and lace - a little girl's dream come true. Young ladies can dress up in gowns and accessorize with feather boas, hats, gloves, parasols, and jewelry. Next comes a hair style befitting the new look, plus make-up, and even having the nails done. (Forget about little girls - this sounds like a mom's dream come true!) Each party-goer then participates in a fashion show and gets her picture taken. In the dining room, "tea" (lemonade) is served along with hors d'oeuvres (bite-size pizza and cocktail wienies), finger sandwiches (turkey, tuna, and peanut butter and jelly), and dessert (candy assortments, brownies, and a cookie). Then party favors are doled out. What a memorable party for young ladies!

Hours: Open for parties by reservation only.

Admission: Parties start at $250 for 7 girls; additional children are $25 each.

Ages: 4 years and up.

PETER PIPER PIZZA

Commerce - (323) 728-8249; Covina - (626) 858-0202; Huntington Park $$$
- (323) 589-9000; Los Angeles - (323) 773-5502; National City - (619)
477-1788; Pacoima - (818) 899-4848; Sylmar - (818) 837-5996; Whittier
- (562) 692-5563. / www.peterpiperpizza.com

Commerce - 5730 E. Whittier Boulevard; Covina - 1459 N. Citrus Avenue;
Huntington Park - 2661 E. Florence Avenue; Los Angeles - 6207 Atlantic
Boulevard; National City - 3007 Highland Avenue; Pacoima - 13200 Osborne
Street; Sylmar - 12902 Foothill Boulevard; Whittier - 11885 Whittier Boulevard

This huge, fun-filled pizza place is very similar to Chuck E. Cheese. Obviously the main food offered here is pizza (a large cheese pizza is $10.99), but chicken wings and a salad bar are also available. For entertainment, there are ball pits, arcade games, lots of skee ball lanes, and a merry-go-round that is free (yea!). The mascot, a green-spotted purple dinosaur, comes on stage a few times throughout the day/night to put on a show. You will have to purchase tokens for the games - twenty tokens for $5. Bring in a good report card for extra, free tokens. The kids love coming here - just cover your ears to block out the din. Note that for a minimum of ten kids, tours are offered where youngsters see the kitchens and top their own 7" pizza. A drink and two tokens are included in the $2.69 per child price. Adults, you're on your own!

Hours: Open Sun. - Thurs., 10am - 10pm; Fri. - Sat., 10am - 11pm.
Admission: Free, but bring money for food and tokens.
Ages: 1½ years and up.

RAINFOREST CAFE

Anaheim - (714) 772-0413; Costa Mesa - (714) 424-9200; Ontario -
(909) 941-7979 / www.rainforestcafe.com
Anaheim - 1515 S. Disney Drive at Downtown Disney;
Costa Mesa - 3333 Bristol Street, South Coast Plaza;
Ontario - 4810 Mills Circle in Ontario Mills Mall

$$$

Deep in the heart of the Rainforest Cafe, realistic-looking animatronic beasts come to life - gorillas beat their chests, elephants trumpet, and parrots squawk. Periodic thunder and lightening "storms" explode through the restaurant. This is not a quiet place to eat. Cascading waterfalls, fake dense foliage, and "rock" walls add to the atmosphere, as do the jaguars and cheetahs that are partially hidden in the banyan trees. Rain drizzles down from the ceiling around the perimeter of the cafe, ending in troughs of misty waters. You'll enter the cafe under a 6,000 gallon fish tank archway that holds a colorful array of saltwater fish. Two more aquariums are inside the cafe and one contains beautiful, but poisonous, lionfish. There is always something to grab your attention here!

Savor your meal at a table, or on a bar stool that is painted to look like a giraffe, zebra, frog, or another animal. The delectable menu offers everything from salmon, flatbread pizza, Oriental chicken salad, and Jamaica Me Crazy! porkchops to hamburgers, meatloaf, and lasagna. Prices start at $8.95 and portions are huge. Children's meals average $5.50 for a choice of a grilled cheese sandwich, catfish, chicken nuggets, hamburger, pasta linguine, or pizza, and include a drink with a souvenir cup. Desserts are deliciously unique. My favorite was Monkey Business - coconut bread pudding with bits of apricots, topped with shaved chocolate and whipped cream.

The adjacent Rainforest Cafe Retail Village (i.e. store) is themed with equal attention to detail. In the front of the store a (pretend) life-size crocodile resides in a small swamp. He moves around and roars every few minutes. Live macaws and cockatoos are on perches just above the crocodile. A knowledgeable animal care specialist will tell your inquisitive little ones all about the birds. Ask about educational programs that take students on a half-hour safari through the restaurant to learn about endangered species, conservation, and the environment. Tours include lunch and a lesson plan. Catch jungle fever and experience the Rainforest Cafe! The location in Anaheim is in DOWNTOWN DISNEY (see the Potpourri section), is multi-level, and doesn't have a crocodile. The location in Ontario is in ONTARIO MILLS MALL (see the Potpourri section).

Hours: Open Mon. - Thurs., 11am - 9:30pm; Fri., 11am - 10pm; Sat., 11am - 9pm; Sun., 10:30am - 9pm.

Ages: All

RUBY'S

(800) HEY RUBY (439-7829) / www.rubys.com
Call for the one nearest you.

These 1940's-style diners offer good food and have a terrific atmosphere for kids. They've readily become one of our favorite places to eat. Old-fashioned-looking jukeboxes that play favorite oldies; red vinyl booths and bar stools; decorations that matches the time period ambiance; and the kind of attentive service that all but disappeared years ago, are some of Ruby's trademarks. Since the restaurants are franchised, each one is slightly different in decor (some have trains going around on tracks overhead), and in their choice of menu items. Most breakfast choices include omelettes ($4.89), waffles ($3.79), etc. Lunch and dinner foods include a wide selection of burgers (beef, turkey, veggie, or chicken), for an average cost of $5. Salads, sandwiches, and soups are available, too. The delicious concoctions from the soda fountain, including flavored sodas and old-fashioned ice cream desserts, keep us coming back for more. Kids' meals range from $3.39 to $4.59 for a choice of a grilled cheese sandwich, corn dog, hamburger, or chicken fingers. Their meals come with fries, a small drink, and a kid-size ice cream cone. Note: You'll find Ruby's at the end of several Southern California piers, kind of like a pot of gold.

Hours: Open daily for breakfast, lunch, and dinner.

Ages: All

BEN BOLLINGER'S CANDLELIGHT PAVILION

(909) 626-1254 / www.candlelightpavilion.com
455 W. Foothill Boulevard, Claremont

See BEN BOLLINGER'S CANDLELIGHT PAVILION, under the Shows and Theaters section, for details.

THE CANDY FACTORY

(818) 766-8220
12508 Magnolia Boulevard, Hollywood
(Exit Ventura Fwy [101] N. on Laurel Canyon Blvd., L. on Magnolia. The cross street is Whitsett. [TG-562 F2])

How sweet it is! The Candy Factory is one of the largest and oldest candy-making suppliers on the West Coast. The store does not actually have a lot of the finished product to purchase, but it has an abundance of the supplies needed such as a wide variety of molds, flavorings, chocolates (to melt), and lollipop sticks.

Hour-and-a-half candy-making classes are offered for families on Saturdays three times a month. Classes often focus on a theme that the whole family can work on together such as making a chocolate house, trimmed with assorted candies ($30 per house); creating chocolate heart-shaped boxes and chocolates to fit in them for Valentine's Day ($17.50 per box); and concocting a bouquet of chocolate flowers for Mother's Day ($25). Note: This type of candy-making doesn't involve the use of an oven, so it's a safe project for most ages. Groups of fifteen to forty people can create edible projects to take home on weekdays. Groups can request a particular theme and learn additional parts of the candy business, such as making clusters and soft centers, hand-dipped candies, and more. Prices begin at $5 per person. Two-hour birthday parties are people-pleasers as the kids get deliciously messy making about a dozen candies, using molds and candy coatings, to sample and bring home. Cake and punch (more sugar!) are also included in the $17.50 per child price. My children offered (begged) to live at the Factory for a while - imagine that!

Hours: The store is open Mon. - Fri., 10am - 5pm; Sat., 10am - 4pm. Closed Sun. for private parties and closed on Mon. Family classes are offered on Sat. afternoons. Call to schedule a group class.

Admission: Some prices are listed above - call for more information.

Ages: 6 years and up.

DALE'S DINER
(562) 425-7285

4229 E. Carson Street, Long Beach

(Exit Riverside Fwy [91] S. on Lakewood Blvd., L. on Carson St. It's on the corner of Carson and Norse Way. [TG-766 A6])

Hey daddy-o! This small 50's diner is a really happenin' place. It's decorated with black and white checkered tile floor, turquoise vinyl seats, and a few special booths that look like they were made from the back section of cars from this era. Each table has its own small jukebox. At 25¢ for two songs, your kids can now be introduced to such classics as *Chantilly Lace* and *Purple People Eater*. For breakfast, try a five-egg omelette stuffed with bacon and cheese and served with hash browns or fruit, and toast or a cinnamon roll, for $5.95. Blueberry flapjacks ($4.25) or cinnamon raisin french toast ($3.80) make tasty morning choices, too. Kids' meals, for ages 9 and younger, include two oreo pancakes (about $3.25), or one egg and one pancake and a piece of bacon (about $3). The lunch and dinner menu offers a Cobb salad ($7.45), pork chops ($7.25), sirloin tip steak kabob ($7.95), deli sandwiches (average $6), hamburgers (average $5), and more. Top off your meal with a chocolate, vanilla, or cherry soda. Kids can choose a burger and fries, grilled cheese with fries, chili, or a pepperoni pizza for about $3.25. Beverages are extra. Come in just for dessert sometime and try a piece of fresh-baked pie ($2.25), or a scrumptious Brownie Saturday, which is alternating layers of brownies with vanilla ice cream, topped with hot fudge and whipped cream ($4.75).

Hours: Open Mon. - Thurs., 6am - 9pm; Fri., 9am - 10pm; Sat. - Sun.,
7am - 10pm; Sun., 7am - 9pm.

Ages: All

EMERALD BBQ GARDEN

(310) 534-5492 $$$$

2795 Pacific Coast Highway in Airport Plaza, Torrance

(Exit San Pedro Fwy [110] W. on Pacific Coast Highway. It's one block west of Crenshaw Blvd.
[TG-793 F4])

The phrase "have it your way" takes on a new meaning at this Korean-style
barbeque buffet restaurant that features interactive dining. For lunch, choose
from marinated portions of beef, pork, chicken, and beef ribs. Dinner selections
also include crab legs, rib eye steak, shrimp, fish, and more exotic items such as
beef tongue and octopus. (Might as well be adventuresome!) Cook these items
on a grill that's built into the middle of your table. While the main course is
grilling, go back to buffet tables to fill up your plate with sushi, white rice,
tempura, noodles, salads, pastas, soups, fresh fruit, Jell-O, and soft serve ice
cream. Parents, this is a night off from cooking, kind of.

Hours: Open daily for lunch 11am - 4pm; dinner 4pm - 10pm.

Admission: Lunch during the week for adults is $8.95; Sat. - Sun. it's $11.95.
Daily lunch prices for kids are $5.95 for ages 8 -12; $3.95 for
ages 5 - 7; children 4 and under are free. Dinner is $15.95 for
adults; $7.95 for ages 8 - 12; $5.95 for ages 5 - 7; children 4 and
under are free. Beverages are extra.

Ages: 4 years and up.

ENCOUNTER RESTAURANT

(310) 215-5151 $$$$

209 World Way, Los Angeles

(Exit Imperial Fwy [105] N. on Sepulveda Blvd. and follow the signs that say "arrivals." It's at L.A.X.
[airport] [TG-702 F5])

Seemingly from a galaxy far, far away comes (a close) Encounter
Restaurant that looks like a space station. It is located at the hub of the Los
Angeles airport. Earthlings need to take the elevator, with its mood lighting and
other-worldly music, up to the restaurant, which overlooks the immediate L.A.
area. Note: The nighttime ambiance is almost surreal as hundreds of twinkling
lights fill the skyline.

I can't decide if the interior decor, designed by Walt Disney Engineering, is
futuristic or from the 60's. The carpet's predominant colors are lime green, dark
red, and blue. The booths are white and oblong. The ceiling has blue and purple
lights shining through oval and odd-shaped holes. My boys and I sat around the
bar and were entertained by the lava lamps. (We are easily amused!) The
servers, who are dressed in space uniforms (think *Star Trek*), used hand held
drink dispensers shaped like laser guns. A main attraction in this circular
restaurant is the windows. They are slanted outward, from the floor to the
ceiling. Although looking down out the window made me dizzy, my boys
thought it was cool (and a little scary).

The food (and prices) are out of this world. The lunch menu includes buckwheat soba noodles in a spicy sesame ginger dressing with prawns ($13); Peking-style duck, shiitaki mushroom pizza with a honey-hoisin-cilantro sauce ($14); and Mahi-Mahi sandwich on a bun with mango relish ($15). The dinner selection includes Caesar salad ($8); tuna sashimi with Japanese cucumber salad ($26); linguine with tiger shrimp, mushroom, and spinach ($24); New York steak with peppercorn cream sauce and mushroom risotto; and sea bass with coconut orange essence, mango salsa, asparagus, and saffron basmati ride ($26); plus chicken, pork chops, and more. Sophisticated children's entrees allow kids 12 years and under to indulge in linguine ($8), filet of beef ($10), chicken breast ($10), or linguine with tomatoes and shrimp ($18). Dessert choices include lemon honey sesame crisps with creme brulee with berries ($8), and cheesecake ($8).

Make sure to take the separate "observation deck" elevator (it's labeled) to go above the restaurant to the open air observation deck. Free telescope viewing is available up here through the partial glass barriers.

Hours: The restaurant is open daily 11am - 4pm for lunch; 4pm - 5pm for cocktails and a light dinner. It is open for dinner Sun. - Thurs., 5pm - 10pm and Fri. - Sat., 5pm - 11pm. The observation deck is open daily.

Admission: Prices are mentioned above. The observation deck is free.

Ages: 3 years and up.

FAIR OAKS PHARMACY AND SODA FOUNTAIN

(626) 799-1414 / www.fairoakspharmacy.net   *$$*

1526 Mission Street, Pasadena

(Exit the Pasadena Fwy [110] S. on Fair Oaks Blvd., R. on Mission. [TG-595 H2])

Fair Oaks is a small "store" with a quaint ambiance, located in the midst of Old Town Pasadena, which has lots of shops and restaurants. It is part pharmacy, that also sells retro collectables, jewelry, and home accents, and part 1900's restaurant and soda fountain, complete with a marble counter top and antique fixtures. Both sides of the store are decorated with memorabilia, unique toys, and fun stuff to look at.

Lunch items include chicken sandwiches ($6.25), deli sandwiches ($5.50), burgers ($5.95), chili cheese dog ($3.95), and either chicken Caesar salad or Cobb salad ($6.25). Now for the good stuff - dessert. Ask the soda jerk (who is actually quite nice) to fix you an old-fashioned phosphate ($1.95); a chocolate, pineapple, or raspberry ice cream soda ($3.95); a clown sundae ($2.50); a hot fudge brownie topped with ice cream and whipped cream ($4.95); or a specialty drink, like a New York egg cream ($1.95). There is a small eating area inside, as well as a few tables and chairs outside.

Hours: Open Mon. - Thurs., 11am - 10pm; Fri. - Sat., 11am - 11pm; Sun., 11pm - 9pm. Lunch is served Sun. - Thurs., 11am - 5pm; Fri. - Sat., 11am - 8pm.

Admission: Prices are mentioned above.

Ages: All

FARMERS MARKET   ☼
!/$$

(323) 933-9211 / www.farmersmarketla.com

6333 W. 3rd Street, Los Angeles

(Going S. on Ventura Fwy [101], exit S. on Vermont Ave., R. on 3rd. Going N. on 101, exit E. on Beverly Blvd., L. on Vermont, R. on 3rd. From the Santa Monica Fwy [10], exit N. on Fairfax. From the San Diego Fwy [405], exit E. on Santa Monica Blvd., R. on Wilshire Blvd., L. on Robertson Blvd., R. on 3rd. It's on the corner of Fairfax and 3rd. [TG-633 B1])

This unique outdoor market, originally founded in 1934, is an eclectic mixture of more than sixty fresh food and produce vendors, and over twenty kitchens that make and sell all sorts of homemade domestic and international favorites. The market can be crowded, but it is a fun place to shop or enjoy lunch. Patrons can order their favorite ethnic food and eat at an outdoor table. Kids love stopping by Littlejohn's English Toffee House stall to watch (and sample) mouth-watering candy being made. At Magee's House of Nuts, they can also see peanuts steadily pouring into a large machine behind glass, being churned around to make very fresh-tasting peanut butter. Across the way from the main marketplace, more than sixty-five retail stores offer unique clothing items and specialty gifts.

Hours: Open in the summer Mon. - Sat., 9am - 7pm; Sun., 10am - 6pm. Open the rest of the year Mon. - Sat., 9am - 6:30pm; Sun., 10am - 5pm. Closed major holidays.

Admission: Free, but bring spending money.

Ages: 2½ years and up.

FRILLS   ☼
$$$$
🎂

(626) 303-3201

504 S. Myrtle Avenue, Monrovia

(Exit Foothill Fwy [210] N. on Myrtle Ave. [TG-567 G4])

Entering through the doors of Frills is like taking a step back in time. The front Victorian boutique sells vintage clothing and a variety of hats, plus gift items like cards and unusual buttons.

The back part of Frills is a tea room. If you feel inappropriately attired, choose a feather boa and/or a glamorous hat from the dress-up trunk. What fun! The room is charmingly decorated with lacy tablecloths, old-fashioned clothing and hats, and tea sets that are for sale. There are over forty types of tea to choose from, with cinnamon vanilla and cherry being the two most popular with the younger set. Order a meal fit for a king with King's Tea, which includes a hearty meat pie or sausage roll, a variety of tea sandwiches, fresh fruit, cheese, dessert, and of course, tea - $12.50. Other teas (meals) fit for a queen, princess, or peasant are available. All meals are served with fresh-baked bread and a delicious dessert. Children's Tea - a peanut butter sandwich, shortbread, fresh fruit, and tea, costs $9.50. Ask about Frills' special children's programs.

Hours: Open Tues. - Sat., 11am - 4pm; Fri., 11am - 7:30pm.

Admission: Prices range from $8.50 - $12.50.

Ages: 4 years and up.

FRISCO'S CAR HOP DINER (City of Industry)

(626) 913-FOOD (3663) / www.friscos.com   *$$$*

18065 Gale Avenue, City of Industry

(Exit Pomona Fwy [60] N. on Fullerton Rd., L. on Gale [TG-678 J4])

Pop quiz: What are skateresses? Answer: Waitresses on skates! Frisco's has them and lots more. The restaurant's prominent colors are hot pink and cool turquoise, along with white and black checked flooring. The walls and ceilings are painted blue with clouds that feature artists from the 50's (i.e. Jimmy Dean, Elvis, Marilyn Monroe, and others) with wings, as in heavenly angels. There are also some neon thunderbolts and a few 3-D images popping out. Other decor includes parking meters, traffic signals, dice, drive-in movie speakers, a juke box, and an old gas pump. Many of the booths have the front or back end of a car incorporated in them.

The food is a combination of American and Greek, served in a fifties-themed restaurant - and somehow it works! Breakfast selections include three eggs, bacon or sausage, home fries or hash browns or fresh fruit, a toast or muffin for $4.50; ribeye steak and eggs, $6.50; breakfast burrito, $4.95; and Belgian waffles, $3.50. Kids 12 years and under can choose from two pancakes or french toast, eggs, and bacon or sausage plus a small drink for $2.75. Lunch options include a variety of burgers starting at $4.25; Greek salad, $5.95; pepperoni pizza, $4.95; turkey avocado melt, $5.95; chicken souvlaki, $5.75; beef fajita pita, $5.50, and more. Kid's meal are $3.95 for a choice of burger, hot dog or corn dog, chicken strips, or grilled cheese, plus fries and a soft drink. Adult dinner choices, which are served with soup or salad, baked potato or rice or french fries, vegetable, and either garlic bread or pita bread, include half rack baby back ribs, $8.95; Grecian platter for two, $22.95; spaghetti with meat balls, $5.95; chicken or beef shish kabob, $9.95; and a carne asada burrito, $5.95. Desserts include blueberry sundaes, $4.45; hot fudge and banana sundae, $3.75; and freezes and floats, $2.95. Keep on cruisin'! Note: There is another Frisco's in Downey.

Hours: Open Mon. - Thurs., 9:30am - 10pm; Fri. - Sat., 8am - midnight. Ask about specials.

Admission: Menu prices are mentioned above.

Ages: All

FRISCO'S CAR HOP DINER (Downey)

(562) 928-FOOD (3663) / www.friscos.com

12050 Woodruff Avenue, Downey

(From the Glenn Anderson Fwy [105], exit N. on Bellflower Blvd., R. on Imperial Hwy, L. on Woodruff. From the San Gabriel River Fwy [605], exit W on Imperial, R. on Woodruff. [TG-706 D7])

See FRISCO'S CAR HOP DINER (City of Industry) in this section for more details. This location is a smaller.

GOSPEL BRUNCH (Hollywood)

(323) 848-5100 / www.hob.com   *$$$$$*

8430 Sunset Boulevard, Hollywood

(From the Hollywood Fwy [101], exit W. on Sunset Blvd. From the Santa Monica Fwy [10], exit N. on La Cienega, R. on Sunset. [TG-593 A5])

Got the blues? Gospel Brunch at the renown House of Blues is the cure. With its corrugated tin roof and weathered walls this unique building looks (deceptively) like an old shack, like something found in the deep South. The three-story house's eclectic decor consists of bottlecaps imbedded in the walls, folk art done in various mediums, African designs on the wood beams, 3-D reliefs on the ceiling depicting Blues' artists (e.g. Aretha Franklin, Billy Holiday, and others), earth tone colors mixed with splashes of bright colors, broken-in wooden tables and chairs, and lots more ambiance. The bars also have African masks and other cultural renderings.

The two-hour gospel brunch is a feast for the body, mind, and spirit. Indulge in eating some of the finest Mississippi Delta cuisine this side of, well, the Mississippi. The buffet includes roast beef, shrimp, biscuits and gravy, fried chicken, macaroni and cheese, omelettes fixed any way you like 'em, mini waffles with a variety of toppings, and desserts. Finger-licking good!

The food is a precursor to the uplifting, high energy, hour-long concert that follows. The stage is on the first floor with a curtain that resembles a patchwork quilt. Above it are symbols of world religions. The upstairs section actually separates (think parting of the Red Sea) so visitors can look down onto the stage. If you are seated on the second floor towards the buffet area, you can either view the concert on the monitors, or get up and move toward the center railing that oversees the stage. Most people do not remain seated throughout the concert, anyway. They are standing up, dancing around, clapping their hands, singing along, and at times, even joining the musicians on stage.

Every week features different artists or groups, from traditional ensembles and choirs to contemporary gospel; from nationally known singers to locally famous ones. It's a great way for a family to spend a Sunday afternoon.

The House of Blues is home to numerous headliner concerts during the week. Check out the BLUES SCHOOLHOUSE in the Educational Presentations section for school kids.

Hours: Brunch is every Sun. at 10am and 1pm. Holiday Sun., such as Easter and Mother's Day, it's served at 9:30am, noon, and 2:30pm. Reservations are highly recommended.

Admission: $33 for adults; $17 for ages 5 - 12; children 4 and under are free. Parking is $5.

Ages: 3 years and up.

GOURMET CAROUSEL RESTAURANT

$$$$

(323) 721-0774 - Chinatown Center event planner / www.chinatown.com

911 N. Broadway, Los Angeles

(Going N.W. on Hollywood Fwy [101], exit N. on Alameda, L. on Alpine, R. on Broadway. Going S.E. on 101, exit N. on Broadway. [TG-634 G2])

Get ready for China Night, a wonderful dinner show that is a cultural and culinary experience offered at least once a month. The same show is usually performed several times a month at brunch. The shows consists of acrobatics, colorful folk dances (such as the lion dance), a martial arts demonstration, meeting the "Emperor of China", live instrumental music, and a delicious nine-course Chinese dinner (or brunch). The cost is $42 for adults; $25 for seniors; $28 for ages 11 and under.

The Brunch and Magic Show is another fabulous entertainment / dining experience. Dim-sum is a traditional Chinese meal where carts filled with finger foods are rolled from table to table. Enjoy a dim-sum brunch followed by a forty-minute magic and comedy show. These brunches are offered several times a month, starting at 11:30am for eating and 12:30pm for the show. Admission is $25 for adults; $20 for seniors; $12.50 for ages 11 and under. Sometimes, the dim-sum and magic show is offered at dinner time, when the price changes to $32 for adults; $25 for ages 11 and under.

Hours:	Call for a schedule. Reservations are suggested.
Admission:	Prices are given above.
Ages:	4 years and up.

GRAND CENTRAL MARKET   ☀

(213) 624-2378 / www.grandcentralsquare.com   *$$*
317 S. Broadway Street, Los Angeles
(Exit Hollywood Fwy [101] S. on Spring St., R. on 3rd St., then a quick L. on Hill. The parking structure is between 3rd St. and Hill St. [TG-634 F4])

This is a fun, aromatic, cultural experience for kids who are used to shopping at grocery stores. There are over forty stalls inside this covered structure that sell everything from exotic fruits and vegetables to octopus and pigs' heads. There are also meat stalls, restaurants, and a bakery. Stop here to shop and/or eat on your way to visit other fun and educational places listed in this book!

Hours:	Open Mon. - Sun., 9am - 6pm; Sun., 10am - 5:30pm.
Admission:	Parking is $1 for every fifteen minutes; $8 maximum. Parking is free for ninety minutes, if you purchase merchandise worth $15 or more.
Ages:	3 years and up.

MALIBU SPEEDZONE

(626) 913-9663 / www.speedzone.com
17871 Castleton Street, City of Industry

See MALIBU SPEEDZONE, under the Family Pay and Play section, for details.

PROUD BIRD RESTAURANT   ☀

(310) 670-3093 / www.calendarlive.com/infosites/proudbird   *$$$$*
11022 Aviation Boulevard, Los Angeles
(Exit Imperial Fwy [105] N. on Aviation. [TG-702 J6])

Several airplanes have landed outside this restaurant, which is fittingly located just a stone's throw from the Los Angeles International Airport. The planes include a P-38 Lightning, P-51 Mustang, and Bell X-I. Inside this elegant restaurant are hallways lined with aviation pictures and flight artifacts. The rectangular-shaped main dining room has windows to see the field of planes in the "backyard", as well as planes actually landing and taking off from the airport. Tip: Choose a table near a window not just for the view, but also because they have headsets so diners can listen to the L.A.X. control tower!

Adult entree lunches include blackened chicken, grilled salmon, hamburgers, and club sandwiches. Prices range from $5.95 to $11.95. Lunch buffets have themes that change daily. Dinner choices include catfish, filet mignon, salmon, London broil, shrimp, lamb shank, chicken, ribs, and lobster. Prices range from $12.95 to $22.95. Appetizers include oysters, crab-stuffed mushrooms or escargot for $7.95 each. The kids' menu has grilled cheese sandwiches, hamburger, or chicken strips for $4.95. Their meals include an ice-cream cone. Beverages are extra.

Hours: Open for lunch Mon. - Sat., 11am to 3pm. Open for Sun. brunch 9am - 3pm. Open for dinner Mon. - Thurs., 4pm - 10pm; Fri. - Sat., 4pm to 11pm.

Admission: See above for menu prices.

Ages: 5 years and up.

QUEEN MARY

(562) 435-3511 / www.queenmary.com
Pier J, Long Beach

See QUEEN MARY under the Museums section for more details.

SHOGUN

(626) 351-8945 $$$$
470 N. Halstead Street, Pasadena
(Exit Foothill Fwy [210] N. on Rosemead Blvd. It's on the corner of Rosemead Blvd. and Halstead St. [TG-566 G3])

This Japanese-style restaurant has built-in tabletop grills where chefs prepare the food with rapid slicing and dicing movements (and cool tricks) in front of your eyes. (See BENIHANA, under this section, as it is a similar type of restaurant.) The "entertainment" is great and the food is delicious. Kids get a real kick out of the presentation, and are more likely to try "new" foods now that they've seen the unique way it has been prepared. Chicken, seafood, and steak are some of the menu selections. Lunch ranges from $6 to $12; dinners from $13 to $30. Kids' meals usually run between $6.95 to $8.95. (Kids are served the same meals as adults, just smaller portions.)

Hours: Open Mon. - Fri., 11:30am - 2pm and 5pm - 10pm; Sat., 5pm - 10:30pm; Sun., 4:30pm - 9:30pm.

Ages: 4 years and up.

TWIN PALMS

(626) 577-2567 / www.twin-palms.com $$$
101 W. Green Street, Pasadena

(Exit Foothill Fwy [210] (just S. of the Ventura Fwy [134]) E. on Colorado Blvd., R. on De Lacey St. It's on the corner of Green and De Lacey. Parking is available on the street (metered parking) or in a parking garage on De Lacey for free for the first 90 minutes, $2 per hour after that. [TG-565 H5])

Come get spiritually filled up, as well as physically satiated, at the gospel brunch served on the first Sunday of every month. The large outdoor patio and the stage area are enclosed in an expansive white tent (reminiscent of a big tent revival?) that is much more elegant than I've just described. Two palm trees (hence the name of the restaurant) protrude from the top of the tent. In cold weather, in-ground heaters warm up the atmosphere, as does moving to the music. The inside, more traditional dining area, does not have a view of the stage. Past featured gospel musicians have included choirs, bands, and soloists; some that raise the roof with the way they rock and roll, and some that simply sing sweet harmonies.

Food selections are from the menu, so choices and prices vary. A western omelette for example, is $7.95; Julian apple pancakes, $8.95; berry-filled french toast, $8.95; sea bass with new potatoes, $15.95; and artichoke ravioli, $12.95. The children's menu includes two eggs, $4.25; waffle, $4.95; chicken fingers with fries, $4.95, and hamburger with fries, $4.95. Delectable desserts include a giant eclair hot fudge sundae, $6.95; lemon meringue tart with fresh berries, $5.95; or chocolate souffle cake, $5.95.

On the other three Sunday brunches the live music might include jazz, calypso, or some other style. Background jazz is offered at night during the week and higher energy music is played on the weekends.

Hours: Brunch is served from 10:30am - 3pm. Music is played 11am - 2:45pm, with a few breaks.

Admission: $5 - $16, depending on what you order.

Ages: 4 years and up.

VINTAGE TEA LEAF

(562) 435-5589 / www.vintagetealeaf.com   *$$$$*

969 E. Broadway, Long Beach

(Exit the Long Beach Fwy [710] E. on Broadway. [TG-825 F1])

Classical music, bone china, lacy tablecloths, and a homey atmosphere make an afternoon tea at Vintage Tea Leaf a real treat. Offerings here include eighteen different kinds of tea "meals." The staples include soup, fresh-baked scones, cakes, and more than ten varieties of dainty sandwiches. Only at tea places do you find such sandwich combinations as salmon, cream cheese, and lemon capers; mayonnaise and mixed berry jam on cranberry bread; etc. I need to be more adventurous while making sandwiches at home! Ask about specific teas for young children, such as the Teddy Bear Tea, with its chocolate chip scones, chocolate tea (de-caf), bear-shaped sandwiches, and biscuits, served with honey of course. The Leaf also features almost 100 kinds of tea to drink, each brewed just right.

Hours: Open Thurs. - Mon., 11:30am - 6pm.

Admission: Prices range, depending on the tea, between $10 - $20 per person.

Ages: 3 years and up.

ALICE'S BREAKFAST IN THE PARK ☼

(714) 848-0690 / www.beachcalifornia.com/alices.html $$$
6622 Lakeview Drive, Huntington Beach
(Exit the San Diego Fwy [405] W. on Warner Ave., L. on Edwards St., L. on Central Park Dr. It's the red building at the end of the parking lot in HUNTINGTON CENTRAL PARK. [TG-857 G3])

Since breakfast is the most important meal of the day, why not start your day at Alice's Breakfast in the Park?! The red, barn-like building has a small dining room packed with antiques and Alice's varied collections, giving it a homey atmosphere. We also enjoy eating outside at the patio tables by the lake's edge. This is a delightful treat, especially for kids who don't always like to sit down throughout a meal. Watch out for the ducks, geese, and other birds that are usually waddling around, hoping for a handout.

Mmmmm - fresh baked bread or buns are served at all of Alice's breakfasts and lunches. Try an "outrageously delicious" cinnamon roll; at $2.25, it's (almost) big enough for a meal. Breakfast averages $5.95 for two eggs, home fries, and fruit. The menu offers a wonderful variety of other breakfast favorites, too, as well as fresh-squeezed orange juice. The lunch menu includes large sandwiches (average $4.50), salads, burgers, chili, and more. Breakfast and lunch kids' meals range from $1.95 to $3.95 and include a choice of grilled cheese sandwich, cheese omelet and fruit, hamburger, corn dog, fish sticks, or peanut butter and jelly. Fries and a drink cost an additional $1.25.

The restaurant is located in Huntington Central Park, so after your meal - go play! See HUNTINGTON CENTRAL PARK / SHIPLEY'S NATURE CENTER under the Great Outdoors section.

Hours: Open daily 7am - 2pm.
Ages: All

ANGELO'S AND VINCI'S RISTORANTE ☼

(714) 879-4022 / www.angelosandvincis.com $$$
550 N. Harbor Boulevard, Fullerton
(Exit Riverside Fwy [91] N. on Harbor Blvd. [TG-738 H6])

Attenzione - this ristorante and full bar not only bears the names of two of Italy's finest artists, but the cuisine and atmosphere is sure to please any *palette*. The dimly-lit restaurant creates a cozy ambiance by its eclectic decor packed around a main square room and upstairs mezzanine. Look up to see re-created Italian marketplace stalls along the walls. The fruit store, meat market, wine shop, etc., display realistic-looking fruit, hanging sausages, jars of pasta, hanging grapes and grapevines, and more, all with toddler-sized dolls dressed as merchants. There are also small knights in shining armor, framed art work, angel mannequins, signs, posters of the Mona Lisa, banners, a doll-sized stage, and bottles of wine all around, as well as trapeze figures and white Christmas lights suspended from the ceiling - always something to keep one's attention. A chapel wall holds statues, including a replica of the David, and old family photographs. There are a few uniquely-decorated banquet rooms at the restaurant.

Menu specialties include Old World-tasting pizza with a huge variety of toppings ($17.95 for a medium), extra large calzone ($15.95), spaghetti (average $7.95), tortellini ($11.95), and linguini and clams ($12.50), plus veal, chicken, shrimp, salads, and more. The all-you-can-eat buffet lunch is $5.95 for chicken wings, pasta Alfredo, chicken cacciatore, lasagna, salad, soup, and breads. There isn't a children's menu, but young ones can easily share a meal.

    Hours: Open Sun. - Thurs., 11am - 10pm; Fri. - Sat., 11am - midnight.

    Ages: All

BREAKFAST WITH CHIP AND DALE

(714) 956-6755 / www.disneyland.com   *$$$$*

1600 Disneyland Drive, Storytellers Cafe, Grand Californian Hotel, Anaheim

(Going S. on Santa Ana Fwy [5], exit R. on Disney Way. Going N. on the 5, exit L. on Disneyland Dr. Follow the signs. [TG-798 H2])

    Which one is Chip and which one is Dale? Only kids know for sure. The two chipmunks, often accompanied by Pluto or another Disney character, walk around to greet each guest at this special breakfast, sign autographs, and hug (or high five) little guests. Order the buffet, which consists of egg dishes, fresh bakery items, fruit, and juice, or order a la cart. Menu choices include a three-egg omelet served with country potatoes and toast - $9.25; eggs Benedict - $10.50; Mickey-shaped waffles - $8.25; and a Japanese breakfast of grilled salmon, miso soup, rolled egg, toasted seaweed, fruit, and steamed rice - $17.

    The restaurant is done up in turn-of-the-century style and decorated with storytelling murals. Ask your server to tell you a few of the stories. Visit the adjacent DISNEYLAND HOTEL and DOWNTOWN DISNEY (both are listed under the Potpourri section) for more fun things to do and see. DISNEYLAND and CALIFORNIA ADVENTURE (both are listed under the Amusement Parks section) are just next door.

    Hours: Open 6:30am - 11:30am

  Admission: The buffet is $17.95 for adults; $9.95 for ages 3 - 11; $3.95 for children 2 and under. Menu prices vary.

    Ages: All

BREAKFAST WITH MINNIE AND FRIENDS

(714) 956-6755 / www.disneyland.com   *$$$$*

1717 S. West Street, Paradise Pier Hotel, Anaheim

(Going S. on Santa Ana Fwy [5], exit R. on Disney Way. Going N. on the 5, exit L. on Disneyland Dr. Follow the signs. [TG-798 H2])

    This breakfast is described as "character dining." I'm still not sure if the "character" reference refers to Disney characters or to my children! The colorful, art-deco-styled restaurant offers a breakfast buffet with an array of delicious foods: omelets made any way you like 'em (my boys considered watching the cook make omelets part of the entertainment), cereal, yogurt, fresh fruit, hash browns, Danish (hungry yet?), mouse-shaped waffles, and smoked salmon. You may also order a la carte from the menu. A traditional Japanese breakfast is also available.

    Minnie Mouse makes an appearance, dispensing hugs to all the kids. She, along with Daisy and Max, get guests involved with doing the limbo (how low can you go?) and the Conga line. Join in the fun and don't forget to bring your camera!

Take some time, before or after your meal, to ride the glass elevator in the lobby to the top of the hotel. It's not much of a view, but the ride was a thrill for my kids. Sometimes, it's the simple things in life that are the most pleasurable. Visit the adjacent DISNEYLAND HOTEL and DOWNTOWN DISNEY (both are listed under the Potpourri section) for more fun things to do and see. DISNEYLAND and CALIFORNIA ADVENTURE (both are listed under the Amusement Parks section) are just next door.

Hours: Open daily 6:30am - 11am.

Admission: The buffet costs $16.95 for adults; $9.95 for ages 4 - 12; $3.95 for children 3 and under. A la carte menu prices range from $4 to about $11. Parking is free for first three hours, with validation.

Ages: All

ELIZABETH HOWARD'S CURTAIN CALL DINNER THEATER

(714) 838-1540 / www.curtaincalltheater.com
690 El Camino Real, Tustin

See ELIZABETH HOWARD'S CURTAIN CALL DINNER THEATER, under the Shows and Theaters section, for details.

GOOFY'S KITCHEN

(714) 956-6755 / www.disneyland.com   *$$$$*
1150 W. Cerritos Avenue, at the Disneyland Hotel, Anaheim
(Going S. on Santa Ana Fwy [5], exit R. on Disney Way. Going N. on the 5, exit L. on Disneyland Dr. Follow the signs. Trams go from the parking lot to Disneyland. [TG-798 H2])

For a special, Disney-style meal, come to Goofy's Kitchen for an all-you-can-eat breakfast, lunch, or dinner buffet. Your children's favorite characters come by the tables for a hug. We were visited by Pluto, Minnie Mouse, Chip (or was it Dale?), John Smith, Miko and, of course, Goofy. Kids even eat a bite or two in between hopping up to touch the costumed characters. Remember to bring your camera (and your autograph book)!

We stuffed ourselves at the dinner buffet with prime rib, ham, chicken, seafood, fruit, salad, and scrumptious desserts. (The way my family suffers just to be able to share with you!) The kids have their own food bar that offers familiar favorites like macaroni and cheese, mini-hotdogs, spaghetti, breaded shrimp, and chicken strips. The lunch buffet consists of salads, fruit, vegetables, pastas, chicken, BBQ beef ribs, and more. The kids' lunch buffet is similar to their dinner selection. The breakfast buffet has equally delicious offerings of Mickey-shaped waffles, pancakes, home fries, cereal, oatmeal, fruit, and omelets.

Goofy's Kitchen offers good food in a fun, family atmosphere. Make your outing even more of a treat by coming early, or staying after mealtime, to walk around and enjoy the hotel grounds. Visit the adjacent DISNEYLAND HOTEL and DOWNTOWN DISNEY (both are listed in the Potpourri section) for more fun things to do and see. DISNEYLAND and CALIFORNIA ADVENTURE (both are listed under the Amusement Parks section) are just next door.

Hours: Open daily for breakfast 7am - 11:30am. Open daily for lunch
noon - 2pm. Open daily for dinner 5pm - 9pm.
Admission: Breakfast buffet is $16.95 for adults; lunch is $17.95; dinner is
$26.95. All meals are $9.95 for ages 3 - 11; $3.95 for children 2
and under. Parking is free for the first three hours, with
validation.
Ages: 1½ years and up.

GOSPEL BRUNCH (Anaheim)

(714) 778-2583 / www.hob.com
1530 S. Disneyland Drive at the House of Blues, Anaheim
(Going S. on Santa Ana Fwy [5], exit R. on Disney Way. Going N. on the 5, exit L. on Disneyland
Dr. Follow the signs. It's in the Downtown Disney venue. [TG-798 H1])

See GOSPEL BRUNCH (Hollywood) under this section for details. This
location's building doesn't resemble a shack and it is located in DOWNTOWN
DISNEY. (See the Potpourri section for details.)

MCDONALD'S (with a train theme)

(714) 521-2303 / www.mcdonalds.com
7861 Beach Boulevard, Buena Park
(Exit Artesia Fwy [91] S. on Beach Blvd. It's just N. of Knott's Berry Farm. [TG-767 H3])

We've nicknamed this "Train McDonald's" because the center of the eating
area has a large model train exhibit with seating available all around it. Kids
(and adults) are enthralled as the train goes around the mountains, through the
tunnels, and past villages. Tracks and a train also run overhead.
Hours: Open daily. The drive-through is open 24 hours.
Ages: All

MEDIEVAL TIMES

(714) 521-4740 / www.medievaltimes.com
7662 Beach Boulevard, Buena Park

See MEDIEVAL TIMES, under the Shows and Theaters section, for details.

PLAZA GARIBALDI DINNER THEATER

(714) 758-9014
1490 S. Anaheim Boulevard, Anaheim

See PLAZA GARIBALDI DINNER THEATER, under the Shows and
Theaters section, for details.

POFOLKS

(714) 521-8955 / www.pofolks.com
7701 Beach Boulevard, Buena Park
(Exit Artesia Fwy [91] S. on Beach Blvd. [TG-767 H3])

PoFolks is a great place to come for home-style cooking and a nice, family
atmosphere. The walls are decorated with pictures, toll-paintings, and other
things that make it look homey. A model train is running on tracks overhead and

there are a few table games to keep kids entertained. Menu choices include soup ($2.49), salads ($5.29 for a chef's), country ham steak ($8.49), home-style dinners like pot roast ($8.99), plus chicken, ribs, and fish. Kids' meal choices include chicken, fish, a burger, a corn dog, or a grilled cheese sandwich for $3.29. Beverages are extra. Tip: McDonald's, just down the street, has a free magazine called "Welcome" that usually contains discount coupons for PoFolks.

    Hours: Open Sun. - Thurs., 7am - 9:30pm; Fri. - Sat., 7am - 10:30pm.

    Ages: All

PRACTICALLY PERFECT TEA WITH MARY POPPINS ☼

(714) 956-6755 / www.disneyland.com   *$$$$*

1717 S. West Street, Paradise Pier Hotel, Anaheim

(Going S. on Santa Ana Fwy [5], exit R. on Disney Way. Going N. on the 5, exit L. on Disneyland Dr. Follow the signs. [TG-798 H2])

Get the kids dressed up and enjoy a spot of tea in this supercalifragilisticexpialidocious tea room. Half of the cozy room is done like a Victorian parlor, with couches and ornate chairs in rose pink hues, while the other half looks like a garden room, with white wicker furniture, climbing green vines, and bird cages. I don't know if it was the somewhat subdued atmosphere, soft music, bone china, or the presentation of dainty finger foods, but when we entered the tea room, my boy's demeanor changed (thankfully) from rambunctious to a bit more proper and gentlemanly-like.

When Mary Poppins appears, her presence lights up the room. Everyone's favorite nanny makes sure she chats with each person, addressing them entirely in character. She is witty, states that "hugs are most definitely allowed," and periodically entertains with stories and songs. Children especially like the rendition of *Chim-Chiminey* because she powders her nose with soot as she sings. A highlight is dressing up in feather boas and hats (top hats for males) and having your picture taken with Mary Poppins. Tip: Bring your camera!

For adults the breakfast tea consists of selections of fresh scones, mini quiche, scrambled eggs and ham, fresh fruit, an apple crepe, wild rice pancakes, and a wide assortment of tea. Children receive scones, a Mickey Mouse waffle, scrambled egg and ham, and tea, taken with just a spoonful of sugar. Afternoon teas include a tasty assortment of finger sandwiches (the mango and turkey combination, and the sun-dried tomato and cream cheese sandwiches were surprisingly good), soup du jour, sweets to nibble on, and, of course, tea. Children's sandwiches are peanut butter and jelly, and ham and cheese, plus some chicken salad, sweets, and tea. Other beverages are available. Etiquette tips for children: 1) Just one lump of sugar, not five; and 2) Don't sip tea with your spoon still in the cup. Note: The Tea is an hour and a half long and my boys and the young girl with us did get a little antsy.

Take the time, before or after your tea, to ride the glass elevator in the lobby of the hotel. It's not much of a view, but the ride was a thrill for my kids. (Sometimes it's the simple things in life that are the most pleasurable.) Visit the adjacent DISNEYLAND HOTEL and DOWNTOWN DISNEY (both are listed under the Potpourri section) for more fun things to do and see. DISNEYLAND and CALIFORNIA ADVENTURE (both are listed under the Amusement Parks section) are just next door.

Hours: Tea is served Wed. at 12:30pm; Sat. at 10am, 12:30pm, and 3pm; Sun. at 12:30pm and 3pm. Additional teas are served in the summer Mon. and Fri. at 12:30pm. Call for special holiday hours. Reservations are required.

Admission: $21.95 for adults; $13.95 for children 12 and under. Parking is free for the first three hours, with validation.

Ages: 3 years and up.

RITZ-CARLTON HOTEL TEA   ☼

(949) 240-2000 / www.ritzcarlton.com $$$$$

1 Ritz-Carlton Drive, Dana Point   ☷

(Exit San Diego Fwy [5] W. on Camino Los Ramblas, turns into Pacific Coast Hwy [1], L. at Ritz-Carlton Dr. [TG-971 F4])

The Ritz-Carlton is an incredibly classy hotel. Celebrate your child with a special afternoon of tea in an elegant room that overlooks the ocean. The Traditional Tea offers a delectable variety of pastries, scrumptious finger sandwiches, a fruit platter, and tea (of course) for $30 per person. Get the royal treatment with the Royal Tea, which comes with champagne or a non-alcoholic cocktail, a choice of teas, finger sandwiches, pastries, and strawberries and cream, all for $35 per person. Come early or stay a bit afterwards to explore the gracious hotel and beautiful grounds. Teddy Bear Teas, for families, are offered on selected days in December and include a marionette show. Call for times and details.

Hours: Seatings for tea are Mon. - Fri. every half hour between 2pm - 4pm; Sat. - Sun. at 2pm and 4:30pm. Call to make reservations.

Admission: Prices are quoted above.

Ages: 5 years and up.

RIVERBOAT RESTAURANT   ☼

(949) 673-3425 / www.newportbeach.com/riverboat $$$

151 E. Coast Highway, Newport Beach

(Take Costa Mesa Fwy [55] to end, where it turns into Newport Blvd., L. on E. 17th St., R., at end, on Dover Dr., L on E. Coast Hwy., on Newport Bay [TG-889 B7])

Dine Mark Twainish style in an intimate room on board a Mississippi riverboat. The view of the harbor is nice and the food is a cut above. Dinner selections range from $15 to $25 and include prime rib, filet mignon, chicken specialties, a selection of fish, St. Louis ribs, jumbo prawns, and more. Come early for the sundown specials. Enjoy live entertainment, via a pianist and vocalist, on Friday and Saturday evenings.

The luncheon fare is equally delicious. Kid's lunches are $4 for grilled cheese, cheese quesadilla, or a burger, plus fries and a beverage. Children's dinners range from $5 to $6 for a burger, fish and chips, or macaroni and cheese, plus fries and a beverage. Brunch is served only on Sundays. Note: The restaurant shares the boat with the NEWPORT HARBOR NAUTICAL MUSEUM. Look under the Museums section for more details.

Hours: Open Tues. - Thurs., 11am to 9pm; Fri. - Sat., 11am - midnight; Sun., 9am - 9pm.

Ages: All

SAM'S SEAFOOD "POLYNESIAN SPECTACULAR" ☼

(562) 592-1321 / www.menusunlimited.com/samsseafood $$$$
16278 Pacific Coast Highway, Huntington Beach   ⊞
(Exit San Diego Fwy [405] S. on Seal Beach Blvd., L. on Pacific Coast Highway. [TG-826 J6])

Aloha! Imagine a balmy evening where Hawaiian music plays softly in the background while you're savoring delicious seafood. Welcome to . . . not Hawaii, but Sam's! This tropically themed restaurant offers all this, plus beautiful South Seas murals, a waterfall decorated with flowers and real volcanic rocks, carved wood totem poles, and (padded) bamboo furniture. Dining here is a treat for the senses and palate. Lunch choices include fried clam strips ($4.95), fried jumbo shrimp ($6.50), broiled salmon ($14.95), swordfish steak ($14.95), shrimp Louie ($9.95), and steak sandwich or hamburger ($4.95 each). Dinner selections include calamari ($13.95), steamed clams ($8.50), prime rib ($14.95), lobster tail ($21.95), and teriyaki steak or barbeque ribs ($13.95 each). The childrens' menu is the same for both lunch and dinner, although the prices are not. It includes fish 'n chips, fried chicken, a grilled cheese sandwich, or a burger, plus fries, for $3.50 for lunch; $4.25 for dinner. Beverages are extra.

If you want to spend more time vacationing at the Pacific islands (via Sam's), come to the three-hour Polynesian Spectacular offered in a "hidden" room just off the main dining area. Seating begins at 7pm, with each party being seated at individual tables. Live music accompanies your meal - feel free to sway along. Although the traditional music is good, two hours of this pre-show fare, including songs sung in native languages, can make a younger child antsy. Dinner selections include prime rib, Mahi Mahi, baby back BBQ ribs, Snow Crab legs, teriyaki shrimp, or Hawaiian-style chicken, accompanied by salad, rice, and dessert. Beverages are served with little paper parasols.

The featured one-hour-and-fifteen-minute show starts at 9pm on a stage that has a waterfall surrounded by rocks and flowers. The singers, dancers, and musicians have Polynesian roots. The variety of performers' costumes include colorful print shirts and dresses, grass skirts, bandeau tops, and feather headdresses. The costumes authentically reflect the islands represented throughout the show - Hawaii, Tahiti, Samoa, and New Zealand. Highlights include the Samoan body slap dance (ouch!), graceful hula dances, belly dances (how do they move like that?), and fierce-looking Maori warriors, complete with face paint and spears, who stomp around and stick out their tongues.

Tip: If you're celebrating a birthday, anniversary, or other special event, tell your waiter upon arrival so that the emcee can include it during her announcements. Also, hang loose and go native by wearing a tropical outfit!

Hours: Sam's is open daily 11:30am - 10pm. The Polynesian Spectacular is offered Fri. nights April through November, 7pm - 10:15pm.

Admission: Meal prices are listed above. The Polynesian Spectacular is $31.95 for adults; $26.95 for ages 4 - 11; children 3 and under are free.

Ages: 5 years and up.

SPAGHETTI STATION

(714) 956-3250 / www.spaghetti-station.com   *$$$*

999 W. Ball Road, Anaheim

(Going S. on Santa Ana Fwy [5], exit Ball Rd. It's on the corner of the off ramp and Ball Rd. Going N. on 5, exit N. on Harbor Blvd., L. on Ball Rd. [TG-768 H7])

For a taste of the Old West, come eat at Spaghetti Station. The lobby area has a stuffed mountain lion and deer, Butch Cassidy's saddle (yes, it really belonged to him), wooden Indians, and cowboy statues. Either before or after your meal take a "tour" through the rustic restaurant. Lots of terrific Western memorabilia is displayed in glass cases in the rooms, such as lanterns, cowboy boots, woman's lace-up shoes, saddles, musical instruments, guns, arrowheads, tomahawks, and arrows, plus statues of bulls, cowboys, and stagecoaches. Upstairs is a small game room with a billiard table.

Each room has a stone fireplace in a house-like setting. The menu has fun facts about the gold rush and other important Western dates and happenings. Food choices include spaghetti, fixed with a wide variety of sauces, plus ribs, chicken, pizza, salad, and more. Prices range from $7.95 to $15.95. The kids' menu offers pizza, spaghetti, cheese ravioli, or chicken tenders for $3.95 to $5.95. Beverages are $1.50. Although there is a bar toward the front, the rest of the restaurant is great for your little cowhands.

Hours: Open Mon. - Fri., 11am - 11pm; Sat., noon - 11pm; Sun., noon - 10pm.

Admission: Menu prices are listed above.

Ages: 2 years and up.

TIBBIE'S MUSIC HALL

(888) 4TIBBIES (484-2243) / www.tibbiesmusichall.com

7530 Orangethorpe Avenue, Buena Park

See TIBBIE'S MUSIC HALL under the Shows and Theaters section for details.

VICTORIAN MANOR TEA ROOM

(714) 771-4044 / www.victorianmanor.com   *$$$*

204 N. Olive Street, Old Towne, Orange

(Exit Costa Mesa Fwy [55] W. on Chapman Ave., R. on Olive [TG-799 G4])

Simply enchanting! This turn-of-the-century Queen Anne Victorian home, including a charming garden, has been lovingly restored and embellished. Each of the five intimate tea rooms are painted a different color. Every one is uniquely decorated (to the hilt!) with old-fashioned women's hats, tea pots and cups, antique boots, period clothing, stencils, and/or an amazing assortment of knick knacks, some of which are available to purchase. The tablecloths are lacy, checkered, or velvety; the centerpieces are traditional (flowers) or whimsical (ornamental teapots); and individual chairs are artistically painted with clouds, a garden scene, polka dots, and other designs. Soothing music plays in the background in each room.

Besides a wide variety of teas, such as apricot, vanilla cream spice, jasmine flower, raspberry cream pecan, and Earl Grey, the Manor offers a menu with sandwiches, soups, and Chef, Ceasar, or chicken salads, as well as scones and confections. Your choice of sandwich - tuna salad, egg salad, turkey, ham and cheese, BLT, roast beef or club - is $7.95, and includes potato salad, fruit, apple sauce or pudding. High teas are also served, such as Lady Tiffany Tea, consisting of a pot of tea, scones with cream and jam, soup of the day, tea sandwiches, vegetables, fruit, cookies, and other confections for $15.98. Children, up to 12 years old, can partake of teas, too (or tea for two?) such as the Victorian Tinkerbell Tea, comprised of tea, pink lemonade, or hot chocolate; scones with cream and jam; four tea sandwiches of peanut butter and jelly, egg salad, cheese, and tuna (or ask the waitress for other choices); and the dessert of the day all for $12.98. Special teas are also available. Friday night dinners consist of a preset menu and are offered by reservation only. What a *tea*lightful stop!

Hours: Open Mon. - Fri., 10am - 5pm; open Fri. until 8pm for dinner; Sat. - Sun., 10am - 6pm.

Admission: Prices are mentioned above.

Ages: 4 years and up.

VILLA PARK PHARMACY

(714) 998-3030 / www.villaparkpharmacy.com   *$*

17821 Santiago Boulevard, Villa Park

(Going S. on Costa Mesa Fwy [55], exit E. on Lincoln, R. on Santiago (right after the Fwy). Going N. on 55, exit E. on Nohl Ranch Rd., R. on Santiago. [TG-770 B7])

Chocolate phosphates, sorbet, dot candy - if these things bring back fond memories, or just make you hungry, head to the Villa Park Pharmacy, where old-fashioned fun is not out of date. The soda fountain is right out of the 1800's, with an old marble counter-top and brass bar stools, plus ornate ceiling tiles and ceiling fans. There are a few booths here, too. Sip a Green River, or another specialty juice, or just have an ice-cream cone.

The candy "store" has big glass display cases, just like in an old-time general store, filled with a delicious assortment of candy. Sometimes creamy fudge or caramel apples are being made on the nearby counter-top.

The rest of the store is a wonderful blend of antique fixtures and modern products. For instance, a 1938 ticket agent's booth is now used to sell lotto tickets, while an old-fashioned Post Office in the back is still used as a real Post Office. An old red phone booth from London adds a wonderful touch of whimsy. The store also carries a full line of cards, books, videos, cosmetics, and gifts. And yes, there is a pharmacy here, too.

Hours: Open Mon. - Sat., 9am - 7pm; Sun., 11am - 5pm.

Ages: 2 years and up.

WATSON DRUGS AND SODA FOUNTAIN

(714) 633-1050 - restaurant; (714) 532-6315 - pharmacy /   *$$$*
www.menusunlimited.com/watsondrug

116 E. Chapman Avenue, Orange

(Exit Costa Mesa Fwy [55] W. on Chapman Ave. It's just E. of the shopping center circle. [TG-799 G4])

Watson Drugs and Soda Fountain, built in 1899, has the distinction of being the oldest drugstore in Orange County. Located in the wonderful shopping center of Old Town, it is a great place to stop for a meal, or just a treat. Part of Watson Drugs is a pharmacy/gift shop. Look up at the eclectic, old-fashioned items on the overhead shelves.

The other half is a retro 40's diner, with a big jukebox, red vinyl seats, and lots of memorabilia, including old license plates that decorate the walls. Breakfast, such as omelets, pancakes, or french toast, costs about $5. Lunch, like chicken salad, roast beef, burgers, or tuna melts, costs about $4.75. Dinner, such as steak, fish, or chicken, costs, on the average, $7.75. The kids' menu includes a choice of a hot dog, tuna fish sandwich, or a grilled cheese sandwich for $2.95. Fries are included in the kids' meals, but drinks are extra. Let's not forget the most important food item - dessert! Ice cream floats, sundaes, shakes, and more, are yours for the asking (and the paying). Eat inside and enjoy the ambiance, or choose one of the tables outside, and watch the world go by.

Hours: Open Mon. - Sat., 6am - 9pm; Sun., 8am - 6pm.
Ages: 2 years and up.

WILD BILL'S WILD WEST DINNER EXTRAVAGANZA

(800) 883-1546 or (714) 522-6414

7600 Beach Boulevard, Buena Park

See WILD BILL'S WILD WEST DINNER EXTRAVAGANZA under the Shows and Theaters section for details.

BIG TOP FOOD 'N' FUN RESTAURANT

(909) 785-3090 / www.castlepark.com   *$$$*

3500 Polk Street, Riverside

(Exit Riverside Fwy [91] N. on La Sierra Ave., R. on Magnolia Ave., R. on Polk St. It's adjacent to CASTLE PARK. [TG-744 F1])

For big time fun, come eat at Big Top Restaurant! The good-sized restaurant resembles a circus big top, complete with a lifelike statue of a circus elephant outside. The inside feels like a circus, too. (Then again, meal times at our house always feel like a circus what with balancing plates of food, kids acting clownish, etc.) Red and white are the predominant colors. Overhead are stuffed animals in acrobatic poses.

The food is good, with pizza being the featured item - $14.95 for a medium, two-topping pizza. A salad bar, burgers, hot dogs, chicken nuggets, and sandwiches are also available. Kids love to be entertained at meal time (any time!), so the Big Top bear mascot occasionally appears on stage for a short show. There are a few kiddie rides, and a small arcade room with "G-rated" games, plus a redemption center.

Big Top also offers educational tours. For example, a half-hour Pizza Tour is given where kids learn how pizza fits into the four basic food groups, see how pizza is made, and make their own. Then, they get to eat it! $2.50 per person includes the tour, a slice of pizza, a soft drink, and five tokens. For an additional $1.50 each, children can also play a round of miniature golf. A minimum of ten kids are needed for this tour. See CASTLE PARK, under the Amusement Parks section, for a description of the adjacent park.

Hours: Open daily in the summer 10am - 9pm. Open the rest of the year Fri., 5pm - 9pm; Sat., 10am - 9pm; Sun., 10am - 8pm.

Ages: 2 years and up.

FARRELL'S ICE CREAM PARLOUR (Temecula)

(909) 296-0668
$$$

40820 Winchester Road, Temecula

(Exit the Temecula Valley Fwy [15] N.E. on Winchester Rd. [79]. It's near the shopping mall next to Edwards Cinema. [TG-958 G3])

See FARRELL'S ICE CREAM PARLOUR in San Diego in this section for more details. This location is very similar, serving up the same kind of food in the same fun atmosphere. Kid's meal here are $5.25 for your choice of hamburger, cheese pizza, fish 'n chips, grilled cheese, or hot dog, plus fries and a drink.

Hours: Open Sun. - Thurs., 11am -9pm; Fri. - Sat., 11am - 10pm.

Ages: All

TOM'S FARMS

(909) 277- 9992 - general info; (909) 277-4012 - Tom's Hamburgers   !/$

23900 Temescal Canyon Road, Corona

(Exit Corona Fwy [15] S. on Temescal Canyon Rd., past the fast food restaurants at the corner. [TG-804 D5])

Tom's Farms consists of five separate buildings, each one selling different products. The front building has farm fresh produce, dried fruit, nuts, and candies. This is a delicious stop. The adjacent Bird's Nest is unusual with its various live birds and related bird items for sale. The small restaurant, Tom's Hamburgers, offers large portions of food. Tasty hamburgers start at $2.95. Kids have their choice of a corn dog, grilled cheese sandwich, or a burger, plus fries and a drink for $2.25. An outside eating area is set up around a small pond that has black swans. Beyond the pond are a few penned farm animals to pet. A wine and cheese store also offers baked goods. On weekends only, although not during the month of January, a few craft booths are set up here, too. Grab a snack or eat a meal at this "farm" with a folksy ambiance.

Hours: Open in the summer daily 8am - 8pm. Open the rest of the year daily 8am - 8pm.

Admission: Free

Ages: All

BARSTOW STATION

(760) 256-0366 / www.barstowstation.com   *$$*
1611 E. Main Street, Barstow
(Exit Mojave Fwy [15] E. on Main St. [TG-3680 B3])

Several retired railroad cars are grouped together to form a unique, albeit brief, shopping and eating experience. Eating McDonald's food in an old train car might taste the same as eating it elsewhere, but the atmosphere here makes it fun. Other rail cars offer bakery goods, ice cream, candy (these are all the important things in life!), souvenirs, and knick knacks. The Station fulfills its goal of being an interesting edible adventure.

Hours: Open Mon. - Thurs., 9am - 8pm; Fri. - Sun., 8am - 10pm. McDonald's is open Sun. - Thurs., 6am - 10pm; Fri. - Sat., 6am - 11pm.
Admission: Free to enter; bring spending money.
Ages: All

OAK GLEN / APPLE PICKING & TOURS

(909) 797-6833 / www.oakglen.net   *$$*
Oak Glen Road, Oak Glen
(From the San Bernardino Fwy [10], exit N.E., on Yucaipa Blvd., L. onto Oak Glen Rd. In about 6 miles, you'll see the sign, "Welcome to Scenic Oak Glen." Orchards and shops dot the long and winding road. From the 60 Fwy exit N. on Beaumont, which turns into Oak Glen Rd. after quite a few miles. This entry names the attractions in order, via exiting the 10 Fwy. [TG-610 J7])

Your *delicious* journey into Oak Glen takes you through a town that is *ripe* with fun things to do. Several orchards offer U-Pic, which means you pick your own apples, raspberries, blackberries, pears, and pumpkins, all in season, of course. Apple varieties range from the exotic, such as Ida Red and Pearmain, to the more familiar ones of Jonathon, Granny Smith, Pippin, Braeburn, and Red Delicious. Most orchards also have wonderful country stores with all sorts of apple concoctions and apple-related items for sale. Although berry-picking season starts in late July and apple season runs from the end of August through the middle of November, there are many year-round reasons to visit Oak Glen. Tips: Although weekends (especially in October) can be crowded, some orchards will only let you pick apples then, so get an early start on your day's adventure. Call the orchards to find out when your favorite type of apple will be ripe. Buy an apple-recipe book, as kids get a little carried away with the joy of picking apples! Here are a few of our favorites stops:

Parrish Pioneer Ranch, 38561 Oak Glen Road, (909) 797-1753 / www.parrishranch.com: The Ranch has a picnic area, pre-picked apples for sale, a few gift shops, and a restaurant. Llamas, goats, and emus are in pens by the parking lot. Harvest season entertainment includes Johnny Appleseed, Yodeling Merle (who sings cowboy songs), and Stunt Masters of the Old West shows. These half-hour shows take place at the outside theater at 1pm, 2:30pm, and 4pm on weekends, weather permitting. Performances always first include a talk on firearm safety, followed by stunts, a melodrama, or a farce on life in the 1800's. Admission is $2 for adults; $1 for ages 7 to 15; children 6 years and under are free. The shops are open daily 10am to 6pm.

Oak Tree Village, (909) 797-4020 / www.oaktree-village.com: Located in the center of Oak Glen is the Village, a wonderful place to shop, play, and eat. Kids enjoy walking on the hilly trail through the good-sized animal and nature park. Penned deer, sheep, llamas, goats, and birds are in here, plus a lot of squirrels that are running around freely. Admission is $2 per person; children 1 year and under are free. On the weekends only during harvest time, the Village offers pony rides ($3); scale model train rides ($2); panning for (and keeping) real gold ($1 per pan); and fishing at the small Trout Pond inside the animal park. Fishing costs the $2 entrance fee into the nature park plus the price per inch of whatever fish you catch. Poles and bait are available for rent for $3. Up the walkway is Mountain Town, a store with a small cave-like museum that displays taxidermied wildlife as well as a few live reptiles. Entrance is 50¢ for adults and children; 25¢ for seniors. Along the perimeter of the museum are mini-stores that display merchandise tempting to shoppers young and old.

Snow Line Orchard, 39400 Oak Glen Road, (909) 797-3415: This short drive up a dirt street offers rows and rows of U-Pic raspberries in season. (We pick basketfuls and freeze them.) In the store, purchase fresh apples and tasty blends of raspberry/apple cider and cherry/apple cider. Tip: On weekends watch the doughnut machine at work providing sweet concoctions. The orchard is open daily September through mid-December from 9am to 5pm.

Los Rios Rancho / Wildlands Conservancy, 39610 Oak Glen Road, (909) 797-1005 - Los Rios; (909) 797-8507 / www.wildlandsconservancy.org - Wildlands Conservancy: This working apple ranch has acres of orchards, a store, a delicious bakery, U-Pic fruit, wonderful nature walking trails, and two picnic areas. One picnic area is the large, grassy front lawn that has picnic tables. The other is a pretty, wooded area, with picnic tables, located behind the store.

An almost two-mile dirt nature trail, with several off shoots and dead-ends, loops around on one section of the ranch land. It leads alongside a stream, through chaparral, and past two ponds where ducks flock, when the pond water is not being used to irrigate the apple orchard. One trail branch, the California tree trail, even has a few redwoods and Giant Sequoias along the route. The trails are open to the general public on weekends only from 9am to 4:30pm and for tour groups during the week.

Los Rios offers hour-long tours during harvest season for groups of ten or more. The tour includes pressing (and sampling) cider, taste testing and comparing the different types of apples, eating fresh-dipped caramel apples (for an additional $1.50 per person), peeking into the packing house/cider mill, hearing the history of local families, and going into the apple orchards to learn about agriculture, particularly the organic aspects of farming. Tours are $4.25 per person. A petting zoo with sheep, goats, ponies, a llama, a donkey, an ostrich, and an emu is also open in harvest season. Admission is $2 per person. The Rancho is open January through August, Wednesday through Friday from 10am to 5pm, and Saturday and Sunday from 10am to 5pm. It's open September through December daily from 9am to 5pm.

Schoolhouse Museum (see this entry under the MUSEUMS section.)

Riley's Log Cabin Farm and Orchard, 12201 S. Oak Glen Road, (909) 797-4061: This orchard looks like it is set in the same time period as *Little*

House on the Prairie and has a delightful store that offers old-fashioned toys, books, and other items. On weekends in July and August come pick berries and a few other types of fruit. In the fall, thirteen different vanities of apples, plus pumpkins, are ripe for visitors to harvest.

A bountiful crop of spring and fall tours includes a colonial or farm Bible study; participating in frontier skills such as chopping wood, washing clothes through a wringer, writing with a quill pen, starting a fire with flint and steel, pumping water, and gardening and harvesting crops; building a log cabin; learning old-fashioned dances such as the minuet and/or square dancing; grinding corn and baking Johnny cakes; archery; tomahawk throwing; and pressing apple cider. Tours are offered May through June, on weekends only, for groups of 120 or more. Fall tours begin Labor Day weekend until the end of November and are offered Tuesday through Friday, usually between 10am to 2pm, to groups with a minimum of thirty people or $165. Tour options range from two to six hours and cost between $5.50 and $10 per person. Rope making and candlemaking are just a few of the other activities offered. Bring a sack lunch to enjoy by the pond picnic area. Riley's is also open on weekends during the fall from 10am to 4pm for group tours, no minimum needed, and for family and individual tours. Advanced reservations are necessary. Tours are $5 per person. The two-hour weekend tour includes participating in the above mentioned frontier skills, from chopping wood to harvesting, plus making corn husk dolls, and one other selected activity. Visitors are welcome to add on other options, such as pressing cider at $6.50 a gallon, practicing archery for $1 for four arrows, tomahawk throwing for $1 for six throws, eating hot-dipped caramel apples for $1.75, and of course, picking apples. Weekend entertainment includes "Johnny Appleseed" playing his fiddle. Ask for Sharon or Marcy to book tours. The farm hosts occasional musical and living history events and hoedowns, and in conjunction with the Riley's listed below, outstanding Civil War encampments and reenactments in June and November (see the Calendar section). Riley's is closed December through April.

Riley's Farm and Orchard, 12253 S. Oak Glen Road, (909) 790-2364 / www.rileysbarn.com: Neighboring in-laws own this Riley's farm that also has U-Pic apples and berries, and a general store with colonial-times toys and games, and more modern purchases. Two-hour tours, for a minimum of twenty-five people, include a horse-drawn hayride, making cider (a fascinating process), drinking cider, eating hot-dipped caramel apples (a personal favorite), and your choice of buttermaking, candlemaking, doing farm chores, tin smithing, making a small wooden toy, or access to the petting farm. A blacksmith area is also available. $5.50 per person for this tour is a great deal! Bring a picnic lunch or grab a bite to eat from the barbecue. Food selections include tri-tip, chicken, hamburgers, and hot dogs. Riley's is open for group tours and private bookings only, April through July daily from 10am to 5pm. These tours do not include apple-related activities. It is open for tours as well as to the general public August through mid-December, Tuesday through Sunday, 10am to 5pm. Pears, blackberries, and raspberries are ripe in late summer. Apples are ready to be picked, baked, sauced, and pressed in the fall. Riley's, in conjunction with the above-mentioned Riley's, hosts outstanding Civil War encampments and reenactments in June and November (see the Calendar section). The farm is closed mid-December through March.

Hours: Apple-picking season is September through November, with most U-Pics open on the weekends only. Stores, tours, and many other activities are usually open year round.

Admission: Pay for U-Pic fruit by the pound. See Los Rios and both Rileys Farms for tour prices and hours.

Ages: All ages for most activities; 5 years and up for the educational tours.

PEGGY SUE'S 50's DINER (Victorville)

(760) 951-5001 / www.peggysuesdiner.com

16885 Stoddard Wells Road, Victorville

(Exit Mojave Fwy [15] N.W. on Stoddard Wells Road. [TG-4296 F2])

See PEGGY SUE'S 50's DINER (Yermo) in this section for a description. This location's building, however, is much smaller and is not as extensively decorated.

Hours: Open Mon. - Thurs., Sat. - Sun.,7am - 9pm; Fri., 7am - 10pm

PEGGY SUE'S 50's DINER (Yermo)   ☀

(760) 254-3370 / www.peggysuesdiner.com   *$$$*

35654 Yermo Road, Yermo   ♨

(Exit Mojave Fwy [15] S. on Ghost Town Rd / Daggett - Yermo Rd., L. on Yermo Rd. [TG-3681 F2])

If your cruisin' for good food served in a really happening place, head over to Peggy Sue's. This diner has several rooms, including small ones packed with booths and a larger room with chairs and tables. The walls feature an impressive and eclectic array of movie and television personality memorabilia, including Lucille Ball, Ricky Ricardo, Cary Grant, Marilyn Monroe, Elvis, James Dean, Buddy Holly, Laurel and Hardy, and the gang from the Wizard of Oz, all portrayed in pictures, posters, masks, dolls, and paintings. Gaudy decor (i.e. paintings on black velvet and cheesy trinkets) is interspersed with nicer mementos (i.e. fine portraits of celebrities and expensive-looking memorabilia). An occasional mannequin dressed in period clothing adds to the kitschyness. The jukebox plays 50's music every night except Friday nights when live music is performed. The diner also features a pizza parlor towards the back, a soda fountain, and a very small outdoor park with a pond, fountains, grass, and a few trees. An attached Dime Store and Curios Shop sells touristy television and movie souvenirs, as well as a number of collector items.

Breakfast options include three eggs any style with ham ($6.49) or pancakes ($3.99). Lunch fare includes a burger ($4.89), club sandwich ($6.69), or meatloaf ($5.49). For dinner, try a New York steak ($9.79), ham steak ($7.79), Southern fried chicken ($8.49), or chef salad ($6.49). Desserts include Green River or cherry phosphates ($1.09), malts or shakes ($2.99), berry pie ($1.99) or cheesecake ($3.29). Kid's menu choices for breakfast include an egg with toast ($1.99); one egg, two strips of bacon or sausage ($2.99); french toast and two strips of bacon or sausage ($2.49); or a hot cake with bacon or sausage ($2.49).

Lunch and dinner selections, which all include french fries, range from grilled cheese sandwich or chicken nuggets to a hot dog or a hamburger. Each meal is $2.99 and drinks are an additional 79¢.

Hours: Open Mon. - Thurs., Sat. - Sun., 7am - 9pm; Fri., 7am - 10pm.
Admission: Prices are listed above.
Ages: All

ANTHONY'S FISH GROTTO

(619) 463-0368 / www.gofishanthonys.com
9530 Murray Drive, La Mesa
(Exit 8 Fwy N. on Severin/Fuerte, R. on Murray Dr. [TG-1251 C7])

$$$

Shell I tell you about this restaurant that resembles an underwater sea cave? It's a pearl of a place. Enter through a giant clam shell. Fish are "swimming" around on the ceiling. Octopus-covered lamps are at the front desk and a fish mosaic covers the wall here. The booths are upholstered with fish designs. Waist-high coral barriers separate the restaurant into sections. (Look for eel and other creatures peeking out from the coral rocks.) The bar is in a cave-like setting. Even the restrooms maintain the theme!

Dining is available inside, or outside under shade trees on patio tables and chairs. Both seating arrangements allow guests to overlook the grotto's small lake. Duck feed is available from the restaurant. A dry-docked boat on the lawn houses a small video arcade.

The Fish Grotto specializes in a wide variety of fresh fish and shellfish, of course, although it also offers chicken and steak as well. Here's a sampling of the menu: Crab stuffed mushrooms ($6.95); clam chowder ($3.20 a pint); shrimp, scallop and swordfish kabobs ($8.95); hand-battered oysters ($11.50); coconut fried shrimp ($14.95); and Alaskan King crab legs ($24.95). The kid's menu offers fish dippers ($3.50), grilled cheese ($2.50), pasta ($3.50), cod ($4.95), and chicken ($4.95). Drinks are extra. Note: Take some of Anthony's fish home as this location also has a retail market.

Although this is the only Anthony's so wonderfully themed, other Anthony's locations have the same great food and most have some sort of view. Other locations are San Diego Bay at 1360 N. Harbor Drive at Ash Street - (619) 232-5103 - a waterfront restaurant overlooking the San Diego Bay; Chula Vista at 215 W. Bay Boulevard off Hwy 5 at 'E' Street - (619) 425-4200 - an open and airy atmosphere with a fish aquarium, fish sand castings, and more; Rancho Bernardo at 11666 Avena Place at Bernardo Center Drive - (619) 451-2070 - has the beautiful Webb Park as its backdrop.

Hours: Open daily 11am - 10pm. Call for hours of other locations.
Ages: All

AVIARA FOUR SEASONS RESORT

(760) 603-6800 / www.fourseasons.com
7100 Four Seasons Point, Carlsbad
(Exit San Diego Fwy [5] E. on Poinsettia Ln., R. on Aviara Pkwy., R. on Four Seasons Point. [TG-1127 C6])

$$$$

All dressed up and nowhere to go? Indulge in an elegant repast of tea time at this fine resort hotel. Tables in the Tea Lounge are covered with white linen, sprinkled with rose petals, and set with fine china. A three-tiered silver cake plate bears scrumptious edibles of finger sandwiches; scones with rose petal jelly, lemon curd, and Devonshire cream; and petit fours. Sip your choice of teas, including herbal and fruit infusions.

Hours: Tea is served daily 2pm - 4:30pm.
Admission: $18 per person. Valet parking is complementary, with the tea.
Ages: 4 years and up.

CALICO RANCH

(858) 586-0392 - during the week. / www.julianfun.com   *$$*
4200 Wynola Road and Hwy 78/79, Wynola
(Off Hwy 78/79, between Julian and San Ysabel [TG-1135 F5])

This twenty-acre apple orchard is one of the only U-pick orchards left in the Julian area. It boasts of 130 different kinds of apples, although the rarer types have only one tree here. Visitors may enter the orchards to pick apples, or purchase a wide variety of just-picked apples, as well as gallons of fresh apple cider. Purchase pre-picked pecks at less per peck than personally picking them (say that five times fast), but then you lose out on the joy of actually picking the apples. The season is short, but tasty - it begins towards the end of September and most of the crop is gone by the beginning of November.

Just down the road are two other fun stops - a shop called Manzanita, which is a general store selling country antiques, apple cider, and lots of fun gift items, and FARMERS MOUNTAIN VALE RANCH (see the Potpourri section for details).

Hours: Open end of September through beginning of November, Fri. - Sun., 9am - 5pm.
Admission: $1 per person admission to the U-pick orchards plus the cost of the apples.
Ages: All

CORVETTE DINER

(619) 542-1476 / www.cohnrestaurants.com   *$$$*
3946 5ᵗʰ Avenue, Hillcrest, San Diego

(Going S. on Cabrillo Fwy [163], exit W. on Washington St., L. on 4ᵗʰ Ave., L. on University St., L. on 5ᵗʰ Ave., which is a one way street. Going N. 163, exit E. on Robinson Ave., L. on Vermont St., L. on University St., R. on 5ᵗʰ Ave. Valet park or circle around the block for self parking. [TG-1269 A5])

This 50's style diner is a really bebopping place to eat! The music played from the deejay's booth; the license plates, neon signs, and hub cabs that decorate the walls; the old gas pumps; the Bazooka bubble gum displays; and the red Corvette (parked inside) all add to the atmosphere of the restaurant. The rest of the decor incorporates black and white checked tiles with blue marbleized vinyl booths. Waiting for a table here can be more fun than usual as you sit on a bench made from the back seat and the fins of an old Cadillac. On Tuesday and Wednesday evenings, from 6:30pm to 9:30pm, be entertained by "Magic Mike," who plies his tricks of the trade and his jokes at your table. (Ask him to show your children how to magically stretch their arms.) On Friday and Saturday evenings, from 6pm to 9pm, balloon artists use more than hot air to entertain customers.

The food here is great! A Hawaii 5-O burger (burger with pineapple) or a Philly steak sandwich is $7.50. Other food choices include fish tacos, grilled Reubens, ribs, meatloaf, blackened chicken pasta, salads, and more. Desserts are delectable. They range from Green Rivers to peppermint smoothies to Snickers Pie to Death by Chocolate Cake. Kids' meals are $4.95 for their choice of spaghetti, burger, corn dog, grilled cheese sandwich, or chicken fingers, plus fries, a soft drink, and an ice cream bar. Was life really this good in the fifties?!

Hours: Open Sun. - Thurs., 11am - 10pm; Fri. - Sat., 11am - midnight.
Admission: Prices are listed above.
Ages: All

FAIROUZ RESTAURANT AND GALLERY

(619) 225-0308 / www.alnashashibi.com/site/cafe.htm $$$
3166 Midway Drive, #102, San Diego
(Exit Ocean Beach Fwy [8] S. on Mission Bay Dr., which turns into Midway. It's in a small shopping center. [TG-1268 D5])

The aroma of Greek and Lebanese cuisine tantalizes your tastebuds the moment you step into this small, storefront restaurant. Ethnic music plays in the background. The booths and tables are surrounded by murals, paintings, and other artwork adorning the walls, as well as clothing items for sale. There is even a small library of books to peruse while eating. Food choices include Greek salad ($3.99), lamb kafta sandwiches ($4.99), falafels ($4.25), moussaka ($8.99), stuffed grape leaves ($6.50), and lots more. The ambiance, the food, the art - it's all Greek to me!

Hours: Open Sun. - Thurs., 11am - 9pm; Fri. - Sat., 11am - 10pm.
Admission: Prices are listed above.
Ages: 5 years and up.

FARRELL'S ICE CREAM PARLOUR (Mira Mesa)

(858) 578-9895 / www.farrellsicecreamparlor.com $$$
10606 Camino Ruiz #10, Mira Mesa
(From Jacob Dekema Fwy [805], exit E. on Mira Mesa Blvd. From Escondido Fwy [15], exit W. on Mira Mesa. It's on the corner of Mira Mesa and Camino Ruiz, in the Target shopping center. [TG-1209 B4])

Remember Farrell's from your high school days? Nostalgia is slightly updated with a few video arcade games and kiddie rides, but there are still rows of candy to tempt children, an old-fashioned player piano, and the ice-cream specialty desserts. Try the Zoo - a five-flavor, myriad topping, ice-cream extravaganza carried to you on its own litter, accompanied by sirens and bells - $33.99; the Volcano with thirty (count 'em, thirty!) scoops of vanilla ice-cream and hot fudge overflowing down the sides, brought out while it's still erupting (bring a friend, or ten, to help you eat this) - $33.99; or the Trough, which is two banana splits piled high with goodies, eaten from a trough as the waiter exclaims, "This person made a pig of himself at Farrell's" and awards the consumer a ribbon - $8.99. There are, of course, numerous other, single-serving choices, such as a Tin Roof, mudslide (coffee ice cream on devil's food cake drenched in hot fudge and Oreo cookie crumbles), and malts.

This very family-oriented restaurant serves all-American food in a fun atmosphere. Hamburgers start at $5.59; patty melt, $6.19; tuna salad, $6.39; and chicken club sandwich, $6.69. Kid's meals, for ages 10 and under, which average $3.09, offer a choice of grilled cheese, hamburger, hot dog, peanut butter and jelly sandwich, or chicken nuggets, and come with fries. Save room for a clown sundae. Ask about weekday specials, such as paying for one adult, and getting one child's meal free. Lunch time can be quiet here, so I actually prefer the rowdier, dinner hour. Note: The birthday party prices are very reasonable. If you don't have a party here, show proof it's your birthday and you receive a free sundae. Note: There is another FARRELL'S ICE CREAM PARLOUR in Temecula. See this section for more details.

Hours: Open Mon. - Thurs., 11:30am - 10:30pm; Fri., 11:30am - midnight; Sat., 11am - midnight; Sun., 11am - 10:30pm.
Admission: Menu prices noted above.
Ages: All

HORTON GRAND HOTEL / IDA BAILEY'S RESTAURANT

(619) 544-1886 / www.hortongrand.com $$$$
311 Island Avenue, San Diego

(Going S. on San Diego Fwy [5], exit W. on Imperial Ave., R. on 12th Ave., L. on Island Ave. Going N. on 5, exit at 'J' St, continue straight off the off ramp and turn L. at Island. [TG-1289 A4])

Put on the lace gloves, extend your pinky, and enjoy a delicious afternoon tea at this Victorian-style hotel. Afternoon Tea consist of petit fours, finger sandwiches, scrumptious scones, cake, and an assortment of teas. High Tea is a bit more formal and also includes sherry, a sausage roll, and truffle. Brunch includes a buffet of anyway-you-like-them omelettes, waffles with various toppings, breakfast potatoes, steak, ham, salads, pastas, and desserts.

As this hotel is in the heart of the historic Gaslamp District, take a stroll around before or after your tea to soak in the district's ambiance. There are many unique stores, so both window shoppers and "real" shoppers will be appeased.

Hours: Teas are served Fri. and Sat., 2:30pm - 5pm; Sun. brunch is 10am - 2pm.
Admission: $11.95 per person for Afternoon Tea; $14.95 for High Tea; $16.95 for adults for brunch; $9.95 for ages 9 and under.
Ages: 5 years and up.

HOTEL DEL CORONADO - TEA TIME

(619) 435-6611 / www.hoteldel.com $$$$
1500 Orange Avenue, Coronado

(Exit San Diego Fwy [5] W. on 75 and cross over the Coronado Bridge, L. on Orange Ave. The toll is $1 to Coronado and the return trip is free. If you are car pooling, cross the bridge using the right lane, at no charge. [TG-1308 J1])

This hotel is the creme-de-la-creme of hotels (personal opinion), and tea time here is a true taste of elegance. (Note: You must make some time before or after your tea to explore this incredible hotel and its grounds!) Teas consist of bay shrimp and celery salad on puff pastry; triple-layered cucumber, cream cheese, and watercress sandwiches; New York sirloin carpaccio on ciabatta toast; brie with apple and grape slices decorated with walnuts; smoked salmon with dill on rye bread (it's amazing what kids will try in an etiquettely-correct atmosphere); an assortment of delectable pastries; and a variety of teas, of course.

Hours: Tea is served Sun. at noon, 12:30pm, 2pm, 2:30pm, and 3:30pm.

Admission: $15.95 includes the food described above. $22.95 also includes champagne, Belgium truffles, and a chocolate dipped strawberry. Parking in the hotel lot costs $2.50 per hour; street parking, which is limited, is free.

Ages: 5 years and up.

JULIAN TEA & COTTAGE ARTS

(760) 765-OTEA (0832) / www.juliantea.com

2124 3rd Street, Julian

(From Hwy 78, which turns into Main St., go N.E. on Washington St., R. on 3rd. [TG-1136 B7])

This quaint (what in Julian isn't quaint?), 100-year-old house is a *tea*lightful place to take your daughter for an afternoon of one-on-one time. The traditional and popular Afternoon Tea ($10.95) includes finger sandwiches, scones with jam and whipped cream, desert, and, of course, a pot of tea. Add a cup of homemade soup or a salad for just a $1.50 per item. Another option is Cream Tea ($5.95), with two scones with whipped cream, jam, and a pot of tea. More filling teas that include lunch (yea!) include the Drew Bailey Tea ($9.95) that comes with a sandwich, cup of soup or a salad, dessert, and tea, and the Ploughman's Lunch ($9.95) with green salad, cheese wedges, fruit, bread or cheese scone, cookie, and of course, tea. Or, just come for dessert. Holiday teas, such as ones offered for Valentines' Day and Mother's Day, are always extra special.

Although tea is served in the tea room and the front porch, the cottage also has a few other rooms which contain items for sale - china, tea pots, baby gifts, bridal gifts, books on teas, cards, teas, and cottage arts such as weaving. Each room is decorated with a variety of tea paraphernalia. The upstairs room, which is decorated to resemble a garden, is reserved for private parties.

Hours: The shop is open Mon. - Sat., 10am - 5pm; Sun., 11am - 5pm. Tea and other foods are served daily from noon - 3pm.

Admission: Prices vary depending on the tea.

Ages: 4 years and up.

NIEDERFRANK'S ICE CREAM SHOP/FACTORY

(619) 477-0828 / niederfranks.signonsandiego.com

726 A Avenue, National City

(Going S. on San Diego Fwy [5], exit E. on 8th Street, L. on A Ave. Going N. on 5, exit E. on Plaza Blvd., L. on A. [TG-1309 H1])

This family-owned store dishes up delectable, all-natural, home-made ice cream that tastes smooth and creamy. The mouth-watering flavors, besides the usual ones, include Washington Red Peach, Lemon Custard, Brownies and Cream, and Coconut Almond Joy. Besides licking an ice-cream cone, another reason to visit is to take a twenty-minute-or-so tour of the small ice cream factory located in the back of the shop. Watch ice cream being made the old-fashioned way with machines that are seventy-five years old. Once all the ingredients are blended it takes ten more minutes for the ice cream to be ready to consume. Samples can be tasted, but you'll want to purchase a full scoop of whatever flavor tickles your taste buds. The shop also makes its own fudge.

Hours: Retail hours are Mon. - Fri., 11am - 6pm; Sat. - Sun., 1pm - 5pm. Call to make a reservation for a tour.

Admission: A single scoop costs $1.65. Tours are free.

Ages: All for ice cream; 10 years and up for the tour.

PLANET HOLLYWOOD

San Diego - (619) 702-7827 / www.planethollywood.com   *$$$*

197 Horton Plaza, San Diego

(Going S. on San Diego Fwy [5] exit S. on Front St., L. on Broadway. Going N. on the 5, exit S. on 6th Ave. R. on Broadway. It's on the corner of 4th and Broadway. [TG-1289 A3])

This very Hollywood restaurant literally has the handprints of once-owners Demi Moore, Arnold Schwarzenegger, Bruce Willis, and Sly Stallone all over them. Film and television memorabilia abound such as costumes, parts of sets, and photographs. Just a few of the featured items are a life-size Turbo man from *Jingle All the Way*, spears and other props from *Raiders of the Lost Ark*, and artifacts from *Titanic* and *Roger Rabbit*. Although memorabilia is definitely a main attraction, the food is good, too. The menu features California cuisine, which actually encompasses everything - pizza, pasta, burgers, ribs, chicken, salads, etc. Prices range from $6.95 to $16. The kids' menu offers pizza, cheeseburgers, chicken fingers, spaghetti, hot dogs, or cheese quesadilla for $5.95. Their meals include fries and a beverage.

Hours: Open daily 11am - 11pm.

Admission: Prices are listed above. Parking is validated for 4 hours.

Ages: 4 years and up.

REUBEN E. LEE RIVERBOAT

(619) 291-1880   *$$$$*

880 E. Harbor Island Drive, San Diego

(Going S. on San Diego Fwy [5], exit W. on Sassafras, L. on Pacific Hwy., R. on Laurel St. Going N. on 5, exit N. on Brant, L. on Laurel. From Laurel, go R. on Harbor Dr., L. onto Harbor Island, L. on Harbor Island Dr. Park. [TG-1288 G2])

Harken back to the days of river boats along the Mississippi. Nowadays, you can still enjoy the ambiance of a riverboat (but in Southern California!) aboard the Reuben E. Lee. The elegant rooms in this permanently anchored, multi-deck, replica paddle-wheeler overlook the picturesque San Diego Bay.

Half of the boat operates under the name Jared's and specializes in steak. Menu selections include filet mignon, $29.95; rib eye steak, $28.95; lamb t-bones, $25.95; and appetizers of exotic mushroom strudel, $6.50 and a five onion tart for $6.25. The Reuben E. Lee side of the boat offers some steak and chicken, but specializes in seafood. Menu selections include salmon, $20; swordfish, $22; and tuna, mahi-mahi, and catfish at various prices. Appetizers include crab cakes or oysters for $11 and deep fried clams for $9. The children's menu, only available at Reuben's, offers fish 'n chips, hamburger, cheeseburger, or fried shrimp for $6.95 per entree.

Hours: Open Mon. - Thurs., 5pm - 9pm; Fri. - Sat., 5pm - 10pm; Sun., noon - 9pm.

Admission: Prices are listed above.

Ages: 3 years and up.

SEAU'S, THE RESTAURANT

(619) 291-SEAUS (7328) / www.seau.com $$$

1640 Camino Del Rio North, #1376, in the Mission Valley Shopping Center, San Diego

(From Mission Valley Fwy [8], exit N. on Auto Circle / Mission Center Rd., R. on Camino Del Rio Rd. It's next to Robinsons-May, towards the east end of the mall. [TG-1269 C2])

San Diego Charger's All-Pro linebacker, Junior Seau, has a two-story restaurant for the good sports in your family to enjoy. Notice how the outside of the restaurant resembles a coliseum. The inside decor is equally eye-catching with a huge mural of Junior Seau, model sports figures in action poses, and signed sports paraphernalia all around such as surfboards, football helmets, baseballs, bats, jerseys, hockey sticks, and lots more. Suspended T.V. monitors show sporting events, and the huge main screen shows the sports channel. (What a surprise!)

The black table tops have sports plays drawn on them. Don't try to erase them, however, because even though it looks like they were done in chalk - they weren't. (We saw others try to do this, too!) Our kids enjoyed watching the pizza maker toss pizzas, and then cook them in the wood-burning stove. The simplest entertainment is sometimes the best kind.

The food goes the whole nine yards - everything we ate was scrumptious. Menu choices run the gamut from burgers ($6.95) and pizza ($9.95) to rib-eyed steak ($15.95) and lobster ravioli ($12.95). The generously-portioned kids' meals range from $3.95 (choice of hot dog, pizza, or burger) to $6.95 (jr. shrimp). They come with fries, Haagen Dazs ice cream, and a beverage in a small take home sports bottle. Ah, to be 12 years old (or younger) again!

Hours: Open Sun. - Thurs., 11am - 10pm; Fri. - Sat., 11am - midnight.

Ages: All

U.S. GRANT HOTEL

(619) 232-3121 / www.grandheritage.com $$$$

326 Broadway, San Diego

(Going S. on San Diego Fwy [5] exit S. on Front St., L. on Broadway. Going N. on the 5, exit S. on 6th Ave. R. on Broadway. [TG-1289 A3])

Old-time elegance permeates tea time in the Grant Hotel lobby. Amid crystal chandeliers, polished mahogany furniture, and beautiful floral arrangements, little girls and boys transform into young ladies and gentlemen, respectively. Savor an assortment of finger sandwiches, scones with fresh cream and preserves, crumpets and pastries, and a fine selection of teas. What a delightful treat! Note: If your children don't care for tea, just request hot chocolate, or juice, for them. Reservations are required.

Hours: Tea is served Tues. - Sat., 3pm - 6pm.
Admission: $14 per person.
Ages: 5 years and up.

VICTORIA STATION

(858) 793-4135
315 S. Coast Highway 101, Solana Beach
(Exit San Diego Fwy [5] E. on Lomas Santa Fe Dr., L. on S. Coast Hwy. [TG-1187 E1])

$$$

Take a "trip" to the British Isles via a visit to these actual train cars that are connected to one another. The restaurant, Victoria Station, takes up a few of the cars, while a store selling British goods is in another, and a pub is in yet another. The restaurant includes freshly cooked authentic British fare such as Thomson's Scotch Pies, steak and kidney pies ($7.75), sausage rolls, Cornish pastries ($5.75), banger and mash ($4.25), fish and chips (&.95), and shepherd's pie ($5.25), plus shortbread, scones, pastries, soups, and sandwiches. A full English breakfast, served on weekends from 10am to 1pm, features bacon, an egg, banger, beans, potato scone, fried bread, tomato, fried mushrooms, and black pudding for $7.25. Order a delightful and delicious afternoon tea which consists of a pot of tea, finger sandwiches, sausage rolls, scones with cream and jam, and a selection of cakes for $7.25 per person.

Experience just a bit o' Britain at the store that has life-sized mannequin palace guards. Shelves are stocked with a wide array of British canned and packaged goods, including biscuits, candies, trinkets, collectibles, tea sets, Scottish and English dolls, bobby hats, and souvenirs.

Hours: Open daily 10am - 8pm.
Admission: Prices listed above
Ages: 4 years and up.

WESTGATE HOTEL

(619) 557-3650 / www.westgatehotel.com
1055 2nd Avenue, San Diego
(Going S. on San Diego Fwy [5] exit S. on Front St., L. on Broadway. Going N. on the 5, exit S. on 6th Ave. R. on Broadway. From Broadway, go N. on 1st Ave, R. on C St, R. on 2nd. [TG-1289 A3])

$$$$

Fashioned after an anteroom at Versailles, children will feel like royalty as they sip their tea and nibble on fancy finger sandwiches, truffles, petit fours, strawberries and cream, and scones topped with preserves, honey, seasonal berries, or Grand Marnier cream. Reservations are requested. (I wanted to write that the food is lip-smacking good, but the refined atmosphere here dictates a more decorous choice of words.) The luxurious surroundings include a Steinway piano, rich tapestries, gilded mirrors, and crystal chandeliers.

Hours: Tea is served Mon. - Sat., 2:30pm - 5pm. Harp music starts at 2:30pm.

Admission: $14 for adults; $9.95 for ages 3 - 12 from the above set menu.
                 You may also order items a la cart.
Ages: 5 years and up.

FILLMORE & WESTERN RAILWAY
(800) 777-TRAIN (8724) / www.fwry.com
351 Santa Clara Avenue, Central Park Depot, Fillmore

See FILLMORE & WESTERN RAILWAY under the Transportation section for more details.

TIERRA REJADA FAMILY FARMS
(805) 523-8552 - food farm; (805) 523-2957 - animal farm / www.tierrarejadafamilyfarms.com
3370 Moorpark Road, Moorpark
(Exit 23 Fwy W. on Tierra Rejada Rd., L. on Moorpark Rd. [TG-496 H4])

Tierra Rejada is both a huge working produce farm, as well as an animal farm. Let's talk food, first. There are two ways to enjoy the crops: 1) Stop by the on-site roadside market to purchase fresh produce (tasty, but boring), or 2) Let the kids pick their own fruits and vegetables. (Ya-hoo - we've got a winner!) There are rows and rows (and rows and rows) of seasonal crops including artichokes, strawberries, blackberries, peaches, squash, potatoes, green beans, apricots, apples, onions, garlic, tomatoes, eggplant, peppers, cabbages, pumpkins, melons, corn, and herbs. My boys were excited to eat strawberries they picked from the vines, carrots they pulled from the ground, beans they harvested from the stalks, and other good-for-you foods they won't normally eat, proving that kids really enjoy the fruits (and vegetables) of their labor.

Heavy-duty pull wagons are available to transport your prize pickings (or tired little ones) at no extra charge. A grassy picnic area, with tables, is located at the front of the farm, near the restroom facilities. Tips: Wear sunscreen and walking shoes; prepare to get a little muddy if you visit here after a rain; and bring a cooler to store your fresh produce.

The farm offers numerous guided tours of the fields for groups of twenty or more. The tours entail learning about a designated crop (or crops) - care, growth cycle, and more - as well as picking some to take home. What a great combination of fun and education! Crops do grow seasonally, so call to see what is currently ripe.

Tierra Rejada also owns an adjacent animal farm. Wander the dirt grounds to see pens of chickens, sheep, ducks, rabbits, goats, pigs, calves, ponies, and horses. Some of the animals come close enough to touch, especially if you purchase feed in the nearby food machines. (Bring quarters!) Pony rides around a small rink are offered for riders up to seventy-five pounds. You are welcome to wander around on your own, making a trip here a pleasant, rural experience. You may also take a half-hour, guided tour, which includes feeding the animals while learning about them. The tour is by reservation only and your group must consist of at least ten people.

Tractor-drawn (and sometimes Clydesdale-drawn) hayrides for up to thirty people go all around the farms. On-site birthday parties in the animal farm area include unlimited pony rides, a tour, and use of a covered party shelter that has grills and a few picnic tables. Bring your own food.

Hours: The food farm is usually open daily mid-February through November, 9am to about 6pm. Call first! The animal farm is usually open daily April through October, 10am - 5pm. It's open March and November Sat. - Sun., 10am - 5pm, weather permitting.

Admission: The food farm is technically free. Crop prices are charged per pound and change per season/availability. Tours on the food farm average about $4 per person, depending on the activity and length of the tour. Admission to the animal farm is $1 per person. Guided tours of the animals are an additional $2 per person. Pony rides are $2.50 per ride. Hayrides are $1.50 per person for a group of at least twenty people. Rental of the party shelter is $150 for two hours for ten children; additional children are $10 each.

Ages: All for a visit; 5 years and up for food tours; 4 - 11 years for animal tours.

FAMILY PAY AND PLAY

The family that plays together, stays together! Indoor play areas, outdoor miniature golf courses, rock climbing centers, laser tag arenas, paint ball fields, skate parks, and more are great places to go to spend some special bonding time. Note: Check this website -www.skateboardparks.com to keep up on new skateboard parks.

CHUCK E. CHEESE

Look under this entry in the Edible Adventures section.

GAMEWORKS
☼

Irvine - (949) 727-1422; Ontario - (909) 987-4263; Orange - (714) 939-
$$$$
9690 / www.gameworks.com

Irvine - 31 Fortune Drive at the Irvine Spectrum Center; Ontario - 4541   ⒨
Mills Circle at Ontario Mills Mall; Orange - 20 The City Drive at The Block
of Orange.

GameWorks is a high-tech entertainment venue dedicated to the latest (and greatest) interactive virtual reality and video games, and motion simulator rides. It also has a full-service restaurant and a bar. There are numerous games here created just for GameWorks, including Jurassic Park - the Lost World (where participants go head to head with dinosaurs) and lots of sports-oriented games. Motion simulator rides, such as the roller coaster, put the participant in the seat with controls as he/she interacts with the screen and moves all around. Vertical Reality, featured at the Irvine and Ontario locations, employs movable seats in front of a twenty-four-foot screen and simulates a three-story free fall, as well as navigating around obstacles - you can ride the game. At the Indy 500, hop in a full-size race car and zoom around the curves shown on the screen. Monster trucks are another way to experience a hair raising ride through a virtual obstacle course. Sounds like a lot of virtual fun. Other motion simulator games include Top Skater and Wave Runner, or play the "classics" such as PacMan, air hockey, and pool. Note: The Irvine location also has a 10,000 square foot indoor go-kart race track.

Food selections include Cobb salad; chicken tortilla soup; cheese pizza, as well as specialty combos of barbeque chicken or shrimp pesto; burgers; steak sandwiches; linguine; ribs; and grilled meatloaf.

Hours: Most locations are open Mon. - Thurs., 11am - midnight; Fri., 11am - 2am; Sat., 10am - 2am; Sun., 10am - midnight. Only adults, ages 18 years and up, are allowed here after 10pm.

Admission: Free. A debit-style game card costs about $25 for 2 hours of play. The Vertical Reality, Monster Truck, and Indy 500 rides cost extra.

Ages: 8 years and up.

ARROYO MINIATURE GOLF
☼

(323) 255-1506 / www.arroyoseco.com
$

1055 Lohman Lane, South Pasadena

(Going S. on Golden State Fwy [5], exit S. on Orange Grove, R. on Mission. Go straight past Arroyo onto Stoney Dr. Going N. on Pasadena Fwy [110], exit N. on Marmion Way, R. on Pasadena, L. on Arroyo, L. on Stoney Dr. From Mission St., Stoney Dr. winds around to the (big) Arroyo golf course. [TG-595 F2])

This miniature golf course, adjacent to a real golf course, is very simple (i.e. no fancy castles, difficult obstacles, etc.). It does, however, offer itself as a good little course for practicing your short stroke game at an inexpensive price. So, for the price, practice, and fun of it, why not bring the kids and come play a couple

of rounds?!
Hours: Open daily 7am - 10pm.
Admission: $1.50 per person per round.
Ages: 3 years and up.

BRIGHT CHILD ☼

(310) 393-4844 $$

1415 4ᵗʰ Street, Santa Monica

(Exit Santa Monica Fwy [10] N. on Lincoln, L. on Wilshire, L. on 4ᵗʰ. It's next door to Toys R Us. Parking is available in structure #5 and #3, on 4ᵗʰ St. [TG-671 E2])

This large indoor play land offers big time fun for your little ones. One of the best of its kind, Bright Child has six slides, four zip lines, a few themed ball pits, a wind tunnel, a mini putting green, a basketball court (with an adjustable rim height), an arts and crafts room, a music room with a karaoke stage and several keyboards, and a toddler room. Whew! Your kids will not want to leave. Classes, geared for particular age groups, are available throughout the week. Instructors encourage learning and agility through activities, games, and using equipment. Outside food is not allowed in, but the cafe here serves good food, such as fresh sandwiches that range between $3.50 to $6.50, and kids' meals that include a sandwich and a drink. Socks must be worn by everyone, including adults. I hope a visit here *bright*ens your day!

Hours: Open daily 10am - 6pm.
Admission: $8 per child for up to two hours of play; each additional hour is $4. One adult is free with one paid child's admission; additional adults are $4 each. Children 20 months and younger are $4. Parking is free for the first two hours in structure #5 or #3.
Ages: 6 months to 9 years.

CHILDREN'S TIME MACHINE EDU-TAINMENT ☼
CENTER

(877) TIMEMAC (846-3622) or (818) 788-4779 / $$$
www.childrenstimemachine.com

14652 Ventura Boulevard, Sherman Oaks

(Exit Ventura Fwy [101] S. on Van Nuys Blvd., R on Ventura. It's on the L. Validated parking is available at Borders across the street. [TG-561 J4])

Enter through a make-believe time machine and explore four themed areas that flow into each other. All entrants wear bar coded wristbands so parents can't leave without kids and vice versa. Each room is interspersed with free activities and games, as well as token-taking games. Kids can redeem the tickets they win at the games for prizes. Take a walk on the Wildside in the jungle-decorated room which features a beautiful mural, plants on the ceiling, vines hanging down with attached stuffed animals, climbing structures, a rope bridge, a short slide, and a small rock climbing wall. Go through a tunnel to the Spaced Out room. The ball pit here has a target board with a bull's-eye and a neat contraption that lets the balls be sucked up, spun around the pit, and thrown back down into it. Climb aboard a spacecraft with "realistic" sounds and light. Tokens pay for a ride on a kiddie spaceship. An adjoining room features small carnival-type mirrors. Walk through a lit up portal with mist coming out to enter the Submerged room. Look at more wonderful murals, plus an aquarium with colorful fish and a wall of bubbles. Play some board games. Touch fake sea stars and coral. Sit in a small submarine. For a few tokens, move back and forth on a dolphin ride. The Castle room contains lots of great costumes pertaining to the medieval time period, and a few games. An arts and crafts room is towards the back of the building prepared for artists with crayons, pens, paper, and other supplies. A presentation area offers a stage for puppet shows, storytelling, and sing-a-longs, plus karaoke with appropriate kids' music!. The room also contains some drums, air hockey, and a few other games. Play in a virtual playground in which visitor's images are projected onto a television screen to it appears they are playing soccer or volleyball or swimming with dolphins. In a separate room, kids can sit on bean bag chairs, don special glasses, and watch a six-minute, 3-D movie that is shown every hour. The show is included with the price of admission.

Adults can play with their kids and/or enjoy the Sports Den where they can watch sporting events on a large-screen TV while monitoring kids through a one-way mirror. An upstairs Time Out room is for adults and contains massage chairs. A party room is also located upstairs.

Bring your own food to enjoy at the indoor tables and chairs. Snacks and beverages are available to purchase. An attached, fully-stocked retail store offers quality educational toys, books, and games.

Hours: Open July through August, Tues. - Thurs. and Sat - Sun., 10am - 8pm; Fri. 1-am - 9pm. Open the rest of the year; Wed. - Thurs., 11am - 8pm; Fri., 11am - 9pm; Sat. - Sun., 10am - 8pm.

Admission: $8 for ages 2 - 18; adults, and children under 2, are free. $1 buys 4 tokens (and you will want to purchase tokens).

Ages: 3 - 10 years.

CLOSE ENCOUNTERS PAINT BALL   ☼
(800) 919-9237 or (323) 656-9179 / www.paintballusa.org $$$$$
22400 The Old Road, Newhall   ♨
(Exit Golden State Fwy [5] L. on Roxford St., under the freeway to the dead end. Turn R. on Sepulveda Blvd. and follow it along the freeway for 1 mile to the first stop sign. Turn L. on San Fernando Rd., which turns into The Old Road. Travel a little over 2 miles and on the R. above a ranch, look for the field, not necessarily the address. [TG-4641 B7])

Play this version of Capture the Flag while armed with markers (i.e. guns) filled with paint. This makes the game a bit more colorful! You'll be placed on one of two teams. The object of the game is to get the flag from your opponent's base, while dodging paintballs by hiding behind bunkers and trees. The three-a-half-acres of mountainside is a perfect setting to play this rugged game. A referee is on the playing field to insure fair play and help out. Each game lasts about twenty minutes. After you're rested, go for another round. Food is available to purchase, or bring your own, as there is a shaded grove of trees with picnic tables. Tip: Wear pants and other clothing you don't care about, and shoes with good traction. Getting hit stings, so wear a padded shirt or multiply layers to help absorb the hits. Participants under 18 must have a waiver signed by a parent or guardian.

Hours: Open to the public Sat. - Sun. and holiday Mon., 9am - 4pm. Groups of thirty or more can reserve play time during the week.

Admission: $40 for all-day play, which includes a pistol, goggles, and face mask. There are two types of upgraded guns to rent - constant-air pump rifles at $20 a day, or a semi-automatic, constant-air machine gun at $25, which includes free CO_2 for the day. Paintballs cost $10 for 100 or $25 for 500. Call to inquire about discount packages for junior players, ages 10 to 15, such as a Ninja Special. This special includes all-day play, an air rifle, and 100 paintballs for $30.

Ages: 10 years and up.

FUNLAND U.S.A.

(661) 273-1407 / www.funlandusa.com

$$$

525 W. Avenue P-4, Palmdale

(Exit Antelope Valley Fwy [14] W. on Ave. P, L. on 10th St. W., L. on Marketplace, which turns into Ave. P-4. [TG-4195 H5])

This land of fun offers three, themed, ten-hole **miniature golf** courses - $5.95 per course for adults; children 5 years and under play for free. **Go-karts** are $5.95 for a five-minute ride. Drivers must be at least 10 years old and 58" or taller and passengers, who may ride for free, need to be at least 4 years old and 40". **Bumper boats** are $5.95 per ride and drivers must be at least 4 years old and 44". Other attractions here include **batting cages**, a large game arcade area, and a snack bar.

Hours: Open Sun. - Thurs., 10am - 10pm; Fri. - Sat., 10am - 11pm. Open in the summer one hour later.

Admission: Individual attractions are listed above, or purchase a park pass - one round of golf, two rides, twelve tokens, and a soda for $16 per person.

Ages: 4 years and up.

FUN TOWN

(818) 776-8309

$

18411 Sherman Way, Reseda

(Exit Ventura Fwy [101] N. on Reseda Blvd., R. on Sherman Way, L. on Cannby (for parking). [TG-530 J5])

This clean, large, one-room indoor play place resembles a friendly city. Wonderful murals create different sections in the room. Each "room" has play materials that pertain to its theme - the library has books; the grocery store has play food and a cash register; and the barbershop has a salon chair (no scissors, thank goodness!). Other rooms include a hospital, fire station, a restaurant, and even a farm and a fake lake. In the middle of Fun Town are Little Tykes™ slides, a parking lot for Little Tyke™ cars, and some other play equipment. Socks must be worn by adults and children in the play area. Mats cover the floor. Bring your own food to enjoy at the picnic tables located inside near the front of the "town".

Hours: Open Mon., Wed., Fri., 9am - 5pm; Tues. and Thurs., 9am - 8pm

Admission: $5 for children 9 months and older; infants 8 months and under and adults are free.

Ages: 6 months to 8 years.

GO KART WORLD AND SLICK CART RACING

(310) 834-3800 or (310) 834-3700

21830 Recreation Road, Carson

(Exit San Diego Fwy [405] E. on Carson, take an immediate R. on Recreation Rd. [TG-764 F6])

$$

Go full speed ahead on the six race tracks here. The Kiddie Track has battery-operated cars that go about three m.p.h. on an L-shaped track. This ride is for children over 3 years old and under 75 pounds. Mini Indie is for drivers at least 45" and goes about nine m.p.h. on a B-shaped track. A double-seater car can hold a driver who is at least 16 years old with a passenger who is at least 32". The Bumper Car track is for drivers at least 45" and the cars can be individually manipulated to go forwards, backwards, and even spin all the way around. For a slick ride, drivers at least 54" can race on the Slick Track. We vote the Turbo Track the most-like-a-real-race-track ride. Race over and under passes and around banked hairpin turns. Drivers must be at least 58". The one-third mile track is for drivers at least 18 years old, as the cars go thirty-five m.p.h. All rides last four minutes. If you have a group of ten or more, you may rent the track for a private party. A large video and arcade game area, with redemption-playing games, are inside.

Hours: Open daily 11:30am - 11pm.

Admission: Each of the rides listed cost $3.50 per ride, or purchase 7 rides for $20.

Ages: 3 years and up.

GOLFLAND ARCADE

(626) 444-5163

1181 N. Durfee Avenue, South El Monte

(Exit Pomona Fwy [60] S. at Peck Ave., R. on Durfee. [TG-637 C5])

$$

What course of action will you take? Choose from four, well-kept miniature golf courses with lots of fun holes designed with whimsical buildings and challenging obstacles. The arcade area is clean and has games, such as air hockey, as well as video games. Tip: McDonald's is only a few buildings away.

Hours: Open Sun. - Thurs., 10am - 11pm; Fri. - Sat., 10am - 1am.

Admission: Miniature golf is $5 for adults; $2 for seniors; $3 for ages 7 - 12; $2 for children 6 and under.

Ages: 4 years and up.

GOLF 'N STUFF - FAMILY FUN CENTER (Norwalk)

(562) 863-8338 / www.golfnstuff.com

10555 E. Firestone Boulevard, Norwalk

(Exit San Gabriel River Fwy [605] E. on Firestone. [TG-706 D7])

$$$

This big family fun center offers several different ways to have fun, with three themed **miniature golf** courses - $6.50 for adults, children 6 years and under are free; plus **Li'l Indy, bumper boats,** and **bumper car** rides - $4 per ride. Height restrictions apply. Yes, there are also lots of arcade games to be played here. This can keep you and the kids busy for hours - just bring quarters!

Hours: Open Sun., 10am - 11pm; Mon - Thurs., 10am - 10pm; Fri. - Sat., 10am - midnight. The rides close a half hour before the park.

Admission: Attractions are individually priced above, or buy an all-park pass for $15 per person that entitles you to a round of miniature golf, 4 rides, and 4 tokens.

Ages: 4 years and up.

HOLLYWOOD SPORTS COMPLEX   ☼
(949) 489-9000 / www.scvillage.com $$$$
9030 Somerset Boulevard, Bellflower   ♨

(From the Artesia Fwy [91], exit N. on Lakewood Blvd. From the San Gabriel River Fwy [605], exit E. on Alondra Blvd. R. on Lakewood. It is on the corner of Lakewood Blvd. and Somerset Blvd. [TG-736 A4])

This twenty-three acre Hollywood-themed recreation and entertainment complex is scheduled to open in 2001, so the following information is facts and designs in the works. The multi-faceted area is comprised of several different venues, combining Hollywood movie sets and some of the most popular and some of the most "extreme" sports, including rock climbing, skateboarding, paintball, a BMX raceway, a slick track speedway, volleyball, basketball, an in line skate plaza, a tennis center, a virtual reality arcade, and a restaurant. Many of the venues are designed for amateurs, as well as professionals competing in televised events.

Hollywood Mount Rock Climbing looks like a huge, mountain of rock with different faces simulating the French Alps, Andes, and Himalayas. The scenic landscaping here includes waterfalls. The large, Freestyle Zone Skateboard Park has stairs, grind poles, pools, ramps, half pipes, and more on smooth cement. There are two very different paintball (or spatball) courses: Wasteland and Space. Both arenas are designed to look like movie sets and contain actual props from Sony and MGM studios. This very physical game contains buildings, bridges, rocky terrain, ditches, towers, and more obstacles. The BMX Bicycle Raceway track is for biking enthusiasts of all levels. The Slick Track Speedway uses quarter-scale bantam stock cars, so riders feel like they are doing some genuine NASCAR racing. Signed racing equipment and memorabilia are at the track, too. If you're ready to volley, set, and spike, head to Muscle Beach Volleyball, a beach-like setting for players and for fans who can relax under beach umbrellas. The 3 on 3 Basketball Challenge Arena is for guests to shoot some hoops and for tournament players. Gotta *love* the Tennis Center, for private matches and professionals. The two-story, 7,000 square feet arcade center features high-tech video games and simulator rides. (Obviously, it features a lot of them!) The decor, as everywhere else in the complex is themed with movie props and sets. The restaurant, referred to as the Soundstage Building, has a spooky, castle-like interior and contains numerous set pieces from sci-fi, suspense, and horror movies. Appetizers to full-course meals are served and live entertainment is often featured.

Hours: Call for hours.

Admission: Call for admission prices.

Ages: Call for age recommendations.

IRWINDALE SPEEDWAY ☼

(626) 358-1100 / www.irwindalespeedway.com *$$$$*

13300 Live Oak Avenue, Irwindale

(Going N. on San Gabriel Fwy [605], exit W. on Live Oak Ave. Going S. on 605, exit W. on Arrow Hwy., L. on Live Oak Ave. [TG-597 J2])

If your family likes fast cars, speed on over to a NASCAR, Speed Truck, Winston West, or USAC Midget and Sprint Cars event. This banked one-half mile super speedway track packs in thrills a minute for the racing enthusiast.

Hours: The season runs mid-March through November. Races are held on Saturdays.

Admission: Admission fees for regular events are $15 for adults; $5 for ages 6 - 12; children 5 and under free. Special event nights are $20 - $35 for adults; $10 for ages 6 - 12; children 5 and under are free.

Ages: 5 years and up.

KID CONCEPTS U.S.A. ☼

(310) 465-0075 / www.kidconceptsusa.com *$$*

22844 Hawthorne Boulevard, Torrance

(Exit San Diego Fwy [405] S. on Crenshaw Blvd., R. on Sepulveda, L. on Hawthorne. It's on the L., beyond the buildings located right on the street. [TG-793 D1])

What a concept! The main feature within this 9,000 square-foot room is a multi-level play structure. It has tubes (large enough for adults to crawl through), slides, ball pits, a bounce room, a mini-zip line, a small room with huge balls to roll on, and lots of nooks and crannies to discover. Note: The black slide is <u>really</u> fast. Kids can also sit in a child-sized rocket ship or helicopter and "fly" away to parts unknown. (Doesn't that sound appealing sometimes?!) Although this area is well-ventilated, my kids got sweaty having such a good time. Wearing socks is a must!!

The large room has several other sections distinguished by various play equipment and/or colorful murals that represent different regions of the U.S. The toddler area, for ages 3 and under, has a tot-sized ball pit, a short slide, and large foam blocks. Under the dinosaur and rock mural, children can unearth "fossils" in the archaeological sand pit. A Hollywood backdrop showcases a stage, complete with karaoke and costumes. The "quiet room" has two computer terminals and a nice selection of children's books. Drive to the little market, that has lots of play food, using pedal cars. For nominal additional fees, guests can play air hockey, work on a craft project, or climb up the four-foot-high, rock-climbing wall that rotates vertically and can tilt at various angles.

The sitting area is centrally located with themed red, white, and blue tables. The restaurant serves up delicious food including regular pizzas ($4.95 for an individual slice), specialty pizzas such as barbecue chicken ($13.95 for a twelve inch), a variety of salads, hamburger or turkey burgers with fries ($6.25), angel hair pasta ($7.99), bagels ($1.00), and brownies (65¢). Kid's meals are $4.95 for their choice of pizza, ham and cheese sandwich, chicken strips, burger, or a hot dog, plus fries and a drink.

Two other features worth mentioning are the cutely-decorated party rooms (party-goers can create their own sundaes) and the separate room for gym classes which contains all the latest equipment for future gymnasts.

Hours: Open Mon. - Sat., 10am - 8pm; Sun., 10am - 6pm.
Admission: Two-hour sessions are $8 for ages 2 and up, with one adult free per child; additional adults are $4; $5 for 1 year olds; children under 1 are free. Ask about prices for gym classes.
Ages: 9 months - 10 years.

L.A. ROCK GYM

(310) 973-3388 / www.larockgym.com

4926 W. Rosecrans Avenue, Hawthorne

(Exit San Diego Fwy [405] E. on Rosecrans Ave. Just past the cross-street of Ocean Gate Ave., pull into the second driveway on the R. The gym is located towards the back. [TG-733 B4])

Climb every mountain - or, at least every indoor rock wall at the Rock Gym. This nice-sized facility has realistic-looking boulders and high walls, two of which are at intense angles, plus multi-colored hand and foot holds that create over 100 different routes. Beginners to experienced rock climbers will be challenged here, as well as enjoy the physical excursion. (Have you ever noticed how most rock climbers don't have an ounce of fat on their bodies? After attempting the sport - I know why!) Harnesses and helmets are the norm here.

The gym holds classes in basic climbing, intermediate techniques, and advanced lead climbing techniques. Birthday parties can utilize the provided tables and chairs for the really important stuff like cake and gifts.

Hours: Open Mon. - Thurs., 11am - 10pm; Fri., 11am - 8pm; Sat. - Sun., 9am - 6pm.
Admission: A day pass is $15. An introductory lesson is $25. A supervised climb, with a belayer, is $10 an hour for a minimum of 2 people. Ask about class and membership rates. Equipment rental is $5.
Ages: Children must be 6 years old to climb.

LASER DREAMS

(310) 823-9256 / www.laserdreams.com

13456 Washington Boulevard, Marina Del Rey

(Exit San Diego Fwy [405] W. on Washington Blvd. It's 1 block E. of Lincoln [TG-672 B5])

A convenient place for locals, this small, outer-space-themed laser tag arena has cardboard cutouts with neon markings. During each game, members of one team try to tag opposing team members with a laser light by shooting across a divider that separates the two teams. A target on each players' vests lets the players know if they've been hit by the "enemy." There are also a few free games and activities here, including ping pong, table soccer, a miniature golf putting green, a basketball hoop, and air hockey. Ninety percent of the time, Laser Dreams hosts birthday parties, utilizing the arena, games, and its few picnic tables, so call before you come if you are interested in open play. Note that Costco and fast food places are just across the street.

Hours: Open Mon. - Fri., 4pm - 7pm; Sat., 11am - 9pm; Sun., 11am - 7pm

Admission: $6 for the first game, an additional $5 for the second game.

Ages: 5 years and up.

LASER STORM (Torrance)

(310) 373-8470 / www.gablehousebowl.com
22535 Hawthorne Boulevard, Torrance

(Going S. on San Diego Fwy [405], exit S. on Hawthorne Blvd. Going N. on 405, exit W. on Sepulveda Blvd., L. on Hawthorne Blvd. [TG-763 D7])

Laser tag is taking kids (and adults) by storm! Power up your laser gun as two teams compete against each other and "shoot" it out in a darkened room. Take cover behind neon-colored partitions, decorated with gak splats, as an opponent aims at you. Or, use the partitions as cover to stealthily sneak up on someone. The ten-minute games are action-packed, and all the running around can literally take your breath away!

Hours: Open during the school year Mon. - Wed., 3pm - 9pm; Thurs., 3pm - 10pm; Fri., 3pm - 11pm; Sat., 10am - 11pm; Sun., 10am - 8pm. Open in the summer Sun. - Thurs., 10am - 10pm; Fri. - Sat., 10am - 11pm.

Admission: $4 per game, Mon. - Fri.; $5, Sat. - Sun.

Ages: 5 years and up.

LASERTREK

(310) 325-7710 / www.lasertrek.com
2755 Pacific Coast Highway, #D, Torrance

(Exit Harbor Fwy [110] W. on Pacific Coast Highway. It's just past Crenshaw Blvd., in a shopping center. [TG-793 F5])

Unlike most laser tag lobbies, which are usually dark and filled with loud video games, LaserTrek's lobby is brightly lit and has just a few games. It also has two birthday party rooms. A space theme is prevalent throughout the actual playing arena. Astronauts, rocket ships, and other-world cities, painted with glow-in-the-dark paint, decorate the walls, angled partitions, and ramps. Even so, it's dark in here. Fog swirls around the up to twenty-five players as they run after (and from) opposing team members who are likewise trying to "shoot" them with laser guns. Each "hit" registers on that person's vest and he/she is out of the game for a few seconds. Then the action, enhanced by mood music, picks back up again. Each pulse-pounding game lasts ten minutes.

Hours: Open Mon. - Thurs., 11am - 10pm; Fri., 11am - midnight; Sat., 10am - midnight; Sun., 10am, - 10pm.

Admission: $5 for one game; $9 for two.

Ages: 5 years and up.

LAZER CRAZE

(818) 889-6633

30135 Agoura Road, Suite A, Agoura Hills

(Exit Ventura Fwy [101] S. on Reyes Adobe, L. on Agoura Rd. It's on the corner. [TG-557 H6])

Kids are crazy about Lazer Craze. The darkened lobby is packed with video and arcade games, including skee ball and air hockey. The walls are decorated with old, junky car parts and road signs. A small upstairs room has more video games, and a party room with a balcony that overlooks the laser arena. The snack bar sells soft pretzels, sodas, churros, and the other important foods.

The barely-lit arena looks like a junk yard for cars. It contains a few old cars, oil drums, a robot (!), and other themed stuff. The obstacles scattered all around are splattered with black and neon paint and graffiti-style markings. Depending on the number of players here, the fast-paced, twelve-minute games can be played with two teams of up to twenty-four people, or every man for himself. This unique atmosphere, coupled with the thrill of laser tag, makes Lazer Craze an exciting pit stop.

Hours: Open during the school year Mon. - Thurs., 3pm - 9pm; Fri., 3pm - 11pm; Sat., 10am - 11pm; Sun., 11am - 8pm. Summer and holiday hours are Mon. - Thurs., 11am - 10pm; Fri., 11am - midnight; Sat., 10am - midnight; Sun., 11am - 10pm.

Admission: $6 per player for one game; $11 for two games.

Ages: 5 years and up.

LAZERSTAR (Glendora)

(626) 963-9444 / www.hottaco.com/lazerstar

1365 S. Grand Avenue, Glendora

(Exit Foothill Fwy [210] S. on Grand Ave. It's in a mall. [TG-599 D1])

See LAZERSTAR (Oxnard), in this section, for details.

MALIBU CASTLE (Redondo Beach)

(310) 643-5167

2410 Marine Avenue, Redondo Beach

(Exit San Diego Fwy [405] N. on Hawthorne, L. on Marine. Or, exit 405 E. on Rosecrans, R. on Inglewood, R. on Marine. [TG-733 B5])

Hold court at Malibu castle as your little subjects play either one of the two wonderful **miniature golf** courses here. There are video and arcade games inside the castle walls, plus a ticket redemption area, a full-service snack bar, and party rooms. **Batting cages** just outside.

Hours: Open Mon. - Thurs., noon - 9pm; Fri., noon - 11pm; Sat., 10am - 11pm; Sun., 10am - 9pm. Call for summer hours.

Admission: Miniature golf is $6.25 a round for adults; $3 for seniors; $5.25 for children 12 and under.

Ages: 4 years and up.

MALIBU SPEEDZONE

(626) 913-9663 / www.speedzone.com

17871 Castleton Street, City of Industry

(Exit Pomona Fwy [60] S. on Fullerton Rd., R. on Colima, R. on Stoner Creek. It's on the corner of Stoner Creek and Castleton. [TG-678 H4])

Ahhhh, the smell of gasoline and the sound of engines being revved! Although SpeedZone is advertised as a racing park for adults, kids can go full throttle here, too. The huge mural and formula race cars on the outside of the massive black and white checkered building reinforce the park's intentions of being dedicated to speed, racing, and competition. Drivers must be at least five feet tall and have a valid driver's license. If you do not have a license, but are at least 58" tall, you may drive a two-seater sidewinder racer on the Turbo Track during daytime hours. The four tracks consist of Top Eliminator Dragsters, with cars powered by 300 hp; Grand Prix, with custom-scale-designed Formula One Racers; Turbo Track, which allows wheel-to-wheel racing with up to nineteen other drivers; and Slick Trax, for a spin around the concrete track. SpeedZone is the closest thing to professional racing available to the public.

Two, eighteen-hole miniature golf courses are done in the racing theme motif and include paraphernalia such as gas pumps, tires, and guard rails, plus waterways and bridges. Inside, SpeedZone decor consists of racing flags, murals, photos, a few cars (on the floor and suspended from the ceiling), and signed memorabilia such as helmets and jumpsuits. Even the restaurant table tops are designed to look like race tracks!

The Terrace Bar and outdoor grill offer open seating, or enjoy full-service dining in the Cafe. For $5.95 each, your menu choices include burgers, turkey or cheddar melt sandwiches, hoagies, Cobb salads, and individual pizzas. A chicken or steak meal is available for a few more dollars.

Keep the adrenaline pumping with over 100 video, virtual reality, and arcade games in the Electric Alley, plus a prize redemption area. Play basketball or skee ball, or try virtual jetskiing, motocross, or downhill skiing. At the Daytona simulators, up to eight drivers can race against each other on the same track. A day at SpeedZone is not just another day at the races!

Hours:	Open Sun. - Thurs., 11am - 11pm; Fri. - Sat., 11am - 1am. Open one hour earlier in the summer. All visitors at SpeedZone after 10pm must have a valid California driver's license.
Admission:	Free entrance. Top Eliminator - $12 for 3 runs; Grand Prix - $3 a lap with a 2 lap minimum; Turbo Track and Slick Trax are $6.25 for 5 minutes. Speedway miniature golf is $6.50 a round for adults; $5.50 for children 12 and under.
Ages:	4 years and up for the restaurant and miniature golf; see above restrictions for driving cars.

MOUNTASIA FUN CENTER ☼

(661) 253-4FUN (4386) / www.mountasiafuncenter.com $$$

21516 Golden Triangle Road, Santa Clarita

(Exit Golden State Fwy [5] E. on Valencia Blvd. which turns into Soledad Canyon Rd., R. on Golden Oak Rd., L. on Golden Triangle Rd. [TG-4551 B3])

Mountasia offers a mountain of fun for your family! Play either one of two **miniature golf** courses that feature a cascading waterfall. (Note: The zebra course has a hole that goes under the waterfall and inside a cave.) Prices are

$6.25 for ages 4 and up; $5.25 for seniors; children 3 years and under are free. Zip around the race track in **go karts** - $4.75 for a single or double car. Drivers must be at least 54" and passengers must be 42". Try to avoid getting wet (or go for it) in the **bumper boats** - $4.75 a ride; a passenger can ride for free. Height and age restrictions apply. Kids at least 48" tall and 6 years old can improve their batting average at the **batting cages**.

Inside Mountasia, skate around the **RollArena** with its constant light and music shows. Ask about their roller hockey games. Day skating sessions go from opening to 4pm and are $4 per skater; night sessions go from 6pm to closing and are $5.50. Friday and Saturday night sessions are $6.50. Skate rentals are $2. Experience the speed of car racing or the thrill of riding roller coasters via Mountasia's dual-seat motion simulators, that actually flips over 360 degrees - $8 for two people. Family-oriented video and arcade games, a redemption center, a playland and ball pit for youngsters (which are free), and a Perky's Pizza place are located inside, too. Attention students - good grades on your report card earns free tokens!

Hours:	Open in the summer Sun. - Fri., 10am - 10pm; Sat., 10am - midnight. Open the rest of the year Mon. - Thurs., noon - 9pm; Fri., noon - 11pm; Sat., 11am - 11pm; Sun., 11am - 9pm.
Admission:	Attractions are individually priced above, or purchase a $12 pass that includes one round of miniature golf, one ride on the go-karts, and one ride on the bumper cars. Ask about other specials.
Ages:	4 years and up.

MULLIGAN FAMILY FUN CENTER (Torrance)

(310) 325-3950 $$$

1351 Sepulveda Boulevard, Torrance

(Exit Harbor Fwy [110] W. on Sepulveda past Normandie. It's on the R. Look for the sign, as it is easy to miss. [TG-793 J1])

This center features **batting cages** - $1 for twenty pitches; two wonderful **miniature golf** courses - $6.50 for adults, $4.50 for seniors and kids ages 5 to 10; children 4 years and under play for free; **Slic Track** racing - $3.75 for a five minute ride (height restrictions apply); a Jungle Gym **play area** with tubes, slides, and ball pits just for children under 60" - $2 for unlimited time; and the ever-present arcade games.

Hours:	Open Mon. - Thurs., noon - 10pm; Fri., noon - 11pm; Sat., 10am - 11pm; Sun., 10am - 10pm.
Admission:	Attractions are individually priced above.
Ages:	2 years through 60" for the play area; 4 years and up for miniature golf.

PEPE'S KARTLAND

(818) 892-9309 $$

8300 Hayvenhurst Place, North Hills

(Exit San Diego Fwy [405] W. on Roscoe Blvd., R. on Hayvenhurst Ave., L. on Hayvenhurst Pl. [TG-531 D2])

Kids at least 4'2" and 7 years old can race around the curvy, asphalt track for an exhilarating, six-minute ride.

Hours: Open Mon. - Thurs., 4pm - 10pm; Fri., 3pm - 11pm; Sat., noon - 11pm; Sun., noon - 10pm.

Admission: $5 a ride or 6 rides for $20.

Ages: 7 years and up.

POWER STATION

(562) 497-1197 / www.powerstationgames.com

7589 Carson Boulevard, Long Beach Town Center, Long Beach

(Going N. on San Gabriel River Fwy [605], exit W. on Carson Blvd. Going S. on 605, exit at Carson and proceed across Carson into the Long Beach Towne Center. It's near the movie theaters. [TG-766 G6])

Power up at the laser tag arena inside this very noisy (and dark) arcade. Games last ten, pulse-pounding minutes as opponents search for one another in over 2,000 square feet of playing room. The room is set up like a maze, making it challenging to find your way in and out of different sections. The walls are decorated with neon colors that show up under the black lights. My boys and I love these fast action games. Note: The Power Station is part of a large outdoor mall which includes Edwards Cinemas, plenty of restaurants and a food court, and lots of fun shops.

Hours: Open Sun. - Thurs., 11am - 11pm; Fri., 11am - midnight; Sat., 10am - midnight.

Admission: $5 per person; $15 per person for 3 hours with a group.

Ages: 5 years and up.

Q-ZAR

(661) 260-3480 / www.q-zar.com

23460 Cinema Drive #C, Valencia

(Exit Golden State Fwy [5] E. on Valencia Blvd., R. on Cinema Dr. [TG-4550 H3])

Q-ZAR laser tag is played in a huge, futuristic-looking arena with lots of corridors and obstacles to make the game challenging (and to give me a chance to hide, until someone sneaks up and shoots me from behind!). Two teams, consisting of twenty players each, can be in here at one time. Games are about twelve minutes long. Run, duck, hide, point, and shoot - it's time for laser tag!

Hours: Open Sun. - Thurs., 11am - 10pm; Fri., 11am - midnight; Sat., 10am - 1am.

Admission: $7 per game. Call for specials.

Ages: 5 years and up.

THE ROCK GYM

(562) 981-3200 / www.therockgym.com

2599 E. Willow Street, Long Beach

(Exit San Diego Fwy [405] S. on Cherry/Temple, L. on Temple, R. on Willow. [TG-795 H3])

Go rock climbing at the beach, Long Beach, that is. The Rock Gym is one of Southern California's largest indoor rock climbing facilities. The huge lead climbing roof, unique bouldering tunnel, and walls jutting out at various angles prove a fitting challenge for your young athletes, and for those who are not so athletically inclined. Both seasoned climbers and those new to the sport will experience a sense of accomplishment as they conquer the rocky obstacles and terrain. Staff is on hand to harness, belay, and encourage climbers. Classes are offered where you can learn to belay your kids and other people. Belay means to stand on the ground, as an anchor, attached to the climber. The multi-colored rocks, embedded in the realistic-looking granite walls, are marked so they can be used as trail guides, though the routes are changed every few months to stimulate your mind and body. Ask about the variety of classes and programs offered. So, if you're feeling caught between a rock and a hard place, come to the Rock Gym for safe, fun exercise for the whole family!

Hours: The gym is open Mon., noon - 10pm, Tues. - Thurs., noon - 11pm; Fri., noon - 8pm; Sat. - Sun., 10am - 7pm.

Admission: $15 for adults for an all-day pass; $11 for ages 11 and under. Equipment rental is an additional $6 a day. An two-hour introduction class for belaying for kids 12 and up (this includes adults) is $35, which also includes a week pass to the gym.

Ages: 5 years and up.

ROCKREATION (Los Angeles)

(310) 207-7199 / www.rockreation.com
11866 La Grange Avenue, Los Angeles
(Exit San Diego Fwy [405] W. on Olympic Ave., N. on Bundy, R. on La Grange. [TG-632 A6])
    See ROCKREATION (Costa Mesa) for details.

Hours: The gym is open Mon. and Wed., noon - 11pm; Tues. and Thurs., 6am - 11pm; Fri., noon - 10pm; Sat. - Sun., 10am - 6pm. Kids' Climb, for ages 5 - 15, is offered Mon., Wed., Sat., and Sun., 4pm - 6pm.

Admission: $15 for adults for a day pass; $10 for ages 11 and under, but they must have a belayer. Rental equipment - shoes, harness, and chalk - is an additional $5. Kids Climb is $20 per participant, which includes the necessary equipment. Reservations are needed.

Ages: 5 years and up.

SHERMAN OAKS CASTLE PARK

(818) 756-9459 / www.shermanoakscastle.com
4989 Sepulveda Blvd., Sherman Oaks
(Going E. on the Ventura Fwy [101] exit N. on Sepulveda. From the San Diego Fwy [405], exit E. on Ventura Blvd., L. on Sepulveda. [TG-561 H3])
    This Castle Park offers royal fun for the whole family. There are three majestic **miniature golf** courses to putt around on, nine **batting cages** (kids must be 8 years old, or at least 4'6", to play in the batting cages), over 100 arcade games, a redemption center, and a full-service snack bar.

Hours: Open Mon. - Thurs., 10am - 11pm; Fri., 10am - 1am; Sat., 9am - 1am; Sun., 9am - 11pm.

Admission: Miniature golf is $5.50 for the first round for adults; $4 for seniors; $4.50 for children 12 and under; $2 for replays for all ages. Pay only $2 a round for early bird specials on Sat. and Sun. morning 9am - 10am.

Ages: 4 years and up.

ULTRAZONE (Alhambra)

(626) 282-6178 / www.playthezone.com

231 E. Main Street, Alhambra

(Exit San Bernardino Fwy [10] N. on Garfield Ave., R. on Main St. [TG-596 B4])

See ULTRAZONE (Sherman Oaks) for details.

Hours: Open most of the year Mon. - Thurs., 4pm - 9pm; Fri., 4pm - midnight; Sat., 11am - midnight; Sun., 11am - 10pm. Summer hours are Sun. - Thurs., noon - 10pm; Fri., noon - midnight; Sat., 11am - midnight; Sun., 11am - 10pm.

Admission: $5 a game.

Ages: 5 years and up.

ULTRAZONE (Sherman Oaks)

(818) 789-6620 / www.ultrazone.com

14622 Ventura Boulevard, Suite 208, Sherman Oaks

(Exit Ventura Fwy [101] S. on Van Nuys Blvd., R. on Ventura Blvd. It's on the S. side of the street, upstairs. Two hours of parking free with validation. [TG-561 J4])

It's almost pitch black. You're going through mazes and tunnels trying to find your way to the enemy's base before your enemy finds you. Suddenly, ZAP - you get hit! You realize you've lost your power and now you have to recharge. Where *is* the recharging site? After getting lost several times you find it, and now your infrared sighting helps spy one of "them"! You fire, hit, and score one for your team!

Ultrazone, with over 5,000 square feet of excitement, is the ultimate in laser tag. You carry your own equipment - a vest and laser gun - and play with up to thirty people, or three teams. After a five-minute briefing, you'll play for fifteen intense minutes. The first game will wear you out, but it's just practice. Now that you've got a handle on how the game is played, go for a second round. Or, just play some video games and grab a bite to eat from the full-service snack bar. Three party rooms are available. Laser tag - there is fun to be had with a game this rad!

Hours: Open Tues. - Thurs., 3pm - 10pm; Fri., 3pm - midnight; Sat., 10am - midnight; Sun., 10am - 10pm.

Admission: Games are $7 each; $18 for all day play. Volume discounts, role playing, and advanced access membership are also available.

Ages: 5 years and up, or not afraid of the dark.

UNDER THE SEA (Northridge)

(818) 772-7003 / www.choicemall.com/underthesea

19620 Nordhoff Street, Northridge

(From San Diego Fwy [405], exit W. on Nordhoff, stay R. on Nordhoff St. as Nordhoff Wy. goes L. From the Ventura Fwy [101], exit N. on Winnetka Ave., R. on Nordhoff St., L. on Corbin Ave., R. again on Nordhoff St. [TG-500 F7])

See UNDER THE SEA (Woodland Hills) for details.

UNDER THE SEA (Woodland Hills)

(818) 999-1533 / www.choicemall.com/underthesea
20929 Ventura Boulevard, Woodland Hills
(Exit Ventura Fwy [101] S. on De Soto Ave., R. on Ventura. [TG-560 C3])

Murals of mermaids and octopuses submerge your children in a world of play Under the Sea. This indoor play area has a bounce house, a ball pit, soft play mats, Little Tykes™ cars, a playhouse, free standing slides, and a Baby Corner. Socks are required in the play area. Ask about classes, including modern dance and Mommy & Me. You are welcome to bring your own food in and enjoy a meal at the picnic tables toward the entrance. There are two other UNDER THE SEA locations.

Hours: Open Mon. - Fri., 10am - 6pm. Open Sat. and Sun. for private parties.
Admission: $5 per child; adults are free.
Ages: 6 months to 7 years.

BALBOA FUN ZONE

(949) 673-0408 / www.thebalboafunzone.com
600 E Bay Avenue, Newport Beach
(Take Costa Mesa Fwy [55] to the end, which turns into Newport Blvd., which turns into Balboa Blvd., L. on Main St. Park and walk. [TG-919 B2])

This strip called the Fun Zone is across the road from the pier. (See BALBOA PIER under the Piers and Seaports section.) The carousel, Ferris wheel, bumper cars, and Scary Dark Ride (that's its real name) are the main attractions here. Rides require one to two tickets, and tickets are $1.25 each. Arcade games and a clown bounce for younger children ($1 for a few minutes of bouncy fun) are also here. Craft activities in the Zone include making spin art pictures and other fun projects.

Kids also enjoy walking around, shopping, or eating a famous Balboa Bar, an ice-cream bar with various toppings. If you're looking for physical activity, bike rentals are available at Bayside Sun and Sport on Palm Street. Rentals are $5 for the first hour for children's bikes, and $12 for tandems. They also have in-line skates and more. Parasailing, (949) 673-3372, is between $55 to $75 for ten minutes of air time and an hour boat trip. Call for hours of operation. See the Transportation section for harbor cruises launched from this immediate area.

Take the historic Balboa ferry which runs Monday through Friday from 6am to midnight (longer on the weekends) to Balboa Island. At only 50¢ per person one way, free for children 4 years and under, or $1.25 for car and driver - the ferry is a fun, affordable way to get to the island and kids love this mini-adventure. Once on the man-made island, there is not a lot for kids to do. Enjoy a walk on the paved pathway along the beach or perhaps head east toward the main shopping street. Note: The Island can also be reached by exiting Pacific

Coast Highway [1] S. on Jamboree Road, where it turns into Marine Ave.

Hours: Stores and attractions along the Balboa Fun Zone are open most of the year Mon. - Thurs., 11am - 8pm; Fri. - Sat., 11am - 10pm; Sun., 11am - 8pm. Summer hours are Mon. - Thurs., 11am - 11pm; Fri., 11am - 11pm; Sat., 10am - 11pm; Sun., 10am - 10pm. Most parking along the street is metered.

Admission: Attractions are individually priced above.

Ages: All

CAMELOT

(714) 630-3340

3200 Carpenter Avenue, Anaheim

(Exit Riverside Fwy [91] N. on Kraemer/Glassell, R. on La Palma, R. on Shepard, L. on Carpenter. It's next door to FAMILY FUN CENTER (Anaheim). [TG-769 G3])

This huge castle has dragons, knights in shining armor, and anything else your prince or princess might consider fun decor. Choose from five exciting **miniature golf** courses - $7 for adults, $6 for ages 5 to 11, children 4 years and under are free with a paid adult; **Lazer Tag**, which is an exciting game of tag using laser guns - $5 for the first game Monday through Thursday, $6 for the first game Friday through Sunday, with all replay games costing $3; four **waterslides** (usually open from May to September) - $4 for ten rides, $6 for twenty rides, and $8 for an all-day rides pass; over 300 video and arcade games; and the mandatory snack bar, serving pizza and Dryer's ice cream.

Hours: Most of Camelot is open in the summer Sun. - Thurs., 10am - midnight; Fri. - Sat., 10am - 1am. The rest of the year it's open Sun. - Thurs., 10am - 11pm; Fri - Sat., 9:30am - midnight. The water slide is open seasonally, daily 11am - 6pm.

Admission: Attractions are individually priced above.

Ages: 2½ years and up.

CLIMBX

(714) 843-9919 / www.climbxhb.com

18411 Gothard Street, Unit I, Huntington Beach

(Exit San Diego Fwy [405] W. on Talbert Ave., L. on Gothard. It's in an industrial section. [TG-857 J3])

This indoor rock climbing facility is not as large as others we've found, but it has all the essential ingredients - several contoured wall structures built at angles that look and climb like real rock; colorful hand and foot holds that mark a variety of "trails"; a small bouldering cave; twenty-six top ropes; and enough challenges for seasoned climbers, along with lots of encouragement and easier routes for beginners. It's encouraging to know that athletic prowess is not necessary when learning how to climb. This is a sport that teaches balance and thinking while instilling a sense of confidence. Climbers are in a safety harness which is attached to a belayer, so even if one should misjudge a hand or foot hold (which my kids sometimes did on purpose), the climber will not fall, but merely swing in the air. ClimbX marks the spot for indoor fun! Note: This facility has a separate party room.

Hours: Open Mon. and Fri., 11am - 8pm; Tues. - Thurs., 11am - 10pm;
Sat. - Sun., 11am - 6pm.

Admission: An all day pass is $13 per person. Shoe or harness rentals are $3
each, per person, or $5 for both. Introductory classes are $55 for
two hours, one night a week for three weeks, and includes a
week of free climbing.

Ages: 5 years and up.

DROMO 1

(714) 744-4779 / www.dromo1.com *$$$*

1431 N. Main Street, Orange

(Exit the Orange Fwy [57] E. on Katella Ave., L. on Main. [TG-799 F1])

Put the pedal to the metal at this 45,000 square feet indoor karting facility.
Enjoy challenging, high performance racing with up to seven other drivers in a
safe, controlled environment. Each session is about twenty laps or twelve
minutes. Drivers must be over five feet tall and are supplied with a driving suit,
helmets with fullface goggles, and a neck brace. Please wear close-toed shoes.
Participants under 18 years old must be accompanied by their parent, who must
sign a liability waiver.

Hours: Open Mon. - Thurs., 1pm - 10pm; Fri. - Sat., 1pm - 11pm; Sun.,
1pm - 9pm.

Admission: $20 per session.

Ages: At least 5 feet tall.

FAMILY FUN CENTER (Anaheim)

(714) 630-7212 / www.boomersparks.com *$$$*

1041 N. Shepard, Anaheim

(Exit Artesia Fwy [91] N. on Kraemer/Glassell, R. on La Palma, R. on Shepard. It's next door to
CAMELOT, miniature golf. [TG-769 G2])

This is a fun center, but bring your money because fun costs. The many
attractions include **bumper boats** - $4 for kids over 44", $2 for kids under 44";
batting cages; go-karts - $5 for a five-minute ride and children must be at least
58" to drive; **Nascars** - $5 a drive (height restrictions apply); and an **outdoor
roller-skating rink** - $4, which includes skate rentals. The giant **maze craze** is
amazing. Walk around the six-feet high partitions and try to find your way out.
To actually play the challenging maze game, purchase a card, punch the time
clock, and try to find the eight numbers hidden throughout the maze - they could
even be up at any of the four towers! The game costs $4 per player. Tip: Keep
younger children with you. **Big Top Fun Zone** has six carnival rides, including a
Ferris wheel, carousel, pirate ship, and some kiddie rides. All rides are $3.75
each or purchase an unlimited rides pass for $10 for 57" and under. Arcade
games and a snack bar are available, too.

Hours: Big Top Fun Zone is open Mon. - Fri., 11am - 9pm; Sat. - Sun.,
11am - 11pm. The rest of the attractions are open Mon. - Fri.,
10am - 10pm; Sat. - Sun., 10am - midnight.

Admission: Attractions are individually priced above.

Ages: 2 years and up.

FAMILY FUN CENTER (Fountain Valley)

(714) 842-1011 / www.boomersparks.com
16800 Magnolia Street, Fountain Valley
(Exit San Diego Fwy [405] S. on Magnolia. [TG-828 C7])

    Family Fun Center is fun for the whole family. The attractions here include **miniature golf** - $6.25 for adults, $5 for seniors and kids 12 years and under; **bumper boats** - $4.50 for a six-minute ride, and kids must be at least 44" to ride by themselves (children under 40" can ride with an adult for $1.50); **batting cages** - eighteen pitches for $1; and **go karts** - $5 for a five-minute ride, and kids must be at least 58" to drive by themselves, $1.50 for additional passengers who must be at least 40". The **Kiddie Big Top** has four carnival rides, such as a Ferris wheel, a roller coaster, and train ride geared for ages 7 and under. Each ride takes four to five tickets and tickets are 50¢ each, or purchase twenty-four tickets for $6; forty-four tickets for $10. BULLWINKLE'S RESTAURANT (look under the Edible Adventures section) is adjacent to this Family Fun Center.

    Hours: Miniature golf is open Sun. - Thurs., 10am - 10pm; Fri. - Sat., 10am - midnight. Batting cages are open Mon. - Thurs., noon - 9pm; Fri. - Sun., 9am - 11pm. Go karts are open daily 2pm - 10pm. The Kiddie Big Top is open Mon. - Fri., noon - 10pm; Sat. - Sun., 9am - 10pm. Family Fun attractions are open extended hours during the summer.

    Admission: Attractions are individually priced above, or $18 for 44" and taller; $10 for 43" and under.

    Ages: 2 years and up.

LASER QUEST

(714) 449-0555 / www.laserquest.com
229 E. Orangethorpe Avenue, Fullerton
(Exit Riverside Fwy [91] N. on Harbor Blvd., R. on Orangethorpe Ave. [TG-768 H1])

    This large arena, with gothic decor, sets the stage for an exciting game of laser tag. Armed with laser guns, and vests with target lights, enter the multi-level maze. Amid the strobe lights, ramps, catwalks, partitions, fog, and pulse-pounding music (which covered up my heavy breathing from being out of shape), race against the clock to "tag" the opposing team members with laser shots, and score. The fifteen-minute games are fast-paced, and leave you either tired or fired up to play another round! The lounge has video games and there is a separate party room.

    Hours: Open Tues. - Thurs., 6pm - 10pm; Fri., 4pm - midnight; Sat., noon - midnight; Sun., noon - 8pm. Open on holiday Mon. Open extended hours in the summer.

    Admission: $7.50 per game.

    Ages: 5 years and up.

PALACE PARK

(949) 559-8336 / www.boomersparks.com
3405 Michelson Drive, Irvine

(Exit San Diego Fwy [405] S. on Culver Dr., R. on Michelson. Or, exit San Diego Fwy [405] S. on Jamboree, L. on Michelson. [TG-859 J6])

This purple palace, which can be seen from the freeway, is definitely a kids' kingdom. There is an almost overwhelming amount of video and arcade games, or, to quote my boys, "Wow!" There is also a ticket redemption center and an Express McDonald's Restaurant. The two **simulator** rides offer different adventures for $4 each. Riders must be at least 42" tall. Also inside the castle walls are activities for the younger set, such as kiddie arcade games and **Palace Playland**, which is a two-tiered, soft play area with soft-play mazes, ball pits, tunnels, and slides - $3.50 for all-day play for kids 48" and under.

Outside, are three, terrific, themed **miniature golf** courses with windmills, castles, houses, and other buildings - $6.25 a round for adults, children 5 years and under are free. **Rock climbing** is $6 for two climbs up the wall. Splash Island **bumper boats** are $4.25 a ride, $1.50 for additional riders and riders must be over 42" tall. I allowed my 11-year old to steer the boat and he did so gleefully - right under the fountain's waters. Oh, the joy of spending time together! **Go-carts**, where drivers must be a minimum of 58", are $6.50 per ride, $1.50 for additional riders who must be at least 42". Younger speedsters, at least 42", can drive their own cars at **Kiddie Go-karts** for $3.75 a ride, while tots can try their hand at driving **Tot Wheels** for $2.75 a ride. **Bumper cars** are $2 a bump, I mean ride. **Batting cages** are here, too. In **Laser Storm**, you and your at least 5-year-old child (personal recommendation) enter a darkened, maze-like room with walls that are three-feet high and lit by fluorescent markings. For ten minutes you'll engage in laser tag, which entails alternately safeguarding your base while shooting at the players on the opposing team. It's a blast. The cost is $6 per game.

Last, but not least to skaters and BMX riders, is the **Gravity Games Skate Park**, a 21,000 square foot outdoor skate park with several wooden ramps, quarter pipes, a half pipe, grinding boxes, and other street skate features, plus some skating (or biking) room, all on a base of smooth concrete. Two-hour sessions cost between $7 to $9 for members; $11 to $14 for non-members, depending on the day and time. Helmet, elbow, and knee pads are required and can be rented for $5 for everything. Participants under 18 must have a waiver signed by a parent or legal guardian.

If the urge strikes, next door is the Irvine Recreation Center with plenty of bowling lanes.

Hours: Open Sun. - Thurs., 10am - 11pm; Fri. - Sat., 10am - midnight. Hours may fluctuate.

Admission: Attractions are individually priced above or purchase a park pass, which includes everything but the skate park, $19 for adults; $9 for younger children.

Ages: 2 years and up.

PHARSIDE
(949) 574-9966
1644 Superior Avenue, Costa Mesa

$$

(Take Costa Mesa Fwy [55] S. to the end. Proceed to Newport Blvd., R. on 18th St. L. on Superior Ave. It's near 16th St. There is no parking on the lot. During the week, park at "Public" parking places. On weekends only, you may use the Model Glass's lot, across the street. [TG-888 H4])

This is a place for after school and weekend skateboarders, in-line skaters, and BMX riders to practice and hang out. There are a few ramps inside toward the back, through the pro shop, such as a six-foot spine connected to a nine-foot half pipe and a four-foot half pipe. Outside on the asphalt is a six-foot half pipe and a grind box. (Your kids will understand this terminology if you don't.) It isn't anything fancy, but skaters and bikers just want a place to do their thing. A small snack shop is available. Helmet, knee pads, and elbow pads are required and so is a parent-signed waiver.

Hours: Open Mon. - Fri., 11am - 7pm; Sat., 10am - 6pm; Sun., 11am - 5pm. There are specific times for skateboarding, blading, and for BMX riding. (All BMX riders must be 16 years old.)

Admission: $10 for non-members for the day; $5 for members. Ask about specials for any given day. Equipment rents for $2 per item, or $5 for the set.

Ages: 8 years and up.

PLANET KIDS (Fountain Valley)
(714) 378-8733 / www.planet-kids.com
18081 Magnolia Street, Fountain Valley
(Going S. on San Diego Fwy [405], exit S. on Magnolia St. Going N. on 405, exit N. on Euclid St., L. on Talbert Ave., L. on Magnolia. It's on the corner of Magnolia and Talbert. [TG-858 C2])

See PLANET KIDS (Laguna Hills) for details.

PLANET KIDS (Laguna Hills)   ☼
(949) 831-3500 / www.planet-kids.com   *$$*
26538 Moulton Parkway, Laguna Hills   🎂
(Exit San Diego Fwy [5] S.W. on La Paz Rd., R. on Moulton Pkwy. It's in a shopping center. [TG-921 G5])

Bring your earthling offspring to Planet Kids for indoor fun that is out of this world! Adventure Crater is the main play structure, where kids will run orbits around you. It has a wooden walkway all around, padded slides, tube slides, and a ball pit. Go through the tunnel under crater rock and peek out the windows into a desert diorama.

The Globe Theater has costumes and karaoke for your budding star. It also shows (mostly Disney) movies. Mission Control is a space-like shuttle room, with the few computers programmed to play educational games. Take "pictures" in the Eclipse room against a photo-sensitive wall as the strobe-like light flashes. A few arcade games are offered on this planet, too.

You'll hear the "music" (i.e. loud noises) before you actually enter the Lunar Tunes room. For band member "wannabes," or for kids who like to play with drums and other instruments, this is the place to be. A floor piano has keys that light up when stepped (or jumped) on (as in the movie *Big*).

The Tot Spot, designed for kids five years and under, has a little beach-like area (sans the sand) and a climbing play structure with a ball pit and soft foam animals. It also has a mini-schoolhouse room with toys, books, and a computer. The snack bar has food ranging from pizza and soft pretzels to chef salad and baked potatoes. If you have places to go and things to do (and want to do it ten times faster without your kids), check into the Blast-Off program. It enables parents to enroll their children, ages 5 to 13, to stay here for up to four hours of supervised play for $15.95 for one child, which includes a meal and a drink, and $10.95 for a sibling. Note: Socks are required in all play areas.

Hours: Open Tues. - Thurs., 11am - 7pm; Fri., 11am - 9pm; Sat., 10am - 9pm; Sun., 11am - 7pm. Closed Mon.

Admission: $5.95 for ages 1 - 3; $8.95 for ages 4 - 17. Adults play for free with a paid child's admission.

Ages: 1½ - 13 years.

PLANET KIDS (Orange)

(714) 288-4090 / www.planet-kids.com

1536 E. Katella Avenue, Orange

(Exit Costa Mesa Fwy [55] W. on Katella Ave. [TG-799 J1])

See PLANET KIDS (Laguna Hills) for details. This location shows signs of being well loved.

ROCKCITY   ☼

(714) 777-4884 / www.rockincity.com $$$$

5100 E. La Palma, suite 108, Anaheim   🎂

(Going E. on the Riverside Fwy [91], exit N. on Lakeview, R. on La Palma, R. on Kellogg to park. Going W. on 91, exit N. on Imperial Hwy., L. on La Palma, L. on Kellogg. [TG-770 C1])

I'm gonna rock 'n roll all night! Well, I'll at least rock for a good portion of the day. This large indoor rock climbing gym is very family oriented. It has thirteen top ropes, numerous lead routes on variously-angled walls, a bouldering wall, and a bouldering cave. Perfect for first time climbers and still very challenging for experts, RockCity offers the best of both worlds. Parents, learn to belay your kids or just relax (remember, they *are* wearing harnesses) and watch them go at it during kid's climbs when the staff does all the work.

Hours: Open Mon. - Fri., noon -10pm; Sat., 10am - 6pm; Sun., noon - 6pm. Kids are welcome to climb anytime, but times especially for them are Thurs., 6pm - 8pm; Sun., 1pm - 3pm.

Admission: $12 for an adult day pass; $10 for a day pass for ages 3 -14. The harness and shoes are an additional $5 per person. Kid's climb is $20 for two hours, which includes the rental equipment and a belayer.

Ages: 5 years and up.

ROCKREATION (Costa Mesa)   ☼

(714) 556-ROCK (7625) / www.rockreation.com $$$$

1300 Logan Avenue, Costa Mesa   🎂

(Exit San Diego Fwy [405] S. on Fairview Rd., R. on Baker St., L. on McClintock Wy., R. on Logan Ave. [TG-859 A5])

Get the kids geared up - it's time to *rock* and roll at Rockreation! This huge indoor warehouse/rock climbing gym is a great place for beginners to learn climbing techniques in a safe and controlled environment. It also provides enough rocky terrain for serious climbers to train. The multi-colored rocks of various shapes and sizes jut out from the twenty-seven-foot geometrical walls for handholds and footholds, offering over 150 different climbing routes. Some of the walls are straight up and down, others have slight inclines, while still others have very challenging angles and overhangs. Belayers, those who hold the rope so if you slip you don't fall, are provided during specific Climb Time hours, for ages 6 and up. Even if you were to hit rock bottom (which you won't), it's "carpeted" with black foam padding. Kids warm up using a short practice wall. Although my boys were a bit intimidated at first, by the end of our time here, they were really climbing the walls - all the way to the top. Enroll your child in a summer camp or one of the year-round classes offered for various levels and ages. Hang out with your kids here, or better yet, tell them to go climb a rock! Also see ROCKREATION (Los Angeles).

> **Hours:** The gym is open Mon. - Thurs., noon - 10pm; Fri., noon - 9pm; Sat. - Sun., 10am - 6pm. Climb Time, for kids 6 and older, is offered Tues. and Thurs., 6pm - 8pm; Sat. - Sun., noon - 3pm.
>
> **Admission:** $15 per person for an all-day pass. Equipment rental - shoes, harness, and chalk - is an additional $5. Climb Time is $10 per person per hour, which includes equipment rental. Reservations are required.
>
> **Ages:** Depending on your child's agility - 5 years and up.

SEAL BEACH SKATEBOARD PARK

(562) 431-2527 / sbrecreation.tripod.com
12th St. and Landing, Seal Beach
(Exit San Diego Fwy [405] S. on Seal Beach Blvd., R. on Landing (just past Pacific Coast Hwy.), enter at the gate near Zoeter Field park. Adjacent to a child care center [TG-826 F4])

This local, outdoor skate park just has a few wooden quarter-pipes, a funbox, and a half pipe all on asphalt. It's just for the fun of it! Safety equipment - helmet and knee and elbow pads - must be worn. A parental waiver must be on file for skaters under 18 years old.

> **Hours:** Open traditional school days Wed. - Fri., 3pm - 6pm; Sat. - Sun., noon - 4pm. Open in the summer and holidays, Tues. - Sun., noon - 6pm.
>
> **Admission:** $2 per two-hour session.
>
> **Ages:** 6 years old and up.

SOUTHLAND HILLS GOLFLAND AND PIZZA

(714) 895-4550
12611 Beach Boulevard, Stanton
(Exit Santa Ana Fwy [5] S. on Beach. Or, exit Garden Grove Fwy [22] N. on Beach. [TG-797 J6])

*Fore*tunately for miniature golf lovers, Southland Hills has two great courses enhanced by a scaled down windmill, pagoda, fort, and other fun landmarks - $6 for adults; $4 for seniors; $5 for ages 11 and under. There are also video arcades, a redemption center, and a snack bar that serves pizza and other food. Monday night, after 5pm, is family night, when everyone can play miniature golf for only $4 a round.

Hours: Sun. - Thurs., 10am - 11pm; Fri. - Sat., 10am - midnight.
Admission: Prices are listed above.
Ages: 4 years and up.

VANS SKATEPARK (Orange)   ☼

(714) 769-3800 / www.vans.com $$$
20 The City Boulevard West, Orange   ⛹
(Exit Garden Grove Fwy [22] N. at The City Drive, near the intersection of I-5. It's in The Block mall. [TG-799 C5])

Wow! Awesome! Incredible! And these were just the first few words out of my boys' mouths. This part-indoor, part-outdoor skate park has 46,000 square feet of wooden ramps, concrete bowls, half pipes, street scene ramps, and more, all at a mega mall. Rollerbladers, skateboarders, and cyclists can all use the park at various times. It is a training "camp" for competitors as well as a practice place for enthusiasts of all levels. Beginners have certain areas that are recommended just for them. Observers can sit anywhere on the multi-level stadium seats that semi-surround the main skate area. Our first few times here we just watched before my older boys actually ventured out on the ramps. Participants under 18 must have a waiver signed by a parent or legal guardian.

An attached pro-shop hawks Vans brand merchandise and everything that a skateboarder needs and more. It also provides rentals of helmets, knee pads, and elbow pads, which are all mandatory. See THE BLOCK AT ORANGE, under the Malls section, for a description of what stores and restaurants are at the surrounding mall.

Hours: Open daily 10am - 11pm.
Admission: Free to observers. Sessions are two hours long and cost between $7 - $14, depending on the time of day and if you are a member or not. Gear rentals are $2 per item or $5 for all of it, per session.
Ages: 3 years and up to watch; 6 years and up to participate.

ADAMS KART TRACK   ☀

(800) 350-3826 / www.adamskarttrack.net $$$$
5292 24ᵗʰ Street, Riverside
(Exit Pomona Fwy [60] N. on Market St. It's on the corner of 24ᵗʰ St. and Market. [TG-645 F7])

The main track, which is six-tenths of a mile of turns, twists, and straight track, is a great introduction to real racing. This race track school offers classes for kart racing, available for kids 5 years and up. Call for a class schedule.

Hours: The track is open Mon. - Fri., 10am - 5pm; Sat. - Sun., noon - 5pm.
Admission: Bring your own kart for the main track - $25 a day for non-members; $20 for members; $20 for an extra passenger; $8 for pit person/spectator. Classes start at $75 for two hours of instruction and racing.
Ages: 5 years and up.

ILLUSIONZONE

(909) 296-9431 / www.illusionzone.com　　$$$$

42188 Rio Nedo, Temecula

(Exit Temecula Valley Fwy [15] W. on Winchester Rd. [79], L. on Diaz Rd., R. on Rio Nedo. [TG-958 F5])

Splat! This indoor paintball facility incorporates the fun of paintball, minus the outdoor rocky terrain. But, you'll still work up a sweat. Squat behind painted-splattered wood obstacles scattered throughout the large room to hide from your opponents. (And hope that you don't get hit by friendly fire!) Layer up and wear shoes with good traction.

Hours: Open Fri., 4pm - 10pm; Sat. - Sun., 8am - 8pm.

Admission: Players with their own equipment pay $5 for one hour; $15 for 6 hours; $25 for twelve hours. Players without equipment pay $10 for one hour; $25 for 6 hours; $40 for twelve hours.

Ages: 8 years and up.

OLLIE HOUSE

(909) 699-1145 / www.olliehouse.com　　$$

43300 Business Park Drive, Temecula

(Exit Temecula Valley Fwy [15] W. on Rancho California Rd., R. on Business Park Dr. [TG-958 G7])

Your kids can practice ollies, kickflips, shoveits, manuals, nosegrabs, and all the other death-defying skateboard maneuvers at this terrific, two-story indoor skateboard park. Several wooden ramps, quarter and half pipes, fun boxes with ledges and rails, a pyramid, a large vert wall, and mini street courses for beginners are situated on a smooth cement floor in the 32,000 square foot arena. Spectators are invited upstairs to watch. All participants under 18 years must have a parent or legal guardian sign a waiver. Helmets and elbow and knee pads are necessary.

Hours: Open during the school year Mon. - Thurs., 2pm -10pm; Fri., 2pm - 11pm; Sat., 9am - 11pm; Sun., 10am - 10pm. Open in the summer extended hours. Sessions are 2 hours each. There are special sessions for ages 8 and under.

Admission: Mon. - Thurs., $6 for members, $8 for non-members; Fri. - Sun., $8 for members, $10 for non-members. Ask about specials. Rental equipment is $5 for the set.

Ages: 6 years and up.

S.C. VILLAGE PAINTBALL PARK

(949) 489-9000 / www.scvillage.com　　$$$$$

Hellman Road & River Road, Corona

(From Riverside Fwy [91] exit N. on Lincoln Blvd., L. on River Rd. From Ontario Fwy [15], exit E. on 6th, which turns into Norco Dr., which turns into Corydon Ave., R. on River Rd. From River Rd., make sure to stay L. on River Rd. as the main road turns into Archibald Ave. [TG-712 J5])

Rambos, Terminators, Xenas, and people from all other walks of life are invited to play paintball on this massive, sixty-acre playing field with twenty different settings. Battle it out in desert terrain, jungle tracts, or even in the city of Beirut. Each field has special props which may include a downed helicopter, ambulance, tents, tanks, radar towers, huts, bridges, tunnels, swamp, camouflage netting, and acres of woods or brush. In this updated version of Capture the Flag, paintball guns and non-toxic gelatin capsules (i.e. paintballs) are used. Two teams compete against each other using the props to run around and hide behind. The object of the game is to somehow capture your opponents' flag and return it to your team's flag station. However, if you are hit with a paintball (which can sting), you are out of the game. Games last between twenty to thirty minutes. All games have referees to insure safe and fair play. There are two levels of play - beginner and advanced. Come by yourself or with a group of friends. All amenities, including a food concession, equipment, and supplies are on-site. Participants under 18 must have a waiver signed by a parent or guardian.

Hours: Open to the public Sat. - Sun., 7:30am - 4pm. Weekday games are by appointment only.

Admission: General admission is $20 per person for half day; $25 for all day. Rental equipment varies in price according to what you want. Goggles/face masks (mandatory) are $5; jumpsuits are $7; guns range from $10 - $15; and paintballs start at $6 for 100 rounds. Package deals are available. For instance, a $45 starter package includes half day admission, full mask, pump rifle, 100 rounds of paintball, four CO_2 cartridges, and ten paint holders.

Ages: At least 10 years old.

BRICKYARD SKATEPARK

(909) 792-5093 / www.brickyardskate.com
21 W. Stuart Avenue, Redlands

(Going E. on San Bernardino Fwy [10], exit S. on Orange St., R. on Stuart. Going W. on 10, exit S. on 6th St., R. on Pearl Ave., L. on Orange, R. on Stuart. [TG-608 B7])

This unique skate park is one-third indoors, two-thirds outdoors, and great for all level skaters. The 7,000 square foot indoor facility has brick walls and features two forty-feet wide back-to-back mini ramps and a six-feet deep wooden bowl. The larger, 14,000 square foot outside street course is spread out around the building. It has bank ramps, rails, launches, quarter pipes, pyramids, and an eleven-foot vert wall. All ramps are made of wood. Non-skaters can pull up a seat and just watch. All participants under the age of 18 must have a parent or legal guardian sign a waiver/liability release form.

Hours: Open Tues. - Fri., 3:30 - 10pm; Sat., noon - 10pm; Sun., noon - 6:30pm. Summer hours may change.

Admission: $7 per session on Tues.; $8 Wed. - Thurs., $10 Fri. - Sun. Each session is about three hours long.

Ages: Must be at least 7 years old.

FAMILY FUN CENTER (Upland)

(909) 985-1313 / www.boomersparks.com
1500 W. 7th Street, Upland

(Exit San Bernardino Fwy [10] N. on Mountain, L. on 7th. [TG-601 H4])

Upland Family Fun Center offers fun for everyone in your family! This giant fun center has four, themed **miniature golf** courses with all the whimsical decorations that make each hole fun. Two of the courses, the Old West and Storybook Land, are indoors so rainy days won't put a damper on your swing. Numerous arcade games are also inside the building. Golf prices are $6 a round for adults, $4 for children 12 years and under. Take a spin on a **go kart** at $5 a ride (no sandals allowed) - drivers must be over 58". An additional passenger under this height is $2. **Bumperboats** are always fun - $4.50 for kids over 44", $2 for riders under this height. There are six **kiddie rides** here, including a Ferris wheel, roller coaster, and mini-airplanes. Each ride or attraction costs three to five tickets. Tickets cost $6 for a book of twenty-four; $10 for a book of forty-four; and $20 for a book of 100. Kids can also practice for the big league at the **batting cages,** or play at the over 100 video and arcade games.

If you've worked up an appetite, BULLWINKLE'S FAMILY RESTAURANT (see the Edible Adventures section for more info on this restaurant) is right next door. Your choice of hamburgers, pizza, chicken, or ribs is served in a fun atmosphere, where there are more arcade games to play. (There is no escape from them.)

Hours: Open Sun. - Thurs., 10am - 10pm; Fri. - Sat., 10am - midnight.

Admission: Attractions are individually priced above, or purchase an all-day pass which includes unlimited use of everything, except the arcade games; $17 for 58" and taller; $10 for 57" and under. The pass is only offered on Fri. after 5pm and all day Sat., Sun., and on holidays. Ask about its daily availability during the summer.

Ages: 3 years and up.

FIESTA VILLAGE   ☼

(909) 824-1111 $$$

1405 E. Washington Street, Colton   ♨

(Exit Riverside Fwy [215] E. on Washington. [TG-646 F2])

Come party at Fiesta Village! There are two, Western-motif **miniature golf** courses - $5 for adults, $4.50 for children 12 years and under; **go karts**, where drivers must be at least 53" tall - $4.50 for a five-minute ride; **batting cages**; **laser tag** - $4.50 for seven minutes of action-packed fun; **bumper cars** - $2.50; and three **waterslides** with a lounging area for spectators - $6 for an all-day pass for ages 4 years and up; $2 for a spectator. Note: There isn't any pool here, just slides. Video arcades are in the lobby.

A full snack bar with pizza, hot dogs, corn dogs, chips, popcorn, and candy, is adjacent to Fiesta Village. If you're in the mood to play, there are video and arcade games, air hockey, and a pool table in here, too.

Hours: The dry land activities are open Sun. - Thurs., 10am - 10pm; Fri. - Sat., 10am - 11pm. The waterslides are open weekends only in May and September 11am - 5pm, and daily in the summer noon - 6pm.

Admission: Attractions priced above.

Ages: 4 years and up.

HANGAR 18 INDOOR ROCK CLIMBING

(909) 931-5991 / www.climbhangar18.com

256 Stowell Street, Suite A, Upland

(Exit San Bernardino Fwy [10] N. on Euclid Ave., R. on Stowell (just after 8th St.). It's on the R. [TG-602 C3])

Love a good cliffhanger? Hangar 18 boasts of 10,000 square feet of overhangs, twenty-five top ropes, and textured climbing walls dotted with numerous multi-colored stones that represent different routes. Lead climbing is available as is a bouldering area, which gives both seasoned climbers, as well as beginners, the opportunity to practice their bouldering technique. Come with a friend (i.e. a fellow belayer) or call beforehand to see if a belayer will be at the gym. Classes in belaying are also available for ages 10 and up. This fun and safe activity builds confidence and stamina. A party room is available. In the after school programs, offered for students in 4th through 12th grades, children learn basic rock climbing technique, knot tying, and belaying. The program includes rental equipment, supervision, and instruction.

Hours: Open Mon. - Thurs., 10am - 10pm; Fri., 10am - 8pm; Sat. - Sun., 10am - 7pm.

Admission: Day passes are $14 for adults; $9 for children 14 and under. Rental equipment - shoes and a harness - is $5. Kids that need a belayer are $15 per hour, $20 for 2 hours.

Ages: 5 years and up.

MULLIGAN FAMILY FUN CENTER (Murrieta)

(909) 696-9696

24950 Madison Avenue, Murrieta

(Exit Temecula Valley Fwy [15] S.W. on Murrieta Hot Springs Rd., R. on Madison Ave. [TG-928 B6])

Calling all ranch hands: Git along to Mulligan Family Fun Center for some family fun! This western-themed miniature golf center has two impressive **miniature golf** courses. (Note: You can see the red rock boulders, small western buildings, and stagecoaches from the freeway, when you're heading southbound on the I-15.) A round of golf costs $6 for ages 13 and up; $5 for ages 5 to 12; children 4 years and under are free. Other attractions include **batting cages**; **bumper boats** - $4 for the driver, $2 for passengers; **go-karts** - $4.50 for drivers, $2 for passengers (height restrictions apply); and **kiddie go-karts** - $3 for those 40" to 54". Complete your day (or night) on the town by coming in the spacious "town hall," which is done up right fine. First, though, take a look at all the fun props outside, like cowboy mannequins literally hanging around. Inside, the old west motif continues with a jail and kids' saloon (cafe). The cafe serves salads, pizza, hot dogs, chicken strips, and other food essentials. There are also plenty of modern-day shoot out games (i.e. arcade and video games).

Hours: Open Mon. - Thurs., 11:30am - 10pm; Fri., 11:30am - 11pm; Sat., 10am - midnight; Sun., 10am - 10pm. Closed Thanksgiving and Christmas.

Admission: Attractions are individually priced above. Unlimited all-day passes are available Fri. after 4pm and all day Sat. - Sun., $19.95 for 56" and taller; $15.95 for 55" and under.

Ages: 3 years and up.

SCANDIA AMUSEMENT PARK   ☼

(909) 390-3092 / www.scandiafun.com $$$

1155 S. Wanamaker Avenue, Ontario   ♨

(Exit Ontario Fwy [15] W. on Jurupa, R. on Rockefeller, R. on Wanamaker. [TG-643 E2])

Vikings might have come to this country just to play at this amusement park! Well, maybe not, but it is a lot of fun and very well kept up. Attractions include two **miniature golf** courses with unlimited play at $6.95 for 54" and taller, $5.95 for 53" and under, 36" and under are free with a paying adult; **batting cages;** sixteen **amusement rides** - some for big kids such as a roller coaster, bumper boats, and scrambler, and some for little kids such as a small semi-truck ride around a track, a carousel, and a slide. Tickets cost $1 each or $11.95 for fifteen tickets. Children's rides require two tickets; big kids' (or adult) rides require three to six tickets. Arcade games and a full service snack bar are here, too.

Hours: Open in the summer Sun. - Thurs., 10am - 11pm; Fri. - Sat. 10am - 1am. Open the rest of the year Sun. - Thurs., 10am - 10pm; Fri. - Sat., 10am - midnight.

Admission: Attractions are individually priced above, or purchase an unlimited pass (excluding arcade games) - $18.95 for 54" and taller; $14.95 for 53" to 36"; $9.95 for kids 35" and under. Inquire about weekday specials.

Ages: 3 years and up.

SCANDIA FAMILY FUN CENTER   ☼

(760) 241-4007 $$$

12627 Mariposa Road, Victorville   ♨

(Exit Mojave Fwy [15] E. on Bear Valley Rd., L. on Mariposa. [TG-4386 A5])

Enjoy some high-desert fun at Scandia Family Fun Center. There are two Scandinavian-themed, **miniature golf** courses, with castles, bridges, and other small buildings that add interest - $4.95 for adults, children 5 years and under play for free; **go-karts** and **bumper boats** - $3.95 per ride (must be at least 54" to drive); and **batting cages**. A full-service snack bar, arcade and video games, and prize redemption center are also here for your enjoyment.

Hours: Open Sun. - Thurs., 10am - 11pm; Fri. - Sat., 10am - midnight.

Admission: Attractions are individually priced above, or buy a pass for $10.95 per person that allows you to play on each attraction once, as well as receive 5 tokens. An unlimited pass is $15.95 per person.

Ages: 4 years and up.

VANS SKATEPARK (Ontario)

(909) 476-5914 / www.vans.com

4758 E. Mills Circle, Ontario

(From San Bernardino Fwy [10], exit N. on Milliken Ave., R. on Mall Dr. From Ontario Fwy [15], exit W. on 4th St., L. on Franklin Ave. [TG-603 E6])

See VANS SKATEPARK (Orange) for a complete description. This location, at ONTARIO MILLS MALL (see the Malls section for details), is surrounded by great shops, restaurants, food courts, movie theaters, and fun!

BELMONT PARK   ☼

(619) 491-2988 - general information; (858) 488-1549 - amusement $$$
rides; (858) 488-3110 - The Plunge / www.giantdipper.com

3146 Mission Boulevard, San Diego

(Exit San Diego Fwy [5] W. on Sea World Dr. and follow the signs to W. Mission Bay Dr. Take Mission Bay Dr. to end. [TG-1267 J2])

Shops and restaurants encircle the ten or so amusement rides at Belmont Park. In the center, is the Giant Dipper Roller Coaster which doesn't have any loops, but has plenty of ups and downs! A replica of the Looff Liberty wooden carousel has horses as well as an ostrich, giraffe, and tiger to ride on. Other amusement rides include bumper cars (drivers must be at least 52"), a Tilt-A-Whirl, and five kiddie rides such as Baja Buggies, Thunder Boats, Submarines, and the Sea Serpent. Rides require between three to five tickets, with tickets costing 50¢ each, or $25 for fifty-six tickets. Jumpstart your heart with Trampoline Bungee, where you can safely do flips because you're harnessed in - $3 per jumping session. Steer remote-controlled boats around a nifty little harbor, complete with mini docks and houses. Kid-friendly attractions around the perimeter of the rides include virtual reality at Cyber Station, movies at the Venturer Theater, and PIRATE'S COVE, and indoor play area for younger children. (Look under this section for information on the cove.)

While at Belmont Park, take a plunge at The Plunge. This large indoor swimming pool, located on the other side of the movie theater, boasts a beautiful underwater/whale mural, painted by renown marine artist, Wyland. The enclosed pool, kept at 83 degrees, is surrounded by huge windows looking out on palm trees, suggesting a tropical atmosphere. Swim sessions are $2.75 for adults; $2.50 for seniors and children 6 months to 17 years.

Too nice a day to go swimming inside? Go for a dip outside, as the ocean is just a few steps away. The surf and sand, and bike trail on the beach are "shore" to help make your day at the park a good one!

Hours: The stores and restaurants are open daily, usually 10am - 7pm. In the summer, the rides are open Sun. - Thurs., 11am - 10pm; Fri. - Sat., 11am - 11pm. The rest of the year the rides are open Mon. - Thurs., 11am - 6pm; Fri. - Sun., 11am - 10pm. Call first as hours fluctuate. The Plunge is open daily to the public with swim sessions held at various times.

Admission: Attractions are priced above. Tuesday nights during the summer, beginning at 4pm, all rides at the amusement park are 75¢ each. Ask about a special deal offered during the week for unlimited kiddie rides plus entrance to Pirate's Cove.

Ages: All

BOARDWALK

(619) 449-7800 / www.boardwalk-parkway.com

1286 Fletcher Parkway, El Cajon

(Going E. on 8 Fwy, exit N. on Johnson Ave., L. on Fletcher Pkwy. Going W. on 8, go N. on San Vicente Fwy [67] and then immediately exit W. on Broadway, which turns into Fletcher Pkwy. Going S. on 67, exit W. on Fletcher Pkwy. [TG-1251 D4])

This Boardwalk is not made of boards, nor is it by the seaside; it is, however, a large indoor amusement center for kids. It's clean with brightly colored games and rides that elicited several, "This is FUN!" comments from my kids. Each token costs 25¢. The main attractions are the **carousel** (three tokens), **castle bounce** (three tokens), **bumper cars** (six tokens), **barrel of fun**, which is similar to the teacups ride (three tokens), **frog hopper** (six tokens), **Himalaya** (six tokens) and **soft play gym** (eight tokens). This two-story soft play gym area, for kids 60" and under, has balls pits, a mini zip line, slides, and obstacle courses, plus tubes to crawl through. There are numerous arcade and video games here. The full-service snack bar offers salads, pizza, pasta, and more, and weekly family deals. Kids meals are $2.75 for a choice of corn dog, chicken nuggets, or pizza, plus fries and a drink. If you feel like scoring more fun, strike out to Parkway Bowl, the connecting bowling alley.

Hours: Open Sun. - Thurs., 11am - 10:30pm; Fri. - Sat., 11am - midnight.

Admission: Attractions are individually priced above. An unlimited play pass is $5.45 Mon. - Thurs., and $6.45 Fri. - Sun. and holidays.

Ages: 1½ years - 12.

BORDERLAND PAINTBALL PARK

(800) 988-8447 / www.borderlandpaintball.com

San Diego

(Call for location)

Childhood games of hide and seek and tag have now "grown up" into the controlled, yet wildly fun, game of paintball. Two opposing teams try to capture the other team's flag, while protecting their own, and try to eliminate "enemy" players by shooting them with gelatin-covered paintballs. Games are usually played in fifteen minute increments, but you may be shot a lot sooner than that. Goggles cover your face and neck, but make sure to cover the rest of your body with padded clothing that you don't mind getting dirty, or paint-marked. Fun? Yes. Painful? A bit - but only if you get hit. Participants under 18 must have a waiver signed by a parent or guardian.

Hours: Open Sat. - Sun., 9am - 4:30pm

Admission: $18 includes all-day play, but no equipment; $35 includes all-day play with equipment.

Ages: 10 years and up.

FAMILY FUN CENTER (El Cajon)

(619) 593-1155 / www.boomersparks.com $$$

1155 Graves Avenue, El Cajon

(Going N. on San Vicente Fwy [67], exit at Broadway, at the end of off ramp, turn L. on Graves. Going S. on 67, exit E. on Fletcher Pkwy, go under fwy and make immediate L. on Graves. [TG-1251 F3])

Come to this Family Fun Center to play for just an hour, or have fun all day. Green fees pay for two rounds at any of the three nine-hole, themed **miniature golf** courses. Choose Memory Lane (fairy tale motif), Iron Horse (western), and/or Lost Crusade (Egyptian) - $6 for adults; $4.50 for seniors and kids 12 years and under. Other attractions include **bumper boats** - $4.25 for adults, $1.50 for passengers (height restrictions apply); **go-karts** - $5 for drivers who must be at least 58", $1.50 for passengers who must be at least 40"; **batting cages**; and the **Kids' County Fair**. The latter is comprised of four rides - a roller coaster, train ride, Ferris wheel, and mini-planes. Each ride costs $1.50, or purchase a book of twenty-four tickets for $6, or forty-four tickets for $10. **Kidopolis** is a multi-level, soft play area with ball pits, slides, and climbing ladders. It's for kids 44" and under and it's free! Socks are required. The two-story arcade and video game building is attractively set up. Try virtual reality rides such as skiing the slopes with the Alpine Racer, or jet skiing on Wave Runner. A full snack bar/restaurant is also at this fun center. Food and fun - what more could you want?!

Hours: Kids' County Fair is open Mon. - Fri., 10am - 8pm; Sat. - Sun., 10am - 8pm. Other attractions are open Sun. - Thurs., 10am - 11pm; Fri. - Sat., 11am - midnight. Hours fluctuate, so please call before you come.

Admission: Attractions are individually priced above, or purchase an unlimited use pass for $20 for 58" and taller; $10 for 57" and under.

Ages: 2½ years and up.

FAMILY FUN CENTER (Escondido)

(760) 741-1326 / www.boomersparks.com $$$

830 Dan Way, Escondido

(Going E. on Hwy 78 Fwy, exit S. on Centre City Pkwy., R. on W. Mission Ave., R. on Dan. Going W. on Hwy 78, turn L. on W. Mission, R. on Dan. [TG-1129 G2])

This Family Fun Center, just one in a chain of several, is packed with fun activities. The three **miniature golf** courses offer interesting embellishments such as a double-headed dragon, a castle, a windmill, fountains, and miniature housing structures - $6 a round for adults; $4.50 for seniors and kids 12 years and under. The **Giant Maze** is an amazing (and confusing) game to play. Use a game card, punch the time clock, and then walk/run through the maze, which has numerous partitions and some towers. The object is to find all eight numbers and four letters on your card that are hidden throughout the maze. Not only is it fun - it's free! **Laser tag** is like playing tag while using laser guns to "tag" (i.e. shoot) your opponents. The five-minute games cost $4 per player. The five rides in **Kiddieland** include a kiddie swing, train, Ferris wheel, and mini airplanes. Each ride takes four to six tickets. Twenty-four tickets cost $6; forty-four costs $10. Other attractions here are the **batting cages**; **go-karts** - $5 per (drivers must be at least 58"), $1.50 for passengers under 36"; **bumper boats** - $4.50 (drivers must be at least 44"), $1.50 for passengers under 44"; and video and arcade games. A full-service snack bar is available to take care of the inevitable hunger pangs. If you haven't had enough of kids running around, Chuck E. Cheese is right next door!

Hours: In the summer, Kiddieland is open daily 10am - 8pm. The rest of the attractions are open Sun. - Thurs., 10am - 11pm; Fri. - Sat., 10am - midnight. The rest of the year, Kiddieland is open daily 11am - 6pm. The rest of the attractions are open Sun. - Thurs., 11am - 10pm; Fri. - Sat., 11am - 11pm.

Admission: Attractions are individually priced above. All day/all play passes (not including batting cages and video and arcade games) are $18 for 58" and taller; $8 for 57" and under. During the school year, the passes can be purchased Fri. after 4pm, or all day Sat., Sun., and on major holidays. They can be purchased daily during the summer.

Ages: 2 years and up for Kiddieland; 4 years and up for most of the other attractions.

FAMILY FUN CENTER (San Diego)   ☼

(858) 560-4211 / www.boomersparks.com   *$$$*

6999 Clairemont Mesa Boulevard, San Diego

(Exit Jacob Dekema Fwy [805] E. on Clairemont Mesa Blvd. [TG-1248 J1])

So much fun can be had at just one place! Choose from two, themed **miniature golf** courses: Storybook Land with a castle, Cinderella's pumpkin, the shoe from the old woman who lived in one, and more, or Western Town, with a bank, jail, storefront facades, a livery stable, and wagons - $6 a round for adults, $4 for seniors and children 12 years and under. Other attractions include **go karts** - $4.25 for a five-minute ride (drivers must be at least 58"), $1.75 for a passenger; **Naskarts** - $5 per ride (height restrictions apply); **bumper boats** - $3.75 per driver, who must be at least 44", $1.50 per passenger; **batting cages**; and **Lazer Runner**. This last game is laser tag played inside an inflated, spaceship-looking big bounce. With six to eight players, it's every kid (or adult) for himself/herself. Although this game is played with the usual laser tag equipment of a vest with flashing lights and a laser gun, running around inside a bounce (with obstacles, even!), adds a whole new element of fun. Five minutes of sweaty fun costs $4 per person, and players must be at least 5 years old. The **Fun Zone** has seven rides, including teacups, a Ferris wheel, a train ride, a swing, and a fire engine that goes in the air and around and around. Rides cost $2 each or take between four to seven tickets at a cost of $7 for 28 tickets; $10 for 44. Of course there is a video and arcade game area and a prize redemption center. There is also a separate section for less violent kiddie video games. For those making every nickel count, a special video arcade area has games to play for only 5¢. F*amoose* Bullwinkle's food is on hand, although it is purchased at a snack bar, not at the usual sit-down restaurant. Ask about group rates and how good grades can translate into free tokens.

Hours: The Fun Zone is open daily in the summer 10am - 9pm. The rest of the attractions are open daily 10am - midnight. The rest of the year, the Fun Zone is open Fri., 4pm - 9pm; Sat. - Sun., 10am - 10pm. The rest of the attractions are Mon. - Fri., noon - 10pm; Sat. - Sun., 10am - midnight.

Admission: Attractions are individually priced above or call about an unlimited activity pass, which is based on height.

Ages: 2 years and up.

FAMILY FUN CENTER (Vista)

(760) 945-9474 / www.boomersparks.com
1525 W. Vista Way, Vista
(Exit 78 Fwy N. on Emerald Ave., R. on W. Vista Way. [TG-1107 D1])

$$$

This Family Fun Center really has it all! If you're in a mutinous mood, play the **miniature golf** course with a pirate ship and fountains. If you're feeling rather noble, play King Arthur's course with its huge (relatively speaking) castles and dungeons, and a bridge over water. Golf prices are $6.25 for adults; $4.25 for seniors and kids 12 years and under. **Laser Runner** is an every man/woman/child for himself laser tag game played inside an inflatable battleship bounce. There are soft obstacles to hide behind (or jump on) and even small rooms to run around in. The game is action-packed, sweaty, and fun. The cost is $4 for a five-minute game, and children must be 5 years old to play. **Kidopolis** is a huge, four-story soft-play area with slides, obstacle courses, ball pits, tubes and tunnels. This major gerbil run was a major hit with my boys. The cost is $3 for kids, who must be 56" or under; two adults can play for free with each paid child's admission. Other attractions here include **batting cages; go karts** - $6 for drivers, who must be at least 58", $1.50 for passengers, who must be at least 40"; and **bumper boats** - $3.50 a driver, who must be at least 44", $1.50 for passengers.

The noisy, but attractive, main two-story building houses numerous video and arcade games. A nickel arcade section is upstairs. Bullwinkle's Restaurant is also here serving up its tasty family fare, along with a fun atmosphere. Rocky and Bullwinkle cartoons play on the television monitors and a spotlight flashes colored lights on a fountain in front of the stage while the water "dances" to the music. (See BULLWINKLE'S RESTAURANT under the Edible Adventures section for more details.)

Hours: Kidopolis is open Mon. - Fri., noon - 8pm; Sat. - Sun., 10am - 8pm. The other attractions are open Mon. - Fri., 11am - 10pm; Sat., 10am - 11pm; Sun., 10am - 10pm.

Admission: Attractions are individually priced above, or purchase an unlimited pass for $19 for 58" and taller; $10 for 57" and under.

Ages: 2 years and up.

FUN-4-ALL   ☀
(619) 427-1473 $$$
950 Industrial Boulevard, Chula Vista   🍴

(Going S. on San Diego Fwy [5], exit E. on J St., R. on Colorado Ave., R. on L St., L on Industrial. Going N. on 5, exit at L. St. [TG-1330 A3])

This small, family amusement park has an older, well-used, **miniature golf** course with a nautical theme - $5.25 a round for adults, $4.25 for kids 12 years and under; a fun **bumper boat** ride around a few islands - $3.75 per person; **go-karts** - $4.25 for drivers and $1.50 for passengers (height restrictions apply); and **batting cages.** There are also several video and arcade games inside the main building, and a full-service snack bar.

> **Hours:** Open in the summer daily 9am - midnight. Open the rest of the year daily 9am - 10pm.
> **Admission:** Attractions are individually priced above, or play one of every attraction, plus receive a soda, for $18 per person.
> **Ages:** 4 years and up.

FUN FARM GO-KARTS AND ARCADE   ☀
(619) 423-0793 $
408 Hollister Street, Otay   🍴

(Exit San Diego Fwy [5] E. on Main St., R. on Hollister. It's near Otay Valley Regional Park [TG-1330 B6])

Like the title suggests - the Fun Farm is for go-karting and arcading. Drivers must be 54" tall.

> **Hours:** Open Sun., Tues. - Thurs., noon - 9pm; Fri. - Sat., noon - 11pm. Closed Mon.
> **Admission:** $4 per six-minute ride in a go-kart.
> **Ages:** 54" tall and up.

HIDDEN VALLEY PAINTBALL   ☀
(760) 737-8870 / www.mrpaintballfield.com $$$$$
Lake Wohlford Road, Escondido   🍴

(Going N. on Escondido Fwy [15], exit E. on Via Rancho Pkwy, which turns into Bear Valley, R. on Valley Center Pkwy., R. on Lake Wohlford Rd. Drive about 2.2 miles to the top of road, the entrance is on L. [TG-1110 H3])

Armed with a semi-automatic paint gun and dressed in mask, goggles, and layers of clothing (to reduce the somewhat painful impact of the paintballs), you are now ready to play the wildly exhilarating and intense game of paintball. Teams are pitted against each other while running around the 100-acre outside playing area where hills, valleys, and trees are used for both offensive and defensive tactical maneuvers. Games last between fifteen to thirty minutes. Bring running shoes, a water bottle, lunch, and most of all - stamina. Note: Participants under 18 must have a signed waiver.

> **Hours:** Open Sat., Sun., and federal holidays 8:30am - 4:30pm.

Admission: $39 for all-day play includes camouflage clothing, a semi-
automatic marker, full face and head protection, all-day supply
air for your gun, and 200 paintballs. Other equipment is also
available for rent.

Ages: 10 years and up.

IMPERIAL BEACH SKATE PARK / CURB BONEZ
SKATE PARK

(619) 423-8615 / www.ci.imperial-beach.ca.us $

425 Imperial Beach Boulevard at the Sports Park Recreational Complex,
Imperial Beach

(Exit San Diego Fwy [5] W. on Corona Ave, which turns into Imperial Beach Blvd. [TG-1349 F1])

This community building has been taken over by skaters and bikers. The
indoor facility has a few wooden ramps, fun boxes, and a slider bar. Helmet,
knee pads, and elbow pads are required, as is a parent/guardian signed
permission slip and liability waiver. An adjacent room has an air hockey
machine and a few couches for lounging around. There is also a pro shop/food
area selling snacks, beverages, and ice cream cones. This is a good place for
neighborhood kids to hang out. The outside park has a playground, baseball
field, picnic tables, and open grassy areas.

Hours: The park is open sunrise to sunset. The skate park is open Mon. -
Fri., 2pm - 6pm; Sat. - Sun., 11am - 6pm. Hours are extended
during the summer and on holidays. Each session is two-hours.

Admission: The park is free. The skate park is $5 per session for non-
members. Annual membership is $10, and then admission is $3
per session. Rental gear is $2 for everything.

Ages: Must be at least 7 years old.

MAGDALENA YMCA ECKE FAMILY SKATE PARK

(760) 942-9622 / ecke.ymca.org $$

200 Saxony Road, Encinitas

(Exit San Diego Fwy [5] E. on Encinitas Blvd., L. on Saxony Rd. [TG-1147 C6])

This great, outdoor, 32,000-square foot skate park is adjacent to the YMCA.
An eleven-foot high vert bowl ramp and six-foot high double-bowled and
double-hipped ramp, plus a full street course with a handrail station, quarter-
pipes, bank ramps, pyramids, roll-in's, and slider station. Street course ramps are
layered in Masonite and half pipes are layered in steel. The course is challenging
for experienced skaters, yet allows less-experienced ones the opportunity to try
some more difficult maneuvers. Younger (or beginning) skaters have a separate,
gated area with lower ramps so they can build confidence as they attempt trickier
moves. Helmet, elbow, and knee pads are mandatory and skaters must supply
them. A parent consent form must be signed, on-site, for participants under 18.

Hours: Open December through February, Mon. - Fri., 2:30pm - 5pm;
Sat. - Sun., 9am - 12:45pm (session one); 1pm - 4:45pm (session
two). Open March through mid-June and September through
November, Mon. - Fri., 3:30pm - 6pm. The weekend schedule is
the same as above. Open mid-June through August, Mon. - Fri.,

3:15pm - 5:30pm (session one); 5:45pm - 8pm (session two). There are camps in the morning hours in the summer.

Admission: Weekday sessions are $4 for members, $10 for non-members. Weekend sessions are $6 for members, $10 for non-members. Membership is $20 a year and comes with a t-shirt and photo ID card.

Ages: 7 years and up.

MISSION BAY GOLF COURSE / AHA MINI GOLF

(858) 490-3370

2702 N. Mission Bay Drive, Mission Bay

(Exit San Diego Fwy [5] W. on Clairmont Blvd., R. on Mission Bay Dr. and follow it around the bend. The mini golf course is adjacent to the regular golf course and driving range. [TG-1248 C6])

The Aha miniature golf course is different than other mini golf courses we've played. It's not fancy in the way that most other courses have small buildings and decorated objects adorning each hole. This one is situated in a garden-like, and sometimes even forest-like, setting and has a subtle Native American/missions theme. Some of the holes are incredibly challenging and unique, such as the multi-layered hole, the one with the spinning wheel, and a few others that bend and curve almost wickedly. A nice restaurant adjacent to the real golf course is also on the grounds.

Hours: Open daily 6:30am - 9pm.

Admission: $4 for adults; $2 for children

Ages: 4 years and up.

MR. PAINTBALL FIELD

(760) 737-8870 - office; (760) 751-2931 - field /
www.mrpaintballfield.com

Office: 525 N. Andreasen Drive, #C, Escondido
Field: Lake Wohlford Road, Escondido

(Going N. on 15 Fwy, exit R. on Via Rancho Pkwy for about 8 miles. The names changes into Bear Valley Rd., then Valley Rd. R. on Lake Wohlford Rd. about 2.2 miles, the field is on the L. Heading S. on 15 Fwy, exit E. on Hwy 78 to the freeway end, straight ahead on Lincoln, R. on Citrus, L. on Washington, L. on Valley Rd., R. on Lake Wohlford. [TG-1110 H3])

Hundreds of acres of outdoor, adrenaline-pumping action is in store for paintball players here. Several different fields offer a variety of "scenes". Run, hide, and position yourself behind hills with trees and props, man-made huts and spools, villages, natural obstacles, and in the trenches (via France during WWI). Try to zap your opponents with paintballs, without getting hit yourself.

Hours: Open Sat. - Sun., 8am - 5pm.

Admission: $39 per person includes all day play, camouflage clothing, face mask, a semi-automatic air rifle, 200 paintballs, air, and even lunch. Ask about other prices.

Ages: 10 years and up.

PENDLETON PAINTBALL PARK

(800) 899-9957 / www.cppaintball.com $$$$$

Camp Pendleton, Oceanside

(Exit San Diego Fwy [5] W. on Camp Pendleton/Ocean Harbor Drive. Go to the main gate and show the MP guard your license, registration, and car insurance. Drive about 7.5 miles and look for the sign. [TG-1085 J6])

I think I would be at a definite disadvantage playing paintball against marines! Actually although the paintball park is on in the marine base, anyone can play. The park is seventy-five acres big with seven tournament-size fields that boast of bunkers, buildings, trenches, big trees, and sandbag fortifications to keep play interesting and challenging. Capture the Flag is the most common game played although alternatives include Center Flag, where two teams go for just one flag, and Elimination, where the winning team must annihilate (figuratively speaking) all members of the opposing team. Wear a long sleeve shirt and long pants even on summer days. Protective gear is included with the price. Note: Gatorade and candy bars are available to purchase and a McDonald's is only a mile down the road. You are welcome to bring in your own food. Participants under 18 must have a waiver signed by a parent or guardian.

Hours: Open Sat. - Sun., 9am - 4:30pm. Call ahead to check on gear availability.

Admission: $9 per person if you have your own equipment; $28 per person with rental equipment (goggles with full face mask, semi-automatic paint gun and CO_2 refills) included. 100 paintballs are an additional $6.

Ages: 10 years and up.

PIRATE'S COVE

(858) 539-7474 / www.giantdipper.com $$

W. Mission Bay Drive and W. Mission Boulevard, San Diego

(Exit San Diego Fwy [5] W. on Sea World Dr. and follow the signs to W. Mission Bay Dr. [TG-1267 J2])

At one end of BELMONT PARK (look under this section for more information) there are two buildings with wonderful pirate murals that comprise an indoor family playland called Pirate's Cove. One building has air hockey, a few video games, and kiddie rides. Downstairs, is an underground cave-like tunnel that connects the two Cove buildings. This second building, with costumed pirate mannequins, is where most of the swashbuckling action takes place. Here are the ball pits, soft play areas, obstacle courses, and big plastic tunnels and tubes that your mateys dream of! There is also a separate area for younger buccaneers to pillage, I mean play on. Note: Socks are required at Pirate's Cove.

Hours: Open in the summer Sun. - Thurs., 10am - 9pm; Fri. - Sat., 10am - 10pm. Open the rest of the year Mon. - Thurs., 10am - 7pm; Fri. - Sun., 10am - 9pm. Call first as hours fluctuate.

Admission: $6.50 for ages 3 to 12; $4.50 for children 2 and under; two
parents can play for free for each paying child. Note: If you
come play here for just the last hour, admission is $3 per child.
Ask about combo prices for Pirate's Cove and the kiddie rides at
Belmont Park.

Ages: 6 months - 12 years.

POWAY FUN BOWL
$$

(858) 748-9110

12941 Poway Road, Poway

(Exit Escondido Fwy [15] E. on Poway Rd. [TG-1190 D4])

If you have some *spare* time, score some fun at this thirty-lane bowling
alley. It also features bumper bowling for younger children and Rock-n-Roll
Bowl, where bowling balls, pins, and lanes light up with bright neon colors
while rock music plays in the background. The latter is usually offered after 9pm
on weekdays and on certain weekends. Have a blast in the laser tag room which
has tall partitions covered in futuristic-looking neon splatterings. The sharp
angles of the partitions and the occasional ramp make the ten-minute game more
challenging - the chase is on!

Hours: Call for open bowling times. Laser tag is open daily from 6pm -
10pm.

Admission: Rock-n-Roll Bowl is $15 per hour per lane or $3.50 per person
per game after 6pm. Laser tag is $5 per game.

Ages: 3 years and up for bumper bowling; 5 years and up for laser tag.

RANDY JONES BIG STONE LODGE
$$$

(858) 748-1617

12237 Old Pomerado Road, Poway

(Exit Escondido Fwy [15] E. on Poway Rd., R. on Pomerado Rd., stay straight on Old Pomerado
Rd. as Pomerado Rd veers L. [TG-1190 B6])

Bring your achy breaky heart and your cowboy boots to join in some down-
home fun at Randy Jones. This rustic, stone lodge features a small dance floor
and country-western music played by a deejay on one side and a restaurant and
full bar on the other. Sunday are family days where kids can join adults and learn
to country line dance (i.e. join people on the dance floor).

The food menu ranges from top sirloin ($14.95) to salmon ($17.95) to
barbecue ribs ($16.95 for a full rack) to chicken breast ($10.95). The buckaroo
menu (for ages 2 to 10 years) offers a choice of burger, chicken fingers ($4.95
each), shrimp ($5.95), or ribs ($7.95), and comes with french fries.

Hours: Sunday family day hours are 3pm - 9pm. Open other days for
bigger cowboys Wed. - Sat., 4pm - midnight.

Admission: Meal prices are listed above. $3 admission per person is charged
if you come just for the dancing. There is no cover charge if you
dine here.

Ages: 3 years and up.

ROLLERSKATELAND AND LASER STORM

(619) 562-3791 / www.rollerskatelandlaserstorm.com

9365 Mission Gorge Road, Santee

(Going N. on San Vicente Fwy [67], exit W. on Prospect Ave., R. on Cuyamaca St., L. on Mission Gorge Rd. Going S. on 67, exit W. on Woodside Ave., which turns into Mission Gorge Rd. Going E. on Fwy 52, go to the end, E. on Mission Gorge Rd. It's behind Jack-in-the-Box. [TG-1231 B6])

Take two opposing teams, arm them with laser phasers and vests, let them loose in a darkened arena with neon-colored partitions, and let the games begin! A dividing line separates the teams. When you shoot the "enemy," you deactivate his phaser. He has to go to the energy pod and reactivate it to get back into the game. Of course, if you get hit, you must do the same thing. A scoreboard keeps track of which team is ahead, and which team ultimately wins. Each exciting game lasts for about ten minutes. But just like potato chips, it's hard to stop at just one (game). Roller skating is a separate activity from laser tag. Call for skate sessions.

Hours: Laser Storm is open Thurs., 7:30pm - 10pm; Fri., 6:30pm - 11pm; Sat., 10am - 4; 6:30pm - 11pm; Sun., 1:30pm - 5:30. Call for extended summer hours. The arena can be reserved at other times for groups. Call for skate sessions.

Admission: Laser Storm costs $3.50 for the first game; $2.50 for additional games. Skate sessions vary in cost depending on the date and time. In-line skate rentals are an additional $3.

Ages: 5 years and up.

SOLID ROCK GYM (Poway)

(619) 299-1124 / www.solidrockgym.com

13026 Stowe Drive, Poway

(Exit Escondido Fwy [15] E. on Poway Rd., R. on Pomerado Rd., L. on Stowe. [TG-1190 E6])

See SOLID ROCK (San Diego) for details.

SOLID ROCK GYM (San Diego)

(619) 299-1124 / www.solidrockgym.com

2074 Hancock Street, San Diego

(Going S. on San Diego Fwy [5], exit at Old Town Ave. off the off ramp onto Hancock St. Going N. on 5, exit at Moore St., L. on Old Town Ave, L. on Hancock St. [TG-1268 G6])

Experience the thrill and physical challenge (i.e. you'll get sweaty) of rock climbing in a safe, indoor, controlled atmosphere. Novice climbers can learn the basic skills and importance of a well-placed foot and/or hand, while experienced climbers will enjoy the opportunity to continue training by sharpening their skills. This is a great sport to introduce kids to because it builds confidence, physical fitness, and strategic thinking. (All this just by rock climbing - and we thought school was important!) Staff members are experienced climbers and are always around to instruct and encourage, although everyone must bring their own belayer.

Multi-colored stones mark various routes on the walls, overhangs, and the bouldering cave. Although a child may be tentative at the beginning, by the end of the first time, he/she is usually literally climbing the walls, and having a great time doing it. So, if you're looking for a creative way to channel your child's excess energy, turn off the cartoons and come *rock* and roll on Saturday mornings! Note: A party room is on the premises.

Hours: Solid Rock is open Mon. - Fri., 11am - 7pm; Sat., 9am - 9pm; Sun., 11am - 7pm.

Admission: An all-day pass Mon. - Fri. is $10 for any age; weekend prices are $14 for adults; $12 for ages 16 and under. Harness and equipment costs and additional $6.

Ages: 5 years and up.

SURF AND TURF

(858) 481-0363

15555 Jimmy Durante Boulevard, Del Mar

(Exit San Diego Fwy [5] W. on Via de la Valle, L. on Jimmy Durante Blvd. [TG-1187 G2])

Next to this driving range are two, eighteen-hole, miniature golf courses. The courses have the mandatory embellishments of small structures and other objects to putt through and around, plus plenty of twists and turns to keep the holes interesting and fun. Note: Older kids might want to try out a bigger back swing at the driving range.

Hours: Open daily 8am - 9pm.

Admission: $5 per person - for as many rounds as you want to play.

Ages: 4 years and up.

ULTRAZONE (San Diego)

(619) 221-0100 / www.ultrazonesandiego.com

3146 Sports Arena Boulevard, San Diego

(Going W. on Ocean Beach Fwy [8], exit before the end of the freeway S. on Midway Dr. / Mission Bay Dr., L. on Sports Arena Blvd. [TG-1268 E5])

Come play laser tag - the tag of the future! Put on your vest, pick up your laser gun, and for fifteen minutes you'll play hard and fast. Laser tag is action-packed, and the thrill of the chase really gets your adrenaline pumping! This Ultrazone, with its dark, cave-like setting, is themed "Underground City." The multi-level city, or playing arena, is huge. Run up and down ramps; seek cover behind floor-to-ceiling walls; duck into partly-hidden doorways; and zap your opponents. Tip: The best time for younger kids to play is weekday afternoons and early evenings, or during the day on weekends. Older kids come out here in hordes at nighttime.

Hours: Open Mon. - Thurs., 4pm - 11pm; Fri., 2pm - 2am; Sat., 10am - 2am; Sun., 10am - 11pm. Summer hours are Mon. - Thurs., noon - 11pm; Fri., noon - 2am; Sat., 10am - 10pm; Sun., 10am - 11pm.

Admission: $6.50 a game. Sat. and Sun. from opening until 2pm is Kids Zone, where kids 11 and under pay $5 per game. Note: Games must be completed by 2pm.

Ages: 6 years and up.

VERTICAL HOLD SPORT CLIMBING CENTER, INC. ☼

(858) 586-7572 / www.verticalhold.com $$$$

9580 Distribution Avenue, San Diego

(Exit Jacob Dekema Fwy [805] E. on Miramar Rd., L. on Distribution Ave. Or, exit Escondido Fwy [15] W. on Pomerado Rd. / Miramar Rd., R. on Distribution Ave. [TG-1228 J1])

Indoor rock climbing is rapidly becoming one of the fastest growing indoor sports in America. This physically challenging and mentally stimulating activity is a great way to redirect a child growing up in our couch potato/video game society. Vertical Hold has over 200 routes that are changed every few months. Climb vertical walls (of course!), overhangs, and chimney routes, or try your hand (and feet) at bouldering. You need to bring your own belayer (i.e. the person who stays on the ground attached to your rope so if you should slip or fall, you won't fall far). If you, as an adult, don't know how to belay, an instructor can show you the ropes. Don't just crawl out from under a rock - go climb it! Note: A party area is available here.

Hours: Open Mon. - Fri., 11:30am - 10pm; Sat., 10am - 9pm; Sun., 10am - 8pm. Kids are welcome to climb at any time with a belayer.

Admission: Adults (or children) with their own equipment - $12 a day; $95 for 10 visits; or $6 per visit at lunchtime (between 11:30am - 1:30pm). Otherwise, it's $18 a day with equipment rental of a harness, rope, shoes, and chalk included in this price. Sat. - Sun. prices are $12 per child, which includes equipment.

Ages: 5 years and up.

VISTA ENTERTAINMENT CENTER / LASER STORM ☼

(760) 941-1032 $$

435 W. Vista Way, Vista

(Exit 78 Fwy N. on Melrose Dr., R. on W. Vista Wy. [TG-1087 G7])

(Laser) lights! Action! Laser Storm is a quick, action-packed game of laser tag. The arena is designed with cardboard hanging partitions painted with neon-colored "gak" splats. There are no solid walls to hide behind, so you need to be constantly on your guard and ready to fire. The ten-minute games, played nearly in the dark, are played by shooting laser guns at the opposite team members' vests and/or at their base, to score points. When you are hit - not "if" because you will get hit - you'll be unable to shoot for just a few seconds while your gun is being recharged. Laser Storm might not be as elaborately set-up as other laser tag places, but it is less expensive and a lot of fun!

Score more fun when you bowl in the lanes just outside the Laser Storm doors. The Entertainment Center has a large bowling alley, a small video games room, a full-service snack bar, and a nice-sized nursery/childcare room.

Hours: Laser Storm is open Fri., 6pm - 10pm; Sat. - Sun., noon - 10pm. Hours do fluctuate. Call for open bowling times.

Admission: Call for a schedule of prices for Laser Storm. Costs vary from $1 per game on Dollarmania nights, to $3 per game, to $10 for a whole night of fun called "Fire Til' You Tire."

Ages: 5 years and up.

WEEKEND WARRIORS

(619) 445-1217 / www.paintballfield.com

$$$$$

25 Browns Road on the Viejas Indian Reservation, Alpine

(Exit Interstate 8 N. on Willows, R. on Browns Rd. [TG-1235 A5])

True to its name, you look like (and probably feel like) a warrior in this game of paintball. Suited up with a full, wrap-around face shield and a paint ball gun (and maybe even some camouflage clothing), you are ready to play a combination of Tag, Hide-and-Go-Seek, and Capture the Flag, at one of eighteen outdoor "battlefields." Moving stealthily through the trees, using rocks as covers, you spy an opponent, then pull the trigger, and splat - he/she has been tagged (ouch!) with a paint ball and is out of the game. (Realize that this can happen to you, also.) Each game lasts about fifteen minutes. Strategizing and staying focused are key elements. (Oh yea, and having fun, too.) Your admission fee includes all day play, which is about fifteen games, and one tank of CO_2. Wear dark clothing that you don't care much about, and expect it to get very dirty. Ask about kids-only events. Participants under 18 must have a waiver signed by a parent or guardian. Tip: Paint ball is a great way to burn calories! Note: Next to the field is a full-service grocery store, two restaurants, and an R.V. park and campground with a pool, showers, and Jacuzzi.

Hours: Open Sat. - Sun. and certain school holidays, 8am - 4pm.

Admission: $20 field entrance fee per person. Gun rentals range from $10 - $15 and include a tank of CO_2, and full face shields. Paintballs cost $7 per 100. Spectators are $3. Prepaid groups of ten or more save a lot of money on entrance and rental equipment. Parents play free with a paying child, although parents must purchase their paintballs here.

Ages: As young as 10 years old with a parent; 12 years and up on their own.

GOLF 'N STUFF

(805) 644-7132 / www.golfnstuff.com

$$$

5555 Walker Drive, Ventura

(Exit Ventura Fwy [101] N. on Victoria Ave., take a quick L. on Walker St. The Golf 'N Stuff sign is visible from the freeway. [TG-492 C5])

If you and the kids are in the mood for a little golf 'n stuff, here's the place for you. There are two, **miniature golf** courses with windmills, a tower, and other fanciful buildings, to putt around on at $6.75 per round for adults; $5.75 for seniors; children 5 years and under play for free. **Indy cars** have a height requirement for drivers of 52", while **bumper cars** and **water boats** both have height requirements for drivers of 48". Inside, there are arcade games and a snack bar.

Hours: Open Sun. - Thurs., 10am - noon; Fri. - Sat., 10am - 1am.

Admission: $4.50 per ride or buy an limited pass for $17 per person.

Ages: 4 years and up.

LAZERSTAR (Oxnard)

(805) 983-0333 / www.lazerstar.bizland.com

$$$

921 E. Ventura Boulevard, Oxnard

(Exit Ventura Fwy [101] N. on Rose Ave. and make an immediate L. on Ventura Blvd., which parallels the freeway. [TG-522 J2])

Reach for the stars at Lazerstar, a galactic adventure in laser tag. The entrance hallway is decorated with a moon and planets mural. The large, noisy, dark lobby has numerous video games, including virtual reality games (e.g. skateboarding and alpine racer), and arcade games, such as Wack-A-Mole and skee ball, along with a prize redemption center. The stool seats are on big, black coils, adding to the other-worldly atmosphere. A few smaller rooms, branching off the main lobby, are for eating or for hosting a party. The full-service snack bar sells hot dogs, pizza, and other food.

Two teams, of up to twenty individuals each, compete against each other armed with laser guns and a lighted vest. The foggy arena, illuminated only by black lights, has ceiling, walls, and barriers that are painted with fluorescent markings and space-related murals. Because the arena is so large (over 5,000 square feet), with numerous obstacles, expect to run around a lot during your fifteen-minute game. Stalk, dodge, hide, and fire laser beams in an effort to score against your opponents, while having fun, of course. When your mission is completed, return to Mission Command Center to pick up your score sheet because it details who scored on who and how many times. Tip: Ask Lazerstar about their great deals for team parties and their various monthly specials.

Hours: Open Mon. - Thurs., noon - 10pm; Fri., noon - midnight; Sat., 10am - midnight; Sun., 10am - 10pm. Open in the summer and on holidays Sun. - Thurs., 10am - 10pm; Fri. - Sat., 10am - midnight.

Admission: $5.75 per player for one game; $3.75 for each additional game. Ask about specials.

Ages: 5 years and up.

SKATELAB

(805) 578-0040 / www.skatelab.com

$$

4226 Valley Fair Street, Simi Valley

(Exit Ronald Reagan Fwy [118] S. on Tapo Canyon Blvd., L. on Cochran, R. on Tapo St., R. on Valley Fair. [TG-498 F2])

Yeowser! This huge (14,000 square feet) indoor skate park has it all, and then some. It has a street section with two half pipes - one is six feet high and the other is 4 feet high, plus grinding boxes, a really large bowl, and more. It's definitely for the advanced skater. It also has a museum devoted to skateboard paraphernalia. I never knew there was so many "extras" in skateboarding! Your kids will think the stuff is so cool.

All skaters must have a waiver signed by their parent or legal guardian at the time of registration. A helmet, and elbow and knee pads are mandatory. Rentals are available here.

Hours: Open Mon., 7pm - 10pm; Tues. - Fri., 3pm - 10pm; Sat., 10am - 10pm; Sun., 10am - 5pm.

Admission: Mon. - Thurs., $8 a session; Fri. - Sun., $10. Sessions are three
                hours long.
Ages: 7 years and up.

SKATE STREET   ☼
(888) 85 - SKATE (857-5283) / www.skatestreetusa.com   *$$$*
1954 Goodyear Avenue, Ventura   ⛟
(Exit Ventura Fwy [101] S. on Telephone Rd., L. on Market St., just a few streets down and R. on
Goodyear (this street sign is hard to see!) [TG-492 A5])

This huge, airy, and very "tight" (according to skateboard lingo, this
translates as "cool") indoor skate park became an instant favorite. It has several
intense ramps, verts, half pipes and more crafted from a smooth wood-composite
atop a cement floor. The street skate park caters to experienced skateboarders, in
line roller-bladers, and even BMX riders, as well as offering a section with less
dramatic half pipes for those who haven't been skating (or biking) as long or
who want to work (somewhat safely) on trickier maneuvers. Some of the inclines
make me twinge, but the kids ate it up; and sometimes they just ate it. My middle
child finally realized that not everyone else is watching him, at least not all the
time, and he really got into it. The city scape murals and hard rock music add to
the ambiance.

An observation area and two party rooms are on the second story. Vending
machine snacks and beverages and a pro-shop are on the first floor. Note: All
participants must wear a helmet. Those under 18 are also required to wear elbow
and knee pads. Equipment is available for rent. Special sessions are available
just for BMX riders. All participants under 18 years old *must* be accompanied by
a parent the first time here to have a parent's signature and liability waiver on
file, or have a parent's signature and a notary republic sign the waiver form.
Note: There are special sessions for ages 13 years and under.

Hours: Open Mon. - Wed., noon - 10pm; Tues., noon - 6pm; Thurs. -
                Fri., noon - 9pm; Sat., 9am - 11pm; Sun., noon - 6pm. Summer
                and school vacation hours may differ. Each session is almost 3
                hours long.
Admission: $12 per skater per session; $8 for members. The last 90 minutes
                costs only $7, or $5 for members. Rental equipment is $5 for
                everything. Membership is $45 for a year.
Ages: 7 years and up.

UNDER THE SEA (Thousand Oaks)
(805) 373-5580 / www.choicemall.com/underthesea
1182 E. Thousand Oaks Boulevard, Thousand Oaks
(Going W. on Ventura Fwy [101], exit N. on Hampshire Rd, L. on Thousand Oaks. Going E. on
101, exit N. on Moorpark Rd., R. on Thousand Oaks. [TG-556 H1])

See UNDER THE SEA (Woodland Hills) for details.

GREAT OUTDOORS

Botanical Gardens, Nature Centers, Parks, and Skate Parks

Contrary to popular belief, Southern California cities consist not only of concrete buildings, but also of the great outdoors. So, come and explore the natural beauty of city life, and take a hike (with your kids)!

Tip: If you and your family are Orange County beach bunnies, consider purchasing a parking pass for $50. The pass price is $30 for seniors. An annual pass for the beach, all Orange County Regional Parks, and a Wilderness pass is $75 per car, $60 for seniors. For more information, call the South Coastal Operations at (949) 661-7013 / www.oc.ca.gov/hbp. If you frequent California State Parks (and there are over 200), annual passes are a great deal at only $35, which is transferable to different cars.

For a complete list of state-run parks, call (916) 653-6995 / parks.ca.gov, to receive a copy of California State Parks Magazine.

Hikers: Be prepared for the trails by wearing appropriate foot gear, and by packing water, snacks, sunscreen, and a small first aid kit. A cell phone doesn't hurt either.

Bikers: Bike trails are interspersed throughout the great outdoors locations, but for a list of specific, paved bike trails (and to order bike maps) look in the Transportation section.

CHILDREN'S NATURE INSTITUTE

(310) 364-3591 / www.childrensnatureinstitute.org

From Los Angeles through Ventura Counties.

Children's Nature Institute provides guided walking tours for groups and families with babies, toddlers, and children up to 10 years old. With over sixty locations throughout the Los Angeles and Ventura counties, you're almost guaranteed to find a walk at a park near you. Some of the hikes are very easy, while others are longer and more strenuous. Tour guides usually encourage strollers, and they gear exploratory walks specifically towards kids. This is a tremendous opportunity for young children to be exposed to the beauty of nature, and to learn to respect the environment at a tender age. Note: Slightly older children who have gone on several Nature Adventures for Kids walks can help lead their peers, with adult assistance, on walks, too!

Bring your camera, sunscreen, and snacks, and enjoy the pitter patter of little feet next to yours on the nature trails!

Hours: Nature walks are given almost daily at various locations, and usually start at 10am.

Admission: $5 per family. Some parks also have parking fees.

Ages: Birth up to 10 years.

SIERRA CLUB

(213) 387-4287 / www.sierraclub.org

3345 Wilshire Boulevard, #508, Los Angeles

Sierra Club's goals are to preserve our unspoiled wilderness, safeguard endangered species, and clean up our environment. One way they achieve these goals is to take people on hikes so that they, too, can experience nature at its finest, and be moved to protect it. You may sign up to become a Sierra Club member, or simply enjoy their hikes, many of which are geared specifically for children. The *Tiny Trailblazer* newsletter comes out three times a year and lists the hikes for the upcoming months, including the meeting place, the length of the hike, and any "extra" activities. A one-year subscription is $6. All of the hikes are free! (We like free.) There are numerous Sierra Club chapters throughout Southern California. Call the above phone number for more information.

Admission: Free

Ages: Varies, according to the hike.

IMPERIAL SAND DUNES

(760) 337-4400 / www.ca.blm.gov

On Highway 78, Glamis

(Exit State 78, between Highway 111 and Highway S34, near the city of Glamis, which is near the borders of Mexico and Arizona. North of the 78 is the dunes wilderness; south is open for off-road vehicles. [TG-431 H1])

The expansive Imperial Sand Dunes, also referred to as the Algodones Dunes, extend for over forty miles - almost as far as the eye can see. They change in appearance from smooth surfaces to rippling waves, depending on the prevailing winds. They conjure up images of science fiction flicks, or of a lone sunburnt person clothed in rags crawling across them desperately crying out,

"Water, water!" Tip: Bring your own water.

Stop off first at the Osborne Overlook, located two miles east of Gecko Road along SR78. Here you'll see a great view of the dunes and the surrounding Imperial Valley. The appropriately named "wilderness" area is north of the 78, between Ted Kipf Road and the Coachella lands. A viewing area is two miles north of Glamis along Ted Kipf Road. Awe-inspiring dunes are towards the west side, while the east side has mostly smaller dunes and washes. The region is open for you to walk, run, jump, and roll down the dunes. Horseback riding is also allowed. Note that summer temperatures can rise to 110 degrees, so the most favorable months to visit are between October and May. Bring your sunglasses, camera, and a bucket and shovel.

The area south of the highway is open for tent and RV camping, off-highway vehicles (OHVs), and all-terrain vehicles (ATVs). Dune buggies are not readily available for rent, so you must bring your own vehicle. Camping is primitive, and trash must be packed out. For more information and an area map, call the BLM (i.e. Bureau of Land Management) at the above number.

Hours: Open daily sunrise to sunset.

Admission: Free

Ages: It depends on how far you want to hike, or if you are content with just playing in the sand.

FORT TEJON STATE HISTORIC PARK

(661) 248-6692 / www.forttejon.org

Fort Tejon Road, Lebec

(Exit Golden State Fwy [5] on Fort Tejon Rd. The park is on the W. side of the fwy, about 30 miles S. of Bakersfield.)

A long time ago battles were fought, and the U.S. Dragoons were garrisoned at this fort. Near the entrance is very small museum with several informational panels and a few military uniforms. Come and explore the long barracks building, walk through the officers' quarters that display war time memorabilia, and pretend to shoot the cannons at unseen enemies. Portions of the fort are still intact, such as a few foundational remains of buildings and a small cemetery. There are plenty of picnic tables and wide open grass areas, plus a few trails for hiking. Note: Primitive overnight camping is permitted here.

I highly recommend coming here when Dragoon Era Programs/Living History Days are presented or during Civil War Reenactments. Dragoon program activities include adobe brick making, playing old-fashioned games, participating in chores from days of yore, and more. Visitors will also see a blacksmith in action, open hearth cooking, military drills, and the everyday life of a soldier. During Civil War reenactment days, troops of the Union and Confederate armies are authentically uniformed and equipped. Meet soldiers and civilians and tour their camps. See demonstrations of weapons and watch battle skirmishes at 10:30am and 1:30pm. Guided tours of the fort are given in between battles. Come see history in action. Come live history in action by participating in day and/or overnight program for students. Kids will live life as it was in the 1800's.

Hours: The fort is usually open daily 9am - 5pm. Closed New Year's Day, Thanksgiving, and Christmas. Dragoon Era Programs are the first Sun. of most months, 10am - 4pm. Civil War Reenactments are held the third Sun. of the month, April through October, 10am - 4pm.

Admission: $1 for adults; ages 16 and under are free. Special programs and reenactments are $5 for adults; $3 for ages 6 - 12; children 5 and under are free. Call for student programs. Camping is $10 a night for a family; $50 a night to rent the entire group campground.

Ages: 3 years and up.

ABALONE COVE SHORELINE PARK

(310) 377-1222 - park; (310) 377-0360 ex. 309 - guided hikes $

5907 Palos Verdes Drive South, Rancho Palos Verdes

(Exit Harbor Fwy [110] W. on Pacific Coast Hwy., L. on Western Ave., R. on Palos Verdes Dr. S. [TG-823 A4])

This beautiful cliff-side park on the Palos Verdes Peninsula has a grassy park area at the top and plenty of picnic tables. The ocean view (and sighting of Catalina on a clear day) is spectacular. This park is the only way down to Abalone Cove and the great tidepools at Portuguese Point, which you are welcome to explore on your own. (Ask for a tidepool map at the entrance.) A paved pathway follows along the street for a short while before veering downward. The quarter mile dirt path is a bit more direct, as well as a bit steeper. Be prepared to carry your gear (chairs, towels, food, fishing poles, etc.). Fishing is allowed as long as participants ages 16 years and up have a California fishing license, which is not sold here. Bring your own bait, too. Lifeguards are on duty at the cove during the summer months. Note: The WAYFARER'S CHAPEL (look under the Potpourri section) is directly across the street.

A variety of outdoor, educational, guided tours and hikes are offered including a two-hour tidepool tour to discover small creatures native to California waters. Wear shoes with good tread as you must first hike down the trail, then cross a cobblestone beach to get to the rocky tidepool. And remember - wet rocks are slippery rocks! Your guide will explain all about the animals you see and ones that you may gently touch. Look for sea stars, sea slugs, sea urchins, crabs, octopuses, and mussels, and scan the ocean for seals and sea lions. Tours are given on days when low tides are one foot above sea level, or lower. Tips: Wear sunscreen and bring a water bottle.

Other two-hour habitat hikes include a good amount of hiking and information about the environment. Topical hikes deal with native animals, geology, plants, ecology, and Indian use of natural resources, or any combination thereof. Depending on the topic emphasized or being studied, hikers will see and learn about coastal sage scrub, bluffs, active landslides, and an Indian site.

Hours: Gates are open most of the year Mon. - Fri., noon - 4pm; Sat., Sun., and holidays, 9am - 4pm. Gates are open Memorial Day through Labor Day daily 9am - 4pm. Tours are given by reservation only and require a three-week advance notice.

Admission: Parking is $5 per car; $15 per bus. Tours are $2 for adults; $1 for children 13 and under; with a minimum of $15.

Ages: 6 years and up.

APOLLO PARK

William J. Barnes Avenue, Lancaster

(Exit Antelope Valley Fwy [14] W. at Ave. G, R. on William Barnes Ave. [across from 50th St. W.], past the General Fox Airfield, into the park. [TG-3924 J7])

This *space*ious park has three man-made lakes, named after the astronauts from Apollo XI: Lake Aldrin, Lake Armstrong, and Lake Collins. The lakes are stocked with trout, and while there is not a fee for fishing, you do need a California state fishing license if you are over 16 years of age. The park, though surrounded by the desert, is picturesque with its shade trees, bridges over portions of water, and plenty of run-around room. There is also a small playground. My kids were intrigued by the glass-enclosed, well-built mock-up of a command module. The placard describes the dedication of the park to the Apollo program. (Don't you love sneaking in a history lesson?) Tip: Bring bread to feed the relentlessly friendly ducks and geese. This ritual alone took us over half an hour!

Hours: Open daily dawn to dusk.

Admission: Free

Ages: All

ARBORETUM OF LOS ANGELES COUNTY

(626) 821-3222 / www.arboretum.org

301 N. Baldwin Avenue, Arcadia

(Going W. on Foothill Fwy [210], exit S. on Baldwin. Going E. on 210, exit E. on Foothill Blvd., R. on Baldwin. [TG-567 B4])

Do you have a budding horticulturalist in your family? Come visit this awesome arboretum and explore the more than 127 acres of plants and trees from around the world. The blooming flowers and the variety of gardens are astounding. We walked along the southern (and most interesting) route first. There are numerous paved pathways as well as several dirt pathways leading through trees, bushes, and jungle-like landscape which makes the walk an adventure for kids. Ducks and geese loudly ask for handouts at Baldwin Lake. (Look for the turtles in the lake's water.)

For your history lesson for the day, peek into the spacious Hugo Reid Adobe house where each room is furnished with period furniture. The adobe grounds are beautiful and reflective of the mid-1800's. Peer into the gracious Queen Anne "Cottage" for another glimpse of the past. You'll see mannequins dressed in old-fashioned clothes, elegantly furnished rooms, and a harp in the music room. The nearby immaculate Coach Barn has stalls ornately decorated with wood paneling and iron grillwork. Instead of horses, they now hold farm tools, blacksmith tools, and a coach. Also see the Santa Anita Depot with a train master's office and railroad paraphernalia.

The lush greenery around the waterfall makes it one of the most enchanting spots in the arboretum. Walk up the wooden stairs for a panoramic view and "discover" a lily pond. Back down on Waterfall Walk you'll see a serene woodland area and rock-lined stream. I was utterly content to sit while the kids let their imaginations kick into gear and play. Colorful Koi fish are just around the "corner" at the Tule Pond.

The northern section has a few greenhouses with exotic flowers and plants. An African and Australian section at this end has an abundance of trees.

Peacocks are everywhere - strutting their stuff and calling out in plaintive-sounding wails. (Peacock feathers are available at the gift shop for $1 each.)

Picnicking is not allowed on the grounds, but there is a shaded, grassy area between the parking lots. Or, eat at the Peacock Cafe which has reasonably priced food. Tip 1: Take a half-hour tram ride around and through the extensive arboretum, or get off at any one of the seven stops along the way and reboard at a later time. Trams run from 11am to 3pm, and passes cost $2 for ages 3 and up. Tip 2: It gets hot here during the summer, so bring water bottles (and look for the sprinklers to run through).

Wonderful, family-geared events are held here several times throughout the year. In the summer, Science Adventure Day Camps, which include classes on space and rocketry, magic, and more, are offered.

Hours: Open in the summer Mon. - Fri., 9am - 6:30pm; Sat. - Sun., 9am - 4:30pm. Open the rest of the year daily 9am - 4:30pm. Closed Christmas.

Admission: $5 for adults; $3 for seniors, students with ID, and ages 13 - 17; $1 for ages 5 - 12; children 4 and under are free. The third Tues. of every month is free for everyone. Free parking.

Ages: 2 years and up.

BLUFF'S PARK / PAPA JACK'S SKATE PARK

(310) 317-1364 / ci.malibu.ca.us   *!/$*

24250 Pacific Coast Highway, Malibu

(Exit Ventura Fwy [101] S. on Las Virgenes Rd., which turns in to Malibu Cyn Rd. Malibu Cyn ends at Bluff's Park on PCH. [TG-628 H7])

Bluff's Park overlooks the Pacific Ocean. Besides the gorgeous view, it also has soccer fields, baseball diamonds (the concession stands are open on game days), picnic tables, and a pathway that leads down to the beach.

Skateboarders and bladers must come to the park office at Bluff's first to sign up for a skate session at Papa Jack's, just down the road at 23415 Civic Center Way, next to city hall. This 10,000 square-foot paved park has fun boxes, a half pipe, a capsule, pyramid, grind rails, and a smooth surface to just skate around. All participants must have a signed parental waiver and wear safety equipment - helmet and knee and elbow pads.

Hours: Bluff's Park is open daily. The skate park is open Mon. and Wed., 3pm - 5pm; Fri. - Sat., noon - 5pm. Tues. and Thurs. are reserved for lessons. Call for summer hours.

Admission: Free to Bluff's Park. The skate park is $2 per two-hour session.

Ages: All for the park. 6 years and up for the skate park.

CASTAIC LAKE RECREATION AREA

(661) 257-4050 - lake information; (661) 775-6232 - boat rentals /
parks.co.la.ca.us

32100 Ridgeroute Road and Lake Hughes, Castaic

(Exit Golden State Fwy [5] E. on Lake Hughes. It's about 7 miles N. of Magic Mountain. [TG-4279 G4])

There are so many ways to play in the great outdoors at the massive (8,000 acres) Castaic Lake Recreation Area. The lake and lagoon are stocked with trout and bass. A California state fishing license is needed if you're over 16 years old. All kinds of boating activities are available. A lifeguarded swimming area at the lagoon (available seasonally), picnicking, and playgrounds can all be found in the park. Ask about their Jr. lifeguard program. The scenery is beautiful with shade and pine trees, plenty of grassy areas, and of course, the lake. Nature trails, for both hiking and biking, are as short as one mile and as long as seven miles. The trails range from an easy stroll to rugged hikes. Maps are available. Come spend the night in sites reserved for RV and tent camping. However long you choose to visit, an escape to Castaic Lake fits all your recreational desires!

Hours: Open daily sunrise to sunset.

Admission: March through October, $6 per vehicle per day. November through February, $6 per vehicle on weekends and holidays only. Camping starts at $12 a night. A fourteen-foot aluminum, nine-horse-power boat rents for $25 for the first two hours; $5 an hour thereafter.

Ages: All

CASTRO CREST

(818) 880-0367 / www.csp-angeles.com

Corral Canyon Road, Malibu

(Exit Pacific Coast Highway N. on Corral Canyon Rd., go about 5.2 very windy miles until it dead-ends. It's a part of Malibu Creek State Park. [TG-628 B1])

My kids jumped out of the almost-stopped car and made a bee-line for the rock formations directly in front of us, the tallest of which they dubbed Pride Rock. A variety of moderately difficult trails lead hikers past just a few more formations. The trails roller-coaster either along the ridgeline offering panoramic views, on fire roads, or on roads that cut through a gorge. Although the green velvety-looking hills were covered with trees when we visited, we found relatively little shade along the trails we walked. Note: There are no restroom facilities here, but there are some off the main entrance at Los Virgenes. Tip: Bring your own water.

Hours: Open daily 8am - sunset.

Admission: Free

Ages: 6 years and up.

CERRITOS REGIONAL PARK / SPORTS COMPLEX

(562) 824-5144 - regional park; (562) 916-8590 - sports complex /
www.ci.cerritos.ca.us

19900 Bloomfield Avenue, Cerritos

(From the San Gabriel Fwy [605] exit E. on Del Amo, L. on Bloomfield. From the Artesia Fwy [91], exit S. on Carmenita, R. on Del Amo, R. on Bloomfield. From Bloomfield, turn R. in the driveway where the sign states "Sports Complex", just past Target. [TG-767 A3])

Thirteen lighted tennis courts, several baseball diamonds with stadium seating and lights, soccer fields, playgrounds, a small lake, a swimming pool (open seasonally), large open grassy areas, cement pathways throughout, and a large, outdoor skate park make this park a delight for the whole family. The gated, 10,000-square-foot concrete skate park has a grinding pole, pools, ramps, bowls, and a small fish bowl. The posted rules (enforced by patrolling policemen who <u>do</u> give out citations) state that skaters (no bikes allowed) must wear helmets and elbow and knee pads. Aluminum benches are available for visitors and tired skaters. My kids love to skate and blade here - I just don't like the foul language that is often prevalent.

Hours: The park is open daily dawn to dusk. The skate park is open
               Mon. 11am - dusk, Tues. - Sun., 8am - dusk. The pool is open in
               the summer.
Admission: Free, including the skate park, tennis, and pool.
Ages: All

CHANTRY FLAT / STURTEVANT FALLS ☼

(818) 790-1151 / www.r5.fs.fed.us/angeles $

Santa Anita Avenue, Los Angeles

(Exit Foothill Fwy [210] N. on Santa Anita Ave., drive 6 miles to Chantry Flat picnic area. [TG-537 E4])

Take the Gabrielino Trail about a mile and a half into the tree-lined Big Santa Anita Canyon. Cross the Winter Creek Bridge up the trail and go straight through the three-way junction. Ford the creek, then recross it where it takes a sharp bend to the left, and scramble over boulders to reach the foot of Sturtevant Falls, a fifty-five foot cascading waterfall. Caution: Climbing up the waterfall can be dangerous! The small rocky pool at the falls end is just right for wading or even a dip. The canyon is beautiful - oak trees line the streambed, along with maples and spruce trees. There are numerous other hiking trails to take in the immediate area, depending on how far you want to go. Note: The Lonergan Pack Station, just up the road, has very limited parking.

Hours: Open daily dawn to dusk.
Admission: $5 per vehicle for an Adventure Pass.
Ages: 5 years and up.

CHARLES WILSON PARK ☼

(310) 618-2930   !

2200 Crenshaw Boulevard, Torrance

(From San Diego Fwy [405], exit S. on Crenshaw Blvd. Going S. on Harbor Fwy [110], exit W. on Carson St., L. on Crenshaw Blvd. Going N. on 110, exit at 220th, L. on Figueroa St., L. on Carson St., L. on Crenshaw Blvd. [TG-763 F7])

This large, elongated park has a delightful playground for younger children, several baseball diamonds, grassy "fields," gently rolling hills lined with shade trees, stroller-friendly pathways that crisscross throughout, and a fountain in the middle. A hockey rink is available by reservation. On the first Sunday of each month, the Southern California Live Steamers Club offers free rides on their scale electric, steam, or diesel-powered trains. Call (310) 631-3845 for more train information.

Hours: The park is open daily 6am - 10pm. Train rides are offered on the first Sun., 11am - 3pm.
Admission: Free
Ages: All

CHATSWORTH PARK ☼

(818) 341-6595   !
22360 Devonshire (South) or 22300 Chatsworth (North), Chatsworth
(Exit Simi Valley/San Fernando Valley Fwy [118] S. on Topanga Canyon Blvd., R. on Devonshire for the south park, or R. on Chatsworth for the north park. [TG-499 H3/J3])

There are two Chatsworth parks; a north and a south. The north park has shade trees, baseball diamonds with stadium lights, a play area, a basketball court, volleyball court, and some pathways to explore.

My family is partial, however, to Chatsworth Park South. It has two tennis courts, a basketball court, a playground, open grassy areas, a community center building that offers lots of activities (including a wheelchair hockey league), a small natural stream running throughout, and picnic tables. Best of all, it has several hiking trails around the perimeter of the park with our favorite ones leading up to, through, and on top of the surrounding rocks! I love climbing rocks and my kids share this passion, so we think this park is "boulderdacious"!

At the southern end of the south park, at 10385 Shadow Oak Drive, is the historic Hill-Palmer House. Take a tour through the old house while visiting the park. It is open the first Sunday of every month from 1pm to 4pm, and admission is free.

Hours: The parks are open daily sunrise to 10pm.
Admission: Free
Ages: All

CHESEBRO CANYON ☼

(818) 597-9192 / www.nps.gov/samo   !
Chesebro Canyon Road, Agoura Hills
(Going E. on Ventura Fwy [101], exit at Agoura Rd., L. on Palo Comado Canyon Rd., R. on Chesebro. Going W. on 101, exit N. on Chesebro Rd. When you're on Chesebro Rd., look for Chesebro Canyon Road on your R., after you pass Old Agoura Park. [TG-558 E4])

Hike or bike on the numerous dirt trails here that go through canyons, grasslands, and riparian areas. The road most traveled is the one immediately accessible, the Chesebro Canyon Trail. The hike starts off moderately easy along a streambed and through a valley of oak trees. A picnic area is about a mile-and-a-half from the parking lot. Stop here, or continue on to more strenuous hiking. Bring your own water! You'll reach Sulphur Springs (almost another two miles), where the smell of rotten eggs will let you know you've arrived. This particular trail goes on for another mile through a variety of terrain. Several trails branch off and connect to the Chesebro Trail. Pick up a trail map at the SANTA MONICA MOUNTAINS NATIONAL PARK HEADQUARTERS (see this entry in this section), which is down the road a bit.

Hours: Open daily sunrise to sunset.

Admission: Free

Ages: 3 years (for shorter hikes) and up.

CHEVIOT HILLS RECREATION AREA

(310) 837-5186 - park; (310) 202-2844 - pool   !/$

2551 Motor Avenue, Los Angeles

(Going W. on Santa Monica Fwy [10], exit at National. Drive past National, up Manning and go R. on Motor Ave. Going E. on 10, exit N. on Overland, R. on Pico, R. on Motor. Going S. on San Diego Fwy [405], exit E. on Pico, R. on Motor. [TG-632 E5])

This large park really fits the bill of a recreation area with its basketball courts, baseball diamonds, tennis courts, and nice playground. During the hot summer months, when kids have played hard and need to cool off, they can take a dip in the municipal swimming pool.

Hours: The park is open Mon. - Fri., 9am - 10pm; Sat. - Sun., 9am - 6pm. Summer sessions for the pool are Mon. - Fri., 10am - 1pm and 2pm - 5pm; Sat. - Sun., 1pm - 5pm.

Admission: The park is free. Each swim session costs $1.25 for adults; ages 17 and under are free.

Ages: All

CLAREMONT SKATE PARK

www.ci.claremont.ca.us   !

1717 N. Indian Hill Boulevard, Claremont

(Exit San Bernardino Fwy [10] N. on Indian Hill. Or take the 30 Fwy E. to the end and continue E. on Foothill Blvd., L. on Wheeler Ave., R. on Base Line Rd. [30], R. on Indian Hill. [TG-601 C1])

This medium-sized, concrete skate park has a bowl, grinding poles, grinding boxes, and some flat area to skate and gain momentum. Lights make it one of the few skate parks available at nighttime. Wearing helmet and knee and elbow pads is required. The rest of the park offers shade trees, picnic areas, and other amenities.

Hours: Open daily 6am - 10pm.

Admission: Free

Ages: 7 years and up.

COLDWATER CANYON PARK / TREEPEOPLE

(818) 753-4600 or (818) 753-4631 / www.treepeople.org   !

12601 Mulholland Drive, Los Angeles

(Exit Ventura Fwy [101] S. on Coldwater Cyn Ave., which merges with Mulholland Dr. near the park. [TG-562 F7])

Coldwater Canyon Park is beautiful, with large oak and California Bay Laurel trees shading the meandering trails. Most of the five miles of hiking trails are covered with sawdust and small broken twigs, making it bumpy for strollers. Picnic tables are available toward the park entrance.

If you and your kids are concerned about environmental issues, come visit the TreePeople, whose headquarters are in the park. This organization is dedicated to replenishing the diminishing number of trees and to encouraging recycling. In a garage-type building, the Recycling Education Center shows how plastic, glass, and aluminum can be recycled and reused in clothing, fiberfill, etc. Kids can turn a crank to see a beautiful canyon transformed into a dirty landfill. Practical recycling tips are shown by neighbors Dirty and Desperate, who create waste by throwing out everything, versus Clean and Cool, who recycle everything possible and are earth-conscious shoppers. Visit the small garden and the adjacent compost pile, which is a smelly, but a fascinating resource tool.

Hour-long, guided tours of the park are given for school groups or other organizations, such as scouts, with reservations. Tours include in-depth information about conservation, as well as the importance of planting trees in areas damaged by pollution. Children, 4 to 12 years, play interactive games as they explore the environmental exhibits and hike the trails.

Hours: The park is open daily. Call to make a reservation for a TreePeople tour.

Admission: The park is free, and the tours are usually free, too.

Ages: 6 years and up.

DENNIS THE MENACE PARK

(562) 904-7127

9125 Arrington Avenue, Downey

(Exit Golden State Fwy [5] S. on Lakewood Blvd., L. on Gallatin Rd., L. on Arrington Ave. [TG-706 D3])

This park has nothing to do with the character, Dennis the Menace, but it has everything to do with fun, imagination, and Camelot. The age of chivalry is not dead as your kids become knights and ladies in King Arthur's court. A big cement castle is the main play structure, complete with an "upstairs," slides, and a wooden bridge for crossing over the pretend moat. Kids can also climb up a sea serpent, try pulling out the sword in the stone, or just play on the other equipment of slides and swings.

The front part of the park has huge shade trees and lots of grass. The community center building is open after school, and has board games and sports equipment to lend. This park has readily become a favorite.

Hours: Gates are usually open Mon. - Fri., 10am - 5pm; Sat. - Sun., 10am - 6pm. The community center is open daily during the summer 10am - 6pm; the rest of the year Mon. - Fri., 3pm - 5pm; Sat. - Sun., 10am - 6pm.

Admission: Free

Ages: All

DESCANSO GARDENS

(818) 952-4400; (818) 790-5571 / www.descanso.com   *$$*

1418 Descanso Drive, La Canada

(Exit Foothill Fwy [210] S. on Angeles Crest Hwy, R. on Foothill Blvd., L. on Verdugo Blvd., L. on Alta Canyada Rd., which turns into Descanso Dr. [TG-535 A4])

Descanso Gardens is over sixty acres of incredible beauty. It's not just a bed of roses here as lilacs, camellias, tulips, dogwood, and other flowers, also bloom.

Although flowers bloom here year round, you can call for a specific bloom schedule. A network of stroller-friendly trails wind through the grounds. One trail that is particularly delightful goes through a forest of California oaks. There are also open grassy areas to run around.

The Japanese garden is intriguing because of its unique, maze-like layout. It also has ponds and a stream. Be on the lookout for squirrels, and land and water birds, as this is a haven for more than 150 species.

Take the forty-five-minute guided tram tour to see all of Descanso Gardens. Hop aboard the five-minute model train ride for a more kid-oriented trip. Either way, bring your camera and enjoy your fragrant outing. Food is available at the cafe daily 9:30am to 3pm; at the Japanese Tea Garden on weekends (the restaurant is closed December and January); or bring your own and use the picnic grounds adjacent to the parking lot.

Hours: The gardens are open daily 9am - 4:30pm. Closed Christmas. Tram tours are offered Tues. - Fri. at 1pm, 2pm, and 3pm; Sat. - Sun. at 11am, 1pm, 2pm, and 3pm. Train rides are available every Sat. and Sun.

Admission: $5 for adults; $3 for seniors and students; $1 for ages 5 - 12; children 4 and under are free. On the third Tuesday of each month, admission is half price. The tram tour and train ride each cost $2 per person.

Ages: 2½ years and up.

DEVIL'S PUNCHBOWL

(661) 944-2743 / parks.co.la.ca.us

28000 Devil's Punchbowl Road, Pearblossom

(Exit Antelope Valley Fwy [14] E. on Ave S., R. on Pearblossom Hwy [138], R. on Longview, L. on Tumbleweed Rd., which turns into Devil's Punchbowl Rd. [TG-4559 F3])

The "punchbowl" is a spectacular geological formation that looks like a huge, jagged bowl created from rocks. The 1,310-acre park consists of rugged wilderness rock formations along the San Andreas Fault, plus a seasonal stream. The hiking trails vary in degrees of difficulty. We hiked down into the punchbowl and back up along a looping trail in about half an hour. The terrain is diverse, ranging from desert plants to pine trees, as the elevation changes from 4,200 feet to 6,500 feet. Rock climbing is a popular sport here, whether you prefer climbing on boulders or scaling sheer rock walls.

The small nature center museum contains a few taxidermied animals and displays that pertain to this region. Outside the center a few live birds, such as owls and hawks, live in cages. The park also offers picnic areas and equestrian trails, and is host to many special events throughout the year. Ask about school field trips.

Hours: Open daily sunrise to sunset.

Admission: Free

Ages: 5 years and up.

EARL BURNS MILLER JAPANESE GARDENS ☀

(562) 985-8885 / www.csulb.edu/~jgarden !

Earl Warren Drive at California State Long Beach, Long Beach

(Exit San Diego Fwy [405] S. on Bellflower, L. on State University Dr. Or, take Garden Grove Fwy [22] to the end, turn R. on Bellflower, R. on State University Dr. From State University Dr., go through the campus gates, turn L. on Earl Warren. The garden is on the L. [TG-796 D5])

This beautiful one-acre Japanese garden has two waterfalls, a meditation rock garden, a quaint teahouse (to look in), and a koi pond. Kids can help feed the koi, so bring 25¢ for the food dispenser. As you cross over the zig-zag bridge into the gardens, share with your kids that it was built in this shape to side-step spirits because, according to Japanese tradition, spirits can only travel in straight lines!

Hours: Open Tues - Fri., 8am - 3:30pm; Sun., noon - 4pm. Closed Mon. and Sat.

Admission: Free. There is metered parking (to your right) in Student Lot D on weekdays; free parking on weekends.

Ages: 3 years and up.

EAST AND RICE CANYONS ☼

(661) 255-2974 / www.smmc.ca.gov !

Off The Old Road, Newhall

(Exit Golden State Fwy [5] on Calgrove and go W. back under the freeway, S. on The Old Road about 1 mile. The trailhead is S. of the entrance to Towsley Canyon, just past the Church of Nazarene - look for signs. [TG-4640 G5])

A year-round stream and a wide variety of plants and trees line trails that lead hikers away from city life and straight into nature. The Rice Canyon trail is a little over two miles round trip. It is a moderate walk that gets harder toward the end as it goes uphill. The trail follows along the stream and crosses over it a few times. If you smell petroleum, it's not coming from cars, but from natural oil seeps near the creek. This area was once part of an oil boom town. The East Canyon trail is almost four miles round trip. As you go steadily up in elevation, you'll pant harder, but you'll also see big-cone Douglas-fir trees and vistas of the Santa Clarita Valley. Be on the lookout for wildlife such as deer, foxes, skunks, and an abundance of birds. Neither trail loops, so I hope you like the way you came, because you get the opportunity to see it all again! Also look up TOWSLEY CANYON in this section.

Hours: Open daily sunrise to sunset.

Admission: Free

Ages: 3 years and up.

EATON CANYON COUNTY PARK ☼

(626) 398-5420 or (626) 794-1866 / www.ecnca.org !

1750 N. Altadena Drive, Pasadena

(Going W. on Foothill Fwy [210], exit at Sierra Madre Blvd. The off ramp turns into Maple. Stay on Maple and turn R. on N. Altadena Dr. Or, going E. on 210, exit N. on Altadena Dr. [TG-536 E6])

Located in the foothills of the mountains, this 190-acre wilderness park has several rugged dirt trails leading up into the mountains. One of the most popular hikes starts at the nature center and continues a little over a mile on an easy trail through oak and sycamore trees to the Mt. Wilson toll bridge. If you feel like pushing it a bit, take the ½ mile stretch past the bridge up to Eaton Falls. Hardy hikers can take a trail up to Mt. Wilson, a "mere" ten-mile hike. Approximately two-thirds of this park was burned in a 1993 brush fire. As the slopes and flats continue to recover from the fire, new plant growth is restoring the park's beauty.

There are shorter trails in the immediate vicinity of the nature center. One such trail is only a quarter of a mile and has a self-guiding pamphlet (pick it up from the nature center) that helps identify the plants. The first, and most important, plant to recognize is poison oak.

The Eaton Canyon Wash (river bed) is filled with rocks and is fun to explore - when it's dry, of course. Eaton Creek flows through the canyon, except during the summer months. Pretty, shaded, and almost hidden picnic areas are found just off the parking lot. Remember to B.Y.O.W. - Bring Your Own Water.

The nature center contains display cases that hold live snakes and other reptiles. A 3-D map of the park shows the areas' trails. Outside, a 150-seat amphitheater is the setting for environmental programs. The park offers many special events, such as free family nature walks which are given every Saturday from 9am to 11am.

Hours: The park is open daily sunrise to sunset. The nature center is open daily 9am - 5pm.

Admission: Free

Ages: 3 years and up.

ECHO PARK

(213) 250-3578

1632 Bellevue Avenue, Los Angeles

(Going N. on Hollywood Fwy [101], exit on Echo Park Ave./N. Glendale Ave. Going S. on 101, exit L. on Alvarado, R. on Santa Ynez which runs into the lake on Glendale Blvd. [TG-634 E1])

This long lake, which is occasionally stocked with trout, is between the freeway and an older, lower income Los Angeles neighborhood. Paddle boat rentals are available daily during the summer and on weekends only the rest of the year. Beside the cement pathway all around the lake, there are some shade trees, a few palm trees, a small playground, picnic tables, and some run-around space. The north end also has a bridge with Chinese-looking decorations on it that reaches over to a small island. The real reason I'm writing about this park is that this end also holds huge seasonal lotus plants that are contained in this area by a rope. Every July, Echo Lake, actually one of the largest lotus ponds in the United States, undergoes a spectacular transformation as the lotus flowers explode into blossom. See the July Calendar section for information about the Lotus Festival.

Across the street and right next to the freeway is the Echo Park Recreation Center and a park. The park boasts a large sand box, a playground, an old basketball court, a few picnic tables with shade trees, a small swimming pool with a lifeguard (open seasonally), and six lighted tennis courts. Note: Just down the street at 1419 Colton Street, (213) 481-2640, is an indoor swimming pool that is open year round.

Hours: The park is open daily sunrise to sunset. Call for hours for a specific activity.

Admission: Free

Ages: All

EL DORADO EAST REGIONAL PARK   ☼

(562) 570-1771 / www.ci.long-beach.ca.us $

7550 E. Spring Street, Long Beach

(Exit San Gabriel River Fwy [605] W. on Spring St. El Dorado Park is on the N. side; the Nature Center on the S. side. If going E. on Spring, use the Nature Center entrance and drive around to park. [TG-796 G2])

El Dorado has 450 acres of lush green park with lots for kids to do! There are three stocked fishing lakes, that also have ducks clamoring for handouts; pedal boat rentals at $7 per half hour - open daily in the summer and 11am to 4pm on weekends the rest of the year; an archery range where targets are provided, but you must bring your own equipment; a model glider field; several playgrounds; a Frisbee golf course; four-and-a-half miles of biking trails, including access to the San Gabriel River cement embankment; and a one-mile, gasoline-powered scale train ride that runs Thursday through Sunday year round (weather permitting) from 10:30am to 4pm. The cost is $2 for ages 2 and up; children 1 and under ride free. Call (562) 496-4228 for more information. Hayrides are also available in the park for $100 for up to ten people, $7.50 for each additional person, and a maximum of twenty-five people. Call (562) 865-3290 for information and reservations. Organized youth groups are invited to camp here overnight. You can be as active or relaxed as you want (or as the kids let you!) at El Dorado Park. Also see EL DORADO NATURE CENTER and EL DORADO PARK WEST.

Hours: Open daily 7am - dusk.

Admission: $3 per vehicle Mon. - Fri.; $5 on Sat. - Sun. and holidays. Entrance fee is good for same-day visit to the Nature Center located across the street. Annual passes are $35.

Ages: All

EL DORADO NATURE CENTER   ☼

(562) 570-1745 / www.ci.long-beach.ca.us $

7550 E. Spring Street, Long Beach

(Exit San Gabriel Fwy [605] W. on Spring St. El Dorado Park is on the N. side, the Nature Center is on the S. side. If going W. on Spring, use the park entrance and drive around to the nature center. [TG-796 G2])

The eighty-five-acre El Dorado Nature Center is part of the El Dorado East Regional Park. When crossing over the wooden bridge leading to the museum and trail-heads, look down to see the many ducks and turtles swimming in the water below.

The Nature Center Museum has skulls, antlers, and other artifacts to touch; bugs to look at under a magnifier; a few cases of live insects and reptiles; a display of feathers and wings; and a huge book depicting various animal habitats. Contact the Center for information on their many special programs, like the Turtle and Reptile Show, or summer camps.

Walk on a short, quarter-mile paved trail, or hike a two-mile, stroller-friendly dirt trail that goes under the pine trees. The longer trail winds around two lakes and a stream. I love being in God's beautiful creation! Picnicking is not allowed inside the Nature Center, but picnic tables and shade trees can be found outside the gates at the end of the parking lot. The Nature Center is truly "an oasis of greenery and woodland in the middle of Long Beach." Also see EL DORADO EAST REGIONAL PARK and EL DORADO PARK WEST.

Hours: The trails and park are open Tues. - Sun., 8am - 5pm. The museum is open Tues. - Fri., 10am - 4pm; Sat. - Sun., 8:30am - 4pm. The Nature Center is closed on Christmas.

Admission: $3 per vehicle Tues. - Fri.; $5 on Sat. - Sun. and holidays. Entrance fee is good for a same-day visit to El Dorado Regional Park located across the street. Annual passes are $35.

Ages: All

EL DORADO PARK WEST

(562) 570-3225 - park; (562) 425-0553 - tennis courts /
www.ci.long-beach.ca.us
2800 Studebaker Road, Long Beach
(Exit San Gabriel River Fwy [605] W. on Spring St., L. on Studebaker. [TG-796 F2])

This city park is just around the corner from its neighbors, EL DORADO EAST REGIONAL PARK and EL DORADO NATURE CENTER. Sprawling across both sides of Willow Street, this park features lots of grassy areas, picnic tables under shade trees, a couple of ponds with ducks, baseball diamonds, playgrounds, a large library, fifteen tennis courts, and an outdoor skate park. The concrete skate park offers street type of skating with ramps, bowls, grinding boxes, and more. Wearing safety equipment - helmet and elbow and knee pads - is enforced.

Hours: Open daily sunrise to sunset. The tennis courts are open Mon. - Fri., 7am - 9pm; Sat. - Sun., 7am - 7:30pm.

Admission: Free to the park and skate park. Tennis courts are $4 per hour during day light hours; $6 per hour after 4pm. (No additional fee if lights are used.)

Ages: All

EXPOSITION PARK

Exposition Park, Los Angeles
(Exit the Harbor Fwy [110] W. on Exposition Blvd., L. on Flower, L. on Figueroa. Or, exit Santa Monica Fwy [10] S. on Vermont, L. on Exposition, R. on Figueroa. Parking is available by entering the first driveway on the right. [TG-674 A2])

The expansive Exposition Park encompasses the AIR AND SPACE GALLERY, CALIFORNIA AFRICAN AMERICAN MUSEUM, CALIFORNIA SCIENCE CENTER, IMAX THEATER, L.A. MEMORIAL COLISEUM and L.A. Sports Arena, and NATURAL HISTORY MUSEUM OF LOS ANGELES. (Look up capitalized attractions individually under the

Alphabetical Index.) Up until now, most of park has simply been grassy areas surrounding these attractions. Exposition Park is currently undergoing development that is transforming it into a more family-oriented park. The perimeters of the park will be lined with trees and each of the four corners of Exposition Park will become distinct parks in their own right, with picnic table, barbecue grills, and playgrounds, as well as open grassy areas. A Community Center, with recreational facilities, will be located in the Southwest quadrant of the park. While paved pedestrian areas will provide easy access to and from the Coliseum, spacious lawns will provide a great place for picnics and tailgate parties.

The sunken Rose Garden, adjacent to the California Science Center, has always been a *scent*ral part of the park. Enjoy its seven acres of beauty where 16,000 specimens of 190 varieties of roses are cultivated. (I bet your kids didn't know there are so many different varieties.) The gardens are wonderful for walking, smelling the perfumed air, and picture taking, plus it's stroller accessible. Often on weekends, people of various nationalities have their wedding ceremonies in the garden. (We like looking at the different types of wedding attire.)

Hours: Open daily.
Admission: Free
Ages: 3 years and up.

FOX HILLS PARK

(310) 253-6650 / www.culvercity.org
6161 Buckingham Parkway, Culver City
(Exit San Diego Fwy [405] N. on Sepulveda Blvd., R. on Green Valley Circle. It's on the corner of Birmingham and Green Valley. [TG-672 H6])

This attractive little park, surrounded on the street level by office buildings and condos, is tucked away on a hill and offers a pleasant respite from city life. The hillside is landscaped with flowers, bushes, and trees and has a packed-dirt jogging/walking trail winding all around it. Exercise equipment, such as pull up bars and rings, are along the track. For kids, and those who work nearby and have extended lunchtime, the top of the hill has a playground, sand volleyball court, a basketball court, several tennis courts, a large flat grassy area (baseball field!), climbing trees, and picnic tables. My boys enjoyed the playground with its slides, climbing structures, and a cement dolphin. When the recreation center building is open, the staff offers board games and sometimes arts and crafts activities.

Hours: The park is open daily 7am - 10pm. The rec center building is open daily in the summer 10am - 7pm. It's open the rest of the year Mon. - Fri., 3pm - 6pm; Sat. - Sun., 10am - 6pm. The tennis courts are open park hours, except for 6am - noon on Wed., and Tues., 3:30pm - 5:30pm, when they are closed.
Admission: Free
Ages: All

FRANK G. BONELLI REGIONAL COUNTY PARK / ☼
PUDDINGSTONE LAKE
(909) 599-8411- park information / parks.co.la.ca.us $$
120 E. Via Verde, San Dimas
(Take San Bernardino Fwy [10] or Orange Fwy [57] to the 210 Fwy, exit on Raging Waters Dr. It's just S. of RAGING WATERS. [TG-600 D6])

This sprawling park is centered around the huge man-made Puddingstone Reservoir, which is an ideal water hole for all your fishing and boating desires. A fishing license is required for those over 16 years old. If the fish are biting, catch bass, catfish, and trout. Boat rentals, (909) 599-2667, are available daily during the summer and on weekends the rest of the year - reservations are required at any time of the year. Rental prices start at $15 an hour for a four-passenger boat. Life jacket rentals are an additional $5. You can also launch your own boat here, but it must pass an inspection here first. Jet skiing, fast boating, and water skiing are allowed on alternate days. Visitors can also feed the ducks and observe the wildlife. (We saw a heron and a crane, which my kids thought was pretty cool.) Picnic areas are plentiful with tables, barbecue pits, and playgrounds, too.

There are a few hiking trails here, but you can really rein your children in with a horseback ride. Horse rentals are available Tuesday through Sunday 9am to 4pm (later on weekends), for $20 an hour for adults; $15 for ages 7 to 12. Younger children can take a pony ride around the compound for $5. Call (909) 599-8830 for more information. The scenery along the equestrian trail changes and ranges from cacti to pine trees - only in California!

Just outside the park grounds, treat yourself and the kids to a relaxing time in a hot tub. (Or just indulge yourself after spending a day with the kids!) Choose from fifteen private, hilltop tubs. Tub rentals are available daily from noon to midnight for $22.50 an hour. Celebrate "Happy Hour" from 5pm to 7pm, when rentals are half price. Call Puddingstone Hot Tubs Resort at (909) 592-2222 for reservations. To reach the hot tubs, exit the 10 Fwy at Fairplex Drive, turn left on Via Verde Drive, right on Camper View Drive.

Hours: Open daily March 1 through October 31, 6am to 10pm. Open November 1 through February 28, sunrise to 7pm. Boat rentals are available Fri., 7am - 4pm; Sat. - Sun., 6:30am - 4pm.
Admission: $6 per vehicle; $6 for a daily boat permit.
Ages: All

FRANKLIN CANYON ☼
(310) 858-3834 / www.smmc.ca.gov   !
Franklin Canyon, Los Angeles
(From L.A., exit San Diego Fwy [405] E. on Sunset Blvd., L. on Beverly Dr. [past Beverly Glen Blvd.], follow signs "to Coldwater Canyon Drive" to the stoplight at Beverly Hills Fire Station #2, turn L. - staying on Beverly Dr. Go 1 mile to Franklin Cyn. Dr., turn R. and go 1 1/2 miles to Lake Dr., and follow signs to the canyon. From the Valley, exit Ventura Fwy [101] S. on Coldwater Cyn. Dr., R. on Franklin Cyn. Dr. [cross over Mulholland Dr.] to the canyon. [TG-592 E1])

Franklin Canyon, almost 600 acres large, proves that there is more to Los Angeles than just skyscrapers. The lower canyon is the site of an old ranch house, which is now an office. A big green lawn and a few picnic tables are the only things down here. Follow the creek along the mile-and-a-half trail leading to the Upper Canyon, and the Nature Center. Inside the Sooky Goldman Nature Center are mounted displays of the type of animals that live in the canyon, such as mountain lions; a scale model of the Santa Monica Mountains; an interactive exhibit and dioramas on Native Americans; and an exhibit on the importance of water conservation. For your tactile child, there are fossils, antlers, furs, bones, and even a few nests to touch.

This Center is also the headquarters of the William O. Douglas Outdoor Classroom, which is really the name for numerous, on-going, free nature programs. Docent-led tours are open for the general public on weekends, with titles like Incredible Edibles. There are programs for all ages that range from Babes in the Woods, which is a stroller-friendly walk on a paved trail, to Full Moon Hikes, geared for older kids to have a howling good time. Tours are available for school groups Tuesday through Friday between 10am and noon.

The canyon has a variety of trees such as California live oaks, black walnuts, and sycamores. Wildlife here includes deer, bobcats, coyotes, rabbits, and lizards. The Upper Reservoir has reverted to a natural lake, and is a wetland area for herons and other waterfowl. Enjoy your day in the wilds of L.A.!

Hours: The canyon entrance is open daily 7:30am to dusk. The Nature Center is open daily 10am - 4pm.

Admission: Free

Ages: All

GATES CANYON
(818) 880-6461
25801 Thousand Oaks Boulevard, Calabasas
(Exit Ventura Fwy [101] N. on Las Virgenes Rd., R. on Thousand Oaks. [TG-558 J3])

Beside the playground, tennis courts, basketball court, and picnic area here, skateboarders have their own little haven. The portable skate park (i.e. wooden ramps, etc. on top of asphalt) is available at certain times throughout the week. Parental waivers are required and all participants must wear a helmet and elbow and knee pads.

Hours: Open Tues. and Thurs., 3pm - 6pm; Sat., 1pm - 5pm. Call for summer hours.

Admission: The park is free. Skating is $2 a day or $20 a month.

Ages: 6 years and up.

GLENDALE SKATEPARK
(818) 548-6420
229 S. Orange Street, Glendale
(Exit Golden State Fwy [5] E. on Colorado St., L. on Orange. In front of the Glendale Galleria [TG-564 E5])

This good-sized skate park has ramps, slide rails, quarter pipes and more on a blacktop surface. The park is fenced-in and staff is on hand at all times. Skaters under 18 years must have a parent or legal guardian sign a waiver. Wearing helmet and knee and elbow pads is a requirement. No rentals are available. This is supposed to be temporary location, with a permanent facility built at Verdugo Park. The above number works for both facilities.

Hours: Open during the school year Mon. - Fri., 3pm - dark; Sat., 10am - noon for 12 year olds and under; noon - dark for all ages; Sun., noon - dark. Open during the summer longer hours.
Admission: Free
Ages: 6 years and up.

GREYSTONE MANSION AND PARK

(310) 550-4654

905 Loma Vista, Beverly Hills

(Exit Santa Monica Fwy [10] N. on Robertson Blvd., R. on Santa Monica Blvd., L. on San Vicente Blvd., L. on Sunset Blvd., R. on Mountain Dr., R. on Loma Vista. Look for park signs. [TG-592 G5])

Edward Doheny made an oil discovery that enabled him to become one of the world's largest oil producers. In 1927 he put a great deal of his wealth into constructing the fifty-five room Greystone mansion, designed in Gothic and neo-classical styles. It was built using mainly grey stones (hence the name), plus limestone facing, a slate roof, and seven magnificent brick chimneys. The basement used to house a bowling alley and billiards room. This multi-story, castle-like mansion is the epitome of opulence and, although you may not go into it, you are welcome to peer into the windows. Opened, iron gates at the end of a stone driveway lead to an outside porch that's made of marble. We looked in the windows at the elegant entry way and saw black and white checkered tiles, a gorgeous chandelier, elaborately carved wooden banisters, and several archways that are followed by incredibly long hallways. There isn't any furniture inside. Quite a few shows have been filmed here including episodes of *Murder She Wrote* and the movie, *Ghostbusters II*. Walk around to the front sundeck for a gorgeous view of Beverly Hills and the Los Angeles area.

Behind the mansion is a dungeon (according to my boys) built into the hillside. The adjacent, closed, control room has levers and a high voltage sign, which clinched the dungeon notion. Imagination definitely reigns here!

Tiered, lush gardens and extensive grounds lavishly landscaped into and around the hillside are immaculately maintained. Go up the stone steps or walk the pathways to see the acres of grassy areas, courtyards surrounded by trimmed hedges, shade trees, some koi fish ponds, reflecting pools, fountains, and a few park benches. A highlight for my kids was simply running down the long, sloping stone driveway - then panting their way back up.

Hours: Open most of the year daily 10am - 5pm; open in the summer 10am - 6pm.
Admission: Free
Ages: All

GRIFFITH PARK

(323) 913-4688 or (323) 913-7390 / www.laparks.org

4730 Crystal Springs Drive, Los Angeles

(Going N. on Golden State Fwy [5] or W. on Ventura Fwy [134], exit at Zoo Dr. and follow the signs. Going E. on 134, exit S. on Victory Blvd., L. on Zoo Dr. Going S. on 5 Fwy, exit S. on Western, L. on Victory Blvd. to Zoo Dr. [TG-564 B4])

The vast 4,100 acres of the eastern Santa Monica Mountains, known as Griffith Park, is really several parks in one. One part consists of enormous stretches of grassy lawns with picnic areas and children's attractions, such as the merry-go-round and playground equipment near Park Center. A particularly interesting picnic area is the Old Zoo Picnic area, on Griffith Park Drive, that has tables in obsolete caves that were once part of the original zoo. Another part of the park has the zoo, museums, and observatory. (Look up AUTRY MUSEUM OF WESTERN HERITAGE, GRIFFITH OBSERVATORY AND PLANETARIUM, and LOS ANGELES ZOO for more information. Note: The Greek Theater, a nationally-renown venue for concerts and other events, is just down the road.) The largest part of the park, two-thirds of it, is the wilderness area with fifty-three miles of trails for hiking and horseback riding. One of the most popular hikes is three-miles round trip, beginning at the Observatory and extending up to the one of highest points in the park - Mt. Hollywood. On a clear day the view is unbeatable. Call or visit the ranger's station in the park for all trail information. Also check out the LA. Orienteering Club which offers monthly nature walks for all skill levels that incorporate learning survival skills such as map and compass reading.

Some noteworthy attractions from the northern end of the park to the southern end include: 1) Los Angeles Live Steamers - located west of the Victory Boulevard entrance to the park. (Also see TRAVEL TOWN under the Museums section.) This club offers free twelve-minute, large scale model train rides on Sundays from 11am to 3pm. Call (323) 669-9729 for more information. 2) Merry-go-round - located off Griffith Park Drive, south of the Zoo. The antique carousel offers rides daily in the summer, and on weekends and holidays the rest of the year from 11am to 5pm. Rides are $1 per person. Shane's Inspiration Playground is also here and really worthy of a separate write-up. The boundless playground, constructed for children with disabilities, has six age-appropriate play areas with paved pathways, lowered monkey bars, high-backed swings, a rocket ship and airplane, signs in Braille, a sand castle with raised sand tables, courts with lowered basketball hoops, and stainless steel slides for hearing-impaired kids. At Shane's Inspiration, able-bodied and disabled children can play side-by-side. 3) Pony rides and covered wagon rides - located at the Los Feliz entrance to the park. Each ride is $1.50 per person and available Tuesday through Sunday from 10am to 4pm. 4) Train rides and simulator - located at the Los Feliz entrance to the park. The eight-minute, mini-train ride costs $2 for adults and $1.25 for seniors; $1.50 for children 19 months to 13 years. Call (323) 664-6903 for more information. The simulator, which simulates bobsledding, riding a roller coaster, or being in an airplane, costs $1.25 per person. Both are open daily from 10am to 4:30pm. 5) Tennis courts, a soccer field, and a swimming pool - located at the Los Feliz entrance to the park. (The cross street is Riverside.) The pool is open mid-June to September, Monday through Friday, 2pm to 6pm; Saturday and Sunday, noon to 3pm and 4pm to 7pm. Adults are $1.25 per session; kids 17 years and under are 75¢. Call (323) 644-6878 seasonally, for pool information. 6) Bird Sanctuary - located on Vermont

Canyon Road, northeast of the Observatory. This verdant area has a short, stroller-friendly nature trail that crosses over a creek and loops around. A wide variety of birds flock here and make it their home. It's open daily from 10am to 5pm. 7) Ferndell - located near the Western Avenue entrance. This is a pretty spot to rest and picnic. Ferns and flowers growing along the brook make it an attractive, cool haven on hot days and nature trails take you into the heart of the park. A snack stand, open seasonally, is also available here. There are refreshment stands located throughout the park, as well as restaurants at golf courses and at the Autry Museum.

Some of the equestrian centers around the park include: Bar S. Stables, (818) 242-8443 at 1850 Riverside Drive, Glendale - open Monday through Friday, 8am to 4pm; Saturday through Sunday, 8am to 4:30pm. Riding costs $15 per hour for adults and $12 for children 13 years and under. J.P. Stables, (818) 843-9890, 1914 Mariposa Street, Burbank - open daily 7:30am to 6pm. Riding costs $15 per hour. L.A. Equestrian Center, (818) 840-8401, 480 Riverside Drive, Burbank - open daily 8am to 5pm. Riding costs $15 per hour. Also see SUNSET STABLES in a separate listing under the Zoos and Animals section.

    Hours: The park is open daily 6am - 10pm.
  Admission: Free
     Ages: All

HANSEN DAM RECREATION AREA

(323) 906-7953 or (213) 236-2357; (818) 899-3779 aquatics center /   **$**
www.laparks.org
11798 Foothill Boulevard, Lake View Terrace
(Exit Golden State Fwy [5] E. on Osborne St, R. on Foothill, R. on Dronfield Ave. [TG-?502 H2])

This large, somewhat run down park offers a few hiking trails, a picnic area, ball fields, and a few scattered playgrounds. Its best features are a small man-made lake and an adjacent year-round swimming pool. The recreation lake, with cement sides, offers paddle boat and kayak rentals. Kayakers must first take a safety class to be eligible to rent the boats. Catfish and bass fishing are also available. A fishing license is needed for ages 16 years and up. Bait is sold at the entrance.

The non-heated, gated pool, which is referred to as the swimming lake, is four-feet deep all around, very large, and extremely long. Lifeguards are on duty when it's open. Coarse sand all around the pool, a sand volleyball court, and no shade offers a quasi-beach-like atmosphere. A snack stand is open in the summertime. Note: The Los Angeles Children's Museum is planning to open a 60,000 square foot, hands-on museum in this recreation area in 2002. It should be absolutely wonderful!

    Hours: The park is open daily dawn to dusk. The pool is open in the
           summer daily 9am - 7pm; open the rest of the year Sat. - Sun.,
           noon - 4pm. Pedal boat rentals are usually open 10am - one hour
           before sunset.

Admission: Park entrance is free. Pool admission is $1.25 for adults; free for seniors, and ages 17 and under. Youths 7 and under must be accompanied by an adult. Pedal boat rentals are $5 a half hour, $7 an hour.

Ages: 3 years and up.

HERITAGE PARK (Cerritos)

(562) 916-8570 / www.ci.cerritos.ca.us

18600 Bloomfield, Cerritos

(From San Gabriel Fwy [605], exit E. on South St., L. on Bloomfield. From Artesia Fwy [91], exit S. on Bloomfield. [TG-767 A1])

One if by land, two if by sea . . . . The most unique feature of this noteworthy park is an island with a kid-size version of an old New England town. Cross the covered bridge and be transported back in time. (Not actually, it's just the atmosphere of the island.) This "town" has a replica of Paul Revere's house, a cemetery, and the North Church Tower, which has two slides coming out of it. (Creative parents can reinforce a Paul Revere history lesson here.) Next to the cement slide are rocks to climb up. Kids can pull themselves back up to the tower via a short tunnel that has an anchored rope through it. The town has little buildings with more slides in them, firehouse-like poles to slide down, and small cannons to sit on or "fire." Two small replicas of British ships are harbored nearby. They're designed for pint-sized merchants to climb aboard. The island has a brook running through it and plenty of shade trees, so it is refreshingly cool even on hot days.

The ducks swimming in the "moat" surrounding the island are always looking for a handout, so be sure to bring old bread. Across the water is a wonderful play area. The park also has picnic tables, a few barbecues, basketball courts, large grass areas, climbing trees, and a baseball diamond with stadium-type benches.

Hours: The park is Mon. - Fri., 9am - 10pm; Sat. - Sun., 8am - 6pm (until 8pm in the summer.)

Admission: Free

Ages: All

HOPKINS WILDERNESS PARK

(310) 318-0668 / www.redondo.org

1102 Camino Real, Redondo Beach

(Exit Harbor Fwy [110] W. on Sepulveda, which turns into Camino Real. [TG-763 A7])

Escape to the wilderness of Redondo Beach. This gated, eleven-acre, hilltop park has two streams running through it, two ponds, and a wonderful view of the city. Hike along the nature trail that will take you through California Redwood and pine trees; through a meadow - be on the lookout for butterflies and lizards; and to the small waterfall and pond where turtles, crayfish, and bullfrogs have made their homes. Wilderness Park also has a campground and is a popular spot for local, overnight camping.

Hours: Open Thurs. - Tues., 10am - 4:30pm. Closed Wed., New Year's Day, Thanksgiving, Christmas, and in bad weather. November through April the park closes at 4pm.

Admission: The park is free. Tent camping (no stakes allowed) is $5 a night for non-resident adults (residents are $4); $3 a night for non-resident kids 17 and under (residents are $2). Residency is proven by bringing a utility bill. Picnic tables and BBQ pits are available for campers.

Ages: 3 years and up.

HUNTINGTON LIBRARY, ART COLLECTIONS AND BOTANICAL GARDENS

(626) 405-2125 / www.huntington.org
1151 Oxford Road, San Marino

See HUNTINGTON LIBRARY, ART COLLECTIONS AND BOTANICAL GARDENS under the Museums section.

JOHNNY CARSON PARK

Bob Hope Drive and Parkside Avenue, Burbank
(Going W. on Ventura Fwy [134], exit N. at Hollywood Wy., go right at end of off ramp on Alameda Ave., R. on Bob Hope Dr. Going E. on 134, exit N. on Bob Hope Dr. It's across the street from NBC STUDIO TOURS and just down the street from WARNER BROS. STUDIOS VIP TOUR. [TG-563 E4])

Despite the proximity of the freeway, this pleasant park offers a refuge, of sorts, in downtown Burbank. Kids will enjoy the large grassy areas, small woods, climbing and shade trees, and stroller-friendly dirt pathways that run throughout the park. The Tonight Show Playground, for today's kids, has slides, swings, and climbing apparatus. Picturesque bridges go over what I first thought was a seasonal stream, but it is only a drainage "creek." Come enjoy a picnic here before or after you take the NBC or WARNER BROS. studio tours. (Both are listed under the Tours section.)

Hours: Open daily.
Admission: Free
Ages: All

KENNETH HAHN STATE RECREATION AREA

(323) 298-3660 / parks.co.la.ca.us
4100 S. La Cienega Boulevard, Los Angeles
(Exit Santa Monica Fwy [10] S. on La Cienega Blvd., exit E. at the turnoff with signs for Kenneth Hahn. [TG-673 A2])

This spacious, 320-acre natural parkland in the heart of Baldwin Hills has hilly grasslands, forest areas, and several dirt hiking trails. It also features a large lake that is stocked with trout in the winter, and catfish, bluegill, and bass in the summer. Swimming in the water is not allowed. You may, however, feed the ducks who are always looking for a handout. There are seven picnic areas (which were a bit run down when we visited), complete with barbecue grills, for families to enjoy as well as a few scattered playgrounds, and basketball and volleyball courts.

Hours: Open daily sunrise to sunset.

Admission: Free during the week; $3 per vehicle on the weekends and on county holidays.

Ages: All

LACY PARK

(626) 304-9648

3300 Monterey Road, San Marino

(Exit Foothill Fwy [210] S. on Sierra Madre Blvd., R. on Huntington Dr., R. on Virginia Rd. The park is on the L. [TG-596 B1])

This is one of the prettiest parks we've visited - so well maintained and beautifully landscaped. In the center is a large expanse of immaculately-kept grass. Encircling it are several varieties of trees, including oak, pine, and palm. An outside dirt track is designated for joggers and walkers. An inside paved loop trail is designated for cyclists and rollerskaters. The playground has the normal play equipment plus talking tubes (i.e. where two people can talk through a long tube to each other) and a few patches of trees to play hide and seek. There are also a few scattered benches and picnic tables.

Hours: Open year-round Mon. - Fri., 6:30am - sunset. Open on weekends May through October, 8am - 8pm; November through April, 8am - 6pm.

Admission: Free on weekdays for everyone, and on weekends for residents, too. Entrance is $3 for ages 5 and up on weekends for non-residents.

Ages: All

LADERA LINDA COMMUNITY CENTER

(310) 541-7073 - park; (310) 377-0360, ex. 309 - guided hikes / www.palosverdes.com/rpv

3201 Forrestal Drive, Rancho Palos Verdes

(Exit Harbor Fwy [110] W. on Pacific Coast Hwy., L. on Western Ave., R. on Palos Verdes Dr. S. (NOT Palos Verdes Dr. N.), R. on Forrestal. [TG-823 D5])

This park features wilderness areas, two grass volleyball courts, a basketball court, a small playground, and, closer to where the additional parking lot is located, two tennis courts and (up the wooden stairs) soccer and baseball fields. There are picnic tables and a few shade trees, too. The community center building is home to Montessori school classes, game rooms, and a Discovery room. The small Discovery room has a few live animals, displays of rocks and fossils, photos of the area, and information regarding this area. Ask about the REACH programs for the developmentally disabled.

Two-hour, docent-led hikes offered by the center enable groups of kids, minimum ten, to explore the coastal habitat of the Palos Verdes Peninsula. Look out for and learn about coastal sage scrub, native trees, and wildflowers, as well as important critters such as lizards, butterflies, and birds. Hikes are moderately difficult, so bring a water bottle and wear sunscreen. The hike/tours can focus on a topic of your choice, such as plants, animals, fossils, or the geology of the area, including a visit to a rock quarry. A visit to the Discovery Room, with explanations about the exhibits, is included in your time here.

Hours: The park is open daily dawn to dusk. The Discovery Room is open during the summer daily 10pm - 5pm. It's open the rest of the year Mon., Wed., and Fri. - Sun., 1pm - 5pm. Tours are set up by reservation.

Admission: Free to the park. Tours are $2 for adults; $1 for children 13 and under; with a $15 minimum.

Ages: All for the park; 7 years and up for the tours.

LIBERTY PARK (Cerritos)

(562) 916-8565 / www.ci.cerritos.ca.us

19211 Studebaker Road, Cerritos

(Exit San Gabriel River Fwy [605] W. on South St, L. on Studebaker Rd. [TG-766 F2])

Experience the freedom at Liberty Park to do almost anything. The park offers long grassy areas to run around, three playground areas, picnic tables, barbeque pits, three picnic shelters, three sand volleyball courts, a 330-yard walking/jogging track, a softball field, a disc (Frisbee) golf course, outside exercise clusters equipped with pull up bars and more, and six lighted tennis courts. Tennis is free for Cerritos residents (show a driver's license or utility bill for proof of residency) and $5 per hour for non-residents. A bike path runs along the Los Angeles River just outside the park gates. (See BIKE TRAIL: SAN GABRIEL RIVER TRAIL in the Transportation section for more information.)

Inside the community building are four racquetball courts ($5 per hour for residents, $8 for non-residents); a weight room (free to residents, $2 per day for non-residents); and a Walleyball court (indoor volleyball that uses walls) on Monday nights ($10 per hour for residents, $15 for non-residents). Summertime offers the refreshing pleasures of a wading pool that has a water sprayer, Monday night family time at the movies ('G' rated), and Wednesday night family entertainment consisting of puppets, magicians, or storytellers.

Hours: Open Mon. - Fri., 9am - 10pm; Sat. - Sun., 9am - 6pm. Call for times for special programs.

Admission: Free to the park. Fees for activities are listed above.

Ages: All

LINCOLN PARK / PLAZA DE LA RAZA

(213) 847-1726 - park; (323) 906-7953 - aquatic center /

www.angelfire.com/ca4/lincolnpark

3501 Valley Boulevard, Los Angeles

(From Golden State [5] (just above the 10 Fwy) exit E. on N. Main St, R. on Marengo, L. on Mission, R. on Selig. Park entrance is a block east of the intersection of Valley Blvd. and Mission Rd. at Plaza de la Raza [TG-635 B2])

This older park in an older section of town has an Aztec-themed playground with two slides coming down from a temple, although the really tall one is made of cement, so it's not very slick. An adjacent playground has more slides and swings. There are rows of picnic tables here under huge pine and oak trees. Other features include paved pathways that crisscross throughout, a big lake with a large fountain that is stocked with fish and home to numerous ducks, four nice tennis courts, another playground with a sand base for younger children, grassy expanses, a community building, and a swimming pool that is open seasonally. We also enjoyed the large, grass-covered hill - walking up it and running back down Kamikaze-style!

Hours: The park and community center are open daily 9am - 10pm. The pool is open mid-June to Labor Day.

Admission: The park is free, as are several of the classes offered at the center. Admission to the pool is $1.25 for adults; free for seniors and ages 18 and under.

Ages: All

LIVE OAK PARK

(310) 545-5621 / www.ci.manhattan-beach.ca.us
Valley Drive N. and 21ˢᵗ Street, Manhattan Beach
(Exit San Diego Fwy [405] W. on Rosecrans Ave., L. on Pacific Coast Highway, next R. on Valley Dr. [TG-732 F5])

This park is formed around a bend in the road and is divided into various, gated sections. The northern section has baseball diamonds, picnic tables, and some short, bent gnarled trees for climbing. One particular threesome of trees bends in and down so much that they form a kind of hideout. Other sections have playground equipment, soccer fields, places just to run and play, and tennis courts. The six courts are open weekdays from 7am to 4pm for $4 per court, and weekdays 5pm to 10pm and all day on weekends for $5 per court. Call (310) 545-0888 to make reservations.

Hours: Open daily from dawn to dusk.

Admission: Free

Ages: All

LOST ADVENTURES CORN MAZE

(818) 787-7038 / www.mazeofcorn.com $$$
6335 Woodley Avenue, Van Nuys
(Exit San Diego Fwy [405] W. on Burbank Blvd., R. on Woodley. On the E. side of Woodley, between Victory and Burbank in the Sepulveda Dam Recreation Area. [TG-561 F1])

Without trying to sound *corny*, this maze is *amaizing*! Eight acres of cornstalks are cut in a particular design; one year it was the bear and star from the California state flag. The object is twofold: Go through the entire maze as quickly as you can (you are timed), and find all the map pieces at certain stations throughout the maze. The pieces are supposed to fit together to help you find your way around, but I am not a map reader. I think the third objective should be to simply find your way out. Note: For an extra challenge, come after dark and go through the maze. Bring your own flashlight!

At the entrance, participants are given a tall flag to carry with a number on it so they can be identified by the maze master, a guy who sits in a tower above the maze helping lost souls. The maze pathways are wide enough to accompany a stroller or wheelchair. Groups are given discounts. School groups receive a twenty minute lesson on corn and mazes before actually going through. A hay bale maze is set up for little ones just outside the main entrance. Make a day of it by bringing a sack lunch and exploring the rest of the huge park area. Look up SEPULVEDA DAM RECREATION AREA in this section for more details.

Hours: Open August through October, Wed. - Sun., 10am - 10pm. Call first as hours fluctuate.

Admission: $9 for adults; $7 for seniors and ages 4 - 12; children 3 and under are free.

Ages: 5 years and up.

MADRONA MARSH   ☼

(310) 32 MARSH (326-2774) / www.tprd.torrnet.com/marsh.htm   !/$$

3201 Plaza Del Amo, Torrance

(From San Diego Fwy [405], exit S. on Crenshaw Blvd., R. on Carson St., L. on Madrona Ave., L. on Plaza Del Amo. Going S. on Harbor Fwy [110], exit W. on Carson St., L. on Madrona Ave., L. on Plaza Del Amo. Going N. on 110, exit at 220th, L. on Figuroa St., L. on Carson St., L. on Madrona Ave., L. on Plaza Del Amo. [TG-763 E7])

The Madrona Marsh hosts educational nature walks for kids (and adults) of all ages. During the hour, or so, guided tour you'll see and learn mostly about birds, plus ground animals, like tree frogs, and several varieties of plant life. Summer field study tours are also given. A Nature Center holds a few displays concerning marsh animals, and is open during scheduled walks. The forty-three acre marsh and pond is located in the middle of an industrial section. If it's not big enough to make you feel like you've gotten away from it all, it's at least big enough to make you feel like you've gotten away from some of it.

Hours: The marsh is open sunrise to sunset to explore on your own. Guided walks are given the fourth weekend of every month, and field study tours are given at various times. Call for details.

Admission: Free; donations gladly accepted. Summer field study tours are $5 per person or $10 per family.

Ages: 6 years and up.

MALIBU CREEK STATE PARK   ☼

(818) 880-0350 - park; (800) 444-7275 - camping reservations / $

parks.ca.gov

1925 Las Virgenes Road, Calabasas

(Exit Ventura Fwy [101] S. at Las Virgenes Rd. The park is S. of Mulholland Hwy. [TG-588 G5])

Of the many hiking, mountain bike, and horseback riding trails to choose from in the Santa Monica Mountains, one of our favorites is the Malibu Creek Trail. Starting at the broad fire road, veer to the right as the trail forks onto Cragg Road. The scenery keeps getting better the further in you hike. Oak trees shade part of the trail as you follow the high road along the creek. Man-made Century Lake is a great place to stop for a picnic, take in the beauty of your surroundings, and/or fish. This spot marks a four-mile round trip. Continue on an additional two miles (round trip) to the former M*A*S*H* set. Being here might not have any meaning for your kids, but they'll at least think the rock formation, named Goat Buttes and used in the opening scene of the show, is worth a "wow."

Malibu Creek Park has many other interesting things to see and do. A mile in from the parking lot is the Visitor's Center, which also has a small museum. Each room in the museum is different. One contains taxidermied animals, another contains M*A*S*H* memorabilia, and yet another is a room for school groups to work on craft projects.

Feel like taking a dip in cool, refreshing water? Just beyond the Visitor's Center, over the bridge to the left, and over a short trail of rocks, is a rock-lined swimming hole. It's like a hidden oasis and my boys thought jumping off the boulders into the "pool" formed by the creek was the ultimate.

Take advantage of all that the park offers by spending a night or two here. Each of the sixty-two campsites, some of which are shaded, has a picnic table and charcoal-use fire pit. Eight people per campsite are allowed.

Hours: The park is open daily 8am to sunset. The Visitor's Center is open Sat. - Sun., noon - 4pm.

Admission: $2 per vehicle. Camping prices are seasonal, and start at $10.

Ages: 3 years and up.

MARIE KERR SKATEPARK ☼
(661) 267-5611 !
39700 30th Street West, Palmdale
(Exit Antelope Valley Fwy [14], W. on Ave. P., R. 30th St. [TG-4195 C5])

Airborne! At least my kids keep hoping for this state when they skate. I just hope they land unharmed. This 8,500 square foot skatepark has all the necessary ramps, grinding boxes, and other street skate elements to make it fun. A helmet and knee and elbow pads are required. A parent or guardian must sign a waiver if the participant is under 18 years old.

The surrounding park has tennis courts, basketball courts, a playground, soccer field, baseball diamonds, and picnic areas.

Hours: The park is open daily. The skatepark is open Mon. - Fri., 3pm - 9pm; Sat. - Sun., 10am - 9pm.

Admission: Free

Ages: 7 years and up.

MATHIAS BOTANICAL GARDEN AT U.C.L.A.
(310) 825-3620 / www.botgard.ucla.edu $$
U.C.L.A. Campus, Westwood
(Exit San Diego Fwy [405] E. on Wilshire Blvd., L. on Westwood Blvd. to the information kiosk. [TG-632 A2])

See U.C.L.A. under the Potpourri section.

MAYFAIR PARK ☼
(562) 866-9771 - park; (562) 804-4256 - pool (in season) !
5720 Clark Street, Lakewood
(Exit Artesia Fwy [91] S. on Lakewood Blvd., L. on South St. It's on the corner of South and Clark Sts. [TG-766 B2])

Mayfair Park is a very fair park indeed! The two enclosed playgrounds have fun equipment for younger children. The best attractions (judging by my kids playing on them for a long time) are the wooden train to climb on and in, and a sand play area that has a small climbing structure with buckets attached to pulleys on the outside of it. Open grassy fields are plentiful here, plus there are basketball courts, tennis courts, baseball diamonds with lights and stadium seating, barbecue pits, a swimming pool, a wading pool, and an Express McDonald's that's usually open in the summer and during special events.

Hours: The park is open daily. The pools are open mid-May through mid-June, weekends only; open daily in the summer. Swim sessions are 1pm to 2:30pm and 2:45pm to 4:15pm. Call for extended nighttime hours.

Admission: Free to the park. Each pool session costs $1.25 for adults; 75¢ for children 17 and under. The wading pool is free.

Ages: All

MENTRYVILLE / PICO CANYON
(661) 259-2701 / www.smmc.ca.gov
Pico Canyon Road, Santa Clarita
(Exit Golden State Fwy [5] W. on Lyons Ave. which turns into Pico Canyon Road. Go about 3 miles, staying to the L. at the Y intersection when the road forks, up a bumpy, semi-paved road. [TG-4640 A1])

Mentryville was once an oil boom town. Of the few old buildings that remain, the Felton schoolhouse, originally built in 1885, is the only one open to the public. Inside are wooden school desks, a pot bellied stove, blackboards, and a very small library room that no longer contains books. A dual-seat outhouse and a tire swing are just outside. Other structures on the grounds include Mr. Mentry's house, a barn and chicken coop, and a jail that was built just a few years ago for a movie. Picnic tables are set up under shade trees. A seasonal creek runs through this area. Take a short hike on a service road that is stroller/wheelchair accessible. The road leads to Johnson Park, a picnic spot featuring a replica of a wood oil derrick. Hike a bit further through the surrounding hills of Pico Canyon, past foundation remains and up to some overlooks. After a few miles the trail changes. Only experienced hikers should continue as the trail now contains several very steep and strenuous sections. Tip: Bring your own water.

Creative teachers can plan a field to Mentryville that incorporates activities such as a school lesson in the schoolhouse, making butter, taking a nature walk, etc. A park ranger will come to give the class a history talk about the area.

Hours: Open daily sunrise to sunset. Explore Pico Canyon on your own on these days as well. Short, guided tours of Mentryville are offered the first and third Sun. of each month between noon and 4pm. School groups may call to reserve a time during the week.

Admission: Free

Ages: All

MILLARD CANYON FALLS
(818) 790-1151 / www.r5.fs.fed.us/angeles
Chaney Trail, Los Angeles

(Exit Foothill Fwy [210] N. on Lincoln Ave., R. on Loma Alta Dr., L. on Chaney Tr., continue as it curves until it ends at Millard campground. [TG-535 H2])

Past the picnic tables and camping area is a fire road. Follow it for about a mile - the walk is fairly easy. There are some boulders to climb over, but that's part of the fun. The falls are beautiful. The pool at the bottom is not very deep, so use caution if you want to get wet.

Hours: Open daily dawn to dusk.
Admission: $5 per vehicle for an Adventure Pass.
Ages: 5 years and up.

NEW OTANI HOTEL AND GARDENS

(213) 629-1200 / www.newotani.com

120 S. Los Angeles Street, Los Angeles

(Exit Harbor Fwy [110] E. on 4th St., L. on Los Angeles. Going W. on Hollywood Fwy [101], exit at Alameda, stay straight to the next street, L. on Los Angeles. Going E. on 101, exit S. on Los Angeles. [TG-634 G4])

Amid the hustle and bustle of downtown Los Angeles, take a quick breather at the New Otani Hotel gardens. Ride the elevator up to the small, but beautiful, Japanese garden located just outside the Thousand Cranes Restaurant. The garden's waterfall give it a sense of serenity. We loved its unique location - on top of a roof! Enjoy your short break from the busy world not far below.

Hours: Open daily - hotel hours.
Admission: Free; metered parking is available.
Ages: 2 years and up.

NORWALK PARK

(562) 929-5702 / www.ci.norwalk.ca.us

12203 Sproul Street, Norwalk

(Exit Santa Ana Fwy [5] S. on Pioneer Blvd., L. on Firestone Blvd., L. on San Antonio Dr., R. on Sproul. [TG-736 J2])

This park has a nature center/mini farm located in the back corner, near the freeway. A little stream and benches under shade trees, make it a nice place to visit the farm friends living here. The animals, all in pens, include spotted goats, sheep, a donkey, pot-bellied pigs, geese, and steer.

The park itself is spacious with lots of open grassy areas, a playground for younger kids, tennis courts, basketball courts, and a small museum. The Sproul Museum contains artifacts from early Norwalk, including pictures, a few articles of clothing, and some furniture. A pool with a shallow end, and a diving board at the deep end, is open seasonally. A snack bar is in the pool area.

Hours: The park is open daily sunrise to sunset. The nature center/mini-farm is open Sat. - Sun., 1pm - 4pm. Call for hours during the week when it is open by appointment for tours for younger children. Call for museum hours. The pool and snack bar are usually open daily mid-June through August. Swim sessions are daily 1pm - 2:45pm and 3:15pm - 5pm. An additional Sunday session is 11am - 12:30pm.
Admission: Free to the park. Swim sessions are $1 per person.

Ages: All

ORCUTT RANCH HORTICULTURE CENTER

(818) 883-6641 / www.laparks.org
23600 Roscoe Boulevard, West Hills
(Exit Ventura Fwy [101] N. on Valley Circle Ave., R. on Roscoe Blvd. [TG-529 F2])

The horticultural center was originally created in the early 1900's. A stroll through these nostalgic gardens is a delightful way to pass a half an hour or so. A short, wide, stroller-friendly, dirt trail leads into a grove of shady oak trees and through grounds that are lush with greenery and wildflowers. The adjacent pathway along Dayton Creek, which borders one side of the Ranch's perimeters, is not for strollers. It does have stone benches for resting and leads to a few bridges that extend over the water. On the other side of the creek is a cozy picnic area. Look for ancient live oaks throughout the ranch; one is over 700 years old (and still growing)! Also on the grounds are a picnic table in the small bamboo grove, a grassy picnic area near the gazebo, and more formal gardens consisting of maze-like hedges around the rose gardens. A statue of Father Serra is in the courtyard, by the fountain, near a small stone grotto. Note: Visitors may not walk through the adjacent acres of citrus trees.

The adobe building, once the Orcutt's home, is now used for park offices and group rental functions. A quick walk around and through the mostly unfurnished building allows you to see the Mexican-influence architecture and hand-painted, South-of-the-Border tiles.

Hours: The grounds are open daily 8am - 5pm. Many private functions are held here, however, so call first. (But you would do that anyhow, right?) Docent-guided tours are given the last Sun. of the month, except in the summer, between 1pm - 4pm.

Admission: Free

Ages: All

PALOS VERDES PENINSULA LAND CONSERVANCY

(310) 541-7613 / www.pvplc.org
Various locations throughout the Palos Verdes and San Pedro areas.

Once-a-month guided Nature Walks, most of them family oriented and suitable for children, are given by naturalists, historians, and geologists. Tour guides share information about the history of the area, wildlife, plants, and more. The walks range from one to three hours and from easy to more difficult. All are on dirt paths. Starting points include Abalone Cove, the Cabrillo Marine Aquarium, Ladera Linda, Madrona Marsh, and Malaga Dunes, most of which are listed separately in this section. Call for a calendar of events.

Admission: Free, but donations are often requested.

PARAMOUNT RANCH

(805) 370-2300 / www.nps.gov/samo
On Cornell Road, Agoura Hills
(Exit Ventura Fwy [101] S. on Kanan Rd., L. on Troutdale Dr., L. on Mulholland Hwy., L. on Cornell Rd. [TG-588 B3])

Howdy partners! You've come to the right ranch if you're looking for some action. Western Town in Paramount Ranch was once owned by Paramount Studios and used as a western movie set. The "town" still stands. The most recent television show filmed here was *Dr. Quinn, Medicine Woman.* Walk the dusty roads and inspect the town buildings from the outside. These buildings include a blacksmith shop, general store, a jail, and even a train depot with railroad tracks. It all looks so real! Dress up your cowboy or cowgirl and bring your camera. Better yet, bring your video camera, props, and script and do your own western mini-movie. Free, guided walking tours that describe the set and history of the area are usually given on the first and third Saturdays of each month at 9:30am.

Over the bridge next to the main part of town, is a huge meadow with a few picnic tables. At the end of the meadow is a wonderful, wooded trail that follows along a creek, and is only one-eighth of a mile round trip. If the kids are in the mood for hiking into the mountains, go up Coyote Canyon Trail, just behind Western Town. This uphill, three-quarters of a mile round-trip trail goes through green chaparral-covered canyons overlooking the valley. The picnic spot up here has a view that is worth the effort. The 5K Run Trail is longer, obviously. It traverses a variety of scenery from the Oak Restoration Area, through Western Town, and down near the creek. Ranger-led naturalist programs are also offered at the park. Call regarding the many special and seasonal events that the ranch hosts.

Hours: Open daily 8am - sunset.
Admission: Free
Ages: All

PETER STRAUSS RANCH

(805) 370-2300 / www.nps.gov/samo
3000 Mulholland Highway, Agoura
(Exit Ventura Fwy [101] S. on Kanan Rd., L. on Troutdale Dr., L. on Mulholland Hwy. [TG-599 D4])

This sprawling park, once owned by actor Peter Strauss, goes for miles and miles, with great hiking trails amongst the chaparral and oak trees. One of the smaller trails is only a three-quarter-mile loop, but there are several other trails for more ambitious walkers.

Hours: Open daily 8am - sunset.
Admission: Free
Ages: 4 years and up.

PIONEER PARK

(909) 394-6230 / www.ci.san-dimas.ca.us
225 S. Cataract Avenue, San Dimas
(Going S.E. on 210 Fwy, exit E. on Arrow Hwy., L. on Cataract. Going N.W. on 210, exit E. on Covina Blvd. and stay on it as it bends to the left and turns into Cataract. [TG-600 B2])

This park offers a playground, basketball courts, picnic tables, and, most importantly for my boys, an 8,000 square foot concrete skate park. It has all the elements of a good skate park - ramps, a grinding box, and more. A helmet, and knee and elbow pads, are required.

Hours: Open daily dawn to dusk.
Admission: Free
Ages: 7 years and up.

PLACERITA CANYON NATURE CENTER AND PARK   ☼

(661) 259-7721 / parks.co.la.ca.us   !
19152 Placerita Canyon Road, Newhall   🎂
(Exit Golden State Fwy [5] N. on Antelope Valley Fwy [14], S. on Placerita Canyon Rd. [TG-4641 G1])

Placerita Canyon was the site of one of the first gold discoveries, small though it was, in California. In fact, the famed oak tree where gold was first discovered, "Oak of the Golden Dream," is just a short walk from the parking lot. There is a wealth of history and wilderness to be found at this Nature Center and park.

The Center has live animals, such as snakes and lizards, on display outside. One of the rooms inside has exhibits regarding the circle of life - predators, prey, and plants. Other exhibits include equipment that monitors weather conditions; dirt samples comparing texture and content; and taxidermied animals. Another room has live snakes and spiders (in glass cases), and a touch table with nests, pine cones, and bones.

The hiking is great here, especially for more experienced hikers. Canyon Trail is a gradual climb, following along a stream. The left fork leads to the Scout campground. The right fork leads to the Waterfall Trail, where yes, about two-thirds of a mile back, is a waterfall. Canyon Trail also hooks up to Los Pinetos Trail, which is a hardy, eight-mile hike.

A large picnic area on the hillside of the park is nestled in a huge grove of oak trees. Play equipment is here, although the main attractions are the beauty of the area and a small hiking trail. Call to find out more about the Saturday nature hikes, the animal demonstrations, astronomy club, summer camps, and other special programs.

Hours: Open daily 9am - 5pm.
Admission: Free
Ages: 2 years and up.

POINT FERMIN PARK   ☼

(310) 548-7756   !
807 S. Paseo del Mar, San Pedro   🎂
(Take Harbor Fwy [110] to the end, turn L. on Gaffey St., L. on 9th St., R. on Pacific Ave. to the end, then R. on Paseo del Mar. [TG-854 B2])

This corner park has lots of green grassy areas, shade trees, and a few play structures. Its two best features are the wonderful view of the California coastline, and a nineteenth-century lighthouse. The lighthouse is not open for tours, but it is very picturesque, with a wide variety of flowers and other plants surrounding it. I mention this park mainly because its large size and its proximity to several fun places in San Pedro makes it ideal for picnicking.

Hours: Open daily sunrise to sunset.
Admission: Free

Ages: All

POLLIWOG PARK ☼

(310) 545-5621 - park; (310) 374-757 - museum

Corner of Manhattan Beach Boulevard and Redondo Avenue, Manhattan Beach

(Exit San Diego Fwy [405] S. on Inglewood, R. on Manhattan Beach Blvd. [TG-732 J6])

This expansive park is wonderfully deceptive. The part seen from the street is beautiful, with a play area and lots of grass and trees. Some of the trees have low branches that beckon to climbers. There is also an exercise area, with wood benches and handles for pull-ups, sit-ups, and other physical activities. A huge portion of the lawn is graded for summer concerts in the park. The original red beach cottage in the park is a small historic museum. It features photos, old-fashioned bathing suits, and other artifacts of the olden days.

As you take the stroller-friendly pathway leading down toward the interior of the park, you'll discover some "hidden" delights, such as a pond where marshy reeds and ducks abound. (Signs ask that you don't feed the ducks.) Tip: Watch your children around the water as there are no guard rails. Kids, ages 6 to 12, have a play structure here that looks like part of an ark. This big boat was built so kids can climb on it and slide down it, but hopefully not jump ship. Younger kids, ages 2 to 5, have a playground designed especially for them with rope bridges, tires, slides, and swings.

Across the street from the main park is a baseball diamond and four lighted tennis courts.

Hours: The park is open daily dawn to dusk. The museum is open weekends noon - 3pm.

Admission: Free to the park and museum.

Ages: All

PYRAMID LAKE ☼

(661) 295-1245 - lake; (805) 257-2892 - bait shop; (661)248-6575 - campground / www.rmrc-recreation.com

Off Interstate 5, 20 miles N. of Santa Clarita Valley.

(Exit Golden State Fwy [5] W. on Smokey Bear Rd.)

This huge sparkling reservoir lake, surrounded by hills, offers a myriad of activities for families. Year-round boating, including waterskiing, canoeing, rowboating, and rubber rafting, is allowed. B.Y.O.B. (Bring Your Own Boat), as only aluminum fishing boats, which seat up to four people, are available to rent. Shaded picnic shelters and barbeques are near the docks. Some of the beach and picnic sites across the lake are reachable only by boat. Fish for seasonal bass, trout, catfish, crappie, and bluegill. A bait and tackle shop is on the grounds. A California state fishing license is required for those 16 years old or older. The waveless swim beach is open during the summer and is patrolled by lifeguards on the weekends. Outdoor showers are available here. Meander on trails along the lake, enjoy a picnic meal, visit the nearby VISTA DEL LAGO (see the Museums section), and/or camp at your choice of two campgrounds near the lake. Los Alamos Campground, two miles up the road, has room for ninety-three family units and three group units. Hard Luck Campground, on Piru Creek, has twenty-two family units.

Hours: The lake is open daily November through March, 7am - 5pm; April through October, 6am - 8pm. The swim beach is open the same hours, seasonally.

Admission: $7 per vehicle, plus an additional $7 if you are bringing in your own boat. Fishing boat rentals November through March, are $30 for the day; in the summer, $28 for 2 hours, $6 per hour after that. Fishing poles are $5 for a half day. Camping is $10 per night. The swim beach costs $1 for adults; 50¢ for children 11 and under, but only when a lifeguard is on duty. Swim at your own risk, for free, during the week when a lifeguard isn't on duty.

Ages: All

RANCHO SANTA ANA BOTANIC GARDEN

(909) 625-8767 / www.rsabg.org

1500 N. College Avenue, Claremont

(Exit San Bernardino Fwy [10] N. on Indian Hill Blvd., R. on Foothill. Go 3 blocks, then turn L. on College Ave. [TG-571 D7])

This eighty-six-acre botanic garden is beautiful in scope and sequence, and abundant with plants native only to California. Thousands of different kinds of plants grow in our state, so this garden covers a lot of ground with its giant sequoias, fan palms, California live oak, manzanitas, cacti, wildflowers, and more.

The numerous trails, many of which are stroller friendly, afford good walking opportunities. Since the diverse vegetation attracts a wide variety of birds, bird lovers can pick up a bird check list at the gift shop, or join an organized bird walk on the first Sunday of each month. I don't know how much horticulture my kids take in when we visit botanic gardens, but it's a good introduction to the variety and importance of plant life, plus a beautiful walk is always enjoyable.

Hours: Open daily 8am - 5pm. Closed New Year's Day, Independence Day, Thanksgiving, and Christmas.

Admission: Free; donations of $2 per person or $5 per family are suggested.

Ages: 3 years and up.

ROBERT E. RYAN PARK

(310) 377-2290 - park site; (310) 541-4566 - city parks / www.palosverdes.org/rpv

30359 Hawthorne Boulevard, Rancho Palos Verdes

(Exit Pacific Coast Highway [1] S. on Hawthorne Blvd. It's S. of Crest Rd., near Vallon Dr. [TG-822 H3])

From the parking lot of this nine-acre park, you get a glimpse of the California coastline, and on a clear day, Catalina Island. Steps lead down into the park itself. Note: Strollers and wheelchairs can take a ramp only a short distance down toward the park. The main play area is then accessible by going over a grassy slope.

The community center has some play equipment to check out, as long as you leave your driver's license in exchange. Play a game of basketball or baseball or romp around on the large, open, grassy areas. Set sail on a metal ship, with masts, that looks like something Columbus would have used for his explorations. Shipmates can climb from stern to bow, go down a slide, and slide down a pole at the end of a gangplank. The playground also has climbing apparatus, swings, and slides, all in a big sand pit. Stroll under shade trees on cement pathways that go through a good portion of the park. Bring a sack lunch to enjoy at the picnic tables, or grill food at the barbecues.

Hours: Open July through Labor Day daily and on holidays 10am - dusk. Open the rest of the year usually Mon. - Fri. and Sun., noon - dusk; Sat., 10am - dusk. Closed New Year's Day, Thanksgiving, Christmas Eve, and Christmas Day.

Admission: Free

Ages: All

ROXBURY PARK

(310) 550-4761 - park; (310) 550-4979 - tennis / www.ci.beverly-hills.ca.us

471 S. Roxbury Drive, Beverly Hills

(Exit Santa Monica Fwy [10] N. on Robertson, L. on Olympic. It's on the corner of Olympic and Roxbury. [TG-632 F3])

This beautiful park fits right in with its surroundings of well-manicured lawns and stately homes. Although it is off a main street, it still seems somewhat removed from city life. The park offers a wealth of activities to choose from such as tennis (four courts plus backboards), grass volleyball, basketball, baseball, and soccer. Along with a few picnic tables, barbecue pits, and some large shaded grassy areas, there is a good-sized playground. One of the wooden structures is designed for slightly older kids with a big slide to go down, bridges to cross, and ropes to climb. The other is designed with younger kids in mind. It has swings, slides, and fun cement shapes to crawl through.

Hours: The park is open daily 6am - 11pm. The community center is open Mon. - Fri., 9am - 10pm; Sat. - Sun., 9am - 6pm.

Admission: Free. Tennis courts are $6 an hour for residents; $8 an hour for non-residents.

Ages: All

RUNYON CANYON PARK

(323) 666-5004 / www.laparks.org

2000 Fuller Street, Hollywood

(Exit Hollywood Fwy [101] W. on Sunset Blvd., N. on Franklin St. all the way to the top. [TG-593 C3])

Hike the hills of Hollywood in the popular Runyon Canyon. The dirt trail starts off at an upward slant, leading past ruins where house foundations and a few chunks of wall still remain. We walked the scenic, mostly woodland, main trail all the way up the mountain, as it affords a spectacular view of the famed city. The hike is strenuous as it goes up and along the rim of the hills. The trail eventually levels off, then loops back down. The two-mile round trip hike is not stroller/wheelchair accessible. Nor is the slightly longer hike out to Mulholland. Bring water! Note: Look where you walk as this is a popular park for walking dogs. Inquire about periodic guided hikes.

Hours: Open daily dawn to dusk.

Admission: Free

Ages: 5 years and up.

RUSTIC CANYON RECREATION CENTER

(310) 454-5734

601 Latimer Road, Pacific Palisades

(Exit San Diego Fwy [405] W. on Wilshire Blvd., R. on 7th St., which turns into Entrada Dr., R. on Mesa Rd., L. on Latimer Rd. [TG-631 B6])

This pretty park is nestled in a somewhat secluded area of Pacific Palisades, but it's worth making the effort to visit here. Shade trees line the perimeter of a paved pathway that leads down into the park. A baseball field, basketball court, playground, grassy area, climbing trees (always a hit with my family), a wooden pyramid structure (to climb on and around), two picnic areas, and barbeque pits make up the central part of the park. Several tennis courts are located in one corner. Up near the parking lot is an older-style recreation center which offers a variety of classes. An adjacent, medium-sized community swimming pool is open seasonally.

Hours: The park is open daily sunrise to sunset. The pool is open the mid -June through Labor Day. Swim sessions are Mon. - Fri., 10am - noon and 1pm - 5pm; Sat. - Sun., 1pm - 5pm.

Admission: Free to the park. Swim sessions are $1.25 for adults; 75¢ for kids 17 and under.

Ages: All

SADDLEBACK BUTTE STATE PARK

(661) 942-0662 / www.calparksmojave.com

17102 Avenue 'J' East, Lancaster

(Going N. on Antelope Valley Fwy [14], exit N. on 20th St. W., N. to Ave. 'J'. Going S. on 14, exit E. on Ave. 'J'. It's quite a few miles out to the park. [TG-4109 H1])

This state park is 3,000 acres of desert landscape, with Joshua trees scattered throughout and a huge granite mountain top, Saddleback Butte, jutting up almost a 1,000 feet above the valley. Be on the lookout for wildlife such as desert tortoises, rabbits, coyotes, kit foxes, kangaroo rats, and lots of reptiles and birds. Several hiking trails are available here, including a two-and-a-half-mile trail that leads to the top of the Butte, and a view that makes the hike worthwhile. Springtime is particularly beautiful at the park because the wildflowers are in bloom. Near the entrance and park headquarters are several covered picnic areas, complete with barbecues. Please remember that desert weather is hot in the summer and cold in the winter, so dress accordingly. Overnight camping is available here. Saddleback is located just a few miles down the road from the ANTELOPE VALLEY INDIAN MUSEUM (look under the Museums section).

Hours: Open daily sunrise to sunset.
Admission: Free for day use. Camping is $8 per night.
Ages: 5 years and up.

SAND DUNE PARK

(310) 545-5621
At the corner of 33rd Street and Bell Avenue, Manhattan Beach
(Exit San Diego Fwy [405] W. on Rosecrans Ave., L. on Bell. [TG-732 F4])

This little park has a big surprise. While there is a small playground for younger children, the park is really "beachy" because of its steep wall of sand that is perfect for running, jumping, or rolling down. Steps lead to the top of the hill, or just climb up it. Bring your own bucket and shovel to play with at the bottom. Here is a local's favorite tip: After it rains, take a snow sled down the hill!

Behind the playground is a green grassy stretch. Picnic tables and a few barbecue pits under a shelter are also available. Parking is limited.

Hours: Open daily dawn to dusk.
Admission: Free
Ages: All

SAN DIMAS COUNTY PARK

(909) 599-7512 / parks.co.la.ca.us
1628 Sycamore Canyon Road, San Dimas
(From Foothill Fwy [210], take the 30 Fwy E. go N.W. on Foothill Blvd., R. on San Dimas Canyon Dr., L. on Sycamore Canyon Rd., up the hill to the park office. [TG-570 D6])

Nestled in the foothills of the San Gabriel Mountains, adjacent to Angeles National Forest, is a wonderful county park/museum/wildlife sanctuary. The nature museum is fairly comprehensive. It contains live snakes, such as rosy boas and rattlesnakes; taxidermied animals, such as California gray squirrels, birds, and raccoons; and several small collections including rocks, arrowheads, insects, and butterflies.

The outside wildlife sanctuary offers a caged home to several injured or non-releasable native animals. Hawks, heart-faced barn owls, and great-horned owls are part of the bird rehabilitation area; not part of the bird "rebellion" area as my son misread the sign. (Hmm - could be something to do with his childhood. . . .) Other live animals here include a deer, raccoon (his little paws were busily cleaning his food when we saw him), possum, a fox, pheasants, and tortoises, plus many squirrels running around freely.

A one-mile, self-guiding nature trail begins in the oak woodland just behind the nature center building and loops around. There are several other trails to choose from which satisfy both novice and experienced hikers. There are plenty of picnic tables here under the cover of shady oak trees. Some of the picnic areas have barbeques. The area below the museum has a baseball diamond, a few playgrounds, and large grassy areas. An equestrian center is next to the park, and a portion of a long bike route goes through part of the park. Come visit the park on your own, or via a Jr. Ranger Program, offered through the park system. A visit to the San Dimas County Park is a great for temporarily escaping city life.

Hours: The park is open daily 8am - sunset. The nature center is open daily 9am - 5pm.

Admission: Free

Ages: All

SANTA FE DAM RECREATIONAL AREA

(626) 334-1065 - park; (626) 334-9049 - boat rental / parks.co.la.ca.us

15501 Arrow Highway, Irwindale

(North entrance: exit Foothill Fwy [210], S. on Irwindale, R. on 1st St. South entrance: from San Gabriel River Fwy [605], exit E. on Live Oak Ave. which turns into Arrow Hwy. - from Foothill Fwy [210], exit S. on Irwindale, R. on Arrow Highway. [TG-568 C7 - 598 E2])

Though located in the middle of an industrial section, city sounds fade away while at this enormous recreational area that sports a mountainous backdrop. Our first stop was at the nature center trail, at the northern end of the park. The rock-lined, three-quarter-mile looping trail is paved, level, and a delight to walk. Desert is the predominant theme. We observed an abundance of cacti and other plant life, and animals such as jackrabbits, lizards, roadrunners, and hummingbirds.

The huge lake toward the entrance offers a nice-sized beach with a lifeguarded swimming area. A small water play area for children 52" and under is located by the picnic area. It has a few slides and some climbing apparatus in shallow waters. Other attractions in the park include a playground; fishing - a California state license is required for those 16 years of age and older; quiet boating activities (no gasoline powered boats allowed), with rentals of kayaks and paddle boats available; a snack bar (usually open in the summer); picnic facilities; and unpaved walking trails. This lakeside area, with its shade trees and acres of green grass, is vastly different from the northern desert area.

Ready for a bike ride? Choose your route and go the distance all the way north to San Gabriel Canyon, or south to Long Beach, using various trails that go through this park. Parts of the trail are paved, while other parts are not.

Hours: Open sunrise to sunset. The swim beach and water play areas are open seasonally. Boat rentals are available on weekends most of the year, and daily during the summer.

Admission: $6 per vehicle; $3 for a senior citizen's or a disabled person's vehicle. There is no extra charge to use the swim beach. The water play area, however, is $1 per person for each hour-and-a-half swim session.

Ages: All

SCHABARUM REGIONAL COUNTY PARK

(626) 854-5560 / parks.co.la.ca.us

Colima Road, Rowland Heights

(Exit Pomona Fwy [60] S. on Azusa Ave., L. on Colima [TG-678 G4])

650 acres huge with lots of green rolling hillsides, this country park is seemingly removed from city life. Towards the entrance are scattered picnic tables, barbeque pits, a playground featuring a pirate ship, shade trees, and open

space to run around. About a mile of paved trail follows along a creek as it winds through part of the park. There are twenty miles of dirt hiking and equestrian trails that weave through the rest of the sprawling countryside, leading past shrub, groves of trees, wild flowers (in the spring), and cherry trees, which are beautiful in bloom.

Ray's Equestrian Center, located inside the park, (626) 810-4229, offers guided horseback rides at $20 an hour for adults; $15 for children 7 to 12 years. Pony rides, for younger children, are $20 for a half-hour guided ride.

Hours: The park is open May through September, Mon. - Fri., 6am - 8pm; weekends 8am - 8pm. Open October through April, Mon. - Fri., 6am - 6pm, weekends, 8am - 8pm. The equestrian center is open in the summer Wed., Thurs., Fri., 11am - 5:30pm; Sat. - Sun., 9am - 5:30pm. It's open the rest of the year Wed. - Fri., 11am - 4pm; Sat. - Sun., 9am - 4pm.

Admission: The park is free during the week. $3 per vehicle is charged on weekends and holidays.

Ages: All

SEPULVEDA DAM RECREATION AREA - BALBOA ☼ PARK and BALBOA LAKE

(818) 756-9743 - Balboa Lake and boat rentals; (818) 756-9642 - sports ! center; (818) 756-8189 - skate park / www.laparks.org/dos/aquatic/balboa.htm

6300 Balboa Boulevard, Van Nuys

(Exit Ventura Fwy [101] N. on Balboa Blvd. It's between Burbank Blvd. and Victory Blvd. [TG-531 D7])

Is there anything you can't do at the massive Sepulveda Dam area? Balboa Park, which comprises a major portion of the area is very spread out: On the east side of the street are three golf courses; on the west side is an enormous field with sixteen soccer fields, four lighted baseball diamonds, sixteen lighted tennis courts (and a backboard), lighted basketball courts, and lots of open space and gently sloping hills. The Encino Velodrome is also in this vicinity. A paved, relatively easy, ten-mile round trip bike trail encompasses the east and west side of the park

Our favorite place to play is a little further north, just south of Victory Boulevard, at Balboa Lake. The huge playground has large flat rocks around its perimeters (which is almost all my boys need) and a few play areas for both toddlers and older kids. The play grounds feature slides, climbing apparatus (some with steering wheels), and wooden bridges, plus large (relatively speaking) model camels, elephants, and turtles to climb on. The twenty-seven acre man-made lake, made from reclaimed water and patrolled by lifeguards, offers pedal boat rentals. The boats hold up to four passengers (with the smallest person weighing at least thirty pounds), and take some muscle power, but are a lot of fun. Bring some old bread for the always-hungry ducks swimming around here. Numerous walkers take advantage of the cement pathway that loops around the scenic lake - no bikes, blades, or skateboards are allowed.

At Pedlow Field, on Victory Boulevard, an enclosed 8,500 square-foot cement skate park is another highlight. It includes handrails, steps, a funbox, plenty of ramps, a pyramid, and a waterfall (which is just a name of a ramp - there is no actual water.) Safety gear - a helmet and knee and elbow pads - are required. Plans for the skate park include doubling it's size and adding an exhibition area and a concession stand.

Drive east through the park, past a golf course and you'll reach Anthony Beilenson Park. Its outstanding feature is a model aircraft flying field. Members of the San Fernando Valley Flyers club are often seen here, using (and fixing) their remote-controlled aircraft on a scale runway, and then flying them. See if you can tell the difference between the models and the real planes coming to and from the nearby Van Nuys airport.

Hours: Most parts of the park are open daily sunrise to sunset. Pedal boat rentals are available daily during the summer 10am - 6:45pm; available the rest of the year on weekends and holidays only 10am - sunset. The skate park is open Mon. - Fri., noon - dark; Sat. - Sun., 10am - dark.

Admission: Free to the park. Pedal boats are $7 a half hour; $10 an hour.

Ages: All

SOLSTICE CANYON   ☼

(805) 370-2301   !

Corral Canyon Road, Malibu

(Exit Pacific Coast Highway N. on Corral Canyon Rd. It's through a gated entry, just off the highway. [TG-628 C7])

This canyon offers a variety of trail lengths and terrain, from huge shady oak woodlands to shrubs to an intermittent stream. Short easy trails include the 1.2 mile round trip on Dry Canyon Trail which ends near a seasonal waterfall, or the Solstice Canyon Trail, a 2.1 mile round trip paved road for bikers as well as hikers. Longer trails include the 3.9 miles Sostomo Trail/Deer Valley Loop. We found the canyon to be a peaceful and beautiful place to explore nature. A few picnic tables are located near the parking lot. Note: There are restroom facilities. Tip: Bring your own water.

Hours: Open daily 8am - sunset.

Admission: Free

Ages: 4 years and up.

SOUTH COAST BOTANICAL GARDENS   ☼

(310) 544-6815 / parks.co.la.ca.us $$

26300 S. Crenshaw Boulevard, Rolling Hills Estates   ⛫

(Exit San Diego Fwy [405] S. on Crenshaw Blvd. It's a few miles to Rolling Hills Estates. [TG-793 D6])

This attractive, eighty-seven-acre garden is a breath of fresh air for Southern Californians. It's planted with exotic trees (redwoods, palms, and others), shrubs, and flowers from Africa, New Zealand, and all over the world. There are several different specialty areas here including a cactus garden, a rose garden (we love taking pictures of roses here - such color and variety), a woodland walk, and a Garden for the Senses. In the latter, vegetation with unique fragrances, textures, and color schemes flourish. A fanciful children's garden features fairy tales figures and structures as well as plants.

Stroll along the cement and dirt pathways through the gardens, under shade trees, and up and down the gently rolling hills and grassy areas. It feels good to be surrounded by such beauty! Feed ducks at the man-made lake and look for koi, turtles, and heron and other waterfowl who make their home here. Enjoy a half-hour narrated tram tour on the weekend. Outside food can't be brought in, but a picnic area is just outside the gates.

Hours: Open daily 9am - 5pm. The tram tour is available Sat. - Sun. at 11am, 1pm, and 3pm. The gardens are closed on Christmas.

Admission: $5 for adults; $3 for seniors and students; $1 for ages 5 - 12; children 4 and under are free. Admission is free the third Tues. of every month. The tram tour costs $1.50 per person.

Ages: 3 years and up.

STONEY POINT ☼

Topanga Canyon Boulevard, Chatsworth !
(Exit Simi Valley/San Fernando Valley Fwy [118] S. on Topanga Canyon Blvd. It's the first big rock on your left. [TG-500 A2])

Do you have a rock-climber "wannabe" in your household? Stoney Point is a famous (at least locally) rock climbers' delight. Practice repelling on this small mountain of stone, or just hike the trail up to the top. Either way, it can be an exhilarating way to spend part of the day.

Hours: Open daily sunrise to sunset.

Admission: Free

Ages: 4 years and up to hike; your discretion about rock climbing.

SWITZER FALLS ☼

(818) 790-1151 / www.r5.fs.fed.us/angeles $
Angeles Crest Highway, Los Angeles
(Exit Foothill Fwy [210] N.E. on Angeles Crest Hwy [State 2], go about 10 miles and Switzer Picnic area will be on your R. Drive down a somewhat steep road to park. You'll pass by a ranger station - stop to purchase an Adventure Pass. [TG-505 H1])

Ah - the rewards of a hike! Follow the moderately-graded Gabrielino Trail on the west end of the picnic area about a mile to the remnants of Switzer's Camp, which is a backpacker's campground, to reach the top of the falls; a fifty-foot chute. To reach the bottom, and your destination of a refreshing, rock-line swimming hole, continue hiking on the Gabrielino Trail, along the right-hand side (or west) of the canyon wall and over some boulders. Note: Please use caution around any waterfall - wet rocks are slippery rocks.

Another alternative is to take the three mile or so hike to Bear Canyon. Once you've hiked down the initial trail and reached Switzer's Camp, go up the canyon to Bear Canyon trail. A primitive campsite, a seasonal stream, and careful boulder hopping await. Bring a water bottle. Note: The small parking lot fills up early on the weekends.

Hours: Open daily 8am to dusk.

Admission: $5 per vehicle for an Adventure Pass.

Ages: 5 years and up.

TEMESCAL GATEWAY PARK   ☼

(310) 454-1395 / www.smmc.ca.gov $
15601 Sunset Boulevard, Pacific Palisades   ⛄
(From Pacific Coast Highway [1], head N. on Temescal Canyon Rd., cross Sunset Blvd. into the park. [TG-631 A4])

This comely wilderness park is particularly pretty in the spring when the wildflowers are blooming profusely. Dirt trails meander throughout. Follow the one-and-a-half-mile trail that winds uphill, under shade trees, back through the canyon along the seasonal creek and to a bridge and waterfall. Picnic tables are scattered throughout the park, so bring a sack lunch.

Hours: Open daily sunrise to sunset.
Admission: $5 per vehicle.
Ages: All

TOPANGA STATE PARK   ☼

(818) 880-0350 / parks.ca.gov $
1501 Will Rogers State Park Road, Pacific Palisades   ⛄
(From Pacific Coast Highway [1], exit N. on Sunset Blvd., L. on Will Rogers State Park Rd. From San Diego Fwy [405], exit W. on Sunset Blvd., R. on Will Rogers State Park Rd. [TG-631 C4])

Believe it or not, this massive state park, actually a huge natural preserve, is all contained within the Los Angeles city limits. Thirty-six miles of hiking trails goes through canyons, hills, and cliffs of the Santa Monica Mountains. The trailhead for the park is at WILL ROGERS STATE HISTORIC PARK. (Look under the Museums section.)

Hours: Open daily 8am - sunset.
Admission: $3 per vehicle; $2 for seniors.
Ages: 5 years and up.

TOWSLEY CANYON   ☼

(661) 255-2974 / www.smmc.ca.gov   !
24255 The Old Road, Newhall
(Exit Golden State Fwy [5] on Calgrove and go W. back under the freeway, S. on The Old Road. Look for entrance signs. [TG-4640 F4])

This beautiful mountain wilderness park contains some spectacular geological structures. First, visit the nature center located at Canyon View trailhead, which contains displays on the history of the park. These include old photographs, taxidermied animals, and artifacts from the days when this area was an oil boom town. A picnic area and restrooms are here, too. Hiking trails range from easy to difficult. The two-mile Canyon View loop trail is a mostly moderate hike with a few short, steep grades. The five-and-a-half-mile Towsley View loop trail has more strenuous grades. This trail, which hooks up to Wiley Canyon, parallels the creek as it goes past grassy areas, the Narrows (where there are unique rock formations), and old oil drilling grounds. Be on the lookout for seasonal wildflowers, plus valley and coastal live oak trees, and animals that share this habitat. The Wiley Canyon trail is two miles round trip and a fairly easy walk. Also see EAST AND RICE CANYON, listed in this section, as that park is just down the road.

Hours: Open daily sunrise to sunset.

Admission: Free

Ages: 3 years and up.

TROUTDALE

(818) 889-9993   *$$$*

2468 Troutdale Drive, Agoura Hills

(Exit Ventura Fwy [101] S. on Kanan Rd., L. on Troutdale Dr. [TG-587 H3])

"Fishy, fishy in a brook/ Daddy caught him with a hook./ Mammy fried him in a pan/ And baby ate him like a man." (Childcraft, Poems and Rhymes, 1966)

Troutdale is in a woodsy setting with two small ponds to fish from - perfect for beginners. There are logs to sit on around the perimeter of the ponds. The entrance price includes a bamboo fishing pole and bait. For an extra 50¢, you can get your fish cleaned. Munch at the snack bar or bring a picnic lunch to eat while you're catching dinner. Be sure to pick up a flyer that has recipe ideas.

Hours: Open Mon. - Fri., 10am - 4pm; Sat. - Sun., 9am - 4pm. Weekend hours are extended during the summer.

Admission: $3 per person, fishing or not. Fish prices vary depending on its length. For instance, a rainbow trout that is 10" - 11" long costs $4.25.

Ages: 3 years and up.

VASQUEZ ROCKS

(661) 268-0840 / parks.co.la.ca.us   *!*

10700 E. Escondido Canyon Road, Agua Dulce

(Exit Antelope Valley Fwy [14] N. on Agua Dulce Canyon Rd., R. on Escondido Canyon Rd. Follow the signs along the way. [TG-4373 F4])

This park became an instant favorite with my boys. The Ranger Station, housed in a barn with corralled horses outside, sets the mood for this all-natural, rustic park. Some of the unusual rock formations are almost triangular in shape, jutting practically straight up from the ground. They have ridges along their sides making them moderately easy to climb, although my kids also climbed much higher (to the tops!) than my heart could take. For those who don't like heights, there are several smaller rocks to conquer, and plenty of walking trails.

If you experience "deja vu" while here, it's probably because this park has been used in numerous commercials and films, such as *The Flintstones*, as well as westerns and science fiction thrillers. Tip: Call before you come because sections of the park are closed when filming is taking place.

Vasquez Rocks, named for an outlaw who hid among the rocks here, also contains Tatavian Indian sites and a seasonal stream. Be forewarned - drinking water is not available in the park. Camping for organized youth groups is allowed.

Hours: Open daily 8am to sunset.

Admission: Free

Ages: 3 years and up.

VINCENT LUGO PARK

(626) 308-2875 / www.sangabrielcity.com
Wells Street, San Gabriel
(Exit San Bernardino Fwy [10] N. on Ramona St., R. on Wells St. [TG-596 D6])

There are three great play areas immediately visible here: A small enclosed one for toddlers; one with a rocket structure to climb up and slide down; and another that is just fun. In the summertime a very small enclosed wading pool is open. A sand pit, lots of grassy running space, and picnic tables help classify this park as a good one.

According to my "park-smart" kids, however, the best part of the park is across the service road and to the south, almost hidden from sight. Children can play on the oversized cement sea creatures that have surfaced here, such as an octopus and whale. Shouts of, "this is the best!" came from my kids as they slid down the sea serpent that is wrapped around a lighthouse. Another giant sea serpent is curled around a rocky hill, which has a huge shade tree growing from it, plus a slide to go down. Like a chest filled with gold on the bottom of the ocean floor, this nautical park was a treasure of a find!

Hours: Open daily 7:30am - 10pm.
Admission: Free
Ages: All

WHITTIER NARROWS RECREATION AREA

(626) 575-5526 or (626) 444-1872 / parks.co.la.ca.us
Rosemead Boulevard and Santa Anita Avenue, South El Monte
(There are a few different entrances - Exit Pomona Fwy [60] N. on Rosemead Blvd. to the athletic facilities; exit S. on Santa Anita Ave. to the lake and park; exit S. on Peck, R. on Durfee to the nature center. [TG-636 J5])

Whittier Narrows will broaden your horizons with the scope of its recreational activities. This expansive 1,100-acre park offers something for every age, interest, and activity level in your family. The section of park on the northern side of the freeway is for the sports-oriented with sixteen lighted tennis courts, six soccer fields, seven baseball diamonds, an archery range, a trap and skeet shooting range, a model plane airfield, a model car track, playgrounds, bike trails, and a bicycle motocross (BMX) track - (626) 575-5521. Check out the adjacent AMERICAN HERITAGE PARK / MILITARY MUSEUM, listed under the Museums section.

Don't want to make waves? Visit the placid Legg Lake, (562) 434-6121, which is south of the freeway. Pedal boat rentals are available here at $15 a half hour and available only on the weekends. Kids can have a "reel" fun time fishing here, too. Model boat races usually take place on Sunday afternoons. The pretty parkland surrounding the lake has shade trees, large grass areas, and playgrounds. A very pleasant, three-plus mile, hard-packed dirt hiking/biking trail goes around the odd-shaped lake and can actually be finished, or started, at the nature center down the road, or entirely within the park.

For those who hear nature calling, the nature center is located at 1000 Durfee, (626) 575-5523. The center is small, but it has live frogs, snakes, and turtles as well as a few taxidermied animals. We saw cardinals and blue jays at the bird feeders just outside. Ask about the center's hour-and-a-half guided school tours. Knowledgeable docents lead the kids on a hike, pointing out and explaining about the plants and animals seen along the way. Students will also listen to a ranger talk regarding the displays in the nature center building. Another tour option is taking a forty-five-minute tractor-drawn hayride around the area. The ranger talk is included in this tour, too. Bring a sack lunch to enjoy at the picnic site here. Note: Hayrides are available for individuals and families every Saturday, too, at 10am. Inquire about other park programs, such as the Jr. Ranger program for ages 7 to 12 years old.

Hours: The park is open daily sunrise - sunset. The nature center is usually open Mon. - Sat., 9:30am - 5pm; Sun., 11am - 5pm. Closed Christmas. Call to make tour reservations.

Admission: Parking is free on weekdays; $3 on weekends and holidays. Admission and parking are free at the nature center. The hiking tour is $10 total for up to sixty students. The hayride is $50 total for up to fifty children. The Sat. hayride is $2 for adults; $1 for children.

Ages: All

WILDERNESS PRESERVE
(626) 355-5309
2240 Highland Oaks Drive, Arcadia
(Exit Interstate Fwy [210] N. on Santa Anita Ave., R. on Elkins Ave., L. on Highland Oaks. [TG-537 E7])

This wilderness park/preserve is in the foothills of the mountains, on the same street as residential housing, A short dirt trail through the shade trees loops around a large grassy area. Plenty of picnic tables are scattered among the woods. A picnic shelter with enough picnic tables for a busload, or two, is on the grounds, next to the kitchen facility that has two sinks, a freezer, a refrigerator, and an oven. This shelter area is available for group rental and also has a fire ring with amphitheater-type seating. Call before you come to ask if the Santa Anita creek, kept in check by controlling the water from the Santa Ana dam, is flowing. If so, get at least your feet wet - so refreshing on a hot summer's day. A swimming hole at the north end of the creek usually has three or four feet of water, regardless if the dam is flowing or not.

The nature center contains quite a few glass-encased, taxidermied animals. We looked at barn owls, ravens, a gold eagle, black bear, mountain lion, coyote, raccoon, and lots more. The building also has a mounted insect collection and a few live snakes. Ask about the many classes that the park offers, including merit badge classes.

Hours: Open January through May and October through December on Fri. only 8:30am - 4:30pm, weather permitting. Open the summer months and September, Mon. - Fri., 8:30am - 7pm. Weekend admission is by advanced reservation only.

Admission: Free

Ages: All

WILLIAM S. HART MUSEUM AND PARK
(661) 254-4584 - museum; (661) 259-0855 - park and camping /
www.hartmuseum.org
24151 San Fernando Road, Newhall

See WILLIAM S. HART MUSEUM AND PARK under the Museums
section.

ADVENTURE PLAYGROUND
(949) 786-0854
1 Beech Tree Lane, Irvine
(Exit San Diego Fwy [405] S. on Jeffrey, which turns into University Dr., R. on Beech Tree. It's in
the University Community Park. [TG-890 C1])

This park is a dream come true for children, as they are actually encouraged
to play in the mud! In warm weather, they can go down a waterslide (i.e. a tarp-
covered hill with a hose) into the mud, and ooze their way through an obstacle
course. Tip: Call to make sure that the water is being turned on the day you plan
to come - no water, no mud. Bring a change of clothes for the kids (and you).
There is an outdoor shower.

Drier play equipment includes kid-size buildings and a big wooden climbing
structure. Kids 6 years and older can add on to the little shanty town here. After
completing a safety course (yea!) they are free to use the wood, hammer, and
nails provided by the park to build onto existing forts, clubhouses, and castles -
whatever they imagine the structures to be. If your child is a regular here, he/she
can stake a plot of land and construct his/her own building.

Some of the special classes offered (for a small fee) include Woodworking,
Crafts, Campfire Cooking, and many different others.

Shade is scarce in Adventure Playground, but fun isn't. Bring a picnic lunch
to enjoy either in here or just outside the gates at University Community Park.
This spacious grassy park has non-muddy playgrounds, a Frisbee golf course,
and open areas for field sports and roller hockey, which is offered a few days a
week.

Note: Close-toed shoes are required at Adventure Playground. The best
times to come are on Saturdays or after 2pm during the week as day campers
often ~~invade~~ visit this unique play area. Note: Look under the June Calendar
section for details on the Adventure Playground in Huntington Beach. It is only
open, however, for five weeks in the summer.

Hours: Open in the summer Tues. - Sat., 10am - 5pm. Open the rest of
the year Tues. - Fri., 2:30pm - 5pm; Sat., 10am - 5pm.

Admission: Free. Groups must call for reservations, and they are charged a
fee.

Ages: 5 - 14 years. Note: Kids under 6 years must be accompanied by
an adult at every activity.

ALISO AND WOOD CANYONS REGIONAL PARK
(949) 831-2790 / www.oc.ca.gov/hbp
Alicia Parkway and Aliso Creek Road, Laguna Niguel

(Exit San Diego Fwy [5] W. on Crown Valley Pkwy., R. on La Paz Rd., L. on Aliso Creek Rd., L. on Alicia Pkwy., R. on Awma. The entrance is 500 ft. S. of Alicia Pkwy. and Aliso Creek Rd. [TG-951 F1])

This regional park has 3,400 acres of wilderness sanctuary to explore by hiking or biking. You and your child will see everything that patience allows - coastal sage, chaparral, oak woodlands, open grassland meadows, canyons, and creeks, plus wildlife such as deer, possums, coyotes, bobcats, and lizards.

This huge park is like life, offering many paths to choose from. Take a trail from here into the adjacent Laguna Niguel Regional Park; ride the twelve-mile Aliso Creek Bikeway, which basically follows along Alicia Parkway; or choose from several other paths inside the park. We walked the Aliso Trail. The first part is paved and rather bland, scenically speaking. As we reached the dirt pathway and went into the hills, the terrain and scenery became much more interesting. (Strollers and bikes can go here, but it does get a bit bumpy.) Just down the road a bit is the Nature Center which houses Indian artifacts, taxidermied animals, photographs of wild flowers in blooms, and maps.

There are numerous caves, or overhangs, throughout the park. A few are open to the public. Past the Nature Center, or Gate 2, is Cave Rock. Kids enjoy climbing up into Cave Rock, and sliding back down. Further back on the trail, is Dripping Cave, also called - and this has much more kid-appeal - Robbers Cave. Legend has it that bandits used this cave as a hideout after a robbery! At one time the holes inside supposedly had wooden pegs to hold their saddle bags, and bags of booty. Tell this to your kids and let their imaginations take over. If you have the time and energy, keep on going to Coyote Run, deeper into the heart of the park. Tip: Bring water!

Look up the ORANGE COUNTY NATURAL HISTORY MUSEUM, under the Museums section, for information on this museum that's located at the trailhead of the park.

> **Hours:**   The park is open 7am to sunset. The Nature Center is open Wed. - Sun., 11am - 5pm.
> **Admission:** $2 per vehicle.
> **Ages:**   2 years and up.

AROVISTA SKATE PARK

(714) 990-7100 / www.ci.brea.ca.us
Elm Street and Sievers Avenue, Brea
(Exit Orange Fwy [57] W. on Imperial Hwy., L. on Brea Blvd., R. on Elm. [TG-739 A1])

This 10,000 square-foot cement skate park has a kidney pool, pyramid, table top, quarter pipes, rails, and street section. Skateboarders and rollerbladers only - no bikes allowed! Spectators are welcome to gather 'round and watch the show! Wearing a helmet and knee and elbow pads is strictly enforced. The surrounding park also has baseball diamonds, a playground, and open grassy areas.

> **Hours:**   The skate park and park are open daily 7am - dusk.
> **Admission:** Free
> **Ages:**   7 years and up.

ATLANTIS PLAY CENTER

(714) 892-6015

9301 Atlantis Way, Garden Grove

(Exit the Garden Grove Fwy [22] S. on Magnolia, L. on minster, L. on Atlantis Way. It's N. of the Garden Grove Park. [TG-828 C1])

This "lost island" park is quite a find. Atlantis Play Center is a wonderful, large, enclosed play area for kids of all ages. Several different playgrounds are scattered around the park that feature slides, tubes, swings, sand pits, grassy expanses, and big, concrete aquatic creatures to play on. The sea serpent slide is a favorite. The green rolling hills are perfect for picnicking. Numerous shade trees make the park surprisingly cool, even in the heat of the summer. A full-service snack bar is open daily during the summer, and usually on the weekends the rest of the year.

One of my boys' favorite things to do is to play in and amongst the bushes that go around the perimeter of the park. The bushes become hideouts, forts, a pirate's landing, or whatever - a little imagination goes a long way!

Just outside Atlantis is the Garden Grove Park, with more play equipment and wide open grassy areas.

Hours: Open in the summer Tues. - Sat., 10am - 4pm; Sun., noon - 4pm. Open the rest of the year Tues. - Fri., 10am - 2pm; Sat., 10am - 4pm; Sun., noon - 4pm.

Admission: $1 for ages 2 and older; children under 2 are free. Adults are not admitted without a child.

Ages: 1½ - 12 years.

BEEBE PARK / MISSION VIEJO SKATE PARK

(949) 470-3061 / www.ci.mission-viejo.ca.us

24190 Olympiad Road, Mission Viejo

(Exit San Diego Fwy [5] N.E. on La Paz Rd., go to end and turn L. on Olympiad. [TG-892 F7])

This 9.8 acre sports park also sports the "latest" in sports - a skateboard park. This 9,000 square foot unsupervised concrete park has bowls, a vert wall, bauer box, rails, spine, pyramid, hips, steps, and ramps. Helmet and elbow and knee pads are required.

Hours: Open 7am - dusk.

Admission: Free

Ages: 7 years and up.

BOLSA CHICA ECOLOGICAL RESERVE

(714) 846-1114 - interpretative center; (714) 840-1575 - tour info /
www.bolsachica.org

17851 Pacific Coast Highway, Huntington Beach

(Exit San Diego Fwy [405] S. on Bolsa Chica Rd., R. on Warner Ave., L. on Pacific Coast Highway. The reserve is opposite Bolsa Chica State Beach. [TG-857 B2])

This 300-acre, saltwater wetland reserve is home to a variety of plant and waterfowl such as avocets, egrets, plovers, sand pipers, ducks, and terns. We also saw herons, and a few brown pelicans that swooped down to scoop up fish. Bird lovers should bring binoculars. Although the nesting and breeding islands are protected by a chain link fence, you may cross over the wooden bridge to walk along an easy and stroller-friendly, mile-and-a-half trail that loops through the reserve, and partially along the highway. No bikes are allowed. My little explorers especially liked walking down to inspect the water and its inhabitants, a little closer than I felt comfortable with. Free, guided tours are given the first Saturday of every month beginning at 9am.

A small Interpretative Center is housed in a trailer on the corner of the reserve, at 3842 Warner Avenue and Pacific Coast Highway. Inside are local ecology displays such as pictures of birds in the area, a rattlesnake skin, a preserved stingray and leopard shark, a touch table, and information panels on the value of wetlands. Interested in helping take care of this area? Clean-up Saturday, where volunteers pick up trash and remove non-native plants, is held the last Saturday of each month. Note: For more fun in the sun, BOLSA CHICA STATE BEACH is directly across the street from the reserve. (See the Beaches section for details.)

> **Hours:** The Reserve is open daily 8am to sunset. The Center is usually open Tues. - Fri., 10am - 4pm; Sat. 9am - noon; Sun., 12:30pm - 3:30pm.
>
> **Admission:** Free
>
> **Ages:** All

BOYSEN PARK / ANAHEIM TENNIS CENTER

(714) 991-9090 - tennis center

975 S. State College Boulevard, Anaheim

(Exit Artesia Fwy [91] S. on State College Blvd. The park is at the intersection of State College Blvd. and Wagner. [TG-769 C6])

Take off to this park whose main attraction is a large gray cement airplane. The wings are tipped just enough so kids can climb up on them (wingwalkers!) and into the instrumentless cockpit. Other park amenities include picnic tables, a playground, baseball fields, and sand volleyball courts. The adjacent schoolyard, available to use when school is not in session, has basketball courts, a few scattered playgrounds, and more baseball diamonds. The park wraps around the Anaheim Tennis Center. Get in the swing of things by playing on one of the Center's twelve lighted courts and/or the ball-machine court.

> **Hours:** The park is open daily. The Tennis Center is open Mon. - Thurs., 8am - 10pm; Fri., 8am - 9pm; Sat. - Sun., 8am - 6pm.
>
> **Admission:** The park is free. Tennis costs vary from $3 an hour for adults to $7 an hour, depending on the time of day. Children 11 and under are $1.50 an hour.
>
> **Ages:** All for the park.

BROOKHURST COMMUNITY PARK

2271 W. Crescent Avenue, Anaheim

(Going S. on Santa Ana Fwy [5], exit S. on Brookhurst St, R. on Crescent. Going N. on 5, exit W. on La Palma Ave., L. on Brookhurst, R. on Crescent. From Crescent, turn R. on Ventura, which turns into Greenacre. The park is right there. [TG-768 D4])

Baseball diamonds, basketball courts, a few picnic tables, and barbecue pits are here, but more importantly, your kids can come to this park and walk on the moon! "Crater Park," our nickname for it, resembles the surface of the moon with play equipment inside crater-shaped areas. There are slides, swings, climbing structures, a rocket ship (for blasting off to parts unknown), and a big white cement walkway that interconnects the play areas. Being here almost eclipses playing at other parks.

Hours: Open daily sunrise to sunset.
Admission: Free
Ages: 2 years and up.

CARBON CANYON REGIONAL PARK

(714) 996-5252 / www.ocparks.com
4442 Carbon Canyon Road, Brea
(Exit Riverside Fwy [91] N. on Imperial Hwy., R. on Valencia Ave., R. on Carbon Canyon Rd. [TG-709 J7])

Talk about recreational opportunities! Carbon Canyon is 124 acres big and offers everything for the sports-minded and fun-loving family. There are tennis courts, volleyball courts, horseshoe pits, softball fields, a huge open field for whatever other sport you feel like playing, and five great playgrounds scattered throughout the park.

Other activities include taking a hike to the ten-acre Redwood Grove, cycling on the one-and-a-half-mile paved trail, or riding the equestrian trail that accesses Chino Hills State Park. The beautiful four-acre lake in the middle of the park has two fishing piers, but it is not stocked. Bring suntan lotion and food, and have a great day.

Hours: Open November through March 7am - 6pm. Open April through October 7am - 9pm.
Admission: $2 vehicle entrance Mon. - Fri.; $4 on Sat. - Sun.; $5 on holidays.
Ages: All

CARL THORNTON PARK

(714) 571-4200 / www.goodtime.net/sfsan.htm
1801 W. Segerstrom Avenue, Santa Ana
(Going E. on San Diego Fwy [405], exit N. on Fairview Rd., R. on Segerstrom Ave. Going S. on Costa Mesa Fwy [55], exit E. on Dyer Rd., which turns into Segerstrom Ave. [TG-859 C1])

The front part of this park is a huge open area, great for kite flying because the trees are short (at least right now). A small creek runs through this area, ending in a big pond that attracts a lot of ducks, geese, and sea gulls. (Don't get goosed by the geese!) For your sporting pleasure, there are also two baseball diamonds.

At the northeast corner of the park, accessible by paved pathways, is an enclosed "barrier free" playground. This means that it has special apparatus designed for disabled children. One of the swings can hold a wheelchair-bound child. A sand play area, with water fountains to make sand castles, is elevated for kids in wheelchairs. Other play areas are great for all kinds of kids, as there are slides, tunnels, and things to climb. Stone turrets give the playground a castle-like setting. A large grassy area is inside the enclosure for safe, run-around play.

Hours: Open daily 8am - 10pm.
Admission: Free
Ages: All

CEDAR GROVE PARK

(714) 573-3325 / www.tustinca.org
11385 Pioneer Road, Tustin
(Exit Santa Ana Fwy [5] N. on Jamboree Rd., L. on Tustin Ranch Rd., R. on Pioneer Way. It's located at the intersection of Pioneer Way and Pioneer Rd. [TG-830 H2])

This park is unique in that it has play equipment for all ages, plus a half-circle basketball court. Starting at the parking lot, follow the winding pathway (reminiscent of a snake's trail), back to three interconnecting playgrounds which are geared for ages 2 to 5, 6 to 10, and 10 years and up, respectively. The toddler playground, built in the sand, has a wooden train to board, a castle play structure (complete with a drawbridge), a heavy-duty sand digger, and an area that has a few water spigots for making wet sand creations. Tip: Bring a change of pants for your child. Go over or under a wooden bridge to reach the next play area which is padded with dense foam. Kids can pretend to sail the seas on the wooden Adventure Ship, as well as play on the swings, wavy slides, monkey bars, rings, climbing structure, and cargo net. Older kids have their own small play area. It has several colorful metal ladders and geometric shapes for kids to climb on or across. (Being practical minded, I wondered if the shapes had a particular function or purpose, but my imaginative kids had a great time just playing on them.) Other fun things here include trying to balance yourself on a rope ladder without it twisting you around and holding on to S-shaped poles as their bases spin around. Plenty of picnic tables line the playground's pathway.

The huge, adjacent grassy area has numerous cedar trees around its perimeters. Next to this is a grove of shady pine trees with picnic tables nestled underneath.

Hours: Open daily sunrise to sunset.
Admission: Free
Ages: All

CRAIG REGIONAL PARK

(714) 990-0271 / www.ocparks.com
3300 N. State College Boulevard, Fullerton
(Exit Orange Fwy [57] W. on Imperial, L. on State College. [TG-739 C2])

124 acres and three separate playgrounds make this an ideal park for all ages. The upper area is hilly and woodsy, blessed with lots of pine trees. The lower slopes flatten out, with alder and willow trees. One of the playgrounds meets the ADA (Americans with Disabilities Act) Standards; one is geared towards little ones; and another is designed for slightly older kids, as it has steeper slides.

There are picnic gazebos, baseball diamonds, volleyball courts, tennis courts, racquetball courts, and a lake. Fishing is allowed in the lake, but it isn't stocked so bring your wiggliest worms. The Nature Center has dioramas depicting the changing environment of animals in Craig Park and the surrounding areas.

Hours: Open daily April through October from 7am - 9pm. Open daily November through March from 7am - 6pm. The Nature Center is open Sat. - Sun., 10am - 3pm.

Admission: $2 per vehicle Mon. - Fri., $4 Sat. - Sun.; $5 on holidays.

Ages: All

CROWN VALLEY COMMUNITY PARK

(949) 362-4350 / www.ci.laguna-niguel.ca.us
29751 Crown Valley Parkway, Laguna Niguel
(Exit San Diego Fwy [5] W. on Crown Valley Pkwy. The park is W. of La Paz Rd. [TG-951 G4])

This delightful park has something that will appeal to each member of your family. Several short trails wind through the hillside botanical garden. Some of the trails are cement, and therefore stroller-friendly (although uphill), and some are dirt paths with wooden steps. Hike up to the picturesque viewpoint and enjoy beautiful landscaping along the way. A playground at the base of the hill has swings, slides, and a wooden ship to climb aboard. Picnic tables are scattered throughout the park. Summer concerts are given on an outdoor stage with tiered seating on a grassy hill. At the top of another hill is a soccer field and baseball field. Between the park office and the adjacent Y.M.C.A. is a regulation-size swimming pool that is open year round to the public and for swim meets. Diving competitions also take place on the two low diving boards, two high dives, and a (really high) diving platform. Cement stadium seats are on one side of the pool. The canopied-covered wading pool is great for your little tadpoles. Finally, a three-quarter-mile bike path here connects to Laguna Niguel Regional Park. This park is a *crown* jewel in Laguna Niguel.

Hours: The park is open daily 6am - 10pm. The pool is open for public swim sessions year round Mon. - Fri., 1pm - 4pm; Sat. - Sun., noon - 4pm. It's open in the summer for an additional session Mon. - Fri., 9am - noon.

Admission: Free to the park. Swim sessions are $2 for adults; $1.50 for seniors and children 2 - 12.

Ages: All

CRYSTAL COVE STATE PARK

(949) 494-3539 / parks.ca.gov
E. Coast Highway, between Laguna Beach and Newport Beach, Laguna Beach
(Take the San Diego Fwy [405] or the Costa Mesa Fwy [55] to the Corona Del Mar Fwy [73], which turns into MacArthur Blvd. Exit MacArthur Blvd. S. on E. Coast Highway. A gated entrance is just opposite Newport Coast Dr. The visitor center and ranger station are farther down on Coast Hwy., on the L. [TG-920 C7])

This 2,800-acre, largely undeveloped state park encompasses everything from coastal and canyon areas on one side of the freeway, to three-and-a-half miles of sandy beach on the other side. The size of the park allows a variety of programs and fun things to do, such as guided tidepool tours (when the tide is low), whale watching, fishing, hiking, and camping, or just enjoying the beach! An eighteen-mile round trip, moderate mountain bike trail winds through the park also. Bikers share the back country hills with deer, roadrunners, and other wildlife. Ask for a trail map.

Environmental camping - meaning whatever you backpack in you take out - is an adventure in the "back country" of the park. The closest campsite is a two-and-half-mile hike. No open fires are allowed. With twenty miles of trails on relatively untouched land, hiking and/or camping here is a real opportunity to commune with nature! Pick up a map at the headquarters.

If you get hungry, the Crystal Cove Shake Shop, serving shakes (try their date shakes) and sandwiches, is across the way at 7408 Pacific Coast Highway, (949) 497-9666. It's open daily 11am to 4pm.

Hours: Open daily sunrise to sunset.

Admission: $3 per vehicle. Camping is $7 a night.

Ages: All

EDISON COMMUNITY CENTER

(714) 960-8870 or (714) 536-5486

21377 Magnolia Street, Huntington Beach

(Exit San Diego Fwy [405] S. on Magnolia. [TG-888 C2])

Although the park is not outstandingly pretty to look at, it is packed with fun things to do. Within its forty acres it has four lighted tennis courts, open to play on a first come first *serve* basis; six racquetball courts; four full basketball courts and several half courts, with lights; two baseball diamonds; lots of open space; a paved trail throughout; a covered picnic area with barbeque pits; a community center building; sand and grass volleyball courts; horseshoes pits (bring your own horseshoes); and a large, sand-based play area complete with slides, swings, tot swings, climbing apparatus, and a section boasting a ship motif.

Hours: The park is open daily dawn to dusk. The community center is open Mon. - Fri., 9am - 9:30pm; Sat., 9am - 5pm.

Admission: Free. Tennis costs only when you want to make a reservation. Reservations are taken beginning at 5pm nightly and are $2 an hour.

Ages: All

EISENHOWER PARK

(714) 744-2225 / www.cityoforange.org

3894 N. Tustin Avenue, Orange

(Exit Costa Mesa Fwy [55] W. on Lincoln, R. on Oceanview, R. at Main to the park. The actual address does you no good in finding the park! [TG-769 J4])

Driving down Lincoln Boulevard, it's easy to miss Eisenhower Park, but it's worth looking for. This park has a stream running through it with almost irresistible stepping stones. You may fish in the lake, although it is not stocked. There are two small play areas for slightly older kids. One area is especially "cool" with a rocket ship play structure, wavy slides, swings, and a big sand area. This big park offers plenty of green rolling hills, plus a few scattered picnic tables and barbecue pits to make your day picnic perfect. Cement pathways make the entire park stroller accessible.

Hours: Open daily sunrise to sunset.
Admission: Free
Ages: All

ENVIRONMENTAL NATURE CENTER   ☼

(949) 645-8489 / www.encenter.org   !
1601 16th Street, Newport Beach
(Take Costa Mesa Fwy [55] S.W. to the end, continue on Newport Blvd., L. on 17th, R. on Irvine Ave., L. on 16th. [TG-889 A6])

This three-and-a-half acre nature center is an almost hidden gem that has been here for more than twenty-five years! Walking back to the trailhead, notice the rocks along the path containing imbedded fossilized shells. Although buildings are around the perimeters of this wooded area, you'll still feel like you're in the midst of nature while walking along the various crisscrossing trails. You'll see a cactus garden, pine trees, woodland trees, and a small rock-lined stream. You can purchase a pamphlet (25¢) at the center to help identify the various plants and animals found here.

The small nature center building has shelves and tables that contain rocks, shells, animals skins, turtle shells, skulls, feathers, and bird's nests, plus many nature-inspired craft ideas. My boys also liked seeing the live snakes, crickets, and lizards in here.

Hours: Open Mon. - Fri., 8am - 4pm; Sat., 8am - 3pm. Closed Sun. and school holidays.
Admission: Free
Ages: 2½ years and up.

FAIRVIEW PARK   ☼

(949) 548-7246 - engineers; (714) 962-5052 - b-day party info /   !
www.livesteamclubs.com/Ocme/Ocme.html
2525 Placentia Avenue, Costa Mesa   ⛫
(Going S.E. on San Diego Fwy [405], exit S. on Brookhurst St., L. on Adams Ave., R. on Placentia., Going N.W. on 405, exit S. on Harbor Blvd., R. on Adams, L. on Placentia. [TG-888 G1])

This spacious park hosts one of the largest model layouts of its kind in Southern California. The Orange County Model Engineers run two miles of track and offer rides for free to park-goers. Bring a picnic, play at the other park amenities, and make a day of it.

Hours: The train is here on the third weekend of each month, 10am - 3:30pm.
Admission: Free
Ages: All

FULLERTON ARBORETUM

(714) 278-3579 - arboretum; (714) 278-2843 - house/museum /
www.arboretum.fullerton.edu

1900 Associated Road, Fullerton

(Exit Orange Fwy [57] W. on Yorba Linda, L. on Associated Rd. [or Campus Dr.] onto California State Fullerton campus. [TG-739 C4])

This twenty-six-acre botanical garden is a delightful, verdant refuge, with flower-lined pathways, a small lake, a stream, and a few bridges. It's big enough to let the kids run loose a little. Take a whiff - the air is perfumed with the scent of roses, mint, and citrus. Garden benches offer a picturesque resting spot, underneath shade trees in the midst of the plants and flowers. Idea: Have your kids dress up and bring your camera for some potentially great shots in a garden setting.

An 1894 Victorian Heritage House, that was the home and office of the first physician in Orange County, is also on the grounds. Older kids will appreciate a tour through the house that has turn-of-the-century furnishings.

There are many special events going on at Fullerton Arboretum throughout the year, including Science Adventure programs, volunteering opportunities, and much more. Please call for details.

Hours: The Arboretum is open daily 8am - 4:45pm. Closed New Year's Day, Thanksgiving, and Christmas. The house is open for tours Sun., 2pm - 4pm. Call to make an appointment for other days and hours. The house is closed for tours in January and August.

Admission: The Arboretum has a donation box by the entrance gate. The house tour is a $2 for adults; $1 per child.

Ages: All

GENERAL THOMAS F. RILEY WILDERNESS PARK

(949) 459-1687

30952 Oso Parkway, Coto De Caza

(Exit San Diego Fwy [5] E. on Oso Pkwy. It's 6 1/2 miles off the freeway right before Oso dead-ends at Coto De Caza Dr. There are also entrances to the park on Coto De Caza. [TG-923 B5])

This hilly wilderness preserve is a sanctuary for native wildlife - coyotes, mountain lions, raccoons, mule deer, a multitude of birds, and lots more. It's comprised of hills with protected sagebrush, oak trees, and other plant life, plus a pond and seasonal creek. Rugged dirt trails (stroller occupants would have a bumpy ride) loop throughout the park and visitors are asked not to stray from them. Although housing developments border part of the park, miles of undeveloped canyons, tree groves, and Santa Ana Mountain peaks can still be seen from the viewpoints.

Take a self-guiding nature hike, or sign up for a guided walk or program. The park makes a wonderful outdoor "classroom" and offers students of all ages firsthand knowledge about the environment. Some of the programs offered include merit badge classes, which could include a topical game and craft; Bat Habits, which includes a slide show and short hike into bat country; Star Watch, designed for viewing and learning about the stars and moon; Jr. Rangers, which is a six-week, springtime class; special classes for toddlers; and more. Most of the programs have a minimal fee.

The small nature center contains a few taxidermy animals and a game that kids can take on the trail to help them identify objects they find along the way. A few picnic tables are under shade trees in front of the nature center. Note: The rangers are very friendly and dedicated to enabling children to learn more about the wilds of Orange County.

Hours: Open daily 7am - sunset.
Admission: $2 parking fee.
Ages: 3 years and up.

HART PARK

(714) 744-7272 / www.cityoforange.org
701 S. Glassell Street, Orange
(Exit Garden Grove Fwy [22] N. on Glassell. [TG-799 G6])

Stone walls add to the beauty of this spacious park. The northern section has lots of picnic tables and barbecue pits, a playground, trees to climb, a few tennis courts (although kids were roller skating on them when we visited), a sand volleyball court (or, for younger kids, a sandbox with a net), and a swimming pool.

The southern section has a large open grassy area lined with trees, plus soccer fields and a few baseball diamonds. One of the diamonds has stadium seating and lights.

Hours: The park is open daily 8am - 10pm. The pool is open in the summer daily, with one-hour-and-fifteen-minute swim sessions, Mon. and Wed., 2:30pm - 8:15pm; Tues., Thurs. - Sun., 1pm - 5:15pm.
Admission: The park is free. Each swim session costs $2 for adults; $1.50 for ages 17 and under.
Ages: All

HARVARD COMMUNITY ATHLETIC PARK

(949) 551-0601 / www.ci.irvine.ca.us
14701 Harvard Avenue, Irvine
(Exit Santa Ana Fwy [5] S.W. on Jamboree Rd., L. on Walnut Ave., R. on Harvard. [TG-860 E1])

This expansive park has three soccer fields, six lighted baseball/softball fields, picnic tables, barbecue grills, and open play areas. The big attraction for skateboarders is the concrete corner skate park which has a pool, ramps, verts, grind boxes, grinding poles, and other standard skate street equipment. Safety equipment - helmet and knee and elbow pads - is required.

Hours: The park is open daily dawn to dusk. The skate park is open during school hours, Mon. - Fri., 2pm - 8pm; Sat., 10am - 9pm; Sun., noon - 8pm. During the summer and on school breaks, it is open daily 10am - 9pm.
Admission: Free
Ages: All for the park; 7 and up for the skate park.

HERITAGE PARK (Irvine)

(949) 724-6750 - youth services center; (949) 559-0472 - Aquatics
Complex; (949) 552-8218 - athletic field / www.ci.irvine.ca.us

14301 Yale Avenue, Irvine

(Going S. on Santa Ana Fwy [5], exit S.W. on Culver Dr., L. on Walnut Ave., L. on Yale Ave. Going N. on 5, exit S.W. on Jeffrey Rd., R. on Walnut Ave., R. on Yale Ave. [TG-860 G2])

Heritage Park is large community park with the emphasis on community. The park has a wooden water tower slide that is almost as tall as a real water tower - whoosh on down!! There are two terrific playgrounds here. One has a pirate ship with bridges, slides, and a ropes obstacle course - kid heaven! Several buildings line the perimeter. The center area has a beautiful small lake (with numerous ducks) to skate or stroller around, and lots of grassy, gently rolling hills to play on. There are also basketball courts, twelve lighted tennis courts, and four lighted fields for organized sports play.

Several buildings line the perimeter of the park, such as the youth services center, which has a few billiard tables and other games; the library; and the IRVINE FINE ART CENTER (look under the Arts and Crafts section). The Heritage Park Aquatics Complex is just around the corner on Walnut Avenue. Two of their pools are open for recreational swim in the summer.

Hours: The park is open daily. The pools are open daily in the summer Mon. - Fri., 1pm - 3pm; Sat. - Sun., 1pm - 4pm.

Admission: The park is free. Swimming costs $2 for adults; $1 for ages 17 and under.

Ages: All

HILLCREST PARK

Brea Boulevard, Fullerton

(Exit the Riverside Fwy [91] N. on Harbor Blvd., R. on Brea Blvd., R. into the park. [TG-738 H5])

For some Fullerton fun, try Hillcrest Park. This huge hilly park has a winding road throughout, with parking lots in several different spots along the way. We saw some creative kids using cardboard to slide down a hill, which probably isn't great for the grass, but it looked like fun. Hillcrest has a few woodland areas with dirt paths for hiking. There are also some play areas, picnic tables, and barbecue pits. The wooden structure at the base of the hill, on Lemon Street, is in the shape of a ship.

Hours: Open daily.

Admission: Free

Ages: All

HUNTINGTON CENTRAL PARK / SHIPLEY'S NATURE CENTER

(714) 960-8847 / www.stockteam.com/centpk.html

Goldenwest Street, Huntington Beach

(Exit San Diego Fwy [405] S. on Goldenwest St. It's between Slater and Ellis Ave. [TG-857 H2])

This gigantic park offers many options for all kinds of fun: Fish at the un-stocked lake, which is tucked in the corner; let the kids go wild on the playgrounds; ride bikes along the cement pathways that crisscross all over; enjoy the sports fields; play the Frisbee golf course on the west side of Goldenwest Street, which offers instructions, maps and an opportunity to purchase your own disc; see a weekend polo match or horse show at the Equestrian Center (call [714] 848-6565 for details); check out books from the huge library off Talbert Street (see HUNTINGTON BEACH CENTRAL LIBRARY under the Potpourri section); play at Adventure Playground for summertime fun (see the June Calendar section for details); or go for a nature walk anytime at Shipley's Nature Center at the northern end of the park.

We turned the easy, fifteen-minute walk around Shipley's Nature Center into over an hour of delightful exploration. The dirt trail, which is not stroller-friendly, leads around a small pond that supports diverse animal life - frogs, turtles, and butterflies. We hiked the trail through tall grass, to the pine trees, and looped back around to the small Nature Center building. Inside the building are a few taxidermied animals and other nature exhibits.

If you'd like to have breakfast or lunch in the park, eat at ALICE'S BREAKFAST IN THE PARK. (Look under the Edible Adventures section for details.)

Hours: The park is open daily sunrise to sunset. The Nature Center is open daily in the summer 8am - 6pm; open the rest of the year 8:30am - 5:30pm.

Admission: Free

Ages: All

IRVINE LAKE

(714) 649-9111 / www.fishinghotpage.com/irvine

4501 Santiago Canyon Road, Orange

(Exit Costa Mesa Fwy [55] E. on Chapman; Chapman turns into Santiago Canyon Rd. [TG-801 E6])

Casting around for fun places to go with your little fisherman? Irvine Lake is not picturesque with its huge dredges, but it is a large lake stocked seasonally with a variety of fish such as bass, trout, catfish, crappie, and bluegill. There is a five fish limit per person. (I wish I had this problem!) The dryer areas of the lake bed serve as a terrific place to bird watch. We saw herons, pelicans, cranes, and at least a half dozen other birds I feel like I should be able to identify.

Towards the entrance is a small playground, a grassy area, a horseshoe pit, a volleyball court, a few picnic tables under shade trees, and a very small, almost-guarantee-you'll-catch-something Catch Out Pond stocked with trout. Conveniently, a bait and tackle shop, and even a breakfast and sandwich cafe counter, are also on the grounds. No fishing license is needed. Ask about overnight camping for organized youth groups.

Boat rentals are available. Motorboats are $30 on weekdays (Monday through Thursday), $45 weekends (Friday through Sunday) or holidays; rowboats - $20 on weekdays, $25 on weekends and holidays; and pontoons - $85 on weekdays, $100 on weekends and holidays.

Hours: Open daily 6am - 4pm. Summer twilight hours are Fri. - Sat., 2pm - 11pm. (Hours do fluctuate.)

Admission: Fishing Mon. - Thurs. is $13 for adults; $12 for seniors; $7 for ages 4 - 12; children 3 and under are free. Fishing Fri. - Sun. is $15 for adults; $12 for seniors; $8 for ages 4 - 12. Rates include the entrance fee and up to five fish. Call about twilight rates. The Catch Out Pond is $3 for the gate entry and $4 per pound of each fish that your catch.

Ages: 4 years and up.

IRVINE REGIONAL PARK   ☼

(714) 633-8074 / www.ocparks.com $

1 Irvine Park Road, Orange   🎂

(Exit Costa Mesa Fwy [55] E. on Chapman, N. on Jamboree, which ends at Irvine Regional Park. [TG-800 J3])

Entire days can be spent exploring all there is to see and do at this 477-acre regional park. The middle area is "carved out," with lots of grass for picnic areas, playgrounds, and baseball diamonds. Toddlers through about 8 years old can ride ponies around a track that is open weekdays 11am to 4pm and weekends 10am to 4:30pm. Rides are $3 each. Call (760) 956-8440 for more information. Kids 8 years and older can take a guided horseback ride inside the park Tuesday through Sunday for $25 an hour. Call Country Trails at (714) 538-5860 /www.ctriding.com for further horse back riding rental information. More fun can be had with pedal boat rentals, which are available weekends 10am to 5pm at $9 per half hour. Bike rentals are available weekends 10am to 5pm at $12 per hour for side-by-sides. For more information on the pedal boats and bikes, call (714) 997-3968. Ten-minute, one-third-scale model train rides around the park are available daily 10am to 5pm at $3 per person. This is a fun little trip! Call (714) 997-3968 / www.irvineparkrr.com for more information.

The Interpretive Center, (714) 289-9616, has taxidermied animals to look at; skulls, furs, and animal pelts to touch; a grinding rock to try out; plus displays and information about the wilderness part of the park. Biking, hiking, and equestrian trails are plentiful in Irvine Regional Park with creeks, sagebrush, and animals throughout. Rangers are available for school and scout tours. Also, look up ORANGE COUNTY ZOO, under the Zoos and Animals section, as it's located inside the park.

Hours: Irvine Park is open daily April through October 7am - 9pm. It's open the rest of the year daily 7am - 6pm. The Nature Center is usually open Sat. - Sun., 11am - 3:45pm.

Admission: $2 per vehicle, Mon. - Fri., $4 on Sat. - Sun; $5 on holidays.

Ages: All

LAGUNA HILLS SKATE PARK   ☼

(949) 707-2600 / www.ci.laguna-hills.ca.us   !

25555 Alicia Parkway, Laguna Hills   🎂

(Exit San Diego Fwy [5], S.W. on Alicia Pkwy. [TG-921 H3])

The skate park is part of a community parks and sports center. Skateboarders and bladers can skate at the lighted, 10,000 square-foot cement park that features a pyramid, cones, steps, grinding rails, volcano, and ramps. All participants must wear helmet and knee and elbow pads.

Hours: Open daily 8am - 10pm.
Admission: Free
Ages: 7 years and up.

LAGUNA LAKE PARK

Lakeview Drive and Euclid, Fullerton
(Exit Riverside Fwy [91] N. on Euclid, R. on Lakeview Dr. [TG-738 F2])

Leaping frogs! This lake is literally covered with large lily pads. In contrast to my earlier thinking, I now know that parks don't require a playground to make it "good." It simply must have kid-appeal, and this one does. The dirt path around the long lake is bike and stroller friendly. The marshy reeds are a great place for dragonfly hunting. Bring bread for the ducks, bait for your fishing pole, and enjoy this unusual park. Barbecue pits and picnic tables are here, too.

Hours: Open daily sunrise to sunset.
Admission: Free
Ages: All

LAGUNA NIGUEL REGIONAL PARK

(949) 831-2791 - park; (949) 362-3885 - fishing / www.ocparks.com;
www.lagunaniguellake.com
28241 La Paz Road, Laguna Niguel
(Exit San Diego Fwy [5] W. on Crown Valley Pkwy., R. on La Paz. [TG-951 G1])

This park is 236 acres of adventures waiting to be had. It offers volleyball courts, horseshoe pits, tennis courts, bike trails, an area for flying remote-controlled airplanes, toddler-friendly playgrounds, open grass areas, barbecue pits, and picnic shelters, plus a forty-four acre lake for fishing and boating. No fishing license is required, but day use permits are. The lake is seasonally stocked with catfish and bluegill, with a limit of five fish per person, per day. Bass are strictly catch and release. Fish from the floating docks or rent a boat at $8 an hour. A bait and tackle shop are conveniently located on the park grounds. The shop rents poles for $6 a day. The park tends to get crowded on weekends and holidays, so get an early start!

Hours: Open daily April through October 6am - 9pm. Open daily
November through March 6am - 6pm.
Admission: $2 per vehicle Mon. - Fri.; $4 on Sat. - Sun.; $5 on holidays.
December through April fishing permits cost $14 for adults; $12
for seniors; $10 for ages 16 and younger; May through
November, permits are $12 for adults; $10 for seniors; $8 for
ages 16 and under.
Ages: All

LIBERTY PARK (Westminster)

(714) 895-2860
13900 Monroe Street, Westminster
(Exit Garden Grove Fwy [22] S. on Beach Blvd., L. on Westminster, L. on Monroe. [TG-828 A1])

The park is a typical, medium-sized park with open grassy areas, a few trees, a few picnic tables, a basketball court, and a playground. The real draw, I think, is for skateboarders and bladers. Their play area is a mid-size cement skate park which has a mini-pool, kidney pool, stair-rail plaza, funbox, and a street course. Wearing safety gear - a helmet, knee and elbow pads - is enforced!

Hours: The park and skate park is open daily sunrise to sunset.
Admission: Free
Ages: 6 years and up for the skate park.

MILE SQUARE PARK

(714) 962-5549 - park; (562) 431-6866 - Surrey Cycle Rentals /
www.oc.ca.gov/hbp
16801 Euclid Street, Fountain Valley
(Exit San Diego Fwy [405] N. on Euclid St. [TG-828 F7])

Mile Square Park has everything you need for a full day of family fun, so be there or be *square*. There are picnic areas with barbecue grills, bike trails, baseball fields, a hobby area for flying model planes and rockets, blacktop for racing cars, an archery range (bring your own equipment), and four playgrounds. One of the playgrounds is on an island in one of the lakes. Kids can take the bridge across and have fun climbing up and down the tower. You may fish in the two man-made lakes - no license is needed unless your child is over 16 years old.

Get physical on the weekends with various pleasure rentals - surrey bikes are between $12 (for two adults and two small children) to $22 (for a limo - up to eight people) an hour; funcycles or tandems are $8 an hour; and peddle boats are $12 an hour. All rentals are usually available 11am to 7pm.

Hours: Open daily in the summer 7am - 9pm. Open daily the rest of the year 7am - 6pm.
Admission: $2 per vehicle Mon. - Fri; $4 on Sat. - Sun.; $5 on holidays. Some free street parking is available on Warner Ave.
Ages: All

NORTHWOOD COMMUNITY PARK

(949) 552-4352 / www.ci.irvine.ca.us
4531 Bryan Avenue, Irvine
(Exit Santa Ana Fwy [5] N. on Culver, R. on Bryan. [TG-860 H1])

The focal point of this park is the big, fortress-like structure which is great for climbing on and around. It has a slide, steps, and a rocky wall that completes the fortress image. The playground also has tire swings, a balance beam, slides, a wooden and cement pirate ship, and sand boxes.

The surrounding park has soccer fields, tennis courts, a basketball court, shuffleboard, a handball court, and baseball diamonds, plus a paved pathway around the fields. You can check out play equipment, free of charge, at the information building.

Hours: The park and information building are open Mon. - Fri., 9am - 9pm; Sat. - Sun., 9am - 6pm.
Admission: Free
Ages: All

OAK CANYON NATURE CENTER

(714) 998-8380 / www.anaheim.net

6700 Walnut Canyon Road, Anaheim

(Exit Riverside Fwy [91] S. on Imperial Hwy, L. on Nohl Ranch Rd., L. on Walnut Canyon. It's next to the Anaheim Hills Golf Course. [TG-770 J4])

    This rustic Nature Center is a fifty-eight-acre natural park nestled in Anaheim Hills. Surrounded by such beauty, it doesn't seem possible that there is a city nearby. Take a delightful, easy hike along the wide pathways along the stream and through the woods that boast of huge oak and other shade tress. Or, opt for more strenuous hiking on the six miles of trails offered here. No bikes or picnicking are allowed so that the animals and plants that consider this canyon their home can continue to live here unharmed.

    The good-sized, Nature Center building houses live critters, plus several trays of mounted butterflies and other insects. The small stage area is great for putting on shows using the animal puppets.

    The Nature Center offers many different programs. One-hour programs for preschoolers, like Feed the Critters or Mudpies and Stone Soup, include a guided nature walk and related activities and perhaps a craft. The fee is $3 per child. Every Saturday morning a family program is offered that incorporates learning about nature with doing a craft together. This program is usually free. On Wednesday evenings throughout the summer, Nature Nights for families begin at 7pm with a twilight walk through the canyon. A formal presentation is given at 7:30pm at the outdoor amphitheater. Ask about their summer day camps.

    Hours: Open daily 9am - 5pm.

  Admission: Free

     Ages: All

O'NEILL REGIONAL PARK

(949) 858-9365 / www.oc.ca.gov

30892 Trabuco Canyon Road, Trabuco Canyon

(Exit Santa Ana Fwy [5] N.E. on El Toro Rd., R. on Live Oak Canyon Rd., which turns into Trabuco Canyon Rd. [TG-863 B7])

    As we explored parts of this over 2,000-acre park, I kept thinking of how absolutely gorgeous it is. O'Neill Park is a canyon bottom and so filled with trees, it's like being in a forest. A creek runs throughout, creating lush greenery. The abundant nature trails are mostly hilly dirt trails, though a few are paved "roads."

    The playground has a log cabin-like building with slides and swings and such around it. Inside the small Nature Center are taxidermied animals around the perimeter of the room. A few tables in the middle display skulls, furs, and rocks to touch. The park also has beautiful campgrounds.

    Hours: The park is open daily 7am to sunset. The Nature Center is usually open Sat. - Sun., 2pm - 4pm; Open Sat. - Sun., 11am - 1pm if staff is available.

  Admission: $2 per vehicle on Mon. - Fri.; $4 on Sat. - Sun; $5 on holidays. Camping starts at $12 a night.

     Ages: All

PETERS CANYON REGIONAL PARK   ☼

(714) 227-1780 / www.ocparks.com   !

Canyon View Avenue & Jamboree Road, Orange

(Exit Costa Mesa Fwy [55] E. on Chapman., R. on Jamboree, R. on Canyon View. [TG-800 J4])

My boys and I have decided that this huge, 354-acre undeveloped park is for rugged hikers. The lake by the parking lot is one of the most scenic spots here. The narrow dirt trails are lined with sage scrub, grassland areas, and willow and sycamore trees. The upper Lake View Trail guides you through the reservoir, while the lower East Ridge Trail provides a panoramic view of the canyon and the surrounding area. The park, and its seven miles of trails, are closed for two or three days after a rain.

Hours: Open daily 7am - sunset.

Admission: Free

Ages: 5 years and up.

RALPH B. CLARK REGIONAL PARK   ☼

(714) 670-8045 / www.ocparks.com $

8800 Rosecrans Avenue, Buena Park   🏛

(Exit Santa Ana Fwy [5] N. on Beach Blvd., R. on Rosecrans. [TG-738 A4])

This sixty-five-acre park is one of the most aesthetically pleasing parks we've seen. It has all the things that make a park great - a lake to fish in, ducks to feed, tennis courts, horseshoe pits, three softball fields, a baseball diamond, volleyball courts, and a few small playgrounds. Take a short hike around Camel Hill, or let the kids climb on the small, therefore ironically named, Elephant Hill. A paved bicycle trail goes all around the perimeter of the park.

The Interpretive Center has a working paleontology lab where kids can look through a big window and observe the detailed work being done. The Center also houses a twenty-six-foot Baleen whale fossil; a skeletal saber-tooth cat "attacking" a skeletal horse; fossils of a ground sloth and a mammoth; shells; and more.

Kids really dig the marine fossil site across the street where a *bone*afide paleontologist conducts "Family Fossil Day" four times a year, usually in February, May, September, and December. This three-hour class is geared for youngsters 6 years and up. They can practice their fossil-finding skills by looking for fossilized shells at the marine site, then study and classify fossils back at the lab at the Interpretive Center. They'll also make a craft related to that day's theme. The price for the field trip is simply the price of admission to the park.

Hours: The park is open November through March 7am - 6pm; April through October 7am - 9pm. The Interpretative Center is usually open Tues. - Fri., 12:30pm - 5pm; Sat. - Sun., 10am - 4:30pm. Call first to make sure staff is available.

Admission: $2 vehicle entrance Mon. - Fri.; $4 on Sat. - Sun.; $5 on holidays.

Ages: All

RANCHO MISSION VIEJO LAND CONSERVANCY

(949) 489-9778 / www.theconservancy.org   *!/$$*

Off Ortega Highway, San Juan Capistrano

(Exit San Diego Fwy [5] E. on Ortega Hwy. [74]. It's about 5.1 miles. Look for signs for Rancho Mission Viejo on the R. [TG-973 E1])

The Land Conservancy manages a 1,200 acre wilderness reserve in the coastal foothills. They offer an incredible array of special programs to the general public and to school groups that give intimate glimpses into the wilderness of Orange County. Programs include guided nature walks, bird watching (and finding), wildlife workshops, astronomy nights, owl outings, bat walks, butterfly classes, butterfly counting (for research purposes), trail maintenance, and much more. The programs are given by trained docents, or professionals in that field of study. What a wonderful opportunity for kids to become aware of wildlife, and what they can do to help protect it.

Hours: Call for program hours or to receive a calendar of events.
Admission: Depending on the program, the fees range from free to $8.
Ages: Varies, depending on the program.

RONALD W. CASPERS WILDERNESS PARK

(949) 728-0235 / www.ocparks.com   *$*

33401 Ortega Highway, San Juan Capistrano

(Exit San Diego Fwy [5] E. on Ortega Hwy. It's about 7 miles. [TG-953 G3])

Orange County's largest park is massive, and consists mostly of canyon wilderness such as seasonally verdant valleys, groves of live oak and sycamore trees, meadows, and running streams. We saw mule deer and jackrabbits scampering through the woods and quail walking/running alongside the dirt road. The over forty miles of hiking trails range from easy walks to strenuous, mountain-man hikes. (Pick up a trail map at the front entrance.) Give kids the freedom to hike, but beware that mountain lions sometimes roam this area, too. Mountain bike usage is permitted on designated roads only. Visitors can also enjoy a barbecue under shade trees; play on the large wooden playground with swings and slides, surrounded by trees; and check out the Nature Center that has a few taxidermied animals and hands-on activities.

The numerous camp sites are picturesque, wonderful for enjoying nature. Campsites have picnic tables, charcoal-burning stoves, fire rings, and a nearby water source.

Hours: Open daily 7am to sunset.
Admission: $2 per vehicle Mon. - Fri.; $4 Sat. - Sun; $5 on holidays.
Camping is $12 a night; $10 for seniors and handicapped.
Ages: All

SANTIAGO OAKS REGIONAL PARK

(714) 538-4400 / www.ocparks.com   *$*

2145 N. Windes Drive, Orange

(Exit Costa Mesa Fwy [55] E. on Katella, which turns into Villa Park, then into Santiago Canyon Rd., L. on Windes, to the end. [TG-770 G6])

Get back to nature at this 350-acre park that has beautiful hiking and equestrian trails that connect to the Anaheim Hills trail system. Take a short path along the creek leading to a waterfall at the dam, or travel more rugged terrain into the heart of the park. Be on the lookout for animals such as lizards, squirrels, deer, and birds. Mountain lions have been seen on rare occasion, too.

A favorite activity here is cooking breakfast over the charcoal barbecues early in the morning, while it's still quiet and cool. A small playground and a few horseshoe pits round out the facilities under a canopy of oak trees. The small Nature Center has taxidermied animals, pictures, and a few hands-on activities. Free, ranger-led tours are given on the weekends beginning at 10am by reservation only.

Hours: The park is open daily 7am - sunset. The nature center is open daily 8am - 4pm.

Admission: $2 per vehicle Mon. - Fri., $4 Sat. - Sun.; $5 on holidays.

Ages: All

SANTIAGO PARK

(714) 571-4200 / www.ci.santa-ana.ca.us

2535 N. Main Street, Santa Ana

(From S. of Santa Ana, exit the San Diego Fwy [5] N. at Main St. North / Broadway, R. on Main St. From N. of Santa Ana, exit San Diego Fwy [5] S. at Main St. North / Broadway (look for signs to Discovery Science Center), L. on Santa Clara, L. at Main St., then an immediate R. Or, go a street further and turn R. on Memory Lane for another entrance. It's directly across from the Discovery Science Center. Tip: Park here and walk through the underpass to the Center, saving a $3 parking fee. [TG-799 F6])

You can literally stroll along Memory Lane here, simply because that's the name of the street adjacent to the park. This long park, located directly across the street from the DISCOVERY SCIENCE CENTER (look under the Museums section), has several areas with play equipment, plus scattered picnic tables, shade trees, grassy patches, and barbecue pits. We usually spend most of our time at the first play area, with its slides, swings, sand area, wooden bridges, tunnels, and a green, wooden fort-like structure. A little further east is a slightly sunken grassy area (perfect for a group party), a lawn bowling center, a baseball diamond, an archery range, tennis courts, and more play equipment. A rocky riverbed path follows along one side of the park. The pathway actually leads all the way to HART PARK (look under this section), although it is a half hour, non-stroller friendly walk to get there.

Hours: Open daily sunrise to sunset.

Admission: Free

Ages: All

TEWINKLE MEMORIAL PARK

(714) 754-5300 / www.ci.costa-mesa.ca.us

970 Arlington Drive, Costa Mesa

(Going E on the San Diego Fwy [405], exit S. on Fairview Rd., L. on Arlington. Going W. on 405, exit S. on Bristol St. R. on Newport Blvd., R. on Arlington. Going N. on the Costa Mesa Fwy [55], exit N.W. on Del Mar Ave., R. on Newport, L. on Arlington. [TG-859 B7])

This fifty-acre park has something for everyone. There is a play area with a big tire to climb on, volleyball courts, baseball fields, and a utility field.

I think nature-loving kids will enjoy this park most. A stream goes around a good portion of it, with ducks and geese having a swimmingly good time. They also populate the small lake. A hike up the hill yields the treasure of a pond in a small, forest-like setting. This park is cool, even on a hot day.

Hours: Open daily dawn to dusk.
Admission: Free
Ages: All

TUCKER WILDLIFE SANCTUARY

(714) 649-2760 / www.fullerton.edu
29322 Modjeska Canyon Road, Modjeska
(Exit Costa Mesa Fwy [55] E. on Chapman, which turns into Santiago Canyon Rd. Turn L. on Modjeska Canyon Rd., drive about 2 miles, veer to the right at the fork. [TG-832 H7])

Tucker Wildlife Sanctuary is tucked in the mountainside at the end of a long and winding road. The Nature Center has a small, one-room museum with live snakes, lizards, and turtles. It also contains taxidermied animals and a touch table with skulls, fossils, and bird's nests.

There are several short - one-fifth or so of a mile - nature trails to walk. Along the Riparian Woodland Trail you'll find a small pond and an enclosed observation porch. The porch, located over a creek, has birdseed scattered on it so kids can sit and readily observe wild birds. The hummingbirds, attracted by the brightly-colored sugar water in their feeders, are our favorites. There are picnic tables along the trail.

Hours: Open daily 9am - 4pm. Closed Christmas.
Admission: $1.50 donation requested per person.
Ages: All

TURTLE ROCK NATURE CENTER

(949) 854-8151 - nature center; (949) 854-8144 - park /
www.ci.irvine.ca.us
1 Sunnyhill Drive, Irvine
(Exit Corona Del Mar Fwy [73] S. on Jamboree, L. on University Dr., R. on Culver Dr., L. on Bonita Cyn., L. on Sunnyhill. [TG-890 D4])

This small, five-acre nature preserve has both a desert habitat and pine trees, so the stroller-friendly trail is partially in the sun and partially in the shade. A ranger here said that going around a little pond, over a few bridges, and looping back around takes "ten minutes if you don't see anything, thirty minutes if you follow the trail guide. The longer you're here, the more you'll learn."

Inside the Center, test your knowledge on a quiz board that lights up if the right answer button is pushed. Kids can also reach in discovery boxes to feel for animal pelts or bones. Visit the small Animal Room (50¢) to see live snakes, bunnies, turtles, crows, and a raccoon. Note: The animals on exhibit do change. Find out why the animals are here and what we can do to take better care of their homes. The room is open every hour on the hour between 11am to 3pm.

The surrounding park has tennis courts, a basketball court, sand volleyball courts, and a playground, plus a nature trail that goes over a creek.

Hours: The nature center is open most of the year Mon. - Sat., 10am - 4pm; Sun., noon - 4pm. It's open in the summer, Mon. - Sat., 10am - 5pm; Sun., noon - 4pm. The park is open daily sunrise to sunset.

Admission: Free

Ages: 2 - 13 years.

UPPER NEWPORT BAY ECOLOGICAL RESERVE AND ☼ REGIONAL PARK

(949) 640-6746 / www.newportbay.org   !/$$

600 Shellmaker, Newport Beach

(Take Costa Mesa Fwy [55] S.W. to end, which turns into Newport Blvd., L. on W. Coast Hwy., L. on Jamboree Rd., L. on Backbay Dr. to Shellmaker. Or, from Corona Del Mar Fwy [73], exit S.W. on Jamboree R., R. on Backbay Dr. to Shellmaker. [TG-889 C6])

This reserve, a remnant of a once-extensive wetland, is part of an endeavor to conserve wildlife in the Upper Bay. Although surrounded by urban development, the bay and small islands are home to hundreds of waterfowl, sea critters, and a variety of plants. The reserve is ringed by roads, but only hikers, bikers, and boaters have access inside the reserve. Introduce your children to the valuable natural resources that God originally put on the earth by involving kids in a variety of interactive and interpretive programs offered here. As you "Canoe the Back Bay," you'll see herons, egrets, and numerous other birds. This program is available every Saturday and costs $13 per person. Free walking tours are given November through March on the second Saturday at 9am. All this plus kayak tours, youth fishing programs, and shark studies are mere samplings of what the reserve has to offer.

The small Peter and Mary Muth Interpretive Center, tucked in the bluff of the Upper Newport Bay at 2301 University Drive, is distinctive in design - it's constructed out of old plastic bottles, lumber scrap, and other recyclable materials. Inside are stuffed herons, owls, and other birds, as well as literature and photographs. Call (714) 973-6820 for more information.

Hours: Hours vary, depending on the program.

Admission: Prices vary, depending on the program.

Ages: 3½ years and up.

WHITING RANCH WILDERNESS PARK   ☼

(949) 589-4729 / www.oc.ca.gov/hbp $

Santiago Canyon Road, Portola Hills

(Exit San Diego Fwy [5] E. on Lake Forest, go 5 miles and turn L. on Portola Pkwy., R. on Market, first driveway on the left. Or, from Lake Forest, turn R. on Portola Pkwy., L. on Glenn Rd. and into the large dirt parking area. This section leads into Serrano Canyon. [TG-862 C5])

"Real" hikers can explore the hills of Trabuco Canyon via Whiting Ranch Wilderness Park. Follow the trails through forested canyons, along streams, and past huge boulders. A moderate hike starts at the Borrego Trail and leads to the Red Rock Canyon trail, which is five miles round trip and loops back around. Note: This trail is more easily reached from the Market Street entrance. The scenery is outstanding. The size and beauty of this park offers the opportunity to

enjoy some good, back-to-nature time with your kids.
>   **Hours:**   Open daily 7am - sunset.
>   **Admission:** $2 per vehicle.
>   **Ages:**   5 years and up.

WILLIAM R. MASON REGIONAL PARK

(949) 854-2490 / www.ci.irvine.ca.us
18712 University Drive, Irvine
(Exit San Diego Fwy [405] S. on Culver Dr., R. on University Dr. [TG-890 A1])

This 350-acre park is serene (even with kids!) and beautiful. The picturesque lake is a central feature. Fishing, with a license, is allowed, but be forewarned - the lake isn't stocked. Honking gaggles of geese will vie for your attention (and bread crumbs). There are four different playgrounds with modular plastic equipment such as tunnels, slides, swings, forts, etc. The park also boasts of volleyball courts, a ball field, horseshoe pits, a disc golf course, picnic shelters, open grassy expanses, large shade trees, and two miles of lovely paved walking/biking trails that crisscross throughout.
>   **Hours:**   Open daily November through March 7am - 6pm. Open daily
>   April through October 7am - 9pm.
>   **Admission:** $2 per vehicle Mon. - Fri.; $4 Sat. - Sun.; $5 on holidays.
>   **Ages:**   All

YORBA REGIONAL PARK

(714) 970-1460 / www.ocparks.com
7600 E. La Palma Avenue, Anaheim
(Exit Riverside Fwy [91] N. on Imperial Hwy, R. on La Palma [TG-740 G7])

This pleasant, 166-acre elongated park follows along the Santa Ana River. It offers a myriad of activities including trails for bike riding (along the river bank), hiking, and horseback riding; four softball fields and a lighted baseball diamond; an exercise course; lakes for fishing, with a valid fishing license for fishermen over 16 years; a lake for operating model boats; paddle boat rentals at $10 a half hour (usually available on the weekends only); a few playgrounds; horseshoe pits; and several volleyball courts.
>   **Hours:**   Open April through October 7am - 9pm; November through
>   March 7am - 6pm.
>   **Admission:** $2 per vehicle.
>   **Ages:**   All

ARLINGTON PARK

(909) 715-3440 / www.ci.riverside.ca.us
3860 Van Buren Boulevard, Riverside
(Exit Riverside Fwy [91] N. on Van Buren Blvd. It's just past Magnolia, on the W. side of the street. [TG-714 H6])

This nice corner park has an older style playground and well-used shuffleboard courts. It also has basketball courts, tennis courts, barbecue pits, and a swimming pool.

Hours: The park is open daily. The pool is open in the summer Mon. - Sat., 1pm - 5pm; plus Tues. and Thurs., 6pm - 8pm.

Admission: Free to the park. Swim sessions are $2.25 for adults; $1 for ages 6 - 17; 75¢ for children 5 and under.

Ages: All

CALIFORNIA CITRUS STATE HISTORIC PARK

(909) 780-6222 / parks.ca.gov

Van Buren Boulevard and Dufferin Avenue, Riverside

(Exit the Riverside Fwy [91] S. on Van Buren Blvd., L. on Dufferin Ave., R. into the park. [TG-745 B2])

The park, with its acres of citrus groves, captures the spirit of Riverside's slogan, "The land of citrus and sunshine." The main section is beautifully landscaped, has a big, grassy area for running around and for picnicking, a small visitor's center, and a gift shop / museum in a restored home. The museum features mostly historical photographs with narrative.

There are two, mile-long hiking trails. The Arroyo Trail goes through a wooded area and creek bed, up towards the dam. The Knolls Trail takes the high, non-shady road, past Grower's Mansion (a soon-to-be restaurant) towards the dam. Neither trail is very strenuous; just good, short nature hikes. Don't forget to stop and smell the oranges along the way!

Hours: The park is open daily in the summer 8am - 7pm; open the rest of the year 8am - 5pm. The nature center is open weekends 11am - 3pm.

Admission: Free

Ages: 2 years and up.

DIAMOND VALLEY LAKE

(800) 273-3430 - recorded info; (800) 211-9863 - visitors center / www.mwd.dst.ca.us

300 Newport Road or Domenigoni Parkway, Hemet

(To get to the overlook: Going S. on Escondido Expressway [215], exit E. on Hwy 74, S. on Hwy 79 / Winchester Rd., L. on Domenigoni / Construction Rd. Going N. on Temecula Valley Fwy [15], exit N. on Hwy 79 / Winchester Rd., R. on Domenigoni / Construction. To get to the visitors center: Exit 74 S. on State St., R. on Newport Rd. From San Diego, after turning R. on Domenigoni, R. on State St., R. on Newport. [TG-870 H1])

In the process of being completed, this enormous, man-made lake (i.e. reservoir) will hold 260 billion gallons of water - enough to secure a six month supply in case of an earthquake emergency. I knew you wanted to know that. With its twenty-six miles of shoreline, this premium lake will have two marinas that can be home to 500 boats; incredible fresh water fishing - perch, catfish, bass, and trout; sailing and other boating opportunities; two large dams to contain the water, one on the west end of the lake, one on the east, and small one on the north side; and two large community parks under the dam areas. The parks will have picnic areas, swimming pools, ball fields, and even tennis court. Over seventy miles of as biking, hiking, and equestrian trails will connect to Lake Skinner and the Multi-Species Reserve. Camping will also be available.

The visitor's center, on Newport Road, contains information as well as a few exhibits, such as the fossils uncovered during the excavation and displays on water conservation. Educational programs offer in-depth information and hands-on activities to do with water preservation and dams.

Hours: The visitors center is open Fri. - Mon., 10am - 4:30pm. The overlook is open Mon. - Fri., 7:30am - 3:30pm; Sat. - Sun., 9am - 4:30pm.

Admission: Free, right now.

Ages: All

FAIRMOUNT PARK

(909) 715-3440 - park; (909) 715-3406 - boathouse /
www.ci.riverside.ca.us
2624 Fairmount Boulevard, Riverside
(Exit Pomona Fwy [60] S. on Market St. The park is on the immediate R. [TG-685 H2])

This lush park has a lot to offer. The huge playground has swings, slides, bridges, and lots of other fun things. The surrounding grassy area is large, with plenty of shade trees and picnic tables. With all this, plus tennis courts, basketball courts, and horseshoe pits, kids can play here all day! The park's rose garden is located at the corner of Redwood and Dexter drives.

Take a very windy drive around the lakes, and watch out for the ducks - they're everywhere! Don't forget your fishing poles as you can stop almost anywhere to fish, including from a small, horseshoe-shaped pier. A fishing permit is required. Pedal boat and rowboat rentals are available seasonally.

The Information Center is open Monday through Friday 8am to 5pm and on the weekends 10am to 5pm. It has exhibits of local history and environmental projects. You'll have a better than fair day at Fairmount Park!

Hours: The park is open daily sunrise to 10pm. The boathouse is open weekends only 10am - 4pm.

Admission: Free. Boat rentals are $5 per half hour.

Ages: All

HIDDEN VALLEY WILDLIFE AREA

(909) 785-7452 / www.riversidecountyparks.org
Near end of Arlington Avenue, Riverside
(Exit Riverside Fwy [91] N. at La Sierra, keeping L. as it turns into Arlington. The wildlife area is on the R. before Arlington turns into North Ave. [TG-714 A1])

Aptly named, this 1,300-acre wildlife area is indeed off the beaten path. There are several options to see at least parts of this "park": Drive along the ridge to see vast expanses of treeless stretches that are close to the road, and wooded areas that are further back into the park; hike along the numerous trails and view the wildlife closer up; or horseback ride, which is obviously a popular option judging from the number of horse trailers we observed.

As Hidden Valley is located along the Santa Ana River, much of the wildlife encouraged and seen here are migratory birds. There are many ponds, too, as you'll discover if you hike into this sprawling park. A small Nature Center is up the road a bit.

Hours: Open daily 7am - 4:30pm. The Nature Center is open Tues. - Fri.
by appointment, and open to the public Sat., 8am - 4pm.
Admission: $4 per vehicle.
Ages: 4 years and up.

HUNTER PARK
(909) 715-3440 - park; (909) 779-9024 - Live Steamers train rides /   !
www.ci.riverside.ca.us
14 96 Columbia Avenue, Riverside
(Exit Riverside Fwy [215] E. on Columbia Ave. It's just N. of 91/60/215 Jct., on the corner of Iowa
and Columbia. [TG-686 B1])

Hunter Park is comprised mostly of grassy playing fields. Its best feature
occurs on the second and fourth Sunday of each month when scale model train
rides are offered. Kids love taking a ride on the track that encircles the park.

Hours: Steam train rides are on the second and fourth Sun., 10am - 3pm.
Admission: Free
Ages: All

LAKE PERRIS STATE RECREATION AREA
(909) 940-5603 - general info; (909) 657-2179 - marina; (909) 940-5656 $$
- Home of Wind Indian Museum / parks.ca.gov
17801 Lake Perris Drive, Perris
(Exit Escondido Fwy [215] E. on Cajalco Expressway/Ramona Expressway, L. on Lake Perris Dr.
[TG-748 A6])

Come for at least a day of play at the popular Lake Perris! This gigantic
(8,800 acres!), man-made lake supports a multitude of water activities. (It's hot
out here in the summer, so you'll need them.) For your boating pleasure, choose
from four- or six-seat passenger boats, ranging from $19 to $54, or pontoon
boats, ranging from $40 to $180 a day. Waterskiing is available, if you bring
your own boat. A cove is also here for non-motorized boats, such as sail boats
and kayaks. Fish at the lake and catch a big one, or at least try to. A license and
day permit is required for those over 16 years. There is a swim beach here with a
playground, grassy areas, barbecue pits, and most importantly, three waterslides.
All-day use of the water slides cost the lake entrance fee, plus $5; half-day is $3.

Drier activities include listening to a concert at the amphitheater, picnicking,
hiking, biking (a ten-mile fairly level, mostly paved trail goes around the lake),
rock climbing (outside - you're on your own), and a visit to the small, regional
Indian museum. The museum contains stuffed animals, displays on native plant
life, exhibits of Indian art, and a beautiful view of the lake out the glass
windows. What more could nature-loving kids want?! Camping! There is so
much to do at Lake Perris, that you'll want to spend a night, or two, here. Ask
about their summer programs, such as campfire times held on Saturday evenings
and the Jr. Ranger program for ages 7 to 12.

Hours: The recreation area is open in the summer, 6am - 10pm; open the rest of the year 6am - 8pm. The marina is open 6am - 8pm year round. The waterslides are open daily in the summer, 11am - 4pm; open weekends only April through mid-June and September through October, 11am - 4pm. The museum is usually open Mon. - Fri., 10am - 2pm; Sat. - Sun., 10am - 4pm. Call first. School tours of the museum are given Tues. and Fri. by reservation only.

Admission: $3 per vehicle. The museum is free with paid admission. Tent camping is $8 a night; RV camping is $14 with hook-ups - prices include vehicle admission. Waterslides and boat rentals are priced above.

Ages: All

LAKE SKINNER COUNTY PARK   ☼

(909) 926-1505 - recorded info.; (909) 926-1541 - park ranger; (800) $
234-7275 -camping reservations. / www.riversidecountyparks.org
37701 Warren Road, Winchester   ⛺
(Exit Temecula Valley Fwy [15] N.E. on Rancho California Rd. About 12 miles from the fwy, turn R. on Warren Rd at the second big bend. There are signs for Lake Skinner. [TG-930 D3])

Here's the skinny on Lake Skinner. The main attraction is fishing, either from a boat, or from the shore. A California state license is required for ages 16 and up. Day permits are $5 for adults; $4 for children 12 years and under. The well-equipped marina offers all sorts of fishing supplies as well as a cafe/restaurant for those who didn't have much luck catching their own meal. Other activities include hiking, picnicking, playing on the small playground, swimming in the pool, and overnight camping.

Hours: The park is open daily 6am - dusk. Fishing is available daily 6am - dark. The pool is open daily in the summer 11am - 6pm.

Admission: $2 for adults; $1 for children 12 and under. The pool is an additional $1 per person. Tent camping is $15 a night; RV camping is $18 a night.

Ages: All

LOUIS ROBIDOUX NATURE CENTER   ☼

(909) 683-4880 / www.riversidecountyparks.org   !
5370 Riverview Drive, Riverside   ⛺
(Exit the Pomona Fwy [60] S. on Rubidoux Blvd., R. on Mission St., L. on Riverview Dr. As Riverview turns into Limonite Ave., turn L., staying on Riverview. [TG-685 A4])

This nature park is wonderful for kids who have an adventuresome spirit. A grouping of big rocks in front of the nature center is fun for climbers. A pond is at the trailhead of Willow Creek Trail, which is an easy, half-mile loop to walk around. Other pathways veer off in all directions, allowing some real hiking excursions. Walk along a tree-lined creek; explore the woodlands and water wildlife along the Santa Ana River; or go farther into the Regional Park system along the horse trail that has extensive chaparral. No biking is allowed, and only off-road strollers will make it. Pick up a self-guided trail map, which also has nature questions for kids to answer.

The main building, or Interpretive Center, houses live animals such as snakes, taxidermied animals, and an extensive butterfly and insect collection. Kids are welcome to touch the various animals pelts; use the discovery boxes that contain skulls, seeds, or feathers; or just play with the puzzles. As with most nature centers, special programs are offered throughout the year. Note: The trail by the parking lot leads into RANCHO JURUPA REGIONAL PARK (look just a few entries down).

Hours: The park and trails are open daily sunrise to sunset. The Interpretive Center is open to the public on Sat., 10am - 4pm. With advanced reservations, it's open Tues. - Fri. for school groups and other large groups.

Admission: Free

Ages: All

MOUNT RUBIDOUX
(909) 715-3440 / www.riverside-ca.org

Off Buena Vista Drive, Riverside

(Exit Riverside Fwy [91] W. on University Ave., R. on Redwood Dr., L. on Buena Vista Dr. Just S. of the Santa Ana River, turn in where you see a small green picnic area and park at the base of the mountain. [TG-685 F3])

For kids who enjoy a somewhat rugged hike, climbing Mount Rubidoux is a great adventure. The steep, two-and-a-half-mile trail winds around the hill that is barren except for boulders and cacti. Reaching the top is a climax. "The trail is two miles up and one mile down." There are rocks to climb on, and on a clear day, the panoramic view of the San Gabriel and San Bernardino Mountains is beautiful. On the western slope of the hill, watch vintage planes take off and land at Rubidoux's Flabob Airport. Hiking here in the summer gets hot, so bring a water bottle. Plan on about an hour-and-a-half round trip. Next door, along the river, is the Mount Rubidoux Park. The bike trail at the base of the mountain goes a few miles back to Martha McClean/Anza Narrow Park and beyond.

Hours: Open daily.

Admission: Free

Ages: It depends how far up you want to hike!.

RANCHO CALIFORNIA SPORTS PARK AND COMMUNITY RECREATION CENTER / TEMECULA SKATE PARK
(909) 694-6410 - park; (909) 695-1409 - skate park /   *!/$*
www.ci.temecula.ca.us

30875 Rancho Vista, Temecula

(Exit Temecula Fwy [15] E. on Rancho California Rd., S. on Ynez Rd., L. on Rancho Vista. [TG-959 C6])

Have a ball at this terrific sports park! It has twelve ball fields, seven soccer fields, lots of open grassy areas for running around, two great playgrounds, shade trees, picnic shelters, and barbecue grills. The roller hockey rink has some open time, although it is used mostly by leagues. Bring your Tony Hawk wannabes (i.e. Tony Hawk is a pro skateboarder) to practice at the gated, one-acre, outdoor cement skate park which is equipped with all the "necessary" features. The sixty-foot diameter bowl has ramp entry which also leads to an upper bowl with a street plaza that consists of a pyramid, fun box, curbs, ramps, stairs, and a hand rail. All participants must have a signed waiver form prior to park entry. Proper safety equipment is mandatory and may be rented on site - helmet, elbow pads, and knee pads.

The indoor gym offers basketball, and can be set up for volleyball. Keep your cool in the twenty-five-meter outdoor swimming pool that has a diving board and a waterslide. There is also a shallow pool just for tots. The Teen Center is a great place for 12 to 18 year olds to hang out. It offers pool, air hockey, Carom, Nintendo, and more. This park offers everything active kids need - my boys would be very happy living there!

Hours: The park is open sunrise - 10pm. During the school year the skateboard park is open Mon. - Fri., 4pm - 9:30pm; Sat., 10am - 9:30pm; Sun., 1pm - 6:30pm. It's open during the summer, Mon. - Sat., 10am - 9:30pm; Sun., 1pm - 6:30pm. Sessions last for 2 ½ hours. The roller hockey rink is usually available for open play Mon. - Fri. before 4pm. After 4pm and on most weekends, it's booked for league play. The pool is open weekends only in April, May, September, and October, 1pm - 5pm. During summer it's open Mon., Wed., Fri., 2pm - 5pm; Sat. - Sun., 1pm - 5pm. The Teen Center is open Mon. - Fri., 2pm - 8:45pm during school hours. Weekends and off-school hours, it's open noon - 8:45pm.

Admission: The park is free. Skateboard sessions are $2 for residents; $5 for non-residents. Bring your own equipment, or rent everything needed for $5. Pool rates for residents are $2.25 for adults; $1.75 for ages 8 - 17; $1 for kids 7 and under. Pool rates for non-residents are $3 per person. The Teen Center asks that a resident card be purchased - $1 for a year's membership.

Ages: All ages for the park. Skateboarders under 7 years must be accompanied by an adult. Kids must be between 12 - 18 years to hang out inside the Teen Center.

RANCHO JURUPA REGIONAL PARK   ☼
(909) 684-7032 / www.riverside-ca.org $
4800 Crestmore Road, Riverside   ♨
(Exit Pomona Fwy [60] S. on Rubidoux Blvd., L. on Mission Blvd., R. on Crestmore Rd., about 1 mile. [TG-685 D4])

This huge mountain-wilderness park, which is part of the even bigger Santa Ana River Regional Park system, provides a delightful escape from the city. The two small lakes are stocked with trout in the cooler months and catfish in the summertime. Fishermen (and women) 16 years and older must have a state fishing license. Near the lake is a big wooden play structure with slides, swings, and monkey bars. Enjoy a day (or two or three) here by camping in one of the eighty camp sites that are slotted in a big, open space near one end of the lake.

Horseshoe pits are located over here, too.

On the other side of the main lake are a few smaller lakes, big grassy open spaces for baseball or whatever, plenty of picnic tables, and barbecue pits. Enjoy an easy hike along the river trail to the adjoining LOUIS ROBIDOUX NATURE CENTER (see a previous entry in this section), where more trails, an Interpretive Center, and rocks to climb on await your kids.

Hours: Open Sun. - Thurs., 7am - 5pm; Fri. - Sat., 7am - 10pm. Call for extended summer hours.

Admission: $2 per person for ages 13 and up; $1 per person for children 12 and under. Dogs are $2 each. Fishing is $5 for ages 16 and older; $4 for ages 6 - 15; children 5 and under fish for free with a paid adult. A campsite with one vehicle and two people costs $16. Each additional person is $1; up to six people allowed in one campsite. Group rates are available.

Ages: All

SANTA ROSA PLATEAU ECOLOGICAL RESERVE

(909) 677-6951 / www.santarosaplateau.org

22115 Tenaja Road, Murrieta

(Exit Interstate 15 W. on Clinton Keith Rd. and go about 6 miles to the trailhead. You'll see entrance signs. Another trailhead is located further down the road, where Clinton Keith / Tenaja Rd. turns into Via Volcano. [TG-957 C3])

From riparian stream sides to basalt-capped mesas, this gigantic 8,300-acre reserve covers the gamut of topography. The thirty-plus trails range from one mile to five miles round trip. Depending on which one you choose, you'll hike through oak woodlands, acres of grasslands, chaparral, up the Santa Ana mountains, and down to creek beds. Look for treefrogs and turtles in the water, and ground squirrels, woodpeckers, hawks, and horned lizards along the wooded pathways. There is a picnic spot at the vernal pools, which is a four-mile round trip hike. Pick up a trail map from the visitors center at 39400 Clinton Keith Road.

Hours: Open daily sunrise to sunset. The visitor's center is open Sat. - Sun., 9am - 5pm.

Admission: $2 for adults; $1 for children 2 - 12.

Ages: 3 years and up.

UNIVERSITY OF CALIFORNIA AT RIVERSIDE BOTANIC GARDENS

(909) 787- 4650 / cnas.ucr.edu

Campus Drive, University of California, Riverside

(Exit Moreno Valley Fwy [215] E. on University Ave. to the entrance of the campus, follow Campus Dr. to parking lot 13. [TG-686 E5])

Riverside's climate ranges from subtropical to desert to mountains, all within forty acres and five miles of hilly trails! A gently sloping walkway provides access to the gardens main areas for wheelchairs and strollers. Explore the botanic gardens to see rose gardens, fruit orchards, an herb garden, saguaros, barrel cacti, pine trees, giant sequoias, and so much more.

Besides the diverse plant life, numerous animals share this habitat. Be on the lookout for bunnies, lizards, squirrels, snakes, coyotes, and numerous bird species. A main trail loops around, and is walkable in forty-five minutes. At the far end of the trail is a pond supporting more wildlife such as frogs, turtles, dragonflies, and koi. A dome-shaped building made of cedar that houses a "living fossils" collection, and a greenhouse are more discoveries you'll make along the way.

Come with your kids to enjoy the beauty of the gardens, and/or come for an educational field trip. Ask for a self-guiding tour booklet, such as *Outdoor Classroom* or *Deserts of the Southwest*, which will greatly enrich your day of exploring and learning.

Hours: Open daily 8am - 5pm. Closed New Year's Day, Independence Day, Thanksgiving, and Christmas.

Admission: Free; donations appreciated.

Ages: All

AFTON CANYON

(760) 252-6000 / www.ca.blm.gov

Afton Rd., Afton

(Exit Mojave Fwy [I-15] to Afton Rd. It's 36 miles NE of Barstow between Afton Rd. and Rasin Rd. [TG-350 B6])

Referred to as the "Grand Canyon of the Mojave", the canyon is at the site where the river surfaces after being underground for more than fifty miles. Since this is one of the few places in the desert where water is available, several wildlife species consider the canyon home, including bighorn sheep, migratory birds, and birds of prey. There are a few established roads through the multi-colored canyon as well as hiking and equestrian trails. Washes and dry stream beds make for good hiking trails, too, although not during a flash flood. Hobby rock collecting is permitted. Primitive camp sites are available with a picnic table and single tap. Bring your own firewood and water.

Hours: Open daily 7:45am - 4:30pm.

Admission: Free to the park. $6 to camp.

Ages: 6 years and up.

AMBOY CRATER

(760) 326-7000 / vulcan.wr.usgs.gov

National Trails Highway (Old Route 66), Amboy

(Going E. [from Barstow] on the Needles Fwy [40], exit S.E. on National Trails Hwy [just past Ludlow]. Going W. on 40, exit S. on Kelbaker Rd. and drive for 11 miles, R. on National Trails Hwy. It's located about 1 hour between Barstow and Needles just W. of the town of Amboy. [TG-370 J4])

What do volcanoes look like? Well, instead of seeing one erupt (which would be thrilling, but potentially deadly), you can see the aftermath by hiking around this cinder cone. The surrounding lava flows surface is black with specks of green-colored, olivine crystals. The surface texture is alternately rough like jutting rocks or smooth like glass. There are twelve, bowl-shaped depressions that add even more variety to the volcanic features.

The Bureau of Land Management suggests a minimum of three hours hiking time to hike around the entire crater rim. The cone is about one mile from the parking lot and it is one mile in circumference. If you follow the trail to the right of the cinder cone, you'll head up to its wide opening where an eruption breached the crater wall. From here the climb to the top is only an eighty-foot incline. There are a few, scattered picnic tables and some informational kiosks. A favorite time to visit is between March and May when the desert flowers are blooming and the sunrises and sunsets are often pink and purple hued. Tips: Carry water! Wear tough boots or tennis shoes as the lava rock can cut bottoms of shoes. Winters can be really cold here, and summer is blazing hot. Note that the town of Amboy is only five miles to the east of the crater.

    Hours: Open daily sunrise to sunset.
Admission: Free
    Ages: 7 years and up.

CALICO EARLY MAN ARCHAEOLOGICAL SITE

(760) 252-6000 / www.ca.blm.gov
Minneola Road, Calico
(Exit Mojave Fwy [I-15] N on Minneola Rd., follow the signs and drive 2 1/2 miles along graded dirt road to the site. It's about 15 miles from Barstow, and 6 miles east of Calico Ghost Town. [TG-393 A2])

At this brief natural pit stop, visitors hike a half-mile to look into this "in-place museum" of Pleistocene archaeology. In other words, look down into excavated pits to see artifacts on the walls and floors made by early man. There are two master pits where most of the findings have been made, one training trench, and four test pits. On your guided tour, which is the only way to see the pit, you'll learn about the area's geography and history. A very small museum shows some of the pottery shards and other artifacts that have been excavated.

    Hours: Tours are offered Wed. at 1:30pm and 3:30pm; Thurs. - Sun. at 9:30am, 11:30am; 1:30pm and 3:30pm.
Admission: $5 for the first 2 adults in your group, $2.50 for each adult thereafter; $2 for seniors; $1 for ages 12 and under.
    Ages: 7 years and up.

CUCAMONGA-GUASTI REGIONAL PARK

(909) 481-4205 / www.county-parks.com
800 N. Archibald Avenue, Ontario
(Exit San Bernardino Fwy [10] N. on Archibald Ave. [TG-602 J6])

Guasti Regional Park offers seasonal catfish and trout fishing at its nice-sized lakes. Pedal boat rentals are available in the summer. The playground has a tire swing, monkey bars, and cement tubes with holes to climb through, plus open grassy areas for running around.

During the summer have some wet fun by going down the two waterslides and/or swimming in the pool. You can also just beach it on the sandy area around the pool and grassy area beyond that. A snack bar, open seasonally also, sells hot dogs, burritos, chips, and ice cream, and is located next to the bait shop - make sure you choose the right food place for you!

Hours: The park is open Fri. - Wed., 7:30am - 5pm. Closed on Thurs. Call for extended summer hours.

Admission: $5 per vehicle. Pedestrians are $2. Fishing permits are $5 for ages 8 and older; $2 for 7 and under. Pedal boat rentals are $5 a half hour, and available in the summertime only. Swimming is $2 weekdays for ages 4 and up, plus the entrance fee; $3 on weekends. An all-day swim and waterslide pass costs $8, plus the entrance fee.

Ages: All

GLEN HELEN REGIONAL PARK

(909) 887-7540 / www.county-parks.com

2555 Glen Helen Parkway, San Bernardino

(Going W. on San Bernardino Fwy [215], exit S. on Devore Rd., which turns into Glen Helen Pkwy. Going E. on 215, exit E. on Cajon Blvd. (just after 15 jct.), R. on Devore. From Ontario Fwy [15], exit N.E. on Glen Helen Pkwy. [TG-545 C1])

This scenic 1,340-acre park, nestled in the mountains, is worth the drive. It offers an assortment of year-round fun, such as catfish and trout fishing in the sizeable lake (a license is needed for those over 16 years old), volleyball courts, a baseball diamond, horseshoe pits, wide open grassy areas, playgrounds, and lots of trails for hiking up and down the mountain. Favorite summer activities include renting pedal boats, swimming in the pool, slip-sliding down the two waterslides that end in a small pool, and sunbathing on the surrounding beach area. Replenish your energy at the nearby snack bar. Many special events occur at the huge pavilion including concerts and other programs. Note: See the April Calendar section for details about the annual Renaissance Pleasure Faire held here.

Camping is available just across the road. The close-together camping sites are just off the freeway and are comprised mostly of dirt and very few trees, but it is a place to stay.

Hours: Open daily in the summer 6:30am - 8pm; open the rest of the year daily 6:30am - 5:30pm. Water activities are open Memorial Day through Labor Day, Wed. - Sun. from 10am - 5pm.

Admission: $5 per vehicle, or $2 for pedestrians. All-day swimming and use of the water slides is $4 per person in addition to the entrance fee. Pedal boat rentals are $5 for a half hour and are available on weekends only. Camping starts at $10 a night for 4 people, $3 extra per person.

Ages: All

JURUPA HILLS REGIONAL PARK / MARTIN TUDOR

(909) 428-8360

11660 Sierra, Fontana

(Exit San Bernardino Fwy [10] S. on Sierra Ave. [TG-644 J3])

Jurupa Hills is another terrific park nestled into a rocky mountainside. It has a great wooden playground for slightly older kids, with wavy slides, a big spiral slide, swaying bridges, and swings. The playground is just outside the water play area. A 418-foot long, gently winding waterslide helps cool off sweaty bodies during the hot summer months. There is also a pool with a small slide. The lower level of the park has a grassy picnic area, along with a baseball diamond, and a few swings.

Hours: The park is open daily dawn - dusk. The pool and slide are open weekends only Memorial Day through mid-June, noon - 6pm; open daily in the summer through Labor Day, 11am - 6pm.

Admission: $2 per vehicle is charged on weekends only. An additional $5 per person includes admittance to all the water activities (groups of ten or more are $4 per person); kids 39" and under are free.

Ages: All

LAKE GREGORY ☼
(909) 338-2233 / www.co.san-bernardino.ca.us/parks $$
24171 Lake Drive, Crestline
(From Rim of the World Hwy [18], go N. on Hwy 138, stay straight on Lake Drive when 138 forks left and follow signs to Lake Gregory. It's about 7 miles off the hwy. [TG-516 J3])

Crestline is a little mountain town that crowds usually just pass through on their way to stay at Lake Arrowhead or Big Bear. Lake Gregory, toward the east end of Crestline, is a large, beautiful lake with clear blue water and a stretch of white sandy beach. It's nestled in the San Bernardino mountains and surrounded by pine and oak trees. One section of the waveless water is roped off for swimmers and paddle boarders, and is patrolled by lifeguards. The long, thin paddle boards rent for $2 a half hour and must be handled with some degree of finesse if you want to stay topside. Another fun aquatic option is a 300-foot-long, twisting waterslide that ends in a small pool. Barbecue pits and picnic tables are available at the swim beach. You may bring in ice chests, but no glass containers or alcohol. A snack bar is here, too.

The rest of the lake is open year round for boating and fishing. The on-site bait and tackle shop rents poles. Rowboat rentals are available for $5 an hour, with a $10 minimum, plus a $25 deposit. Seasonal boat rentals include canoes, kayaks, and windsurfers. Pedal boats, which seat four people, and Aqua Cycles, big-wheel-type water cycles that seat two people, both use pedal power and rent for $6 a half hour, each. They are available daily in the summer, and on weekends through October.

Hours: The lake is open daily sunup to sundown for fishing. The swim beach and waterslide, and most boating activity is open daily Memorial Day through Labor Day 10am - 5pm.

Admission: $3 for ages 4 and up for the swim beach; children 3 and under are free. In addition to the entrance fee, an all-day waterslide pass is $6; five rides on the slide is $4. A permit is needed for fishing for ages 16 and up - $10.75. A California state license is not necessary.

Ages: All

MOJAVE NARROWS REGIONAL PARK

(760) 245-2226 - park / (760) 244-1644 - horse rentals / www.county- $
parks.com

18000 Yates Road, Victorville

(Exit Mojave Fwy [I-15] E. on Bear Valley, N. on Ridgecrest Rd. Ridgecrest turns in to Yates. [TG-4386 H1])

    This delightful park hosts the annual Huck Finn Jubilee in June and, indeed, it looks like it belongs in Huck Finn country. There are two lakes. The larger one, Horseshoe Lake, is great for fishin' (no license needed for ages 15 years and under), has a bait shop near the entrance, and an island in the middle of it. A stream runs through part of the park which boasts of wide open grassy spaces; lots of trees, including willow thickets and patches of cottonwoods; some hiking and riding trails; a paved nature trail for the physically disabled; and pasture land for the numerous horses boarded at the on-site stables. Decent tent and full hookup camp sites (with showers), an equestrian campground, a few playgrounds, pedal and row boat rentals, an archery range, hay rides, and picnic shelters complete the park.

    Hours: Open daily 7am - dusk. Horse rentals are available during the summer Tues. - Sun., 9am - 6pm; during the rest of the year, weekends and holidays only, 9am - 5pm.

Admission: $3 per car. Camping is $10 a night. Horseback riding is $20 an hour for ages 6 and up. Pedal boats rentals are $5 a half hour. Row boats are $5 an hour.

    Ages: All

MOUNT BALDY TROUT PONDS

(909) 982-4246 $$$

Mount Baldy Road, Mount Baldy Village

(Exit San Bernardino Fwy [10] N. on Monte Vista Ave., which turns into Padua Ave., R. on Mount Baldy Rd. It's about 11 miles past Montclair, just N. of Mt Baldy Village. [TG-512 B4])

    No waders are needed to catch fish at this delightful fishing spot up in the mountains. The clear, spring water ponds are surrounded by shady oak trees. The first pond stocks fish 13" through 18"; the second holds smaller fish, 9" through 13". The fish are abundant here, so chances are your young fisherboy/girl will make at least one catch of the day! All fish caught must be kept and paid for. After you've caught your fill, or the kids need more action, take a hike through the woods on the surrounding trails. During the summertime, enjoy a refreshing dip in the nearby stream.

    Hours: The ponds are open Sat., Sun., and holidays (including week-long school holiday breaks) 9am - 4:30pm. Additionally, they are open July through August, Tues. - Sun., 10am - 4pm. Note: You must be here at least a half hour before closing time. Closed Thanksgiving and Christmas.

Admission: $1 if your bring your own pole; $2 to rent a pole. Price includes bait, cleaning, and packing fish in ice. You may share poles. Fish prices range from $2.15 for 9" to $16.45 for 18".

    Ages: 3 years and up.

PRADO REGIONAL PARK

(909) 597-4260 - park information; (909) 597-5757 - horse rentals. /
www.co.san-bernardino.ca.us/parks

16700 S. Euclid Avenue, Chino

(Exit Riverside Fwy [91] N. on Corona Exp [71], which turns into Chino Valley Fwy, exit N.E. on Euclid [83]. From the Pomona Fwy [60], exit S. on Euclid [83]. [TG-712 C2])

This is another, has-it-all regional park! Besides the three softball diamonds, two soccer fields for tournament games or family fun, and year-round fishing at the huge lake (over 16 years old needs a license), there are four playground areas. One playground has assorted cement shapes to climb up and through, while the others have newer equipment with more traditional activities.

For those of you with delicate noses, you have correctly detected the nearby presence of horses, cattle, and sheep, as this is farm country. There are herds and ranches all up and down Euclid Street. The Prado Equestrian Center is located at the northern end of the park. Children 7 years old and up can take a one-hour, or more, ride on a trail through the park and to the basin. Kids 2 to 7 years can be led inside the arena for a minimal charge.

Get physical on the weekends in the summer by renting a row boat, pedal boat, or aqua cycle. There is a special area for radio-controlled boats, too. A snack bar is also open in the summer. The paved street that winds all around the park will have to suffice for most skating or hiking desires. Across Euclid Street, the park also has trap and skeet fields.

If you like it here so much that you don't want to go home, stay and camp. The campgrounds are at the far end of the park and are nice-looking. While a few of the sites have small shade trees, the majority of the campsites are near barren, gently sloping hills.

Hours: The park is open daily 7:30am - 5pm; open extended hours during the summer. Boat rentals are available in the summer only. Horseback riding is available Tues. - Sun., 8am - 5pm.

Admission: $5 per vehicle during the week; $6 on weekends. Pedestrians are $2. Boat launches are $2. Fishing, ages 7 and older, is $5 a person; $2 for children 6 and under. Horseback riding is $20 an hour. Pedal boats rentals are $5 for half an hour; aqua boats are $6 for half an hour; and rowboats are $4 an hour Mon. - Fri.; $5 an hour Sat. - Sun., with minimum rental hours required. Camping starts at $16 a campsite.

Ages: All

RAINBOW BASIN

(760) 252-6000 / www.ca.blm.gov

Fossil Canyon Loop Road, 8 miles N. of Barstow

(Exit Mojave Fwy [15] N. on Barstow Rd., L. on Main St., R. on First St., L. on Fort Irwin Rd. Go about 6 miles, turn L. on Fossil Bed Rd. and go about 2 miles, R. toward Owl Canyon Campground. The 4 mile, narrow, bumpy, one-way dirt road loops around. [TG-349 B6])

ROY G BIV (red, orange, yellow, green, blue, indigo, and violet) and all the in between, somewhat muted, colors of the rainbow are represented at the aptly named Rainbow Basin. Note: Although the dirt roads are a bit bumpy, the destination is worth the jolting. (Four-wheel drive vehicles are recommended, but our van made it without any problems.) The colorful sedimentary rock formations are eye catching. We stopped the car several times to get out and look more closely at the variety of rocks and to hike among the formations, even though there are no developed trails. We didn't find any, but we read that this area is rich with mammal fossil remains as mastodons, pronghorns, "dog-bears", and horses have been found here. Collecting fossils, however, is forbidden. Tip: Bring water!

Owl Canyon Campground has thirty-one fairly primitive sites. Facilities include fire rings, grills, and vault toilets. Bring your own firewood and water. Remember that, as with any desert area, extreme temperatures occur.

Hours: Open daily dawn to dusk.
Admission: Free. Camping is $6 a night.
Ages: 4 years and up.

YUCAIPA REGIONAL PARK
(909) 790-3127 / www.co.san-bernardino.ca.us/parks
33900 Oak Glen Road, Yucaipa
(Going E. on San Bernardino Fwy [10], exit N.E. on Yucaipa Blvd., L. on Oak Glen Rd. Going W. on 10, exit N. on Live Oak Canyon / Oak Glen. It's W. of the Oak Glen apple orchards. [TG-649 J1])

Nestled in the rocky San Bernardino Mountains is this huge, beautiful oasis of a park offering year-round fun. Fish in any one of the three, very large, picturesque lakes to catch seasonal bass, trout, or catfish. A fishing license is required.

During the summer months, get in the swim of things in the one-acre swim lagoon, and/or go for the two long waterslides! White sandy beaches frame the water's edge, with grassy areas just beyond them. A few steps away is a full-service snack bar, plus pedal boat and aqua cycle rentals. A wonderful playground is right outside the swim area. Another playground, designed specifically for disabled children, is across the way.

RV and tent camping is available for those who really want to get away from it all for a weekend or so. The grassy areas, trees, and mountains are a scenic setting for the camp sites. There are plenty of picnic tables and shelters, as well as barbecue pits. Hiking is encouraged on either paved trails or along the few dirt pathways. (See OAK GLEN / APPLE PICKING & TOURS, under the Edible Adventures section, for nearby places to go.)

Hours: The park is open most of the year daily 7:30am - 5pm; open in
                 the summer daily 7:30am - 8pm. Swimming is available in the
                 summer Tues. - Sun.,10am - 5pm.
Admission: $5 per vehicle. Pedestrians are $2. A fishing license is needed for
                 those over 16 - available here for $10.75. Fishing is $5 a day for
                 ages 8 and older; $2 for ages 7 and under, plus park admission.
                 Entrance to the swim lagoon Tues. - Fri. is $2 per person for kids
                 4 and up, plus park admission; $3 on Sat. - Sun. An all-day
                 waterslide and swim pass is $8 per person, plus park admission.
                 Pedal boat and aqua cycle rentals are $6 for a half hour. Camping
                 prices range from $11 to $18 per night, for up to six people.

Ages: All

AGUA CALIENTE SPRINGS COUNTY PARK   ☼
(858) 694-3049 - park; (619) 565-3600 - reservation / www.co.san-
diego.ca.us/parks

*39555 Great Southern Overland Stage Route of 1849, Agua Caliente Hot
Springs*
(From 8 Fwy head E. to Ocotillo, N. on Imperial Hwy [S2]. It's about 25 miles to the park. From
Route 78 head E. through Julian, S. on S2. [TG-430 D3])

For a more therapeutic take on life, come visit Agua Caliente Springs
County Park. It features a big, glass-enclosed pool with water temperature
maintained at 102 degrees as it is fed by underground hot mineral springs.
Ahhhh - feels so good! However, only kids 56" and up and adults may use the
indoor pool. The fifteen-foot by thirty-foot shallow outdoor pool is fun for
children to use, though.

The park also has a general store, shuffleboard courts, horseshoe pits, play
areas, hiking trails and over 140 campsites. There are several trails to choose
from, including a half-mile loop called Ocotillo Ridge Nature Trail and a more
arduous two-and-a-half-mile trail called Moonlight Canyon Trail. The park is
pretty and parts of it are lush with lots of plants and trees fed by the natural
springs running throughout. Look for the many species of birds, and other
wildlife, that call it home.

Hours: The park is closed for the summer. It is open Labor Day through
Memorial Day, Mon. - Thurs., 9:30am - 6pm; Fri. - Sun., 9:30am
- 9pm. The indoor pool is open daily for day use and over night
campers, 10am - 5:30pm. It is open just for adults at other times.
The outdoor pool is open March through May daily, 9:30am -
5pm; September through February daily, 9:30am - sunset.

Admission: $2 per vehicle for day use. Use of the pools are included in this
fee. Camping costs between $10 (tents) - $16 (full hook-ups) a
night. There is an additional $3 fee for camping reservations.

Ages: 3 years and up.

ANZA BORREGO STATE PARK   ☼
(760) 767-5311 - state park; (760 767-4205 - visitor center; (760) 767- $
4684 - wildflower hotline; (800) 444-7275 - camping reservations. /
www.anzaborrego.statepark.org

200 Palm Canyon Drive, Borrego Springs
(From San Diego - Exit 8 Fwy N. on Cuyamaca Hwy [79], through Julian, go E. on San Felipe Rd
[S-2] about 4.5 miles, L. on Montezuma Valley Rd. [S-22] into Borrego Springs, L. at first stop
sign, Palm Cyn. Dr., which dead-ends into the Visitors Center. Look for the flagpole as the Visitors
Center building is hidden. From Escondido Fwy [15] exit E. Rt.79 through Warner Springs, S. on
S-2, then look at the directions from San Diego for the park entrance. From San Diego Fwy [5],
exit E. on 78 Fwy to Julian. Take 78 E. out of Julian, N. on Yaqui Pass Rd. [S-3], L. on Borrego
Springs Rd., L. on Palm Cyn. Dr. [S-22], stay on Palm Canyon to the end. [TG-410 B8])

This massive state park is over 600,000 acres of living desert, which
includes palm trees, flowers, oases, bighorn sheep, and lizards, plus sand, rocks,
mountains, and much more. The following description merely touches on a few

of the activities and places that this park has to offer. Remember that this is a desert and the temperatures can reach over 125 degrees during the summer - always bring water!!! Nighttime temperatures can drop drastically, no matter what time of year, so be prepared for anything!

As with any major park, your best bet is to start at the Visitors Center. Get familiar with the park by watching the slide show that is presented upon request, and looking at the exhibits such as taxidermied animals and photographs. Be sure to pick up trail guides and a map.

Anza Borrego has some of the most incredible scenery in Southern California and although much of it can be seen by driving through the park, the really awe-inspiring vistas and landscape can only be seen by hiking. Within the park, take your choice of hiking trails which range from easy loops to arduous "mountain man" trails. One of the most popular hikes is a one-and-a-half-mile nature trail from the Borrego Palm Canyon campground up through Borrego Palm Canyon. The end of the trail is a sight for sore eyes (and hot bodies) - a refreshing waterfall with a pool! Parking is available near the trail entrance for $5 per vehicle.

There are several campsites available in this gigantic park, including one for campers with horses. Tip: Try to choose a site that has some shelter from the desert winds that blow in seemingly at random. Prices for camping run the gamut from the $5 per vehicle entrance fee for back country camping to $22 a night, depending on location and facilities. For more information call the park office at the number above.

See the previous entry, AGUA CALIENTE SPRINGS COUNTY PARK, as it located at the southern part of Anza Borrego park, as well as OCOTILLO WELLS STATE VEHICULAR RECREATION AREA under the Transportation section.

Hours: The park is open 24 hours a day, 365 days a year. The Visitor's Center is open October through May daily 9am - 5pm. It's open June through September on weekends and holidays only, 9am - 5pm.

Admission: $5 per vehicle. Camping prices range from $5 - $22 a night.

Ages: 3 years and up.

BALBOA PARK
(619) 239-0512 / www.balboapark.org
Balboa Park, San Diego

See BALBOA PARK under the Museums section.

BATIQUITOS LAGOON ECOLOGICAL RESERVE   ☀
(760) 943-7583; (760) 845-3501 - Fri. - Sun., 10am - 2pm. /   !
www.batiquitosfoundation.org
E. Batiquitos Drive, Carlsbad

(Going N. on San Diego Fwy [5], exit E. on La Costa Ave., L. on El Camino Real [S-11], L. on Aviara Pkwy, L. on Batiquitos Dr. Going S. on 5, exit E. on Poinsettia Ln, R. on Batiquitos. From Batiquitos, follow lagoon and look for parking. [TG-1127 D7])

Although we parked at an overlook point, this pretty walking trail (no bikes allowed) is mostly a fairly level hard dirt pathway. The trail is sandwiched between a golf course on one side (that boasts a beautiful waterfall) and the lagoon on the other. There is even a branch of the trail that goes closer to the water for a short ways. Bring binoculars for a more up-close look at the wide variety of birds that flock here. Along the almost two-mile, non-looping trail, are trees, benches, and interpretative signs that describe the critters that call this salt marsh their home.

Hours: Open daily dawn to dusk.
Admission: Free
Ages: All; strollers/wheelchairs are O.K. for a good part of the path.

BELL GARDENS

(760) 749-6297 / www.bellgardensfarm.com
30841 Cole Grade Road, Valley Center
(Going S. on Escondido Fwy [15], exit E. on Gopher Canyon Rd. (near Escondido) and cross the freeway. Turn R. onto Champagne Blvd., L. on Old Castle Rd. until it joins with Lilac Rd. Continue S.E. on Lilac Rd., L. on Valley Center Rd., L. on Cole Grade Rd. and look for entrance on R. Going N. on 15, exit E. on Valley Pkwy and follow it through Escondido until it becomes Valley Center Rd., L. on Cole Grade Rd. [TG-1070 F3])

What Mexican fast food restaurant rings a bell with your kids? Yes - Taco Bell! Glen Bell, founder of Taco Bell, is also the founder of this delightful garden, a real working farm that encompasses 115 acres of cultivated fields, a greenhouse, a creek bed, walking trails that are stroller/wheelchair friendly, lawns for picnicking and play, a free tractor-drawn hay wagon ride, and a free quarter-scale train ride. Your rides, depending on the season, take you past cornfields, tomato plants, various other vegetables, and a pumpkin patch, plus a small lake (stocked with catfish - no fishing allowed), and through an oak grove. The on-site produce stand sells fresh-picked, seasonal fruits and veggies, such as artichokes, beans, carrots, garlic, Indian corn, melons, peas, rhubarb, spinach, and strawberries, plus some newer food combos such as yellow seedless watermelon and lemon cucumbers. Gourds and dried flower arrangements are also available for purchase. In the barn, which is shaped like the front of a Taco Bell restaurant, you're invited to watch video clips of Mr. Bell describing and showing his garden.

Bell Gardens also offers seasonal events and activities, guided school tours during the week, and farm-related classes and workshops. For instance, the general farm tour, which is offered year round, consists of a veggies show-and-tell, samples to taste, and a walk through Ghost Canyon to visit the demonstration gardens - $3 per person. At the Strawberry Pick, offered April through June, visitors learn all about the crop and then pick a basket full of berries - $5 per child. Adobe brick making, offered year round, includes the recipe and making mini-bricks to take home (participants will get muddy) - $10 per person. A walk through a corn maze and exploration of the pumpkin patch is offered in October. The maze is free; pumpkins are $5 per child. Most of the tours also include the hay ride and train ride, too. Note: For your information, you'll pass an Arabian Horse Farm on the way into Bell Gardens.

Hours: Open November through March, 10am - 4pm; open April
                 through October, 10am - 6pm. Closed Thanksgiving, Christmas,
                 and during inclement weather. Farm tours are offered on
                 weekends for the general public, or for groups of 10 or more
                 during the week.
Admission: Free. See the last paragraph for tour prices.
Ages: All

BLUE SKY ECOLOGICAL RESERVE   ☼
(858) 679-5469 / users.abac.com/bluesky   !
Espola Road & Green Valley, Poway
(Exit Escondido Fwy [15] E. on Rancho Bernardo Rd., which turns into Espola. [TG-1170 G3])

Head for the hills! From the parking lot, that is your only option. The large,
mostly hard-packed dirt fire road follows along a seasonal creek into the hills.
The main trail leading to 700 acres of nature is surrounded by tall, leafy oak and
sycamore trees, and shrubs. One trail branches off to hook up at the neighboring
LAKE POWAY. (See this entry in this section for more details on the lake.)
Bring your own water. No bikes allowed. Guided groups hikes, such as Owl
Prowl and Star Party, are offered several times throughout the year.
Hours: Open daily sunrise to sunset.
Admission: Free
Ages: 4 years and up.

CIVIC CENTER PARK / VISTA SKATE PARK   ☼
(760) 726-1340 / www.ci.vista.ca.us   !
600 Eucalyptus Avenue, Vista   ⏚
(Going W. on 78 Fwy, exit N. on Escondido Ave., R. on Eucalyptus. Going E. on 78, exit N. on
Vista Village Dr., R. on Escondido, L. on Eucalyptus. [TG-1087 J6])

This outdoor, 9,000 square foot cement skate park has curbs, small ramps,
stairs, rails, platforms, all in bowl-shaped sides. Spectators watch from a slightly
elevated standpoint. All participants must wear a helmet and knee and elbow
pads. Picnic tables and a playground are also on the grounds.
Hours: Open Mon. - Fri., 10am - dusk; Sat. - Sun., 8:30 - dusk.
Admission: Free
Ages: 7 years and up.

CUYAMACA RANCHO STATE PARK / LAKE   ☼
CUYAMACA
(760) 765-0755 - park; (800) 444-7275 - camping reservations / $
parks.ca.gov
12551 Cuyamaca Highway [79], Descanso, San Diego County
(Exit 8 Fwy N. on Hwy. 79, about 9 1/2 miles up; or exit Hwy 78 [from Julian] S. on Hwy. 79.
[TG-1196 G6])

Retreat from the buildings, noise, and general busyness of city life to this
outstanding state park with its 25,000 acres of pristine wilderness - a balm to the
mind and soul. Take in the forests, grassy meadows, streams, peaks, and valleys
that this park has to offer. There are over 120 miles of hiking trails and forty

miles of biking trails along the fire roads and access roads. As the terrain varies, hiking trails vary in their degree of difficulty. Be on the lookout for birds, mule deer, lizards, coyotes, and other critters. Pick up a trail map (50¢) at the park headquarters. While at the headquarters, go through the adjacent museum, which features Native American artifacts, and other exhibits regarding the history and the plant and animal life of this area.

Seasonal changes at this altitude of 4,000 feet are often drastic and beautiful: Autumn bursts on the scene with its rich colors of gold, red, and orange; winter brings a white blanket of snow; spring explodes with a profusion of brilliant wildflowers; and summer offers refreshment, by sitting near a stream, under a canopy of trees.

Want to go horseback riding through the mountainside, but don't own a horse? Call Holidays on Horseback riding stables, (619) 445-3997 / www.holidaysonhorseback.com, and enjoy a one-and-a-half-hour ($40 per person) or two-hour ($50 per person) excursion. Riders must be at least 7 years old. Ask about the half-day buffet ride - four hours of riding, plus lunch. Reservations are needed for all rides - no walk-ins.

Campgrounds in the park, and some near rivers, are available for families at either Paso Picacho or Green Valley. You can hike to waterfalls from the latter campground. The cost is $12 per night, maximum eight people per campsite. Most of the camp grounds have picnic tables, fire rings, and heated showers (25¢). Paso Picacho also has a few one-room cabins available for $15 to $22 a night. Camp with your horse at specific campgrounds for $17 a night.

Fishing or boating at Lake Cuyamaca, (877) 581-9904 / www.lakecuyamaca.org, is another way to enjoy this area. Motorboat rentals are $26 a day *oar* rent a row boat at $13 a day. Canoes are $7 an hour. Fishing permits are $5 for adults; $2.50 for kids 8 to 15 years; children 7 years and under are free with a licensed adult. A California license is also required for ages 16 and up for $10.75. Depending on the season (and your luck), you can catch trout, catfish, bass, bluegill, and crappie. The lake is at the northern end of the park. There is also a full-service restaurant at the lake - in case you don't catch your own meal!

Hours:	The park is open daily sunrise to sunset. The gift shop and museum are open Fri. - Mon., 10am - 4pm. Fishing and boat rentals are open daily 6:30am - sunset. Call for extended summer hours.
Admission:	$2 for day use parking. Other prices are mentioned above. There are several scenic turn-outs along Hwy. 79 that offer picnic tables and hiking trails.
Ages:	2 years and up.

DALEY RANCH
(760) 741-4680 or (760) 839-6266 / www.ci.escondido.ca.us
La Honda Drive, Escondido
(Exit Escondido Fwy [15] E. on El Norte Pkwy., L. on La Honda Dr. It's next to Dixon Lake. [TG-1110 C3])

This 3,058-acre ranch is a hiking/mountain biking wilderness habitat preserve that offers a variety of terrain, from meadows to open grasslands to hills with rugged boulders. Twenty miles of main trails and offshoots traverse the property and range from wide, easy paved fire roads to narrow, up and down, dirt trails. We hiked the somewhat steep East Ridge route (1.6 miles) and reached two decent-sized ponds. Boulder Loop Trail (2.5 miles) offers a great view and rock "gardens." The wide Ranch House Loop Trail (2.5 miles) passes the site of Daley's original (unrestored) log cabin. The ranch house, built in 1927, will eventually become an interpretative center. On Sunday, a free shuttle service that runs every half hour, takes visitors from the parking area up a dirt road to the ranch house. Note: DIXON LAKE is just "next door". See this section for details.

    Hours: Open dawn to dusk.
Admission: Free
    Ages: 5 years and up.

DISCOVERY PARK / DISCOVERY LAKE

www.san-marcos.net
Foxhall Street, San Marcos
(Exit Highway 78 S.W. on San Marcos Blvd., L. on S. Bent Ave., which turns in to Craven, R. on Foxhall. [TG-1128 G3])

    This attractive small park has a younger children's play area by the parking lot with two wooden trains to climb on, a grassy area, and a covered picnic pavilion. A little lake is ringed by a 3/4 mile smooth trail; half of which is paved in asphalt, the other half is hard-packed dirt. The pathway makes for a nice stroll or bike ride. Fishing is allowed, although one has to be fairly optimistic or incredibly lucky to catch anything, as the lake is not stocked.

    Hours: Open dawn to dusk.
Admission: Free
    Ages: All

DIXON LAKE

(760) 741-3328 / www.ci.escondido.ca.us
La Honda Drive, Escondido
(Exit Escondido Fwy [15] E. at El Norte Pkwy, L. at La Honda Drive. Dixon Lake is to the R.; Daley Ranch is to the L. [TG-1110 C3])

    This beautiful get-away offers year-round fishing with promising areas of the reservoir titled Trout Cove, Catfish Cove, and Bass Point. Fish off the shoreline, off the piers, or rent a motor boat or row boat to try your luck. Paddle boat rentals are also available. The lake is cradled in pines, poplars and other vegetation along the surrounding hillsides. There are a few short walking trails along the lake. (For longer hikes, go "next door" to DALEY RANCH. See this section for details.) One picnic area, with a small playground and a patch of grass, is at the entrance of the park. Another, larger one, with some picnic shelters and more play equipment, is farther in. A concession stand is open seasonally.

    Camping spots are up on the mountain ridge and overlook the valley on one side, the lake on the other. Some of the sites are a very short hike down from the parking area and therefore a bit more private than other sites. All in all - Dixon Lake is scenic and peaceful. Note: No swimming or biking is allowed.

Hours: Open daily dawn to dusk.

Admission: $1 per vehicle. Camping is $12 a night, plus an advance registration fee of $5. Fishing is $5 for ages 16 and up; $4 for seniors; $3 for ages 8 - 15; children 7 and under are free. A fishing license is also required. Night fishing is available during summer months. Row boat rentals are $8 for half a day; $10 a full day. Motor boats are $14 for half a day; $18 a full day. Paddle boats are $6 a half hour for up to 4 people.

Ages: All

DOS PICOS REGIONAL PARK ☼

(858) 694-3049 / www.co.san-diego.ca.us/parks $

17953 Dos Picos Park Road, Ramona

(Exit Hwy 67 S. on Mussey Grade Rd., R on Dos Picos Rd. [TG-1171 H5])

This is my kind of "secluded" wilderness - close to a small town, yet seventy-eight acres that are mostly al natural. Huge boulders dot the hillsides and a trail leads up amongst them. The valley of the park is filled numerous oak trees that provide wonderful shade, as well as open grasslands and chaparral. The park also provides a pond (those over 16 years old need a fishing license), play area, horseshoe pit, picnic area, exercise course, open play areas, and tent and RV camping. There are other wilderness attractions (such as LAKE POWAY) not far away, and the town of Ramona is just around the bend.

Hours: Open daily 9am - sunset.

Admission: $2 per vehicle per day. Tent camping is $10 a night; RV, $14.

Ages: All

KIT CARSON PARK / ESCONDIDO SPORTS CENTER ☼

(760) 741-4691 - park; (760) 839-5425 - sports center /   !/$$

www.ci.escondido.ca.us

3333 Bear Valley Parkway, Escondido

(Exit Escondido Fwy [15] E. on Via Ranch Pkwy which turns into Bear Valley Pkwy. [TG-1150 B2])

Come to where the action is! A "state-of-the-art" outdoor sports center is located in the heart of Kit Carson Park. It has an arena soccer field with bleachers, a roller hockey arena, a 20,000 square-foot skate park, and a pro shop and concession stand. The fully-lighted skate park is complete with variously-sized ramps, a full street course with rails, spine, pyramids, quarter pipes, a bowl, and more - impressive! At times the skate park is open for bikers as well as skaters. Bring your own equipment, or borrow a helmet, elbow pads, and knee pads from the park at no charge, but know that it is first come, first served. Sign up for leagues, camps, and/or skate sessions, or just come to watch the action. A pond is located across the way from the Sports Center.

Just north of the center is the Humane Society and the rest of Kit Carson Park with its 185 undeveloped acres and 100 developed acres. It's very family-friendly with pretty landscaping, bridges over a creek, plenty of picnic tables, barbeque pits, green grassy areas for running around, nine ball fields (some with stadium seating), tennis courts, soccer fields, an amphitheater, a fitness course, a fitness trail with markers, hiking trails, a few playgrounds (plus one just for tots). Whew! The playgrounds feature a gigantic multi-arched cement snake, a Paul Bunyan-sized wagon tilted to slide down, a few climbing tree, and some paved pathways. This park handily accommodates all of your family's different activities.

Hours: The park is open daily dawn to dusk. Call for hours on the various sporting center activities. The skate park is open during the school year Mon. - Fri., 4pm - 9:30pm; Sat. - Sun., 9am - 9:30pm. It's open for an additional session in the summer, Mon. - Fri., 9am - 11:30am. The first session on Wed. and Sat. is for kids 6 - 12 years only. The second session on Wed. and the last session on Sun. is for bikers only.

Admission: The park is free. Skate/bike sessions are $10 per two-a-half-hour session. Year memberships are available at $15 per person, which brings the cost of each session down to $4 during the week, $6 on weekends.

Ages: All for the park. 6 years and up for skating.

LA JOLLA INDIAN RESERVATION CAMPGROUND / ☼
TUBING ON SAN LUIS REY RIVER

(760) 742-1297 or (760) 742-3771 / www.lajollaindians.com $$$

22000 Highway 76, on the La Jolla Indian Reservation, Pauma Valley

(Going S. on Escondido Fwy [15], exit E. on Rt. 76 and up about 28 mountain miles. Going N. on 15, exit N.E. on Valley Pkwy, which turns into Valley Center., R. on 76 and go about 8 miles. It's 100 yards N. of Segnme Oaks Rd., R. at the Texaco Gas Station. [TG-409 G7])

Come to the campground just for the day, or spend a night or two here in the lush, semi-wilderness of the foothills of the beautiful Palomar Mountains. Hike amongst the beautiful foliage along the San Luis Rey River; climb the rocks on the river banks; try your luck at fishing; or wade in the river waters.

For more wet thrills, go inner tubing down the river. Cruise down the two mile stretch, which takes about an hour, as many times as you're willing to hike back up it. Parts of the river are idyllic, while other parts are a bit more exciting (and bumpy). Be prepared for this adventure by wearing a hat, tee shirt, sunscreen, and sneakers (for painlessly stepping on the rocks on the river bottom). B.Y.O.T. (Bring Your Own Tube) or rent an inner tube here for $6. Tip: Tie your inner tube to your child's so you can stay together!

Almost all of the camping sites are located right by the river. (The water can be soothing or loud, depending on how you interpret its sound.) Chemical toilets are scattered throughout the camp, and hot showers are available at designated places. Campfires are allowed. Firewood, tackle, supplies, and food are available at the small Trading Post on the grounds.

Hours: Open March through November, sunrise to sunset. Tubing is available daily during the summer 8am - 6pm.

Admission: $10 per vehicle for day use for up to four people. Additional passengers are $1 per person. River tubing is included in this price. Tube rentals are $6. Camping is $15 per vehicle for tent campers; $18 for R.V.s.

Ages: 4 years and up.

LAKE JENNINGS COUNTY PARK ☼ $

(619) 466-0585 or (858) 565-3600; (858) 565-3600 - camping; (619) 667-6293 - boating / www.co.san-diego.ca.us/parks

10108 Bass Road, Lakeside

(Exit San Vicente Fwy [67] E. on Mapleview St., which turns into Lake Jennings Park Rd., L. on Bass Dr. [TG-1232 E4])

Fishing is the main draw here with trout, catfish, bass, and bluegill yours for the catching, depending on the time of year (and your luck). Fish from the shore seven days a week at the various coves, or venture out on the sprawling lake via boat Friday through Sunday only. Boat rentals are available for $8 a half day for a row boat; $20 for a motorized boat. The concession stand also sells bait. A daily permit and a California fishing license for those 16 years old and over are required. Permits are $4.75 for adults; $4.50 for seniors; $2.75 for ages 8 to 16; children 7 and under are free with a paying adult. Picnic tables overlook the lake. Miles of hiking across the chaparral-covered hills is another reason to visit Lake Jennings. And don't forget about tent and RV camping. There are some walk-back tent sites, too, which offer a bit more seclusion.

Hours: The park is open daily 9am - sunset. Fishing is allowed Mon. - Sat., 6am - dusk.

Admission: $2 per vehicle. Camping starts at $12 a night, plus a $3 reservation fee.

Ages: All

LAKE POWAY RECREATION AREA ☼ $

(858) 679-4393; (858) 679-5465 lake info; (858) 486-1234 concession stand / www.ci.poway.ca.us

14164 Lake Poway Road, Poway

(Exit Escondido Fwy [15] E. on Rancho Bernardo Rd., which turns into Espola, L. on Lake Poway. [TG-1170 H4])

Nestled between mountains, this pretty park features green grassy rolling hills, two playground areas, ball fields, a sand volleyball court, picnic tables overlooking the lake, horseshoe pits, an archery range, and miles of dirt pathways and hiking trails. One trail, great for hardy hikers and mountain bikers, is a scenic, three-mile rocky trail that goes a good distance around the lake. More rugged trails include the two-and-a-half-mile hike up to Mt. Woodson, and trails leading into the adjacent BLUE SKY RESERVE. (See this section for more details.) Be on the lookout for wildlife such as red-tail hawks, raccoons, and even deer.

The large Lake Poway is seasonally stocked with trout or catfish. Bait, fishing permits, and fishing licenses (for ages 16 years and up) can be purchased at the concession stand. Looking for something fun to tackle on summer nights?

Try night fishing any Thursday, Friday, and/or Saturday night from 4pm to
11pm, Memorial Day through Labor Day. Boats rentals are available here:
rowboats - $10 a day; motorboats - $15 a day; paddle boats - $8 an hour; and
canoes - $8 an hour.

Hours: Open daily 7am to dusk. The lake is open for fishing and boating
Wed. - Sun., sunrise to sunset.

Admission: Free for Poway residents; $4 per car for non-residents is charged
April through October on weekends and holiday Mon. (It's free
the rest of the year.) Fishing permits are $4.50 for adults; $2 for
ages 8 - 15; free for ages 7 and under.

Ages: All

LAS POSAS AQUATIC CENTER

(760) 599-9783 or (760) 744-9000 / www.san-marcos.net

N. Las Posas and W. Borden Road, San Marcos

(Exit Hwy 78 N. on Rancho Santa Fe Rd., R. on Mission Rd., L. on Las Posas Rd. [TG-1108 E5])

The park has two tennis courts, a huge treeless field, a soccer field, and a
baseball diamond. The main attraction here is summertime fun in the heated pool
that has a shallow water area for children and handicapped access ramp. A small
water play "sprayground" on the deck adjacent to pool adds to the fun for
younger children and a water play area for slighter older kids aids them in
having a "cool" time. Restrooms and showers are here, too.

Hours: The park is open daily. The pool and sprayground are open
seasonally, May to mid-September.

Admission: The park is free. Admission is $2 per person to the pool.

Ages: All

MIRAMAR RESERVOIR

(619) 668-2050 or (619) 465-3474; (619) 390-0222 concessionaire
/ www.sandiegocity.org/water

Scripps Lake Drive, Mira Mesa

(Exit Escondido Fwy [15] E. on Mira Mesa Blvd., R. on Scripps Ranch Blvd., L. on Scripps Lake Dr.
[TG-1209 G4])

Take a gander at all the geese and ducks waiting for a hand out at the
reservoir. B.Y.O.B. (Bring your own bread!) This lovely lake offers paddle boat
and rowboat rentals, fishing, and lakeside picnic tables and barbecue areas. An
almost five-mile paved trail loops around the lake and, judging by the number of
people we saw, it's ideal for walking, biking, rollerblading, and skateboarding.
November through September families can enjoy fishing and boating. Fishermen
16 years and older need a fishing license and a permit which are available to
purchase here. Rowboat rentals are $12 a day or $8 for just the afternoon. Two-
seater paddle boats rent for $8 an hour; four-seaters are $10 an hour.

Hours: The park and perimeter trail is open daily sunrise to sunset. The
lake is open for fishing and boating Sat. - Tues., sunrise to
sunset. The lake is closed for the month of October.

Admission: Free. Fishing permits are $5 for adults; $2.50 for ages 8 - 15;
children 7 and under don't need a permit.

Ages: All

MISSION BAY PARK ☼

www.sandiegocity.org !/$

2581 Quivira Court, San Diego

(Exit San Diego Fwy [5] W. on Clairemont Dr. to drive the Mission Bay loop - go S. on E. Mission Bay Dr. to Sea World Dr. to Mission Bay Dr. [or N. on Ingraham St.] to Grand Ave. [TG-1268 A4])

Mission Bay Park is not a singular bay or park like the name implies - it is thousands of acres of incredibly beautiful vistas, and of beaches, water, pathways, playgrounds, grassy areas, and various attractions. Generic things to do include jogging, cycling, in-line skating, swimming (there are nineteen miles of beaches here!), picnicking, fishing, kayaking, sailing, paddle boating, and camping. Park at any one of the scenic spots you see along Mission Bay Drive, or Ingraham Street, and enjoy. Hot spots include: <u>Pacific Beach</u>, just north of Mission Beach on Mission Boulevard - a favorite hang out for surfers, swimmers, joggers, and others; <u>Fiesta Island</u>, just northeast of Sea World, and <u>Vacation Isle</u>, on Ingraham Street north of Sea World Drive - both have numerous biking trails, delightful picnic areas, and a few playgrounds; <u>South Mission Beach</u> and <u>North Mission Beach</u>, both along Mission Boulevard - popular beaches for swimming and laying out; and <u>De Anza Cove</u>, on E. Mission Bay Drive - a nice area for swimming.

A few helpful names and phone numbers in the Mission Bay area include: Campland on the Bay, (800) 4BAY-FUN (422-9386), for camping, with over 650 sites; Mission Beach Club, which is a building shaped like a castle, (858) 488-5050, for rentals of bikes, skates, boogie boards, and more; San Diego Sailing Center, (858) 488-0651 / www.kayaksandiego.com, for rentals of sailboards and kayaks; and Windsport Kayak & Windsurfing Center, (858) 488-4642 / www.windsport.net, for kayak and windsurfing rentals.

Attractions listed separately in Mission Bay Park are: BELMONT PARK, PIRATE'S COVE, SAN DIEGO VISITOR INFORMATION CENTER, SEA WORLD, and TECOLOTE SHORES PLAY AREA.

Hours: Open daily
Admission: Free
Ages: All

MISSION TRAILS REGIONAL PARK ◑

(619) 668-3275 / www.mtrp.org !

One Father Junipero Serra Trail, San Diego

(There are several entrances to the park. From Mission Valley Fwy [8], exit N. on Mission Gorge/Fairmount and go 4 miles N. on Mission Gorge Rd. The Visitor and Interpretive Center entrance is on the L. between Jackson Dr. and Golfcrest Dr., on Father Junipero Serra Trail. From Route 52, exit S. when it ends on Mission Gorge Rd. If visiting the Old Mission Dam area, the Old Mission Dam entrance is about 1/2 mile down Mission Gorge Rd. The Visitor and Interpretive Center is about 2 miles further down Mission Gorge Rd. See directions from Fwy 8. [TG-1250 D2])

This massive, almost 6,000-acre recreational area is comprised of several major areas and points of interest: 1) The Visitor and Interpretive Center - This architecturally beautiful building blends in with the natural rock setting of the park, and is a great starting place for an adventure. Every thirty minutes the small theater presents a film on the park. Pick up trail guides, program information, and/or enjoy some interactive exhibits inside. Kids gravitate to the Indian faces carved from "rocks." Several touch screens offer information about the park - where to go, and all about the plants and animals. Walk to the upper story of the center amid bird and animal sounds. See ancient volcanic rock and a great view of your surroundings. Outside the center is a small stage and rocks that are almost irresistible for kids to climb. The kids sweated (I glowed) as we hiked on the moderate looping trail around the Visitors Center, which took us a good hour. Our mission, should we decide to accept it, is to come back to Mission Trails and experience more of what it has to offer!; 2) Lake Murray (619) 668-2050 / www.sandiegocity.org/water - At the southern part of the park this beautiful, stocked lake allows fishing and boating activities from sunrise to sunset on Wednesdays, Saturdays, and Sundays between November and Labor Day. A paved trail goes partly around the lake. Picnic tables are also available; 3) Cowles Mountain - Hiking is the main sport here. For an outstanding 360 degree view of the city, take the one-and-a-half-mile trail (about two hours) to the top of the mountain; 4) Old Mission Dam Historic Area - This is a starting point for several hikes. Picnic tables are here, too. People of all abilities can go on a self-guided paved pathway from the parking lot to the footbridge across the San Diego River, lush with foliage. Further along is the gorge with rock cliffs. Press buttons along the trail to listen to explanations of the area. Take a longer hike, too. So many trails - so little time!; 5) East Fortuna Mountain - This area offers some of the most diverse environments of the park. Check out some of the canyons! The smallish Kumeyaay Lake, accessible from Father Junipero Serra Trail, is fun for shoreline fishing. A relatively flat one-and-a-half-mile trail goes around the lake; 6) West Fortuna Mountain - You can hike or mountain bike up plateaus and series of canyons.

Hours: The trails and park are open daily sunrise to sunset, although the car entry gates are open 9am - 5pm. The Center is open daily 9am - 5pm. Closed on Christmas.

Admission: Free

Ages: 3 years and up.

MISSION VALLEY SKATE PARK

(619) 281-7885

3250 Camino del Rio North, Mission Valley

(Going W. on Jacob Dekema Fwy [805], exit N. on Mission Gorge Rd., L. on Camino del Rio. Going E. on 805, exit N. on Texas St. / Qualcomm Wy., R. on Camino Del Rio N. The park is next to the YMCA. [TG-1269 F1])

Skateboarders and roller bladers flip (not literally) for this huge, gated outdoor skate park that is just off the freeway. It has numerous, and variously-sized, wooden ramps and half pipes, plus grinding boxes, rails, and other street skate equipment, as well as areas to simply skate on asphalt. Skaters under 18 must have a waiver signed by a parent or legal guardian.

Hours: Sessions run daily 11am - 2pm; 2pm - 5pm.

Admission: $10 per person per session.

Ages: 7 years and up.

OCEAN BEACH ATHLETIC AREA / ROBB FIELD ☼
SKATEBOARD PARK

(619) 525-8486 / www.sandiegocity.org $

2525 Bacon Street, Ocean Beach

(Exit Ocean Beach Fwy [8] S. on Sunset Cliffs, R. on W. Point Loma, R. on Bacon. [TG-1267 J5])

This huge park has something for every athlete in the family. It boasts eight baseball diamonds, soccer fields, racquetball courts, several tennis courts, a football field, lots of grass areas, picnic tables, a bike path that follows along the adjacent San Diego River, and a terrific skate park at the east end.

In front of the skate park are a few very shallow cement pools (more like a toe dip area than pool) and cement area. This area is free and a good place for young skaters to practice. The gated, outdoor, smooth concrete-surface skate park has numerous pools of varying depths along with ramps, steps, a split fun box, ledges, blocks, an octagon volcano, and pump bump, plus a few flat areas and a pathway around the perimeters. Benches are just outside for ~~anxious~~, I mean, observing parents. Vending machines carry snacks and beverages. Note: All participants must have a liability release form on file signed by a parent or guardian for skateboarders under 18 years old. Helmet, elbow and knee pads are required (and available here to use at no extra charge). Parents who drop off kids take note: If a green flag is flying, the session is open. If a red flag is flying, the session is closed.

Across the street, Dusty Rhodes Park offers more picnic and run around area, plus a playground. To the west is Dog Beach, where furry visitors from all over come to romp and play frisbee on this stretch of beach. Tip: Watch where you walk.

Hours: The park is open daily sunrise to sunset. The skate park is open mid-February through mid-June daily 9am - 5:15pm; mid-June through Labor Day daily 10am - 7:30pm; after Labor Day through October, Mon. - Fri.,11am - 5pm, Sat. - Sun., 9am - 5pm; November through mid February. Mon. - Fri., 11am - 4:30pm, Sat. - Sun., 10am - 4:30pm. Sessions are 2 ½ hours each.

Admission: The park is free. The skate park is $5 per session (or all day if it's not busy); $30 for an annual pass.

Ages: All for the park; 6 years and up for the skate park.

OLD POWAY PARK

(858) 679-4313 / www.ci.poway.ca.us; www.powaymidlandrr.org

14134 Midland Road, Poway

See OLD POWAY PARK, under the Potpourri section, for details.

OTAY LAKE COUNTY PARK

(858) 694-3049 - park; (619) 668-2050 - lake /   !/$$
www.co.san-diego.ca.us/parks; www.sandiegocity.org/water
Wueste Road, Chula Vista

(Exit Jacob Dekema Fwy [805] E. on Telegraph Canyon Rd., which turns into Otay Lakes Rd., R. on Wueste Rd., L. at the fork in the road where the sign says Eastlake. If you continue straight, you'll end up at the ARCO OLYMPIC TRAINING CENTER. [TG-1332 B3])

The view from atop this small park is beautiful as it overlooks lower Otay Lake. The playground has slides, swings, and climbing equipment, plus talking tubes and a mini zip line. A grassy area, picnic tables, and three short hiking trails up the hillside complete this scenic park. Enjoy motor or row boating and fishing in the lake that is stocked once a year with catfish. Note: Visit the nearby ARCO OLYMPIC TRAINING CENTER (look under the Potpourri section) on your way to or from the park.

Hours: The park is open daily dawn to dusk. Fishing and boating are available February through September, Wed., Sat., and Sun., sunrise to sunset. No fishing or boating is allowed October through January. (It's duck season.)

Admission: The park is free. Fishing is $5 for adults, plus a fishing license; $2.50 for ages 8 - 15 (no license necessary); children 7 and under are free. Row boats are $12 for the day; motor boats are $35 for the day.

Ages: All

PALOMAR MOUNTAIN STATE PARK / PALOMAR OBSERVATORY

(760) 742-2119 - observatory; (760) 742-3462 - state park; (800) 444- $
7275 - camping reservations. / parks.ca.gov;
www.astro.caltech.edu/palomarpublic
S6, Palomar Mountain

(Exit Escondido Fwy [15] E. on Pala Rd. [Route 76], L. [N.E.] on S6 about 26 miles up the mountain to the observatory. [TG-409 G6])

Up in the Palomar Mountains, at the end of a long and winding road, is the Palomar Observatory. A short hike up to the observatory allows you to see the famed 200" Hale telescope. But forewarn your children - you can only look <u>at</u> the telescope which is housed behind glass panes; you cannot look through it. The telescope is magnificent in size and scope and seeing it is almost worth the drive here! The small one-room museum displays outstanding photos of star clusters, galaxies, and clouds of glowing gas. It also shows a continuously running video about the workings of the telescope and about our universe.

Just a few miles down the road is Palomar Mountain State Park. If you're planning on coming to the observatory, I suggest making the park a destination, too, as just walking around the observatory and museum took us only half an hour. Palomar Mountain General Store, (760) 742-3496, is at the junction of S7 and S6, making it a natural stopping place before going on to the park. The store has a bit of everything, including fossils, gems, Indian jewelry, and artifacts.

Continue about three miles on S7 to reach the park. At 2,000 acres, this

Sierra Nevada-like park is incredibly beautiful. It also can get snow in the winter. You'll find several hiking trails through the scenic mountainside. The Boucher Hill Lookout trail, for instance, is a looping two-mile hike with marvelous vistas. Fishing is available at Doane Pond, which is stocked with trout regularly. There is a five fish limit per day, and those 16 years old and older need a California state license. The park also provides areas for picnicking and overnight camping. Each of the thirty-one family campsites have fire rings and picnic tables, plus community coin-operated hot showers. Call the ranger station (park office) for more information.

Gravity Activated Sports, (800) 985-4427/ www.gasports.com, offers the Palomar plunge, or downhill biking. A van takes bikers and equipment up to the observatory. Then participants, who must be at least 12 years old, can zip down the sixteen miles and enjoy a well-deserved lunch at Mother's Kitchen. Daily departures are at 10:30am. The $80 per participant fee includes a bike, helmets, gloves, lunch, a photo, a t-shirt, and water. Bring your own sunscreen and sunglasses.

Hours: The museum and the observatory are open daily 9am - 4pm. Closed Christmas Eve and Christmas Day. The state park is open sunrise to sunset.

Admission: Free to the observatory and museum. A $2 vehicle entrance fee is charged for day use of the park. Overnight camping is $12 a night.

Ages: 8 years and up for the observatory and the museum; ages 3 and up for the park.

QUAIL BOTANICAL GARDENS

(760) 436-3036 / www.qbgardens.com   *$$*
230 Quail Gardens Drive, Encinitas
(Exit San Diego Fwy [5] E. on Encinitas Blvd., L. on Quail Gardens Dr. There are signs along the way. [TG-1147 D6])

We didn't see any quail on our visit to the Quail Botanical Gardens, but we did see (and hear) woodpeckers plus a variety of other birds such as wrens, finches, scrub jays, and hermit thrushes. The thirty landscaped acres here include desert, exotic tropical, palm, bamboo, and native California plants. The lush foliage; the incredible array of flowers; the meandering trails (some dirt, some paved); the beautiful waterfall; and the benches under shade trees, all invoked the sensation of visiting a secret garden. Some of our highlights included seeing the Sausage Tree, with its large and very heavy pods that really do resemble sausages; walking up to the Overlook Pavilion for a 360-degree view of the gardens, mountains, ocean, and surrounding community; and taking pictures of the unique flowers. Our favorite flowers were the white and yellow upside-down bellflowers. Strolling around the botanical gardens is a delightful way to spend the day! Ask about guided tours.

Hours: Open daily 9am - 5pm. Closed New Year's Day, Thanksgiving, and Christmas.

Admission: $5 for adults; $4 for seniors; $2 for ages 5 -12; children 4 and under are free.

Ages: 2 years and up.

RANCHO BERNARDO COMMUNITY PARK &   ☼
RECREATION CENTER
(858) 538-8129 - park; (858) 487-9698 - tennis club /   !
www.rbernardo.com
18402 W. Bernardo Drive, Rancho Bernardo
(Exit Escondido Fwy [15] S.W. on W. Rancho Bernardo Dr./Pomerado Rd. [TG-1150 A6])

This community park has a playground, six baseball diamonds, basketballs courts, the Bernardo Tennis Center, picnic tables, barbecue pits, and lots of grassy areas and paved pathways throughout for all kinds of wheels. All of this is nice, but what makes this park stand out is the adjoining open area with some fairly easy dirt hiking trails. The area has hard-to-resist-climbing-on large rocks scattered throughout, gentle hills, and a trail that leads to Lake Hodges, a lake within visual range from the park.

Hours: The park is open daily sunrise to sunset. Play tennis daily 7am - 9pm. (Of course you'd be tired if you played that often.)
Admission: Free. Tennis is $5 per hour and a half.
Ages: All

SAN PASQUAL BATTLEFIELD STATE HISTORIC   ☼
PARK
(760) 737-2201 / parks.ca.gov   !
15808 San Pasqual Valley Road (SR78), San Pasqual
(Going S. on San Diego Fwy [5], or Escondido Fwy [15], exit E. on Hwy 78, which turns into San Pasqual Valley Rd. Going N. on 15, exit E. on Via Rancho Pkwy., which turns into Bear Valley Rd., R. on San Pasqual Rd., which turns into Via Rancho Pkwy., go to end, R. on San Pasqual Valley Rd. It is just E. of San Diego Wild Animal Park. [TG-1131 B7])

This is the site of the worst (i.e. bloodiest) battles in California during the Mexican-American War. Kids need to know this fact for its historical significance, and because it will make their visit here more exciting. The grounds have picnic tables and a quarter-mile, looping trail. The visitors center overlooks the battlefield, which is actually across the highway, on private land. The small center has interpretive panels, a few uniforms, weapons, and a ten-minute video entitled *Mr. Polk's War*. Living History Days are held the first Sunday of each month from 11am to 2pm., but not during the summer. Docents are dressed in period costume and do old-fashioned chores, crafts, and other activities. Periodically, you can also see a cannon being fired. Note: The battle is reenacted in December. See the Calendar section for details.

Hours: The park is open Sat. - Sun., 10am - 5pm. Guided school tours are given during the week, by appointment.
Admission: Free
Ages: 6 years and up.

SANTEE LAKES REGIONAL PARK AND CAMPGROUND

(619) 448-2482 or (619) 596-3141; (619) 596-3141 reservations /
www.padredam.org/santee.htm

9040 Carlton Oaks Drive, Santee

(Take the 52 Fwy E. to the end, go E. on Mission Gorge Rd., L. on Carlton Hills Blvd., L. on Carlton Oaks Dr. Going N. on San Vicente Fwy [67], exit W. on Prospect Ave., R. on Cuyamaca St., L. on Mission Gorge Rd., R. on Carlton Hills Blvd., L. on Carlton Oaks Dr. Going S. on 67, exit W. on Woodside Ave., which turns into Mission Gorge Rd., R. on Carlton Hills Blvd., L. on Carlton Oaks Dr. [TG-1231 A6])

This regional park is made up primarily of a series of lakes that are seasonally stocked with trout, catfish, bluegill, and bass. A California state fishing license is required and available for purchase at the park entrance. No swimming is allowed. Boating and paddle boat rentals are available. The park also contains playgrounds, campgrounds, a swimming pool (for campers only), a general store, laundry facilities, and a recreation center. Full hook-up campgrounds start at $27 a night. Primitive campgrounds, open Friday and Saturday only, are available for $18 a night. Each campsite has a picnic table and barbeque pit.

Hours: The park and fishing are open Mon. - Thurs., 8am - sunset; Fri. - Sun., 6am - sunset. The pool is open seasonally.

Admission: $2 per vehicle during the week; $3 per vehicle on the weekends. Catch and release fishing permits are $4 for adults; $2 for ages 7 - 15; children 6 and under fish for free. Catch and keep permits are $7 for adults; $4 for ages 7 - 15; children 6 and under are free. Camping prices are listed above.

Ages: 2 years and up.

SOUTH CLAIREMONT RECREATION CENTER / POOL

(858) 581-9924 - recreation center; (858) 581-9923 - pool /
www.sandiegocity.org

3605 Clairemont Drive, Clairemont

(Going N on San Diego Fwy [5], exit E. on Balboa Ave., R. on Clairemont. Going S. on 5, exit S. on Mission Bay Dr., L. on Garnet Ave., which turns into Balboa Ave., R. on Clairemont. [TG-1248 E5])

This large community park offers various activities for families to enjoy. Green grassy areas and scattered picnic tables provide a picnic atmosphere, while the older-style playground, complete with hopscotch, slides, swings, and climbing apparatus, provides the fun. Check at the community center building for special classes, programs, and events. There are also two tennis courts and a good-sized, outdoor swimming pool that is open year round. During the week, only half of the pool is open for public use because the swim team uses the other half. On weekends, the whole pool is open for the public to use.

Hours: The park is open daily sunrise to sunset. The pool is open Mon. - Fri., 10am - 3:45pm (shallow end only); Sat. - Sun., 11am - 3pm (whole pool). Call for hours as they do fluctuate.

Admission: The park is free. Swimming sessions cost $2 for adults; $1.50 for seniors and ages 15 and under.

Ages: All

STELZER PARK

(619) 561-0580 - park; (619) 390-7998 - Discovery Kit Program / $
www.co.san-diego.ca.usparks
11470 Wild Cat Canyon Road, Lakeside
(Exit San Vincente Fwy [67] E. on Mapleview, L. on Ashwood, which turns into Wild Cat Canyon, drive up a few miles. [TG-1212 C7])

What a delightful respite! The 314-acre back country park has two playgrounds and several clusters of picnic tables, with barbeques, under sprawling oak and sycamore trees. (My boys also found a few good climbing trees, of course.) The park is disabled-friendly with a wheelchair exercise par course, incorporating specially designed and standard play equipment, and pathways that are wheelchair/stroller accessible. A series of short hiking trails almost form a full loop. The .7 mile Riparian Trail begins near the ranger/visitor center and goes over a series of bridges as it follows along the seasonal creek. It connects to the Wooten Loop and then you have a choice. Go left onto the .6 mile Stelzer Ridge Trail, which meanders through oak groves, or go straight, which is a relatively quick climb up to the summit and promontory point.

The small visitor center has a few taxidermied animals and a Discovery Kit Program. Each kit features pre and post visit materials for teachers and involves hands-on, interactive learning for elementary-aged children to learn about Native Americans, geology, birding, or general ecology.

Hours: Open daily sunrise to sunset.
Admission: $2 per car; bring quarters.
Ages: All

SWEETWATER REGIONAL PARK / ROHR PARK

(619) 691-5071 - park; (619) 422-3175 - Chula Vista Live Steamers, Inc. *!/$*
/ www.co.san-diego.ca.us/parks
4548 Sweetwater Road, Bonita
(Exit Jacob Dekema Fwy [805] E. on Bonita Rd., L. on Willow, R. on Sweetwater Rd. [TG-1310 H2])

Sweetwater Regional Park is a long stretch of land that runs between Sweetwater Road and Bonita Road. Fred Rohr Park is a nice oblong park, within Sweetwater Park, that parallels a golf course. The lake here is home to numerous ducks. Picnic tables are scattered throughout the park along with a few barbecue pits. Entertainment is provided by using swing sets, jungle gyms, volleyball courts, softball fields, basketball courts, grassy areas, shade trees, and cement bike and blade paths. A monthly highlight is a ride on a scale model steam locomotive around the park. The Live Steamers, who run the locomotive, also operate 1/8-scale diesel and electric trains.

Hours: The park is open daily. The trains run on the second full weekend of each month (except September) between noon and 3pm.
Admission: Free to the park. Train rides are 25¢ per person.
Ages: All

TECOLOTE SHORES PLAY AREA   ☼

www.sandiegocity.org   !

1600 E. Mission Bay Drive, San Diego   ⛹

(Exit San Diego Fwy [5] W. on Clairemont Dr., L. on E. Mission Bay Dr., past the Hilton. [TG-1268 D2])

Head for some big time fun at the large Tecolote Shores Play Area. This wonderful playground has a great combination of old and new equipment. In the main area, with its sand-covered grounds, there are slides, swings, and cement turtles to climb on (and under). Other sections include aquatic cement creatures, a pirate ship, mini-obstacle ropes course, bridges, and various other climbing apparatus. There are plenty of picnic tables and grassy areas here, too. As the playground is right on the bay, the view is beautiful. Tip: There aren't many tall trees here, at least right now, so this is a great place to fly a kite.

Hours: Open daily sunrise to sunset.
Admission: Free
Ages: All

TIDELANDS PARK   ☼

(619) 686-6225 - park; (619) 522-7342 - skate park /   !

www.portofsandiego.org

Glorietta Boulevard, Coronado   ⛹

(Exit San Diego Fwy [5] onto Coronado Bridge, first R. onto Glorietta. You'll see the park from the bridge. [TG-1289 A6])

This delightful, large, corner park offers a spectacular view of San Diego across the bay, plus pathways, a bike path, playgrounds, a fitness course, picnic tables, ball fields, grassy areas, and a sandy beach for swimming (no lifeguards). A good-sized, gated skate park near the beach has several concrete pools along with steps and grinding boxes. Fun tip: Check out the Marriot Hotel next to the park as it has real flamingos outside in its front fountain.

Hours: The park is open 6:30am - 10:30pm. Call for skate park hours.
Admission: The park is free. Call for prices for the skate park.
Ages: All

TIJUANA ESTUARY and VISITORS CENTER / BORDER ☼ FIELD STATE PARK

(619) 575-3613 - Estuary and Visitors Center /   !

inlet.geol.sc.edu/TJR/home.html

301 Caspian Way, Imperial Beach   ⛹

(Exit San Diego Fwy [5] W. on Coronado Ave., which turns into Imperial Beach Blvd., L. on 4th St., R. on Caspian Wy. [TG-1349 F1])

First things first - an estuary is: "The wide part of a river where it flows near the sea; where fresh water and salt water mix." (That's why this book is called "Fun and *Educational* . . .") The Visitors Center has several wonderful interactive exhibits. One of our favorite displays are ordinary-looking, black and white sketched pictures of habitats that magically revealed brightly colored birds, insects, fish, and other animals when viewed through a polarized filter. The touch table contains snake skin, nests, skulls, and a dead sea turtle. The food chain is portrayed through pictures and graphs. Beneath the Sand exhibit entails pressing the bill of bird puppet heads into holes in various levels of "sand." A light on the side panel displays what birds with shorter beaks, that reach only shallow levels, eat (insects and plant seed), compared to what birds with longer beaks, that can reach deeper levels, eat (crabs and worms). Upon request, a small theater shows films such as *Timeless River* and *Tide of the Heron*.

Eight miles of walking trails are interspersed throughout the reserve. Ask for a map at the center, as there are different entrance points. Some of the trails follow along the streets, while others go deeper into the coastal dunes and near the Tijuana River. Be on the lookout for terns, egrets, herons, curlews, and other birds and wildlife. On a very short loop around the center, my boys and I saw interesting plants and birds, plus thirteen bunnies! Take a guided walking tour to learn more about the flora and fauna at the estuary, or sign the kids up for one of the numerous programs available. The Jr. Ranger Program, for students 7 to 11 years old, is offered every Thursday from 3:15pm to 4:45pm. During the program kids will enjoy a walk, earn patches or buttons, and/or make a craft - all free of charge!

Just south of the estuary is Border Field State Park, which borders Mexico. A marker shows the United States - Mexico boundary. The cliffs provide an awesome view of the ocean, and of the whales during whale-watching season, which is January through March. You can even see some of Tijuana from here, including a bullfighting ring. Picnic tables, grassy areas for running around, and pathways for hiking into parts of the estuary are all parts of the park.

An exciting way to see more of the park is by taking a horseback ride on the beach. Wear long pants, a windbreaker, and close-toed shoes before saddling up for a one -to three-hour adventure. Call Sandy's Rental Stables, located at 2060 Hollister Street (go east on Coronado Avenue, right on Hollister), at (619) 424-3124 / www.sandysrentalstable.com. The stables offers other rides too, such as going on the wildlife trail in the estuary, or mounting up for a Chuckwagon Meal Ride. Children 7 years and up may join in a horseback ride; younger children may take a parent-led pony ride around the arena.

Hours: The Visitors Center is open daily 10am - 5pm. Closed Thanksgiving and Christmas. The stables are open daily 9am - 5pm.

Admission: Free to the Visitors Center. Horseback riding is $25 an hour; $55 for a 3-hour beach ride; $10 for a half-hour pony ride around the parking lot.

Ages: 3 years and up.

TORREY PINES STATE RESERVE   ☼

(858) 755-2063 / www.torreypine.org $

Torrey Pines Park Road, La Jolla

(Exit San Diego Fwy [5] W. on Del Mar Heights Rd., L. on Camino Del Mar, turns into N. Torrey Pines Rd., R. on Torrey Pines Park Rd. past the beach and up the hill. [TG-1207 H3])

The Torrey pine tree grows only in this and one other reserve (that's also in Southern California) in the whole world! My kids were impressed with this fact and by the beauty of the park. Our favorite trail was the Guy Fleming Trail. It's an easy loop, only two-thirds of a mile, and incredibly scenic through the trees out to a cliff overlooking the ocean. Tip: Hold on to younger children! Other trails include the half-mile, Parry Grove looping trail; the two-thirds-of-a-mile, Razor Point Trail with dramatic views of gorges; the steep, three-quarters-of-a-mile (one way) Beach Trail which ends at the San Diego - La Jolla Underwater Park; and the two, demanding, Broken Hill Trails.

The Visitors Center shows a short film that gives an overview of the reserve - just ask to see it. The exhibits here offer good visual information regarding the plants and animal wildlife of the reserve. On display are taxidermied raccoons, skunks, and birds; a pine cone display; a pine needle display; and more. We appreciated Torrey Pines Reserve for its glorious nature trails and its breath of fresh air! A lifeguarded State Beach is right below the reserve for those who are into sand and surf.

Hours: Open daily 8am - sunset.
Admission: $2 per vehicle.
Ages: 3 years and up.

VOLCAN MOUNTAIN NATURE PRESERVE   ☼

(760)765-0650 / www.co.san-diego.ca.us/parks   !
Near the intersection of Wynola and Farmer Roads, Julian
(On Hwy 78, just N. of town, take Main St., which becomes Farmers Rd., turn R. at the 4-way intersection with Wynola, then take an immediate L. The entrance is on your R. [TG-1136 B3])

The three-mile trail up the mountain encompasses spectacular wilderness scenery. You'll pass through meadows, high chaparral, and forests of oak and pine, to eventually reach a 360 degree panoramic view of the surrounding area, including the Salton Sea.

Hours: Open daily sunrise to sunset.
Admission: Free
Ages: 3 years and up.

WILLIAM HEISE COUNTY PARK   ☼

(858) 694-3049 / www.co.san-diego.ca.us/parks $
4945 Heise Park Road, Julian   ▦
(From Hwy 78, take Pine Hills Rd. S. for 2 miles, head E. on Frisius R. for another 2 miles, R. on Heise. [TG-1156 C5])

Consider this forest-like park a family destination. With eight miles of hiking trails to choose from, there is bound to be a trail, or two, suitable for each member of the family. Select an easy pathway that leads through a cedar forest, a moderate trail that goes through canyon live oak, or choose a rugged trail for more experienced hikers.

Over forty tent sites, sixty RV sites, and two cabins with electricity and a few furnishings, provide overnight camping in this beautiful area. The campgrounds have piped-in water, showers, barbeques and fire rings, and a playground. The one-room cabins each have a fireplace and sleep up to six people.

Hours: Open daily 9am - 5pm.

Admission: $2 per vehicle. Camping starts at $12 a night. The cabins are $35 a night and have electricity.

Ages: All

WOODLAND PARK AND AQUATIC CENTER

(760) 746-2028 - pool complex; (760) 744-9000 - community services /
www.san-marcos.net

672 Woodland Parkway, San Marcos

(Going E. on Highway 78, exit E. on Barham, L. on Woodland Pkwy. Going W. on 78, exit E. on Rancheros Dr. L. on Woodland Pkwy. [TG-1109 C6])

A large, picturesque fountain and a small, man-made, rock-lined pond decorates the corner section of this park. A short paved walkway winds around the pond and up through the park inviting strollers to use it. A children's play area and a long grassy area, plus picnic tables and barbecue pits, make the park a fun outing. Up the small hill from the park are a few pools, one of which is a wading pool. One of the pools has a fifty-foot waterslide that makes a 270-degree loop. High dives and low diving boards are other attractive features. Showers are available here, too.

Hours: The park is open daily dawn to dusk. The pool is open seasonally.

Admission: Free for park facilities. $2 per person for pool use.

Ages: All

WOODS VALLEY KAMPGROUND

(760) 749-2905 / www.woodsvalley.com

$$$$

15236 Woods Valley Road, Valley Center

(Exit Escondido Fwy [15] E. on Old Castle Rd., which turns into Lilac Rd., R. on Valley Center Rd., L. on Woods Valley Rd. about 3 miles on a gently winding country road. Look under the BATES NUT FARM in the Potpourri section for a fun nearby place to visit. [TG-1090 H5])

Kamp (or camp) in pretty, back woods country, seemingly far removed from city life. Eighty-nine camp sites are available for either tent or RV use. The campground contains fun amenities such as a swimming pool, a kid's fishing catch and release pond, a playground, a recreational hall, a general store, and nearby (not in the campground) hiking trails. Woods Valley is not open for day use.

Admission: Tent camping is $22 during the week; $28 on the weekend. RV camping is $25 during the week; $30 on the weekend.

Ages: All

AMAZING MAIZE MAZE

(805) 495-LOST (5678) / www.americanmaze.com

$$$

305 W. Hueneme Road, Camarillo

(Exit Ventura Fwy [101] S. on Las Posas Rd. Drive 1.5 miles. It's at the corner of Las Posas and Hueneme Rds. [TG-554 A4])

Plant it and they will come. One of several cornfield mazes cropping up all over the nation, this one is built on a four-acre site with two miles of twisting, turning pathways blazed through nine-foot high stalks which still have corn on them. Each year the cornfield is cut in a new design. One year depicted a California Mission; another year, an Aztec calendar. (The themes are rendered most clearly from aerial photos.)

At the entrance, players may pick up tall flags attached to PVC pipe to carry throughout their journey. The flags can help the Maze Master, who sits on a twenty-five-foot chair and has a microphone, to identify and direct flag holders. Before beginning the maze, players are told some important rules, such as no picking of the corn, how to wave the flag in case you need help, and no running because you simply get lost faster!

You can go through the maze to complete one or a combination of objectives: 1) Make it through from start to finish, which is an accomplishment in itself. 2) Time yourself. 3) Find each of the twelve puzzle pieces that are in the twelve mailboxes scattered throughout the maze. Tape the pieces together (tape is provided) on the game piece to complete the puzzle and see how the finished maze actually looks. (We found most of the pieces, but I still couldn't tell where I was or where to go next. Mazes are not my strong point.) 4) Find the twelve "kernels of knowledge" located at various dead-ends throughout the maze. This entails reading the information plaque - each one gives theme-related information - and filling in the answer on the crossword puzzle on your game sheet. We found almost all the dead-end kernels, and one of them several times!

The pathways are lined with variously-colored ribbons that represent what part of the maze you are in. For instance, in walking through the mission maze, the sky section had blue ribbons, the mission building had yellow, and the grass green. A victory bridge covers a good portion of one end of the maze. Up top, non-participants can watch the activity and parties that split up can meet again. After an hour and a half of walking, having had a great time exploring, finding most of the kernels of knowledge and nine puzzle pieces, we opted to head to the Victory bridge and call it a day. We gathered the rest of the kernels and puzzle pieces there from a staffer. Now we felt victorious!

A few side notes: Wear sunscreen. Although the Maze Master helps direct lost souls, my kids and I had split up so we used our walkie talkies to keep in contact with each other and meet up at the end. The pathways are stroller/wheelchair friendly. Water fountains are located throughout the maze. There are picnic grounds outside the maze and full-service snack bars. Younger children also enjoy the several, very low walled "practice" mazes located in the courtyard in front of the big maze. These are free.

School groups can learn the value of agriculture as well as participate in lessons on map reading, math, a history of the maze, and navigation via supplemental curriculum sent to your group ahead of their scheduled "tour" time. Special events occasionally featured here include hay rides, a petting zoo, a pumpkin patch, and moonlight and flashlight jaunts.

Hours: Open the end of June through November, Thurs. - Mon., 10am - 6pm. Call first.

Admission: $10 for adults; $7 for seniors and ages 4 -12; children 3 and under are free. $1 off per ticket for groups of 20 or more.

Ages: 5 years and up.

CHANNEL ISLANDS NATIONAL PARK   ☼

(805) 658-5730 - National Park; (805) 642-7688 - recorded information $$$$$
for Island Packers; (805) 642-1393 - Island Packers reservations /
www.islandpackers.com

The park headquarters is at 1901 Spinnaker Drive; Island Packers is at 1867
Spinnaker, Ventura

(Going W. on Ventura Fwy [101], exit S.W. on Seaward Ave., L. on Harbor Blvd. Going S.E. on
101, exit at Seaward Ave. and go straight onto Harbor Blvd. From Harbor Blvd., go R. on
Spinnaker Dr. - all the way to the end. There are also departures from Oxnard Harbor Channel
Islands. [TG-491 F7])

The Channel Islands comprise eight islands off Southern California, five of
which make up Channel Islands National Park and marine sanctuary. Prepare
your kids for a half or whole day excursion to an island by first obtaining
information from the park service. The islands were originally the home of
Chumash Indians. Then, hunters came and killed certain otter, seal, and sea lion
species almost to extinction. Finally, ranchers settled here. Some parts of the
islands are still privately owned. It's important to emphasize to your child that
Channel Islands is a national preserve, so "take only memories, leave only
footprints."

Climate on the islands is different from mainland climate, even during the
summer. The harsher conditions have produced various terrains within the
relatively small parcels of land, from sandy beaches to rocky hills. Cruise to the
islands and explore nature at her best and wildest. Kids get especially excited
about seeing the numerous seals and sea lions that are plentiful because they
breed on many of the islands. Be on the lookout for blue sharks and dolphins and
note that whale watching is included with all cruises from the end of December
through March. Once on an island, be on the lookout for some unusual birds, and
animals like the island fox. Bring jackets and your camera; wear sneakers; pack
a water bottle; and have a terrific outing!

Here is a very brief overview of the islands (enough to whet your
adventuring appetite), along with cruise prices from Island Packers. Note that
whale watching is part of any cruise offered from the end of December through
March:

Anacapa - This is the closest island to Ventura, only fourteen miles away. It is
five miles long. On East Anacapa, climb up the 153 steps to a sweeping
panoramic view. Enjoy a small visitor's center and nearly two miles of hiking
trails. There is no beach here, but swimming is allowed at the landing cove on
calm summer days, as is scuba and skin diving. Picnicking is welcomed. This is
one of the most popular islands to visit. Round-trip takes about seven hours,
including about three hours on the island. Adult fare is $37; children 12 years
and under are $20. A half-day cruise around the island, with no island landing, is
about three-and-a-half hours long. Adult fare is $21; children 12 years and under
are $14. Take an express run - a five-hour day, including two hours on the
island, for $32 for adults; $20 for kids. On days of low tide, visit the tidepools at
West Anacapa. The price for this cruise is the same as an all-day cruise.

Santa Cruz - At twenty-four miles long, this is the largest island off California.
Topography varies from sea caves and steep cliffs to rolling hills and grasslands.
Offered year-round, round-trip takes eight to nine hours, including about three-

and-a-half hours on the island. Adult fare is $42; children 12 years and under are $25. Overnight camping here is $54 for adults; $40 for children 12 years and under.

Santa Rosa - This island is fifteen miles long and, although eighty-five percent of it is grasslands, there are still canyons, volcanic formations, and fossil beds that vary the landscape. There is plenty to see and do here for those who thrive on being in the midst of nature. Offered April through November, round-trip takes about twelve hours, including about four hours on the island. Adult fare is $62; children 12 years and under are $45. Overnight camping is $80 for adults; $70 for children 12 years and under.

San Miguel - This eight-mile-long island has beaches and an incredible number of seals and sea lions. The most popular destination here is the Caliche Forest (i.e. mineral sand castings), which is a three-and-a-half-mile hike from the beach. Be prepared for strong winds, plus rain and fog any time of the year. The varying island terrains reflect the assault of weather upon San Miguel. Weekend camping, offered May through November, and round-trip transportation costs $90 for adults; $80 for children 12 years and under. Day trips leave only from the city of Santa Barbara, and entail spending the night before on the boat. The day visits to San Miguel, offered April, and June through October, are recommended for hardier kids.

Santa Barbara - This is the smallest island, only 640 acres, and is the farthest away from mainland Ventura. It has steep cliffs, a small "museum," and hiking trails. There are no shade trees on the island, so load up with sunscreen. Round-trip, offered April through November, takes about eleven hours, including about four hours on the island. Adult fare is $49; children 12 years and under are $35. Camping is $75 for adults; $65 for children 12 years and under.

If you prefer to fly, check out Channel Islands Aviation, (805) 987-1301 / www.flycia.com, located in the Camarillo Airport. Following a half-hour scenic flight over Anacapa and Santa Cruz Islands, you'll land on Santa Rosa Island and be here for about five and a half hours. A ranger drives around the island where you'll see a century-old cattle ranch and other island highlights. You can hike around a bit, have a picnic lunch (which you supply), and explore more of the island before you fly back to Camarillo. Adult fare is $106 round trip; children 2 to 12 years cost $84. Horizons West Adventures, (562) 799-3880, offers three-day fly-in camping trips three times a month from March to November for about $400 per person - camping equipment and a tour guide are included.

Also check out CHANNEL ISLANDS NATIONAL PARK VISITOR CENTER under the Museums section, and VENTURA HARBOR and VILLAGE under the Piers and Seaports section.

Hours: Listed under each island.
Admission: Listed under each island.
Ages: 6 years and up.

CONEJO COMMUNITY PARK and BOTANIC GARDEN ☼
(805) 495-2163 / www.crpd.org
400 Gainsborough Road, Thousand Oaks

(Exit Ventura Fwy [101] N. on Lynn Rd., R. on Gainsborough Rd. [TG-526 E6])

This nature park is delightful in size and scope. There are acres and acres of green rolling hills, and a creek running throughout. The creek, by itself, is a major attraction. My boys loved looking for crawdads and, of course, stepping on the rocks, with the possible thrill of slipping and getting a bit wet. Almost a full day's adventure can be had by climbing the gnarled, old oak trees. There are cement pathways throughout the park, making much of it stroller accessible. The ambiance here is peaceful, unless you bring your kids, of course!

The upper field sports a baseball diamond, while a basketball court is across the way. A playground is located in front of the community center building. A covered picnic area with barbecue pits is also available here.

The Botanic Garden is bigger than it first appears. One short path traverses through a variety of landscapes, looping around and covering most of the garden. Another nature trail goes up and around the hillside, following a creek through oak and willow trees before looping back around. I don't know how much actual plant knowledge my kids gained from our garden walk, but I'm always hopeful that just spending time in such an environment will help them develop an appreciation for the beautiful gift of nature.

Hours: The park is open daily dawn to dusk. The community center is open Mon. - Fri., 9am - 7pm; Sat., 9am - 4pm; Sun., noon - 4pm.

Admission: Free

Ages: All

CONEJO CREEK NORTH LIBRARY PARK

(805) 495-6471 - park; (805) 449-2660 - library / www.crpd.org

1401 E. Janss Road, Thousand Oaks

(Exit the 23 Fwy E. on Janss Rd. [TG-526 H5])

Around the back of the library, near the freeway, is a long strip of land that is a delightful park. Trees block the view of the freeway, and some of its sound. A rock-lined creek runs through most of the park. (My boys could spend hours playing just here, and getting a little wet.) There are also walkways, a few nice playgrounds, sand volleyball courts, picnic shelters, grassy areas, shade trees, an ornamental fountain, and quite a few bridges, one of which leads directly to the library. A visit to the library and/or adjacent senior/teen community center can round out your trip.

Hours: Open daily sunrise to sunset. Call for library hours.

Admission: Free

Ages: All

LAKE CASITAS RECREATION AREA

(805) 649-2233 / www.fishinghotpage.com/casitas.htm

11311 Santa Ana Road, Ventura

(Exit the Ojai Fwy [33] E. on Casitas Vista Rd., R. on Santa Ana Rd. It's at the junction of Baldwin Rd. [150] and Santa Ana Rd. [TG-450 G4])

A day at Lake Casitas is pure pleasure. The main attractions at this beautiful huge lake, which is stocked seasonally with bass, rainbow trout, crappie, and catfish, have traditionally been fishing, biking, and camping. The bait and tackle shop, (805) 649-2043, has boats for rent. A four-passenger aluminum motor boat is $30 an hour and a ten-passenger pontoon boat is $65 an hour. No waterskiing is allowed. A fishing license is needed for those 16 years and older. A day license is available here for $9.70. Bike on the five miles or so of paved trail, and a few dirt paths, that run throughout the park. Cycles for Rent, (805) 652-0462, is located just inside the recreation area. Bike rentals start at $7 an hour for a mountain bike and $9 an hour for a tandem. Over 450 campsites range from basic tent camping to full RV hookups. Each site has a picnic table and fire ring. Ask for a schedule of events, such as the Renaissance Fair, Pow Wows, Bass Tournaments, and more.

Beat the summer heat with the lake's Blue Heron Water Playground, designed for children 10 years and under. Kids on the upper end of this spectrum, however, will probably find this wading pool too tame. (The park is in the process of expanding its water attractions to accommodate more age groups.) This spacious, colorful water play area has six slides, chutes, climbing structures, wheels to turn to adjust the water spray, anchored squirt guns, and water spurting out of its pipes - all in only eighteen inches of water. Several lifeguards patrol the pool. Parents can cool off in the water or relax on the adjacent grassy areas that surround this aquatic playground. Note: If your younger child is not quite potty trained, swim diapers are available to purchase here for $10. The water is tested throughout the day and if someone has used it instead of the restrooms, the play area will be shut down for the day for cleaning.

Hours: The lake and most amenities are open daily sunrise to sunset. The water playground is open on weekends only in May, September, and October 10am - 5pm. It is open daily during the summer 10am - 6pm, or so. Sessions are a little over one hour long.

Admission: Entrance to the lake is $6.50 per vehicle; $12 with a boat. Camping prices range from $15 - $39.75, depending on the site and time of year. The water playground is $1.50 per person per session. For walk-ins (i.e. those not paying the vehicle entrance fee), the water playground costs $3 per person for the first session; $1.50 for additional sessions.

Ages: 1 - 10 years for the water playground; 3 years and up for the rest of the park.

LIBBEY PARK
Ojai Avenue [33] & Signal Street, Ojai
(Enter directly off either Ojai Ave. [33], where Signal is the nearest cross street, or from Ojai Ave., then turn S. on Montgomery St. [TG-441 H7])

This sprawling park is really a combination of several kinds of parks. The playground area, accessible from Ojai Avenue, is terrific. It has heavy-duty, plastic tubes to crawl through, and suspension bridges to cross, plus slides and swings. Kids love squishing the wonderfully fine sand between their bare toes. A thirty-five-foot long talking tube is mostly underground, with just the funnel-shaped ends above ground, at kid-level. Have your child talk into one end while you listen at the other.

An abundant number of tennis courts are here, some with stadium seating as this is the home of an annual spring tournament that attracts the country's top-ranked collegiate players. The half-dome-shaped Libbey Bowl has graded seating for concerts, or for your young stars to make their (pretend) debut.

Further back, or entering from Montgomery Street, is the nature section of the park. Kids naturally gravitate to the creek that is surrounded by glorious old oak and sycamore trees. For just a little while, you'll feel refreshingly removed from civilization. The OJAI VALLEY NATURE TRAIL, listed later in this section, also begins (or ends) here. Tip: Top off your time with a visit to the ice cream store across Ojai Street, in the Antique Mall.

> **Hours:** The park is open daily dawn to dusk.
> **Admission:** Free
> **Ages:** All

MARINA PARK ☼

Pierpont Boulevard, Ventura

(Exit Ventura Fwy [101] S. on Seward Ave., L. on Pierpont Blvd., which dead-ends into the park. [TG-491 F5])

This very cool park is part beach, part grass. The beach part has rock jetties, a small cove (with waves) for swimming, a surfing area, and a paved pathway that goes out to a point. A relatively large cement replica Spanish galleon is on the beach and filled with sand. The "ship" has a zipline, or pulley, that goes from the ship to a post about thirty feet away on the sand. The adjacent grassy knolls have a few palm trees (no shade trees), picnic tables, and a playground with swings, toddler swings, slides, and other apparatus.

> **Hours:** Open daily sunrise to sunset.
> **Admission:** Free
> **Ages:** All

MORANDA PARK ☼

(805) 986-6555

Moranda Parkway, Port Hueneme

(Exit Ventura Fwy [101] S. on Ventura Rd., L. on Port Hueneme Rd., R. on Moranda Pkwy. [TG-552 F6])

This hilly green park is spread out and diverse with eight tennis courts, two softball fields, horseshoe pits, a sand volleyball court, a basketball court, and a nice playground. A paved path goes around and through the park making it a great place to stroll, jog, or bike. Stop to play here, or have a picnic while exploring Oxnard and Ventura!

> **Hours:** Open daily dawn to dusk.
> **Admission:** Free
> **Ages:** All

POINT MUGU STATE PARK

(805) 488-5223 or (310) 457-1324; (800) 444-7275 - camping reservations

9000 W. Pacific Coast Highway at Sycamore Cove and Sycamore Canyon, Malibu

(Exit P.C.H. N. on Sycamore Canyon Rd. Another trailhead, the La Jolla Valley Loop Trail is reached by exiting P.C.H. N. on La Jolla Canyon Rd. [TG-585 A4])

This westernmost park in the Santa Monica Mountain Recreation Area consists of miles of beach and thirty more miles of inland hiking and biking trails. A passageway under the highway allows visitors access to both parts of the park. The beach is a popular spot for swimming, seasonal whale watching (end of December through March) and viewing flocks of monarch butterflies (November through December). The inland, mountainside trails vary in length, difficulty, and scenery. Some trail heads are found at the campground.

The La Jolla Valley Loop Trail is about seven miles round trip. It is a relatively easy walk (about 3/4 of a mile) to a waterfall, then the trail gets more strenuous. This trail also leads past a small pond before entering valley grasslands. You can follow the Loop trail to reconnect to the canyon or continue to Mugu Peak Trail and the 1,266-foot summit (an additional three miles). Other trails offer high-walled canyons, oak trees groves, fields of wild flowers (in the spring), and more.

Camping is available in Sycamore Canyon, which is part of the Point Mugu State Park system. Most of the sites nestled in the mountainside have trees and are very nice. Adjacent to the campground is the Sycamore Nature Center with exhibits housed in a 1928 mission style bungalow. Beach camping is available just one mile north at the Thornhill Broome exit.

Hours: Open daily 7am - sunset. The nature center is open Sat. and Sun., 10am - 3pm.

Admission: $3 per vehicle for day use. There is limited street parking available. Camping at Sycamore Canyon, which has showers and running water, starts at $12 a night. Camping at Thornhill Broome starts at $7 a night. A $7.50 camping reservation fee is also charged. Admission is free to the nature center.

Ages: All

RANCHO SIERRA VISTA / SATWIWA NATIVE AMERICAN CULTURE CENTER

(805) 370-2300 or (818) 597-9192 / www.nps.gov/samo

Potrero Road, Newbury Park

(Exit Ventura Fwy [101] S. on Campino Dos Rios/Wendy Dr. about three miles, R. on Potrero about 1 mile. [TG-555 E4])

The chaparral-covered hillsides and oak and sycamore trees make this an ideal place for some great hiking and/or picnicking. (Bring your own water.) Several trails radiate from the cultural center. The Satwiwa Loop Trail branches out and loops back around. If you continue straight on the trail before looping back, you'll hook up to the Boney Mountain trail, which crosses a stream several times and eventually leads to a waterfall. Other trails from the center hook up to

Pt. Mugu State Park.

Come on a Sunday to the culture center, located in the park, to listen to a traditionally-dressed Native American tell stories or talk about aspects of his ancestor's life and culture, or watch a craft demonstration. The Center also has Chumash exhibits such as gourds, pictures, and text. Outside, there are picnic tables and a replicated Chumash round dwelling made of willow and tule.

Hours: The park is open daily dawn to dusk. The Culture Center is open weekends during the summer, and Sun. the rest of the year, 10am - 5pm.

Admission: Free

Ages: 8 years and up.

SANTA MONICA MOUNTAINS NATIONAL PARK HEADQUARTERS/VISITORS CENTER

(818) 597-9192 / www.nps.gov/samo

401 W. Hillcrest Drive, Thousand Oaks

(Exit Ventura Fwy [101] N. on Lynn Rd., R. on Hillcrest, L. on McCloud, R. on Civic Center Dr. [TG-526 E7])

From the thousands of acres of mountains to the coastline beaches to the inland grounds, the enormous Santa Monica Mountain National Park covers a major part of the wilderness and parkland in Southern California which includes hiking, biking, and equestrian trails, plus camping, swimming, scenic drives, ranger-led programs, and more. The center has a few interpretative displays and a gift shop containing hiking and nature books. I am really writing about this place because maps and a calendar schedule of events for the numerous parks within the Santa Monica Mountains Park system can be found here. The parks, most of which can be found listed individually under the Great Outdoors Section, include Circle X Ranch, Coldwater Canyon Park, Franklin Canyon Ranch, Leo Carrillo State Park, Malibu Creek State Park, Malibu Lagoon State Beach, Paramount Ranch, Peter Strauss Ranch, Rancho Sierra Vista, Temescal Gateway Park, Topanga State Park, Will Rogers State Historical Park, and the U.C.L.A. Stunt Ranch.

Hours: Open daily 9am - 5pm.

Admission: Free

Ages: 5 years and up.

WILDWOOD REGIONAL PARK

(805) 381-2741 or (805) 495-2163 / www.crpd.org

W. Avenue de los Arboles, Thousand Oaks

(Exit Ventura Fwy [101] N. at Lynn Rd., L. at Avenida de los Arboles, all the way to the end. [TG-526 B2])

Take a walk on the wild side at Wildwood Regional Park. The narrow, dirt trails and service roads are great for real hiking. There are two major trail heads that lead to an extensive trail system for hikers, bikers, and equestrians. Come prepared by bringing water bottles, sunscreen, and backpacks with food for designated picnic areas. Although hiking downhill is easy, plan twice as much time for the hike back up.

Some highlights along the somewhat shorter trails, which are still an almost all day event, include the Nature Center; Little Falls; and Paradise Falls, which is a forty-foot waterfall that you'll hear before you actually reach it. As you walk along the creek or throughout the chaparral and woodlands, be on the lookout for wildlife, such as mule deers or lizards.

Hike here during the spring months and you'll see an abundance of wildflowers. I encourage you to get a trail map, as different routes have different highlights that you'll want to explore. The park offers wonderful, fun, and educational programs like Saturday Night S'Mores, Full Moon Hikes, and Outdoor Experiential Workshops. Enjoy nature, almost in your backyard!

Hours: Open daily dawn to dusk.

Admission: Free. Some of the programs cost between $3 - $4.

Ages: 4 years and up. Kids will tire easily.

MALLS

This section is not to tell you necessarily where to go shopping, but rather to inform you of free kids' clubs, programs, events, and "shoppertainment" features that your local mall has to offer. We included just a few of our favorite, unique malls. Be entertained, enjoy, and create - and maybe get a little shopping in, too!

Kamdon Yanelli

DEL AMO FASHION CENTER - KID'S CLUB ☼

(310) 542-8525 / www.ci.torrance.ca.us/city/delamo/dafc.htm !
Carson Street at Hawthorne Boulevard, Torrance 🏛

(Exit Harbor Fwy [110] W. on Carson. [TG-763 D6])

Join in an hour of fun and frivolity every Thursday morning by the Food Court. Kids' entertainers encourage your children to laugh, sing, and dance along with them as they tell stories, sing songs, juggle, and more.

    Hours: Every Thurs. at 10:30am.
    Admission: Free
    Ages: 2 - 8 years.

EAGLE ROCK PLAZA - KIDS CLUB ☼

(323) 256-2147 / www.shoppingtowns.com !
2700 Colorado Boulevard, Los Angeles 🏛

(Going E. on Ventura Fwy [134] exit S. on Harvey Dr., immediate L. on E. Wilson Ave., which becomes W. Broadway, which turns into Colorado. Going N. on Glendale Fwy [2], exit E. on Colorado. [TG-564 J5])

One-hour shows feature comedy, juggling, puppets, live animal presentations, arts and crafts, singers, or dancers! Call for a specific show schedule. Come to the lower level center court and join in the fun.

    Hours: In the summer, it's held the first and third Wed. at 11am; the rest of the year, it's the first and third Wed. at 6pm. No show in December.
    Admission: Free
    Ages: 2 - 13 years.

FALLBROOK MALL - WEDNESDAYS ARE FOR KIDS ☼ CLUB

(818) 340-5871 / www.mallibu.com !
6633 Fallbrook Avenue, West Hills 🏛

(Going W. on Ventura Fwy [101], exit W. on Ventura Blvd., R. on Fallbrook. Going E. on 101, exit E. on Ave. San Luis, L. on Fallbrook. [TG-529 H6])

Every week a different, forty-five-minute children's performance is featured near the food court. Performances can include music, storytelling, or anything else that's fun and entertaining.

    Hours: Every Wed. at 11am, January through October.
    Admission: Free
    Ages: 1 ½ - 8 years.

FOX HILLS MALL - KID'S CLUB ☼

(310) 390-7833 / www.shoppingtowns.com !
294 Fox Hills Mall, Culver City 🏛

(Going N. on San Diego Fwy [405], exit N.E. on Sepulveda. Going S. on 405, exit E. on Slauson Ave. Or take Marina Fwy [90] E. to the end and turn L. on Slauson. It's on the corner of Sepulveda and Slauson. [TG-672 H6])

The first and third Wednesdays feature "name" entertainment, showcasing puppetry, music, juggling, and more. The second and fourth (and the occasional fifth) Wednesday usually offer a time of arts and crafts, and perhaps a story or two. All programs are about an hour in length. The club takes place in the community room on the second level next to Robinsons May. Lunch and shopping seem like a natural follow up!

Hours: Every Wed. at 11am.
Admission: Free
Ages: 1 - 7 years old.

THE GALLERIA, AT SOUTH BAY - KIDS CLUB

(310) 371-7546 / www.southbaygalleria.com
1815 Hawthorne Boulevard, Redondo Beach
(Exit San Diego Fwy [405] W. on Artesia Blvd., L. on Hawthorne. [TG-763 C1])

Twice a month kids can come to the Galleria and enjoy an hour of entertainment such as stories, puppets, animal shows, bubbles, sing-alongs, or seasonally-oriented arts and crafts activities presented near the food court. After each show, raffles drawings are held for mall certificates. Make new friends as you and your child become regulars! Make sure you sign up to become a Kids Club member (membership is free) because a postcard is mailed out once a month listing a schedule of events and offering free give-aways from retailers, such as a small piece of jewelry or a coupon for an ice cream cone.

Hours: The Club is held on the first Tues. of each month at 10:30am and the third Tues. at 6:30pm. No shows in December.
Admission: Free
Ages: 2 - 10 years.

GLENDALE GALLERIA

(818) 240-9481 / www.glendalegalleria.com
Colorado Boulevard and Central Avenue, Glendale Galleria, Glendale
(Exit Golden State Fwy [5] E. on Colorado Blvd. [TG-564 D5])

This mall often hosts special events, programs, and displays. Past happenings have included Radio Disney's sponsoring of interactive booths and auditioning kids for emcee spots, and a re-creation of the set from the movie *Babylon 5: Thirdspace*, which included a props display, touch screens, and even star appearances. Call for a current schedule.

Hours: The mall is open Mon. - Fri., 10am - 9pm; Sat., 10am - 8pm; Sun., 11am - 7pm. Call for special program dates and times.
Admission: Free
Ages: Varies with programs offered.

LAKEWOOD CENTER MALL - A2Z KIDZ CLUB

(562) 531-6707 / www.shoplakewoodcenter.com
200 Lakewood Center Mall, Lakewood
(Exit Artesia Fwy [91] S. on Lakewood Blvd. [TG-766 A3])

The first 225 kids are invited to participate in a fun, usually seasonal craft, like decorating a Father's Day barbecue apron in June, or sand buckets in August. It's a great club to belong to because kids love to make projects, and all the materials are supplied for free! There are also member discounts on various products and restaurants in the mall. As an added benefit, the mall mails your child a certificate redeemable for a few little birthday presents during the month of his/her birthday. Note: Make sure your child is registered with the club by simply filling out a registration form. The mall also hosts occasional special event such as live animals presentations or Civil War reenactor speakers.

    Hours: The second Tues. of every month from 4pm - 7pm. Call for holiday availability.

Admission: Free

    Ages: 3 - 12 years.

MEDIA CITY SHOPPING CENTER - KID CITY

(818) 566-8617

201 E. Magnolia Boulevard, Burbank

(Exit Golden State Fwy [5] E. on Burbank Blvd., R. on 3rd St., R. on Magnolia. [TG-533 G7])

    Kids gather together on Thursdays on the first level at Macy's Court for an hour of puppetry, music, storytime, and other kinds of entertainment.

    Hours: Every other Thurs. at 10:30am. No shows in December.

Admission: Free

    Ages: 1 ½ to 6 years.

NORTHRIDGE FASHION CENTER - KIDS CLUB

(818) 885-9700 / www.mallibu.com

9301 Tampa Avenue, Northridge

(From San Diego Fwy [405], exit E. on Nordhoff St. From Ventura Fwy [101], exit N. on Tampa Avenue. It's on the corner of Nordhoff and Tampa. [TG-500 F6])

    Become a NFC kid and get in on all the fun! Forty-five-minutes of storytelling, singing, dancing, art workshop, circus acts, or even short plays are on the morning's agenda at Bullock's Court. The Club also gives its young members discounts at participating mall stores, and a free gift on their birthday.

    Hours: The first and third Thurs. of each month at 10:30am.

Admission: Free

    Ages: 2 - 12 years.

PLAZA AT WEST COVINA - KIDS CLUB

(626) 960-1881 / www.shoppingtowns.com

112 Plaza Drive, West Covina

(Going W on San Bernardino Fwy [10], exit S. on Sunset, mall is on the L. Going E. on 10, exit S. on West Covina Pkwy., mall is on the L. [TG-598 F7])

    The hour-long kids club consists of a wide variety of seasonal craft activities that include decorating calendars, making Valentines, and so on. Discounts at certain mall stores and the food court are offered to all participants. Bring a friend!

    Hours: Once a month, usually on the second Sat. at 11am.

Admission: Free

    Ages: 3 - 10 years.

PUENTE HILLS MALL - MOMMY/DADDY AND ME CLUB

(626) 965-5875

449 Puente Hills Mall, City of Industry

(Exit Pomona Fwy [60] S. on Azusa Ave. Mall is immediately on L. [TG-678 G4])

    Mommy/daddy and me holiday-themed arts and crafts activities are offered in the Center Court. Borders bookstores then invites all participants (and whoever else would like to join in the fun) to a time of storytelling and other book-related events at 1:30pm. In the summertime, these same activities are geared for a wider variety of ages, preschool through elementary.

    Hours: Every Wed. from 11:30am - 1pm and on the second Sat. of each month from noon - 2pm.

    Admission: Free

    Ages: 2 - 6 years during the week; preschool through elementary on weekends and during the summer.

SANTA ANITA - KIDS CLUB

(626) 445-3116 / www.shoppingtowns.com

400 S. Baldwin Avenue, Arcadia

(Exit Foothill Fwy [210] S. on Baldwin. [TG-567 A6])

    Thematic (and just for the fun of it!) arts and crafts activities are offered here such as decorating flower pots (Mother's Day), making calendars, and decorating cookies.

    Hours: Once a month on Wed., 4:30pm - 6:30pm. No club meeting in July.

    Admission: Free

    Ages: 12 years and under.

SOUTHBAY PAVILION - LI'L SHOPPERS CLUB

(310) 327-4822 / www.southbaypavilion.com

20700 S. Avalon Boulevard, Carson

(Exit San Diego Fwy [405] N. on Avalon Blvd. [TG-764 E4])

    Encourage your little shoppers to join the Li'l Shoppers Club, which meets at center court. Children enjoy the forty-five-minute shows put on by some great children's entertainers.

    Hours: Every Thurs. at 6pm, February through November.

    Admission: Free

    Ages: 1½ - 8 years.

STONEWOOD CENTER - KIDS CLUB

(562) 861-9233 / www.shopstonewoodcenter.com

9066 Stonewood Street, Downey

(Exit San Gabriel River Fwy [605] W. on Firestone Blvd. Mall is on the corner of Firestone and Lakewood Blvd. [TG-706 C5])

    Join Kids Club, held near Robinsons May, for one hour of fun and entertainment. The shows feature singers, dancers, puppets, or magicians. What a great family outing! Register your children for the club and they will receive a free gift on their birthday.

Hours: Every Thurs. at 6pm. No shows in December.
Admission: Free
Ages: 1½ - 8 years.

THIRD STREET PROMENADE

(310) 393-8355 / www.downtownsm.com
3rd Street, Santa Monica
(Exit Santa Monica Fwy [10] N. on Lincoln Blvd., L. on Wilshire Blvd. Park wherever you can. [TG-671 D2])

This three-block pedestrian walkway is a fascinating outdoor mall experience. It rates an A+ for people-watching as the international mix of people, converging here from the nearby Los Angeles International Airport, make it a cultural adventure. Nighttime and weekends bring out performers who want to show off their talents, however glorious or dubious they might be. We've seen and heard African drum playing, tap dancing, folk songs, acrobatics, men acting like robots, clowns making balloon animals, and an Organ grinder monkey begging - all within the span of an hour. Benches are plentiful, so if you really enjoy some of the entertainment, sit down and watch. A plethora of artsy and unique stores and boutiques, plus movie theaters line the "street." Vendor carts are along the sidewalks. Choose from a multitude of restaurants that range from upscale to grab-a-bite, or snack at a bakery or ice cream shop. A few fountains, featuring dinosaurs spouting water, complete the eclectic ambiance at the promenade. If you haven't gotten enough shopping in, at the other end of the promenade is Santa Monica Place, which is three levels of indoor shopping at 140 stores. Note: The Big Blue Bus, (310) 451-5444 / www.bigbluebus.com, runs a loop from Main Street to Third Street Promenade every fifteen minutes at a cost of 50¢ per person.

Hours: Most stores and restaurants are open daily 10am - 9pm.
Admission: Free, but bring spending money.
Ages: All

TOPANGA PLAZA - FAMILY FUN NIGHT and KIDS CLUB

(818) 594-8740 / www.shoppingtowns.com
6600 Topanga Canyon Boulevard, Canoga Park
(Exit Ventura Fwy [101] N. on Topanga Canyon Blvd. [TG-530 A7])

Families can enjoy free shows and/or craft time every Thursday night near the food court. Past shows have included clowns and dancing. Craft projects are usually themed, such as creating Valentines near Valentine's Day. After the show, shop at the more than 150 stores, but not all of them on one visit.

Hours: Every Thurs., 5pm - 7pm. No shows in December.
Admission: Free
Ages: 4 - 11 years.

VALENCIA TOWN CENTER - KIDSTOWN

(661) 287-9050 / www.valenciatowncenter.com
24201 W. Valencia Boulevard, Valencia
(Exit Golden State Fwy [5] E. on Valencia Blvd. [TG-4550 F3])

Kidstown comes to town every other Thursday morning by the Sears court. Join in the forty-five-minute show of puppetry or song and dance - it's all interactive fun for young kids.

> **Hours:** Every other Thurs. morning at 10:30am, March through November.
> **Admission:** Free
> **Ages:** 1½ - 6 years.

WESTSIDE PAVILION - KIDS' CLUB

(310) 474-6255 / www.westsidepavilion.com
10800 W. Pico Boulevard, Los Angeles
(Exit San Diego Fwy [405] E. on Santa Monica Blvd., R. on Westwood Blvd., Mall is on corner of Westwood and Pico. Or, exit Santa Monica Fwy [10] N. on Overland Ave. The mall is on corner of Overland and Blythe Ave. [TG-632 D6])

Parents and kids can enjoy a half hour together on Wednesday nights at Westside Pavilion. Shows can consist of puppetry, magicians, musicians, and more.

> **Hours:** Every Wed. night at 6pm. No shows in December.
> **Admission:** Free
> **Ages:** All

WHITTWOOD MALL - KIDS CLUB

(562) 947-2871 / www.whittwoodmall.com
15603 Whittier Boulevard, Whittier
(From San Gabriel River Fwy [605], exit E. on Whittier Blvd. From Santa Ana Fwy[5], or Artesia Fwy [91], exit N. on Beach Blvd. L. on Whittier. [TG-707 H4])

This Kids Club meets once a month, sometimes for a time of entertainment, such as music, puppetry, or live animals shows, and sometimes for a time of making arts and crafts projects. The mall also provides special events throughout the year. Past activities have included taking a train through a teddy-bear wonderland and riding in a stationary hot-air balloon for youngsters.

> **Hours:** Once a month at 6pm. Call for the exact dates.
> **Admission:** Free for the Kids Club. Most of the special events are free, too.
> **Ages:** 2 -10 years.

THE BLOCK AT ORANGE

(714) 769-4000 / www.theblockatorange.com
20 City Boulevard West, Orange
(Exit Garden Grove Fwy [22] W. at City Drive, near intersection of I-5. [TG-799 B5])

This mega mall (over 100 shops!) offers unique shopping, entertainment, and dining experiences. Just some of our favorite stops here include the AMC Theaters; Ben & Jerry's (ice cream!); Hilo Hattie (Hawaiian clothing); GAMEWORKS (see this separate entry under the Family Pay and Play section);

Borders (we love bookstores!); VANS SKATE PARK (see this separate entry under the Family Pay and Play section), and Dave and Buster's. The latter is a restaurant and games place geared mostly for adults, but kids can play here, too, when accompanied by an adult. Some highlights in here are Turbo Ride, a 3-D simulation theater; billiards; Ground Zero, a futuristic laser shoot out game; virtual golf; a shoot-out in an Old West setting; tabletop shuffleboard; and Million Dollar Midway, another virtual reality game complete with headgear.

The mall also offers a wonderful variety of restaurants including Cafe Tu Tu Tango, an art-themed restaurant with original artwork for sale, artists painting at their canvases in the restaurant, and sometimes an art activity for children; Wolfgang Puck, an art deco pizzeria plus; and Alcatraz Brewing Co., which looks like a jail.

If you can't see it all on one visit, just remember that sometimes you have to go more than once around 'The Block'!

Hours: Most stores are open daily 10am - 11pm.
Ages: All

IRVINE SPECTRUM CENTER   ☼

(949) 789-9180 / www.irvinespectrumcenter.com   !/$
At the junction of the 405 and 5 Fwy, Irvine

(Going S. on Santa Ana Fwy [5], exit at Alton Pkwy. At the end of the off ramp, go straight into the Spectrum. Going N. on 5, exit W. on Alton Pkwy, L. on Gateway Blvd. Going S. on San Diego Fwy [405], exit N. on Irvine Center Dr., R. on Pacifica. [TG-891 B2])

Just two of our favorite stores in this outside mall include a gigantic Barnes and Noble Bookstore and the Houdini's Magic Shop, a small shop that sells magic tricks. For interactive fun, try GAMEWORKS (see the Family Pay and Play section); or NASCAR Silicon Motor Speedway, (949) 753-8810. Nascar has twelve, incredibly realistic racing car simulators geared for teens on up as the jolting motion and virtual power of the cars make them hard to manage. The center also has a Dave & Busters, an eatery/arcade/virtual game play place for adults. Hungry? Choose from four outstanding restaurants - Bertolini's, Champps Americana, P. F. Chang's China Bistro, or Wolfgang Puck. A wonderful food court is also here, complete with a Ben and Jerry's and a sweet shop. As usual, kids enjoy the simple pleasures, like playing (and getting wet) on the turtle statues in the fountain outside the food court. See EDWARDS IMAX 3-D THEATER, under the Shows and Theaters section, for information on the large screen and 3-D format theater here.

Hours: Open daily 11am - 11pm.
Admission: Technically free.
Ages: All

WESTMINSTER MALL   ☼

(714) 898-2550 / www.westminstermall.net   !
Bolsa Avenue and Goldenwest Street, Westminster   ♨

(Exit San Diego Fwy [405] S. on Goldenwest St. [TG-827 G3])

Special exhibits are presented here at various times throughout the year. For instance, in celebration of Project Earth, giant sea creatures (up to forty feet long!) came alive via Dinamation - they roared and thrashed their tails. Other exhibits in conjunction with this theme included a display from Sea World's wild arctic, weekend stage shows, and a rivers and oceans wetlands exhibit. Who knew that malls could be so fun and educational?!

Hours: Call for a schedule of special events.
Admission: Free
Ages: All

ONTARIO MILLS MALL   ☼

(909) 484-8300 / www.ontariomillsmall.com   !/$
One Mills Circle, Ontario

(From San Bernardino Fwy [10], exit N. on Milliken Ave., R. on Mall Dr. From Ontario Fwy [15], exit W. on 4th St, L. on Franklin Ave. [TG-603 E6])

Ontario Mills is California's largest outlet mall with over 200 outlet, speciality, and off-price retail stores. The mall also offers various forms of "shoppertainment." AMC features thirty movie screens and Edwards has the EDWARDS IMAX 3-D movie theater (see the Shows and Theaters section) for both 2-D and 3-D shows. Other entertainment offered at the mega mall includes GAMEWORKS (see the Family Pay and Play section); Dave & Buster's, a combination restaurant/bar and game/arcade center geared for adults; and VANS SKATE PARK (Ontario). (See the Family Pay and Play section.)

The food court is fancifully decorated with large, colorful, inflatable foods. Other tantalizing eating experiences, in unique surroundings, are Wolfgang Puck's Cafe and RAINFOREST CAFE (Ontario) (look under the Edible Adventures section). Krispy Kreme Doughnuts (a personal favorite!) is located just outside the mall.

Hours: The mall and most attractions are open Mon. - Sat., 10am - 9:30pm; Sun., 10am - 8pm.
Admission: Technically, free.
Ages: All

HORTON PLAZA   ☼

(619) 238-1596 - plaza; (619) 236-1212 - San Diego Visitor's Bureau /   !/$
www.hortonplaza.com
324 Horton Plaza, San Diego

(Going S. on San Diego Fwy [5] exit S. on Front St, L. on Broadway. It's on the corner of 4th and Broadway. Going N. on the 5, exit S. on 6th Ave. R. on Broadway. [TG-1289 A3])

This outdoor mall is seven city blocks of shopping, dining, and entertainment. Colorful and unique architecture, with buildings designed at various, odd angles, contain over 125 places to shop. Favorite kid-friendly stopping places include FAO Schwarz (a gigantic toy store), the Nature Company, and the Disney Store. Other attractions are the numerous movie theaters and over twenty places to dine, including PLANET HOLLYWOOD. (See the Edible Adventure's section.) Stop by the visitor's bureau to pick up a coupon booklet, information, and/or maps on the area.

Hours: Open Mon. - Fri., 10am - 9pm; Sat., 10am - 7pm; Sun., 11am - 6pm.

Admission: Technically, free.
Ages: All

NORTH COUNTY FAIR - KIDS CLUB
(760) 489-0631 / www.shoppingtowns.com
272 E. Via Rancho Parkway, Escondido
(Exit the Escondido Fwy [15] E. on Via Rancho Pkwy. It's near Beethoven Rd. [TG-1150 B3])

Come and join the fun at center court for an hour of craft time or wonderful, kiddie entertainment such as storytelling, song and dance, puppetry, and more. The mall also has 180 stores and restaurants, including a McDonalds with a play center.

Hours: Every Wed. at 9:30am.
Admission: Free
Ages: 1 - 6 years

PARKWAY PLAZA - KIDS CLUB
(619) 579-9932 / www.shoppingtowns.com
415 Parkway Plaza, El Cajon
(Going E. on 8 Fwy, exit N. on N. Johnson Ave. It's on the corner of Fletcher Pkwy and Johnson. Going W. on 8, exit N. on Mollison Ave., L. on Broadway, which turns in to Fletcher. Going S. on San Vicente Fwy [67], exit W. on Fletcher. [TG-1251 F4])

Have fun with bubbles, puppets, magicians, or musical groups once a week for an hour at center court. This could be the highlight of you child's week!

Hours: Every Tues. at 3:30pm
Admission: Free
Ages: 3 - 10 years.

PLAZA BONITA MALL - KIDS CLUB
(619) 267-2850 / www.shoppingtowns.com
3030 Plaza Bonita Road, National City
(Exit Jacob Dekema Fwy [805] E. on Bonita Rd., L. on Plaza Bonita Rd. From the 54 Fwy, exit S. on Reo Dr., which turns into Plaza Bonita Center Wy., R. on Sweetwater Rd. [TG-1310 D4])

Have some fun while making new friends at the Kids Club at Plaza Bonita. Free, hour-long, weekly entertainment could include puppet shows, toe-tapping music, storytelling, and/or singing. Each club "meeting" starts with Kid Aerobics or jazzercise. Meet in the Center Court near J. C. Penney.

Hours: Every Wed. at 3:30pm, February through November.
Admission: Free
Ages: 1 -10 years.

PLAZA CAMINO REAL MALL - KIDS' CLUB
(760) 729-7927 / www.shoppingtowns.com
2525 El Camino Real, Carlsbad
(Exit 78 Fwy, S. on El Camino Real [TG-1106 G3])

Come join in the Kids' Club fun at the Center Court, lower level. Clubs usually begin with an action warm-up of Kid Aerobics or jazzercise. Free, forty-five-minute, weekly entertainment can include laughing with kids' comedians, dancing, singing, storytelling, and general silliness.

Hours: The first Tues. of every month at 10am. No shows in December.
Admission: Free
Ages: 1 - 8 years.

U.T.C. - KIDS CLUB

(858) 453-2930 / www.shoppingtowns.com
4545 La Jolla Village Drive, San Diego
(From Jacob Dekema Fwy [805], exit W. on La Jolla Village / Miramar Rd. From San Diego Fwy [5], exit E. on La Jolla Village. [TG-1228 D2])

This outdoors mall offers kid's activities once a month across from Nordstrom, weather permitting. Past activities have included arts and crafts, educational plays, musicals, live animal presentations, and more. Call for a specific event schedule.

Hours: Once a month, March through October. Call for times and dates.
Admission: Free
Ages: 3 - 11 years.

VIEJAS OUTLET CENTER

(619) 659-2070 / www.shopviejas.com
5005 Willows Road, Alpine
(Going W. on 8 Fwy, exit N.E. on Willows. Going E. on 8, exit at Alpine Blvd., go L. on the end of the off ramp on Via La Mancha, R. on Willows. The mall is directly across from the Viejas Casino. [TG-1234 J5])

This factory outlet outdoor mall is located on an Indian reservation and has a Native American theme. Adobe-style stores decorated with wooden beams and large boulders border the walkways. A small stream runs through one section while a grassy expanse of lawn, the Viejas Park, is integrated at the east end of the mall. The stores include Gap Outlet, Liz Claiborne, London Fog, Tommy Hilfiger, Leather Loft, Nike Factory, Vans, Black and Decker, Paper Outlet and many more, plus a few eateries, such as Rubio's and McDonalds. There is a large fountain that shoots up water from its ground holes in some sort of pattern (although I couldn't figure it out). Kids love getting wet here in warmer weather.

Although the shopping is great and the aesthetics of the center is pleasant, I've really included this entry because the mall offers two nightly shows, weather permitting, at the outside show court near the fountain. Rows of chairs encircle the large water fountain to allow guests to watch the "dancing" waters that move to the beat of music and pulsating lights. It's quite mesmerizing. Although the second feature changes three times a year, each twenty-minute show incorporates music, lasers, lights, videos on the huge screens above the audience's seats, and pyrotechnics - it's a mini spectacular. One show, usually running February through April, is called "Splashtrack - A Musical Journey" which used the fountain while presenting a rock and roll review of music from the 40's through the 90's. We saw "Spirit of Nightfire", a tale of Native American heritage starring a costumed dancer in the fountains, and several special effects. It is shown April through October. "Legend of the Ice Princess", running November through January, again incorporates a live performer with a flashy show. The shows might not be a main destination, but if you're in the neighborhood, they are a worthwhile addition to your itinerary.

Hours: Mall hours are Mon. - Sat., 10am - 9pm; Sun., 10am - 7pm. The dancing waters "show" usually starts at 7:30pm in the fall and winter; 8:30pm in the spring and summer. The main presentation starts a half hour later. Call for hours.

Admission: Free

Ages: All

THE OAKS - OK KIDS CLUB

(805) 495-2031 or (805) 376-3515

222 W. Hillcrest Drive, Thousand Oaks

(Exit Ventura Fwy [101] N. on Lynn Rd., R. on Hillcrest. [TG-556 E1])

A variety of half-hour shows are presented every week at the lower level court near Robinsons May. Shows could include marionettes, singers, dancers, magicians, and other entertainment. This mall often hosts special events, such as Kid's World in August. This particular event usually features hands-on exhibits, kids' concerts, small pet races, and a Safety Zone where kids learn about safety in an interactive manner.

Hours: Every Thurs. at 10:30am. No shows in December.

Admission: Free

Ages: 1½ - 7 years.

MUSEUMS

While children are (almost) never too young to start appreciating art, there is a whole new world of kid-friendly museums that captivates their imaginations, hearts, and even their hands! A few tips about museums:

• Exhibits rotate, so be flexible in your expectations.

• If you really like the museum, become a member. You'll reap benefits such as visiting the museum year round at no additional fee, being invited to members-only events, receiving newsletters, and lots more.

• If you're looking for a special gift, most museum gift shops carry unique merchandise that is geared toward their specialty.

• Museums offer a wide array of special calendar events. Get on mailing lists!

• Take a tour! You and your kids will learn a lot more about the exhibits.

• You can $ee L.A. or you can ¢.E.E. L.A.! The Cultural Entertainment Events card (C.E.E. L.A.) is an incredible way to explore sixteen top museums, including AUTRY MUSEUM OF WESTERN HERITAGE, HOLLYWOOD ENTERTAINMENT MUSEUM, JAPANESE AMERICAN NATIONAL MUSEUM, KIDSEUM, MUSEUM OF FLYING, RICHARD NIXON LIBRARY AND BIRTHPLACE, REAGAN LIBRARY AND MUSEUM, SOUTHWEST MUSEUM, and more for only $44 a year for your family! This card also offers 50% off some major sporting events, and theater and concert venues. Call (818) 957-9400 / www.cee-la.com for more details.

AIR FORCE FLIGHT TEST CENTER MUSEUM   ☼

(661) 277-8050 / www.edwards.af.mil   !
405 Rosamond Boulevard, Edwards Air Force Base, Kern County
(Exit the Golden State Fwy [5] N. on the Antelope Valley Fwy [14] Fwy. Exit [14] E. on
Edwards/Rosamond and drive for a few miles. [TG-3835 H4])

Edwards Air Force Base is the premier site for flight research and flight testing. You'll drive by a huge dry lake which is the main landing site. At the museum, walk around the thirteen, or so, aircraft on display outside the museum. The planes vary in design, shape, size, and maneuverability. Some of the planes currently on display include a B-52D, T-33A, and an F-104A.

Inside the museum are two airplanes that are grounded, an F-16 and A-7, and two others suspended in the air, as if in flight. The museum is packed with memorabilia fitting for the birthplace of supersonic flight. One section is dedicated to "Mach Busters," the men who broke sound barriers, including, of course, Chuck Yeager. It shows and tells how planes (and men) were tested for this significant breakthrough. The "First Flights Wall" is a model display of the more than 100 aircraft that completed their first flight at Edwards AFB. Other items on exhibit include aircraft propulsion systems, engines, life support equipment, photographs, flight jackets, and personal memorabilia. Ask to see the film on the history of Edwards and on flight testing. While here, check out the NASA DRYDEN FLIGHT RESEARCH CENTER tour and/or the AIR FORCE FLIGHT TEST CENTER tour. Both are listed under the Tours section. Note: Just down the street at the base exchange, which is open to the public, is a food court which has a Baskin Robbins. Also note that the Aerospace Walk of Honor, in downtown Lancaster between 10th Street W. and Sierra Highway, displays biographical plaques that honor forty aviation pioneers.

    Hours: Open Tues. - Sat., 9am - 5pm.
Admission: Free
     Ages: 6 years and up.

BORAX VISITOR CENTER   ☀

(760) 762-7588 or (760) 762-7432 / www.borax.com $
Borax Road, Boron
(Exit Highway 58 N. on Borax Rd. This facility is E. of Edwards Air Force Base.)

Borax isn't something that my family normally spends a lot of time thinking about. However, visiting this center made us realize how widely this mineral is used. As you drive past the active mine (and past the sign that states the speed limit as 37 ½ m.p.h.), you'll see what appears to be a little city, complete with buildings, trucks, and Goliath-type machines used to extract and process the borax. This area supplies nearly half the global need for the mineral!

Up the hill is a state-of-the-art visitors' center. Outside are original twenty mule team wagons, with harnessed mule statues, that were once used to haul the ore over 165 miles through desert and rocky terrain. Inside is a large sample of kernite, a type of borate ore, plus a pictorial history of the Borax company, and an exhibit that shows the process of raw ore being transformed (crushed, actually) into fine dust. The "Borax at Home" display shows examples of everyday staples made from borax, including glass, ceramic glazes, detergent, shaving creams, and plant fertilizer. For products closer to a child's heart, the display features footballs, Play Doh™, and nail polish. Borax is also added to commodities to make them sparkle, including toothpaste and fireworks. An adjacent room shows continuously running videos of Borax commercials starring Ronald Reagan, Dale Robertson, Clint Eastwood, and others. The front room (or back room, depending on your point of view) has an all-glass wall for an unobstructed panorama of the entire open pit mine. High powered microscopes are available for closer inspection of borax and other crystals. Free, organized school tours of the center are given, and fun, supplemental materials are available to aid learning. Don't forget to stop off at the TWENTY MULE TEAM MUSEUM (look at the next entry), which is just down the road.

> **Hours:** Open daily 9am - 5pm, excluding major holidays and during inclement weather.
> **Admission:** $2 per vehicle.
> **Ages:** 4 years and up.

TWENTY MULE TEAM MUSEUM ☀
(760) 762-5810 / www.rnrs.com/20MuleTeam   !
Twenty Mule Team Road, Boron
(Exit Highway 58 S. on Boron Ave., R. on Twenty Mule Team Rd. The city of Boron is N.E. of Edwards Air Force Base.)

This small-town museum is built around its claim to fame - the Twenty Mule Team wagons. Beginning in 1883, these wagons were used for five years to haul borate ore 165 miles through the desert and rocky outcroppings, from Death Valley to the Mojave railhead. The museum displays the history of the surrounding area from the late nineteenth century up to the present day via enlarged photographs, a continuously running video, and four small rooms that contain artifacts. Some of the items on exhibit include samples of kernite and borate ore (components of Borax); mining equipment, such as replica scale mine cars, and caps that held candlesticks and lamps; models of planes tested at Edwards Air Force Base; clothing worn during the turn-of-the-century; and handcuffs and prison garb from the nearby federal prison.

Stroll around outside to see more exhibits, such as rusty agricultural and mining equipment, a large granite boulder with holes (because it was used for drilling contests), water pumps, an ore bucket, a surrey, and a miner's shack. There is also a shade area with a few picnic tables. Just across the street is a small park with a roadside display that includes an antique fire engine and an F-4 fighter jet. Make sure to visit the nearby BORAX VISITOR CENTER, listed in the above entry.

> **Hours:** Open daily 11am - 4pm
> **Admission:** Free; donations appreciated.
> **Ages:** 4 years and up.

ADAMSON HOUSE AND MALIBU LAGOON MUSEUM ☼
(310) 456-8432 - museum; (310) 456-1770 - docent, during museum   !/$
hours; (818) 880-0363 - lagoon tour
23200 Pacific Coast Highway, Malibu

(Exit Ventura Fwy [101] S. on Las Virgenes Rd., which turns into Malibu Cyn. Rd. Go to the end, L. on P.C.H.. It's on P.C.H., W. of Malibu Pier, near Serra Rd. [TG-629 B7])

The Adamson House, and its adjacent museum, is on beautifully landscaped grounds just a few feet away from the Malibu Surfrider Beach and lifeguard station, and Malibu Lagoon - definitely beach front property. The outside of the house and the fountains integrate the colorful Malibu tiles in their design. We wandered around the grounds on flagstone walkways that wove through grassy lawns, beneath shade trees, along several gardens (including a rose garden), past a pool that was once filled with salt water from the ocean, and to the chain-link fence which marks the house boundaries. Here, just a short distance from the pier, we watched surfers do their thing.

The small museum features exhibits pertaining to the history of Malibu including cattle brands, arrowheads, maps, fossilized shells, and numerous photographs. I liked the Malibu Colony of Stars' pictures of Robert Redford, Bing Crosby, Clara Bow, Joan Crawford, and others. Ask for a tour or for explanations regarding the history of the railroad, the dam, and the movie colony.

The two-story house was built in 1929, and the rooms can be seen on a one-hour, guided tour. Adults and older children will appreciate the bottle-glass windows, hand-painted murals, additional tile work (especially in the kitchen), furnishings, and unique decor.

There isn't any direct access to the lagoon (i.e. the parcel of water and land that is a haven for various bird species) from the house. You can get to this area by walking or driving over the bridge and down Cross Creek Road. We observed pelicans, herons, sandpipers, and other birds coming in for a landing before taking to the skies once again. Visit here on your own or make tour reservations to educate your kids (and yourself) about the waterfowl, ecology, the area's Chumash Indian past, and more. The lagoon programs are given by a state park ranger. Note: Although the beach is accessible by going through the museum parking lot, the waters are for surfers only. If your kids want to go swimming, head to Malibu Pier, just up the street.

Hours: The house and museum are open Wed. - Sat., 11am - 3pm. The last house tour begins at 2pm. Call for information on lagoon tours and programs.

Admission: The museum and house tour are free. Parking in the museum lot costs $5 per vehicle. Some free street parking is available. Lagoon tours cost $6 per vehicle for parking.

Ages: 7 years and up for the house tour and museum; 4 years and up for the lagoon tour.

ADOBE DE PALOMARES   ☀
(909) 620-0264 / www.osb.net/pomona $
491 E. Arrow Highway, Pomona
(Exit San Bernardino Fwy [10] N. on Towne Ave., L. on Arrow Hwy. [TG-601 A4])

This thirteen-room restored adobe was originally built in 1854. A guided tour of the house includes seeing the courtyard and authentic period furniture, as well as cooking utensils (how did they live without so many technical doohickeys?!), tools, antique clothing, and children's toys. The grounds are lovely. A blacksmith shop is also on site and features saddles, ranching tools, branding irons, and a horse-drawn carriage circa 1880's. Adjacent to the Adobe is Palomare Park, so bring a picnic lunch and enjoy some running around space.

Hours: Open Sun., 2pm - 5pm
Admission: $2 for adults; $1 for children 12 and under.
Ages: 6 years and up.

AFRICAN AMERICAN FIREFIGHTER MUSEUM

(213) 744-1730 / www.lafd.org/aafm.htm
1401 S. Central Avenue, Los Angeles
(Exit Santa Monica Fwy [10] N. on Central Ave. It's on the corner of Central and 14th St. [TG-634 F7])

This small, beautiful museum is set in a Los Angeles neighborhood. It chronicles the history of black firefighters by honoring them and their white colleagues who pushed for integration. The walls and reference books contain photographs and stories that tell of the once-segregated station. For instance, although black and white men battled fires and fought side-by-side to save lives, they couldn't cook or eat together. African Americans even slept in beds designated "black beds." Exhibits include a fire engine, uniforms, boots, fire extinguishers, badges, helmets, and other mementos.

Hours: Open every Tues. and the second and fourth Sun. of each month, 1pm - 4pm.
Admission: Free
Ages: 5 years and up.

AIR AND SPACE GALLERY

(213) 744-7400 / www.casciencectr.org
Exposition Park, Los Angeles
(Exit Harbor Fwy [110] W. on Exposition Blvd., L. on Flower, L. on Figueroa. Or, exit Santa Monica Fwy [10] S. on Vermont, L. on Exposition, R. on Figueroa. [TG-674 A2])

This building is actually part of the California Science Center. It's hard to miss with a jet fighter perched precariously on its top! The atmosphere is uplifting with planes, such as the 1902 Wright Flyer; jets, such as the Northrop T-38 jet trainer; and a space capsule, the Gemini II, all suspended from the ceiling in mock flight. Four main galleries include Air and Aircraft, Humans and their Spaceships, Mission to the Planets, and Stars and Telescopes. Educating the public on flight technology is accomplished through numerous interactive displays. A favorite is the mock-up of the International Space Station where interactive exhibits encourage visitors to assess neuromuscular responses, bone decalcification, visual queues, and the effects of muscle atrophy that go along with prolonged space flight. You know, normal dinner table topics. Kids glean even more information about our universe by taking a school tour here.

A wonderful way to round out your day is to have a picnic and visit one of the other attractions in this complex - CALIFORNIA AFRICAN AMERICAN MUSEUM, CALIFORNIA SCIENCE CENTER, EXPOSITION PARK, IMAX THEATER, and NATURAL HISTORY MUSEUM OF LOS ANGELES. (Look under the Alphabetical Index to find these attractions.)

Hours: Open daily 10am - 5pm. Closed New Year's Day, Thanksgiving, and Christmas.

Admission: Free. Parking is $5.

Ages: 3 years and up.

AMERICAN HERITAGE PARK / MILITARY MUSEUM ☀

(626) 442-1776 / www.members.aol.com/tankland/museum.htm $$

1918 N. Rosemead Boulevard, South El Monte

(Exit Pomona Fwy [60] N. at Rosemead Blvd. The entrance is on the R. side of the street, at the northern part of WHITTIER NARROWS RECREATION AREA. [TG-636 J3])

Attention! Over 125 pieces of equipment, representing all branches of the United States Military, can be found at this outside museum. The collection contains vehicles and weapons from World War II and the Korean and Vietnam wars. It includes Jeeps, amphibious trucks, ambulances, helicopters, cannons, gun turrets, and thirty-ton Sherman tanks. The vehicles can be looked at, but not sat on or touched.

To the untrained eye it looks like a random compilation of old military equipment. And it is. However, some pieces are in the process of being restored, and some have been used in movies and T.V. shows. The volunteers are knowledgeable and know many of the "inside" stories about the vehicles. Tip: This is an ideal setting if your kids are studying any of the wars and want to make a video.

Hours: Open Sat. - Sun., noon - 4:30pm. Open Wed., Thurs., and Fri. for groups by appointment. Closed on rainy days.

Admission: $4 for adults; $3 for seniors and military; $2 for ages 10 - 16; 50¢ for ages 5 - 9; children 4 and under and weekday groups are free.

Ages: 4 years and up.

ANTELOPE VALLEY INDIAN MUSEUM ☀

(661) 942-0662 - state park; (661) 946-3055 - museum / $

www.calparksmojave.com

15800 Avenue 'M', Lancaster

(Exit Antelope Valley Fwy [14] E. on Ave. 'K', R. on 150th St. East, L. on Ave. 'M'. Or, exit Pearblossom Hwy [138] N. on 165th St. East, which turns into 170th St, L. on Ave. 'M'. [TG-4109 E4])

Built into and around rock formations of the Mojave Desert, the outside of this Indian museum looks incongruously like a Swiss Chalet. The inside is just as unique. Once the home of artist Howard Edward, portions of the interior (e.g. walls, ceilings, and flooring) are composed of boulders. My kids' reaction was simply "WOW!" The large, main room is lined with Kachina dolls on the upper shelves and painted panels of the dolls on the ceiling. (The Hopi People believed that Kachina dolls brought rain.) The unusual furniture and the support beams are made from Joshua trees. A connecting room has several glass-cased displays of pottery shards that were once used for money and jewelry; cradle-boards; baskets; and various items made from plants, such as yucca fiber sandals.

Kids love climbing up the narrow stony steps into a large display room, which is carved out of rock. Exhibits here include arrowheads, whale bone tools, shells, whale ribs, harpoons, and weapons. Go back down a few of the steps. Stop. Look up. You'll see Indian dioramas and re-created cave paintings.

Outside, you'll pass by a series of small cottages that were once used as guest houses. Your destination is Joshua Cottage, a place that has some hands-on activities for kids. They can grind corn with stone mortars and pestles, try their hand at using a pump drill to drill holes, and "saw" with a bow drill to create smoke. Kids can even learn how to make a pine needle whisk broom. (The brooms may not have much practical use now-a-days, but it's a fun and educational project.) Docents will gladly explain the use of various seeds and other plant parts. The small adjacent room is a gallery that's also used for educational programs.

The museum is part of the California Department of Parks and Recreation. Enjoy an easy half-mile nature walk on the trails through the buttes and desert just behind the Indian Museum. A guidebook (50¢) explains the fourteen Native American symbols on the posts along the trail.

Hours: Open mid- September through mid- June, Sat. - Sun., 11am - 4pm. Closed in the summer. Tours are available Tues., Wed., and Thurs. by appointment.

Admission: $1 for adults; ages 15 and under are free.

Ages: 5 years and up.

AUTRY MUSEUM OF WESTERN HERITAGE ☼
(323) 667-2000 / www.autry-museum.org $$$
4700 Western Heritage Way, in Griffith Park, Los Angeles
(Going N. on Golden State Fwy [5] or W. on Ventura Fwy [134], exit at Zoo Dr. and follow the signs. Going E. on 134, exit S. on Victory Blvd., L. on Zoo Dr. Going S. on 5, exit S. on Western, L. on Victory Blvd. to Zoo Dr. The museum is across the parking lot from the L. A. Zoo. [TG-564 B4])

The cowboy lifestyle lassos our imagination. Bryce, my middle son, wants to become a cowboy missionary (yes, he is special), so this museum really spurred on his interest, at least regarding the cowboy part of his career choice. It will also delight fans of the Old West with its complete array of paintings, clothing, tools, weapons (one of Annie Oakley's guns!), and interesting artifacts. Movie clips, videos, and movie posters throughout the museum highlight specific areas of this romanticized period. In the Spirit of Imagination Hall, a big hit is sitting on a saddle and making riding motions to become part of an old western movie showing on a screen behind the rider. My kids particularly enjoyed the hands-on children's Discovery Gallery, set up like the home and workplace of the Sees, a Chinese American family. Visit their parlor and read some books, or listen to an old-fashioned radio. Pretend to prepare a meal in the realistic mini kitchen. Visit the Sees' "antique" store; cook up some Chinese food at a re-created portion of the real restaurant, Dragon's Den; and try on Chinese clothing.

The entire museum is interesting and wheelchair/stroller-friendly, but you do have to keep your kids corralled, as most of the exhibits are not touchable ones. Saturday programs, for ages 6 to 12, are more interactive with storytelling, games, and even sing alongs. Ask about their weekly summer history classes for kids. Autry Museum offers numerous outstanding programs throughout the year. A cafe is on the grounds, as is a wonderful, large, grassy picnic area.

Hours: Open Tues. - Sun. (and certain Mon. holidays), 10am - 5pm; open Thurs. until 8pm. Closed Thanksgiving and Christmas.

Admission: $7.50 for adults; $5 for seniors and ages 13 - 18; $3 for children 2 - 12. Certain discounts available through AAA. Admission is free on the second Tues. (See C.E.E. L.A. for membership savings, pg. 261.) The Hollywood CityPass, $49.75 for adults and $38 for ages 3 - 11, is good for one-time admission to American Cinematheque's Egyptian Theatre in Hollywood, AUTRY MUSEUM OF WESTERN HERITAGE, HOLLYWOOD ENTERTAINMENT MUSEUM, MUSEUM OF TELEVISION AND RADIO, MUSEUM OF TOLERANCE, PETERSEN AUTOMOTIVE MUSEUM, REAGAN PRESIDENTIAL LIBRARY AND MUSEUM, and UNIVERSAL STUDIOS within a 30 day period. (All of the entries mentioned, except for the theater, are listed separately.) Call (888) 330-5008 / www.citypass.com for more information.

Ages: 4 years and up.

BANNING RESIDENCE MUSEUM AND PARK   ☼

(310) 548-7777 / www.banning.org $

401 E. M Street, Wilmington

(Exit Harbor Fwy [110] E. on Pacific Coast Highway, R. on Avalon Blvd., L. on M St. [TG-794 F5])

This huge Victorian museum, where the founder of Wilmington once lived, is reflective of the Banning family lifestyle in the 1800's. The hour-and-a-half guided tours are best suited for older children as there is much to see, but not to touch. First, walk through the photo gallery, past a display of brilliant cut glass, and into the house where each of the seventeen rooms are beautifully decorated with period furniture and eclectic art work. (Note: The house is completely decked out at Christmas time and looks particularly splendid.) Check out the hoof inkwell in the General's office. Get the kids involved with the tour by asking them questions like, "What's missing from this office that modern offices have?" (Answer - a computer, a fax machine, etc. Surprisingly, a copy machine *is* here.) The parlor doubled as a music room and contains a piano, violin, and small organ as well as an unusual-looking chair made out of buffalo hide and horns. Other rooms of interest are the children's nursery; the bedrooms - one has a unique hat rack made of antlers, while another has a stepping stool that is actually a commode; and the kitchen with its pot-bellied stove and all of its gadgets. (Obviously some things never change.) Request to see the Stagecoach Barn, a fully-outfitted, nineteenth-century working barn with real stagecoaches. Ask your children if they can figure out how some of the tools were used.

School groups are given two-hour tours, geared for fourth graders, that include attending class in the one-room schoolhouse, with its old-fashioned desks, slates, and McGuffy primers. Kids don an apron or ascot, get a math or English lesson from that time period, and go out for recess to play games of yesteryear. Ask about Heritage Week in May, when special school programs and a free public weekend event encourages visitors to partake in activities from the 1880's.

The museum is situated in the middle of a pretty, twenty-acre park that has a small playground, a few picnic tables, a rose garden, eucalyptus trees, giant bamboo trees, and grassy areas.

Hours: Tours are given Tues. - Thurs. at 12:30pm, 1:30pm, and 2:30pm; Sat. - Sun. at 12:30pm, 1:30pm, 2:30pm, and 3:30pm.
Admission: $3 per adult; children 12 and under are free.
Ages: 7 years and up.

CALIFORNIA AFRICAN AMERICAN MUSEUM

(213) 744-7432 / www.caam.ca.gov
600 State Drive, at Exposition Park, Los Angeles
(Exit the Harbor Fwy [110] W. on Exposition Blvd., L. on Flower, L. on Figueroa. Or, exit Santa Monica Fwy [10] S. on Vermont, L. on Exposition, R. on Figueroa. Parking is available the first driveway on the R. It's located in the same building complex as the CALIFORNIA SCIENCE MUSEUM. [TG-674 A2])

This museum portrays the works of African American artists documenting the African American experience in this country. The rotating exhibits are interesting to people of all races. The exhibits we saw were various playhouse-size houses and work environments made from recycled materials, along with photographs, and various sculptures. Another room contained lots of Western artifacts, and the fascinating history of James Beckwourth, an explorer, trapper, and businessman who lived from 1798 to 1866. See the nearby AIR AND SPACE GALLERY, CALIFORNIA SCIENCE CENTER, EXPOSITION PARK, IMAX THEATER, and NATURAL HISTORY MUSEUM OF LOS ANGELES. (Look up the attractions listed individually in the Alphabetical Index.)

Hours: Open Tues. - Sun., 10am - 5pm. Closed New Year's Day, Memorial Day, Thanksgiving, and Christmas.
Admission: Free. Parking costs $5.
Ages: 5 years and up.

CALIFORNIA HERITAGE MUSEUM

(310) 392-8537
2612 Main Street, Santa Monica
(Take Santa Monica Fwy [10] W. almost to the end, exit S. on 4th St, R. on Pico, L. on Main. [TG-671 F4])

This two-story house/museum is hard to miss with its giant cowboy sign out front! A grassy lawn welcomes picnickers. Inside, the downstairs living room is cozy and rustic-looking. I like the antler candelabras on the mantel. The dining room atmosphere is more elegant as the table is set with fine china. The restored kitchen is the one Merle Norman originally used to cook-up her cosmetic recipes. (From such humble beginnings . . .)

The upstairs is redecorated each time a new exhibit is installed. Note: The museum is usually closed between installations. Often the exhibits are aimed at appealing to the younger generation. Past themes have focused on cowboys, guitars from all over the world, children's books and illustrations, and model trains. Call for information on the current display.

      Hours: Open Wed. - Sun., 11am - 4pm.

  Admission: $3 for adults; $2 for seniors and students; children 12 and under are free.

       Ages: 5 years and up.

CALIFORNIA SCIENCE CENTER

(323) SCIENCE (724-3623) / www.casciencectr.org

700 State Drive, Exposition Park, Los Angeles

(Exit Harbor Fwy [110] W. on Exposition Blvd., L. on Flower St., L. on Figueroa. Or, exit Santa Monica Fwy [10] S. on Vermont, L. on Exposition, R. on Figueroa. Parking is available in the second driveway on the R. [TG-674 A2])

     Hanging from a very high ceiling that connects the IMAX Theater to the Science Center are hundreds of various-sized gold balls dangling on wires: an intriguing mobile. Inside, the lobby is dominated by another science-oriented piece of art - a fifty-foot, kinetic folding and unfolding structure, suspended by cables and designed by an artist-engineer. The first floor contains the museum store, which has an extensive selection of science experiments, kits, books, and lots more. It also has a McDonald's (which gets <u>extremely</u> busy during lunch hours), and the less-crowded MegaBites eatery. A sit-down restaurant, the Rose Garden Cafe, is located on the third floor.

     The second floor was our favorite. The west wing, titled World of Life, is packed with exhibits that pertain to human and animal lives. Look closely at cells via a microscope and a video. Crank a knob to watch how a model's digestive system unravels to stretch over eighteen feet. Watch a movie of an actual heart transplant as it is beamed onto a statue patient. Drive a simulator car to experience the difference in driving sober and driving drunk. See preserved fetuses in jars ranging from a few weeks old to nine months. View a movie on conception (suitable for older children). Sit on a clear, no-butts-about-it chair filled with over 200 cigarettes and watch a movie on lung cancer. Press buttons to match recorded heartbeats to real hearts that are on display, from the huge elephant's to the medium-sized cow's to the tiny mouse's. Look at real brains - human, monkey, and rat. Learn about the basic needs of plants and animals through other interactive displays. Tess, the reclining, fifty-foot human figure, comes to "life" in a great, fifteen-minute presentation in the BodyWorks room. A large movie screen above her head stars a cartoon character who helps Tess explain how her body parts work together to keep her system in balance (i.e. homeostasis). Periodically, her muscles, organs, and circulatory system are illuminated by fiber optics. An adjacent Discovery Room allows younger children to put on puppet shows, and look at small, live animals such as frogs and mice.

     The east wing, or Creative World, features communication exhibits. Inside the large Creative World room, visitors can play virtual volleyball; whisper into a parabolic dish and have someone across the room hear them; type in telephone or television messages that are then relayed by satellite; play air drums and digitize the sound; construct buildings using scale model parts and then subject them to the shake, rattle, and roll of an earthquake via a shake table; build archways using Styrofoam blocks to learn about the strength of compression; and more. There are several large and small screen videos in both east and west wings that offer enticing and entertaining visual bits of information, although they are often not accompanied by written or verbal data.

Part of the third floor is a continuation of Creative World, focusing on transportation. Fans that blow wind to move model sailboats and a solar-paneled car are a few of the exhibits. The Discovery Room has a play house and game activities that enable younger children to learn more about the displays throughout the center. The west room features special rotating exhibits. It was a geography room when we visited. Kids learned about people, customs, plants, and unique geological formations from all over the world, via interactive displays.

Ever want to join the circus and try the high-wire act? Here's your chance. For $3, you can pedal a weighted bike across a cable wire that is forty feet above the ground. Although you're strapped in and safety netting is in place, it is still a slightly scary venture, especially when the staff person tilts the bike before pushing it across the cable wire!

Ask about the numerous special classes and programs offered for children and adults. For instance, audience-participatory shows, including *Science Comes Alive,* are presented for various age groups. Another program, called Think Science!, sends teachers supplemental materials and activities, for a modest fee, on specific topics related to science and technology. Groups of twenty to fifty students also work with educators in age-appropriate programs. Call the education department at (213) 744-7444 for a schedule of other programs and for more information.

Tips: 1) School kids come in busloads on weekday mornings, so several exhibits require waiting in line to view or use during these peak hours. Therefore, consider either arriving early to watch an IMAX movie and explore the grounds and other nearby museums first, or come here in the early afternoon. 2) Avoid restaurant lunch lines by packing a lunch. There are several shaded grassy areas for picnicking. 3) Locker rentals are available on the first floor. Note: The Center is stroller/wheelchair accessible. Check out the nearby AIR AND SPACE GALLERY (which is actually part of the science center), CALIFORNIA AFRICAN AMERICAN MUSEUM, IMAX THEATER, and NATURAL HISTORY MUSEUM OF LOS ANGELES. (Look under the Alphabetical Index to find each listing.)

Hours: Open daily 10am - 5pm. Closed New Year's Day, Thanksgiving, and Christmas.

Admission: Free. Parking is $5 per vehicle. Membership here is a great deal and reciprocal with the DISCOVERY SCIENCE CENTER in Santa Ana and REUBEN H. FLEET SCIENCE CENTER in San Diego.

Ages: 3 years and up.

THE DOCTORS' HOUSE MUSEUM / BRAND PARK

(818) 242-4290
1601 W. Mountain Street, Glendale
(Exit Golden State Fwy [5] N. on Western Ave., R. on Mountain. It's in Brand Park. [TG-534 B7])

Tour through this delightfully restored Queen Anne Eastlake style home that was once owned by three doctors. (Hence the name.) Docents point out and discuss the doctors' office with its instruments and vials, period furniture from the early 1900's, clothing, and other artifacts from the Victorian time period. One-hour, free, school tours, for third graders and above, are given during the week. In addition to the house tour, students also play outdoor Victorian games. Ask about special functions throughout the year, such as the candlelight tour in December.

Just outside the house is an expansive green lawn and a gazebo. During the week, teas are offered under the gazebo for groups between sixteen to twenty-five adults. Sandwiches are served, along with scones, tea, fresh fruit, cakes, and other goodies that fit with a traditional Victorian tea.

A Japanese tea garden, complete with a waterfall, koi fish, and a Japanese tea house to peek into is also on the grounds.

The Doctors' House Museum and the beautiful Glendale Library are located in Brand Park. The front part of the park is comprised of green lawns, playgrounds, a few basketball courts, volleyball courts, and picnic tables. The back part, behind the museum and library, is a huge, hilly area with miles of dirt and asphalt (for mountain bikers who like a real workout) hiking trails that lead through chaparral into the Verdugo Mountains and around a reservoir. The park sees a lot of action on the weekends.

Hours: The park is open daily sunrise to sunset. The museum is open Sun., 2pm - 4pm, except major holidays, inclement weather, and the month of July.

Admission: The museum is $1 for adults; ages 16 and under are free. The tea is $12 per person.

Ages: 6 years and up.

THE DRUM BARRACKS CIVIL WAR MUSEUM

(310) 548-7509 / www.drumbarracks.org
1052 Banning Boulevard, Wilmington
(Exit Harbor Fwy [110] E. on Pacific Coast Highway, R. on Avalon Blvd., L. on 'L' St., R. on Banning Blvd. [TG-794 F6])

The year is 1861 and the Civil War has broken out. Although most of the fighting was done in the east, troops from Camp Drum, California fought on the Union side. Your forty-five-minute tour of the medium-sized barracks/house/museum starts in the library research room. The first video is six minutes long and tells the history of Camp Drum through reenactments, with a costumed character narrating. Do your kids enjoy a good mystery? The second video features the Drum Barracks in an episode of *Unsolved Mysteries*. Apparently, a few good ghosts from the Civil War still hang out here. Needless to say, my kids heard "ghostly" noises throughout the rest of our visit.

The parlor room is where the officers entertained. Besides period furniture, it also has a stereoscope, which is an early Viewmaster™, to look through. Q: Why didn't people smile for photographs back then? A: Many people had bad teeth, plus it took a long time to actually take a picture.

The hallway shows a picture of the Camel Corps. which is a regiment that actually rode camels. It also has a flag from an 1863 battlefield - have your kids count the stars (states). Upstairs, the armory room has a few original weapons, like a musket and some swords. A rotating exhibit up here has displayed a hospital room with beds, old medical instruments, and a lifelike mannequin of a wounded soldier; a quarter master's quarters; and more. The officer's bedroom has furniture, personal effects, and old-fashioned clothing. Q: Why did women usually wear brown wedding dresses? A: You'll have to take the tour to find out!

Hours: Tours are given Tues. - Thurs. on the hour between 10am - 1pm; Sat. - Sun, 11:30am - 2:30pm.
Admission: $3 for adults; children 12 and under are free.
Ages: 5 years and up.

EL MONTE HISTORICAL MUSEUM
(626) 580-2232
3150 N. Tyler Avenue, El Monte
(Exit San Bernardino Fwy [10] S. on Santa Anita, L. on Mildred St., L. on N. Tyler Ave. It's on the corner, next to El Monte School. [TG-637 C1])

A visit to this adobe-style museum offers fascinating glimpses into the history of the United States, as well as the history of the pioneers of El Monte. There is plenty to see and learn to keep young people's interest peaked, even though no touching is allowed. Items in the numerous glass displays are labeled, making it easy to self-tour. However, I highly recommend taking a guided tour, given for groups of ten or more people, so your family, or school group, doesn't miss out on the many details and explanations of the exhibits.

My kids were captivated by the hallway showcasing Gay's Lion Farm, which was a local training ground in the 1920's for lions used in motion pictures. The photos depict the large cats interacting with people in various circus-type acts. There are also several adorable shots of lion cubs. A lion's tail and teeth are on display, too. The Heritage Room, toward the back, looks like an old-fashioned living room with antique furniture and a piano, plus cases of glassware, ladies' boots, and clothing. The walls are lined with pictures of walnut growers and other first-residents of El Monte.

The Pioneer Room has wonderful collections of typewriters, lamps/lanterns, dolls, toys, books, bells, quilts, army medals, and Bibles. It also contains ornate swords, a flag (with two bullet holes in it) from the battlefield at Gettysburg, a piece of the Berlin wall, George Washington's lantern, and an actual letter written by the Father of our Country who, by the way, had nice handwriting! The Frontier Room is equally interesting with early-day policeman and fireman hats, police badges and guns, a 1911 Model T, a wall of old tools, early Native American artifacts, and a re-created old-time law enforcement office.

The huge Lexington Room is sub-divided into smaller, themed "rooms" such as a turn-of-the-century schoolroom with desks, maps, and schoolwork; an old-time general store filled with shelves of merchandise; a barber shop with a chair; a music shop with ukuleles, violins, a Victrola, and more; and a dressmaker's shop with beautiful dresses, sewing machines, elegant hair combs, and beaded handbags. Most of the rooms also have period-dressed mannequins. This section of the museum also contains re-created rooms that would have been found in a house of the early 1900's such as a parlor, bedroom, kitchen, and library. Each room is fully furnished and complete to the smallest detail. The El Monte Historic Museum, with a plaque that commemorates it as "the end of the Santa Fe Trail", offers a window to the world!

For further study, or just for the joy of reading, the El Monte Public Library is only a few buildings down. Directly across the street from the museum is a park. This pleasant corner park offers plenty of picnic tables and shady oak trees, plus a few slides and some metal transportation vehicles to climb on.

Hours: Open Tues. - Fri., 10am - 4pm; Sun., 1pm - 3pm. Open on Sat. by appointment and during the week for school tours.

Admission: Free

Ages: 5 years and up.

FORT MACARTHUR MILITARY MUSEUM

(310) 548-2631- museum; (310) 548-7705 - Angels Gate Park / www.ftmac.org

3601 S. Gaffey Street, San Pedro

(Exit Harbor Fwy [110] S. on Gaffey St. Drive almost to the end of Gaffey, then R. through the gates on Leavenworth Dr., past Angels Gate Park. [TG-854 B2])

This concrete World War II coastal defense battery building really fires up kids' imaginations as they walk the grounds and tour rooms filled with big artillery guns, cannons, mines, uniforms, pictures, and other war memorabilia. Military history is important to learn, but my boys really loved running through the underground corridors! Starting at the Gun Pit, it's a slightly scary thrill to run from one end of a long narrow darkish tunnel to the other end, then climb up stairs, through an open trap door, and into the Plotting Room. Now this is adventure!

A sixteen-minute video shows recoil guns shooting as well as the history of this museum. In the small Decontamination Room my kids pretended they had come in contact with poisonous gas and stepped on an air pump to blow it off, just like the soldiers of old. Only then could they enter the Communications Room, which has fascinating old radios and transmitters behind glass. Store Room 2 has riveting pictures of battleships being blown up. The pictures also tell stories of soldiers' bravery and hardships. The Barracks Display shows the inside of a soldier's (small) room and typical army articles.

Talking through the elaborate speaking tube system keeps kids busy for a long time, as someone speaks through one end while someone else tries to find the receiving end. Don't forget to take the steps up to the top of the defense building where one of the hideouts, used by lookouts with guns to watch for incoming, attacking ships, is still open to spy from. Picnic tables on the rooftop of the small souvenir shop make a picnic here special. Note: Check the July Calendar section for Old Fort MacArthur Days war reenactments.

Just east of the museum, on a hill in Angels Gate Park, sits the seventeen-ton Korean Friendship Bell set in a traditional, Korean-style pagoda. Let the kids run loose to enjoy the grassy knolls. There are a few pieces of climbing apparatus and a basketball court, too. Since it's a fairly treeless area, it's also ideal for kite flying. On a clear day the coastal view is gorgeous, and you can see Catalina Island.

Hours: The museum is open Sat. - Sun., noon - 5pm. It's also usually open Thurs., noon - 5pm (Call first.) Docent tours are offered Thurs., Sat. - Sun. at 1pm and 3pm. (Call first.) The park is open daily sunrise to 6pm.

Admission: Free; donations suggested.

Ages: 2 years and up, though younger ones will have to be careful not to yell in the corridors, where noise reverberates off the cement walls. The walls are marked "Quiet please" in an attempt to keep the noise level at a minimum.

THE GAMBLE HOUSE

(626) 793-3334 / www.gamblehouse.org   *$$*
4 Westmoreland Place, Pasadena

(Exit Foothill Fwy [210], near where it intersects with the Ventura Fwy [134], W. on N. Orange Grove Blvd., turn R. into the Gamble House. [TG-565 G4])

Wood, and the way various types are crafted and blended, is the primary focus of the Gamble House. Teak, maple, cedar, redwood, and oak were used in the furniture, cabinetry, paneling, carvings, and exterior walls in a way that represents the best of the Arts and Crafts movement from the turn of the century. Not that kids care about these details, but they are impressed by the natural beauty of the rooms, original furnishings, and terraces. A one-hour guided tour explains the history of the house, the era in which it was built, and the architecture's harmonious use of wood and natural light in the home in accord with its environmental surroundings. Highlights, besides the use of wood, include the appealing open porches (used as sleeping porches), and the Tiffany glass throughout. Note: The house is not stroller/wheelchair accessible.

The outside grounds are classy looking, with beautiful landscaping, rolling green lawns, and a brick walkway and driveway.

Hours: Open Thurs. - Sun., noon - 3pm. It's closed on major holidays.

Admission: $8 for adults; $5 for seniors and students with ID; children 11 and under are free.

Ages: 6 years and up.

GEORGE C. PAGE MUSEUM / LA BREA TAR PITS

(323) 857-6311 / www.tarpits.org   *$$$*
5801 Wilshire Boulevard, Los Angeles

(Exit Santa Monica Fwy [10] N. on Fairfax, R. on Wilshire Blvd., L. on Curson St. [TG-633 C2])

Kids boning up on becoming paleontologists will really dig this place. First, take them to see the fifteen-minute movie, *Treasures of the Tar Pits*. It gives an interesting overview and explains that the fossils they'll see in the museum have been excavated from the pits, just outside.

The George C. Page Museum has over thirty different exhibits including saber-tooth cats, an imperial mammoth, dire wolves, mastodons, bison, giant ground sloths, and a variety of birds and plants. (Forewarn your kids that dinosaurs had been extinct for many years before the tar pit entrapments occurred, so the only thing here on dinosaurs is a short film.) The exhibits are comprised of fossils, skeletons, and lifelike murals, plus an animated model of a young mammoth. Kids can pit their strength against the force of asphalt by pulling on glass enclosed cylinders stuck in the sticky stuff. The futility of this effort makes it easier to understand why animals, of any size, couldn't escape the tar pits.

Other highlights include the La Brea Woman, whose image changes continuously, via optical illusion, from a skeleton to a fleshed-out figure; the wall display of over 400 dire wolf skulls; and watching, through the huge windows of a working paleontologist's laboratory, the on-going process of cleaning, studying, and cataloging newly excavated fossils. Kellan, my oldest son, wanted to become a *bone*afide paleontologist until he saw how tedious the work can be. I'm encouraging him to keep an open mind. Toward the exit is a room devoted to the theory of evolution.

Outside, enjoy a walk around the twenty-three acres of beautifully landscaped Hancock Park, otherwise known as the La Brea Tar Pits. The pits are comprised of asphalt that has seeped to the surface to form sticky pools in which the animals got trapped and died. There are several active tar pits in the park, with hundreds more having been dug out and filled in. For two months during the summer, you can see real excavation work going on at Pit 91. The park, with its outdoor amphitheater and picnic facilities, is also a backyard, and has connecting walkways, to the LOS ANGELES COUNTY MUSEUM OF ART. (Look up this entry under the Museums section.) Note: If all else fails, kids will have a great time rolling down the hills outside the museum and climbing on the statues!

Hours: Open Mon. - Fri., 9:30am - 5pm; Sat. - Sun., 10am - 5pm. Closed New Year's Day, Thanksgiving, and Christmas.

Admission: $6 for adults; $3.50 for seniors and students with ID; $2 for ages 5 - 12; children 4 and under are free. Certain discounts available through AAA. The museum is free to everyone on the first Tues. of the month. Parking in the lot behind the museum is $7, with validation, or try parking on 6th Street directly behind the museum, for free.

Ages: 3½ years and up.

THE GETTY CENTER / J. PAUL GETTY MUSEUM   ☼
$

(310) 440-7300 / www.getty.edu
1200 Getty Center Drive, Los Angeles
(Exit San Diego Fwy [405] W. on Getty Center Dr. It is just N. of I-10. [TG-631 G1])

Everything you've heard about the Getty Museum is true! Your adventure begins with a four-and-a-half-minute tram ride up a winding track that seemingly hugs the edge of the road. You may also hike up the 1.9 mile road, but you'll get enough exercise walking around the Getty.

The architecture of the museum is stunning - it elicited several exclamations of admiration from my kids. The all-white marble structures can also be blinding, so bring sunglasses. Once inside the lobby, make your first stop at one of two theaters that show a ten-minute orientation movie regarding the Center. Next, invest $2 for an audio guide that suggests special stops for families, and describes over 250 works in a total of six and a half hours. Simply press the number on your tape machine that corresponds to the number near the work of art to hear commentary and interviews regarding that specific piece. Note: Guided tours and special classes are available for school groups.

Stroll down the courtyard toward the boulder fountain as you aim for your next destination, the Family Room. This small room contains several child-oriented art books, a computer for finding out more art information, and five costumes for children to try on that are originally depicted in paintings found in the Getty. Note: Kids will find these particular paintings in the museum and think it's cool that they dressed up like that, too! You can check out a game kit from the Family Room that enables your kids to go from mere observers to interactive participants in the galleries. Make up your own activities, too, such as having your children imitate portrait poses, or encourage them to be on the lookout for paintings with bridges or dogs or the color red. Note: The museum offers family workshops for ages 5 through 13 years old twice a month that include a guided tour and related art activity.

The four Art Information rooms, staffed with knowledgeable volunteers, are worthy of your time. One shows step-by-step depictions of how bronze statues are made using wax moldings. It also has samples of crushed rocks, plants, insects, charred human bones, and copper corrosion that were used for color in illuminated manuscripts. Another room has easels, paper, colored pencils, and still life objects for aspiring artists to use for drawing their own masterpiece. As pictures can be displayed here for the day, you can truthfully boast that your child had a picture hanging at the Getty.

Now it's time to actually see the world-renown art. Forgive me for not going into detail here about the works - they are too numerous and grand. Suffice to say that the five, multi-level galleries feature paintings, sculptures, drawings, photography, and decorative arts (e.g. elegant gold-gilded furniture, tapestries, vases, and more.) in natural-light conditions, which enhance the beauty of the work. My boys were fascinated with the overhead sun panels that automatically adjust to let in the right amount of light. Many of the works have stories about the pieces printed alongside them, making them more interesting than just another pretty picture. A separate, darkened room features medieval, illuminated (i.e. hand-painted) manuscripts with still-vivid colors painted on vellum (i.e. sheep skin). From Van Gogh to Rembrandt to Renoir, the Getty has something to please every palette.

Hardwood floors and elevators make the Center stroller/wheelchair accessible, although the doors that connect the galleries are heavy to push and pull open. As the Getty is on a hill, the several terraces offer magnificent vistas from Mt. Baldy to Catalina to the surrounding Beverly Hills area. We particularly liked the cactus garden on top of a building outside the South Pavilion. Another outside attraction is the tiered, maze-like, central garden which you may walk in and around.

Hungry visitors have several options. Two cafeterias have both indoor and outdoor seating, and serve a variety of prepacked cold or hot lunch and dinner items for an average of $7. The on-site restaurant is an elegant, sit-down dining experience, and entrees range from $9 to $25. You may also bring a lunch to enjoy at the large picnic area by the base of the tram ride. It has grassy green lawns and numerous covered picnic tables. This last choice entails taking the electric tram down to the parking lot and then back up to the museum.

Here are a few tips to make your day more memorable: 1) Consider pre-purchasing (through the Getty bookstore or elsewhere) *A is for Artist*, a Getty Museum pictural alphabet book that inspires children to be on the lookout for certain works of art. (Familiarity, in this case, breeds pleasurable recognition.) Or, buy *Going to the Getty* by J. otto Seibold and Vivian Walsh, a book that gives a solid and fun overview of the museum, as well as a look at a few pieces in particular. 2) Look for fossils embedded in the Getty walls, particularly at the plaza where the tram arrives. 3) Pre-warn your children to stand 6" to 12" away from the art. There are no ropes in front of the pieces, and while the security guards are friendly, they are also insistent. 4) A free coat/bag check is available in the entrance hall. 5) Going outside, just to another building, is almost unavoidable, so if it's raining bring an umbrella. 6) Wear comfortable walking shoes! 7) Parking reservations are required on weekdays only up until 4pm. You may arrive here, however, without reservations, by bike, taxi, or bus. MTA bus No. 561 and the Santa Monica Blue Bus No. 14 stop at the entrance.

Our eyes were glazed over when we left the Getty, but our minds and hearts were filled with wondrous works of art.

Hours: Open Tues. - Wed., 10am - 7pm; Thurs. - Fri., 10am - 9pm; Sat. - Sun., 10am - 6pm. Closed Mon. and major holidays. Parking reservations are needed up to 4pm on weekdays.

Admission: The museum is free. Parking is $5 per vehicle.

Ages: 3 years and up.

GORDON R. HOWARD MUSEUM / MENTZER HOUSE ☼
(818) 841-6333 $

1015 W. Olive Avenue, Burbank

(Exit Ventura Fwy [134] N. on Victory Blvd., L. on Olive Ave. Or, exit Golden State Fwy [5] W. on Olive Ave. The Museum is located at 115 N. Lomita St. and the Mentzer House is connected to the museum by a walkway. [TG-563 G1])

Make sure to save a Sunday afternoon to come and explore the Gordon Howard Museum. The hallway has old toys and dishes on display, plus a drawing room and a music room. The salon contains wedding dresses, old dresses (that are now back in style), and a stunning 1898 dress with beads and lace, plus ladies boots, jeweled hat pins, and dolls.

The Historical Room is large and filled with interesting slices from Burbank's past. Along one wall are glass-enclosed rooms, each one complete with furniture and period-dressed mannequins. Look into the rooms, pick up an old-fashioned telephone receiver, press a button, and listen to stories about Dr. Burbank (does that name ring a bell?), a family-owned winery, a 1920's hotel lobby (when $1 paid for a room!), a country store, and the *Jazz Singer*, Al

Jolson. Other exhibits in this room include military uniforms, flags, and other war memorabilia; a display devoted to Lockheed, comprised of numerous pictures and model airplanes; a tribute to Disney featuring animation cells, photographs, and posters; and an ornate desk used by Spanish noblemen.

The Vehicle Room is packed with lots of antique "stuff," such as an old switchboard, tools, parking meters, a huge Gramophone, a hotel telephone booth, and fire hats. It also showcases classic cars in mint condition, and several vintage vehicles including a 1922 Moreland Bus, a 1909 Ford horseless carriage with a crank, and a 1949 fire engine with a huge target net that my kids thought was a trampoline. The small upstairs gallery has pictures and paintings as well as a complete collection of old cameras. A video on the history of Lockheed is shown at 1:10pm and again at 2:30pm.

Follow the walkway from the museum courtyard to the reconstructed Mentzer House, which was originally built in 1870. On your walk-through tour you'll see two bedrooms, a dining room, and a living room containing period furniture, plus old-fashioned items such as a phonograph, an old telephone, and a vacuum cleaner. The kitchen has a beautiful coal stove, china dishes, and cooking gadgets.

Right next door is the Olive Recreation Center, easily identified by the model F-104 Starfighter in the front. The park has picnic tables and a playground, plus tennis and basketball courts.

> **Hours:** Open Sun., 1pm - 4pm.
> **Admission:** $1 donation per person is requested.
> **Ages:** 5 years and up.

GRIER MUSSER MUSEUM

(213) 413-1814 / people.we.mediaone.net/gmuseum

403 S. Bonnie Brae Street, Los Angeles

(Exit Harbor Fwy [110] W. on 3rd St, L. on Bonnie Brae. The house/museum is in a L.A. neighborhood, with parking behind the building. [TG-634 C2])

This thirteen-room, two-story, green and rust-colored Queen Anne-style house/museum was built in 1898. It was the Grier Musser family home. Since the tour guides are family relatives, they know and share the history and interesting stories of the memorabilia. The house is literally packed with personal ~~stuff~~ treasures accumulated over the years. The front parlor contains an original chandelier, Delph plates, a grandfather's clock, and other antiques. The family room has a 1950's television set, a piano, and a fainting couch for women who did just that. The dining room's fireplace is decorated with ornate tiles and beautifully carved wood work. The kitchen has a wood-burning stove, a gas stove, a beaded chandelier from the 1915 Exposition Fair, dishes from the Depression era, a collection of cookie jars, kitchen gadgets, and china cabinets filled with original boxes of Ivory Soap, Morton's Salt, etc. At the foot of the stairs is a red velvet chaperone's seat. While a gentleman courted his lady love, a chaperone would sit out of the way, but within eyesight.

An upstairs study contains a desk, grandma's diploma from high school, and a pictorial history of the Red Cross, plus a closet full of nursing uniforms from WWII. The master bedroom and adjoining bedroom have maple furniture, and closets full of hats, dresses, and boots. The children's bedroom is filled with toys, stuffed animals, dolls, and dollhouses. The dresser displays old bottles and hairbrushes as well as a more unique sign of the past - a container of leg makeup from WWII. Women would put this makeup on their legs to make it look like they were wearing nylons - seams and all. The sundeck is a favorite room for kids because of the numerous games and toys, and extensive Disney collection. Open the printer drawers to see even more treasures, such as jewelry.

Using the maid's stairway, go down to the basement to see pictures of the family and the Los Angeles area, and an extensive postcard collection from around the world. A visit here makes you wonder if maybe you should have kept that bottle cap collection, or at least your great grandfather's fishing pole as a potential museum piece.

Hours: Open Wed. - Sat., noon - 4pm.

Admission: $6 for adults; $4 for seniors and students; $3 for ages 5 - 12; children 4 and under are free.

Ages: 5 years and up.

GRIFFITH OBSERVATORY AND PLANETARIUM ☼

(323) 664-1191 / www.griffithobservatory.org

2800 E. Observatory Road, in Griffith Park, Los Angeles

(Exit Golden State Fwy [5] W. on Los Feliz Blvd., take Hillhurst Ave. N. past the Greek Theater to the Observatory. [TG-593 J2])

The Observatory is one of the best places to get an overview of the city on a cloudless day, and to view the city lights and stars on a clear night. Coin-operated telescopes are here to get that "closer" look that kids insist they need. The largest public telescope in California is available to use (for free) every clear evening in the summer from dusk to 9:45pm. It's available the rest of the year Tuesday to Sunday from 7pm to 9:45pm. Call the Sky Report, (323) 663-8171, for twenty-four-hour recorded information.

The Hall of Science in the Observatory has some fascinating and interactive exhibits that explore astronomy and the physical sciences. The West Hall emphasizes light and stars. The solar telescope allows viewing of the sun, through filters, on clear days, so kids can actually see sun spots or solar flares. Have the kids step on a scale and see how much they would weigh on Mars or Jupiter. (The moon scale is my personal favorite.) The computer terminals have astronomy quiz games like astronomer's hangman.

The East Hall's emphasis is on more down-to-earth sciences. The weather exhibit has an earth and moon globe, plus a seismograph exhibit where kids can stomp on the floor and measure the size of their own "earthquake." The space telescope here is one-fifth the size of the Hubble. Out on the rotunda, kids enjoy the huge Foucault pendulum that knocks big pegs over, as it illustrates the rotation of the earth. Note that the observatory has limited handicapped accessibility. (See GRIFFITH PLANETARIUM AND LASER SHOWS, in the Shows and Theaters section, for show information.) Note: The Greek Theater, a nationally-renown venue for concerts and other events, is just down the road.

Hours: Open daily in the summer 12:30pm - 10pm. Open the rest of the year Tues. - Fri., 2pm - 10pm; Sat. - Sun., 12:30pm - 10pm.

Admission: Free
Ages: 4 years and up.

GUINNESS WORLD OF RECORDS MUSEUM ☼

(323) 463-6433 *$$$*
6764 Hollywood Boulevard, Hollywood ⛟
(Exit Hollywood Fwy [101] W. on Hollywood Blvd. [TG-593 E4])

There are over 3,000 facts, feats, and world records told about and shown at this very Hollywood museum, so there is something to astounded all ages. See life-size models, pictures, videos, and special effects of the tallest, smallest, most tattooed, most anything and everything. (The kids should be great at Trivial Pursuit after this visit.) We were enthralled with the domino exhibit, which shows a video of an incredible domino run.

Prep your children before their visit: Q: Do you know who holds a record for the most fan mail in one day? A: Mickey Mouse. He received 800,000 letters one day in 1933. Q: What animal had the smallest brain in proportion to his body? A: Stegosaurus. Q: What was the longest length a human neck was stretched using copper coils? And why? A: Fifteen and three-quarter inches. I don't know why, though. Watch some fascinating footage of intriguing and bizarre facts about our world and the people and animals in it: *The Human World*, *The Animal World*, *Planet Earth*, *Structures and Machines*, *Sports World*, and a salute to *The World of Hollywood*.

Hours: Open daily 10am - midnight. Closed major holidays.
Admission: $10.95 for adults; $8.95 for seniors; $6.95 for ages 6 - 12; children 5 and under are free. Combination tickets with HOLLYWOOD WAX MUSEUM (see this entry in this section) are $15.95 for adults; $10.95 for seniors; $8.95 for ages 6 - 12.
Ages: 4½ years and up.

HACIENDA HEIGHTS YOUTH SCIENCE CENTER ☼

(626) 854-9825 / www.youth.net/ysc *!*
16949 Wedgeworth Drive, Hacienda Heights
(Exit Pomona Fwy [60] S. on Azusa, R. on Pepper Brook, R. on Wedgeworth. It's located in classroom 8 at the Wedgeworth Elementary School. [TG-678 F4])

The Youth Science Center functions as a museum and a classroom. Actually, the museum is in a classroom decorated with colorful, informative posters, at Wedgeworth Elementary School. Although it's not state-of-the-art, a lot of science is contained in this room: A sand pendulum creates patterns depending on how you swing it; a heat-sensitive, liquid crystal display leaves colored impressions when touched; a Jacob's ladder of electricity is on display; a cow's heart and a pig embryo are in jars; a case of fossils and drawers of butterflies and other insects can be examined; and a tank with fish in it shares shelf space with a few other live critters like snakes, frogs, tortoises, a tarantula, and a scorpion. Also here are computer stations with game cartridges, Geo Safaris, puzzles, books, construction toys, and numerous scientific videos to borrow. The retail store area is a small space packed with rocks, shells, science books, and experiments.

For a minimal fee, children can attend classes like "The Great Paper Airplane Race," where they'll learn about aerodynamics and wind, while making and flying paper airplanes. Several field trips, such as nature hikes and tours, are offered throughout the school year. A terrific array of science-related classes, from model rocket-building to hands-on, physical science, are available during the summer. Call for a schedule.

> **Hours:** Open in the summer, Mon. - Fri., 8am - noon. Open during the school year Tues. and Fri., 11:30am - 3:45pm; Sat., 10am - 2pm.
>
> **Admission:** Free
>
> **Ages:** 4 years and up.

THE HATHAWAY RANCH MUSEUM ☼

(562) 944-6563 / www.alumni.caltech.edu/~remy/HRM/HRM.html $
11901 E. Florence Avenue, Santa Fe Springs
(From Santa Ana Fwy [5] or San Gabriel River Fwy [605] exit E. on Florence Ave. The driveway is just east of Pioneer Blvd. [TG-706 H5])

Drive up the driveway and into the past where great grandma Nadine Hathaway still lives on the premises of this five-acre ranch. Dogs bark their greeting outside the small visitor's center that houses saddles, old pictures, and a collection of irons. Check out the 1930's machine shop next door, filled with tools, tractor pistons, and even some working lathes.

All of the antiques on display in the house/museum have been accumulated from three generations of Hathaways; things used until they couldn't be fixed, and kept because the family couldn't bear to throw anything away. (So, if I start saving all my "stuff" and my children's stuff, someday their children could open up a museum!) The first room inside the museum is a fully furnished living room. The adjacent kitchen contains a coal and a wood burning stove, ice box, old baby buggy, high chair, and a myriad of labeled gadgets such as butter molds, old graters, and more. A 1920's girl's bedroom holds dolls, pictures of movie stars from that era, and tennis racquets. Another bedroom displays Nadine's grandmother's wedding dress, feather boas, and more. Upstairs is a hideaway room that kids immediately want duplicated in their own homes. The small "secret" room now holds model trains and old-fashioned toys. A bedroom holds dresses from different eras including a prom dress, plus fur coats, shoes, hats, and sewing machines. The hallway has a display of once-stylish hats and beaded handbags. The "military room" is packed with personal belongings from several wars. It contains uniforms, medals, a forty-eight star flag, a Civil War hat, and a WWII helmet. See history close up!

The grounds are equally fascinating - so much machinery in one place! If your group is small, a golf cart is used to show you around. If your group is larger, or you come on a Sunday, a tractor wagon is used. You'll see and learn about old John Deeres, combines, numerous tractors, oil well engines, gas shovels, old trucks, farming equipment, a wagon originally used on the Oregon Trail, a steam roller, a filling station with gas pumps, and lots more. Though it may resemble a large junkyard, much of the machinery is in the process of being restored. While on the ranch grounds you'll also see ducks and chickens and a garden growing of its own accord.

Hours: The grounds are open Mon. - Tues. and Thurs. - Fri., 11am -
4pm. The museum is open and a tour of the grounds is available
the first Sun. of the month 2pm - 4pm. Call to make an
appointment if you're interested in a tour during the week.
Admission: A donation of $1 per person is appreciated.
Ages: 4 years and up.

HERITAGE JUNCTION HISTORIC PARK ☼

(661) 254-1275 / www.scvhs.org   !
24101 San Fernando Road, Santa Clarita
(Take Golden State Fwy [5] to Antelope Valley Fwy [14], exit N.W. on San Fernando Rd. [TG-4641
A2])

A steam locomotive is on the tracks out in front of this restored, late 1800's
train station/museum. Inside the museum are photographs, information, and
artifacts that show and tell the history of this valley, including the Spanish era,
the petroleum and mining areas, and its rich film history. Several other buildings,
in various stages of restoration, comprise the rest of the junction. You can walk
back and peek in through the windows of the little red school house, the Ramona
chapel, and the Edison house. On the first Sunday of the month, you may take a
tour through the small Kingsburry house that contains nineteenth-century
furniture. We weren't here long, but it was an interesting, historical stop. Note:
The junction park is right next to the WILLIAM S. HART MUSEUM AND
PARK. (Look under the Museums section for details.)

Hours: Open daily just to walk the grounds. The buildings are open Sat.
- Sun., 1pm - 4pm. Open for school tours during the week by
appointment.
Admission: Free
Ages: 6 years and up.

HERITAGE PARK (Santa Fe Springs) ☼

(562) 946-6476 / www.santafesprings.org   !
12100 Mora Drive, Santa Fe Springs   ⛪
(Exit San Gabriel River Fwy [605] E. on Telegraph Rd., past Pioneer, R. on Heritage Park Dr. to the
end. [TG-706 H5])

Heritage Park is like a breath of fresh air among the historical parks. Its six
acres of beautifully landscaped grounds make any length visit here a pleasure.
The high-ceilinged, wood Carriage Barn, which holds turn-of-the-century
exhibits, is a must-see. Two carriages from horse and buggy days take the center
floor. Behind glass is a large display of period clothing, including a wedding
dress, plus dolls, toys, and books. The small touch and play area has clothing to
try on, an old telephone to dial (not touch tone), and a few other articles to play
with. Inventing a Better Life display features old phonographs, typewriters,
bikes, roller skates (not in-line skates), plus cameras and other equipment. It's
interesting to see how the inventions of yesteryear benefit us today.

A thirty-two-foot dome-shaped dwelling is the centerpiece of a recreated
Native American (Tongva) village. A small creek, a granary, and a sweatlodge
are also featured. This area often showcases storytellers, a craft time, and

demonstrations.

Grab a bite to eat at The Kitchen, an outside, full-service snack bar. It's open Monday through Friday from 8am to 3pm. The average cost of a sandwich or salad is $4. Or, bring your own lunch, and enjoy the garden setting with beautiful old shade trees and wooden picnic tables. A walk-through aviary has parakeets, canaries, and a few other birds. A small window to an archeological pit shows excavated trash such as cattle bones and pottery. There are remain sites marking original fireplace and basement foundations, but kids cannot go down in them to explore. A hedge around the beautiful formal gardens gives way to an old fig tree with huge roots that are irresistible for kids to climb on. An immaculate wood-paneled tank house, once used to store water, is at the far end of the park. On a school tour, kids can go inside the tank house and walk up the crisscross stairs to the top, then go outside, and take in the view.

I can't emphasize the beauty of this park enough. It's clean, green, and the walkways throughout make every area accessible. Ask about the park's special programs throughout the year, including a Pow Wow in November.

Just outside the park gates are three restored railroad cars on a track. Take a tour of the engine car and ring the bell, then go through the caboose and see where coal was stored. Exceptional, two-hour, school tours of Heritage Park include lots of historical information, presented in a kid-friendly way, plus hands-on activities. Tours are free.

Hours: The park is open daily 7am - 10pm. Railroad exhibit and Carriage Barn hours are Tues. - Sun., noon - 4pm. School tours are given Wed. and Thurs. between 9am - noon. Call for a reservation.

Admission: Free

Ages: All

HERITAGE SQUARE MUSEUM

(626) 796-2898 / www.heritagesquare.org

3800 Homer Street, Montecito Heights

(Exit Pasadena Fwy [110] S.E. on Avenue 43. Take an immediate R. on Homer St. [TG-595 B5])

This little "town" behind a gate at the end of a residential street has five houses, plus a carriage barn (used for storage), a church building, and a train depot. The elegant Victorian homes, originally built between 1865 to 1914, have been relocated here and are in various stages of restoration. Each one has a different architectural style. One is white with columns, almost colonial-looking, while another is green, gingerbreadish in style, and has a brick chimney. The octagon-shaped house is the most unique-looking house here. Its unusual configuration makes it interesting to look at as well as walk through.

Only on the one-hour guided tours can you go through some of the homes. The Queen Anne house on the tour is the only one furnished. The grassy grounds are ideal for picnicking. Two-hour school tours are offered Monday through Thursday and include a tour with a period-dressed docent, a craft from the era, and a short play involving the students. Tours are geared for either third through fifth graders or older students who are studying architecture.

Hours: Open Fri., 10am - 3:30pm; Sat. - Sun. and holiday Mon.,
11:30am - 4:30pm. Guided tours are given Sat. - Sun. on the
hour, noon - 3pm.
Admission: Fri. admission is free, but only the grounds are open. Admission
to the buildings and the grounds on weekends and holiday Mon.
is $5 for adults; $4 for seniors and ages 13 - 17; $2 for ages 7 -
12; children 6 and under are free. Tours are a minimum of $75.
Ages: 6 years and up.

HOLLYWOOD BOWL MUSEUM

(323) 850-2058 / www.hollywoodbowl.org
2301 N. Highland, Hollywood
(Exit Hollywood Fwy [101] at Highland and follow signs to Hollywood Bowl. [TG-593 E3])

While at the Hollywood Bowl for a concert, or if you're in the area, stop by
the Hollywood Bowl Museum. This 3,000 square foot museum offers a history
of the Bowl via displays of musical instruments and pictures of performers and
conductors. Touch screens show concerts featured at the Bowl. The second story
has rotating exhibits focusing on various aspects of music. A music education
program is offered for school groups where kids learn about music, as well as try
their hands at playing some instruments. The program specifics change from
season to season.

Hours: Open during the summer Tues. - Sat., 10am - 8:30pm. Open the
rest of the year Tues. - Sat., 10am - 4:30pm. It's also open during
intermission on concert evenings.
Admission: Free. Parking is free.
Ages: 7 years and up.

HOLLYWOOD ENTERTAINMENT MUSEUM

(323) 465-7900 / www.hollywoodmuseum.com   *$$$*
7021 Hollywood Boulevard, Hollywood
(Exit Ventura Fwy [101] W. on Hollywood Blvd. [TG-593 D4])

The main room in this entertaining museum is done up dramatically in true
Hollywood style with movie posters, old movie cameras, microphones, lighting
equipment, a Hollywood time line, and video screens that show the history and
background information of particular exhibits. Listen to Walt Disney talk about
animation, or see Buster Keaton in action. Other exhibits include the armor,
sword, and helmet from *Ben Hur*; a gown worn by Marilyn Monroe; a Max
Factor display showing stars at their most glamourous; and the opportunity to
become a Star Trek character, via a mirrored reflection. A central screen
intermittently shows a montage of film clips and/or a mini-documentary. The
stage below the screen has a model of the town of Hollywood built into the floor
and covered with plexiglass so you can walk on it. Note: Flash photography is
not allowed in the museum.

Take the behind-the-scenes tours which are included in your admission
price. One enables you to see a prop room filled with masks, desks, stuffed
animals, clocks, sports equipment, musical instruments, and lots more, plus
closets stuffed with costumes and outfits categorized by color and season. *Star*

Trek fans (and others) can beam aboard the Enterprise's bridge, sit in the captain's chair, and watch clips from the original and *Next Generation* series. Picard's ready room is also here. Look closely at the diagrams and technical jargon on the display panel in the hallway. You'll see a hamster on a wheel, "slippery when wet" signs, and sayings such as, "In space no one can hear you scream." The cameras never shot close enough to catch these details! Another Trekker room follows, with masks and items that would be found on a Klingon vessel. For a change of scenery, walk through the entire original *Cheers* bar, where everybody knows your name.

The second tour is a fascinating Foley Room. Station one shows how sound effects bring life to motion pictures. Horses clopping, kissing, even putting on a leather jacket are all sounds later incorporated into a film using a variety of creative props, such as trash can lids. Kids (and adults) can try out their new-found knowledge at station two where a silent clip is shown once, and then again. The second time the audience is invited to add dialog and use the provided props of a doorbell, typewriter, telephone, and more, at the proper spots. The clip is played for a third time with the (hilarious) results recorded.

The museum also offers school programs to students who are interested in learning about the entertainment industry.

The museum is located in a complex with a theater and several shops and restaurants. It is also in the heart of Hollywood's Walk of Fame, so look down to see the stars' names adorning the sidewalks. Just a few blocks down is Disney's El Capitan Theater, the famous Mann's Chinese Theater (with stars' handprints and footprints), plus other Hollywood museums and activities.

Hours: Open Thurs. - Tues., 11am - 6pm. Closed Wed., New Year's Day, Thanksgiving, and Christmas. Open daily in the summer the same hours.

Admission: $7.50 for adults; $4.50 for seniors and students; $4 for ages 5 - 12; children 4 and under are free. Metered parking is available wherever you can find it, or park for $2 around the corner on Sycamore Street. The Hollywood CityPass, $49.75 for adults and $38 for ages 3 - 11, is good for one-time admission to American Cinematheque's Egyptian Theatre in Hollywood, AUTRY MUSEUM OF WESTERN HERITAGE, HOLLYWOOD ENTERTAINMENT MUSEUM, MUSEUM OF TELEVISION AND RADIO, MUSEUM OF TOLERANCE, PETERSEN AUTOMOTIVE MUSEUM, REAGAN PRESIDENTIAL LIBRARY AND MUSEUM, and UNIVERSAL STUDIOS within a 30 day period. (All of the entries mentioned, except for the theater, are listed separately.) Call (888) 330-5008 / www.citypass.com for more information.

Ages: 6 years and up.

HOLLYWOOD WAX MUSEUM

(323) 462-5991 / www.hollywoodwax.com

6767 Hollywood Boulevard, Hollywood

(Exit Hollywood Fwy [101] W. on Hollywood Blvd. [TG-593 E4])

Hundreds of celebrities from the world of television, movies, sports, politics, and religion are presented in waxy lifelikeness, surrounded by appropriate and realistic settings. Kids will enjoy "seeing" their favorite stars like Sylvester Stallone as Rambo, Clint Eastwood dressed in his "make my day" attire, Dorothy and her companions in the Wizard of Oz, Kareem Abdul Jabbar, Elvis, and hundreds more. A permanent exhibit here includes over 100 original movie costumes such as Christopher Reeve's *Superman*, Esther Williams' bathing suit, etc. A word of caution: There is a House of Horrors which might frighten younger children, though thankfully it has a separate walking loop.

Hours: Open Sun. - Thurs., 10am - midnight; Fri. - Sat., 10am - 2am. Closed major holidays.

Admission: $10.95 for adults; $8.95 for seniors; $6.95 for ages 6 - 12; children 5 and under are free. Combination tickets with GUINNESS WORLD BOOK OF RECORDS (see this entry in this section) are $15.95 for adults; $10.95 for seniors; $8.95 for ages 6 - 12.

Ages: 4 years and up.

HOLYLAND EXHIBITION ☼
(323) 664-3162 $
2215 Lake View and Allesandro Way, Los Angeles
(Going S. on Golden State Fwy [5], exit R. on Fletcher Dr., make a quick L. on Riverside Dr., R. on Allesandro St., R. on Oak Glen Pl. [across a bridge], R. on Allesandro Way. The house is on the corner of Lake View and Allesandro. Going N. on [5], exit at Stadium Way, make a quick L. on Riverside Dr., L. on Allesandro St. Then follow the above directions. [TG-594 E5])

Wow! I could take this tour at least three more times and still not see and learn everything this museum has to offer! The Holyland Exhibition is an inconspicuous two-story corner house that was built in the late 1920's. It contains an incredible collection of priceless Egyptian and biblical items. The two-hour tour is not hands on. It does involve a lot of listening and learning. An incredibly well-informed, costumed docent will take you first to the tapestry-rich Bethlehem/Egyptian room which, like all the rooms, is not large, but packed with artifacts. You'll feel transported to a different time and country. Some of the items explained in depth are the 2,600-year-old mummy case; the hand-made brass art pieces and plates; papyrus; shoes made of camel hide and ram skin; headdresses; and a lunch bag made of goat skin. Each item is presented with its history and its biblical connection. You'll also see jewelry, engraved leather goods, a 2,000-year-old lamp, and much more.

The Bible Art and Archaeology Room has stones, shells, pottery, spices, and more from Nazareth, Bethlehem, the Jordan River, and surrounding areas. You'll view the type of large thorns used in Christ's crown of thorns; a big chunk of salt called Madame Lot; a very comprehensive family tree detailing lineage from Adam to Jesus; the kind of stones crushed and used for pitch on Noah's ark; a picture of Mt. Ararat where *ark*eologists believe the ark landed; and a re-created Ark of the Covenant. Make sure your tour guide explains how Mr. Futterer, the museum founder, went on an expedition to find the ark and how this was the basis for the movie *Raiders of the Lost Ark*. (This will definitely spark your children's interest.) Again, amazing amounts of Bible references are given with the presentation of each article.

The Damascus Room has an intricate game table inlaid with mother-of-pearl that took fifty man-years to make - kids may not play games on it! The room also contains beaded lamps, musical instruments, a camel saddle, animal skin (to write on), and many unique pieces of furniture. In another room, enjoy a taste of Israel while sitting on oriental rugs around low tables, as you're served small samples of Holy Land refreshments. The Jerusalem Bazaar is a gift shop with souvenirs (and great teaching aids) made of olive wood, mother-of-pearl, and other materials, at bargain prices. With all that I've just written, I've barely scratched the surface of what this museum features. So, come, take a trip to the middle east, via the Holyland Exhibition, and learn about its peoples and customs. The interdenominational museum is frequented by Christians, Jews, Muslims, and people of various other faiths.

Hours: The museum is open to tour seven days a week, including holidays and evenings. Call at least a week ahead of time, and choose the most convenient time for your family or group.

Admission: $2.50 for adults; $2 for ages 3 - 16; children 2 and under are free.

Ages: 6 years and up.

THE HOMESTEAD MUSEUM   ☼

(626) 968-8492 / www.homesteadmuseum.org   !

15415 E. Don Julian Road, City of Industry

(Exit Pomona Fwy [60] N. on Hacienda Blvd., L. on Don Julian Rd. [TG-678 C1])

The Homestead Museum resides on six acres of land. A major portion of the property is an open, grassy area between the main group of buildings and the old mausoleum. A shady picnic area is here, too. A one-hour guided tour, starting at the water tower, will take you behind the gates. Kids will see and learn about the history of the United States, and about California in particular. They'll learn, for instance, that our state was once Mexican territory, and how that influence has factored in the development of our culture. They will also learn about the Art and architecture of the 1830's through the 1930's.

The tour goes into the two residences on the premises. The Workman adobe home has no furniture inside, but outside are a few artifacts that kids can touch. The Temple house is spacious with twenty-five rooms, mostly furnished in 1920's decor. Kids will also get information about the onsite pump house, tepee, and mausoleum.

Hours: Open Wed. - Sun., 1pm - 4pm. Tours are given on the hour. Open for tour groups, minimum ten people, at other times throughout the week. Call for a reservation. Closed major holidays and the fourth weekend of every month.

Admission: Free

Ages: 6 years and up.

HUNTINGTON LIBRARY, ART COLLECTIONS AND ☼ BOTANICAL GARDENS

(626) 405-2141 / www.huntington.org $$

1151 Oxford Road, San Marino

(Exit Foothill Fwy [210] S. on Sierra Madre Blvd., R. on California, L. on Allen Ave., go straight ahead into park. [TG-566 D7])

The Library houses one of the world's greatest collections of rare books, manuscripts, and documents including a Gutenberg Bible; Ellesmere Chaucer's *The Canterbury Tales*; Benjamin Franklin's autobiography, in his own handwriting; original works by Whitman and Dickens; and letters written by George Washington, Thomas Jefferson, and Abraham Lincoln.

The Huntington Art Gallery is the epitome of opulence. This mansion contains sculptures, rare tapestries, miniatures, period furniture, and famous paintings, including Gainsborough's *Blue Boy*. Watch the interesting, thirteen-minute video about this painting first, then see if you can find some of the hidden elements in the painting. Get kids involved with observing the paintings by pointing out the ones with children and ones with different styles of dress. Tell them stories about the subjects. For instance, sweet-faced *Pinkie* died soon after her portrait was finished, and the boy in *Lavina, Countess Spencer and her son Viscount Althorp* was one of Princess Diana's great great (great, etc.,) grandparents. This is a gentle way to introduce children to some truly great works of art.

The botanical gardens are comprised of twelve separate, amazing gardens that cover 150 acres of the 200-acre estate. As Lisa Blackburn, a museum associate says, "The gardens . . . have wide open spaces and vast rolling lawns; great for running, somersaulting, cartwheeling, shrieking, and releasing all that boundless energy that is sometimes stifled in traditional museum settings." There are waterfalls, lily ponds, koi, ducks, turtles, and frogs to capture kids' attention - almost more than can be seen in one day. The Desert Garden has, again to quote Lisa, "twelve acres of some of the most bizarre, colorful, creepy-crawly plants that a child could imagine." Another favorite garden is the Japanese garden, which is a quarter-mile west of the main entrance. This has a traditionally furnished Japanese house, stone ornaments, an old temple bell, a moon bridge, and a bonsai court. My little Tarzans said the best part of coming to the Huntington, though, is hiding in the bamboo groves in the Jungle Garden.

Discovery Carts can be found throughout the grounds. The carts contain a variety of small projects for children. For example, water samples collected from the pond can be examined under a microscope.

Be sure to pick up a "Family Guide", a brochure that helps lead children on an educational expedition through the galleries and gardens. Look for a 25-acre Botanical Research and Education complex to open in 2003. It will include a children's garden.

Picnicking is not allowed on the grounds. However, a special treat for you and your daughter, as it's not really a boy's cup of tea, is to dress up and sip English tea in the Rose Garden Tea Room, (626) 683-8131. The all-you-can-eat buffet includes a variety of finger sandwiches, tea, scones, cheeses, fresh fruit, and delightful English desserts and cost $12.95 for adults, $6.50 for children 6 years and under. A restaurant is on the grounds, too. Ask about the numerous special classes and programs, including the Kid's Nature Crafts, which is offered the first Saturday of every month.

Hours: Open in the summer Tues. - Sun., 10:30am - 4:30pm. Open the rest of the year Tues. - Fri., noon - 4:30pm; Sat. - Sun., 10:30am - 4:30pm. Self-guiding tour brochures are available. Garden tours depart Tues. - Sun. at 1pm. Closed major holidays. The tea buffet is served Tues. - Fri., noon - 3:30pm; Sat. - Sun., 10:45am - 3:30pm.

Admission: $8.50 for adults; $8 for seniors; $6 for students with ID; children 11 and under are free. Admission is free the first Thurs. of every month.

Ages: 4 years and up.

INTERNATIONAL PRINTING MUSEUM   ☼
$$$
(714) 529-1832 / www.printmuseum.org
315 Torrance Boulevard, Carson
(Exit Harbor Fwy [110] E. on Torrance Blvd. [TG-764 C5])

A visit to this museum helps kids to understand the history and importance of the printed word, and how printing presses changed the world of reading. Visitors will see a working wooden press from 1750, a replica of Gutenberg's first press, printing artifacts, and demonstrations of bookbinding and papermaking. They will also have the opportunity to fold their own book as a keepsake. General tours are offered for the public and specific tours are offered for groups of up to fifty people. As a parent and a readaholic, I appreciate all that this fine museum has to offer, especially the presentations that encourage kids to realize the joy of reading.

Two, ninety-minute group tours, which also include a general museum tour, are *The Pages of Invention: The Communication Tour*, and *The Pages of Freedom: The Constitutional Convention*. The Invention Tour is a fascinating journey that begins thousands of years ago when the Chinese first invented paper and "wrote" on it using carved blocks of wood. Children continue traveling to the period when Egyptian scrolls were written on papyrus, then on to the time of Gutenberg's invaluable contribution of the printing press. Students learn about the tools of the trade while listening to anecdotes and information on bookbinding. They also learn about the time it took to make a hand-written book (three to five years); the price; the increase in availability of books to the common people because of the press; and a lot more. A costumed appearance by Benjamin Franklin - well, not the real one, but one who is a dead ringer - then follows. Utilizing slides and equipment, Ben explains his numerous inventions and discoveries, such as electricity, an unsteady chair (i.e. rocking chair), markers called milestones, and more. Eager audience members participate in experiments that demonstrate static electricity and electricity generated through a replica 1750 electro static generator. He regales listeners about his life in Colonial America and encourages children to get educated by reading.

The Pages of Freedom Tour is a reenactment of the Constitutional Convention. Divided into thirteen groups (colonies), students use pre-written cards to debate foundational issues such as representation taxation, election of the president, and slavery. Ben Franklin presides over the meeting which ends with the colony deputies signing the Constitution. This is an outstanding, experiential history lesson/tour!

If your group comprises more than fifty students, reserve a *History in Motion: A Museum on Wheels* presentation, where the museum comes to your site. Host a slightly expanded version of the Inventions tour, or invite just Ben Franklin for a fifty-minute presentation/"show." Again, I can't recommend this tour highly enough.

Hours: Open to the public Sat., 10am - 4pm. Open for groups by reservation.

Admission: $8 for adults; $6 for seniors and ages 5 - 18; children 4 and under are free. In-house group educational tours are $150 for up to 25 people; $6 per person over that number. The traveling tours, for up to 150 students, are a flat fee of $500 for the two-hour presentation; $350 for the talk with Ben.

Ages: 6 years and up.

JAPANESE AMERICAN NATIONAL MUSEUM

(213) 625-0414 / www.janm.org   *$$$*

369 E. 1ˢᵗ Street, Los Angeles

(Exit Harbor Fwy [110] E. on 1ˢᵗ St. Or, exit Hollywood Fwy [101] S. on Alameda, R. on 1ˢᵗ St. It's on the corner of 1ˢᵗ St. and Central Ave. in Little Tokyo. Park in the lot across the street for $2 or $3 for the day. [TG-634 G4])

During World War II, more than 120,000 people of Japanese ancestry, most of whom were American citizens, were incarcerated in American relocation/concentration camps from 1941 to 1946. This museum is dedicated to preserving the memory of that time period, and learning from it. There are two buildings to this one museum, located across the pedestrian walkway from each other.

The newer glass building is nicely laid out and has seven gallery rooms, plus a research library, classrooms, and a theater room. The exhibit rooms holds rotating displays, varying from art exhibits, to the history of Japanese Americans, to athletes of Japanese ancestry. Permanent displays include authentic wooden barracks from an internment camp in Wyoming and a gallery reminiscent of an Ellis Island tribute with suitcases and immigrants' belongings, such as clothing (i.e. wedding dresses, uniforms, and everyday clothing), personal articles, board games, and numerous photographs. Articles on discrimination in the 1920's and on the loss of citizens' rights during WWII offer both shameful and fascinating information. Videos in several galleries complete the museums' offerings.

The historic brick building across the way contains the Legacy Room, which displays photographs of Japanese families, the Japanese-American time line, uniforms, and scale models of the layout of the camps. A craft table is available, too, where volunteers show visitors how to create origami art. The second floor features rotating exhibits that touch upon various aspects of Japanese culture, whether the exhibits focus on art or Sumo wrestlers.

The museum anchors the east end of Little Tokyo Historic District which is comprised of ethnic shops and restaurants. Try an unusual flavor of ice cream here, such as green tea or red bean.

Hours: Open Tues. - Sun., 10am - 5pm (open Thurs. until 7:30pm). Closed New Year's Day, Thanksgiving, and Christmas.

Admission: $6 for adults; $5 for seniors; $3 for ages 6 - 17; children 5 and under are free. Admission is free the third Thurs. of every month.

Ages: 7 years and up.

JUSTICE BROTHERS RACING CAR MUSEUM

(626) 359-9174 / www.justicebrothers.com

2734 E. Huntington Drive, Duarte

(Exit San Gabriel Fwy [605] E. on Huntington Dr. It's just past Las Lomas St. [TG-568 D5])

Justice Brothers is an established name in car care products. In the main lobby of their headquarters office building is a slick exhibit of their collection containing thirteen-plus cars and a few motorcycles. Featured models include gleaming and colorful vintage Kurtis midget and sprint cars dating back to the 1930's, a 1968 Ford GT-40 LeMans, a Ford Model T, and a classic Corvette and Thunderbird. Other memorabilia includes numerous gasoline pumps, a great display of lights from the top of old gasoline pumps, models, photographs, engines, and even a biplane "flying" overhead. The winner for most unique motorcycle goes to an ice motorcycle, or "icycle", with its steel spikes on the tires to grip ice in Russia and a few other cold countries. There are two other, smaller display areas in adjacent buildings that showcase a few more race cars and a Chevy truck.

Hours: Open Mon. - Fri., 8am - 5pm.

Admission: Free

Ages: 6 years and up. Visitors under 18 must be accompanied by an adult.

KENNETH G. FISKE MUSICAL INSTRUMENT MUSEUM

(909) 621-8307 / cucpo.cuc.claremont.edu/fiske

747 N. Dartmouth Avenue, Claremont College, Claremont

(Exit San Bernardino Fwy [10] N. on Indian Hill Blvd., R. on 4th St. The College is at the corner of 4th St. and College Way. The museum is on the lower level of the Bridges auditorium. [TG-601 D3])

This museum is like music to your ears. The gallery contains a comprehensive collection of several hundred rare, historic, and ethnic musical instruments. The instruments in display cases and lining the wall, range from the 1600's to the twentieth century. They include exotic drums, a Russian bassoon with a dragon's head, an armonica (invented by Benjamin Franklin), a walking cane violin, mandolins, Civil War bugles, a seven-foot trumpet, square pianos, player pianos, and lots more. On the half-hour tour, the curator explains the various instruments and even plays a few of them. This museum can be instrumental in teaching your kids about music! Tip: To continue your musical adventure, check out the nearby Folk Music Center shop, (909) 624-2928, at 220

Yale Avenue, which has an array of interesting folk instruments.

Hours: Call for an appointment.

Admission: Free; donations accepted.

Ages: 7 years and up.

KIDSPACE CHILDREN'S MUSEUM
(626) 449-9143 / www.kidspacemuseum.org

390 S. El Molino Avenue, Pasadena

(Take Pasadena Fwy [110] to end, R. on California Blvd., L. on El Molino. Or, exit Foothill Fwy [210] S. on Lake Ave., R. on Del Mar, L. on El Molino. [TG-566 A5])

As soon as kids enter this great participatory museum they immediately get immersed in the professions and activities offered as they sit behind a desk at a "TV studio" and become newscasters; dress up as firefighters and man (or woman) the hoses and ladders, which are (thankfully) attached to walls; learn how they get things letter-perfect at the Post Office by playing Postmaster; get sand between their toes at the beach play area; discover architecture as they build bridges; and play in, on, and under the indoor treehouse play area, called Critter Caverns. Kids go buggy at InterAntics, a simulated giant ant hill to crawl up and an oversized leaf to climb on and over. Young shoppers or cashiers-in-the-making have a mini-market with baskets, food, and a (play) cash register. Little ones have a wonderful area just for them that offers various activities.

Saturday and Sunday craft times, for ages 5 and up, are weekend bonuses. During the week, "No Nap" storytelling and craft times are offered for toddlers. The museum also features many special programs, exhibits, and workshops throughout the year, as well as traveling exhibits. We have thoroughly enjoyed school field trips here as students learn about insects (or other subject matter) in depth, complete a related craft project, and play. Note: The museum is planning on moving within Pasadena in 2002, or so.

Hours: Open in the summer Sun. - Thurs., 1pm - 5pm; Fri. and Sat., 10am - 5pm. Open the rest of the year Tues., 1:30pm - 5pm; Wed. - Fri. and Sun., 1pm - 5pm; Sat., 10am - 5pm. Closed Mon. Open for school tours during the week, with advanced reservations.

Admission: $5 for ages 3 and up; $3.50 for seniors; $2.50 for children 1 - 2. Certain discounts available through AAA. School tours are $2.50 per person. Admission is free on the last Mon. of every month (except October), 5pm - 8pm.

Ages: 1½ - 11 years old.

THE LEONIS ADOBE
(818) 222-6511 / www.leonisadobemuseum.org

23537 Calabasas Road, Calabasas

(Exit Ventura Fwy [101] S. on Valley Circle Blvd. / Mulholland Dr., take a quick R. onto Calabasas Rd. [TG-559 F4])

Step back over 100 years in time when you visit the Leonis Adobe. The restored buildings help kids to picture the wealthy ranchero as it once was. The rustic grounds, complete with grape arbors, old farm equipment, windmills, and a corral containing longhorn cattle, horses, sheep, and goats, enhance the yesteryear atmosphere. Officially Los Angeles' Historic Cultural Monument No. 1, the adobe was once owned by Miguel Leonis, a Basque who led a very colorful life, and Espiritu, his Native American wife. Both the museum and its owners have a rich and fascinating history that kids will enjoy hearing.

The Visitor's Center is actually the re-located Plummer House, the oldest house "in" Hollywood. It contains a few glass-cased displays of mannequins dressed in period clothing. Outside, a huge, 600-year-old oak tree dominates the grounds. You are welcome to explore the barn, complete with wagons and buggies; a blacksmith's shop that is outfitted with saddles and tools; and the adobe. The bottom story of the adobe has a kitchen with a wood-burning stove and other old-fashioned kitchen implements; a pantry for preserving and drying food (kids like the hanging cow with fake blood); and a dining room - notice the dirt floors. Upstairs is the Leonis' elegant bedroom that has a red velvet bedspread over the canopy bed, plus ladies' boots, and leather trunks. You'll notice that the hallway floor tilts at a downward angle, slanting away from the house. It was built like that to ensure that rains would run away from the walls, not seep into them. The Juan Menendez (bed) Room has a ghost story associated with it. (Every good historical home has at least one such story!) Also up here is an office, complete with desk, ledger, and guitar. Elsewhere on the ranch grounds are penned turkeys, ducks, and chickens; a covered beehive oven which was used for baking bread; and steps leading up to the tank house, or worker's bedroom. The Leonis Adobe is a classy reminder of the relatively brief, but pivotal Mexican/California era.

Just a short walk eastward, past the Sagebrush Cantina restaurant, is the small, but beautiful Calabasas Creek Park. It offers a pleasant picnic area and respite with a rose garden out front, wrought-iron benches throughout, massive shade trees, and bridges over the duck pond. The only drawback to this serene scene is the ever-present freeway noise.

Hours: The Leonis Adobe is open Wed. - Sun., 1pm - 4pm.
Admission: $2 for adults; $1 for children 12 and under.
Ages: 4 years and up.

LOMITA RAILROAD MUSEUM
(310) 326-6255 / www.lomita-rr.org
250th Street and Woodward Avenue, Lomita
(Exit Harbor Fwy [110] W. on Pacific Coast Hwy., R. on Narbonne, R. on 250th St. [TG-793 H4])

Stop, look, and listen! This small, re-created, turn-of-the century train depot is as charming to look at - with its decorative wrought iron, gingerbread molding, and brick patio - as it is to tour. Inside the depot museum/souvenir shop, visitors will see various train memorabilia such as an old-time station agent ticket office, scale model train cars, telegraph equipment, locomotive whistles, marker lights, an exhibit of railroad ties, and glass cases filled with photographs, and more artifacts. Hanging from the ceiling and the walls is a collection of hand-lanterns.

Outside, on real train tracks, are two railcars: An all-wood, 1910 Union Pacific "bobber" (i.e. caboose) to look around in and a 1902 Southern Pacific

Steam locomotive with a cab that the kids can climb in and let their imaginations go full steam ahead. Note that the valves and handles are labeled with explanations for their use, but they are not for touching.

The museum annex park is just across the street. This pretty little grassy spot, with a few picnic tables under shade trees, boasts a real wood box car and a 1923 Union Oil tank car that are for display purposes only.

Hours: Open Wed. - Sun., 10am - 5pm. Closed Thanksgiving and Christmas.

Admission: $2 for adults; $1 for children 12 and under.

Ages: 1 ½ years and up.

LOS ANGELES COUNTY MUSEUM OF ART and ☼ L.A.C.M.A. WEST

(323) 857-6000 / www.lacma.org $$$
5905 Wilshire Boulevard, Los Angeles
(From Santa Monica Fwy [10], exit N. on Fairfax Ave., R. on Wilshire Blvd. From San Diego Fwy [405], exit E. on Wilshire Blvd. [TG-633 B2])

Art, according to Webster, is: "The use of the imagination to make things of aesthetic significance; the technique involved; the theory involved." This leaves the interpretation of what constitutes art wide open! The Los Angeles County Museum of Art is composed of five buildings, plus the Bing Center of theater and movies for older audiences. Each building features a different style of art.

The Anderson building is a favorite with its twentieth-century art, which translates as "anything goes." We started in the *Garage* (our title for the exhibit). Open the door to this walk-through exhibit, and it's like being in your grandfather's garage. It's crammed with old, rusted tools hanging up on the walls, other storage-type incidentals, and a car that needs more work than it will ever get. (I can now tell my husband that our garage is not a mess - it's art.) Throughout the Anderson building, kids are attracted to and puzzled by the larger-than-life sculptures, abstract paintings on gigantic canvases, and common objects that express artistic creativity, like a kitchen sink, or an arrangement of cereal boxes. Two particularly eye-catching pieces are the life-size, faceless monks sitting around in a circle, and *The Black Planet*, which is a huge black disc with long strands of black tubing (think Cajun spaghetti) coming out of it.

In contrast, the Ahmanson Building has more traditional works of art from Medieval European, the Romantic, and the Renaissance periods. Classic paintings and portraits hang in various galleries throughout the stately, three-story building. Gilbert gold and silver pieces, such as elaborate bowls and candelabras, are on display here, as are incredibly detailed, inlaid stone pictures. Other exhibits include Korean, Chinese, and American art.

The Pavilion for Japanese Art is architecturally unique, inside and out. It houses mostly paintings and a few sculptures in a serene, natural-light setting. The Samurai warrior statue, dressed in eighteenth-century black chain mail armor, gets our vote for the most interesting exhibit here. The stairs spiral downward, toward the small waterfall and pond on the lowest level. The Hammer Building specializes in photography, impressionism, and prints. The permanent and temporary exhibits here portray another medium of artistic endeavor.

Although many docents are on hand to insure that nothing is touched, the atmosphere is not stifling. Contact the museum about their great art classes, school tours, and family tours offered throughout the year. For instance, our school group took the free sculpture tour where we went on a guided tour of the sculptures here and then went to the on-site classroom to make sculptures out of the provided clay. Family Fun Days are held on the last Sunday of the month and include art workshops, live performances, and a family gallery tour. For your information, a cafe, serving good food, is in the courtyard. Enjoy walking around the museum's spacious backyard, Hancock Park. The parks hosts concerts and presentations at the amphitheater, has picnic tables, grassy areas, trees, and is home to the La Brea Tar Pits and adjacent to the GEORGE C. PAGE MUSEUM.

The L.A.C.M.A. West is a satellite building of the huge main museum and is on the corner of Fairfax and Wilshire, just down the street from L.A.C.M.A. (One admission fee pays for entry to both museums.) One gallery rotates exhibit pieces from the central art museum's massive permanent collection, and showcases traveling exhibits. The most interesting galleries for kids is the "experimental gallery", where family members enjoy themed rotating hands-on exhibits, corresponding games, crafts, and perhaps some computer activities.

Hours: Open Mon., Tues., and Thurs., noon - 8pm; Fri., noon - 9pm; Sat. - Sun., 11am - 8pm. Closed Wed., Thanksgiving, and Christmas. School tours are often given in the morning hours.

Admission: $7 for adults; $5 for seniors and students; $1 for ages 6 - 17; children 5 and under are free. Admission is free on the second Tues. of each month, except for ticketed events. Parking costs $5 in the lot at the S.E. corner of Wilshire Blvd. and Spaulding, or at Hancock Park at Sixth St. and Curson Ave.

Ages: 6 years and up.

LOS ANGELES MARITIME MUSEUM

(310) 548-7618 / www.lamaritimemuseum.org

Berth 84, San Pedro

(Take Harbor Fwy [110] to the end. It turns into Gaffey St. Turn L. on 9th, L. on Harbor Blvd. It's at the foot of 6th St. [TG-824 C5])

If you have older children who dream of sailing the oceans blue, they will enjoy walking through the six galleries of this maritime museum, which is housed in an old ferry building. There are hundreds of ship models to look at, ranging from real boats to ones inside a bottle. (How do they do that?) An impressive twenty-one-foot scale model of the Queen Mary and two cut-away models, of the Titanic and Lusitania, give your kids the inside scoop on ocean liners.

A highlight is the Amateur Radio Station where your child might be able to talk to someone on the other side of the world.

Hours: Open Tues. - Sun., 10am - 5pm. Closed New Year's Day, Thanksgiving, and Christmas.

Admission: $1 donation for adults.

Ages: 5 years and up.

MARTYRS MEMORIAL AND MUSEUM OF THE HOLOCAUST

(323) 761-8170

6006 Wilshire Boulevard, Los Angeles

(From Santa Monica Fwy [10], exit N. on Fairfax Ave., R. on Wilshire Blvd., R. on Ogden Drive. Museum is at SW corner of Ogden and Wilshire. Fee parking at rear of Museum or metered parking nearby. From San Diego Fwy [405], exit E. on Wilshire Blvd. It's located on Museum Row diagonally across from LACMA. [TG-633 B2])

The first story of this building, which is run by the Jewish Federation, houses the fairly extensive Jewish Community Library of Los Angeles, as well as a side room that is the museum. The museum consists mainly of photographs and information panels on the walls, plus artifacts, part of a (human) cargo train car to walk through, a model layout of the Sobibor death camp, and touch screens that show newsreels from WWII Germany and interviews with survivors. Note: Several of the photographs are necessarily graphic (i.e. piles of naked bodies). A few display cases exhibit typical family belongings, religious items, and cultural arts memorabilia. Guided school/group tours can be arranged. The museum can provide speakers, docents, and survivors who address classrooms on Jewish history by incorporating art, music, and/or writing.

Hours: Mon. - Thurs., 10m - 5pm (Tues. until 8pm); Fri., 10am - 2pm; Sun., noon - 4pm. Closed Sat.

Admission: Free. Ask about tour information.

Ages: 4th graders and up.

MISSION SAN FERNANDO REY DE ESPAÑA

(818) 361-0186

15151 San Fernando Mission Boulevard, Mission Hills

(From San Fernando Valley Fwy [118] exit N. on Sepulveda Blvd., R. on San Fernando Mission Blvd. Going N. on San Diego Fwy [405], exit E. on San Fernando Mission Blvd. Going S. on 405, exit E. on Rinaldi St., R. on Sepulveda Blvd., L. on San Fernando Mission Blvd. [TG-501 H2])

What was life like in the early days of California? Take a self-guided tour of one of my family's favorite missions to find out. Mission San Fernando Rey, founded in 1797, was the seventeenth mission in the chain of outposts along the coast of California. It has a beautiful, large courtyard, with a small sundial at the north entrance, and west gardens that are surrounded by numerous rooms. These rooms lead to small, alcove rooms - what delightful exploration! The Museum Room is a good place to begin as it's filled with old photos (including one of a bathroom that looks like a small indoor pool), statues, bows and arrows, peace pipes, a bell collection, and several more artifacts. The Madonna Room is fascinating as it contains over 100 representations of the Madonna, each depicted by different nationalities and cultures. From simplistic versions to ornate ones, there are Chinese, African, and Indian Madonnas, plus one that looks like a prairie woman, another like an Eskimo, and more.

Other rooms and items of interest we saw include a hospice that held beds made with rope supports (pre-box springs); simply furnished bedrooms; plain wooden tables and chairs; the Convent, where meat was hung to dry; mission vestments; a library containing shelves of very old books including a colorful, hand-illuminated liturgical book with large Gothic lettering; brick ovens; and pipe organs. The workshop and weaving rooms are interesting because they hold, respectively, blacksmith tools, saddles, and scythes, and a large wooden loom with cowhide chairs. The church, which still holds regular worship services, has adobe walls and an ornately decorated altar with gold-leaf overlay. A small cemetery behind the church opens into a huge, neighboring cemetery. In the midst of all this history, my boys loved seeing the many peacocks that wandered the grounds. They even "discovered" a few roosters that were tame enough to pet.

Brand Park, once a part of the mission, is just across the street. This grassy park has lots of shade trees, plenty of picnic tables, and running around space, but no playground. It also has vats where mission wines were once produced.

Hours: Open daily 9am - 4:30pm. Closed Thanksgiving and Christmas.
Admission: $4 for adults; $3 for seniors and ages 7 - 15; children 6 and under are free. Admission to Brand Park is free.
Ages: 5 years and up.

MISSION SAN GABRIEL ARCHANGEL
(626) 457-3048 $$
537 W. Mission Drive, San Gabriel
(Exit San Bernardino Fwy [10] N. on Del Mar Ave., L. on Mission Rd. [TG-596 D4])

Located in the Mission District, California's fourth mission is aptly nicknamed "Queen of the Missions." The graceful buildings and pleasant grounds transport you back to 1771, when the mission was founded. They also offer a wonderfully visual way to learn about California's Spanish/Mexican heritage.

In the midst of the cactus garden are tanning vats, with a placard describing the tanning process. Walk up a few stone steps to see four large holes in the ground, which were once the soap and tallow vats. The San Gabriel Mission supplied soap and candles to most of the other missions. There are several fountains and statues distributed throughout the mission gardens. In the cemetery, for instance, is a life-size crucifix - a memorial to the 6,000 Indians buried on the grounds.

The Mission Church is still in use. The wall behind the altar is eye-catching as it is ornately decorated. The small baptismal room is equally impressive. Next to the church, the small and somewhat dark museum contains only a few articles that were of interest to my kids - big, old books covered in sheepskin dating from 1489 and 1588, and a Spanish bedroom set. Knowing that the museum was once a series of rooms, such as sleeping quarters, weaving rooms, and carpenter shops, made it a bit more interesting.

Located in the center of the mission is the Court of the Missions. Models of each of California's twenty-one missions, varying in size and layout, but similar in style, are on display here. Vaya con Dios! (Go with God!)

Hours: Open daily 9am - 4:30pm. Closed Easter, Thanksgiving, and Christmas.

Admission: $5 for adults; $4 for seniors; $2 for ages 6 - 12; children 5 and under are free.

Ages: 5 years and up.

MONTEREY PARK HISTORICAL MUSEUM   ☼
(626) 307-1267   !

781 S. Orange Avenue, Monterey Park

(Exit San Bernardino Fwy [10] S. on Garfield Ave., L. on Graves Ave., R. on Orange Ave. The museum is situated in Garvey Ranch Park. [TG-636 D3])

This small museum's claim to fame is its twenty-one scale models of the California missions. The adobe-like museum has three reconstructed rooms that also house Indian artifacts, household items (such as toys and a phonograph), tools, period clothing, photographs, and a corner dedicated to Laura Scudder (who lived in Monterey Park).

Adjacent to the museum is a small observatory that is open for public viewing on Wednesdays at about 7pm. Garvey Ranch Park is a nice park with grassy areas, trees, a few covered picnic areas, paved pathways, two lighted baseball diamonds with stadium seating, basketball courts, playgrounds, and two tennis courts just up the hill.

Hours: The museum is open Sat. - Sun., 2pm - 4pm. The park is open daily.

Admission: Free

Ages: 5 years and up.

MUSEUM OF CONTEMPORARY ART / GEFFEN   ☼
CONTEMPORARY
(213) 626-6222 / www.moca.org   *$$$*

250 S. Grand Avenue, Los Angeles

(Going W. on Hollywood Fwy [101], exit S. on Grand Ave. Going E. on 101, exit E. on Temple St., R. on Grand Ave. From Harbor Fwy [110], exit E. on 4th St., L. on Broadway, L. on 1st st. L. on Grand. [TG-634 F3])

The elegant Museum of Contemporary Art (MOCA), located on top of a plaza, presents rotating exhibits of eclectic art work - paintings, sculptures, photos, etc. This type of museum is a fun one to bring kids to as an introduction to art because the pieces are unusual, imaginative, and sometimes puzzling. Idea: After visiting the museum, have the kids come home and create their own contemporary or abstract piece of art. As we looked at the huge paintings on canvas, my boys and I took the liberty of renaming several pieces. (I think some of their title choices were more apropos than the ones the artists chose.) This involved the kids in studying the art and therefore enhanced our visit here. Downstairs in the museum is a reading room with several books, many geared for children, that pertain to the art and artists currently featured at the MOCA.

A satellite building of MOCA, the Geffen Contemporary, is located one mile away at 152 N. Central Avenue in Little Tokyo, across the plaza from the JAPANESE AMERICAN NATIONAL MUSEUM. The Museum of Contemporary Art is actually one museum in two buildings!

Hours: Open Tues. - Sun., 11am - 5pm (Thurs. until 8pm). Free public
tours are given at noon, 1pm, and 2pm. Closed New Year's Day,
Thanksgiving, and Christmas.

Admission: $6 for adults; $4 for seniors and students with ID; children 11
and under are free. Thurs. from 5pm - 8pm is free admission.
Paid admission is good for both locations of the museum, if
visited on the same day. Parking in the plaza costs about $5.

Ages: 6 years and up.

MUSEUM OF FLYING   ☼

(310) 392-8822 / www.museumofflying.com $$
2772 Donald Douglas Loop North, Santa Monica   �📶
(Exit Santa Monica Fwy [10] S. on Bundy Dr., R. on Ocean Park Blvd., L. on 28ᵗʰ St. It's adjacent to
the Santa Monica Airport. [TG-672 A2])

Ready to take-off to a place where the sky is the limit? This airy museum
has three stories of vintage aircraft, models, and air-related exhibits. Take the
catwalk-like stairs to the second level, which has an observation window
overlooking the airport. Kids can listen to the control tower via the headphones.
My boys liked the mock-up of a war-briefing room up here, too.

Some of the planes are maintained in flight-ready condition. In fact, a
hangar door is open for kids to watch WWII planes and other small aircraft
taxiing, flying, and landing on the runway. Want to feel the jolting of a "real"
flight? Take a simulator ride for $2.

A replica of the Voyager, which flew non-stop around the world in 1986, is
on display at the entrance to Airventure. So is a slightly older flying model - a
Pterodactyl. Airventure is designed just for kids as they can sit in a real Vietnam
War-era helicopter, pilot the controls at a real cockpit, and play in various
pretend planes. Workshops for kids ages 5 and older are offered on the
weekends. Call for specific times and details. Kindergarten through twelfth
grade students who get an 'A' on their report card are treated like Top Guns
here; they can take a free, fifteen-minute flight in a two or four seater airplane.
The program is offered once a month and reservations are required.

Hours: Open Wed. - Sun., 10am - 5pm.

Admission: $7 for adults; $5 for seniors; $3 for ages 3 -17; children 2 and
under are free.

Ages: 3 years and up.

MUSEUM OF LATIN AMERICAN ART   ☼

(562) 437-1689 / www.molaa.com $$
628 Alamitos Avenue, Long Beach
(Exit Long Beach Fwy [710] E. on Anaheim St., R. on Alamitos. [TG-795 F7])

This museum has a nicely laid out main gallery and surrounding gallery
rooms. Rotating exhibits feature art, sculpture, and paintings by Latin American
artists. The museum regularly hosts hands-on art workshops for children, usually
geared for ages 6 and up, that tie in with the present exhibit. Explore Latin
American culture and heritage while experiencing its art. Note: The gift shop is
filled with wonderful, cultural items to purchase.

Hours: Open Tues. - Fri., 11:30am - 7:30pm; Sat., 11am - 7:30pm;
Sun.,11am - 5pm.
Admission: $7 for adults; $5 for seniors and students; children 12 and under
are free.
Ages: 6 years and up.

MUSEUM OF NEON ART

☀
$

(213) 489-9918 / www.neonmona.org
501 W. Olympic, Los Angeles
(Exit Harbor Fwy [110] E. on 9th St., R. on Grand Ave., R. on Olympic. It's on the corner of Olympic and Hope, with the entrance on Hope. Free underground parking is available at the Renaissance Tower on Grand Ave., just N. of Olympic Blvd. [TG-634 E5])

For an enlightening experience, bring your kids to the Museum of Neon Art. Only here can you see Mona Lisa's smile really light up. Walk through the rainbow arch and into the warehouse-like rooms that display rotating exhibits of artists who use kinetic and electric art as an outlet for their creative endeavors. In other words, there are some funky-looking, 3-D reliefs and sculptures in here! Most of the pieces are fragile, but some of them have buttons to push that make parts light up or move around.

Just outside the museum is Hope Grant Park, which is the front lawn to the Fashion Institute of Design and Merchandise. This haven of greenery in the middle of downtown Los Angeles is a welcome respite. It has a small playground, a few picnic tables, a mosaic clock tower, colorful mosaic art forms, and a large fountain with steps around its perimeter that kids love to climb.

Hours: The museum is open Wed. - Sat., 11am - 5pm; Sun., noon - 5pm.
On the second Thurs. of each month, the museum is open until
8pm. The park is open daily 7am - 6pm.
Admission: $5 for adults; $3.50 for seniors and students; children 12 and
under are free. Admission is free on the second Thurs. of every
month from 5pm - 8pm. The park is free.
Ages: 4 years and up.

THE MUSEUM OF TELEVISION AND RADIO

☀
$$
⛪

(310) 786-1000 / www.mtr.org
465 N. Beverly Drive, Beverly Hills
(Exit Santa Monica Fwy [10] N. on Robertson, L. on Wilshire, R. on Beverly Dr. Or, exit San Diego Fwy [405] E. on Santa Monica Blvd., R. on Beverly Dr. Two hours of free valet parking, with validation, is available under the museum, just off Little Santa Monica Blvd. [TG-632 F1])

Tune in to the Museum of Television and Radio, which houses the ultimate collection of broadcasting programs. Inside the upscale, contemporary-looking building are various rooms to watch and listen to shows, with just the touch of a button. The lobby has rotating exhibits of art, mementos, storyboards, costumes, sets, and more. The Radio Listening Room is just what its name implies. The room is quiet as visitors use headphones to choose from five preset radio channels. A sampling of the rotating selections can include comedy, rock 'n roll, history of radio, witness to history (e.g. historic speeches), etc. There is also a fully equipped radio station in here to do live broadcasts. Next door, watch a pre-selected show in the fifty-seat Screening Room, or watch a film in the 150-seat Theater Room. Call to see what's playing.

Use the upstairs computer library to select your choice of radio or television show. For example, key your television selection into the computer, then view it in the adjacent Console Room. This room has individual monitors as well as family consoles which accommodate up to four people. Your child is in couch potato heaven here, able to choose his own television programs from literally thousands of titles available.

Some of the benefits of this museum include viewing (and listening to) historic shows both for school-aged children and for researchers. Ready access to programs is also great if you just want to choose a favorite show. Call for information on special children's events. Hot tip: On most Saturdays from 10am to 11:30am kids ages 9 to 14 years old can partake in an old-time radio workshop called Re-creating Radio. Participants use scripts, sound effects, and music to produce a broadcast, and they even get a copy of the tape to bring home. The cost is $5 and reservations are required. What a fun (and unique) birthday party idea!

Hours: Open Wed. - Sun., noon - 5pm (open Thurs. until 9pm). Closed Mon., Tues., New Year's Day, Independence Day, Thanksgiving, and Christmas.

Admission: $6 for adults; $4 for seniors and students; $3 for children 12 and under. Ask about the Hollywood CityPass, which is valid for 30 days from when it is first used. The Hollywood CityPass, $49.75 for adults and $38 for ages 3 - 11, is good for one-time admission to American Cinematheque's Egyptian Theatre in Hollywood, AUTRY MUSEUM OF WESTERN HERITAGE, HOLLYWOOD ENTERTAINMENT MUSEUM, MUSEUM OF TELEVISION AND RADIO, MUSEUM OF TOLERANCE, PETERSEN AUTOMOTIVE MUSEUM, REAGAN PRESIDENTIAL LIBRARY AND MUSEUM, and UNIVERSAL STUDIOS within a 30 day period. (All of the entries mentioned, except for the theater, are listed separately.) Call (888) 330-5008 / www.citypass.com for more information.

Ages: 6 years and up.

MUSEUM OF TOLERANCE / SIMON WEISENTHAL ☼ CENTER

(800) 900-9036 or (310) 553-8403 / www.wiesenthal.com   *$$$*
9786 W. Pico Boulevard, Los Angeles
(Exit San Diego Fwy [405] E. on Santa Monica Blvd., R. on Westwood Blvd., L. on Pico. [TG-632 F4])

The Simon Wiesenthal Center's Beit Hashoah Museum of Tolerance is unique in its format of numerous technologically advanced, interactive major exhibits, and in its focus on personal prejudice, group intolerance, the struggle for civil rights in America, and the Holocaust. After orientation, enter through the door marked Prejudiced or the one marked Unprejudiced to begin your journey in the American Experience/Tolerancenter. A computer exhibit of the

L.A. riots asks visitors for a personal profile - age, gender, ethnicity - then asks thought-provoking questions about social justice and responsibility. In a mock 50's diner visitors use a monitor to answer questions about personal responsibility regarding drinking, drugs, and other unhealthy habits. A replicated courtroom, called Crime and Punishment, allows students to serve on juries that examine global crimes. You'll be riveted and affected by the sixteen-screen video Civil Rights Wall, an interactive U.S. map that discloses 250 hate groups in America, an intense movie called *Genocide*, and a short walk through the Whisper Gallery. Voices in here whisper racial slurs and derogatory remarks, and then encourage you to think twice about the words you use.

The Holocaust "tour" begins as you print out a child's passport. You then witness a series of chronological vignettes, while listening to narration that explains the events leading up to the Holocaust. This factual and emotional forty-five-minute tour is one of the most informative and visual ways to begin to understand what happened. After walking through a replica of the gates of Auschwitz, your tour culminates in the Hall of Testimony, where you'll discover the fate of the child whose passport you hold.

The second floor of the museum contains a multimedia learning center with over thirty work stations. Numerous films - on Anne Frank, Harriet Tubman, Helen Keller, and others - are available for viewing. Also housed here are original letters of Anne Frank, a bunkbed from a concentration camp, and medical instruments. Holocaust survivors speak here several times throughout the day. The third floor displays rotating exhibits. Call for a current schedule. The fourth floor has a cafeteria. Note: Cameras are not allowed in the museum.

Hours: Open Mon. - Thurs., 11:30am - 4pm; Fri., 11:30am - 3pm; Sun., 11:30am - 5pm. Closed Sat., Thanksgiving, Christmas, and Jewish holidays. School tours are offered as early as 9:15am.

Admission: $8.50 for adults; $6.50 for seniors; $5.50 for students with ID; $3.50 for children 3 - 10. Free validated underground parking is available on Pico Blvd. The Hollywood CityPass, $49.75 for adults and $38 for ages 3 - 11, is good for one-time admission to American Cinematheque's Egyptian Theatre in Hollywood, AUTRY MUSEUM OF WESTERN HERITAGE, HOLLYWOOD ENTERTAINMENT MUSEUM, MUSEUM OF TELEVISION AND RADIO, MUSEUM OF TOLERANCE, PETERSEN AUTOMOTIVE MUSEUM, REAGAN PRESIDENTIAL LIBRARY AND MUSEUM, and UNIVERSAL STUDIOS within a 30 day period. (All of the entries mentioned, except for the theater, are listed separately.) Call (888) 330-5008 / www.citypass.com for more information.

Ages: 10 years and up - it's too intense for most younger children.

NATIONAL HOT ROD ASSOCIATION MOTORSPORTS MUSEUM
(909) 622-2133 / www.nhra.com   *$$*
1101 W. McKinley Avenue, Pomona

(Going E. on San Bernardino Fwy [10] exit N. on White Ave., L. on McKinley. Going W. on 10, exit S. on Orange Grove Ave., R. on McKinley. It's adjacent to Pomona Raceway, near Gate 1. [TG-600 G5])

To see some really hot wheels, visit this stylish hot rod museum that showcases over sixty very cool cars in mint condition. The cars chronicle the colorful history of drag racing, from its days as an illegal street activity to its current status as a major spectator event. Some of the legendary cars on display include Kenny Bernstein's 1992 Budweiser King Top Fuel Dragster, the first car to break the 300mph barrier in NHRA competition; Warren Johnson's 1997 GM Goodwrench Pontiac Firebird, the first Pro Stock machine to break the 200 mph barrier; "Big Daddy" Don Garlits' 1971 Swamp Rat 14, the first successful rear-engine dragster; and the "Bean Bandit" dragster from the early 1950s; plus Indy roadsters, midgets, and much more. With all of this inspiration, what kid (or man) wouldn't dream of being behind the wheel of any one of these cars and racing towards the finish line?!

Glass cases that run almost the length of the museum contain trophies, photographs, helmets, driving uniforms, and more. Murals and paintings decorate the other walls. One wing, sponsored by Auto Club, is an interactive area for kids. It has three big screen monitors that show races, vignettes on careers in motor sports, and the history of motor sports; a jr. dragster to sit in and "drive"; a Christmas tree reaction timer; a fuel flow bench that, once activated, shows how quickly fuel flows into the engine; a race seat with a safety harness and a fire suit; and other activities that incorporate science and math "lessons". So, don't be a drag; race to this museum. Note: Ganesha Park is just east on McKinley Avenue. It offers picnic tables, grassy areas to run around, basketball courts, and a community swimming pool.

Hours: Open Wed. - Sun., 10am - 5pm.
Admission: $5 for adults; $3 for ages 6 - 15; children 5 and under are free.
Ages: 3 years and up.

NATURAL HISTORY MUSEUM OF LOS ANGELES ☼ COUNTY

(213) 763-3466 / www.nhm.org. $$$

900 Exposition Boulevard, Los Angeles

(Exit the Harbor Fwy [110] W. on Exposition Blvd., L. on Flower, L. on Figueroa. Or, exit Santa Monica Fwy [10] S. on Vermont, L. on Exposition, R. on Figueroa. Metered parking is available on the street across from U.S.C., or park in the lot on Menlo Blvd. [TG-674 B1])

This museum has a lot of a little bit of everything. Four long halls show North American, African, and exotic mammals mounted in a backdrop of their natural habitat (i.e. huge dioramas). The gigantic walrus, buffalo, and elephant are the most impressive. Take a walk through time in the American history rooms. They contain early vehicles, such as tractors, stagecoaches, and a streetcar; mannequins dressed in period clothing; early weapons; and other pioneer artifacts. An adjacent, outstanding rock and mineral collection includes fluorescent minerals (that shine neon colors under black light), and rocks that are so brilliant in color or so oddly shaped that they look unreal. Some of our favorite exhibits at the museum are the dinosaurs in the Din-O-Scovery room.

On display, in life-like poses, are some of the massive animals in skeletal form, while others are fleshed out, so to speak. Other exhibits on this floor include a real mummy; a preserved, unusually long, and flat-looking fish - the oarfish; a Megamouth shark; and a room devoted to pre-Columbian archaeology.

The second floor has an entire wing devoted to our fine feathered friends. There are taxidermied penguins, vultures, ostriches, ducks, turquoise cotingas (guess what color they are?), and more. Pull out the drawers of the cabinets in the hallway to see a variety of feathers and bird eggs. A large part of the ornithology (study of birds) exhibit is interactive. Turn a disk to get a magnified view of wings, feathers, and bones. Step on a scale to see how much just your bones weigh - they make up 17% of your body weight. (Although I'm sure my bones weigh more than that.) Exit through a dark, two-story rain forest that resounds with bird noises and has a waterfall. Another room upstairs presents an in-depth look at marine life via murals, mounted animals, and information.

"Hands-on" is the motto at the wonderful Discovery Center. This includes putting on puppet shows; making rubbings from fossilized shells (you'll take home a lot of these papers); playing on computers; going for a fossil dig at the small sandpit; and touching rocks, shells, bones, and skulls of an alligator and polar bear. Kids can also touch (or wrap themselves in) skins of deer, fox, skunk, opossum, sheep, and other animals. There are live animals in here, too, such as iguanas, toads, a python (he gets fed once a week), and fish. Forty different Discovery Boxes offer different activities with varying degrees of difficulty: "Sharks" simply has shark teeth and fossil vertebrae to look at and study, plus books on sharks to read. "Native Games" gives directions and materials to play with walnut shells, dice, and Indian darts. "Listen Up" is a game where the same objects that are in clear jars are also in black jars. Shake them, listen, and then match the sounds and the jars.

Just up the stairs is the Insect Zoo, which has cases swarming with live insects! Show no fear (or disgust) in front of your kids - some of the little buggers are quite interesting. You'll see scorpions, millipedes, tarantulas, beetles, and more (than you've ever wanted!).

The museum also features wonderful rotating exhibits, usually downstairs, such as "Cats, Mild to Wild," which featured house cats to lions in dramatic pictures, interactive animated figures, and more. Call to see what is currently showing. Also, ask about the museum's numerous, in depth field trips, for various age groups, as well as their special events held on site. April through June the butterfly pavilion makes its annual appearance in a tented room just outside the museum. Walk through as hundreds of winged creatures flutter all about.

Picnic tables and lots of grassy areas surround the museum. Also see the nearby AIR AND SPACE GALLERY, CALIFORNIA AFRICAN AMERICAN MUSEUM, CALIFORNIA SCIENCE CENTER, EXPOSITION PARK, and IMAX THEATER. (Look up the attractions listed individually under the Alphabetical Index.)

Hours: Open Mon. - Fri., 10am - 5pm; Sat. - Sun., 10am - 5pm. Closed New Year's Day, Thanksgiving, and Christmas.

Admission: $8 for adults; $5 for seniors and students; $2 for ages 5 - 12; children 4 and under are free. Certain discounts are available through AAA. Special exhibits raise the admission price a few dollars. The first Tues. of every month is free admission day. Entrance to the butterfly pavilion is an additional $3 for adults; $2 for ages 5 - 12; children 4 and under are free. Parking in the lot costs $5.

Ages: 2½ years and up.

NETHERCUTT COLLECTION / NETHERCUTT   ☼
MUSEUM

(818) 367- 2251 or (818) 364-6464 / www.ktsmotorsportsgarage.com   ǃ
15200 Bledsoe Street, Sylmar

(Exit Golden State Fwy [5] N.E. on Roxford St., R. on San Fernando Rd., L. on Bledsoe St. [TG-481 H4])

There are two buildings that hold an impressive array of vintage automobiles, hood ornaments, mechanical musical instruments, and time pieces collected by J. B. Nethercutt, the co-founder of Merle Norman Cosmetics. The Nethercutt Collection, housed in a five-story box-like building, offers two-hour guided tours. The inside is opulently decorated with marble floors and columns in the Grand Salon room, plus chandeliers, elegant wood paneling, and spiral staircases elsewhere. The Salon features more than thirty classic American and European luxury cars in pristine condition, including a 1934 Packard Dietrich Convertible Sedan, a one-of-a-kind 1933 Dusenberg Arlington Torpedo Sedan, and a few Rolls Royces and Cadillacs. The Louis XV-style dining room has a chandelier similar to the one in Versailles, a stunning grandfather clock, and collection of musical pocket watches. The third floor mezzanine showcases over 1,000 "mascots" (i.e. hood ornaments), including some made out of crystal, and ornate eighteenth-century French furniture (both originals and reproductions). The spacious fourth floor displays mechanical musical instruments such as music boxes, reproducing (i.e. player) pianos, nickelodeons, and the crown jewel - the Mighty Wurlitzer Theater Pipe Organ. The tour guide describes the mechanical system of each instrument and also plays a few of them. Dress appropriately for your tour here - no jeans or shorts.

The Nethercutt Museum is another building, across the street, that displays over 150 more antique and immaculate automobiles in beautiful surroundings. Outside are a few train cars on tracks. Another, 40,000 square foot addition is in the works to open in 2002. This will hold "black iron cars", examples of the best of the mass-production vehicles made in America. It will also provide a bigger home for the automotive restoration facility, the shop where classic cars are striped to the bare "bone" and then painstakingly rebuilt according to original specifications.

Hours: The Collection is open for guided tours only, Tues. - Sat., at 10 and 1:30. Reservations are required, usually about 6 weeks in advance. The Museum is open Tues. - Sat., 9am - 4:30pm - peruse at will. Closed Sun., Mon., and holidays.

Admission: Both buildings have free admission.

Ages: Must be at least 12 years old for a tour of the Collection; ages 8
years and up will enjoy the Museum.

NORTON SIMON MUSEUM   ☼

(626) 449-6840 / www.nortonsimon.org $$
411 W. Colorado Boulevard, Pasadena
(Exit Foothill Fwy [210] (just south of the Ventura Fwy [134]) W. on Colorado. It's on the R. [TG-565 G5])

The museum brochure describes some of the masterpieces as "highly
important works" and "glorious compositions", which lets astute readers know
that this is not a hands-on museum for younger children. A visit to the museum
and observing the numerous museum employees/security guards confirms this
impression.

The Norton Simon is, however, a treasure for art connoisseurs as the pieces
are truly outstanding and tastefully displayed in an atmosphere of quiet elegance.
The permanent collection of this thirty gallery, two-story, fine arts museum
consists of seven centuries of European art, from the Renaissance to the
twentieth century. A sampling of the featured artists includes Raphael, Botticelli,
Rembrandt, Renoir, Monet, van Gogh, Goya, Picasso, and Matisse. Western art
and Asian sculpture are also well represented. A special exhibits section presents
more of the permanent collection on a rotating basis. Tip: Ask for the family
guide as you check in. Beginning at 12:30pm and showing every hour, the
museum theater presents a thirty-minute orientation documentary movie on the
life and collections of Norton Simon. The theater room is also a venue for
concerts and lectures.

Educational tours are available by reservation for students in grades sixth
through twelfth. Personally, I benefit greatly from the "insider" information and
explanations.

Hours: Open Wed. - Sun., noon - 6pm. Open Fri. until 9pm. Closed
Mon., Tues., New Year's Day, Thanksgiving, and Christmas.
Admission: $6 for adults; $3 for seniors; free for ages 18 and under.
Ages: 10 years and up.

PASADENA HISTORICAL MUSEUM / FEYES   ☼
MANSION

(626) 577-1660 / www.pasadenahistory.org $
470 W. Walnut Street, Pasadena
(Exit Foothill Fwy [210], near where it turns into Ventura Fwy [134], W. on W. Walnut St., L. on N.
Orange Grove Blvd., and turn L. into the first driveway past the mansion on the corner. [TG-565 G4])

Pasadena's stately heritage landmark mansion/museum showcases gracious
living at the turn of the century. A one-hour guided tour, which is the only way
to see the mansion, allows visitors to see original memorabilia and furnishings
which came from all over the world. Some of the highlights downstairs include
several clocks, such as the grandfather clock in the foyer that has rotating,
colored-glass slides of early Pasadena; old-fashioned utensils in the kitchen (my
boys needed an explanation about the rug beater); china in the butler's pantry;

numerous volumes of books in the hallway and office; the solarium; fine, wooden tables and chairs; and chests in the living room and studio ornately finished with tortoise shell, ivory, and mother-of-pearl. The stories about the artifacts are intriguing, especially the legend of flying carpets, which is thought to come from prayer rugs supposedly endowed with magical powers. A prayer rug is located in the studio.

The elegantly-decorated master bedroom and a child's bedroom are upstairs. So are a few bathrooms, which always appeal to kids.

A few small rooms adjacent to the lower level gift shop hold old tools, a piano, an old bike with one large front wheel, a collection of old cameras, and several military uniforms. Pasadena is a city with rich cultural history that is well represented by this mansion/museum. The grounds are beautifully landscaped and steps lead down to the research library and the Finnish Folk Art Museum, just next door. This homey three-room replica of a Finnish farmhouse contains handmade furniture, plus utensils and folk costumes.

Hours: Open Thurs. - Sun., 1pm - 4pm. Tours are given every hour on
            the hour.
Admission: $5 for adults; $4 for seniors; free for children 12 and under.
Ages: 6 years and up.

PETERSEN AUTOMOTIVE MUSEUM   ☼
(323) 930-CARS (2277) / www.petersen.org $$$
6060 Wilshire Boulevard, Los Angeles   ♨
(Exit Santa Monica Fwy [10] N. on Fairfax, R. on Wilshire. [TG-633 B2])

The driving force behind this 300,000 square foot, state-of-the-art museum is dedication to the art, culture, and history of the automobile. Streetscape, on the first floor, takes you on a chronological walk through time via cars, from horse and buggy, vintage automobiles, and an exhibit of gas pumps, to prototypes, solar-powered, and other, futuristic-type cars. Each car is displayed in its own walk-through setting, complete with asphalt, manholes, sidewalks, fake plants - whatever surroundings fit the car - as well as mannequins dressed in period outfits. Sounds, like birds chirping where a Model T is "Stuck in the Mud," help children enter into the spirit of the lifestyles represented here. Kids can climb aboard the trolley car used in old Laurel and Hardy movies, although other cars on this floor are not hands-on.

The second floor has six galleries, including a terrific collection of hot rods, roadsters, race cars, and classics in prime condition. A glitzy Hollywood Gallery stars cars that were featured in movies and television shows, and/or that were owned by celebrities. Biking enthusiasts will appreciate the adjacent Otis Chandler Motorcycle Gallery. However, the ultimate in kid-cool is putting on a helmet and getting behind the wheel of a real Indianapolis 500 race car!

The third floor, the Discovery Center, will really get kids revved up with its 6,500 square feet of motor vehicle interaction! They can ride on a real Highway Patrol motorcycle, complete with sirens blaring and flashing lights. Have your children dress up in a motoring duster, cap, and scarves and "drive" a Model T. A Sparklett's water truck contains plastic jugs filled with a variety of games, puzzles, costumes, and construction toys all pertaining to the car motif. A play area is set up for toddlers to race mini-cars around on tracks and play mats. Older kids can get behind the wheel of a virtual reality simulator called Driver's Ed. (Now I know why they don't allow 11 year olds to have a license!) Another large room is for the mechanically minded. It has a giant dashboard, which visitors can manipulate; a display that traces the route an engine takes to come to life, from ignition to the voltage regulator; and other learning stations that allow kids to push, pull, steer, or observe different facets of how a car actually works. Our favorite exhibit is Power of the People. This car seat, on huge wheels, can actually be moved across the room when you (and some strong-legged friends) push down on oversized pistons that pop up at regular intervals. (Fun, but tiring.)

Take a pencil Treasure Hunt and/or ask about the other special activities and classes, such as the hands-on workshop the first Saturday of the month. Hour-long school tours are offered during the week for all ages at $1 per person. Know that a visit here will definitely accelerate your child's interest in cars!

Hours: Open Tues. - Sun. 10am - 6pm. The Discovery Center closes at 5pm.

Admission: $7 for adults; $5 for seniors and ages 5 - 12; children 4 and under are free. Enter the museum parking structure from Fairfax - $6 for all-day parking. The Hollywood CityPass, $49.75 for adults and $38 for ages 3 - 11, is good for one-time admission to American Cinematheque's Egyptian Theatre in Hollywood, AUTRY MUSEUM OF WESTERN HERITAGE, HOLLYWOOD ENTERTAINMENT MUSEUM, MUSEUM OF TELEVISION AND RADIO, MUSEUM OF TOLERANCE, PETERSEN AUTOMOTIVE MUSEUM, REAGAN PRESIDENTIAL LIBRARY AND MUSEUM, and UNIVERSAL STUDIOS within a 30 day period. (All of the entries mentioned, except for the theater, are listed separately.) Call (888) 330-5008 / www.citypass.com for more information.

Ages: 5 years and up.

PETTERSON MUSEUM

(909) 621-9581 / www.pilgrimplace.org

660 Avery Road, Claremont

(Exit San Bernardino Fwy [10] N. on Indian Hill Rd., L. on Harrison Ave., R. on Mayflower Rd., L. on Avery. It's at Pilgrim Place. [TG-601 C3])

This small, folk art museum is housed on the grounds of a community of retired pastors, missionaries, and other church professionals. Those who shared the gospel in far corners of the globe often returned with significant mementos of their host culture and crafts, covering many centuries of human history. Some of the exotic artifacts in display cases include costumes, textiles, masks, statues, dolls, shells, and pottery. The docent-guided tours give insight into the exhibits. Note: Check the November Calendar section for the annual Pilgrim Place Festival.

Hours: Open to the public Fri. - Sun., 2pm - 4pm. Call to make a reservation to take a tour at another time.

Admission: Free

Ages: 6 years and up.

POINT VINCENTE INTERPRETIVE CENTER AND PARK   ☼

(310) 544-5260 $

Palos Verdes Drive W., Rancho Palos Verdes

(From Pacific Coast Highway [1] in Redondo Beach, turn S. on Palos Verdes Dr. W. and drive the winding coastal road just past Hawthorne Blvd. Turn R. into the park. Or, exit Harbor Fwy [110] W. on Anaheim, L. on Palos Verdes Dr. N., L. on Crenshaw to end, R. on Crest Rd., L. on Hawthorne to end, L. on Palos Verdes Dr. W. Or, exit San Diego Fwy [405] S. on Crenshaw, go to the end, R. on Crest Rd., L. on Hawthorne to end, L. on Palos Verdes Dr. W. [TG-822 F5])

This small museum has a variety of natural wonders on display, such as fossils of ocean animals, a side-by-side comparison of fossilized shells with recent shells of the same type, and taxidermied animals such as the great horned owl, a gray fox, and a peacock.

Whales are the main focus here as this is a prime site for whale watching. The museum has an overhead model of a gray whale, a continuously running video on whales, and a telephone so kids can literally listen to the call of the whales. There is a small enclosed area upstairs and an outside area that are good spots to either watch the whales as they migrate, January through March, or just to see a terrific view of the coastline. The Point Vincente Lighthouse is close by and on foggy days, you'll hear the horn blast its warning signal.

A quarter-mile paved trail winds around the Interpretive Center and the few picnic tables that are here. If your family is in a hiking or biking mood, there is a three-mile, or so, narrow dirt trail leading from the Center and looping back around. This main pathway and its offshoots are alternately flat and hilly, so be prepared for some real exercise! Have a whale of a time at this small museum and at the park.

Hours: The Center is open daily in the summer from 10am - dusk. It's open daily the rest of the year from 10am - 4:30pm. Closed New Year's Day, Thanksgiving, Christmas Eve, and Christmas Day. The park is open daily from dawn to dusk.

Admission: The museum entrance fee is $2 for adults; $1 for seniors and ages 4 - 14; children 3 and under are free. There is no admission for the surrounding park and trails.

Ages: 2½ years and up.

QUEEN MARY   ☼

(562) 435-3511 / www.queenmary.com $$$$

Pier J, Long Beach

(Take Long Beach Fwy [710] S. to the end, R. on Queen's Way Bridge and follow signs. [TG-825 E3])

Cruise over to Long Beach Harbor to see the Queen, Queen Mary I mean - one of the largest luxury passenger liners ever built. Take a one-hour guided Behind-the-Scenes tour and learn about the ship's fascinating history. Only on this tour can you see the dining room/ballroom, boiler room, and an original first class suite. Younger children will get antsy. We thoroughly enjoyed our self-guided Shipwalk tour. Starting on the lower decks, we watched a video called *The Queen Mary Story* about its construction, maiden voyage, and service during WWII. The Hall of Maritime Heritage, a small museum, displays navigating instruments, ship models, and pictures and stories of famous doomed ships, including the Titanic. Everything in the engine room is clearly marked, making it easy to explain the machinery's function to youngsters. The last remaining propeller on the ship is in an open-top, propellor box in water. It looks like a shark fin at first. Tell your kids that the life-size diver in the water is just a model. We toured the bridge, the wheel house where officers were quartered, and the state room exhibits. A highlight for my boys was playing on the gun turrets on the bow of the ship, as they fought off invisible enemies.

Did you see that? It looked just like a . . . ghost! Capitalizing on the numerous ghost reports, the half-hour guided Ghosts and Legends attraction takes visitors through lower decks including the forward work areas, six-story boiler room, and swimming pool (which is empty) area. Special effects designed to make the paranormal experiences come alive, so to speak, include changes in temperature in certain rooms, ghostly images against ceilings and walls, electrostatic charges, and the finale - a shudder like two ships colliding and a deluge of water that seemingly bursts through the hull of the Queen Mary.

The wooden upper decks are great for ~~running~~ strolling around. Note: As an older ship, there are many narrow staircases, but not many ramps on board. Elevators enable those using strollers or wheelchairs to get from deck to deck.

Queen Mary's Seaport, adjacent to the ship's berth, has the Queen's Marketplace for your shopping and dining pleasures. There are also several fine shops and restaurants on the ship that run the gamut from the very elegant and expensive Sir Winston's, open daily 5:30pm to 10pm, and Chelsea, open Monday through Friday from 11:30am to 2:pm and Wednesday through Sunday from 5:30pm to 10pm, to a more family-style and family-priced eatery, Promenade Cafe, which is open daily 6am to 10pm. Inquire about the buffet-style champagne Sunday brunch in the Grand Salon of the ballroom. Here's a good deal: If you have a reservation at either Sir Winston's or Chelsea, where entrees average between $20 to $30, you don't pay the ship's admission fee although you're free to then tour it, and your parking is validated.

Other tips: 1) For a ~~cheap~~ inexpensive family date, come on board after 6pm (during the school year) when there isn't an admission charge, only a parking fee. Although the stores and many parts of the ship are not open then, some restaurants are open, so you can grab a dessert. Plus, it's fun for kids to walk around, and the sunsets are beautiful. Don't miss the ship! 2) Watch the fireworks on board the Queen Mary on Saturday nights at 9pm during the summer. (Or, watch them for free just outside the ship or from a nearby vista point.) 3) Remember, that you can sleep on board the Queen Mary, as it functions as a floating hotel, too. 4) See SCORPION, under this section, and LONG BEACH AQUARIUM OF THE PACIFIC, under the Zoos and Animals section, for information on these nearby attractions.

Hours: Open most of the year daily 10am - 6pm. Open daily in the summer 9am - 9pm.

Admission: General admission, including the self-guided tour, is $17 for
adults; $15 for seniors; $13 for ages 4 - 11; children 3 and under
are free. The Behind-the-Scenes guided tour is an additional $10
for adults and seniors; $8 for ages 4 - 11. A package which
includes general admission, the Behind-the-Scenes tour, and
admission to the Scorpion is $27 for adults; $25 for seniors; $24
for ages 4 - 11. (Ask about AAA discounts.) Parking is $8 per
vehicle. Beat parking prices by catching the free Passport shuttle
that runs from downtown Long Beach to the Queen Mary.

Ages: 3 years and up.

RANCHO LOS ALAMITOS   ☼
(562) 431-3541 / www.ci.long-beach.ca.us   !
6400 E. Bixby Hill Road, Long Beach
(Exit San Diego Fwy [405] S. on Palo Verde Ave. to the end. Go through the gated entrance [tell
the gate employee you are going to the museum], L. on Bixby Hill. [TG-796 E6])

This beautiful, historic ranch appeals to kids of all ages. The barn has
several horse stalls, a few of which have been converted into small rooms, or
self-contained history lessons. They display photographs, animal pelts, branding
irons, and (our favorite) a suspended horse harness, showing how a horse was
hooked up to help plow. Other buildings of particular interest, in this area,
contain a blacksmith shop filled with old tools, and a room with lots of saddles
and branding irons. A ranch is not complete without animals, so goats, sheep,
chickens, ducks, and Shire horses are in outside pens.

An hour-long tour includes going inside the adobe ranch house. It's always
fun to try to guess the name and use of gadgets in old kitchens. The bedroom,
library, music, and billiards rooms are interesting to older children.

The front of the house has a garden and two, 150-year-old Moreton Bay fig
trees with huge roots. An Artifacts Room is open at certain times so kids can
touch - that's right - artifacts! Most of the site is wheelchair/stroller accessible.
Ask about the rancho's terrific school tours.

Hours: Open Wed. - Sun., 1pm - 5pm. Tours are offered on the half
hour. School tours are given at various times throughout the
week. Call to make reservations. The rancho is closed on
holidays.

Admission: Free; donations appreciated.

Ages: 3 years and up for the outside grounds; 6 years and up for a tour
of the house.

RANCHO LOS CERRITOS   ☼
(562) 570-1755 / www.bixbyland.com/rancho.htm   !
4600 Virginia Road, Long Beach
(Exit San Diego Fwy [405] N. on Long Beach Blvd., L. on Roosevelt, then make a quick R. on
Virginia Rd. [TG-675 D5])

This picturesque historic rancho is situated almost at the end of Virginia
Road. The visitors center has a clever exhibit of big puzzle pieces representing
different eras with pictures and information on them, that attempt to fit together

pieces of our past. The information is interesting and some of the window-type "pieces" offer glimpses into the past by displaying old pottery, equipment, and other artifacts.

The perimeter gardens are beautifully landscaped around a grassy center area. There is also a huge old Moreton Bay fig tree with tremendous roots. A one-hour tour takes you through the house which is furnished as it was in the late 1870's. This is a terrific way to see and learn about our Mexican-California heritage. Kids can more easily relate to the bigger picture of state history when they explore a small part of it.

School group tours include hands-on fun, such as candle-dipping and playing old-fashioned games. Students also have the opportunity to do chores, such as butter churning and washing clothes, the way they were done years ago. The tour might also include seeing a blacksmith's demonstration.

Ask for a Kids' Activity Treasure Hunt, where young visitors use pencil and paper as they look for particular items throughout the museum - it makes a visit here that much more interesting. Bring a sack lunch as there are picnic tables on the grounds. Ask for a schedule of the Rancho's special family events - they are great. (See Mud Mania in the August Calendar section.)

Hours: Open Wed. - Sun., 1pm - 5pm. Guided tours are given on the weekends only, on the hour. School tours are given on Wed. and Thurs., 9:30am - noon.

Admission: Free; donations appreciated.

Ages: 7 years and up.

RAYMOND M. ALF MUSEUM

(909) 624-2798 / www.alfmuseum.org $

1175 W. Baseline Road, Claremont

(Exit the San Bernardino Fwy [10] N. on Towne Ave., L. on Baseline Rd., R. up the hill. It is part of the Webb Schools. [TG-571 A7])

Make no bones about it, this unique museum displays dinosaur skeletons and skulls, plus fossils and archaeological finds from all over the world. As you enter this circular museum you'll see Footprints in the Sands of Time, an unusually large rock slab containing numerous reptile footprints that is reportedly 250 million years old. Next to the display on Egyptology is a skull cast of a Purussaurus, an animal with jaws that are almost as big as the upper part of my body. The touch table has mastodon tusks, vertebrae, rocks, and a fossilized turtle shell, which is surprisingly heavy.

The exhibits downstairs consist mainly of trackways, which are rock slabs with castings of dinosaur, camel, horse, and bear-dog footprints. The trackways are displayed on the walls, and around the room, under glass-encased coffee tables (albeit, priceless ones). A kid's area has computer games, books, dinosaur puzzles, and a small sandpit for archaeologists-in-training to "dig" for fossils (and they are guaranteed to find them - not quite like being out in the field).

Good-sized rock and mineral specimens, like geodes and petrified wood, abound, as do fossils such as mammoth molars, and fern imbedded in rock. Have your kids look at the rocks on the table near the exit and take the "test" - do they know which is a fossil and which is a mineral?

This museum is great for older kids who are interested in paleontology, or for younger ones to just see the sheer size of some of the animals from long ago. Month-long research expeditions, which combine fossil collecting and camping, are available for high school students during the summer. Hour-and-a-half long school/group tours are offered Monday through Thursday at 9:30am, with reservations, for second graders and up. Travel presentations are also available.

Hours: The museum is open Mon. - Thurs., 8am - noon and 1pm - 4pm. It is also open the first Sun. of each month 1pm - 4pm. Closed major holidays.

Admission: $1 for ages 5 and up; children 4 and under are free. Admission is free every Wed. Tours are $20 for up to 35 students.

Ages: 4 years and up.

RIPLEY'S BELIEVE IT OR NOT! MUSEUM (Hollywood) ☼
(323) 466-6335 / www.ripleys.com   *$$$*
6780 Hollywood Boulevard, Hollywood

(Exit Hollywood Fwy [101] W. on Hollywood Blvd. [TG-593 E4])

See the description under RIPLEY'S BELIEVE IT OR NOT! MUSEUM (Buena Park). This museum displays nearly 300 unusual and amazing items and facts collected from around the world.

A few doors down is Mann's Chinese Theater, where many past and present stars have left their imprints in the concrete courtyard in front of the theater. See if your child can fill the shoes of his favorite stars!

Hours: Open Sun. - Thurs., 10am - 10pm; Fri. - Sat., 10am - 11pm.

Admission: $9.95 for adults; $8.95 for seniors; $6.95 for ages 5 - 12; children 4 and under are free. Certain discounts are available through AAA.

Ages: 5 years and up.

SCORPION ☼
(562) 435-3511 / www.queenmary.com   *$$$$*
1126 Queens Highway, Long Beach

(Take Long Beach Fwy [710] S. to the end, R. on Queen's Way Bridge and follow the signs to the Queen Mary, as it is docked adjacent to the famous ship. [TG-825 D3])

Do your kids like to play spy? The 300-foot-long Scorpion, technically known as the Povodnaya Lodka B-427, is a Soviet-built, Foxtrot-class submarine that is docked here until 2004. In service for twenty-two years, it was once equipped with low-yield nuclear torpedoes. (That information alone makes it interesting to kids.) It was assigned mainly to gather intelligence on Allied naval activities. Now a tourist attraction, the Scorpion inspires spy game ideas, at least with my kids, as well as being a vessel of education and intrigue. Note: You may view the submarine, topside, without going on a tour.

Before you board, go into a holding room that contains labeled artifacts from the sub, such as an emergency escapes suit, flags, pressure gauges, manuals in Russian, and more. Get your feet wet, so to speak, by watching a thirteen-minute reenactment video on the history of the submarine and its "warriors beneath the waves."

Your actual tour inside the Scorpion is self-guiding, with a Russian-accented narration piped into each compartment. Begin by going down a narrow staircase to the forward torpedo room. The room contains six torpedo tubes and replicas of the warheads once loaded inside them. Then, think thin and squeeze through several porthole-style hatches, walk down narrow hallways, and look into (through glass-covered doorways) very small sleeping quarters, a control room, a dining room, the galley, and various other rooms. The tour has its own momentum as there is not a lot of room for the people behind you to pass. Visitors can peer through a periscope to the outside world, push the numerous buttons, and turn the wheels on board. My boys would have liked to stay down here for hours. Down another staircase is the engine room filled with gadgets that helped churn the water to power the sub. The last stop on your tour is the aft torpedo room which held four torpedoes. It is a relatively short tour for your money, but it is historic and fascinating.

Note that strollers aren't allowed on the Scorpion, nor may you carry children on the tour. If you get claustrophobic, this isn't the place to be. Ladies, stepping up through hatch openings and down narrow ladders doesn't lend itself to wearing dresses or heels.

See LONG BEACH AQUARIUM OF THE PACIFIC, QUEEN MARY, and SHORELINE VILLAGE under the Alphabetical Index for attractions in the immediate vicinity.

Hours: Open Mon. - Fri., noon - 6pm; Sat. - Sun., 10am - 6pm. Open in the summer daily 10am - 9pm.

Admission: $10 for adults; $8 for seniors and military personnel; $9 for ages 3 - 11; children 2 and under are free. Parking is $3 for the first half hour, then it jumps to $8 for the day. Take a free Passport shuttle from downtown Long Beach to save on parking fees.

Ages: 4 years and up.

SHERIFFS TRAINING AND REGIONAL SERVICES (STARS) CENTER ☀

(562) 946-7081

11515 S. Colima Road, Whittier

(Going N. on Santa Ana Fwy [5], exit N. on Carmenita Rd., R. on Leffingwell, L. on Colima. Going S. on 5, exit E. on Imperial Hwy., L. on Colima. [TG-707 E6])

This 5,000 square foot museum depicts the history of the Los Angeles County Sheriffs Department from 1850 through the present day. A classic 1938 Studebaker police car can not be touched, but kids can "ride" on the police motorcycle next to it and push a button to make the red lights flash. (I hope this won't bring back any bad memories!)

A westernized room has a replica of a nineteenth-century sheriff's office, complete with a model sheriff and a prisoner behind bars. The Vice Exhibit showcases how different carnival-type games can be rip-offs, as well as illegal. The back room, which can be bypassed, contains a gun case, a display of gang weapons, and graphic scenes of some infamous cases.

Another room contains an entire helicopter. It also has the side of a Search and Rescue helicopter mounted on a wall, with a dangling child mannequin being air-lifted in a basket. The live-video footage shows the awesome job that Search and Rescue teams perform.

Outside, a wall too filled with plaques memorializes officers killed in the line of duty. For your information: Every May a memorial ceremony is held here that commemorates the lives of peace officers who have died in the line of duty in L.A. County in the past year. This moving ceremony, attended by numerous officers, families of slain officers, and government officials, is also open to the public.

Hours: Open Mon. - Fri., 9am - 4pm. Closed on major holidays.
Admission: Free
Ages: 5 years and up.

SKIRBALL CULTURAL CENTER   ☼
(310) 440-4500 / www.skirball.org   *$$*
2701 N. Sepulveda Boulevard, Los Angeles
(Exit San Diego Fwy [405] W. on Skirball Center Dr. [TG-591 F1])

This Cultural Center tells the story of the Jewish people, from post-biblical days and journeys, to present day life in America. The exhibits of Jewish heritage include ancient and modern artifacts, photographs, art, film, and video screenings all housed in a building beautifully designed with archways and high-ceilings. The variety of the unique Torah mantles and Hanukkah lamps on display is outstanding. One of our favorite menorahs has each of its eight branches fashioned like the Statute of Liberty.

The Coming to America room features a reproduction of the hand and torch of the Statue of Liberty at seventy percent of full scale. It's huge! This room also contains documents from past United States Presidents that supported non-discrimination. The Lincoln display has a lifemask of his face (i.e. a mold of his actual face), which is one of only six ever made.

Each of the five Gallery Exploration kits, for ages 4 to 8, contains games, books, related objects and activity cards that ask questions about the items in the galleries. Usage of the free kits allows the children to get more involved with the articles in the museum.

In the Discovery Center, geared for ages 8 and up, kids can uncover the wonders of the archaeological world. Upstairs is a re-creation of a dig site, a hands-on tool area, and a great computer game called "Dig It." The stairway is lined with lamps behind glass displays. The downstairs has a reproduction of a tomb in a rock; displays that show the new condition of an animal or object, and then its remains after years have gone by; and over twenty "discovery" game boxes containing great activities that reinforce the concepts presented. Kids can also learn about the history of writing and try different forms of it at the rubbing table. Students on school tours will gain a tremendous amount of insight into the archaeological world as docents teach and guide them through the Discovery Center. They'll also go outside where they can excavate roads, walls, an alter, and more, at a small mock dig site.

Zeidler's is a full-service restaurant within the Center. Offering reasonable prices, it's open for lunch and afternoon coffee. Menu choices include pizza, pasta, sandwiches, omelettes, salads, fish, house-baked breads, and chocolate desserts.

As you enter and exit the Skirball Center you'll see, etched in stone, words fit for everyone - "Go forth . . . and be a blessing to the world." (Genesis 12: 1 - 3)

Hours: Open Tues. - Sun., noon - 5pm. Closed Mon.

Admission: $8 for adults; $6 for seniors and students; children 11 and under are free.

Ages: 7 years and up.

SOUTHWEST MUSEUM

(323) 221-2164 / www.southwestmuseum.org

234 Museum Drive, Highland Park

(Exit Pasadena Fwy [110] N.E. on Avenue 43, R. on Figueroa St., L. on Ave. 45, R. on Marmion Way, L. on Museum Dr. [TG-595 B4])

There are three ways to enter this museum on a hill: One is an unadventurous walk up the driveway; another is walking up the steep Hopi trail, which is a stone stairway. Catch your breath at the top, and take a look at the view of the city and beyond. The third is walking (running) through a 250-foot tunnel - which echos every footstep and shout - burrowed into the museum hillside. It's lined with twenty Indian dioramas. From here, take the elevator up into the museum.

The Southwest Museum collection represents Native American cultures from Alaska to South America. The two-story building has displays of Indian clothing, some of which are decorated with elk's teeth or bone; costumes; boots; beautifully beaded moccasins; an extensive collection of baskets; rabbit-skin blankets; weapons; turquoise and silver craft jewelry; early baby snugglies (cradleboards); musical instruments such as a flute, drum, and rattle; and Kachina dolls, which are supposedly rain-bringing spiritual beings. The exhibits are mostly behind glass.

A rotating exhibit room featured, for example, Spirit Horses, the entrance of which was a simulated cave, with horses painted on its walls. The room itself, which doubles as a (small) auditorium, had statues of horses, paintings of horses, a mural of horses, beautiful saddles, etc. *Neigh* doubt about it, this room embodied the American Indian legend that the horse is a spiritual gift of the gods.

Another room has an eighteen-foot Cheyenne tepee (just to look at), and a big rock with reproduced pictographs. Kids can crawl through a doorway (think dog door) that has photographs on the other side. Also on display in this room are headbands, arrowheads, bows, and rattles made of cocoons and rattlesnakes. Outside, an archeological dig site is a bit further up the hill. A small botanical garden is in the front of the museum.

How do you learn more about Native Americans? An extensive research library on the museum grounds is open to the public Wednesday through Saturday, 1pm to 5pm. If you're looking for a place to picnic, just drive north on Figueroa Street to Highland Park.

Hours: Open Tues. - Sun., 10am - 5pm. Closed Mon. and major holidays.

Admission: $6 for adults; $4 for seniors and students; $3 for ages 6 - 17;
children 5 and under are free.
Ages: 5 years and up.

S. S. LANE VICTORY
(310) 519-9545 / www.lanevictoryship.com $
Berth 94, San Pedro
(Exit Harbor Fwy [110] or Vincent Thomas Bridge on Harbor Blvd. Cross Harbor Blvd. onto
Swinford St. and follow signs to Berth 94. [TG-824 D4])

This fifty-five-year-old ship served as a cargo ship during World War II, the
Korean War, and the Vietnam War. The large Victory ship is not only
seaworthy, but it is also a museum, with one-hour tours given by retired
merchant marines. We sensed adventure, though, and decided to explore the ship
unaccompanied.

You and your kids will get ship-shape by climbing up and down ladders
from the bridge and crew's quarters to the radio room, and into the huge engine
room. The multi-level engine room is a bit spooky, with the noises and bulky
machinery, but this added to the excitement of being on our own.

Guns and superstructures make the decks interesting to investigate. (Tell
your kids that they are on a poop deck - it will make your outing a big hit!)
Below deck, the ship's museum room features memorabilia such as flags,
whistles, photographs, and cannons. The Gift Shoppe sells wonderful nautical
items from clothing to medals to model ship kits. Batten down the hatches and
be sure to wear tennis shoes for your ship-to-shore adventure.

A few times a year the S.S. Lane Victory hosts an all-day cruise to Catalina
where a "Nazi spy" is discovered on board. Nazi fighters are soon attacking the
ship, but American aircraft come to the rescue. The mock aerial dogfight uses
blanks, but the World War II planes are real. This is more exciting than any
Hollywood movie! The cruise also includes continental breakfast, live music,
and a buffet luncheon. The cost is $100 for adults; $60 for kids 15 years and
under.
Hours: Open daily 9am - 4pm.
Admission: $3 for adults; $1 for ages 5 - 15; children 4 and under are free.
Parking is free for the first two hours.
Ages: 5 years and up.

TOURNAMENT HOUSE / THE WRIGLEY GARDENS ☼
(626) 449-4100 / www.rosebowl.com   !
391 S. Orange Grove Boulevard, Pasadena
(Take Pasadena Fwy [110] N. to the end, where it turns into Arroyo Pkwy., L. on California, R. on
Orange Grove. Going W. on Foothill Fwy [210], exit S. on Fair Oaks, R. on Colorado, L. on Orange
Grove. Going E. on Ventura Fwy [134], exit E. on Colorado, R. on Orange Grove. [TG-565 G5])

The Tournament House, more aptly referred to as a mansion, is used
throughout the year as the meeting headquarters for committees, float sponsors,
and practically everything else associated with the annual Tournament of Roses
Parade. Once owned by Wrigley, of the chewing gum fame, each room is
simply, but elegantly furnished. The downstairs contains a spacious living room,

a library, meeting rooms, and the Eisenhower bathroom - so named because when the president was Grand Marshall, he got stuck in here and no one knew where he was, not even the Secret Service agents.

The second floor is interesting to kids who have some knowledge and interest in the Rose parade and Rose Bowl games. Each former bedroom is dedicated to various elements of Tournament of Roses' traditions. The Rose Bowl Room showcases pennants and football helmets from Rose Bowl teams, plus photographs, trophies, and other memorabilia dating back to the first game in 1902. The Queen and Court Room is femininely decorated to allow the reigning Queen and her Court, who attend over 100 events a year, a place to recuperate. A display case in here features past winners' crowns, tiaras, and jewelry. The Grand Marshall's Room shows photographs of past Grand Marshals like Bob Hope, Shirley Temple Black (do your kids know who she is?), Hank Aaron, Walt Disney, Charles Schultz, and others. Out in the hallway is an impressive 240-pound sterling silver saddle - heigh ho, Silver, away! The President's Room has pictures and other mementos of past presidents of the Rose Parade, plus models of the current year's winning floats. You are also invited to watch an interesting fifteen-minute behind-the-scenes film on how the floats and parade are put together.

The beautifully-landscaped grounds have a fountain surrounded by one of the rose gardens. Another huge rose garden at the north end also blooms seasonally.

Hours: Tours of the house are given February through August, on Thurs., 2pm - 4pm. The grounds are open throughout the year, except December 31 through January 2.

Admission: Free

Ages: 7 years and up.

TRAVEL TOWN

(323) 662-5874 / www.lacity.org

5200 W. Zoo Drive, Los Angeles

(Going N. on Golden State Fwy [5] or W. on Ventura Fwy [134], exit at Zoo Dr. and follow the signs. Going E. on 134, exit at Forest Lawn Dr., L. on Zoo Dr. Going S. on 5, exit S. on Western, L. on Victory Blvd. to Zoo Dr. It's near the L. A. Zoo. [TG-563 J4])

"All aboarrrrrd!" This wonderful outdoor "town" has a "trainriffic" atmosphere. There are real boxcars, a few cabooses, and some steam locomotives to climb into (but not on top of). Grassy areas invite you to rest (one can always hope), play, and/or picnic. A scaled model train takes you for a ride around the small town - $2 for adults, $1.25 for seniors, $1.50 for ages 2 to 12, and free for ages 18 months and under.

Inside the buildings are old-fashioned carriages, wagons, period automobiles, and early fire-fighting equipment. It's tempting to touch the vehicles, but don't give in to temptation. Note: Live Steamers, located just west of Travel Town, offers free, twelve-minute rides through a part of Griffith Park on Sundays from 11am to 3pm. Call (323) 669-9729 / www.trainweb.org/girr/lals/lals.html.com for more information.

For a listing of other things to do in this area see AUTRY MUSEUM OF

WESTERN HERITAGE, GRIFFITH PARK, GRIFFITH PARK
OBSERVATORY, and LOS ANGELES ZOO listed separately in the
Alphabetical Index.

Hours: Open Mon. - Fri., 10am - 4pm; Sat. - Sun. and holidays, 10am -
5pm. Closed Christmas.

Admission: Free; donations appreciated.

Ages: 2 years and up.

VISTA DEL LAGO VISITORS CENTER   ☼

(661) 294-0219 / www.dwr.water.ca.gov
Vista del Lago, Gorman
(Exit Golden State Fwy [5] on Vista del Lago. It is 20 miles north of Santa Clarita Valley and 5
miles S. of Gorman.)

Overlooking Pyramid Lake is a hexagon-shaped building showcasing
California's liquid gold - water. This surprisingly interesting museum features
many educational and interactive exhibits that show the State Water Project's
water supply and delivery systems throughout California. Step on special scales
in the first room and find out how much of your body is comprised of water
(60%), and how much you actually weigh. Visual displays show the amount of
water needed daily to grow and process food, manufacture household items, do
laundry, and so on. Video presentations and information panels point out that
although water is abundant in the north, most of the population is in the south, so
we need ways to transport it down. At the "Big Lift," visitors can turn a crank to
lift up a full bucket of water, which translates into learning how much energy it
takes for a pumping plant to lift water over the mountains. Learn how water is
treated before it is delivered to homes and how it is tested for quality. Thirsty
yet? Go with the flow by playing the computer games and using the touch
screens in each of the seven display rooms. The theater room shows several short
films, ranging from five to seventeen minutes, that present various aspects of
water, for instance *Water for Farming, Save Water*, and *A Visit to the Feather
River Hatchery*. Educators take note: Not only can the videos be rented, but
there is a lot of information given here on a field trip. Pamphlets, comic book-
style booklets, teacher's guides, and lots more add to a guided tour of the
facility.

The Visitors Center is a great place to quench your child's desire to learn
about irrigation, flood control, and water conservation. Tip: After your visit here,
enjoy the rest of the day at PYRAMID LAKE (look under the Great Outdoors
section), where you can boat, fish, swim, picnic, hike, and even camp.

Hours: Open daily 9am - 5pm. Closed New Year's Day, Thanksgiving,
and Christmas.

Admission: Free

Ages: 4 years and up.

WELLS FARGO HISTORY MUSEUM   ☀

(213) 253-7166 / www.wellsfargohistory.com
Wells Fargo Center, 333 S. Grand Avenue, Los Angeles

(From Harbor Fwy [110], exit E. on 4th St., L. on Olive St., L. on 3rd St., R. on Grand. Going N. on Hollywood Fwy [101], exit S. on Grand. Going S. on 101, exit E. on Temple, R. on Grand. [TG-634 F4])

Discover the Old West in the middle of downtown Los Angeles. The history and development of the West (and of Wells Fargo) is laid out like booty in this museum. Highlights include an 100-year old stagecoach, which kids may not climb on; a replica stagecoach, that they are welcome to climb in; a replica of an 1850's agent's office; a mining display with yes, real gold; a gold miner's rocker; a telegraph machine to try out; photographs; and a twenty-minute film that depicts the hardships of a journey taken in 1852 from St. Louis to San Francisco. Buy a pan and some gold here so kids can try their hand at working a claim in their own backyard!

Hours: Open Mon. - Fri., 9am - 5pm. Closed bank holidays. Tours are available with advanced reservations.
Admission: Free. Parking starts at $5 on Hope and 3rd Sts.
Ages: 4 years and up.

THE WESTERN HOTEL MUSEUM

(661) 723-6260 / www.cityoflancasterca.org
557 W. Lancaster Boulevard, Lancaster
(Going N. on Antelope Valley Fwy [14], exit N. on 20th St. West, R. on Ave J, L. on 10th St. W., R. on Lancaster Blvd. Going S. on 14, exit E. on Ave. J, L. on 10th St. W., R. on Lancaster Blvd. [TG-4015 H5])

This small, quaint Western Hotel/Museum has been restored to look like it did when it was originally built in the late 1800's, when room rentals were only $1 a day. The downstairs has a few bedrooms and a parlor that contains old furniture, a wheelchair, and a phonograph that belonged to the last owner, Myrtie Webber. Kids are interested in hearing some of the stories about her, and are impressed that she lived until she was 110 years old! (She doesn't look a day over 70 in her photographs.)

Upstairs is a dinosaur/fossil/artifacts room; a life-size diorama of early Antelope Valley residents and housing facilities, which translates as Native Americans and their huts; a furnished office; and Myrtie's bedroom, which displays some of her clothing and hats, along with her bedroom furniture. The highlight for my boys was seeing the vivid black-and-white pictures of jack rabbit hunts. The rabbits were hunted, corralled, and then clubbed to death. Although it is not a pretty sight, it is an interesting slice of Lancaster history.

Hours: Open Fri. - Sat., noon - 4pm.
Admission: Free
Ages: 4 years and up.

WESTERN MUSEUM OF FLIGHT

(310) 332-6228 / www.wmof.com
12016 S. Prairie Avenue, Hawthorne
(From the San Diego Fwy [405], exit E. on El Segundo, L. on Prairie. From the Glenn Anderson Fwy [105], exit S. on Prairie. It's in the Hawthorne airport, on the corner of Prairie and 120th. [TG-733 D1])

A rendition of "Off we go, into the wild blue yonder, flying high into the sky. . ." goes through one's mind when visiting this museum. The Western Museum of Flight "houses" between twelve to fifteen rare planes like the YF23A, YF17, a Freedom Fighter, and an exact replica of the first controlled aircraft, an 1883 glider. Most of the planes are outside, braving the elements, although several are inside the hanger. The ones inside are in the process of being restored, so kids have the opportunity to see this process. Also in the hanger, which resembles a workshop, are displays of engines, model planes, medals, leather helmets and jackets, and other memorabilia from WWI and WWII. This museum is for the more serious students of flight. For those interested in doing aeronautical research, a library is available. Call for more details.

    Hours: Open Tues. - Sat., 10am - 3pm.
  Admission: $3 for adults; $2 for children 12 and under.
      Ages: 6 years and up.

THE WHITTIER MUSEUM

(562) 945-3871 / www.whittiermuseum.org
6755 Newlin Avenue, Whittier
(Exit San Gabriel River Fwy [605] E. on Whittier Blvd., L. on Philadelphia, L. on Newlin. It's on the corner of Philadelphia and Newlin. [TG-677 C6])

    Journey back in time to the early days of Whittier, circa 1900. Stroll along a wonderfully re-created, full-size Main Street. The Victorian style is predominate in both the store and home fronts, and in the fully-furnished, walk-through rooms. A stereoscope and an old-fashioned stove and bathtub are some of our favorite items. Authentically-dressed mannequins all around make the visitors feel a part of this era.

    The next few rooms feature an outhouse, a water pump that kids can actually try, photos, murals depicting early Whittier as a farming community, a tractor, old farm tools, and a big model of an oil derrick. Sitting on old church pews, kids can watch a video that shows the history of Whittier. The transportation room has photos and an encased display of old medical instruments and medicine vials, plus a doctor's buggy, a racing plane, and a replicated front end of the historic Red Car. Walk up through the Red Car into the children's room filled with hands-on delights, such as old typewriters, adding machines, telephones, and a switchboard. There are also old-fashioned toys to play with and clothes for dressing up. The Library Room is an archival room housing documents on the history of Whittier. Upstairs is a large gallery room with changing exhibits. Call to see what's currently showing. Kids enjoy walking through history at this museum.

    Hours: Open Sat. - Sun., 1pm - 4pm. Group tours are also given Tues. -
                 Fri., by appointment.
  Admission: Free
      Ages: 3½ years and up.

WILLIAM S. HART MUSEUM AND PARK   ☼

(661) 254-4584 - museum; (661) 259-0855 - park and camping /   !
www.hartmuseum.org

24151 San Fernando Road, Newhall   ⛺

(Take Golden State Fwy [5] N. to Antelope Valley Fwy [Hwy 14], exit W. on San Fernando Rd., approximately 1 1/2 miles to the park, after the railroad tracks. [TG-4640 J2])

William S. Hart was a famous western star of the silent films - a bit before my time. His Spanish, colonial-style home is now a museum. It is a short, but tough hike up a winding trail to reach the house/museum on the hill. Note: Seniors and physically disabled people can get a pass from the park ranger to drive up the side street to the house. The half-hour guided tour of his home is quite interesting, as the house is filled with western and Indian art and furnishings. Kids can look at, but not touch, the saddles, guns and other weapons, forty-pound buffalo coat, bear skin rug, stuffed buffalo head, paintings, and western movie memorabilia.

The park covers over 265 acres, with almost 110 acres set aside for wilderness area. A herd of buffalo roam the grounds (which definitely adds to the Old West ambiance), within an enormous fenced-in enclosure. Many deer consider this area home, too. Hiking and nature trails through chaparral and woodland start behind the museum, and loop back around. Primitive camping is available here, too.

At the bottom of the hill, a large picnic area is located next to a grouping of barracks, which contain period artifacts. A smaller picnic area is behind the on-site "farm." Purchase some animal feed to entice the barnyard animals - sheep, ducks, horses, burros, and cows - to come within petting distance.

Hey pardners, ask about Cowboy Sleepovers and Night Hikes, which are held on special days throughout the year. Crafts, ranch-type activities, and learning about Native American lifestyles are just part of the program. Call for dates and information and ask about other special events. Note: See the adjacent HERITAGE JUNCTION HISTORIC PARK listed under this section.

Hours: Hart park is open daily 7am - sunset. The museum is open in the summer Wed. - Sun., 11am - 3:30pm. It's open the rest of the year Wed. - Fri., 10am - 12:30pm; Sat. - Sun., 11am - 3:30pm. Docent-led tours are given every half hour. The museum is closed New Year's Day, Thanksgiving, and Christmas.

Admission: Free

Ages: All

WILL ROGERS STATE HISTORIC PARK   ☼

(310) 454-8212 / parks.ca.gov $

1501 Will Rogers State Park Road, Pacific Palisades   ⛺

(From Pacific Coast Highway [1], exit N. on Sunset Blvd., L. on Will Rogers State Park Rd. From San Diego Fwy [405], exit W. on Sunset Blvd., R. on Will Rogers State Park Rd. [TG-631 C4])

"I never met a man I didn't like." These famous words were spoken by the "cowboy philosopher," actor, columnist, humorist, and philanthropist - Will Rogers. His ranch house was deeded to the state, and is now a museum. It has been left virtually unchanged from when he lived here in the late 1920's. The rustic, wood-beamed living room features many Indian blankets and rugs, saddles, animal skins, a longhorn steer head over the fireplace, a wagon wheel "chandelier," Western statues, Will's boots, and furniture. You'll also see his library/drawing room, upstairs bedrooms, and an office, which are all simply and comfortably furnished, and decorated with a western flair, of course.

The Visitors Center shows a free, continuously playing twelve-minute film on Will Rogers, featuring some of his rope tricks. Also available at no cost is an audio wand tour. Borrow a wand and place it at the several designated locations throughout the park, and it will tell you information about that area.

Picnic tables are plentiful at the park. The huge grassy area is actually a polo field. Games are held on weekends April through September. So come, have fun, learn a little history about a fascinating man, and if you feel like horsing around, watch a polo match.

There are several trails leading through the park that connect with its "backyard" neighbor, the huge TOPANGA STATE PARK. (See the Great Outdoors section.) One of the most popular hikes is the almost two-mile loop trail to Inspiration Point which, on a clear day, gives an inspirational, breathtaking view.

Hours: The park is open daily 8am - sunset. Tours of the house are available every hour on the half hour from 10:30am - 4:30pm, staff and weather permitting.

Admission: $3 per vehicle; $2 for seniors. House tours and polo matches are free.

Ages: 5 years and up.

ZIMMER CHILDREN'S MUSEUM   ☼
(323) 761-8989 / www.zimmermuseum.org $$
6505 Wilshire Boulevard, suite 100, Los Angeles   ♨
(From Santa Monica Fwy [10], exit N. on Fairfax Ave., L. on Wilshire Blvd. From San Diego Fwy [405], exit E. on Wilshire Blvd. It's on the ground floor of the Jewish Federation Building. [TG-633 A2])

Shalom and welcome to this colorful, two-story, completely hands-on museum, developed for kids to have fun while learning about Jewish history, customs, values, holidays, folklore, traditions, heros, and music, as well as Shabbat, Israel, and the Hebrew language. Oy!

At the entrance is a giant, neo-lit Tzedakah pinball game. Children are given a choice of disks to insert symbolizing giving money, time, or of oneself (the latter disk is mirrored). A Piper aircraft, with real cockpit controls where passengers can watch a video of a flight to and around Israel, and an airport waiting room are in the lobby. Some of the exhibits and things to do in the museum include a theater, complete with a dressing area, costumes, makeup tables and a blue screen backdrop so the video camera can superimpose children over a variety of locales; a mini version of the Jerusalem wall; a Geodesic dome that simulates outer space with a high-tech mock mission control center and astronaut costumes (see how well the kids can actually move in these!); a full size ambulance parked outside the mini-hospital emergency room, which is complete with machinery and doctor's uniforms; a main street with a kid-size home, synagogue, bookstore, cafe, park, puppet theater, and toddler play area.

Seasonal workshops and family day art activities are just a few events offered throughout the year. School and group tours are welcome. The museum is wheelchair/stroller friendly.

Hours: Open Tues - Thurs., 12:30pm - 4pm; Sun., 12:30pm - 5pm. Closed Mon., Fri., Sat., national holidays, and Jewish holidays. Group tours are scheduled between 10am - 12pm on days when the museum is open.

Admission: $5 for adults; $3 for ages 3 - 12; children 2 and under are free. Grandparents are free when accompanied by a grandchild. Free parking is available on the west side of the building.

Ages: 2 - 12 years.

ANAHEIM MUSEUM

(714) 778-3301

241 S. Anaheim Boulevard, Anaheim

(Exit Santa Ana Fwy [5] E. on Lincoln Ave., R. on Anaheim Blvd. [TG-768 J5])

This small museum is housed in Anaheim's restored 1908 Carnegie Library building. The upstairs room displays show the growth of Orange County's oldest city from an orange grove and grapevine-producing society to the opening of Disneyland in 1955 to the present. There are photos, a model of Disneyland, and a display of old tools and machines, as well as orange crate labels.

Downstairs is a small, children's gallery that features rotating, hands-on exhibits such as puppets, toys, musical instruments, and games. It reminds me of a culturally-aware kindergarten classroom, but there are also workshops for older kids.

Hours: Open Wed. - Fri., 10am - 4pm; Sat., noon - 4pm.

Admission: $2 for adults; children 15 and under are free.

Ages: 2 years and up.

BOWERS KIDSEUM

(714) 480-1520 / www.bowers.org

1802 N. Main Street, Santa Ana

(Going S. on Santa Ana Fwy [5], exit S. on Main St. Going N. on 5, exit W. on E. 17th St., R. on Main St. It's located on the corner of Main and 18th St, just S. of the Bowers Museum of Cultural Art. And yes, the building was a bank at one time. [TG-829 F1])

Kidseum is a hands-on, cultural museum designed to assist kids, ages 6 to 12, develop an appreciation of art and the ways of life in African, Asian, and Native American cultures. Cross over the short (symbolic) bridge from the lobby into the main gallery. Your kids will love trying on unusual masks from around the world; playing unique musical instruments, like deer hoof shakers, African drums, and string instruments; and dressing up in a wide variety of ethnic costumes in the theater area.

The Time Vault, which was an actual bank vault, has an incredible mural on the wall. Kids can "saddle up" on the workbench horses in here or grind pretend corn with a stone mortar and pestle. Playing games from foreign lands; working on geography puzzles; and putting on your own puppet show at the small theater

- all this is available at Kidseum, too!

Afternoons and weekends at the museum is a time for telling tales, storytelling tales, that is. The storytelling room also brings to life Asian tales in January, in celebration of the Chinese New Year; African tales in February to celebrate Black History Month; and so on. Stop by the Art Lab, which is usually open about the same hours as the museum, where kids can paint, color, learn how to make Indian rain sticks, experiment with sand art, and more. Most activities are included in the price of admission. School tours here are my favorite combination of hands-on fun and learning. Kidseum proves that learning about other cultures can be exciting!

Note: The Bowers Museum, located just down the street at 2002 N. Main Street, is the parent museum of Kidseum. It contains carvings, pictures, and other art work from African, Asian, and Native American cultures. Older kids might appreciate a walk through the galleries. As admission is reciprocal with Kidseum when visited on the same day, why not visit both?!

Hours: Open in the summer and during school breaks Tues. - Fri., noon - 5pm; Sat. - Sun., 10am - 4pm. Open the rest of the year Sat. - Sun., 10am - 4pm. Call to make a reservation to take a tour during the week.

Admission: $4 for adults; $3 for seniors and students; $2 for ages 5 - 12; children 4 and under are free. There is reciprocal admission with the Bowers Museum if both are visited on the same day. (See C.E.E. L.A. for membership savings, pg. 261.)

Ages: 3 - 13 years. Young children will enjoy the hands-on quality of this museum, though signs do ask for a gentle touch.

CHILDREN'S MUSEUM AT LA HABRA   ☼

(562) 905-9793 / www.lhcm.org $$

301 S. Euclid Street, La Habra   ♨

(Exit Artesia Fwy [91] N. on Euclid. [TG-708 E6])

This museum, housed in a renovated Union Pacific Railroad Depot, has a child's interest at heart. Out front are dinosaur print trackways of a tyrannosaurus, sauropod, and theropod; a sand bed where visitors can make their own tracks; and a replica nest containing unhatched "dino" eggs. Youngsters can also count the rings on a six foot diameter tree slab.

Inside, a small Science Station encourages hands-on exploration with a Dino Dig (i.e. digging in sand for "fossils"), pendulum and marker pictures, and a few science experiments. The adjoining room has a carousel to ride, a mini-market for shopping, and the front end of an Orange County Transit bus to practice driving skills. The next room has wonderful, interactive, changing exhibits. Past themes have included "Cowboys and the Wild West," which featured western gear to try on, a wooden horse with a saddle, and a guitar to strum on the range; and "Would You Look At That?" which featured fun with lenses, light, and optical equipment. This room is always enlightening! Do you hear trains chugging, clanging, and whistling as they come around the mountain? A connecting room contains a large model train layout. The train room then leads to the nature room. Listen to the sounds of nature (e.g. birds chirping) as you look at the taxidermied wildlife, such as bears, mountain lions, a raccoon, and a wart hog. Hanging on the wall are stuffed animal heads of deer, moose, and buffalo. A touch table in here has fur and skulls. A bee observatory gets the kids all a-buzz.

Quiet on the set! The dress-up area, with its stage, numerous costumes (including several fireman uniforms), and even prepared scripts, inspires future actors and actresses. The lighting booth, with all of its working buttons, is perfect for aspiring directors. The adjoining playroom, for children 5 years and under only, has a fake tree to climb, a little puppet theater, a play castle, and a small, separate play room for very little ones. Just outside the museum is a train caboose that is open to walk through at certain times.

On Saturdays, the museum hosts special programs such as craft projects, storytelling, or shows for kids to enjoy and participate in. Call for a schedule of events.

Portola Park is located just behind the museum. It's open daily and features a playground, baseball fields, tennis courts, picnic tables, and barbecue grills.

Hours: Open Mon. - Sat., 10am - 5pm; Sun., 1pm - 5pm. Closed major holidays.

Admission: $4 for ages 2 and up; children under 2 are free.

Ages: 1½ - 12 years.

DISCOVERY MUSEUM

(714) 540-0404 / www.discoverymuseumoc.org

3101 W. Harvard Street, Santa Ana

(Exit San Diego Fwy [405] N.E. on Warner Ave., L. on Fairview, L. on Harvard. [TG-829 A7])

Travel back to Victorian times as you visit the Kellogg House (i.e. Discovery Museum), built in 1898. Take a few moments to walk around the truly lovely grounds. Tours begin in the parlor where kids can play a pump organ, crank an old telephone, listen to music played on an Edison talking machine, and look through a stereoscope - an early version of the modern-day View Master™. The kitchen has wonderful gadgets that kids can learn about as well as touch. The wood dining room is oval-shaped with cabinets specially made to bend with the curves, like the inside of a ship. The twisted, wooden staircase got "cool" raves from all the kids. Upstairs, children play a game that teaches them the parts of a Victorian house. The master bedroom is now a room to dress up in authentic Victorian clothing, with beautiful dresses for the girls and dapper coats and vests for the boys. The hats are great, too. The children's room has old-fashioned toys to play with. Kids may sit at the one-room schoolhouse desks and write with chalk on the slate boards.

Outside, on the back porch, children can practice *real* chores like "washing" clothes on a scrub board and drying them with the clothes wringer. Sometimes visitors are invited to make their own butter or learn how to play Victorian-era games. After the official tour, kids are welcome to go back and explore their favorite rooms, with parental supervision, of course.

Enjoy a picnic lunch in the Gazebo area. A working blacksmith's shop is open on the third Sunday of the month, and sometimes on Thursdays. Demonstrations are given here, such as crafting candlesticks out of iron. Once a month the museum offers special events, such as American Indian Day, or a themed tea, where kids are invited to make crafts and participate in topical programs. Call for a schedule and for pricing. Each Sunday, from October through May, brings a special family activity such as storytelling, a craft, blacksmith demonstrations, or a nature hike. This activity is included in your admission price. School groups, with a minimum of ten students, should inquire about their wide array of programs including gardening, a pirate's treasure hunt (focusing on math, map-making, compass-reading, and other skills), archaeology, ecology themes, and more. Two-hour classes start at $7 per student. Children 12 years and up can even become volunteer youth naturalists.

Of all the historical homes we've toured, and we've been through quite a few, this one has earned one of the highest ratings from my boys. Most houses, while beautiful and worthy of a tour, are understandably hands off. The Discovery Museum has hands-on activities, plus the docents gear the tour towards youngsters, both in the tour length and the way the information is presented. Come here and let your kids touch history!

Hours: Open Wed. - Fri., 1pm - 5pm; Sun., 11am - 3pm. Open Sat. for special events only. Call to book a school tour or scout outing during the week.

Admission: $5 for ages 3 and up; $4 for seniors; children 2 and under are free.

Ages: 3 years and up.

DISCOVERY SCIENCE CENTER   ☼
(714) 542-CUBE (2823) / www.discoverycube.org $$$
2500 N. Main Street., Santa Ana

(From S. of Santa Ana, exit the San Diego Fwy [5] N. at Main St. North / Broadway, R. on Main St., across the intersection. It's on the left. From N. of Santa Ana, exit San Diego Fwy [5] S. at Main St. North / Broadway (look for signs), L. on Santa Clara, L. at Main St. The distinctive ten-story-high cube, which tilts precariously on top of the building, is visible from the freeway. [TG-799 F7])

This two-story, high-caliber science center has over 100 hands-on experiments and displays throughout its eight major exhibits areas: Human Perception, Quake Zone, Dynamic Earth, Principles of Flight, Human Performance, Space Exploration, Exploration Station, and KidStation. The Bed of Nails, a favorite because it's unusual, is a large wooden table with 3500 sharp steel nails embedded in it. Visitors can lie down on the on the bed and not get hurt, due to the equal distribution of body mass. (May your kids never complain about an uncomfortable mattress again!) See yourself in a "new light" inside a room with a camera that takes real time pictures of your movements. Watch your image reflected on a screen in vivid colors and lights. If you can't get enough of the real California quakes, enter the Shake Shack, a room with a platform that simulates major and minor quakes. Walk through an eight-foot-tall artificially generated tornado and even redirect its pattern. Speak through a tube that changes your voice from normal to sound like you're underwater, in an opera, an alien, and more. Use wind to blow sand into dunes or other formations. Create a cloudy day (inside!) by pushing on large rings around a cloud machine which then form various-sized clouds. Experience what you would weigh on the moon or on Mars by hoisting yourself up on a properly weighted pulley system. Take

apart certain machines (with screwdrivers, not hammers) at designated times at
the tool area. You are also invited to create an animated movie (we spent an hour
just doing this!), participate in live science shows, climb a rock wall, log on to
the several computer terminals to play educational games, and so much more.
Don't forget to catch a show at the 3-D Laser Theater!

In the space-themed KidStation, designed for children five years and
younger, kids can suit up as an astronaut, turn and "repair" gears at the Gear
Wall, converse through the Talk Tubes, race balls down a slide at the Ball Run,
fingerpaint electronically (a lot less messy than the real thing), bop around in the
soft play area, play with space-age toys, and read books about the stars and
planets.

Ask about the numerous special programs offered here, including a "Meet
the Scientists" series, science camps, scout programs, school outreach programs,
and more. The Discovery Science Center unites education with entertainment in
an appealing format for all generations.

Note: An on-site Taco Bell and Pizza Hut have an indoor and outdoor eating
area. Also, see SANTIAGO PARK (listed under the Great Outdoors section),
which is across the road, but accessible by an underpass. Parking at the park is
free.

Hours: Open daily 10am - 5pm. Closed New Year's Day, Thanksgiving,
and Christmas.

Admission: $9.50 for adults; $7 for seniors and ages 3 - 17; children 2 and
under are free. Free admission to Santa Ana residents (bring a
valid photo ID with your Santa Ana address) and up to three
additional guests is offered on the first Mon. of every month.
Shows at the 3-D Laser Theater are an additional $1 per person.
Parking is $3 per vehicle. Note: Membership here is reciprocated
at the CALIFORNIA SCIENCE CENTER in Los Angeles and
the REUBEN H. FLEET SCIENCE CENTER in San Diego. Call
around for the best membership deal.

Ages: 2 years and up.

DOLL AND TOY MUSEUM   ☀

(714) 527-2323 $

1238 S. Beach Boulevard, Anaheim

(Exit Artesia Fwy [91] S. on Beach Blvd. Or, exit Garden Grove Fwy [22] N. on Beach. The
museum is in Hobby City, 2 miles S. of Knott's Berry Farm. [TG-797 J1])

Take a walk down memory lane as you go through this museum. It contains
a personal collection of the owner's over five thousand rare and antique dolls
from around the world, all housed in a half-scale model of the White House
(making the museum easy to spot). Some of the more kid-recognizable dolls
include Cupie dolls, Star Wars figures, and an extensive Barbie collection. This
small museum is for the special child who can resist the touching urge. The
attached shop buys, sells, and repairs old and modern dolls. They also carry a
line of doll clothes, shoes, wigs, hats, and books. (Look up the adjacent
attractions - ADVENTURE CITY and HOBBY CITY, listed separately in the
Alphabetical Index.)

Hours: Open daily 10am - 5:30pm.
Admission: $2 for adults; $1 for senior citizens and children 12 and under.
Ages: 3 years and up.

FULLERTON MUSEUM CENTER

(714) 738-6545 - museum; (714) 738-3136 - tour info / $
www.ci.fullerton.ca.us/museum
301 N. Pomona Avenue, Fullerton
(Exit Riverside Fwy [91] N. on Harbor Blvd., R. on Commonwealth, L. on Pomona. It's on the corner
of Wilshire and Pomona. [TG-738 H7])

This small cultural museum has two galleries with rotating exhibits that
often have kid-appeal, plus a video that explains more about what is currently
showing. Past exhibits have included The Nature of Collecting, which featured
different collections ranging from *I Love Lucy* paraphernalia to pencil sharpeners
and old radios; Touchable Sculptures, with over seventy touchable, lifecast
sculptures of contemporary and historic figures such as George Bush, Clint
Eastwood, and Dizzy Gillespie; and Anne Frank, a re-creation of the life and
times of Anne Frank through photographs and facsimiles of her diary, plus
commentary.

One-and-a-half-hour school tours are given that include an in-depth tour of
the museum and a hands-on activity that correlates to the current exhibit.

Super Saturdays are year-round family workshops, held on one Saturday a
month from 1pm to 3pm. The art activity is geared for kids ages 5 through 10.
Super Tuesdays and Thursdays are held on most Tuesdays and Thursdays during
the summer, from 9:30am to 11am. The activities are geared for kids ages 8 to
12 years. These culturally-themed and/or art workshops, like Secrets of Pharaoh,
Papermaking, International Christmas Tree Ornaments, or Day of the Dead,
include an interesting lesson followed by a related craft. Reservations are
needed.

Hours: The museum is open Wed. - Sun., noon - 4pm; open Thurs. until
                8pm.
Admission: $3 for adults; $2 for students; $1 for ages 6 - 12; children 5 and
                under are free. The workshops cost $8 per person. School tours
                are $2 for ages 12 and up; $1 for children 11 and under. Adult
                chaperones are free.
Ages: 5 years and up.

HERITAGE HILL HISTORICAL PARK

(949) 855-2028 / www.ocparks.com $
25151 Serrano Road, Lake Forest
(Exit San Diego Fwy [5] N.E. on Lake Forest Dr., L. on Serrano. It's on the corner. Parking is
available in the adjacent shopping center. [TG-891 J2])

Heritage Hill consists of several restored historical buildings in a beautiful
gated setting. Four buildings are open to tour that reflect part of Orange
County's heritage. The Serrano Adobe dates from 1863 and has furniture from
the late nineteenth-century. The Bennet Ranch House, built in 1908, reflects a
ranching family's lifestyle from the early twentieth century. St. George's

Episcopal Mission, built in 1891, has many of its original interior furnishings. El Toro Grammar School was built in 1890. It is a favorite with kids because it has school books from that era, as well as desks and other school-related items. The Historical Park has a few picnic tables on the grounds.

Two school tours are offered. The third grade tour is one-and-a-half hours long, costs $2 per person, and is designed for ten to seventy students. Groups go through each house and do an activity in each, such as grinding corn in the adobe. In the school house, they participate in a mini school session. The fourth grade tour is two hours long and cost $3 per person. Seventeen to thirty-five students participate in hands-on lessons in the school house. Learning was never so interesting! Reservations for tours are required.

If your kids need more running around space, visit Serrano Creek Park, just behind Heritage Hill. Serrano is a long, narrow, wooded park with a paved walkway and a creek running through it. The big wooden play structure, which looks like a clubhouse, has a bridge, slides, and some huge tires to climb on.

> **Hours:** Heritage Hill is open Wed. - Sun., 9am - 5pm. Guided tours are the only way to see the interior of the buildings. The tours are given Wed. - Fri. at 2pm; Sat. - Sun. at 11am and 2pm. School groups can make reservations for tours at other times throughout the week. Closed major holidays.
>
> **Admission:** Donations.
>
> **Ages:** 6 years and up.

HISTORIC GEORGE KEY RANCH

(714) 528-4260 / www.ocparks.com   *$$*
625 W. Bastanchury Road, Placentia
(Exit Orange Fwy [57], E. on Yorba Linda Blvd., L. on Placentia Ave., L. on Bastanchury. Parking is not permitted on the grounds, but on the adjacent streets of Gilman Circle or Key Drive. [TG-739 D3])

Orange groves, originally planted in 1893, once covered most of the George Key Ranch. On your guided tour here you can still see two remaining acres of producing orange trees. Your one-a-half-hour tour begins with a brief video of the Key family. Then walk through the Key house to see the family furnishings and old photographs; the Kitchen Collection building, which has an extensive collection of kitchen items, dating from the 1890's to the 1940's, that all came from local ranch houses; a workshop shed that contains artifacts related to ranch life, such as a squirrel and gopher smoker, an avocado picker, and an alfalfa/grass chopper for making chicken feed; and a blacksmith and carpentry shop which holds smithing and carpentry tools as well as implements used in picking and packaging oranges. The yard contains a variety of old farm equipment and machinery such as plows, harrows, spreaders, seeders, orchard heaters, a citrus spray rig, and even wagons from the early 1900's. Enjoy a stroll along the brick-lined garden and bring a sack lunch to enjoy at the picnic tables here.

Ask about the ranch's special programs, such as the Civil War Brass Band and the California Battalion - a concert of military music and camp songs with the President and Mrs. Lincoln in attendance; the summer concert series; Open

House, where docents in period dress demonstrate old-fashioned crafts; scout programs; ranch clean up programs; and more.

Hours: Open only for guided tours, by appointment. Tours are limited to thirty people and are usually given on Fri. mornings for school groups, and Fri. afternoons for adults. Note: There is presently no handicapped access.

Admission: $4 per person.

Ages: 6 years and up.

HOUSE OF VICTORIAN VISIONS BRIDAL MUSEUM
(714) 997-1893 / www.victorianbridalmuseum.com   *$$$*
254 S. Glassell Street, Orange
(Exit Orange Fwy [57] W. on Chapman, S. on Glassell, just S. of the traffic circle, in Old Town. [TG-799 G5])

Here comes the bride, all dressed in white . . . . Did you know that the tradition of wearing a *white* wedding dress was started by Queen Victoria? Learn this and numerous other fascinating and educational pieces of information by taking a guided tour of the bridal museum, which is housed in a beautifully decorated, Victorian-style home. Each of the six small rooms feature antique wedding gowns dating from the 1830's - gowns that are mostly white, although there are some colorful ones, too. The rooms also contain pictures, documents, boots, fans, brooches, headpieces, and various other wedding accessories. The thirty-five-minute guided tour is like a class in history/social studies, and the wedding articles are great springboards for discussions. Visitors learn about etiquette (how well women communicated with just a fan!); fashion (those corsets look painful); morality (I appreciate the reasons for orange blossoms in the headpieces); and more. Listen to the history of the women who owned the gowns, from the woman who was friends with President Lincoln to the missionary who never wore her gown. Note: This is a terrific outing for preteen and teen girls, as well as adults. Groups of more than six will be divided into two or more groups.

A small gift shop offers wedding-related articles for sale as well as the opportunity to order a specialized wedding dress or period gown.

Hours: Open Wed. - Sat., 11am - 6pm; Sun., 11am - 3pm.

Admission: $5 per person for a self-guided "tour"; $7.50 per person for a guided tour.

Ages: 10 years and up.

HUNTINGTON BEACH INTERNATIONAL SURFING MUSEUM
(714) 960-3483 / www.surfingmuseum.org   *$*
411 Olive Avenue, Huntington Beach
(Going N. on San Diego Fwy [405], exit E. on Ellis Ave., veer L. past Beach onto Main St. Going S on 405, exit S. on Beach, R. on Main. From Main, go R. on Olive near end of Main. [TG-887 J1])

Surf's up at this small museum that celebrates surfing and surf culture, from its roots in Hawaii to the present day. Get in the mood with beach music playing in the background. Feel like catching a wave? Check out some of the famous and unique surfboards here, like the Batman board and a surfboard made in three pieces. There are also trophies, clothes, and photographs to look at. The Surfer's Walk of Fame, honoring eleven people, is just down the street.

Hours: Open June through Labor Day, daily noon - 5pm. Open the rest of the year Wed. - Sun., noon - 5pm.

Admission: $2 for adults; $1 for kids; children 6 and under are free.

Ages: 6 years and up.

MARCONI AUTOMOTIVE MUSEUM FOR KIDS

(714) 258-3001 / www.marconimuseum.org $

1302 Industrial Drive, Tustin

(Exit Cost Mesa Fwy [55] E. on Edinger Ave., R. on Red Hill Ave., R. on Industrial Dr. [TG-830 A6])

The front hallway of this classy museum is lined with gleaming motorcycles. The museum is for kids in that money raised through it is donated to children's charities. Also, unlike many vintage car museums, there aren't any ropes around the cars and kids are encouraged to (gently) touch the cars on display and peer through their windows. The museum features the private collection of Dick Marconi's automobiles, which are kept in mint condition. He owns seventy-two-plus cars and over fifty of them are housed here at any given time. The cars vary in style, shape, and color. His collection includes a 1929 Ford Model 'A' Cabriolet, a 1937 Ahrens-Fox Fire Engine, a 1954 green Chevrolet, a 1973 canary-yellow convertible Ferrari Daytona Spider (once owned by Cher), a restored 1964 Corvette Sting Ray, and a jet-black 1989 Lamborghini Countach, plus seventeen racing Ferraris, an assortment of motorcycles, and a few kid-size cars. Marconi's prized possession is the last car Mario Andretti drove to victory at the 1993 Phoenix International Raceway. It is signed by Andretti. My boys' favorite was the rather colorful car completely decoupaged with magazine covers featuring boxing champions. Racing flags, trophies, drivers' jumpsuits and helmets, and a huge, shining silver horse constructed out of old car bumpers complete this museum.

Hours: Open Mon. - Fri., 9am - 4pm by appointment only. You may call as little as a few hours before you would like to visit.

Admission: $5 for adults; children 12 and under are free.

Ages: 5 years and up.

MISSION SAN JUAN CAPISTRANO

(949) 234-1300 / www.missionsjc.com $$

Camino Capistrano and Ortega Highway, San Juan Capistrano

(Exit San Diego Fwy [5] W. on Ortega Hwy. [74]. It's on the corner of Ortega Hwy and Camino Capistrano. [TG-972 C1])

The Mission, founded in 1776, is thirteen acres of historic stone buildings and beautifully landscaped gardens, courtyards, and walkways. It's easy to see why the San Juan Mission was considered the "Jewel of the Missions." There are many "parts" to the Mission, so there is something to interest almost any age child. It's a history treat for school kids as they visit and "experience" the early Native American, Spanish, and Mexican lifestyles, depicted in separate rooms. Walk through rooms that contain murals such as Indians hunting, and artifacts such as bone weapons. The Soldiers' Barracks room looks "lived in," just as it did many years ago. It contains life-size models of soldiers and their (few) possessions. Note: Outside, behind the barracks, are some picnic tables.

The extensive grounds are a maze of pathways. The Central Courtyard, the cemetery, the areas of on-going archaeological excavation, and the industrial center are all interesting. For instance, tanning vats in the industrial center were used to turn animal skin into sellable leather, while the ovens were used to turn animal fat into candles, soap, and ointments.

The Mission has two churches. One is the Serra Chapel, the oldest building in California, where mass is still regularly performed. The glittery baroque altar, made of gold leaf overlay, is eye-catching. The Great Stone Church, once a magnificent cathedral, was destroyed by an earthquake in 1812. Scaffolding is around the ruins, holding up the remaining walls while the church awaits restoration.

Mission San Juan Capistrano offers several special, educational activities such as Saturday at the Mission. This program, offered during the school year, is held on the first and third Saturday of the month from 9am to 11:30am. It's geared for kids ages 6 to 12. A topic is introduced and then reinforced, either with a related craft, by playing games, or even by participating in a simulated, archaeological dig. Living History Day occurs on the second Saturday of each month from 10am to 2pm. Authentically costumed docents become living historians. Talk with them to find out about mission life "firsthand."

If you're looking for somewhere fun to eat, RUBY'S (see the Edible Adventures section) is across the street and up the stairs at the shopping district. This 1940's diner has a train going around overhead, red vinyl seats, and kids' meals that are served in a forties-style, cardboard car. Afterwards, take a walk around Camino Capistrano, which is a street with many interesting stores with truly unique merchandise. For example, the Moonrose store sells candles, and visitors can even make their own! Idea: Take a train into town and really make a day of your visit here! The train depot is only two blocks away from the Mission. (Look up JONES FAMILY MINI FARM under the Zoos and Animals section for a fun, close-by adventure.) Check the March Calendar section for the Fiesta de las Golondrinas held at the mission.

Hours: Open daily 8:30am - 5pm. Closed New Year's Day, Good Friday afternoon, Thanksgiving, and Christmas.

Admission: $6 for adults; $5 for seniors; $4 for ages 3 - 12; children 2 and under are free. Saturday at the Mission is $15 per participant.

Ages: 5 years and up.

MOVIELAND WAX MUSEUM

(714) 522-1154 / www.movielandwaxmuseum.com

7711 Beach Boulevard, Buena Park

(Exit Artesia Fwy [91] S. on Beach Blvd. It's 1 block N. of Knott's Berry Farm. [TG-767 H3])

Over 400 movie and television celebrities are immortalized in wax, posed in the settings that made them famous. To insure authenticity, almost every measurement and picture angle imaginable is taken of the star before the sculptor begins his work. Often times the costumes and props adorning the wax figure, and its surrounding settings, are personally donated by the stars.

Kids who are film buffs will probably get more out of this museum, but almost any age child enjoys "seeing" Dorothy and the whole *Wizard of Oz* gang; Robin Williams as Mrs. Doubtfire; and Michael Jackson dressed from his video *Bad*; as well as Whoopi Goldberg, *Star Trek* crew members, Superman, the Little Rascals, and many more. Special lighting, sound effects, and animation are also used throughout the museum to enhance the realism of the exhibits. Halfway through the museum, you are routed through a gift and candy shop and small arcade area. Here you have the choice of whether to go through the Chamber of Horrors or bypass it. (The Chamber of Horrors, which holds scary and sometimes gross figures, could frighten younger children.)

Hours: Open Mon. - Fri., 10am - 6pm; Sat. - Sun., 9am - 7pm.

Admission: $12.95 for adults; $10.55 for seniors; $6.95 for ages 4 - 11; children 3 and under are free. Certain discounts available through AAA. Combo prices with RIPLEY'S BELIEVE IT OR NOT! MUSEUM, which is just across the street, are $16.90 for adults; $13.95 for seniors; $9.75 for ages 4 - 11.

Ages: 4 years and up.

NEWPORT HARBOR NAUTICAL MUSEUM

(949) 673-7863 / www.newportnautical.org

151 E. Coast Highway, Newport Beach

(Take Costa Mesa Fwy [55] to end, where it turns into Newport Blvd., L. on E. 17th St., R., at end, on Dover Dr., L on Coast Hwy., on Newport Bay. [TG-889 B7])

This beautiful, paddlewheel riverboat, now harbored in Newport Bay, looks like it just came down the Mississippi River. Our visit here wasn't long, but it was interesting. An upstairs room is devoted to glass-enclosed model ships. The huge (for a scale model) Fort Victoria is displayed in the center. The U.S.S. Missouri model, built in remembrance of the men who served on her and for the WWII peace treaty which was signed on board, is complete with men and little cannons, plus waves under the bow and stern. Other outstanding models were crafted from sterling silver, intricately carved wood, and bone. In the hallway is a captain's wheel with beautiful stained glass panels - spin it gently. Elegantly displayed exhibits in the other upstairs room consist of artifacts from early California. My boys particularly liked the bowl made from whale vertebrae and the necklace made from fish bones. Downstairs is a wall display of ships in a bottle and a small seashell exhibit. You can also watch a short, grainy, homemade video taken during a real hurricane in Newport Beach in 1939.

If you've worked up an appetite, dine at the classy RIVERBOAT RESTAURANT, located on board. (See Edible Adventures for more details.)

Hours: The museum is open Tues. - Sun., 10am - 5pm. Closed Mon.

Admission: Free

Ages: 6 years and up.

NEWPORT SPORTS COLLECTION
(949) 721-9333 / www.newportsportscollection.org
100 Newport Center Drive, Suite 100, Newport Beach
(Exit San Diego Fwy [405] S. on Jamboree Rd., L. on Santa Barbara, L. on Newport Center Dr. It's near Fashion Island mall. [TG-889 E7])

Name a sport, any sport. Almost any one that you can think of is represented in this 5,000 square-foot sports museum filled with signed memorabilia. The hundreds of game-used and game-worn equipment and clothing on display include jerseys, shoes, helmets, rows and rows of hockey sticks, basketballs, golf clubs, a multitude of footballs, baseballs, bats, and more. Included in this collection is the ball Babe Ruth hit for his last home-run, George Kelly's 1920 first baseman's mitt, and other baseball items signed by Cal Ripken, Joe DiMaggio, Nolan Ryan, Jackie Robinson, and lots more. The downstairs room contains numerous baseball keepsakes and has stadium seats facing a mural of a baseball field. One room upstairs is devoted to baseball, while several other small rooms display boxing gloves honoring Mohammad Ali, hockey items that belonged to Wayne Gretzsky, a football signed by John Elway, and pictures of or equipment used in water polo, tennis, horse racing, etc. An Olympic section contains Olympic memorabilia and paraphernalia.

The Newport Sports Collection Foundation is the non-profit organization who own and operate this facility. It also puts on programs where athletes come in and speak to kids about staying in school and staying off drugs. Call for more information about this program, but come by and see the sports collection any time.

Hours: Open Mon. - Fri., 9am - 6pm; Sat., 10am - 3pm.
Admission: Free
Ages: 6 years and up.

OCEAN INSTITUTE
(949) 496-2274 / www.ocean-institute.org
24200 Dana Point Harbor Drive, Dana Point
(Exit San Diego Fwy [5] N. on Pacific Coast Highway, L. on Dana Point Harbor, all the way to the end of the road. It's a part of Dana Point Harbor. [TG-971 G7])

The Ocean Institute's main purposes are to teach about maritime history and about the marine environment. It offers all levels of wonderful in-house classes, such as the Crab Lab, which is somewhat hands-on, and public and school outings, such as the Bio-Luminescence cruise. This two-and-a-half-hour night cruise highlights glowing worms, glow fish, and plankton. The cost is $20 for adults, $14 for ages 12 and under. Children must be at least 4 years old for this cruise. The four-hour Pelagic and Onshore Field Study is an educational cruise which includes trawling to collect plant and animal samples to dissect and study microscopically. The cost is $24 per person. Several other cruise options, including an overnight Catalina Island Ecology Safari ($125 per person), a four-hour Advanced Floating Lab for high-schoolers through college age ($24), and a one-hour Dana Harbor Cruise for everyone ($11 for adults, $8 for children) are available. Ask about guided tidepool hikes, too.

If, however, you are coming just to see the Institute, there are relatively few things to look at besides a few aquarium tanks and a great gift shop that has educational toys, books, and games. One of the tanks has an octopus. The back room has a touch tank, where a docent holds a starfish or a lobster for your child to touch. Overhead is a skeleton of a gray whale.

A 130-square-foot replica of the historic Tallship "Pilgrim", riggings and all, is moored in front of the building and open to walk through most Sundays. (See the September Calendar section for the terrific annual Tallships Festival.) Want to swab the decks, matey? Pilgrim offers one to eighteen-hour on-board programs which recreate the austere life of a sailor in the early nineteenth century. Students learn sea chanteys, how to raise the sails, load cargo, and other period related activities.

Behind the Institute is a small park overlooking the harbor, with rock jetties, a few picnic tables, and tidepools. (See DANA POINT HARBOR under the Piers and Seaports section.)

Hours: The Institute is open daily 10am - 4:30pm. The touch tank is open Sat. - Sun., 10am - 4:30pm. The Pilgrim is open most Sun., 10am - 2:30pm. Call for school group tours. Everything is closed on major holidays.

Admission: Free to enter the Institute. Call for class fees.

Ages: 3 years and up.

OLD COURTHOUSE MUSEUM

(714) 834-3703 / www.ocparks.com
211 W. Santa Ana Boulevard, Santa Ana
(Going S. on Santa Ana Fwy [5], exit S. on Main St., R. on Civic Center Dr. Going N. on 5, exit W. on 1st St. R. on Main St., L. on Civic Center Dr. Although the address is on Santa Ana Blvd., metered parking is on Civic Center Dr. [TG-829 F2])

Order in the court! Older kids interested in the history of our legal system, or in seeing what an actual courtroom looks like, will enjoy visiting the oldest courtroom in Southern California. Built in 1901, this huge, red sandstone building contains three floors of Orange County history. The bottom floor has glass cases of archaeological artifacts, such as fossils and bones. The second floor, which is the entrance, has two displays containing information about the museum and the court of law.

The third floor is your ultimate, and most interesting, destination. It features a turn-of-the century courtroom, jury room, and judge's chambers, plus a court reporter's room that has original transcribing machines, a candlestick telephone, and an old roll-top desk. My boys and I role-played a bit here so they could get a feel for how the court system is set up. The museum, which is a room of changing exhibits, is across the way from the Superior Courtroom. Past exhibits have included displays of sheriff's badges, war posters, a mock-up of a 1940's living room, and World War II artifacts from Orange County. A visit to the Old Courthouse Museum is a good beginning for future lawyers. I rest my case.

Hours: Open Mon. - Fri., 9am - 5pm. Forty-five-minute guided tours are available by appointment.

Admission: Free

Ages: 6 years and up.

ORANGE COUNTY DENTAL SOCIETY MUSEUM ☼

(714) 634-8944 / www.ocds.org   !

295 S. Flower Street, Orange

(Exit Orange Fwy [57] E. on Chapman Ave., R. on Flower St. [TG-799 D5])

This small museum doesn't floss over America's early dental period. It
contains several old dental chairs, including an 1855 wooden chair with a
straight back and a spittoon - no running water on this device; an 1876 velvet,
rose-colored chair with fringe and a spittoon; and a modern-day chair with all the
amenities. The glass-enclosed display shelves are lined with old dental tools that
made me wince just to look at them, such as extraction forceps, clamps for
separating teeth, and small saws. My 8-year old commented, "I'm going to brush
my teeth ten times a day from now on!" We also saw a lot of false teeth,
porcelain shade guides (used to match teeth for bridge work or capping), metal
swagging sets (for making gold crowns), a buffalo horn mallet (used before
plastic), and numerous steel instruments - some made with ivory and some with
mother-of-pearl handles. The crowning jewel here is in a silver trinket box - a
partial denture of four of George Washington's ivory teeth! You are welcome to
explore the museum on your own, as everything is labeled, or ask for further
explanations across the hall at the Dental Society. This museum is something
you can really sink your teeth into!

Hours: Open Mon. - Thurs., 8am - 3pm; Fri., 8am - 1pm.
Admission: Free
Ages: 4 years and up.

ORANGE COUNTY NATURAL HISTORY MUSEUM ☼

(949) 831-3287 / www.ocnha.mus.ca.us $

28373 Alicia Parkway, Laguna Niguel

(Exit San Diego Fwy [5] S.W. on Alicia Pkwy, cross Aliso Creek Rd., R. on Awma. It is located in a
spacious trailer by Gate One at Aliso and Wood Canyons Regional Park. [TG-951 E1])

This terrific trailer museum has exhibits of fossils and seashells, and an
extensive butterfly and moth collection. It also has a skeleton of a dolphin, the
tooth of a great white shark, whale bones, and the remains of Waldo, a walrus or
sea lion. Children may touch the animals bones and pelts. Many taxidermied
birds are on display - some in flight and others lying down - including owls,
hummingbirds, quail, a scrubjay, and a warbling. Other stuffed native animals
are a coyote, raccoon, opossum, badger, and more. Make tracks of the wildlife
by using life-size paw print stamps in a box of dirt. Live lizards, toads, and
several kinds of snakes, including a huge rattlesnake, take up residence here in
glass cases. Look for fossils in the pile of rocks here, and look at some of the
shells recently gathered from Shellmaker Island and surrounding areas. Kids can
take a pencil safari where they are given a list of things to find and check off.
Picnic tables are just outside the trailer under a few shade trees. See ALISO
AND WOOD CANYONS REGIONAL PARK, under the Great Outdoors
section, for details on exploring the adjacent wilderness park.

Micropals is one of the many programs offered and sponsored through this
museum. It is taught by a geologist and allows kids to extract specimens, process
samples, and go on field trips while learning about the world of

micropaleontology. Call for more information about this and other programs.

Hours: Open Wed. - Sun., 11am- 5pm. Closed Mon., Tues., and holidays.

Admission: $2 for adults; $1 for seniors and children 12 and under; $5 for a family of four or more. Parking is $2.

Ages: 3 years and up.

PRETEND CITY

(949) 553-8790 / www.pretendcity.org

At the 405 Fwy and Sand Canyon Avenue, Irvine

Slated to open in 2002, Pretend City will be a destination for families to learn how a city, albeit a kid-size one, functions. Located on a three-acre parcel of land, it'll contain everything a real city does from an air-traffic control tower to a restaurant.

A construction area will allow kids to learn about infrastructures and buildings by creating bridges, tunnels, houses, and skyscrapers. The transportation area will demonstrates and enlists children's help in getting around a city, whether by car, bus, subway, airplane, or even a surfboard. Design different modes of transportation and make them go! Journalist wanna-bes can practice their career choice by writing newspaper articles, drafting advertisements, adding artwork to the newspaper, and working an actual printing press. Other media-oriented activities include designing a comic strip, working crossword puzzles, and studying the weather via a computer. A 200-seat theater will present kids' programs, demonstrations, storytelling, and other entertainment. An on-site library encourages literacy. Youngsters can work at, or just visit, Pretend City's supermarket, gas station, fire station, and vet's office. Toddlers will have their own enclosed mini-city environment within a mini-city. Like any good city, this one will also have a (real) restaurant and snack bar that offer an array of healthy foods as well as the other kind of foods favored by kids.

Hours: Call for hours.

Admission: Call for admission.

RICHARD NIXON PRESIDENTIAL LIBRARY AND BIRTHPLACE

(714) 993-3393 / www.nixonlibrary.org   *$$*

18001 Yorba Linda Boulevard, Yorba Linda

(Exit Orange Fwy [57] E. on Yorba Linda. Or, exit Riverside Fwy [91] N. on Imperial Hwy [90], L. on Yorba Linda. [TG-740 B4])

This museum/library/grave site/rose garden features nine acres of galleries and gardens, plus the restored birthplace of - here's a quiz - what number president? (The answer is at the end of this description.) Bring a pencil and request a Children's Treasure Hunt to encourage your kids to become more involved with the exhibits in the museum. They'll search for objects like the Presidential Seal, the Woody Station Wagon Nixon used for campaigning, and the piano he practiced on in his younger years.

The theater presents a twenty-eight-minute movie, documenting Richard Nixon's political career. It's a great introduction to who he was, both personally and presidentially. There are several videos and touch screens throughout the museum showing different aspects of his life, including the Kennedy/Nixon debates, footage from his speeches, a tribute to Pat Nixon, and a presidential forum with over 300 questions to choose from. I was surprised at how interested my kids were in all of this.

The exhibit of ten, life-size statues of world leaders (some of whom were very short) is impressive. Touch screens offer comments and biographical summaries on the leaders. Gifts of State are unique treasures to look at. My oldest son, however, thought the pistol from Elvis Presley was the coolest gift. Other pieces of history include a big chunk of the Berlin Wall; the presidential limo that at various times held Johnson, Ford, Carter, and Nixon; a re-creation of the White House's Lincoln Sitting Room; numerous photographs; Nixon's daughters' wedding dresses; and the Watergate Room. In the latter room, excerpts of the "smoking gun" tape can be heard through headsets. A pictorial and descriptive time line of this historic event takes up an entire wall. Tip: At the very least, know how to explain the term "impeach" to your kids. Two-hour, free guided tours are given Monday through Friday for fourth through twelfth graders, with advanced reservations.

Walk outside, through the First Lady's beautiful rose gardens (which look prettier in bloom), to the home where Nixon was born. A tour of the small house only takes fifteen minutes. Richard Nixon was, by the way, our thirty-seventh President.

Hours: Open Mon. - Sat., 10am - 5pm; Sun., 11am - 5pm. Closed Thanksgiving and Christmas.

Admission: $5.95 for adults; $3.95 for seniors and students; $2 for ages 8 - 11; children 7 and under are free. Certain discounts are available through AAA. (See C.E.E. L.A. for membership savings, pg. 261.)

Ages: 6 years and up.

RIPLEY'S BELIEVE IT OR NOT! MUSEUM (Buena Park)   ☼

(714) 522-7045 / www.ripleys.com $$$
7850 Beach Boulevard, Buena Park   ⛪
(Exit Artesia Fwy [91] S. on Beach Blvd. It's just N. of Knott's Berry Farm. [TG-767 H3])

As a reporter, Robert Ripley traveled all over the world visiting over 200 countries and meeting with Kings and Queens, Cannibal Chieftains, and tribesmen to collect interesting, humorous, and bizarre items and facts. There are hundreds of pictures, life-size models, special effects, statues, and assorted odd artifacts throughout the museum. My son, Bryce, summed up the exhibits best by saying, "They're kind of cool and kind of gross."

The "native" section is a little eerie and includes a real shrunken head. The Asian section contains a model of a Chinese man who had two sets of pupils in each eye, and a man who held a real burning candle *in* his head, among others exhibits. (Truth can definitely be stranger than fiction.)

The next section has unusual, rather than weird, displays, such as a sculpture of Marilyn Monroe made from over a quarter of a million "real" dollars (that will make your child's mouth drop open); a miniature violin, which is only five-and-a-half inches long, yet can actually be played; and a complete landscape scene painted on a potato chip. Two of my favorite exhibits here are a rendition of the Last Supper done with 260 pieces of toast (varying from barely toasted to burnt), and the huge portrait made out of dyed clothes dryer lint. How do people think of doing these things, and why?

Videos show amazing feats such as unusual body contortions, swallowing razor blades, and more. (Don't try these activities at home.) Trivia buffs can really study up here. Toward the end of the museum are a few graphic "bloody" exhibits to bypass. Word of warning: If you take an inquisitive child who can't read the explanations, be prepared to read a lot of information and answer a lot of questions!

Hours: Open Mon. - Fri., 11am - 5pm; Sat. - Sun., 10am - 6pm.

Admission: $8.95 for adults; $6.95 for seniors; $5.25 for ages 4 - 11; children 3 and under are free. Certain discounts available through AAA. Combo prices with MOVIELAND WAX MUSEUM, which is just across the street, are $16.90 for adults; $13.95 for seniors; $9.75 for ages 4 - 11.

Ages: 5 years and up.

WESTMINSTER MUSEUM / HISTORICAL PARK ☀

(714) 891-2597

8612 Westminster Boulevard, Westminster

(Exit Garden Grove Fwy [22] S. on Magnolia St., R. on Westminster. It's the gated historic park on the S. side of the street. [TG-828 B1])

Like many other cities who want to preserve their roots for future generations, the city of Westminster has a historical museum. It houses displays from its founding in 1870, to the present day. The museum building, which looks like a converted auditorium, has exhibits, mostly in glass cases, set up in chronological groups. Each grouping has a number that corresponds to an information sheet which explains the memorabilia, thus making for an easy self-guided tour. If you prefer, a docent will explain articles more fully and allow children to touch just a few items - this is a mostly "eyes-on" (as opposed to hands-on) museum. Some of the more interesting items to see include a very small 1897 child's bed; an old stove, washboard, butter churn and other kitchen implements; an antique, wind-up phonograph that still works; old-fashioned ladies' hats and clothing; a collection of dolls from around the world; war posters; and the head of a water buffalo.

Four other buildings grace the park's grounds. A California Crazy, or Shutter Shack, is a little, picture-perfect "store" that looks like a camera. (It was once used for dropping off and picking up film.) A docent will take you through the other buildings. The small, restored McCoy-Hare House was the community's first drugstore as well as a home. The front room contains a pump organ, plus shelves filled with jars of medicine, bolts of fabric, and sundries. The adjacent living room has some period furniture and clothing. Next, walk through the Wayne Family Farmhouse to see the parlor, which holds a 1749 grandfather's clock and a piano; a dining room, with its table set with china; the bedroom that contains a bed (people were much shorter back then!) and a ceramic pot (i.e. port-a-potty); and the kitchen with its stove and old-time telephone. A sink wasn't necessary as water and garbage were simply thrown out the back door to feed the plants and the chickens, respectively. The adjacent large barn contains saddles, large farm equipment, a wooden sugar beet wagon, and tools. Everything is well-labeled. Walk into the part of the barn that has two fire engines and an antique paramedic "van." Kids may climb into the cab of the 1952 white fire engine and "drive" around.

A few grassy areas and a picnic table on the premise complete this park.

Hours: Open to the public the first Sun. of each month, 1pm - 4pm.
School groups may call to book a tour during the week.
Admission: Free
Ages: 5 years and up.

CALIFORNIA MUSEUM OF PHOTOGRAPHY   ☼

(909) 784-FOTO (3686) / www.cmp.ucr.edu   !
3824 Main Street, Riverside
(Exit Riverside Fwy [91] W. on University Ave. and park near Main St. The museum in on the pedestrian walkway. [TG-685 H4])

Expose your kids to the photographic arts at the unique, three-story California Museum of Photography. The main level has rotating photo exhibits, with an emphasis on various photography styles or photographers, such as Ansel Adams. The back area houses a collection of cameras, including working miniature cameras (my boys refer to them as "spy" cameras), old-fashioned cameras with the drape cloth, a Spiderman camera, and one that is part of a radio-controlled car! If you feel like taking up another sport, surf the Internet here.

Take the spiral stairs up to the mezzanine terrace, which is a catwalk-like hallway gallery. The top floor focuses on kids with its small, interactive gallery. Children can use the Zoetropes to draw pictures and spin them around in a drum, creating moving images - early animation! The next exhibit proves that not all shadows are black as the images shadowed here produce a rainbow of colors. Use the next display to visually explain to kids how the aperture of a camera is similar to the pupils in their eyes. Have them look into a light and watch in the mirror as their pupils enlarge or contract, according to the amount of light entering in. The Shadows Room temporarily imprints body outlines on the photosensitive wall when a light flashes. Camera Obscura is a small, dark room with a tiny hole of light that projects an upside down image of the outside scene on its wall. This is a visual demonstration of how a camera lens works. Kids will get a wide angle view of photography at this Museum! Note: Guided school tours are available for 7th through 12th graders.

Hours: The museum is open Tues. - Sun., 11am - 5pm.
Admission: Free
Ages: 3 years and up just to look at things; ages 5 and up will begin to really appreciate it.

GILMAN HISTORIC RANCH AND WAGON MUSEUM ☼
(909) 922-9200 / www.co.riverside.ca.us $
On Wilson Street and 16th Street, Banning
(Exit San Bernardino Fwy [10] N. on 22nd Ave., R. on Sunrise Ave., R on Wilson. [TG-721 J2])

Wagons, ho! Take the dirt road back to the Gilman Historic Ranch and
Wagon Museum, and explore life as it was over 150 years ago. The exhibits are
set up in a chronological order. Over fifteen wagons from yesteryear are inside
the museum including chuck wagons, stagecoaches, and prairie schooners. Some
of the wagons are hitched to large wooden horses. Learn how our pioneer
ancestors traveled across the country, and hear about the hardships that they
endured. Also on exhibit are photographs, saddles, a bedroom set with a ladies'
riding habit and surrey, a blacksmith's shop, and Indian artifacts.

The adjacent ranch has a few historic buildings, shaded picnic grounds, and
hiking trails. Some of the trails go across the creek and to the upper reservoir,
while others go deeper into the canyons. Be on the lookout for rabbits, deer, and
other wildlife.

School groups, with a minimum of twenty students, can take outstanding
and informative two-hour tours, which include a tour of the museum and
grounds, a nature hike, and hands-on activities. The activity choices are creating
a brand (out of a rubber stamp), panning for real gold flakes in sluices set in the
woods (you may keep whatever you pan), and grinding corn meal as part of the
Native American program. Scout groups may use the campfire sites and fire
rings and choose badge-earning activities. Enjoy your day reliving the past!
(Look up Mountain Man Days under the September Calendar section.)

Hours: The museum and grounds are open to the public March through
November on Sat., 10am - 4pm. Tours for school groups are
offered throughout the week by reservation.

Admission: $2 for adults; $1 for children 11 and under. Tour prices range
between $4 - $5.50 per participant, depending on the activities
involved.

Ages: 5 years and up.

HERITAGE HOUSE ☼
(909) 689-1333 / www.ci.riverside.ca.us $
8193 Magnolia Street, Riverside
(Exit Riverside Fwy [91] N. on Adams St., R. on Magnolia St. It's on the N. side of the street. [TG-715 B4])

Heritage House is a beautiful Victorian house built in 1892. It is fully
restored and filled with elaborate, turn-of-the-century furniture. Adding to its
charm is the wrought iron fence in front, the well-kept grounds, the backyard
windmill, and the barn complete with clucking chickens.

Your older children will appreciate the half-hour guided tour as they see and
learn about a different era and style of living. Kids can look through the stereo-
optic, which is an early version of today's View Master™ and view a unique,
old music box. Explaining the Edison phonograph is a lot harder now that record
players are also a thing of the past! The formal oak stairway leads upstairs to the
master bedroom. You'll also find the office/library with trophy animal heads and

a bearskin rug, and the servant's quarters up here. Heritage House graciously displays the life of an affluent citrus grower.

The last Sunday of every month is Living History Day, when the past comes to life in the present. Docents dress up as from the late 1900's owner and have a (pretend) party. Talk to the hostess, maid, cook, and guests to learn about customs from this time period. Call about the House's other special events.

Hours: Open Thurs - Fri., noon - 3pm; Sun., noon - 3:30pm. Closed July through Labor Day, except for regular Sun. hours.

Admission: Suggested donations are $1 for adults; 50¢ for kids.

Ages: 7 years old and up.

JENSEN-ALVARADO RANCH HISTORIC PARK   ☼

(909) 369-6055 / www.co.riverside.ca.us $

4307 Briggs Street, Riverside

(Exit Pomona Fwy [60] S. on Rubidoux Blvd., R. on Mission St., L. on Riverview Dr., L on 42nd St., R. on Briggs St. [TG-685 C3])

This historic site brings the history of the 1880's to life. Costumed docents are on hand to demonstrate farm chores like butter churning, livestock care, and outdoor cooking. The front part of the park is a large, fairly treeless area, with picnic tables. Rusty old farm equipment lines the main pathway. The corral and animal pens, with a few horses, sheep, chicken, and other ranch animals, are located next to the Jensen-Alvarado Ranch House. Behind the house was a winery; it's now a small museum. Inside is period furniture, plus wine-making presses, barrels, and other equipment.

A two-and-a-half-hour school tour includes seeing all of the above, plus hearing a living history presentation; participating in hands-on demonstrations such as making ice cream or tortillas; and maybe, feeding the animals. Tour reservations begin the first week of September; openings are usually filled by the end of the month. Note: Check the September Calendar section for the Cornelius Jenson Birthday Celebration.

Hours: Open September 15 through June 30, Tues. - Fri. for school and large groups only, by reservation. Open to the public September through June on Sat., 10am - 4pm. Closed in the summer and on holidays.

Admission: Sat. admission is $3 for adults; $1.50 for kids 12 and under. School tours are $5 per child; $1 for adults.

Ages: 6 years and up.

JURUPA MOUNTAINS CULTURAL CENTER / EARTH   ☼
SCIENCE MUSEUM

(909) 685-5818 / www.the-jmcc.org   !/$$

7621 Granite Hill Drive, Riverside

(Exit Pomona Fwy [60] S. on Pedley Rd., L. on Mission Blvd., L. on Camino Real, under the freeway. [TG-744 H7])

This center is a rock hound's paradise where kids can either start or add to their rock collection. The main building is a gigantic warehouse with an incredible array of rocks, minerals, dinosaur skeletons, and fossils of all sizes and quality, for display and purchase.

The adjacent Earth Science Museum has outstanding rocks, minerals, fossils, and Indian artifacts displayed according to classification. The large crystals, geodes, carbons, etc., are worthy of a few "oohs" and "aahs." The collection of ancient and modern Native American artifacts includes tools, weapons, a wonderful arrowhead exhibit, an 1100 year-old corn cob, and costumes, in particular, a beautiful fringed and beaded wedding dress. Products, like Borax, are shown in their commercial form next to their original mineral form. Other unique exhibits are the florescent exhibit, which literally highlights rocks with luminescent characteristics; the space exhibit, which includes moon rocks; and the ivory exhibit, which has examples of intricately carved scrimshaw. Note: The outside of the building is comprised of petrified wood and fossils.

If your kids want to take home their own, hand-picked treasures, go Rock Collecting at the Dinosaurs. This drop-in, family field trip starts at the magnetic rock, proceeds to the small petrified wood "forest," and has several other stops along the way, with kid-appropriate explanations about the fascinating plants and rocks you see. (I finally understand that fossil simply means, "something that was once living.") The destination, dinosaur mesa, has eight, giant, non-scary, kid-made dinosaurs. The highlight of the excursion is sorting through the huge spread of rocks and rock chips strewn at the dino's feet, and picking out twelve to take home! Egg cartons are provided. Crystals, jasper, malachite, petrified wood, amethyst, chrysocolla, and sulphur, are some examples of what can be found here. Back at the warehouse/store, you can label each of your treasures, with a geologist's help if needed.

Another great drop-in field trip is Kids' Fossil Shack, geared for ages 6 and up. Kids will learn about fossils, and then clean and prepare one to take home. This is, obviously, a more sit-down activity, but another great way to combine hands-on education and fun.

The Jurupa Cultural Center offers a wide variety of terrific school group and scout programs, such as gold panning, a tour of the Crestmore Mine, lapidary workshops, creating an Indian pictograph, archaeology, and lots more. The Center also comes to schools for on-site classes. Call for information on their periodic Pow Wows and Renaissance Fairs, as well as week-long classes of Nature School in the summer that range from hiking and survival, to dinosaurs and fossils.

Hours: The warehouse store is open Tues. - Sat., 8am - 4:30pm. The Earth Science Museum is open Tues. - Sat., 8am - 4pm. Both are closed on national holidays. Rock Collecting at the Dinosaurs is held every Sat., 9am - 10:30am and 1:30pm - 3pm, weather permitting. During inclement weather, inquire about other Sat. outings. Kids' Fossil Shack is held Sat., 10:30am - noon. Once-a-month public classes include worm composting, gold panning, Indian pictograph, Jr. lapidary, and more.

Admission: Entrance to the warehouse store is free. The Earth Science
Museum admission is by donation. Rock Collecting at the
Dinosaurs and Kids' Fossil Shack are $5 per person, each event.
No reservations are needed. School tours start at $5 per
participant. Call for specific information and a class schedule.
Ages: 3 years and up.

MARCH FIELD AIR MUSEUM
(909) 697-6600 / www.marchfield.org
16222 Interstate 215, March Air Force Base
(Exit Moreno Valley Fwy [215] E. on Van Buren Blvd. [TG-747 B3])

A P-40 Warhawk stands guard at the entrance of March Field Museum,
which is the proud home to one of the most extensive collection of military
aircraft and aviation artifacts in the United States. The walkway is lined with
airplane engines, plus a jeep that kids can get into and "drive" around. Outside,
over fifty historic airplanes are on display, from the smaller F-84 to the massive
B-52 to the sleek Blackbird SR-71. Kids are welcome to look at the planes, but
not to climb in them.

Inside, the huge hanger displays everything possible pertaining to the Air
Force. Airplanes, such as a biplane trainer, have landed in here, as have exhibits
of flight uniforms, a "war dog" memorial, photographs, model planes, engines,
medals, weapons, and equipment from both World Wars, Korea, Viet Nam, the
Cold War, and Desert Storm. This museum defines the word "comprehensive!"

The March Field Story and other informative films are available for viewing
with prior notice. A three-minute jolting simulator ride can be taken for $5.
Although the only touchable activity for kids is to strap themselves into a flight
training chair, they really enjoy the museum, especially your pilots-in-training.

Hours: Open daily 10am - 4pm. Closed New Year's Day, Easter,
Thanksgiving, and Christmas.
Admission: $5 for adults; $2 for ages 5 - 12; children 4 and under are free.
Ages: 3 years and up.

MISSION INN / MISSION INN MUSEUM
(909) 784-0300 - Inn; (909) 788-9556 - museum / www.missioninn.com
3649 Mission Inn Avenue, Riverside
(Exit Riverside Fwy [91] W. on University Ave., R. on Orange St., L. on Mission Inn Ave. Going S.
on 91, exit at University, go W. on Mission Inn. [TG-685 H4])

Is it a European castle? Not quite, but this elegant, old, sprawling Inn is
beautiful to look at and tour. The hour-and-a-half tour shows much of its eclectic
architecture and furnishings. Mediterranean style, emphasized in the colorful
tiles, spiral columns, and bells, is incorporated with an Oriental influence, such
as a hotel kitchen chimney in the shape of a pagoda, plus other unique touches.
Only through the tour can you see all four wings of the hotel with highlights
including the gilded eighteenth-century altar in the wedding chapel; the music
room; the Court of Birds (there are no actual birds still here, but the stories about
them give wings to the imagination); the Taft Chair, that seats up to five kids at
one time; and the open-air, five-story spiral staircase in the rotunda, which is

quite grand looking. If your kids are interested in architecture or hearing about
the Inn's history, they will enjoy the tour. If not, at least take a quick walk
through the grounds.

The small museum is located on the pedestrian walkway, next to the Inn's
gift shop. Frank Miller, the Inn's builder, had an international collection that
reflected his tastes. Housed in the museum are a scale model of a pagoda,
encased figurines, artifacts, and photos. The most appealing exhibit to kids has
old-time barber shop chairs (not to sit in) with mirrors and hair cutting
instruments. A tape of old-timers reminiscing adds to the display's atmosphere.

Hours: The Inn is a functioning Inn so it is open daily. Tours are given
Mon. - Fri. at 10:30am and 2pm; Sat. - Sun., 10am - 3pm,
approximately every hour. The Museum is open daily 9:30am -
4pm.

Admission: You can walk around the hotel at no charge. The tour costs $8
for adults; children 12 and under are free. The Museum is $2 per
person.

Ages: 8 years and up.

ORANGE EMPIRE RAILWAY MUSEUM
(909) 657-2605 / www.oerm.mus.ca.us
2201 S. 'A' Street, Perris

See ORANGE EMPIRE RAILWAY MUSEUM, under the Transportation
section, for details.

RIVERSIDE MUNICIPAL MUSEUM
(909) 826-5273 - museum; (909) 788-2747 - educational tours /
www.ci.riverside.ca.us
3580 Mission Inn Avenue, Riverside
(Going N. on Riverside Fwy [91], exit W. on University Ave., R. on Orange St, L. on Mission Inn.
Going S. on 91, exit at University, go W. on Mission Inn. [TG-685 H4])

This museum contains a wealth of information and fun for both kids and
adults. The natural history exhibits are a natural place to start. Push a button and
the taxidermied mountain lion crouched on the ledge "roars." Other stuffed
animals are also posed in animated positions. For instance, a baby bobcat is
batting at the air and a skunk is doing a handstand on its front paws. The geology
area has a nice display of rocks and minerals, plus a section on earthquakes. The
paleontology exhibits have a saber-tooth cat skeleton, some fossilized elephant
tusks (they are huge!), and a few dinosaur bones. The anthropology section has
displays of Indian clothing, musical instruments, hunting weapons, and a few
dioramas. The local history display features missions, cowboys, tools, and guns,
plus machinery and crate labels of citrus growers.

The upstairs sometimes has rotating displays. We saw exhibits that
emphasized Mexican heritage, with ethnic costumes, and artifacts. The hallway
is lined with small botanical dioramas. A favorite room is the small Nature
Laboratory. Kids can inspect shells and bugs under a microscope. They can also
dissect owl pellets. There is a small sea display with preserved sea horses, and a
few live reptiles in here, too - snakes, lizards, and turtles. The entire museum

rates high on kid-interest! In a program called "First Sunday," free arts and crafts activities are offered on the first Sunday of each month, October through May, 1pm to 4pm. Other museums in Riverside offer free admission and/or arts and crafts on this Sunday, too.

Hours: The museum is open Tues. - Fri., 9am - 5pm; Sat., 10am - 5pm; Sun., 11pm - 5pm. The Nature Laboratory is open Wed., 2pm - 4:30pm; Sat., 1pm - 3pm.

Admission: Free

Ages: 2 years and up.

TEMECULA VALLEY MUSEUM / TEMECULA - OLD ☼ TOWN

(909) 694-6480 / www.ci.temecula.ca.us   !/$

28314 Mercedes Street, Temecula

(Exit Temecula Valley Fwy [15] W. on Rancho California Rd., L. on Front St. to Old Town, or L. on Moreno St. to the museum at Sam Hicks Park. [TG-958 H7])

Mosey on over to Old Town Temecula and enjoy an hour or so shopping along Main Street. This western strip of town looks and feels authentic, right down to its wooden sidewalks. The over 100 antique and specialty shops offer many unique gift items for sale, making it an alluring place to shop, even with children.

The museum is located on a corner park - Sam Hicks Park - that has a small playground, and a large rock inscribed with the names of pioneers. The small museum is an interesting glimpse into Temecula's past. On the first floor a few tools, household goods, guns, saddles, and army equipment portray life on the local ranches and frontier towns. There are also some Native American artifacts, plus memorabilia from Erle Stanley Gardner, the author of the Perry Mason stories and a one-time resident of Temecula. At the more interactive second-floor room, kids can become a part of the Old West mostly by dressing up in vintage clothing and sitting on a pretend horse (bring your camera!), plus looking at facades depicting a frontier town.

Hours: Open Tues. - Sat., 10am - 5pm; Sun., 1pm - 5pm. Closed Mon. and holidays. Main Street shopping is usually open daily 10am - 6pm.

Admission: By donation

Ages: 5 years and up.

WORLD MUSEUM OF NATURAL HISTORY ☼

(909) 785-2209 / www.lasierra.edu/wmnh   !

4700 Pierce Street in Cossentine Hall on the campus of La Sierra University, Riverside

(Exit Riverside Fwy [91] S.W. on Magnolia, R. on Pierce. Go L. on Campus Dr. at the intersection of Pierce St. and Sierra Vista Ave. Park at the end of Campus Dr. in parking lot F on weekends. If you've made arrangements for a special tour, ask the curator to get a parking permit for you. [TG-714 B7])

This quality museum is tremendous in its comprehensive scope of minerals, and freeze-dried animals. Full-grown and young animals are displayed according to species. The old and new world primates - or monkeys, gorillas, and chimps - all look so life like! The size and variety of the Crocodiles of the World is impressive. We had not heard of at least half the ones featured here. The Indian Gavial is especially unique with a snout that resembles a long, thin saw blade. The numerous types of turtles were similarly astounding. They range from the very small to the gigantic alligator snapping turtle. Snakes of the World boasts another record-breaking variety, ranging from boas, pythons, and common garters, to venomous snakes and even a two-headed snake. Other reptiles, including a huge Komodo dragon, are also on display. Birds from all over the world are represented here, such as pelicans, flamingoes, penguins, an imperial eagle, and a blue-hued hunting green magpie. Some of the more unusual animals on display are the flat-headed cat (which, not surprisingly, has a very flat head), bats (one is just the size of a pin), an armadillo, a kangaroo, and an Indian rhino.

An outstanding collection of rocks and minerals are grouped, in one section, according to color. These include large specimens of amethyst, malachite, etc. Other groupings include meteorites, fluorescent minerals, geodes, and huge slabs of petrified wood. There is also a large display of sphere balls or, in kidspeak, "cool-looking bowling balls." Part of this display shows the progression of a chunk of raw rock to a cube and then to the finished, sphere product. A fine display of Indian artifacts, such as arrowheads and headdresses, is also noteworthy. The World Museum of Natural History is a gem of a place!

Hours: Open Sat., 2pm - 5pm, or weekdays by appointment. Tour groups are welcome - Wed. is the best day.

Admission: Free; donations gladly accepted.

Ages: 2 years and up.

THE AIR MUSEUM "PLANES OF FAME"   ☼
(909) 597-3722 / www.planesoffame.org $$$
7000 Merrill Avenue, Chino
(Exit Riverside Fwy [91] N. on the 71, N. on Euclid [or the 83]. Exit Hwy 83 R. on Merrill Ave., R. on Cal Aero Dr., past the National Air Race Museum. [TG-682 D5])

For some *plane* old fun, come see over 100 vintage aircraft (some of which are flyable) that have landed here, including one of the only air-worthy Japanese Zeros in the world. The parking lot boasts of Lucky Lady II, a Boeing B-50A who starred in the first non-stop flight around the world. Many of the planes are touchable without any formal barriers to keep visitors away, making it a comfortable place to take children.

Planes, parts of planes and helicopters, and military vehicles are stationed outside the north hanger. The hanger is dedicated to Japanese and German aircraft from WWII, some of which are "flying" around overhead, while others are grounded. My boys were drawn to the "Wild Grinning Face of the Green Dragon Unit" - a nose of a plane that has machine guns and is decorated with a fire-breathing dragon painted on its side. The "Betty" bomber is displayed looking like it has crashed landed in a jungle, complete with an overgrowth of plants, plus dirt and a background mural. This building also displays airplane engines and small models of Japanese army aircraft, plus news clippings regarding Pearl Harbor.

The two south hangers hold more colorful and historic aircraft. Another hanger is part restoration work area, part model aircraft display, and part hands-on Aviation Center. Visitors are welcome to watch the restoration, but may not touch anything. The model aircraft collection is one of the largest we've ever seen in one place. Kids who are aeronautically inclined will be in their element at the Aviation Center. They can climb into three experimental planes and play pilot; practice their mechanical skills by "using" rivet guns, drills, and control sticks; and take apart (and put together) parts of an engine. This hanger also displays gun turrets, instrument panels, cutaways of aircraft engine, and uniforms.

A B-17 Bomber is available on weekends only to walk through or sit down in and "fly". The first Saturday of every month features a particular plane, or type of planes, and a seminar at 10am with panelists or veteran pilots who were directly associated with that plane. Whenever possible, this event concludes with a flight demonstration.

It's a short drive around the corner to the Fighter Jets Museum and Space Exhibit. The Bell X-1 was used in the movie, *The Right Stuff* and was the first plane to break the sound barrier. Other planes here, including the red "Stinger" Formula One Racer, have descriptions that are equally informative, though some are a bit technical. The Space Exhibit has a full-size model of the Apollo 13 capsule, a test pilot's suit, and a Mercury spacecraft mock up, along with posters, photos of astronauts, and rockets blasting off - all underneath a ceiling painted to look like a starry, nighttime sky.

The Air Museum is in the Chino airport, so kids can experience the thrill of seeing planes take off and land. Don't miss the annual Air Show in October! If you get hungry, pilot your way to Flo's Cafe, which is also on airport grounds.

Hours: Open daily 9am - 5pm. Closed Thanksgiving and Christmas.

Admission: $8.95 for adults; $1.95 for ages 5 - 11; children 4 and under are free.

Ages: 3 years and up.

A SPECIAL PLACE   ☼
(909) 881-1201 $
1003 E. Highland Avenue, San Bernardino   ⚒
(Exit Hwy 30 S. on Waterman, L. on Highland, L. on Harrison St. to park. [TG-577 A3])

A Special Place is ideal for younger children who delight in hands-on activities. (That should include all of the younger population!) Outside, a small covered cement patio enhances disability awareness via a wheelchair maze (those corners are tough!); a swing for kids in wheelchairs; braces to try on; crutches to use; and even prostheses to touch. Your children will get a feel for what it's like to be mobile in different ways. Also out here is western gear, such as boots, cowboy hats, and a few saddles so kids can ride the range.

Inside, two rooms are divided into sections. The drama area has face painting and costumes. It's a hot time in the old town when kids dress up as firefighters and climb up (and down) the fireman pole. The schoolroom area has a few old-fashioned school desks and a thirteen star flag. (See if your kids notice this and know how many stars are on our flag today.) There is also a working traffic light here to play the game Red Light, Green Light.

Along the back wall is a wonderful aquatic mural, plus fish and turtle aquariums, and a cage of birds. Kids can turn a handle at an Edison display to try to generate enough electricity to power a light bulb. At the puppet theater, children make the puppets come to life.

Another section is set-up like a mini-Kaiser clinic, with an X-ray machine, infant incubator, and blood pressure machine. Prepare your child to go to the doctor or to become one! The Shadow Room is always fun. When the light flashes, kids love posing to leave a temporary shadow of their body on the photo-sensitive wall.

The museum is small, but it has a great variety of interactive things to do, making it a special place, indeed.

Hours: Open Mon., 1pm - 5pm; Tues. - Fri., 9am - 5pm; Sat., 11am - 3pm. Call for extended summer hours.

Admission: $2 per person; children 2 and under are free. The first Sat. of each month is free for grandparents who are accompanied by a paying child.

Ages: 6 months to 10 years.

CHINO YOUTH MUSEUM

(909) 464-0499 / www.chinoyouthmuseum.org

13191 6th Street, Chino

(Exit the Pomona Fwy [60] S. on Central Ave., R. on D St., R. on 6th St. [TG-641 G7])

This children's museum has a main corridor with several small rooms that branch off from it. Each room is themed, with a mural or building facade and a prop or two, around a particular function or career choice found within city limits. For instance, kids can sit behind a desk and give a pretend newscast (and watch themselves on a screen); try on firemen clothes, slide down a pole, and sit on a real police motorcycle as they become civil servants for a day; "shop" in a grocery store; work at a bank behind the teller's window; use a judge's costume and gavel to send little criminals to the little jail; and even crawl into a tent at a make believe campsite/park. Ah, to be young again and just have to pretend at working a job! The museum also has a room just for arts and crafts.

Hours: Open Wed., 8am - noon; Thurs. - Fri., 2pm - 6pm; Sat., 10am - 4pm.

Admission: $4 for adults; $2 for seniors and ages 2 - 18.

Ages: 2 - 8 years.

EDWARD-DEAN MUSEUM AND GARDENS

(909) 845-2626 / www.edward-deanmuseum.org

9401 Oak Glen Road, Cherry Valley

(Exit Moreno Valley Fwy [60] N. on Beaumont Ave., which turns into Oak Glen Rd. Look for signs to the museum. [TG-690 J2])

This elegant, medium-sized fine arts museum seems almost out of place in the rural town of Cherry Valley. It is situated on beautifully landscaped grounds with formal gardens, accompanied by grassy lawns and a small pond with lily pads. Just outside the museum is a fountain surrounded by a rose garden.

The two-story museum has several galleries that specialize in art from the late 18th to early 19th centuries. The left wing gallery has rotating exhibits. We saw "Art in Miniature", which showcased buildings, artwork, and scenes in miniature. The permanent upstairs galleries are situated in a home-like atmosphere. They feature furniture, china, a Buddha exhibit in a room with ornate wood wall carvings, silk tapestries, portraits, a beautiful oriental robe, statues, and a music room with a piano and a harp. Downstairs is a small reference library, plus a wing displaying a pope's wooden traveling desk and few other items. The docents we encountered were friendly and readily explained many of the exhibit pieces. Note that the museum is just down the road from all the fun at OAK GLEN. (See the Edible Adventures section.)

Hours: Open Fri. - Sun., 10am - 5pm. Open during the week for hour-long school tours.

Admission: $3 for adults; $2 for seniors and students; children 12 and under are free.

Ages: 7 years and up.

GRABER OLIVE HOUSE

(909) 983-1761 / www.graberolives.com

315 E. Fourth Street, Ontario

(Going E. on San Bernardino Fwy [10], exit S. on Euclid, L. on Fourth St. Going W. on 10, exit W. on 4th St. [TG-602 C6])

This is an unusual pit stop for kids. On the grounds are a small museum, an olive processing plant, a gift shop, and the owner's house, whose Victorian-style living room doubles as a tea room and etiquette classroom for kids and adults. The one-room museum shows a pictorial history of olive processing. It also has an eclectic mix of antiques such as a big wooden olive grader, a Singer sewing machine, a sausage stuffer, and more.

Take a short tour around the working olive plant. The "on-season" is mid-October through December, when the machinery and workers are in full production. This, then, is the best time to take a tour. Walk into the grading room, where olives are sorted by size and quality, and peer into the enormous olive vats. The boiler room, where olives are sterilized, the canning machine, and the labeling machine are all interesting to look at. A ten-minute video, that shows the history of the packing plant, is also available to watch.

The gift shop is very classy with etiquette videos, stationery, delicious jams, and elegant candies. (The chocolate-covered cherries are to die for!) Kids can sample a Graber olive, which might mean more to them after a tour. Family tours are given whenever someone is available. Twenty-minute school or scout tours are given only by the teacher or leader, respectively, and only after he/she has first taken a guided tour.

Hours: Open Mon. - Sat., 9am - 5:30pm; Sun., 9:30am - 6pm.

Admission: Free

Ages: 5 years and up.

JOHN RAINS HOUSE - CASA DE RANCHO CUCAMONGA

(909) 989-4970 / www.co.san-bernardino.ca.us

8810 Hemlock Street, Rancho Cucamonga

(Exit San Bernardino Fwy [10] N. on Vineyard. It's 2 blocks N. of Foothills Blvd., on the corner of Vineyard and Hemlock, in a residential area. [TG-602 G1])

Built with bricks in 1860, this restored rancho residence is a lovely example of a house from this era. Tours are given through the historical home to see period furniture in the bedrooms, living rooms, and other rooms, and around the beautiful grounds, complete with green lawns, trees, picnic tables in the backyard, and the central courtyard. Docents recount stories about the people who once lived here. Their lives were like soap operas, complete with affairs, murders, buried treasure, and more sordid happenings - kids love this! (And they are learning history.) Ask about school and group tours and the special events that the Rancho hosts, such as Old Rancho Days. Note: The house is exquisitely decked out at Christmas time.

Hours: Open Wed. - Sat., 10am - 5pm; Sun., 1pm - 5pm.

Admission: $1 per person.

Ages: 6 years and up.

KIMBERLY CREST HOUSE AND GARDENS

(909) 792-2111 / www.kimberlycrest.com

1325 Prospect Drive, Redlands

(Exit San Bernardino Fwy [10] S.W. on Ford St., R. on Redlands Blvd., L. on Highland Ave., L. on Prospect. [TG-648 D3])

This three-story, rather large, light lime green and gray French chateau, with yellow trim, was originally built in 1897. The turrets add to its eye-catching appeal, as do the formal Italian-style gardens and grounds, complete with lotus blossoms and koi in the lily ponds, plus the gazebo and surrounding orange groves.

The period (and replicated) furniture and decor is as grand as the outside with gilt furniture and silk damask wall coverings. Tour the French parlor, library, living room, dining rooms (set with crystal), bedrooms, and other beautifully accessorized rooms. The gift shop is located in a one-hundred year old carriage house.

The Crest house is nestled in one end of the lush, Prospect Park. After your tour, enjoy a walk on the dirt trails through the park.

Hours: Tours are given Thurs. - Sun., 1pm - 4pm, with the last tour at 3:30pm. Closed holidays and August. The surrounding park is open daily 9am - 5pm.

Admission: $5 for adults; $4 for students; children 11 and under are free.

Ages: 6 years and up.

LINCOLN MEMORIAL SHRINE

(909) 798-7636 - Shrine; (909) 798-7632 - Heritage Room at the Smiley Public Library / www.akspl.org/lincoln.html

125 W. Vine Street, Redlands

(Exit San Bernardino Fwy [10] S. on Hwy 38 [or Orange St.], R. on Citrus Ave., L. on Eureka St.
[TG-608 B7])

"Fourscore and seven years ago. . ." begins the Gettysburg Address. If your
older children are studying our revered sixteenth president, but can't make it to
Washington D.C., bring them to the Lincoln Memorial Shrine in Redlands. The
central, octagon-shaped building also has two wings, all devoted to Lincoln
memorabilia. The building contains research books; surgical instruments; letters
and documents written from and about Lincoln, Lee, and Stonewall Jackson;
Civil War photographs; bullets found on battlefields; officers' uniforms; medals;
and a lifemask (i.e. an exact likeness of a person via a mold) and handcast of
Abraham Lincoln. Mementos from his assassination include his cuff links, a
strand of his hair, mourning bands, and the wreath that laid on his casket. The
shrine also displays other Civil War artifacts such as swords, an 1863
Springfield rifle, hardtack, documents, models, and pictures of Abraham
Lincoln, Robert E. Lee, and Ulysses S. Grant.

Come view the materials here on your own. Better yet, take a guided tour
and benefit from knowledgeable docents who explain the exhibits in more detail.
Exhibits at the memorial rotate because the small shrine cannot contain the
3,000-plus manuscripts and other items in the archives. The outside of the
building is inscribed with excerpts from Lincoln's inaugural addresses and
various other speeches.

The shrine is located behind the Smiley Public Library, with an expanse of
green lawn in between. The multi-level library, established in 1894, is an
architectural and book-lovers delight.

Hours: Open Tues. - Sun., 1pm - 5pm. Closed holidays except for
               Lincoln's birthday. Small group tours can be arranged for
               morning hours.
Admission: Free
Ages: 7 years and up.

MOJAVE RIVER VALLEY MUSEUM / DANA PARK

(760) 256-5452 - museum; (760) 256-5661 - park / mvm.admenu.com
270 E. Virginia Way, Barstow
(Exit Mojave Fwy [15] N. on Barstow Rd. [TG-3679 H4])

This little museum is full of interesting artifacts and displays. My boys liked
hearing the story and seeing the bones of a headless horseman, found astride his
horse. The rock and minerals on display include nice specimens of arrowheads,
quartz, calate, and black and gold forms of chalocopyrite, plus fluorescent
minerals that glow neon colors under black light. Other glass-encased exhibits
are an eclectic mixture, such as lanterns, irons, rug beaters, pottery, clothing, a
collection of glass insulators used by telegraph companies, and more. Kids can
try their hand at grinding corn with stone mortar and pestle. They can also touch
various animal skins, a turtle shell, bones, pinecones, rocks, and cotton. Short
nature films are available to watch upon request. Call to arrange a field trip, and
students will not only learn a lot about local history, but they can pan for real
gold (and keep it!). Classes are usually taught by Mr. Walker, an archaeology
instructor at the college. The outside of the museum has large mining equipment

around its perimeters - ore carts, picks, and other tools. Across the street is the small Centennial Park, which is actually an extension of the museum. It has a caboose, an army tank, and a mining display, which are representative of the three industries that helped formed Barstow.

Dana Park is just across Virginia Way. It has picnic shelters, some grassy hills to roll down, a playground, and a community swimming pool that is open seasonally.

Hours: The museum is open daily 11am - 4pm.
Admission: Free to the museum, though donations are appreciated. The pool is $2 per person, per session.
Ages: 3 years and up.

MOUSLEY MUSEUM OF NATURAL HISTORY ☼
(909) 790-3163 / www.co.san-bernardino.ca.us $
35308 Panorama Drive, Yucaipa
(Exit San Bernardino Fwy [10] N.E. on Yucaipa Blvd., L. on Bryant, R. on Panorama. [TG-650 A1])

This museum contains an extensive mineral collection, a fluorescent mineral display (which shows cool neon colors under black light), rocks and fossils from around the world, and the largest collection of shells on display in the United States. A geologist staff person is usually on hand to explain how the minerals and rocks are used today, their names, and more. Kids who don't know a lot about shells and rocks get excited about seeing such a variety of colors, shapes, etc. A quarter-mile dirt nature trail is in back of the museum. School groups are welcome.

Hours: Open Wed. - Fri. and Sun., 1pm - 5pm; Sat., 9am - 5pm.
Admission: $1 per person
Ages: 5 years and up.

MUSEUM OF HISTORY AND ART, ONTARIO ☼
(909) 983-3198 / www.ci.ontario.ca.us   !
225 S. Euclid Avenue, Ontario
(Exit the San Bernardino Fwy [10] S. on Euclid, L. on Transit. It's on the corner. [TG-642 C1])

The Museum of History and Art captures the flavor of historic Ontario. The hallway leading toward the history section is lined with local school children's art work. The small museum's history galleries feature artifacts from citrus groves and industry, such as a replica of a Graber olive grader and a citrus smudge pot, which was used to warm trees. Other displays, mostly behind glass, include an old-fashioned kitchen exhibit; an iron collection; a section of photographs, uniforms, and information on WWII; and old machinery such as a typewriter and switchboard.

The art rooms contain changing exhibits of local and regional artists, as well as student work. Set in a Mediterranean-style building with a big fountain out front, the museum is a pleasant way to learn more about local roots.

Hours: The museum is open Wed. - Sun., noon - 4pm.
Admission: Free
Ages: 6 years and up.

OAK GLEN SCHOOL HOUSE MUSEUM

(909) 797-1691 $

11911 S. Oak Glen Road, Yucaipa

(Exit 10 Fwy N. on Beaumont Ave., which turns into Oak Glen Rd. It's N. of Riley's Cabin. [TG-651 C2])

This small, one-room school house museum was originally built in 1927. The stone exterior encompasses a room containing old-fashioned desks facing a black board, a pot-belly stove, a phonograph, a stereoscope, newspaper clippings, apple crate labels from ranches, and old pictures. Tours are offered to the public upon request. School groups can take the basic fifteen-minute tour and then add on additional activities, such as making a candle by rolling up a sheet of beeswax, dipping pen in an ink bottle and writing, and taking a short nature walk. Teachers are welcome to bring their own curriculum to teach, too.

The adjacent, picturesque small park has grassy lawns, shade trees, picnic tables, and some play equipment.

Hours: Open to the public Sat., noon - 4pm; Sun., 1pm - 5pm, weather permitting. Call to make a reservation for a school tour.

Admission: $1 for adults; 50¢ for children. School tours cost 50¢ per student, per activity.

Ages: 4 years old and up.

ROY ROGERS - DALE EVANS MUSEUM

(760) 243-4547 / www.royrogers.com $$$

15650 Seneca Road, Victorville

(Exit Mojave Fwy [15] W. on Roy Rogers Dr. and circle 'round to the museum. You'll see it from the freeway. [TG-4296 B7])

The Roy Rogers - Dale Evans Museum is easy to spot from the freeway. It looks like a fort, and has a larger-than-life statue of Roy's horse, Trigger, out front. Step into the museum and step back to a simpler time when cowboys were heroes and family morals were admired and desired. Although you, and certainly your kids, might be too young to remember when Roy Rogers and Dale Evans were household names and he reigned as "King of the Cowboys," this museum is fascinating to all ages. It is an extensive collection of personal memorabilia that is incredibly well-displayed and delightful to explore.

Roy saved a lifetime of things and turned them into a museum. Family albums and celebrity photos abound. There are also many cases of trinkets, letters, and other items sent by fans, including lots of signed sports paraphernalia. After the Roy Rogers Show went on the air, Roy's likeness began appearing on everything from cereal boxes to comic books to lunch boxes. He endorsed almost every kind of child's toy imaginable including cap guns, lassos, rings, hobby horses, and more. A sample of these items are on display here. My middle son (and cowboy "wannabe") loved seeing all the guitars, glitzy saddles, spurs, Western statues, numerous pairs of boots, and the fancy western duds that both Roy and Dale wore. At the kiddie corral, three sturdy wooden horses and a blue sky backdrop make for a great "ride 'em, cowboy!" photo opportunity.

One of the most popular displays features the taxidermied Trigger (Roy's beloved horse), Buttermilk (Dale's horse), and Bullet (the "wonder dog"). There are many more stuffed animals on exhibit including an exotic black Russian Boar, a mountain lion, an albino skunk, and an albino raccoon. Roy was a game hunter, at a time when it was politically acceptable. His collection also includes mounted baboons, a zebra leg stool, a monkey rug, and an elephant feet foot stool. He also amassed a number of guns, pistols, and rifles - some with extravagantly decorated handles.

We enjoyed the Story Theater which shows a film, several times a day, of the family sharing memories of growing up with Roy and Dale, plus movie clips. It's like watching a professional (and entertaining) home video. The back room contains vehicles that are special to the family, including a horse-drawn carriage and a car with show guns mounted on the hood. The outside center courtyard has more displays of large game, such as an elephant's head and a polar bear, as well as Native American displays. The latter includes feather headdresses, beaded clothing, rugs, and more. I'll close this entry with an inevitable, "Happy trails to you."

    Hours: Open daily 9am - 5pm. Closed Easter, Thanksgiving, and Christmas.

Admission: $8 for adults; $7 for seniors and ages 13 - 16; $5 for ages 6 - 12; children 5 and under are free.

    Ages: 3 years and up.

SAN BERNARDINO COUNTY MUSEUM

(909) 307-2669 / www.sbcountymuseum.org

2024 Orange Tree Lane, Redlands

(Exit San Bernardino Fwy [10] N. on California St., R. on Orange Tree Ln. [TG-607 G6])

Spend a day at the incredible San Bernardino County Museum where the hallway exhibits are just as fine as the ones in the exhibit rooms! The distinctive half-dome attached to the main building is the Fisk Gallery of Fine Arts. The Hall of History and Anthropology is down the ramp from the main level. Here you'll find a covered wagon and a Wells Fargo stage coach, along with period clothing. The Anthropology section has Indian artifacts, such as arrowheads and painted rock art.

The hallway going to the Upper Level is lined with exhibits such as old-time medicine bottles, fossilized mammoth tusks, the bones of a ground sloth, and a saber-tooth cat skull. The other side of the hallway is a wonderful prelude to the Upper Level, displaying taxidermied birds and bird eggs. The eggs vary in size from very large elephant bird eggs to very small hummingbird eggs.

If your kids show any interest in ornithology, the study of birds (calling each other bird brain doesn't count), they will be fascinated by the entire Upper Level. The Hall of Water Birds takes you on flights of fancy, although with taxidermied birds you won't get very far. See if your kids can correctly match the birds to their eggs, which are also on display throughout the room. The next wing, Hall of Land Birds, displays birds and eggs according to regional habitat. Look for the "awww, so cute" hatchling exhibit. I have never seen so many birds flocked together.

A large stuffed California Condor guards the entrance to the Upper Dome Gallery. This gallery has rotating exhibits of art work.

An absolutely dazzling display of rocks, minerals, and gemstones line the hallway toward the Lower Level. The doors in the hallway lead out to the Exploration Station, but we'll come back to that. Continue down the ramp into the Hall of Mammals. The walls in here are lined with fossilized animal bones, horns, and teeth. Bug collectors will be bug-eyed at the comprehensive collection of mounted insects of all sizes, shapes, and colors. Also along the walls are dioramas of smaller taxidermied animals and reptiles, such as spotted skunks, possums, and turtles. The Hall of Mammals is unique in that it also has exhibits of larger taxidermied animals, such as a polar bear, an Alaskan brown bear, a mountain lion, a bison, and a gigantic moose. My kids were really impressed by the sheer size of some of the animals.

Outside, between the main building and the Exploration Station, is a patio area designed just for kids. (Check out the F-105 jet just around the corner.) The displays include a mining car carrying "explosives" on track toward a tunnel and a full-size caboose and steam engine that are sometimes open to climb aboard. Picnic tables are here for snack attacks.

The Exploration Station is a learning center that has small, live mammals, such as bunnies and bats, and reptiles, such as iguanas, a boa, and other snakes. Kids can touch fossils, animal furs, and casts of bones and dinosaur fossils. The room also has aquariums.

The Special Exhibit Hall has terrific, changing, usually interactive displays. A past exhibit was rather batty - Masters of the Night - The True Story of Bats. It included entering through the portals of a gothic castle, seeing videos, touching models of bats, and literally hanging around in a bat cave.

Family Activity Day is usually offered once a month and designed to educate the entire family about a particular topic or animal in a fun, hands-on manner. The programs are free with general museum admission. Ask about special events, classes, and tours.

Hours: Open Tues. - Sun., 9am - 5pm. The Exploration Station is open Tues. - Thurs., 10am - 1pm; Fri., 10am - 4pm; Sat. - Sun., 1pm - 4pm. The museum is closed Mon., New Year's Day, Thanksgiving, and Christmas.

Admission: $4 for adults; $3 for seniors and students; $2 for ages 5 - 12; children 4 and under are free.

Ages: 2 years and up.

VICTOR VALLEY MUSEUM

(760) 240-2111 / www.vvmuseum.com

11873 Apple Valley Road, Apple Valley

(Exit Mojave Fwy [I-15 to Hesperia] E. on Bear Valley Rd., go 7 miles, turn R. on Apple Valley Rd. [TG-4387 C6])

This classy, off-the-beaten-track museum is like an oasis in the desert. A landmark two-ton giant tortoise sculpture resides outside the building. The lobby contains a doctor's buggy circa 1890's, a stuffed grizzly bear, and a replica of the Old Woman meteorite. An art wing with rotating exhibits of local and regional art is to the left of the lobby.

The museum contains taxidermied animals in life-like poses such as a cougar, buffalo, muskox, and bear. A wall of mounted heads showcases a pronghorn, buffalo, moose, caribou, and goat. The "Old West" section contains twelve saddles, horseshoes, rope, bronze cowboy sculptures, a stagecoach, farm tools, and great-great-grandma's kitchen and household utensils, such as a butter churn and candle mold. An adjacent workroom contains drills, wrenches, hammers, axes, saws, and more, hanging on the wall. A living room section contains a phonograph, pump organ, radio, an early TV, and various other items. There are also collections of telephones, cameras, pictures (people back then didn't smile because they had to hold absolutely still for an entire minute or so), and real monies from the Bible (i.e. thirty pieces of silver and a widow's mite). The Native American section features baskets, arrowheads, and more.

A children's room, the Imagination Station, features hands-on fun such as an old-fashioned switchboard, a stone mortar and pestle, face painting, panning for gold, a small school "room", some games and puzzles, and a hospital room with an X-Ray machine, an I.V. set-up and clothing for doctors and patients. Other dress-up clothing in the Station includes policemen and firemen uniforms, sailor outfits, and lots more. The room also contains air plane models, dolls and toys from around the world, snake skins, and taxidermied snakes and gila monsters.

A self-guided tour is good, but a guided tour, as usual, is much better. We learned about heros, such as Indians - how they made and did so much with seemingly so little - and Earl Bascom, a local rodeo star. As we inspected Native American baskets we learned how the weaving was so tightly done that the baskets could hold water. And we gained more knowledge about the rocks, minerals, and numerous other artifacts on display. Pre and post-visit lesson packets are available for classrooms.

Hours: Open Wed. - Sat., 10am - 4p.m; Sun., noon - 4 p.m.

Admission: The museum is $3 for adults; $2 for seniors and ages 12 - 21; children 11 and under are free. Entrance to the Imagination Station room is $1 per person.

Ages: 6 years and up.

YORBA-SLAUGHTER ADOBE

(909) 597-8332 / www.sbcountymuseum.org

17127 Pomona Rincon Road, Chino

(Exit Chino Valley Fwy [71] N.E. on Euclid [83], take a quick L. on Pomona Rincon Rd. [TG-712 A4])

Just for the record, the name "Slaughter" refers to a family that once lived here - not the slaughtering of animals. The adobe was built in 1852 and therefore receives the distinction of being the oldest standing residence in San Bernardino. A tour through the adobe, which is fairly well kept up, allows visitors to see its low beam ceilings; a dining room, with a table set for company; a living room and music room with period furniture and artifacts that include a piano, sewing machine, dolls, and a pot-bellied stove; a kitchen; a bedroom; and a few, simply furnished rooms upstairs.

There are a few other buildings on the grounds that are also original, but very weathered in appearance. A shed with a stone chimney, a winery building, a one-ton solid copper pot (used for tallow), a wooden mill, and a few pieces of old farming equipment complete the homestead. Note: Group and school tours are given by appointment.

Hours: Open to the public Wed. - Sat., 10am - 5pm; Sun., 1pm - 5pm. Closed Mon., Tues., New Year's Day, Thanksgiving, and Christmas.

Admission: $1 per person.

Ages: 7 years and up.

ANTIQUE GAS & STEAM ENGINE MUSEUM, INC.

(800) 5-TRACTOR (587-2286) or (760) 941-1791 / www.agsem.com

2040 N. Santa Fe Avenue, Vista

(From San Diego Fwy [5], exit N.E. on San Luis Rey Mission Exwy [76]. From Escondido Fwy [15], exit W. on Pala Rd [76]. From 76. go S. on N. Santa Fe Ave. From Vista Fwy [78], exit N. on Melrose Dr., R. on W. Bobier Ave., L. on Santa Fe Ave. [TG-1087 F2])

California has a museum for almost any interest. This one answers the age-old question, "Where do engines go when they run out of gas (or steam)?" The forty-acre, mostly outdoor museum, has hundreds of tractors, combines, gas and steam engines (that's a given from the name of the museum), horse-drawn carriages, and equipment used in mining, oil drilling, construction, agriculture, and more. The machines have been (or are in the process of being) restored to working condition. In fact, some of the equipment is used to help farm the adjacent lands. Walk around on your own or make a reservation for a tour, which is offered for pre-schoolers through college internship students. Kids will see many of the machines in action and learn a lot about the history of agriculture via harvesting and grounding flour, baking bread in a wood stove, and more. Another option is to visit here on the third and fourth weekends of June and October during Threshing Bees and Antique Engine & Tractor Shows. Watch or take part in planting, harvesting, household chores, early American crafts, blacksmithing, log sawing, parades, and square dancing. It's a good ol' time! See the Calendar section for more details.

Some of the museum's collection is housed in structures that collectively resemble a small town. Featured buildings include a huge (and complete) blacksmith and wheelwright shop, a farm house with parlor, a sawmill, a one-third scale train with a telegrapher's office, and a barn. There are picnic tables here and even a small playground with two small, stationary tractors to climb on. The museum is interesting to visit anytime, but it's exciting to visit at exhibition time!

Hours: Open daily 10am - 4pm.

Admission: $3 for adults; $2 ages 6 - 12; children 5 and under are free.

Ages: 4 years and up.

BALBOA PARK

(619) 239-0512 - Visitors Center; (619) 692-4919 - Morely Field Sports Complex / www.balboapark.org

Balboa Park, San Diego

(Going S. on San Diego Fwy [5], exit at Sassafras/Airport, go straight on Kettner Blvd. L. on Laurel St., which turns into El Prado. Going N. on 5, exit N. on Pershing Dr., L. on Florida Dr., L. on Zoo PL., L. on Park Blvd. Going S. on Cabrillo Fwy [163], exit N. on Park Blvd. (near end). The museums are W. on Park Blvd. [TG-1289 C1])

This massive 1,158-acre park is the cultural and recreational heart of San Diego. Numerous programs and seasonal events are held here - see the Calendar section in the back of the book and/or call for a schedule of events. The park has shade trees, grassy areas, several gardens, picnic areas, and even playgrounds which are located at Pepper Grove Picnic Area on Park Boulevard, south of the San Diego Zoo, and at the north end of Balboa Drive. Morley Field Sports Complex, located off Morely Field Drive in the northeastern section, has twenty-five public tennis courts available for all-day use at $5 per person for adults; $3 for seniors; $2 for ages 17 and under. Call the Balboa Tennis Club at (619) 295-9278 for reservations. It also has a fitness course; boccie ball, which is an Italian sport similar to lawn bowling; a velodrome that hosts races and offers classes; an archery range; baseball diamonds; a frisbee golf course; lawn bowling for adults; playgrounds; picnic areas; and a swimming pool that is open year round - call for hours. Swim sessions cost $2 for adults, $1.50 for seniors and children. Call (619) 692-4920 for more pool information.

Balboa Park is home to a majority of the city's best museums, as well as the world famous SAN DIEGO ZOO (look under the Zoos and Animals section). Individual museum entries are found under this section, listed by their official titles: MINGEI INTERNATIONAL FOLK ART MUSEUM, MUSEUM OF PHOTOGRAPHIC ARTS, MUSEUM OF SAN DIEGO HISTORY, REUBEN H. FLEET SCIENCE CENTER, SAN DIEGO AEROSPACE MUSEUM, SAN DIEGO AUTOMOTIVE MUSEUM, SAN DIEGO HALL OF CHAMPIONS SPORTS MUSEUM, SAN DIEGO MODEL RAILROAD MUSEUM, SAN DIEGO MUSEUM OF ART, SAN DIEGO MUSEUM OF MAN, and SAN DIEGO NATURAL HISTORY MUSEUM. VETERANS MEMORIAL CENTER AND MUSEUM is across the street. Passports can be purchased to visit eleven museums for $30 for adults. (Children's admissions are already discounted or free.) Passes can be bought at the Visitors Information Center and are good for one week from the date of purchase. Below is a list of which museums are free on particular Tuesdays: First Tuesday: S.D. Natural History (permanent exhibits only), Reuben H. Fleet Science Center, and S.D. Model Railroad; Second Tuesday: Museum of Photographic Arts and Museum of S.D. History; Third Tuesday: Japanese Friendship Garden, Mingei International Folk Art Museum, S.D. Museum of Art (permanent exhibits only), and S.D. Museum of Man; Fourth Tuesday: S. D. Hall of Champions Sports, S.D. Aerospace Museum, S.D. Automotive Museum, and Cottages and House of Pacific Relations International whose Hall of Nations films, such as *Children Around the World* show at 11am to 3pm.

The park also offers many other attractions that are worthy of mention. The beautiful, latticed **Botanical Building** is located at the north end of the lily pond next to the San Diego Museum of Art. It has (labeled) tropical and subtropical plants on display. It is open Friday through Wednesday 10am to 4pm. Admission is free. The **Timken Museum of Art** is located next to the Visitors Center. Housed here are collections of works by European Old Masters, eighteenth- and nineteenth-century American paintings, and Russian icons. It is open Tuesday through Saturday, 10am to 4:30pm; Sunday, 1:30pm to 4:30pm. Admission is free. The **Japanese Friendship Garden** is a Japanese-style house with a main room that has a traditional table set with (fake) Japanese food. Children must stay on the short path leading to the small garden. If you are interested in seeing this room and garden, come here when admission is free, on the third Tuesday of the month, as admission is otherwise $3 per person. Free outdoor concerts are given on the famous **Spreckels Pipe Organ** year round on Sundays 2pm to 3pm, plus Mondays, 8pm to 9:30pm during July and August. The organ is located in an architecturally beautiful building set in a huge half circle. My kids think the steps here are a great place for picnicking. The **Spanish Village Art Center**, (619) 233-9050, is just north of the San Diego Natural History Museum. The "village" has retained its old-world charm with its Spanish architecture and colorful courtyard tiles and flowers. The thirty-five art studios and galleries include woodcarvings, sculptures, and gems and minerals, for show and sale. Oftentimes, the artisans demonstrate their craft which makes the Spanish Village Center an intriguing stop for slightly older kids. The **House of Pacific Relations**, (619) 234-0739, is located behind the United Nations Building, across from the Spreckels Organ. The "House" is comprised of fifteen cottages representing thirty-one nationalities. Exhibits in each cottage pertain to specific ethnic groups. Music and dance programs are held on Sundays 2pm to 3pm from mid-March through October 31. The cottages are open Sundays 12:30pm to 4:30pm and on the fourth Tuesday from noon to 3pm. Admission is free. Two other kid-friendly attractions are the **miniature train ride** and the **merry-go-round.** Both rides are located south of the Zoo and north of the Spanish Village Center. They operate weekends and holidays only, 10:30am to 5:30pm and cost $1.25 per person per ride. The old-fashioned carousel has horses and other animals to ride on, and offers a chance to grab at the gold ring. There are a few theaters and places to eat within Balboa Park, too.

At any time during your visit to the park, you are welcome to hop aboard the Balboa Park Tram. This free, intra-park transportation system can take you from Presidents Way and Park Boulevard, up to the carousel, through where the museums are, and up north to 6th Street and the MARSTON HOUSE (look under this section for more details). It makes several stops along the way, so you can catch it coming or going. It operates daily from 9am to 6:15pm, with extended hours in the summer. Plan to visit Balboa Park many times, as you obviously cannot see it all in one, two, or even three days!

Hours: The park is open daily. The Visitors Center is open daily 9am - 4pm. Individual attractions are listed in separate entries.

Admission: Entrance to the park itself is free. Individual attractions are listed in separate entries.

Ages: All ages for the park.

BANCROFT RANCH HOUSE MUSEUM

(619) 469-1480 / www.sandiegohistory.org/societies/springvalley
9050 Memory Lane, Spring Valley
(Exit Martin Luther King Jr. Fwy [94] S. on Bancroft Dr., L. on Memory Ln. [TG-1271 B5])

I love visiting old house/museums because I always learn some history about the original owners and the time period that they lived there. With every new tidbit learned, it's like fitting in another piece of a huge historical puzzle. For instance, in the early 1900's Howe Bancroft, one-time owner of this adobe ranch house, was a renowned historian who wrote and compiled thirty-nine books describing the civilization of the Old West.

A truth window, where visitors here can see the layers of original adobe - mostly mud and hay - is one of the first things the guide points out. One small room contains a few display cases of Native American artifacts such as grinding stones, arrowheads, and baskets. Another room contains a straw bed, Bancroft's history books, and few period household goods. A connecting room has an old school desk and a map. The last room holds display cases of boots, clothing, tools, kitchen implements, and most exciting of all because kids can hold them - ship to shore cannon balls, and tumbler balls used to crush rocks. School groups are encouraged to visit.

There are a few picnic tables under shade trees out front of the house and an indigenous garden. An adjacent parcel of land will hopefully be turned into a park. When we saw it, it had overgrown grass covering uneven ground, a large grouping of very old palm trees, and the surface run off from an underground spring. Although the surrounding area is a bit rundown and the museum grounds are a work in progress, seeing and hearing a potion of history makes the Bancroft Museum a worthwhile visit.

Hours: Open Fri. - Sun., 1pm- 4pm.
Admission: Free, but donations are appreciated.
Ages: 8 years and up.

BARONA CULTURAL CENTER AND MUSEUM

(619) 443-7003 x219 / www.baronatribe.com
1095 Barona Road, Lakeside
(Take the San Vicente Fwy[67] N. to the end and continue on 67 Hwy., R. on Willow Rd., L. on Wildcat Canyon Rd. which turns in to Barona R. About 6 miles from Willow, just past the Barona Casino on the left in the community center. [TG-1192 G7])

The Barona Band Mission Indians's museum reflects their culture and heritage. This small museum has hundred of artifacts in display cases, such as arrows, spears, coiled basket, and jewelry, as well as a few interactive exhibits. Visitors can push buttons to listen to the native language, try on sandals made out of fiber, try on a bark skirt, and shake gourd rattles. School field trips include a tour, a lecture on the history of the Indians, and perhaps playing a traditional game or two.

Hours: Open Wed. - Fri., noon - 5pm; Sat., 10am - 5pm; Sun., noon - 5pm.
Admission: Free
Ages: 8 years and up.

BUENA VISTA AUDUBON NATURE CENTER

(760) 439-BIRD (2473) / members.nbci.com/bvasnaturecenter
2202 S. Coast Highway, Oceanside

(Exit San Diego Fwy [5] W. on Vista Way, L. on S. Coast Highway. It is just N. of the Buena Vista Lagoon. [TG-1106 D4])

This museum is not just for the birds! The exhibits inside this small building consist mainly of taxidermied birds (some in flight) such as a pelican, a great blue heron, a red-tailed hawk, a colorful yellow western tanager, and more. A stuffed owl has a mouse in its beak and a pellet at its feet that contains partially digested animal parts. Other mounted animals on display include a bobcat and a possum. The touch table has a raccoon skin, petrified wood, and whale bones, among other things. Look through a kid-level window on the central display to see fish "swimming" underneath. A book corner for children has a nice selection of nature books to read. Other items of interest are the fish tank with catfish (it's easy to see where they got their name), a small rock and mineral display, and a live tarantula.

Outside, take a walk through the marshy reeds out to the lagoon. This area is home to a wide variety of birds. Guided field trips are one of the best ways to really learn about the abundant wildlife at Buena Vista. Migrate over to the picnic tables which are available to make your day just ducky!

Free, one-hours tours are offered for kindergartners through 4th graders that cover a variety of topics such as what makes a bird a bird, birds of prey, and migration.

Hours: Open Tues. - Sat., 10am - 4pm; Sun., 1pm - 4pm.
Admission: Free
Ages: 3 years and up.

CALIFORNIA SURF MUSEUM

(760) 721-6876 / www.surfmuseum.org
223 N. Coast Highway, Oceanside
(Exit San Diego Fwy [5] W. on Mission Ave., R. on N. Coast Hwy. [TG-1086 A7])

Surfing is the heart of the Southern California beach culture. This small museum aims to preserve the history and lifestyle of surfing so it won't be wiped out. It displays a diverse selection and variety of surfboards. To the inexperienced eye, some might look simply like thick boards, but I'm learning that there is more to the board than meets the eye. Exhibits rotate yearly and have included a tabletop wave, a Hawaiian hut made of palm leaves that paid homage to surfing's roots, and lots of photographs and information regarding surfing.

Hours: Open Thurs. - Mon., 10am - 4pm. Closed Tues., Wed., and holidays.
Admission: Free; donations gladly accepted.
Ages: Surfer dudes 8 years and up.

CAMP PENDLETON

(760) 725-5569 - general information
Oceanside
(Exit San Diego Fwy [5] at Oceanside Harbor / Camp Pendleton exit onto the base. You'll need to show your driver's license and vehicle registration at the main gate. [TG-1085 J6])

Driving on I-5 between Orange County and Oceanside, it's hard to miss the sprawling Camp Pendleton. At the gate, ask for a newspaper that gives self-driving directions, the camp's history, and information on the buildings. This military training camp is one of the largest, especially for amphibious training. My boys like the thought of being on a real marine base, so taking a "windshield tour" (i.e. driving around in here) was a treat for them. We saw the Marines working out, many military vehicles, and even the helicopter landing pad. Camp Pendleton is also on an historical site where early Spanish explorers traveled. For a more detailed understanding of this time period, tour the on-site Rancho Las Flores and the nineteenth-century Santa Margarita adobe ranch house, with a minimum group of twenty people. The houses retain the essence of yesteryear in both landscaping and interior furnishings. Advanced registration is needed.

The one-room Amphibious Vehicle Museum, is located at the southern end of Camp Pendleton at the Del Mar basin. (Head south on Kraus Street.) It contains L.V.T.'s (Land Vehicle Tracks) - amphibious vehicles used in combat. These large relics from WWII are accompanied by war mementoes such as uniforms, weapons, and personal artifacts. You may ask to watch the video on the history of the L.V.T.'s. Note: The CAMP PENDLETON PAINTBALL PARK (see the Family Pay and Play section) is also located on base.

Hours: Drive through Camp Pendleton daily during daylight hours. Call for rancho and adobe house tours. The Amphibious Museum is usually open Tues. - Sat., 9am - 4pm.

Admission: Free

Ages: 6 years and up.

CARLSBAD CHILDREN'S MUSEUM ☼

(760) 720-0737 / www.museumforchildren.org $$

300 Carlsbad Village Drive, #102, Carlsbad

(Exit San Diego Fwy [5] W. on Carlsbad Village Dr. [TG-1106 D5])

After my oldest son understood that we were not going to Carl's Bad Children's Museum, his dread turned into anticipation and we all had a great time. Each room at the museum is themed, appealing to different aspects of your child's personality. Set sail for adventure and catch some pretend fish while skippering a real boat (at least the front end of one), surrounded by a wall with a sea mural. Use a cart to hold all your items while shopping at the well-stocked Kid's Marketplace. The cashier can use the real cash register, with fake money. Things are positively medieval when your kids play at the large replica castle. Girls dress up and turn into princesses (temporarily) while boys (and girls) suit up to become knights in shining (plastic) armor. My oldest son simply declared himself king and ordered everyone else around. Hear and see sound frequencies through the water at the Sounds exhibit. Look at and learn about musical instruments from all over the world and even play a few of them. Every week Creative Corner provides your child with a new art project to create and take home. Aprons are available for those with messier instincts. At the science area, test a hand battery, watch a solar-powered train go around a track, and stand in the center of a bubble that's as tall as you are. There are a few computers in the museum and a small area for toddlers that has books, toys, and a puppet theater.

The Children's Museum is located in Carlsbad Village Faire and Shopping

Centre, directly across from the Status Chocolates Shop, a sweet stop. The fountain in the middle of the Plaza has reclining chairs around it making it a delightful place to rest, unless your child falls in the water!

Hours: Open Sun., Tues. - Thurs., noon - 5pm; Fri. - Sat., 10am - 5pm. Closed Mon. It's open in July and August daily, 10am - 5pm.

Admission: $4 for ages 2 and up.

Ages: 1½ - 11 years.

CHILDREN'S MUSEUM / MUSEO DE LOS NIÑOS

(619) 233-KIDS (5437) - recording; (619) 233-8792 - museum /   *$$$*

www.sdchildrensmuseum.org

200 W. Island Avenue, San Diego

(Going S. on San Diego Fwy [5], exit S. on 1st St., R. on Island. Going N. on the 5, exit S. on 6th Ave. R. on Island. [TG-1289 A4])

The museum's emphasis is "to be a hands-on, minds-on experiential learning environment for people of all ages" and "to be truly bi-national, recognizing Tijuana and Mexico as neighbors." The exhibits here, designed by artists, are all arts and humanities focused.

There are very few permanent exhibits in this innovative children's museum that is housed in a warehouse. They include the Art Studio, which is a place to create wonderful art projects, and is the home of a 1952 Dodge pick-up truck that kids paint, repaint, and paint again; a bubble making machine; a London double deck bus used as a reading "corner"; the Improv Theater, which is a dress up and stage area; and Cora's Rain House, which is a giant tin house featuring a recreated rain forest and recycled water. It is designed for kids to come in and express their thoughts or emotions by talking, drawing, or writing.

The temporary exhibits are all hands-on and great fun. Just a few of the past exhibits include building a prefab house with hammer and nails; the story of making candy told in pictorial renderings; a giant, floor checkerboard, played by using huge red and black foam pillows; a video using a virtual reality game to hook up with kids in a museum in Mexico City, which had an identical system, so the two nations could interact on the screen together; and Pop Art featuring life-size super heroes and other cool guys. Call to see what is currently being featured, although kids will thoroughly enjoy whatever it is. A small park, good for picnicking, is located diagonally across the street from the museum.

Hours: Open Tues. - Sat., 10am - 4pm. Closed Sun. and Mon.

Admission: $6 for ages 3 and up; $3 for seniors; children 2 and under are free. There is limited free parking. Paid parking is available at Front and Island St. The SAN DIEGO TROLLEY (look under Transportation section) also stops at the museum.

Ages: 2 years and up.

COMPUTER MUSEUM OF AMERICA

(619) 465-8226 / www.computer-museum.org   *$*

7380 Parkway Drive, La Mesa

(Exit Mission Valley Fwy [8] N. on Lake Murray Blvd., R. on Pkwy Dr. The museum is on the Coleman College campus. [TG-1270 F1])

From an abacus to PCs, this medium-sized, one-room museum displays about fifty products that show the evolution of computers. The machinery is nicely arranged and a self-guided tour notebook contains explanations for all of the equipment. Some of the items here include 1930's vintage Burroughs calculators, heavy steel IBM card punches, teletypes, an IBM 360 mainframe computer of the 60's, a Royal Precision computer that used 113 vacuum tubes, and even a few typewriters. Some of the machines are cut open so visitors can see the inner workings. My younger, not-interested-in-technology kids enjoyed the interactive exhibits - they played Pong (remember this one?), Space Invaders, and the original Donkey Kong. Note: The adjacent Learning Center is a resource center for qualifying students in seventh through twelfth grades to be utilized for school projects. Note: The museum is planning on moving. Please call first for the current location.

Hours: Open Tues. - Sat., 10am - 5pm
Admission: $2 for adults; $1 for children 2 - 13.
Ages: 8 years and up.

CONFEDERATE AIR FORCE WWII MUSEUM (El Cajon) ☀

(619) 448-4505 / www.cafairgroup1.org $
1850 Joe Crosson Drive, El Cajon
(Exit San Vincente Fwy [67] W. on Bradley, R. on Pioneer Wy. / Floyd Smith Dr., R. on Joe Crosson. The hanger is located just S. of Gillespie Airport. [TG-1251 E2])

This small, but mighty, aviation museum has four planes on display that are in various stages of restoration - an SN-J, a L-5, A-26 and P-82. A wildcat (an airplane, not a cat that's wild) occasionally flies in. The museum, operated by WWII aviation buffs, has a friendly and casual atmosphere. Kids are usually allowed in the airplanes and on the army jeeps equipped with (non-operative!) machine guns. Display cases around the perimeter of the hanger hold artifacts donated to the museum and include model planes, photos, goggles, equipment, and lots of other paraphernalia.

Visitors will also enjoy watching small planes land and take off. The Mayday Cafe is right around the corner. See the May Calendar section for the Wings Over Gillespie Air show.

Hours: Open Wed - Sat., 10am - 3pm.
Admission: $3 for adults; children 12 and under are free.
Ages: 4 years and up.

DEER PARK WINERY AND AUTO MUSEUM ☼

(760) 749-1666 / www.deerparkwinery.com $$
29013 Champagne Blvd., S, Escondido
(Going S. on Escondido Fwy [15], exit S. on Gopher Canyon Rd. Ron on Champagne. Going N. on 15, exit E. on Mountain Meadow exit, L. on Champagne Blvd. It's next to Lawrence Welk Village. [TG-1089 A1])

Pretend you're driving along, feeling the sun on your face and the wind in your hair. Ahh - to be in a convertible (or hanging your head out a window)! This auto museum, with over 112 cars displayed, is devoted to preserving the history of the convertible. It contains cars from the turn-of-the-century, one-cylinder horseless carriages, and fine finned fashions of the 50's (say that last part five times fast!), including little-known names of Crosley Hotshort and Frazer Manhattan. It also exhibits a rich assortment of Americana memorabilia.

Your tour starts in the nice, gift shop/market building that offers wine-related items (including wine tasting), automotive-related keepsakes, books, and other gift items. A delicatessen here provides sandwiches, potato salad, and other picnic foods. The back of the store is like a mini-museum. It showcases thirteen vintage automobiles, including a Model A Ford Sports Coupe and a 1959 Cadillac Eldorado, along with a few motorcycles and some collectable memorabilia, such as old Coca-Cola products.

Walk through the gift shop out through the vineyard to reach the bulk of the museum, which is actually located in two other, separate buildings. Automobiles in the lower level building, are parked (and packed) everywhere. Along the sides are displays containing collections of old radios, TVs, refrigerators, vacuums, other household appliances, cameras, typewriters, gas station "stuff", hubcaps, and lots more. The upper building was the winery building. It now houses more cars, including the triple black 1953 Cadillac Eldorado, plus more radios, neon dealership signs, an array of bicycles, kiddie cars, and some movie-star mementos of Elvis, Marilyn Monroe, and Elizabeth Taylor. An adjoining room contains everything Barbie. Wine production equipment, such as fermenting tanks and grape crush pads, are outside, around the back of the building.

The cars are not to be touched, of course, but we sure got an eyeful and my kids have now put in requests for the type of convertible they want when they can drive. (I told them to work hard and save lots of money!)

Enjoy a picnic on the grassy front lawn of Deer Park, under shady oak trees, by a small creek, near a gazebo.

Hours: Open daily 10am - 5pm.

Admission: Entry to the gift shop and mini museum is free. Museum entrance is $6 for adults; $4 for seniors; children 11 and under are free.

Ages: 6 years and up.

FIREHOUSE MUSEUM

$

(619) 232-3473 /
www.globalinfo.com/noncomm/firehouse/Firehouse.HTML
1572 Columbia Street, San Diego
(Going N. on San Diego Fwy [5], exit E. on Hawthorne St., L. on Columbia. Going S. on 5, exit S. on Front St., R. on Cedar, it's on the L. at Columbia St. [TG-1289 A2])

Have a hot time in downtown San Diego by visiting the Firehouse Museum! Housed inside an old fire station, the museum features ten fire engines from different time periods. Also on display are several antique pieces of fire-fighting equipment such as a water pump and steamer, helmets, axes, and speaking trumpets through which chiefs would shout their orders, plus other items such as a telephone switchboard.

Hours: Open Thurs. - Fri., 10am - 2pm; Sat. - Sun., 10am - 4pm.

Admission: $2 for adults; $1 for seniors and ages 13 - 17; children 12 and under are free. The first Thurs. of every month is free admission day.

Ages: 4 years and up.

GASKILL STONE STORE MUSEUM

(619) 478-5707   *$*

31330 Highway 94, Campo

(Exit 8 Fwy [45 miles from downtown San Diego] S. on Buckman Springs Rd., 10.5 miles to Hwy. 94, bear right [1.5 miles] to the store on the corner. [TG-430 B10])

This small museum is exactly as its name implies - a museum created from an old store built with stones in 1885. The exhibits in the room consist of a stocked, old-fashioned general store; a small, turn-of-the-century kitchen; tools; appliances; and lots of photographs and documents. The back room, once used for storing food and other items, is a man-made cave blasted from rock. Upstairs is a military room with mannequins in uniforms, plus photographs and information about this area's military region. A stream runs in front of the museum and a woods surrounds it. Just around the corner is the SAN DIEGO RAILROAD MUSEUM. (See the Transportation section for more details.)

Hours: Open weekends and selected holidays 11am - 5pm.

Admission: $2 for adults; children 12 and under are free.

Ages: 7 years and up.

GUY B. WOODWARD MUSEUM OF HISTORY

(760) 789-7644   *$*

645 Main Street, Ramona

(From San Diego Fwy [5] or Escondido Fwy [15], take 78 Fwy E. to Ramona, L. on Main St. [also 78]. From 8 Fwy, take San Vicente Fwy [67] N. Stay on Hwy 67 to Ramona, which turns into Main St. [TG-1152 H5])

A complex of buildings make up this small, early western museum "town." The outside courtyard has a stage wagon - no springs made for a bumpy ride! A red barn houses an old medicine car (an RV prototype). The long garage contains a 1920's tractor, old buggies, an antique fire engine, fire fighting equipment, and lots of old tools, such as saws and wheat scythes, in neat rows on the walls. Just around the corner is a Honey House which contains beekeeping equipment. A narrow Millinery Shoppe features a doll collection, real mink stoles, outrageous feather hats, and a few beaded dresses. Other buildings here include a real jail; an outhouse; a re-created Post Office; a Hobby Room, which is really a catch-all room filled with old typewriters, bottles, and one of the first T.V. sets; a Bunkhouse where cowboys used to live; a Tack Room with dusty, rusty saddles; and a Blacksmith Shop complete with all the tools of the trade. Farm machinery is displayed all around the cluster of buildings. See if your kids can recognize washing machines, butter churns, the large incubator, a cream separator, and a machine for bottling milk.

The museum contains the heritage (and furnishings) of the older citizens of Ramona. The main house has roped-off rooms to look into including a turn-of-the-century doctor's office with a bloodied mannequin patient on the bed, and a collection of early medical instruments and vials; a beautifully decorated parlor, which is a combination of living room and music room, with mannequins dressed in period clothing; a library; a bedroom; and a kitchen that is packed with irons, dishes, butter churns, and other implements. The screened in back porch is set up like a bedroom - my kids were ready to move in!

The downstairs used to be a wine cellar, and the temperature is still cool here. The conglomeration of "stuff" now stored and displayed here includes Civil War artifacts, such as uniforms and cannon balls; a collection of cameras; a turkey-feather cape; a six-foot long Red Diamond Rattlesnake skin; Native American artifacts, such as stone mortar and pestle, and pottery; a hair perming machine that looks like something out of a science fiction film; a Casey Tibbs memorial exhibit dedicated to this World Champion rodeo rider; mining equipment; and more.

This unique museum is more than a glimpse into the past - it is a good, long, and interesting look into our ancestors' way of life. While you're here, enjoy a stroll around historic Old Town Ramona, located on both sides and across the street from the museum.

> **Hours:**   Open Fri. - Sun., 1pm - 4pm. Closed the month of September.
> **Admission:** $3 for adults; 50¢ for children 11 and under.
> **Ages:**   5 years and up.

HERITAGE OF THE AMERICAS MUSEUM   ☼

(619) 670-5194 / www.cuyamaca.net/museum   **$**

12110 Cuyamaca College Drive West at Cuyamaca College, El Cajon

(Going W. on 8 Fwy, exit S. on 2nd St. which turns into Jamacha Rd. [Hwy 54], continue on Jamacha Rd., R. on Cuyamaca College Dr. W. Going E. on 8, exit S. on Fwy 125, exit S. on Spring St., immediately get on 94 Fwy E., continue on to end, turns into Campo Rd., L. on Jamacha Rd., L on Cuyamaca College Dr. W. It is on the Cuyamaca College campus. [TG-1271 J5])

This museum makes learning about our heritage much more exciting than simply reading about it in a history book. Four different exhibit halls branch off diagonally from the reception desk. The <u>Natural History Hall</u> contains rocks and minerals, including a lodestone (i.e. a hunk of rock with a magnetic "personality") with nails sticking out from it. The meteorite display is out of this world. Other favorite items in this wing include a fossilized turtle shell, a T-Rex tooth, an Allosaurus claw, trilobites, a rattlesnake skin, a prehistoric bee trapped in amber, shells, coral, and seahorses. The many taxidermied animals include a leopard, deer, coyote, and the head of a cape buffalo.

The <u>Archaeology Hall</u> contains an incredible arrowhead collection, gathered from all over the world, and from different periods of time. Some of them are practical, while others are more ornamental. Other displays in the glass cases include stone artifacts, such as hoes and ax heads; Mayan treasures of stone and clay; necklaces made of jade, quartz, and amethyst; and various forms of money, such as shells and copper. Weapons, of course, are always a hit with my boys.

The <u>Anthropology Hall</u> showcases impressive Native American articles such as eagle feather headdresses, ceremonial costumes, and exquisitely beaded moccasins, gloves, and vests. More intriguing, however, are the elk tooth and eagle claw necklaces; beaded mountain lion paw bag; knife made from a blackfoot bear jaw; shark tooth sword that looks like a small chain saw; and rattles (used for dances) made out of turtle shells and trap door spiders' nests. This section also displays tomahawks, guns from the Old West, and a buffalo robe.

The <u>Art Hall</u> features Western art with cowboys and Indians portrayed in drawings, paintings, photographs, and sculptures. Four different pamphlets are available that give details about exhibits in each of the halls. This hilltop museum also has two small gardens with picnic tables, plus a stunning 360-degree view.

Hours: Open Tues. - Fri., 10am - 4pm; Sat., noon - 5pm. Closed selected holidays.

Admission: $3 for adults; $2 for seniors; $1 for students with ID; children 16 and under are free.

Ages: 5 years and up.

HERITAGE WALK / GRAPE DAY PARK

(760) 743-8207 / www.ci.escondido.ca.us
321 N. Broadway, Escondido
(Exit Escondido Fwy [15] E. on Fwy 78, R. on Broadway which is Hwy 78 [TG-1129 J2])

Grape Day Park has a charming ambiance created by a rose garden, large grassy areas, shade trees, picnic tables, Victorian buildings, a restored train depot, and a unique playground. The small playground has colorful metal configurations that look like interlocking tree branches to climb up, under, and through. It also has a small play structure that resembles the top of a space ship, with enough room at the flat top for just one person to sit - a natural setting to play King of the Hill. The park has horseshoe pits, too. Equipment can be checked out weekdays from 8am to 4pm. (Parental supervision is required.)

The five buildings that comprise the museum complex of Heritage Walk were relocated here in 1976, and are open to the public. They are: 1) Escondido's first library; 2) A quaint, completely furnished, two-story 1890's house with a living room, parlor, and kitchen, plus four small bedrooms upstairs; 3) A 1900's barn containing a 1890's popcorn wagon, a 1935 winery truck, a working printing press, and more; 4) A blacksmith's shop which holds demonstrations when it's open; and 5) An 1888 Santa Fe Depot. The two-story depot building is nice-looking and interesting to explore. Some highlights include a train master's office, a working telegraph station (send a message to someone!), a stuffed grizzly bear, and displays of conductor's hats and dining plates once used on trains. The depot also has a real train car that can be toured. It contains a model train set with an historic layout that makes tracks around realistic looking landscape.

A tank house and a small herb garden can also be seen on the short walk around Heritage Walk. The park is a fun place for kids to play, but bring them sometime to see the museum part of it, also. Call for tour information.

Hours: The park is open daily sunrise to sunset. The museum is open Thurs - Sat., 1pm - 4pm. It's closed Thanksgiving weekend, all major holidays, and during rainy weather.

Admission: Free; donations for Heritage Walk are appreciated.

Ages: All for the park; ages 5 and up for the museum.

JULIAN PIONEER MUSEUM   ☼

(760) 765-0227 / www.julianfun.com $

2811 Washington Street, Julian

(From San Diego Fwy [5] or Escondido Fwy [15], take 78 Fwy E. to Julian. 78 is Washington St. in Julian. From the 8 Fwy, take 79 N. to Julian, at 78 Jct. turn left on Main St., L. on Washington St. [TG-1136 B7])

If I were to clean out my grandparents' and great-grandparents' attics, closets, garages, etc., I would probably find many articles similar to what is inside this pioneer museum. The wide assortment of items here include carriages, guns, saddles, tools, eyeglasses, mining equipment, rocks, bottles, clothing, arrowheads, a ceremonial Indian costume, kitchen implements, a metal bathtub, a pot-bellied stove, an American flag (with forty-five stars), and lots of old, handmade lace. My favorite exhibit was a machine from a 1930's beauty shop. It was supposed to perm hair, but with the wires and rods sticking out all over the mannequin's head, it looks more like something from a science fiction film! Bring a lunch and enjoy a picnic on the tables outside this quaint museum.

Julian is a charming town with unique shops along Main Street. Your kids will enjoy a stop-off at the Julian Drugstore, located at the corner of Main Street and Washington Street, to enjoy an ice cream at its old-fashioned soda counter. Also see EAGLE MINING COMPANY, under the Tours section, to take a tour of a real gold mine.

Hours: Open December - March, Sat. - Sun. and certain holidays, 10am - 4pm. Open April - November, daily 10am - 4pm. Closed New Year's Day, Thanksgiving, and Christmas.

Admission: $1 for adults; children are free.

Ages: 5 years and up.

LA MESA DEPOT   ☼

(619) 595-3030; (619) 697-7762 - depot / www.sdrm.org   !

4650 Nebo Drive, La Mesa

(Going E. on the 8 Fwy, exit at Spring St., at end of off ramp, go straight on Nebo Dr. Going W. on 8, exit E. on El Cajon Dr., L. on Nebo. [TG-1270 J3])

This restored train station, circa 1894, boasts of a few cars still on the tracks - an engine, and caboose. The small depot building is contains several railroad artifacts, including an antique baggage scale.

Hours: Usually open Sat., 1pm - 4pm

Admission: Free

Ages: All

MARINE CORPS RECRUIT DEPOT COMMAND   ☼
MUSEUM

(619) 524-6038 - museum; (619) 524-8727 - graduation info   !

In the Marine Corps Recruit Depot on Pacific Highway and Witherby Street, San Diego

(Going S. on San Diego Fwy [5], exit at Old Town Ave., go straight from off ramp onto Hancock St., R. on Witherby St. Going N. on 5, exit at Moore St., L. on Old Town Ave, L. on Hancock St., R. on Witherby St. You must show a valid driver's license to enter the base. The museum is directly across from the guard entrance. [TG-1268 F6])

The first thing my kids noticed were the Japanese 70mm Howitzers outside the museum. Inside, the downstairs California Room displays numerous paintings of war, including battles involving Native Americans, blue coats verses grey coats, and more. The hallway has photos of movies and television shows that have featured Marines. An on-going, twenty-minute narrated film is presented in the small theater. It shows all the different phases of Marine training, from boot camp to graduation. Naturally, the "coolest" parts of it, according to my boys, were the army maneuvers where rounds and rounds of ammunition were shot, and the nighttime target practice where spots of light were seen when the guns were fired. After the movie my youngest son, with his eyes shining, declared, "I want to be a Marine!" The Visitor's Lounge looks like a large living room with couches and chairs. Around the perimeter of the room are exhibits such as helicopter and ship models, various military hats, and small models of physical fitness courses that make me tired just looking at them.

The upstairs rooms are filled with military memorabilia. The extensive exhibits include uniforms, swords, medals, grenades, posters, pictures, flags, mannequins dressed in camouflage, rocket launchers, jeeps, police motorcycles, a collection of knives (including machetes and bayonets), and a room devoted to guns and ammunition. The China Room focuses on American Marines in Peking. It contains a lot of documents and news articles from this time period, plus photos, traditional Chinese military dress, and a cannon.

The museum encompasses the history of the Marines from its inception 225 years ago, through WWI and WWII, and up to the present day. Always looking for "a few good men and women," the Marine Corps maintains a museum that is historically important, and that will enlist your child's attention.

Forty-four Fridays out of the year the Marine Corps holds a brief "morning colors ceremony," where the flag is raised and the *National Anthem* is played. It begins at 8am sharp. At 9:50am, a "pass and review" parade, mini band concert, and graduation ceremony commence. The public is welcome to attend one or both ceremonies. Call for specific dates.

Hours: Open Mon. - Fri., 0800 - 1600 (8am - 4pm); Sat., 1200 - 1600 (noon - 4pm). Closed Sun. and most federal holidays.

Admission: Free

Ages: 5 years and up.

MARITIME MUSEUM

(619) 234-9153 / www.sdmaritime.com

1306 N. Harbor Drive, San Diego

(Going N. on San Diego Fwy [5], exit E. on Hawthorne St., L. on Harbor. Going S. on 5, exit S. on Front St., R. on Ash. The museum is at the end of Ash St., on Harbor Drive. [TG-1288 J2])

"I saw a ship a-sailing, a-sailing on the sea; and, oh! it was all laden with pretty things for thee!" (An old rhyme.) The three historic ships that comprise the Maritime Museum - the Star of India, the Berkeley, and the Medea - are laden with wonderful, nautical artifacts. The 1863 Star of India is beautiful to behold with its intricate-looking rigging, interesting figurehead, and polished wooden exterior. Inside, kids can look out the portholes; check out the very narrow bunks that once held emigrants; look at the old tools and display of knots; and marvel at the variations of ships in bottles. Not only are the ships unique, but the shapes of the bottles vary, too. Our favorite was the ship in a lightbulb. The fifteen-minute video, *Around Cape Horn* is a bit dry, though it depicts action at sea. Top board is the captain's cabin (which is small enough to give me claustrophobia), a few passengers' cabins (which passengers had to furnish themselves), a dining room, and the chart room.

The 1898 ferryboat, Berkeley, contains a number of fascinating model ships and yachts. A model ship construction and repair shop is on board, and we watched a builder at work. He told us a model takes an average of five years to complete! Such detailed work! One section of the Berkeley has a whaling gun on exhibit and displays of fish (mostly tuna) and fisheries. Downstairs is the engine room which you can explore on your own. The room is intriguing with its huge machinery and gears, narrow walkways, and slightly spooky ambiance. Also below deck is a room showcasing memorabilia from America's Cup. The triple expansion steam engine is put to work and demonstrated at various times throughout the day.

Cross over the bridge from the Berkeley to the 1904 steam yacht, Medea, which is a very small vessel. Peek into the elegant, Edwardian-decorated smoking room and into the galley that contains a coal-burning stove, big copper pots, and a wooden ice box. All in all, we had a merry time at the Maritime Museum.

Hours: Open daily 9am - 8pm. Open one hour later in the summer.

Admission: Admission includes all three ships - $6 for adults; $4 for seniors and ages 13 - 17; $2 for ages 6 - 12; children 5 and under are free. Ask about AAA discounts.

Ages: 5 years and up.

MARSTON HOUSE

(619) 298-3142 / www.sandiegohistory.org   *$$*

3525 7th Avenue, San Diego

(Going S. on San Diego Fwy [5], exit at Sassafras / Airport, go straight on Kettner Blvd., L. on Laurel St., L. on 6th Ave., R. on Upas St. It's at the end of Upas St. on 7th Ave. Going N. on 5, exit N. on 6th Ave., R. on Upas St. Going S. on Cabrillo Fwy [163], exit S. on 6th Ave., L. on Upas St. [TG-1269 B6])

This 1905 mansion was built to provide "function, simplicity and good design." (For an interesting contrast, compare its practical exterior and interior designs to the much more elaborate VILLA MONTEZUMA JESSE SHEPARD HOUSE, which is listed in this section.) The sixteen various rooms, covering four floors, are decorated in American Arts and Crafts, oriental, and Native American styles. What a fun and different way to learn the many facets of American history! This tour is better for older kids who can appreciate the lifestyle changes that occurred during the early twentieth century.

Hours: Open Fri. - Sun., 10am - 4:30pm

Admission: $5 for adults; $2 for ages 6 - 17; children 5 and under are free.

Ages: 8 years and up.

MINGEI INTERNATIONAL FOLK ART MUSEUM

(619) 239-0003 / www.mingei.org $$

Plaza de Panama, Balboa Park, San Diego

(Going S. on San Diego Fwy [5], exit at Sassafras/Airport, go straight on Kettner Blvd. L. on Laurel St., which turns into El Prado. Going N. on 5, exit N. on Pershing Dr., L. on Florida Dr., L. on Zoo PL., L. on Park Blvd., R. on Village Pl. Going S. on Cabrillo Fwy [163], exit N. on Park Blvd. (near end), L. on Presidents Wy. [TG-1289 C1])

"Min" is the Japanese word for "all people"; "gei" means "art," so mingei translates as "art of all people," or folk art. A child's enjoyment of this folk art museum depends on the current exhibits. We saw many tapestries, handcrafted furniture, and beautiful pieces of jewelry. Past exhibits have included toys and dolls from around the world, Mexican folk art, and the horse in folk art. Call first, or go on the third Tuesday of the month when admission is free. The museum's gift shop offers colorful and unique items. (See BALBOA PARK [San Diego] in this section for a listing of all the museums and attractions within walking distance.)

Hours: Open Tues. - Sun., 10am - 4pm.

Admission: $5 for adults; $2 for ages 6 - 17; children 5 and under are free. Admission on the third Tuesday of every month is free. Passports for 11 museums in Balboa Park are available for $30 for adults at the Visitors Center, and are good for one week from the date of purchase. (Children's admissions are already discounted or free.)

Ages: 8 years and up.

MISSION BASILICA SAN DIEGO DE ALCALA

(619) 281-8449 $

10818 San Diego Mission Road, San Diego

(Going W. on Mission Valley Fwy [8], exit N. on Mission Gorge Rd., L. on Twain Ave., which turns into San Diego Mission Rd. From Escondido Fwy [15], exit E. on Friars Rd., R. on Mission Gorge Rd., R. on Twain Ave. [TG-1249 H7])

Father Junipero Serra came to California on a mission - to start missions. The Mission San Diego de Alcala was the first church in California, founded by the Padre in 1769. As with a visit to any of the twenty-one missions, coming here brings the past vividly back to life. The church is long and narrow and, of course, housed in an adobe structure. The gardens here are very small, but pretty. The Padre Luis Jayme Museum, named after the missionary who was killed here by an Indian attack, contains some interesting excavated artifacts such as flintlock pistols, swords, buttons, and pottery. Other exhibits here include vestments, old photos, and small dioramas of all the missions. The monastery ruins have partial walls and the outlines of where the padres living quarters, the library, and other rooms once stood. Tips: Read the pamphlet about the mission as you explore it, because knowing its history makes it much more interesting for kids. Or, use the tote-a-tape tour, which audibly explains more about this mission. The cost is $2 per tape/recorder.

Hours: Open daily 9am - 5pm. Closed Easter, Thanksgiving, and Christmas.

Admission: $3 for adults; $2 for seniors and students over 12; $1 for children 11 and under.

Ages:　7 years and up.

MISSION SAN ANTONIO DE PALA
(760) 742-3317

$

Pala Mission Road, Pala

(Exit Escondido Fwy [15] E. on Pala Rd. [Route 76], go about 6 miles, then L. on 3rd St. R. on Pala Mission Rd. [TG-1029 J4])

This mission, founded in 1816, is the only remaining Spanish California Mission to continue in its original purpose of proselytizing and serving Native Americans. The adjacent school is for Native American children and the gift shop is run by Native Americans. The small mission is located on an Indian Reservation, a fact that greatly enhanced its value in my children's eyes.

The museum part of the mission consists of two small wings. One contains arrowheads, pottery, clothing with intricate beadwork, the Padre's small quarters, and an altar. Hand-carved religious figures and the Southwestern-style painted ceilings are eye-catching. The other wing is the Mineral Room, showcasing nice specimens of jasper, petrified wood slabs, and amethyst. The room also has a marine display that includes a stuffed puffer fish, corral, huge shells, and a giant clam shell.

The small back courtyard has a nicely landscaped garden, an altar, and a fountain with Koi. The old bell tower is around the side of the mission, next to the cemetery.

Hours:　Open Wed. - Sun., 10am - 5pm. Closed most major holidays.
Admission:　$2 for adults; $1 for children 12 and under.
Ages:　6 years and up.

MISSION SAN LUIS REY DE FRANCA
(760) 757-3651 / www.sanluisrey.org

$$

4050 Mission Avenue, Oceanside

(From San Diego Fwy [5], exit N. on San Luis Rey Mission Exwy [76] about 4 miles. From Escondido Fwy [15], exit W. on Pala Rd [76] about 15 miles. From 76, exit N. on Rancho del Oro Dr. [TG-1086 H2])

Founded in 1798, this mission has been nicknamed "King of the Missions" because it is the largest of the twenty-one missions. It is also one of the most interesting. The extensive grounds cover nearly six and a half acres, though not all of it is open to the public. The first series of rooms contain several glass-encased displays that document the history of the mission. Next, is the Friar's small bedroom with a knotted rope bed, and monks' robes. (Twenty-one Franciscan monks still live here in a separate section of the mission.) The weavery and work rooms have a loom, spinning wheel, and implements for leather tooling, respectively. The kitchen contains pots, pans, a brick oven, and glassware typical of the Mission period. The next few rooms display embroidered vestments, statues of angels and the Madonna, and other religious art work. The big Mission Church is gorgeous. Exit the church through the Madonna Chapel into the cemetery which contains a large wooden cross to commemorate the 3,000 Indians buried here.

The grounds are equally interesting to explore. Large grassy areas, with plenty of picnic tables, are outside the mission's front doors. Just past this area are ruins of soldiers' barracks. Further down, toward the street, is an ornate stone arch and a tiled stairway that lead to an old mission laundry area and large sunken garden. The garden looks like it was left over from Babylonian times; once elegantly landscaped, but now overgrown. Mission San Luis Rey de Franca is a great one to cover for those fourth grade mission reports! And of course, guided tours are available.

Hours: Open daily 10am - 4:30pm. Closed New Year's Day, Thanksgiving, and Christmas.

Admission: $4 for adults; $3 for ages 8 - 14; children 7 and under are free. $12 is the family rate for four or more members.

Ages: 5 years and up.

MUSEUM OF CONTEMPORARY ART (La Jolla) ☼ $

(858) 454-3541 / www.mcasandiego.org
700 Prospect Street, La Jolla
(Exit San Diego Fwy [5] W. on La Jolla Village Dr., L. on Torrey Pines Rd., R. on Prospect Pl., which turns into Prospect St. [TG-1227 E7])

I admit two things about contemporary art museums: 1) I enjoy visiting them, and 2) I don't always "get" the art on exhibit. I've learned not to step on things lying on the floor or to touch anything, even things as seemingly innocuous as a pole in the center of the room - it could be an exhibit. Displays here rotate quarterly, so there are new eclectic paintings, sculptures, photos, and other pieces to figure out every few months.

Our favorite past exhibits include a room-size metal spider carrying a nest of eggs; toddler-size figures made out of wax in various stages of melting because of the heat lamps directed on them; the "Reason for the Neutron Bomb," which had 50,000 match tips glued onto nickels on the floor, each one representing a Russian tank; and a darkened room with a large church bell which, when my kids pulled on the rope, triggered a hologram of the Virgin Mary and baby Jesus to appear.

Borrow an audio tape (and player) at the front desk that explains the current exhibits. The M.C.A. offers free school group tours with titles such as Art and Creative Writing and Meaning and Wonder of Art. Pick up a free children's guide (pamphlet) at the reception desk about discovering contemporary art. It asks thought-provoking questions, and gives kids things to do and look for. By the way, the view of the coastline from the museum is spectacular. Also see the following entry, MUSEUM OF CONTEMPORARY ART, San Diego.

Hours: Open Mon. - Tues., and Fri. - Sun., 11am - 5pm; open Thurs. 11am - 8pm. Closed Wed.

Admission: $4 for adults; $2 for seniors, military with ID, and students; children 11 and under are free. Admission is free on the first Sun. and third Tues. of every month.

Ages: 6 years and up.

MUSEUM OF CONTEMPORARY ART (San Diego)
(619) 234-1001 / www.mcasandiego.org
1001 Kettner Boulevard, San Diego
(Going S. on San Diego Fwy [5] exit S. on Front St., R. on Broadway. Going N. on the 5, exit S. on 6ᵗʰ Ave. R. on Broadway. It's at Broadway and Kettner, right by the metro. Parking is hard to come by. [TG-1288 J3])

This artsy-style building sets the right mood for your visit to San Diego's contemporary art museum. What kinds of materials are used in the art that you're looking at? Traditional materials, like paint? Or nuts, bolts, wires, or other improbable materials? These are a few of the questions listed in the (free) children's guide on discovering contemporary art, which is found at the reception desk. The guide helps your child become more involved with the art, and enables him/her to understand the artist's vision in creating their work. Contemporary art is fun because it is eclectic. Some art pieces might be as unusual as a box of cereal, while other paintings, sculptures, and/or photos are a more daring combination of design, light and texture. This small museum, which has quarterly rotating exhibits, is a branch of the main M.C.A. in La Jolla.

> **Hours:** Open Mon - Tues. and Thurs. - Sat., 10am - 5pm; Sun., noon - 5. Closed Wed.
> **Admission:** Free
> **Ages:** 6 years and up.

MUSEUM OF CREATION AND EARTH HISTORY
(619) 448-0900 / www.icr.org
10946 Woodside Avenue North, Santee
(Take the 52 Fwy E. to the end, go E. on Mission Gorge Rd. Just past the intersection at Magnolia, the road turns into Woodside Ave. and forks at a stop sign; go L. on Woodside Ave. North. The museum is 1/4 mile on the left. From San Vicente Fwy [67], exit N. on Riverford Rd., L. on Woodside Ave. North. [TG-1231 F5])

Genesis 1:1: "In the beginning, God created the heavens and the earth." This walk-through creation museum, a part of the Institute of Creation Research, is a richly visual way of seeing how the earth and its inhabitants have developed. Each phase of the earth's history is graphically represented by murals, photographs, models, or audio sounds, plus Biblical references, questions to ponder, and lots of technical information. Start at the beginning, of course, and proceed through to modern day. Day four (when the sun, moon, stars, and planets were created) is the first dramatic depiction of the unfolding wonders of our universe. This room is basically dark, with spotlights on stunning photos of the planets, constellations, and our sun. Each photograph is accompanied by factual explanations. Entering the room for days five and six is like entering a small jungle. Greenery abounds alongside a few cages of small live animals such as birds, fish, snakes, and mice. Accompanied by Psalm 139 ("I am fearfully and wonderfully made. . .") an entire wall shows models of man, his inner workings, diagrams, and pictures of families.

Continue on, and see the fall of man, illustrated by bones, decay, and the sound of crying; a wood-paneled room with a mural depicting Noah's ark, complete with storm sounds and lightning flashing; a room with touchable walls that are layers of the earth and a replicate of Mt. St. Helens' volcano that you can walk through; a blue hallway representing the Ice Age with icicles hanging overhead, and models of woolly mammoths; an Egyptian room with a scale model of the enormous Tower of Babel taking center stage; the Stone Age room; the room of civilization immortalizing (so to speak) Greek and Roman cultures; and finally, the hallway of modern man, including pictures and philosophies of evolutionists and creationists. The Museum of Creation is the ultimate, interactive time line.

Each of the rooms offers various free pamphlets that discuss the ideas and facts presented throughout the museum. Guided tours are available for groups, between fifteen to thirty people, with reservations. The tours are geared for at least first graders and up. Once-a-month classes are also available for upper elementary and older students who wish to delve into creation research and Biblical learning and understanding. The classes and the museum are geared for slightly older children as a lot of the information is very technical, however, the incredible visuals make quite an impact on any age.

> **Hours:** Open Mon. - Sat., 9am - 4pm. Closed holidays. Hour-long tours are offered Tues. - Thurs., at 9:30am and 11am; Sat., 9:30am, 11am, and 2pm. Call to make a reservation.
>
> **Admission:** Free
>
> **Ages:** 5 - 9 years for the visual enjoyment; 10 years old and up to understand the technical information.

MUSEUM OF MAKING MUSIC

(877) 551-9976 / www.museumofmakingmusic.com   *$$*

5790 Armada Drive, Carlsbad

(Exit San Diego Fwy [5] E. on Palomar Airport Rd., L. on Armada. It's inside the NAMM (National Association of Music Merchants) building on the R. [TG-1126 J3])

"It makes no difference if it's sweet or hot, just give that rhythm everything you got." (From *It Don't Mean A Thing* by Irving Mills and Duke Ellington.) This would be a fitting motto for this note-worthy museum. The museum is nicely laid out and chronologically traces the history of music from the late 1800's through present day in an audibly and visually stimulating way. Paintings and wall-sized historic photographs of musicians add to the museum's ambiance.

Each section showcases, behind glass, instruments (over 450 total!) typical for that particular era which could include trumpets, banjos, mandolins, harmonicas, guitars, electric guitars (one signed by Jimi Hendrix), keyboards, pianos (one signed by Henry Mancini), horns, and drums. The sections also have listening stations where visitors can, at the press of a button, hear samplings of popular music, sounds of specific instruments, and even some of the key innovations and inventions that changed the style of music being produced. Expose kids to the sound of ragtime, big bands, jazz, blues, hillbilly, country, and more. Rooms toward the exit emphasize music probably more familiar to them - rock and roll, heavy metal, new wave, jazz infusion, and the Latin scene. Videos, instead of just "audios", accompany the latter years of music.

End your visit on a high note, by letting the kids play the instruments in the small lobby/gift shop. Children are encouraged to try out the drum set, keyboard, and electric guitars whose sound, thankfully, can only be heard through headsets.

Although the gift shop doesn't sell instruments, it does have a wide variety of them on display and it does sell some unique, music-related gifts. Guided tours for the general public and for school groups are available.

Hours: Open Tues. - Sun., 10am - 5pm. Closed Mon., New Year's Day, Independence Day, Thanksgiving, and Christmas.

Admission: $5 for adults; $3 for seniors, active military, and ages 4 - 18; children 3 and under are free.

Ages: 7 years and up.

MUSEUM OF PHOTOGRAPHIC ARTS

(619) 238-7559 / www.mopa.org $$

1649 El Prado, Balboa Park, San Diego

(Going S. on San Diego Fwy [5], exit at Sassafras/Airport, go straight on Kettner Blvd. L. on Laurel St., which turns into El Prado. Going N. on 5, exit N. on Pershing Dr., L. on Florida Dr., L. on Zoo Pl., L. on Park Blvd., R. on Village Pl. Going S. on Cabrillo Fwy [163], exit N. on Park Blvd. (near end), L. on Presidents Wy. [TG-1289 C1])

Your shutterbugs will appreciate this large showroom, with five galleries, that features changing exhibits of photographic works. Some exhibits zoom in on portraiture work or the history of American photography, while others focus more on pictures taken from all over the world. We enjoy the artistry in the pictures as well as comparing styles and choice of subjects. Ask about the Visual Classroom, a student-friendly curriculum supplement. Free, guided tours are given Sundays at 1pm.

A 200-seat theater shows a variety of movies such as *All Dogs Go to Heaven, Angels in the Outfield*, and *Heaven Can Wait*. (See BALBOA PARK [San Diego] in this section for a listing of all the museums and attractions within walking distance.)

Hours: The museum is open daily 10am - 5pm. The theater shows movies usually on Fri. night and the weekends. Call for specific hours.

Admission: Museum admission is $6 for adults; $4 for seniors, military, and students; children 11 and under are free. Admission to the museum is free on the second Tues. of every month. Passports for 11 museums in Balboa Park are available for $30 for adults at the Visitors Center, and are good for one week from the date of purchase. (Children's admissions are already discounted or free.) Theater admission is $7.50 for adults; $6 for MoPA members; $5 for seniors, students, and ages 11 and under.

Ages: 7 years and up.

NATIONAL CITY SANTA FE DEPOT

(619) 474-4400 / www.trainweb.com/sandiegorail/sdera $$

922 W. 23rd Street, National City

(Exit San Diego Fwy [5] W. on Bay Marina Dr., R. on Harrison. The depot sits between 24th and 23rd on Harrison Avenue [TG-1309 G3])

This small historic depot, originally built in 1882, is restored to it's original floor plan, containing ticket offices and upstairs living quarters for the station master. It is now home to the electric railway museum. Across the street is a glassed-enclosed gazebo that protects the restored an 1887 passenger coach No. 1.

The main attraction for little train lovers is the forty-minute round-trip railbus excursion over the Coronado Belt Line on a speeder, gasoline pump car, or open-sided car. The trip starts near the above-mentioned museums on Bay Marina Boulevard and loops around the bay.

Hours: The museum is open Sat. - Sun., noon - 4pm. The train trip runs on the first Sun. of each month, noon - 4pm.

Admission: Call for museum prices. The train ride is $5 for adults; $2 for ages 6 - 12; children 5 and under are free.

Ages: All

OLD TOWN SAN DIEGO AND STATE HISTORIC PARK ☼

(619) 220-5422 - Robinson Rose House and park ranger /   !/$
www.sandiegohistory.org

Taylor, Juan, Twiggs, and Congress Sts., Old Town, San Diego

(Going S. on San Diego Fwy [5] [just south of Interstate 8] exit E. [across the bridge] on Old Town Ave., L. on San Diego Ave. Going N. on 5, exit at Moore St., R. on Old Town Ave., L. on San Diego Ave. or Congress St. Parking is available on the streets if you arrive early, or at several parking lots. [TG-1268 F5])

Old Town is a six-block, closed-to-through-traffic area, bound by Taylor, Juan, Twiggs, and Congress streets. The places mentioned below encompass this area, plus the immediate, walkable vicinity.

Old Town is a wonderful conglomeration of unique shops, scrumptious places to eat, vintage houses, museums, and a Mexican bazaar, all located along dirt "roads" that are closed to automotive traffic, and on paved sidewalks outside of "town". It's a town you'll want to visit more than once to make sure you experience all it has to offer. San Diego is the site of the first permanent Spanish settlement on the California coast, thus it shares a similar historical significance with Jamestown, the first English settlement on the East Coast. Old Town contains many original and restored buildings from San Diego's Mexican period before 1846, and the early California period. A day here is a combination of history lessons and fun shopping! The route for the attractions listed below starts at the Robinson Rose House - the park headquarters - then proceeds east, south, and north before looping back around. Most of the attractions are open daily 10am to 5pm; shops are usually open until 9pm in the spring and summer. Admission is free, unless otherwise noted. All historic buildings are closed on New Year's Day, Thanksgiving, and Christmas. Free maps of the area are available at the park headquarters, in many of the stores in Old Town, and in local hotel lobbies. Free walking tours that cover all of the old buildings, not just the more kid-friendly ones I've listed here, are offered daily at 11am and 2pm beginning at Robinson Rose House.

ROBINSON ROSE HOUSE is located at 4002 Wallace Street, on the other side of the parking lot from Taylor Street. This 1853 adobe structure houses the park headquarters and has walking tour maps available for purchase. It also has a few exhibits, such as photo murals and a scale model of Old Town as it appeared in the mid 1870's.

OLD TOWN PLAZA is located directly in front of the Robinson Rose House. This area is essentially a large grassy area for kids to run around, with olive, fig, cork, and eucalyptus trees providing beauty and shade. A large fountain is in the middle of this park and there are plenty of benches for weary travelers (or shoppers).

The row of stores across from the Plaza are in reconstructed buildings dating from around 1830. Just a few of our favorite stores in Old Town include Miner's Gems and Minerals, Toler's Leather Depot, The Mexico Shop, and of course the ice cream and candy shops! Old Town is truly a shopper's delight.

COLORADO HOUSE/WELLS FARGO MUSEUM is located on San Diego Street in the heart of Old Town. This museum has the appeal of the Old West, with a Concord Stagecoach prominently displayed in the center. Other exhibits include a colorful wall display of Wells Fargo featured in comic books, trading cards, and even a board game; rocks with gold, gold coins, and bags of gold found in treasure boxes; mining tools; Old West posters; and more. A video shows and describes this time period and the history of Wells Fargo.

CASA DE MACHADO Y STEWART is located almost directly behind the Colorado House/Wells Fargo Museum. This plain-looking adobe is an exact replica of the original house, complete with a dirt walkway leading to it. The brick-floored house contains few furnishings, including a dining table, shelves with dishes and pottery, a sparsely furnished bedroom, and some tools. Just beyond the front porch is a beehive oven and open fire stoves, evidence of the outdoor cooking that pioneers once employed.

MASON STREET SCHOOL is located on Mason Street, diagonal to the Casa de Machado y Stewart. This 1865 red schoolhouse is a child's favorite historical stop in Old Town. It was the first public schoolhouse in San Diego and retains its old-fashioned ambiance with twenty school desks, a school bell, flags, a chalkboard, a wood-burning stove, the dunce's corner (and cap), and old pictures and books. It's open daily 10am to 4pm.

THE DENTAL MUSEUM is located on San Diego Avenue in front of the schoolhouse. Kids will enjoy a quick peek at the past here as they see a dentist chair, instruments, and even some molds of teeth.

SAN DIEGO UNION BUILDING is located on San Diego Avenue. The first edition of the San Diego Union came off the presses here way back when. Now, kids can see an old Washington handpress (printing press), typeset letters and tools, and the adjacent small newspaper office.

WHALEY HOUSE - See WHALEY HOUSE, in this Museums section, for details. It's an interesting museum! Take a quick peek into the Old Town Drug

Store Museum, located behind this museum. Kids can see an old-time pharmacy containing bottles, patented medicines, and a mortar and pestle.

HERITAGE PARK, (858) 565-3600, is located north of the Whaley House, on Harvey and Juan Streets. This group of buildings is enchanting to simply look at. Each of the seven Victorian houses now serve other functions: The Sherman Gilbert house, our favorite, was built in 1887 and is now the Old Doll Shoppe, offering dolls, dollhouses, miniatures, and ornaments for sale and the Christian House is now a bed and breakfast.

THE MORMON BATTALION VISITOR CENTER, (619) 298-3317, is located on Juan Street. An informative tour guide will show your family around this small center. The first thing we noticed was a statue as tall as the biblical Goliath - he *really* was tall! Kids can hold a sun-baked adobe brick and learn its historical significance. They'll also learn how people placed copper pennies in an oven (an alternative way of baking bricks) until the pennies began to melt, at 2,000 degrees. This meant the oven was hot enough to bake bricks (and lots of other things, too!)

Although the 500 men of the Mormon Battalion never fought a battle, the 1846 volunteer unit marched 2,000 miles across country to San Diego to help fight in the Mexican/American war. Their arduous trail blazing efforts and accomplishments are reenacted in an interesting fifteen-minute film. The diorama adjacent to the screen is occasionally spotlighted to emphasize portions of the movie. After the film, we were led into another room and shown huge paintings of Jesus during various times of his ministry. As our tour concluded, we were offered a Book of Mormon and asked if we could have someone call on us regarding the Mormon religion. The visitor center is open daily 9am to 9pm. Admission is free.

SEELEY STABLES is located on Calhoun Street. This huge, reconstructed barn contains several exhibit stalls. The saddles, bells, and harnesses, plus at least ten stagecoaches and carriages, are great visual aids for picturing the past. Free slide shows are presented in the downstairs theater throughout the day, so come and rest, and learn a little history. The upstairs loft has more exhibits of the wild, wild west, such as branding irons, spurs, more saddles, a Mexican cowboy hat, and furniture including an unusual chair made out of steers' horns. A native American display features Kachina dolls, a feather headdress, and baskets. Other exhibits up here include an old-fashioned slot machine, a roller organ, an antique telephone, a case of model horses, and a child's room with toys.

The backyard of the stables is an open courtyard with early farm equipment around its perimeters, plus several more carriages and stagecoaches in glass-cased enclosures. Also back here, or accessible from Mason Street, is THE BLACK HAWK LIVERY STABLE AND BLACKSMITH. This large blacksmith workshop holds demonstrations every Wednesday and Saturday 10am to 2pm. Kids might see the hot fires help bend pieces of metal into horseshoes or heavy chains, or they might hear a hammer clank against the anvil to create a sword or branding iron. The stable room is filled with finished pieces and tools.

GEORGE JOHNSON HOUSE is located on Calhoun Street, near Mason Street. This small building has a room to walk through - it took us maybe five minutes. It displays archaeological findings of the area such as bottles and pottery, plus tools of the trade and pictures showing the painstaking work of excavation and cleaning.

BAZAAR DEL MUNDO, (619) 296-3161 / www.bazaardelmundo.com, is located on the corner of Juan and Wallace Streets. This gaily decorated traditional Mexican courtyard is festive in appearance and atmosphere. Mariachi bands play, costumed dancers entertain occasionally, and the colorful storefronts and wares beckon shoppers of all ages. Our favorite shops here include Geppetto's, a wonderful toy store; Just Animals, for the wild (and tame) at heart; Creations and Confections, specializing in old-fashioned candies, chocolates, and party supplies; La Panaderia, serving delectable Mexican breads and pastries, including churros; and Treasures, a store that carries gifts and crafts from exotic lands. If your tummy is saying, "Tengo hambre" (that's Spanish for "I'm hungry"), sample and savor some of the culinary delights at any one of the several restaurants here. Most shops here are open daily 10am to 9pm.

Look up the SERRA MUSEUM / PRESIDIO PARK entry, in this section, which is located just north of Old Town.

Hours: Most "attractions" open daily 10am - 5pm.
Admission: Free, but bring spending money. See individual listings.
Ages: 4 years and up.

RANCHO BUENA VISTA ADOBE / VISTA HISTORICAL ☸ MUSEUM

(760) 639-6164 / www.ci.vista.ca.us $
651 E. Vista Way, Vista
(Exit Vista Fwy [78] N. on Escondido Ave / Sunset Dr., R. on Vista Way. Both are adjacent to Wildwood Park. [TG-1087 J6])

Follow the signs through the park and over the footbridge to the Adobe. Guided tours, the only way to see the inside of the rancho, begin just outside the gift shop, in front of an eye-catching, hand-painted map of the surrounding cities. The brick-paved patio and pathways leading to the eleven-room adobe add to the old-time ambiance. The immaculately kept grounds and adobe are often used for weddings, meetings, and other functions.

The first stop is simply to check out the thickness of adobe walls. Walk into each room, all of which are furnished with items donated by area residents. The kitchen is constantly in use and it contains numerous old-fashioned implements. In one bedroom touch cowhide (which is hard) and calf hide (which is supple) draped on a bed. The bathroom has ornate tiles from the 1930's and a cool bathtub. Another room contains a loom and other workman's tools of trade. A living room contains an old piano with candle holders (used before electricity was invented), a phonograph with cylinder "records", pictures, and paintings. My boys especially liked the light fixtures with wood-carved knight figures on them. Outside are a few neatly arranged washing machines and farm tools.

Listen to the fascinating history and stories of this home, from rancho to Hollywood hangout. A few samples to pique your interest: One room supposedly still contains a skeleton in the wall because when it was discovered years and years ago, it was just covered back up again. Once a bandit came to steal a horse and instead, wound up ordering his gang to protect the owner who had befriended him. A few of the rooms were originally not enclosed and used as a thoroughfare for horses. One owner slept with his prize stallion in his room. And so on.

Two-hour California history programs, offered for groups comprising of ten to thirty-three students, include a forty-minute guided tour and two activities. Choose from candle dipping, cooking, branding, roping, weaving, Native American games, and/or Native American crafts. Activities take place in the adobe or in the backyard. Teachers may request a curriculum notebook with lesson plans and worksheets.

The small park adjacent to the rancho has a few pieces of playground equipment, a grassy area, picnic tables, and a stage.

The Vista Historical Museum is next to the park and parking lot. It contains a little bit of everything such as old clothing, gloves, hats, a collection of typewriters, rock specimens, arrows, a hair curler machine that looks like it's out of a science fiction story, tools, and more. Visitors can request a viewing of the thirty-minute "History of Vista" documentary featuring interviews with residents raised in the city during its formative years.

Hours: The rancho is open Wed. - Sat., 10am - 3pm, although tours are not always given on Sat. afternoons. (Call first.) The museum is open Wed. - Sat., 10am - 3pm. The park is open daily dawn to dusk.

Admission: The rancho is $3 for adults; $2 for seniors and Vista residents; $1 for students; 50¢ for ages 11 and under. School programs are $5.25 per student with one free adult for every 5 students. Extra adults are $3. The museum and park are free.

Ages: 7 years and up.

RANCHO GUAJOME ADOBE

(760) 724-4082 / www.co.san-diego.ca.us/parks $
2210 N. Santa Fe Avenue, Vista
(Exit Fwy 78 N. on Vista Village Dr., L. on Santa Fe Ave. [TG-1087 G2])

This "Cadillac of adobes", built in 1853, contains thirty rooms and is one of the finest examples of early California hacienda architecture. (Count all the archways!) It was built for the same reason missions were built; to protect residents from intruders and maintain a small community of family and servants on the grounds.

Encircling a large inner courtyard, the rancho consists of a schoolroom, spacious family living quarters, dining room, a separate chapel, servants' quarters, the kitchen, sheds, stables, and a Victorian-style garden. It has all been beautifully restored. The furnishings, plus the buggy in the carriage courtyard and the docent's information, make the past seem vividly present.

School groups are offered guided tours that correspond with California state curriculum. One of the highlights for students is making adobe bricks. (Dress accordingly!) Note that the ANTIQUE GAS AND STEAM ENGINE MUSEUM (listed in this section) is next door, and Guajome Regional Park, for picnic and playtime, is just down the street.

Hours: Open for tours Sat. - Sun. at 11am, 12:30pm, and 2pm, except in rainy weather. Open weekdays for groups by reservation.

Admission: $2 for adults; $1 for children. School tours are free.

Ages: 7 years and up.

REUBEN H. FLEET SCIENCE CENTER / IMAX ☼
THEATER

(619) 238-1233 / www.rhfleet.org   *$$$*

1875 El Prado, Balboa Park, San Diego

(Going S. on San Diego Fwy [5], exit at Sassafras/Airport, go straight on Kettner Blvd. L. on Laurel St., which turns into El Prado. Going N. on 5, exit N. on Pershing Dr., L. on Florida Dr., L. on Zoo Pl., L. on Park Blvd., R. on Village Pl. Going S. on Cabrillo Fwy [163], exit N. on Park Blvd. (near end), L. on Space Theater Wy. [TG-1289 C1])

This huge Science Center is a fascinating place for hands-on exploration, experimentation, and discovery. There are numerous permanent exhibits throughout several gallery rooms, including a periscope that literally goes through the roof to view the outside world; a build and play area for children ages 2 to 6; a virtual tour through the heart in Heartflight, where the beat goes on; and ExploraZone®, which contains thirty activities to do with color, sound, and communication. A few favorite exhibits here include the bubble maker; the whisper dishes, where friends sit fifty-feet apart, whisper into a dish, and hear each other; and the "Why is the Sky Blue?" exhibit. (You'll have to visit the museum to find out the answer.) Meteor Storm is a virtual reality game that up to six people can play at a time. They "journey" through a meteor storm to save the earth, of course. SciTours, a simulator ride, offers another way to experience outer space via *Journey to Mars,* a jolting, thrilling eight-minute ride. It holds up to twenty-three people. Riders must be at least 40" tall and children under 10 must be accompanied by a parent. There are also many outstanding temporary exhibits here, too. Check the web site to see what's currently at the museum.

The second floor hosts a few changing displays as well as TechnoVation, the corporate name for numerous, technology-based exhibits. For instance, watch a film showing laser eye surgery being performed; learn the history of computers from punch card to P.C.; have a video conference with someone across the room; see technological breakthroughs; and find out where water comes from and how it gets clean - from rain water to tap water. The CHALLENGER LEARNING CENTER (see this entry in the Educational Presentations section) is also located on this floor. Registered participants take a class in the Mission Control room and use the ten computer stations to experience hands-on learning of all the stages of launching and completing a space mission. Live science demonstrations are also given on this floor.

The geodesic dome-shaped IMAX theater shows one-hour films on a screen several times the size of screens in regular movie theaters, therefore drawing you into the show's action. The shows are usually educational and are always interesting. Other stellar productions include one-hour planetarium shows given on the first Wednesday of every month at 7pm.

Tip or warning: The gift shop appeals to all ages who are even slightly scientific or hands-on oriented. *Star Trek* fans, in particular, will have a field day here. (See BALBOA PARK [San Diego], in this section, for a listing of all the museums and attractions within walking distance.)

Hours: The exhibit gallery is open Sun. - Thurs., 9:30am - 5pm; Fri. - Sat., 9:30am - 9pm. It's open in the summer and on school breaks daily 9:30am - 9pm. IMAX films are shown throughout the day.

Admission: Exhibit gallery entrance is $6.50 for adults; $5.50 for seniors; $5 for ages 3 - 12; children 2 and under are free. Admission to an IMAX show and the exhibit gallery is $11 for adults; $9 for seniors; $8 for ages 3 - 12; children 2 and under are free. Planetarium shows are $5 for adults; $4 for seniors; $3 for ages 3 - 12. Membership here is reciprocal at the DISCOVERY SCIENCE CENTER in Santa Ana and the CALIFORNIA SCIENCE CENTER in Los Angeles. Admission to the exhibits only is free on the first Tues. of every month. Passports for 11 museums in Balboa Park are available for $30 for adults at the Visitors Center, and are good for one week from the date of purchase. (Children's admissions are already discounted or free.)

Ages: 4 years and up.

SAN DIEGO AEROSPACE MUSEUM

(619) 234-8291 / www.aerospacemuseum.org   *$$$*

2001 Pan American Plaza, Balboa Park, San Diego

(Going S. on San Diego Fwy [5], exit at Sassafras/Airport, go straight on Kettner Blvd. L. on Laurel St., which turns into El Prado. Going N. on 5, exit N. on Pershing Dr., L. on Florida Dr., L. on Zoo PL., L. on Park Blvd., R. on Village Pl. Going S. on Cabrillo Fwy [163], exit N. on Park Blvd. (near the end), L. on Presidents Wy. [TG-1289 C1])

Take to the skies in this marvelous museum that visually chronicles the history of aviation from the dawn of flight through the age of space travel. The first few rooms, formally titled the International Aerospace Hall of Fame, give homage to the aero-engineers, pilots, and aviation founders that didn't fly off course in their vision for creating aircrafts and the aerospace industry. The hall is filled with photos, plaques, and medals of these aviation heroes. Portraits of Armstrong, Aldrich, and other astronauts, especially, caught my children's eyes. An Apollo XI display features a replica of the plaque left on the moon, the box used to collect lunar samples, and more.

The next rooms are packed with exhibits of early flying machines and models of inventions such as gliders, "birdmen" who used bicycle tires, bi-planes, and the Wright Brother's flyer, plus narrated videos that show pictures of early flying attempts. Consecutive eras are also well defined and enhanced with colorful wall murals, period-dressed mannequins, and other fine details. Wood-paneled rooms, complete with sandbags and army netting, house WWI and WWII planes and other memorabilia such as helmets, goggles, and uniforms.

The flying aces and the fighter planes that served them, including the Spad, the Nieuport, Spitfires, Hellcats, and Zeros, are well represented. In between wars, the U.S. Mail service was introduced. Displays here include a Curtiss JN-4 Jenny, wall posters of stamps blown up in size that commemorate aviation, and a replicated 1918 mail office. Kids love the next exhibits of barnstormers and pictures of daredevils using planes to entertain. These showmen of the air are doing headstands on wings, transferring from a plane to a speeding car, and other feats.

The next series of rooms honor women aviators, house engines and propellers, and display lots of model airplanes. Enter a pilot's ready room to watch the film *Sea Legs*. The armed forces are saluted with their contributions and a scale model of the U.S.S. Yorktown, and the U.S.S. Langley - the Navy's first carrier.

Enter the Jet Age with the F-4 Phantom, and the spy plane, the Blackbird. This exciting time period is followed by the Space Age. This last set of rooms feature bulky astronaut uniforms, capsules, modules, a moon rock, and more. An adjacent theater room showcases the history of model making.

Soar to new heights as you and your children explore the Aerospace Museum! Behind-the-scenes tours of the aircraft restoration facility are available upon request. (See BALBOA PARK [San Diego], in this section, for a listing of all the museums and attractions within walking distance.)

Hours: Open daily 10am - 4:30pm. Open in the summer daily until 5pm. Closed Thanksgiving and Christmas.

Admission: $8 for adults; $6 for seniors; $3 for ages 6 - 17; active duty military and children 5 and under are free. Admission on the fourth Tues. of every month is free. Passports for 11 museums in Balboa Park are available for $30 for adults at the Visitors Center, and are good for one week from the date of purchase. (Children's admissions are already discounted or free.)

Ages: 4 years and up.

SAN DIEGO AEROSPACE MUSEUM (auxiliary)   ☀

(619) 258-1221- direct line; (619) 234-8291 - Aerospace Museum in   !
Balboa Park

335 Kenney Street, El Cajon

(Going N. on San Vincente Fwy [67], exit W. on Prospect, L. on Magnolia Ave., R. on Kenney. Going S. on 67, exit W. on Mission Gorge Rd., L. on Magnolia, R. on Kenney. It's on the N. side of Gillespie Airport. [TG-1251 E1])

Even I couldn't miss this museum - it has an Atlas missile on the front lawn! This museum is a depository for "work-in-progress" planes from the SAN DIEGO AEROSPACE MUSEUM in Balboa Park as numerous planes here are in the process of being restored or rebuilt. Outside, besides the missile, are an F-14, F-8, F-86, and A-6, plus an army helicopter and other jet fighters. Exhibits do rotate. There are about ten planes inside the two hangars, including an F-16, A-4, and P-51, plus the nose of a B-52. A few engines and aeronautical artifacts are also housed here.

Hours: Open Mon., Wed., and Fri., 8:30am - 3pm.

Admission: Free
Ages: 5 years and up.

SAN DIEGO AIRCRAFT CARRIER MUSEUM

619) 702-7700 / www.midway.org
1335 N. Harbor Drive, San Diego
(Going N. on San Diego Fwy [5], exit E. on Hawthorne St., L. on Harbor. Going S. on 5, exit S. on Front St., R. on Ash, L. on Harbor. On S. side of Navy Pier [TG-1288 J3])

Opening in 2002, the decommissioned USS Midway, a legend of the U.S. Naval carrier fleet that put in forty-seven years of service, is doing a final "tour of duty" as an interactive museum. The first thing children will notice is Midway's size - she's enormous! On board the ship will be flight simulators, a below deck theater, computer kiosks, an educational research center, interactive displays, exhibits depicting carrier battles, real aircraft, and one of the largest collections of U.S. Navy artifacts. The encased artifacts date from the American Revolutionary War, the Civil War, WWI, and WWII, and will include photographs, swords, flags, uniforms, model planes, and lots more. The Midway's flight decks and bays will boast of fifteen-plus historic aircraft including a E-2C Hawkeye, F4-S Phantom, F-14 Tomcat, A-6E Intruder, and SH-53 Helicopter. Tours and educational programs are also offered. There is nothing done half-way on the Midway, so drop anchor and visit this unique nautical museum. Note: The Aircraft Carrier Memorial, honoring those who have defended our country, is nearby. Check out other close-by port activities, too.
Hours: Open daily. Call for hours.
Admission: To be announced.
Ages: 4 years and up.

SAN DIEGO AUTOMOTIVE MUSEUM

(619) 231-2886 / www.sdautomuseum.org $$
2080 Pan American Plaza, Balboa Park, San Diego
(Going S. on San Diego Fwy [5], exit at Sassafras/Airport, go straight on Kettner Blvd. L. on Laurel St., which turns into El Prado. Going N. on 5, exit N. on Pershing Dr., L. on Florida Dr., L. on Zoo PL, L. on Park Blvd., R. on Village Pl. Going S. on Cabrillo Fwy [163], exit N. on Park Blvd. (near end), L. on Presidents Wy. [TG-1289 C1])

Jump start your child's interest in automobiles at this museum that has more than eighty vehicles on display. Most of the gleaming cars are in a line and readily viewable. Some of the vintage automobiles are on display in appropriate settings, such as a fifties car in front of a backdrop of a drive-through. Classics here range from old-fashioned Model A's to futuristic-looking DeLoreans. Other favorites include a 1948 Tucker "Torpedo" (only fifty-one were ever built), a 1934 convertible Coupe Roadster, a 1955 Mercedes Benz (300SL Gullwing), a 1957 Chevrolet, and Packards from 1929 to 1936. Prototypes, model cars, a race car, a re-created mechanics shop complete with tools, and an engine room for those who want the inside scoop on cars, are also found at this museum. "Gentlemen, start your engines" applied to my boys as they raced over to see the over forty motorcycles on display. They were particularly elated by the Harley

Davidsons, the Indian Chief, and an army cycle. (See BALBOA PARK [San Diego], in this section, for a listing of all the museums and attractions within walking distance.)

Hours: Open daily 10am - 4pm. Open in the summer daily 10am - 5pm.
Admission: $7 for adults; $6 for seniors; $3 for ages 6 - 15; children 5 and under are free. Admission on the fourth Tues. of every month is free. Passports for 11 museums in Balboa Park are available for $30 for adults at the Visitors Center, and are good for one week from the date of purchase. (Children's admissions are already discounted or free.)
Ages: 6 years and up.

SAN DIEGO COUNTY SHERIFF'S MUSEUM   ☀
(619) 260-1850   !
2384 San Diego Avenue, San Diego
(Going S. on San Diego Fwy [5] [just south of Interstate 8] exit E. [across the bridge] on Old Town Ave., L. on San Diego Ave. Going N. on 5, exit at Moore St., R. on Old Town Ave., L. on San Diego Ave. It's just S. of Old Town. [TG-1268 F5])

This two-story, innocuous-looking adobe building, fitting right in with the surrounding Old Town architecture, houses two jails and lots of weapons! Actually, these items are part of the displays at the Sheriff's Museum. Other exhibits include the history of law enforcement, particularly in San Diego; a helicopter that visitors can sit in for a bird's eye view of, well, just the rest of the museum; a real police motorcycle; a banged up car that was hit by a drunk driver; a mock court room; a gallery of honor in memory of fallen officers; and a salute to K-9 units, search and rescue teams, and the special forces. A display on gangs, narcotics, and weapons is also here. The two jails are from different eras: one is a replicated 1850's jail and the other is a more modern-day facility. Just a few minutes behind these bars will hopefully make an impact upon kids so that they won't want to do any time anywhere else. Note: School tours are given four times a day that fit in with California fourth grade curriculum.

Patrol the rest of Old Town while you're here. Look up the OLD TOWN SAN DIEGO AND STATE HISTORIC PARK entry (under this section) to check out what else there is to see and do in the immediately vicinity.

Hours: Open Tues. - Sat., 10am - 4pm.
Admission: Free
Ages: 5 years and up.

SAN DIEGO HALL OF CHAMPIONS - SPORTS   ☀
MUSEUM
(619) 234-2544 / www.sandiegosports.org $$
2131 Pan American Plaza, Balboa Park, San Diego   ♨
(Going S. on San Diego Fwy [5], exit at Sassafras/Airport, go straight on Kettner Blvd. L. on Laurel St., which turns into El Prado. Going N. on 5, exit N. on Pershing Dr., L. on Florida Dr., L. on Zoo PL., L. on Park Blvd., R. on Village Pl. Going S. on Cabrillo Fwy [163], exit N. on Park Blvd. (near end), L. on Presidents Wy. [TG-1289 C1])

Give your sports fans something to cheer about by taking them to the Hall of

Champions. Over forty different sports are represented in this eye-catching museum, including baseball, basketball, hockey, boxing, table tennis, surfing, racing, boating, soapbox derby, and a beach game called over-the-line. The exhibits showcase athletes, like Ted Williams and Bill Walton, and teams, like the Padres, all associated with San Diego - what a winning city this is! You'll see photographs, statues outfitted in sports attire, videos, trophies, and lots of sports equipment such as uniforms, balls, and even a racing boat and a motorcycle. The theater presents continuously running sports films and clips, mostly bloopers, which kids love. (See BALBOA PARK [San Diego], under this section, for a listing of all the museums and attractions within walking distance.)

Hours: Open daily 10am - 4:30pm.

Admission: $4 for adults; $3 for seniors; $2 for ages 7 - 17; children 6 and under are free. Admission on the fourth Tues. of every month is free. Passports to 11 museums in Balboa Park are available for $30 for adults at the Visitors Center, and are good for one week from the date of purchase. (Children's admissions are already discounted or free.)

Ages: 5 years and up.

SAN DIEGO HISTORICAL SOCIETY MUSEUM ☀

(619) 232-6203 / www.sandiegohistory.org $$
1649 El Prado, Balboa Park, San Diego

(Going S. on San Diego Fwy [5], exit at Sassafras/Airport, go straight on Kettner Blvd. L. on Laurel St., which turns into El Prado. Going N. on 5, exit N. on Pershing Dr., L. on Florida Dr., L. on Zoo PL., L. on Park Blvd., R. on Village Pl. Going S. on Cabrillo Fwy [163], exit N. on Park Blvd. (near end), L. on Presidents Wy. [TG-1289 C1])

This museum presents the history of San Diego, from the 1850's to the present, via numerous photographs, plus maps, works of art, costumes, household goods, furniture, and other artifacts. An authentic stagecoach is the first item you'll see and it sets the mood for your visit here. We always enjoy seeing history and understanding more about our past generation's lifestyles. (See BALBOA PARK [San Diego] in this section for a listing of all the museums and attractions within walking distance.)

Hours: Open Tues. - Sun., 10am - 4:30pm. Open also the second Tues. of each month.

Admission: $5 for adults; $4 for seniors; $2 for ages 6 - 17; children 5 and under are free. Admission the second Tues. of every month is free. Passports for 11 museums in Balboa Park are available for $30 for adults at the Visitors Center, and are good for one week from the date of purchase. (Children's admissions are already discounted or free.)

Ages: 5 years and up.

SAN DIEGO MODEL RAILROAD MUSEUM �“

(619) 696-0199 / www.sdmodelrailroadm.com $
1649 El Prado, Balboa Park, San Diego

(Going S. on San Diego Fwy [5], exit at Sassafras/Airport, go straight on Kettner Blvd. L. on Laurel St., which turns into El Prado. Going N. on 5, exit N. on Pershing Dr., L. on Florida Dr., L. on Zoo Pl., L. on Park Blvd., R. on Village Pl. Going S. on Cabrillo Fwy [163], exit N. on Park Blvd. (near end), L. on Presidents Wy. [TG-1289 C1])

You won't have to railroad your children into coming to this museum. Just one of the things I learned here was the difference between model trains and toy trains. (Hint: The way they operate and the way they look are very different.) The museum houses the largest operating model railroad exhibits in America. Kids (and short adults) can step up onto platforms to get a closer look at the several huge layouts. Watch scale model trains make tracks through and around authentically landscaped hillsides and miniature towns that are complete with scale cars, trees, and people. Some of the exhibits depicting the development of railroading in Southern California include the Tehachapi Pass, the Cabrillo and Southwestern, and a Civil War era live steam locomotive. One of our favorites is the Pacific Desert Line, which has a model train going through a town, citrus groves, and a gorge, all of which can be seen by looking through real train car windows!

Kids will have the most fun in the Toy Train Gallery, which features Lionel O Gauge trains and more. Turn knobs, push buttons, and pull back on throttles to operate trains, make signal crossers flash, windmills turn, and toy trucks haul "rocks" to a loading dock. A wooden Brio train set for younger children completes this interactive and at*track*tive room. As the railroad museum is always in the process of re*modeling*, it is fun and different every time you visit. (See BALBOA PARK [San Diego], under this section, for a listing of all the museums and attractions within walking distance.)

Hours: Open Tues. - Fri., 11am - 4pm; Sat. - Sun., 11am - 5pm.

Admission: $4 for adults; $3 for seniors; $2.50 students; children 14 and under are free. Admission on the first Tues. of every month is free. Passports for 11 museums in Balboa Park are available for $30 for adults at the Visitors Center, and are good for one week from the date of purchase. (Children's admissions are already discounted or free.)

Ages: 2 years and up.

SAN DIEGO MUSEUM OF ART   ☀

(619) 232-7931 / www.sdmart.com   *$$$*

1450 El Prado, Balboa Park, San Diego

(Going S. on San Diego Fwy [5], exit at Sassafras/Airport, go straight on Kettner Blvd. L. on Laurel St., which turns into El Prado. Going N. on 5, exit N. on Pershing Dr., L. on Florida Dr., L. on Zoo Pl., L. on Park Blvd., R. on Village Pl. Going S. on Cabrillo Fwy [163], exit N. on Park Blvd. (near end), L. on Presidents Wy. [TG-1289 C1])

This ornately-edificed building primarily features European, American, Asian, and twentieth-century art. As with any art museum, my children's interest was sparked by having them look for differences in artistic styles or color, and looking at various choices of subject. Kids need to somehow participate with the art in order to enjoy it. My boys were intrigued most by the statues, especially the fighting Minotaur. The small Image Gallery room has touch screens that introduce and teach children (and adults) more about the paintings and sculptures throughout the museum. (Anything to do with computers draws this generation's interest!) Although the museum has more appeal for older children, Sunday Family Days are geared for ages 4 years and up. These programs focus on a particular aspect or image of art, (e.g. finding dogs in paintings), followed by a game and/or a related craft. Call for dates, times, and prices. Tip: If you're not sure your children will enjoy this museum, come on the third Tuesday of the month, when admission is free. (See BALBOA PARK [San Diego], under this section, for a listing of all the museums and attractions within walking distance.)

Hours: Open Tues. - Sun., 10am - 6pm, open Thurs. until 9pm. Closed Mon. (except Labor Day), New Year's Day, Thanksgiving, and Christmas.

Admission: $8 for adults; $6 for seniors, military, and ages 18-24; $3 for ages 6 - 17; children 5 and under are free. Admission Fri. - Sun. is $1 more for all paying age groups. Admission on the third Tues. of each month is free to view the permanent collection. Passports for 11 museums in Balboa Park are available for $30 for adults at the Visitors Center, and are good for one week from the date of purchase. (Children's admissions are already discounted or free.)

Ages: 8 years and up.

SAN DIEGO MUSEUM OF MAN
(619) 239-2001 / www.museumofman.org
1350 El Prado, Balboa Park, San Diego
(Going S. on San Diego Fwy [5], exit at Sassafras/Airport, go straight on Kettner Blvd. L. on Laurel St., which turns into El Prado. Going N. on 5, exit N. on Pershing Dr., L. on Florida Dr., L. on Zoo Pl., L. on Park Blvd., R. on Village Pl. Going S. on Cabrillo Fwy [163], exit N. on Park Blvd. (near end), L. on Presidents Wy. [TG-1289 C1])

"You've come a long way, baby!" is the best way to rephrase this museum's theme of our ancestors' growth, change, and accomplishments into modern day man. The first floor exhibits that we saw (they do rotate) consisted of tapestry hangings, a weaving demonstration, and plaster casts of stone monuments engraved and dedicated to deities. Toward the stairs is a huge, stuffed mountain gorilla and displays on primate evolution. Upstairs, the theory of evolution theme continues with lots of visuals. There are skeletons of apes and man side by side to compare and contrast; a theoretical time line; and life-size models depicting what some scientists believe early man looked like. Warning: Many of the models are naked (and very hairy). Peoples of the Southwest are represented by displays of pottery, Kachina dolls, and jewelry. Hunters are represented by displays of weapons, tools, and foods. Our favorite exhibits, pertaining to this latter category, were the rabbit skin blanket, eagle feather skirt, shoes from fibers, and a quiver made out of a raccoon. Ancient Egypt is *tut*tilating with a real mummy, dating from around 330 B.C., plus coffin masks covered with symbols of Isis, and exotic jewelry.

The hands-on Children's Discovery Center sometimes rotates its theme. We "experienced" Ancient Egypt by dressing up in appropriate clothing and headwear, building pyramids with blocks, trying our hand at hieroglyphics, and playing ancient games - all in a replicated noble's home. On weekends, for an additional $3 fee, your children can also participate in a take-home, themed craft. (See BALBOA PARK [San Diego], under this section, for a listing of all the museums and attractions within walking distance.)

Hours: Open daily 10am - 4:30pm.

Admission: $6 for adults; $5 for seniors; $3 for ages 6 - 17; children 5 and under are free. Admission on the third Tues. of every month is free. Passports for 11 museums in Balboa Park are available for $30 for adults at the Visitors Center, and are good for one week from the date of purchase. (Children's admissions are already discounted or free.)

Ages: 5 years and up.

SAN DIEGO NATURAL HISTORY MUSEUM   ☼
(619) 232-3821 / www.sdnhm.org $$$
1788 El Prado, Balboa Park, San Diego

(Going S. on San Diego Fwy [5], exit at Sassafras/Airport, go straight on Kettner Blvd. L. on Laurel St., which turns into El Prado. Going N. on 5, exit N. on Pershing Dr., L. on Florida Dr., L. on Zoo PL., L. on Park Blvd., R. on Village Pl. Going S. on Cabrillo Fwy [163], exit N. on Park Blvd. (near end), L. on Presidents Wy. [TG-1289 C1])

Naturally, this huge museum is a favorite for kids to visit! Enter through the south side, across the pedestrian street from the other Balboa Park museums, or through the north side, which leads into a beautiful, multi-story, glass-walled atrium. The hall below the atrium features first class, major, national traveling exhibits. We saw a wild and woolly exhibit with elephants, woolly mammoths, and mastodons. Knowing that elephants (and their ancestors) are the largest land animals still didn't quite prepare my kids for the impact of seeing the towering life-size models. Touching re-created hair, trunk, and feet was unique, as was seeing a live Asian elephant close up (outside, in the "backyard") and learning about its anatomy. Another favorite past exhibit was on dinosaurs.

The permanent exhibits are equally wonderful. Journey through the Past explores dinosaurs through ice-age mammals via fossils, skeletons, models, multi-sensory dioramas, and other interactive exhibits that put visitors in touch with history. Journey through the Present includes walking through some re-created regional habitats, from the mountains, to the prairies, to the oceans white with foam, plus the desert, Baja California, and Sea of Cortes. (Well, not all of these areas, but Southern California is well represented.) Huge walk-through dioramas with caves depict the southwestern desert. Some of the taxidermied animals on display include cougars, coyotes, gold eagles, birds, and saber tooth cats. One wall has a beautiful array of butterflies - some have fantastic fluorescent colors. Dive into another area that contains models and stuffed sea creatures such as sea lions, stingrays, dolphins, sharks, and a pilot whale. Also on display are the menacing jaws of a shark, plus skeletons, a gigantic whale fin bone, and a whale skull. The Discovery Room features live animals for visitors to see and even touch; natural objects to touch and study, such as animal fur; microscopes for closer study; activity kits; and seasonal activities.

The Hall of Minerals has amazing specimens, including petrified logs, a huge jade boulder, and a gigantic amethyst geode. Walk through a re-created mine tunnel and see "holes" that showcase garnets, topaz, and other rocks and minerals. Try the crystal radio and hear how it works. Touch a meteor that is out of this world. Observe fluorescent rocks and glowing minerals. Experiment with radioactive rock. See rainbows through special crystals using a polarizing filter. Don't let the earthquake exhibit shake you up!

The museum offers many classes, tours, guided nature walks, family programs, camp outs, and even camp-ins! Call for a schedule. Join Ms. Frizzle, of Magic School Bus fame, every Sunday at 10am., noon, and 2pm for some wacky science. (See BALBOA PARK [San Diego], under this section, for a listing of all the museums and attractions within walking distance.)

Hours: Open daily 9:30am - 5:30pm. Open in the summer one hour later. Closed New Year's Day, Thanksgiving, and Christmas. During special exhibits, daily museum hours are extended - 9am - 6pm.

Admission: $7 for adults; $6 for seniors; $5 for ages 3 - 17; children 2 and under are free. Special exhibits can cause prices and hours to fluctuate, so always call first. In between special exhibits, admission is half-price for all ages. Admission is free on the first Tues. of every month to the permanent exhibits; half price to the special exhibits. Passports for 11 museums in Balboa Park are available for $30 for adults at the Visitors Center, and are good for one week from the date of purchase. (Children's admissions are already discounted or free.)

Ages: 3 years and up.

SAN DIEGO RAILROAD MUSEUM
(619) 595-3030 / www.sdrm.org
Sheridan Rd, Campo

See SAN DIEGO RAILROAD MUSEUM under the Transportation section.

SAN DIEGUITO HERITAGE MUSEUM
(760) 632-9711 / www.encinitas101.com/sdmuseum.htm
561 S. Vulcan Avenue, Encinitas
(Exit San Diego Fwy [5] W. on Encinitas Blvd., L. on Vulcan Ave. [TG-1147 C7])

This very small museum is a good stop off. Built at an ex gas station, a stagecoach is located where the gas pumps used to be - fill 'er up! There are also a few picnic tables outside.

Inside, the room contains exhibits in chronological order. Display cases around the perimeter hold tools, a variety of barbed wire, household items, dolls, toys, a mock Indian wickiup, Mexican Ranchero costumes, and even a few surfboards. A pseudo shanty room has period-dressed mannequins and a bed. I appreciate the docent's willingness to explain the items and the paper and pencil treasure hunt that got the kids involved with the exhibits.

Hours: Open Wed. - Sat., noon - 4pm. Open the fourth Thurs. until 7pm.
Admission: Free
Ages: 5 years and up.

SERRA MUSEUM / PRESIDIO PARK
(619) 297-3258   *$$*
2727 Presidio Drive, San Diego

(Going E. on Mission Valley Fwy [8] exit S. on Taylor St., L. on Presidio Dr., and L. again to stay on Presidio Dr. Going W. on 8, exit at Hotel Circle/Taylor St. [the exit before Morena Blvd.], go straight off the off ramp and curve over fwy, R. on Taylor St., L. on Presidio Dr., and L. again to stay on Presidio Dr. [TG-1268 F4])

Located just above OLD TOWN SAN DIEGO AND STATE HISTORIC PARK (see entry in this section), picturesque Presidio Park has green rolling hills and lots of old shade trees. Follow the signs and walk along the Old Presidio Historic Trail and you'll be walking in the footsteps of settlers from centuries ago.

On a hilltop in the park sits the mission-style Junipero Serra Museum. It was built in 1929 to commemorate the site where Father Junipero Serra and Captain Gaspar de Portola established California's very first mission and fortified settlement. Outside the museum is an old wine press. Inside, the first floor contains 400-year-old Spanish furniture, some of which is quite elegant. Second story exhibits include clothing, weapons (such as a cannon and cannon balls), art, artifacts from the outside dig site, and housewares that belonged to Native American and early Spanish/Mexican residents. There is also a room dedicated to the founder, Father Serra, that contains personal belongings and items given to him. A seven-minute video is shown throughout the day that describes San Diego's beginnings. Upstairs, in a bell-like tower, look through the windows for an unparalleled view of San Diego.

> **Hours:** The park is open daily sunrise to sunset. The museum is open during the summer Tues. - Sun., 10am - 4:30pm. It's open the rest of the year Fri. - Sun., 10am - 4:30pm. Tours for eight or more people can be given at other times. Call for a reservation.
>
> **Admission:** The park is free. The museum is $5 for adults; $4 for seniors; $2 for ages 6 - 17; children 5 and under are free. AAA members receive discounts.
>
> **Ages:** The museum is best suited for ages 7 and up.

STEPHEN BIRCH AQUARIUM-MUSEUM
(619) 534-FISH (3474) / www.aquarium.ucsd.edu
2300 Expedition Drive, San Diego

See STEPHEN BIRCH AQUARIUM-MUSEUM under the Zoos and Animals section.

VETERANS MEMORIAL CENTER & MUSEUM
(619) 239-2300 / www.sdvets.org
2115 Park Boulevard, San Diego

(From San Diego Fwy [5], exit N. on Pershing Dr., L. on Florida Dr., L. on Zoo PL., L. on Park Blvd., R. on Village Pl. Going S. on Cabrillo Fwy [163], exit N. on Park Blvd. (near end), L. on Presidents Wy. [TG-1289 C1])

"The nation which forgets its defenders will be itself forgotten." (Calvin Coolidge) The Veterans center is a memorial dedicated to honor all the men and women who have served in all branches of the U.S. Armed Services, including the Merchant Marines.

The small museum is located in the former chapel of the Naval Hospital, which was built in the early 1940's and still retains the original stained glass windows. Display cases contain plaques, medals, gas masks, uniforms, and more memorabilia from WWI, WWII, the Korean War, Vietnam War, and Desert Storm. Several mannequins are dressed in military attire. Multitudes of military flags hang from the ceiling, with several versions of the American flag prominently displayed. A display table has a few uniforms and hats for kids to try on, as well as some war time field phones to use. Docents who have served in the military now serve as tour guides, so the information comes from those who have been there, done that. Memorial plaques are on the back lawn of the museum. Note: BALBOA PARK is just across the street.

Hours: Open Tues. - Sun., 10am - 4pm. Closed Mon.
Admission: Free; donations are encouraged.
Ages: 7 years and up.

VILLA MONTEZUMA JESSE SHEPARD HOUSE   ☼

(619) 239-2211 / www.sandiegohistory.org   *$$*
1925 K Street, San Diego
(Going S. on San Diego Fwy [5], exit E. on Imperial Ave, L on 20ᵗʰ St., L. on K St. Going N on 5, exit E. on J St., R. on 20ᵗʰ St., R. on K St. [TG-1289 C4])

Built and designed in 1887 for celebrated author, spiritualist, and musician, Jesse Shepard, this two-story house is by far one of the most interesting and ornamental Victorian houses we've ever seen. The outside is beautiful with its steep roofs, gables, turrets, and bay windows. The rooms inside are paneled with redwood and walnut, and are decorated with intricate wood carvings and moldings. The ceilings are elegantly embossed. There are numerous, gorgeous stained glass windows throughout that depict Beethoven, Mozart, a knight, the Greek poetess Sappho, and more. The furnishings are equally elaborate, and even though much of the furniture is not originally from this house, it is from the same time period. Older kids will enjoy the hour-and-a-half tour. They'll see the large music room, the drawing room, and the downstairs kitchen and laundry room which are filled with "labor saving" devices such as an early washing machine, vacuum cleaner, kitchen gadgets, and more. Upstairs are the bedrooms that, in keeping with the rest of the house, are also stylishly decorated. My 11-year old and I were fascinated by the house, but were bewildered as to why Jesse Shepard designed such a masterpiece and incurred the city's expense to construct it only to live in it for two years! Personally, I could live here for a lot longer.

Hours: Open Fri. - Sun.,10am - 4:30pm. Group tours are available Tues. - Sun. by reservation.
Admission: $5 for adults; $4 for seniors; $2 for ages 6 - 17; children 5 and under are free.
Ages: 8 years and up.

WHALEY HOUSE

(619) 297-7511   *$$*

2482 San Diego Avenue, San Diego

(Going S. on San Diego Fwy [5] [just south of Interstate 8] exit E. [across the bridge] on Old Town
Ave., L. on San Diego Ave. Going N. on 5, exit at Moore St., R. on Old Town Ave., L. on San
Diego Ave. It's on the corner of San Diego Ave. and Harney St. [TG-1268 F5])

Built in 1847, this two-story brick house/museum is definitely worth
touring. It has served in the community as a residence, store, theater, and
courthouse, and is filled with numerous early California artifacts. The first room
you're ushered into, the courthouse room, is fascinating. As you listen to the ten-
minute tape explaining the history of the house and this time period, look
around. Behind the railing is an old wooden judge's desk, and chairs for the jury.
Along one wall is a bookshelf given to Ulysses S. Grant on his inauguration, and
an 1860 lifemask (only one of six in existence) of Abraham Lincoln. Display
cases in this room feature documents, spurs, pistols, Spanish helmets and
swords, clothing, and ornate hair combs and fans. An early copy machine, a
letter press, a handmade U.S. flag from 1864 (how many stars does it have?),
plus pictures and portraits of George Washington, Abraham Lincoln, Ulysses S.
Grant, and Robert E. Lee are also here.

The kitchen, with all of its gadgets, is downstairs, as is the beautifully
decorated parlor, and a small music room that contains a spinet piano used in the
movie, *Gone With the Wind.* There are several bedrooms upstairs that can be
viewed through the protective glass in the doorframes. The bedroom behind the
staircase has a decorative wreath, framed on the far wall. It is made from the
Whaley girls' hair gathered from hairbrushes and then braided - something to
keep the family busy on pre-television nights. The children's bedroom has dolls
and toys, while the other bedrooms contain a soldier's dress uniform,
mannequins clothed in elegant, ladies' dresses, a lacy quilt covering a canopy
bed, and period furniture. The Whaley House is also one of two authenticated
haunted houses in California. I highly recommend taking a guided tour, so you
don't miss out on any of the background information. Ask about guided school
tours.

Exit through the backdoor into a small, picturesque, tree-shaded courtyard.
A quick peek into the Old Town Drug Store Museum allows kids to see an old-
time pharmacy containing bottles, patented medicines, and a mortar and pestle.
Push a button to hear more of the building's history. See OLD TOWN SAN
DIEGO AND STATE HISTORIC PARK, in this section, for details about other
attractions in this immediate area.

Hours: Open Wed. - Mon., 10am to 4:30pm. Closed Tues.
Admission: $4 for adults; $3 for seniors; $2.50 for ages 12 and under.
Ages: 7 years and up.

ALBINGER ARCHAEOLOGICAL MUSEUM

(805) 648-5823 / www.vcmha.org   *!*

113 E. Main Street, Ventura

(Going W. on Ventura Fwy [101], exit N. on California Ave., L. on Main St. Going S.E. on 101, exit
E. on Main. It's on the N. side of the street. [TG-491 B2])

This small, one-room museum has a collection of archaeological finds spanning thirty-five centuries that have been uncovered from this site. Arrowheads, bottles, milling stones, bone whistles, and more are on display. When the kids have seen their fill, which was pretty immediate with my younger ones, head out the back door and look at the site of an actual dig. The foundations of an original Mission (church) are clearly marked here. My kids were more interested after I explained what we were looking at, and how archaeologists found the remains. (Digging in dirt is a popular pastime with our family, too.)

The enticing stone steps back here lead, disappointingly, to a small street, but at least we got in some exercise.

Hours: Open September through May, Wed. - Fri., 10am - 2pm; Sat. - Sun., 10am - 4pm. Open June through August, Wed. - Sun., 10am - 4pm. Closed New Year's Day, Easter, Thanksgiving, and Christmas.

Admission: Free; donations appreciated.

Ages: 6 years and up.

AVIATION MUSEUM OF SANTA PAULA

(805) 525-1109 / www.amszp.org

830 E. Santa Maria Street, Santa Paula

(Exit the Santa Paula Fwy [126] S. on Palm Ave., L. on Santa Maria St. [TG-464 B6])

Take your child to new heights at this aviation museum, adjacent to the Santa Paula Airport. Watch small planes land and take off. The museum consists of a chain of hangers, each one featuring different exhibits. Inside the first hangar, displays pertain to the history of the Santa Paula airport, including a short video. Other hangars showcase restored antique, military, classic, and experimental aircraft. More unusual exhibits (at least unusual for an aviation museum) are vintage and unusual radios, jukeboxes, antique and classic cars, vintage racing cars, paintings, photos, collectibles, and more. Visitors are welcome to climb aboard the educational airplane here and play pilot, or passenger. The museum's goal is to expand to include other hangars and incorporate more historical aircraft, especially from the various war eras. School and other group tours are offered during the week - call to make a reservation.

Enjoy the numerous classic airplanes that come in for a landing on the first Sunday, coinciding with the museum being open. What a great way to spend time with the whole family! Note: Grab a bite to eat at the on-site Logsdon's Restaurant and Lounge, which is open for breakfast, lunch, and dinner. Call (805) 525-1101 for more information. See SANTA PAULA AIRPORT / CP AVIATION and YOUNG EAGLES PROGRAM (Santa Paula), both in the Transportation section, if you're interested in taking airplane rides.

Hours: Open the first Sun. of every month, 10am - 3pm.

Admission: Free

Ages: 4 years and up.

CALIFORNIA OIL MUSEUM   ☼

(805) 933-0076 / www.oilmuseum.net $
1001 E. Main Street, Santa Paula
(Exit the 126 Fwy, N. on State Route 150 [or 10th St.]. The Museum is on the N.E. corner of 10th
and Main St. [TG-464 C5])

The Union Oil Museum is housed in the original headquarters of the Union Oil Company. The interior and exterior of the 1890 building has meticulously been restored to its original luster. Upon entering, kids can punch a keepsake time card in an old time card machine. The walls are covered with great pictures and murals regarding the history and technology of the oil industry.

Quite a few of the exhibits are interactive, such as the Lubricity Exhibit. Kids can turn the gears and see how much easier the figures on bicycles can pedal when the gears are oiled. They can push a button and watch a model rig "drill" for oil through the layers of the earth. With a touch of a button, the Centrifuge Exhibit spins to separate water and other substances from crude oil. A few touch screens here impart interesting information about how the oil industry affects so many aspects of our lives.

Since geology is vital to finding oil, several terrific geological displays are in the museum. Some of the fossils on display include shells, dinosaur bones, and shark teeth.

The upstairs, which can only be seen by a half-hour guided tour, is interesting to older kids. There are restored offices, bedrooms, a kitchen, and fireplaces with ornate tiles around them. A walk-in safe looks like a secret, hidden room.

Walk through the main building and outside to reach the Rig Room. Kids can see a full-size drilling rig, and a huge cable rig in action as the engine turns the sand wheel that turns the band wheel that moves the wooden walking beam and the huge drill bits. I hope you feel like we did when we visited the museum - like we struck oil!

Hours: Open Wed. - Sun., 10am - 4pm. Tours of the upstairs are offered during regular museum hours. Closed major holidays.

Admission: $2 for adults; $1 for ages 6 - 15; children 5 and under are free. The tour of the upstairs costs an additional $1 per person.

Ages: 4 years and up.

CARNEGIE ART MUSEUM   ☼

(805) 385-8157 - exhibit info.; (805) 385-8158 - receptionist during $
museum hours. / www.vcnet.com/carnart
424 S. 'C' Street, Oxnard
(Exit Ventura Fwy [101] S. on Hwy 1 [or Oxnard Blvd.], R. on 4th St. It's on the S. side of the street.
[TG-522 G6])

I mention this small, beautiful museum mainly because of the kid-friendly workshops offered. (Tell your kids the building is done in neo-classical design, though they'll just think the columns look really neat.) I take my kids through art museums, explaining what I can and hoping that some understanding and appreciation for art will take root. However, I think the best way to reach and teach our kids is through guided tours and hands-on workshops.

In a group tour here, kids learn about a particular style, artist, or medium, depending on the current exhibit. Then, they create their own art projects in a workshop taught by a local artist. Reservations are needed. Carnegie occasionally offers family classes, too.

Come see the permanent and rotating exhibits of paintings, photographs, and sculptures at this Museum. Have your children draw a picture of their outing!

Hours: Open Thurs. - Sat., 10am - 5pm; Sun., 1am - 5pm. Closed during public holidays and during installation of new exhibits.

Admission: $3 for adults; $2 for seniors and students; $1 for ages 6 - 16; children 5 and under are free. The museum is free on Fri., 3pm - 6pm.

Ages: 6 years and up.

CEC-SEABEE MUSEUM

(805) 982-5163 / www.seabeehf.org

23rd Avenue and Dodson Street, Port Hueneme

(Exit the Ventura Fwy [101] S. on Ventura Rd., then just S. of Channel Islands Blvd. turn R. on 23rd Ave (it's Sunkist St. on the left). through the gates of the military base in the Naval Construction Battalion Center. The museum has a statue of a huge bee with a machine gun outside the entrance. [TG-552 E3])

This huge museum is dedicated to documenting, preserving, and maintaining public awareness of the contributions of the Seabees and Civil Engineer Corps. The mission statement is formal sounding, but the museum is incredibly rich with fascinating exhibits. There are life-size models and statues of men and women depicted in scenes of battle and peacetime, wearing authentic uniforms and costumes from around the world. Displays of weapons, medals, banners, photos, and equipment, such as gas masks, represent all facets of a Seabee's life in action.

Another wing has model boats and an underwater diving exhibit with small, model scuba divers. Kids can touch a full-size, old-fashioned diving suit and helmet. Wonderful dioramas, such as a Seabee's amphibious landing and establishment of camp, can be easily seen, thanks to viewing platforms.

The Cultural Artifacts section is interesting because of the number of exhibits and international content. On display are unusual musical instruments; foreign currency and coins; tools; Indian weapons, beadwork, drums, and other artifacts; an Alaska exhibit; a China exhibit; and so much more! Although nothing here is hands-on, my kids were captivated by the variety and uniqueness of the items. Each exhibit brought a yell of, "Hey, come over here and check this out!" It's the kind of museum, because of its size and the scope of displays, that you can visit again and again.

Hours: The museum is open Mon. - Sat., 0900 - 1600 (8am - 4pm); Sun., 1230 - 1630 (12:30pm - 4:30pm). Closed federal holidays, Easter, and the week between Christmas and New Year's Day.

Admission: Free

Ages: 4 years and up.

CHANNEL ISLANDS NATIONAL PARK VISITOR   ☼
CENTER
(805) 658-5730 / www.nps.gov/chis   !
1901 Spinnaker Drive, Ventura
(Going W. on Ventura Fwy [101], exit S.W. on Seaward Ave., L. on Harbor Blvd. Going S.E. on
101, exit at Seaward Ave. and go straight onto Harbor Blvd., R. on Spinnaker Dr. - all the way to
the end. [TG-491 F6])

The Channel Islands Visitor Center is worthy of a trip in itself. You'll pass
by beaches and stores (see VENTURA HARBOR and VILLAGE under the
Piers and Seaports section), but pacify the kids with a, "we'll stop there on the
way out." The Center is a good combination of museum, store, and resource
center. The kids will head straight for the indoor tidepool (not a touch tank),
which offers an up-close look at sea stars, anemones, and other small, ocean
creatures. Other eye-catching displays are the taxidermied animals (some of the
birds are in flight), and a topographical model of the islands. My boys also
enjoyed sifting sand in the mini-sand pit and grinding pretend meal with a
Chumash Indian stone mortar and pestle.

The twenty-five-minute movie, *A Treasure In the Sea,* is shown throughout
the day, and is a fun way to learn more about sea life. Tidepool talks are
available on weekends as are free Ranger programs that offer an in-depth look at
a particular animal or habitat. Rangers will also come to local schools for
presentations. (Also look under CHANNEL ISLANDS NATIONAL PARK in
the Great Outdoors section.)

    Hours: Open daily 8:30am - 5pm. Closed Thanksgiving and Christmas.
Admission: Free
     Ages: 2 years and up.

CHUMASH INTERPRETIVE CENTER / OAKBROOK   ☼
REGIONAL PARK
(805) 492-8076 / www.designplace.com/chumash $
3290 Lang Ranch Parkway, Thousand Oaks
(Exit Hwy 23 E. on Avenida De Los Arboles, R. on Westlake, then the first L. on Lang Ranch Pkwy.
[TG-527 C4])

Long ago, the Chumash Indians occupied this area of land, which is now
Ventura County, and other surrounding areas. A small, one-room, Interpretive
Center features artifacts representative of the Chumash way of life. Pictures and
native paintings decorate the walls. Some local plants, and the way they were
used, are on display, such as yucca fibers braided into ropes, and sticks
fashioned into weapons. Rabbit and bear furs can be touched, while other
exhibits are behind glass. My kids liked the musical instruments, such as drums
and rattles, and I admired the jewelry made out of beads. Outside, kids can see a
replicated Chumash village. If kids can handle the one-and-a-half-mile walk,
hike back to see the centuries-old pictographs, or rock paintings, visible from the
caves/overhangs. (The pictographs might not look like much to kids, but their
symbolism and preservation is important to Chumash heritage.) Sign up for a
guided nature walk, given on Saturdays at 1pm and Sundays at 2pm. The cost is
the same as admission to the center. Ask for the dates of the Pow Wows held

here.

School or group tours are two hours long, very informative, and one of the most effective ways to really see and understand what the Center has to offer. The first hour consists of a storytelling, the history of the Chumash, an explanation of the exhibits, and making handcrafts to take home. The second hour is a guided walk through the park and archaeological preserve, from a Chumash perspective. You'll learn about their way of life; inspect a re-created Chumash village complete with a large ap (i.e. roundhouse), two smaller aps, and a sweatlodge, and a ceremonial ground; and hear how different plants and trees were used. As an alternative, the second hour could be a wildlife presentation, learning about the native animals, and how to live with and respect them. You might also play native games and go on a culture hunt (as opposed to a scavenger hunt.)

The park itself is beautiful, and can be visited without going into the Interpretive Center, although they do ask that you sign in. There are picnic tables, shady oak trees, and miles of hiking trails.

> **Hours:** The Center is open Tues. - Sat. from 10am - 5pm. The park is open daily from dawn to dusk.
>
> **Admission:** $5 for adults; $3 for seniors, students, and ages 5 - 12; children 4 and under are free. Tours are $3 per person; teachers are free. Entrance to the park is free.
>
> **Ages:** 7 years and up for the Center.

CONFEDERATE AIR FORCE WORLD WAR II ◐ AVIATION MUSEUM (Camarillo)

(805) 482-0064 / www.orgsites.com/ca/caf-socal   *$$*
Eubanks Street, Camarillo Airport, Camarillo
(Exit Ventura Fwy [101] S. on Las Posas Rd., R. on Pleasant Valley Rd., R. on Eubanks. [TG-523 J4])

Five World War II aircraft, and other items, are on display at this two-hangar museum. Some of the planes are in flyable condition and some are in the process of being restored. See a Japanese Zero fighter, a Curtiss C-46 transport, a Grumman F8F-2 Bearcat fighter, a North American SNJ Navy trainer, a B-25 Mitchell bomber, and other visiting planes. Kids can climb in the cargo airplane and the fighter jet. The docents are affable, knowledgeable, and ready to impart aviation facts whenever asked. All of the artifacts on exhibit date from WWII and include helmets, flags, airplane parts, and more. Outside, children may climb on a cannon that was originally from an aircraft carrier. As the museum is adjacent to the airport, you'll want to spend some time watching small planes take off and land. Tip: At the end of the air field is Freedom Park, so bring a sack lunch.

> **Hours:** Open daily 10am - 4pm. Guided tours are given on request.
>
> **Admission:** $5 for adults; $1 for ages 10 - 16; children 9 and under are free.
>
> **Ages:** 4 years and up.

EARTH SCIENCE MUSEUM
(805) 642-3155 or (805) 646-5976   !
5019 Crooked Palm Road, Ventura
(Exit Ojai Fwy [33] W. on Shell Rd., L. on Ventura Ave., L. on Crooked Palm Rd. [TG-471 C1])

This small museum is run by the Gem and Mineral Society and is open by appointment only. The "dinosaur petting zoo" consists of wonderful casts of dinosaur skulls, bones, and teeth that kids can touch. Other casts and real fossils include a ground sloth, mammoth tusk, sauropod ribs, skull of a cave bear, and lots more. The displays include nice pieces of various rocks and minerals, such as geodes, agates, and others; locally found fossils, including shells, eggs, and bird tracks; petrified wood; and lots of informational posters. Everything not behind glass can be handled. Tours are tailored toward your children's ages and attention spans, and the facts dispensed are fascinating. (i.e. A saber-tooth cat is not a tiger because it had no stripes.)

Hours:	By appointment.
Admission:	Free
Ages:	4 years and up.

GULL WINGS CHILDREN'S MUSEUM
(805) 483-3005 / www.gullwingsmuseum4kids.org $$
418 W. 4th Street, Oxnard
(Exit Ventura Fwy [101] S. on Hwy 1 [or Oxnard Blvd.], R. on 4th St. [TG-522 G6])

Children's museums strive for the right combination of fun and education. Gull Wings has achieved a delightful balance of these goals. The long building has sectioned off "rooms," each one focusing on a different theme. The first room is a delightful toddlers' play area. The next one is for future geologists or paleontologists. It contains rocks, fossils, and skulls to look at and/or touch. (The saber-tooth cat is a particular favorite). Kids can use a microscope to study other elements. This room also teaches engineering principles through play with wooden gears.

My kids played doctor and patient in the next room for over an hour. This complete medical room has gowns, a surgery table with play instruments, an X-ray set up, wheelchairs, and crutches. For hands-on health and science learning, there are plastic models of the body with removable parts, and cloth dolls that kids can unlayer to reveal muscles, bones, and organs.

Further back in the museum is a mini-market with shopping carts, a cash register, and bins of "food" for your little shoppers. A puppet theater allows storytellers to express themselves in creative ways. For more "let's pretend," kids can dress-up in elegant gowns, cowboy duds, firefighter's and sailor's uniforms, and other attire. Backdrops and props, like a fire hydrant and a boat, help complete the scenes your kids act out. Face painting and an Art Nook bring out the creative genius in your offspring. Enter another dimension when you enter the outer space room. With the aid of a video camera and an unearthly backdrop, it appears as though you are on the moon.

Other highlights include playing with a wooden train set, an at*track*tion for kids of all ages; computers with educational games; taking temporary shadow pictures against a photo-sensitive wall; a touch tank with sea stars, sea cucumbers, and sea urchins; and "driving" a kid-proofed Saturn car. Young drivers can get behind the wheel, shift gears, turn on headlights and, via a plexiglass hood, see the inner workings of an engine. A side door panel is also clear. Pet Corner has a few live animals that children can pet or hold, including turtles, garter snakes, a rat, and a guinea pig.

Ask about the numerous craft and educational classes, storytelling hours, and special family nights.

Hours: Open Tues. - Sun., 10am - 5pm.
Admission: $3.50 per person; children under 2 are free.
Ages: 1 to 13 years.

OJAI VALLEY HISTORICAL SOCIETY AND MUSEUM ☼
$
(805) 640-1390
130 W. Ojai Avenue, Ojai
(Take State Hwy 150 into Ojai. The road turns into Hwy 33, then into Ojai Ave. [TG-441 H7])

This museum, located inside an old chapel, has a mission - keeping historic Ojai alive by preserving the valley's cultural and natural heritage. Since most of the exhibits are encased in glass, my kids did a lot of nose pressing. They smudged up the cases containing Chumash Indian artifacts such as arrowheads, beadwork, and rattles made from turtle shells and sea shells. The simulated archaeological pit was interesting, too. Another exhibit area with a lot of kid-appeal is the taxidermied animals, some of which can actually be touched. The stuffed animals on our hit parade include the black bear and the more unusual, platypus and bat. The museum also has a fine collection of taxidermied snakes.

Some of the fossils featured here include a big sea snail and an even bigger rock with at least a dozen sand dollars imbedded in it. (The buck stops here!) The museum has a fairly extensive shell collection, too. I only hope we can remember some of their names the next time we go to the beach.

Hours: Open Wed. - Fri., 1pm - 4pm; Sat. - Sun., 10am - 4pm.
Admission: $3 for adults; $2 seniors; ages 18 and under are free.
Ages: 3 years and up.

OLIVAS ADOBE HISTORICAL PARK
!
(805) 644-4346 /
www.geocities.com/BourbonStreet/Dixie/9959/OlivasAdobeHistoricPar
kCenter.html
4200 Olivas Park Drive, Ventura
(Going S. on Ventura Fwy [101], exit S. on Harbor Blvd., L. on Olivas Park Dr. Going N.W. on 101, exit S. on Victoria, R. on Olivas Park Dr. [TG-491 H7])

The Olivas Adobe is a restored, two-story, adobe home built in 1847. It is representative of the rancho period in California's history. The residence has bedrooms, a living room, and a kitchen to look into that are furnished just as they were over 100 years ago. The grounds are beautifully landscaped. The open courtyard, containing a Chumash Indian oven and some farming equipment, gives younger ones some running-around space. A small exhibit building, across from the rose garden, contains items that relate to this particular time period, such as saddles, pictures, and ranching equipment. While this is not an all day visit, kids enjoy the opportunity to "see" the past.

Hours: The grounds are open daily 10am - 4pm. The Adobe, and tours of it, are available on Sat. and Sun., 10am - 4pm.

Admission: Free

Ages: 6 years and up.

RONALD REAGAN PRESIDENTIAL LIBRARY AND ☼ MUSEUM

(800) 410-8354 or (805) 522-8444 / www.lbjlib.utexas.edu/reagan $

40 Presidential Drive, Simi Valley

(From the Simi Valley/San Fernando Valley Fwy [118], exit S. on Madera Rd., R. on Presidential Dr. From the 23 Fwy, exit N.E. on Olsen Rd, which turns into Madera Rd., L. on Presidential Dr. [TG-497 C4])

The massive, Spanish-style Ronald Reagan Library and Museum is alone on a hilltop. Remember those books that you read about kings and queens and their treasures? Walk down the hallway lined with incredible gifts from heads of states and feel like those storybook pages have come true. Treasures range from an exquisite hand-beaded blouse for the First Lady to an intricately carved, ivory-handled sword that has a gold sheath inlaid with jewels, for the President.

Reagan's heritage and love of the West is evident throughout the museum. One room, in particular, is dedicated to the American west with displays of elaborate saddles, boots, spurs, statues, and an eye-catching cowboy hat with a real rattlesnake head on the band. Even the full-size replica of the Oval Office, which reflects each President's personal style, is decorated with western art.

Two theaters show twenty-minute-plus videos of the Reagan years that include inauguration speeches, tearing down the Berlin wall, and a remembrance of the Challenger crew. My kids were thoroughly captivated by the footage.

The next few galleries depict Reagan's road to the presidency via movie posters, uniforms, costumes, documents, and lots of photos. My oldest child was also impressed by a large nuclear cruise missile on display that was once deployed in Europe. One room contains signed sports paraphernalia. Another displays gifts that range from the elegant to the homemade, such as a jellybean-painted cane, and the Presidential Seal crafted from 6,500 silver nails - what a great kid's project this would make! There are pictures of Nancy Reagan, some of her gowns, and a whole wall devoted to her "Just Say No" campaign.

There are numerous touch screens throughout the museum so kids can learn about Reagan's views on issues by letting their fingers "do the walking." Visitors can become members of Reagan's cabinet (albeit temporarily) while sitting around a table in a re-created White House Room. His image and responses are shown on a big screen in the room. Travel to the Geneva Convention and witness a historic meeting between Gorbachev and Reagan as their images are projected on the screen above the chateau's fireplace.

Out back is a huge, decoratively spray-painted, chunk of the Berlin wall. Note that the gift shop has great aids for teaching history. The Reagan Country Cafe is on-site and open the same hours as the museum.

Hours: Open daily 10am - 5pm. Closed New Year's Day, Thanksgiving, and Christmas.

Admission: $5 for adults; $3 for seniors; children 15 and under are free. The Hollywood CityPass, $49.75 for adults and $38 for ages 3 - 11, is good for one-time admission to American Cinematheque's Egyptian Theatre in Hollywood, AUTRY MUSEUM OF WESTERN HERITAGE, HOLLYWOOD ENTERTAINMENT MUSEUM, MUSEUM OF TELEVISION AND RADIO, MUSEUM OF TOLERANCE, PETERSEN AUTOMOTIVE MUSEUM, REAGAN PRESIDENTIAL LIBRARY AND MUSEUM, and UNIVERSAL STUDIOS within a 30 day period. (All of the entries mentioned, except for the theater, are listed separately.) Call (888) 330-5008 / www.citypass.com for more information.

Ages: 5 years and up.

SAN BUENAVENTURA MISSION

(805) 643-4318 / www.anacapa.net/~mission

211 E. Main Street, Ventura

(Going W. on Ventura Fwy [101], exit N. on California Ave., L. on Main St. Going S.E. on 101, exit E. on Main. It's on the N. side of the street. [TG-491 B2])

Built in 1792, and ninth in the chain of California missions, San Buenaventura exudes old-world charm. Although the mission is readily seen from the street, a tour through the rooms and grounds offer a better picture of life during this historical time period. You'll see a small courtyard, artifacts from mission days in the several rooms, and even a small cemetery around the side. Groups, with a minimum ten people, can take guided tours, for a minimal fee. The tour includes information about the mission's past inhabitants and doing a thematic craft project.

Hours: Open Mon. - Fri., 10am - 5pm; Sat., 9am - 5pm; Sun., 10am - 4pm.

Admission: $1 for adults; 50¢ for children 16 and under.

Ages: 6 years and up.

STAGECOACH INN MUSEUM

(805) 498-9441 / www.toguide.com/stagecoach

51 N. Ventu Park Road, Newbury Park

(Exit the Ventura Fwy [101] S. on Ventu Park Rd. [TG-556 B1])

This beautiful 1870's hotel and stagecoach stop is both interesting and educational, and seen only by guided tour. The downstairs consists mainly of the parlor, dining room, and kitchen. The furniture, decor, and history are interesting to older kids, but younger kids get antsy.

Upstairs, however, it is a different story. A small "cowboy" bedroom has a saddle, bear skin rug, and other western paraphernalia. The Chumash Indian room has a collection of fossils, beadwork, and pictures. Another room has an extensive butterfly and bug collection in glass cases. The Music Room has an old-fashioned, elegant feel to it as antique violins, other instruments, and vintage clothing are fashionably displayed. A child's room is filled with toys of yesteryear (no Nintendo!), and a bed that Todd Lincoln slept in. (I hope kids won't ask, "Who's that?") Oooooo - a man named Pierre was supposedly shot here and his ghost still haunts the Inn. Now, the Inn becomes fascinating to kids!

Outside the hotel, take a short nature trail that leads to other historic points of interest. The Carriage House contains stagecoaches, while further around the bend are the Pioneer Newbury House and the Spanish Adobe House. Both are open to tour. The Chumash Indian Hut and a beehive oven are also interesting. Explain to your kids that the oven is named for its design, not for cooking bees.

When the kids have seen all they want, head out to the small Stagecoach Park above the Inn. It's easier to drive to the park than to walk, as the entrance is on another street.

Hours: The Inn is open Wed. - Sun., 1pm - 4pm. The Carriage House is open only on Sun., 1pm - 4pm.

Admission: $3 for adults; $2 for seniors; $1 for ages 5 - 12; children 4 and under are free.

Ages: 5 years and up.

STRATHERN HISTORICAL PARK AND MUSEUM   ☀

(805) 526-6453 $

137 Strathern Place, Simi Valley

(Exit Simi Valley/San Fernando Valley Fwy [118] S. on Madera Rd., R. on Strathern Place. [TG-497 E2])

This outside museum is several historical buildings inside a gated, park-like setting. Start your one-hour guided tour at the visitor's center. Learn about the early days of Simi by first watching a twenty-minute tape about the Valley's history. Some of the exhibits in here include maps and, a little more exciting, beekeeping equipment such as smokers and hoods. Next, walk through one of the very first local colony houses. Though the inside decor is from the 1930's, the building itself still retains its earlier, original charm. An adobe house, built in the early 1700's, displays an owner's furnishings from the 1950's. The Strathern House, which is a Victorian house built in 1893, has antique treasures throughout including furniture, clothing, and a pump organ.

The library contains some fossils, as well as books. The enclosed barn has eight stalls with different exhibits in each, such as kitchen gadgets, early laundry equipment, an old-fashioned switchboard, Chumash Indian artifacts, farm machinery, and old automobiles such as a truck, a tractor, and a Ford Model A. Another barn contains more farm equipment, such as hay wagons. Around the perimeters of the historical park are pieces of old (rusted) farming equipment, which adds to the rustic ambiance.

Hours: Open to the public Sat. - Sun., 1pm - 4pm and Wed., 1pm - 2pm for tours, weather permitting. Open for school tours upon request.

Admission: $2 for adults; $1 for students.

Ages: 5 years and up.

VENTURA COUNTY MARITIME MUSEUM   ☀

(805) 984-6260 $

2731 S. Victoria Avenue, Oxnard

(Exit Ventura Fwy [101] S. on Victoria St. The museum is located at Channel Islands Harbor at the corner of Victoria St. and Channel Islands Blvd. [TG-552 B2])

Explore the seas without leaving port! This good-sized, nautical museum has original paintings, and various sizes and styles of model ships behind glass cases. What detail! Marine artists from the 1700's to the present have their eye-catching work on display throughout the museum. If your child has the patience, or desire, a docent will gladly explain local nautical history, which gives more meaning to the exhibits.

Hours: Open daily 11am - 5pm.
Admission: Suggested donations of $3 for adults; $1 for children 11 and under.
Ages: 4 years and up.

VENTURA COUNTY MUSEUM OF HISTORY AND ART ☼
(805) 653-0323 / www.vcmha.org $

100 E. Main Street, Ventura

(Going W. on Ventura Fwy [101], exit N. on California Ave., L. on Main St. Going S.E. on 101, exit E. on Main. It's on the S. side of street. [TG-491 B2])

This museum is a great introduction to art for children. The paintings and dioramas are beautiful, and the variety of exhibits is even better. As we followed along the building's circular layout, we saw a wonderful display of fossilized shells and bones. The outside patio area has an impressive collection of large farm machinery. Chumash Indian stone mortars and pestles are out here for kids to try. A section of the museum is set up chronologically, showing the beginnings of Ventura County, featuring Chumash artifacts, to the New West, which is represented by a 1910 car, an old vacuum cleaner, washer, and other household appliances.

The George Stuart Gallery room displays part of his over 200 historical figures. Marie Antoinette, American patriots, and others, are one-quarter life-size (three inches to the foot). The intricate art work and attention to detail makes the finished figures very lifelike. My kids were most intrigued with the models and pictures that explained how Mr. Stuart designs and constructs his figures. They now want to attempt to make similar figures at home.

The museum is well laid out and the kids enjoyed most of the exhibits - a good start for laying a foundation of art appreciation!

Hours: Open Tues. - Sun., 10am - 5pm. Closed Mon.
Admission: $4 for adults; $3 for seniors; $1 ages 6 - 17; children 5 and under are free.
Ages: 4 years and up.

VINTAGE MUSEUM ☼
(805) 486-5929 / www.chandlerwheels.com $$$

1421 Emerson Avenue, Oxnard

(Exit Ventura Fwy [101] S. on Vineyard Ave., L. on Oxnard Blvd., L. on Woodley Rd., R. on Pacific, L. on Emerson. [TG-552 J1])

Retired L.A. Times publisher Otis Chandler's extensive collection of motorcycles, race cars, and classic and antique cars are on display, all lined up, ready to hit the road. But they won't. They are kept in pristine condition for serious collectors and casual enthusiasts to admire.

The over thirty American classic cars include Dusenbergs, Packards, Lincolns, and Cadillacs. Just a few other automobiles in this collection include a 1905 Panhard, 1907 Renault, 1973 Porsche Carrera, 1973 Ferrari 365 GTS/4 Daytona Spider, and 1997 Porsche Turbo. Six rare muscle cars are also here. More than 125 motorcycles are on exhibit, including numerous Harley Davidsons. Other vehicles are the Ahrens-Fox pumper fire truck, a Mack truck, and a 1894 Baldwin steam locomotive. Chandler's big-game hunting trophies are also on display.

Hours: Open one day a month, 10am - 2pm.
Admission: $7 per person.
Ages: Must be at least 11 years old.

PIERS AND SEAPORTS

It ap*pier*s that walking around seaport villages, looking at boats, fishing off piers, taking a cruise, and maybe going on some rides, is a delightful way to spend a few hours with your child!

FISHERMAN'S VILLAGE

(310) 823-5411   *!/$*
13755 Fiji Way, Marina Del Rey
(Take Marina Fwy [90] to the end where it turns into the Marina Exwy, L. on Mindanao Wy., L. on Lincoln, R. on Fiji Wy. [TG-702 B1])

This turn-of-the-century, New England-themed shopping, restaurant, and boating complex is located on the main channel of the Marina Del Rey harbor. It offers pier fishing and boat rentals. (See MARINA BOAT RENTALS under the Transportation section.)

I still say the best things in life are free, or at least relatively inexpensive. It's fun just walking along the pier, looking at the boats, maybe grabbing a snack, and feeling the ocean breeze.

    Hours: The Village is open Sun. - Thurs., 9am - 9pm; Fri. - Sat., 9am - 10pm.
Admission: Free. Two-hours of free parking with validation.
    Ages: All

PORTS O' CALL VILLAGE
(310) 732-7696 / www.portofla.org   *!/$*
Berth 77, San Pedro
(Exit Harbor Fwy [110] S. on Harbor Blvd. and follow the signs. [TG-824 D6])

This picturesque village with seventy-five shops and restaurants has cobblestone streets, making it an interesting (and bumpy) stroll. Harbor tours are available (see the Transportation section), as are Adventure Helicopter rides. Five-minute helicopter rides are $24 - flight time and prices go up from there - and available on weekends and holidays. Call (310) 547-3419 for more information. Tip: The electric, green trolley has several stops in San Pedro and Ports O' Call is one of them. Take the trolley to LOS ANGELES MARITIME MUSEUM, S. S. LANE VICTORY (both listed under the Museums section), or around town. At 50¢, this is a fun, mini-adventure.

    Hours: Most shops are open daily 11am - 6pm. Restaurants are open later in the evenings. Shops and restaurants are open longer in the summer. Closed Christmas.
Admission: Free, but bring spending money.
    Ages: All

REDONDO BEACH INTERNATIONAL BOARDWALK / KING HARBOR
(310) 374-3481 - marina; (310) 374-2171 - visitor's center /   *$*
www.redondo.org
Where Torrance Boulevard meets the sea, Redondo Beach
(From San Diego Fwy [405], exit S. on Western, R. on 190th St., which turns into Anita St., L on Pacific Coast Highway, R. on Torrance. From Harbor Fwy [110], exit W. on Torrance. [TG-762 H5])

This is no ordinary pier, but a fascinating place to explore with your family! Starting at the north end of the harbor, come hungry because enticing food smells waft through the air. Choose from egg rolls, gyros, hamburgers, or pizza as the international restaurants run the gamut from grab-a-bite to elegant. We munched as we watched the ducks and boats in the water, and soaked up the ambiance.

Stop off at Quality Seafood - it's like a mini sea-zoo with tanks of live crabs, lobsters, shrimp, and shellfish. You cannot entirely avoid the Fun Factory, which is a huge, under-the-boardwalk, amusement center. It has over 200 video, arcade, and carnival-style games, plus kiddie rides, which adds up to a lot of noisy stimulus. Come up for a breather and take a boat ride. See the Transportation section for information on cruises and watercraft rentals.

Back on the cement, horse-shoe shaped pier, have your kids look down at the various sea etchings, including blue whales and sting rays. Try your luck at fishing off the pier. The gift shops on the older, wooden boardwalk offer a variety of merchandise for sale. Check out the store Shark Attack. Not only does it sell shark teeth, sea shells, and more, but for an additional $1.50 for adults, $1 for kids 10 years and under, you can go past the curtain and see a sixteen-and-a-half foot, taxidermied, great white shark.

Last, but not least, there are rock jetties here. Deeming them fairly safe for the kids to walk on, my husband and I won the coveted, "You guys are the greatest!" award from our children. Ah, the simple pleasures.

Look for the nearby Whaling Wall. This incredible mural of the California gray whale, painted by marine artist, Wyland, decorates the massive wall of the Redondo Generating Station building located on Harbor Drive at Herondo Street. It's worth a drive by, or a stop and stare.

Hours: Most restaurants are open daily for breakfast, lunch, and dinner. Most of the stores and attractions are open daily 10am - 6pm; open later in the summer.

Admission: Parking is always 50¢ for each 20 minutes. During the summer, it's $5 maximum on weekdays; $7 maximum on weekends. During the rest of the year, it's $3 maximum on weekdays; $5 on weekends.

Ages: All

SANTA MONICA PIER   ☼

(310) 458-8900 / www.santamonicapier.org $$
Foot of Colorado Boulevard, Santa Monica
(Exit Santa Monica Fwy [10] N. on 4ᵗʰ St, L. on Colorado Blvd. It dead-ends at the pier. Park on the pier or just around the corner at 1550 Pacific Coast Highway. [TG-671 E3])

This renowned wooden pier offers a lot to do, including just soaking up the beach atmosphere. There are food stands, restaurants, and great shops that carry a little bit of everything. Peek in the fresh fish store as it has tanks of live lobsters, crabs, and other shellfish. Or, go fishing off the pier to catch your own fresh meal. Rent a pole for $3 an hour at the bait and tackle shop at the end of the pier.

A major kid-attraction on the pier is PACIFIC PARK. (See the Amusement Parks section.) A food court is near the amusement park to service your tummy. A carousel is open Thursday through Sunday 11am to 5pm during the school year and open daily in the summer. Rides are 50¢ for adults; 25¢ for children. The Playland Arcade draws kids like a magnet with its video and arcade games.

A friendly warning: Weekends can be almost overwhelmingly crowded here.

Discover a place where touchable tidepool life is teeming under the boardwalk at the U.C.L.A. OCEAN DISCOVERY CENTER. (See the Zoos and Animals section.) Santa Monica beach offers plenty of long stretches of beach, great surf, and several playgrounds.

Feel like going for a ride? A twenty-mile bike path goes through Santa Monica; from the north at Wills Rogers State Beach to the south at Torrance Beach. If you forget your wheels, call Sea Mist Rentals at (310) 395-7076. They also have in-line skates and boogie boards for rent.

Hours: The stores are usually open 10am - 6pm year round. Open extended hours in the summer.

Admission: Free to the pier. Parking can be hard to find. Parking on the pier is $3 for the first two hours, with a vendor validation, or maximum $7. Parking on P.C.H. is $6 Mon. - Fri.; $7 on the weekends.

Ages: 2 years and up.

SHORELINE VILLAGE   ☀

(562) 435-2668 / www.shorelinevillage.com $
407 Shoreline Village Drive, Long Beach
(Take Long Beach Fwy [710] to the end, E. on Shoreline Dr., R. on Shoreline Village Dr. [TG-852 D2])

This turn-of-the-century coastal "village" has specialty shops and places to eat, including Parker's Lighthouse Restaurant, which is a multi-story "lighthouse" on the water's edge. There are also the all-important candy stores and an ice cream shop. Weekday mornings are a great time to enjoy serenity here. Stroll along the walkways and/or take the cement pathway all the way to the LONG BEACH AQUARIUM OF THE PACIFIC (look under the Zoos and Animals section), and even beyond to a grassy park. Catch a water taxi to the Aquarium, the QUEEN MARY, or SCORPION. (Look under the Museums section for the latter two, which are just across the water.)

Hours: The stores are open daily, usually 10am - 6pm. Open extended hours in the summer.

Admission: Free. Parking is free for the first two hours with validation and a minimum $3 purchase. It is $1 for every half hour after that; $6 maximum.

Ages: 2 years and up.

BALBOA PIER   ☼

Main Street, Newport Beach   !/$
(Take Costa Mesa Fwy [55] to the end, which turns into Newport Blvd., which turns into Balboa Blvd., R. on Main St. to the end of the pier. [TG-991 B2])

Enjoy the miles of sandy beach for sunning and surfing; fish from the pier just for the fun of it; or grab a bite to eat at the small RUBY'S Diner at the end of the pier. (See the Edible Adventures section.) Peninsula Park is on the east side of the pier. This grassy park, shaded only by palm trees, has barbeques, picnic tables, and even a small playground. See BALBOA FUN ZONE, under the Family Pay and Play section, located just across the road, and combine both attractions for a full day of fun.

Hours: Open daily.
Admission: Free. Parking in the lot costs about $3.
Ages: All

DANA POINT HARBOR

(949) 496-1094 / www.danapointharbor.com   *!/$*
34675 Street of the Golden Lantern, Dana Point
(Exit San Diego Fwy [5] N. on Pacific Coast Highway, L. on Dana Point Harbor Dr./ Del Obispo St., L. on Street of the Golden Lantern. [TG-971 J7])

Dana Point Harbor has beaches, tidepools, a seaside shopping village, boat rentals, picnic areas, and more. The shopping village offers many specialty stores, from Indian jewelry to seafaring items. Food choices range from the elegant to the quick bite, plus ice cream and candy shops, of course. Your young sailor can watch boats of all sizes, shapes, and colors sail in and out of the harbor and up and down the coast. Call Dana Wharf Sportfishing, (949) 496-5794, for information on whale-watching cruises and fishing.

At the western end of the harbor, next to the Ocean Institute, is Dana Cove Park, or "Baby Beach." There are a few picnic tables here overlooking the bluffs, a long rock jetty to climb out on, a waveless beach, and a youth group facility which holds classes for water sports. On the other side of the Institute is a rocky patch of beach and tidepools of the marine preserve, which you can explore on your own or call for a guided tour. Tip: Wear shoes with good tread.

Enjoy the day with your family day at Dana Point, whatever you choose to do! (See DOHENY STATE BEACH PARK, under the Beaches section, and OCEAN INSTITUTE, under the Museums section, for other things to do here.)

Hours: Most shops are open daily 10am - 6pm. Open extended hours in the summer.
Admission: Parking is free.
Ages: All

OCEANSIDE PIER AND HARBOR

(760) 435-4000 - harbor; (760) 722-0028 - boat rentals /   *$*
www.oceansidechamber.com
At the end of Pier View Way at The Strand, Oceanside
(Exit San Diego Fwy [5] W. on Mission Ave., R. on Pacific St., L. on Pier View Wy. [TG-1105 J1])

The Oceanside Pier is one of the longest piers in San Diego County, and the majority of it is made from wood planks. It stretches out over the ocean almost 2,000 feet, or twenty minutes of walking, depending on the age of your youngest child. Don't want to walk? There is a Ruby's Scooby Doo golf-cart-like shuttle available for 50¢ one way, free the other way. The spacious RUBY'S Diner (see the Edible Adventures section) at the end of the pier is a 40's diner serving great all-American food at good prices in a very kid-friendly atmosphere. Another pier-related activity is fishing. It doesn't require a license, so reel 'em in! A bait and tackle shop has pole rentals available. The other end of the pier (the land end) offers a McDonald's restaurant, an outdoor amphitheater (used for in-line skating when concerts aren't in session), a playground with wooden climbing structures, sand volleyball courts, and, of course, miles of surf and sand.

Breeze on over to the Oceanside Harbor, just a few streets north of the pier. The Harbor offers your choice of boat rentals at Boat Rentals of America, including single kayaks ($10 an hour), double kayaks ($16 an hour), paddle boats ($15 an hour), and Hobie Mirage - a combination of pedal boat and kayak ($15 an hour). Come on in, the water's fine for swimming and surfing. On the beach are sand volleyball courts, a playground for the younger set, fire rings, and picnic areas with barbecues and covered cabanas. Wear shoes with tread to carefully walk along the tidepools. RV camping only is available along the beach, too. The Cape-Cod-like stores and restaurants entice the shoppers (and the hungry) to indulge.

Hours: Most restaurants are open daily 10am - 6pm. Open extended hours in the summer.

Admission: Parking costs $3 - $5 at the beach.

Ages: All

SEAPORT VILLAGE

(619) 235-4014 / www.spvillage.com $

800 W. Harbor Drive at Kettner Boulevard, San Diego

(Going S. on San Diego Fwy [5] exit S. on Front St., R. on Broadway, L. on Kettner. Going N. on the 5, exit S. on 6ᵗʰ Ave. R. on Broadway, L. on Kettner. [TG-1288 J4])

This delightful harbor-side shopping area is in an expansive, beautiful, park-like setting. There are three themed plazas here representing early California, a New England fishing village, and the Victorian era. There are several wonderful restaurants to choose from as well as numerous places for snackers to eat. Along its boardwalk and cobblestone "streets" the Village offers over sixty-five unique shops, including Magnet Max, Miner's Gems and Minerals, and Fantasy World of Toys. Kids will enjoy riding the 100-year-old carousel located in the West Plaza. The carousel is open daily 10am to 9pm. Rides cost $1 each for ages 4 years and up; children 3 years and under ride for free with a paid adult. See CINDERELLA'S CARRIAGE, under the Transportation section, for another way to see the village.

Hours: Open daily 10am - 9pm. Open in the summer one hour later.

Admission: Technically free. Parking for two hours is free with a validation of any purchase. Otherwise, it's about $1.50 an hour.

Ages: All

CHANNEL ISLANDS HARBOR VILLAGE

Corner of Victoria Avenue and W. Channel Islands Boulevard, Oxnard   !/$

(Exit Ventura Fwy [101] S. on Victoria Ave. [TG-552 B2])

Stroll and shop part of the day away in this quaint-looking, Victorian harbor village. While some stores cater to your taste buds, others have great gift-giving items for sale. Kids enjoy walking the village "streets" and taking in the sights. Stop in at the VENTURA COUNTY MARITIME MUSEUM (look under the Museums section) sometime before you ship out.

Hours: Most stores are open daily 10am - 6pm.

Admission: Free
Ages: All

VENTURA HARBOR and VILLAGE

(805) 644-0169 / www.venturaharborvillage.com

1559 Spinnaker Drive, Ventura

(Going W. on Ventura Fwy [101], exit S.W. on Seaward Ave., L. on Harbor Blvd. Going S.E. on 101, exit at Seaward Ave. and go straight onto Harbor Blvd. From Harbor Blvd., go R. on Spinnaker Dr. [TG-491 F7])

This harbor has a lot to offer. The picturesque "village" has over thirty unusual gift shops and restaurants. Come for lunch or, my personal favorite, dessert! Enjoy a stroll around and look at the boats, check out all the colorful ceramic tiled marine murals, or take a ride on the merry-go-round at $1.50 a ride. Every Saturday and Sunday, weather permitting, join in Kids Harbor Land, which includes pony rides, a petting zoo, a jump, and rock climbing wall, all available for nominal fees. The activities are offered noon to 4pm. Free outdoor concerts are also given on most weekends. The harbor also sponsors numerous annual events, such as the Parade of Lights in December, the tallships in February, and Seafest in June.

Your family can take a cruise (this is always such a treat for kids), walk on the rock jetties located down toward the Channel Islands Visitor Center, and/or play at the nearby MARINA PARK which has a playground, a cement ship, a walkway around a harbor, and more. (Look under the Great Outdoors section for details.) By the way, the rock jetties are not for the faint of heart or for really young kids, as part of the "walkway" on the rocks is washed away. Bring your fishing poles if you have the time and patience. The beach is here, too, of course, along with picnic areas and barbecues. Enjoy your day here with all there is to do and *sea*! (Also see CHANNEL ISLANDS NATIONAL PARK under the Great Outdoors section, and CHANNEL ISLANDS NATIONAL PARK VISITORS CENTER under the Museums section). Tip: The Ventura Trolley tours visitors around the entire city and all of the surrounding places of interest for only $1 per person.

For cruise information, and rentals of kayaks and pedal boats, see BAY QUEEN HARBOR CRUISE under the Transportation section. If you want to experience the thrill of "really" flying like a bird, and you weigh at least 80 pounds, try parasailing with Blue Edge company, (805) 684-0022. The cost is $55 for a ten-minute ride. Passengers may accompany parasailers on the boat for $10. The boat ride out in the ocean and back takes about an hour.

Hours: Most stores are open daily 10am - 6pm. The merry-go-round is open Mon. - Thurs., 10am - 7pm; Fri. - Sun., 10am - 9pm.
Admission: Free, but bring spending money.
Ages: All

POTPOURRI

The dictionary defines potpourri as: "A miscellaneous mixture; a confused collection." This accurately defines this section!!! You'll find a little bit of everything here, so pick through and have fun.

ALLIED MODEL TRAINS

(310) 313-9353 / www.alliedmodeltrains.com   *!/$*

4411 S. Sepulveda Boulevard, Culver City

(Going S. on San Diego Fwy [405], exit on Washington Blvd., turn L. at the end of the off ramp, L. on Culver Blvd., R. on Sepulveda. Going N. on 405, exit N on Sawtelle Blvd., R. on Braddock Dr. It's on the corner of Sepulveda and Braddock. [TG-672 F4])

Chug on over to the world's largest model railroad store to pick up anything one could possibly use or need for trains, tracks, villages, and other accessories. Allied caters to the casual hobbyist, the diehards, and everyone in between. Their stock includes ¼-inch-tall Z-gauge people, Thomas the Tank pieces, and collector's items costing thousands of dollars. We like to gaze at the multitude of marvelous displays. Streets, towns, even entire worlds (well, not quite) are on exhibit with working trains, lights, and animated scenes. Kids may need to be lifted up to see some of them. If you aren't enamored with trains when you first come through the doors, I bet you'll at least be tempted to buy a layout by the time you leave.

Hours: Open Mon. - Thurs. and Sat., 10am - 6pm; Fri., 10am - 7pm. Closed Sun.

Admission: Technically, free.

Ages: 3 years and up.

CAMERA OBSCURA

(310) 458-8644   *!*

1450 Ocean Avenue, Palisades Park, Santa Monica

(Exit Santa Monica Fwy [10] N. on 4th St., L. on Colorado Blvd., R. on Ocean. It's on the corner of Broadway, in front of the Santa Monica Pier. Metered street parking. The entrance to the Camera Obscura is through the Senior Recreation Center. (You'll need to leave a form of ID to use the key to the camera room.) [TG-671 E2])

A visit to the Camera Obscura takes just a little longer than it takes to snap a picture. The Camera's building design involves a revolving metal turret that pokes through the roof of the building with a mirror inside the turret angled at forty-five degrees. The outside surrounding city street and beach scene is reflected through a convex lens down onto a large circular table screen. Artists and drafts people have used this type of camera in years past to sketch landscapes. The bottom line is that kids can see a 360-degree view of the outside world and learn how a camera operates by (kind of) being inside one. Tips: 1) Come on a sunny day as the Camera Obscura depends on sunlight to work effectively, and 2) turn off the light in the small viewing room!

Palisades Park is a long, grassy park above the beach, with a paved pathway that parallels the beach. The park is popular with both joggers and transients.

Hours: Open Mon. - Fri., 9am - 4pm; Sat. - Sun., 11am - 4pm.

Admission: Free

Ages: 6 years and up.

CATALINA ISLAND

(310) 510-1520 - Visitors Bureau / www.catalina.com   *$$$$$*

Across the water! [TG-5923 H4]

Catalina Island is a resort in the truest sense of the word. It's twenty-one miles long, eight miles wide, 85% natural (meaning development is only allowed on 15% of the land), only twenty-two miles from the mainland, and packed with all sorts of things to see and do. The main town, Avalon, has an abundance of shops and restaurants along the beach and harbor. Come here to fish in the deep blue sea; take a glass bottom boat ride; go horse-back riding, hiking, or camping on the untamed side of the island; take an Island safari, where kids thrill at seeing real buffalo; or just enjoy the beach and all the water activities, such as swimming, snorkeling, and canoeing. There are two main beaches in Avalon - the long strip in front of the main harbor, and Descanso Beach Club, which is a short walk away on the other side of the Casino. The latter beach costs $1 per person admission. Kayak rentals are available here. Catalina has a quaint ambiance and is a wonderful family day trip or weekend excursion. I highly recommend ordering the 100-page Visitors Guide as it has all the information you could possibly want about Catalina. (Call the Visitors Bureau at the above number to order it.) The following information covers many of the main attractions and a few of the minor ones:

How much time you have in Catalina will dictate what you should do. Consider taking a tour or two as you'll see more of the island. Both Catalina Adventure Tours, (310) 510-2888 / www.catalina.com and Discovery Tours, (800) 322-3434 / www.scico.com, offer numerous and diverse tours at comparable prices. (Prices quoted are from Discovery Tours.) Get acquainted with Catalina by taking a forty-five-minute, narrated **city tour** to see the Wrigley estate, the city streets, and an unparalleled view of the harbor while hearing about Catalina's history - $9.75 for adults; $8.50 for seniors; $5 for children ages 2 to 11. Note: Children's admission prices are for ages 2 to 11, unless otherwise stated. A longer city tour includes a stop at the **Botanical Garden and Wrigley Memorial** - a nice spot to walk along the pathways - $21 for adults; $18.50 for seniors; $10.50 for children. During the **two-hour inner island bus tour** you'll see canyons to coastlines, plus wild bison and maybe wild turkeys and foxes. A stop at Airport-in-the-Sky is good for stretching your legs, watching small planes land and take-off, trying a buffalo burger at the Buffalo Springs Station, and visiting the (free) Nature Center, (310) 510-0954. This tour costs $21 for adults; $18.50 for seniors; $10.50 for children. Adventure Tours offers a **four-hour Land and Sea Tour** that takes you all around the island by bus, including a stop over at the beach for an hour, then takes you back to Avalon by boat - $75 for adults; $55 for kids. One of my favorite options is the Discovery Tours narrated **three-and-a-half-hour bus tour**, which includes seeing the inner island and wild bison and a visit to the Airport-in-the-Sky, plus a stop at the Pacific side of Catalina (a beach overlook), and at El Rancho Escondido, where refreshments and an Arabian horse performance are part of the deal - $36 for adults; $31.75 for seniors; $18 for kids.

There are several cruise and water taxi options, at about $3 per person, if you want to see Catalina from the water. The two tour companies also offer forty-minute, narrated **glass-bottom boat rides**, which are *clearly* one of the best ways to see the many varieties of fish and underwater gardens off the coast of Catalina. Aboard the Sea View, via Adventure Tours, you can even feed fish through specially designed tubes and watch the feeding frenzy. (It's just like the dinner table at home!) Night excursions are also available. Prices for the Sea View glass-bottom boat tour are about $8 for adults; $7 for seniors; and $5 for children. The Undersea Tour, via Discovery Tours, is given onboard a **semi-submersible boat** which enables guests to see the colorful fish out porthole windows. Feeding time is particularly fun here, too. This trip is $24.50 for adults; $21.50 for seniors; $12.25 for children. Don't miss the Discovery Tours **nighttime flying fish tour**, where yes, the fish really do "fly" across the water as the light from the boats hits and scares them. Excursions cost $14.75 for adults; $13 for seniors; $8.50 for children. Combo tour packages are available for all of the above. Our favorite combo is the **Sundown Isthmus Cruise** with Discovery Tours. The four-hour trip combines a cruise out to Two Harbors, which is on the other side of the island, with an hour stop over to walk the beach, or eat dinner at the restaurant (or pack a picnic meal!), and a Flying Fish "tour" on the way back! The cost is $36 for adults; $31.75 for seniors; and $15 for children.

There are a myriad of other water activities to choose from, too, besides the obvious choice of swimming. Ocean Rafting Trips, (800) 900-RAFT (7238) / www.catalina.com/oceanraft.html, offers **half-day and full-day voyages** to explore coves, beaches, and sea caves. The voyages, which optionally include snorkeling, too, start at $45 per person. Take a **guided kayak excursion** with Catalina Island Expeditions, (310) 510-1226 / www.kayakcatalinaisland.com. A two-hour guided tour, which is really a natural history field trip, is two-plus miles of kayaking - $34 for adults; $16.50 for children 11 years and under. **Parasailing**, (310) 510-1777, offers the thrill of flying - ten minutes air time - for $49 per person. The flying and boat ride takes about an hour total. Additional, non-flying passengers in the boat are $10 each. The ultimate experience for staying dry while in the water is the **Seamobile Submersible**, available June through October. This two-person submarine has a bubble-like top for a 360 view underwater. A diver, outside the vessel, narrates and steers the sub, although riders can maneuver somewhat, too, with a joystick. The hour-long voyage includes a half hour actually under the water. Two people must go on each ride and the cost is $119 per person. Call (909) 252-6262 / www.seamagine.com for more information.

Dryer, land activities are fun, too! Go on a guided **horseback ride**, via Catalina Stables, (310) 510-0478, through the mountains to see the unspoiled countryside, and a great view of Avalon. Children must be at least 8 years old. A one-hour-and-fifteen-minute ride is $50. Get it in gear and rent a **bike** at Brown's Bikes, (310) 510-0986, to explore the island. Take an open **jeep tour** of the rugged inland with Jeep Eco-Tours, (310) 510-2595, starting at $98 per person for a three-hour ride, minimum two people per ride. Play a beautiful and challenging **miniature golf course** at Golf Gardens, (310) 510-1200 - $6 for adults; $3 for children 7 years and under. There are two other noteworthy short stops: The small **Catalina Island Interpretive Center**, (310) 510-2514, which has mostly pictorial and informational displays, such as a marine mural with buttons to push to listen to whale sounds and a large kelp mural with text, plus rocks that were found on the island. The Center is open Tuesday through Sunday, 10am to 4pm, and admission is free. The **Catalina Island Museum**,

(310) 510-2414, is located in the famous Casino building. (If you take a tour of the building, admission to the museum is included). The museum has a wall with trophy fish such as Marlin, a few models of ships, old switchboards, and informational and photographic displays of the island's history. It's open Friday through Wednesday (closed Thursday) 10am to 4pm. Admission is $2 for adults; $1 for seniors; 50¢ for children 5 to 11 years old.

To really get away from it all, explore Catalina by **hiking** and/or **camping**. Off-season camping, mid-November through March, is $6 per person at all the campgrounds. On-season camping, April through mid-November is $12 for adults; $6 for ages 2 to 11 at all the campgrounds. Cabins that sleep up to six people are available at Two Harbors Campground and at Hermit Gulch in Avalon. Cabins are $30 a night, no matter the season, plus the above-mentioned camping fee. Refreshing seaside camping is available at Two Harbors Campground, which is a quarter-mile from the small town of Two Harbors. The town is at the isthmus, down the coast quite a bit from Avalon. It's like being in another part of the world. This is a popular camping site because of its accessibility and water activities. For your information, a two-hour bus drive from Avalon to Two Harbors is $18 one way for adults; $12 for children. Parson's Landing Campground is remote, located at the complete opposite end of the island from Avalon. An optional extra $9 is charged for firewood and water. It is beautiful, and suitable for older kids who like to backpack. Little Harbor Campground is on the other side of the island from Avalon. The campground is near two sandy beaches under small, but somewhat shady, palm trees. It is accessible by taking a shuttle bus. Blackjack Campground, situated among a grove of pine trees, away from the water, toward the interior of the island, is for hardy campers. The surrounding area is great for hiking. Hermit Gulch Campground is the only campground in Avalon. This is getting-away-from-it-all camping, but not too far away. Reservations are always recommended, and are necessary in July and August. For more information regarding campgrounds, for reservations, and to inquire about equipment rental (i.e. tents and such), call Santa Catalina Island Company at (888) 510-7979.

Another way to visit Catalina is via a five-day **Volunteer Vacation**, where campers participate in the ecological restoration of the island and enjoy its beauty. Large tents, padded bunks, hot showers, dinner, and an outdoor kitchen are provided. Ages 12 years and up may participate when accompanied by a parent. The cost is $115 per person. Call (310) 510-2595 for more information.

Note: Catalina's busiest season is the summer. September, however, provides balmy weather and travel discounts.

Channel crossing time takes anywhere from one to two hours, depending on the point of departure and type of boat. Some numbers to call for cruise information, with various points of departure, are: *Catalina Channel Express*, (800) 315-7925 / www.catalinaexpress.com, which offers a just-over-one-hour cruise. Departing from Dana Point, admission is $41.50 for adults, $37.50 for seniors, $31 for ages 2 to 11; $2 for infants under 2. Departing from Long Beach or San Pedro Harbor, admission is $39 for adults; $35.50 for seniors; $29.50 for ages 2 to 11; $2 for infants under 2. A $2 additional per passenger fee is charged. All-day parking is $8. *Catalina Passenger Service*, (949) 673-5245 /

www.catalinainfo.com, departs from Balboa. The hour-and-fifteen-minute cruise costs $38 for adults, $35 for seniors, $22 for ages 3 to 12, $2 for children 2 years and under. All-day parking is $7. If time is of the essence, take a fifteen-minute helicopter ride with *Island Express Helicopter Service*, (310) 510-2525 / www.islandexpress.com, which departs from Long Beach or San Pedro - $67 one way for all ages; children under 2 ride free on a parent's lap. Once on the island, you'll need to walk fifteen minutes to get to town, or take a taxi.

 Admission: Prices given above.

  Ages: All

CHINATOWN   ☼

(323) 721-0763   !/$

N. Broadway Street, Los Angeles

(Going N.W. on Hollywood Fwy [101], exit N. on Alameda, L. on Alpine, R. on Broadway. Going S.E. on 101, exit N. on Broadway. [TG-634 G2])

 Instead of digging a hole to China, hop in the car and drive to Chinatown. Walk along North Broadway to meander through the red and gold decorated stores here (faux palace architecture), or immerse yourself in this Far East experience by entering the pedestrian plaza through a large Chinese-style gate with a sign that announces "Chinatown." (This entrance is just past College Street.) Take along a few coins to toss at the wishing well inside that has signs directing you to throw your money at appropriate desires: love, health, wealth, etc. (And may all your wishes come true!)

 Among the open air booths, small stores tucked away, and stores with neon signs, your kids will see touristy stuff as well as authentic Chinese items. You'll find Chinese-style silk dresses, fortune cookies (which did not originate in China), whole barbecued ducks hanging in windows, robes with beautiful embroidery on them, chopsticks, jewelry, dragon statues, toys, and lots, lots more. The herb shops are fascinating, and many people swear by the concoctions. The bakeries are tantalizing. Hungry for something more substantial? Give your taste buds (and stomach) a surprise by trying ostrich, fried large intestines, or other unusual fare. Or, stop in at the GOURMET CAROUSEL RESTAURANT. (Look under the Edible Adventures section.) Enjoy your cultural adventure!

  Hours: Most stores are open daily 10am - 6pm, or so.

 Admission: Free, but bring spending money.

  Ages: All

EL PUEBLO DE LOS ANGELES HISTORICAL   ☼
MONUMENT / OLVERA STREET

(213) 628-1274 $$$

125 Paseo de la Plaza #400, Los Angeles

(Going N.W. on Hollywood Fwy [101], exit N. on Alameda, L. on Paseo de la Plaza. Going S.E. on 101, exit N. on Los Angeles St., which turns into Paseo de la Plaza. [TG-634 G3])

 This attraction is not a single monument, but the oldest part of the city of Los Angeles. It contains twenty-seven historic buildings, eleven of which are open to the public, and four of those are restored as museums. A traditional

Mexican-style plaza and Olvera Street are also here. Tip: Read up a little on the history of this area, as it will make your visit here more meaningful.

The plaza is the central hub. Usually a docent is on hand giving out maps and other information. If not, check the Visitors' Center at Sepulveda House, which is mentioned a few paragraphs down. The circular plaza has some interesting statues to look at. Across the way is the **Firehouse Museum**. Inside is a restored, old fire engine that was once hooked up to a horse. The walls are decorated with different fire hats. Next door is the **Docent Center**. This is the starting point for two free tours. One is a one-hour, guided walking tour of the highlights of El Pueblo Monument. This is best suited for fourth graders and up. It is offered Tuesday through Saturday at 10am, 11am, noon, and 1pm. Reservations are required for groups, but not individuals. The second tour is a two-hour guided bus tour, for families and/or school-aged kids. Buses are provided. The tour covers the central city and points of historic interest. Stops along the way depends on the docent giving the tour. It starts at 10am on the first and third Wednesdays of each month. Reservations are required.

Olvera Street is one of the oldest streets in Los Angeles. In 1930 it was closed to through traffic and reborn as a Mexican marketplace. It is very commercial and a definite tourist attraction, but it still conveys the flavor of old Mexico. Enjoy a walk down the brick-paved "street" to look at the colorful displays, watch a glassblower at work, see candles being dipped, hear strolling mariachi bands, and munch on bakery goods. There are inexpensive and expensive Mexican handicrafts to purchase both inside the stores and at the center stalls. Note: Kids love the variety of candy that is conveniently placed at their grabbing level.

Olvera Street offers four full-service restaurants. A favorite one is La Luz del Dia, located toward the entrance, because the food is good and kids can climb the ornately tiled steps and peer into the kitchen to see tortillas being made by hand.

The Sepulveda House, which also houses the Visitors' Center, is a few doors down from the entrance on the west side of Olvera Street. You can also enter it from Main Street. It has an encased display of Mrs. Sepulveda's bedroom, and her kitchen as it appeared in the late 1800's. The small Visitors' Center carries gift items, maps, and more. Inside a curtained room is an eighteen-minute film, *Pueblo of Promise* about the early history of Los Angeles. (My kids actually watched and enjoyed the movie.) The small gallery around the corner has some interesting artifacts from the area.

The Avila Adobe is located almost directly across from the Sepulveda House. This is the city's oldest building, constructed in 1818. It has rooms to walk through that reflect the style of a wealthy ranch owner in the 1840's. Some of the more interesting items include a child's bed that used rope and cowhide instead of box springs, a wooden bathtub, and a Chinese shawl that was used as a bedspread. The Courtyard, a packed-dirt patio, was used as a kitchen because most of the cooking was done outside. We enjoyed the side trip here, and learned a little along the way.

As you walk around this historic area, enjoy soaking up the atmosphere of a different country while so close to home!

Hours: Olvera Street is open daily in the summer 10am - 10pm. Open the rest of the year 10am - 7pm. The Sepulveda House is open Mon. - Sat., 10am - 3pm. The Avila Adobe is open daily 9am - 5pm. The Firehouse Museum is open Tues. - Sun., 10am - 3pm.

Admission: The entrance to everything is free. Parking is available at a number of lots that charge between $5 - $10 for the day. The one on Main St., between Hope and Arcadia, charges $7.50 for the day. Some of them are quite a walk to the plaza.

Ages: 3 years and up in general; 7 years and up for the tours.

FOREST LAWN MEMORIAL PARK (Glendale)   ☼

(323) 254-3131 / www.forestlawn.com   !

1712 S. Glendale Avenue, Glendale

(Exit Golden State Fwy [5] N. on Glendale Ave., which turns into Brand Blvd., R. on San Fernando Rd., L. on Glendale Ave. [TG-594 E1])

Most of the Forest Lawn Memorial Parks have outstanding works of art, including beautiful works of stained glass. Tip: Pick up a map at the entrance. The Great Mausoleum at this park contains Leonardo da Vinci's Last Supper re-created in stained glass, as well as replicas of Michelangelo's La Pieta and Moses. Please note that many of the statues are naked. The larger-than-life replica of David is on the grounds, as are other statues and a huge mosaic titled, Signing of the Declaration of Independence.

Make sure to visit the Hall of Crucifixion/Resurrection. A twenty-two-minute "show" features an audio presentation of Christ's last days on earth, complete with various voices, sound effects, and a narrator. As the dramatic story is told, a spot light shines on parts of one of the largest religious oil paintings ever created, a 45-foot by 190-foot painting titled Crucifixion. At the end, the picture is seen in its entirety. The Resurrection painting, a close runner up in size and impact at 51-foot by 70-foot, is also highlighted in the same manner during the re-telling.

Next door, an on-site museum contains stained glass pictures, coins mentioned in the Bible, statues, medieval armor, and the tiny Sotterraneo. The latter is a reconstructed room/cell that Michelangelo hid in for three months because the Pope ordered his death. Photo murals of some of his fifty-six sketches that he drew on the walls in Florence also decorate these walls. Did you ever think there could be so much history and art at a mortuary? Note: Check the Calendar section for Forest Lawn's terrific, free educational programs.

Hours: The museum is open daily 10am - 5pm. The Crucifixion/Resurrection paintings and show can be seen daily on the hour 10am - 4pm. The curtain covering The Last Supper stained glass is raised on the half-hour.

Admission: Free, although $1 donation per adult is requested for the Crucifixion/Resurrection "show".

Ages: 7 years and up.

FOREST LAWN MEMORIAL PARK (Hollywood Hills)

(818) 241-4151 / www.forestlawn.com

6300 Forest Lawn Drive, Los Angeles

(Exit Ventura Fwy [134] S. on Forest Lawn Dr. It's W. of Griffith Park. [TG-563 E5])

    A cemetery might seem like an odd addition to this book, but this Forest Lawn has several impressive art pieces and tributes to American history. There is a huge memorial and statue of George Washington, as well as larger-than-life commemorations of Abraham Lincoln and Thomas Jefferson. A 30-foot by 165-foot tiled mosaic graces the outside of the Hall of Liberty building. The colorful, chronological, mosaic scenes of freedom depict the surrender of General Cornwallis, the crossing of the Delaware, Betsy Ross making the flag, and the signing of the Declaration of Independence. Inside the hall is a replica of the Liberty Bell, models of famous early Americans in period costumes, and a continuously running film regarding the founding of our country called *The Birth of Liberty*. A small Museum of Mexican History is adjacent to the Hall of Liberty. It contains pictures, statues, models, clothing, and artifacts from Mayan, Aztec, and other Indian and Mexican cultures. See the Calendar section for Forest Lawn's fantastic, free educational programs.

    Hours: Open daily 9am - 6pm. Closed during private services.

Admission: Free

     Ages: 6 years and up.

LOS ANGELES AIRPORT OUTING

(310) 646-2911 - Lot B, shuttle info

Los Angeles Airport, Los Angeles

(From Imperial Fwy [105] take the Aviation exit, turn L. on Imperial, an immediate R. on Aviation, R. on W. 111th St. and into parking lot 'B'. [TG-703 A6])

    This conglomeration of things to do makes for a fun, and relatively inexpensive, outing. After parking your car in parking lot B, either walk next door and eat at the elegant PROUD BIRD RESTAURANT (look under Edible Adventures section), or take a free shuttle to the airport.

    After deciding at which airline terminal to be dropped off, take a free shuttle to LAX. Fun things to do at the airport include: buying lunch (choose from Ruby's, McDonald's, or other places), or packing a snack to munch on; shopping at the stores, which often have touristy items, but sometimes have unique gifts items, too; watching planes land and take off; making up stories about the people involved with tearful reunions or departures; exchanging American money for foreign currency; dreaming about where your family could go on vacation (this is referred to as a mind trip); creating an educational field trip regarding the airport; and more! ENCOUNTER RESTAURANT (look under the Edible Adventures section) is just a walk across the very busy street. Besides the expensive food and out-of-this-world decor, this building has a free elevator ride up to an observation deck. Tip: At night the view is quite pretty with all the twinkling lights. Take the shuttle (which my kids consider a fun adventure in itself - go figure) back to parking lot B. I hope you had a nice trip!

    Hours: Shuttles run 24 hours a day, every 20 minutes. Most of the airport shops are open from 10am - 6pm.

Admission: Parking in lot B is free for the first two hours; $1 for each 2-hour
period, or increment thereof; or $5 for each 24-hour period.
Bring spending money if you want.

Ages: 4 years and up.

LOS ANGELES CENTRAL LIBRARY   ☀

(213) 228-7000 - Children's Literature Department; (213) 228-7040 - $
cultural and educational activities / www.lapl.org

630 W. 5th Street, Los Angeles

(Exit Harbor Fwy [110] E. on 6th St, L. on Grand, L. on 5th. It's at Hope and 5th St. [TG-634 E4])

This 125-year old library is a classic. From the unique architecture to the
millions of books to the areas and exhibitions that focus on special interests, it is
an oasis to researchers and readers of all ages who can easily spend hours here.
The Language Learning Center offers audio tapes and instruction manuals in
twenty-eight languages. What a unique adventure for your children's ears. Over
250 newspapers and periodicals are offered in numerous languages. The
children's section is a haven for young book lovers with its comfy furniture and
shelves of books that open their imagination to new worlds.

On the second floor, in the Children's Literacy Department, the KLOS Story
Theater presents a free, one-hour show on Saturdays at 2pm. Various past shows
have featured magic tricks, instructions on how to make a book (followed by
actually making one), and storytelling with puppets. On Sundays at 2pm a free,
one-hour children's video is shown. At least once a month, on the first floor of
the library, at the Mark Taper Auditorium (which seats 225), a free, one-hour,
usually culturally-themed performance, such as folk-dancing, is given. Call for
specific themes and shows. One-hour school tours are given Mondays (for pre-K
to second graders only), and Thursdays and Fridays (for third to fifth graders) at
10am and 11am. Tours consist of a half-hour tour of the library and a half hour
of story time or making a craft. Call (213) 228-7055 to make a reservation.

Hours: The library is open Mon., Thurs. - Sat., 10am - 5:30pm; Tues. -
Wed., noon - 8pm; Sun., 1pm - 5pm. Closed most major
holidays.

Admission: Free. Enter the parking structure under the library on Flower St. -
$1 for the first hour, $2.20 for the second hour - with validation.

Ages: 3 years and up.

MRS. NELSON'S TOY AND BOOK SHOP   ☀

(909) 599-4558   !/$

1030 Bonita Avenue, La Verne

(Going N. on Foothill Fwy [210], exit E. on Bonita. Going S. on 210, exit E. on Arrow Hwy, L. on
Bonita. [TG-600 E2])

Mrs. Nelson has a delightful selection of books, educational toys, games,
puzzles, tapes, and arts and craft supplies. Storytelling, followed by a related
craft, is offered on Tuesdays at 10am, and again on Saturdays at 11am, unless a
special program is being offered. A few times a year, you are invited to bring
your picnic blankets and enjoy a free sing-along or dance-along concert. Sign up
to receive a quarterly newsletter that gives dates and times for these activities as

well as workshop information, author book signings, and more.

Hours: Open Mon. - Thurs. and Sat., 9am - 6pm; Fri., 9am - 7pm; Sun.,
11am - 5pm.

Ages: 2 years and up.

NATURALIZATION CEREMONY

(213) 741-1151 / www.lacclink.com

1201 S. Figueroa Street, Los Angeles Convention Center, Los Angeles

(Going N. on Harbor Fwy [110], exit E. on Pico Blvd., L. on Figueroa. Going S. on 110, exit at Olympic Blvd., turn L. at end of off ramp on Blaine St., L. on 11th St., R. on Figueroa. [TG-634 D5])

Naturalized citizens must meet three requirements: be lawful permanent residents of the United States; have lived here for at least five years; and pass a written citizenship test. Many applicants study our history so intensely that they know it better than those of us who have lived here all our lives.

The naturalization ceremony usually takes place once a month, and as several hundred people can be inducted at one time, it can take a few hours. After green cards are turned in and the applicants seated, each one is given a congratulatory letter from the White House and a small American flag to wave after the swearing in. A district judge pounds the gavel and administers the Oath of Citizenship in which the almost-new citizens renounce any foreign allegiance and promise to uphold the Constitution. Next on the agenda, an INS representative gives a short speech, a patriotic song is sung (with not many dry eyes in the audience), and a short video shows a sweeping overview of America. Ta da - new American citizens have been born! Finally, Certificates of Citizenship are handed out.

I mention this ceremony as an outing because I think older kids who are studying the Constitution or immigration might be interested in seeing this process and perhaps even catch a little national fever. Note that the public is welcome, but they must sit or stand near the back of the huge hall.

Hours: Call for dates.

Admission: $7 for parking

Ages: 10 years and up.

ROSE HILLS MEMORIAL PARK

(562) 699-0921

3900 S. Workman Mill Road, Whittier

(Exit San Gabriel River Fwy [605] E. on Rose Hills Rd., L. on Workman Mill Rd. to the East Park. [TG-677 C1])

This is one of the world's largest memorial parks. The east park features a three-and-a-half-acre rose garden with more than 750 varieties. We enjoyed their fragrance as well as their names: Iceberg, The Doctor, Las Vegas, Confetti, Mister Lincoln, Summer Fashion, etc. The west park has a small, traditional Japanese garden with a meditation house, lake, and a bridge that add to the serene beauty. Again, as with FOREST LAWN (see previous entries in this section), perhaps this is an odd addition to this book, but can be an enjoyable (and obviously different) place to go.

Hours: Open daily from 8am - 5pm. Open extended hours in the summer.
Admission: Free
Ages: 4 years and up.

STORYOPOLIS

!/$

(310) 358-2500 / www.storyopolis.com
116 N. Robertson Boulevard, Plaza A, Los Angeles
(From Santa Monica Fwy [10], exit N. on Robertson. From Hollywood Fwy [101], exit E. on Silver Lake Blvd., which turns into Beverly Blvd., L. on Robertson. Storyopolis is on the E. side of the street, in the Plaza, just N. of 3rd St. [TG-632 H1])

This unique store offers a perfect way to introduce children to art and to encourage a love of reading. Half of Storyopolis has rotating, book-related exhibits. We saw original art work by illustrators of children's books. The art was displayed at kids' eye level. Each book, from which the illustrations were inspired, was on a stand in front of its appropriate picture(s). My 8 year-old budding artist and I first read excerpts from the book and then matched the framed art work to illustrations in the book. He remarked that it gave him the idea to write and illustrate his own book so that "maybe people can see my work here, too."

The other half of this medium-sized store has a cozy reading area and a terrific selection of children's books, with an emphasis on the arts. Storyopolis regularly hosts children's story-times, craft projects, author-signings, presentations, and special events. Call for a schedule of events.

Hours: Open Mon. - Sat., 10am - 6pm; Sun., 11am - 4pm.
Admission: Free
Ages: 4 years and up.

TEDDY BEAR STUFFERS

$$$

(888) 883-8356 / www.teddybearstuffers.com
6600 Topanga Canyon Boulevard, Canoga Park
(Exit Ventura Fwy [101] N. on Topanga Canyon Blvd. It's in the Topanga Plaza. [TG-530 A6])

This mall kiosk offers something special for teddy bear lovers - they can choose just the right furry bear form, or other type of animal, and bring it to life. Well, life as in a stuffed animal to bring home and love. Step on the "stuffery", a pedal that causes a machine to blow fiber stuffing into the bear. Put a red felt heart into your animal before he/she is completely stitched up. When the last of the stitches are sewn, choose a name for your new friend, fill out a birth certificate at a computer, pick out an accessory or two, and take him/her home in its own cardboard cradle. A great *bear*thday party idea is to buy bears to take home with pre-stuffed arms, legs, and head, and have party-goers finish stuffing the bears themselves. (Stuffing is provided.)

Hours: Open mall hours, usually Mon. - Sat., 10am - 9pm; Sun., 11am - 7pm
Admission: Prices start at $11 for the unstuffed animal. Accessories are extra.
Ages: 2 years and up.

U.C.L.A. ☼
(310) 825-4321 / www.ucla.edu $$
U.C.L.A. Campus, Westwood
(Exit San Diego Fwy [405] E. on Wilshire Blvd., L. on Westwood Blvd. to the information kiosk. Make sure you ask for a map. Parking lot 9 is the closest to the garden. [TG-632 A2])

University of California at Los Angeles is a classic campus with huge old brick buildings and stately trees. I hope our visit here planted some dreams in my children's mind of going to college. If, in fact, you have a college-bound high schooler, take the free two-hour walking tour of the campus which highlights housing, academics, financial aid, and, most importantly, social activities. Tours are given Monday through Friday at 10:15am and 12:15pm, and Saturday at 10:15am. The following are some of our "discoveries" as we walked the campus on our own. Tip: There are several places on campus to eat lunch or grab a snack, and since you've paid for parking, you might as well make a day of it!

Mathias Botanical Garden, located on the lower part of the campus, gave us the feeling of being in a secret garden, with its stony pathways through a lush "forest" and a hidden dirt path along a small creek. Trails crisscross through cactus and various other plant sections, all of which are as interesting to study as they are beautiful. The gardens are open Monday through Friday, 8am to 5pm; Saturday and Sunday, 8am to 4pm. Admission is free. Call (310) 825-3620 / www.botgard.ucla.edu for more information.

We took a free shuttle to the north end of the campus to the Murphy Sculpture Garden, which has over sixty sculptures scattered around an open grassy area. My 11-year old summed it up best from a kid's perspective; "I thought this was supposed to be great art. How come it's just a bunch of naked people?"

The U.C.L.A. **Fowler Museum of Cultural History**, (310) 825-4361, is also on the north end of campus. The majority of the exhibits are sophisticated, with a focus on anthropology. Older kids might enjoy them. Call for a current schedule of exhibits showing in the gallery rooms. Inquire about their children's programs and family workshops. The museum is open Wednesday through Sunday, noon to 5pm; open Thursday until 8pm. Admission is $5 for adults; $3 for seniors; ages 17 and under are free. Admission is free every Thursday.

The **Planetarium**, (310) 825-4434 / www.astro.ucla.edu, located at the Math and Science building, offers a free presentation every Wednesday night during the school year at 7pm. The show, which is used as a teaching tool for astronomy students, displays and discusses the night sky in both hemispheres and the configuration of the galaxies. Afterward, view the real sky, weather permitting, through three rooftop telescopes.

X Cape, (310) 206-0829, in Ackerman Union building, Level A, is a game room with video and virtual reality games, and a very high noise level. It's open Friday 7pm to 10pm and Saturday 10am to 1pm. Admission is $6 which pays for unlimited game play. For the last hour, admission is only $3. A small food court and even a gift shop are also in this building.

The **Athletic Hall of Fame**, (310) 206-6662, is a showplace for U.C.L.A. athletes. It houses photos, trophies, and a few pieces of equipment used by Bruin athletes who have excelled at tennis, basketball, football, volleyball, and other sports. A small theater shows a short film of the athletes in action. The hall is open Monday through Friday 8am to 5pm. Admission is free. U.C.L.A. abounds with other forms of entertainment, too. Check out the U.C.L.A. CENTER FOR PERFORMING ARTS, under the Shows and Theaters section, for first-rate theater productions.

Just across the street from the campus, at 10619 Bellaglo Road, is the U.C.L.A. **Hannah Carter Center,** (310) 825-4574 / www.japanesegarden.ucla.edu. This two-acre, almost hidden, beautiful Japanese garden has a teahouse, a shrine, bridges, a pond with koi fish and lily pads, and a "jade rock" brought here from Japan, along with other rocks and boulders. Guided group tours can be arranged, but enjoy it on your own Tuesday through Friday and on the first Sunday of the month 10am to 3pm. It is not stroller/wheelchair accessible. Admission is free. Reservations are required simply because there are only two parking spaces.

Hours: Campus is usually open daily 8am - 5pm. Attractions are usually closed on University holidays.

Admission: Parking is $6 for the day.

UNIVERSAL CITYWALK
(818) 622-4455 / www.universalstudios.com/citywalk
Universal Center Drive, Universal City
(Going N.W. on Hollywood Fwy [101], exit N. at Universal Center Dr. Going SE on 101, exit at Lankershim Blvd., L. on Cahuenga, L. on Universal Center Dr. It's right next to UNIVERSAL STUDIOS HOLLYWOOD. [TG-563 C6])

CityWalk is an outdoor, multi-level mall built in theme-park style with fantastic stores, unique restaurants, and unusual entertainment. Everything here, from the larger-than-life neon signs to the oversized, Disneylandish-decorated storefronts is done with spectacular Hollywood flair, and that's just the outside of the buildings! On weekend nights, live entertainment, such as jugglers, magicians, musicians, and puppeteers, add to the carnival-like atmosphere.

Here are just a few of the major attractions along the walkway: **Jillian's Hi Life Lanes** has a games room downstairs featuring video games and virtual bowling using real balls. Upstairs, ten real bowling lanes have monitors above, showing mostly rock videos. Glow-in-the-dark balls and pins are standard equipment at nighttime and weekends during Cosmic bowl. The **Awesome Atoms** store offers a fine selection of scientific and educational games and toys. Outside the **Hard Rock Cafe** is a gigantic neon guitar. Inside this restaurant, dedicated to the preservation of rock 'n roll, a car spins on a pedestal in the middle. Guitars, costumes, posters, and personal items from famed musicians decorate the walls. (See HARD ROCK CAFE under the Edible Adventures section.) Across the way from the Cafe is an eighteen-screen movie theater and a **3-D IMAX** Theater, (818) 508-0588, that shows both 3-D and 2-D movies on a screen six stories high. Tickets are $9 for adults; $6 for seniors; $5 for ages 3 to 11. Shake, rattle, and roll your way through a five-minute simulator ride in the **Imaginator.** It is open Sunday through Thursday 10am to 8pm, and Friday through Saturday 10am to 1am. Kids must be at least 42" tall to ride. Each ride costs $5. **NASCAR Silicon Motor Speedway,** (877) 633-3773 /

www.SMSonline.com, offers virtual racing in an almost life-sized stock car. Race against the clock or other competitors for $8.50 for a six-minute ride. **Sam Goody** has a giant neon gorilla (think King-Kong) hanging on its sign. Inside, kids like the constant music, the enormous wall posters, going up the grated stairs to the Coffee Cafe, and walking over the bridge to check out the mini-museum that has signed Beatles photos, a Judy Garland letter, record plaques, and costumes of famous performers. Look out for the **water fountain** in the center circle of CityWalk, where water spouts up at unexpected times in hot weather. Two terrific kids' bookstores, **Upstart Crows Nest** and **Golden Showcase**, are decorated as I dream a really large children's room should look like. **Hollywood Freeway** lures people in with Hagen-Daz ice cream. Its entrance sign has the upside down front end of a '57 Chevy crashed through it. On the storefront of **Things From Another World** the back half of a spaceship, which is still emitting smoke, is all that remains from a crash landing. Whew - the extravagant gimmicks alone are worth the price of parking! An outdoor ice-skating rink is here November through February. During other months, concerts and other special events are offered.

Restaurants on the walk aim to please any taste bud, as the wide-ranging food selections indicate. Eat Chinese (including Dim Sun), Mexican, Italian, Cuban, sushi, hamburgers, steaks, or order deli. Check out WIZARDZ MAGIC CLUB AND DINNER THEATER on CityWalk, too. (Look under the Shows and Theaters section for details.) UNIVERSAL STUDIOS HOLLYWOOD, listed in the Amusement Parks section, is at one end this pedestrian thoroughfare. You can experience practically all of Hollywood at CityWalk - all at one time! Note: Weekend nights, especially, with the crowds, activities, music piped in everywhere, and rock videos playing on a large screen outside the movie theaters, are a bit too stimulating for younger children (and sometimes adults!).

Hours: Most stores and restaurants are open Sun. - Thurs., 11am - 10pm; Fri. - Sat., 11am - midnight.

Admission: Free. Parking, in a lot also shared by Universal Studios Hollywood, is $7. Valet parking is $4 for the first two hours with validation; $1.50 for each half hour after that.

Ages: 2 years and up.

WAYFARERS CHAPEL

(310) 377-1650 / www.wayfarerschapel.org
5755 Palos Verdes Drive South, Palos Verdes

(Exit San Diego Fwy [405] S. on Crenshaw Blvd. and stay on this street into the city of Palos Verdes; turn R. on Crest Rd., L. on Hawthorne to the end, L. on Palos Verdes Dr. It's about 2 miles on the L. [TG-823 A4])

This unique, relatively small church, is nicknamed the "Glass Church" because it's built almost entirely of glass, and some stone. It is nestled in a few overgrown trees and looks to be almost a part of them. It was designed by Lloyd Wright, son of Frank Lloyd Wright. The church is built on a bluff overlooking the Pacific Ocean, surrounded by redwoods and gardens. The chapel is unique and charming, and the landscaping is beautiful. This is a short stop off, so look

up ABALONE COVE, REDONDO BEACH INTERNATIONAL
BOARDWALK, or SOUTH COAST BOTANICAL GARDENS - listed
separately in the Alphabetical Index - for other things to do in this area.

Hours: Open daily 7am - 5pm. Church functions take precedence over
public accessibility.

Admission: Free

Ages: 5 years and up.

BUILD-A-BEAR WORKSHOP

(877)789-2327 or (949) 640-0865 / www.buildabear.com

Newport Center Drive at Fashion Island, Newport Beach

(Exit San Diego Fwy [405] S. on Jamboree Rd., L. on San Joaquin Hills Rd., R. on Santa Cruz Dr.,
to Newport Center Dr. and follow the signs to the Fashion Island mall. The store is located
between Macy's and Bloomingdale. [TG-889 E7])

Make your own new best friend at the Build-A-Bear store. First choose a
furry bear, frog, cow, monkey, kitty, or dog body. Then, help stuff it by pressing
on a pedal that (gently!) shoots stuffing into your animal, fluffing him/her until
he/she is just right. After putting a little heart inside your new buddy, have the
last few stitches sewn up, and choose a name to put on a personalized birth
certificate or inside of a storybook. The store also offers over 200 outfits and
accessories to dress up your furry friend. What a fun excursion!

Hours: Open Mon. - Fri., 10am - 9pm; Sat., 10am - 7pm; Sun., 11am -
6pm.

Admission: The "bear" minimum prices are $10 - $25, depending on the size
of the bear. Clothing, accessories, and storybooks are extra.

Ages: 2 years and up.

DISNEYLAND HOTEL

(714) 956-6425 / www.disneyland.com

1150 Magic Way, Anaheim

(Going S. on Santa Ana Fwy [5], exit R. on Disney Way. Going N. on the 5, exit L. on Disneyland
Dr. Follow the signs. [TG-798 H1])

If a day at the "Magic Kingdom" doesn't fit into your budget or energy
level, come spend an hour or two at the magic hotel. One section of the lobby
contains a collection of Disney memorabilia, while around the corner is a huge
wall collage displaying trinkets from Disneyland's past. (Remember 'E' ride
tickets?)

Walk down the eastern part of the hotel complex to connect with
DOWNTOWN DISNEY, a pedestrian street filled with unique shops and
restaurants. (See DOWNTOWN DISNEY in this section for more details.) Of
course DISNEYLAND and CALIFORNIA ADVENTURE, the two Disney
amusement parks, are just a quick tram ride away. Another treat for your kids is
a meal at GOOFY'S KITCHEN, BREAKFAST WITH MINNIE AND
FRIENDS, BREAKFAST WITH CHIP AND DALE, or PRACTICALLY
PERFECT TEA WITH MARY POPPINS - all described under the Edible
Adventures section.

Disney delights in the back courtyard include the waterfalls and water show.

Your kids will thrill at walking down the stony steps (this part is not stroller accessible), and going behind the waterfalls. It does get loud down here for younger ones because of the roar of the waterfall, and it is a little wet, as it's real water (not animated) that spritzes the pathways. After sunset, the underwater lights turn the waterfalls into a rainbow of cascading colors. Back on the surface, check out the koi pond. Call the hotel to find out what time the koi feedings are. Want to indulge in the sweeter pleasures of life? Stop for an ice-cream cone at Croc's Bits and Bites for $2 a single scoop.

Three or four times a night on the hour, usually starting at 7pm, experience the highlight of a nocturnal visit to the hotel - a free, twenty-minute, Fantasy Water show, in an area near the koi pond. The dramatically lit water fountains dance, sway, and pulsate to classic and rock versions of Disney tunes. During summer nights, from this same spot, at 9:30pm, look between the hotel buildings to see a dazzling fireworks display put on by Disneyland Park; a terrific way to end your evening with a bang!

From the end of November through the beginning of January celebrate the ho-ho-holidays with lavish decorations, strolling carolers in Dickens-style dress, and a visit with Santa Claus.

Hours: The hotel is open daily.

Admission: Parking for non-hotel guests is $2 every 20 min., $6 an hour, $30 maximum. If you eat at one of the restaurants, parking is validated for up to three hours.

Ages: All

DOWNTOWN DISNEY
(714) 300-7800 / www.disneyland.com */$*
Disneyland Drive/Disneyland Way, Anaheim
(Going S. on Santa Ana Fwy [5], exit R. on Disney Way. Going N. on the 5, exit L. on Disneyland Dr. Follow the signs. There are 2 self-parking lots for Downtown Disney. The N. on is located just W. of Disneyland Dr. at Magic Way and Downtown Dr. The S. lot is N. of Katella, just W. of Disneyland Dr. [TG-798 H1])

Downtown Disney has an uptown feel. It is a wide, non-gated, beautifully landscaped pedestrian walkway, lined with unique restaurants, shops, nightclubs, and a movie theater.

Top restaurants picks include the Inca temple-styled RAINFOREST CAFE (look this up under the Edible Adventures section); Ralph Brennan's Jazz Kitchen, an upscale French Quarter-look building with Cajun cuisine, a kid's menu, and usually live Dixieland music; Naples Ristorante e Pizzeria, serving Italian cuisine, using a wood burning oven, in an elegant, Mediterranean atmosphere; the ESPN Zone, done in a red-bricked, brewery architectural design, that combines American grill food, live sports telecasts from around the world showing on numerous video monitors all around, and competitive sports games; Y Arriba! Y Arriba!, offering hot Latin music and entertainment coupled with South American menu selections; and HOUSE OF BLUES, featuring Delta-inspired food and live rock, reggae, hip-hop, or blues concerts. (Also see this entry in the Edible Adventures section.) Of course, sometimes it's just as much fun to come downtown for a scoop (or two) of ice cream at Haagen-Dazs.

Favorite stores in this eclectic mixture, include the massive World of

Disney, which is one of the world's largest collections of exclusive Disney merchandise. If you can't find it here, they don't make it! Lego Imagination Center carries a huge variety of Lego products. Department 56 offers collectible, hand-crafted miniature houses and villages. An independent book store, candle shop, surfer's shop, traveler's aide stores, and more round out this area.

Downtown Disney is located in between DISNEYLAND and CALIFORNIA ADVENTURE (see the Amusement Parks section), and connects with the DISNEYLAND HOTEL (look under the Potpourri section) and the Grand Californian Hotel. This gigantic (and expensive) hotel is done in the Arts and Crafts design; a woodsy yet understated elegant theme. Take a walk through and gawk at the high, high beam ceiling and the lobby fireplace that dominates the room because of its size and timber trusses that look like a castle gate door. The hotel does offer free tours. It also has two on-site restaurants; the comfortable, Storyteller's Cafe (see BREAKFAST WITH CHIP AND DALE in the Edible Adventures section) and the more refined Napa Rose, which has three hosts for every table, incredible food fixed in a theater-type of kitchen (the "show" makes it great "eatertainment"), and even a children's menu.

Hours: The "street" is open daily 7am - 2am. Most of the stores and restaurants open at 9am. Closing times vary.

Admission: Free. Parking is free for the first 3 hours. Validate an additional 2 hours from a full-service restaurant or at the movie theaters.

Ages: All

HOBBY CITY   ☼

(714) 527-2323   !/$

1238 S. Beach Boulevard, Anaheim

(Exit Artesia Fwy [91] S. on Beach Blvd. Or, exit Garden Grove Fwy [22] N. on Beach Blvd. It's 2 miles S. of KNOTT'S BERRY FARM. [TG-797 J1])

What did you collect when you were a kid? Hobby City offers twenty-three different hobby, craft, and collector's shops to get your youngster started (or add to) his/her hobby habit. Some of the more kid-oriented shops include the Cabbage Patch Shop, The Bear Tree (in the shape of a tree trunk), Prestige Hobbies & Models (airplanes, ships, cars, etc.), The Little Depot (for all your model train needs and wants), The American Indian Store, Baseball Card Shop, Miniatures, Stamps, Coins, and Treasure Cove (for those hard to find craft supplies). Happy hobbying!

The "city" also has a restaurant (open for breakfast and lunch), a Doll Museum (see DOLL AND TOY MUSEUM under the Museums section) and an amusement park just for younger children (see ADVENTURE CITY under the Amusement Parks section). Hobby City is very kid-friendly - it even has a small picnic area.

Hours: Most stores are open daily 10am - 6pm.

Ages: 3 years and up.

HUNTINGTON BEACH CENTRAL LIBRARY and CULTURAL CENTER

(714) 842-4481

7111 Talbert Avenue, Huntington Beach

(Going N. on San Diego Fwy [405], exit N. on Euclid St., L. on Talbert Ave. Going S. on 405, exit S. on Beach Blvd., R. on Talbert Ave. [TG-857 H2])

When is a library more than just a place to peruse books? When it is the Huntington Beach Central Library! This multi-level facility is delightful to visit. Kids are captivated by the huge center fountain inside and the spiraling paved walkway that encircles it. The fountain is loud, especially on the lower level, in contrast to the normal quiet tones associated with a library. The bottom floor has vending machines and tables and chairs for eating, reading, and/or studying. Look up and see returned books being transferred to be re-shelved via a metal conveyor belt. (Only kids notice this sort of thing.)

One side of the main floor has an incredible number of books organized on several levels within the library. A map is available to help you find your topic of interest. There are even a few small art galleries in this wing.

Just outside the Children's Room is a circular aquarium - look for the eel. The Children's Room has a large selection of books. It also contains a reading area, a toddlers' section, a wooden frame of a boat for tots to play in, and a big screen monitor that intermittently shows children's films. The adjacent Tabby Storytime Theater, which is used for storytelling events, and a media/computer room make this library complete. Pick up a calendar listing of children's events, or call (714) 375-5107 for children's programing information.

The Huntington Beach Playhouse is located on the lower level. Several, mostly adult-oriented performances, are given throughout the year. Children's productions are occasionally offered here, although usually given in the upstair theater room. These can include marionette and puppet shows, musicals, and so on.

HUNTINGTON CENTRAL PARK (look under the Great Outdoors section for details) surrounds the library. Directly behind the library is a trail leading down to a pond. Acres of trails, rolling green hills, shade trees, and picnic areas are all here to enhance your visit. For summertime fun, check out Adventure Playground (see the June Calendar section), just up the hill from the library.

Hours: The library is open Mon., 1pm - 9pm; Tues. - Thurs., 9am - 9pm; Fri - Sat., 9am - 5pm; Sun., 1pm - 5pm. Call for hours for special events, and for the shows.

Admission: Free to the library, although it is $25 a year if you are a non-resident and want to check books out.

Ages: All

INDEPENDENCE HALL

$$

(714) 220-5244 - Knott's Berry Farm education department / www.knotts.com/advinedu/advinedu.htm

Beach Boulevard, Buena Park

(Exit Artesia Fwy [91] S. on Beach Blvd. It's right across the street from KNOTT'S BERRY FARM and adjacent to SOAK CITY U.S.A. [TG-767 J4])

This full-size reproduction of Independence Hall houses, among other things, a replica of the Liberty Bell. Press a button to hear a prerecorded history message about the bell. See the re-created room where the Declaration of Independence was signed. Every half hour, a twenty-minute "show," called *Storm in Philadelphia*, is presented. It consists of sitting in the darkened room while candle lights flicker and a "storm" rages outside, and listening to voices debate the ratification of the Declaration of Independence. It is very well done and stirs up patriotism in an American's heart. The gift shop here has patriotic memorabilia to purchase at good prices. Tip: Bring a dime to put in the machine to watch the miniaturized Spirit of '76 army march around. It also has period-dressed mannequins and artifacts, such as a cannon. Tip: Purchase a copy of the self-guided tour brochure (50¢) before you bring a group here, just to acquaint yourself with all the hall has to offer.

Guided group tours are available, such as the half-hour, Adventures in History tour. The two-hour, Our Early American Heritage tour, has a costumed docent explain the history of our revolutionary times, and students meet with Benjamin Franklin and Patrick Henry. Call the above phone number for information on the over twenty tours offered through Independence Hall and KNOTT'S BERRY FARM.

The surrounding park area has a pond with ducks, shade trees, and grass - perfect for picnicking.

Hours: Open daily 10am - 5pm.
Admission: Free. $7 for parking, or park at the by-the-hour parking for cheaper rates.
Ages: 5 years and up.

ROGER'S GARDENS

(949) 640-5800 / www.rogersgardens.com
2301 San Joaquin Hills Road, Newport Beach
(Exit San Diego Fwy [405] S. on MacArthur Blvd., L. on San Joaquin Hills Rd. [TG-889 F7])

Enter the world of gardening fantasy; a fantasy for me as I have a black thumb. Roger's Gardens sells an enormous variety of plants and shrubs in a beautifully landscaped, garden-like setting. Walk the two-tiered paved trails and fill your eyes with an explosion of color. My kids loved the unusual plants as well as seeing ones that supposedly bloomed in our garden, too. The front patch of grass has a model train set that goes over hill and dale. There are a few good-sized gift shop rooms that sell gardening tools, books, dried flower arrangements, specialty soaps, cards, and other paraphernalia. At Christmas time, one room is completely adorned with decorated Christmas trees.

Hours: Open daily 9am - 5pm.
Admission: Free
Ages: All

SOUTH COAST STORYTELLERS GUILD

(949) 496-1960 / www.storyguild.com
1551 W. Baker Street #A, Costa Mesa
(Exit San Diego Fwy [405] S. on Harbor Blvd., R. on Baker St. [TG-858 J5])

"It is an ancient art, yet it is ever new." (Heinrich Heine) What marvels have been passed down from generation to generation through the ancient art of storytelling! For parents and other educators, as well as students, who aspire to become better storytellers, help is at hand. The Guild offers a wealth of information via meetings (held the third Thursday of each month), workshops, story swaps, special classes for kids, and children's storytelling teas and crafts (often held at KIDSEUM - look under the Museums section). The best advice given to me for obtaining terrific (and inexpensive) selections of stories was, "Look up section 398.2 at your local library for folk tales, fables, and fairy tales." Ask the Guild for their complete set of guidelines, available at a nominal fee, for starting an ImagUtelling Club at your local school or church, or for a group of your children's friends. For more storytelling helps, call the National Storytelling Network at (800) 525-4514, which produces *Storytelling Magazine.*

There are about sixty Guild members. Several of them perform at various locations around the Southland, such as bookstores, museums, schools, children's shelters, and libraries. They also sponsor the annual Southern California Story Swapping Festival. Call for the date and time. So many tales to tell, so little time!

    Hours: Call for a schedule of activities.

Admission: Call for cost on activities.

    Ages: 8 years and up.

CALICO GHOST TOWN

(800) TO CALICO (862-2542) / www.calicotown.com

36600 Ghost Town Road, Yermo

(Exit Mojave Fwy [15] N. on Ghost Town Rd. It's about 10 miles E. of Barstow. [TG-3591 H2])

Once upon a time, a rich vein of silver was found in a mine underneath some multi-colored mountains. Word about the strike spread like wildfire, and pretty soon there were 5,000 people, of twenty different nationalities, living in and around this mining town. The town was called Calico because the varied minerals that created the different colors of the mountains were "as purty as a gal's Calico skirt." Between 1882 and 1907, the 500 mine claims produced eighty-six million dollars worth of silver and forty-five million dollars worth of borax. Then, the price of silver dropped. And the boom town went bust. Thankfully, the story doesn't end here.

Nowadays, this authentic western town has twenty-three unique shops and restaurants (including an ice cream parlor) on both sides of the wide, dirt, main road that snakes up the mountain - put your walking shoes on. Some of the current shops are even housed in original buildings. Topping our list of favorite shops are the rock and fossil shop, the leather works, and an 1890's general store.

There are several other attractions here. Gun fights break out every hour on the half hour starting at 10:30am. Visit the re-created schoolhouse at the end of the road, and an authentically-dressed schoolmarm will gladly teach your kids what going to school was like in the olden days. There is a sturdy wooden teeter-totter and swing outside the schoolhouse. If you want to know more about the town's history, take a free guided tour offered daily at 10am, noon, and 2pm. Don't be a fool when you pan for gold 'cause it's only fool's gold. The Mystery

Shack is a small house of optical illusions where water rolls uphill, a broom stands up at an angle without falling over, and more. Before you walk through Maggie Mine, a real silver mine, look at the mining tools on display, such as a stamp mill, ore cart, re-created assay office, and more. Just inside the mine is a display of rocks and minerals mined from these parts, including fluorescent ones that glow in neon colors when the lights are turned off. Take the short walk through the mine, which has mannequin miners in action and audio explanations of the mining process. The Odessa Railroad is simply an eight-minute train ride on a narrow-gauge railcar. It takes you around part of a mountain where you'll see small cave-like openings that were front doors to miners' homes. On your ride you'll learn that the huge pile of "tailing," from the Silver King Mine, still contains six million dollars worth of silver ore, but it would cost nine million dollars to process. Oh well! Sharpshooters can test their skill at the shooting gallery. Look at and into the house made of bottles - it's the ultimate in recycling.

Call for a schedule of special events, such as a Civil War Reenactment (President's Day Weekend), Hullabaloo Festival (Palm Sunday weekend), and Calico Days (Columbus Day Weekend). Oh, and do explain to your kids that the term, "ghost town" doesn't mean that there are ghosts here, but just that the town went from being inhabited to being deserted.

Tent, RV, or cabin camping (which sleeps four) is available just below the town. The sites are small, but the surrounding area makes it especially attractive for kids because there are (small) caves all over. In fact, seeing and even going into a few caves, was one of the things my children liked best about Calico. If you have a four-wheel drive vehicle, turn left after leaving Calico and head for the hills to explore some of the hiking trails (and mineral deposits) in this area.

Hours: Open daily 9am - 5pm. Closed Christmas.

Admission: Entrance is $6 for adults; $3 for ages 6 - 15; children 5 and under are free. The Mystery Shack and Odessa Railroad train ride are each $2 for adults; $1 for ages 6 - 15; children 5 and under are free. A walk through Maggie's Mine is $1 per person. Gold panning is $1. (This attraction is only open in warm weather.) The Shooting Gallery is $1 for 20 shots. The schoolhouse, shootouts, guided tours, and tram ride up the hill from the parking lot, are free. Tent camping is $18 a night; the cabin is $28 a night.

Ages: All

ARCO OLYMPIC TRAINING CENTER   ☼

(619) 482-6222 / www.usoc.org   !

1750 Wueste Road, Chula Vista

(Exit San Diego Fwy [5] E. on 'L' St, which turns into Telegraph Canyon Rd., which turns into Otay Lakes Rd. Turn S. on Wueste Rd. [TG-1312 A7])

This incredibly beautiful facility is nestled in a mountain range by the blue waters of Otay Lakes. The 150-acre campus is the training grounds for future Olympians (and other athletes) as they prepare for the thrill of victory (not the agony of defeat). Throughout the day, the visitors' center shows a free six-minute video, plus a longer twenty-minute film titled, *Once In A Lifetime*. The movies are great motivators to get you in the spirit of the Olympic games! The gift shop is first class.

Free, guided tours of the facility are offered, or just take a detailed map and stroll along the paved Olympic Path on your own. The path slices through the center of the facility. It is elevated so you get a bird's eye view of the sports being played on both sides, including soccer, field hockey, tennis, track and field, cycling, and archery. Water sports, such as rowing, canoeing, and kayaking can also be observed from this vantage point. Visitors are asked to stay on the path, which is nine-tenths of a mile each way, as it winds through the training center. Call ahead to see which athletes are currently training here because seeing them in action makes the center come alive! The facility also has athlete housing, an athlete dining area, a medical facility, and more.

Future sport venues in development are an aquatics center; a gymnasium for volleyball, basketball, and other indoor sports; and baseball diamonds.

Hours: Open Mon. - Sat., 9am - 5pm; Sun., 11am - 5pm.
Admission: Free
Ages: 6 years and up.

BASIC BROWN BEAR FACTORY

(877) 234-BEAR (2327) / www.basicbrownbear.com
2375 San Diego Avenue, Old Town, San Diego
(Going S. on San Diego Fwy [5] [just south of Interstate 8] exit E. [across the bridge] on Old Town Ave., L. on San Diego Ave. Going N. on 5, exit at Moore St., R. on Old Town Ave., L. on San Diego Ave. [TG-1268 F5])

This is a beary good outing! The store contains a myriad of non-stuffed, furry bear bodies - black, brown, white, and tri-colored - as well as sheep, dragons, moose, and bunnies. Kids (and adults) can purchase a bear (or whatever) body and then participate in stuffing it via a machine that swirls the stuffing around like a dryer. Choose your bear and as a worker puts it in on a pole connected to the machine, press down on a foot lever that shoots stuffing into the bear (and occasionally onto the floor). You can choose to have the bear really packed or slightly stuffed. The bear owner (your child) must initiate the hug test to make sure his/her bear is just right. After an employee quickly sews up the seam, your child can send the bear through the "bear bath", a machine that squirts air on the bear to get off extra stuffing or threads. The store also has a wide selection of clothing for all the stuffed animals.

Tours are given for a group of eight or more that include a twenty-minute talk on the history of teddy bears (kudos to Theodore Roosevelt) and how bear patterns are designed and put together.

Hours: Open Mon. - Sat., 10am - 6pm; Sun., 11am - 6pm.
Admission: Technically free. Bears start at $12.00.
Ages: All

BATES NUT FARM

(760) 749-3333 / www.batesfarm.com   !/$

15954 Woods Valley Road, Valley Center

(Exit Escondido Fwy [15] E. on Old Castle Rd. which turns into Lilac Rd., R. on Valley Center Rd., E. on Woods Valley Rd. about 3 miles on a gently winding country road. Look under the WOODS VALLEY KAMPGROUND in the Great Outdoor section for a nearby place to camp. [TG-1091 B5])

Is your family a little nutty? Then join nuts from all over the world at the Bates Nut Farm. This eight-acre farm features acres of open green grassy areas with shade trees and picnic tables. It is a welcoming and charming place to stop and relax. Nice-sized pens hold a variety of animals to feed (bring your own) and pet through the fences - sheep, goats, llamas, an emu, ducks, and ponies. You are invited to seasonally pick your own pumpkins at the huge pumpkin patch on site.

The larger store here has rows and rows of nuts (almonds, cashews, walnuts, and more), dried fruits, and candies, plus antiques, baskets, country crafts, and more. Grind your own peanut butter from unsalted Spanish peanuts for $1.85 a cupful. The smaller, adjacent Farmer's Daughter gift boutique sells books, dolls, collectibles, jewelry cards, and more country crafts.

Free, fifteen-minute tours of the Bates Nut Farm are given January through August. The tours show and tell a more in depth look at the growing and processing of nuts by going through the roasting room, cold storage room, and packaging room. Call to make a reservation. Call, also, about the many seasonal events held here, such as the cornfield maze, hayrides, choose n' cut Christmas trees, and arts and crafts fairs. You've got *nut*in' to lose by coming here for a visit!

Hours: Open daily 9am - 5pm.
Admission: Free, unless you purchase something.
Ages: All

CABRILLO NATIONAL MONUMENT

(619) 557-5450 / www.nps.gov/cabr $

Located at the southern end of Point Loma, on Cabrillo Memorial Drive, San Diego

(Take Ocean Beach Fwy [8] to the end, L. on Sunset Cliffs Blvd., L. on Nimitz Blvd., S. on 209. Follow the signs. [TG-1308 A2])

In 1542 Juan Rodriguez Cabrillo sailed into San Diego Bay and claimed it for Spain. A huge statue of Cabrillo, commemorating his epic voyage along the western coast of the U.S., resides on the tip of the peninsula at this national park. Press the button near the monument to hear the history of Cabrillo and the bay area.

Older kids will appreciate the exhibit hall in the building behind the monument. Displays include maps and drawings of the areas Cabrillo and other explorers "discovered"; lots of written information; examples of food eaten on board ship, like dried fish and hardtack; and models of ships. The adjacent Visitors' Center offers pamphlets, film programs, and guided walks of this area, plus a book shop and an incredible view.

Before walking out to Point Loma Lighthouse, which was used from 1855 to 1891, listen to its history by pressing an outside storyboard button. We listened to it in Japanese and German [as well as English] - just for the fun of it. Kids think it's great to actually climb up the spiral staircase inside the refurbished lighthouse. The odd-shaped bedrooms are fully furnished with period furniture and knickknacks, as is the small living room, kitchen, and dining room. The entrance to the top floor is closed by a grate, but you can look through it and see the huge light that was a beacon to so many sailors.

Take the Bayside Trail, about three kilometers round trip, to walk further out to the point. Along the way look for remnants of a coastal artillery system used during both world wars. The trail goes down through a coastal sage scrub "forest." Topside of the trail, behind plexiglass, is a whale overlook. From late December through March, catch a glimpse of the gray whales during their annual migration southward. Audio information is, again, available at the touch of a button. (This time we listened to explanations in French and English.) Even if you don't see a whale, the view is spectacular.

From this viewpoint, look down to see the rocky marine environment of the tidepools. A driveable road from the monument leads down to them. Check with a park ranger for dates and times of low tides. Exploring tidepools is always a wondrous adventure for my kids. See and touch (but don't bring home) sea stars, anemones, and limpets, and be on the lookout for crabs and even octopus. Tip: Be sure to bring your camera, wear rubber-soled shoes (the rocks get slippery), and keep a close eye on your little ones! Ask about guided school tours for third to fifth graders for the tidepools and the monument park.

Hours: Open daily 9am - 5:15pm.
Admission: $5 per vehicle; $2 for walk-ins; seniors are free.
Ages: 3 years and up.

FARMERS MOUNTAIN VALE RANCH

(760) 765-0188 / www.julianfun.com

4510 Hwy 78 / 79, Julian

(From San Diego Fwy [5] or Escondido Fwy [15], take 78 Fwy east. From the 8 Fwy, take 79 N. toward Julian. It's off Hwy 78/79, 2 1/2 miles E. of Santa Ysabel, N.W. of Julian. [TG-1135 E4])

This ranch is a delightful stop. The small store offers delectable home-made goodies, such as jams and jellies, fresh ice cream, fruit, and fresh-baked apple and berry pies. Kids enjoy the small petting farm, with llamas, goats, pigs, turkeys, pheasants, and ducks. Feed is available to purchase. You are invited to walk around the ranch, through the rose garden and on the walking trails on the property. Short tours of the facility are given to groups of at least ten or more to see a cider press, apple peeler, water wheel, and duck pond. U-Pic apple picking is offered just down the road at CALICO RANCH (see the Edible Adventures section for details). Another fun stop is Manzanita, a general store that's almost next door.

Hours: Open daily September through May, 9am - 5pm. Open weekends only the rest of the year 9am - 6pm.
Admission: Free; bring money for the store.
Ages: All

KNORR CANDLE FACTORY

(858) 755-3361 / www.knorrcandleshop.com   *!/$*

14906 Via De La Valle, Del Mar

(Exit San Diego Fwy [5] E. on Via De La Valle. [TG-1188 C1])

Candlelight. Just the word conjures up all kinds of images. Maybe not ones usually associated with kids, but the Knorr Factory is a candle shop for all ages to enjoy. It offers the largest selection of candles I've ever seen under one roof. It also has an adjacent small factory outlet building with overruns from special orders and sale items at great prices.

Up the driveway, a small museum on the premises shows a seven-minute video of the history of candlemaking. The museum also features displays of beekeeping equipment, bee hives (uninhabited), crude wax (that's brown or yellow, depending on what the bees were fed), enclosed live bees, and candlemaking equipment, including a variety of molds. Free, twenty-minute tours are offered Monday through Friday which include making a small candle from a sheet of beeswax. This section of the Factory also carries numerous candle-making supplies, including beeswax sheets that come in thirty-eight colors, plus molds, paraffin, wicks, scents, and more. Several types of candle-making workshops are offered here, too.

Outside the shop are a few wrought-iron tables and chairs in a tiny, garden-like setting. Bring your own picnic lunch to enjoy here.

Hours: Open daily 9am - 5pm. Closed major holidays.

Admission: Free. Call for workshop prices.

Ages: 6 years and up. Tours are recommended for second graders and up.

OBSERVER'S INN

(760) 765-0088 / www.observersinn.com   *$$$$$*

3535 Highway 79, Julian

(Exit Hwy 8 N. on Hwy 79 or exit Hwy 78 S. on Hwy 79. It's 1 1/2 miles S. of the main town of Julian. [TG-1156 D2])

Star light, star bright, first star I see tonight; I wish I may, I wish I might, have this wish I wish tonight. Fulfill a wish by visiting this unique Inn located in the mountains of Julian. Observant guests will see and appreciate the *star* attraction - the night sky displaying all its heavenly beauty. Us city folk rarely get the full picture of the vast array of celestial bodies, but in the mountains the people-manufactured lights fade away and God's lights take over in a dazzling display. A nineteen-foot by twenty-three-foot observatory, with a retractable roof, houses several research grade telescopes, although visitors are invited to bring their own, also. Take a one-hour "sky tour", as the Inn's owner acts as a guide around the visible universe. (I still have trouble "seeing" the constellations, tho!) The observatory is carpeted, has heat, a stereo system, and couches, and is decorated with lots of astronomical photos. Beverages and cookies are offered in here.

This is an Inn, too, which means you may spend the night here and spend hours on the concrete observing pads just outside the observatory using your own telescope. Bring your 35mm camera to attach to a telescope for great moon pictures. Dress warmly, even during summer months, as nighttime temperatures can drop rapidly.

Single night booking is allowed on weekdays; weekend guests must stay for a two-night minimum. A detached guesthouse has two private rooms (although the rooms can be adjoining) with queen-size beds and full baths decorated with celestial photographs. Other activities include hiking on nearby trails, picnicking, resting in a hammock under oak trees (although technically, this isn't an activity), and seasonally sledding down hills. (B.Y.O.S. - Bring your own sled.). An on-site gift shop is an authorized Meade dealership.

Hours: Call for hours.

Admission: $20 per person for just the sky tour. Nightly rates are $148 for double occupancy, which includes a one-hour sky tour each night and a continental breakfast each morning of your stay.

Ages: 7 years and up.

OLD POWAY PARK ☼

(858) 679-4313 - park; (858) 486-4575 - Hamburger Factory / !/$
www.ci.poway.ca.us; www.powaymidlandrr.org
14134 Midland Road, Poway
(Exit Escondido Fwy [15] E. on Camino del Norte, which turns into Twin Peaks Rd., R. on Community Rd., L. on Aubrey St. It's on the corner of Aubrey and Midland. [TG-1190 F2])

This charming park is set up like a small historic western village, complete with its own train depot. The two-acre grassy park boasts of shade trees, a gazebo, picnic tables, barbeques, crisscrossing pathways, and bridges over the creek. Come during the week to simply enjoy the park. Come on a weekend, however, for some action, because that's when the "town" is open and everything comes to life! Regular weekend activities include a farmer's market on Saturday mornings, arts and crafts booths, tours through the museum and house, and train rides. The small Heritage Museum has glass-encased displays from olden times in Poway such as pictures, clothing, a guitar, glassware, and a piano. The small Nelson House contains a turn-of-the-century, fully furnished kitchen, living room, music room, and bedrooms. The blacksmith's shop puts on demonstrations of its craft on the third and fourth Saturdays of each month. Last, but not least, take a short ride around town on a genuine steam engine train, or one of the other train cars. Take a look into the train barn which houses the steam engine, a 1938 Fairmont Speeder, ore cars, and a 1894 Los Angeles Yellow Trolley. Don't forget to check out the many special events that go on here throughout the year!

Bring a picnic lunch, or enjoy good old American food at the on-site Hamburger Factory. The Factory has wood-paneled walls that are decorated with buffalo heads, steer skulls, and more, giving it a rustic ambiance. The restaurant is open daily for breakfast, lunch, and dinner. Kids' meal are served starting at 11:30am. Choices include hamburger, chicken nuggets, a hot dogs, or a grilled cheese sandwich. Meals come with fries and a drink for an average of $4.

Hours: The park is open daily. Rail cars operate Sat., 10am - 4pm; Sun., 11am - 2pm. - closed the second Sun. of each month. The museum and Nelson House are open Sat., 9am - 4pm; Sun., 11am - 2pm. Attractions are closed on Christmas. The restaurant is open Sun. - Thurs., 7am - 8pm; Fri. - Sat., 7am - 9pm.

Admission: The park is free. Train rides vary from $1 to $2 for adults depending on the rail car; children 12 and under are 50¢. Donations are requested for the museum and Nelson House.

Ages: All

SAN DIEGO POLO CLUB   ☀

(858) 481-9217 / www.sandiegopolo.com   *$$*

14555 El Camino Real, Rancho Sante Fe

(Exit San Diego Fwy [5] E. on Via De La Valle. [TG-1188 A2])

Question: Marco? Answer: Polo! Observe the fast paced, high-energy game of polo (not water polo), where eight players from junior leagues on up to the pros compete on horseback. The gated playing field is on seventy-eight-acres of unobstructed, beautiful green grass. Watch the hour-long game from the tail gate of your car and bring a picnic, or bring a lawn chair field side or sit at a table by the Player's Club, which is a restaurant and concession area. (No outside food is allowed in the Player's Club.) Admission includes entrance to the Club plus play time in the party jump that is usually on the grounds.

Hours: Open mid-June through mid-October on Sun. afternoons.

Admission: $5 per person or $15 per vehicle.

Ages: All

SAN DIEGO VISITOR INFORMATION CENTER   ☀

(800) 892-VALU (8258) or (619) 276-8200 / www.sandiego.org   *!*

2688 E. Mission Bay Drive, Mission Bay

(Exit San Diego Fwy [5] W. on Clairemont Dr., into the Visitor Center. [TG-1248 D7])

I don't normally mention visitor centers as attractions, although they are always a good source for maps and brochures. This one, however, is located right on the bay so both the scenery and the actual building are picturesque. There are basketball courts just outside the center, plus picnic tables, a small playground, and a paved biking/walking trail. Just down the street is the TECOLOTE SHORES PLAY AREA. (See this entry under the Great Outdoors section.)

Inside the center you'll find a wealth of information on things to do in San Diego (actually it's all covered in this book!), plus maps, and discount coupons on attractions and hotels. This center and another, larger San Diego visitors center, at (619) 236-1212, carry a free coupon booklet that offers discounts on hotels, main attractions around San Diego, harbor cruises, trolley rides, restaurants, and more. Call for information on receiving it through the mail.

Hours: Open daily 9am - 5pm. Closed Thanksgiving and Christmas.

Admission: Free

Ages: All

SUMMERS PAST FARMS

☀
!/$

(619) 390-1523 / www.summerspastfarms.com
15602 Olde Highway 80, Flinn Springs
(Exit 8 Fwy N. on Dunbar Ln., L. on Olde Hwy. 80. [TG-1233 C3])

Experience a genteel way of life (yes, even with kids) at Summers Past Farms. Although the Farm is not large, its beautifully-landscaped gardens, blooming with a variety of flowers and herbs, almost ensure a delightful (and fragrant) *thyme* here. The plants are both for show and sale. One of the small gardens has a little creek with a bridge over it. There is a grassy area with trees, trellises, and white wrought-iron benches.

One of the retail shops, housed in a big red barn, offers potpourri, wreaths, baskets, teas, essential oils, lotions, dried and fresh flowers, and more. Craft classes are available. The other shop is Ye Old Soap Shoppe offering a wide variety of *scent*sational herbal soaps. Pick up a free sample (I chose Lavender/French Vanilla), and maybe you'll even get to see (and smell) the owner mixing essences for his soaps. You may purchase soap-making supplies, or a complete soap-making kit that includes <u>everything</u> you need to make twenty-eight aromatic bars for about $65.

Hours: Open Wed. - Sat., 8am - 5pm; Sun., 10am - 5pm.
Admission: Free
Ages: 5 years and up.

SUNNY JIM CAVE STORE

☀
$

(858) 459-0746
1325 Coast Boulevard, La Jolla
(Exit San Diego Fwy [5] W. on La Jolla Village Dr., L. on Torrey Pines Rd., R. on Prospect Pl., R. Cave St., stay L. for Coast Blvd. [TG-1227 F6])

Coffee, tea, and other beverages, plus antiques and artwork, are for sale here, but the real centerpiece, literally in the center of the store, is natural sea cave that is accessible via a 145-step "tunnel" that was dug in 1902. Once in the small cave, the only things to see are a view of the ocean through the cave openings, and crabs crawling around on the rocks below. The trip down the steps, which get slippery toward the bottom, was the primary adventure. My boys were excited to tell everyone that they had been inside a real sea cave, though, so it was worth it.

Hours: Open daily 9am - 5pm
Admission: Free to the store; going down to the cave cost $2 for adults; $1 for ages 16 and under.
Ages: 3 years and up.

TIJUANA, MEXICO

☼
$$$

www.tijuana.com; www.seetijuana.com
(Across the border.)

Hola! Come spend the day in a foreign country without the European price tag (or luxuries, majestic sights, etc.). There are several ways you can arrive at and enter into Mexico: 1) Drive into Mexico; 2) Take a tram from downtown San Diego to the border, and then take a taxi or walk across; or 3) Drive your own car almost to the border, park on the U.S. side, and then walk or take a shuttle across. Following are more details about the above options: Option 1 - If you drive into Mexico you must buy Mexican automobile insurance because American insurance doesn't mean anything over there. The border town of San Ysidro has several places to purchase Mexican insurance. The cost depends on the coverage you are buying and the value of your car. A few other things to take into account if you drive into Mexico: You will experience lines getting into and especially getting out of Mexico in the afternoon - it's rush hour traffic (actually this occurs no matter what mode of transportation you use); parking can be a problem (I mean challenge); and if you think that Los Angeles drivers are scary - you ain't seen nothing yet! For those who like to live life on the edge - drive into Tijuana. Option 2 - Take a trolley into Mexico from downtown San Diego, which costs $2 one way for ages 6 and older. Trolleys run every twenty minutes, from 5am to midnight. You can pick one up at the corner of First and Broadway at the Transit Store, or call (619) 233-3004 or (619) 231-8549 for more locations and information. There is paid parking available (about $7 for the day) at the downtown location; parking is free at Old Town San Diego. The trolley takes you to the border where you can walk across the bridge or take a taxi into Mexico. It's a long walk from the border, about a mile, to the main shopping area in Tijuana. Even if you walk into Tijuana, you might consider taking a cab or shuttle out because you'll be carrying shopping bags, and your children will be tired (and so will you!). Taxis are plentiful, but determine exactly where you are going first, and decide on a price before you get into the cab. The fare is usually $5 to Avenida Revolucion. Option 3 - This was our personal choice, and it was fairly hassle-free. We parked on this side of the border at Border Station Parking - signs off the freeway direct you to the huge parking lots - which was $7 for all-day parking, and attendants are on duty twenty-four hours. Tip: Just behind Border Parking are factory outlet stores. Then we took a Mexicoach shuttle ($1.50 per person), which runs every half hour, from the parking lot into the heart of the oldest Tijuana shopping district - Avenida Revolucion, which is seven blocks of tourist-shopping heaven. You may buy up to $400 of duty free goods in Tijuana.

Shopping along Avenida Revolucion is an experience. The numerous small shops, most of which are open daily 10am to 9pm, have goods almost overflowing onto the sidewalks that practically scream at your children to buy them. Vendors are constantly hawking their wares, enticing you, begging you, to come into their store. Be tough. Tips to keep in mind when shopping: 1) Don't feel obligated to buy just because you asked the price. 2) I can almost guarantee that you will see that exact same item at least ten more times. 3) Never pay the original asking price. Bargaining is expected. As a rule of thumb, pay around half (or a little more) of the asking price. Be willing to go higher if it's something you really want or can't live without. (Decide beforehand how much the item is worth to you.) Haggle if you want it, but be prepared to walk away in order to get a better price, or if it isn't the price you want. 4) Prepare your children beforehand that they won't always get the item being bargained for, if the price is still too high, etc. Lastly, and most importantly - 5) Teach your children to not say, "I love it - I must have it!" in front of the merchants.

Merchandise that appeals most to kids includes leather vests, hats, boots, purses, gold and silver jewelry, kids' guitars, gaudy ceramic figurines, watches, blankets, ponchos, and knickknacks. The more mature shopper will enjoy leather goods and jewelry, too, as well as perfumes, pharmaceutical supplies, clothing, and more. On every street corner you'll find the touristy-looking carts hooked up to donkeys (painted to look like zebras) along with gaudy sombreros available for you to wear while having your picture taken - $5 for a Polaroid, $1 with your own camera. (Our pictures turned out nice!)

There are other places to shop in Tijuana besides Avenida Revolucion. Try Avenida Constitucion, which is the next street over, and Plaza Rio Tijuana Shopping Center - near the Cultural Center - which has a few major department stores and specialty shops. The latter is a long walk, or a short drive, from Avenida Revolucion. Mercado Hidalgo is only five minutes from the border and often overlooked. It is a true Mexican marketplace where locals shop for produce and specialty items, such as spices and cookware.

We walked around downtown Tijuana, just beyond the shopping district. Tijuana has been cleaned up and renovated in certain areas, but we also saw a lot of poverty, broken sidewalks, and people setting up shop in much less healthy environments than would be allowed in the States. It was an eye-opener for my kids. And, since they couldn't read any of the signs, it gave them an understanding of how difficult it is for foreigners in America to get around. Tip: Bring your own water, still.

There are several nearby attractions in Tijuana. Note: The 01152 number designates making an international phone call; (66) is the area code; the other digits are the actual phone number. **Bullfights** at Plaza Monumental de Playas, near the border, and on Agua Caliente Blvd. at the Tijuana Bullring. Fourteen fights are held May through September on Sunday afternoons. Tickets range from $15 - $38. Call 01152 (66) 80-1808, 01152 (66) 86-1510, or (619) 232-5049 for more info. **Centro Cultural Tijuana** at Paseo de los Heroes y Mina. The Museum of the Californias is good, although the art gallery wasn't that exciting to my kids. The Centro also has a planetarium/Omnimax theater. (The shows, of course, are in Spanish.) Call 01152 (66) 87-9600 for more info. **Hipodromo Caliente** at Blvd. Agua Caliente y Tapachula. Greyhound races takes place here and there is a small zoo on the grounds. Call 01152 (66) 81-7811 for more info. **Jai Alai** at Avenida Revolucion at Calle 7. The beautiful old building has a Jai Alai player out front, showing kids what to expect. The fast-moving court game is played with a ball and a long, curved wicker basket strapped to the player's wrist. Games are played on various days and at various times. Tickets range from $2 to $5. Call 01152 (66) 85-2524 or (619) 231-1910 for more info. **Mexitlan** at Calle 2 and Avenida Ocampo. This city-block-long attraction houses about 200 scale models of Mexico's most important monuments, buildings, churches, plazas, archaeological sites, and more. This is a great way to get an overview of the country. Open May through October, Wed. - Fri., 10am - 6pm; Sat. - Sun., 9am - 9pm. Open November through April daily 10am - 5pm. Admission is $4 for adults; children 11 years and under are free. Call 01152 (66) 38-4101 or (619) 531-1112 for more info. **Mundo Divertido** (Family Entertainment Center) at 2578 Paseo de los Heroes y Jose Ma. This

Family Fun Center offers the same fun, and at comparable prices, as the Family Fun Centers in the States - miniature golf, batting cages, bumper boats, go karts, video and arcade games, and amusement rides such as a roller coaster and a kiddie train. Call 01152 (66) 34-3213 for more info. **Rodeos** at Lienzo Charro and Avenida Bravlio Maldonado. Call 01152 (66) 80-4185 for dates, times, and prices. **State Park Jose Maria Morelos Y Pavon** at Blvd. Insurgentes 16000. This state park and ecological reserve has large open spaces, grassy lawns for picnicking, and a Creative Center for children that offers an aquarium, a lake, an open-air theater, botanical gardens, children's rides, and games. Call 01152 (66) 25-2469 for more info. **Q-Zar** at Via Oriente Local #9. This indoor laser tag arena is huge and located at the shopping Mall of Puerto Amigo. Phone 01152 (66) 83-6183 for more info. **Wax Museum of Tijuana** at 8281 Calle 1 near Avenida Revolucion. This museum is home to over sixty waxy, lifelike historical figures and movie stars such as Mikhail Gorbachev, Emiliano Zapata, Elvis Presley, Marilyn Monroe, and Christopher Columbus. It's open daily from 10am - 10pm. Admission is $5 for adults; $3 for ages 6 to 12; children 5 years and under are free. Call 01152 (66) 88-2478 for more information.

    Hours: Most shops are open 10am - 8pm.
    Ages: 5 years and up.

BART'S BOOKS   ☼
(805) 646-3755   *!/$*
302 W. Matilija, Ojai
(Exit State Highway 33 [or Ojai Ave.] N. on Canada, L. at Matilija. [TG-441 H6])

    This unique, outdoor, used bookstore is worth at least a browse-through, weather permitting. Your reader-child will delight in this big, Bohemian-style store. It's like exploring an old, comfortable (albeit roofless) house, except that most of the "rooms" are created by bookshelves. There are hundreds of books here on every subject, including a small, but packed, children's section. Sit down on an assortment of benches and chairs, or in a recliner by a fireplace, and peruse your purchase.

    Books that are on shelves facing the outside of the store are available for purchase any time of day or night. The trusting (or hopeful) store sign reads: "When closed please throw coins in slot in the door for the amount marked on the book. Thank you." The atmosphere here is worth the trip.

    Hours: Open Tues. - Sun., 10am - 5:30pm.
  Admission: Free
    Ages: All readers.

SHOWS AND THEATERS

How about a day (or evening) at the theater? The listings here range from theaters that have productions specifically for children, to planetarium shows, to dinner and show combinations, to musical extravaganzas!

ALEX THEATRE

(800) 233-3123; (818) 243-2611 - box office / www.alextheatre.org

216 N. Brand Boulevard, Glendale

(Going E. on Ventura Fwy [134], exit Central/Brand Blvds. and go straight over Central, R. on Brand. Going W. on 134, exit Central/Brand Blvds. and go L. on Brand. [TG-564 E4])

The gorgeous Alex Theatre seats 1,450 and offers a wide variety of performances and programs. These include Peking Acrobats, folk dance ensembles, holiday shows, music theater (such as *The Music Man* and *Ain't Misbehavin'*), and even classic films. Special kid's presentations given on Sunday afternoons at 2pm and 5pm, have featured *Parachute Express, Beakman's World, Gizmo Guys*, and more.

Hours: Call for a complete schedule.

Admission: Prices vary depending on the show. Sun. afternoon kid's shows are $14 per person.

Ages: 4 years and up, depending on the show.

BEN BOLLINGER'S CANDLELIGHT PAVILION

(909) 626-1254 / www.candlelightpavilion.com

455 W. Foothill Boulevard, Claremont

(Exit San Bernardino Fwy [10] N. on Indian Peak Rd., L. on Foothill Blvd. [TG-601 C2])

This family-owned, elegant dinner theater serves gourmet cuisine along with its ninety-minute, professional musical productions. Families dress up in their Sunday best, and sit down in padded booths with linen tablecloths, or larger groups may sit at equally nice, long tables. Tiered seating is available on the main floor, or choose terrace seats. Candlelight wall chandeliers and candles on the table add to the ambiance. (My oldest son liked the draped stage curtains, too.)

Dinner is served for almost two hours before the show begins. (If kids get antsy, wander outside on the cement pathways, near the fish pond.) Entrees differ with each show but usually include variations of tri tip, chicken, fish (we had grilled salmon with shrimp mousse strudel), or a vegetarian dish. Meals come with vegetables and delicious hot rolls. The children's menu offers chicken strips with french fries. Full waiter service makes dining here a real treat. The dessert selection includes cheesecake, honey orange ice cream in an almond phyllo nest, and (my personal favorite) chocolate strawberry euphoria - brownies topped with ice cream, fresh strawberries, chocolate mousse, and chocolate. Note: The show and dinner are included in the admission price, but appetizers, beverages, and desserts are extra. Champagne brunches are served Sundays at the matinee seating. A performance is included with the brunch.

The six, yearly musical productions are first rate, and most of them are suitable for children. Past shows have included *Secret Garden, Joseph and the Amazing Technicolor Dreamcoat, Ben Bollinger's Broadway, The Sound of Music*, and the annual *Wonderful World of Christmas*. Reservations are required for all shows. Appropriate attire is requested.

Ask about school group productions, when children can see a show and bring a sack lunch to eat at the picnic tables outside. Also inquire about their Children's Series.

Hours: Dinner seatings are Thurs. - Sat., 6pm; Sun., 5pm. Enjoy brunch on Sun. at 11am. Shows begin at 8:15pm, 7:15pm, and 12:45pm, respectively.

Admission: $33 - $65 per person, depending on where you sit (terrace is the most expensive) and your entree selection. Children's rates for Fri. evenings and Sat. matinees are $22 in section A and the main floor, only. Children must be 12 or under to order a children's entree. (If a child's entree is desired at another show time, you must call ahead of time.)

Ages: 6 years and up.

BIOLA YOUTH ARTS

(562) 906-4574 / www.biola.edu/academics/community $$

13800 Biola Avenue, La Mirada

(Going N.W. on Santa Ana Fwy [5], exit N. on Valley View Ave., R. on Rosecrans Ave., L. on Biola. Going S.E. on 5, exit E. on Rosecrans, L. on Biola. It's in Biola University. [TG-737 F2])

Young children and teens present one full-length, popular musical or theater production each semester. Past productions have included *Oliver, Joseph and the Amazing Technicolor Dreamcoat, Anne of Green Gables*, and *The Lion, the Witch, and the Wardrobe.* Two different casts perform; a home school cast and an after-school cast. Maybe your child will enjoy the performance so much that he/she will want to audition for the next production!

Hours: Call for a schedule of performances.

Admission: $8 for adults; $5 for students. Daytime school presentations are less expensive.

Ages: 5 years and up.

BOB BAKER MARIONETTE THEATER

(213) 250-9995 $$$

1345 W. 1ˢᵗ Street, Los Angeles

(From Hollywood Fwy [101], exit S. on Glendale, L. on 1ˢᵗ St, which is just before the bridge. From Harbor Fwy [110], exit E. on 3ʳᵈ St, R. on Lucas, R. on 1ˢᵗ. [TG-634 E2])

The Bob Baker Marionette Theater has been around since 1963, proving its staying power in this ever-changing world. Interactive marionette performances are given while children sit on a horseshoe-shaped carpet around the stage, and parents sit in chairs behind them.

The musical revues feature marionettes, and some stuffed animals, that range in size from very small to the size of a two-year-old. They "sing" and "dance" their way right into your child's heart. The puppeteers, dressed in black, become invisible to the audience as the kids get swept away in the magic of the show. The performance is done within touching distance of the kids, and sometimes the marionettes even sit in their laps! This is a great way to keep short attention spans riveted. If the story line seems a little thin to you and your attention drifts, watch the puppeteers manipulate the strings - it's a good show in itself. If it's your child's birthday, for an additional $6, he/she will get special recognition with a crown, a song just for him/her, and a little present.

After the hour-long show, chat with the puppeteers and enjoy a sack lunch (that you supply) at the picnic tables in the lobby. Reservations are required for all shows.

Hours: Performances are given Tues. - Fri. at 10:30am; Sat. - Sun. at 2:30pm. There are additional shows given during the month of December.

Admission: $10 for ages 2 and up; $8 for seniors; children under 2 (lap sitters) are free. Free parking next to the theater.

Ages: 2½ - 11 years.

CARPENTER PERFORMING ARTS CENTER ☼

(562) 985-7000 / www.csulb.edu/~cpac $$$$

6200 Atherton Street, on the campus of California State University of Long Beach, Long Beach

(From San Diego Fwy [405], exit S. on Palo Verde Ave. Follow CSULB signs, R. on Atherton St. From San Gabriel River Fwy [605], exit W. on 7th Street [22], R. on Bellflower Blvd., R. on Atherton St. Enter the Carpenter Center parking lot on your L. [TG-796 D5])

Lovers of musical theater, dance, dramatic theater, and children's performances will enjoy shows given at this center. One-hour-plus family matinees are given four to six times during the season. Troupes have entertained youngsters with magic, comedy, circus-type acts, dance, storytelling, ballet, and more. Ask about their annual, Wide-Screen Film Festival (where classic and popular films are shown), usually held in October. Come join the fun!

Hours: Family matinees are given on selected weekends at 2pm. Call for other show dates and times.

Admission: Tickets for the family matinees are $8 - $11 per person, depending on your seat. Call for prices for other shows.

Ages: Some shows are for ages 5 and up; some shows are recommended for older kids.

CERRITOS CENTER FOR THE PERFORMING ARTS ☼

(800) 300-4345 / www.cerritoscenter.com $$$$$

12700 Center Court Drive, Cerritos

(Going W. on Artesia Fwy [91], exit W. on Artesia Blvd., L. on Bloomfield. Going E. on 91, exit S. on Bloomfield. From Bloomfield, turn L. on Town Center Dr., R. on Center Court Dr. [TG-767 A1])

Every season this absolutely beautiful Center (with grounds that are equally lovely) features four or five top-rate performances specifically for families, such as puppetry, dance, circus acts, or dramatic theater. Cerritos also features star-studded headliners such as Bill Cosby; Peter, Paul, and Mary; the Moscow Ballet; and numerous others. Call for times and dates. Check the Calendar section in June for information about the annual Family Arts Festival. Call (800) 300-4345 to inquire about receiving a kids-and-music newsletter. Educators - call the aforementioned number to ask about the free or minimal cost professional performances given especially for students throughout the year.

Hours: Call for a schedule.

Admission: Show prices usually range from $35 - $85.

Ages: 5 years and up.

DEAF WEST THEATER ☼

(818) 762-2773 - voice; (818) 762-2782 - TTY / www.deafwest.com $$$$

5112 Lankershim Boulevard, Hollywood

(Exit the Hollywood Fwy [170], E. on Magnolia, R. on Lankershim. [TG-562 J3])

This unique theater puts on adaptations of classic, contemporary, children's, and original plays featuring deaf and/or hard of hearing actors, directors, costume designers, and others. A children's play is performed at least once a season. Hour-and-a-half shows are performed in American Sign Language, while a spoken version can be heard through headsets. Under-the-seat subwoofers enable deaf patrons to actually feel the music and the sound effects. Past shows include *Cinderella*, *A Christmas Carol*, and *Aladdin and the Wonderful Lamp*. Older patrons have enjoyed *Romeo and Juliet*, *Oliver*, and *Saint Joan*, among other productions. What a great opportunity for both hearing-impaired and hearing guests to enjoy a show together! Inquire about children's twelve-week workshops.

Hours: Call for show times.

Admission: Prices range, depending on the show, from $15 - $20 for adults; $12 - $15 for seniors, students, and kids high-school age and under.

Ages: 6 years and up.

EL CAPITAN ☼

(800) DISNEY6 (347-6396) or (818) 845-3110 / $$$$

www.elcapitantickets.com

6838 Hollywood Boulevard, Hollywood 🏛

(Exit Hollywood Fwy [101] W. on Hollywood Blvd. [TG-593 E4])

This Disney-owned theater puts on elaborate productions of new Disney releases such as *Bug's Life* and *Toy Story*. First, watch the movie in the ornately-decorated, tiered theater. After the screening, partake in special interactive attractions that pertain to the theme of the movie in the adjacent, multi-level entertainment center building. Characters from the movie are usually on hand to greet visitors and have their pictures taken. Other activities have included playing a variety of arcade games where participants win trading cards (based on the movie they've just viewed); running obstacle courses; watching a stage show; playing in a playroom; digging for "fossils"; and joining in a song and dance time geared for younger children. The movies and following activities generally run for a few months, a few times a year.

In the interim between new movies releases, the theater features live stage shows and/or Disney classics often with an added fun, audience participation activity or two.

Hours: Call for show dates.

Admission: Ticket prices vary according what is playing. The first-run movies with all the activities usually cost $15 for ages 12 and up; $12 for seniors and ages 3 - 11; children 2 and under are free. Group rates are discounted. Disney classics usually cost about $9 for adults; $5.95 per child.

Ages: 4 years and up.

EXCALIBUR THEATER

(818) 760-PLAY (7529) / www.kelrik.com   *$$$*

12655 Ventura Boulevard, Studio City

(Going E. on Ventura Fwy [101], exit S. on Coldwater Cyn. Ave., L. on Ventura. Going W. on 101, exit S. on Laurel Cyn. Blvd., R. on Ventura. [TG-562 E5])

This sixty-five-seat theater presents youth actors, with an adult lead, in one-hour fairy tales that encourage audience participation. Past productions have included *Pinocchio*, *Snow White and the Seven Dwarfs*, *Jungle Book*, and *Aladdin and the Wonderful Lamp*. Stay for a double feature as on most Sundays one show is performed at 1pm and a different one at 3pm.

Hours: Most Sun. at 1pm and 3pm.
Admission: $12 for adults; $8 for ages 12 and under.
Ages: 2 years and up.

FALCON THEATRE

(818) 955-8101 / www.falcontheatre.com   *$$$*

4252 Riverside Drive, Burbank

(Going E. on Ventura Fwy [134], exit S. on Pass Ave, R. on Alameda, which turns into Riverside. Going W on 134, exit at Hollywood Way, at the bottom of the off ramp, go L. on Alameda, which turns into Riverside. [TG-563 D4])

This professional theater produces at least four shows a year aimed at high-school kids and adults; another four are geared for kindergartners through middle schoolers. Just a few of the past productions have included *Rumpelstiltskin*, *Hansel and Gretel*, and *The Lion, the Witch and the Wardrobe*.

Hours: Adult productions usually run Thurs. - Sun. at 8pm, with matinees on weekends. Children's programs generally run on Sat., 1pm and 3pm; Sun. at 1pm. Call for a complete schedule.
Admission: Tickets range between $10 (for the children's show) up to $35 for adult shows.
Ages: K and up - depending on the show.

GLENDALE CENTRE THEATRE

(818) 244-8481 / www.glendalecentretheatre.com   *$$$*

324 N. Orange Street, Glendale

(Going E. on Ventura Fwy [134], exit S. on N. Central Ave., L. on Lexington Dr., R. on Orange St. Going W. on 134, exit S. on N. Brand Blvd., R. on Lexington Dr., L. on Orange St. [TG-564 E4])

This theater puts on terrific, one-and-a-half-hour shows for children. Past productions have included *The Little Mermaid*, *Sleeping Beauty*, *Hansel and Gretel*, and *Jack and the Beanstalk*. The season begins in March and ends in November. Many block-buster musicals and comedies suitable for the family are also performed throughout the year.

Hours: Children's shows are usually performed Sat. at 11am. Call for other show times.
Admission: $10 for adults; $8 for children 12 and under.
Ages: Depends on the show.

GOURMET CAROUSEL RESTAURANT

(323) 721-0774 - Chinatown Center event planner /
www.chinatown.com
911 N. Broadway, Los Angeles

See GOURMET CAROUSEL RESTAURANT under the Edible
Adventures section.

GRIFFITH PLANETARIUM AND LASERIUM SHOWS ☼

(323) 664-1191 - Planetarium; (818) 997-3624 - Laserium /   *$$/$$$*
www.griffithobservatory.org; www.laserium.com
On the slope of Mount Hollywood, in Griffith Park, Los Angeles
(Exit Golden State Fwy [5] W. on Los Feliz Blvd., take Hillhurst Ave. N. past the Greek Theater to
the Observatory. [TG-593 J2])

The Planetarium has a gigantic projector that fills the dome ceiling with
realistic views of the nighttime sky, even though you're inside and it might be
daytime. The hour-long show is an eye-opener for citified kids (and adults) who
have not seen such starry wonders. Children 4 years and under are admitted only
to the 1:30pm show on Saturdays and Sundays, but do take them then as the
show, *Voyage to the Planets* is geared for young kids. A friendly, green,
animated space alien is the tour guide, "talking" with the real-life lecturer, and
taking the intrigued audience on a trip to different planets.(See GRIFFITH
OBSERVATORY AND PLANETARIUM, under the Museums section, for
other things to do here.)

The Laserium shows are laser-beam concerts with rock, classical, or other
music, and incredible special effects. Your audio, visual, and kinesthetic child
will love this illuminating production. A variety of different shows are offered
each week. Note: The Laserium is moving to a new venue in 2002.

Hours: Planetarium shows are given in the summer Mon. - Fri., 1:30pm,
3pm, and 7:30pm; Sat. - Sun., 1:30pm, 3pm, 4:30pm, and
7:30pm. Shows are given the rest of the year are Tues. - Fri.,
3pm, and 7:30pm; Sat. - Sun., 1:30pm, 3pm, 4:30pm, and
7:30pm. Laserium shows are presented Tues. - Thurs. and Sun.
at 6pm and 8:45pm; Fri. - Sat. and various holidays at 6pm,
8:45pm, and 9:45pm.

Admission: The Planetarium show is $4 for adults; $3 for seniors; $2 for
ages 5 - 12. Children 4 and under are admitted free to the 1:30pm
weekend show with a paying adult. The Laserium show is $7 for
adults; $6 for senior citizens and ages 5 - 12; children 4 and
under are not admitted. Certain discounts are available through
AAA.

Ages: 3 years and up for the Saturday planetarium show; 5 years and
up for all other shows.

HARRIET AND CHARLES LUCKMAN FINE ARTS COMPLEX

(323) 343-6610 / www.calstatela.edu $$$$

5151 State University Drive, on the California State Los Angeles campus, Los Angeles

(Exit San Bernardino Fwy [10] N. on Eastern Ave., stay to the R. on Paseo Rancho Castilla, then immediate R. on State University Dr. [TG-635 F2])

The Luckman Fine Arts theater presents modern dance, ballet, opera, and other musical performances. Many of them are suitable for families, such as the *Nutcracker Suite.*

Hours: Call for show dates and times.
Admission: Prices vary greatly depending on the show. Parking is about $5.
Ages: Depends on the show.

IMAX THEATER

(213) 744-2014 / www.casciencectr.org $$$

700 State Drive, Exposition Park, Los Angeles

(Exit the Harbor Fwy [110] W. on Exposition Blvd., L. on Flower, L. on Figueroa. Or, exit Santa Monica Fwy [10] S. on Vermont, L. on Exposition, R. on Figueroa. It's adjacent to the California Science Center. Parking is available the first driveway on the R. [TG-674 B1])

Moviegoers can enjoy both traditional 2-D and newer 3-D film formats at this large screen IMAX Theater. In the 3-D format, the use of polarized glasses, a surround sound system, and the seven-story high, ninety-foot-wide screen shows films take you and your child on wonderful adventures. You'll explore the depths of the ocean and swim with fish (watch out for the sharks!); river raft through the Grand Canyon; enter the world of outer space; and more. In other words, you'll feel like you actually experience whatever is on the screen, without ever leaving your seat. "Edutainment" is what this theater all about! See nearby attractions listed individually in the Alphabetical Index: AIR AND SPACE GALLERY, CALIFORNIA AFRICAN AMERICAN MUSEUM, CALIFORNIA SCIENCE CENTER, EXPOSITION PARK, and NATURAL HISTORY MUSEUM OF LOS ANGELES.

Hours: Call for show titles and show times. Shows run Mon. - Fri., 10am - 6pm; Sat. - Sun., 10am - 8pm.
Admission: 2-D movies are $6.50 for adults; $4.50 for seniors and ages 4 - 12; $5 for students 13 - 21; children 3 and under are free. 3-D movies are $7.50 for adults; $5.50 for seniors and ages 4 - 12; $6 for students. Parking is $5.
Ages: 3 years and up.

JAMES ARMSTRONG THEATRE

(310) 781-7171 or (310) 781-7150 / www.tcac.torrnet.com $$$

3330 Civic Center Drive, at the Torrance Cultural Arts Center, Torrance

(From Harbor Fwy [110], exit W. on Carson St., R. on Madrona Ave., R. on Civic Center Dr. From San Diego Fwy [405], exit E. on Artesia, L. on Prairie Ave., which turns into Madrona Ave., L. on Civic Center Dr. [TG-763 E5])

The Arts Center has a 500+ seat theater that is host to a variety of professional and community productions, as well as film screenings. Five special programs featuring professional performers, titled the Peanut Gallery Theatre Series, are given for youngsters and their parents usually in the months of January, February, September, November, and December. The programs feature dance, music, drama, comedy, or a combination thereof. Past shows have included *Jim Gamble Puppets*, *Sleeping Beauty*, *Dan Crow* (zany music and comedy), the *Ugly Duckling* (musical theater), and children's concerts.

Hours: Call for show times and dates. Peanut Gallery series' shows are given Sat. at 10am.

Admission: Prices vary for each show. Peanut Gallery shows are $7.50 per person

Ages: 3 to 8 years old.

L. A. CONNECTION COMEDY THEATER

(818) 710-1320 / www.laconnectioncomedy.com

13442 Ventura Boulevard, Sherman Oaks

(Exit Ventura Fwy [101] S. on Woodman, L. on Ventura Blvd. [TG-562 C5])

Tickle your children's funnybones and bring them to the Comedy Theater for comedy improv performances by kids, for kids. The almost hour-long improvisational show is given in a small room with tiered, theater-type seating. The performers consist of one adult and usually six kids that are between 5 to 14 years old. The kids are members of the Comedy Improv for Kids and are trained in the L.A. Connection's Improv Workshops.

Audience participation is mandatory as the actors ask for help in creating characters, or supplying ideas to use in a skit. Your children love to see their suggestions acted out. Remember, the performers are kids, so there is a lot of kid-type humor. As with any improv show, the success of a skit depends on the improvisationalists and the audience. The L.A. Connection really connected with my kids!

If your child thinks the whole world is a stage, then maybe he should be on it. Sign him up for comedy improv classes and the next performance you see could be his.

Hours: Performances are Sun. at 3:30pm.

Admission: $7 per person.

Ages: 5 years and up - younger ones won't get the humor.

LA MIRADA THEATER FOR THE PERFORMING ARTS

(562) 944-9801 / www.cityoflamirada.org

14900 La Mirada Boulevard, La Mirada

(Exit Artesia Fwy [91] or Santa Ana Fwy [5] N. on Valley View, R. on Rosecrans, R. on La Mirada. [TG-737 G4])

Golden State Children and Programs for Young Audiences are two production companies that present children's programs here three to five times a year.

Hours: Call for show dates and times.

Admission: Tickets are usually $8 per person.

Ages: 5 years and up.

LANCASTER PERFORMING ARTS CENTER

(661) 723-5950 / www.lpac.org $$$

750 W. Lancaster Boulevard, Lancaster

(Exit Antelope Valley Fwy [14/138] E. on Ave. J., N. on 10th St. West, R. on Lancaster. [TG-4015 G5])

Theater productions run the gamut of musicals, dances, and dramas. The Arts for Youth program usually stages five plays a year. Past productions have included *Rumpelstiltskin, Nutcracker, Sleeping Beauty*, and *Revenge of the Space Pandas*.

Hours: Call for show dates and times.

Admission: $5 - $75 per person, depending on the show.

Ages: 3 years and up, depending on the production.

LOS ANGELES CENTRAL LIBRARY

(213) 228-7000 - Children's Literature Department; (213) 228-7040 - cultural and educational activities / www.lapl.org

630 W. 5th Street, Los Angeles

See LOS ANGELES CENTRAL LIBRARY under the Potpourri section for details.

LOS ANGELES PHILHARMONIC TOYOTA SYMPHONIES FOR YOUTH SERIES

(323) 850-2000 / www.laphil.org $$$$

135 N. Grand Avenue, Dorothy Chandler Pavilion in the Music Center, Los Angeles

(From Harbor Fwy [110], exit E. on 4th St., L. on Olive St., go to end, L. on 1st St., R. on Grand. Going N. on Hollywood Fwy [101], exit S. on Grand. Going S. on 101, exit E. on Temple, R. on Grand. [TG-634 F3])

Six times a year the Los Angeles Philharmonic offers one-hour concerts under the collective title of Toyota Symphonies for Youth. They are designed to excite kids, particularly between the ages of 5 to 12, about the wonderful world of orchestral music. Meet in the lobby first for a variety of pre-concert activities. Different stations can include arts and crafts, storytellers, dance, and/or meeting with musicians who will demonstrate their instruments. All the activities help to introduce (and reinforce) the morning's concert theme. Move into the grand hall for the concert. Past concerts include *Magical Melodies*, *Fun with Bach*, and *Peter and the Wolf*.

Hours: Pre-concert workshop activities begin at 10am. Concerts begin at 11am on selected Sat., usually in the months of November, December, February, March, April, and May.

Admission: $8 - $10 per person, depending on your seat. Parking is available in the Music Center Garage for $7 or at the Department of Water and Power for $5.

Ages: 5 to 12 years.

MAGICOPOLIS

(310) 451-2241 / www.magicopolis.com

$$$$

1418 4ᵗʰ Street, Santa Monica

(Exit Santa Monica Fwy [10] N. on Lincoln Blvd., L. on Wilshire, L. on 4ᵗʰ St. [TG-671 E2])

Abracadabra - make a magical place appear. Poof! Magicopolis, meaning "City of Magic," was actually created by veteran magician, Steve Spill, to make first-class magic shows available to the whole family. He has succeeded wonderfully. Penn and Teller have even given their blessings to Magicopolis by having their hands and feet cast in cement inside the lobby. While waiting for the shows to begin, watch what a resident magician has up his sleeve, and grab a bite to eat from the inside cafe that serves muffins, coffee, and juice.

The magic is executed in two main rooms. In the Hocus Pocus room, an intimate setting of thirty-four seats, three different magicians perform in a ninety-minute show integrating quicker-than-the-eye and "mind-reading" acts. Being close-up to the performers, however, does not insure that audience members will "get" the trick; at least it usually doesn't in my case. The Abracadabra room has 150 theater-style seats and a comfortable atmosphere. Professional, featured magicians perform in ninety-minute shows that entertain and mystify visitors with larger-scale illusions. Comedy and sleight-of-hand acts are often part of the show, too. My kids and I sat watching with mouths opened and asked, "How did he do that?" Each show incorporates some audience participation, adding to the overall enjoyment. For those who want to try a little magic of their own, check out the in-house retail shop.

Hours: Performance schedules vary, although shows are usually given in the Hocus Pocus room on Fri. at 8pm and in the Abracadabra room Sat., 2pm and 8pm; Sun., 2pm. Call for a complete schedule.

Admission: $20 per person for an evening performance; $15 for a matinee.

Ages: 6 years and up.

METROPOLITAN EDUCATIONAL THEATRE NETWORK (Northridge)

(818) 706-9884

18111 Nordhoff Street, at the California State University of Northridge, Northridge

(From San Diego Fwy [405], exit E. on Nordhoff. From Ronald Regan Fwy [118], exit S. on Reseda Blvd., L. on Nordhoff. From Ventura Fwy [101], exit N. on Reseda, R. on Nordhoff. [TG-501 A7])

See METROPOLITAN EDUCATIONAL THEATRE NETWORK (San Diego) for details. Numerous other performances are also given at this theater.

METROPOLITAN EDUCATIONAL THEATRE NETWORK (Torrance)

(310) 376-1740

3330 Civic Center Drive, James Armstrong Theatre at the Torrance Cultural Arts Center, Torrance

(From Harbor Fwy [110], exit W. on Carson St., R. on Madrona Ave., R. on Civic Center Dr. From San Diego Fwy [405], exit E. on Artesia, L. on Prairie Ave., which turns into Madrona Ave., L. on Civic Center Dr. [TG-763 E5])

See METROPOLITAN EDUCATIONAL THEATRE NETWORK (San Diego) for details. This theater also offers numerous other family-oriented, as well as adult, productions.

MORGAN-WIXSON THEATRE

(310) 828-7519 $$$

2627 Pico Boulevard, Santa Monica

(Going W. on Santa Monica Fwy [10], exit S. on Cloverfield, L. on Pico. Going E. on 10, exit S. on 20th St., L. on Pico. [TG-671 J1])

Several times a year the Rainbow Factory, a teenage resident children's theater company, produce show specifically for young audiences. Past shows include *Frog Prince*, *The Emperor's New Clothes*, *Midsummer Night's Dream*, and *Rumpelstilskin*. There are other theater shows for the whole family, as well as comedies, musicals, and dramas for older audiences. Some of these titles are *Sherlock's Last Case*, *Oliver*, *Fiddler on the Roof*, and *Cat on a Hot Tin Roof*.

Hours: Call for shows hours.

Admission: Prices for children's series are $7 per person. Call for prices for other shows.

Ages: Depends on the show.

MUSIC CENTER

(213) 972-7211 - general info; (213) 972-7483 - tours / $$$$$
www.musiccenter.org

135 N. Grand Avenue, Los Angeles

(From Harbor Fwy [110], exit E. on 4th St., L. on Olive St., go to end, L. on 1st St., R. on Grand. Going N. on Hollywood Fwy [101], exit S. on Grand. Going S. on 101, exit E. on Temple, R. on Grand. Parking is available on Grand Ave. and, on the evening and weekends only, at the Dept. of Water and Power on Hope St. [TG-634 F3])

This sprawling, two-city block Los Angeles complex features three (soon to be four) powerhouse entertainment venues, each with a resident company. The **Ahmanson Theater**, (213) 628-2772 or (213) 972-7200, puts on world-class, big-name, mainstream and Tony-award winning musical productions, many of which are terrific for the whole family. The **Dorothy Chandler Pavilion**, (213) 972-7211, is home to the Los Angeles Philharmonic, the Los Angeles Opera, and Los Angeles Master Chorale. The fabulous **Walt Disney Concert Hall** will be the new home of the Philharmonic. The 750-seat **Mark Taper Forum**, (213) 628-2772, produces spectacular theater. Note: Free guided tours of all the buildings, for third graders and up, are offered during the week. Call for tour dates and times.

Call, or check the website, for the numerous family and educational events, some of which are free. One of my favorite events is the once a year Spotlight, where the stars of tomorrow (i.e. incredibly talented high schoolers) compete in six categories in a variety show format. Ask about the Saturday Family Series, where two, hour-long show series are geared for young children: The Pillow Theatre series is for ages 3 to 6 and held at the Dorothy Chandler Pavilion on selected Saturdays at 10am for $6 per person; the Young Arts series is for ages 7 to 12 and held at Zipper Concert Hall (just down the street) on selected Saturdays at 10am for $6 per person.

Hours: Call for show dates and times.

Admission: Varies, depending on the show. Parking is $7 on Grand Ave., $5 on Hope St.

Ages: 5 years and up.

NORRIS CENTER ☼

(310) 544-0403 / www.norristheatre.org $$$$

27570 Crossfield Drive, Rolling Hills Estates

(Exit San Diego Fwy [405] S. on Hawthorne Blvd. Drive about 8 miles and turn L. on Indian Peak Rd., L. on Crossfield Dr. [TG-793 A7])

Ballet, big band, off Broadway shows, Chinese acrobats, storytelling, puppetry, and comedy are just a few examples of the assortment of programs and shows put on at the Norris theater. Past productions specifically for kids, called the Children's Series, include *Carnival of the Animals, Ramona Quimby, Ugly Duckling, Heidi,* and the *Nutcracker.*

Hours: Call for show dates and times. Children's productions are on certain Sun. at 1pm and 4pm.

Admission: Various shows cost different prices. Tickets for the Children's Series are usually $14 per person.

Ages: 2 years and up, depending on the show.

OLD TOWN MUSIC HALL, INC. ☼

(310) 322-2592 $$$

140 Richmond Street, El Segundo

(Take Century Fwy [105] W. to the end; it turns into Imperial Hwy, turn L. on Main St., R. on Grand, L. on Richmond. [TG-732 E2])

Step back in time, to the golden era of film where silent movies and "talkies" dominated the screens. The rich red drapes, chandeliers, intimate seating, and the sound of the mighty Wurlitzer pipe organ, which is like a one-man band, create an atmosphere of yesteryear. The proprietors, two older gentlemen who have been in business together here for over thirty years, share organ duty and run the movies. The audience gets warmed up with four or five sing-alongs while on-screen slides provide lyrics and hokey cartoons. The Wurlitzer is played at every showing and accompanies silent epic and comedy films. Past films have included *The General, Wings, Phantom of the Opera,* and the original *Ben Hur.* Talkies have included *The Firefly* with Jeanette MacDonald, *Donkey Serenade, Roaring Twenties* starring James Cagney and Humphrey Bogart, and *The Little Princess* with Shirley Temple. Grand pianos are on hand for ragtime and jazz concerts. What a great this-it-the-way-it-was experience for kids (and adults!).

Hours: Show times are Fri. - Sat., 2:30pm and 8:15pm; Sun., 2:30pm. Call to see what's playing.

Admission: $6 per person for a matinee; $7 for a nighttime show.

Ages: 2 years and up, depending on the show.

PALMDALE PLAYHOUSE
(661) 267 - ARTS (2787) or (661) 267-5685 /
www.cityofpalmdale.org/events/playhouse.html
38334 10th Street E., at the Antelope Valley Community Arts Center,
Palmdale
(Exit the Antelope Valley Fwy [14], E. on Palmdale Blvd., R. on 10th St. E. [TG-4286 B1])

Comedy, drama, music, magic, improv, and more is yours to experience throughout the year at the Playhouse. Past performances have included a smorgasbord of shows from *A Victorian Holiday* to *1776* to *The Lion, the Witch, and the Wardrobe*. Annual festivals include the Shakespeare Festival and the Children's Festival, which is a day of arts, crafts, and storytelling.

Hours: Call for show hours.
Admission: Prices vary according to the show.
Ages: It depends on the show.

PANTAGES THEATER
(323) 468-1770 / www.nederlander.com
6233 Hollywood Boulevard, Hollywood
(Going N. on Hollywood Fwy [101], exit W. on Hollywood Blvd. Going S. on 101, exit S. on Vine St., L. on Hollywood. [TG-593 F4])

Outstanding productions - musical, drama, and comedy - are performed here regularly. Call for a current schedule. A few of our favorite past productions include *Peter Pan*, which starred Cathy Rigby, and *Phantom of the Opera*.

Hours: Call for show dates and times.
Admission: Varies, depending on the show.
Ages: 5 years and up.

PASADENA PLAYHOUSE
(626) 356-7529 / www.pasadenaplayhouse.org
39 S. El Molino Avenue, Pasadena
(Exit Foothill Fwy [210] S. on Lake Ave., R. on Colorado Blvd., L. on El Molino. [TG-566 A5])

The Playhouse has two areas of interest for kids. The first is the plays themselves. The Playhouse does not have a family series, but often the plays are appropriate for middle-school-aged children and older. The best bargain for students are matinees, offered during the week to school groups or other children. After the play, join in a post-play discussion with some of the actors. The second area of interest is a one-hour tour. See the Tours section for details.

Hours: Call for dates and times of shows.
Admission: Matinees are $10 per person (although some scholarships are available). Student rush tickets, available about 20 minutes before curtain time, are also $10 per person. (Must show student ID) For other shows, tickets range from $33 - $42 per person.
Ages: 4th graders and up.

PASADENA SYMPHONY MUSICAL CIRCUS
(626) 793-7172 / www.pasadenasymphony.org
300 E. Green Street, at the Pasadena Civic Auditorium, Pasadena

(Exit Pasadena Fwy[110] N. on Fair Oaks Ave., R. on Green. [TG-565 J5])

Eight, one-and-a-half-hour interactive and educational presentations of the Musical Circus are given throughout the year. The first half hour is spent in the lobby of the auditorium for the "Petting Zoo", where children are invited to try out the various instruments - clarinets, flutes, trumpets, violins, and cellos - and ask questions of the musicians. During the next hour, a soloist or a small group of musicians give a mini concert, and this is followed by a final rehearsal of the Pasadena Symphony. I bet this show will strike a chord with some of your children!

Hours: Presentations are given on selected Sat. starting at 8:30am.
Admission: Free
Ages: 2 - 10 years.

PEPPERDINE CENTER FOR THE ARTS

(310) 456-4522 / www.pepperdine.edu $$$
24255 Pacific Coast Highway, Malibu
(Exit Ventura Fwy [101] S. on Las Virgenes Rd., which turns into Malibu Cyn. Rd. Go to the end, R. on Pacific Coast Hwy. [TG-628 G7])

The Childrens Series consists of five different, one-hour shows performed throughout the season. Past titles include *Jungle Book, Treasure Island,* and *Ugly Duckling.* Pepperdine offers just a few other presentations geared for all ages, including magic shows and concerts.

Hours: The Childrens Series is presented one Sat. a month at 11am and at 1pm, usually in the months of October, January, February, March, and April. Call for other show dates and times.
Admission: $10 per person for the Childrens Series. Inquire about prices for other shows.
Ages: 3 years and up.

PIERCE COLLEGE

(818) 719-6488 / www.lapc.cc.ca.us $$$
6201 Winnetka Avenue, Woodland Hills
(Exit Ventura Fwy [101] N. on Winnetka Ave. It's in the Performing Arts Building. [TG-530 E7])

The college usually performs at least one children's show a year, such as *Willy Wonka and the Chocolate Factory* or *Wind in the Willows.*

Hours: Call for a program schedule.
Admission: Prices vary according to show.
Ages: 6 years and up.

PUPPET AND MAGIC CENTER

(310) 656-0483 / www.puppetmagic.com $$$
1255 2ⁿᵈ Street, Santa Monica
(Exit Santa Monica Fwy [10] N. on Lincoln Blvd., L. on Arizona, R. on 2ⁿᵈ St. Parking is on the R. The center is near the Third Street Promenade. [TG-671 D2])

What do you get when you mix Harry Houdini with Edgar Bergen? Steve Meltzer! Steve puts on forty-five minute, musical, one-man puppet/ventriloquist/magic shows that intrigue youngsters, confound older kids, and entertain everyone. The intimate theater, tastefully decorated with pictures and posters of magic and puppeteer greats, seats up to fifty people in comfortable theater-style chairs. The first half of the show consists of puppets and marionettes that speak, sing, tell jokes, and even dance, with Steve's help, of course. (Remember that only person is doing this show, so it may lag a bit in places.) This former elementary school teacher has a delightful range of voices and "personalities." I was surprised my children didn't clap more during the second part of his performance, the magic show, until I realized that they were amazed at the tricks and kept trying to figure out how he did them, usually to no avail. Audience interaction throughout the show is an added highlight. Tip: It's no illusion - this is a great place for a birthday party!

After the performance, you'll get the opportunity to see (with your eyes, not your hands) Steve's hundreds of puppets. You may also peek into his puppet workshop where you might see one of his creations in process. A small Magic Shop is here, too where puppets and magic tricks are for sale. Anytime you are in the neighborhood, make sure you stop off at the Puppet and Magic Center - no strings attached. Note: The Center is near the THIRD STREET PROMENADE. (Look under the Malls section for details.)

Hours: Shows are usually performed Wed. at 1pm and Sat. - Sun., 1pm and 3pm. Please call first. Call, also, for Magic Shop hours, which are usually Mon. - Fri., noon - 5pm, and call for special performance times.

Admission: $6.50 per person.

Ages: 1½ to 12 years.

SANTA MONICA COLLEGE PLANETARIUM ☀

(310) 434-4223 or (310) 434-3000 / www.smc.edu/planetarium   *$$*

1900 Pico Boulevard, Santa Monica

(Going W. on Santa Monica Fwy [10], exit S. on Cloverfield, R. on Pico. Going E. on 10, exit S. on 20th St., R. on Pico. [TG-671 H2])

Do your kids have stars in their eyes? Bring them to the planetarium, then lean back, look up at the nighttime sky, and watch some of the mysteries of the heavens unfold. The lecture and changing fifty-minute shows, with titles like *Alien Skies*, focus on space exploration, astronomy, and the possibility of extra-terrestrials.

The December show, *Star of Wonder*, resets the nighttime sky to the time of Jesus' birth. Explore the possibilities of the origin of the Star of Bethlehem as the astronomer/lecturer incorporates Bible passages and the research known to astronomers from that time period.

Hours: Shows are most Fri. nights at 7pm and 8pm. (The latter time is the feature presentation.) Note: There are no shows in August.

Admission: $4 for adults for a single show; $7 for both shows; $2 per show for ages 12 and under.

Ages: 6 years and up.

SANTA MONICA PLAYHOUSE

$$$

(310) 394-9779 / www.santamonicaplayhouse.com

1211 4th Street, Santa Monica

(Exit Santa Monica Fwy [10] N. on Lincoln Blvd., L. on Wilshire, L. on 4th St. [TG-671 D2])

This ninety-two seat Playhouse offers original, one-hour, family-style musicals every weekend. Most of the productions are based on well-known characters and have titles like *Alice's Wonderful Teapot* and *Captain Jack and the Beanstalk*. There is a cookies and punch intermission. Young and old will enjoy this theater experience. Ask about their special classes and workshops.

Hours: Every Sat. and Sun. at 12:30pm and 3pm.

Admission: $9 for ages 2 and up.

Ages: 3 years and up.

SHUBERT THEATER

$$$$$

(800) 233-3123

2020 Avenue of the Stars, Los Angeles

(Exit San Diego Fwy [405] E. on Santa Monica Blvd., R. on Avenue of the Stars. [TG-632 E3])

This first-class theater presents the finest in Broadway musicals, hit plays, and hot comedies. Many of the productions are great for the entire family. This is one of our favorite places for "real" theater shows.

Hours: Call for show dates and times.

Admission: Varies, depending on the show.

Ages: 5 years and up.

SILENT MOVIE THEATRE

$$$

(323) 655-2520 / www.silentmovietheatre.com

611 N. Fairfax Avenue, Los Angeles

(Going S. on Ventura Fwy [101], exit S. on Highland Ave., R. on Melrose Ave., L. on Fairfax. Going N. on 101, exit E. on Melrose, L. on Fairfax. From the Santa Monica Fwy [10], exit N. on Fairfax. From the San Diego Fwy [405], exit E. on Santa Monica Blvd., R. on Melrose, R. on Fairfax. [TG-593 B7])

Douglas Fairbanks, Clara Bow, Alfred Hitchcock, Boris Karloff, Lillian Gish, Mary Pickford, Charlie Chaplin, and Fred Astaire - these once-household names are back in vogue again at the Silent Movie Theatre. Come to enjoy two hours of old-time dramas, which are usually shown on Thursday evenings, or for comedies, with the likes of Laurel and Hardy, The Marx Brothers, or Buster Keaton, that play on the weekends. Sunday matinees, in particular, are aimed toward the younger generation. And yes, kids laugh uproariously at clean, classic comedy - even if it's in black and white. The 224-seat theater usually plays live organ music during the feature presentation. Shorts or cartoons precede the feature film classic.

Upstairs is a lounge, a cafe that sells beverages and snacks, and a silent movie stars' photo gallery to use during intermission or for a birthday party. Come here not to just watch a movie, but to experience the Hollywood of old.

Hours: Movies are shown Thurs. - Sun. at 8pm (doors and box office open at 6pm); Sun., 1pm and 4pm.

Admission: $9 for adults; $6 for seniors and children 11 and younger.

Ages: 7 years and up.

SOUTHERN CALIFORNIA CONSERVATORY OF MUSIC
(818) 767-6554 $$
8711 Sunland Boulevard, Sun Valley
(Exit Golden State Fwy [5] N. on Sunland Blvd. [TG-533 A1])

Four operas a year are performed fourteen times each in this small theater. The children's operas (i.e. every word is sung) are performed by children, ages 8 to 14 years. Most of the musicals have been designed and composed for this group. Past show titles include *Snow White and the Seven Dwarfs*, *Robin Hood*, and *Mother Goose*. Come to watch, or sign up your future star to be in the next production!

   Hours: Call for a schedule.
Admission: $5 for adults; $2.50 for ages 4 - 11; children 3 and under are free.
      Ages: 3 - 13 years.

STORYBOOK THEATER AT THEATRE WEST
(818) 761-2203 / www.theatrewest.org $$$
3333 Cahuenga Boulevard West, Los Angeles
(Going S. Hollywood Fwy [101], exit at Lankershim Blvd., S. on Cahuenga. Going N. on 101, exit E. on Lankershim, L. on Cahuenga. [TG-563 C7])

Every Saturday, Storybook Theater presents a fun, musical, audience-participatory play geared for 3 to 9 year olds. Classics are re-done to appeal even more to children (with all the violence eliminated), like *Little Red Riding Hood* and *Jack In The Beanstalk*. There is an apple juice intermission in this hour-long show. Afterward, the cast stays around to talk with the kids. What a wonderful "first theater" experience! Call to find out what's playing.

   Hours: Sat. at 1pm.
Admission: $10 for adults; $8 for ages 12 and under.
      Ages: 3 - 9 years.

SYMPHONY IN THE GLEN
(213) 955-6976 or (800) 440-4536 / www.symphonyintheglen.org   !
Griffith Park, Los Angeles
(Going N. on Golden State Fwy [5] or W. on Ventura Fwy [134], exit at Zoo Dr. Going E. on 134, exit S. on Victory Blvd., L. on Zoo Dr. Going S. on 5 Fwy, exit S. on Western, L. on Victory Blvd. to Zoo Dr. It's at the Old Zoo picnic area, S. of the L.A. Zoo. [TG-564 B5])

Three or four times a year during the warmer months (beginning in May), families can tote a blanket, picnic lunch/dinner, and sunscreen to the park's grassy expanse to listen to an hour-and-a-half of classical music. Past performances have included *Peter and the Wolf*, *Birds and Beasts,* and *Divine Mortals* featuring Beethoven's Fifth. Make sure you come for one of two pre-concert activities, offered on alternating dates. One activity is the Jr. Maestro conducting class where children and parents learn the basics of tempo and how to conduct an orchestra. Six youngsters are chosen to help lead the forty-piece orchestra. The other activity allows audiences to learn and identify how different instruments sound - flutes, violins, French horns, trumpets, etc. - and perhaps play one or two of them. Note: You have to walk the equivalent of two city blocks to reach this site. Remind your children gently that although they're at a park, this is time to sit down and soak in the ambiance of beautiful music played in a natural, outdoor setting, not run around screaming.

Hours: Pre-concert activities usually begin at 1:30pm. Concerts usually start at 3:15pm

Admission: Free. Canned good donations are requested.

Ages: 4 years and up.

U.C.L.A. CENTER FOR PERFORMING ARTS ☼

(310) 825-2101 / www.performingarts.ucla.edu $$$$$

University of California in Los Angeles, Los Angeles

(Exit San Diego Fwy [405] E. on Wilshire Blvd., L. on Westwood Blvd. to the information kiosk. Make sure you ask for a map. [TG-632 B2])

Name it, and it plays at U.C.L.A. There are several different concert and theater venues such as Royce Hall and Freud Playhouse, that feature 200 performances a year including a wide variety of musicals, dance, theater, concerts, and for-the-family shows. One of our favorites was *Stomp,* a high-energy show where performers created rhythm and music using brooms, trash can lids, and other unusual "instruments."

Hours: Call for a schedule of current shows.

Admission: Prices vary depending on the show. Parking is $5.

Ages: It depends on the show.

WILL GEER THEATRICUM BOTANICUM ☼

(310) 455-2322 - more info; (310) 455-3723 - box office / $$$
www.theatricum.com

1419 N. Topanga Canyon Boulevard, Topanga

(From the Ventura Fwy [101], exit S. on Topanga Canyon. Go about 5 1/2 miles and it's on the R. From Pacific Coast Highway, go N. on Topanga Canyon Blvd. about 6 miles. It's on the L. [TG-590 C3])

A professional, resident acting company uses repertory to perform several classics and at least one Shakespeare play during its season at this outdoor amphitheater. Past productions have included *Taming of the Shrew*, *Our Town, A Midsummer Night's Dream,* and *Harold and Maude.* During the summer, a kids' concert series is also presented. Dress warmly for evening shows, bring a blanket, and pack a picnic lunch/dinner, or buy something from the Cafe which offers tuna salad, grilled chicken breast, Greek salad, pastries, cold drinks, and snacks.

Besides ongoing classes for both children and adults and a summer youth drama camp, the Botanicum presents two other theater options for children. One option is the School Days Educational Program offered during the month of May. Prior to the actual field trip to the theater, students receive a Shakespeare resource packet and have an in-class visit by an actor/teacher who explains the language and the story. Participating classroom teachers are also offered an in-service day for further understanding, ideas, and preparation. Once at the theater, students meet costumed actors such as Queen Elizabeth I and William Shakespeare, or President and Mrs. Lincoln, depending on what time period is being studied. Some students rehearse for the play, which is performed later on, while others participate in two, thirty-minute workshops. Some of the workshops offered are Stage Illusion, Mime, Elizabethan Dance, and Singing and Improvisation. After lunch, students watch a Shakespearean or American History play. The second option is the Classroom Enrichment series. In the Acting series, an actor/teacher will visit the classroom seven times to direct students (in song, dance, stage combat, or acting) in a play that will ultimately be performed before the entire school. In Classics-off-the-Page, the actors/teachers perform excerpts from great plays or novels by William Shakespeare, Mark Twain, Victor Hugo, F. Scott Fitzgerald, Nathaniel Hawthorne, and others. Living History programs are assemblies where the actors/teachers portray historical figures and reenact history-making events.

Hours: Call or check the website for a schedule.

Admission: Prices for the plays range from $13 - $20 for adults; $9 - $14 for children, depending on the seats. Ages 6 - 12 are $7, no matter where the seat is located. Children 5 and under are free. The School Days Educational Program is $13 per student for the full day and all the preliminaries; $6 per student for most of the program and the play. Call about other program offerings.

Ages: Plays - 8 years and up. Programs can be adapted for K - 12 graders.

WIZARDZ MAGIC CLUB AND DINNER THEATER   ☼

(800) 882-8729 or (818) 506-0066 / www.wizardzmagic.com   *$$$$$*
Universal CityWalk, Universal City
(Going N.W. on Hollywood Fwy [101], exit N. at Universal Center Dr. Going SE on 101, exit at Lankershim Blvd., L. on Cahuenga, L. on Universal Center Dr. [TG-563 C6])

For an evening, or afternoon, of magical entertainment and good food, visit Wizardz. Hint: Getting here a little early might ensure getting better seats. The first floor features a magic shop, offering tricks that you can do at home to amaze your friends. Take the elevator up to the second level to wait in the lounge area before dinner and the show. A full bar here also serves "mystic" kiddie drinks, which looks like they use dry ice in the concoctions. A strolling magician entertains small groups. People who do psychic readings are in the corner, easy to bypass if you're not into this type of thing.

The tri-level dinner theater seats 300. The star-studded ceiling, velvet drapes, and background music playing songs that have the word magic in them, add to the ambiance. Seating is mostly at long tables, so you might share a bread basket with new friends. The first hour is consumed with eating dinner. Adult entree choices include grilled chicken breast, sirloin steak, or vegetarian lasagna in Alfredo sauce, plus salad, vegetables, bread, and rainbow sherbet. All of the selections are delicious! Children are served chicken strips, french fries, salad, bread, and rainbow sherbet. And yes, guests may keep the plastic, neon-colored beverage cups that are emblazoned with "Wizardz". Note: If you are celebrating a birthday or anniversary, make sure you let the staff know ahead of time so the celebrants can have their names flash across the screen on stage.

A short, but engaging laser light show, accompanied by music, gets everyone prepped for the main event. The second hour is pure magic. Three very different types of professional magic acts, ranging from audience participatory sleight-of-hand; to comedian/magicians or novelty acts, such as combining juggling with magic; to illusionists, take center stage and hold guests spellbound amid murmurs of "How did he do that?" The emcee is also a magician and does a splendid job of entertaining while keeping the show flowing smoothly. After reading this entry, I hope you, too, will be off to see the Wizardz! Note: See UNIVERSAL CITYWALK, under the Potpourri section, for other fun, close by attractions.

Hours: Show times are Mon. - Thurs., 7pm; Fri., 6:30pm and 9pm; Sat., 5:30pm and 8:30pm, Sun., 3pm and 6:30pm.

Admission: For adults: Mon. - Thurs., $38.95; Fri. - Sat., $42.95; Sun. matinee, $33.95. Children 12 and under are $23.95 at any show. Groups of 15 or more receive a discount. Gratuity and tax is not included. Parking is $7.

Ages: 5 years and up.

BALLET PACIFICA

(949) 851-9930 / www.ocartsnet.org/ballet_pacifica *$$$$*

650 Laguna Canyon Road, Festival of Arts Forum Theater, Laguna Beach

(Exit San Diego Fwy [405] or Santa Ana Fwy [5] S. on Laguna Canyon Rd. [Hwy 133]. It's on the R., on the Festival of the Arts grounds. [TG-950 G2])

Ballet Pacifica has a Children's Series, consisting of four productions a year, at the Forum Theater. The ballet productions are held in September or October, February, March, and April. Past performances include *The Emperor's New Clothes, Winnie-the-Pooh,* and *Puss in Boots.* Note: The *Nutcracker* is performed over fifteen times in December. Each show is a winner for the whole family, especially your blossoming ballerina. Check for time and location, as the company also performs at other locations, such as the Irvine Barclay Theater.

Hours: Call for a schedule.

Admission: Tickets for the Children's Series are $12 for adults; $10 for seniors and ages 12 and under. Nutcracker prices are $23 for adults; $21 for seniors; $19 for ages 12 and under.

Ages: 5 years and up.

BROADWAY ON TOUR CHILDREN'S THEATER

(714) 542-6939 / www.broadwayontour.org *$$$*

625 French Street, Santa Ana

(Going N. on the Santa Ana Fwy [5], exit S. on Grand Ave., R. on Santa Ana Blvd., R. on French St., R. on Civic Center Dr., R. into parking lot. Going S. on 5, exit S. on Main St., L. at Civic Center, past French St., R. into the parking lot. [TG-828 F2])

At this 300-seat theater, kids 10 to 18 years old put on presentations for younger children who delight in seeing just slightly older versions of themselves on stage. The one-hour musicals are usually based on classic fairytales, and they run for six weeks. Longer, full-length Broadway musicals, still performed by kids, are offered for the whole family. Broadway on Tour's motto is, "Children bringing theater to children." Call for show information and to find out how your child could become a performer.

Hours:	One-hour shows are usually performed on the weekends. The full-length musicals are usually performed on Fri. evening, and Sat. - Sun. afternoons. Call for hours.
Admission:	$6 per person for the one-hour shows; $9 for adults; $6 for seniors and children on the full-length productions.
Ages:	4 - 12 years.

BROWN BAG PLAYERS

(949) 581-5402 / www.childrenstheatreworkshop.org

21801 Winding Way, Lake Forest

(Exit San Diego Fwy [5] N.E. on Lake Forest Dr., L. on Serrano Rd., L. on Winding Way. It's held across the street from Heritage Park at Rancho Canada School. [TG-891 H2])

The Brown Bag Players are sponsored by the Children's Theater Workshop. The Workshop teaches theater to children ages 7 to 16, who then put on a production. Other Brown Bag Players are seasoned actors whose goal is to make theater accessible to children via interaction. Kids are invited to bring their own brown bag lunch (hence the name of the company) between 11:30am and noon to eat while watching the actors prepare for the performance. As the actors put on their make-up, children are invited to join in by putting on make-up (or face paint). During the show, kids are intermittently invited on stage to help tell the story. Afterward, the actors answer questions about scenes, scenery, costumes, technical equipment, or other things kids wonder about. What a great way to encourage kids to be involved with theater! Past one-hour presentations have included *Tale of the Frog Prince, Jungle Book,* and *Treasure Island.*

Hours:	Each of the 3 yearly productions are put on for 3 consecutive weekends. The doors for lunch are open at 11:30am; the play starts at 12:15pm.
Admission:	$6 per person.
Ages:	2 - 12 years.

CALIFORNIA STATE FULLERTON PERFORMING ARTS

(714) 278-3371 / www.arts.fullerton.edu/events

800 N. State College, Fullerton

(Exit Orange Fwy [57] W. on Nutwood. The college is on the corner of Nutwood and State College. [TG-739 C6])

The Kaleidoscope Players put on special presentations every February, just for kids.

Hours:	Call for show date and time.
Admission:	Call for prices.
Ages:	5 years and up.

CURTIS THEATER / CITY OF BREA GALLERY

(714) 990-7722 - theater; (714) 990-7730 - gallery / www.ci.brea.ca.us
1 Civic Center Circle, Brea
(Exit Orange Fwy [57] W. on Imperial, R. on Randolf, R. on Birch, R. on Civic Center Circle. [TG-709 C7])

Curtis Theater boasts Brea's Youth Theater and Kids Culture Club. The Youth Theater is comprised of a talented cast of young actors and actresses (i.e. kids) who put on two musical extravaganzas a year. Past productions include *Peter Pan* and *Joseph and the Amazing Technicolor Dreamcoat.* Call for information about signing your kids up to be in a future production. The terrific Culture Club is comprised of a wide variety of eight professional productions a year. Previous year's forty-five-minute headliners have included a music and laser show, a magic show, the *Nutcracker Suite*, cowboy trick roper, Highland fling, and Jim Gamble's puppets. Call for a current schedule.

Across from the theater, the Civic Center also has a small gallery called City of Brea Gallery where exhibits change periodically. The gallery also has a Children's Art Space where young visitors may create their own masterpiece that is related to the current exhibit. The Brea Gallery is usually open on performance nights and gives kids something to look at while waiting for the theater doors to open.

Hours: Call for a schedule of shows. The gallery is open Wed. - Sun., noon - 5pm (open Thurs. and Fri. until 8pm). The Children's Art Space is open Wed. - Thurs., 3:30pm - 4:30pm; Sat. - Sun., 2:30pm - 3:30pm.

Admission: Tickets for the Youth Theater usually run $9.50 for adults; $7.50 for children 12 and under. Tickets for the Culture Club and other family shows generally run between $5 - $10 per person. The gallery is $1 for adults; free to youth 17 and under.

Ages: 5 years and up.

EDWARDS IMAX THEATER (Irvine)

(714) 832-IMAX (4629); or (949) 450-4900 /
www.edwardscinemas.com
At the junction of the 405 and 5 Fwy., at the Irvine Spectrum Center, Irvine
(Going S. on Santa Ana Fwy [5], exit at Alton Pkwy. At the end of the off ramp, go straight into the Spectrum. Going N. on 5, exit W. on Alton Pkwy, L. on Gateway Blvd. Going S. on San Diego Fwy [405], exit N. on Irvine Center Dr., R. on Pacifica. [TG-891 B2])

For your viewing pleasure, Edwards Theater has a twenty-one screen theater complex in the heart of the Irvine Spectrum entertainment center. The crown jewel of this Hollywood-looking building is a 3-D IMAX theater. The giant screen is six stories high and ninety-feet wide. The lightweight headsets, which look like heavy duty sunglasses, help create three-dimensional images that look incredibly real. You become part of the forty-five-minute movie as you swim with fish, fly in an airplane, etc. You feel like you're really living the adventure! Watch your kids reach out to try to touch objects that seemingly jump right off the screen. The movies can be a terrific educational tool, too. If you make reservations to come on a class field trip, request a Teacher's Resource Guide for the group. The theater also shows wonderful 2-D movies on the huge screen. See IRVINE SPECTRUM CENTER, under the Malls section, for information on the rest of the mall.

Hours: The first show starts daily at 10am.

Admission: The 3-D IMAX is $9 for adults; $7.50 for seniors and ages 12 and under. 2-D prices are $8 for adults; $6.50 for seniors and ages 12 and under.

Ages: 4 years and up.

ELIZABETH HOWARD'S CURTAIN CALL DINNER THEATER ☼

(714) 838-1540 / www.curtaincalltheater.com $$$$$

690 El Camino Real, Tustin

(Going S.E. on Santa Ana Fwy [5], exit N.E. on Newport Ave., L. on El Camino Real. Going N.W. on 5, exit N.E. on Red Hill Ave., L. on El Camino Real. [TG-830 B4])

Prepare for an evening of fine dining and a terrific Broadway musical when you come to this dinner theater. The restaurant/theater holds up to 300 people, and tiered seating insures that every seat has a good view of the stage. Seating for your three-course meal begins two hours prior to show time, although younger kids will get antsy if you actually arrive this early. The main entree selections include baked chicken with herbs, ham, New York roast, or prime rib. A vegetarian lasagna, may be pre-ordered. Soup, salad, and vegetables come with the meal, while desserts and beverages cost extra. Savor the food and enjoy the service! (It's just like the kind of meals we have at my house. Oh, never mind, that's Martha Stewart's house I'm thinking of.)

The ninety-minute musicals are enthralling, especially for children who appreciate the opportunity of seeing live theater. Most of the shows are suitable for the family, but call first and ask to see what is currently playing. Five different shows are performed each year. Past titles include *Camelot, Sound of Music,* and *The King and I.*

Hours: Meal seating begins Tues. - Sat. at 6:15pm; Sun. at 11:15am and at 5:15pm.

Admission: $28.95 - $38.95 per person, depending on the night you visit. (Tues. is the least expensive.)

Ages: 6 years and up.

IRVINE BARCLAY THEATER ☼

(949) 854-4646 / www.thebarclay.org $$$

4242 Campus Drive, Irvine

(Exit San Diego Fwy [405] S. on Culver Dr., R. on Campus Dr. [TG-889 J2])

This theater offers four to five family-oriented shows a year, plus several touring shows geared for kids. The various types of shows include circus acts, folk singers, Indian dancers, acrobats, and the *Nutcracker Suite.* Applause, applause - not a seat in the house is more than sixty feet away from the stage.

Hours: Call for show dates and times.

Admission: Tickets range from $5 - $50.

Ages: 5 years and up.

THE LAGUNA PLAYHOUSE ☼

(949) 497-9244 / www.lagunaplayhouse.com $$$$

606 Laguna Canyon Road, Laguna Beach

(Exit San Diego Fwy [405] or Santa Ana Fwy [5] S. on Laguna Canyon Rd. [Hwy 133]. It's on the R., in the Laguna Moulton Theater, on the Festival of the Arts grounds. [TG-950 G2])

"Orange County's Award-Winning Theater for Young People and the Young at Heart!" Four, great-for-the-kids plays are presented here each year. Past productions include *Wind in the Willows*, *How to Eat Like a Child*, and *The Best Christmas Pageant Ever*.

Hours: Call for show dates and times.

Admission: Tickets are usually between $14 - $17.

Ages: 5 years and up.

MEDIEVAL TIMES ☼

(714) 521-4740 / www.medievaltimes.com $$$$$

7662 Beach Boulevard, Buena Park

(Exit Artesia Fwy [91] S. on Beach Blvd. [TG-767 H3])

"Joust" the sight of this eleventh-century-style castle sets the mood for a "knight" to remember. Upon entering the castle hall, wear the crowns to given ye, good Lords and Ladies, as the color designates which of the six knights you'll cheer for. The Lord of the Castle has invited you, and hundreds of your closest friends, neighbors, and foes to a two-hour royal tournament. Tiered, spectator seating encircles the arena. First, silky-maned horses prance and high-step, delighting horse fans young and old. These elegant displays of horsemanship are the highlight of the pre-show activities.

Then comes the main event - the tournament, which the castle Lord presides over. Six knights on horseback compete against one another as they perform feats of real skill during several medieval games before a wildly cheering crowd. (It's O.K. if the kids yell here!) After every game, the winning knight throws flowers out to his rooting section. As the show progresses, the knights engage in battle, with their swords actually sparking as they strike each other. The knights fight on horseback, and then on foot, until there is just one knight left "alive" - the victor. (Reassure younger kids that this is just a show.)

Throughout the evening serfs and wenches serve a four-course feast, eaten without utensils, of course. The delicious meal consists of vegetable soup, a whole roasted chicken, spare ribs, potatoes, pastries, and a drink. We enjoyed the food and were riveted by the action. After the show, the gift shop selling medieval memorabilia is open, or dance at the in-house Knight Club. Note: The Museum of Torture is open before the show. This unusual museum displays over thirty reproductions of instruments of torture and ridicule used during the Middle Ages, like the Rack, and the Stock and Pillories. Each instrument is explicitly labeled as to its use. Personally, I wouldn't go through the museum again. Admission is $2 for adults, $1 for kids 12 years and under.

Student Matinees are offered January through August, on certain Tuesdays and Thursdays, 11:30am to 1pm for grades kindergarten through twelfth. A medieval history lesson is given by a Master of Ceremonies on horseback, in place of some of the pageantry of the nighttime show. Kids still see, though, the knights engaging in period games and sword fights. This educational "tour" includes a lunch of chicken, potato, apples, cookies, and drink. The cost is $19.50 per person.

One-hour, educational Castle Tours are offered for a minimum of twenty students. Kids are guided by a costumed Master of Ceremonies through the decorated halls. Life in the Middle Ages is explained as they look at authentic medieval artifacts, and learn about chivalry and knighthood. The highlights are meeting a "real" knight, and seeing demonstrations of horsemanship and actual medieval weapons. Tours are given Monday through Thursday, at 10am and 11:30am. Call to make a reservation. The cost is $5 per person. The castle is also open during the day, except on matinee days, for those who want to simply come in and look at the horses and the arena.

Hours: Call for times for the knightly performances.

Admission: The price, including dinner, show, and tax, is $39.95 for adults; $26.95 for ages 12 and under. Reservations are required. Certain discounts available through AAA, but not on Sat. Note: If three people pay in full, the fourth person, (i.e. the birthday person, who must show proof of his/her birthday) gets in for free during the month of his/her birthday.

Ages: 3 years and up.

ORANGE COUNTY PERFORMING ARTS CENTER / ☼ MERVYN'S MUSICAL MORNINGS

(714) 755-5799 - symphony; (714) 556-2787 - center / www.ocpac.org $$$$
600 Town Center Drive, Costa Mesa
(Exit San Diego Fwy [405] N. on Bristol St, R. on Town Center. [TG-859 D3])

Six Saturdays a year, Pacific Symphony puts on Mervyn's Musical Mornings, which are concerts designed for kids. The performances vary in content, but aim to be pieces that children are familiar with, such as music from *Nutcracker Suite,* or even from cartoons. They are always fun for kids, as well as interactive. Activities can include a musical treasure hunt through the lobby, a "petting zoo" (touch, and perhaps play, a few instruments), a computer center, and participation in a dance or theater number. On other selected Saturdays, the Center hosts family-oriented musical performances. Of course, the Center also offers first-class performances geared for adults, too. Note: One hour prior to each performance in the Dance, Jazz, and Chamber Music Series, a noted expert gives a free informative talk, open to all ticket holders, to share insights about the performance. See the Tours section for information on taking a tour of this center.

Hours: Mervyn's mornings and other family shows are offered on select Sat. at 10am and 11:30am.

Admission: Mervyn's mornings are $12 for adults; $10 for children 12 and under. Family Saturday tickets range from $11 - $16, depending upon the seating.

Ages: 5 years and up.

PLAZA GARIBALDI DINNER THEATER

(714) 758-9014 $$$$

500 N. Brookhurst Street, Anaheim

(Going S.E. on Santa Ana Fwy [5], exit S. on Brookhurst. Going N.W. on 5, exit W. on La Palma, L. on Brookhurst. [TG-799 A1])

Experience the finest Mexican entertainment and cuisine this side of the border. Your almost two-hour dinner/show features a variety of acts such as Mariachis, singers, folkloric dancers, cowboy ropers, tango dancers, and more. The fiesta atmosphere, authentic costumes, and colorful decor enhance your visit here. Adults can choose from numerous entrees, ranging from traditional Mexican fare to seafood. Kids can choose from hamburger with fries, carne asada, or chicken with rice. Beverages are extra. Sunday brunches are all-you-can-eat buffets that come with champagne. Ole!

    Hours: Shows are given Fri. - Sun., at 7:30pm, 9:30pm, and 11:30pm. Sunday brunches are at 12:30pm and 2:30pm.

Admission: $16.95 for adults; $8.95 for children 12 and under. The price includes dinner and the show.

    Ages: 4 years and up.

ROBERT B. MOORE THEATER

(714) 432-5880 / www.occtickets.com $$$

2701 Fairview Road, at Orange Coast College, Costa Mesa

(Exit San Diego Fwy [405] S. on Fairview. [TG-859 A7])

This college puts on <u>fourteen</u> children's productions throughout the year, which is two or three favorites for each person in my family!

    Hours: Call for show dates and times.

Admission: $7 for adults; $5 for ages 12 and under.

    Ages: 5 years and up.

SAM'S SEAFOOD "POLYNESIAN SPECTACULAR"

(562) 592-1321 / www.menusunlimited.com/samsseafood

16278 Pacific Coast Highway, Huntington Beach

See SAM'S SEAFOOD "POLYNESIAN SPECTACULAR", under the Edible Adventures section, for details.

SOUTH COAST REPERTORY

(714) 708-5577 or 5555 / www.scr.org $$$

655 Town Center Drive, Costa Mesa

(Exit San Diego Fwy [405] N. on Bristol, R. on Town Center Dr. [TG-859 D3])

Come to this acclaimed theater for year-round professional productions, or invite the theater to come to your child's school. Musicals and dramatic presentations correlate with school curriculum on a variety of subjects, including multi cultural themes, dealing with relationships, and even Shakespeare. Call for a schedule and pricing information.

    Hours: Call for show dates and times.

Admission: Varies, depending on the show.

Ages: 6 years and up, depending on the show.

TESSMANN PLANETARIUM AT SANTA ANA ☀
COLLEGE
(714) 564-6356 / www.sacollege.org   *$$*
1530 W. 17ʰ Street, Santa Ana
(Exit Santa Ana Fwy [5] W. on 17ᵗʰ St., L. on Bristol and enter at the south side of the campus. Park in lots 7, 8, or 9. Parking is $1. It is a brisk, at least 5-minute walk through campus to the north end to the planetarium. [TG-829 C1])

Twinkle, twinkle little star, how I wonder what you are? Your kids can begin to find the answers to this question, and many more, in the ninety-seat planetarium. Several, hour-long shows, such as *Introduction to the Sky*, are wonderful trips around the galaxy, as you see and learn about planets, constellations, our solar system, comets, and more. All the shows have live narrations given by an astronomer. The various programs appeal to different age groups, from 5 year olds up to 95 year olds. There is time after the presentation for questions and answers. For more information on the wonderful Christmas show, *Star of Bethlehem,* look in the Calendar section under November.

Hours: Shows are presented mid-September through Mid-May, Mon - Fri., at 9:30am. A second show is offered Tues. and Thurs. at 11am. Call for summertime hours. Reservations are needed. School, or other groups, are welcome to make reservations, too, and large groups can book the planetarium at other times.

Admission: $3 per person.

Ages: 5 years and up.

TIBBIE'S MUSIC HALL   ☼
(888) 4TIBBIES (484-2243) / www.tibbiesmusichall.com   *$$$$$*
7530 Orangethorpe Avenue, Buena Park   ♨
(From Riverside Fwy [91], exit N. on Beach Blvd. [39], L. on Orangethorpe. From the Santa Ana Fwy [5], exit S. on Beach Blvd., R. on Orangethorpe. It's at the Sequoia Conference Center. [TG-767 H2])

More than just dinner, and more than just a show - Tibbie's is a wonderful two-hour, dinner, musical song and dance revue. The eight waiters and waitresses are also the entertainers. They start the show by singing as they bring in the salad, and they entertain all the way through dessert. They perform on the stage, as well as all around you. Their high energy, beautiful voices, numerous costumes changes, and well-choreographed dance moves make any show here a delight. Past show titles have included *From Stage to Screen* (favorite Broadway show tunes and movie music), *Solid Gold* (songs from the 70's), and the fantastic, annual Christmas show, *Holiday Follies*. Audience participation and other surprises throughout the evening add to your family's enjoyment.

The delicious dinner selections for adults include prime rib, salmon, a chicken entree, or chef's vegetarian special. Children are offered a hamburger or chicken strips. The topsoil (i.e. chocolate cookie crumbs) and dirt (i.e. vanilla ice cream) served in a pot with a silk flower isn't your garden variety dessert; it's much tastier. If your child or another member of your party is celebrating a birthday, graduation, or other special occasion, be sure you tell Tibbie's beforehand so they will mention it sometime during the show. Enjoy your night out on the town where the food is good and the entertainment is clean and fun. One to two week reservations are suggested. Five or six different shows are presented throughout the year, so call for particular show titles.

Hours: Shows are Fri. at 7:30pm; Sat. at 7pm; and selected Sun. at 3pm.
Admission: The show, dinner, and dessert are $39.95 for adults; $25.95 for children 12 and under.
Ages: 6 years and up.

TRINITY CHRISTIAN CITY INTERNATIONAL ☼
(714) 708-5404 / www.tbn.org !
3150 Bear Street, Costa Mesa
(Exit San Diego Fwy [405] S. on Bristol St., R. on Paularino Ave., R. on Bear St. [TG-859 C4])

A lavish fountain outside, surrounded by beautiful landscaping and white archways, enhances the serene garden setting. The lobby of T.C.C.I.'s international headquarters is opulently decorated in whites and golds, along with beveled mirrors on the walls and around the columns. (I kept wishing for my own bottle of Windex™, so my children's visit here wouldn't be *so* obvious, although they were never looked at disparagingly. I've rarely encountered friendlier staff.) A powerful-looking angel at the top of the ornate central staircase immediately draws your attention. He is made out of white marble, brandishes a real sword, and is stepping upon a representation of Satan. The ceiling of the rotunda, just over his head, depicts heavenly scenes painted in a Victorian style.

Take the stairs, or a glass-enclosed elevator, to the second floor where you'll see a non-traditional church setting and a broadcasting room. Check out all the lighting and camera equipment! You are invited to attend free broadcasts and tapings of the Trinity Broadcast Network programs that air from either room. Call for dates and times.

After my boys and I stopped gaping, we went back downstairs into a small theater room. Tip: Just before you enter, note the "mirror room" where you look through several sets of beveled mirrors, seemingly into infinity. A fifteen-minute preview, hosted by Paul Crouch, president and founder of T.B.N., presents the history and Christian heritage of Orange County and T.B.N. Afterward, as the screen and curtain rise, you are invited to walk along an excellent re-creation of Via Dolorosa, the cobblestone street in the city of old Jerusalem where Jesus carried his cross to Calvary. The street ends at the entrance of another theater.

Four, one-hour-long movies are shown in this forty-nine seat Virtual Reality Theater. (Virtual Reality, or "surround" sound, means that you literally feel the rumblings of earthquakes and thunder, and that the loud noises and music are amplified.) Three of the movies are outstanding reenactments that vividly bring Biblical events to life. Each film, shot on location in Israel, is presented a few times throughout the day. Note that the films powerfully and realistically portray their subject, so certain scenes are necessarily graphic and thereby intense for younger children. *The Revolutionary* shows the life of Christ, from His birth to His resurrection. Graphic scenes include a demon being cast out and Christ being nailed on the cross. *The Revolutionary II* is about the miracles of Jesus' ministry. Graphic scenes include a demon being cast out and Christ being nailed to the cross. (I know that last part sounded familiar.) *The Emissary* depicts the Apostle Paul's life, his conversion, his subsequent new life of faith, and his struggles. Graphic scenes include the stoning of Stephen, beatings, and a shipwreck. The fourth movie, the *Omega Code,* is more modern. It deals with Bible prophecy and end times. It's definitely geared for older kids as the storyline is somewhat complex and there is on-screen violence.

A beautiful, fully-stocked gift shop is also on the premises. See TRINITY BROADCAST NETWORK, under the Tours section, for an associated attraction. Tip: Pack a sack lunch because Shiffer Park is just across the street. The park has a few playgrounds, large grassy areas, shade trees, and picnic tables.

Hours: The building is open Mon. - Thurs., 10am - 6pm; Fri. - Sat., 10am - 7pm; Sun., 1pm - 6pm. Movies, beginning on the half hour, run Mon. - Thurs., 10:30am - 4:30pm; Fri. - Sat., 10:30am - 7:30pm; Sun., 1:30pm - 5:30pm. Call for a program schedule.

Admission: Free

Ages: 6 years and up.

WILD BILL'S WILD WEST DINNER EXTRAVAGANZA ☼

(800) 883-1546 or (714) 522-6414   *$$$$$*

7600 Beach Boulevard, Buena Park

(Exit Artesia Fwy [91] S. on Beach Blvd. [TG-767 H3])

Put on your best cowboy or cowgirl duds and see how the West was fun. Stagecoaches are outside, while posters, a saloon-door entrance (great for picture taking), a few stuffed buffalos, and steer's horns decorate the inside.

The two-hour, non-stop, high-energy show features Wild Bill as the host, who also sings and plays guitar; Miss Annie, Bill's co-host, who also sings and dances; dancing girls; Indian dancers; and specialty acts. The Native American dancers in full regalia, especially the one who usually perform the always-captivating hoop dance, are incredible. Another favorite is Bonnie, a trick rope artist, who twirls ropes, cracks whips, and spins guns like you've never seen - what a show! One of the specialty acts that we saw, and these rotate, was a hilarious and talented comedic magician. The music, dancing, costume changes, and special effects, are wonderful, and the audience participation is a lot of fun. (How often are your kids encouraged to yell at the top of their lungs in public?!) On a personal note, Wild Bill and Miss Annie have a very flirtatious relationship, with numerous nuances. Also, Miss Annie's outfits and the dancing girl's costumes are saloon style, pleasing for cowboys.

A four-course, finger-lickin', all-American meal is served throughout the performance. The food includes delicious chicken, ribs, salad, biscuits, baked potato, corn on the cob, apple pie a la mode, and a beverage.

Terrific, hour-and-a-half-long educational programs, for kindergartners through sixth graders, are offered several times throughout the year, and almost weekly in the summer. Wild Bill welcomes the guests, sings a little, and teaches about the Old West, as well as explains the artifacts in the banquet hall. An

Indian dancer, dressed in full costume, explains his heritage and performs some intricate dances. Bonnie performs her lariat-twirling, whip-cracking (always a hit), and gun-slinging. Again, kids are encourage to hoot and holler. Audience members help put on a Wild Bill Show at the end and it is a highlight. Lunch is fried chicken legs, potato chips, a biscuit, seasonal fruit, ice cream, and soda.

Hours: Shows are performed Sun. - Thurs., 7pm; Fri., 7:30pm; Sat., 5pm and 8pm. School programs are given at 11:30am on selected days.

Admission: $38.95 for adults; $24.95 for ages 3 - 11. School programs are $9.95 per person, which includes tax and gratuity.

Ages: 4 years and up.

RIVERSIDE COMMUNITY COLLEGE PLANETARIUM ☀

(909) 222-8090 / www.opencampus.com $

4800 Magnolia Avenue, Riverside

(Exit Riverside Fwy [91] W. on 14th St., L. on Market St./Magnolia Ave. [TG-685 G5])

Come see a truly star-studded show at the college planetarium! The theater seats sixty people and each presentation has a live narrator. Different shows study various aspects of astronomy such as constellations, revolutions (the earth's, not a country's), galaxies and measuring distances between them, lunar eclipses, and what makes the sun shine.

School groups, or other groups, can schedule a time to see fifty-minute shows such as *Sun's Family*, or *Finding Your Way in the Sky*, or others. These shows are geared specifically for elementary-aged kids. There are several shows and programs geared for secondary grade levels, too. *Christmas Star* is offered only in the month of December. It explores the possible origins of the Star of Bethlehem utilizing Biblical passages and astronomer's technology and understanding of the heavens.

Hours: Public shows are offered year round, usually on Fri. nights at 7pm. Groups can see shows Mon. - Thurs. at noon. Reservations are required.

Admission: Public shows are $3 for adults; $2.50 for students; $1.50 for children 11 and under. Group shows are $75 for up to sixty people.

Ages: 6 years and up.

CHAFFEY COLLEGE PLANETARIUM ☀

(909) 941-2758 / www.chaffey.cc.ca.us $$

5885 Haven Avenue, Rancho Cucamonga

(Exit San Bernardino Fwy [10] N. on Haven, turn into the college at Amber Ln., and park in the lot just after Myrtle Dr. The Planetarium is across the lot from Amber Ln. [TG-573 B3])

A forty-five-minute introduction to celestial bodies is given most Friday nights here at the college. See and learn about our solar system and other galaxies as you gather under the indoor nighttime stars. School tours are given during the week with advanced registration. Some of the show titles to choose from include *Our Solar System*, *Finding Your Way in the Sky*, and *Eclipses*.

Hours: Shows for the general public are given most Fri. nights at 7pm.
Call to book a weekday school tour.

Admission: $4 for adults; $3 for Chaffey students; $2 for ages 6 - 10. Most
shows aren't geared for younger children. School groups are $60
for up to seventy-six people.

Ages: 6 years and up.

EDWARDS IMAX THEATER (Ontario)   ☼

(909) 476-1525 or (909) 941-4487 / www.edwardscinemas.com $$$
4900 E. 4th Street, Ontario

(From Ontario Fwy [15], exit W. on 4th St. From San Bernardino Fwy [10], exit N. on Milliken, R. on 4th St. It is just outside Ontario Mills Mall. [TG-603 E5])

Going to the movies is a lot more fun if you are part of the action, not just watching it happen. Besides the twenty regular movie screens, this Edwards allows you to "experience" a movie on the giant IMAX screen by using lightweight headsets that create three-dimensional images. Objects will jump out at you, float around you, and seemingly become a part of your immediate surroundings. (Watch your kids try to reach out and touch the objects.) Live whatever adventure you see on the screen, whether it's underwater with fish, in the sky with birds, etc. Use your visit as an educational tool if you come with a group of students, and request a Teacher's Resource Guide, which are very well put together. Note that the theater also offers excellent 2-D movies on its huge screen. See ONTARIO MILLS MALL, under the Malls section, for other nearby attractions.

Hours: The first show starts at 10am.

Admission: Prices for 3-D movies are $8 for adults; $6 for seniors and ages
12 and under. 2-D movies are $7 for adults; $5.50 for seniors and
ages 12 and under.

Ages: 4 years and up.

THEATER AT THE GROVE   ☼

(909) 920-4343 $$$$
276 E. 9th Street, Upland   ⛰

(Exit San Bernardino Fwy [10] N. on Euclid, R. on 9th. [TG-602 C3])

Fine, professional, dramatic live theater is performed at the grove, along with comedies, concerts, six musicals per season, and children's workshops. Past shows have included *Jesus Christ Superstar* and *Barnum*.

Hours: Call for show dates and times.

Admission: Varies, depending on the show.

Ages: Varies, depending on the show.

CALIFORNIA BALLET COMPANY   ☼

(858) 560-5676 / www.californiaballet.org $$$$
San Diego

This professional ballet company tours throughout San Diego, including in-school performances, out-reach performances, backstage tours, and Girl Scout Patch programs. They perform three to four, ninety-minute ballets a year. Past family-oriented shows, usually put on in the spring, have included *Alice in Wonderland* and *Snow White*. The associated junior ballet company, with performers between the ages of 12 and 17 years, put on a yearly show, usually in January. The company also offers dance classes of ballet, jazz, and modern dance for children 3 years and up.

    Hours: Call for a schedule.

Admission: Prices depend on the theater venue.

    Ages: 6 years and up.

CALIFORNIA CENTER FOR THE ARTS

(800) 98-TICKETS (988-4253) / www.artcenter.org   *$$$*

340 N. Escondido Boulevard, Escondido

(From the Escondido Fwy [15], exit E. on Valley Pkwy; take the east bound lane which turns into Grand Ave., L. on Escondido. Going E. on the 78 Fwy, exit S. on Centre City Pkwy., L. on Washington Ave., R. on Escondido. [TG-1129 H2])

    All the world's a stage and kids are invited to come watch the world, or at least a production or two. Several of the yearly performances given at the center are perfect for the entire family. Past productions have included *The Sound of Music*, *The Magic Schoolbus*, and *The Hobbit,* which was performed with large puppets.

    Hours: Call for the names and dates of productions.

Admission: Tickets are usually about $10 for children's productions, but prices vary.

    Ages: 5 years and up.

CHILDREN'S CLASSICS

(858) 268-4494 / www.sdactorstheatre.com   *$$*

1540 Camino del Mar at the L'Auberge del Mar Hotel Garden Amphitheater, Del Mar

(Exit San Diego Fwy [5] W. on Del Mar Heights Rd., R. on Camino Del Mar. [TG-1187 F5])

    An entertaining, thirty-five-minute presentation of classic children's literature, such as fairy tales, Shakespeare's works, or modern adaptations of well-known stories, is performed by the San Diego Actors Theater a few times each month. Past productions of the audience participatory shows have included *The Giving Tree*, *Snow White and the Seven Dwarfs* (where kids came up on stage to help be the dwarfs), *Hansel and Gretel*, and *Goldilocks*. These theater presentations are great for the younger (and older) set! Sometimes acting workshops are offered after the shows. Workshops are geared for kids 4 to 9 years old and cost $10 per child.

    Hours: Performances are given the second and fourth Sat. of each month at 11am.

Admission: $4 per person.

    Ages: 3 years and up.

CHRISTIAN YOUTH THEATER

(800) 696-1929 or (619) 588-0206 / www.cctcyt.org/cyt   *$$$*

San Diego

Enjoy live, musical theater, performed by students 8 through 18 years, put on at seven locations throughout San Diego County. Past productions have included *Aladdin, Jungle Book, The Secret Garden, Tom Sawyer, Willy Wonka & the Chocolate Factory,* and *Alice in Wonderland.* The theater presents wholesome entertainment for the whole family!

Hours: Call for show locations, dates, and times.
Admission: Tickets usually cost about $8 for adults; $6 for ages 12 and under. At North County Inland, prices are $9.75 for adults; $9 for ages 12 and under.
Ages: 4 years and up.

IMAX DOME THEATER
(619) 238-1233 / www.rhfleet.org
1875 El Prado, Balboa Park, San Diego

See REUBEN H. FLEET SCIENCE MUSEUM for more details. The museum houses the IMAX Theater.

LAMB'S PLAYERS THEATER
(619) 437-0600 / www.lambsplayers.org   *$$$$*
1142 Orange Avenue, Coronado
(Exit San Diego Fwy [5] on Hwy 75 [the Coronado Bridge], L. on Orange Ave. [TG-1288 H7])

This 350-seat theater offers five great, usually musical, productions a year and most of them are very kid-friendly. Past shows include *Joseph and the Amazing Technicolor Dreamcoat, You're a Good Man, Charlie Brown, Dracula,* and *American Rhythm,* a journey across America through music. On Forum Friday shows, the audience is invited to stay after the performance and participate in an informal discussion with cast members. Lamb's Players also put on productions in National City, Escondido, and Horton Plaza. Inquire about immersion programs the theater offers for school groups and about summer camps for children aspiring to the stage and screen.

Hours: Call for show dates and times.
Admission: Tickets usually range from $16 - $36 for adults, depending on the date and time. Ages 5 - 17 are half price in section A and $4 off in section B on selected shows. Children 4 and under are not admitted. Rush tickets, 10 minutes before curtain time, are $10 in section B.
Ages: 5 years and up.

MARIE HITCHCOCK PUPPET THEATER
(619) 685-5045   *$*
Balboa Park, San Diego
(Going S. on San Diego Fwy [5], exit at Sassafras/Airport, go straight on Kettner Blvd. L. on Laurel St., which turns into El Prado. Going N. on 5, exit N. on Pershing Dr., L. on Florida Dr., L. on Zoo Pl., L. on Park Blvd., R. on Village Pl. Going S. on Cabrillo Fwy [163], exit N. on Park Blvd. (near the end), L. on Presidents Wy. [TG-1289 C1])

This intimate theater, located behind the San Diego Automotive Museum, presents kid-approved, half-hour, puppet shows. The type of puppets vary from show to show, and can include hand puppets, marionettes, dummies (for ventriloquists), and puppets made from anything and everything found around the house. The shows themselves are similar in that they never fail to capture a child's imagination. From *Cinderella* to *The Ugly Duckling* to *The Frog Prince*, stories are told as only puppets can tell them! Shows change weekly so watch out - bringing the kids here can become habit forming. (See BALBOA PARK [San Diego], under the Museums section, for a listing of all the museums and attractions within walking distance.)

Hours: Performances are usually given Wed., Thurs., and Fri. at 10am and 11:30am; Sat. - Sun. at 11am, 1pm, and 2:30pm.

Admission: $3 for adults; $2 for children 2 - 12.

Ages: 1½ - 10 years.

METROPOLITAN EDUCATIONAL THEATRE ☼ NETWORK (San Diego)

(619) 238-8280 $$$$

Performed at Lyceum Theater at Horton Plaza, Broadway Circle & 4ᵗʰ Avenue, San Diego; and the Center for Performing Arts, 15498 Espola Road, Poway

(San Diego: Going S. on San Diego Fwy [5], exit S. on Front St., L. on Broadway. Going N. on the 5, exit S. on 6ᵗʰ Ave. R. on Broadway. Poway: Exit Escondido Fwy [15] E. on Rancho Bernardo Rd., which turns into Espola Rd. [TG-1289 A3 / 1170 G5])

This terrific, everyone-gets-a-role, theater group is comprised of kids 4 years old through college-age, as well as a few adult performers. What a great "first-theater" exposure for kids who are acting, and those in the audience. Past productions have included *Joseph and the Amazing Technicolor Dreamcoat*, *The Wiz*, *Peter Pan*, *Aladdin*, and *Fiddler on the Roof*. If your child is a thespian "wannabe", call about enrolling him/her for the next production. The twelve-week Saturday course costs $160, which includes rehearsal workshops, training, and productions. Participants also have the opportunity to go abroad once a year. There are two other locations of the theater network: Northridge and Torrance.

Hours: Call for show locations, dates, and times.

Admission: Tickets are usually $15 for adults; $12 for children 4 - 12.

Ages: 4 years on up to watch or participate.

POWAY CENTER FOR THE PERFORMING ARTS ☼

(858) 748-0505 / www.powayarts.org $$$

15498 Espola Road, Poway   ⚒

(Exit Escondido Fwy [15] E. on Rancho Bernardo Rd., which turns into Espola Rd. [TG-1170 G5])

This 800-seat capacity theater offers a variety of family entertainment throughout the year, as well as a few outstanding children's programs. Past productions have included Jim Gamble puppets; a troop that performed juggling, acrobatics, and comedy combined with a laser light show; the Boys Choir of Harlem; *The King and I*; *Cinderella;* and a kid-friendly opera, *The Barber of Seville*.

Hours: Call for performance times.

Admission: Tickets usually run between $10 for adults; $5 for ages 17 and under.
Ages: 4 years and up.

SAN DIEGO JUNIOR THEATER   ☼
(619) 239-1311 or (619) 239-8355 / www.juniortheatre.com $$$
Performed in Balboa Park, Casa del Prado Theater, San Diego   ⏛
(Going S. on San Diego Fwy [5], exit at Sassafras/Airport, go straight on Kettner Blvd. L. on Laurel St., which turns into El Prado. Going N. on 5, exit N. on Pershing Dr., L. on Florida Dr., L. on Zoo Pl., L. on Park Blvd., R. on Village Pl. Going S. on Cabrillo Fwy [163], exit N. on Park Blvd. (near the end), L. on Presidents Wy. [TG-1289 C1])

The San Diego Junior Theater is a comprehensive workshop program, for students 4 to 18 years old, that presents six family-oriented shows a year that range from Broadway classics to locally developed pieces. Past performances of the for-kids-by-kids group have included *The Miracle Worker*, *Schoolhouse Rock*, *Master Prince and the Pauper*, and *The Adventures of a Bear Named Paddington*. Ask about special performances that are interpreted for the deaf. Midweek matinees are given for schools and other large groups, and curriculum supplements are provided for classrooms.
Hours: Call for show dates and times.
Admission: Prices range from $7 - $9 for adults, depending on the seat; $5 - $7 for seniors and ages 2 - 14.
Ages: 4 years and up.

SAN DIEGUITO PERFORMING ARTS ASSOCIATION   ☼
(760) 752-5078 / www.sdpaa.com $$$$
El Camino Real and Dove Lane, Carlsbad
(Exit San Diego Fwy [5] E. on La Costa Ave., L. on El Camino Real. In the Ruby G. Schulman Auditorium, at the new Carlsbad City Library. [TG-1127 E6])

Community concerts showcase the talent of local musicians. Many of the concerts are arranged to inspire children to develop a passion for music. Past performances have included a Baroque concert, the Pacific Trio, and an ensemble of traditional Irish singers, dancers, and musicians. The theater seats 200.
Hours: Concerts are given October through May and usually begin at 7pm.
Admission: $15 for adults; $12 for seniors; $8 for ages 12 and under.
Ages: 8 years and up.

VIEJAS OUTLET CENTER
(619) 659-2070 / www.viejas.com
5005 Willows Road, Alpine

See VIEJAS OUTLET CENTER under the Malls section for details.

WELK RESORT THEATER   ☼
(888) 802-7469 / www.welkresort.com $$$$$
8860 Lawrence Welk Drive, Escondido   ⏛

(Going S. on Escondido Fwy [15], exit S. on Gopher Canyon Rd., R. on Champagne. Going N. on 15, exit E. on Mountain Meadow exit, L. on Champagne Blvd. From Champagne, go E. on Lawrence Welk Dr. [TG-1089 B2])

This "wannaful" (i.e. that's the way Lawrence Welk used to say "wonderful") theater offers five different, full production Broadway musicals a year. Audiences in the intimate 330-seat theater have seen the likes of *My Fair Lady, The King and I, Seven Brides for Seven Brothers,* and its annual, *Welk Musical Christmas Show.* As you can tell by the titles, many of the musicals are family-oriented.

Before or during intermission, take a short "tour" around the elegant lobby/museum. It features portions of Welk's life in chronological order via pictures, and actual props, bandstands, and instruments from the Lawrence Welk Show.

Grab a bite to eat at one of the restaurants, like the pizzeria, in the Welk Village shopping area. Personally, I was glad we arrived early enough to also shop in the village. The restaurant up the hill from the theater, Mr. W's, offers a decent buffet lunch and dinner, which is always a good choice for picky eaters. Combined with a theater show, a meal here is only a few dollars more.

Hours: Matinee performances are given Tues. - Thurs., Sat. - Sun. at 1:45pm. Evening performances are given Tues., Thurs., and Sat. at 8pm. No performances are given on Fri. or Mon. The buffet lunch is served 11:15am - 1:15pm; the buffet dinner, 5:30pm - 7:30pm.

Admission: $29 - $36, depending on the time and day, for adults for just the show; $32 - $40 for adults for a buffet meal and show; $15 for ages 3 - 12 for just a show; $21 for children for a buffet meal and show.

Ages: 6 years and up.

PERFORMING ARTS CENTER

$$$

(805) 486-2424 or (805) 385-8147 /
www.west.net/~oxnardcty/performingarts.html
800 Hobson Way, at the Performing Arts Center, Oxnard
(Exit Ventura Fwy [101] S. on Hwy 1 [or Oxnard Blvd.], R. on 9th St., R. on Hobson. [TG-522 F7])

Shows performed here for the general public have included *Sesame Street, Nutcracker,* and *Anne Frank.* School groups often rent the theater for special performances put on by American Theater for Youth, or other touring groups. Call for a schedule.

Hours: Call for show dates and times.
Admission: Varies, depending on the show.
Ages: 3 years and up, depending on the show.

THOUSAND OAKS CIVIC ARTS PLAZA

$$$

(805) 449-ARTS (2787) / www.civicartsplaza.com
2100 E. Thousand Oaks Boulevard, Thousand Oaks
(Going W. on Ventura Fwy [101], exit N. on Hampshire Blvd., L. on Thousand Oaks. Going E. on 101, exit N. on Rancho Rd., R. on Thousand Oaks. [TG-556 J2])

This arts plaza offers two theaters: the Forum, which seats 500 people, and the Kavli, which seats 1,800. Professional local and national touring production groups put on numerous, first-class shows ranging from ballet, to musicals, to dramas. A variety of family and children's concerts are offered, as well as several different children's series. Past programs include Jim Gamble's Marionettes, *Do Jump! Acrobatic Theater*, *Freedom Train*, *The Music Man*, *Oregon Trail*, and *Sesame Street Live*. Call for a complete schedule.

Hours: Call for show dates and times.
Admission: Prices vary, depending on the show.
Ages: Varies, depending on the show.

TOURS

Insight into ordinary and unique places is what this section is all about. Many tours are offered under the Museums, and other sections, too. Tip: See the Ideas / Resources section toward the back of the book for general tour ideas regarding a particular profession or subject.

RESTAURANTS

Many restaurants, especially chain restaurants, offer tours of their facility. The tours usually require a minimum number of participants (usually school-aged children), and include a tour of the kitchen, and a partial or full meal. Tours are usually free. Participating restaurants that I know of (although there are no guarantees) include Bristol Farms (I know it's not really a restaurant, but it does have food), California Pizza Kitchen, Chevy's Restaurant, In and Out Burgers, Krispy Kreme Doughnuts (I know, another not-restaurant, but you get milk and one of their incredible doughnuts), and Outback Steakhouse. My suggestion is that if you see a place you're interested in taking a tour of, call! They might not be set up to do it for the general public, but they might be willing to take your group around.

A.D. EDMONSTON PUMPING PLANT

(661) 858-5509 / www.water.cal.gov
Edmonston Road, Grapevine
(Exit Golden State Fwy [5] E. at the Grape Vine exit, past Denny's and continue on Edmonston Rd. (or The Pump Plant Rd.) for about 6 miles. It's about a half hour S.E. of Bakersfield.)

Edmonston pumping plant is located at the foot of the Tehachapi Mountains and is the largest pumping facility of the State Water Project. A ninety-minute tour, given for a minimum of twelve people and maximum of thirty-five, begins with a twenty-minute video on water safety. Visitors start the walking tour at the top floor, which contains the control room, then go down into the depths of the plant, five stories underground. On the fourth floor, you'll see the top of pump motors, where 80,000 (hp) electric motors turn the pumps. The enormous machinery is impressive, and a bit overwhelming. (Water pipes weigh 220 tons!) The fifth floor is the electrical gallery, where numerous power lines enter the building. On the lowest level, water enters the plant from the bottom of the fore bay. As kids see plant machinery, they learn about water conservation, water safety, and how the pumping plant lifts water over the mountains. It gives them a lot to think about the next time they drink tap water or take a long, hot shower.

Hours: Tours are given by request.
Admission: Free
Ages: 8 years and up.

AIR FORCE FLIGHT TEST CENTER

(661) 277-3510 or (661) 277-3512 / www.edwards.af.mil
Edwards Air Force Base
(Exit the Golden State Fwy [5] N. on the Antelope Valley Fwy [14], E. on Edwards/Rosamond and drive for a few miles. [TG-3835 H4])

Your ninety-minute tour starts off with a half-hour film on the history of flight testing, called *First Flights*. The movie has general public appeal, but it is geared for those who are aeronautically inclined. The hour-long, narrated bus tour takes visitors past the hangers and to the flight line, along the taxiway and to the edge of the dry lake beds that are fondly referred to by everyone on base as "the greatest natural landing fields." Ride the length of the flight line and, weather and operations permitting, get out to take a closer look at the lake beds.

Along the way, you'll see test planes taking off, several unmanned vehicles, and whatever else is on base that particular day. The tour is comprehensive and, when coupled with a visit to the AIR FORCE FLIGHT TEST CENTER MUSEUM (see the Museums section) and/or the NASA DRYDEN FLIGHT RESEARCH CENTER (see this section), you have a thorough overview on aeronautics and flight testing.

Hours: Tours are given on Fri. at 10am. Reservations are required.
Admission: Free
Ages: 8 years and up.

NASA DRYDEN FLIGHT RESEARCH CENTER ☼

(661) 258-3446 / www.dfrc.nasa.gov   !
Lilly Avenue, Edwards Air Force Base
(Exit the Golden State Fwy [5] N. on the Antelope Valley Fwy [14], E. on Edwards/Rosamond., R. on Lilly Ave., almost to Hwy. 58 [TG-3835 H4])

A mural of twenty aircraft that reflects the aeronautical heritage of NASA Dryden is in the lobby of the Visitors' Center. This is the primary research and test center for flight research and the space shuttle program, as well as a backup landing site. The tour begins with a fifteen-minute, somewhat technical film that gives insight to the importance and accomplishments of the space program. During your ninety-minute guided walking tour you'll go into a large hanger to see and learn about past research aircraft, particularly the 'X' series of experimental aircraft; some of the current planes being tested; the massive dry lake bed used for a runway and NASA landing site; and, time permitting, the control tower. Admittedly, my children also liked seeing the doors to the office building because it was a shot frequently used in the TV show, *I Dream of Jeannie*. We saw a lunar aircraft (LLRV), too, that helped train Apollo astronauts how to land on the moon. Note: Neil Armstrong was a research pilot here before joining the space program. Much of the information on the tour is technical, so I was a little surprised how much my boys (as they range in ages) enjoyed it. Any and all questions (and my kids had a lot) are fully answered, and the knowledge that does sink in make this a memorable tour. Outside, next to the parking lot, are several more test planes to look at.

The large gift shop is also part mini-museum. An aircraft display features phones in front of model planes so visitors can hear explanations on the history and achievements of particular planes and pilots. In another section, panels light up according to the planes being discussed by a recording. The last display has mannequins modeling pressure suits used by test pilots, including one worn by Neil Armstrong, and an Apollo suite worn on the moon.

Combine your visit here with a trip down the street to the AIR FORCE FLIGHT TEST CENTER MUSEUM (under the Museums section) and the AIR FORCE FLIGHT TEST CENTER tour (under this section).

Hours: Tours are given Mon. - Fri. at 10:15am and 1:15pm.
Reservations are required.
Admission: Free
Ages: 8 years and up.

CALIFORNIA INSTITUTE OF TECHNOLOGY - ☼
SEISMOLOGY TOUR

(626) 395-6327 or (626) 395-6811 /   !
www.gps.caltech.edu/seismo/seismo.page.html
1200 E. California Boulevard, Pasadena
(Exit Foothill Fwy [210] S. on S. Lake Ave., L. on California Blvd. It is on the Caltech campus in the Mudd Building, on the N.E. corner of Wilson Ave. and California Blvd. [TG-566 B6])

Too often in Southern California there is a whole lot of shakin' going on. What causes this? Find out by taking a seismology tour. Much of the information is technical, but older children can appreciate it. The one-hour tour starts in the lobby, which has a time line that shows how information comes into the lab. The lobby also has a computer that shows recent earthquake activity around the world and a computer with a touch screen that shows (with sound and animation) information on the Northridge quake and others. From here you go through the seismology lab to see giant drums where seismic data are recorded, and learn how to read the seismographs. You also go through the media center, where press conferences are held after a quake. Note: This is not a hands-on tour.

Tours are given for groups of at least ten people, maximum twenty-five. If your group has less than ten, you will be assimilated in with another group, if possible. Students must be at least 12 years old or in the sixth grade. All tours must book the date at least one month in advance so participants have time to receive and read the provided educational materials before coming. Note: It is a requirement that all tour participants be familiar with the materials prior to taking a tour as this outing is meant to supplement, not introduce, knowledge of seismology.

    Hours: Tour are offered on the first Tues. and first Thurs. of the month at 10am, 11am, 1:30pm, 2:30pm, and 3:30pm. They are not offered during the months of January, July, August, or September.

  Admission: Free

    Ages: At least 12 years old or 6th grade and up.

FEDERAL RESERVE BANK OF SAN FRANCISCO ☼

(213) 683-2900 / www.frbsf.org $
950 S. Grand Avenue, Los Angeles
(Exit Harbor Fwy [110] on 9th St., R. on Grand. Look for public parking close by or park at a lot at the corner of Olympic Blvd. and Olive St. [TG-634 E5])

What actually happens to our money once it's deposited in a bank? Find out by taking a tour of the Los Angeles branch of the Federal Reserve Bank. The ninety-minute tour starts with a fifteen-minute video that describes the bank and the role of the Federal Reserve System in the U.S. economy. The rest of the tour focuses on the cash and check processing operations. You'll see how coin, currency, and checks are processed by high speed machines and robots. You may also peruse the World of Economics exhibit in the lobby of the bank. The exhibit attempts to simplify the complex ideas of American economics by using a time line, computer games, videotapes, and colorful murals. Over 100 free publications are available to render further aid.

Rules are enforced at the bank as a matter of security. Visitors must wear badges at all times, pass through a metal detector, and stay with the tour. No cameras are allowed. Tours need a minimum of eight participants, a maximum of thirty, and must be arranged in advance.

Hours: Tours are given Tues., Wed., and Thurs. at 10am and 1pm. The lobby is open to the public Mon. - Fri., 8am - 5pm.
Admission: Free. Parking costs about $3.
Ages: 9th graders and up.

GOODWILL INDUSTRIES (Long Beach)   ☼

(562) 435-3411 / www.goodwill.org   !
800 W. Pacific Coast Highway, Long Beach
(Exit Long Beach Fwy [710] E. on Pacific Coast Hwy. [TG-795 C5])

See GOODWILL INDUSTRIES (Santa Ana) in this section for details. This facility also has a cafeteria that visitors may use. The minimum number for the tour is ten people.

Hours: Tours are offered Mon. - Fri., 9am - 2pm.
Admission: Free
Ages: At least 8 years old.

GOODWILL INDUSTRIES (Los Angeles)   ☼

(323) 223-1211 / www.lagoodwill.org   !
342 San Fernando Road, Los Angeles
(From the Golden State Fwy [5], exit E. on Broadway/Spring, R. on Ave 20, which turns into San Fernando. Going N. on Pasadena Fwy [110], exit W. on Figueroa, L. on San Fernando. Going S. on 110, exit N. on Ave 26, L. on Figueroa, L. on San Fernando. [TG-594 J7])

See GOODWILL INDUSTRIES (Santa Ana) in this section for details. This facility doesn't have a shrink wrap machine on the premises, but it does have a computer recycling center, which techno kids love. Note that a cafeteria, open to the public, is here also. The minimum number for this tour is five.

Hours: Tours are offered Mon. - Fri., 9am - 3pm.
Admission: Free
Ages: Preferably 5th graders and up.

GUIDE DOGS OF AMERICA   ☼

(818) 362-5834 / www.guidedogsofamerica.org   !
13445 Glenoaks Boulevard, Sylmar
(From Golden State Fwy [5], exit N. on Roxford St, R. on Glenoaks Blvd. From Foothill Fwy [210], exit S. on Roxford St, L. on Glenoaks Blvd. [TG-481 H3])

Guide Dogs of America is a center that breeds, raises, and trains Labrador Retrievers, Golden Retrievers, and German Shepherds for the blind. It is also a school that teaches blind men and women how to use guide dogs. These services are offered free of charge. Free tours, which last about an hour and a half, are given of the facility.

First you'll watch a twenty-minute video that shows puppies frolicking, plus students getting to know their dogs and testimonies on their lives being changed by being mobile. The film tugs at your heart. You'll walk past the administrative offices and hallways lined with photos of graduates and tour the dormitories where students stay for a month while receiving training. Note: If students are in residence, this part of the tour is bypassed. The best part, according to kids, is seeing the kennels and whelping bays of future guide dogs. Tip: Call first to see if there is a puppy litter because seeing them makes the field trips extra special. Tours are offered for groups of ten or more people with an advance registration of thirty days. Walk-in tours, for individuals, are also available.

Have you ever thought about being a foster parent - for a dog? Guide puppies, or future guide dogs, need temporary homes for the first eighteen months of their life. If you are willing to teach them basic obedience, love them, and encourage them to be well socialized (sort of like raising children), call for more information. The heartbreak of separation from your pup comes in the knowledge that your family enabled a blind person to be mobile and independent. You're invited to attend the graduation ceremony of your dog and the student you've helped.

Hours:	Group tours are given Tues. and Wed. at 10am and 2pm, by reservation only.
Admission:	Free
Ages:	Geared for fourth graders and up, but younger children may come, also.

JET PROPULSION LABORATORIES   ☼
(818) 354-9314 / www.jpl.nasa.gov/faq/tours   !
4800 Oak Grove Drive, Pasadena
(Going N.W. on Foothill Fwy [210], exit S.E. on Foothill Blvd., go to end and turn L. on Oak Grove Dr. Going S.E. on 210, exit S. on Gould Ave., L. on Foothill Blvd., go to end and turn L. on Oak Grove Dr. [TG-435 E5])

"Space, the final frontier." JPL is a leading research and development center for NASA, with 160 buildings on 177 acres of land. Its mission is to observe earth, explore new worlds (via unmanned spacecraft), send back pictures, and ultimately, find the answer to the question, "Are we alone?" A twenty-minute film, *Welcome to Outer Space,* shows spectacular pictures of stars, moons, and various planet surfaces. It made my family aware of the incomprehensible vastness of our universe. My boys were awed by this realization - I just felt very small and insignificant. (Did you know that one light year translates as six trillion miles?) The theater room/auditorium contains vivid photographs of star fields and pillars of gas; replica models of the Voyagers; and a Voyager gold record made for other intelligent life forms to listen to and learn about planet earth. Press the display button and listen to a sampling of the recording. The actual recording contains greetings in fifty-nine languages as well as photographs of our culture, and sounds of music, the rain forest, a heartbeat, and much more.

The adjacent museum has replicas of early and modern space craft including the 1958 Explorer, the Mars Pathfinder, the 1989 Galileo, and the Cassini. Our tour guide talked extensively about the models and their actual missions. Although some of it was a bit too technical for my kids (and me - I guess I'm no rocket scientist), we learned a lot.

Trekking over to another building, we watched Mission Control in action. The viewing room allows visitors to see the Operations Chief tracking and (maybe) listen to him communicate with spacecraft - it depends on what's going on. The last stop is the assembly area where, again, depending on what is in process, you might see actual spacecraft being assembled. Maybe you'll see a piece of history in the making!

JPL facilities can only be seen on a two-hour walking tour, although the center is also wheelchair accessible. You are welcome to take pictures. Reservations are required. Individuals should make reservations at least five weeks in advance. Groups need to make reservations about five months in advance. Bring your space cadets here and have a blast! Note: See the May Calendar section for details about JPL's annual Open House.

Hours: Tours are offered for individual or family members comprising less than 9 people, on alternating Mon., Wed., and Fri., usually at 1pm. Tours are offered to groups comprising 10 to 40 people Mon. - Fri., 10am -noon and 1pm - 3pm. Reservations are required for all tours.

Admission: Free

Ages: 7 years and up.

LONG BEACH AIRPORT TOUR

(562) 570-2611

4100 Donald Douglas Drive, Long Beach

(Exit San Diego Fwy [405] N. on Lakewood Blvd., L. on Donald Douglas Dr. [TG-796 A1])

Invite your preschool-aged kids (and older) to come to the airport and take a pretend trip. (No minimum group number is required.) A customized, forty-five to seventy-five-minute tour answers all their questions about what goes on here. They'll see lots of different things, depending on the busyness of the airport. Kids can talk to skycaps, go to the boarding lounges, and walk through the screening area where monitors show items going through the conveyor. Be prepared to answer questions like, "How does it take pictures of the insides of things?" and "Why?"

The Observation Deck is great for, well, observing planes landing and taking off. Your trip might include a visit to the baggage area (you just never know what your child might find interesting), and for smaller groups of older kids, the Control Tower, where air-traffic controllers are at work. Kids might even get to see an Airport Fire and Rescue truck with all of its heavy-duty equipment. Lastly, they'll board a mock wooden aircraft and watch a video that simulates a flight. Afterwards, the kids are given little souvenirs of their "trip." Flexibility is a key for this high-flying tour.

Hours: Tours are available at your convenience, but preferably given Mon. - Fri. Two week reservations are needed.

Admission: Free

Ages: 4 years old and up.

LOS ANGELES TIMES

(213) 237-5757 or (213) 237-3178   !
202 W. 1ˢᵗ Street, Los Angeles
(Exit Harbor Fwy [110] E. on 4ᵗʰ St, L. on Main St, L. on 1ˢᵗ St. Or, exit Hollywood Fwy [101] S. on
Alameda, R. on 1ˢᵗ St, L. on Spring to park at 213 S. Spring, the "employee" parking garage. To
reach the Olympic plant from the 101, continue S. on Alameda St. and turn L. on 8ᵗʰ St. [TG-674
B2])

Children, who are at least 10 years old or in the fifth grade, with journalistic tendencies will enjoy seeing how a newspaper is put together. The beautiful, historic building with marble flooring has a lobby that contains old printing artifacts, as well as an informational and visual time line which chronicles the inception of the Times through present day. The forty-five-minute tour goes through the editorial offices, where news from all over the world is gathered, written, and edited; the composing room, where news stories and advertisements are put together in page format and computer-generated graphics are used; and the Sports area. Visitors can look into the library, the photography department, and the test kitchen, where recipes are tested and photographed for the Food Section.

Groups may also go down the street to 2000 E. 8ᵗʰ Street and take a one-hour tour through the aptly-named Olympic plant, the enormous warehouse facility where over half a million copies of the newspaper are made each evening and temporarily stored. Pass through a pressroom, which is twice the size of a football field; the newsprint storage area, where robot-like automated vehicles carry rolls of newsprint weighing 2,500 pounds; the plate-making area, where newspaper pages go from photographic negatives to aluminum printing plates; and the mail room, where an automated distribution system takes newspapers from presses to the delivery trucks. Depending on the day of your visit, you might view the presses actually running, from the lobby.

Tip: Our group took both tours and found plenty to see and do in between tour times. From the Times, walk through the GRAND CENTRAL MARKET (look under the Edible Adventures section), take a ride up ANGEL'S FLIGHT (look under the Transportation section), walk to the LOS ANGELES CENTRAL LIBRARY (look under the Potpourri section), and/or shop downtown L.A.!

Kids (and adults) rarely realize what it takes, on a daily basis, to put together the internationally acclaimed newspaper that gets read with a cup of coffee every morning. Individuals and groups, which must consist of ten to twenty people, need to make reservations at least a week in advance. Also see LOS ANGELES TIMES, ORANGE COUNTY, for a tour of the Orange County edition.

Hours: Tours of the Times building are offered to individuals Tues. and Thurs. at 1:30pm. Individuals may tour the Olympic plant Mon. - Fri., 11am, and on selected days at 9:30am and 1:30pm. Tours for groups are offered at both facilities Mon., Wed., and Fri. at 9:30am and 1:30pm; Tues. and Thurs., 9:30am. No tours are given on major holidays. Reservations are required for all tours!

Admission: Free. Parking is free at the Times garage.

Ages: Children must be at least 10 years or older.

MUSIC CENTER (tour)

(213) 972-7483 - tours / www.musiccenter.org *$$*

135 N. Grand Avenue, Los Angeles

(From Harbor Fwy [110], exit E. on 4ᵗʰ St., L. on Olive St., go to end, L. on 1ˢᵗ St., R. on Grand. Going N. on Hollywood Fwy [101], exit S. on Grand. Going S. on 101, exit E. on Temple, R. on Grand. Parking is available on Grand Ave. and, on the evening and weekends only, at the Dept. of Water and Power on Hope St. [TG-634 F3])

This two-city block Los Angeles complex features powerhouse entertainment venues - the Ahmanson Theater, Dorothy Chandler Pavilion, Walt Disney Concert Hall (opening soon), and Mark Taper Forum. Free guided tours of all the buildings, for third graders and up, are offered during the week. Call for tour dates and times. See MUSIC CENTER in the Shows and Theaters section for details about the buildings.

Hours: Call for tour dates and times.

Admission: Free. Parking can cost up to $7.

Ages: 8 years and up.

NBC STUDIO TOURS ☼

(818) 840-4444 / www.nbc4.tv *$$$*

3000 W. Alameda Avenue, Burbank

(Going E. on Ventura Fwy [134], exit S. on Pass Ave., L. on Alameda. Going W. on 134, exit at Hollywood Way, R. on Alameda. [TG-563 E3])

Start your seventy-minute walking tour of the NBC Studios by, fittingly enough, watching TV. A six-minute film depicts the history of NBC, including clips of classic shows. Then, walk through huge warehouses filled with props from past and present shows. It helps to be a fan of either *Days of Our Lives* or *The Tonight Show* since the tour emphasizes these particular shows. You might see, depending on availability, *The Tonight Show* set, the wardrobe department, a video demonstration of make-up, an NBC Sports Presentation, set construction, production studios, and maybe even a star or two. It's all contingent on what is going on at the studio that day, but it's usually a wonderful opportunity to see behind the scenes of a working studio. In the last room, a few visitors are asked to stand against a blue background. Via screen magic, on the video monitor they look like they are flying. Note: Free tickets for *The Tonight Show,* for ages 18 years and older, are available at the studio, so you can combine a behind-the-scenes tour with watching a live show all in the same day. Be forewarned that the tickets go fast.

Bring a sack lunch and go to the JOHNNY CARSON PARK (look under the Great Outdoors section), right across the street from the studio.

Hours: Tours are given Mon. - Fri., 9am - 3pm, every hour on the hour. Tours are also given Sat., 10am - 2pm during the summer.

Admission: $7 for adults; $3.75 for ages 5 - 12; children 4 and under are free.

Ages: 6 years and up.

NORWALK DAIRY

(562) 921-5712
13101 E. Rosecrans, Santa Fe Springs
(Going N.W. on Santa Ana Fwy [5], exit N. on Carmenita Rd., L. on Rosecrans Ave. Going S.E. on 5, exit E. on Rosecrans. [TG-737 B3])

California once boasted of numerous dairies, but they've become more rare with urbanization. This family-owned and operated working dairy shows city slickers how their over 200 cows are cared for, fed, and milked. Visitors also see the processing room for the milk, the homogenizer, and how milk is bottled and cartoned. Norwalk Dairy produces and bottles their own brand of milk - homogenized, whole, low-fat, and most important, chocolate. The forty-five minute tour needs a minimum group of fifteen.

      Hours: Call to schedule a tour.
Admission: Free
       Ages: 4 years and up.

PARAMOUNT PICTURES

(323) 956-4848 / www.paramount.com   *$$$$*
5555 Melrose Place, Hollywood
(Exit Hollywood Fwy [101] W. on Santa Monica Blvd., L. on Gower. [TG-593 G6])

Paramount Pictures offers a two-hour, guided walking tour of its studio for ages 10 and up. This tour includes a historical and informative behind-the-scenes look of a major motion picture and television facility during its day-to-day operations. This is great insight for actor/director/producer "wannabes"!

      Hours: Tours leave every half hour Mon. - Fri., 9am - 2pm.
Admission: $15 per person.
       Ages: 10 years and up.

PASADENA PLAYHOUSE (tour)
(626) 356-7529 / www.pasadenaplayhouse.org
39 S. El Molino Avenue, Pasadena
(Exit Foothill Fwy [210] S. on Lake Ave., R. on Colorado Blvd., L. on El Molino. [TG-566 A5])

The renowned Playhouse offers one-hour tours. Visitors see first hand what the audience normally doesn't see - behind-the-scenes. The tour may include seeing the green room, dressing rooms, and other rooms of interest, while hearing the history of the theater as well as this particular area. See PASADENA PLAYHOUSE under the Shows and Theaters section for details about the shows presented here.

      Hours: Call to book a tour; a minimum of 5 people is necessary.
Admission: Free
       Ages: 4th graders and up.

RIO VISTA WATER TREATMENT PLANT

(661) 297-1600 / www.clwa.org
27234 Bouquet Canyon Road, Santa Clarita
(Exit Golden State Fwy [5] E. on Valencia Blvd., L. on Bouquet Canyon Rd. [TG-4461 A7])

Aaah - nothing like a drink of cold water to refresh your body. But how does the water magically appear in our tap? Take a one-hour tour of this plant to learn about the need for water, Santa Clarita Valley water sources, and water conservation. Climb up stairs and walk around to see filters, huge generators, and containers of liquid oxygen and the chemical ozone. At the small conservation garden outside, see and learn about water-conserving plants and drip irrigation. The tour is bested suited for older children, but the docents, who are educators, will tailor the talk for whatever age and interest group is represented, including youth service organizations trying to meet merit badge requirements. Between ten to thirty participants comprise a group. Note: School buses to and from the plant will be provided for students within the Santa Clarita Valley school district.

Hours: Public tours are conducted Thurs. at 1pm and the third Sat. at 1pm. Groups may take tours Mon. - Fri. Call to make a reservation.

Admission: Free

Ages: 3rd graders and up.

SEBASTIAN INTERNATIONAL RAIN FOREST

(800) 829-7322 / www.sebastian-intl.com
6109 DeSoto Avenue, Woodland Hills
(Exit Ventura Fwy [101] N. on DeSoto Ave., L. on Erwin. It's on the corner. [TG-530 C7])

    Sebastian International is a beauty care company that really cares about the environment and in particular, stopping the depletion of the rain forest. The corporate headquarters is in an angular, artsy building and has a room with displays pertaining to the rain forest. The Wall of Life has holes with objects in it, such as fake plants or animals, to pull out, look at, and read their descriptions. Its purpose is to demonstrate how species depend upon each other. Other exhibits include a big globe that shows how much of the earth used to be covered by rain forests compared to now-a-days, and a wall-size aquatic terrarium containing live fish and plants. Walk through the exhibits on your own, or take a guided, forty-minute tour for groups between ten to twenty-five people, that includes some hands-on reinforcements. Use Sebastian as a supplemental aid in teaching your kids about the rain forest.

Hours: Open to the public daily 9am - 3:30pm. Open for group tours Mon. and Fri., 9am - noon; Wed., 9am - 3pm. Call for an appointment.

Admission: Free

Ages: 7 years and up.

SONY PICTURE STUDIOS TOUR

(323) 520-TOUR (8687)
10202 W. Washington Boulevard, Culver City
(Exit Santa Monica Fwy [10] S. on Overland Ave., L. on Washington Blvd., R. on Madison Ave. Park under the Sony Plaza on the L. [TG-672 G1])

    Catch a glimpse of great moments in movie and television history that have been made on this forty-four-acre lot. The two-hour walking tour begins in the lobby of the architecturally gorgeous Sony Plaza building. Some of the costumes we saw on display behind glass here included Captain Hook's pirate outfit, Tinkerbell's dress, and dresses (and furniture and a stagecoach) from the 1994 version of *Little Women.*

First watch a twenty-minute movie on the history of Columbia/Tristar/Sony, including some classic film footage. Then, walk across the street to the main cluster of buildings. In a park-like setting, visit the Thalberg building which houses two original Oscars, as well as several others made for the studios, for "Best Picture" awards. The tour continues past numerous buildings that were once dressing rooms to stars and are now less-glamorous editing or business offices. You'll hear a little bit about Louis B. Mayer, Judy Garland, Joan Crawford, and other famous alumni.

Because this is a real working studio, what you see next differs from tour to tour, depending on the day, the time of day, and what shows are being filmed. We saw the scoring stage, with chairs and microphones ready for musicians to record; the wardrobe department, where seamstresses were busy at work and where the clothes "closet" was almost as big as my house; and we walked through many of the sound stages, including the one housing the Jeopardy set. The huge sound stages, which have padded walls that block out 98% of sound, are in a constant state of flux - either under construction, being torn down, or containing sets of shows currently on the air. Not to take away from the magic of Hollywood, but we saw a lot of equipment, free-standing doorways, stairs that led nowhere, props of all kinds, and lots of stuff (i.e. nails, trash, and boards) just left around. Watch your step! Our tour guide pointed out the sound stage where the yellow brick road once wound through Munchkinland, the one where agents from *Men in Black* battled outlaw aliens from outer space, and another one that holds a pool (i.e. tank) where Ethel Merman swam. Tip: Call ahead to get a schedule of shows being filmed to combine a tour with the possibility of being part of a studio audience. Finish your time here by shopping on Main Street, which is the only place picture-taking is allowed. The "street" is comprised of a row of stores, including an emporium stocked with Sony products, and a few places to grab a bite to eat.

    Hours: Tours depart Mon. - Fri., at 9:30am, 11am, noon, and 3pm.
Admission: $20 per person.
      Ages: 12 years and up only.

VAN NUYS AIRPORT TOUR

(818) 785-8838 / www.lawa.org
Roscoe Boulevard, Van Nuys
(Exit the San Diego Fwy [405] W. on Roscoe Blvd. The actual address is on Sherman Way, but this is where visitors meet for a tour. [TG-531 D2])

Here's a way to stay grounded while touring an airport - take the ninety-minute bus tour of the Van Nuys airport. Groups must provide their own bus, or ask if the airport has one available. There are several stops along the way, depending on what's available on the day of your visit. You will cruise along the service road and runway, and look inside hangers. Stops could include seeing the fire station and the radar facilities, and boarding a Highway Patrol helicopter, a commercial plane, and/or smaller aircraft. Visit "Vinny", the airport's kid-friendly educational airplane. As the children watch planes land and take off, they'll learn the history of the airport and gain some high-flying knowledge. Bring a sack lunch and eat at the observation site while watching the planes in flight.

Hours: Tours are offered for groups of fifteen or more people, Mon. - Fri., 9:30am and 11am. Reservations are required.

Admission: Free

Ages: Must be at least in the 1st grade, and up.

WARNER BROS. STUDIOS VIP TOUR

(818) 972-TOUR (8687) / www.studio-tour.com $$$$$

4000 W. Warner Boulevard, Burbank

(Going E. on Ventura Fwy [134], exit S. on Pass Ave., L. on Olive/Warner. Going W. on 134, exit at Hollywood Way, L. on Alameda., L. on Hollywood Way to Warner. [TG-563 D4])

Kids must be at least 8 years old to participate in this two-hour, part walking, part cart tour that gives an intimate and educational look at how a studio works. Start off your tour in the waiting room which has props from *Casablanca* and *Batman*. What you see, exactly, depends on what is happening that day at the studio. You'll see numerous exterior sets from classic to current movies and television shows; interior sets from *Friends* and *Norm* (the sets rotate, depending on what is currently being filmed here); and the wardrobe department, with its miles of costume racks. You also might see a set being constructed, or even filming in a sound studio. No matter what, this tour affords visitors a great opportunity to see what actually goes go on behind the scenes. It will also either take some of the romance out of picture-making, or make your child want to be involved in the process! Reservations are required.

Hours: Tours, for no more than 12 people at a time, leave every hour Mon. - Fri., 9am - 4pm., October through May, and every half hour Mon. - Fri., 9am - 4pm, June through September.

Admission: $32 per person.

Ages: 8 years and up.

WILDLIFE SANCTUARY TOUR

(909) 594-5611 / www.mtsac.edu !

100 N. Grand Avenue, Mount San Antonio College, Walnut

(Exit Pomona Fwy [60] N. on Grand Ave., R. on Temple Ave., L. on Bonita Dr. The entrance is on Bonita. [TG-639 H3])

A forty-five-minute guided tour of this fairly small gated wildlife environment includes walking the dirt footpath, which is not stroller-friendly, to see and learn about the plants and animals. Look for the turtles in the pond and the variety of birds that visit. A guide from the college explains why the plants and animals need protection and what visitors can do to help. Also see FARM TOUR (under the Zoos and Animals section) for another tour given by Mount San Antonio College.

Hours: Tours are offered Tues. and Thurs. at 9am, 10am, 11am, 2pm, 3pm, and 4pm. Reservations are required.

Admission: Free, but donations are appreciated.

Ages: Elementary-school age kids.

BODEGA FUDGE AND CHOCOLATES   ☀

(714) 429-1057 - tour; (714) 432-0708 - store /   !
www.bodegachocolates.com

3198-A Airport Loop Drive, Costa Mesa

(Exit San Diego Fwy [405] S. on Bristol St., L. on Paularino Ave., L. on Red Hill Ave., R. on Airport Loop. [TG-859 F4])

My middle son has never met a chocolate he didn't like, so he *really* loved Bodega. This family-owned and operated retail store has received numerous awards for their fudge truffle confectionary concoctions. Groups of ten or more preschoolers through elementary-school-aged children are invited, along with their parents, to take a half-hour tour of the Bodega "factory", which is really like a large kitchen. (Tours are also offered for senior citizens.) Visitors will learn how the chocolates are made, what makes the products kosher, how the machines run, and how quality control is maintained by making small batches at a time. Best of all, samples are given out. (You know how vital it is to taste test.) Children may also draw their initials, with chocolate, in a candy bar that they can take home to eat. The store sells several different flavors of truffle bars, including rocky road and butter vanilla, plus chocolate truffle sauce and traditional English toffee. How sweet it is!

Hours: The store is open Mon. - Sat., 9am - 5pm. Tours are given by
appointment February through June.

Admission: Free

Ages: 4 years old to 6th graders, and senior citizens.

CRYSTAL CATHEDRAL OF THE REFORMED   ☀
CHURCH IN AMERICA

(714) 971-4013 / www.crystalcathedral.org   !

4201 Chapman Avenue, Garden Grove

(Exit Santa Ana Fwy [5] E. on Chapman Ave. [TG-799 B4])

This spectacular sanctuary, enclosed by 10,000 mirrored windows, is an impressive place to see. The windows are panes of glass that overlay a massive amount of steel trestled framework. Kids (and adults) look up and around in amazement at this church. Tour on your own, or take a forty-minute guided tour which goes through the church and around the other facilities. The tour guide will explain how and why the cathedral was built, as well as offer information about the different ministries going on here. The grounds are beautiful, with a fountain between the office buildings and a large gift/book shop. Look down at the concrete floor panels to read various Bible verses. The tower of the Cathedral contains a fifty-two bell carillon that rings every fifteen minutes. Look in the Calendar section for details on the spectacular shows, *Glory of Christmas* in December, and *Glory of Easter* in March.

Hours: Tours are given Mon. - Sat., 9am - 3:30pm. (Church functions
affect tour times.) Closed major holidays.

Admission: Donations are accepted.

Ages: 6 years and up.

FULLERTON MUNICIPAL AIRPORT

(562) 691-6280 or (714) 738-6323 / www.ci.fullerton.ca.us

4011 W. Commonwealth, Fullerton

(Exit Artesia Fwy [91] or Santa Ana Fwy [5] N. on Magnolia to end, L. on Commonwealth, 1 block to the Tower. [TG-738 A7])

Help navigate your kindergartner or older child on this one-hour walking tour. A docent, who is a member of the Fullerton's Pilot Association, will show your group, of at least five people, around the airport.

Tours are modified to fit your particular children's interests and questions. A highlight is sitting in a small Cessna plane and in a helicopter owned by the Fire Department. Small groups of older kids may visit the Control Tower - depending on how busy the air traffic is. They'll get a bird's eye view of planes landing and taking off, and see how radar works. The tour ends on a high note as souvenirs, like plastic wings for future pilots, are given out.

Hours: Hours and days are flexible, although Mon. - Fri. is preferred.

Admission: Free

Ages: 5 years and up.

GOODWILL INDUSTRIES (Santa Ana)

(714) 547-6308 / www.ocgoodwill.org

410 N. Fairview Street, Santa Ana

(Going E. on Garden Grove Fwy [22], exit S. on Fairview St. Going W. on 22, exit S. on Haster St., L. on Garden Grove Blvd., R. on Fairview St. From the Santa Ana Fwy [5], exit W. on 1st St., R. on Fairview St. [TG-829 A3])

Learn how to spread goodwill as you accompany your kids on a half-hour tour of this facility. You'll get an overview of what Goodwill Industries does by observing people, including many disabled people, being trained to work in several different areas. Watching assembly lines are interesting, as things are put together and packages are shrink wrapped. Kids will also see recycling in action, as old stuffed animals and toys get fixed up for someone else to play with and love. Check out the receiving dock where the donations are piled. Idea: Clean out your closets and have your kids bring their old toys and clothes to Goodwill on your tour date. Tip: Next door to this facility is a thrift store and an "as is" store where kids can hunt for treasure amidst the junk. (I think we bought as much as we brought!) There is no minimum number of people required for a tour, but a week's notice is requested. Also see other GOODWILL INDUSTRIES locations listed under this section.

Hours: Tours are given Tues. and Thurs., 10am - 2pm.

Admission: Free

Ages: At least 7 years old.

GOURMET LOLLIPOP CO.

(714) 841-2000

7351 Heil Avenue, Sweet J, Huntington Beach

(Exit San Diego Fwy [405] S. on Beach Blvd., R. on Heil Ave. [near Gothard]. [TG-827 J6])

Suckers are born every minute; lollipops, however, are made here daily. The Gourmet Lollipop Company is a small, family-owned retail store that offers a wide variety of tasty candies, most of them made on the premises. It also sells candy molds, flavors, toppings, and everything else needed to make sweet treats. What a fun family activity!

One of the attractions here, besides the obvious one of purchasing (and eating) candy, is taking a twenty-minute candy-making class in the back room kitchen where the concoctions are created. As you make a chocolate lollipop, you might even see them making their flavored lollipops (they make forty-eight different flavors!), from the stirring of ingredients to pouring the mixture in the mold to putting on the wrappers. The class, which is short, sweet, and to the point, is offered for a minimum of ten people and participants must be at least 5 years old. Reservations are recommended.

Hours: The store is open Tues. - Fri., 9am - 6pm; Sat., 9am - 4pm. Candy-making classes are offered Wed., Thurs., and Fri. at 3pm and 4pm.

Admission: The class is $5 per person, minium 10 people or $50.

Ages: Children must be at least 5 years old for the class.

JOHN WAYNE AIRPORT TOUR

(949) 252-5168 or (949) 252-5219 / www.ocair.com

3151 Airway Avenue, Costa Mesa

(Exit San Diego Fwy [405] S. on Bristol St., L. on Paularino, R. on Airway. [TG-859 E5])

This terrific, one-hour tour is tailored toward the participants' ages. It shows how the airport is similar to a small city, with different people doing different jobs, each one making a contribution to the community. Kids see the public access places while learning about the history of the airport and some basic information on aviation. The knowledgeable docents are involved in aviation in one form or another; most are retired pilots. The tour goes all around the terminal, to the departure and arrival levels to see the various activities that happen at each one, including baggage claims areas, and more. There are huge windows all along the field, and a V-shape one jutting into it that offers a wonderful view of the planes landing and taking off, planes being serviced, and baggage being loaded and unloaded. A fun remembrance, such as an airplane coloring book, is given out at the end of the tour. Happy landings! A minimum of ten people and maximum of twenty-five are needed for a tour.

Hours: Tours are available Mon. - Sat., 10:30am - 3:30pm. Reservations are required. No tours are given in August.

Admission: Free; parking is $1 per hour.

Ages: 6 years and up.

KOCE-TV

(714) 895-5623 / www.koce.org

15751 Gothard Street, at Golden West College, Huntington Beach

(Going S. on San Diego Fwy [405], exit S. on Goldenwest St., L. on Edinger Ave., L. on Gothard. Going N. on 405, exit S. on Beach Blvd., R. on Edinger, R. on Gothard. Park in the lot advertising KOCE. [TG-827 H5])

At KOCE, Southern Californians have the opportunity to look at the behind-the-scenes workings of a television station, not just what viewers see on air.

Orange County's first television station and Public Broadcasting System member produces the "Real Orange" news show as well as several other shows. The first stop on the one-hour guided tour is the actual studio set, with sound absorbing walls and lots of lights, camera equipment, and Teleprompters. The tour goes at a relaxed pace, so we saw and learned about the consoles, master control room, make up room, newsroom, editing room, and post production office, and asked questions along the way. We dubbed the tour "insightful". Well, I dubbed it insightful and the kids learned a new word. Groups between ten to fifteen people are welcome.

Hours: Tours are offered Mon. - Fri., 9am - 3pm.
Admission: Free
Ages: 8 years and up.

LOS ANGELES TIMES, ORANGE COUNTY ☀

(714) 966-5960 / www.latimes.com !
1375 Sunflower Avenue, Costa Mesa
(Exit San Diego Fwy [405] N. on Fairview Ave., L. on Sunflower. [TG-858 J3])

Walk through the photo, graphic, sports, and features departments and hear a representative from each (depending on the day and circumstances) explain a little about his or her work and the function of that particular department. Learn how the paper is laid out, the plates are made, the actual printing is done, and how the paper is distributed. It's a thrill for any news buff to see how this working facility puts together the front page, sports, comics, and even the classifieds. Note: Although morning and afternoon tours are basically the same, the presses (which are incredibly loud!) usually run in the afternoon. The one-hour tour is open for groups only, consisting of ten to twenty people. Children must be at least 10 years old.

Hours: Tours are given Mon. - Fri., 10am - 4pm by appointment only.
Admission: Free
Ages: 10 years and up.

ORANGE COUNTY PERFORMING ARTS CENTER (tour) ☀

(714) 556-2787 / www.ocpac.org !
600 Town Center Drive, Costa Mesa
(Exit San Diego Fwy [405] N. on Bristol St., R. on Town Center. [TG-859 D3])

All the world's a stage! Get a behind-the-scenes look at the 3,000-seat Segerstrom Hall, a beautiful facility, where major symphony concerts, operas, ballets, and Broadway musicals are presented. Take a tour, beginning at the ticket box office, through the theater, to the star's dressing rooms and wardrobe area, and finishing up backstage. Tour routes may vary due to rehearsal and performance schedules and backstage construction. For show information, please see ORANGE COUNTRY PERFORMING ARTS CENTER under the Shows and Theaters section.

Hours: Guided tours are offered Mon., Wed., and Sat. at 10:30am.
Reservations are required for a group of 10 or more people.
Closed on some holidays.

Admission: Free
Ages: 8 years and up.

TRINITY BROADCASTING NETWORK   ☼

(714) 832-2950 / www.tbn.org   !
14131 Chambers Road, Tustin

(Exit Santa Ana Fwy [5] S. on Tustin Ranch Rd., L. on Walnut Ave., L. on Franklin Ave., L. on Michelle Dr., L. on Chambers. Trinity owns several buildings in this section, but the tour starts in the main lobby. [TG-830 D6])

This forty-minute walking tour starts in the plush lobby of T.B.N. The docent takes visitors to the prayer room on the third floor, a room that has cushioned benches around the perimeters and ornately-painted Biblical scenes on the ceilings and walls. In another building across the street, you'll see another prayer room with more of the colorful scenes from the Old and New Testament. The tour guide explains the scenes as well as the work that T.B.N. does. Walk down a hallway lined with photos of Paul and Jan Crouch - hosts of the *Praise the Lord!* program and co-founders of T.B.N. - along with many of their celebrity guests. The studio contains a beautiful living room set for programs that are sometimes filmed before a live audience. The tour ends back across the street in the attractive T.B.N. library where oak shelves are filled with books that the public is welcome to use, but not check out. Tip: See TRINITY CHRISTIAN CITY INTERNATIONAL, under the Shows and Theaters section, for their other, much larger facility which features four of their production movies.

Hours: Call for an appointment to take a tour.
Admission: Free
Ages: 6 years and up.

RIVERSIDE PRESS-ENTERPRISE   ☼

(909) 782-7765 / www.press-enterprise.com/nie   !
3512 14th Street, Riverside

(Exit Riverside Fwy [91] E. on 14th St. [TG-685 G5])

School, scout, or other groups interested in the workings of a newsroom and how a newspaper is put together can get a behind-the-scenes look on this one-hour tour of the Enterprise. The tour begins with the history of this paper. The group then walks through the various departments, seeing and learning how each one functions along the way. The departments include advertising, the newsroom, editing, production or composing, the color lab, plate making, inserts and packaging, and the pressroom. The latter is more interesting when the presses are actually running, although it does get loud. Lots of interesting facts about newspapers are given and students will be surprised at how much paper is used for just one edition. Tours are open to a minimum of ten students and maximum of twenty; groups over twenty will be divided into smaller groups. Ask about their Newspaper In Education program.

Hours: Tours are offered year-round on Tues. and Fri. during normal business hours. Call to make a reservation.
Admission: Free
Ages: 3rd grade or above.

WINCHESTER CHEESE CO.

(909) 926-4239 / www.winchestercheese.com $$
32605 Holland Road, Winchester

(Going S. on Escondido Fwy [215], exit E. on Hwy 74, S. on Winchester Rd. [79], R. on Holland. A sign says Wesselink Dairy on the corner. Going N. on Temecula Valley Fwy [15], exit N.E. on Winchester Rd. [79], L. on Holland. [TG-685 G5])

Smile and say "cheese"! The Winchester Cheese Co. is a family-owned dairy that produces fresh Gouda cheese in trailers located on this large tract of farm land. During the almost two-hour outdoor tour visitors learn a lot about the dairy process and about the 400-plus cows here. They learn what cows eat and how often, when they are milked, and ultimately, how cheese is made from the raw milk. Visitors see the feed; walk around the pens to pet and even bottle feed newborn calves; peek into the windows to see the cheese being made; and go into the trailer to look at how and where the cheese and cheese wheels are kept refrigerated for future consumption. A wonderful amount of information dispensed and, for us city folk who rarely see a real dairy "in action", the hands-on, eyes-on activities strengthens the retention. (I hope!) The last activity is also the tastiest - sampling a variety of cheese with flavors that range from sharp to mild to spicy hot. Snack time is complete with apples wedges, crackers, pretzels, and a beverage that is all provided. Feel free to bring a picnic lunch, too. Tip: Bring extra money to purchase some cheese to take home!

Hours: Tours are given Wed. and Thurs., 9:30am - 11:30am by reservation only. Groups must constitute a minimum of 30 people or $75; $3 per person is charged after 30 people, the maximum number is 50.

Admission: $3 per person.

Ages: 5 years and up.

WRIGHT WORM FARM

(909) 928-1485 / www.wrightwormfarm.com $
32205 Meadow Blossom, Neuvo

(Exit the Escondido Fwy [215], E. on Ramona Exwy, R. on Hansen, L. on Meadow Blossom (a dirt road). It's on the R. [TG-779 D4])

Traditionally used as bait, worms actually play an equally important role in farming, as well as fishing. Find out more interesting information about these slimy little critters on a half-hour tour. The Wright farm has long rows of red worms living in dirt mounds called windrows (this is not a misspelling of the word window). Two other types of worms, Pheretimas and euros (i.e. European night crawlers), live in boxes full of dirt and castings (i.e. worm poop). Castings make terrific fertilizer. After the tour, purchase a few worms to start your own compost area.

Hours: Tours are given by appointment for a minimum of 10 people and maximum of 35.

Admission: $1.75 per person, which can be applied toward a purchase of worms or castings.

Ages: 4 years and up.

GOODWILL INDUSTRIES (San Bernardino)

(909) 885-3831 / www.goodwillic.org
8120 Palm Lane, San Bernardino
(Exit 215 Fwy E. on 6ᵗʰ St., R. on E St., L. on 5ᵗʰ St., R. on Waterman Ave., L. on 3ʳᵈ St., L. on Palm Ln. [TG-607 A1])

See GOODWILL INDUSTRIES (Santa Ana) in this section for details. This location is a main donation center, where goods get consolidated and processed. It also has manual production lines, the work activity area, plus a retail store next door.

Hours: Tours are offered Mon. - Fri., 8am - 4pm by reservation.
Admission: Free
Ages: 7 years and up.

OAK GLEN / APPLE PICKING & TOURS

www.oakglen.net
Oak Glen Road, Oak Glen

See OAK GLEN / APPLE PICKING & TOURS under the Edible Adventures section for details.

ONTARIO INTERNATIONAL AIRPORT

(909) 937-2883 or (909) 937-2700
Vineyard Avenue, Ontario
(From San Bernardino Fwy [10], exit S. on Vineyard. From Pomona Fwy [60], exit N. on Grove Ave., R. on Holt Blvd., R. on Vineyard. [TG-642 G1])

Your youngsters can pretend to fly the friendly skies on their hour-and-a-half, guided tour of the airport. They will see the hustle and bustle as passengers arrive and depart; walk through a metal detector; see the baggage claim area and, find out, maybe, where luggage actually goes; learn about the people who work at an airport; watch planes land and take off; and more. Tours are given for school or organized groups only.

Hours: Tours are offered year-round, Mon. - Fri., 9:30am - noon.
                Reservations are needed.
Admission: Free
Ages: Children must be of kindergarten age or older.

BUCK KNIVES

(619) 449-1100 / www.buckknives.com
1900 Weld Boulevard, El Cajon
(Going E. on Ocean Beach Fwy [8], exit N. on Johnson Ave., L. on Bradley Ave., R. on Cuyamaca, L. on Weld. Going W. on 8 Fwy, exit N. on San Vicente Fwy [67], W. on Bradley, R. on Cuyamaca, L. on Weld. [TG-1251 C1])

The Buck stops here, or starts here, actually. The lobby is decorated with numerous mounted animal heads (deer, moose, etc.), as well as a full bear skin rug and lots of knives in display cases. The forty-minute, casual and informative factory tour takes visitors through the large plant where *sharp* kids will learn how knives are made. Radio headsets are worn so the tour guide can be heard over the din of the machinery. See and hear machines grind steel to specified thicknesses, lasers cut steel into knife parts, heat-treating ovens harden steel, and vibrating bins give blades a consistent surface. Knives are assembled along a conveyor belt type of equipment then sharpened, buffed, packaged, and finally, shipped. Males (of all ages) especially, will ooh and aah over the machinery and the process, and will want to possess their own finished product. Conveniently, a small gift shop is on the premises and is open after your tour. Items here include fishing knives, pocket knives, numerous fixed blades, a few multi-purpose tools, and articles of clothing with the Buck logo. Note: Tour groups are limited to twelve persons per guide. Reservations are required. Photography is permitted in certain areas.

Hours: Tours are offered Mon. - Thurs. at 10am, noon, 1pm, and 2pm. Closed for tours Fri., holidays, or during company shutdown periods.

Admission: Free

Ages: Must be at least 7 years and up.

CALLAWAY GOLF

(760) 931-1771 / www.callawaygolf.com

2285 Rutherford Road, Building 1, Carlsbad

(Exit Interstate 5 E. on Palomar Airport Rd., L. on College, R on Aston, R. on Rutherford. [TG-1127 D2])

Fore golf lovers of all ages, Callaway is considered a premier name in club manufacturing. Trivia: Their "Big Bertha" drivers are named after the German WWI cannon that shot cannonballs straight and far, hence. . . . The half-hour tour, geared for small groups, takes visitors into the warehouse/factory where shafts, club heads, and grips are assembled, glued, and adjusted to precise alignments and weights with the help of computers, then buffed, and packaged. I was struck by the relatively large number of people working here - my family is used to factory tours where the relatively few workers act more as assistants to the machinery rather than the other way around. My kids especially enjoyed watching the workers employ a machine that, in a matter of seconds, grinds off the part of the shaft that sticks out from the bottom of the club head. The presentation is detailed and interesting, with plenty of opportunities for questions. Note that visitors are invited to purchase the scrumptious cafeteria food usually reserved for employees and to shop in the small gift shop. Golf clubs, however, are not sold here.

Hours: Tours are offered Mon. - Fri. at 9:15am, 11am, 1pm, 2pm, and 3:30pm. Reservations are required.

Admission: Free

Ages: 6 years and up.

EAGLE MINING COMPANY

(760) 765-0036 / www.julianfun.com

North end of 'C' Street, Julian

(From San Diego Fwy [5] or Escondido Fwy [15], take 78 Fwy E. to Julian. From the 8 Fwy, take 79 N. to Julian. From Main St. in Julian, go N. on 'C' St. Follow the signs. [TG-1136 B6])

Eureka! There's gold in them thar hills! Original mining equipment and a few old buildings make it look like time has stood still here. One of the buildings is a small museum/store with rock specimens, mining tools, and a glass-cased display of memorabilia from the early 1900's.

Trek through time on your one-hour, guided, walking tour through two genuine gold mines that were founded in 1870: the Eagle Mine and the connecting, High Peak Mine. My kids studied about the forty-niners, but to actually go through a gold mine, walk on ore-cart tracks, see stone tunnels hand carved by picks, and learn the hardships of mining, really made a lasting impact on them. We saw the vein that the miners worked and realized, along with hundreds of other people both past and present, that gold wasn't easily obtainable. It took one ton of rock to yield a sugar-cube-size amount of gold! We went up two of the eleven levels in the mines, saw the hoist room where ore buckets were used as olden-day elevators, and experienced darkness so black that we couldn't see our hands in front of our faces. I admire the fortitude of our early engineers. It's interesting to note the difference between the earlier smooth rock tunnels that were hand drilled and the later jagged edges left from blasting with charges. Don't forget to look up at the amazing shaft tunnels (and duck your head)!

Outside, we saw the milling equipment used to crush rocks, and learned the tedious process of extracting gold. Try your hand at panning for gold (it's harder than it looks) in a "stocked" water trough on the premises, but warn kids that they can't keep the gold. And just remember: All that glitters isn't gold.

Julian is a quaint town with unique shops along Main Street. Your kids will enjoy a stop-off at the Julian Drugstore for an ice cream at its old-fashioned soda counter. The drugstore is located on the corner of Main and Washington Sts. Look up Julian under the city index for other, close-by attractions.

Hours: Open daily 10am - 2:30pm.
Admission: $8 for adults; $4 for ages 5 - 15; $1 for children 4 and under.
Ages: 4 years and up.

GOODWILL INDUSTRIES (San Diego)
(619) 225-2200
3663 Rosecrans Street, San Diego
(Going S. on San Diego Fwy [5] exit E. on Old Town Ave. Going N. on 5, exit at Moore St., R. on Old Town Ave. From Old Town go L. on San Diego Ave., L. on Congress St., L. on Taylor St., which turns into Rosecrans. [TG-1268 E5])

See GOODWILL INDUSTRIES (Santa Ana) in this section for details. This facility does not have a shrink wrap machine.

Hours: Tours are offered Mon. - Fri., 9am - 3pm by reservation only.
Admission: Free
Ages: 7 years and up.

HILLIKER'S EGG RANCH
(619) 448-3683
11329 El Nopal, Lakeside
(Exit San Vincente Fwy [67] N. on Riverford, L. on El Nopal. [TG-1231 G3])

What came first - the chicken or the egg? 22,000 chickens, housed in five, long rectangular buildings containing rows and rows of chickens, produce an egg a day. The eggs are gathered twice a day and then processed through the egg machine. The machine first uses suction cups to pick up the eggs by the dozen. The eggs are then carried along on an automated tray where they are washed, inspected via a back light (for imperfections), graded (by size and color), sorted, and boxed. It's a fascinating process for us city folks to watch.

On a half-hour or so tour, given only for school groups, students see the machine being put through its paces, step into the refrigerator room, look into the chicken houses, learn how and why these chickens are raised, where the eggs are sold, and generally learn about farm life. A few other animals live on this family-owned "ranch" - a few pigs, several ducks, some cows, and peacocks. Be sure to purchase some fresh eggs on your way out!

Hours: Tours are offered Tues. - Fri. at 9:30am. Call to make an appointment.

Admission: Free

Ages: All

MCCLELLAN-PALOMAR AIRPORT

(800) 759-5667 or (760) 431-4646 / www.co.san-diego.ca.us
2198 Palomar Airport Road, Carlsbad
(Exit San Diego Fwy [5] E. on Palomar Airport Rd., L. on Yarrow Rd. [TG-1127 D3])

Visitors won't get airborne on this airport tour, but they can experience flight vicariously. Small airplanes are constantly landing and taking off as guides tell about the different type of aircraft here. If a grounded plane is available, children can sit inside it and check out all the controls in the cockpit. After the tour, kids are given a memento - an airplane coloring book, a Styrofoam airplane, and/or "wings."

The adjacent Airport Cafe, which is open daily 7am to 5pm, has both indoor and outdoor seating. For those who feel the need to actually experience flight, twenty minute to hour-long biplane and cruiser rides are available. See BIPLANE AND AIR COMBAT ADVENTURES under the Transportation section.

Hours: Tours are given by appointment.

Admission: Tours are free. Call for biplane or cruiser flights. Two hours of free parking.

Ages: 4 years and up.

NAVY SHIPS TOURS

(619) 437-2735 or (619) 437-2735
U.S. Navy Pier of Harbor Drive, near Broadway on the Embarcadero, San Diego
(Going N. on San Diego Fwy [5], exit E. on Hawthorne St., L. on Harbor. Going S. on 5, exit S. on Front St., R. on Ash, L. on Harbor. [TG-1288 J3])

The Navy offers a unique opportunity for the public to tour a destroyer, frigate, amphibious cruiser, submarine, aircraft carrier, or other naval craft. A forty-five-minute or so tour is given for a minimum group of twenty, maximum of 100. Groups must sign up at least four weeks in advance. The type of ship you

actually see depends on what is in the harbor on the day you plan to visit. A
military tour guide will take you through the ship and answer any questions, and
we all know that kids always have plenty of those. Note that the tour isn't
stroller/wheelchair accessible and that there are incline ladders to climb. (Don't
wear dresses or skirts, ladies!) A favorite room is the combat information center,
where radar equipment is on display.

Hours: Tours are offered Tues. and Thurs., 9am - 3pm.
Admission: Free
Ages: 5 years and up.

NIEDERFRANK'S ICE CREAM SHOP/FACTORY

(619) 477-0828 / niederfranks.signonsandiego.com
726 A Avenue, National City

See NIEDERFRANK'S ICE CREAM SHOP/FACTORY in the Edible
Adventures section for details.

SAN DIEGO INTERNATIONAL AIRPORT   ☼
                                                                        !

(619) 686-8014 / www.portofsandiego.org
Harbor Drive at Lindbergh Field, San Diego
(Going S. on San Diego Fwy [5], exit W. on Sassafras. Going N. on 5, exit W. on Hawthorne St., N.
on Harbor. Follow the signs to the airport. [TG-1288 G1])

Pilot your way to the airport for a two-hour tour of the San Diego
International Airport. Tours include a walk through a majority of the facility
while learning about architecture, travel, communications, career opportunities,
and the history of aviation. Hear about Charles Lindbergh while looking at a
replica of the Spirit of St. Louis. See some of the works of art on display and a
demonstration of what the on-site fire station does. Take a tram tour that runs
parallel to the runway and wave at the various workers. Go through the baggage
claim area, find out about courtesy phones, and how to use the maps on the
walls. The tour enables children and adults to find out all about travel without
experiencing jet lag, or the cost of a trip! Groups must consist of a minimum of
ten people and a maximum of thirty-five.

Hours: Tours are offered Wed. - Fri., 10am - noon.
Admission: Free
Ages: Kids must be at least 7 years and up.

SAN DIEGO UNION-TRIBUNE   ☼
                                                                        !

(619) 221-7215 - tour; (619) 299-3131 - general /
www.signonsandiego.com
350 Camino de la Reina, San Diego
(Going W. on Mission Valley Fwy [8], exit E. at Mission Center Rd., go L. on Camino Del Rio,
which turns into Camino de la Siesta, L. on Camino de la Reina. Going E. on 8, exit E. on Hotel
Cir. S., R. on Camino de la Reina. [TG-1269 A3])

A one-hour tour to see how a newspaper is put together may be just the
thing to spur your child's interest in journalism. Tours may include walking
through the newsroom to see reporters and editors at work, seeing the production
area where composing and paste-up work is done, and learning about circulation,

advertising, and numerous other newspaper components. Tours are given to groups between twenty to thirty-five students and require advance registration. If you, as an individual, would like to take the tour, you may join in with a pre-registered tour group that is usually comprised of students. The facilities are wheelchair accessible.

Hours: Tours are given Tues., 10:30am and 1:30pm; Wed. - Thurs., 10:30am.

Admission: Free. A school group may be charged a minimal fee to cover the cost of materials which are sent to the school before the visit.

Ages: Children must be 9 years and up.

ST. VINCENT DE PAUL VILLAGE

(619) 233-8500 / www.svdpv.org

1501 Imperial Avenue, San Diego

(Going S. on San Diego Fwy [5], exit W. on Imperial. Going N. on 5, exit N. on Crosby St., L. on 25ᵗʰ St., L. on Imperial. From Escondido Fwy [15], exit E. on Ocean View Blvd., R. on 28ᵗʰ St., L. on Imperial. [TG-1289 C4])

". . . Give me your tired, your poor, your huddled masses yearning to be free. . ." (Part of a poem that is engraved on the pedestal of the Statue of Liberty.) St. Vincent's Village is a "network of residential centers providing a continuum of care to over 2,000 men, women, and children daily." This incredible, state-of-the-art, self-contained facility aids the poor and homeless in very practical ways. It offers them a new lease on life with homes, meals, life-skills programs, counseling, and medical programs.

A one-hour tour takes your group or family through most of the facility - the lobby, office, kitchen courtyard, residential buildings, food storage, and medical buildings. This is quite an operation, so a behind-the-scenes tour is eye opening. If you are seeking to instill compassion in your children and/or if they are looking for a venue to help those less fortunate, a visit to this village is a good starting point. Coming here will make an indelible mark upon hearts because the homeless are then no longer faceless or nameless, but real people with real needs.

Hours: Tours are offered Mon. - Fri. on the hour 9am - 2pm. Please call at least a week ahead of time to reserve a tour date and time.

Admission: Free

Ages: 8 years and up.

TAYLOR GUITARS

(619) 258-6957 / www.taylorguitars.com

1980 Gillespie Way, El Cajon

(Exit Interstate 8 N. on Johnson Ave., L. on Bradley, R. on Cuyamaca, L. on Gillespie Way. [TG-1251 C1])

What do Aerosmith, Pearl Jam, President Clinton, and Garth Brooks have in common? They each own Taylor guitars. This over-an-hour-long tour is Taylor-made for guitar fans. Starting in the lobby, which features an informational and pictorial time line of the guitar company, visitors see and learn how a guitar is put together, from start to glossy (or satin) finish. Cherry, Sapele mahogany,

Sitka spruce, Big Leaf maple, cedar, Indian rosewood, Hawaiian koa, and walnut are just a few of the common and exotic woods used in Taylor guitars. Once the wood is cut to precise specifications, it is kept in climate controlled rooms and containers, then carved, sanded, and assembled. Specially designed (loud!) machines, such as the ones that slice grooves in the neck of the guitar, are fascinating to watch as are the workers who are involved in each step of the process. Note: It takes a week to ten days to complete just one guitar.

The tour is geared for real guitar afficionados (we had some people on ours who asked lots of "technical" questions), but kids will appreciate the different shapes, woods, colors, and sounds of the guitars. After the tour, guests are given a "soundhole coaster" actually made from wood used to make guitars. They are invited to purchase a wide selection of merchandise (guitar picks, jackets, etc.) imprinted with the Taylor logo. Guitars are not sold on the premises. The tour is geared for small groups, is not wheelchair friendly, and visitors must stay within specified lines and resist the temptation to touch anything in the factory warehouses. Photography is permitted.

Hours: Tours are offered at Mon. - Fri., at 1pm. Reservations are not required, but suggested. Tours are not given for a week towards the end of June, at the beginning of July, and for a week before Christmas through New Year's Day.

Admission: Free

Ages: 7 years and up.

TIME WARNER CABLE   ☀
(858) 635-8464 / www.timewarnersandiego.com   !
8949 Ware Court, Miramar
(From Escondido Fwy [15], exit W. on Miramar Rd., R. on Carroll Rd. (past the pyramid building), cross over Camino Santa Fe, R. on Ware Ct. From Jakob Dekema Fwy [805], exit E. on Miramar Rd., L. on Camino Santa Fe, L. on Carroll Rd, immediate R. on Ware Ct. [TG-1208 J7])

Hour-long tours, which are limited to twenty people, meet in a functioning TV studio that is used by the community. An eight-minute promotional video about Time Warner introduces guests to this tele-communications company. Visitors walk through and into several rooms including editing rooms (with lots of console equipment), the sales floor, customer service, and my children's favorite - the network center. In the latter, a huge wall of small television screens display concurrently all the shows that Time Warner helps air, such as H2O, Travel Network, Nickelodeon, sports, the SCI-Fi channel, etc. While our guide explained to the adults how every show was monitored for troubleshooting, the kids stood transfixed, staring at all the shows. The next room was an impressive display of millions of dollars of equipment used for television, cable network, computers, and more.

Along the tour (which is not wheelchair friendly) we walked up and down stairs, outside to look at the satellites, and across the street to another one of Time Warner's buildings. We learned about fiber optics, the latest technological advances, and the entertainment industry. The tour was partially a commercial for Time Warner and partially technical information about telecommunications. We all enjoyed the goodie bags given out at the end.

Hours: Tours are offered the first and third Mon. of each month at noon and 3:30pm; and the last Sat. at 9am, 11am, 1pm, and 3pm. Reservations are requested. Note: Special tour dates can be arranged for school and Scouting groups.

Admission: Free

Ages: 9 years and up.

VAN OMMERING DAIRY

(619) 390-2929

14950 El Monte Road, Lakeside

(Exit San Vincente Fwy [67] E. on Mapleview St., which turns into Lake Jennings Park Dr., L. on El Monte Rd. Drive for a few miles and then look for a sign that announces Van Ommering Dairy or Circle V Dairy and turn L. [TG-1212 J7])

For a really moooving tour, visit this family-owned dairy. The hour-long tour starts in the commodities shed where seed is stored for the 600 cows that live on the premises. Guests then go through the showers (not literally!) where the cows are washed down before they're milked. From the milking barn, with all of its fascinating modern machinery, the tour visits the maternity pen. You might even be lucky enough to see a calf being born. Another pen is home to newborns and kids are welcome to gently pet them. Information is dispensed throughout the tour about the workings of a dairy, cows' eating habits, where the milk goes after it's outside the cows, and more. Visitors leave with lots of knowledge about these milk/meat/leather-producing animals, a greater understanding of how farmers' work affects everyone, and an informational pamphlet about the dairy industry. Note: The WILLIAMS WORM FARM, mentioned in the Tours section, is right next door.

Hours: Tours are offered April and May on Mon., Tues., and Thurs. at 9:30am, 10:30am, and 11:30am. Groups from 15 to 100 people are welcome.

Admission: Free

Ages: All

WASTE MANAGEMENT

(619) 596-5100

1001 W. Bradley Avenue, El Cajon

(Exit San Vincente Fwy [67] W. on Bradley. [TG-1251 D2])

Have your younger children ever stood riveted, watching the garbage men take trash from the curb and toss it into the garbage trucks? Now you can find out where the trash goes and see how it's processed. Waste Management offers interesting one-hour tours of one of its main facilities. We went through the offices; saw the huge trash trucks (and learned how expensive they are!); sat in a cab, tooted the horn, and "played" with the computer; saw the recycling area; and saw and smelled tons and tons (literally) of trash being scooped up and dumped onto another truck that takes the waste out to landfills. We learned how many tons make a compressed bundle, where the landfills are and how much longer they should be available, and that we should waste not, want not.

Hours: Tours are offered Tues. and Thurs. at 9:30am for up to 30
people. Call to make a reservation.
Admission: Free
Ages: 4 - 10 years.

WILLIAMS WORM FARM

(619) 443-1698 / www.williamswormfarm.com
14893 El Monte Road at Willows Road, Lakeside
(Exit San Vincente Fwy [67] E. on Mapleview, which turns into Lake Jennings, L. on El Monte and
drive a few miles, L. at the sign that announces Van Ommering Dairy or Circle V Dairy, L. at the
fork in the road. The farm is just past the dairy. [TG-1212 J7])

"Worms are the intestines of the earth." (Aristotle) A half-hour tour of this
red worm (not earthworm) farm leads credence to that visual picture. Bill, the
owner, has two, 250-foot long chicken barns that now contain rows of dirt
packed with worms. The worms become visible only when Bill scoops up a
shovel full of earth. It takes worms thirty days to make castings (i.e. worm poop
that makes great dirt). Twenty-five percent of these worms are sold for fish bait,
while another portion is added to dog and cat food. A major portion of the "dirt"
is sold to gardeners and composters. All this and more is yours to learn on a tour.
And yes, you may even hold a handful of the wiggly critters. Note: Since the
farm is next to the VAN OMMERING DAIRY (see this section) try to schedule
a tour here for the same day.
Hours: Tours are given Mon. - Fri. Call to schedule.
Admission: Free
Ages: All

VENTURA COUNTY COURTHOUSE

(805) 650-7599 - the bar association/tour
800 S. Victoria Avenue, Ventura
(From Ventura Fwy [101], exit N. on Victoria. From Santa Paula Fwy [126], exit S. on Victoria.
[TG-492 C3])

Now kids can have their day in court! This two-and-a-half-hour tour, for
groups between twenty to thirty-five people, explains the process of the Ventura
County court system. The tour consists of seeing the courthouse, the
administration building (where residents pay property taxes and obtain licenses),
the sheriff department, and the jail. Here visitors learn what happens when an
inmate is incarcerated - from frisking, to showers, to where they eat and sleep.
At the courthouse, visitors see and learn about the law library, the ceremonial
courtroom, traffic court, and the jury room. They usually get to sit in on a civil
and/or criminal case, too.

A highlight of the tour is a grade-appropriate, one-hour mock trial of an
actual court case. Participants read from scripts as they become members of the
jury, lawyers, the bailiff, and even the judge (along with a robe and gavel). I
think this is a fascinating tour, but I'll let you be the judge!
Hours: Tours are given Mon. - Thurs. at 10:30am with advanced
reservations only.
Admission: Free
Ages: 6th graders and up.

TRANSPORTATION

Take a journey with your child by bike, plane, train, automobile, ship, carriage, etc., for a truly "moving" experience together. Note: There are numerous boating companies up and down the coastline. I've mentioned only a few, giving just some pertinent facts. Anchors away!

ALFREDO'S
(562) 434-6121

   Alfredo's has seventeen concessions throughout Southern California, along the beach and in many parks. They rent kayaks - $5 an hour for single, $15 an hour for double; pedal boats - $15 a half hour; as well as bikes, skates, and boogie boards. The boat rentals are available usually daily in the summer, and on weekends only the rest of the year. Call for their locations.

BIKE TRAILS
   There are numerous bike trails throughout Southern California. (Really - not everyone drives a car!) Please note that these paved pathways are also wonderful for joggers, strollers, scooters, skateboarders, etc. I've just called them bike trails. I mention a few of our favorites later in this section - look under BIKE TRAIL, under the county you're interested in. I feel like the best way I can be of service to you in this area is to give you phone numbers and web sites so you can order bike trail maps and make your own choices about routes. The county maps are wonderfully marked with colorful lines delineating if the trail is a completely separate right-of-way for the exclusive use of non-motorized travel (my personal favorite), beach trails, or a bicycle route that is a separate, marked lane along the street. Many parks also have bike paths, so please look in the Great Outdoors section.

   For the Los Angeles area, call (213) 244-6539 for a map. They are still working on doing an update, but they'll be done sometime! You might also try (213) 922-3068 - the Los Angeles County Metropolitan Transportation Authority, or even the State of California Caltrans Office of Bicycle Facilities at (916) 653-0036.

   For the Orange County area, call (800) 636-RIDE (7433) or (714) 636-BIKE (7433) / www.octa.net for a bike map. This is the number for the Orange County Transportation Authority. For your information, many Orange County buses are now equipped with bike racks, too. To inquire about trail closures and detours on county-operated off-road trails (i.e. mountain biking) call the EMA-Harbors, Beaches, and Parks Operation at (714) 567-6222 or (714) 834-2400.

   For the San Diego County area, call (619) 231- BIKE (2453) or (800) COMMUTE (266-6883) / www.sdcommute.com/bicycle.htm for a map. Bike racks are also available on many bus routes and on the Coaster commuter train. Call Coaster information at (800) COASTER (262-7837) / www.sdcommute.com for a route schedule and prices.

   For the Ventura County area, call (805) 642-1591 / www.goventura.org. This is the number for the Ventura County Transportation Commission.

   Mountain bikers can also call the U.S. National San Bernardino Forest Service, (909) 383-5588 and Cleveland National Forest, (858) 673-6180 for information.

   Be wise when biking. Carry water bottles, a cell phone, change to make a call or for snacks, a small bike pump, a patch kit, sun screen, a small first aid kit, and anything else useful. Most pathways are safe, but bike with a buddy, just in case.

THE CALIFORNIAN   ☼
(800) 432-2201 / www.californian.org $$$$$

   Set sail in this full-scale re-creation of the 1848 vintage *Revenue Cutter*
tallship, once one of the fastest ships of its kind. It's magnificent to look at. The
primary purpose of the *Californian* is to serve students and adults as a unique
training vessel. On board the ship, participants will learn maritime history, the
art of sailing tallships, and how shipmates must work together as a team.
   The *Californian* offers three programs. In the Sea Chest program, for fourth
through eighth graders, a container that looks like an old sea chest is sent to the
classroom about a month before the sail date. The chest holds a workbook for
each student, a teacher's guide (thank goodness!), a video tape of the ship's
sailing adventures, an audio tape of sea chanteys, and line for students to
practice knot-tying techniques. On the sail date, the student crew receives
dockside orientation before their three-hour tour; that's right - their three-hour
tour. Hoisting all the sails takes quite a bit of time. Once out at sea, students
attend twenty-minute workshops at each of the three stations: One emphasizes
what a sailor's life was like in the 1850's; a second teaches basic navigation
skills and how to chart a ship's course; and the third allows attendees to
participate in actually sailing the ship, by raising sails, steering, etc. Tip: Bring
snacks on board and have lunch waiting for the kids afterwards! A minimum of
thirty-five students and maximum forty-five students are required for this cruise.
Smaller groups can be combined together to reach the necessary numbers.
   The Cadet Cruise is a five-day experience for ages fifteen to nineteen years.
Program topics include earth sciences, environmental awareness, California
history, applied sciences, and, of course, learning how to sail a tallship. Besides
receiving hands-on learning on these topics, the cadet crew members will learn
teamwork and responsibility, and how to sleep next to someone who might
snore. A group of sixteen students is required for this cruise.
   The Tallship Day Sail program is a four-hour excursion where the public
can just enjoy the ride, or participate in sailing the ship - hauling on lines to raise
sails, taking a turn at the ship's helm to steer the ship, etc. Passengers will also
learn the history of tallship vessels and all about the life of a sailor. Lunch is
provided on board. The recommended age for this cruise is at least ten years old.
   Note: About ten days a year the *Californian* docks at a harbor and is open to
the public, for free, to board and simply look around. Guided tours are not given.
   Hours: Call for program dates. The *Californian* docks at Oxnard, Marina
                del Rey, Long Beach, Dana Point, Oceanside, San Diego, and
                Chula Vista at various times throughout the year.
   Admission: The Sea Chest program is $38 per person; the Cadet Cruise is
                $495 per person; and the Tallship Day Sail is $75 per person.
   Ages: 10 years and up; certain programs have other age requirements.

METROLINK   ☼
(800) 371-5465 / www.metrolinktrains.com $$
Serves almost all of Southern California

   The metro commuter train links several counties in Southern California,
from Ventura, to San Bernardino, to the Antelope Valley (and everything in

between). Dial the above phone number for specific route information. It's a fun excursion and saves the hassle of driving in traffic.

Hours: The rail runs Mon. - Fri. from early morning until evening. Only the San Bernardino - Santa Clarita/Antelope Valley line runs on Sat.
Admission: Varies, depending on starting point and destination.
Ages: All

VOYAGES OF REDISCOVERY   ☼
(800) 200-LADY (5239) / www.ladywashington.org;   *$$/$$$$$*
www.hawaiianchieftain.com

The *Lady Washington* is a faithful replica of the first American square rigged ship to round Cape Horn and come to the Pacific Northwest. The *Hawaiian Chieftain* is an authentic replica of a typical European merchant trade ship, similar to those used by Spanish explorers in the late eighteenth century. Both ships set sail from their base in northern California and travel together to our southern harbors for a few months in the winter. They will dock in Ventura, Marina Del Rey, Long Beach, and San Diego, periodically during the months of December, January, and February. Boarding the ship, kids can experience first hand the life of sailors, coastal explorers, traders, missionaries, and Native Americans. This is accomplished by a dockside tour or sailing expedition. In preparation for either tour, Voyages will send the class a packet of suggested pre-trip activities and a bibliography. Costumed, docent educators are the instructors on the tours, both of which are geared specifically for fourth and fifth graders.

At the one-hour dockside tour, students visit each of three learning stations. The first one teaches line handling and the life of a sailor; the second, navigation and the work of officers; and the third, the history of the many cultures along the coast over 200 years ago. The three-hour expedition incorporates the same kind of "classes" as in the dockside tour, as well as actually setting and trimming the sails, steering the ship, and using traditional navigation tools. Kids will be learning mathematics, cartography, astronomy, and other sciences, and most of all, how to work together as a team.

Programs run rain or shine, just like sailors of old, who sailed (almost) no matter what the weather conditions were like. Each tour must have a minimum of thirty participants (this number includes chaperones and teachers) for either ship, with a maximum of forty-five, or ninety, for both ships. Smaller groups may be able to share their tour with another group.

Individuals and families wishing to explore the ships may do so in three ways. One is by going sailing on a three-hour, battle reenactment trip led by period-dressed crew members. The passengers are spectators as the two ships try to out maneuver each other by sailing furiously. A highlight is the firing of the cannons. (The cannons don't use real ammunition, just lots of noise and smoke.) The second way is to go on a sunset cruise and enjoy the sea breeze and the sun setting on the horizon. The third opportunity to explore the ships is offered when they are docked. A formal tour is not given, but docents are on hand to answer questions. Whatever you choose to do, come sail the high seas of adventure!

Hours: All tours take place from the above mentioned ports during the months of December through February. Dockside tours for school groups are given Mon. - Fri. at 9am, 10am, and 11am. Sailing expeditions for groups are offered once a day, Mon. - Fri. from 12:30pm - 3:30pm. Battle reenactments are conducted Sat. from 2pm - 5pm; Sun. from 10am - 1pm and 2pm - 5pm. Dockside exploration for individuals and families is available Mon. - Fri. between 3pm - 6pm; Sat. between 10am - 1pm.

Admission: Dockside tours for groups are $5 per participant. Sailing expeditions are $30 per participant. Battle reenactments are $40 for adults; $20 for children 12 and under. Sunset cruises are $30 for adults; $15 for children. Dockside exploration for individuals is $7 for a family (i.e. immediate family members), or $3 for adults; $2 for seniors and students; $1 for children 12 and under.

Ages: 4th and 5th graders for tours; 6 years and up for battle reenactments; 3 years and up for dockside exploration for families.

AMTRACK - ONE-DAY TRAIN RIDES

(800) USA RAIL (872-7245) / www.dot.ca.gov/hq/rail/ $$$$
800 N. Alameda Street, Union Passenger Station, Los Angeles
(Exit Hollywood Fwy [101] N. on Alameda. [TG-634 G3])

A train ride is a treat for any age child! The Union Station in Los Angeles is a wonderful starting place for this exciting journey. The station is grandly old, and with its high ceiling, arched doorways, marble floors, and wood and leather seats (and a little imagination), it is a nostalgic and romantic reminder of the era when train travel was the only way to go. By incorporating a train trip into your day's excursion, whether it's simply to a park, to a special restaurant, or to a major destination, you make your outing and time together more memorable. The train cars have bathrooms and most have snack cars, too. Note: Amtrack leaves from various other cities.

The prices quoted are for unreserved round trips; reserved seats are at least an additional $7 per rider. Reserved summer rates are slightly higher. Always ask for special promotions. Certain discounts are available through AAA. The age definition for children is 2 through 15 years. Listed below are just six Amtrak routes, departing from L.A. and arriving at various cities. Call for destinations closer to you, and please always call for current departure times and prices:

L. A. -   Fullerton; a thirty-three-minute ride that ends five miles north of Knott's Berry Farm.
Departs at 8:30, 10:30, etc. Adults are $14; children are $7.

L. A. -   Anaheim; a forty-two-minute ride, where you can walk across the street to Katella Street, and take a commuter rail to Disneyland, or the Disneyland Hotel.
Departs at 8:45, 10:45, etc. Adults are $16; children are $7.

L. A. -   Santa Ana; a fifty-two-minute ride.
       Departs at 6:45, 8:45, 10:45, etc. Adults are $16; children are $8.

L. A. -   San Juan Capistrano; a one-hour and fifteen-minute ride. (It lets off
       two short blocks from Mission San Juan.)
       Departs at 6:45, 8:45, 10:45, etc. Adults are $24; children are $12.

L. A. -   San Diego; a two-hour and forty-five-minute ride.
       Departs at 8:45, 10:45, etc. Adults are $46; children are $23.
       Ages: All

ANGELS FLIGHT RAILWAY   ☀

(213) 626-1901 or (800) 371-5465   *$*
351 S. Hill Street, Los Angeles
(Exit Hollywood Fwy [101] S. on Alameda St, R. on 3ʳᵈ St, L. on Hill. [TG-634 F4])

       A ride on the world's shortest, restored wooden railway is one of those cool
little excursions that kids (and adults) enjoy. Starting at the restored station
house, with Victorian carvings, the funicular (vocabulary word for the day) takes
passengers up and down the steep hill. Go for the brief thrill of it, or go shopping
at the bottom of the hill. Add this "trip" onto another local attraction, such as
GRAND CENTRAL MARKET listed under the Edible Adventures section.
       Hours: Open daily from 6:30am to 10pm.
       Admission: One-way fare is 25¢.
       Ages: All

BEACH CITIES WATERCRAFT RENTALS

(310) 372-7477 / www.beachcitywatercraft.com   *$$$$*
Where Torrance Boulevard meets the sea at Redondo Beach Pier, Redondo
Beach
(From San Diego Fwy [405], exit S. on Western, R. on 190ᵗʰ St, which turns into Anita St, L on
Pacific Coast Highway, R. on Torrance. From Harbor Fwy [110], exit W. on Torrance. [TG-762 H5])

       Open April through October for watercraft fun: Ocean pedal boats are $20
an hour (you can take them outside the harbor); double or single kayaks are $25
for two hours; a small glass bottom boat (which you maneuver) that seats four
adults is $45 an hour; jet skis are $75 or $85 an hour, depending on the model;
runabouts are various prices; and parasailing is $45 per person. Charter boat
rentals are also available here. See REDONDO BEACH INTERNATIONAL
BOARDWALK for adjacent activities.
       Hours: Open April through October. Call for more specific hours.
       Admission: Prices listed above. Parking at the pier is always 50¢ for each 20
                  minutes. During the summer, it's $5 maximum on weekdays; $7
                  maximum on weekends. During the rest of the year, it's $3
                  maximum on weekdays; $5 on weekends.
       Ages: 6 years and up.

BELMONT PIER
(562) 434-6781 $$$$
29 39th Place, Long Beach
(From Long Beach Fwy [710], exit E. on Broadway, R. on Redondo Ave., L. on Ocean Blvd., R. on 39th Pl. From San Diego Fwy [405], exit S. on Lakewood Blvd. [19], go E. on Pacific Coast Hwy [1] at the traffic circle, L. on Redondo, L. on Ocean, R. on 39th. [TG-825 J2])

Take a whale-watching cruise, available January through March.

Admission: During the week, fare is $15 for adults for a three-hour tour; $12 for children 12 and under. Call for weekend prices.

BEVERLY HILLS TROLLEY
(310) 285-2551 / www.ci.beverly-hills.ca.us $$
Departs from the corner of Rodeo Drive and Dayton Way, Beverly Hills
(Exit San Diego Fwy [405] E. on Santa Monica Blvd., R. on Dayton Wy. There is parking just past Rodeo Dr. on the R. [TG-632 F2])

This is the best bargain in Beverly Hills! If you're in the area and want to give your kids a taste of the posh lifestyle, at an affordable price to you, hop on board a trolley for your choice of mini-adventures. A forty-minute Sites and Scenes narrated tour shows riders some of the most famous sights in Beverly Hills, including a few celebrity homes, film locations, some of the high-priced boutiques, and the elegant hotels. The ninety-minute Art and Architecture tour points out some of the most significant art and architectural locations around town, including City Hall, galleries, Creative Artists Agency, Museum of Television and Radio, and more. Note: Parking in the structure on the corner is free for the first two hours, so after your ride, spend some time window shopping on Rodeo Drive!

Hours: The Sites tour usually runs July through Labor Day and the latter part of December, Tues. - Sat. every hour noon - 5pm. It runs May through June, and September through November on Sat. only on the hour noon - 4pm. The Art tour is offered July through New Year's on Sat. at 10:30am. All tours are canceled if it is raining.

Admission: $5 for adults per tour; $1 for children 11 and under. Tickets are available from the trolley driver on a first come, first serve basis.

Ages: 5 years and up.

BIKE TRAIL: LONG BEACH SHORELINE
Bay Shore Avenue to Shoreline Village, Long Beach   !/$
(Take San Diego Fwy [405] or San Gabriel River Fwy [605] to 22 Fwy W. Exit S. on Studebaker, R. on Westminster, which turns into 2nd St, L. on Bay Shore Ave. Or, start at the other end by exiting the Long Beach Fwy [710] E. on Shoreline Dr. and into Shoreline Village. [TG-826 B3 / 825 D2])

This 3.1 mile (one-way) easy, paved riding path follows along the Pacific Ocean. An ocean breeze and practically no hills makes it a delightful ride for the family. Stop and shop at SHORELINE VILLAGE (see the Piers and Seaports section) with its nice array of quaint-looking restaurants and stores. Also, check out other places nearby - LONG BEACH AQUARIUM OF THE PACIFIC (see the Zoos and Animals section) and QUEEN MARY and SCORPION (see the

Museums section).

> **Hours:** Open daily dawn to dusk.
> **Admission:** Free, although parking at Shoreline Village costs up to $6 maximum.
> **Ages:** 5 years and up.

BIKE TRAIL: LOS ANGELES RIVER TRAIL ☼

(323) 913-4688 or (323) 913-7390 - Griffith Park;   !
(213) 381-3570 - Friends of the L.A. River

Griffith Park, Los Angeles

(Going N. on Golden State Fwy [5] or W. on Ventura Fwy [134], exit at Zoo Dr. and follow the signs. Going E. on 134, exit S. on Victory Blvd., L. on Zoo Dr. Going S. on 5 Fwy, exit S. on Western, L. on Victory Blvd. to Zoo Dr. The bike trail extends from Victory Blvd. in Burbank to Fletcher Drive at Atwater Village. The best place to park is inside Griffith Park, near the bike trail entrance where Zoo Drive meets Riverside Dr. / Victory Blvd. [TG-564 B4])

The first five miles of this urban bikeway are not always quiet, as some of it parallels the Golden State Freeway, even though the paved bike trail is entirely off-road. Although the riverbed is up against concrete slopes, there are now trees, flocks of birds, and even a few ponds along the way, plus portions of it are lit at night. The next forty-seven miles are still in the planning and making-it-work stage, although the next three-mile stretch, heading through Elysian Valley towards downtown L.A., has already begun. Eventually, the pathway will stretch from the mountains all the way to sea along the Los Angeles River. For now, the bike path goes along GRIFFITH PARK, so enjoy a side trip into the park. (See the Great Outdoors section for more details about the park, its zoo, and its museums.)

> **Hours:** Open daily sunrise to sunset.
> **Admission:** Free
> **Ages:** 6 years and up.

BIKE TRAIL: SAN GABRIEL RIVER TRAIL ☼

Lakewood, Long Beach, Seal Beach   !

(Exit San Gabriel Fwy [605] W. on South St. (by Cerritos Mall), L. on Studebaker, turn R. into Liberty Park to park. [TG-766 F2])

This two-way, concrete river trail, a right-of-way for bicyclers and skaters, actually travels almost the whole length of the San Gabriel River (i.e. flood control waterway). It begins (or ends, depending on how you look at it) in Seal Beach at Marina Drive, just west of 1st Street, and ends (or begins) in Azusa at San Gabriel Canyon Road, north of Sierra Madre. The pathway has several access points along the way. The route sometimes follows along main streets, although it just as often veers completely away from them. Depending on where you catch the trail, it passes under bridges; goes through some scenic areas that are a delight to behold; past parks; past people's backyards; and even through sections that don't feel as safe as I'd like.

One of our favorite stretches starts at LIBERTY PARK - Cerritos (look under the Great Outdoors section) and goes all the way to SEAL BEACH (look under the Beaches section). Along the way, we often stop off at Rynerson Park, which has playgrounds and paved pathways throughout; the Long Beach Mall (just east of the Auto section along the pathway), which has restaurants, fast food places, a movie theater, Barnes and Noble, Sam's Club, and lots more stores; and EL DORADO NATURE CENTER and EL DORADO PARK (look under the Great Outdoors section). The latter park is beautiful and there is no admission fee from the bike path. Sometimes we actually make it to Seal Beach! We then ride to the ocean's edge and go along Main Street into the quaint town of Seal Beach, where there are plenty of shops and a RUBY'S restaurant (look under the Edible Adventure section) at the end of the pier. (We also cheat sometimes and invite my husband to meet us for lunch or dinner, and then have him drive us all home in the van!) Non-stop from Liberty Park to Seal Beach takes my older children and I about an hour. This section of the riverbank route is also great for birdwatching, as we've seen numerous herons, egrets, and pelicans.

  Hours: Open daily dawn to dusk.
Admission: Free
  Ages: 4 years and up.

BIKE TRAIL: SOUTH BAY

Torrance County Beach to Pacific Palisades   !

(Torrance Beach: Exit Harbor Fwy [110] W. on Pacific Coast Hwy., L. on Ave I when PCH turns north, R. on Esplanade Ave. Find an entrance to the beach and start pedaling. Pacific Palisades: Take Santa Monica Fwy [10] W. to the end and go N. on Palisades Beach Rd. [1], which turns into Pacific Coast Hwy. The north end of Will Rogers State Beach is located by the intersection of Pacific Coast Highway and Sunset Blvd. [TG-792 H1 / 630 H6])

  Life's a beach and this twenty-mile, two-lane, relatively flat concrete bike trail emphasizes that by cruising mostly right along the sandy shores of California's beaches. It passes through Venice beach, the Santa Monica Pier, and other state treasures. There are many stores and eateries (and restrooms!) to stop off at along the strand. Of course weekends, especially in the summer, are very crowded. Don't forget your sunscreen.

  Hours: Open sunrise to sunset.
Admission: Free
  Ages: 4 years and up.

CALIFORNIA AQUATICS

(562) 431-6866 - office; (562) 434-0999 - beach #   *$$$*
Bay Shore Avenue and 2nd Street, Long Beach

(Take San Diego Fwy [405] or San Gabriel River Fwy [605] to 22 Fwy W. Exit S. on Studebaker Rd., R. on Westminster, turns into 2nd. Bay Shore is just over second bridge. [TG-826 B2])

  Kayak rentals are $5 to $7 an hour, and peddle boats are $15 an hour. California Aquatics also offers weekend water field trips for the family. Another option is to sign up to become a member of the Snorkeling By Kayak Club. The $35 membership fee is good for four years, entitling the card bearer and family members (best suited for junior high schoolers and up) to rent kayaks, peddle boats, wetsuits, and skindiving equipment for only $10 per day! There is another Aquatics location on Appian Way, by Mother's Beach.

  Hours: Open weekends only in the winter. Call for all hours.
  Ages: 5 years and up.

GONDOLA AMORE

(310) 376-6977 / www.gondolaamore.com   *$$$$$*

260 Portofino Way, at the Portofino Hotel and Yacht Club, Redondo Beach

(From San Diego Fwy [405], exit S. on Western, R. on 190th St., which turns into Anita St., L. on Pacific Coast Hwy. From Harbor Fwy [110], exit W. on Torrance, R. on Pacific Coast Hwy. From P.C.H., turn W. on Beryl, which turns into Portofino Way. Your gondolier will meet you in the lobby. [TG-762 H4])

O solo mio! This one-hour gondola cruise is a unique way to see the Redondo harbor and shoreline. During the day you'll also see Catalina Island (on a clear day), sailboats, waterfowl, and maybe a few seals. Nighttime rides bring about their own magic (and romance). The two gondolas, operated by the owner and by lifeguards, seat up to four people, have canopies for privacy, and small twinkling lights around the boat and canopies. Amore provides blankets, as the ocean air can get chilly even on a summer night, cups for your drinks, fresh fruit, and bread and cheese. Your list of things to bring includes jackets, a music cassette, beverages, and your camera. Tips: Before or after your cruise, check out the nearby Cheesecake Factory for scrumptious food and/or walk around the pier. (Look up REDONDO BEACH INTERNATIONAL BOARDWALK under the Piers and Seaports section.)

Hours: Open daily noon - 9pm. Reservations are required. Note: Holiday seasons book quickly.

Admission: $75 for two people; $10 for each additional person. Note: AAA members receive a substantial discount.

Ages: 4 years and up.

GONDOLA GETAWAY

(562) 433-9595 / www.gondolagetawayinc.com   *$$$$$*

5437 E. Ocean Boulevard, Long Beach

(Exit San Diego Fwy [405] S. on Cherry Ave., L. on Ocean Blvd. [TG-762 H4])

Long Beach, California is transformed into Venice, Italy when you take your child on a gondola ride. I know this attraction is thought of as a romantic excursion, and it is. It is also a wonderful treat for your child. Step into a Venetian gondola and for one hour, gently slip in and out through the waterways and canals of Naples. Your gondolier will serenade you with Italian music, regale you with interesting tales, or quietly leave you alone. After our kids plied my husband and I with questions about the possibility of sharks and whales, they settled down to enjoy the ride and look at the incredible homes along the waterfront. Christmas time is particularly spectacular, as many of the houses are decked out with lights, animated figures, etc. Make reservations for this time period far in advance.

Bread, cheese, salami, and a bucket of ice are provided, as is a blanket for the colder nights. Bring your own liquid refreshment. Your child will now be dreaming of visiting a tiny little town far away in a boot-shaped country. Ciao!

Hours: Open daily for cruises 11am - 11pm. Suggested reservations are two weeks in advance.

Admission: Gondolas carry two to six people - $55 for the first two passengers; $10 for each additional person. The Carolina carries eight to fourteen people - $17 per person. Fleet cruises carries twenty to fifty-six people - $15 per person.

Ages: 4 years and up.

HORNBLOWER (Marina Del Rey)

(310) 301-6000 / www.hornblower.com

13755 Fiji Way, Marina Del Rey

(Take Marina Fwy [90] to the end where it turns into the Marina Exwy, L. on Mindanao Wy., L. on Lincoln, R. on Fiji Wy. [TG-702 B1])

See HORNBLOWER (San Diego) for details.

LONG BEACH MARINE INSTITUTE

(714) 540-5751 / www.longbeachmarineinst.com

5857 Appian Way, Long Beach

(Take San Diego Fwy [405] or San Gabriel River Fwy [605] to 22 Fwy W. Exit S. on Studebaker, R. on Westminster, which turns into 2ⁿᵈ St., R. on Appian Way, near the bridge, first L. in the Marina lot parking, on the Sea Explorer Base. [TG-826 D2])

"The Long Beach Marine Institute, formerly the Newport Institute of Oceanography, is an association of researchers and educators dedicated to bringing marine field research into the classroom and the classroom into the field." (A quote from the institute's brochure.) L.B.M.I. offers a myriad of different programs to encourage hands-on learning about marine life and their habitats. Most programs are offered for groups of twenty-five or more. If your group number is smaller, the L.B.M.I. workers will hook you up with another group. Besides going on the guided kayak tours, snorkeling excursions, and guided tidepool tours, being on board the *Conqueror* is a main attraction. This ninety-foot, ship-shape vessel is the host and means of transportation for several field trips.

The three-hour Sea Creature Trawl is a popular expedition. After a slide presentation and boat orientation, set sail for adventure. Organisms from the sea floor are gathered (by use of a trawl) on board to be inspected and sorted through. Kids love being able to put their hands in this fascinating pile of gunk to find "treasures." They can also examine their findings under a microscope. Combine the Sea Creature Trawl with the Marine Mammal Safari (more than just a whale-watching cruise) for only a few dollars more. Another special outing combines a sleep-over on the boat with the Sea Creature Trawl, and a morning kayak trip in the back bay. Life doesn't get any better than this!

Hours: Call for times for various excursions.

Admission: Prices range from $5 per person for a tidepool tour to $15 for a Sea Creature Trawl to $73 for the sleep over, and so on.

Ages: 4 years and up, depending on the activity.

LONG BEACH SPORT FISHING

(562) 432-8993

555 Pico Avenue, Long Beach

(Exit Long Beach Fwy [710] W. on Anaheim, L. on Santa Fe Ave., L. on 9ᵗʰ St., which turns into Pico. [TG-825 C2])

Fishing and whale-watching cruises (January through March) are offered here.

Admission: $13 for adults for the two-and-a-half hour whale-watching cruise; $10 for children 12 and under.

Ages: 4 years and up.

LOS ANGELES SIGHTSEEING CRUISES　　　☀

(310) 831-0996 / www.lasightseeingcruises.com　　　　　　　*$$$*
Berth 78, Ports O' Call Village, San Pedro
(Exit Harbor Fwy [110] S. on Harbor Blvd. and follow the signs. [TG-824 D6])

Enjoy a one-hour cruise of the inner and outer harbor, past supertankers, cruise ships, a Coast Guard station, Terminal Island, a Federal Prison, and Angels Gate Lighthouse. Two-hour coastline cruises along the Palos Verdes Peninsula, and whale-watching cruises are also available. Two-and-a-half hours cruises go all the way to Long Beach, past the Queen Mary and Scorpion, under bridges and through canals.

Hours: One-hour cruises depart from the Village Boat House on the hour, Mon. - Fri., noon - 4pm; Sat. - Sun. and holidays, noon - 5pm. Two-hour cruises (and longer) depart on the weekends at 11:30am, 1:30pm, and 3:30pm. Closed Thanksgiving and Christmas.

Admission: One-hour cruises are $8 for adults; $4 for ages 6 - 12; children 5 and under are free. Two-hour cruises are $12 for adults; $6 for ages 6 - 12. Two-and-a-half hour cruises are $15 for adults; $8 for ages 6 - 12.

Ages: 4 years and up.

MARINA BOAT RENTALS　　　☀

(310) 574-2822 / www.boats4rent.com　　　　　　　*$$$$*
13719 Fiji Way, Marina del Rey
(Take Marina Fwy [90] to the end where it turns into the Marina Exwy, L. on Mindanao Wy., L. on Lincoln, R. on Fiji Wy. [TG-702 B1])

Located in FISHERMAN'S VILLAGE (see the Piers and Seaports section), Marina Boat Rentals includes kayaks - $10 per hour for a single, $16 an hour for a double; sailboats - $35 an hour for a fourteen footer; motor boats - $40 an hour for a six-passenger boat that doesn't leave the harbor, and $75 an hour for a six-passenger boat that does; and electric boats - $60 an hour.

Hours: Open in the summer daily 9am - 9pm. Open the rest of the year daily 10am - 5pm or so, depending on the weather.

Admission: Prices listed above.

Ages: 4 years and up.

METRO RAIL　　　☀

(213) 626-4455 / www.mta.net　　　　　　　*$*
Los Angeles

This rail mode of transportation is a work-in-progress, but the rail lines that are complete make going to a destination an adventure. The Blue Line runs north and south between Long Beach and downtown Los Angeles. Trains run every ten minutes. The Green Line runs east and west, connecting Norwalk, so far, to El Segundo and Redondo Beach. Trains run alongside, but separate from, the 105 freeway. The Red Line runs two lines from Union Station in downtown Los Angeles; one to Wilshire Boulevard and one to North Hollywood. The advantages of riding the rails are numerous, such as it's inexpensive, you don't have to fight traffic, you don't have to try to find a parking spot, and kids consider it a treat. Pick up a map of the route at Union Station or ask for a copy to be mailed directly to you.

Hours: Trains usually run daily 6am - 11pm.
Admission: $1.35 for adults, plus 25¢ for a transfer; children 4 and under are free.
Ages: All

REDONDO BEACH PIER BOAT CRUISES ☼

(310) 374-3481 - marina / www.redondo.org   *$$$*

Where Torrance Boulevard meets the sea at Redondo Beach Pier, Redondo Beach

(From San Diego Fwy [405], exit S. on Western, R. on 190th St., which turns into Anita St., L on Pacific Coast Highway, R. on Torrance. From Harbor Fwy [110], exit W. on Torrance. [TG-762 H5])

The Ocean Racer is a high-speed racer that seats about 140 people. Half-hour rides are $10 for adults; $5 for ages 11 and under; $1 for infants. The Voyager is a double deck wooden boat ideal for those who like viewing the ocean at a slower pace. Be on the lookout for the colony of sea lions that usually hangs around. Half-hour Voyager rides are $5 for adults; $3 for ages 5 and under. See REDONDO BEACH INTERNATIONAL BOARDWALK for adjacent activities.

Hours: Open weekends and holidays only.
Admission: Prices are listed above. Parking at the pier is always 50¢ for each 20 minutes. During the summer, it's $5 maximum on weekdays; $7 maximum on weekends. During the rest of the year, it's $3 maximum on weekdays; $5 on weekends.
Ages: All

SHORELINE VILLAGE CRUISES / SPIRIT CRUISES ☼

(562) 495-5884 / www.spiritmarine.com   *$$*

401 E. Shoreline Drive, Long Beach

(Take Long Beach Fwy [710] to the end, E. on Shoreline Dr. [TG-825 E1])

Enjoy a forty-five-minute cruise through Queen's Way Bay, past the QUEEN MARY, SCORPION, and LONG BEACH AQUARIUM. Whale-watching cruises are also available the end of December through March.

Hours: Summertime departures are daily at 1pm, 2pm, 3pm, and 4pm. Wintertime departures are usually weekends only.

Admission:	$7 for adults for the harbor cruise; $3 for children 12 and under. $15 for adults for the two-and-a-half whale-watching cruise; $8 for children.
Ages:	4 years and up.

SPIRIT CRUISES (Ports O' Call)

(310) 548-8080 / www.spiritmarine.com

$$

Berth 77, Ports O' Call Village, San Pedro

(Exit Harbor Fwy [110] S. on Harbor Blvd. and follow the signs. [TG-824 D6])

Cruise through the main channels and see the sights! Reservations are suggested.

Hours:	Forty-five-minute cruises are offered on Sat. and Sun. One-and-a-half-hour cruises are offered daily May through October; weekends only the rest of the year.
Admission:	$7 for adults for the shorter cruise; $3 for children 12 and under; $12 for adults for the longer cruise; $6 for children.
Ages:	5 years and up.

YOUNG EAGLES PROGRAM (Lancaster)

(661) 940-1709 or (661) 258-3674 / www.youngeagles.com

!

4555 W. Avenue G, Fox Field, Lancaster

(Exit Antelope Valley Fwy [14] W. on Ave. G and drive for about 3 miles. This program alternately uses the Cal City airport in Mojave and Rosamond airport. [TG-3924 H7])

See YOUNG EAGLES PROGRAM (Pacoima) under this section for details. Reservations are needed. Note: The Young Eagles Program is scheduled to end December, 2003.

Hours:	Usually offered on the second Sat. of the month, starting at 8am.
Admission:	Free
Ages:	8 - 17 years.

YOUNG EAGLES PROGRAM (Pacoima)

(818) 725-4AIR (4247) - Pacoima; (800) 843-3612 - national number /

!

www.youngeagles.com

12653 Osborne Street, Whiteman Airport, Pacoima

(Exit the Golden State Fwy [5] N.E. on Osborne, past San Fernando Rd., turn L. [TG-502 E4])

"They will soar on wings like eagles." (Isaiah 40:31) I think all kids (and adults) dream of flying, and the Young Eagles Program helps those dreams become a reality. Young Eagles is a national program sponsored by the E.A.A. (Experimental Aircraft Association), who desire to introduce children to the joy of aviation. There are several Young Eagle chapters throughout Southern California who offer aviation camps, educational programs, and more, as well as an opportunity to actually fly (for free!) in a two or four-seater airplane. Kids, between the ages of 8 and 17 years, are invited to participate, one time only, in this unique flying experience. Please remember that everyone here is volunteering their time, including pilots, so be patient with a process that might take a few hours. Although the following information is fairly standard, call the particular program you're interested in for specific dates, times, and other details. Reservations are highly suggested, and necessary at some of the airports. A signed consent form by a parent or legal guardian is required for each child.

At the airport, after your child registers, he/she will (in no particular order): • Participate in a pre-flight inspection training, which means looking over an airplane to make sure it's mechanically sound while learning some technical aspects of how to fly a plane. • Fly! The flight is usually twenty minutes round trip. What a thrill! If it becomes too thrilling for your child, airsick bags are provided. The planes are either two-seaters or four-seaters. • Take a tour of the control tower if available. Kids will need to keep their voices low so they don't disturb the tower operators. Two more wonderful freebies are a certificate upon completion of the flight, and a magazine called *Sport Aviation for Kids* that comes later in the mail. Plan on bringing something to munch on as many airports have picnic tables available. Kids who are grounded will enjoy watching the planes take off and land. Blue skies and tail winds to you!

At the Pacoima airport, kids will fly over Magic Mountain, which makes their flight extra special. Note: The Young Eagles Program is scheduled to end December, 2003.

Hours: One Sat. a month, starting at 10:30am. Call for specific dates.
Admission: Free
Ages: 8 - 17 years old.

YOUNG EAGLES PROGRAM (Santa Monica)   ☼

(310) 390-8000 - program; (310) 458-8591 - airport /   !
www.youngeagles.com
3200 Airport Avenue, Santa Monica Airport, Santa Monica   ⏛
(Exit Santa Monica Fwy [10] S. on Bundy Dr., R. on Airport Ave. [TG-672 A2])

See YOUNG EAGLES PROGRAM (Pacoima) under this section for details. This airport features the program three or four times a year on selected Saturdays. When kids have flown with the eagles, so to speak, they can get into the nearby MUSEUM OF FLYING (look under the Museums section) for free! Ask about this chapter's other Young Eagle events and educational programs. Note: The Young Eagles Program is scheduled to end December, 2003.

Hours: Three or four selected Sat. throughout the year.
Admission: Free
Ages: 8 - 17 years.

YOUNG EAGLES PROGRAM (South Bay)   ☼

(310) 374-4812 / www.youngeagles.com   !
Compton Airport, Long Beach Airport, and Torrance Airport   ⏛

See YOUNG EAGLES PROGRAM (Pacoima) under this section for details. Most pilots at this program try to let the kids have a turn at the controls, for just a short period of time. They fly out of the above airports when they have a group of thirty, or so, young pilot "wannabes." Note: The Young Eagles Program is scheduled to end December, 2003.

Hours: Offered about seven times a year on selected Sat., starting at
          noon.
Admission: Free

Ages:　8 - 17 years.

ADVENTURES AT SEA YACHT CHARTERS

(800) 229-2412 / www.gondola.com　　　　　　　　　　*$$$$$*

3101 W. Coast Highway, Suite 209, Newport Beach

(Take Costa Mesa Fwy [55] S. to end where it turns into Newport Blvd. After about 2 miles take right lane which exits to Coast Hwy [1]. Don't go over the bridge, but turn L. on W. Coast Hwy. Adventures at Sea is about 250 yards down on the right. [TG-672 A2])

These luxurious, electric gondolas are made out of mahogany, have leather seats, a canopy, and are operated by gondoliers either dressed in a tuxedo (depending on the occasion), or in the traditional, Venetian outfit. Take a peaceful cruise along the waterways of Newport Beach Harbor and Newport isle to view the boats and waterfront homes. The gondoliers will begin your cruise from the harbor office, or pick you up at one of several harbor-side restaurants. Adventures at Sea provides a chilled bottle of Martinellis and Godiva chocolates, or it can provide a complete dinner served on china. This is definitely an upscale adventure!

Hours:　Open daily, call for reservations.
Admission:　$125 for two people, $10 each additional person.
Ages:　4 years and up.

AIR COMBAT USA, INC.

(800) 522-7590 / www.aircombat.com　　　　　　　　　　*$$$$$*

230 N. Dale Place, Fullerton

(Exit Artesia Fwy [91] or N. Santa Ana Fwy [5] N. on Magnolia, L. on Commonwealth, R. on Dale St., veer right for Dale Pl. Or, exit S. on the Santa Ana Fwy [5], E. on Artesia, R. on Dale Pl. (just after Dale St.). It's at Beach/Aviation, on the N. side of airport. [TG-738 A7])

If being a Top Gun is your top dream, here's the opportunity to make it a reality. You, perhaps being an unlicenced pilot and leading an otherwise normal life, will actually fly and fight air-to-air combat. "The SIAI Marchetti SF260 is a current production, Italian-built, fighter aircraft. It has 260 horsepower, can fly at 270 MPH, FAA certified to +6 to -3 G's and can perform unlimited aerobatics. It was originally designed to transition student pilots to jet fighters. It is maneuvered by the stick grip complete with gun trigger, identical to the F4 Phantom. The pilot and guest pilot sit side-by-side with dual controls." (Excerpted from Air Combat's brochure.) If all this has your adrenaline pumping, go for it!

You'll be prepped for your flight in a one-hour ground school, which covers the basics, with emphasis on tactical maneuvers. After being fitted with a flight suit, helmet, and parachute, you'll soar for one hour with the birds over Catalina waters. You're actually in control of the aircraft 90% of the time, while receiving constant instruction on how to get the "enemy." After practicing maneuvers, you'll engage in six "g-pulling" (i.e. gut wrenching) dogfights against a real opponent (e.g. friend, spouse, etc.) A direct hit registers through an electronic tracking system, complete with sound effects and smoke trailing from the other aircraft. This is as close to the real thing as you can possible get without being in the military. I will confess that after a few high/low yo-yos and roll overs, I used that special white bag and became part of the 10% that share in this ritual.

After you've landed, and come down from your high, you can view the videos, complete with sound, that were simultaneously recorded from each aircraft. Relive your flight and your "hits" again and again on the copy you receive to take home. This is an unforgettable experience!

Hours: Four classes/flights that accommodate two people each, are offered every day. Class times are 7am, 9:30am, noon, and 2:30pm.

Admission: $895 a flight. Ask about specials, such as discounts for two people, or ready/alert, which means you'll be called to come over A.S.A.P. if there is a cancellation.

Ages: 8 years old and up - large enough to wear a parachute and in good health.

BALBOA BOAT RENTALS

(949) 673-7200 *$$$*

510 E. Edgewater, Newport Beach

(Take Costa Mesa Fwy [55] to the end, which turns into Newport Blvd., which turns into Balboa Blvd., L. on Island Ave, R. on Edgewater. [TG-919 B1])

Kayaks and eight-seater electric boat rentals are offered here.

Admission: $10 an hour for a single kayak; $15 an hour for a double. Boats that seat up to 8 passengers are $45 an hour; up to 12, $55 an hour.

Ages: 4 years and up.

BIKE TRAIL: SANTA ANA RIVER

7600 E. La Palma Avenue in Yorba Regional Park, Anaheim to Pacific !
Coast Highway, Suset County Beach, Huntington Beach

(Anaheim: Exit Riverside Fwy [91] N. on Imperial Hwy, R. on La Palma. Huntington Beach: Exit San Diego Fwy [405], S.E. on Warner, go to the end and turn R. on PCH. [TG-740 G7 - 826 J7])

The twenty-three mile, mostly easy-riding trail extends from beautiful Yorba Linda Regional Park to a premiere beach, Huntington Beach. Starting at the park, the first few miles are park-scenic, then meander through an adjacent wilderness area with shade trees and flocks of birds. A good stopping point (and maybe turning around area?) is the ten-mile mark, just before the Arrowhead Pond, where a pocket park has the necessary amenities. (Bring your own snacks, though.) Hearty bikers - bike on!

Hours: Open daily sunrise to sunset.

Admission: Free

Ages: 5 years and up.

DAVEY'S LOCKER

(949) 673-1434 / www.daveyslocker.com *$$$*

400 Main Street, Newport Beach

(Take Costa Mesa Fwy [55] to the end, which turns into Newport Blvd., which turns into Balboa Blvd., L. on Main St. [TG-919 C2])

Skiff rentals, fishing, and whale-watching cruises (January through March)

are offered here.
  Admission: $45 for a half day for skiffs. $15 for adults for the two-and-a-half
              whale-watching cruise; $9 for ages 4 - 12.
  Ages: 4 years and up.

FUN ZONE BOAT COMPANY   ☼
(949) 673-0240 / www.funzoneboats.com   *$$*
600 E. Edgewater Avenue, Newport Beach
(Take Costa Mesa Fwy [55] to the end, which turns into Newport Blvd., which turns into Balboa
Blvd., L. on Island Ave, R. on Edgewater. [TG-919 B1])

    Board the Pavilion Queen or Pavilion Belle for a forty-five-minute cruise
that is perfect for kids as they'll go around Balboa Island and, hopefully, see
some sea lions. On the other forty-five minute cruise see several star's homes
and hear the history of Balboa Island Peninsula. The ninety-minute cruise is a
combination of both cruises - the best of both worlds. One-hour sunset cruises
and whale watching cruises (December through March) are also available.
  Hours: Daily departures for the forty-five-minute cruises are at 11am,
            1pm, and 3pm. Daily departures for the ninety-minute cruise are
            on the hour between 11am - 6pm in the summer, 11am - 3pm the
            rest of the year.
  Admission: $6 for adults for the forty-five-minute cruise; $2 for ages 5 - 11;
            children 4 and under are free. $8 for adults for the ninety-minute
            cruise; $2 for ages 5 - 11; children 4 and under are free. Sunset
            cruises are $7 for adults; $2 for kids. Whale-watching cruises are
            $14 for adults; $8 for kids. Closed December 24 - 25.
  Ages: 4 years and up.

HORNBLOWER (Newport Beach)
(949) 646-0155 / www.hornblower.com
2431 W. Coast Highway, Newport Beach
(Take Costa Mesa Fwy [55] to end, where it turns into Newport Blvd., L. on E. 17th St, R., at end,
on Dover Dr., R on W. Coast Hwy. [TG-889 A7])

    See HORNBLOWER (San Diego) for details.

NEWPORT HARBOR TOUR, BALBOA PAVILION   ☼
(949) 673-5245 / www.funzoneboats.com   *$$*
400 Main Street, Newport Beach
(Take Costa Mesa Fwy [55] to the end, which turns into Newport Blvd., which turns into Balboa
Blvd., L. on Main St. [TG-919 C2])

    Forty-five and ninety-minute cruises are available here. Depending on the
length of your cruise, you'll see stars' homes such as George Burns and John
Wayne; Pirate's Cove, where Gilligan's Island was filmed; and tour around six
of the eight islands in the immediate area.
  Hours: Daily departures are 11am - 7pm in the summer; 11am - 4pm the
            rest of the year. Closed Christmas.

Admission: $6 for adults for the forty-five-minute cruise; $4 for seniors; $1 for ages 5 - 12; children 4 and under are free. $8 for adults for the ninety-minute cruise; $4 for seniors; $1 for ages 5 - 12; children 4 and under are free. Certain discounts available through AAA.

Ages: 4 years and up.

NEWPORT LANDING SPORTFISHING

(949) 675-0550

309 Palm, Suite F, Newport Beach

(Take Costa Mesa Fwy [55] to the end, which turns into Newport Blvd., which turns into Balboa Blvd., L. on Palm. [TG-919 B2])

Whale-watching cruises January through mid-April are available here.

Hours: Call for hours.

Admission: $14 for adults for the two-and-a-half hour cruise; $10 for seniors and children 12 and under.

Ages: 4 years and up.

OCEAN INSTITUTE

(949) 496-2274 / www.ocean-institute.org

24200 Dana Point Harbor Drive, Dana Point

See OCEAN INSTITUTE in the Museums section for details about boat outings.

PADDLEPOWER

(949) 675-1215 / www.paddlepowerkayaks.com

500 W. Balboa Boulevard, Newport Beach

(Take Costa Mesa Fwy [55] to the end, which turns into Newport Blvd., which turns into Balboa Blvd. [TG-919 B2])

Kayak rentals are available here.

Admission: Prices start at $10 an hour for a single, $14 an hour for a double.

Ages: 6 years and up.

RESORT WATERSPORTS

(800) 585-0747 or (949) 729-1150

1131 Backbay Drive, Newport Dunes Resort, Newport Beach

(Take Newport Fwy [55] S.W. to end, which turns into Newport Blvd., L. on W. Coast Hwy., L. on Jamboree Rd., L. on Backbay Dr. Or, from Corona Del Mar Fwy [73], exit S.W. on Jamboree Rd., R. on Backbay Dr. before E. Coast Hwy. [TG-889 D6])

Located in NEWPORT DUNES RESORT (look under the Beaches section), this rental facility has everything you need to make your day at the beach more exciting. Going rates are: $15 an hour for pedal boats, $45 for electric-powered boats, $18 an hour for windsurfers, $17 an hour for sail boats, $13 an hour for single kayaks, and $16 an hour for double kayaks. Bike rentals, skate rentals, and California chariots (a cross between a skateboard and scooter) start at $6 an hour. They also offer guided kayak tours of an adjacent wildlife estuary reserve every Sunday at 10am, weather permitting. In the estuary, you can see crabs, blue herons, snowy egrets, and other birds and animals in their natural habitat. We took this tour and learned why this reserve is becoming endangered, as well as some of the clean up projects that we can get involved with. A two-hour tour is $20 per person; $15 for ages 12 years and under. What a work-out for those of us not physically fit! But it is also a fun and educational way to spend some family time together.

Hours: Open daily in the summer from 9am - 8pm. Open year round on the weekends, usually from 10am - 5pm. Call for other hours of operation.

Admission: Prices are stated above, plus a $7 per vehicle entrance fee.

Ages: 6 years and up.

THE CARRIAGE HOUSE
(909) 781-0780   *$$$$*
Mission Inn District, Riverside

Take a ride in a beautiful horse-drawn carriage through the historic Mission Inn district. The carriage holds four adults comfortably or two adults, three kids. With horses named Cinderella and Belle, children feel like they are living out a storybook fantasy, if only for a short ride.

Tea parties are a perfect occasion to incorporate a carriage ride. Or, rent the wagon, which seats up to sixteen people, for a cowboy party. At Christmas time, even though there isn't any snow to glisten, the carriage sleigh bells ring if you're listenin', plus Christmas lights are even more dazzling when seen from this old-fashioned vantage point. Note: Take a ride around the block with Santa Claus for only $3 per person at Christmas time, weather permitting.

Hours: Carriages can often be found along the Mission Inn district, but calling for a reservation is your best bet.

Admission: A twenty-minute ride is $35, inclusive, for everyone in the entire carriage; an hour ride is $70.

Ages: All

CARRIAGES BY MARGARET
(909) 789-1620   *$$$$*
Riverside

What Cinderella or Prince Charming child hasn't dreamed of riding in a horse-drawn carriage, if only because of fairy tales? Take a ride in an immaculate white or black carriage pulled by a beautiful silky horse that is gentle enough to pet. The carriages seat up to six people, four adults comfortably. If you have a party, reserve a formal, horse-drawn trolley, or reserve a hay wagon. Choose your own route for a ride or call to use the carriage for special events

Hours: Call to make a reservation.

Admission: Prices vary, depending on the length of the ride and the destination.

Ages: All

ORANGE EMPIRE RAILWAY MUSEUM

(909) 657-2605 / www.oerm.mus.ca.us   *!/$$$*

2201 S. 'A' Street, Perris

(Exit Escondido Fwy [215] W. on 4th St. A more direct route than following the signs is to turn L. on 'A' St, then go down a few miles until you reach the museum on the L. [TG-807 G6])

If you love trains, make tracks to the Orange Empire Railway Museum where you can really go full steam ahead! This 65-acre, unique, outdoor museum is best described as a work-in-progress. Railcars from all over the country, in various states of disrepair, find their way here. Some are being restored while others are just stationed here. Walk around to see which railcars the volunteers are working on.

The museum is open daily, but weekends are the prime time to visit as this is the only time when train and trolley rides are available. Purchase an all-day ride ticket, which is good for rides on a locomotive, electric trolley, streetcar, freight car, and/or passenger car. (Three types of cars are usually running.) Each ride lasts about fifteen minutes and a conductor explains the history of the vehicles and the museum, and the impact of train transportation in Southern California. The train's whistle, the clickety-clack of its wheels, and the clanging of streetcar bells add excitement to your adventure.

Walk through the several car houses (i.e. buildings that house railcars) to see historic Yellow Cars (which my kids thought looked like school buses); a San Francisco cable car; electric railway streetcars and locomotives dating from 1900; steam engines; and wood passenger cars. The car houses are usually open on weekends. They are open during the week whenever volunteer staff is available.

Check out the Middleton Collection that includes old toy and scale model railroad cars, and others. There is an ongoing video that shows how tracks are laid. We got derailed at the gift shop, which offers videos, books, and all sorts of train paraphernalia. There are also a few picnic tables and grassy areas on site.

Hours: The grounds are open daily 9am - 5pm. Train and trolley rides are available only on weekends and major holidays 9am - 5pm. Closed Thanksgiving and Christmas.

Admission: The museum is free. All-day ride passes are $7 for adults; $5 for ages 5 - 11; children 4 and under ride free.

Ages: All

YOUNG EAGLES PROGRAM (Riverside)

(909) 683-2309 / www.youngeagles.com   *!*

4130 Mennes Street at Flabob Airport, Riverside

(Exit Pomona Fwy [60] S. on Rubidoux (not the Valleyview/Rubidoux exit), go to the end, turn L. and a quick R. through the airport gates. [TG-685 C3])

See YOUNG EAGLES PROGRAM (Pacoima) in this section for a complete description. This particular airport also features a twenty-five minute video on aviation starring Cliff Robertson, plus hot dogs and soft drinks for $1 each, t-shirts for $10, and perhaps a chance at the controls while in the air. If time permits, adults may get an opportunity to fly for a $15 donation. Call to make reservations. Note: The Young Eagles Program is scheduled to end

December, 2003.
> **Hours:**   The second Sat. of the month, except August and December,
>   starting at 8am.
> **Admission:** Free
> **Ages:**   8 - 17 years old.

CALIFORNIA SPEEDWAY   ☼

(800) 944-RACE (7223) / www.californiaspeedway.com   *$$$$$*
9300 N. Cherry Avenue, Fontana
(Exit San Bernardino Fwy [10] N. on Cherry Ave. [TG-604 C4])

   The best in NASCAR racing roars to life in Southern California! Located on
over 525 acres, this state-of-the-art speedway features a two-mile, D-shaped oval
super speedway with a 1.3 mile infield road course. The track can accommodate
three to four cars side by side. (Racers clock average speeds of up to 180mph!)
The two major race weekends occur in April for the NASCAR / Winston Cup
series and October/November, for the CART Series. The stadium seats allow
great views of the races. Gigantic screens and hundreds of smaller monitors
show the action to spectators, too. Thirteen huge message boards, an incredible
speaker system, a car-themed children's play area, sometimes live entertainment,
and "real" food (including lobster), as well as standby's of hot dogs and
hamburgers, all aid in making this a very fan-friendly speedway.
> **Hours:**   Major races occur in April and October/November. Call for a
>   race schedule.
> **Admission:** Fri. practices are $10; Sat. assigned seating is $35 - $45 (AAA
>   members are given certain discounts); Sun. assigned seating is
> $39 - $105. Pay an additional $45, in addition to a grandstand
>   pass, for a pit pass (only for those 18 and older).
> **Ages:**   5 years and up.

YOUNG EAGLES PROGRAM (Chino)   ☼

(714) 758-7035 / www.youngeagles.com   !
Merrill Avenue, Chino Airport, Chino   ♨
(From Riverside Fwy [91], exit N. on the 71, N. on Euclid [83]. Exit Hwy 83 R. on Merrill, R. on
Airport Way. From Pomona Fwy [60], exit S. on Euclid [83], L. on Merrill, R. on Airport. It is near
hanger #3, by the Fighter Jets Museum part of the Air Museum. [TG-682 D5])

   See YOUNG EAGLES PROGRAM (Pacoima) under this section for
details. This program allows kids the opportunity to control the aircraft - for a
short period of time! Each young pilot gets a Polaroid picture taken of
himself/herself, too. The program gives boy scouts half of what they need for
their aviation merit badge. Since you are here, check out the adjacent AIR
MUSEUM "PLANES OF FAME" museum. (Look under the Museums section
for details.) Note: The Young Eagles Program is scheduled to end December,
2003.
> **Hours:**   Offered four times a year on selected Sat., starting at 10am.
> **Admission:** Free
> **Ages:**   8 - 17 years.

YOUNG EAGLES PROGRAM (Redlands)

(909) 798-3933 / www.youngeagles.com

1745 Sessums Drive, Redlands Airport, Redlands

(Going E. on San Bernardino Fwy [10], exit N. on University Ave., R. on Colton Ave., L. on Wabash Ave. Going W. on 10, exit N. on Wabash. Wabash dead-ends into the airport. [TG-608 G3])

   See YOUNG EAGLES PROGRAM (Pacoima) under this section for details. Reservations are needed. Note: The Young Eagles Program is scheduled to end December, 2003.

  Hours: Offered four or five times a year on selected Sat., starting at 9am.

Admission: Free

  Ages: 8 - 17 years.

YOUNG EAGLES PROGRAM (Upland)

(909) 982-8048 / www.youngeagles.com

1749 W. 13th Street, Cable Airport, Upland

(Exit San Bernardino Fwy [10] N. on Central, R. on Foothill, L. on Benson, L. on 13th into the airport. [TG-601 H1])

   See YOUNG EAGLES PROGRAM (Pacoima) in this section for details. At this location, a forty-minute video is viewed that shows the history and goals of E.A.A. (Experimental Aircraft Association). Reservations are required for this program; please call at least a week ahead of time. Note: The Young Eagles Program is scheduled to end December, 2003.

  Hours: Offered on the Sat. following the second Fri. of each month, except January and December. Be here by 8am.

Admission: Free

  Ages: 8 - 17 years.

BIPLANE AND AIR COMBAT ADVENTURES

(800) 759-5667 / www.barnstorming.com   *$$$$$*

2198 Palomar Airport Road, McClellan Palomar Airport, Carlsbad

(Exit San Diego Fwy [5] E. on Palomar Airport Rd. [TG-1127 D3])

   Flying in a restored open-cockpit biplane, wearing helmet, goggles, and a pilot scarf reminds me of another flying ace, Snoopy, and his adventures with the Red Baron. (Yes, I do know that Snoopy isn't real.) You'll fly over the stunning San Diego coastline for twenty minutes, side-by-side with another passenger (this could be your child!), while the pilot sits behind you. It's like riding a motorcycle in the sky!

   Another adventure offered here is Air Combat. After a crash course, so to speak, on general aviation and specifically, tactical maneuvers during combat, you'll suit up and take off for the wild blue yonder. When you've gotten a feel for the controls, get ready for combat with a real "enemy." You'll fly for over thirty minutes, experiencing high/low yo-yos (where the plane dips abruptly downward and zooms upward and your stomach heads in the opposite direction), and other maneuvers in a dogfight - let the fur fly! This exhilarating experience is one that you'll remember and talk about for the rest of your life.

  Hours: Call to schedule a flight.

Admission: Biplane Adventures start at $49 for one person, although two people are required for twenty minutes of flight time. Air Combat starts at $249 per person, or $199 if you B.Y.O.E. (Bring Your Own Enemy). Ask about current specials. Reservations are highly recommended.

Ages: 6 years and up.

CAJON SPEEDWAY

(619) 448-8900 / www.cajonspeedway.com $$$

1888 Wing Avenue, El Cajon

(Exit San Vicente Fwy W. on Bradley, R. on Wing. It's adjacent to Gillespie Field [airport]. [TG-1251 F2])

NASCAR Winston Racing Series, Coors Light Series, and stock cars - if these terms make your heart race just a little faster, you'll enjoy the races at the speedway.

Hours: The season runs mid-March through mid-October.

Admission: $10 - $12 per adults; $5 for ages 6 - 12; children 5 and under are free.

Ages: 5 years and up.

CINDERELLA'S CARRIAGE

(619) 239-8080 / www.cinderella-carriage.com $$$$$

In front of the Harbor House Restaurant at Seaport Village, or in front of Crowces Restaurant at 5ᵗʰ Avenue and 'F' Street in the Gaslamp Quarter, San Diego

(Seaport Village: Going S. on San Diego Fwy [5], exit S. on Front St, R. on Broadway, L. on Kettner. Going N. on the 5, exit S. on 6ᵗʰ Ave. R. on Broadway, L. on Kettner. Gaslamp Quarter: Going S. on San Diego Fwy [5], exit W. on Ash St., L. on 6ᵗʰ Ave., R. on 'F' St. Going N. on 5, exit S. on 6ᵗʰ Ave., R. on 'F' St. [TG-1288 J4 / 1289 A3])

The largest carriage company on the coast still makes every ride feel special and intimate. Enjoy the waterfront from a different vantage as you take a carriage around Seaport Village, or explore the historic and romantic Gaslamp Quarter. The one-horse powered carriages are pulled by a large draft horse (e.g. a Clydesdale or a Belgium horse). Kids (and adults) get a thrill out of clip-clopping along the streets of downtown San Diego. And don't worry, your Cinderella's carriage won't turn into a pumpkin before your ride is over.

Hours: Carriages are available at Seaport Village daily noon - 11pm, and at the Gaslamp District nightly 6pm - 11pm. You may just show up, or make reservations.

Admission: Forty-five minute rides cost $60 for up to four people.

Ages: All

COASTER

(619) 685-4900 - automated system for the coaster, bus, and trolley / $$$
(800) 262-7837 - transit office / www.sdcommute.com

San Diego County

Coast stress-free from Oceanside to Old Town to further south in San

Diego, with stops at Carlsbad, Encinitas, Solana Beach, and Sorrento Valley via the sleek transit express rail line. Pick out a destination in the above-mentioned cities, or let the ride be the adventure. Automated fare machines at the Coaster stations make obtaining a ticket a breeze, although calling to find out the schedule on the automated number can drive one a little nuts.

Hours: It operates Mon. - Sat., except major holidays, starting at about 5:30am and ending at about 6:30pm - depending on destination.

Admission: Prices range from $3.25 - $3.75 per person one way. One child 5 and under travels free with a paid accompanying adult.

Ages: All

COUNTRY CARRIAGES

(760) 765-1471   *$$$$*

2134 Main Street, Julian

(From San Diego Fwy [5] or Escondido Fwy [15], take 78 Fwy E. to Julian. From the 8 Fwy, take 79 Fwy N. to Julian.78/79 becomes Main St. in Julian. [TG-1136 B7])

Clip clop, clip clop - a horse-drawn carriage ride through Julian fits in perfectly with the ambiance of this quaint town. Most of the tours begin in front of the Julian Drug Store, a fun place to stop for a treat at an old-fashioned soda fountain. A thirty-minute ride costs $25 per couple, or a family consisting of two adults and one to two small children; for three adults and two small children the price is $30. A one-hour ride is $50 per couple on the weekdays.

Hours: Look for the carriage Mon. - Thurs., 11pm - 4pm; Fri. - Sun., 11am - 7pm, weather permitting. Reservations are recommended.

Admission: Prices are listed above.

Ages: All

GONDOLA COMPANY

(619) 429-6317 / www.gondolacompany.com   *$$$$$*

4000 Coronado Bay Road, Coronado

(Exit San Diego Fwy [5] W. on Palm Ave. [75], stay R. to go on Silver Strand Blvd., R. on Coronado Bay. It's at Loews Coronado Bay Resort and Marina. [TG-1309 E7])

This part of Coronado becomes a part of Italy via an authentic gondola cruise through the exclusive waterway of the Coronado Cays. Romantic? Yes, but it can also be a peaceful, hour-long adventure with children. The gondolier dresses in the traditional costume of striped shirt and black pants. Italian music plays in the background. The cruise includes either antipasto appetizer or chocolate-covered strawberries. An ice bucket and glasses are provided, and you supply your own choice of beverage. Each of the three gondolas can take up to six people.

Hours: Open daily 11am - 11pm.

Admission: $60 for two people; $15 per additional person. For more of a memorable outing (and more $), enjoy a four-course meal - appetizer, salad, entree, and dessert - for $195, offered Tues. - Sun.

Ages: 4 years and up.

H & M LANDING   ☼
(619) 222-0427 / www.hmlanding.com   *$$$$*
2803 Emerson, San Diego
(Going S. on San Diego Fwy [5], exit S. on Rosecrans St., L. on Emerson. Going N. on 5, exit at
Hawthorne St., go straight on Brant St., L. on Laurel, R. on N. Harbor Dr., L. on Rosecrans St., L. on
Emerson. [TG-1288 B2])

San Diego's oldest whale-watching expedition company offers two, three, and even five-hour cruises during whale-watching season, which is January through March. Three-hour cruises depart at 10am and 1:30pm and head to the coastal waters of Point Loma. Five-hour trips depart at 10am and travel to the Coronado Islands and Mexico's marine wildlife sanctuary. Be on the lookout for whales, sea lions, dolphins, and elephant seals.

Hours: Stated above.
Admission: The three-hour whale watching excursion is $20 for adults; $15
               for ages 13 - 17; $13.50 for ages 12 and under.
Ages: 6 years and up.

HORNBLOWER (San Diego)   ☼
(619) 725-8888 / www.hornblower.com   *$$$$*
1066 N. Harbor Drive, San Diego
(Going S. on San Diego Fwy [5], exit S. on Front St., R. on Broadway., L. on Harbor Dr. Going N.
on 5, exit L. on Hawthorne St., L. on Harbor Dr. Go to the Cruise Ship Terminal. [TG-1288 J3])

Hornblower offers three-and-a-half-hour whale watching cruises that include narration by the Captain; watching a documentary on whales; viewing sea lions, birds, and whales; indoor/outdoor seating; and a snack bar with hot food and drinks available. Whale sighting is guaranteed or your receive a Whale Check, good for another cruise. This yacht company also offers other specialty cruises throughout the year, as well as harbor tours.

Hours: Cruises are offered the end of December through March. Tours
               depart daily at 9:30am and 1:30pm. Reservations aren't
               necessary, but call first (of course!).
Admission: $23 for adults; $21 for seniors and military; $11.50 for ages 4 -
               12; children 3 and under are free.
Ages: 5 years and up.

OCOTILLO WELLS STATE VEHICULAR   ☼
RECREATION AREA
(760) 767-5391 / parks.ca.gov   *!*
(Take 78 E. out of Julian about 35 miles, beyond Ocotillo Wells. [TG-1121 J2])

For a little off-roading fun, try Ocotillo Wells Recreation Area where you can go up hills, over sand dunes, and through dry washes! You must provide your own vehicles (and have them registered), but the entrance is free and so are primitive camping sites.

Hours: Open daily.
Admission: Free
Ages: 6 years and up.

OLD TOWN TROLLEY TOURS

(619) 298-8687 / www.historictours.com $$$$
4040 Twiggs Street, San Diego
(Going S. on San Diego Fwy [5] [just south of Interstate 8], exit E. [across the bridge] on Old Town Ave. Going N. on 5, exit at Moore St., R. on Old Town Ave. From Old Town Ave., go L. on San Diego Ave., R. on Twiggs St. [TG-1268 F5])

Really get to know the city of San Diego by taking a narrated tour on board an old-fashioned looking trolley. The tour guide will tell you about the history of San Diego, plus lots of fun stories. One of the best features about this tour is that you can take a continuous two-hour tour, or jump off (so to speak) and rejoin the tour at any time throughout the day. There are eight locations covered on the loop, including Old Town, Seaport Village, Horton Plaza, Hotel Del Coronado, San Diego Zoo, and Balboa Park. Appropriately nicknamed "transportainment," we enjoyed the commentary, the freedom of stopping at attractions, staying for a bit, and getting back on board when we were ready. Hassle-free parking is another plus. Ask about their specialty tours, such as the three-hour, Navy tour, where you'll see various aspects of the military in San Diego. Also see SAN DIEGO TROLLEY, under this section, for another way to get around San Diego.

Hours: Trolleys run daily 9am - 6pm. They do not run on Thanksgiving or Christmas. The Navy tour departs every Fri. at 9:15am.
Admission: The prices for all tours are $24 for adults; $12 for ages 4 - 12; children 3 and under are free.
Ages: 5 years and up.

POINT LOMA LANDING

(619) 223-2390 / www.pointlomasportfishing.com $$$$
1403 Scott Street, San Diego
(Going S. on San Diego Fwy [5], exit S. on Rosecrans St., L. on Harbor Dr., R. on Scott St. Going N. on 5, exit at Hawthorne St., go straight on Brant St., L. on Laurel, R. on N. Harbor Dr., L. on Scott St. [TG-1288 C2])

Three-hour, whale-watching cruises are offered twice daily during the whale-watching season.

Hours: Open daily January through March. Call for times.
Admission: $20 for adults; $18 for ages 12 - 18; $12 for ages 12 and under.
Ages: 6 years and up.

SAN DIEGO BAY FERRY / OLD FERRY LANDING

(619) 234-4111 / www.sdhe.com $$
1050 N. Harbor Drive at the Broadway Pier in downtown San Diego, and the Ferry Landing Marketplace in Coronado
(Going S. on San Diego Fwy [5], exit S. on Front St., R. on Broadway to end. Going N. on 5, exit L. on Hawthorne St., L. on Harbor Dr. [TG-1288 J3])

Take a fifteen-minute ride over to Coronado (and back) on the San Diego Bay Ferry. Enjoy the Ferry Landing Marketplace on the Coronado side, with its Victorian-style shopping and eating complex. Bike, blade, or walk along the waterfront paved pathways. You can also romp in the grassy lawns along the pathways, or sunbathe on the beach. A farmer's market is held on the island on Tuesdays 2:30pm to 6pm. TIDELANDS PARK (look under the Great Outdoors section) is next to the Marketplace. If you want to go to Hotel Del Coronado, take the Coronado shuttle, (619) 427-6438, from the landing. It runs approximately every hour from 9:20am to 6pm, with a few stops along the way. The shuttle costs $1 a ride per person. Or, enjoy a scenic walk to the hotel (one-and-a-third miles), though it might get a little long for younger children. See SAN DIEGO HARBOR EXCURSION, under the Transportation section, for longer, and more scenic, boat rides.

Hours: The ferry departs from the pier every hour on the hour, Sun. - Thurs., 9am - 9pm; Fri. - Sat., 9am - 10pm. It leaves Coronado every hour on the half hour, running the same hours.

Admission: $2 for adults (one way); children 3 and under are free; bikes are an additional 50¢. Parking at the Broadway pier is $1 per hour; $3 maximum.

Ages: All

SAN DIEGO HARBOR EXCURSION   ☼
(800) 442-7847 or (619) 234-4111 / www.sdhe.com $$$$
1050 N. Harbor Drive, Broadway Pier, San Diego

(Going S. on San Diego Fwy [5], exit S. on Front St., R. on Broadway to end. Going N. on 5, exit L. on Hawthorne St., L. on Harbor Dr. [TG-1288 J3])

Enjoy a one or two-hour narrated cruise along San Diego's coast in a nice excursion ship. A snack bar is on board. During a one-hour cruise, you'll see the Star of India, the Naval Air Station, and the San Diego shipyards that hold merchants' vessels, fishing boats, and more. During the two-hour cruise, you'll also travel by the Cabrillo National Monument. Whale-watching trips are given January through March and a sighting is guaranteed or you ride again for free. Tip: Bring a jacket or sweater on any journey by sea!

Hours: One-hour cruises depart daily, starting at 10am. Two-hour cruises depart Mon. - Fri. at 2pm; Sat. - Sun., 9:45am, 12:30pm, and 2pm. Call first as hours may change in the winter. Three-hour whale watching cruises depart daily at 10:15am and 1:30pm.

Admission: One-hour cruises cost $13 for adults; $11 for seniors and active-duty military; $6.50 for ages 4 -12; children 3 and under are free. Two-hour cruises are $18 for adults; $16 for seniors and military; $9 for ages 4 - 12. Whale watching is $23 for adults; $21 for seniors and military; $15 for ages 4 - 12. Parking at the Broadway pier is $3 all day.

Ages: 3 years and up.

SAN DIEGO PARASAIL ADVENTURES   ☀
(619) 223-4386 / www.goparasailing.com $$$$$
1617 Quivira Road, Suite 101, Mission Bay   ▥

(Exit San Diego Fwy [5] W. on Sea World Dr. and follow the signs to W. Mission Bay Dr., turn L. on Quivira Rd. and go R. at the end on Quivira. [TG-1268 A3])

Experience the thrill of soaring up in the air, "flying" over San Diego waters, and getting a bird's eye view of this lovely city. Rides last about eight minutes, although participants are in the boat for about an hour, to ensure that everyone gets their turn. Take off and land directly on the boat. Single or tandem flights are available. All riders must weight at least 80 pounds.

Hours: Open April through mid-June and mid-September through October, weekends only. Open daily mid-June through mid-September. Closed November through March. When open, the hours are 9am - 6:30pm (weather permitting).

Admission: $59.95 per person

Ages: At least 80 lbs.

SAN DIEGO RAILROAD MUSEUM ☼ $$$
(619) 595-3030 / www.sdrm.org
Sheridan Road, Campo
(Exit 8 Fwy [45 miles from downtown San Diego] S. on Buckman Springs Rd., travel 10.5 miles to junction Hwy 94., bear R. [1.5 miles] to Old Stone Store, L. after railroad tracks on Forest Gate Rd., L. on Sheridan Rd. and follow signs to the Museum. [TG-1318 A7])

The sound of a train whistle blowing has always been a signal for adventure! Come abooooard the San Diego Railroad Museum train for an hour-and-a-half ride your children will never forget. You'll ride in restored classic steam or diesel locomotives, depending on what is available. My boys loved the freedom of moving about while traveling. They walked in between the cars (parents are asked to accompany minors), watched the scenic mountains and meadows roll past, saw a few cows, and played cards. Tip: We brought a picnic lunch, as only snack food is available to purchase on the train. At the halfway point, kids can view (from the windows) the engine being switched around to pull you back the way you came. The conductors were friendly and shared a lot of information about railroads and the history of the area.

Free walking tours are offered one stop before the end of the excursion. You'll see numerous old and restored rail cars such as passenger, Pullman, and freight cars; learn about the historical significance of the railways; and walk through a caboose. The forty-five minute tour leads you back to the Campo Depot.

At the museum (depot) there are a few stationary pull carts to climb on, a Box Car Theater that shows continuously running videos about the railway system, a gift shop, and picnic tables. In addition to weekly rides, special trips are arranged to Tecate in Mexico, and Jacumba in California.

Hours: The Museum hours are 10am - 5pm on weekends and holidays. Trains depart at 10am and at 2:30pm on Sat., Sun., and most holidays. Closed Thanksgiving and Christmas.

Admission: To simply come and look at the trains is free. Train rides cost $12 for adults; $10 for seniors and active military; $3 for ages 6 - 12; children 5 and under are free.

Ages: 3 years and up.

SAN DIEGO TROLLEY   ☼
(619) 685-4900 - 24-hour information line; (619) 233-3004 - office; $$
(619) 234-5005 - for persons with hearing impairments. /
www.sdcommute.com
San Diego

The San Diego Trolley (and bus) line is a great way to get around San Diego. The Blue line extends from Mission San Diego all the way down to San Ysidro. From this last stop at the border, you can either walk into Mexico, or take a cab. Park for free at the Old Town Transit Center, or all day at the MTS tower garage at 12th and Imperial for $6. The Orange line goes from Santee to Seaport Village. There are several places to catch the trolley line along the routes, with many of the stops being at major attractions. Part of the fun for a child is just the ride. Also see OLD TOWN TROLLEY TOURS, under this section, for another way to get around San Diego.

Hours: It runs daily 5am - 1am, with service every fifteen minutes most of the day.

Admission: One-way fares range from $1 - $2.25, depending on how far you go. Children 4 and under ride for free. Tickets are usually dispensed from machines.

Ages: All

TORREY PINES GLIDER PORT   ☼
(858) 452-9858 / www.flytorrey.com   !/$$$$$
2800 Torrey Pines Scenic Drive, La Jolla
(Exit San Diego Fwy [5] W. on Genesee Ave., L. on N. Torrey Pines Rd., R. on Torrey Pines Scenic Dr., to the end onto the dirt parking lot. [TG-1207 H7])

Man has had dreams and aspirations to fly since the beginning of time. Hang gliding and paragliding are the closest things we'll get to it in this lifetime (and they are much better than Icarus' attempt!) Kids may participate in this uplifting sport, or come to just watch. We brought a picnic lunch, as there are tables at the cliff tops, although a full-service snack bar is here, too. Besides the exhilarating sight of gliders soaring and dipping along the coastline, there is a breathtaking view of the ocean and beach. The small planes you see flying overhead are really remote control planes that have a take-off/landing site right next "door."

Hours: Flights are scheduled daily, although if you're coming to watch, you might want to call first to see if anyone is actually flying that day. Closed Christmas.

Admission: Free, unless you're flying! Tandem introductory lessons, starting at $125, usually take about a half hour, which includes ground school instruction and about 20 minutes of flight time. Solo lessons start at $350 for two days of lessons.

Ages: All to come and watch; 5 years and up for tandem; at least 100 pounds for solo flights.

YOUNG EAGLES PROGRAM (San Diego)

(619) 661-6520 - airport / (619) 276-3251 / www.youngeagles.com
1409 Continental Avenue, Brown Field, San Diego
(From San Diego Fwy [5] and Jakob Dekema Fwy [805], exit E. on Route 905 (only 1 1/2 miles from the border) and drive about 3 miles. Look for airport and E.A.A. signs. [TG-1351 E2])

See YOUNG EAGLES PROGRAM (Pacoima) under this section for details. At this location, the flight is over the city of San Diego and over the ocean. Younger children who are grounded can ride in a simulator that has a radio, earphones, and all the instruments that are in a cockpit. The ride moves and turns as the wheel is turned. Ask about this chapter's other Young Eagle programs. Note: The Young Eagles Program is scheduled to end December, 2003.

Hours: Usually offered the second Sat. of each month.
Admission: Free
Ages: 8 - 17 years.

BAY QUEEN HARBOR CRUISE

(805) 642-7753
1691 Spinnaker Drive, Ventura
(Going W. on Ventura Fwy [101], exit S.W. on Seaward Ave., L. on Harbor Blvd. Going S.E. on 101, exit at Seaward Ave. and go straight onto Harbor Blvd. From Harbor Blvd., go R. on Spinnaker Dr. [TG-491 F7])

Enjoy a forty-minute cruise out of the harbor, past the boats and homes along the coastline. See VENTURA HARBOR and VILLAGE, under the Piers and Seaports section, for other things to do in this area. Kayak and pedal boat rentals are also available here.

Hours: Cruises depart Sat. - Sun., noon - 4pm, every hour on the hour.
Admission: Cruises are $6 for adults; $3 for ages 12 and under. Single kayaks are $12 an hour; doubles are $20. Pedal boats are $12 an hour.
Ages: All

BIKE TRAIL: OJAI VALLEY TRAIL / VENTURA RIVER TRAIL

(805) 654-3951 - parks; (805) 646-8126 - Chamber of Commerce
One end begins on Ojai Avenue in Ojai; the other at San Buenaventura State Beach in Ventura. Or, start in the middle at Foster County Park in Casitas Springs
(The Ojai starting point is off State Highway 33 / Ojai Ave. Catch the trail on the east side of town at Soule Park or just behind LIBBEY PARK [look under the Great Outdoors section]. You can also park your car at the park-and-ride lot at Ojai Ave. and Fox St. To reach San Buenaventura State Beach, exit Ventura Fwy [101] S. on California St., L. on Harbor Blvd. To reach Foster Park, exit State Highway 33 at Casitas Vista Rd. and go underneath the freeway to the park. Foster is 6 miles N. of Ventura. [TG-441 H7 / 461 A6])

This scenic, paved route is about sixteen miles long one way. The Ojai Valley Trail, from Libbey Park to Foster Park, is about nine miles. Although it follows along the major street of Ventura Avenue (Highway 33), oak and sycamore trees adorn it, making it pretty while shading good portions of it, plus major sections are hidden from the main thoroughfare and give it a ride-in-the-country feel. The trail is frequented by bikers, skaters, strollers, equestrians, and joggers. The six-mile trail from Foster Park to the ocean, is not all easy on the eyes, as it goes through industrial areas, but pathway artists have enlivened it somewhat with murals. As you head toward your final destination, the Pacific Ocean, you'll connect with the Omer Rains Trail (i.e. Ventura River Trail) which goes along the coastline. Go north to reach Emma Wood State Beach or south to San Buenaventura Beach, (805) 648-4127, and the Ventura Pier. Note: The grade of the trail is a gentle slope from north to south, and therefore noticeably easier to pedal than vice versa.

Forgot your wheels? Bicycle rentals are available at Bicycles of Ojai, (805) 646-7736 at 108 Canada Street, Ojai for $6 an hour. Note: No child-size bikes are available here. Cycles 4 Rent, (805) 652-1114 at 239 W. Main Street, Ventura charges $5 to $9 an hour depending on the type of bike.

    Hours: The trail is open dawn to dusk.

Admission: Free at the Ojai end; $5 parking at San Buenaventura Beach; $1 parking at Foster Park during the week, $3 on the weekends.

    Ages: 4 years and up, depending on how long and far you want to ride.

CHANNEL ISLAND'S LANDING

(805) 985-6059

3821 S. Victoria Avenue, Oxnard

(Exit Ventura Fwy [101] S. on Victoria Ave. [TG-552 B4])

$$$$

Set sail on sailboats that rent for $18 to $25 an hour, or on an electric boat that seats up to ten people and rents for $40 an hour. (Somehow it doesn't sound right to say, "Set sail on an electric boat" - oh well!)

    Hours: Open daily 8:30am - 5pm.

Admission: Prices listed above.

    Ages: All

FILLMORE & WESTERN RAILWAY

(800) 773-TRAIN (8724) or (805) 524-2546 / www.fwry.com

351 Santa Clara Avenue, Central Park Depot, Fillmore

(Exit State Route 126 N. on Central Ave. [TG-456 A6])

$$$$

"More powerful than a locomotive"; *The Great Train Robbery*; *The Little Engine that Could* - what does this potpourri of things bring to mind? A train ride, of course! Riding on a train is a real adventure for children. The countryside is scenic along this route with citrus groves and beautiful landscapes. This railway line is also a favorite Hollywood location, so many of the trains you'll see and ride on have appeared in movies and television shows. A snack bar and gift shop are on board.

There are several types of weekend excursions offered. Hop on board for a two-and-a-half-hour round-trip ride between Fillmore and Santa Paula, which includes a half-hour stopover in Santa Paula. Ride the rails in an open air railcar, a restored passenger coach (circa 1930), a 1929 parlour car, or a more modern car. Lunches are offered in the restored 1950's Streamlined diner before your ride or en route. Meal prices range between $4 to $10. Spirit of the West train rides (adults only) include a stop at a private location for a barbecue dinner (which is provided), musical entertainment, and dancing to live music. The Spaghetti Western ride is offered the third Friday of every month and includes the two-and-a-half hour ride, dinner (guess what they serve?), and entertainment by actors dressed in western attire. Other specialty rides, such as murder/mystery rides (adults only), are offered throughout the year. Ask about the School Trains, where students ride the rails and learn about the workings of a train, vintage cars, the scenery, and more.

Hours: Trains depart from Fillmore January through March on weekends at 2pm. They depart the rest of the year Sat. at 2pm; Sun., 11am, and 2pm. Spirit of the West rides depart at 6pm and return at 9:30pm. Spaghetti Western rides depart at 7pm and return at 9:30pm.

Admission: Round-trip fare is $18 for adults; $16 for seniors; $8 for ages 4 - 12; $5 for ages 3 and under. Spirit of the West rides are for adults only: $51 for adults; $45 for seniors. Spaghetti Western rides are $40 for adults; $20 for ages 4 - 12; $5 for ages 3 and under. School Trains are $6 per person.

Ages: 3 years and up.

JIM HALL RACING SCHOOL   ☼
(805) 654-1329 / www.jhrkartracing.com $$$$$
675 N. Harbor Boulevard, Oxnard
(Going W. on Ventura Fwy [101], exit S. on Victoria, R. on Olivas Park Dr., L. on Harbor Blvd. Going S.E. on 101, exit at Seaward Ave. and go straight onto Harbor Blvd. [TG-521 H5])

What child doesn't like racing around? Now he/she can learn how to do it in karts! Besides the adult classes, this racing school offers Day One Sprint Kart programs for ages 13 and up. Classes range from half-day instruction to a week, or more. Drivers learn safety (yea!), how to drive, braking techniques (this could be especially valuable in just a few years), and they'll even get timed. Watch out, Mario Andretti!

Hours: Call for class hours.

Admission: Varies, depending on the length of class. The Day One Sprint Kart program, which is four hours of instruction and driving, starts at $150.

Ages: 8 years and up.

SANTA PAULA AIRPORT / CP AVIATION, INC.   ☼
(805) 933-1155 or (805) 525-2138 / www.cpaviation.com $$$$$
830 E. Santa Maria Street, Santa Paula
(Exit the Santa Paula Fwy [126] S. on Palm Ave., L. on Santa Maria St. [TG-464 B6])

This small airport is kid-friendly; partly because of its size, and partly because it's always fun to watch planes land and take off. Instead of just watching, however, why not take the kids up for a spin, literally! At the instructor's discretion, if your child is at least 12 years old (and doesn't get motion sickness), he/she can take an exhilarating half-hour aerobatic ride with loops, rolls, and G's (better than a roller coaster!) for $120 per person. For those who enjoy a calmer scenic ride, a Cessna 172, which seats three passengers, is only $50 (total) for a half-hour flight. Other aircraft are available for flights, too. Lunch at the airport restaurant will complete your lofty adventure.

If you're visiting on the first Sunday of the month, take a walk through the adjacent hangars that houses the AVIATION MUSEUM OF SANTA PAULA. See the Museums section for details. Also check the YOUNG EAGLES PROGRAM (Santa Paula) in this section.

Hours: The airport is open daily. Call for hours for a flight.
Admission: Prices listed above.
Ages: 4 years and up for a look around the airport and a scenic flight.

YOUNG EAGLES PROGRAM (Camarillo)   ☼

(805) 647-6994 or (805) 482-0064 / www.youngeagles.com;   !
www.eaa723.org
Eubanks Street, Camarillo Airport, Camarillo   ♨
(Exit Ventura Fwy [101] S. on Las Posas Rd., R. on Pleasant Valley Rd., R. on Eubanks. [TG-523 J4])

See YOUNG EAGLES PROGRAM (Pacoima) under this section for details. Reservations are necessary! The Young Eagles Program is scheduled to end December, 2003. Also check out the CONFEDERATE AIR FORCE WORLD WAR II AVIATION MUSEUM (Camarillo) at the airport. (Look under the Museums section.)

Hours: Offered the first Sat. of every month 9:30am - 11:30am.
Admission: Free
Ages: 8 - 17 years.

YOUNG EAGLES PROGRAM (Santa Paula)   ☼

(805) 647-6994 or (805) 525-1100 / www.youngeagles.com   !
830 E. Santa Maria Street, Santa Paula   ♨
(Exit the Santa Paula Fwy [126] S. on Palm Ave., L. on Santa Maria St. [TG-464 B6])

See YOUNG EAGLES PROGRAM (Pacoima) under this section for details. Reservations are needed. Note: The Young Eagles Program is scheduled to end December, 2003.

Hours: Offered the first Sun. of every month 10am - noon, which coincides with the AVIATION MUSEUM OF SANTA PAULA being open. (See the Museums section for more detail.)
Admission: Free
Ages: 8 - 17 years.

ZOOS AND ANIMALS

Kids and animals seem to go hand-in-hoof - both are adorable and neither is easy. Animal lovers - this section is for you! Tip: Take a trip to a pet shop. See "Pets" in the Ideas and Resources section for some of our local favorites.

EXOTIC FELINE BREEDING COMPOUND

(661) 256-3793 / www.cathouse-fcc.org

Rhyolite Avenue, Rosamond

(Exit Antelope Valley Fwy [14] W. on Rosamond Blvd. [to the E. is Edwards Air Force Base], R. on Mojave-Tropico Rd., L. on Rhyolite Ave.)

This place is the cat's meow! There are fifty exotic wild cats living here, representing over fifteen different species. Since it is a breeding compound, you're almost guaranteed to see a few kittens, too. Unlike traditional zoos, the safety fences keep you only a few feet (not yards) away from the caged animals. This allows for plenty of up-close viewing and photo opportunities.

Stroll along the cement pathways to see jaguars, panthers, pumas, lynxes, fluffy Amur leopards, regal-looking servals, weasel-like jaguarundi, and lots of Chinese leopards. Ask for a guided tour to learn about the animals - what they eat, how much they weigh, their life span, and more - and about the importance of this breeding compound. Three huge Siberian tigers live in the back (in cages) and will be back on exhibit when their homes are rebuilt.

The gift shop has a few displays showing some of the reasons these cats are facing extinction - one fur coat was made from fifteen bobcats, and another was made from over fifty leopards. Tip: Late afternoon and cooler months are the best times to visit the compound as this is when the felines are more active. Please call if you want to schedule a tour for ten or more people. Educational outreach programs are also available.

Hours: Open Thurs. - Tues., 10am - 4pm. Closed Wed. and Christmas.
Admission: $3 for adults; $1.50 ages 3 - 18.
Ages: 4 years and up.

CABRILLO MARINE AQUARIUM

(310) 548-7562 / www.cabrilloaq.org

3720 Stephen M White Drive, San Pedro

(Take Harbor Fwy [110] to the end, L. on Gaffey St., L. on 9th St., R. on Pacific Ave. almost to the end, L. on 36th St. which turns into Stephen M White. [TG-854 C2])

Explore the underwater treasures of Los Angeles Harbor without ever getting wet! Cabrillo Marine Aquarium specializes in the marine life of Southern California. It features quite a few tanks, mostly at kids' eye-level, filled with a wide variety of sea life.

The front courtyard has full-size killer whale, shark, and dolphin models, plus a full-grown gray whale outlined on the cement. Kids are welcome to touch the whale bones in the adjacent Whale Graveyard.

The exhibit halls have tanks filled with live jellies (usually referred to as jellyfish), crustaceans, octopuses, fish, leopard sharks, moray eels, and other sea animals. There are numerous displays of preserved animals, such as seals and sea lions; bones, skeletons, jaws, and teeth of sharks and whales; pictures; and other models of sea life. My boys liked pushing the button to hear the recording of a whale singing, although their renditions of it were more grating than musical. We also watched a shark blend into the sandy ocean floor; touched a sample of shark skin and compared it to a sample of sandpaper; and saw a slide presentation at the auditorium. Call to see what's currently showing.

As most kids have this inherent need to explore the world with their hands and not just their eyes, a definite favorite is the tidepool touch tank. Here kids can gently touch sea anemones, sea stars, and sea slugs.

The Cabrillo Aquarium offers seasonal events such as whale watching (January through April) and grunion hunting (March through July), plus various workshops and programs, such as Sleep With the Fishes. At low tide - call for particular times and seasons - tidepool tours are given at the beach in an area called Pt. Fermin Marine Life Refuge. A paved, wheelchair-accessible trail runs from the parking lot to the aquarium, across the beach, and to the water's edge at the tidepools. You are welcome to explore this area on your own, too.

Don't forget to pack your swimsuits and beach towels as Cabrillo Beach is right outside the aquarium. Wonderful sandy stretches and a play area await your children. For more adventuresome kids (or whosoever's parents will let them), there are rock jetties to explore. Enjoy your day playing by the ocean, and learning more about it.

Hours: The Aquarium is open Tues. - Fri., noon - 5pm; Sat. - Sun., 10am - 5pm. Closed Thanksgiving and Christmas. The touch tank doors open for twenty minutes at a time Tues. - Fri. at 1:30pm, 2:30pm, and 3:30pm; Sat. - Sun. at 11:30am, 1:30pm, 2:30pm, and 3:30pm. Slide shows are presented Tues. - Sun. at 11am and 2pm. The beach is open daily 6am - 10pm.

Admission: The aquarium is free; donations are appreciated. Parking is $6.50 per vehicle in the summer; the rest of the year, Mon. - Fri., $4.50; Sat.- Sun., $5.50. If you get here early enough, you can park on the street and just walk through the beach/aquarium entrance gate.

Ages: All

ECO STATION ENVIRONMENTAL SCIENCE AND WILDLIFE RESCUE CENTER

(310) 842-8060 / www.theecostation.org

$$$

10101 W. Jefferson Boulevard, Culver City

(Exit San Diego Fwy [405] E. on Jefferson Blvd., L. on Sepulveda Blvd., and go straight as Sepulveda then turns into another Jefferson Blvd. [TG-672 H2])

Done in the style of a Mayan temple, complete with archways, wall friezes, and (fake) greenery all around, the ECO Station's message of teaching kids the importance of preserving the environment and protecting wildlife comes across in an inviting manner. This place is, in fact, a designated wildlife sanctuary and works with the Department of Fish and Game. Illegal articles, seized from people trying to smuggle them into the country via airports, seaports, and over the border, are displayed here for show and tell.

The first room is the Gallery of the World, displaying art, food, and clothing from various countries. In the Oceania gallery half of the Heal the Bay tank is polluted by urban run off, cigarette butts, and trash. The other half is clean. Aquariums here contain a tropical reef tank, newts, eels, colorful angelfish, blue tangs, coral that's been harvested, a unique pillow starfish, lionfish, and dogface pufferfish, and other aquatic creatures taken from people attempting to bring them into the U.S. Another marine-oriented room holds turtles and a touch tank with horseshoe crabs, sea stars, and sea slugs. A tank displays small sharks and rays. Look for the poisonous arrow frogs. Walk through a faux kelp forest while learning about the food chain and how to keep the ocean healthy. Turn a corner and see (gasp!) a life-size stuffed leopard that looks very real. Confiscated goods here, that children may touch, include boots made out of rattlesnakes; a purse made out of an alligator, including its head and paws; animals' skins such as tiger, zebra, and cheetah; an elephant foot stool; and more. Again in here, visitors will be educated about endangered species. Another room provides temporary housing for animals such as primates, pot-bellied pigs, and others. The Lost Reptile Kingdom room holds Nile monitors, Komodo dragons, and tortoises. The chameleons in here may be touched and held. Kids (and adults) are invited to wrap the pythons around themselves, or for the more squeamish, to merely stroke them (or not). Environmental Marketplaces are small rooms containing clothing, tools, weapons, and other artifacts from several Native American tribes. Toucans, parrots, cockatoos, and other species dwell in the Bird Kingdom.

School or group tours generally run two hours and provide comprehensive information. During public hours, although visitors may roam around on their own, staff personal is on hand to answer any questions and assist in holding the animals.

Hours: Open to the public Sat., 10am - 4pm. Open for school/group tours, minimum 40 students and maximum 80, Mon. - Fri., 9am - 3pm.

Admission: $7 for adults; $6 for seniors; $5 for ages 2 - 12; children under 2 are free. For a school/group tour the cost is $3.50 per child; $5 for adults; one adult is free for every ten children.

Ages: 2 years and up.

THE FARM

(818) 341-6805 - recording; (818) 885-6321 - The Farm on the weekends.

8101 Tampa Avenue, Reseda

(Exit Ventura Fwy [101] N. on Tampa. [TG-530 G2])

This Farm reminds me of Old MacDonald's place in that song with all those vowels. There are over 100 animals to pet, and even a few to hold. The llamas, cows, chickens, bunnies, turkeys, sheep, ducks, pigs (including Babe, from the movie), peacocks, and goats are readily accessible to pet through the fence pens. If you come at the right time of year, you'll also see baby animals and have the opportunity to cuddle lambs and kids (i.e. baby goats). Animal feed is available for purchase for an additional 50¢. Old tractors, bales of hay, and the aroma of farm animals add to the barnyard atmosphere. Riding lessons and/or pony rides around a track are available, too. And yes, The Farm does birthday parties.

Hours: Open Sat. - Sun. and holidays, 10am - 5pm, weather permitting. Open in the summer one hour later.

Admission: $5 for ages 1 and up; $2 for seniors. Pony rides are an additional $2. Call for horse riding lessons.

Ages: All

FARM TOUR (Pomona)

(909) 869-2224 / www.csupomona.edu

Kellogg Drive, California State Polytechnic University, Pomona

(Going E. on San Bernardino Fwy [10], exit S. on Kellogg Dr. Going N. on Orange Fwy [57], exit W. on Temple, R. on S. Campus Dr., L. on Kellogg Dr. Parking is on the R. in the campus parking lot. Cross the street to the university farm. [TG-640 B2])

Cal Poly campus is beautiful, set in the hillside and surrounded by pastureland. One-hour farm tours of the horse center (please see KELLOGG ARABIAN HORSE CENTER in this section) and of the sheep and swine area are given by a student. The tour guide tells visitors about animal husbandry and all about the animals on the farm here. It's a fun tour, especially for younger children.

Hours: Tours are given whenever a student is available.
Admission: Free
Ages: Pre-K through 6th grade.

FARM TOUR (Walnut)

(909) 594-5611 / www.mtsac.edu

100 N. Grand Avenue, Mount San Antonio College, Walnut

(Exit Pomona Fwy [60] N. on Grand Ave., R. on Temple Ave., L. on Bonita Dr. The entrance is on Bonita.([TG-639 H3])

Take a forty-five-minute guided tour of the farm animals on this college campus. You'll see cows, horses, goats, and sheep, and depending on your guide, learn about what the animals eat, how to take care of them, and more. The tour is geared for younger children and is simply a fun introduction to farm animals. Pack a sack lunch to enjoy at a picnic area under nearby shade trees, adjacent to a hilly, grassy field. Check out WILDLIFE SANCTUARY TOUR, under the Tours sections, for another tour offered by the college.

Hours: Tours are given Mon. - Thurs., 9am, 10am, and 11am.
Admission: Free, but donations are appreciated.
Ages: 3 - 10 years.

GENTLE BARN

(818) 705-5477 / www.gentlebarn.com

6050 Corbin Avenue, Tarzana

(Going W. on Ventura Fwy [101], exit N. on Tampa Ave., L. on Hatteras St., R. on Corbin. Going E. on 101, exit N. on Winnetka Ave., R. on Hatteras, L. on Corbin. It is at a residence. [TG-560 F1])

In a large backyard with well-maintained stalls the sheep, goats, chickens, horses, ducks, cows, turkeys, and pigs coexist with the human owners who live in the adjacent house. Gentle Barn's purpose is to introduce children to barnyard animals, as well as teach them to respect the animals and how to care for them. Time spent here is fun, interactive, and educational as visitors feed and pet animals, as well as learn about where eggs and wool come from, what animals eat, and how they communicate.

Hours: Open to the public Sat., 10am - 2pm. Groups and school field trips may take tours during the week, with advanced reservations.

Admission: $5 per person.

Ages: All

HOLLYWOOD PARK

(310) 419-1500 / www.hollywoodpark.com

1050 S. Prairie Avenue, Inglewood

(Exit San Diego Fwy [405] E. on Century, L. on Prairie. Or, exit Century Fwy [105] N. on Prairie. [TG-703 D4])

$$

Do your kids like horsing around? At Hollywood Park they can see thoroughbred horses and enjoy a children's play area located at the north end of the park. The play area has a grassy lawn for picnicking as well as some playground equipment. Arcade games are also available here. The landscaping of the park, with its lagoons and tropical trees, is pleasing to the eye.

Hours: The season goes from mid-April through mid-July, and November through mid-December. Call for racing information and times.

Admission: $6 for adults (which includes parking and a program); ages 17 and under are free with a paid adult.

Ages: 4 years and up.

INTERNATIONAL CENTER FOR GIBBON STUDIES

(661) 296-2737 / www.izoo.org/icgs

$$$

Esquerra Road, Santa Clarita

(Exit Golden State Fwy [5] E. on Valencia Blvd., L. on Bouquet Canyon [about 5 1/2 miles], R. on Esquerra Rd., which is a dirt road on the right-hand side that is easy to miss - it is before you enter the Angeles National Forest. Go through the stream bed (hard to cross if it's raining), a quick R. on Galton, which is another dirt road, to a dirt driveway outside the six-foot high chain-link fence. [TG-4461 G3])

What's the difference between a monkey and an ape? If you answered, "Monkeys have tails," you are correct. Next question: Are gibbons monkeys or apes? Hint - they have no tails. A one-hour guided tour of this outdoor facility takes you past sixteen enclosures that hold over thirty-five gibbons in their natural family groupings. The enclosures are sizable, chain-link cages, scattered over the hard-packed dirt grounds and under shade trees. The tours are informative, entertaining, and vary according to the interests and ages of the participants in the group. Note: To ensure the safety of the gibbons, visitors must be in good health, not have had any recent contact with a person or animal with an infectious disease, and stay a minimum of five feet away from all enclosures.

Gibbons are arboreal apes - they swing from tree to tree - and are found in the rain forests of Southeast Asia. This research facility, which has six out of the eleven species, studies their behavior and helps to increase their endangered gene pool, which means you could see babies on your visit here. Gibbons are the only primates to walk upright and they have earned the name of loudest land mammal. Every species has a different way of singing (that's the technical name - I call it screaming) to each other, usually in the morning hours. They can project their voices a distance of up to two miles. We heard them. I believe it. The kids loved it. Siamangs have vocal sacs that inflate to the size of a large grapefruit (reminiscent of a bullfrog) when they sing. This is fascinating to listen to and watch. Males and females in certain species are born one color and change colors as they mature. (Is this the same thing as humans "going gray"?) We also learned about gibbons' nutrition, why they are dying off, preventative medical care, and more. My boys went ape over this center!

Hours: Open by appointment for groups of twenty or more people.
Admission: $7 for adults; $5 for ages 12 and under.
Ages: 4 years and up.

KELLOGG ARABIAN HORSE CENTER

(909) 869-2224 / www.csupomona.edu/~equine/Kellogg.htm
Kellogg Drive, California State Polytechnic University, Pomona
(Going E. on San Bernardino Fwy [10], exit S. on Kellogg Dr. Going N. on Orange Fwy [57], exit W. on Temple, R. on S. Campus Dr., L. on Kellogg Dr. Parking is on the R. in the campus parking lot. Cross the street to the university farm. [TG-640 B2])

The Kellogg Arabian Horse Center at Cal Poly houses over eighty-five purebred Arabian horses. The center's thirty-eight scenic acres are set in the hills and encompass a huge pasture, three barns, foaling stalls, a breeding area, a veterinary clinic, a farrier shop, an arena, and a covered grandstand that seats 900.

Staff members and students of horse husbandry and equine sciences present hour-long shows that put the horses through their various paces. Guests see demonstrations of English and western riding, with riders in appropriate costumes, as well as drill team and precision maneuvers, and horses jumping over small fences. Riders in silver and gold flowing Arabian dress are crowd pleasers as their horses, decorated in jewel-toned brocade and tassels, prance around the ring. Our favorite act was the horse that performed several tricks, including walking a baby carriage and rocking a cradle.

After the show, children can ride a horse around a path for $3; watch a thirty-minute video on the history of Kellogg's center (note that the small video room contains a horse skeleton); and walk around the stables. Tip: Bring carrots to feed the horses. Families can pet the beautiful horses, watch them being bathed and groomed, and simply enjoy the ambiance. Springtime is the best time to visit as there are newborn colts to see.

See FARM TOURS in this section for information on the Farm Tour. Ask about rodeos presented at the college, as well as those sponsored by Cal Poly, but performed off campus.

Hours: Shows are offered October through June on the first Sun. of each month at 2pm. Shows are also offered five Thurs. in both the spring and fall at 10:30am. Just the show is offered on these selected Thurs. (no horse rides around the path, etc.) and reservations are required.
Admission: Sun. shows are $3 for adults; $2 for ages 6 - 17; children 5 and under are free. Thurs. shows are $1 per person.
Ages: 3 years and up.

LAKEWOOD PONY RIDES AND PETTING ZOO ☼
(562) 860-1108 $
11369 E. Carson Street, Lakewood   ♨
(Exit San Gabriel River Fwy [605] W. on Carson. It's in the Lakewood Equestrian Center. [TG-766 G6])

If you're in the *neigh*borhood, saddle-up for a pony ride in this small, attractive, park-like riding center. Choose from either a pony sweep, a parent-led walk around the track, or a trotting track (for ages 3 years and up). There is also a small petting zoo with a llama, a turkey, a pot belly pig, goats, rabbits, and sheep. Ponies and/or the petting zoo can be brought to your home, school, church, or fair for a party, too.

Hours: Open Wed. - Fri., 10am - 4:30pm; Sat. - Sun., 10am - 5pm.
Admission: Pony rides are $2.50 each. The petting zoo is 50¢ per person.
Ages: Children 1 year old and up to 100 pounds may enjoy the pony rides. All ages for the petting zoo.

LONG BEACH AQUARIUM OF THE PACIFIC ☼
(562) 590-3100 / www.aquariumofpacific.org $$$$
100 Aquarium Way, Long Beach
(Exit San Diego Fwy [405] S. on the Long Beach Fwy [710] to the end of the Downtown exit, which will turn into Shoreline Dr., R. on Aquarium Way. [TG-825 D1])

Something fishy's going on at the fourth largest aquarium in the United States. The first stop in this multi-level aquarium is the spacious entryway, or **Great Hall of the Pacific**, where your attention is immediately riveted by a life-size, eighty-eight-foot blue whale (no way can a creature be so large!) hanging overhead with her calf "swimming" beside her. This hall also contains preview tanks of the main exhibit regions. Watch a short video about the aquarium in the theater, or one of several other sea-related films. Description cards, with the names and color photos of all the creatures, accompany each gallery. Information and breath-taking footage on the audio/video screens throughout the aquarium answer many of the questions visitors have about the animals here. Note that almost everything in the tanks, besides the fish, is man-made, although it is incredibly realistic looking. Note, too, that small Discovery Labs are located in each area of the main areas and staffed with docents to answer questions, give demonstrations, and allow you to touch selected sea creatures. All exhibits are handicapped accessible. Now it's time to view the three main exhibit areas: California/Baja, Northern Pacific, and Tropical Pacific.

The natural flow of the aquarium leads visitors toward the back of the building, to the **California/Baja** area. Watch the enthralling moon jellies and other exotic drifters float gracefully around in their tanks. Peek at the Swell Shark egg cases where baby sharks are getting ready to be born. A kelp display shows those of us who aren't marine biologists that kelp is used as an ingredient in lipstick, Jell-O, toothpaste, and other household items. Catch an underwater look at the seals and sea lions splashing around. (Ask about feeding times, when divers often come in and play with the animals.) Walk up the stairs and outside to see these mammals sun themselves on the surface of the rocky "shoreline." Tiered cement seating allows good viewing for everyone. This outdoor plaza also features sea turtles, shore birds (who are unable to fly away), and a touch tank that holds stingrays and batrays. They feel like rubber. The Discovery Lab here contains sea urchins, anemones, sea stars, and crabs to gently touch. Back inside, on the second floor of the gallery, you'll see aptly-named garden eels and a rocky reef that holds unusual looking fish, particularly the Lookdowns, which are a vertically flattened fish.

For a change in venue and temperature, enter the **Northern Pacific** gallery. The most popular attraction here are the playful sea otters in a tank with underwater and above-water viewing. Ample information is given about their fur (for which they've been voraciously hunted), their food, their habitats, and more. Other draws include the tank of anchovies (no pizza!), diving puffins (seabirds), monstrous-looking Giant Japanese Spider Crabs, and a Giant Pacific Octopus, which is not menacing, but so shy that you might not even see him.

The **Tropical Pacific** is one of the most colorful sections here. It's set up so you'll "travel" through the reef and into deeper waters as you venture deeper into this gallery. The coral lagoon showcases brilliantly-colored fish - electric blue, canary yellow, jade green, and vivid purple. The largest tank, containing a tropical reef and its 1,000 inhabitants, offers various levels of viewing which is interesting because of the diversity of life shown in here. You'll see clown fish, zebra sharks, giant groupers, and more. At feeding time the divers are equipped with aquaphones to answer any questions. A partial water tunnel allows visitors to see sharks, and every parent knows that an aquarium visit is not complete without seeing sharks. Other outstanding exhibits in this gallery include deadly sea snakes; sea horses; the strange-looking leafy sea dragons and weedy sea dragons; upside-down jellies, who were created to live like this; orange-spined unicorn fish; sex reversal fish (mainly wrasses) who change from females to males as they mature or undergo stress - go figure; and beautiful, but venomous or poisonous fish, such as the lionfish.

The **Kids' Cove**, outside by the California/Baja gallery, is a semi-enclosed area with ocean-themed murals and several hands-on activities for kids. The activities include a huge whale to crawl under, a larger-than-life octopus sculpture featuring informational panels and an arm that is a mini slide, a canopied-covered theater for presentations, and a sand play area.

Cafe Scuba has good food and indoor tables, plus outdoor tables that overlook the seal and sea lion exhibit and Rainbow Harbor. And yes, fish is on the menu.

Ask about the multitude of special events and programs offered to families and school groups including sleep overs, behind-the-scenes tours, and studies of a particular animal or species. Two classrooms in the educational wing are fully stocked with lab equipment, live systems (touch-tank animals), terrestrial aquariums, craft projects, and other good stuff. An educator's room, available for teachers, contains computers, books, arts and crafts resources, and more.

Note: Weekend and holidays are peak attendance times, which translates as lots of people and waiting in line to get in. You can purchase pre-sell tickets and at least avoid the wait in line.

The aquarium is adjacent to Rainbow Harbor. In between the aquarium and harbor is an esplanade and a large green lawn. Feel free to bring a blanket and a picnic lunch. Head out on the esplanade (i.e. cement walkway) to the colorful-looking buildings of SHORELINE VILLAGE, a shopping and eating complex. Head the other way around the harbor toward a quasi park (i.e. an expanse of green lawn with a few picnic tables) where you can view the QUEEN MARY and SCORPION just across the waters. (Look under the Museums section for more details.) Aquabuses (i.e. boats), which leave about once an hour, will take you to and from those attractions for $2 per person one way. Call (800) 429-4601 for more information.

Hours: Open daily 9am - 6pm. Closed Christmas.

Admission: $14.95 for adults; $11.95 for seniors; $7.95 for ages 3 - 11; children 2 and under are free. Parking is $6. Catch a free ride to the aquarium on a bright red Long Beach Passport shuttle bus that cruises Pine Ave., Shoreline Dr., and Ocean Blvd. in the downtown area, and connects to the Metro Blue Line at the Transit Mall on First Street. Passport buses will also deliver you to the Queen Mary and Scorpion.

Ages: All

LOS ANGELES ZOO   ☼

(323) 644-4200 / www.lazoo.org   *$$$*

5333 Zoo Drive, Los Angeles

(Going N. on Golden State Fwy [5] or W. on Ventura Fwy [134], exit at Zoo Dr. and follow the signs. Going E. on 134, exit S. on Victory Blvd., L. on Zoo Dr. Going S. on 5, exit S. on Western, L. on Victory Blvd. to Zoo Dr. [TG-564 B4])

All the big-name animals star at the Los Angeles Zoo - elephants, tigers, mountain lions, giraffes, bears, kangaroos, polar bears, and rhinoceros. Our favorites are the gorillas, apes, orangutans, chimps, and other primates - they provide entertainment that tops television any day! The chimps have their own play area and the orangutans are living in the rain forest, at least a re-created one here at the zoo. An aquatic area features otters and seals. The darkened Koala House has koalas in their nighttime environment, since they are supposed to be more active at that time. Don't forget to ssssstop by the Reptile House to see the snakes and lizards. A playground is located at the far end of the zoo, too.

Zoo keys can be purchased for $3 and are good for a year. Insert a key in boxes at various animal enclosures to hear more information (and a jingle) about that particular species. If you get tired of walking around this huge and hilly zoo, purchase an all-day shuttle pass for $3.50 for adults, $1 for seniors, $1.50 for ages 2 to 12. The shuttle goes around the perimeter of the zoo, and will drop you off or pick you up at various stops along the way.

The Children's Zoo has a few barnyard animals to pet through the fence pens, such as goats and sheep; baby animals to observe through nursery windows; some great interactive displays that teach about various zoo inhabitants and their habitats; and two animal demonstrations areas that allows visitors to see, maybe touch, and definitely learn about an assortment of animals in an intimate setting. At the amphitheater area, keepers introduce "larger" animals, such as an alpaca. At the indoor kids' place, close-up encounters involved smaller animals, such as ferrets and chickens. Storytelling and puppet shows are also offered here. Young spelunkers can explore a man-made cave, which offers tunnels to crawl through, exhibits on cave creature dwellers to look at, and (pretend) stalactites and stalagmites to see.

At the prairie dog exhibit kids can pop their heads up from underneath the ground into a plexiglass dome while real prairie dogs are looking at them! This is a fun photo opportunity. Look - it's a bird, it's a plane, it's Superman! No, it's a bird! The World of Birds shows feature free-flying birds - a flight, sight not to miss.

In the summer months, join in a Sundown Safari where your family can join numerous others and sleep in tents on the zoo grounds. Enjoy a delicious dinner, campfire snack, and breakfast, plus enjoy special nighttime and early morning behind-the-scenes tours of the animals. What a great experience! Ask about their numerous other special programs and events, including free guided tours given to mid and upper elementary school-aged kids.

Hours: Open daily 10am - 5pm. Closed Christmas. Call for show times.
Admission: $8.25 for adults; $5.25 for seniors; $3.25 for ages 2 - 12. Certain discounts are available through AAA. Sundown Safari costs $75 per adult; $50 per child.
Ages: All

MARINE MAMMAL CARE CENTER AT FORT MACARTHUR   ☀

(310) 548-5677 - center; (310) 547-9888 - tours / www.mar3ine.org   !
3601 S. Gaffey Street, San Pedro
(Exit the Harbor Fwy [110] S. on Gaffey St. Go almost to the end of Gaffey, turn R. through the gates on Leavenworth Dr., just past the FORT MACARTHUR MILITARY MUSEUM. [TG-854 B2])

Injured or sick marine mammals, like sea lions and seals, are brought here, doctored, and taken care of until they can be released back into the wild. Rehabilitation can take one to three months, depending on the case. We saw one seal that was severely underweight and another that had numerous shark bites. This small facility can house between five to forty-five marine mammals outside in chain link fence pens, depending on the season. Stormy weather and pupping season (February through July) bring in more injured or abandoned animals. However, the staff has more time to spend during non-busy times. Your children have an opportunity to learn more about these animals as knowledgeable volunteers are on hand to answer any questions kids might ask. And they do ask!

A variety of educational tours and classes are offered for all ages that incorporate a visit with the animals, a video, reinforcement activities, and pre- and post-visit materials. Fourth graders and up may also utilize the laboratory inside the adjacent building, operating the microscopes and computers and looking at the aquarium. Tours are an hour for pre-k through kindergartners and two hours for older children, with an emphasis on the academics. Inquire about the International Day of the Seal festival in April. Note that building next to the center, Oiled Bird Care Center, often has birds that need cleaning and care from oil on the oceans. Look up FORT MACARTHUR MILITARY MUSEUM, under the Museums section, as it is located just across the street.

Hours: Open daily 8am to 4pm.

Admission: Free. The educational tours and classes cost $25 for curriculum materials for up to 60 people.

Ages: All - younger ones will just enjoy seeing the animals, while older ones can learn about them and appreciate what the Center does.

MONTEBELLO BARNYARD ZOO / GRANT REA PARK ☀
(323) 887-4595 - park; (323) 727-0269 - pony and horse rides   !/$
600 Rea Drive, Montebello   ⛫
(Exit San Gabriel River Fwy [605] E. on Beverly Blvd., R. on Rea Dr. [TG-676 F1])

A small Barnyard Zoo is at one corner of the Grant Rea Park. It has a small pond for ducks, an aviary with doves and peacocks, and pens holding goats, pigs, a cow, llamas, horses, and sheep that kids can pet through the fences. Visiting this "zoo" makes a stop at the park a little more special. Other activities include a short, truck-drawn hayride around part of the park for $1 per person (this is offered in the summer only); train rides around the same "track" for $1.50 per person; a merry-go-round for $1.50 per person; and pony rides, for younger children, twice around the walking track for $2. Forty-five-minute guided tours, minimum ten kids, include visiting with each of the animals, plus a train, pony, and merry-go-round ride.

The surrounding, nice-sized park is pretty. It has baseball diamonds, batting cages (open at certain times), picnic tables under shade trees, barbeques, a playground, and bike trails along the river bed.

Hours: The park is open daily 7am - dusk. The zoo is open daily 10am - 4pm. Specialty rides are usually available during zoo hours. Tours are offered daily. Call first.

Admission: Free to the park and zoo. Prices for rides are given above. Tours are $6 per child.

Ages: 1 - 10 years.

ROUNDHOUSE AQUARIUM ☀
(310) 379-8117 / www.commpages.com/roundhouse   !/$
Manhattan Beach Boulevard, at the end of Manhattan Beach Pier,   ⛫
Manhattan Beach
(Exit San Diego Fwy [405] W. on Rosecrans Ave., L. on Pacific Coast Highway. Take the next R. on Valley Dr., R. on Manhattan Beach Blvd. [TG-732 E6])

Come see the stars of Manhattan, sea stars that is. The Roundhouse Aquarium is a very small marine learning center, but packed with information and exhibits. The various tanks contain leopard sharks, horn sharks, and moray eels; a fifty-year-old, and a seventeen-pound spiny rock lobster (God definitely created some odd-looking creatures). A touch tank contains mostly sea stars. A few other aquariums with tropical fish and local invertebrates round out the collection at Roundhouse Aquarium. There are also whale bones and shark's teeth to examine.

Upstairs is a play and study center, set up like a kelp forest, that is complete with sea animal puppets, books, and videos. Note: It gets crowded quickly inside the aquarium.

The aquarium offers marine science programs and field trips for students.

For example, the one-hour Ocean Discovery class, for at least eight or more people of any age, includes learning about the marine environment and teaching time by the touch tanks. The cost is $4 per person. A three-hour class, given for kindergartners through twelfth graders, includes a lot of fa*sea*nating information, as well as hands-on fun such as touching sea stars and even petting a shark. The cost is $180 for forty students. Sleeping with the Sharks is an overnight field trip that includes a pizza party (i.e. similar to a shark feeding frenzy), touching sharks and shark teeth, dissecting parts of a shark, and more. The cost is $50 per person.

On your way out to the aquarium, which is located at the end of a concrete pier, check out all the beach activity - sand volleyball, surfing, swimming, and of course, sun bathing. You can also, ironically, fish from the pier. Sidewalk shops are just down the street.

Hours: Open Mon. - Fri., 3pm to sunset; Sat. - Sun., 10am - sunset. Call for tour and program times.

Admission: Free entrance to the aquarium; donations encouraged. Tour prices are given above. Metered parking is available on Manhattan Beach Blvd. by the stores, or wherever you can find it!

Ages: 2 years and up.

SANTA ANITA PARK

(626) 574-7223 / www.santaanita.com   *!/$$*

285 W. Huntington Drive, Arcadia

(Exit Foothill Fwy [210] S. on Baldwin Ave., L. into the parking lot for Gate 8. The park is located next to a shopping mall. [TG-567 A5])

Hold your horses! One of the most famous thoroughbred horse racing parks in the United States is surprisingly family-friendly. Watch the horses being put through their paces during their morning workouts from 4:15am (this is a little too early for me!) to 10am. Grab a bite to eat at Clocker's Corner Cafe breakfast counter which offers inexpensive items that can be eaten at the outside patio area overlooking the track. On Saturdays and Sundays, weather permitting, between 8am and 9am take a free, fifteen-minute, behind-the-scenes, narrated tram ride. Catch the tram near Clocker's Corner Cafe in the parking lot near the west side of the grandstands. You'll ride along dirt "roads", through a hub of horse activity, and past rows of stables where walkers, trainers, and jockeys are exercising, bathing, and grooming horses. Tip: Call first as the tram ride is not offered on days of major races.

Walk in the beautifully landscaped Paddock Gardens, located just inside the admission gate, to look at the flowers, statues, and equine-themed topiary plants. In the gardens, twenty minutes prior to post time, there is a brief "show" as jockeys, in their colorful silks, walk and ride their mounts around the walking ring before going on to the race track. Note: The first race usually begins at 1pm Monday through Friday and on 12:30pm on Saturday and Sunday. Weekends bring special events such as mariachi bands and dancers, costumed park mascots strolling about, and more. Ask for a schedule of their numerous, family-oriented events, such as Family Fun Days and the annual Irish Faire.

Go through a paved tunnel from the gardens to the infield (i.e. interior of the racetrack) to reach a playground. Kids can horse around on the large play structure that has wavy slides, metal domed monkey bars, a merry-go-round, and a circular swing set. The infield also features large grassy areas for running around and picnicking, so pack a lunch. Note: You may stay in the infield during races.

From the time the starting gates (which are portable) and jockeys are in position, to the finish line, enthusiasm runs rampant through the crowd. The actual races, although over quickly, are thrilling, even for non-betters. (The numerous manned windows and wagering machines receive a lot of frantic activity.) My boys "scientifically" deduced who to root for - according to the horse's name and/or the color of the jockey's silks. Tip: Sitting in grandstand seats is the best way to see the action as the slanted cement standing area in front of the seats fills up quickly with people who are always taller than you. Note: It is almost a half an hour between races.

Lunchtime food can be purchased at snack bars, the cafeteria, the casual, but nice Turf Club, or the posh Club House, where appropriate dress is required. Prices vary according to venue.

I wager your kids will have a good time watching the "Sport of Kings."

Hours:	The season runs the month of October to mid-November, and the end of December through April.
Admission:	Free admission before 9:30am includes watching the daily horse workouts and, on weekends, going on the tram ride. If you arrive after 9:30am, admission is $5 for adults; free for kids 17 and under when accompanied by an adult. Parking is $3 after 9:30am.
Ages:	4 years and up.

SUNSET RANCH HOLLYWOOD STABLES   ☼

(323) 464-9612 / www.sunsetranchhollywood.com $$$$$
3400 N. Beachwood Drive, Los Angeles

(Going N.W. on Ventura Fwy [101], exit N. on Beachwood. Going S.W. on 101, exit N. on Vine St., R. on Franklin Ave., L. on Beachwood Dr. Take Beachwood all the way up to the top. [TG-563 G7])

Many places offer scenic horseback riding during the day, including this one, but this stable also offers guided, moonlit rides. You'll leave around 6pm and ride over the hills of Griffith Park. Parts of this trail are very secluded, and beautiful. At 8pm or so, you'll arrive at Vivas Mexicas restaurant. After dinner, head back to arrive at the stables around 11pm. It's a long night, but a special one, too.

Hours:	The stables are open daily 9am - 3:30pm. Open for individuals for the sunset ride on Fri. nights 5:30pm - 11pm; open for groups of 10 or more for the sunset ride any other night.
Admission:	$20 an hour for daytime horseback riding; $40 per person for the sunset ride, plus $6 - $12 for dinner.
Ages:	7 years and up for daytime rides; must be at least 16 years for the sunset ride.

U.C.L.A. OCEAN DISCOVERY CENTER ☼

(310) 393-6149 / www.odc.ucla.edu $$

1600 Ocean Front Walk, Santa Monica

(Exit Santa Monica Fwy [10] N. on 4th St., L. on Colorado Ave. It is at the foot of the Santa Monica Pier. [TG-671 E3])

Discover what really lives in the Santa Monica Bay at the Ocean Discovery Center, located under the Santa Monica Pier. This small, but fascinating center has several tanks of live sea creatures to look at and touch. The changing exhibit is the open ocean tank. We saw moon jellies that were mesmerizing to watch as their milky white bodies floated gracefully around in their tank. Another large aquarium holds crabs, sea stars, and various fish. Use the flashlight provided to see tiny Swell Sharks developing inside their hanging egg cases. Mature Swell Sharks (which aren't necessarily wonderful sharks, it's just the name of that shark species), sand crabs, sand dollars, leopard sharks, and batrays are too fragile for fingers, but they are easily seen in shallow tanks placed at a child's eye level. Kids can, however, gently touch tidepool life such as sea stars, sea anemones, and sea slugs. A touch table displays a shark's jaw and individual teeth. It also has a microscope for closeup look at scales, shells, etc.

Another prime attraction in the center is the numerous Discovery boxes that are filled with age-appropriate activities, games, and/or books. Choose from Diving Deep, Knot Relay, Ocean Life Puzzles, Beach Bingo, and more. Computer terminals offer software featuring the marine environment. On weekends a variety of short, ocean-related films are shown throughout the day. The beautiful, marine-muraled classroom was designed for the instructional use of the school programs that are offered here. These informative, wonderful, and interactive one-hour-plus programs are offered year round.

Make a day of your visit to the Discovery Center by taking a walk on the pier (see SANTA MONICA PIER under the Piers and Seaports section), enjoying some rides at PACIFIC PARK (see this entry under the Amusement Parks section), or just playing at the beach!

Hours: Open most of the year Sat. - Sun., 11am - 5pm. Call for holiday hours. It's open in the summer Tues. - Fri., 3pm - 6pm; Sat., 11am - 6pm; Sun., 11am - 5pm. School programs are offered Mon. - Fri., at 9:30am, 11am, and 12:30pm.

Admission: $3 for adults; children 2 and under are free. School programs are $120 for up to sixty students.

Ages: 3 years and up.

WILDLIFE WAYSTATION ☼

(818) 899-5201 / www.waystation.org $$$

14831 Little Tujunga Canyon Road, Angeles National Forest

(From Golden State Fwy [5], go N.E. on San Fernando Fwy [118], E. on Foothill Fwy [210], and take the Osborne off ramp. turn L. at the bottom of the ramp, go under the overpass to the first signal, which is Osborne and turn L. up the winding road (approximately 5 miles) that turns into Tujunga Canyon Rd. You'll see the signs. [TG-4643 B5])

This donor-supported waystation is in existence to help wild animals with the three "r's": rescue, rehabilitation, and refuge. Our tour guide told us that they sometimes rehabilitate and release baby animals in the wild and, when appropriate, they release adults in the wild, too. My 8-year-old heard this, and with an incredulous look said, "They release adults in the wild?"

This can be a wonderful wildlife experience as long as you and your children follow the necessarily stringent rules. The shelters here provide homes to over 1,000 animals - lions, tigers, the rare ligers (a cross between a lion and a tiger), bears, wolves, bobcats, jaguars, leopards, raccoons, deer, and other animals. A primate center houses orangutans, chimpanzees, monkeys, baboons, and more. We were in awe of seeing so many "zoo" animals up close, separated by almost nothing more than a chain link fence. This is where the rules come in. Since carnivores tend to look at children as dinner, and the unpaved trails are narrow, parents must keep a really close eye, and/or hand, on their kids.

We learned fascinating facts about the animals and their habitats on our forty-five-minute walking tour. Note: Not all of the paths, especially the ones with wooden steps, are stroller/wheelchair friendly. The tour guides are committed and knowledgeable volunteers, but they do vary greatly in their ability and desire to relate to kids.

Make sure to spend time at the Waystation either before or after your tour to watch the animal presentations. Every half hour, or so, individual animals are brought out on a small stage by a learned handler who provides excellent opportunities to learn more about particular species. We have seen and learned about rattlesnakes, birds of prey, wolves, lions and, even the unusual binturong (i.e. "bear/cat").

Feed the animals at the petting zoo for an additional 50¢, or just pet them for no additional cost. The zoo contains pigs, goats, llamas, emus, and donkeys. Snacks for humans are available for purchase, but bringing outside food is not allowed. If you are interested in supporting the Waystation, ask about being a financial donor and/or call before your visit to see what items you can bring that are on their wish list, such as shovels, toilet paper tubes, towels, etc.

Two-hour educational tours are given for second graders up to pre-vet students and are tailored for the specific age. Tip: Don't bring a wide variety of age groups for a single tour! Students learn what country the animals are from, why they don't make good pets, why the animals are important in the environment, how to keep animals from getting bored or depressed, and more. Twenty is the minimum number of participants.

Hours: In the spring and fall, tours are offered every hour between 10am - 5pm on the first and third Sun. of each month, weather permitting. In the winter, tours are between 10m - 3pm, on the first and third Sun. In the summer, between 2pm - 5pm only on the first Sun. Also in the summer, one Sat. each month, tours are given in the evening for ages 16 and up and include dinner. Educational tours are offered year-round, Mon. - Fri., 10am - noon. Reservations are required for all tours.

Admission: Sunday admission is $12 for adults; $9 for seniors; $6 for ages 3 - 11; children 2 and under are free. (Your "donation" is tax deductible.) Sat. evening tour/dinner is $50 per person. Educational tours are $5 per person.

Ages: 3 years and up.

CASA DE TORTUGA ☼ !
(714) 962- 0612

10455 Circulo de Zapata, Fountain Valley

(Going N. on San Diego Fwy [405], exit N. on Brookhurst, R. on Slater, L. on Ward, L. on Circulo de Zapata. Going S. on 405 , exit E. on Warner, R. on Ward, R. on Circulo de Zapata. Casa De Tortuga is in a residential section and is actually outside [and inside] a large house. [TG-858 F1])

Come out of your shell to see the wonderful variety of turtle and tortoise species - over 100 - at this "House of Turtles." A favorite is the large Galapagos Island tortoise. In this one-hour, outdoor tour children walk around the turtle pens, within touching distance of the turtles. Kids will hear what tortoises like to eat, which are endangered species, what "endangered species" means, and the difference between a turtle and a tortoise. Docents welcome questions, which makes your curious child very happy.

We also loved the "really neat" pond in the backyard filled with turtles. If your child is interested in adopting a turtle, he/she will be given information to help make the best choice. Note: Narrow pebbled walkways make strollers difficult to push.

Slow and steady might win the race, but tours here fill up almost a year in advance, so hurry and make your reservation. (No more than twenty-five people are allowed in any group.) Casa De Tortuga has a free, annual open house, usually held the third weekend in August - no reservations are needed (or accepted).

Hours: Tours are given Mon. - Sat. at 10am.
Admission: Free
Ages: 3 years and up.

CENTENNIAL FARM ☼ !
(714) 708-1618 / www.ocfair.com

88 Fair Drive, Costa Mesa

(Exit Costa Mesa Fwy [55] S.W. on Newport Blvd., R. on Fair Dr., through Gate #1. It's on the Orange County Fair Grounds. [TG-859 B7])

This outdoor working farm has pigs, chickens, sheep, bunnies, ducks, Clydesdale horses, llamas, and a buffalo. During the springtime, in particular, be on the lookout for the many animal babies that are born here. The bee observatory is fascinating and with their nonstop motion, it's easy to see where the term "busy boys" oops, I mean "busy bees," came from.

Walk around the grounds to learn about other aspects of farming. Younger kids will probably be amazed to see vegetables such as carrots, zucchini, lettuce, and corn being grown, not already picked and packaged as in the grocery stores. (Please do not pick the vegetables or feed the animals.) The Millennium Barn has horse stalls, a tack room, a small museum area, and a milking parlor. A few picnic tables are here at the farm too, so pack a sack lunch. The huge parking lot is usually empty at this time, so bring skates or bikes.

A ninety-minute tour of the farm is available for grades kindergarten and up, for groups of ten or more students. One day a month is reserved for preschoolers.

The tour includes walking all around the farm, milking a cow, going into the main building and seeing chicks hatch in the incubator, planting a seed (and then taking it home), and learning about the food groups. Reservations are required. The four-hour "Agademics" tour, for fourth through sixth graders is a more in-depth look at farming and includes more hands-on activities. Students attending this tour need to bring a lunch.

Hours: The farm is open to the public August through May, Mon. - Fri., 1pm - 4pm; Sat. - Sun., 9am - 4pm. Tours for kindergartners and up are given October through May, Mon. - Fri. at 9am and 11am. Agademics is offered Mon. - Fri. at 9am. The farm is closed to the public in June. It's open in July only with paid admission to the Orange County Fair. (See the July Calendar section.)

Admission: Free. All tours are also free.

Ages: 2 years and up during public hours; K - 6th graders for most tours; Pre-K for their once-a-month tour.

FRIENDS OF THE SEA LION MARINE MAMMAL CENTER

(949) 494-3050 / www.fslmmc.org
20612 Laguna Canyon Road, Laguna Beach
(Exit San Diego Fwy [405] or Santa Ana Fwy [5] S. on Laguna Canyon Rd. [Hwy 133]. It's just S. of El Toro Rd. [TG-920 J5])

This Center is a small, safe harbor for sea lions and harbor seals that are abandoned, ailing, or in need of medical attention. The animals are kept outside in bathtub-like pens until they are ready to be released back into the wild. This is a good opportunity for kids to see these animals up-close, while learning more about them and the effect that we have on our oceans (i.e. their habitats). The volunteers are great at answering the numerous (and sometimes off-the-wall) questions kids ask.

Feeding time, usually around 3pm or 4pm, is lively as the sea lions go wild, barking in anticipation of a meal. (It sounds like mealtime at our house.) There are usually between five to twelve mammals here, but more arrive toward the end of pupping season, which is the end of February through July. One-hour educational programs that feature a slide presentation and a guided tour are $20 plus $3 per child. If your child really loves seals, ask about having a birthday party here as it includes a visit with the animals and crafts. (Also see LAGUNA KOI PONDS, in this section, located just north of the center.)

Hours: Open daily 10am - 4pm.

Admission: Free; donations gladly accepted.

Ages: 3 years and up.

JONES FAMILY MINI FARM / LOS RIOS DISTRICT

(949) 831-6550
31791 Los Rios Street, San Juan Capistrano
(Exit the San Diego Fwy [5] W. on Ortega Hwy [74], L. on Del Obispo, over the railroad tracks, R. on Paseo Adelanto, which is the backside of the farm. [TG-972 C1])

This working "mini-farm" will become a favorite stopping place whenever you visit San Juan Capistrano. Inside the barn is a small petting pen with goats, sheep, rabbits, and guinea pigs. The farm also has a few other animals to pet through the fence pens, such as horses, sheep, and a pot-bellied pig. Chickens, geese, and a few cats roam the grounds. Feed is available to purchase for the animals for $1. Starting at 8 months old, kids up to eighty pounds can ride a pony around a track. Scale model train rides around the farm and hay rides around historic Los Rios street are also available. For a birthday party with a real farm, or western flavor, rent the large outside picnic area for $100 for two hours.

In front of the farm is the 100-year-old Olivares Home, and next door is the O'Neill Historic Museum, (949) 493-8444. Older kids might enjoy a walk through these Victorian homes to see antique furniture and clothing. You can park your car at MISSION SAN JUAN CAPISTRANO (see the Museums section), which is just down the street. Note that the Amtrack depot is just a block away, if you're interested in taking a train to this city. Either way, enjoy a short walk to the farm and around this quaint, historic area.

Hours: The Farm is open Wed. - Sun., 11am - 4pm. O'Neill Historic Museum is open Tues. - Fri., 9am - noon and 1pm - 4pm; Sun., noon - 3pm.

Admission: Free to walk around outside of the farm. $1 entrance to go inside the petting farm; children under 2 are free. Pony rides start at $2. Train rides are $1.50 per person. Hay rides are $2 per person. O'Neill Museum is free; donations of $1 per person are appreciated.

Ages: All

LAGUNA KOI PONDS

(949) 494-5107 / www.lagunakoi.com
20452 Laguna Canyon Road, Laguna Beach
(Exit San Diego Fwy [405] or Santa Ana Fwy [5] S. on Laguna Canyon Rd. [Hwy 133]. It's just S. of El Toro Rd. [TG-920 J5])

This fun little stop off has several cement tanks filled with Koi fish, and a store carrying fish supplies. We enjoy just looking at these colorful fish with their beautiful patterns. Who knows, you may want to purchase a few to raise at home. You may also feed them - 25¢ for a handful of pellets. It's fun to watch their large mouths open quickly and bite at the food. Combine a trip here with a visit to the FRIENDS OF THE SEA LION MARINE MAMMAL CENTER (see this section), which is located just south of the ponds.

Hours: Open Mon. - Sat., 9am - 5pm; Sun., 11am - 5pm
Admission: Free
Ages: All

LOS ALAMITOS RACE COURSE

(714) 995-1234 / www.losalamitos.com
4961 E. Katella Avenue, Los Alamitos
(From San Gabriel River Fwy [605], exit E. on Willow/Katella. From San Diego Fwy [405] or Garden Grove Fwy [22], exit N. on Valley View, L. on Katella. [TG-797 C3])

Thoroughbreds, quarter horses, Arabian horses, and harness racing are the attractions here. Have your child cheer for his favorites! Call for schedule information.

Hours: Open year round - call for specific races and hours.

Admission: $3 for adults, or $5 for the clubhouse; kids 15 and under are free. Free parking.

Ages: 4 years and up.

MAGNOLIA BIRD FARM (Anaheim)   ☼
                                                   !
(714) 527-3387

8990 Cerritos, Anaheim

(Going N. on Santa Ana Fwy [5], exit W. on Ball Rd., L. on Magnolia, R. on Cerritos. Going S. on 5 or E. on Artesia Fwy [91], exit S. on Magnolia, R. on Cerritos. It's on the corner of Cerritos and Magnolia. [TG-798 B1])

Take your flock of kids to visit their fine feathered friends at the Magnolia Bird Farm pet shop. Birds here range from common doves and canaries to more exotic cockatoos and macaws. A small-bird aviary is located just outside the main building.

The Bird Farm has bird accessories, including a wide assortment of bird cages. Here's a craft idea: Buy a simple wooden cage for your kids to paint and decorate, then fill it with bird seed, and hang it up in your backyard. While you're here, have your kids take the bird challenge - see if they can get one of the talking birds to actually speak to them! (Also see MAGNOLIA BIRD FARM, Riverside.)

Hours: Open Tues. - Sat., 9am - 5pm.

Admission: Free

Ages: All

ORANGE COUNTY ZOO   ☼
                                       $
(714) 633-2022 / www.netreality.com/oczoo   ♨

1 Irvine Park Road, Orange

(Exit Newport Fwy [55] E. on Chapman, N. on Jamboree, which ends at Irvine Regional Park. [TG-800 J3])

Take a trip to the zoo while you're in the park! Tucked away in the massive IRVINE REGIONAL PARK (see the Great Outdoors section) is the eight-acre Orange County Zoo. The zoo has barnyard animals such as cows, sheep, goats, and pigs to pet through fence pens. Food dispensers are here, too. The main section of the zoo features animals native to the southwestern United States, such as mountain lions, bobcats, deer, coyotes, brown pelicans, a black bear, porcupines, and a variety of birds.

Hours: Open daily 10am - 3:30pm.

Admission: $1 for ages 6 and up; children 5 and under are free. This admission is in addition to the vehicle entrance fee to the park.

Ages: All

SANTA ANA ZOO   ☼
                                   $$
(714) 835-7484 / www.santaanazoo.org   ♨

1801 E. Chestnut Avenue, Santa Ana

(Going S. on Santa Ana Fwy [5], exit at 4th St. go straight on Mabury St., which turns into Elk Ln., L. on Chestnut. Going N. on 5, exit W. on 1st St., L. on Elk Ln., L. on Chestnut. It's at Prentice Park. [TG-829 H3])

Lions and tigers and bears - not here! This small zoo, however, is perfect for young children. They can easily walk around it, see all the animals, and still have of time to play on the playground, all within just a few hours. The Santa Ana Zoo houses llamas; cavies; small mammals, such as porcupines; birds, including bald eagles; fruit bats; sloths; and a wide variety of monkeys - our personal favorites. The cages and animals are not far off in the distance, but right along the pathways. Walk through the wonderful aviary where you can see beautiful and exotic birds close up. The Children's Zoo has pigs, goats, and sheep to pet through pens, plus reptiles and amphibians to look at.

Kids can ride a real elephant once round a small trail between 11am to 3pm on most weekends, and holiday Mondays, October through May for $3 per person. Scale model train rides around part of the zoo are available Friday through Sunday from 11am to 3pm for $1 per person. The on-site playground has a small climbing hut, slides, and turtle statues. The gift shop has a wonderful variety of animal-oriented merchandise. Purchase lunch at the snack bar, which is usually open, or enjoy a sack lunch right outside the zoo gates at the adjoining Prentice Park which offers picnic tables, grassy areas, and shade trees.

Breakfast with the Beasts is a once-a-month Saturday morning program offered for ages 3 and older. It includes a light breakfast, a guided tour, and a chance to feed some animals in the Children's Zoo. The fee is $8 per person. A variety of other educational and interactive programs for kids are also offered throughout the year.

Hours: Open Mon. - Sun., 10am - 4pm. Closed New Year's Day and Christmas.

Admission: $4 for adults; $2 for seniors and ages 3 - 12; children 2 and under and the physically impaired are free. AAA discounts are available.

Ages: All

MAGNOLIA BIRD FARM (Riverside)

(909) 278-0878

12200 Magnolia Avenue, Riverside

(Going N.E. on Riverside Fwy [91], exit S.E. on Pierce, R. on Magnolia. Going S.W. on 91, exit S.W. on Magnolia. [TG-744 C3])

See MAGNOLIA BIRD FARM, Anaheim, for a more complete description of the bird farm. The main difference between the two is size, with this location being almost three times as large. The aviary here includes parakeets, love birds, finches, and quail, as well as doves and pigeons.

As springtime brings the birth of new baby birds, kids can sometimes see them being hand fed through the glass walls. Tour groups, of at least ten or more people, will learn about seed, such as which kind is best for what species; see and study a (live) white dove; and more.

Hours: Open Tues. - Sat., 9am - 5pm. Reservations are needed for the free, half-hour tour.

Admission: Free

Ages: All

MOJAVE STATE FISH HATCHERY

(760) 245-9981

12550 Jacaranda Avenue, Victorville

(Exit Mojave Fwy [15] E. on Bear Valley Rd., about 6 miles, L. on Mojave Fish Hatchery Rd. By the corner of Mojave Fish Hatchery and Jacaranda. [TG-4387 A5])

This facility is the largest trout production hatchery in California. Six raceways (i.e. holding tanks for the fish) at 1,000 feet long each, hold four strains of rainbow trout that supplies seven counties. Tempting though it may be, you may not bring your fishing pole.

      Hours: Open daily 7am - 3:30pm.

   Admission: Free

       Ages: 2 years and up.

TIGER RESCUE

(909) 825-3311 / hometown.aol.com/catigerrescue   *$*

1350 W. Agua Mensa Road, Colton

(Exit San Bernardino Fwy [10] S. on Rancho Ave., R. on Agua Mensa. [TG-646 A1])

This family-owned and operated rescue is a grrrrrreat place to observe over forty tigers and twenty other big cats. All of the animals here have been born in captivity and placed here instead of being destroyed. Most of them are "leftovers", animals once used in movies, T.V. shows, music videos, and magic acts, and now put out to pasture, so to speak. (Maybe you'll recognize some of them.)

A paved pathway leads past several enclosures of groupings of exotic felines, such as Siberian tigers, Bengal tigers, leopards, and panthers. Cement pools are available for them to cool off in the hot summer months. A two-acre parcel of land is being transformed to a free roaming natural habitat.

A petting zoo with farm animals, a deer, and a llama is also on the premises. Thirty flightless birds are on the outside of the compound, including emus, rheas, and ostriches. Don't forget to check out the small gift shop.

Half-hour guided school tours are offered during the week for a minimum of twenty students. As kids see the animals, they'll learn why exotic animals don't make good pets, what species of animal they are seeing and where it naturally lives, their eating habits, and much more.

      Hours: Open Sat. - Sun., 10am - 4pm. Summer hours may fluctuate.

   Admission: $5 for adults; ages 11 and under are free. School tours are $4 per person.

       Ages: All

WOLF MOUNTAIN SANCTUARY

(760) 248-7818 / www.wolfmountain.com   *$$$*

7520 Fairlane Road, Lucerne Valley

(Exit Mojave Fwy [15] E. on Bear Valley Rd. At the first Y stay R. and continue on Hwy 18. At the next Y (intersection of 18 and Hwy 247), stay R. and go about 6 miles. You will see a white picket fence on your R., turn L. on Fairlane. The Sactuary is the first house you come to on your left. Call first. [TG-4571 J2])

Twelve, or so, wolves that have been discarded from movie makers or put out to pasture by wolf breeders now roam the enclosures here. Visitors are invited to first watch a video to understand the ways of wolves, listen to a talk about the owner's first hand experiences, and then visit the magnificent-looking creatures. Some of them are friendly enough to allow guests to pet them. According to the owner, many people also come for the healing powers attributed to wolves. The types of wolves here include British Columbia Black, McKinsley Timber, Alaskan Tundra, and Alaskan Grey.

Hours: Call in the morning or evening to schedule a tour.
Admission: $10 per person.
Ages: 3 years and up.

CALIFORNIA WOLF CENTER ☼

(619) 234-WOLF (9653) / www.californiawolfcenter.org $$$
Highway 79, Julian

(Exit Highway 79, 4 miles S. of Julian at the K.Q. Ranch Campground. [TG-1156 G5])

Who's afraid of the big bad wolf? And why? Clear up many misconceptions about North American and Alaskan Gray Wolves at the wolf center during a two-hour presentation/tour. First, gather in a room filled with wolf paraphernalia for a twenty-minute slide show. See and learn about what wolves eat; how they communicate (yes they howl, but not at the moon); the pack's pecking order, starting with an alpha (i.e. dominant) male and female; and their predators (man). Then watch a fifteen-minute portion of the video, "Return of the Wolves", shown on PBS, which showcases wolves in the wild as they hunt and capture their prey, and what happens when a new wolf tries to join an established pack. Learn the difference between a fox, a coyote, and a wolf (this being the largest of the three) via a touch table with skins, skulls, teeth, and plaster footprints. Also hold and learn about tracking collars that researchers use on wolves.

A highlight is going out to the enclosures to actually see these majestic creatures. There are currently two packs here, totaling about twenty-eight wolves. The ones used in the education programs are very curious and come close up to the fence where visitors line up - all the better to see you, my dear. Bring your camera. Take a short hike up a hill to see the other wolves who may, or may not, come over to check out the group.

The center also offers Wolf Encounters, a program for kids held either at the center or at a school. The presentation is similar to the one held here on Saturdays, except that the slide show is tailored specifically for kids and, if the encounter is at a school, two of the wolves are brought along for show and tell. Curriculum supplements are provided. Have a howling good time here!

Hours: Open Sat. at 1:45pm - do not be late!! Reservations are required. Call to set up a time for group programs during the week.
Admission: $7 per adult; $5 for seniors; $3 for ages 3 - 10. Wolf Encounters start at $125 for up to 35 participants, plus fuel charges if any.

Ages: 7 years and up for the Sat. program; kindergartners and up for educational programs.

CHULA VISTA NATURE CENTER

(619) 409-5900 / www.chulavistanaturecenter.org

1000 Gunpowder Point Drive, Chula Vista

(Exit San Diego Fwy [5] W. on 'E' St. to park, or exit E. on 'E' St., to park at the Visitor's Center and take the free trolley into the Nature Center. [TG-1309 J6])

Putting their hands in a pool of hungry sharks is only one of the special things that kids (and adults) are invited to do at the Chula Vista Nature Center, located in the Sweetwater Marsh National Wildlife Refuge. You'll start your visit by taking an old-fashioned trolley (free of charge) into the refuge - cars are not allowed. The medium-sized center is full of interactive exhibits such as using a bioscanner (i.e. a mounted camera with a zoom lens) to see anemones close up on a monitor, and poking your head up into a glassed-enclosed exhibit to watch mice run around. (Mice use the refuge to look for food.) The touch table has pelican bones, bird skulls, whale vertebrae, and shells. There are several tanks with live sea creatures, such as seahorses, halibut, lobsters, and rainbow trout. Listen for the snapping sounds of the snapping shrimp as they try to frighten predators away. Like a good mystery? Then try to find the California scorpionfish, who are hiding in plain sight.

My boys proudly boast that they've touched a shark, and lived! The outside petting pool contains leopard and horn sharks as well as batrays, stingrays, and the odd-looking shovel-nose guitarfish. (These creatures actually come within petting distance.) Join in the feeding fun, which usually takes place around 4pm.

An outside overlook affords an opportunity to observe migrating shore birds such as terns, killdeer, plovers, sandpipers, and more wetlands wildlife. A walk-through bird aviary features water birds, as well as some interactive exhibits such as rubbing tables and an oversized clapper rail nest for kids to crawl inside. Other bird enclosures contain non-releasable birds of prey, such as owls and hawks. A hummingbird and a butterfly garden are also on the grounds. Stroller-friendly trails in front of the Center branch off in various directions and allow kids to get close to the bay to see geese, egrets, or smaller water inhabitants. Look for other wildlife along the trail such as bunnies and lizards. Visit the bird blind which raises visitors up to get a bird's eye view of, well, birds.

The Nature Center offers a variety of on-site special programs, such as Make It Take It craft workshops for ages five and up, given on Saturdays and Sundays from 1pm to 2pm for 50¢. Call to get a complete schedule, or to sign up for a guided group tour.

Hours: Open Tues. - Sun., 10am - 5pm. Closed New Year's Day, Easter, Thanksgiving, and Christmas. Trolleys run approximately every 25 minutes.

Admission: $3.50 for adults; $2.50 for seniors; $1 for ages 6 - 17; children 5 and under are free.

Ages: 3 years and up.

DEL MAR FAIRGROUNDS / RACETRACK

(858) 755-1141 or (858) 793-5555 / www.delmarracing.com
Jimmy Durante Boulevard, at Del Mar Fairgrounds, Del Mar
(Exit San Diego Fwy [5] W. on Via de la Valle. [TG-1187 G2])

Horse racing season at the famous Del Mar Fairgrounds begins in July and runs through mid-September. Kids have good horse sense - they aren't here to bet, but to enjoy the races. On most weekends, the infield is transformed to a fun zone for children with pony rides, face painting, an inflatable jump, obstacle course, and more. Admission is free for children, when accompanied by a parent. Also inquire about horse shows, rodeos, and polo games.

Hours: Gates are open July through mid-September, Mon., and Wed. - Fri. at noon; Sat. - Sun., 11:30am. Post time is usually 2pm, although it's at 4pm for the first five Fri. The track is closed on Tues.

Admission: General admission is $4 for adults for the grandstands; $7 for clubhouse seating (which is closer to the finish line); free for children 17 and under.

Ages: 5 years and up.

FREEFLIGHT

(858) 481-3148
2132 Jimmy Durante Boulevard, Del Mar
(Exit San Diego Fwy [5] W. on Via de la Valle, L. on Jimmy Durante, follow around the fairgrounds. It's located next to the Vet and Bird Hospital, just past the racetrack. Turn in at the 2126 address. [TG-1187 G3])

This boarding house is for the birds, literally. It is also a breeding facility with baby birds available for sale. There are more than thirty perches along the short pathway in this jungle-like backyard. Look at and even gently touch some of the brilliantly-colored cockatoos, macaws, parrots, and other exotic birds. It's a good place to get some great picture of birds! Note: Loud squawking of the birds is set off by loud kids who are set off by the loud squawking, etc. Young children might be startled. Also, many of the birds have strong talons which could scare or hurt visitors, so young ones are better off simply looking at and not holding the birds. Bring 25¢ to purchase peanuts to feed the birds. Freeflight offers half-hour tours that explain the different types of birds, their habitats, and more. Please note that children under 13 years must be accompanied by a parent. Tip: Bring a sweater because the beach weather is often cool.

Hours: Open daily 10am - 4pm. Closed on rainy days.

Admission: $1 per person.

Ages: 3 years and up.

FUND FOR ANIMALS WILDLIFE REHABILITATION CENTER

(760) 789-2324 / www.fundwildlife.org
18740 Highland Valley Road, Ramona
(Exit the Escondido Fwy [15], E. on Hwy 78. Stay on 78 into Ramona, go R. on 67. R. on Highland Valley Rd. [TG-1172 A2])

Just off the beaten path is a rehabilitation center specializing in the rescue and medical treatment of abused and discarded exotic pets, confiscated (i.e. illegal) animals, or injured mountain lions, bobcats, coyotes, and birds of prey. If possible, when some of the animals have recovered, they are released into their original habitats. These animals are kept away from people (therefore you cannot see them) to minimize human contact. Other animals live here permanently, such as the declawed mountain lion.

A guide walks each group of people around the enclosures, explaining where the animals came from, their behaviors, and what they eat. Although the types of animals here rotate, we saw two llamas, some goats, bobcats, lynx, a turkey vulture, a gold eagle, Arctic foxes, a hedgehog, and several old house cats. Note: There are more animals here in the spring when orphaned babies are rescued. Also note that the felines tend to be napping in the afternoon (doesn't that sound wonderful?!), thus they are not very active.

Hours: Open Sat. - Sun., 10am - 4pm, weather permitting.
Admission: Free
Ages: All

HELEN WOODWARD ANIMAL CENTER

(858) 756-4117 ext. 318 / www.animalcenter.org
6461 El Apajo Road, Rancho Santa Fe

(Going N. on San Diego Fwy [5], exit E. on Del Mar Height Rd., L. on El Camino Real, R. on San Dieguito Rd., L. on El Apajo. Going S. on 5, exit E. on Via De La Valle., R. on El Camino Real, L. on San Dieguito Rd., L. on El Apajo. [TG-1168 F6])

This unique facility, whose motto is "people help animals and animals help people", is part animal shelter and part training center. It is a temporary home to cats and dogs, as well as long term homes to horses, llamas, rabbits, turtles, birds, and a few other critters. The training part of the center has many components, but all are designed for people, especially children, to experience the unconditional love and tactile benefits of animals. People with a variety of disabilities interact and ride gentle horses as they participate in the therapeutic riding program. Other programs include pet encounter therapy for abused children, seniors, and others; Camp EdVenture (day camps); family fun nights with storytelling and crafts; educational assemblies, either on-site or at a classroom; "edu-taining" birthday parties; and forty-five-minute tours of the twelve-acre campus. Most of the programs incorporate playing games and up-close animal presentations to teach animal behavior, pet responsibility, and proper pet care.

The center also contains a riding arena and stables for horses used in the programs, boarding facilities, a large and a small animal veterinary hospital, a grooming center, and classrooms.

Hours: Call for a current program schedule.
Admission: Call for prices for the activity of your choice.
Ages: Depends on the program.

LEELIN LLAMA TREKS

(800) LAMAPAK (526-2725) / www.llamatreks.com
1645 Whispering Pines Drive, Julian

$$$$$

(Take 78 Hwy E., from Julian. After 78 turns N., go R. on the second (not the first) Whispering Pines Dr. It's just N. of the town of Julian. [TG-1136 C5])

Looking for an unusual outing? Sign up for a llama trek! Choose from a variety of destinations - to the lake, through the mountains, or through the town of Julian. Each member of your group leads his/her own llama that carries trekkers' lunches and other necessities. Most kids, and adults, aren't used to being around llamas, so the intrigue, as well as the scenery, makes the four to six-hour expeditions unique experiences. The animals are gentle, enjoy being pet, and by the end of the trek, your children will want to take theirs home. They can't. A deli sandwich, cold salad, cookie, and cold drink are included in your outing. The best bet for kids is the Eagle Mine Trek, which takes about five hours round trip. The trip includes a tour of the gold mine, EAGLE MINE (see the Tours section for more detail). Children 8 and older are eligible to go on overnight trips to the Sierras. The latter excursion includes four to ten nights of camping in the mountains, hiking, and delicious, home-cooked food!

LeeLin Wikiup is a bed and breakfast, geared for couples, owned by LeeLin Llama Treks. (The llamas actually live on the grounds here.) Each room of the Wikiup, although adjacent to each other, has its own unique, completely themed decor - Native American, Victorian, or rustic.

Hours: Call for reservations. At least two people must sign up for any of the treks.

Admission: Prices start at $75. The Eagle Mine trek is $75 for adults; $60 for children 3 - 10. Overnight Sierra trips are $150 per day per person. Wikiup rates start at $155 per couple during the week.

Ages: 4 years and up.

THE MONARCH PROGRAM

(760) 944-7113 / www.monarchprogram.org
450 Oceanview Avenue, Encinitas
(Exit San Diego Fwy [5] W. on Encinitas Blvd., R. on Vulcan, R. on Orpheus, R. on Union, R. on Oceanview. [TG-1147 C5])

I'm not particularly fond of most insects, so I think butterflies should be in a classification by themselves, called beautiful winged creatures, or something. This facility, located in a residential neighborhood, has two rooms devoted to our fluttery friends. The education room is in a garage that is set up like a classroom. It contains maps that show the path of butterfly migrations, books, and a few real caterpillars and chrysalides in various stages of metamorphosis. A docent is on hand to answer any questions. A video, showing the life cycle of a butterfly, can be watched upon request.

The second "room", or vivarium, is a relatively small outside enclosed area with plants, flowers, a few trees, and several butterflies flying around. Most of the butterflies in here are native to California, except the zebra butterfly. We saw a few monarchs, a swallowtail, a California dogface (which doesn't look like its namesake), and a few others. Children can hold out a piece of fruit (provided by the Monarch Program), such as a watermelon, to attract the butterflies. But, please, don't try to catch the butterflies - it could hurt them.

School/group tours are welcome during the week. A one-hour tour consists of a half-hour slide show and talk and another half hour in the vivarium. It also includes a take-home booklet that has butterfly body parts to identify and color, plus information on several species. Note: Caterpillars are available for purchase.

Bring a sack lunch to enjoy at Orpheus park, which is just down the street. The park has picnic tables, grassy areas, shade trees, and a playground.

Hours: Open April through June and mid-September through October, Sat., 11am -3pm. Open July through mid-September, Thurs. - Sat., 11am - 3pm. Open for school tours April through October, Mon. - Fri. Call to make a reservation. The program is closed November through March.

Admission: $5 for adults; $3 for ages 6 - 18; children 5 and under are free. Group tours are a flat fee of $85 for up to thirty children.

Ages: 2 years and up.

SAN DIEGO WILD ANIMAL PARK   ☼
(619) 234-6541 - general info; (760) 738-5049 - special programs / $$$$$
www.sandiegozoo.org
15500 San Pasqual Valley Road, Escondido
(Going S. on San Diego Fwy [5] or Escondido Fwy [15], exit E. on Hwy 78, which turns into San Pasqual Valley Rd. Going N. on 15, exit E. on Via Rancho Pkwy., which turns into Bear Valley Rd., R. on San Pasqual Rd., which turns into Via Rancho Pkwy., go to end, R. on San Pasqual Valley Rd. [TG-1130 J6])

Go on a safari and see the exotic animals that live in the African veldt and Asian plains, without ever leaving Southern California. The 2,000-acre San Diego Wild Animal Park has tigers, rhinos, elephants, giraffes, antelope, etc., in atypical zoo enclosures. The animals here roam the grasslands freely, in settings that resemble their natural habitats. The best way to see a majority of the animals is via the Wgasa Bush Line monorail, a five-mile, fifty-minute, narrated journey (tour). Tip: Sit on the right-hand side (not the driver's side) of the monorail car as most of the animals are on this side. This fascinating ride is included in your admission price. I suggest going on the monorail first as the lines get longer later in the day.

The ride ends back at Nairobi Village, which is a great starting point for the rest of your wild animal adventure. Walk through some of the thirty acres that comprise the Heart of Africa. A paved, circuitous path in this section is three-quarters-of-a-mile long and can take at least an hour. The trail will take you into the forest where antelope and the unusual-looking okapi roam; along a stream - look for warthogs and foxes; near waterfalls; and to a large watering hole where rhinos, waterbuck, and other animals congregate. Cross over a bridge to the one small island (out of five islands total) that has a mock research station and see dart guns and lab equipment. A live aardvark and hornbill dwell here, too. The plains are home to wildebeest, cheetahs, and even a station, open at designated times, where visitors can hand-feed giraffes for an additional fee.

There are numerous other attractions at the wild animal park. Watch the antics of the monkeys and gorillas. The Petting Kraal has small deer, goats, sheep, and other animals to pet and feed. Check the time for the animal shows performed (or presented) here. Hand-feeding rainbow-colored lorikeets, which look like small parrots, is a thrill. Bring your camera to capture your child's expression as the birds land on his arms or even his head. Check for feeding times. I was enchanted by the Hidden Jungle. This "room" is filled with lush green plants and colorful butterflies fluttering all around. Look through telescopes on the observation deck of Condor Ridge to see the habitats of dozens of endangered species, including, obviously, California condors. Special zoo keys can be rented for $3.75 which are used on boxes in front of many enclosures. The keys unlock audio messages that provide additional information about the particular animal's habitats, reproduction, behaviors, and more.

Mombasa Lagoon is a terrific, interactive way to experience animal behavior "firsthand": Put on a furry pair of bat ears and look silly, but hear acutely; sit in a large turtle shell (and maybe hatch an idea or two); explore the inside of the weaver bird dwelling; climb a giant spider web; hop from one huge lily pad to another; and more! Enjoy all your travels through the animal kingdom.

Want to make your day picture perfect? The Photo Caravan (ages 8 and up) offers two photo opportunities to go on an open, flat-bed truck into some of the animal enclosures. The cost ranges from $95 to $115, depending on the length of the adventure. Your kids can feed some of the animals, take pictures of them, and learn all about them. Call for tour dates and more information. Roar and Snore overnight tent-camping safaris include nature hikes, a campfire and food, photo opportunities, and close-up encounters with wild (and more mild) beasts! The cost is $115 for adults; $95 for kids, who must be at least 8 years old. These are just a few of the special programs offered - call for a complete schedule.

Hours: Open daily in the summer 7:30am - 8pm. Open daily the rest of the year 9am - 5pm.

Admission: $23.95 for adults; $21.55 for seniors; $16.95 for ages 3 - 11; children 2 and under are free. Certain discounts are available through AAA. Parking is $6. A combination ticket with the SAN DIEGO ZOO (to be used once at each location within five days) is $40.75 for adults; $25.55 for ages 3 - 11. Admission to the Wild Animal Park is free one day in May in celebration of Founder's Day.

Ages: All

SAN DIEGO ZOO ☼

(619) 234-3153 / www.sandiegozoo.org $$$$

2920 Zoo Drive, San Diego

(Going S. on San Diego Fwy [5], exit N. on Cabrillo Fwy [163], E. on Richmond St. (Zoo/Museums exit), follow signs. Going N. on 5, exit N. on Pershing Dr. L. on Florida Dr. L. on Zoo Place, cross Park Blvd. to parking. Zoo entrance is off Park Blvd. at Zoo Place. [TG-1269 C7])

The world-famous San Diego Zoo is home to some of the rarest animals in captivity, and almost every animal imaginable, at least that's what it seems like. Put your walking shoes on because this zoo covers a lot of ground! In fact, you'd be hard pressed to try to see all 4,000 animals in one day, at least with young children in tow. The flamingos, just inside the entrance, are a colorful way to start your day. Tiger River, Elephant Mesa, the Horn and Hoof Mesa, Gorilla

Tropics, and the Reptile House are just a few of the exhibit areas to visit. The two-acre Ituri Forest follows a path under a canopy of trees, past a tropical jungle that houses forest buffalo, exotic okapis, monkeys, and several other species of mammals and birds. Be amazed at how enormous hippos really are and the size of polar bears in two underwater viewing exhibits - Hippo Beach and Polar Bear Plunge, respectively. Experience panda-monium and see the two giant pandas that are visiting from China - what unique-looking animals! Enjoy a walk through the Rain Forest Aviary to see brilliantly colored jungle birds amidst tropical foliage; watch the antics of the bears at Sun Bear Forest; see koalas in their trees; and take the opportunity to observe kangaroos, camels, primates, and other animals in enclosures that simulate their natural habitat. If you want to find out more about particular animals and plants, and hear stories about the zoo, as well as test your zoo trivia, rent an audio guide for $4.

A forty-five-minute, double-decker, narrated bus tour is not only fun and informative, but it's a great way to get a good overview of most of the animals here. Another narrated bus ride, the Kangaroo Bus Tour, also covers about seventy-five percent of the zoo, but you can hop on and hop off (hence the name), at eight locations, as often as you want throughout the day. The Skyfari Aerial Tram ride is another way to view a portion of the zoo at $1.50 per person, each way.

The *Sea Lion Show* and the *Wild Ones Show*, presented twice daily, are an entertaining and interesting way to see some favorite animals close up. The Children's Zoo is always a highlight as there are animals to pet; mole-rats and other unique animals to look at; and an animal baby nursery that shows off the newest zoo additions. Ask about the many special programs the zoo offers during the year, including zoo sleepovers and Close Encounters of the Zoo Kind.

    Hours: Open daily in the summer 9am - 10pm. Open daily the rest of the year 9am - 5pm.

Admission: $18 for adults; $8 for ages 3 - 11; children 2 and under area free. Certain discounts are available through AAA. The bus tour is an additional $5 for adults; $3 for ages 3 - 11. The Kangaroo bus tour is an additional $12 for adults; $6 for kids. A combination package with the SAN DIEGO WILD ANIMAL PARK (to be used once at each location within 5 days) is $40.75 for adults; $25.55 for children. Admission is free on the first Monday of October in celebration of Founder's Day.

      Ages: All

SEAL ROCK MARINE MAMMAL RESERVE   ☀

(619) 221-8901; (619) 687-3588 - docent program /   !
www.lajollaseals.org

1180 Coast Boulevard, La Jolla

(Exit San Diego Fwy [5] W. on La Jolla Village Dr., L. on Torrey Pines Rd., R. on Prospect Pl., R. Cave St., stay L. for Coast Blvd. [TG-1227 E6])

From a distance, we saw what looked like lots of lumpy rocks on the beach. As we got closer, however, we could see that they were really seals sprawling on the sand and on the nearby rocks. The seals have taken over what used to be known as Children's Pool Beach, so named because the rocks form a breakwater. My boys and I were thrilled that we were almost close enough to touch the seals, although doing so and getting too close is forbidden. (Even seals are protected by harassment laws!) A normal family might be here for just a few minutes; we were here for an hour because we were enthralled. Warning: Seals are not sunbathing here constantly, so seeing them is a hit or miss deal. Also see LA JOLLA SHORES BEACH and COVE (under the Beaches section) for more about this immediate area.

Hours: Open daily.
Admission: Free
Ages: All

SEAWORLD ADVENTURE PARK   ☼
(619) 226-3901 / www.seaworld.com $$$$$
500 Sea World Drive, San Diego   ♨
(Exit San Diego Fwy [5] W. on Sea World Dr. [TG-1268 B4])

Sea World entertains and educates people of all ages with its wide variety of sea animal exhibits. The dazzling dolphin and silly sea lion shows get top ratings. The killer-whale show, starring Shamu and friends, is a crowd-pleaser with its thrills - a trainer riding a whale gets catapulted - and chills - those sitting in the splash-zone bleachers get drenched. Trainer For a Day is a special program that allows visitors to wade into shallow water, reach over an acrylic panel, and touch the killer whales. Real trainers also invite a few volunteers to help out and train the whales by holding targets, carrying food buckets, and rewarding the giant mammals for a behavior correctly performed. View the animals underwater at the viewing gallery. A similar program with dolphins allows visitors, who must be at least 6 years old, to put on a wet suit, wade into shallow water for about twenty minutes with the dolphins, to touch, feed, and interact with them while learning about their anatomy and personalities. The cost is $125 per person.

There are several other unique attractions, such as Shark Encounter, which culminates in a fifty-seven-foot-long enclosed people-mover tube that takes you through shark-infested waters(!), and Rocky Point Preserve, where kids can actually touch and feed bottlenose dolphins. They feel rubbery. If you stretch your arms far enough, you can touch bat rays and other marine animals at Forbidden Reef and the California Tide Pool. The penguin exhibit also features the penguins' cousins, the funny-looking puffins who fly through the air and sea. *Pirates 4-D* is a seventeen-minute, multi-sensory adventure film on a 3-D screen. The audience becomes involved with the (mostly) funny antics of hapless pirates. Be forewarned that as a swarm of hornets chase the pirates on screen, a buzzing device in audience's seat cushions is activated, and as a bird flies overhead in the movie, sprays of water are dropped on viewers' heads. A simulated helicopter ride at Wild Arctic lands you at a remote research station. (Actually, you're still at Sea World.) Blasts of Arctic air greet you as you view beluga whales, harbor seals, walruses, and polar bears. The year-round high-flying bird show is terrific, as are some of their other seasonal shows.

Shamu's Happy Harbor is two acres of pure kid delight. This play area has tubes, slides, ropes, balls, a sandy beach, a moon bounce, an outdoor theater for kid-oriented entertainment, and a Funship for pretend pirates to climb aboard. For those who want (or are allowed) to get wet, there are a few water fountains to splash in, and water tubes to go through. Tip: Bring a towel or change of clothing.

Another wet activity is the Shipwreck Rapids ride. A nine-passenger raft swirls past several realistic-looking shipwrecks, real sea turtles, through "rapids", and semi under a roaring waterfall. Lunch or dinner at the adjacent island cafe offers a tasty selection of food and even eater-tainment in the form of a trainer coming by with a sea lion, otter, or penguin for a brief presentation. For an additional $2.75 per person, each attraction (or $3.75 for both), the Skytower, which offers a panoramic view, and the Bayside Skyride, which is a gondola ride over Mission Bay, are fun treats. Dine with Shamu at a pool-side buffet luncheon (dinners are only offered during the summer) where the great whale may even come out of the water to greet you. The luncheon is $25.49 for adults; $12.95 for ages 3 to 11. Sea World also offers various outstanding educational tours, such as a sleep over with sharks or other animals. What fun! A ninety-minute, behind-the-scenes tour is an additional $10 for adults, $8 for seniors and ages 3 to 11. Call for information on the times, hours, and admission for other unique field trips. Also ask about the monthly school days specials where admission is greatly reduced for students. Special summertime highlights at Seaworld include fireworks, and special ice skating, gymnastics, or music shows. Note: Although no outside food is allowed inside, a picnic area is set up just outside the park. Spending a day (or night) here is a great way for the whole family to "sea" the world!

Hours: Open daily in the summer Mon. - Fri., 9am - 10pm; Sat. - Sun., 9am - 11pm. Check for seasonality. Open daily the rest of the year 10am - 5pm.

Admission: $41.95 for adults; $31.95 for ages 3 - 11; children 2 and under are free. Certain discounts are available through AAA. A two-day package, where you may visit Sea World twice within a 7 day period, is a great deal at $44.95 for adults; $34.95 for ages 3 - 11. Parking is $7 per day.

Ages: All

STEPHEN BIRCH AQUARIUM-MUSEUM   ☼
(858) 534-FISH (3474) / www.aquarium.ucsd.edu $$$
2300 Expedition Way, San Diego

(Exit San Diego Fwy [405] W. on La Jolla Village Dr. Stay to the right as La Jolla Village Dr. turns into N. Torrey Pines. Take the next L. on La Jolla Shores Dr. and follow it to Scripps Institute of Oceanography. Stephen Birch is at the University of California, Scripps Institute of Oceanography. [TG-1227 H3])

Statues of leaping, large gray whales are in the fountain outside the entrance of the Stephen Birch Aquarium - Museum. This outstanding, sizable, aquarium-museum has three main exhibit areas. The aquarium section contains over thirty-three large tanks filled with an incredible variety of creatures found in the Earth's oceans - from eels to sharks to flashlight fish that glow in the dark. Just some of our favorite sea animals showcased here include the almost mesmerizing moon jellies; chocolate chip starfish; garden eels that look like hoses "standing" upright in the sand; bizarre-looking, weedy sea dragons (related to the seahorse); the amazing giant octopus; and the beautiful, but venomous, striped lionfish. The largest tank has a huge kelp forest which makes it easy to view animals that are normally hidden on ocean floors. See divers feed the fish in the forest Tuesdays and Thursdays at 12:20pm and Sundays at 10:30am. (These times may change.)

Outside, the rocky Tidepool Plaza connects the aquarium and the museum. A wave machine gently creates natural water motion in a simulated tidepool. Kids will see up close (and can gently touch) sea stars, sea urchins, sea cucumbers, and more. Also, take in the magnificent panoramic view of the La Jolla coastline (and the world famous Scripps Institute).

The museum features Exploring the Blue Planet, a fantastic oceanographic exhibit with seven different, interactive display areas. Each area incorporates touch screens or an activity that shows and explains the integral part that oceans play in relation to how the Earth functions. Kids will learn about various aspects of ocean sciences from the displays on currents, tides, and waves; from earthquakes and plate tectonics; and as they experience a simulated, submersible ride to the ocean floor. My kids really enjoyed the Ocean Supermarket, where they used scanners on common household products to see which ingredients came from the ocean. (Did you know that ice cream uses carrageenan [i.e. red seaweed] to make it smooth and creamy?!)

The above is a sampling of what the Stephen Birch Aquarium- Museum has to offer - come "sea" it for yourself! There is also an Aquarium Bookshop, and outdoor picnic areas that are stroller and wheelchair accessible. Call about the many special activities and programs offered through the aquarium-museum including tidepools tours, whale-watching cruises, grunion hunting, and snorkeling.

Hours: Open daily 9am - 5pm. Closed New Year's Day, Thanksgiving, and Christmas.

Admission: $8.50 for adults; $7.50 for seniors; $6 for students; $5 for ages 3 - 17; children 2 and under are free. Parking is $3.

Ages: 3 years and up.

AMERICA'S TEACHING ZOO

(805) 378-1441 / www.vcnet.com/gwhiz
7075 Campus Road, at Moorpark Community College, Moorpark
(Exit Simi Valley/San Fernando Valley Fwy [118] N. on Collins Dr. Continue all the way up Collins, behind the college, R. into the dirt parking area where you'll see signs for the zoo. [TG-477 A5])

Students attend this teaching zoo, that contains 130 exotic animals, to become zoo keepers, veterinarians, and animal trainers. If your child aspires to one of these professions, or is just intrigued with animals, come visit. As this is a teaching zoo and not just here for public enjoyment, many of the caged animals are in rows, making it difficult, or impossible, to see a lot of them. However, the animals that are readily viewed can be seen more up close than at a typical zoo. Note: Picnic tables are here for your lunching pleasure.

Twenty-minute demonstrations, featuring three to five animals per show, such as primates, hoofed animals, or reptiles, are given every hour on a small outdoor stage. The student trainers talk about the animal's habitats, nutrition, and training. Afterward, kids can come up, ask questions, and usually touch the animals. One of the reptiles we saw and touched was a boa. We were amazed at its strength and its under-belly softness. Trainer talks, where one animal is showcased and discussed more in depth, are given in the morning.

Don't miss the 3:45pm feeding of the carnivores! Actually, get there a little early and see animals being fed that aren't on the scheduled program. We saw a trainer go inside a cage to feed the tigers and to "show-off" the tigers' learned behavior. The trainers and students willingly answered all the questions they were asked. My kids and I learned so much here! One-hour school tours are given during the week and include a few demonstrations or tour or both.

Watch out for a type of monkey called langurs. One growled and leapt at the bars toward my kids. We were told that this species considers eye contact to be a sign of aggression, and smiling children to be teeth-baring, aggressive adversaries. As parents, we often feel the same way.

Hours: The Zoo is open weekends 11am - 5pm. Trainer talks are given throughout the day. The demonstrations are every hour on the hour noon - 3pm, weather permitting. You can call to see what animals will be shown. Feeding of the carnivores is at 3:45pm.

Admission: $4 for adults; $3 for seniors and children 12 and under. School tours start at $100 for up to 30 people; additional people are $1 each.

Ages: All

FILLMORE FISH HATCHERY
(805) 524-0962   !
612 E. Telegraph Road, Fillmore
(Exit Hwy 23 R. on Ventura St. [126], which turns in to Telegraph. Look for signs. [TG-456 H6])

Stop off and take a look around the fish hatchery to see hundreds of thousands of rainbow trout. This hatchery supplies fish to lakes and streams through San Luis Obispo, Santa Barbara, Los Angeles, and Ventura counties. The long, narrow, concrete tanks have compartments that are labeled with the various species names. Coin-operated fish food dispensers are here and the fish always seem to be hungry. Note: Just east down the road is Cornejo's produce stand offering great, in-season produce.

Hours: Open daily 7:30am - 3:30pm
Admission: Free
Ages: 2 years and up.

TIERRA REJADA FAMILY FARMS
(805) 523-8552 - food farm; (805) 523-2957 - animal farm /
www.tierrarejadafamilyfarms.com
3370 Moorpark Road, Moorpark

See TIERRA REJADA FAMILY FARMS under the Edible Adventures entry for details about its animal farm.

BIG BEAR (and the surrounding area)

This four-season mountain resort is close enough to escape to for a day or a weekend, though it offers enough activities for at least a week's vacation. The pine trees and fresh air that beckon city-weary folks, plus all the things to do, make it an ideal family get-away. November through March (or so) the mountains become a winter wonderland with lot of opportunities for snow play and skiing. This section, however, also covers a broader base of activities because Big Bear is great any time of year! For specific information on events held during the time you plan to visit, call (909) 866-573 - chamber of commerce / www.BigBeartodaymag.com. For lodging information call (800) 4BIG BEAR (424-4232) / www.bigbearinfo.com.

General directions to Big Bear are as follows: Head E. on the Riverside Fwy [91] or San Bernardino Fwy [10], N. on the 215 Fwy; E. on Hwy 30, N. on 330 to Hwy 18.

ALPINE SLIDE at MAGIC MOUNTAIN
(909) 866-4626 / www.bigbear.com/alpineslide
Big Bear Boulevard, Magic Mountain Recreation Area, Big Bear
(1/4 mile W. of Big Bear Lake Village. [TG-4811 D2])

$$$

Alpine Slide lifts family fun to new heights! Take the chairlift up the mountain. Then, you and your child sit on heavy-duty plastic toboggans and rip down the quarter-mile, cement, contoured slide that resembles a bobsled track. Control your speed by pushing or pulling on the lever. We were cautious only on our first ride. Your child can go down by himself if he's at least 7 years old.

If you don't succumb to motion sickness, take a whirl on the Orbitron. You'll be harnessed to the inside of this big sphere and spun around in all directions. Doesn't that sound like fun? The miniature golf course, Putt 'N Around, has just a few frills, but kids still enjoy puttin' around on it. Go karts are available here, too. Inside the main building are a few video games, of course, and a snack bar. That delicious food you smell is a burger or hot dog being barbecued right outside, or maybe a bowl of soup or chili served in a bread bowl.

Summer play is enhanced by two zippy waterslides. You'll end with a splash in the three-and-a-half-feet deep pool, but it's not for swimming in. Winter allows you and the kids a chance to cultivate the fine art of throwing snowballs or to inner tube down the snowplay hill on four, side-by-side runs that resemble a snake's trail. Instead of trudging back up the hill, with tube in hand, take the Magic Carpet, which is similar to a moving conveyor belt. You'll have mountains of fun any season you come to Alpine Slide at Magic Mountain.

Hours: The Alpine Slide, Orbitron, miniature golf, and go karts are open mid-June through mid-September and November through Easter, daily 10am - 5pm (weather permitting). In the summer, these attractions are often open later on weekends. The rest of the year they are open the same hours, but on weekends only. The waterslide is open mid-June to mid-September, daily 10am - 6pm. The snow play area is open as long as snow is available daily 10am - 4pm.

Admission: Alpine ride - $3.50 for one ride; $15 for a five-ride book. Orbitron - $4 a ride. Miniature golf - $4 a round for adults; $3 for kids. Go karts - $3.50 a single car; $5.50 a double car. Waterslide - $1 for one ride; $7 for a ten-ride book; $12 for an unlimited day pass. Snow play - $15 for an unlimited day-pass with a tube; $10 for an unlimited day-pass using your own tube. Fri. and Sat. night tubing sessions, 5pm - 9pm, are $10 per adult. Children 2 - 6 are free with a paying adult on the Alpine slide, waterslide, and snow play area, as long as they are accompanied by a paying adult.

Ages: 3 years and up.

ALPINE TROUT LAKE
(909) 866-4532
440 Catalina Road, Big Bear
(Exit Big Bear Blvd. S.E. on Catalina, just N.E. of Moonridge Rd. [TG-4811 J1])

$$$

Tall pine trees line the perimeters of this small stocked lake, making it a beautiful place to fish. And catching a fish is (almost!) guaranteed, which is great for kids (and adults) who get discouraged easily, like the author of this book! Two-pounders are quite common. Make a day of your time here as picnic tables and barbecue pits are also on the grounds, so catch your meal and eat it, too. In fact, the owners also sell fixings for the trout as well as barbecue coals. You are also welcome to bring in your own food and beverages. This is a private lake, so a fishing license is not required. Tip: Bring a cooler in case you want to take some fish home.

Hours: Open Mon. - Fri., 10am - 5pm; Sat. - Sun., 9am - 6pm, weather permitting.

Admission: $5 for a family or group of up to 6 people. Rod rentals, reel, and bait are an additional $3.50 per person. Fish cost $4.89 per pound.

Ages: 3 years and up.

BALDWIN LAKE STABLES

(909) 585-6482 / www.baldwinlakestables.com $$$$

E. Shay Road, Big Bear

(Go E. on Big Bear Blvd., past the Hwy 38 turnoff, and follow it as it turns into Shay Rd., then watch for sign on the R. The stables are right where Shay Rd. turns into Baldwin Lake Rd. [TG-4743 A5])

Leave the city behind and horseback ride through the scenic national forest. The breathtaking mountain views, and sore bottoms for those unused to trotting, are all included in your ride price. Enjoy a one- to- four- hour ride along the Pacific Crest Trail, or see things in a different light by taking a sunset ride! Ask about the over night camp ride, which includes a ride, a traditional western dinner, sleeping in a tent, and a hearty campfire breakfast. Hand-led pony rides for young bronchos are $5 per child for three laps around the track. A petting zoo here has bales of hay all around and a barn-like small building. For $3 per person, enter the pen to pet and/or feed llamas, bunnies, goats, sheep, and ducks.

Hours: Open daily most of the year, weather permitting, 9am - 5pm. Winter hours are daily 10am - 4pm. Call before you come.

Admission: $20 an hour per person. Sunset rides are $40 per person - no children allowed.

Ages: At least 7 years old and 4' tall.

BEAR MOUNTAIN RIDING STABLES

(909) 878-4677 $$$$

At the top of Lassen Drive, Big Bear

(Exit Big Bear Blvd. S.E. at Moonridge Rd. Go to the end of Moonridge and turn L. on Lassen Dr. It's at the foot of Bear Mountain Ski Resort. [TG-4812 C4])

There is only so much you can see of Big Bear from the car! A horseback ride is an ideal way to experience the beauty of the mountains. Children 7 years and up can take a one or two-hour guided horseback ride through the pine trees and over mountain ridges. At the stables, younger children can take pony rides around the track.

Hours: Open daily May through September, 9am - 5pm, during good
weather. Call first, just in case.

Admission: $20 per hour per person for horseback riding. $5 for three laps
around the track on a pony.

Ages: 1 - 6 years for pony rides; 7 years and up for horseback rides.

BEAR VALLEY BIKES

(909) 866-8000 / www.bearvalleybikes.com   *$$$*

40298 Big Bear Boulevard, Magic Mountain Recreation Area, Big Bear

(It's 1/4 mile W. of Big Bear Lake Village, on top of Red Ant Hill, across from the Alpine Slide at
Magic Mountain. [TG-4811 D2])

Pedal your way around town or sign up for a guided tour. Bear Valley has
mountain bikes, tandems cycles, BMX bikes, trailers for children, toddler bikes,
and even helmets. An adjacent BMX track is open Wednesday evenings at
5:30pm to practice. Races are held on Sunday afternoons. Sign up and join in the
fun!

Hours: Open daily 10am - 5pm. Call for winter hours.

Admission: Mt. bikes are $6 an hour; tandems are $10 an hour; BMX bikes
are $5 an hour. $8 to race on the BMX tracks.

Ages: All

BIG BEAR BIKES

(909) 866-2224 / www.burrobikes.com   *$$$*

41810 Big Bear Boulevard, Big Bear

(On Big Bear Blvd., near Snow Summit Blvd. [TG-4811 H1])

Need some wheels to get around town? Big Bear Bikes offers, fittingly
enough, mountain bikes and suggests trying out the beautiful North Shore bike
path. This bike shop also rents snowshoes and can suggest numerous
destinations for putting them to good use. (Note: This is a winter-time activity.)
They also host three-hour, guided moonlight snowshoe tromps for $20. The price
includes equipment rental, hiking for a few hours, and stopping off to warm
yourselves near a campfire. (Bring your own munchies.)

Hours: Open Mon. - Fri., 10am - 5pm; Sat. - Sun., 10am - 6pm; weather
permitting.

Admission: Bike rentals, available in the summer only, start at $6 per hour.
Tandems are $10 an hour. Snowshoe rentals begin at $10 a day.

Ages: All for bikes; 6 years and up for snowshoes.

BIG BEAR DISCOVERY CENTER

(909) 866-3437 / www.bigbeardiscoverycenter.org   *!/$*

Highway 38 (North Shore Drive), Big Bear

(Between Fawnskin and Stansfield Cutoff, at the Ranger Station [TG-4741 G5])

This ranger station is the best place to call or visit for trail maps, camp sites,
and special program information. Some programs include weekend campfire
programs offered in the amphitheater behind the center, nature programs on
Thursday nights (summer hours vary), canoe tours around the lake, and
numerous other activities. The center has informational and pictorial panels

regarding the forest and the lake and their inhabitants. Pick up an Adventure Pass here, too. An Adventure Pass is required for all vehicles parking on National Forest property for recreational purposes.

Pick up your free *Eagle Discovery Guide and Games* booklet at the center. The guide will help you find eagles on your own, plus it offers fun ways to learn about eagles and their habitats. Another option to "hunt" for eagles during their winter season in the mountains is to board the Eagle Discovery Tour bus for a three-hour journey through Big Bear. There are several stops along the way. A professional naturalist will aid you in identifying eagle habitats and the surrounding eco system, while informally teaching interesting facts about our national symbol. You'll receive the use of binoculars and a spotting scope. A light snack is included, too.

Hours: Open daily in the summer 8am - 6pm; open in the winter 9am - 5pm. Closed New Year's Day, Thanksgiving, and Christmas. Eagle tours are given December through March on weekends and daily during holiday periods, Sat., 9am - noon and 1pm - 4pm; Sun., 10am - 1pm. Reservations are required.

Admission: The Adventure pass is $5 per day or $30 for an annual pass. The Eagle Discovery Tour is $25 for adults; $20 for youth.

Ages: All

BIG BEAR HISTORICAL MUSEUM

(909) 585-8100 or (909) 866-5753
Greenway Drive, Big Bear
(Exit W. Big Bear Blvd. N. on Greenway. The museum is in the N.E. portion of the Big Bear City Park, E. of the airport. [TG-4742 D5])

The past is definitely present at the Eleanor Abbott Big Bear Valley Historical Museum. The buildings that comprise the museum are very old (and old looking). The small main building contains a good assortment of taxidermied animals such as a golden eagle, skunk, red fox, badger, and others, displayed mostly behind glass in "natural" settings. Other exhibits include birds' nests, eggs, arrowheads, rocks, fossils, unique leather carvings, old photographs of old Big Bear, and old-fashioned toys. Outside on the porch are turn-of-the-century post office boxes, plus mining equipment and mining artifacts. An old barn and lots of old, rusted agriculture equipment are also on the grounds.

An on-site, furnished, 1875 one-room log cabin offers a real look into the pioneer lifestyle. The docents in here are wonderful at explaining to kids how pioneer families lived, and the uses of some of the household items. My boys couldn't believe that chamber pots were really used as portable potties. It finally dawned on them that entire families lived together in this one room; sleeping, cooking, eating, and playing together. I hope they'll be more thankful about their own living arrangements!

An adjacent park has a few pieces of play equipment and some old tennis courts. The park is good mostly for visitors to just run around in its overgrown fields. Shade is scarce, but there are a few picnic tables here.

Hours: Open May through October only, Sat. 10am - 4pm; Sun. and holidays, 11am - 2pm.

Admission: $1 per person donation.
Ages: 3 years and up.

BIG BEAR JEEP TOURS   ☼
(909) 878-5337 / www.bigbearjeeptours.com   *$$$$$*
40977 Big Bear Boulevard, Big Bear
(Big Bear Blvd., just E. of Pine Knot Blvd. [TG-4811 F1])

For rugged kids, who like bumpy adventures, jeep tours are the way to go. There are so many historical, beautiful places to explore in these mountains and some of them are only accessible via four-wheel drive. Take a one-hour trip to the top of the ridgeline, or go for several hours to explore Holcomb Valley where kids will learn about the Gold Rush, a ghost town, and gold mines. What a great way to see and experience a bit of golden history!

Hours: Open May through mid-October. Call for tour times.
Admission: Prices range from $40.95 per person for a one-and-a-half-hour tour, to $89.95 per person for a five-hour tours.
Ages: 4 years and up.

BIG BEAR MARINA   ☼
(909) 866-3218 / www.bigbearmarina.com   *$$$*
500 Paine Road, Big Bear
(Exit Big Bear Blvd. N. on Paine Rd. [TG-4811 E1])

The Marina offers a boatload of fun for the family. Motorized fishing boats start at $15 an hour and seat up to five people. Pedal boats, kayaks, and canoes are $10 an hour per. Jet skis are $95 an hour for up to four people. Wave runners are $65 an hour for up to two people. Rent a small pontoon, a flat-bottomed boat that is almost seasick proof, for $35 an hour. It seats up to eight people. A larger pontoon, which seats up to twelve people, is $45 an hour. Take an hour-and-a-half, narrated tour around Big Bear Lake on the Big Bear Queen. Tours are given daily, in season, always at 2pm, and sometimes at 10am, noon and 4pm, if at least fifteen people are signed up. Prices are $10 for adults; $8.50 for seniors; $5 for ages 3 to 12; children 2 years and under are free.

Where can your family go for dinner that is a fun, kid-friendly treat (and I don't mean McDonald's)? Somewhere that is exotic, yet cost efficient? Different, but agreeable to all? The answer to all these questions is - on a pontoon sunset dinner cruise! Big Bear Queen offers dinner cruises in the summer on Tuesday and Thursday nights starting at about 7pm for $16.50 per person, which includes a guided tour and a dinner of enchiladas or chicken or another menu choice. Reservations and prepayment are required.

Hours: Open daily, seasonally, usually spring through October, 7am - 7pm.
Admission: Prices are listed above.
Ages: 3 years and up.

BIG BEAR PARASAIL   ☼
(909) 866-IFLY (4359) / www.pineknotlanding.com   *$$$$$*
At the north end of Pine Knot Boulevard, Big Bear

(Exit Big Bear Blvd. N. on Pine Knot Blvd. [TG-4811 F1])

Ever had dreams where you can fly? Parasailing is the next best thing. Start off on dry land, attached by a harness to the parasail and by a tow rope to the boat. As the boat pulls away, you are lifted into the air for ten minutes of flight. You can stay dry if you want, and if all goes well, or take a quick dip (more like a toe touch) in the lake before being airborne again. This is a thrill-seeking experience for kids and adults.

Hours: Seasonal only - late spring through early fall - Mon. - Fri., 9am - 5pm; Sat. - Sun., 8am - 6pm.
Admission: Single - $40 weekdays; $45 weekends. Tandem - $70 weekday; $80 weekends.
Ages: 90 pounds and up.

BIG BEAR SOLAR OBSERVATORY

(909) 866-5791 / www.bbso.njit.edu
40386 North Shore Lane, Big Bear
(Exit North Shore Dr. on North Shore Ln. It's past Fawnskin. [TG-4741 D6])

The small, thirty-foot dome solar observatory offers a unique way to study the often sunny skies in Big Bear. Three telescopes monitor and record images of the sun, which are then displayed on video monitors. Cameras can show sharper details than the unaided eye can see. Take a forty-five-minute tour to get the hot facts about the sun.

Hours: Open July 4th through Labor Day, Sat., 4pm - 6pm.
Admission: $2 for adults; $1 for children.
Ages: 8 years and up.

CHILDREN'S FOREST
(909) 337-5156 / www.sbnfa.org
Off Highway 18, between Running Springs and Arrow Bear Lake
(Exit Highway 18 on Keller Peak Rd. for the information center, interpretive trail, and lookout tower. [TG-519 D7])

The Children's Forest is 3,400 acres within the San Bernardino National Forest. Maintained primarily by youths, its purpose is to encourage children to develop a passion for the environment. Using a self-guided brochure, walk the only established trail, which is a three-quarter-mile paved trail. Or, choose any other place to wander around in the forest. Among the pine trees and along the mountain stream be on the lookout for wildlife such as birds, deer, squirrels, unusual insects, etc. Youth naturalists lead free walks along the interpretive trail at various times during the summer. With a minimum of twenty participants, you can schedule an appointment for special programs, such as Finding Wildlife, Charting Your Course, and Rappers and Raptors. These programs are the same ones offered to school groups - see below for descriptions. Most programs are recommended for ages 6 and up, although younger children will especially enjoy the program, Preschool Small Worlds of Wonder. Don't forget to pack lunch, water, sunscreen, and binoculars.

The Keller Peak lookout tower is open to the public daily in the summer and during fire season from 9am to 5pm - what a view! On a clear day you can see all the way to the ocean. When the tower is open, you may drive out to it or hike to it. The trail to the tower is four miles from the highway.

School exploration programs are offered Monday through Friday, year round. Each program is four hours long. The majority of the time is spent in the forest, plus there are games and hands-on activities. Groups are limited to two classes and all age students are welcome. Note that smaller groups generally see and do more. A sampling of topical studies includes Finding the Wild Things - learn how animals adapt to their environments, where they live, what they eat, and how to read the signs of their presence; Birds - Rappers and Raptors - learn to identify many species by their markings, habits, and songs; Get Green and Growing - learn to identify plants and their function in the ecosystem; and Charting Your Course - learn elementary map and compass reading techniques. Seasonal snowshoe field trips are available to aid in learning about winter ecology. Get a workout while following animal tracks!

Other programs include training youths between fifteen to eighteen years to become naturalists and conduct Investigation Days, where conservation topics such as survival skills, birding, art/music, and more, are taught. With all that it offers and set in such beautiful surroundings, I'm glad the Children's Forest is open to adults, too!

Hours: The paved trail and the forest is open in the spring and summer daily sunrise to sunset. Program times vary - call for a schedule or to make an appointment.

Admission: $5 per vehicle per day to stop anywhere in the forest. Public and school programs cost $150 for minimum twenty participants; $300 for twenty-one to forty participants.

Ages: All for the paved trail and walking around; other age requirements depend on the program.

COWBOY EXPRESS STEAK HOUSE

(909) 866-1486

40433 Lake View Drive, Big Bear

(Exit Big Bear Blvd. N. on Lake View. It's 3 blocks W. of the village [TG-4811 D1])

Rustle up some good lunch or dinner grub in this rustic, cowboy-themed restaurant. Some enticing entrees include T-bone steaks, $14.95; chicken steak, $9.95; beef back ribs, $12.95; beef, chicken, or pork tortilla wraps, $7.95; and burgers, $7.50. Children can choose chicken strips, cheeseburger, corn dog or pork ribs for $6.95. Steak or shrimp is $7.95. All kids' meals come with fries, a drink, and a small sundae.

Hours: Open daily 11am - 9pm.

Admission: Prices mentioned above.

Ages: All

HIKING

(909) 866-3437 / www.sbnfa.org

There are many, *many* places to go hiking in the Big Bear area. See BIG BEAR DISCOVERY CENTER, in this section, for information on the ranger station. Note: Anywhere you park in the national forest for recreational reasons, you must pay for an Adventure Pass. Just two of the places my family has enjoyed trekking include:

CASTLE ROCK:
(From Highway 18, the trailhead is about one mile east past the dam.)

The trail is only eight-tenths of a mile, but it is an uphill walk over some rocky terrain. The destination is Castle Rock, a large rock that kids love to climb on. Its name gives lead to a lot of imaginative play time here. All of my kids wanted to be king - what a surprise! If everyone still has the energy, keep hiking back to the waterfalls, and/ or to Devil's woodpile. The scenery along the way is spectacular.

WOODLAND TRAIL:
(On Highway 38, parking is almost directly across the street from M.D. Boat Ramp, just west of the Stanfield Cutoff Road.)

This one-and-a-half-mile loop is an easy walk, as the dirt trail follows more along the side of the mountain, rather than into the mountain. Although you can hear the traffic from certain sections of the trail, the changing landscape, from pine trees to coastal shrub to cactus, still offers the sense of being immersed in nature. An interpretative trail guide is available through the Ranger Station. Make it an educational field trip as well as a nice walk!

> **Hours:** Open daily.
> **Admission:** $5 a day for an Adventure Pass.
> **Ages:** 4 years and up.

HOLLOWAY'S MARINA and RV PARK

(800) 448-5335 / www.bigbearboating.com $$$
3 miles to the east of the dam at Metcalf Bay, Big Bear
(Exit Big Bear Blvd., N. on Edgemoor, about 1 1/2 miles E. of the village. [TG-4811 C1])

Holloway's rents almost anything that is water worthy. Two-seater paddle boats are $6 a half hour, $10 an hour; four seaters are $7 a half hour, $12 an hour. Eight to ten people flat bottom pontoons are $40 an hour, $65 for two hours; twelve to fourteen people pontoons are $50 an hour, $75 for two hours. Aluminum motorized fishing boats are $18 an hour. Kayaks and canoes are $14 an hour, $24 for two hours. Sailboats and wave runners, and even fishing poles are also available for rent.

> **Hours:** Open year round, weather permitting.
> **Admission:** Prices are mentioned above.
> **Ages:** 2 years and up, depending.

THE HOT SHOT MINIATURE GOLF COURSE

Corner of Catalina and Big Bear Boulevard, Big Bear $$
(On Big Bear Blvd., just N. of Moonridge. [TG-4811 J1])

Putt around under shady pine trees at this basic, but fun miniature golf course. Encourage your kids to be hot shots here!

> **Hours:** Open daily seasonally, weather permitting, 10am - 6pm. Closed during the winter.
> **Admission:** $4 for adults; $3 for ages 12 and under. Replays are $1 per person.

Ages: 3 years and up.

LAKE ARROWHEAD CHILDREN'S MUSEUM

(909) 336-1332 - recorded information; (909) 336-3093 - front desk / $$
www.mountaininfo.com/kids

Highway 18, in the Village Shopping Center, Lake Arrowhead

(Exit San Bernardino Fwy [10] N. on the 215, E. on the 30. Take the Waterman Ave. [Hwy 18]
exit 'up the hill' to Lake Arrowhead. The museum is located in the lower level of the Village, at the
end of the peninsula, just past the G.R. Toy Shop and Rocky Mt. Chocolate Factory. [TG-518 A1])

In the Lake Arrowhead Village shopping center, kids now have a place of
their own to "shop" for fun. This museum is comprised of a large room,
decorated with beautiful nature murals, divided into interactive exhibit areas.
Some of the permanent exhibits include the Ant Wall - where children are the
ants, climbing up and down carpeted ramps and tunnels; Inventor's Workshop -
where recyclable "trash" is crafted into take-home treasure; a Bubble Area -
where bubbles can be kid-size; a Theater - with face paint; a Toddlers' Room -
with several toys, and Peter Pan's ship to climb aboard and sail off to Never
Land; Science Stations - where kids can throw a ball and clock its speed, speak
through tubes to each other, and experiment with magnets, hand batteries, and
more; Space - which has glow-in-the-dark chalk and a chalkboard, black
lighting, and control panels of a space ship; a Funzone with tubes to crawl
through and ball pits; and Village Merchants - with playhouse-size "stores" like
a fire station, a post office, a photo shop with a photosensitive shadow room, a
Vet's office with lots of stuffed animals, and a mini-mart with cash registers,
carts, and pay food. Technologically-minded children enjoy playing educational
games on the computers. Check out the imaginative temporary exhibits here, too.
There is always something fun to do at this children's museum!

Hours: Open in the summer daily 10am - 6pm. Open the rest of the year
daily 10am - 5pm. Closed Thanksgiving and Christmas.

Admission: $4 for ages 3 and up; $3 for seniors; children 2 and under are
free.

Ages: 2 - 10 years.

MCDILL SWIM BEACH / MEADOW PARK

(909) 866-0130 $$

Park Avenue, Big Bear

(Exit Big Bear Blvd. N. on Knight St. to the end. [TG-4811 F1])

This waveless lagoon, with a lifeguard on duty, offers a refreshing respite
during the hot summer months. Kids can play in the water, or build castles on the
sandy beach. Swimmers enjoy going beyond the roped area, out to the floating
dock that they can lay out on or dive off. A small playground, a volleyball court,
and a snack bar round out the facilities at this beach. And the view of the
mountains is spectacular! Children 10 years and under must be supervised by an
adult.

Meadow Park is just outside the Swim Beach gates. This large, grassy park
has a small playground, nice tennis courts, volleyball courts, baseball diamonds,
and horseshoe pits. Bring a picnic dinner to cook at the barbecue pits, and enjoy

the sunset.

Hours: The swim beach is open seasonally on weekends noon - 6pm, and daily in the summer noon - 6pm. The park is open sunrise to sunset.

Admission: The swim beach is $3.50 for adults; $2.50 for ages 5 - 10; children 4 and under are free. The park is free.

Ages: All

MOONRIDGE ANIMAL PARK
(909) 584-1171 or (909) 866-0183 / www.moonridgezoo.com
18012 Goldmine Drive, Big Bear
(Exit Big Bear Blvd. S.E. on Moonridge Rd. The Animal Park is at the end of the road, on Goldmine Dr. [TG-4812 C3])

Get a little wild up in the mountains! Animals from the surrounding mountains that need extra care, whether they are orphaned or hurt, find sanctuary in this small animal park. Grizzly bears, snow leopards, black bears, wolves, bison, coyotes, bobcats, raccoons, deer, and birds of prey such as eagles, hawks, owls and other birds and animals now consider the animal park their home. It's just the right size for kids to walk around easily, and since the enclosures are not too large, it's easy to see the animals up close. Walk through a flight enclosure that holds shore and other aquatic birds. And don't missss the walk-through reptile housssse!

Special daily events include animal presentations at noon, where an animal is brought out and talked about, and a feeding tour given at 3pm daily (except on Wednesdays) most of the year and on weekends only in the winter. The latter, a forty-five-minute educational feeding tour, takes place at each cage. As the animals are fed (mush, dead chicks, and other stuff) a staff member explains why the animal is here, its habits, and more. We've always found the docents and trainers willing, even eager, to answer our kids' questions, so it makes our visit here more memorable. The Animal Park also offers seasonal special programs, such as flashlight tours and tasty ice cream safaris. After a snowfall, come take a guided "snow tour" through the Animal Park from 11:30am - 1:30pm. Admission is then reduced to $2.50 per person. Call first and dress warmly! Traveling exhibits are offered to school groups. Call (909) 584-1299 for more information.

A small grassy picnic area inside the zoo has a few picnic tables. A small education center in the lobby has a few nature exhibits such as bird eggs and nests, fossils, and animal jawbones.

Hours: Open daily mid-May through October, 10am - 5pm; open November through mid-May, 10am - 4pm, weather permitting.

Admission: $4 for adults; $3 for seniors and ages 3 - 10; children 2 and under are free.

Ages: All

PINE KNOT LANDING
(909) 866-BOAT (2628) / www.pineknotlanding.com
439 Pine Knot Avenue, Big Bear Lake

(Exit Big Bear Blvd. N. on Pine Knot Blvd. [TG-4811 F1])

Boat rentals here are *knot* a problem! Come on board the double decker Sierra Belle paddle wheel boat for a one-and-a-half-hour narrated excursion. Learn the history of the lake, famous people who have or still live here, and general information about Big Bear Valley. Sunset cruises are another special way to tour the lake. Cruise around on your own via an eight-passenger pontoon boats at $40 an hour, or a fifteen-passenger pontoon at $50 an hour. Motorized fishing boats start at $13 an hour for four passengers. Speedboats start at $50 an hour for seven passengers.

Hours: Open April through December, Mon. - Fri., 6am - 7pm; Sat., Sun., and holidays, 6am - 8pm. Always call first! The Sierra Belle tour is available daily, if there is a minimum of fifteen passengers. Tours depart on weekends and holidays at 10am and 2pm, regardless. Note that reservations are necessary for most outings.

Admission: The narrated tour is $10 for adults; $8.50 for seniors; $5 for ages 4 - 12; children 3 and under are free. Other prices are listed above.

Ages: 4 years and up.

SCENIC SKY CHAIR

(909) 866-5766 / www.snowsummit.com
880 Snow Summit Boulevard, at Snow Summit ski area, Big Bear
(Exit Big Bear Blvd., S. on Summit Blvd. [TG-4811 H2])

Do your kids appreciate the awesome scenery of mountains, trees, and Big Bear Lake, plus breathing clean air? If not, they'll still enjoy the mile-long, thirteen-minute (each way) chair ride up the mountaintop. At the top, there is a picnic and barbecue area, so bring your own food, or purchase a burger, chicken sandwich, etc., from the snack bar. As there are over forty miles of trails through the forest and wilderness areas, hikers and biking enthusiasts are in their element up here. The terrain varies, meaning that trails range from easy, wide, forest service roads to arduous, single-track, dirt trails. What better way to spend a day than up here in a place readily described as "God's country."

Bike rentals are available at the base of Snow Summit at Team Big Bear Mountain Bikes, (909) 866-4565 / www.teambigbear.com. Mountain bikes are the recommended cycle, and helmets are required for all riders. The store has maps for all the Big Bear trails.

Hours: The sky chair operates May through mid-June and mid-September through October (or the beginning of ski season) on weekends only, 9am - 4pm. It's open daily, mid-June through mid-September, Mon. - Fri., 9am - 4pm; Sat., 8am - 5pm; Sun., 8am - 4pm, weather permitting.

Admission: One-way ride (no bike) - $6 for adults; $3 for ages 7 - 12; children 6 and under are free when accompanied by a paying adult. One-way ride with a bike or a round trip no bike - $9 for adults; $4 for ages 7 - 12. An all-day pass with a bike - $21 for adults; $9 for kids. Ask about half-day prices.

Ages: 3 years and up.

SKIING and SNOW PLAY ☼
$$$$$

The following is a list and quick bites of information on ski slopes and snow play areas in and around the Big Bear area. I found www.onthesnow.com/skireport/SouthernCalifornia.html helpful for up-to-the-minute ski conditions. Ask each resort about beginner specials, special promos, and even a free lift ticket on your birthday:

Big Bear Mountain: from Hwy 18 to Big Bear Lake, R. on Moonridge Rd. and follow the signs - (909) 585-2519; (800)BEARMTN (232-7686) - ski conditions / www.bearmtn.com. Big Bear has 12 lifts and 32 runs on 200 acres, with the longest run being 2 miles. Top elevation is 8,800 feet. Admission is $35 (non-holiday) adults; $12 for ages 6 - 12 on weekends; children 5 and under are free. Ask about weekday specials for kids. The tubing area is $5 an hour per person and they supply the tube.

Mountain High: 24510 Hwy 2 in Wrightwood - (760) 249-5808; (888) 754-7878 (ski conditions) / www.mthigh.com. Mt. High has 10 chairs and 47 runs on 220 acres. The elevation is 8,200 feet. Ski both east and west mountains with free shuttles going in between. Night skiing, 5pm - 10pm, is available. Day skiing is $35 for adults; $12 for children ages 7 - 12; ages 6 and under are free with a paying adult.

Mount Baldy: from 10 Fwy, exit N. on Mountain Ave. and go N. (909) 981-3344 / www.mtbaldy.com. Mt. Baldy has 4 lifts and 26 runs. The elevation is 8,600 ft. Admission is $40 for adults; $25 for ages 10 - 15; $10 for ages 9 and under.

Mount Waterman: exit 210 Freeway N. on 2 Fwy; it's E. of Wrightwood - (626) 440-1041; (818) 790-2002 / www.rideacr.com. Waterman has 3 lifts and 23 runs on 150 acres. It does not have a snow-making machine. The top elevation is a little more than 8,000 feet. Skiers can also go "tree skiing", meaning they can venture off the marked runs and go through the forest. Admission is $30 (non-holiday) for adults; $10 for children; free for ages 6 and under with a paying adult.

Ski Sunrise: off Hwy 2, N. on Table Mt. Rd. in Wrightwood - (760) 249-6150 / www.skisunrise.com. Sunrise has 4 chairs and 16 runs on 100 acres. The elevation is 7,600 feet. Admission is $28 for adults on weekends, $25 on weekdays; $20 for ages 7 - 17 on weekends; $17 on weekdays. Children 6 and under ski are free with a paying adult.

Snow Summit: exit Big Bear Blvd. R. on Summit Blvd. in Big Bear Lake - (909) 866-5766; (909) 866-5841; (888) summit-1 (for ski conditions) / www.snowsummit.com. Summit has 12 chairs and 32 runs on 230 acres. The elevation is 8,000 feet. Night skiing is available on Friday, Saturday, and holidays, 3pm - 9:30pm. Non-holiday, day rate admission is $39 for adults; $33 for ages 13 - 19; $12 for ages 7 - 12 years; children 6 and under are free with a paying adult. Holiday rates are $48 for ages 13 and up; $20 for ages 12 and under.

Snow Valley: on Hwy 18, 5 miles E. of Running Springs - (909) 867-2751;

(909) 867-5151; (800) 680-SNOW (ski conditions) / www.snow-valley.com.
Snow Valley has 11 lifts and 27 runs on 230 acres. The elevation is 7,440 feet.
Night skiing is available on Thursday, Friday, and Saturday nights and holidays,
4pm - 9pm. Snow Valley also has an adjacent snow play area. Lift tickets are
$35 for adults; $12 for ages 6 - 12; children 5 and under are free with a paying
adult.

SUGARLOAF CORDWOOD CO.   ☀
(909) 866-2220   !/$
42193 Big Bear Boulevard, Big Bear
(At the corner of Big Bear Blvd. and Stanfield Cut-off [TG-4741 J7])

The gigantic, wooden, chain-saw carvings of bears, Indians, and other
figures, will attract your attention as you drive along Big Bear Boulevard. This
unique store is worth a stop. Take a walk through the lot and inside the rooms to
see smaller carvings and other unusual, artistic, gift items.

> **Hours:**   Usually open Mon. - Fri., 10am - 5pm; Sat. - Sun., 9am - 6pm.
> **Admission:** Free
> **Ages:**   3 years and up.

SUGARLOAF PARK   ☼
Baldwin Lane and Maple Lane, Big Bear   !
(Exit Big Bear Blvd. [38] S. on Maple Ln., L. on Baldwin. [TG-4742 F7]) ♨

It is a beautiful drive to this well-worn park, but where up here isn't the
scenery beautiful? Sugarloaf Park has a softball field, a few tennis courts, a sand
volleyball court, a basketball court, and older metal playground equipment, plus
picnic shelters and barbecue pits. It also has a small grouping of short trees that
could feel like a mini forest to younger kids.

> **Hours:**   Open daily sunrise to sunset.
> **Admission:** Free
> **Ages:**   All

THE TIME BANDIT   ☼
(909) 878-4040 / www.bigbearboating.com $$$$
398 Edgemoor Road at Holloway's Marina, Big Bear   ♨
(Exit Big Bear Blvd., N. on Edgemoor About 1 1/2 miles E. of the village. [TG-4811 C1])

If it's adventure you're seekin' matey, then climb aboard and hoist the sails!
This jet black, one-third-scale replica of a 16th century pirate ship comes
complete with its own crew of pirates, well at least a captain. Sail across Big
Bear Lake (it's kind of like sailing the seven seas, just a shorter trip) on an over
one-hour narrated cruise and stop by the Discovery Center and Whaler's Pointe
restaurant. *The Time Bandit*, named after the 1981 movie in which it was
featured, often offers live entertainment at night. Overnight charters are available
as the ship is equipped with a stateroom and bed, and bunk beds for kids.

> **Hours:**   Usually open June through October, with tours leaving daily at
>   2pm. If enough people are signed up (the ship holds 25), tours
>   also depart at 10am, noon, 4pm, and 6pm.

Admission:	$12.50 for adults; $10.50 for seniors; $9.50 for ages 12 and under. Infants or lap-sitting toddlers are free.
Ages:	All

VICTORIA PARK CARRIAGES, LTD

(909) 584-2277 / www.buggies.com

Big Bear

There is no more elegant, storybook way to explore Big Bear than by horse and carriage. The carriage can usually be found in the heart of the Village, across from Chad's, on the weekends. Take a fifteen or twenty-minute ride through the Village, and down to the lake. Carriages seat between four to seven people. Ask about taking a hayride, too.

Hours:	Call to make a reservation.
Admission:	$25 a couple during the day; $30 a couple at nighttime; no charge for small children. Additional adults are half-price.
Ages:	2 years and up.

PALM SPRINGS (and the surrounding desert cities)

A collage of words and images used to come to mind when I thought about Palm Springs - desert; hot; resort; homes of the rich and famous; golf; and shopping mecca. Now that my family has thoroughly explored it, I can add to this list - kid-friendly; fun; beautiful; great hiking opportunities; and educational treasures. This area is one oasis that is no mirage!

KENAN

AGUA CALIENTE CULTURAL MUSEUM   ☀

(760) 323-0151 / www.prinet.com/accmuseum   !
219 S. Palm Canyon Drive, Palm Springs
(Exit Interstate 10 S. on Indian Canyon Dr., which turns into Palm Canyon Dr. [Hwy 111] [TG-786 D2])

This small tribal museum relates the history and culture of the Agua Caliente Band of Cahuilla Indians via changing exhibits. School tours feature an explanation of the exhibits, demonstrations, and a video presentation. The museum also offers classroom visits and field trips.

Hours:	Open Memorial Day through Labor Day, Wed. - Sat., 10am - 4pm; Sun., noon - 4pm. Open Labor Day through Memorial Day, Fri. - Sat., 10am - 4pm; Sun., noon - 4pm.
Admission:	Free
Ages:	7 years and up.

BIG MORONGO CANYON PRESERVE   ☼

(760) 363-7190 / www.bigmorongo.org   !
11055 East Drive, Morongo Valley
(Exit Interstate 10 N. on Route 62, R. on East Dr. [TG-615 J6])

The quietness of this peaceful preserve was broken only by shouts from my kids whenever they spotted a lizard, bunny, roadrunner, or other animals. The trails are relatively easy to walk, and many of them go in and through the canyon and the fire-blackened trees. There are several short looping trails, as well as a longer hike of five-and-a-half miles along the Canyon Trail, which extends the length of the canyon. Fresh water marshes and a variety of trees and plants add to the otherwise more traditional desert landscape. Wildlife here includes Bighorn sheep, raccoons, coyotes, and so many species of birds that people come just to observe them. Bring binoculars!

Hours:	Open daily 7:30am - sunset. No dogs or pets allowed.
Admission:	Free
Ages:	3 years and up.

CAMELOT PARK FAMILY ENTERTAINMENT CENTER   ☼

(760) 770-7522 / www.boomersparks.com $$$
67-700 E. Palm Canyon Drive [111], Cathedral City   ⬛
(Exit Interstate 10 S. on Gene Autry Tr., L. on E. Palm Canyon Dr. [Hwy 111] [TG-787 C7])

In short, there's simply not a more congenial spot for happy ever aftering than here in Camelot! This huge family fun center (the first castle off Highway 111), offers a variety of entertainment for everyone. Choose from three themed **miniature golf** courses - $6.25 per round for ages 6 and up, $4.25 for seniors, children 5 and under are free; **go carts** - $5.25 a ride for drivers, $1.50 for passengers; **bumper boats** (avoid the shooting fountain waters or get refreshed) - $4.50 a ride for drivers, $1 for passengers; **bumper cars** - $3 per driver, $1 for passengers; a **simulator** ride with different "experiences" - $4.75; a **rock climbing wall** - $2 for a few climbs; **batting cages;** and over 200 video and sport games, plus a prize redemption center. Note that height restrictions apply on some rides.

Hours: Open Mon. - Thurs., 11am - 10pm; Fri., 11am - midnight; Sat., 10am - midnight, Sun., 10am - 10pm.

Admission: Attractions are individually priced above, or purchase one of the super saver packages.

Ages: 4 years and up.

CHILDREN'S DISCOVERY MUSEUM OF THE DESERT ☼

(760) 321-0602 / www.cdmod.org *$$*

71-701 Gerald Ford Drive, Rancho Mirage

(Exit Interstate 10 W. on Ramon, L. on Bob Hope Dr., R. on Gerald Ford Dr. [TG-788 B6])

The desert, well known for golf and retirement living, boasts of a terrific museum for children. The building is deceptive. Its architectural style befits an art museum, and its high ceilings are complemented by numerous windows and tall, pastel, modular room dividers. Upon entering the lobby, my 11-year old whispered, "Are you sure this is a hands-on place for kids?" Most definitely!

The exhibits flow easily from one to another. Note that no strollers are permitted. Some of the scientific exhibits in the front include a music machine of sorts, where a touch on a metal sculpture produces a jazz or percussion musical sound, and a stroboscope, which is a display where kids can draw their own design, attach it to the fan, and watch it "dance" in the strobe light. Follow any one of three colored ropes through a kid-size, spider-web-looking rope maze. A reading corner has several books, tables and chairs, and colorful wooden pattern pieces. Indigenous rock and flora displays add local color to one section. Put together a life-size skeleton in another area. Get properly suited up with a safari hat, goggles, and gloves and use the tools provided to find faux artifacts in a simulated dig. Climb a (fake) rock wall, complete with hand and foot holds. The relatively large Make-It-Take-It work area is a real treat for kids who like to take apart radios, computer components, and other household gadgets. They can even use the screwdrivers, glue, pieces of wood, and recycled materials to make a new creation to take home. Design a home with drafting boards and a magnetic wall that utilizes stick on furniture. Painting a car is not normally allowed, but the VW Beetle here is a much-decorated canvas on wheels. Smocks, paints, and brushes are supplied. The Art Corner has paper, markers, a computer with art programs, and even a giant loom for young weavers. Toward the back of the museum is a well-stocked grocery store with mini-carts and a checkout counter. Pizza, every child's favorite food, can be made to order just next door. This pizzeria has all the ingredients (made from cloth) to make pizzas, as well as aprons, hats, and a pretend brick oven, plus tables and chairs for customers. An enclosed toddlers' play area and a real CHP motorcycle are also located in this wing.

Walk up the snake-like, winding ramp to the second story Grandma's Attic Room. This area is decorated with old trunks, hat boxes, fishing poles, pictures, and adding machines and telephones. One of the best features is the quality costumes in which to play dress up. They range from princess dresses with sequins to military uniforms to suits and everything in between. Lots of hats, an assortment of shoes and boots, plus boas and ties are some of the accessories.

The above merely lists the highlights of the museum! Parental supervision is required at all times but, as each activity was so much fun, I was delighted to comply. Both the adjacent Dinah Shore theater and the outdoor amphitheater put on a variety of performances year round. Ask about numerous special programs and classes offered for children, such as art classes, ballet lessons, manners classes, and lots more.

Hours: Open January through April, Mon. - Sat., 10am - 5pm; Sun., noon - 5pm. Open the rest of the year Tues. - Sat., 10am - 5pm; Sun., noon - 5pm. School field trips here are offered Tues. - Fri. at 9:30am - 11:30am and 12:30pm - 2pm.

Admission: $5 per person; children under 2 are free. Yearly membership is a great deal at $15 per person. School groups, consisting of a minimum of ten students, are $3.50 per student; teachers and chaperones are free.

Ages: 1 year and up.

COACHELLA VALLEY MUSEUM & CULTURAL CENTER ☼

(760) 342-6651 $

82-616 Miles Avenue, Indio

(Exit Interstate 10 S. on Monroe, L. on Miles Ave. [TG-5410 F7])

Each city desires to preserve its history and make it available for future generations. The Coachella Valley Museum has displays inside the small 1928 adobe home that reflect Indian and pioneer heritage. Some of the permanent displays include Indian pottery and arrowheads; dioramas of date picking, and an interesting thirteen-minute video about growing dates; old-fashioned clothing; original kitchen appliances; and a large panel displaying various fire alarms.

Outside, on the beautiful grounds, are lots of old agricultural tools and machinery. Peek inside the blacksmith shop to see forges, anvils, tongs, and other tools. Take a guided tour to learn background information on the items here or, although nothing is hands-on, look around by yourself to get a rich, visual sampling of history.

Hours: Open October through May, Wed. - Sat., 10am - 4pm; Sun., 1pm - 4pm. Open weekends only in June and September. Closed July and August.

Admission: $2 for adults; $1 for seniors and ages 5 -1 4; children 4 and under are free.

Ages: 5 years and up.

COACHELLA VALLEY PRESERVE ☼

(760) 343-1234 / www.cnlm.org   !

29-200 Thousand Palms Canyon Road, Coachella

(Exit Interstate 10 E. on Ramon Rd., L. on Thousand Palms Canyon Rd. [TG-759 D5])

This 18,000-acre preserve is not only immense, but it is diverse in topography and wildlife. The preserve straddles Indio Hills and the infamous San Andreas Fault. Thousand Palms Oasis (yes, it contains at least this many palm trees) is at the heart of the Coachella Valley Preserve. The oasis is supported by water constantly seeping along the fault line.

Kids begin to appreciate the many faces of the desert as they hike through here. It is sandy, dry, and rocky, and these elements create sand dunes, bluffs, and mesas. It is also mountainous and interspersed with dense palm trees, cacti, and various other vegetation. Some of the trails are as short as one-quarter mile, while others are longer at one-and-a-half miles, and more.

Start at the rustic Visitors Center that has natural history exhibits behind glass. The displays include arrowheads, mounted insects, birds' nests, and eggs. Bring a water bottle and/or a picnic lunch and have a delightful time exploring desert wilderness at its finest.

Hours: Open daily sunset to sunrise.
Admission: Free
Ages: 4 years and up.

COACHELLA VALLEY WILD BIRD CENTER
(760) 347-2647

46-500 Van Buren Street, Indio

(Exit Interstate 10 S. E. on Golf Center Pkwy and turn R. at the off ramp, L. on Ave. 45 and go about 1 mile. Turn L. on the driveway at the pink and blue flags - the center is off the road. [TG-5470 J1])

This center offers a wonderful opportunity to learn about native wild birds in a variety of ways. The small inside exhibit room has taxidermied animals, literature, and a few other displays, as well as several snakes (i.e. rosy boas, racers, and king snakes) and iguanas. Outside are enclosures that hold birds that have been injured, imprinted, or abused. Some are releasable; some are not. The enclosures hold hawks, geese, great horned owls, and others. Docents talk about the birds - why they are here, what they eat, why they are not good to have as pets, and lots more good information. Beyond this area are fenced in wetlands with reeds, a few ponds, and more life-sustaining elements. Sandpipers, mallards, pelicans, and other waterfowl nest here, or at least drop in for a visit. Bring binoculars. Bring a sack lunch to take advantage of the on-site picnic area. Tours are given by reservation. Call beforehand and ask what supplies you can bring to help out the center, such as trash bags, paper towels, film, etc.

Hours: Open daily 10am - 5pm. The wetlands area is open Thurs. - Sat., 7:30am - sunset.
Admission: Free; donations are appreciated.
Ages: 4 years and up.

COVERED WAGON TOURS
(800) 367-2161 or (760) 347-2161 / www.coveredwagontours.com   *$$$$$*

Washington Street, Thousand Palms

(Going E. on Interstate 10, exit E. on Ramon Rd., which turns into Washington at Thousand Palms Cyn Rd. Going W. on 10, exit N. on Washington St. The tour begins off a dirt road about 1/2 mile E. of Thousand Palms Cyn. A sign is there when the tour is open. [TG-390 C8])

Travel in a mule-drawn, covered wagon for a two-hour, narrated tour of the Coachella Valley Preserve. You'll go along the San Andreas fault, and see three oases and lots of wildlife, and occasionally get out along the way. The wagons are not the primitive ones your pioneer ancestors used, as these have padded seats, springs, tires, and other amenities, although part of the fun is the bumpiness of the ride. Take just the tour, or add on a chuck wagon cookout dinner and sing-a-long for the full western experience.

Hours: Call for tour times.

Admission: Tours are $36 for adults; $18 for ages 7 - 16; children 6 and under are free. Tour and dinner costs $60 for adults; $30 for ages 7 - 16; children 6 and under are free.

Ages: 5 years and up.

DESERT ADVENTURES ☼

(888) 440-JEEP (5337) or (760) 864-6530 / www.red-jeep.com $$$$$

67-555 E. Palm Canyon Drive, suite A104, Cathedral City

(Exit Interstate 10 S. on Gene Autry Tr., L. on E. Palm Canyon Dr. [Hwy. 111] It's In Canyon Plaza. [TG-787 C6])

Explore the natural wonders of the desert by choosing from several different excursions via a two- to four-hour, seven-passenger jeep ride. All the guides are knowledgeable in history, geology, animals, Native American heritage, and more. The Indian Cultural Adventure takes you through archaeology sites; an authentically re-created Cahuilla Indian village; a hidden, lush oasis; and a stream, all the while learning about the history of Cahuilla Indians and the Palm Springs area. Lost Legends of the Wild West Adventure is for cowboys and cowgirls as passengers explore a replica of an old Wild West Mining Camp, complete with a walk-through mine and the necessary equipment. Through no fault of their own, visitors may also straddle the San Andreas Fault line, as well as inspect a fossil bed and look at the great geography. The Mystery Canyon Adventure is a great combination of an off-road adventure and a naturalist tour. Travel through a rich agricultural area to steep-walled canyons and ravines, fantastic and colorful rock formations, and cross the San Andreas Fault. The Sunset - Nightwatch Adventure is special - there really are millions of stars in the sky (at least out here in the desert!). See God's masterpiece sunsets on an original canvas.

Some of the tours involve hiking around the area. Bighorn sheep, coyotes, and other wildlife are abundant along the back roads, so keep your eyes open. Bring your camera! Dress appropriately with closed-toed shoes and a hat, and bring sun block, sunglasses, and a water bottle.

Hours: Open year-round, weather permitting. Call first to make a reservation.

Admission: Two-hour tours are $59 for adults; three-hour tours are $89; four-hour tours are $109. Seniors and ages 6 - 12 are $5 off. Sunset tours are $99 per person.

Ages: 6 years and up.

DESERT IMAX THEATER ☼

(760) 324-7333 $$$

68-510 E. Palm Canyon Drive, Cathedral City

(Going E. on Interstate 10, exit S. on Date Palm Dr., R. on Palm Canyon [Hwy111]. Going W. on 10, exit W. on Ramon Rd., L. on Date Palm, R. on Palm Canyon. [TG-787 E7])

Larger than life! That's the images shown on the huge IMAX screen, which features several films on any given day. Some of the films are entertaining and some are educational. I am personally partial to the 3-D format, also available here, as viewers get more involved with the on-screen action. Ask about double feature specials and school group discounts.

Hours: Movies are shows daily 11:30am - 8:45pm.
Admission: 2-D format is $7.50 for adults; $6.50 for seniors; $5.50 for ages 3 - 12. 3-D format is $8.50 for adults; $7.50 for seniors; $6.50 for ages 3 - 12.
Ages: 3 years and up.

DINOSAURS / WHEEL INN RESTAURANT
(909) 849-8309 - dinos; (909) 849-7012 - restaurant   *!/$*
50-900 Seminole Drive, Cabazon
(Exit Interstate 10 N. on Main St., R. on Seminole. It's E. of Hadleys, about 20 minutes N.W. of Palm Springs. [TG-723 E3])

While cruising down the desert highway, looking out the window, your kids see the usual things, such as big trucks, cactus, and dinosaurs. Screech go the brakes! The gigantic (150-feet long) Apatosaurus, with fiery eyes, is almost triple the size of the actual dinosaur that roamed the earth long ago. The same goes for the Tyrannosaurus behind him. Enter the steel and concrete Apatosaurus through its tail. Along the cave-like stairway are a few fossils and rocks behind glass displays, plus information and explanations regarding these two huge time travelers. Up in the Apatosaurus' belly is a gift shop, specializing in everything dinosaur. The fun for a child is just being inside here. The T-Rex, however, can only be looked at.

Wheel Inn Restaurant is a folksy truck-stop cafe with merchandise for sale, such as gift items and sculptures, which are also displayed throughout. Retail pictures on the walls range from Disney to the Southwest. (Note: There are pictures of scantily-clad women toward the back.) Note: A Denny's restaurant and Burger King are also at this stop. All in all, it's a *dino*-mite little stop!

Hours: The dinosaur gift shop is usually open daily 9am - 8pm. The restaurant is open twenty-four hours.
Admission: Free to look and walk around the dinosaurs.
Ages: All

EL DORADO POLO CLUB
(760) 342-2223 / www.polobarn.com   *!/$$$*
50-950 Madison Street, Indio
(Exit Interstate 10 S. on Monroe St., R. on 50ᵗʰ, L. on Madison. [TG-5470 C6])

The exciting game of polo is played on ten fields at this large club and visitors are welcome to watch. Practice matches are generally held during the week. On weekends, especially on Sundays, top players often compete in tournament matches that last about an hour. An announcer is brought in for Sunday's games. Bring a picnic lunch to enjoy on the grass or have a tailgate party.

Hours: Games are played November through April, Fri - Sun., 10am -
2pm.

Admission: Free for practices matches and Fri. and Sat. games; Sun. games
are $6 per person.

Ages: 3 years and up.

GENERAL PATTON MEMORIAL MUSEUM

(760) 227-3483

Chiriaco, Chiriaco Summit

(Exit Interstate 10 at Chiriaco Summit. The museum is right off the freeway, 30 miles east of Indio.
[TG-5477 A6])

Any study of World War II includes at least one lesson on war hero,
General George Patton. Even if kids don't know who he is yet, they will like all
the "war stuff" at the museum. Outside the memorial building are over a dozen
tanks. Kids can't climb on them, but they can run around and play army!

Inside, the front room is dominated by a five-ton relief map depicting the
Colorado River Aqueduct route and surrounding area. The large back room is
filled with General Patton's personal effects, and WWII memorabilia such as
uniforms, weapons, flags, and artillery. Our favorite exhibits include a jeep, a
lifelike statue of General Patton (who looks amazingly like George C. Scott),
and rounds of machine gun bullets. Special displays showcase Nazi items taken
from fallen Nazi soldiers; a small, but powerful pictorial Holocaust display; and
items found on the battlefield of Gettysburg.

Over one million servicemen and women were trained at this huge Desert
Training Center site during WWII. If your child is especially interested in this
period of military history, take him to the remnants of the training camps,
accessible by four-wheel vehicles. Call the museum for directions and more
details.

Hours: Open daily 9:30am - 4:30pm. Closed Thanksgiving and
Christmas.

Admission: $4 for adults; $3.50 for seniors; children 11 and under are free.

Ages: 3 years and up.

GUIDE DOGS OF THE DESERT

(760) 329-6257 / www.guidedogsofthedesert.com

60-740 Dillon Road, Whitewater

(Exit Interstate 10 N. on Highway 62 [Twenty-nine Palms], go about 1 mile, L. on Dillon Rd. [TG-
725 F2])

Thirty or so dogs consider this place their temporary home as they are
trained to become guide dogs for their blind owners. Visitors learn about the
program which takes pups, places them in loving homes for eighteen or so
months then brings them back for serious training as guide dogs, and matches
them with a new master or mistress. Explore the kennels where the puppies are
raised (call first to see if any puppies are currently here); tour the dormitories (if
they are unoccupied) where owners stay for their orientation; watch dogs being
trained; learn how to treat guide dogs (i.e. when it's acceptable to touch them

and when it's not); and learn how to put a harness on the dogs. Tours can last a half hour up to an hour and a half, depending on the interest of the visitors.

Hours: Tours are given by reservation, Mon. - Fri., 9am - 3pm; Sat., 10am - 1pm.

Admission: Free; donations appreciated.

Ages: 3 years and up.

HI-DESERT NATURE MUSEUM

(760) 369-7212 / www.yuccavalley.com/organization/museum

57-116 Twentynine Palms Highway, Yucca Valley

(Exit Twentynine Palms Highway [62] N. on Dumosa, just E. of Sage Ave. [TG-4957 J2])

I highly recommend the Hi-Desert Nature Museum. It offers lots of activity, and has fascinating exhibits on wildlife, geology, culture, and science.

Just some of the rotating exhibits in the front room have included Wild on Wildflowers; Shake, Rattle & Roll, Living With Earthquakes, and Holiday Traditions (from around the world). We saw Black Widow. Arachnophobia aside, the fantastic photographs, video, and information combined with live and dead specimens made learning about this feared insect interesting. The far wall in this room contains encased displays of Indian baskets, arrowheads, pottery, and Kachina dolls.

Another room has taxidermied waterfowl plus animals that are unique to the desert such as mule deer, quail, roadrunners, jack rabbits, and coyotes. A hands-on area in here has skulls and soft fur to match with the stuffed animals.

Fossils, shells, and a wonderful rock and mineral collection comprise the earth science room. The petrified logs are unusual, as are the sphere balls. Rocks such as amethyst and malachite are shown in their rough, natural state, and also in a polished version. Original minerals are shown next to their commercial counterpart such as fluorspar next to toothpaste, and talc next to baby powder; this helps kids to make connections and understand that man-made products were first God-created resources.

A mini-zoo has live squirrels, lizards, snakes, and a tarantula. A docent is often on hand to assist your child in holding one of the animals. I'm proud to write that after recovering from my cold sweat, I held the (large!) tarantula.

The Kids' Corner is action packed. There is a small sand pit (I mean archaeological dig); animal puppets; a butterfly and insect collection; stone mortar and pestles with corn kernels to grind; discovery boxes to reach in and guess what you're touching; animal tracks to match with animals; a touch table with whale bones, rocks, and shells; books; and containers of construction toys. The Hi-Desert Nature Museum also offers themed traveling classroom programs on recycling, insects, wildflowers, a particular animal, and more.

The community center/park just behind the museum is equally fine. It has four basketball courts, a baseball field, a skateboard park with cement ramps and steps, a sand volleyball court, a covered picnic area, grassy areas, and three playgrounds complete with slides, climbing apparatus, and swings. All this and a few shade trees are against the backdrop of Joshua trees and the desert mountains.

Opening an oyster and finding a pearl that's been created by a grain of sand, is like opening the doors to this museum and finding a part of the sandy desert that has been transformed to a treasure of great worth.

Hours: Open Tues. - Sun., 10am - 5pm. Closed Mon. and major holidays.

Admission: Free

Ages: 1 year and up.

INDIAN CANYONS

(800) 790-3398 or (760) 325-3400 / www.indian-canyons.com
S. Palm Canyon Drive, Palm Springs
(Exit Interstate 10 S. on Indian Canyon Dr., which turns into Palm Canyon Dr. [Hwy 111] Keep going S. for a few miles. [TG-816 F3])

Vast, spectacular, and awesome are three words that come to mind when exploring Indian Canyons. Long ago, ancestors of the Agua Caliente Cahuilla Indians made their homes in these canyons and the surrounding area. Today, a large number of Indians still reside on the reservation here. The Tribal Council has opened the canyons for the public to explore.

A mile or so past the entrance gate is the trading post. Kids enjoy looking at the trinkets, jewelry, and Indian art work. Beyond the store are picnic grounds, and hiking and horse trails.

Palm Canyon is fifteen miles long and abundant with palm trees; a stark contrast to the surrounding rocky hills. The moderately-graded, paved walkway into this valley leads you along a stream, and to a picnic oasis. The scenery almost makes you forget that you're hiking! Andreas Canyon is unexpectedly lush with fan palms and more than 150 species of plants, all within a half-mile radius. Walk along a stream and see unusual rock formations. Challenge your kids to look for shapes or people in the rocks. There are also Indian caves back in the canyon and old grinding stones. Hike to Murray Canyon from Andreas Canyon. Murray is smaller and less accessible, but no less beautiful. There are caves here also, which always sparks a child's imagination. Tahquitz Canyon, at 500 W. Mesquite, has a visitor's center and is only open for two-hour guided walking tours at $10 for adults; $5 for children. Call (760) 416-7044 to make reservations. Hiking in Indian Canyons is a wonderful opportunity to explore the desert wilderness surrounded by the stunning backdrop of the rocky mountains.

Hours: Open daily 8am - 5pm. Summer schedule may vary.

Admission: $6 for adults; $3.50 for seniors, military, and students; $1 for ages 12 and under.

Ages: All, but older kids for real hiking.

JOSHUA TREE AND SOUTHERN RAILROAD MUSEUM

(760) 366-8503 / www.jtsrr.org
8901 Willow Lane, Joshua Tree
(Exit Highway 62 S. on Park Blvd., which turns into Quail Springs Rd., R. on Rincon, immediate L. on Willow Lane. [TG-4959 D6])

This site is great for those who are loco about trains! Both the Live Steam Club and the railroad museum are located here. Model railroad enthusiasts can not only work on their hobby, but some have engineered it so that they live here, too. The trains range from two-and-a-half-inch scale models to full-size rail cars. If it's running, you're invited to ride on Uncle Bert's gasoline-powered model train, which covers about a mile of track, over bridges and through desert terrain. Take a tour of the full-size cars including a diner, with its old-fashioned stove and icebox; a mail car, with small pigeonholes that are labeled with city names; a Pullman sleeping car, which always makes sleeping on a train seem romantic; and the grand finale - a caboose.

Camping is available here, too, including RV hookups, tent camping, and even "camping" inside an on-site rail car. The dormitory-style bunks come furnished with a mattress only. Small groups may also use the cooking facilities in the caboose.

Inside the museum are model steam engines and lots of railroad memorabilia from Francis Moseley's collection. Ask to watch the video which shows how a model train operates.

Hours: Open to the public on the second and third Sat. - Sun. of the month, 10am - 4pm. Call to reserve a tour at other times.

Admission: $1 per person. Camping is $15 per adult for RVers, $10 per adult for tent or train camping; ages 11 and under are free.

Ages: 3 years and up.

JOSHUA TREE NATIONAL PARK ☼

(760) 367-5500 / www.nps.gov/jotr $$

Joshua Tree

(The south entrance: Exit Interstate 10 N. on Cottonwood Springs, 25 miles east of Indio. The north entrance: Exit Twentynine Palms Highway [62], S. on Utah Trail, in the town of Twentynine Palms. The west entrance: Exit Twentynine Palms Highway [62], in the town of Joshua Tree, S. on Park Blvd., which turns into Quail Springs Rd. This is the best way to reach Keys View and Hidden Valley. [TG-390 K10 / 4962 H6 / 4959 H5])

This over 900,000-acre park gets its name from the unique Joshua trees that Mormon visitors likened to the biblical Joshua reaching up to God. Explore the riches of this national treasure by car, by foot, and/or by camping.

Entire books are written on Joshua Tree National Park, so consider the following information a very condensed version. Just a few phrases attributed to this enormous park are "wind-sculpted boulders"; "massive granite monoliths"; "five fan palm oases dotting the park"; "wildflowers and wildlife"; "mountainous"; and "rugged." Start your visit at the main headquarters/Visitors Center in Oasis of Mara, located off the north entrance. You can get a map here, look at the botanical displays, and watch a slide show that gives a good overview of the park.

If you are automobile adventurers, which is a good way to get a lay of the land, there are many roads to travel. Keys View is the most popular destination because of its breathtaking view of the valley, mountains, and deserts. (Bring a panoramic camera.) If you don't mind a few bumps along the way, and kids usually don't, there are many dirt roads accessible only by four-wheel drive. Particularly outstanding is the eighteen-mile Geology Tour Road, which showcases some of the most incredible landscape the park offers.

Hiking runs the gamut from easy, one-tenth-of-a-mile trails, to strenuous, over thirteen-mile long trails. Three of the trails that offer fascinating terrain also lead to special destinations. The first one is Hidden Valley, with trails winding through massive boulders. It leads to and through legendary cattle rustlers' hideouts. The second is Barker Dam, which was built almost 100 years ago, and is now a reservoir that many desert animals frequent. Approach it in whispers, if possible, so as not to scare away any critters. Encourage your children to look for some of the "hidden" wildlife in the water. The third is Lost Horse Mine, which is a rugged one-and-a-half-mile hike. This mine was used for prospecting and gold mining. Maybe there still is gold in them thar hills! **Bring water** no matter which trail you take because it is not supplied in the park.

Rock climbing is a popular sport here. Even if your kids are too young to participate, they'll get a vicarious thrill at watching more experienced climbers. Boulder hopping is also fun, and that can be done by kids of all ages.

Camping is primitive at most of the 500 sites in Joshua Tree. Many campsites are located in the shelter of rocks, while others, at higher elevations, offer spots of shade. It is hot during the day, much cooler at night (even cold), and at times quite windy, but kids revel in it all. Water is only provided at Cottonwood and Black Rock Canyon campgrounds, so other sites are really back to basics.

National parks are sometimes called "universities of the outdoors." Joshua Tree National Park is an outstanding university to attend. Everyone will go home with a special memory, and a different reason for wanting to come back.

Hours: Open daily sunrise to sunset.

Admission: $10 per vehicle, which is good for 7 day's admittance. Most of the visitors centers are open daily 8am - 5pm. Camping starts at $10 a night.

Ages: All

LAKE CAHUILLA

(760) 564-4712 - lake; (800) 234-PARK (7275) - camping reservations
58-075 Jefferson, La Quinta
(Exit Interstate 10 S. on Monroe St., R. on Avenue 58., L. on Quarry Ln. [TG-5530 A7])

Escape from the heat at Lake Cahuilla recreation park. The gigantic, stocked lake is a prime spot for fisherboys and girls to reel in the catch of the day. Kids over 16 years need a state fishing license. Night fishing is open Friday and Saturday during the summer. Although swimming in the lake is prohibited, there is a pool open for your aquatic pleasure. A wooden playground is located behind the pool - youngsters always have energy to play, no matter what temperature it is!

The park is not abundantly blessed with shade trees, but there are large grassy areas and palm trees to enhance its beauty. Hiking trails traverse the park, so make sure you've got plenty of sunscreen and water. Over 150 campsites are available here, complete with barbecues and other amenities. Come escape the city life, if just for a day or night!

Hours: The park is open mid-October through April daily sunrise to sunset, May through mid-October, Fri. - Mon., sunrise to sunset. The pool is open weekends only April through May, and September through October, 11am - 5:45pm. It is open during the summer Fri. - Mon., 11am - 5:45pm.

Admission: $2 for adults; $1 for children 10 and under. The swimming pool is an extra $1 per person. Primitive camping (space and a table - no shade trees) is $12 a site; an upgraded site is $16 a night. The camping reservation fee is $6.50. Fishing is $5 for ages 16 and up; $4 for ages 5 - 15; children 4 and under are free. A California state fishing license is necessary.

Ages: All

LIVING DESERT WILDLIFE AND BOTANICAL ☼
GARDEN PARK

(760) 346-5694 / www.livingdesert.org $$$
47-900 Portola Avenue, Palm Desert   ▥
(Exit Interstate 10 S. on Monterey Ave., L. on Palm Canyon [Hwy 111], R. on Portola. [TG-848 G4])

Kids can experience a lot of living in the 1,200-acre Living Desert! Choose one of three areas of interest - botanical gardens, wildlife, or hiking - or partake in some of each.

The nocturnal (this can be your child's new word for the day) animals exhibit is to your immediate left through the entrance gate. Bats are always a highlight in here. Behind this exhibit is the good-sized Discovery Room. Children can get a real "feel" for desert life as they touch live snakes, turtles, and a big hairy tarantula, plus feathers, bones, rocks, and fur. They can also put on animal puppet shows at the box theater, put together puzzles, or make crayon rubbings of desert animals.

The northern section of this "like a zoo, only better" park is mostly botanical. The pathways weave in and out amongst an incredible variety of desert floral including saguaros, yuccas, and towering palm trees. Caged bird life is abundant along the walkways, too. We took the time to really watch our feathered friends' activities and learned quite a bit.

Eagle Canyon houses twenty desert animal species living in their natural element. Powerful mountain lions, Mexican wolves, and the small fennec foxes dwell in their own craggy retreats that are easily viewed through glass. Don't miss the tree-climbing coyote!

The three-acre African Village, Wa Tu Tu, has hyenas, camels, leopards, and a petting zoo (but not with the aforementioned animals!).

A trail system lies to the east, traversing through some of the 1,000-acre wilderness section of the park. Three loops offer something for every level hiker: An easy three-quarter mile hike; a moderate one-and-a-half-mile hike; and a strenuous five-mile, round-trip hike to the base of Eisenhower Mountain. Don't get me wrong, however, the walk around the park is a hike in itself. If you get tired, take the fifty-minute, narrated tram tour that goes all around the park. A pick up and drop off shuttle is available for $3 per person. (This service is also included in the tram price.)

Animals in the Living Desert dwell in outdoor enclosures that resemble their natural habitat. A rocky mountain is home to the Bighorn sheep. Look for them leaping among the boulders. Other exotic animals include Arabian oryx, aardwolves, zebras, cheetahs, small African mammals, and birds. We saw several other animals in the wild, too, such as a snake slithering across our path and the ever-speedy roadrunner darting out of the bushes. Seeing them authenticated the unique setting of this park. Want to see more animals, more up close? See Wildlife Wonders, a live animal presentation at the outdoor theater, featuring your favorite desert critters. Also check the schedule for "Meet the Keeper", where the animal keepers visit the enclosures and talk about five different critters each day, such as cheetahs, hyenas, big horn sheep, and more.

Visit here during the spring when the desert flowers and trees explode in a profusion of colors, or come in the winter to see Wildlights (see the December Calendar section for more information). Anytime you choose to visit the Living Desert will be a time of wonder, relaxation, and education.

Hours: Open September through June 15 daily, 9am - 5pm. Open June 16 through August 31 daily, 8am - 1:30pm. Closed Christmas. The Children's Discovery Room is open daily 10am - 4pm, but closed the first Tues. of the month. The weekend Wildlife Wonders show is usually given at 11am and 2pm most of the year; at 10am in the summer.

Admission: $8.50 for adults; $6.50 for seniors; $4.25 for ages 3 - 12; children 2 and under are free. The tram tour is $5 a person. School groups, with reservations, are free, however, spaces fill up fast so make your reservation soon.

Ages: All

MCCALLUM THEATRE

(760) 340-ARTS (2787) / www.mccallumtheatre.org

73-000 Fred Waring Drive, Palm Desert

(Exit Interstate 10 W. on Ramon Rd., L. on Bob Hope Dr., R. on Fred Waring Dr. It's in the Bob Hope Cultural Center. [TG-818 E7])

This beautiful theater seats over a thousand people and has three levels of seating, including box seats. Several one-hour, just-for-kids plays and musicals are put on throughout the year. Past titles include *Romana Quimby*, *Pippi Longstocking*, and *Pinocchio*. There are also several productions that are enjoyable for the entire family.

Hours: Call for a program schedule.

Admission: Tickets for the kids' shows range between $5 - $15 per person, depending on the seat.

Ages: 4 years and up.

MOORTEN BOTANICAL GARDEN

(760) 327-6555

1701 S. Palm Canyon Drive, Palm Springs

(Exit Interstate 10 S. on Indian Canyon Dr., which turns into Palm Canyon Dr. [Hwy111]. When the main road turns L. and becomes E. Palm Canyon Dr., make sure to stay R. on S. Palm Canyon. The garden will be on your R. [TG-786 E5])

This place has plenty of prickly plants along pleasurable pathways. In other words, this compact botanical garden, specializing in cacti, is a delightful stroll and an interesting way to study desert plant life. There are over 3,000 varieties of cacti, trees, succulents, and flowers, plus lots of birds! You'll see giant saguaros, ocotillos, and grizzly bear cactus, and you may walk through a greenhouse (or cactarium). Toward the entrance are petrified logs, and a few, small desert animals in cages. Enjoy this spot of greenery in the midst of the sandy, brown desert.

Hours: Open Mon. - Tues., Thurs. - Sat., 9am - 4:30pm; Sun., 10am - 4pm. Closed Wed.

Admission: $2.50 for adults; $1 for ages 5 - 15; children 4 and under are free.

Ages: All

OASIS WATERPARK   ☼

(760) 325 - SURF (7873) or (760) 327-0499 /   *$$$$*
www.oasiswaterresort.com

1500 Gene Autry Trail, Palm Springs   ▥

(Exit Interstate 10 S. on Gene Autry Trail. Or exit 10 W. on Ramon Rd., L. on Gene Autry. [TG-787 B4])

This twenty-two-acre waterpark is truly an oasis in the desert. Built in and on top of a rocky hill, with an adjoining resort health club, the surroundings are luxurious. Eight waterslides for big kids range from mild uncovered slides, to an enclosed forty-m.p.h. slides, to a seventy-foot free fall slide. Catch a wave, dude, in the wave pool where kids can body or board surf. Get carried away in the gentle, three-foot-deep, circular Lazy River inner tube ride. Younger children can take the plunge in their own small water play area. Tots have a place to call their own with a wading area, kiddie slides, inflatable toys, and even a bounce. Oasis Waterpark also offers locker rentals, private cabana rentals, full-service snack bars, and an indoor restaurant for all your creature comforts. Note: You cannot bring your own food inside the park. And yes, there is a video arcade here, too.

Tip: For a rocky mountain high in the desert, try your hand (and foot) at the UPRISING ROCK CLIMBING CENTER (described later in this section), which is located right next door.

Hours: Open daily mid-March through mid-June, 11am - 5pm. Open daily mid-June through Labor Day, 11am - 6pm. Open weekends only Labor Day through October, 11am - 5pm.

Admission: $13.95 for local residents (bring proof of residency). For non-residents - $20.95 for adults; $13.95 for seniors and kids 36" - 60" tall; kids under 36" are free. After 3pm, admission is $20 for two people. Body boards rentals are $6. Parking is $4, or $6 for preferred (i.e. closer) parking.

Ages: All

OFFROAD RENTALS   ☼

(760) 325-0376 / www.offroadrentals.com $$$$$

59-511 Highway 111, Palm Springs

(Exit Interstate 10 S.W. on White Water, which turns into Tipton Rd., go L. at the intersection of Wendy Rd. to stay on Tipton, then L. on Hwy. 111. It's 4 miles N. of the Palm Springs Aerial Tramway. The office is in a white train caboose. [TG-725 D6])

Come ride the sand dunes in Palm Springs! After watching a ten-minute video on safety in a cave-like setting, put on helmet and goggles (provided by Offroad), hop on your single-seater, four-wheel ATV, and go for an exhilarating ride. An expansive, flat area immediately in front of the rental facility is great for beginners, and it is the only place children may ride. The "course" has tire obstacles, too. More experienced riders (i.e. older) can venture out on the large sand hills beyond this area. Machines are suited to the age and size of the rider, and speed limits are built into the vehicles. (Yea!) For instance, children 6 to 10 years, or so, are assigned vehicles that can't exceed four mph. The ride here was a highlight for all of us. A beverage is included in your admission price, but bring your own sun block.

> **Hours:**   Open daily 10am - sunset. Hours might vary during the summer.
> **Admission:** Forty-five-minute rides start at $30 per person.
> **Ages:**   6 years and up.

THE OLD SCHOOLHOUSE MUSEUM   ☼

(760) 367-2366   !

6760 National Park Drive, Twentynine Palms

(Exit Interstate 10 E. to Twentynine Palms Hwy [62]. Go approximately 42 miles to the town of Twentynine Palms. Once in town, look for National Park Dr. - one block east of Adobe Rd. (1st stop light), turn R. [TG-4892 F6])

Originally built in 1927, the old schoolhouse now houses historical exhibits of the early settlers, mostly via pictures and written information. The books on display are on Native Americans, gold miners, cowboys, and homesteaders. A re-created schoolroom, complete with wood desks, a flag, and a blackboard, is now a small research library. The gift shop carries pamphlets on the history of this area as well as cards and gift items. Call if you would like information on a school field trip.

> **Hours:**   Open Wed. - Sun., 1pm - 4pm.
> **Admission:** Free
> **Ages:**   7 years and up.

PALM DESERT TOWN CENTER - KIDS CLUB   ☼

(760) 346-2121 / www.shoppingtowns.com   !

72840 Palm Canyon Drive, Highway 111, Palm Desert

(Exit Interstate 10 S. on Monterey. It's on the corner of Monterey and Hwy 111. [TG-848 D1])

Calling all kids! This mall has it all. The kids club is a wonderful blend of craft activities, such as designing calendars, picture frames, aprons, and more, and a storytime or another fun form of entertainment. The mall also has a Kids Corner on the upper level behind the food court. A scale model train ride, a few other kiddie rides, arcade games, rotating exhibits (from the Children's

Discovery Center), and interactive murals, such as doing chalk drawings on the wall, are all in this area. There is also an indoor ice skating rink adjacent to the mall. Call Center Ice at (760) 776-6560 for more information.

Hours: The club runs the second Fri. of each month, except December, 5pm - 7pm.

Admission: Free

Ages: 11 years and under.

PALM SPRINGS AERIAL TRAMWAY ☼

(760) 325-1391 / www.pstramway.com   *$$$$*

1 Tramway Road, Palm Springs

(Exit Interstate 10 S. on Palm Canyon Dr. [Hwy.111], R. on Tramway Rd., 3 1/2 miles up the hill. [TG-755 F7])

In fourteen minutes an eighty-passenger, enclosed car, carries you seemingly straight up the side of Mount San Jacinto. The scenery change in this short amount of time is almost unbelievable - from cactus and desert sand below, to the evergreen trees and cool air up above. (Call ahead to see if there is snow.) The altitude up at Mount San Jacinto State Park is 8,516 feet.

The Mountain Station at the top has the Top of the Tram Restaurant, which is open 11am to 9pm, plus a snack bar, a game room, a gift shop, and observation areas where you can see the entire valley, including the Salton Sea which is forty-five miles away. The bottom floor of the Station has a few taxidermied animals and an interesting twenty-two-minute film on the history of the tramway.

Behind and down the Mountain Station building is Mount San Jacinto Wilderness State Park, with fifty-four miles of great hiking trails, campgrounds, and a ranger station. Call (909) 659-2607 for camping information. Though we just walked along the easier trails, the mountain scenery anywhere up here is unbeatable! Just remember that the trail you go down, you must also come back up to catch the tram. Horse rentals are available for a guided tour. Snow equipment rentals are available in the winter, November 15 through April 15, conditions permitting. There are plenty of areas to go sledding, snow-shoeing, snow-tubing, and cross country skiing. Guided nature walks are offered weekends during the summer.

Catch the package deal called Ride 'n' Dine, which includes tram fare and buffet-style dinner. The meal is your choice of chicken, ribs, or vegetable lasagna, with a salad bar, bread, and dessert served from 4pm to 9pm at the restaurant. Tickets may be purchased after 2:30pm; no advanced reservations are accepted. Otherwise, the cost of a buffet dinner, served 4pm to 10pm, is $11.95 for adults; $8.95 for children. The lunch menu, served daily from 11am to 3:30pm, is a la carte. Tip: Bring jackets for everyone and wear closed-toed shoes - it **really** does get cold up here!

Hours: Cars go up every half hour Mon. - Fri., starting at 10am; Sat. - Sun., starting at 8am. The last car goes up at 8pm, and the last car comes down at 9:45pm.

Admission: $20.25 for adults; $18.25 for seniors; $13.25 for ages 3 - 12;
children 2 and under are free. Discounts are offered to AAA
members and military personnel. Ride 'n' Dine costs $25.95 for
adults; $16.80 for ages 3 to 12; children 2 and under can eat off
your plate, or you can purchase a meal for them.
Ages: 3 years and up.

PALM SPRINGS AIR MUSEUM   ☼
(760) 778-6262 / www.air-museum.org $$$
745 Gene Autry Trail, Palm Springs
(Exit Interstate 10 S. on Gene Autry Trail. [TG-787 B3])

Enjoy happy landings at this classy air museum, conveniently located next
to the Palm Springs Airport. Three hangers house between fifteen to thirty
vintage WWII aircraft that are being restored or are in flight-ready condition.
The collection includes Hellcats, Tomcats, B-17's, a P-40 Warhawk, and more.
The planes are not cordoned off, making it easier to look at them close up,
although touching is not allowed. Walk under and look up into the belly of an A-
26 Invader attack bomber. My kids were thrilled to see the places where it
actually held real bombs! The planes are fascinating for the part they've played
in history, and visually exciting for kids because most have decorative emblems
painted on their sides. Bunkers and displays around the perimeter of the airy
hangers honor different eras of flight by featuring various uniforms, flight
jackets, photographs, patches, combat cameras, and more. Other exhibits include
gleaming antique cars, maps of missions, and touch screens. Tour the inside of a
B-17 for a donation of $3 per person, or just admire it from the outside.

Starting at 10am, the Wings Theater continuously shows war movies,
combat videos, or interviews with war heroes. Kids always enjoy watching small
planes land and take off at the adjacent runway. For more entertainment with an
altitude, every other Saturday hear a special guest speaker in a program that
almost always concludes with a fly-over.
Hours: Open daily 10am - 5pm.
Admission: $8 for adults; $6.50 for seniors and military with ID; $3.50 for
ages 6 - 12; children 5 and under are free.
Ages: 4 years and up.

PALM SPRINGS DESERT MUSEUM   ☼
(760) 325-7186 / www.psmuseum.org $$$
101 Museum Drive, Palm Springs
(Exit Interstate 10 S. on Indian Canyon Dr., which turns into Palm Canyon Dr. [Hwy 111], R. on
Tahquitz Canyon Way, R. on Museum Dr. [TG-786 D2])

There are many facets of this museum jewel. The lobby displays an
impressive giant ground sloth. The Natural Science Wing has wall murals and
life-size dioramas featuring taxidermied desert animals. Pick up an adjacent wall
phone to hear about their habits and habitats. A rock "wall" with windows
allows visitors to see live animals such as a variety of snakes (e.g. sidewinders
and kings), gila monsters, scorpions, and kangaroo rats. An adjacent room has
rotating science exhibits that often include hands-on experiments.

The left wing is a fine arts gallery with changing exhibits of paintings, sculptures, and other forms of art. As the gallery is not overwhelmingly large, exploring the art world is a feasible journey for youngsters. My middle son has an artistic temperament, so I'm hoping art exposure will develop the talents, too!

Further back on the main floor are a few rooms devoted to Western and Native American art. One room consists mainly of paintings, blankets, and numerous baskets. Another, called the George Montgomery Collection, features the western star's movie posters, furniture, paintings, and bronze sculptures of cowboys and Indians. The William Holden Collection offers some of Holden's prized art pieces. Also in this area is a Miniature Room, which displays miniature dioramas in the perimeter of the walls.

The upper level room and mezzanine level have rotating exhibits of twentieth century art, which means expect the unexpected. I love seeing what's new up here.

The downstairs Annenberg Theater presents shows mostly for adult audiences, such as plays, ballets, operas, and concerts. Even if you don't eat here, take a stroll through the Gallery Cafe to check out its colorful mobiles and funky decor. Outside, all-age visitors will enjoy the small, twentieth-century sculpture garden. Ask about the variety of free guided on-site adult and school tours. The Eyes On/Hands On is a favorite with kids.

The classy Palm Springs Desert Museum is an interesting way to learn about natural history and different art styles, plus it's a respite from the heat!

Hours: Open Tues. - Sat., 10am - 5pm; Sun., noon - 5pm. Closed Mon. and major holidays. Docent guided tours are conducted each day at 2pm.

Admission: $7.50 for adults; $6.50 for seniors; $3.50 for ages 6 - 17; children 5 and under are free. The first Fri. of each month is free admission day.

Ages: 3 years and up.

PALM SPRINGS VILLAGEFEST
(760) 325-1577 / www.pschamber.org   */$
Palm Canyon Drive, Palm Springs
(Exit Interstate 10 S. on Indian Canyon Dr., which turns into Palm Canyon Dr. [Hwy 111] It's between Barristo Rd. and Amado Rd. [TG-786 D2])

It's Thursday night and you're in Palm Springs with the kids, wondering what to do. You pick up this terrific book called *Fun and Educational Places to go With Kids and Adults* and read about VillageFest - problem solved! The VillageFest, or international old-time street fair, is held along several blocks on Palm Canyon Drive in the heart of Palm Springs. There is food, arts and crafts vendors, boutiques, cafes, and entertainment, such as live music. For kids, various attractions could include pony rides, magic shows, a party bouncer, a gyroscope, school band competitions, and a stage for children's productions.

Hours: Thurs. nights, usually 6pm - 10pm.

Admission: Free entrance.

Ages: 4 years and up.

SUNRISE PARK / SWIM CENTER
(760) 323-8278   !/$$
On Sunrise Way and Ramon Road, Palm Springs
(Exit Interstate 10 S. on Indian Canyon Dr., which turns into Palm Canyon Dr. [Hwy 111], L. on
Ramon Rd., L. on Sunrise Way. [TG-786 G3])

This park has activities that will keep your family busy and refreshed from
sunrise to sunset. Besides the wonderful grassy areas and big playground with
bridges, slides, and swings, the most important feature here is the Olympic-size
swimming pool. (It has a shallow end for younger kids to cool off.) The deck has
lawn chairs and a picnic area.

After spending a day at the park, take your kids out to the ball game next
door. The baseball stadium has night lights.

Hours: The park is open daily from sunrise to sunset. The pool is open
year-round, Mon., Wed., and Fri., 11am - 5pm; Tues., Thurs.,
Sat. - Sun., 11am - 3pm. Night swimming is available in the
summer.

Admission: The park is free. Swim sessions are $3.25 for adults; $2.25 for
ages 4 - 12; children 3 and under are free with a paid adult. Such
a deal - pay a $20 one-time fee for membership and then pay an
additional $20 for a card worth twenty-five swims!

Ages: All

UPRISING ROCK CLIMBING CENTER
(760) 320-6630 / www.uprising.com $$$$
1500 S. Gene Autry Trail, Palm Springs
(Exit Interstate 10 S. on Gene Autry Trail. Or exit 10 W. on Ramon Rd., L. on Gene Autry. It's in the
same complex as OASIS WATERPARK. [TG-787 B4])

Do your kids have you climbing the walls? Then you'll feel right at home at
Uprising Rock Climbing Center. The three, outdoor climbing structures have
micro mists systems and are covered with an awning to block out direct sunlight.
Kids can test their rock climbing skills here and train to reach new heights. The
tallest wall is forty feet high while another, connected structure, has a thirty-foot
repelling tower. There are forty top ropes in all. All climbers are belayed and
wear harnesses, although lead climbing for advanced climbers is available. The
twenty-foot "teaching" wall might not look that high, but it seemed tall to me
when I was at the top! It's a great spot for beginners to get a grip on this sport. A
small bouldering area (i.e. no ropes needed) is also here.

Rental gear is available, or you can bring your own. Climb a few times
during your visit, or make it an all-day workout. Ask about climbing excursions
to Joshua Tree, Idyllwild, and out-of-state sites.

Hours: Usually open Mon. - Fri., 10am - 8pm; Sat. - Sun., 10am - 6pm.
Call for hours.

Admission: Prices vary greatly, depending on your skill level, if you bring
any people with you, and how long you plan on being here. For
instance, an "opener" class includes one hour of climbing,
equipment rental, and a belayer for $25. Harness, shoes, helmet,
and chalk bag are available to rent.

Ages: At least 6 years, and up.

WHITEWATER TROUT CO. / RAINBOW RANCHO ☼
TROUT FISHING

(760) 325-5570   *$$$*

9160 Whitewater Canyon Road, Whitewater

(Exit Interstate 10 N. on Whitewater Canyon Rd, along the Whitewater Cut Off. Across from the
Whitewater Rock Supply Company, L. (N.) on Whitewater Canyon Rd. It's located 5 miles back.
[TG-654 G5])

Grilled, baked, and fried are just a few savory suggestions as to how you
can fix the trout lunch or dinner that you're almost sure to catch. In fact, you can
rent a picnic table in the BBQ area, fix your fish, and eat 'em right there. A state
license is not necessary. Two stone-lined ponds with benches around them,
shade trees, and a grassy expanse offer a visual and physical respite from the
desert surroundings. Tip: Bring your own cooler for your fish. For the non-fish
eaters in the family, a cafe is on the grounds, serving hamburgers and hot dogs.
An RV park is also available here.

Take a half-hour tour of the adjacent fish hatchery, which has been here
since 1939. Call first to make a reservation. Learn about the hatchery's history
and how to raise trout; see the various size fish; and feed them.

Note: Before you turn north on Whitewater Canyon Road and just past the
Rock Supply Company, there is a seasonal stream bordered by big rocks. While
it's not usually deep enough to swim in, it is a great place to at least get your feet
wet. Wear a bathing suit and bring a towel.

Hours:	Open April through Labor Day, Wed. - Sun., 10am - 5pm. Call for off season and school holiday hours. The fish hatchery tour is offered weekends only, 10am - 2pm.
Admission:	50¢ a person entrance fee; $3 per person fishing fee which include a pole, bait, and tackle. (You may not use your own equipment.) Fish start at $3.28 per pound, with a sliding scale. It's 25¢ (per fish) for cleaning. Rent a picnic table for $20 a table, although $10 of that is applied towards fishing. The fish hatchery tour is $1 per person.
Ages:	3 years and up.

WIND MILL TOURS ☼

(760) 251-1997 / www.windmilltours.com   *$$$$*

20th Avenue, Palm Springs

(Exit Interstate 10 N. on Indian Avenue., L. on the frontage road of 20th Ave. 1 1/4 mile to the
trailer buildings. [TG-726 B4])

If you like learning about alternative energy sources and are fascinated by
the power that wind can generate, you'll be (literally) blown away by this tour.
To state the obvious, it is usually very windy out here. Why? Because cool
coastal air comes inland and pushes the hot air through the narrow mountainous
San Gorgonio Pass.

The ninety-minute tour, of one of several wind farms in the world, takes
place via a golf-cart-style electric vehicle, powered by the on-site giant turbines.

During cloudy weather or extreme heat, however, enclosed buses are utilized. You'll be driven around on the grounds and hear the thumping noise created by the huge pinwheels in motion. At selected stops you'll hear about the history and future of the wind machines, and you'll have the opportunity to inspect components (e.g. blades and nacelle [battery covers]) up close. Blades, by the way, can span more than half the length of a football field. You'll see the older style wind turbines, with lattice towers (reminiscent of the Eiffel Tower), and the newer, sleeker, more efficient ones with hollow steel towers. And, yes, you'll finally find out if these wind mills are simply tax shelters or actually producing usable, affordable energy! A lot of information is given and although much of it is technical, even I understand a bit more now about electricity, sources of clean energy, and what comprises a kilowatt hour. Although the tour got a little long winded for my boys, they particularly liked hearing about the wind smiths, those brave people who climb up the 150-foot tower ladders to do maintenance work.

Bring sunscreen, sunglasses, and water bottles. A visitors' center sells wind farm paraphernalia as well as solar-powered products.

Hours: Tours are usually offered Mon. - Sat., at 9am, 11am, 1pm, and 3pm. Reservations are suggested, but not required. Call first.

Admission: $23 for adults; $20 for seniors; $15 for students with ID; $10 for ages 6 - 13; $7 for children 5 and under. Call for group tour prices.

Ages: 9 years and up.

EDUCATIONAL PRESENTATIONS

This section is written for all kinds of educators as most of the programs / presentations travel to schools or offer unique classes for students off site. It is by no means complete, just *some* of the gems we've discovered.

AMUSEMENT PARKS

Amusement Parks are unexpected places to find educational classes. KNOTT'S BERRY FARM has wonderful outreach programs, as well as over fifteen classes offered on-site. (Maybe you can squeeze in a ride or two!) PHARAOH'S LOST KINGDOM also offers classes on site. Look under the main Amusement Park section for more information and ideas.

CALIFORNIA WEEKLY EXPLORER, INC. ☼

(714) 730-5991 / www.californiaweekly.com					$$

This company sends a knowledgeable staff member or two to your school for outstanding, interactive, and educational two-and-a-half-hour presentations. The six different presentations offered are called "walk throughs", as they walk students through particular time periods via costumes, role playing, skits, games, flags, props, music, hands-on quizzes, models, maps, and/or time lines. Each walk through is consistent with California state framework and requires some prior preparation and memorization for participants.

Fourth graders (or so) can take Walk Through California, which covers state geography, history, and people and/or the Walk Along El Camino Real, which emphasizes missions and Native American cultures. Fifth graders (or so) are offered Walk Through the American Revolution, which focuses on participants in the Revolution, the document of the Declaration of Independence, and a greater understanding of freedom and the concept of liberty. Walk With Lewis and Clark, also geared for fifth grade students, presents Lewis and Clark, Jefferson, Sacagawea, and others as well as the story of our country's expansion. Sixth graders (or so) can take a "trip" with Walk Through the Ancient World, which explores ancient Egypt, Greece, and Rome and the people (e.g. Julius Caesar, Socrates, Queen Cleopatra, Rameses II, and Homer) who made this time period so fascinating. This age group can also participate in Walk Through Israel, which covers the history and geography of Israel and its Biblical heritage. Some of Israel's most famous leaders, including Moses, Abraham, and Joshua, are introduced as are this country's traditions, conflicts, and importance.

The program leaders do a great job of keeping children (and adults) interested and yes, even learning during the presentations. Programs are limited to thirty-five students.

Hours:	Programs are offered Mon. - Fri. Reservations are required.
Admission:	$255 per program in the fall; $280 in the spring. All programs pay an additional travel fee.
Ages:	4th - 9th graders.

HISTORY-ALIVE ☼

(626) 810-3397 / www.history-alive.com

This group is comprised of Living Legends presenters who "perform" for your class. Invite one of the following famous leaders to speak with your group: Patrick Henry, Benjamin Franklin, Thomas Jefferson, Harry S. Truman, Golda Meir, Douglas MacArthur, Junipero Serra, Jedediah Smith, Betsy Ross, Susan B. Anthony, Louisa May Alcott, Thomas Paine, or Abraham Lincoln. The web site has the various performer's phone numbers as well as their bios.

Ages: Kindergartners and up.

JIM WEISS - STORYTELLER EXTRAORDINARE ☼
(800) 477-6234 / www.greathall.com

Jim Weiss, with Greathall Productions, is a nationally acclaimed storyteller. He's won forty prestigious awards from American Library Association, Parent's Choice Foundation, NAPPA, Oppenheim Toy Portfolio, and others. He loves history, researches his subject matter completely, and then retells (mostly) classic stories in voices and manners that kids of all ages enjoy. His tape / cd titles include *Arabian Nights, Greek Myths, Fairytales in Song and Dance, Sherlock Holmes, Shakespeare for Children, Three Musketeers*, and more.

As wonderful as he is to listen to on tape, he is even more enthralling in person. Jim does storytelling, as well as workshops for both kids and adults on how to tell stories. He explains the twists and turns all good stories have, plus how to choose a topic, shape a story and map a plot, create and develop characters and their voices, use voice inflections masterfully, and lots more. He gears his presentations according to the age of his audience. Our school had him do a half and half presentation; half of the time was a workshop and the other half was storytelling. It was fascinating and educational for all ages!

Admission: $500 for a two-hour presentation. Half-day and full-day workshop / presentations are also available.

Ages: All

MAD SCIENCE ☼
(877) 900-9996 - call to find your local mad scientist!
/ www.madscience.org

Bubbling potions, rocket launches, magnets, lasers, super bounce ball, cool chemical reactions, slime, and more hands-on learning fun is offered through Mad Science. Forty-five to sixty-minute programs include after school enrichment classes, summer camps, in-class workshops, school assembly demonstrations, and "edu-tainment" birthday parties. (That pretty much covers the gamut!) Programs are themed based and come with pre -and post-packages designed for teachers.

Ages: Pre-school through 6th grade.

MUSEUMS

Numerous museums have "traveling programs", designed specifically for coming to your choice of locale to present great, hands-on educational programs. Generally speaking, the art and science museums are often the ones with this type of program, although some children's museums offer it, too. The following are just a *very few* suggested places that we know have programs. For more information on them, and others, look under the Museums section:

CALIFORNIA SCIENCE CENTER

DISCOVERY SCIENCE CENTER - They offer a wonderful series of science classes that come directly to your location. Class projects include owl pellet dissection, making seltzer-tablet rockets, squid dissection, creating a mini-terrarium, and Starlab, a portable planetarium. They also offer programs at the Science Center.

INTERNATIONAL PRINTING MUSEUM - The extraordinary *History in Motion: A Museum on Wheels* presentation is one of the museum's specialities.

JURUPA MOUNTAINS CULTURAL CENTER - They offer over twenty on-site programs, plus a few outreach programs.

KIDSPACE CHILDREN'S MUSEUM

LA HABRA CHILDREN'S MUSEUM

RAYMOND M. ALF MUSEUM

PRESENTERS OF THE PAST

(626) 795-3397 / www.presentersofthepast.org/

Presenters of the Past offers a variety of living history programs in music, dance, craft, workshops, participatory performances, lectures, and storytelling. Presenters are dressed as people from other places and times - Elizabethan England, America's beginnings, old California, and the Victorian Age. Choose from classroom historical presentations, in-service presentations, historical reenactments, or workshops-in-the-woods.

Choose from over twenty-five classroom historical presentations, representing many different eras, that come to life at the location of your choosing. Costumed educators talk about and reveal slices of everyday life "back then" as kids learn about the language of Shakespeare, spinning, basketry, Early Italian improvisational comedy, uses and meanings of herbs, military life, Sir Francis Drake, Abigail Adams, gold mining, tea and manners, or Victorian carols.

Historical reenactors are talented performers that enliven any history lesson with a-cappella folk songs, an Old West Medicine Show, a half-hour version of Shakespeare's *Taming of the Shrew*, jugglers, or a talk on brass rubbing followed by actually doing one.

Workshops-in-the-woods, geared for third graders through seniors and given on weekdays, is designed to recreate life in a 16th century village at an already established Renaissance Faire. The buildings are all in place, but not the crowds. First, watch a joust to get everyone in the mood. Then students participate in Shakespeare's England via country dance classes, learning early navigation skills, wheat weaving, falconry, and a military battle pageant. Four, half-hour workshop sessions are offered per day. Workshops are $20 per student who must dress in appropriate Renaissance attire, and bring their own lunches.

SCIENCE ADVENTURES

(800) 4SCIENCE (472-3623) or (800) 213-9796 / www.scienceadventures.net

Motorized cars, robots, launching rockets, X-treme science camps, physics, and more fun by learning projects are available through Science Adventures. They put on school presentations, after school classes, scout programs, and birthday parties. Build projects, conduct experiments, and play science related games.

Admission: Prices range widely. Two, forty-five performances are about
$400. Their outstanding week-long camps are $220 per person.
Ages: Pre-school through 6th grade.

SHOWS AND THEATERS

This is another category that often has traveling shows, whether it's a play
presented to children, or it is a theatrical workshop of some sort. A starting point
is WILL GEER THEATRICUM.

ZOOS AND ANIMALS

Many zoos have fantastic in-house programs as well as traveling programs.
Call the one nearest you for more information.

BLUES SCHOOLHOUSE (Hollywood)   ☼

(323) 769-4671 or (323) 848-5100 / www.hob.com/foundation   !/$
8430 Sunset Boulevard at the House of Blues, Hollywood
(From the Hollywood Fwy [101], exit W. on Sunset Blvd. From the Santa Monica Fwy [10], exit N.
on La Cienega, R. on Sunset. [TG-593 A5])

Three days a week this renown House of Blues music clubhouse is
transformed into a Blues Schoolhouse. (For a description of the building, see
GOSPEL BRUNCH under the Edible Adventures section.) The three-hour class
covers the history and evolution of the blues in a unique manner. The class
begins on the third floor, with a description and look at the paintings out of mud,
sculptures, stained glass, ceiling from a castle in England, carvings, collages
using beads, murals, and other folk art that decorates the inside of this "house."

Next, at the main stage downstairs, two to three actresses present dramatic
vignettes as they tell stories of the history of blues and incorporate music
influenced by the blues. They act out, talk, and play music to do with the history
of Africa; spirituals; the slave trade, from kidnaping to selling to emancipation;
work and freedom songs; the Jazz Age; and causes (and cures) for racism. We
were immersed in the events. Kids then get in the act with miming inventions
created by African Americans, such as the roller coaster and ticket dispensers.

The last hour concludes with a live band performance. The band plays
samples of all the music that has been influenced by the blues including jazz,
rock 'n' roll, rap, hip-hop, call and response, rhythm and blues, and even
country. Toe-tapping, hip-hopping, interactive and educational fun - what a great
way to learn!

Notes: Call in the spring to book for the fall; call in the fall to book for the
spring. Curriculum guides are available. School assemblies are a project in the
works. You may stay for lunch at the restaurant, open daily 11:30am to 4:30pm,
for the cost of lunch. This mid-day meal menu includes seafood gumbo ($4.25 a
bowl), Cobb salad ($8.95), blackened chicken sandwich ($7.50), burger ($6.95),
and Cajun catfish tortilla wrap ($7.50), plus a variety of desserts. Note: Another
Blues Schoolhouse / House of Blues location is in Anaheim.

Hours: Offered August through June (not during the summer), Tues.,
Wed., and Thurs., 9am to noon.

Admission: Free to public school students and non-profit youth organizations. The cost for a private group is $700 for up to 100 students.

Ages: 5th through 12th graders.

CHALLENGER LEARNING CENTER (Carson)   ☼

(310) 243-2627 / www.csudh.edu/clc/info.htm; www.challenger.org   *$$$*

1000 E. Victoria Street, at California State University Dominguez Hills, Carson   ⛁

(Exit Artesia Fwy [91] S. on Avalon Blvd., L. on Victoria St. [TG-764 E2])

What did you want to be when you grew up? I'm sure that you, or someone you knew, wanted to be an astronaut, at least once while deciding on a career. The Challenger Center, established in memory of the Challenger crew and sponsored by NASA, allows students the opportunity to live out this dream, while stationed on earth, of course.

Participants solve problems and make decisions at the realistic, mock space station via real computer consoles, communication headsets, continuous messages on the loud speakers, electronic messages, teammates they can sometimes only see on video monitors, and emergency sounds and flashing lights. Working together, the mission specialists (that's their official name) become a part of one of eight teams, critical to the running of a successful mission. The teams are navigation, which uses star charts to locate celestial objects in the star fields and control lunar landings; probe, which gathers data via a probe to relay data for analysis; isolation, which uses robots to handle "hazardous" chemicals and conduct tests, and workers who wear gloves to reach into the glass dome "box" to maneuver and pick up objects; biosphere remote, which uses robots to collect specimens; life support, which monitors and repairs spacecraft's water, air, and electricity; medical, which performs medical tests to monitor health and handle emergencies; communication, which maintains audio and video link; and data team, which transmits diagrams and info through a computer link.

There are several ways to participate in a mission. Families can call for information on weekend missions. Simulations are offered for birthday parties and for school groups. For the latter, the center provides several weeks worth of curriculum, including a mandatory day-long teacher workshop, that culminates in a two-hour, hands-on, simulated space mission inside a "spacecraft" and Mission Control room. The center also offers *challeng*ing, week-long summer camps. Let your space pioneer help explore the final frontier! Note: Also see CHALLENGER LEARNING CENTER (San Diego) for another Southern California location.

Hours: Call to make a reservation. Missions are offered Mon. - Fri., for school groups; weekends for all others.

Admission: $500 per class of 24 - 36 students. Ask for prices for other missions.

Ages: 6th - 12th graders.

A VISIT WITH MR. LINCOLN

(949) 830-7239 / www.lincolnvisit.com
24881 Alicia Parkway, E-146, Laguna Hills

John Kendall portrays Honest Abe, wearing his stove pipe hat and all. Looking every inch a president, he speaks about integrity, working hard for a worthy goal, and the power of a good character, as well as reciting the Gettysburg Address and telling students many historical facts and anecdotes of Abraham Lincoln's life. He makes history come alive in a unique way. Mr. Kendall speaks for forty-five to sixty minutes to individual classes and assemblies.

Admission: $295 for one assembly.
Ages: Kindergarten through 8th grade.

BLUES SCHOOLHOUSE (Anaheim)

(714) 778-2583
1530 S. Disneyland Drive at the House of Blues, Anaheim
(Going S. on Santa Ana Fwy [5], exit R. on Disney Way. Going N. on the 5, exit L. on Disneyland Dr. Follow the signs. It's on the Downtown Disney venue. [TG-798 H1])

See BLUES SCHOOLHOUSE (Hollywood) in this section for a description of the show. Note that this House of Blues is in DOWNTOWN DISNEY, so see this entry under the Potpourri section for details.

SAN JUAN CAPISTRANO RESEARCH INSTITUTE

(949) 240-2010 / www.sji.org
31882 Camino Capistrano, Suite 102, San Juan Capistrano
(Exit San Diego Fwy [5] W. on Ortega Hwy., L. on El Camino Real to the Playhouse, which is where the classes are held. [TG-972 C1])

Funded in part by NASA, this two-and-a-half-hour interactive class gives students a good overview of the solar system, gases, and a few scientific principles, as well as a basic introduction to physics and chemistry. The presiding science teacher lays the foundation in the first forty-five minutes by explaining various gases, the solar spectrum, the order and substance of planets, phases of the moon, and giving information about objects in space. Kids get to hold a piece of a meteor at this point. Students follow along with the lecture by filling out a workbook that is included with the class. A documentary video, *Toys in Space,* shows the difference in playing with toys on earth and in space.

The second part of the class involves smaller groups rotating to different stations. Accompanying parents and teachers help direct the activities with the aid of worksheets. Students are supposed to learn a particular scientific principle at each station, try the corresponding experiment, and again, fill out their workbooks. The experiments include looking through a telescope at sunspots; making vibrating waves with a string and vibrator; playing with magnets; viewing primary colors of lights via a television screen; changing frequencies on a machine to see and hear voice and sound vibrations; looking at a computer with 3-D glasses; and more.

The last segment is comprised of demonstrations, such as adding dry ice to colored water (the mad scientist effect) and attaching a balloon with baking soda onto a bottle containing vinegar (the balloon expands). Overall, although a few more cohesive explanations would have helped me to understand some of the principles better, the kids certainly added to their knowledge about our universe and how it works. Tip: Bring a picnic lunch to enjoy at the adjacent park.

Hours: Classes are offered Tues. and Thurs. at 9am or 9:30am.

Admission: Minimum $250 for a group of up to 50 students; an additional $5 for each additional student.

Ages: 3rd - 6th graders.

CAL-EARTH   ☼
(760) 244-0614 or (760) 956-7533 / www.calearth.org   !/$$
10177 Baldy Lane, Hesperia
(Exit Mojave Fwy [15] E. on Main St, L. on Topaz, L. on Live Oak, R. on Baldy Ln. [TG-4475 H4])

Nestled among Joshua trees, the California Institute of Earth Art and Architecture (aka Cal-Earth) has an educational facility that emphasizes building structures utilizing the four basic elements - earth, water, air, and fire. Domed, igloo-like structures made out of superadobe bricks, which look like sand bags, are on the grounds; prototypes for future buildings. Archways are constructed instead of the typical, box-like corners and doorframes. Both the United Nations and NASA have expressed interest in the designs and environment-friendly building materials.

The general public is invited to come, learn, and tour around. A minimum group of fifteen students are offered three-hour and full-day workshops. In the "class", they learn how, by hearing about and by physically working, to build homes with arches and vaults using the earth (i.e. dirt); how to build emergency housing that is flood and fire-proof; teamwork; and how to live in harmony with the environment, using solar energy for glazing buildings and for cooling them. Deforestation is examined as alternative choices are shown and worked with. Prepare the kids for some hard labor and for out-of-the-box thinking. Note: A museum and nature center are in the process of being built using these methods. They are located a short drive away at the end of Main Street, by Hesperia Lake. Note: This lake offers picnic tables, fishing, a children's play area, and camping.

Hours: Open May through October the first Sat., 9am - 1pm; 4pm - 7pm. Open November through April the first Sat., 10am - 3pm. Call first. Tours are given by appointment Sat. after 2pm or for school groups during the week.

Admission: Free on the first Sat. School tours cost between $5 - $15 per person, depending on the length of time and activities.

Ages: 8 years and up.

RILEY'S FARM - Living History   ☼
(909) 797-7534 or (909) 797-5145 / www.rileysfarm.com $$$$
12261 S. Oak Glen Road, Oak Glen
(Going E. on San Bernardino Fwy [10], exit N. on the Yucaipa exit, L. onto Oak Glen Rd. In about 6 miles you'll reach the "Welcome to Oak Glen" sign. This farm is at the end of the windy road. From the 60 and 10 intersection, go N. on Beaumont Blvd. which turns into Oak Glen Rd., drive up a few miles. It's the 1st turn into the orchards. [TG-651 C3])

The year is 1775. The Revolutionary War is imminent. Students can learn first hand how it felt to be involved with this radical war by participating in a four-hour reenactment. Upon arrival, students are broken into "townships" and each group then visits various stations to experience life in this era. Some of the activities they participate in include visiting a blacksmith, witnessing Colonel Fenton's attempt to bribe Sam Adams, encountering British soldiers, going through a court trial, training with arms (using fake muskets), grinding wheat, churning butter, learning etiquette of the times, and in a grand finale - marching across the orchard lands in a battle re-creation. Kids become a part of the history - living it and learning it. A typical fare of rations is also served: a hunk of bread, slice of cheese, piece of fruit, and beef jerky. Tip: Bring some of your own lunch!

If kids are studying the Civil War, Riley's also has a reenactment for this pivotal time period that is just as engrossing and just as authentic as the Revolutionary War. These tours were a favorite for my troops! Riley's Farm, set in the hills of Oak Glen, has a naturally rural ambiance with running streams, apple orchards, and dirt trails. If your group is too small to meet the minimum number for a reenactment (sixty participants), ask about joining up with another group. See OAK GLEN / APPLE PICKING & TOURS under the Edible Adventures section for more to do in this immediate area.

Hours: Tours are offered February through mid-June and September through mid-December by reservation.
Admission: $12 per student; one adult free with every fifteen students.
Ages: 3rd graders through high schoolers, but not all the grades combined for one field trip.

CHALLENGER LEARNING CENTER (San Diego)

(619) 238-1233 / www.rhfleet.org/RHF/education/challenger.html $$$$
1875 El Prado, Balboa Park, San Diego

(Going S. on San Diego Fwy [5], exit at Sassafras/Airport, go straight on Kettner Blvd. L. on Laurel St., which turns into El Prado. Going N. on 5, exit N. on Pershing Dr., L. on Florida Dr., L. on Zoo PL., L. on Park Blvd., R. on Village Pl. Going S. on Cabrillo Fwy [163], exit N. on Park Blvd. (near the end), L. on Space Theater Wy. It's in Balboa Park, inside the Reuben H. Fleet Science Center. [TG-1289 C1])

See the CHALLENGER LEARNING CENTER (Carson) under this entry for more details about the program. The San Diego center also occasionally holds three-hour public missions. Advanced reservations are required. Also see REUBEN H. FLEET SCIENCE CENTER (under the Museums section) for more information about the museum.

Hours: Call for a schedule.
Admission: $15 per person for the public missions. Call for other prices.
Ages: 5th graders and up.

ICARUS PUPPET COMPANY

(800) 449-4479
San Diego

This eleven-year-old company travels all over San Diego county entertaining audiences with the magic of puppetry. The shows are a dynamic blend of theater, puppetry, music, masks, and even workshops.

Admission: Between $200 - $450.

Ages: Pre-school through 6th grade.

CALENDAR
(a listing of annual events)

Many places listed in the main section of this book offer special events throughout the year. Below is a calendar listing of other annual stand outs. If you are looking for more local events, like fairs and carnivals, check the front pages of your local phone book, call the Recreation Department of your local parks, or call your Chamber of Commerce. The prices and information quoted here are as of March 2001 - please keep in mind that some events change from year to year. **Please call an event a month in advance as dates sometimes fluctuate.**

JANUARY:

CABRILLO WHALE WATCH WEEKEND, Point Loma. (619) 557-5450 / www.nps.gov/cabr, Cabrillo Memorial Dr. at Cabrillo National Monument. On the third weekend in January, come watch for Pacific Gray Whales as they migrate southward. Park rangers give presentations about marine life, exhibit booths are on site, and you can also tour the facilities or visit the tidepools. Open Sat. - Sun., 10am - 5pm. Admission is free; parking is $5.

DISNEY ON ICE. See December entry for details.

EMPIRE EQUESTRIAN CENTER DESERT CIRCUIT, Indio. (760) 775-7731 / www.indiochamber.org, 81-500 Ave. 52 and Monroe St. at the HITS Desert Horse Park. For six weeks, horse-lovers can get an eyeful as more than 2,000 horses and riders, the top hunters and jumpers in North America, compete in America's largest horse show. Professional and amateur riders, both adults and juniors, compete in the show ring. The circuit begins mid-January and ends mid-March. Open Wed. - Sun., 8am - 4pm. Admission is free Wed. - Fri., and costs $5 for ages12 and over on the weekends.

FESTIVAL OF THE WHALES, Dana Point. (949) 496-2274 / www.ocean_institute.org, 24200 Dana Point Harbor Dr. at the Ocean Institute. This three-weekend festival, running the end of Feb. and beginning of March, celebrates the California gray whales' migration southward. The whole family can enjoy a variety of events offered throughout Dana Point, such as parades, art shows, kite flying, sand castle workshops, tidepool explorations, street fairs, kid's coloring contests, film festivals, and whale-watching excursions. Prices vary according to the event. Have a whale of a time!

HOLIDAY OF LIGHTS, Del Mar. See November entry for details.

NATIONS OF SAN DIEGO INTERNATIONAL DANCE FESTIVAL, San Diego. (619) 469-9255 / www.signonsandiego.com or www.gosandiego.com, 79 Horton Plaza at the San Diego Repertory Theatre/Lyceum Stage. For lovers of dance, this two-weekend festival featuring 100 dancers from 14 dance companies representing 14 countries, is a rhythmic and ethnic feast. One weekend showcases the same two-hour performance at each show and the next weekend features a different two-hour show. The theater lobby is transformed into a marketplace before the shows and during intermission. It offers food and arts and crafts from various countries. The shows are Fri., 8pm; Sat., 2pm and 8pm; Sun., 2pm. Admission per show is $15 - $25 for adults, depending on seating; $5 for ages 3 to 12.

POMONA VALLEY AIR FAIR, Upland. (909) 982-8048, 1749 W. 13th St. at Cable Airport. Fly bys, aerobatic maneuvers and demonstrations, remote control plane acrobatics, sky divers, a penny a pound 15-minute airplane rides, community performances (i.e. bands, gymnastics, etc.), an antique car show, vendors, and static displays are all part of this wonderful air fair. There isn't any seating (unless you bring your own), so just wing it! Open Sat., 10am - 4pm; Sun., 11am - 3pm. Admission is $3 for adults; $2 for ages 5 - 17; children 4 and under are free.

TOURNAMENT OF ROSES PARADE, Pasadena. (626) 449-ROSE (7673) - recording; (626) 449-4100 - real person / www.tournamentofroses.com, Pasadena City Hall. This two-hour, world-famous parade of fancifully, elegantly, decorated floral floats, plus bands and equestrian units, is held on New Year's Day. Camp out overnight on the streets to guarantee a viewing spot, (626) 744-4501 - police (ask about camping regulations on parade route); try your luck by arriving in the early morning hours on the actual day; or call Sharp Seating Company, (626) 795-4171 / www.sharpseating.com for grandstand seating. Prices for seats range from $30 - $70. Please make reservations at least two months in advance. The parade begins at 8am. Call for the parade route.

TOURNAMENT OF ROSES VIEWING OF FLOATS, Pasadena. (626) 449-ROSE (7673) or (626) 449-4100 / www.tournamentofroses.com, along Sierra Madre Blvd. and Washington Blvd., near Sierra Madre Villa Ave. The famous floats can be viewed up close for a few days after the parade. Arrive early, in hopes of bypassing some of the hordes of people, to let your kids walk around and "oooh" and "aaah" at the intricate workmanship. Bring your camera! It is a one mile walk to view all the floats. Admission is $4 per person; children 2 and under are free. Expect to pay about $5 for parking. Open Jan. 1, 1:30pm - 4:45pm and Jan 2, 9am - 4:45pm. Open Jan. 2, 7am - 9am for mobility-impaired and srs.

WHALE WATCHING. See the Transportation section in the main portion of the book for places to call to take a whale-watching cruise. The season goes from the end of December through March. Cruises are usually two and a half hours of looking for (and finding!) gray whales as they migrate to Baja. Also, be on the lookout for dolphins, pilot whales, and sea lions. Dress warmly.

FEBRUARY:

CALICO CIVIL WAR DAYS, Yermo. (800) TO CALICO (862-2542) /

www.calicotown.com, 36600 Ghost Town Rd. at Calico Ghost Town. Over the three-day President's Day weekend, the North meets the South in Civil War reenactments complete with drills, music, living history displays, Confederate and Union camps, and two battles a day. Lincoln, Grant, and/or Lee might make an appearance, too. Open 9am - 5pm. Admission, which includes entrance to the Ghost Town, is $7 for adults; $4 for ages 6 - 15; children 5 and under are free. On-site camping is $18 a night; $28 a night for cabins.

CAMELLIA FESTIVAL, Temple City. (626) 287-9150, corner of Las Tunas Dr. and Golden West Ave. at Temple City Park. The festival, held the last weekend in February, is complete with carnival rides, and an art show on Sunday. The highlight, the festival parade, is held on Saturday. Camellia-covered floats (which must be finished only with parts of camellias), are designed and made by youth groups. Prizes, including a Sweepstakes Trophy, are given out. Over twenty marching bands and drill teams, plus other organizations that promote the welfare of children, such as Brownies and Cub Scouts, participate. Carnival rides are open Fri., 4pm - 10pm. The parade begins Sat. at 10pm and festivities go on to 10pm. The festival runs Sun., noon - 8pm. Admission is free. Certain activities cost.

CHINESE NEW YEAR CELEBRATION, Los Angeles. (213) 617-0396 / www.lachinesechamber.org or www.lagoldendragonparade.com, 600 - 900 block Broadway St. in Chinatown. This three-day celebration's main event is the elaborate Golden Dragon Parade on Saturday with floats, bands, and dragon dancers (in wonderful costumes), plus the Little King and Queen contest and the Children's Lantern Procession. Other goings-on include a street fair with arts and crafts, carnival rides, and live music. Open Fri., 5pm - 10pm, Sat., 11am - 10pm; Sun., 11am - 8pm. The parade is Sat., 2pm - 5pm. General admission is free, although certain activities cost. "Gung Hay Fat Choy." (Happy New Year.)

CHINESE NEW YEAR FOOD AND CULTURE FAIR, San Diego. (619) 234-7844 or (619) 234-4447. 3rd and J Street, downtown San Diego. Thousands of people attend these two days of celebrating the Chinese culture. Enjoy demonstrations such as karate and acrobatics; dances such as fire dances, Chinese folk dances, the lion dance, and the dragon dance (the dragon is thirty-five feet long!); a craft area where kids make a Chinese lantern and form a lantern parade; and wonderful food. Open Sat., 11am - 6pm; Sun., 11am - 4pm. General admission is free.

CIVIL WAR REENACTMENT, Anaheim. (714) 772-1363 / www.stcatherinesmilitary.com, 215 N. Harbor Blvd. at St. Catherine's Military School. Tours are given of the camp where participating students and adults live for the weekend, portraying people Rebs and Yanks. A field hospital might be set up and "doctors" explain how medicine was practiced at the time; an officer might discuss the political events leading up to the war; and a camp cook might talk about supplies and feeding the troops. Teachers can request study guides. Two skirmishes a day, complete with cannons blasting, are reenacted - New

Market and Appomattox or Shiloh. Open Sat. - Sun., 9am - 4pm. Skirmishes are at 10am and 1:30pm. Admission is $5 per day for adults; $3 for srs. and 12th graders and under. Note: This reenactment is not always held in Feb.

COIN & COLLECTIBLES EXPO, Long Beach. (805) 962-9939 / www.longbeachshow.com or (562) 436-3661 / www.longbeachcc.com, 100 S. Pine Ave. at the Long Beach Convention Center. A penny for your thoughts! Over 400 vendors buy and sell rare coins, paper money, foreign currency, collectible postcards, autographs, historical documents, jewelry, and stamps. A free coin and stamp are usually given out to younger children at the Young Numismatists and Young Stampers table, respectively. Open Thurs. - Sun., 10am - 7pm. Admission is $5 for adults for all four days; children 6 and under are free. Parking is $7.

DICKENS FESTIVAL, Riverside. (800) 430-4140 or (909) 781-3168 / www.pe.net/dickens, Mission Inn Avenue between Lime and Orange. You'll have a Dickens of a time at this three-day festival! Walk the streets of a re-created London marketplace where the entertainment, costumes, and food are served up Victorian style. A mini fare for kids include making period crafts, storytelling, and scavenger hunt. Other activities and events included dramatic and musical presentations, a costume fashion show, educational workshops, eating fish n' chips, the Gordon Highlanders encampment (catch at least one drill and fire demonstration accompanied by pipes and drums), and even a night out on the town, such as a ball at Mr. Fessiwig's place where you can do the (Oliver) Twist and night at a pub, is in store for all who hold Charles Dickens in high esteem, or who just want to experience something out of the ordinary. Open Fri. at 5:30pm for pub night (adults only - $25). Open Sat. - Sun., 10am - 6pm. Entrance to the marketplace is free. Some shows cost $5 per person.

EMPIRE EQUESTRIAN CENTER DESERT CIRCUIT, Indio. See January entry for details.

FESTIVAL OF THE WHALES, Dana Point. See January entry for details.

FLYING U RODEO, Anaheim. (714) 704-2500 / www. arrowheadpond.com, 2695 E. Katella Ave. at Arrowhead Pond. Not quite the great outdoors, but this two-day rodeo still gives the necessary cowboy atmosphere. Watch bull riding, bareback and saddle bronc riding, kid's mutton bustin', and more. Pre-show fun includes a petting farm and pony rides in the arena. Call for hours. Tickets range from $9.50 - $30; children 11 and under are $2 less.

LINCOLN CELEBRATION, San Juan Capistrano. (949) 234-1300 / www.missionsjc.com, between Camino Capistrano St. and El Camino Real at Mission San Juan Capistrano. Meet President Lincoln, who seems to be everywhere on President's Weekend. Watch a reenactment of him signing documents deeding the mission to the church, and then check out the original documents here as well as other memorabilia. Other Civil War figures also roam the grounds. Open President's Day Mon., 10am - 4pm. Admission is $6 for adults; $5 for srs.; $4 for ages 3 - 12.

PRESIDENT'S DAY, Simi Valley. (800) 410-8354 / www.lbjlib.utexas.edu/reagan, 40 Presidential Dr. at the Ronald Reagan Presidential Library and Museum. On President's Day Monday, Washington and Lincoln are only two of the president's honored. Roving president look-alikes could include Reagan (of course), Jefferson, Theodore Roosevelt, Washington, and Lincoln, as well as a few first ladies. Each year the specific activities change, but there are usually storytellers, music, and few educational presentations for the family, as well as food booths. Open 10am - 5pm. Admission for the activities and to the museum is free on this special day.

PRESIDENT'S DAY, Yorba Linda. (800) 872-8865 / www.nixonfoundation.org, 18001 Yorba Linda Blvd. at the Richard Nixon Presidential Library and Birthplace. Presidential tributes begin on the Sunday before President's Day and continue on Monday. Actors portraying Lincoln and Washington tell stories about their lives and times. Explore the museum to experience another presidential era. Open Sun., 11am - 5pm; Mon., 10am - 5pm. Admission is $5.95 for adults; $3.95 for srs.; $2 for ages 8 - 11 years; children 7 and under are free.

RIVERSIDE COUNTY FAIR & NATIONAL DATE FESTIVAL, Indio. (760) 863-8247 / www.datefest.org or www.indiochamber.org, 46350 Arabia St. at the Desert Expo Center. This ten-day county fair usually begins the Friday before President's Day. There are lots of special exhibits and activities, many with particular kid-appeal. These include the gem and mineral show, carnival-type rides, a model railroad, livestock shows, a petting zoo (we saw the usual array of farm animals as well as llamas, a zebra, and a kangaroo), elephant rides, camel rides, pony rides, and virtual reality rides. The camel and ostrich races (the animals are ridden bareback and also with "chariots") are some of the festival highlights. These races take place twice a day, and you just never know what is going to happen with two such stubborn species of animals. On President's Day Monday there is a colorful Arabian Nights parade. An hour-and-a-half musical Arabian Nights pageant - starring Aladdin, Jasmine, lecherous slave owners, and scantily-clad harem dancers - is put on nightly. The festival is open daily 10am - 10pm. Admission is $6 for adults; $5 for srs.; $4 for ages 5 - 12; children 4 and under are free. Rides and some attractions have additional fees. Parking on the fairgrounds is $3.

SCOTTISH FESTIVAL, Long Beach. (562) 435-3511 / www.queenmary.com, 1126 Queens Hwy, adjacent to and on the Queen Mary. Wear a kilt and bring your bagpipes for this two-day event, although you don't have to. Over fifty Scottish clans are on hand to entertain visitors with a parade, battle reenactments, traditional and contemporary music, Highland games (e.g. tossing the caber, etc.), storytelling, vendors with Scottish wares, a parade of British automobiles, food, and much more. Open Sat. - Sun., 10am - 6pm. Admission, which includes entrance to the Queen Mary, is $17 for adults; $15 for srs. and military personnel; $13 for ages 3 - 11; children 2 and under are free. Parking is $8. Tips: Very limited free parking is available on Queensway Dr. and Harbor Plaza in front of the park. The games, which you may watch for free, take place at the park on the grassy lawn. The opening parade (10am) and reenactments (noon) can also be seen at no cost.

TET FESTIVAL, Westminster. (714) 216-7233; (714) 898-9648; (714) 893-3139, Bolsa Ave., between Magnolia and Brookhurst Sts.. This one-day festival celebrates the start of the Vietnamese lunar new year in a big way. A colorful parade with various costumes, flags, and floats kicks off the festival. Arts and crafts and food booths are just some of the fun "extras". Call for hours. General admission is free.

VISIT WITH WASHINGTON AND LINCOLN, Hollywood Hills. (800) 204-3131 / www.forestlawn.com, 6300 Forest Lawn Dr. at Forest Lawn Memorial Park. Meet Betsy Ross, George Washington, and Abraham Lincoln (i.e. educators dressed in costume) who talk about "their" lives and their accomplishments for about thirty minutes each, near the Court of Liberty. Lincoln recites the Gettysburg Address, along with other speeches, and tells fascinating stories about himself. See the fifteen-minute film called *Birth of Liberty* in the theater, then walk the grounds to see statues other famous people. This wonderful living history program is presented on two weekdays for up to 350 people, every half hour from 9:30am - 11:30am. Reservations are required, but a family could probably just add themselves to a group already there. Admission is free. See the Forest Lawn entry in the main part of the book for more details about the park.

WHALE WATCHING. See January entry for details.

MARCH:

BUNNY DAYS, Mission Viejo. (949) 768-0981 or (949) 460-2713 / www.svusd.k12ca.us/recreation, 23941 Veterans Way at Oso Viejo Park. Join the Easter Bunny and friends the Saturday before Easter for egg hunts, carnival game booths, family crafts, a petting zoo, on-going entertainment, and big wheel races. Open Sat., 11am - 2pm. General admission and the egg hunts are free. Some activities cost.

CIVIL WAR CAMP, Santa Fe Springs. (562) 946-6476 / www.santafesprings.org, 12100 Mora Dr. at Heritage Park. For one weekend, join forces with the 1st N. Carolina Artillery and Calvary and the Taylor's/Hays Brigade. Troops, artillery drills, cannon firings, horses, Civil War surgeons demonstrating their skill on the wounded, and dancing Southern belles are all part of the reenactment. Open Sat. - Sun., 10am - 4pm. Admission is free.

COWBOY POETRY AND MUSIC FESTIVAL, Santa Clarita. (661) 255-4910 /

www.santa-clarita.com, Arch St. and 12th St. at Melody Ranch Motion Picture
Studio. Howdy-doo! Over 12,000 people attend this four-day event that
acknowledges that cowboys are still heroes. Browse in shops at the historic
Melody Ranch (which resembles a western town), grab some chuck wagon grub,
and listen to some of the finest poetry, stories, and music that the west has to
offer. Several specifically family-oriented programs are offered, including
western farces and trick ropers. Off-site events include "gold" panning at
Placerita Canyon Nature Center, watching old Western flicks on Friday night at
the Saugus Train Station, and horseback riding at Mentryville Park. The festival
just gets bigger and better every year! Tip: Dress up in western duds and don't
forget to wear your Stetson. The festival grounds are only open Sat., 10am -
11:30pm; Sun., 10am - 6pm, but off-site activities run Thurs., 8pm - 9:30pm;
Fri., 7pm - 10pm. Trail rides into the ranch begin at 8am on the weekend and
cost $60. Admission to the festival is $10 per person per day, which includes a
shuttle ride to the ranch. Note that while a majority of the shows are included in
the admission price, certain shows are ticketed events and cost extra.

EASTER BUNNY CARNIVAL AND EGG HUNT, Rancho Margarita. (949)
589-4272 / www.rancho-net.com, Antonio Parkway and Las Flores at Trabuco
Mesa Park. Usually held the Saturday before Easter, this event (with over 2,000
participants last year and 17,000 plastic eggs!) is really *egg*citing. Start your
morning off at 7am with a pancake breakfast - $3 for adults; $2.50 for ages 7 to
12. Then join in the Easter egg hunt designed for children 2 to 10 years old.
(Each age group is then given a different starting time.) Don't forget your Easter
basket! Visit the costumed characters of Mr. and Mrs. Bunny, the petting zoo,
and the bounce house, plus make and decorate a child-size kite - all for free!
There are also arts and crafts booths. At the on-site Baby Goods Swapmeet you
can buy good quality used baby and children's clothes and toys. Hours for the
*egg*stra special carnival and hunt are 9am - noon.

EASTER EGG HUNTS. Many parks and schools put on free Easter egg hunts
and/or Easter craft activities the weekend or Saturday before Easter. Call the
Recreation Department of your local park for more information.

EMPIRE EQUESTRIAN CENTER DESERT CIRCUIT, Indio. See January
entry for details.

FESTIVAL OF THE KITE, Redondo Beach. (310) 372-0308 /
www.sunshinekiteco.com, where Torrance Blvd. meets the sea near the Redondo
Beach Pier. On the second Sunday this month watch brilliantly colored kites of
all shapes and sizes fly high above the shoreline. There are contests, activities
for kids, and children 9 years and under receive a free kite kit (quantities are
limited). Come fly 11am - 7pm. Admission is free.

FIESTA DE LAS GOLONDRINAS (Festival of the Swallows), San Juan
Capistrano. (949) 234-1300 / www.missionsjc.com. or (949) 493-4700 /
www.sanjuanchamber.com. This week-long festival celebrating the return of the

swallows from their annual migration to Argentina takes place in different areas throughout San Juan Capistrano, including the mission. The swallows actually return to the mission every year on March 19th, so the major weekend festivities happen around this date. Some of the festivities include parades (like a children's pet parade), pageants, petting zoo, pony rides, carnival rides, carnival games, a kid's hat contest, arts and crafts, music, and more! Certain activities and attractions cost. The mission is open at 7am on the 19th as the birds usually arrive in the morning.

FLOWER FIELDS, Carlsbad. (760) 431-0352 / www.theflowerfields.com, 5802 Paseo del Norte, off Palomar Airport Rd. During March and April, walk through fifty acres of rows of blooming ranunculus. The colors are amazing, and the trails lead to bluffs overlooking the shoreline. Call first to make sure the flowers are in full bloom. Guided educational tours are also available. Open daily 10am - dusk. Admission is $5 for adults; $4 for srs; $3 for ages 6 - 12; children 5 and under are free.

GEM SHOW, Costa Mesa. (760) 931-1410 / www.gemfaire.com or www.ocfair.com, 88 Fair Dr. at the Orange County Fairgrounds. This three-day show for rock hounds brings over fifty vendors that buy, sell, and trade a wonderful variety of rocks, minerals, beads, and jewelry. Open Fri., noon - 7pm; Sat., 10am - 7pm; Sun., 10am - 5pm. Admission is $4 for adults; $3 for srs.; ages 12 and under are free.

GLORY OF EASTER, Garden Grove. (714) 54-GLORY (544-5679) / www.crystalcathedral.org, 12141 Lewis St. at the Crystal Cathedral. This hour-long, spectacular production with live animals and actors, celebrates the resurrection of Jesus Christ in a powerful way. The last days of his life; the events leading up to his death, including the crucifixion; and his resurrection are presented in a dramatic and realistic reenactment. The show runs for about twelve nights, with the curtain rising at 6:30pm and at 8:30pm most nights (there are no shows on Mondays), and an additional show at 4:30pm on selected weekend days. Tickets are $20 - $30 for adults; $2 less for srs. and ages 12 and under. Ask about family days discounts, when tickets are $15 per person.

GREAT AMERICAN TRAIN SHOW, Long Beach. (562) 436-3661 /www.longbeachcc.com, 100 S. Pine St. at the Long Beach Convention Center. Chug over to the weekend show that features operating train models as well as several hundred vendors selling train paraphernalia. Free workshops are offered so you can learn modeling tips and more. Open Sat. - Sun., 11am - 5pm. Admission is $5 for adults; ages 12 and under are free. Parking is $7.

GREAT AMERICAN TRAIN SHOW, Pomona. (630) 834-0652 or (909) 623-3111 / www.fairplex.com, 1101 W. McKinley Ave. at the Pomona Fairplex. Thousands of model trains are for sale and on display, and children are allowed to operate some of them. Models include old Lionel and American Flyer brands and state-of-the-art cars. Note: This show is held on different months every year.

Open Sat. - Sun., 11am - 5pm. Admission is $6 for adults; ages 12 and under are free. Parking is $5.

GREEN MEADOWS FARM, Orange. (800) 393-3276 / www.greenmeadowsproductions.com, 1 Irvine Rd. at Irvine Regional Park. From mid-March through mid-April take a guided, two-hour, walk around this unique, completely hands-on, petting farm. There are over 500 animals to see, touch, snuggle, and sometimes feed, such as rabbits, chicks, ducks, cows, pigs, sheep, goats, turkeys, and a buffalo. Spring is in the air, so kids are almost assured of seeing animal babies. Your admission price also includes milking a cow and taking a pony ride and a tractor-driven hayride. This is a wonderful, informative, and memorable field trip for kids and adults. A nice gift shop is here, too. Open Mon. - Fri., 9:30am - noon (last tour); Sat., 10am - 2pm (last tour). Admission is $9 for ages 2 and up. Admission for groups of twenty or more is $7 per person. Reservations for groups are required. Also see the May and September Green Meadows Farm entries.

GRUNION RUNS, up and down the coast. Call beaches, the Cabrillo Marine Aquarium, the Ocean Institute, or Stephen Birch Aquarium Museum (all listed in the main section of the book) for more details, dates, and times. Grunions are small, silvery fish that venture out of the waters from March to August to lay their eggs on sandy beaches. They are very particular about when they do this - after every full and new moon, and usually around midnight. You may catch them only on certain months and no nets or gloves are allowed; only bare hands. (Did I mention that the fish are slippery?) Eat what you catch, or let them go, and enjoy a unique night of grunion hunting. Cabrillo charges $2 for adults; $1 for children. Ages 16 and up must have a valid fishing license.

HARVEST FESTIVAL, Del Mar. (800) 321-1213 / www.harvestfestival.com, 2260 Jimmy Durante Blvd. at the Del Mar fairgrounds. See October entry for details.

HARVEST FESTIVAL, Pomona. (800) 321-1213 / www.harvestfestival.com, 1101 McKinley Ave. at Fairplex at the Pomona County Fairgrounds. See October entry for details.

LIFE OF CHRIST MOSAIC PROGRAM, Covina Hills. (800) 204-3131 / www.forestlawn.com, at 21300 Via Verde at Forest Lawn Memorial Park. A costumed educator, representing Christ, talks for about a half hour about "his" life and purpose. The talk is given in the forecourt of the Heritage Mausoleum. This living history program is given on a weekday at 9:30am, 10:30am, and 11:30am. Reservations are necessary. Admission is free.

OCEAN BEACH KITE FESTIVAL, Ocean Beach. (619) 531-1527 / www.ci.san-diego.ca.us, between Santa Monica and Newport Sts. at Ocean Beach Elementary School and across the street at Ocean Beach Recreation Center. The first Saturday of the month offers a colorful, high-flying festival celebrating the joy of kiting. You are invited to build, decorate, and fly kites. There are contests for all ages in the morning, a parade in the afternoon, and an on-going crafts fair. There is no charge for admission or for materials for kite making.

OJAI RENAISSANCE FAIR AND SHAKESPEARE BY THE LAKE, Lake Casitas. (805) 496-6036 / www.goldcoastfestivals.com, 11311 Santa Ana Rd. The age of chivalry is not dead! Enjoy a Medieval weekend, via a recreated European village, replete with games, three stages of entertainment, food (such as roasted turkey legs and sausages), and period-dressed performers and participants. A children's area has pony rides, magic shows, and more. Make sure you encourage the kids to watch a Shakespearean play or two, also. Tip: Bring your own chair or blanket. Open Sat. - Sun., 10am - 6pm. Admission is $10 for adults; $5 for ages 5 - 11; children 4 and under are free. Parking is $3.

POINT MUGU'S NAVAL AIR WEAPONS STATION'S AIR SHOW, Oxnard. See April entry for details.

POPPY RESERVE, Lancaster. (661) 942-0662 - state park; (661) 724-1180 - recorded info from the poppy reserve / www.calparksmojave.com, 15101 W. Lancaster Rd., located 13 miles west of the Antelope Valley Fwy (14), off Avenue I. Do you hear echos of the wicked witch's voice in *The Wizard of Oz* cackling, "poppies, poppies"? During the months of March and April our bright orange California state flower blooms in this 1,758 + acre reserve, as do several other types of wildflowers. (You'll also notice wonderful patches of flowers along the roadside, too.) Call first to see how rains have affected the bloom schedule. Hike along the seven miles of hilly trails that run through the reserve, including a paved section for stroller/wheelchair access. Don't forget your camera!! Although poppies only bloom seasonally, the reserve is open year round sun-up to sundown. The Visitors' Center is just open seasonally - mid-March through April, Mon. - Fri., 9am - 4pm; Sat. - Sun., 9am - 5pm. It provides orientation to the reserve and educational information. Parking during poppy season is $5 a vehicle; $2 off season.

POW WOW, Indio. (800) 827-2946 or (760) 342-5000 / www.cabazonindians.com, 84245 Indio Springs Dr. at Fantasy Springs Casino. Hosted by the Cabazon Band of Mission Indians, this Pow Wow brings together Native Americans and non-Indians in a celebration of music, drums, dance, food, and arts and crafts. Don't miss the "grand entrance" where all the Indians, in full costume, dance as they come in. The Pow Wow is usually held Fri., 5pm - midnight (grand entrance at 7pm); Sat., 11am - midnight (grand entrance at 1pm and 7pm); Sun., 11am - 6pm (grand entrance at 1pm). Admission is $4 for adults; $3 for srs.; $2 for ages 6 - 12; children 5 and under are free.

RENAISSANCE FESTIVAL OF PALM SPRINGS, Palm Springs. (800) 320-4736 / www.renaissanceinfo.com, Alejo and Palm Canyon Dr. in Frances Stevens Park. For three days experience a re-creation of a 15th/16th century

European village and meet the type of people that lived there. Join in the merriment and dancing, music, magic, juggling, theater, crafts, and the food! Open Fri., 10am - 6pm; Sat., 10am - 9pm; Sun., 10am - 5pm. Admission is $9 for adults; $6 for srs. and ages 6 - 12; children 5 and under are free.

RIVERSIDE AIRPORT OPEN HOUSE AND AIR SHOW, Riverside. (909) 351-6113 / www.riversideairport.com, Arlington and Airport Drs. Army Golden Knights parachute team, Air force A-10 aerobatics team, and numerous other performances are part of this annual air show. Other activities and events include a Stealth Fighter fly-by, over thirty vintage aircraft plus military helicopters on display, twenty-minute helicopter rides ($35), and a car show with hot rods, cruisers, and custom cars. The Cafe is open. The Open House is Sat., 9am - 4pm. Admission is free. Parking is $4 per car.

ST. PATRICK'S DAY PARADE AND FESTIVAL, San Diego Park. (858) 268-9111 / www.stpatsparade.org, Sixth and Maple near Balboa Park. One Saturday a year, near St. Patty's day, think of little green men, and I don't mean Martians. Leprechauns, Celtic music, marching bands, kiddie rides, arts and crafts booths, and lots of green-colored food are top of the order for this one-day shenanigans. The two-and-a-half-hour parade begins at 11am and goes along Fifth and Ivy up to Sixth Ave. and Maple. The festival is Sat., 10am - 5pm. Admission is free.

SHEEP SHEARING FESTIVAL, Santa Ana. (714) 835-7484 or (714) 953-8555 / www.santaanazoo.org,1801 E. Chestnut Ave. at the Santa Ana Zoo. "Ewe" are wanted here for the shear joy of it! As a variety of sheep get their hair cut, visitors see shearing demonstrations, and spinners and weavers transform raw wool into refined yarn. The one-day festival runs from 10am - 12:30pm, although of course you are welcome to spend the rest of the day here. The festival is free with zoo admission, which is $4 for adults; $2 for srs. and ages 3 - 12.

SPRING RAIL FESTIVAL, Fillmore. (800) 773-TRAIN (8724) / www.fwry.com, off Hwy 126 on Central at Central Park. The Visitors Center has huge model train display and lots of paraphernalia and collectables. Antique tractors and equipment, craft booths, live entertainment, and barbecue cooking are part of the fun. Check out the open-top speeder cars used to maintain railroad tracks. Miniature live steam engine rides cost a minimal fee. Periodically, gunslingers come into down, have a shootout, rob a bank, and make a getaway on a train. Ride an antique steam car for an hour, or go for a 2 ½-hour diesel excursion all the way to Santa Paula and back, including a half-hour stop over. Note: The Santa Paula ride has food services available. General admission is free. Train tickets are $12 for adults and srs.; $8 for ages 4 - 12 years; $5 for ages 3 and under. All aboard Sat. - Sun., 9am - 5pm.

VISIT WITH FATHER SERRA, Long Beach. (800) 204-3131 / www.forestlawn.com, 1500 E. San Antonio Dr. at Forest Lawn Memorial Park. Learn California history from a founding father, or rather, a costumed actor who tells about Father Serra's life and time period from a "first person" perspective. This half-hour talk is interesting and educational. The presentation is on a weekday, geared for school kids. Call to make a reservation. Admission is free.

VISIT WITH MICHELANGELO AND LEONARDO DA VINCI, Glendale. (800) 204-3131 / www.forestlawn.com, 1712 S. Glendale Ave. at Forest Lawn Memorial Park. A costumed Michelangelo and Da Vinci talk to an audience of up to 350 people for about a half hour about "their" lives and achievements - history comes alive! Take a self guided tour around the premises to view "their" art. (Note: The art does contain some nudity.) This two-day, weekday, program is presented at 9:30am, 10:30am, and 11:30am. Reservations are necessary. This event repeats in October. Admission is free. See Forest Lawn in the main section of the book for details about what else this park has to offer.

WHALE OF A DAY FESTIVAL, Rancho Palos Verdes. (310) 544-5264, 31501 Palos Verdes Dr. W. at Pt. Vincente Interpretative Center. Bring your binoculars and look for the Pacific Gray Whales as they migrate south. Other activities include storytelling, arts and crafts, and booths manned by representatives from Cabrillo Marine Aquarium, Marine Mammal Care Center, L.A. Zoo, and others. Tours of the Pt. Vincente Lighthouse are given on a first come first serve basis for ages 7 years and older. The festival commences Sat., 10am - 4pm. Admission is free. Parking is available at Long Point with free shuttles.

WHALE WATCHING. See January entry for details.

WHAT'S UP FOR KIDS EXPO, Rolling Hills Estate at 27570 Crossfield Ave. See April entry for details.

APRIL:

BLESSING OF THE ANIMALS, Los Angeles. (213) 628-1274 / www.cityofla.org/elp, 125 Paseo de la Plaza at El Pueblo de Los Angeles State Historic Park. This event is held on the Saturday before Easter. Children can dress up their pets - all domestic animals welcome - and bring them to the Plaza Church to be blessed by priests. Some participating zoos bring in more exotic animals. This is done to honor the animal's contributions to the world. It gets wild with all different kinds of animals "held" in children's arms! Admission is free.

BUTTERFLY / ECO-ARTS FESTIVAL, Pasadena. (626) 449-9144 / www.kidspacemuseum.org, 390 S. El Molino Ave. at the Kidspace Children's Museum. (See the main section of the book under Museums.) Butterflies are free - well, not quite. Two weeks prior to the festival kids can adopt and nurture, for free, their very own Painted Lady caterpillar. They bring the butterflies to the festival and release them en mass. Other activities and events at the festival include recycling material into arts and crafts, listening to live entertainment, helping plant a butterfly-attracting garden, trying an obstacle course, and learning about the environment from on-site vendors. Come play on Sat., 11am - 2pm. Admission to the festival is free. Admission to the museum is a special price of $3 per person.

CHILDREN'S DAY, Santa Fe Springs. (562) 946-6476 / www.santafesprings.org, 12100 Mora Dr. at Heritage Park. This day of old-fashioned fun is held around Easter. Kids can ride on a fire engine; pet animals in the petting zoo; pump water from a well; dress-up in old-fashioned clothing; hunt for Easter eggs; listen to story-tellers; try square dancing; churn butter; crank a wheel to make ice-cream; take a hay ride; pan for gold; and play turn-of-the-century games and crafts. Open Sat., noon - 4pm. Admission and activities are free.

CIRCUS VARGAS, San Diego. (619) 239-0512 / www.balboapark.org, Park Blvd. at Balboa Park. For one week Circus Vargas, one of the largest circuses under the big top, presents everything a child dreams about in a circus. Animal acts, daring acrobatics, and talented clowns are all part of this extravaganza. Shows begin at 8am and end at 10pm. Tickets are usually $8 for adults; $6 for children.

CIVIL WAR REENACTMENT, Valley Center. (760) 749-9499 / www.batesfarm.com or www.geocities.com/bourbonstreet/2663, 15954 Woods Valley Rd. at Bates Nut Farm. This very civil Civil War reenactment features two days of costumed participants and battle skirmishes. Walk through the encampment and converse with people from that time period, or at least people who stay have researched that time period and stay in character. Open Sat. - Sun., 10am - 4:30pm. Free admission.

CROSSROADS EUROPEAN RENAISSANCE FESTIVAL, Corona. (800) 320-4736; (909) 943-5949 / www.renaissanceinfo.com, River Rd. and Archibald at Riverview Park. Peasants, lords and ladies, merchants, artisans, craftsmen, nobles, knights, travelers, and anyone else is invited to join in the weekend festivities. Archery competitions, horse shows, sheep shearing, weaving and spinning demonstrations, great food, and crafts of old are just part of the fun. Open Sat. - Sun., mid-April through May, 10am - 6pm. Admission is $10 for adults; $6 for ages 6 - 12; children 5 and under are free.

DEL MAR NATIONAL HORSE SHOW, Del Mar. (858) 755-1161 / www.delmarfair.com, 2260 Jimmy Durante Blvd. at the Del Mar fairgrounds. Saddle up for three weeks of exciting horse competition and Olympic selection. Each weekend features a main equestrian category: Western, Dressage, and Hunter/Jumper. Watch the horses being put through their paces during the week. Note: Check the website for exciting horse shows throughout the year. Open weekdays 8am - 5pm with free admission. Open weekends for shows (call for hours) - the cost is $8 for grandstand seats; $12 for box. Parking is $6.

EARTH DAY, San Diego. (619) 239-0512 / www.balboapark.org, Park Blvd. at

Balboa Park. Celebrate the preservation of the environment in this one-day event. Several hundred organizations host booths and exhibits on organic materials; alternatives to lighting, power, and energy; and more. Kids (and parents) who attend Earth Day will hopefully become more planet smart. Activities begin at 10am and end at 6pm. Admission is free.

EASTER. Look at all the Easter-related activities in March, if Easter falls in April this year.

END OF THE TRAIL WORLD CHAMPIONSHIP COWBOY SHOOT OUT AND WILD WEST JUBILEE, Riverside. (714) 998-0209, River Rd. at Raagauge's Ranch at the Prado Dam Recreation Area. For three days, more than 500 authentically-dressed Wild West competitors from around the world compete in this action shooting contest, including a mounted shooting competition. Note: Visitors must wear eye protection (sunglasses are fine) in the shooting area. The festival also celebrates the cowboy lifestyle and features era-appropriate activities for the family such as chuck wagon races, trick ropers, cowboy poetry, and Wild West shows. Over 100 vendors are on site. Happy trails! The activities run 9am - 6pm. Admission is $10 a day for adults; children 12 and under are free. Parking is $2.

FARM FEST, Santa Paula. (805) 525-9293 or (805) 658-7952, 14292 W. Telegraph Rd. at Faulkner Farm. If you have a brown thumb, come learn about gardening and more at the Farm Fest. The demonstration garden also feature composting demonstrations, a storytelling area, and planting vegetables in containers. A 4-H petting zoo and display pens; weaving, spinning, and quilting demonstrations; farm equipment displays; living history by costumed docents; food vendors and a barbecue area; tours of the Faulkner House; and more are all included. Open Sat., 10am - 4pm. Free admission.

FLOWER FIELDS, Carlsbad. See March entry for details.

GLORY OF EASTER, Garden Grove. See March entry for details.

GREEN MEADOWS, Irvine. See March entry for details.

IMAGINATION CELEBRATION, Orange County. (949) 833-8500 / www.icfestival.com. The Orange County Performing Arts Center hosts this fifteen-day event that's held during the latter part of April, and early part of May. At least fifty of Orange County's artistic and educational organizations bring performances, workshops, and exhibitions to over seventy locations. This festival of arts for families takes place at malls, museums, parks, schools, etc. Some of the activities include puppet making, family art days, folk tales, band and theater performances, and dancing. Almost every event is free in this county wide celebration of imagination! Call for a schedule of events.

INTERNATIONAL SPEEDWAY, Costa Mesa. (949) 492-9933 or (714) 708-

3247 / www.cmspeedway.com, 88 Fair Dr. at the Orange County Fairgrounds. The Speedway roars to life every Saturday night from April through September. Note: Racing in July is limited due to the Orange County Fair. This spectator sport of motorcycle racing can include sidecars, go karts, Quads, a kids' class (ages 6 to 12), and more. After the two-hour show, which can get long for younger ones, take the kids into the pits to get racer's autographs, or, when the bikes cool down, to sit on a cycle or two. Wear jeans and t-shirt (and bring a sweatshirt) as dirt tracks aren't noted for cleanliness. Gates open at 6:30pm; races start at 7:30pm. Admission is $10 for adults; $6 for srs. and ages 13 - 17; $3 for ages 6 - 12; children 5 and under are free. Parking is free.

KALEIDOSCOPE, Long Beach. (562) 985-2288 / www.kaleidoscope.csulb.com, 1250 Bellflower at California State Long Beach campus. This open house, sponsored by the various departments of the college, is a wonderful, one-day community event. There is face painting, carnival rides, cultural dances, an African marketplace, a Pow Wow, a Kid Zone, Earth Day celebrations, Fiesta Latina, a solar car (from the Engineering Dept.), and more. Open 11am - 5pm. Admission is free.

LAKESIDE RODEO & WESTERN DAYS, Lakeside. (619) 561-4331 - rodeo / www.lakesiderodeo.com or (619) 561-1031 - parade info, 12854 Mapleview and Hwy 67 at the Lakeside Rodeo grounds. Corral your young broncos and bring them to the two-and-a-half-hour rodeo show the last weekend in April. This fantastic three-day rodeo features the major events - bullriding, team roping, calf roping, buckin' horses, barrel racing, bareback riding, saddle broncs, and steer wrestling. On rodeo Saturday a down-home town parade begins at 9:30am at Woodside and Main. Rodeo shows are Fri., 7:30pm; Sat., 2pm and 7:30pm; Sun., 2pm. Tickets on Fri. are $5 per person or $20 for two adults and three kids 12 and under; weekend shows are $8 for adults, $3 for ages 12 and under, or $10 - $12 for reserved seats.

LOS ANGELES TIMES FESTIVAL OF BOOKS, Westwood. (800) LATIMES (528-4637) / www.latimes.com/events, U.C.L.A. campus. This weekend festival is absolutely the place for book lovers of all ages. Hundreds of publishers have booths in which to sell their books. Well-known authors and celebrity authors sign their books, do book readings, and give seminars. Special programs on-going at the children's stages include storytellers, clowns, musicians, character appearances, and more. Open Sat., 10am - 6pm; Sun., 10am - 5pm. Admission is $5 per vehicle.

PALMS WILD WEST GRAND PRIX, Twentynine Palms. (562) 428-4971 / www.hilltoppersmc.com or (760) 367-3445 / www.29chamber.com, 3 miles east of town at the Moto Sports Arena. This AMA-sanctioned, District 37 competition Grand Prix Series dirt bike race features more than 1,200 participants across seven plus miles of desert. Top racers in the country compete on the course, and kids, of all age groups, compete just around the track. Demonstrations of car equipment and vendors round out the grand prix. Open

Sat. - Sun., 8am - 4pm. Admission is $5 per vehicle.

PASADENA MODEL RAILROAD CLUB'S SPRING OPEN HOUSE, Pasadena. (877) 484-4664 / www.pmrrc.org, 5458 Alhambra Ave. Over a period of several days, make tracks to see the largest model railroad, which covers 5,000 square feet, as well as lots of other railroad paraphernalia. Call for hours. Admission is $3 for adults; $1 for ages 10 - 17; free for ages 9 and under with an accompanying adult.

PET EXPO, Pomona. (800) 999-7295 / www.wwpsa.com, 1101 W. McKinley Ave. at Fairplex at the L.A. County Fairgrounds. Bark, meow, oink, baaa, sssss, neigh - this three-day weekend is for animals lovers. Over 1,000 animals - dogs, cats, reptiles, goats, mini horses, llamas, rabbits, pigs, fish, etc. - are at the expo. See bird shows, cat shows, a petting zoo, Frisbee dogs, celebrity animals, pet products, stage shows, and educational demonstrations. Check out the pet adoption services. (Animals are not for sale here.) Open Fri., 10am - 6pm; Sat., 9am - 7pm; Sun., 9am - 6pm. Admission per day is $8 for adults; $6 for srs.; $3 for ages 6 - 12; children 5 and under are free. Parking is $5.

POINT MUGU'S NAVAL AIR WEAPONS STATION'S AIR SHOW, Oxnard. (805) 989-8786; (805) 989-8548 / www.nbvc.navy.mil, Las Posas near the P.C.H. intersection at the Naval Warfare Station. At this three-day show, the air is filled with flight demonstrations including solo routines, formation flying, the famous Air Force Thunderbirds, and daring acrobatic stunts. The ground displays are equally exciting with exhibits of aircraft, a flight simulator, children's rides, a home show, food booths, and more. Gates are open Fri. at noon (the air show is at 3pm); Sat. - Sun. at 8am; demonstrations begin at 9:30am. Open-air, unreserved seating and parking are free. Reserved seats are between $4 - $35. Bring suntan lotion!

POPPY FESTIVAL, Lancaster. (661) 723-6077 / www.city.lancaster.ca.us, 43011 N. 10th St. W. at Lancaster City Park. The poppy festival, located fifteen miles east of the poppy reserve, is held for one weekend in April. The festival offers carnival rides, a twenty-minute helicopter ride over the reserve ($30 for adults, $25 for children), craft workshops, environmental displays, and more. Open Sat., 10am - 6pm; Sun., 10am - 5pm. General admission is $6 for adults; $3 for ages 6 - 12; children 5 and under are free. Parking is $2.

POPPY RESERVE, Lancaster. See March entry for details.

RAMONA PAGEANT, Hemet. (800) 645-4465 / www.ramonapageant.com, 27400 Ramona Bowl Rd. All the world's a stage, or at least this mountainside in Hemet. A cast of over 300 (including children and animals) use the mountainside as a stage to tell the romantic story of Spanish Ramona and her Indian hero, Alessandro. The tale, which also reflects our early California heritage, is incredibly well told and fascinating. Going into its 78th year, this epic is performed for three weekends. Performances begin at 3:30pm. and end at 6pm.

Tickets range from $15 (upper section) - $25 (lower section) for both adults and children. Bring a blanket and picnic dinner.

RENAISSANCE PLEASURE FAIRE, San Bernardino. (909) 880-0122 / www.renfair.com or www.recfair.com, 2555 Glen Helen Pkwy. at Glen Helen Regional Park. Heare ye, heare ye, this annual faire runs for eight weekends from April to June, bringing the Renaissance time to life, including wenches dressed accordingly, and bawdiness. Eat, drink, and be merry as you cheer on knights; play challenging games from times of yor; be entertained by juggling, dancing, and singing; and enjoy the delicious food and faire. Educational field trips called Workshop-in-the-Woods, put on by Presenters of the Past, (626) 795-3397 / www.presentersofthepast.org, are offered Tues., Wed., and Thurs. from 9:15am - 2:30pm for $20 per student. (Adults chaperones are free.) Geared for 5th graders through high schoolers, students, who must be dressed in period costume, will watch and/or partake in jousting demonstrations, chainmail knitting, Elizabethan country dance, basketry, paper making, and more. Students learn about this time period as they see it being relived before their eyes! The faire is open to the public Sat. - Sun., 10am - 6pm. Admission is $17.50 for adults; $15 for srs. and students; $7.50 for ages 5 - 11; children 4 and under are free. Parking is $8.

SCANDINAVIAN FESTIVAL, Thousand Oaks. (805) 493-3151 / www.clunet.edu, 60 W. Olsen Rd. at California Lutheran University. Valkommen! This two-day festival usually takes place on the third weekend of April. Enjoy a presentation/program of a 16th century Swedish royal court, a Viking encampment, folk dancing, a colorful parade with authentic costumes, arts and crafts booths, and a replica of Tivoli Gardens, though it's not quite as large as the one in Denmark. Kids will particularly enjoy the jugglers, puppet shows, magicians, clowns, and moon bounces. A smorgasbord is served here, too. The festival is open Sat., 10am - 6pm; Sun., noon - 5pm. Admission is $6 for adults; $1 for ages 9 and under. Certain activities cost extra.

SHAKESPEARE FESTIVAL, Palmdale. (888) 4-FILMAV (434-5628) or (661) 267-5684 / www.cityofpalmdale.org, 38334 10th St. This four-day festival features performances that include madrigal singers, enchanters, juggling, and jousting. Join in on a free language workshop on Thursday to familiarize yourself with Shakespearian language and his influence on modern day verbiage. Enjoy English fair food. A different, full-length show is presented at each performance: Fri. and Sat., 7pm; Sun., 2pm. (The matinee performance is an easier to understand play for kids.) Admission is $12 for adults; $10 for srs., students, and military; $8 for ages 12 and under.

SONY ARTWALK, San Diego. (619) 615-1090 / www.sonyartwalk.com, from Juniper St. along Kettner Blvd. to the south in downtown San Diego. Hundreds of visual and performing arts exhibitors strut their stuff in a weekend-long celebration of the arts. (Many events happen throughout the month, too.) In cooperation with Museum of Contemporary Art, San Diego Area Dance

Alliance, Children's Museum, San Diego Performing Arts League, etc., you'll see paintings, dance, ballet, poetry, photography, sculpture, opera, folkloric dance, divas, and more. Just a few specific activities for kids include writing poetry, creating an origami animal, making a 3-D paper model, and molding a sculpture. Open Sat. - Sun., noon - 6pm. Admission is free.

SUNKIST ORANGE BLOSSOM FESTIVAL, Riverside. (800) 382-8202 or (909) 715-3400 / www.orangeblossomfestival.org, near Market and 10th Sts., 20 square blocks in historic downtown Riverside. *Orange* you glad you came to this weekend festival? Traditionally held the third weekend in April, it boasts several stages of live entertainment; a recreated living history town; a Technology Grove; a parade featuring floats, marching bands, and equestrian units; tasty orange treats and cooking demonstrations; a children's grove with magic shows, carnival rides, and a petting zoo; a fireworks display on Saturday night; and arts and crafts booths. Open Sat., 10am - 8pm; Sun., 10am - 7pm. Admission is free, although certain activities cost. Parking is $6.

TOYOTA GRAND PRIX, Long Beach. (562) 981-2600 / www.longbeachgp.com or (800) 752-9524, E. Shoreline Dr. and Seaside Way. This three-day event includes practice and qualifying runs on Friday; celebrity racing and final qualifying runs on Saturday; and final cart car racing on Sunday. Gates are open 7am - 6pm. General admission (unreserved seating) Fri. - Sat. is $28 for adults; Sun., $36; a three-day pass is $46. Children 12 and under are free with a paid adult. Reserved seats on Sun. is $62 for adults; $34 for children; a three-day pass is $108 for adults; $53 for children. See you at the races!

WHAT'S UP FOR KIDS EXPO, Torrance. (310) 544-1042 / www.whatsupforkids.com, 3330 Civic Center Dr. at the Torrance Cultural Arts Center. This one-day event is geared specifically for younger children. Some events and activities include live entertainment by popular children's singers and dancers, moon bounces, face painting, parenting resources, a safety expo, and lots of interactive exhibits sponsored by the Long Beach Aquarium, Los Angeles Zoo, and lots more. Open 10am - 4pm. Admission is $3 for adults; children are free. All activities are included with admission.

YOUTH EXPO, Orange County. (714) 708-3247 / www.ocfair.com, 88 Fair Dr. at the Orange County Fairgrounds. This huge, three-day expo highlights the talents of Orange County kids from elementary through high school age. Their artistic endeavors are showcased in different buildings according to age groups and categories, such as fine arts, photography, woodworking, and ceramics. 4-H Club members also have wonderful exhibits. The Science Fair is a highlight which draws people from all over the United States who offer money and/or scholarships to students whose experimentally-based research designs are outstanding. The Expo is great for admiring other kids' works, and for sparking the creative genius in your child. Open Fri., 9am - 3pm (this day can get crowded with school tours); Sat. - Sun., 9am - 5pm. Admission is free.

MAY:

ANIMAL FAIR, Newhall. (661) 222-7657 / www.hartmuseum.org, 24151 N. San Fernando Rd. at the William S. Hart Museum. (See this museum entry in the main section of the book.) This one-day "educational" fair is geared for children 12 years and under. It features pony rides, a petting zoo, a safari yard, exotic animals used in movies, games, and an entertainment stage. Adopt-a-Pet program staff talk with visitors about animal care, how wild animals don't make good pets, and more. Open the third Sun., 10am - 4pm. Free admission.

ARMED FORCES DAY FESTIVAL, Miramar. (858) 577-1000 / www.mccsmiramar.com, Marine Corps Air Station. This one-day event has a little something for everyone including a car show, craft fair, kiddie rides, Native American Pow Wow, a military history exposition, and military static displays such as planes, jets, helicopters, tanks, and more. The festival is open Sat., 10am - 4pm. Admission is free.

BANNING HERITAGE DAYS, Wilmington. (310) 548-7777 / www.banning.org, 401 East M St. at the Banning Residence Museum. For one week, the museum becomes a living classroom for school groups on weekdays and for the public on the prior Sunday. Intermingle with Victorian-dressed ladies and gentlemen and Civil War encampment reenactors; drill with the war regiment; learn new (actually, old) dance steps; practice tying sailor knots; play hoops and other 19th century games; learn animal husbandry; and take a self-guiding tour of the museum. The school program runs Mon. - Fri., 9am - 12:30pm. Tip: Bring a picnic lunch. Call way in advance for reservations. It's open to the public Sun., noon - 4pm. Admission to both programs is free.

CALIFORNIA STRAWBERRY FESTIVAL, Oxnard. (888) 288-9242 or (805) 385-7578 / www.strawberry-fest.org, 3250 S. Rose Ave. and Channel Island Blvd. at College Park. This big, juicy festival, held on the third weekend of May, offers unique strawberry culinary delights, an arts and crafts show with over 300 artisans, and contests, including a strawberry shortcake eating contest. Kids enjoy Strawberryland, in particular, because it has a petting zoo, puppet shows, clowns, hands-on arts and crafts, and carnival rides. Have a berry good time here! Open Sat. - Sun., 10am - 6:30pm. General admission is $9 for adults; $5 for srs. and ages 5 - 12; children 4 and under are free. Certain activities cost extra.

CHERRY FESTIVAL and CHERRY PICKING, Beaumont and Leona Valley. See June entry for details.

CHILDREN'S DAY (or Kodomo no Hi), Los Angeles. (213) 628-2725 / www.jaccc.org, First St. in Little Tokyo. This traditional Japanese celebration is for families, and particularly children ages 4 to 12. They are invited to participate in a running race, as well as making arts and crafts. Other attractions can include magic shows, sports clinics, kite-making, dancing, displays of traditional costumes, live entertainment, and more. Open Sat., 10am - 6pm. General admission is free, although certain activities cost.

CINCO DE MAYO CELEBRATION, The fifth of May, Mexican Independence Day, is celebrated throughout Southern California. The festival celebrates this Mexican holiday with several days of Mexican folk dancing, mariachi music, parades, puppet shows, booths, piñatas, and fun! In Los Angeles, for instance, call (213) 628-1274 / www.cityofla.org/elp/, at El Pueblo de Los Angeles State Historic Park in downtown. In San Diego County, call Bazaar del Mundo in Old Town San Diego, (619) 296-3161 / www.bazaardelmundo.com; Borrego Springs, (800) 559-5524 / www.borregosprings.com; or Oceanside, (760) 471-6549.

CROSSROADS EUROPEAN RENAISSANCE FESTIVAL, Corona. See April entry for details.

EARLY CALIFORNIA DAYS, Long Beach. (562) 570-1755 / www.ci.long-beach.ca.us/park/ranchlc.htm, 4600 Virginia Rd. at Rancho Los Cerritos. Blend Native American and Hispanic cultures, throw in Yankee seafaring elements, mix it together to re-create the period when California was under Mexican rule, and you'll get a old-time fiesta. Entertainment includes sea shanties, Hispanic songs and dances, roping, blacksmithing, hide scraping and leather working, rope weaving, and knot tying. Hands-on activities include rope making, adobe brick making, candle dipping, stick horse racing, and more. Open 12:30pm - 4:30pm. Admission is $3 per person; children 2 and under are free.

FERN STREET CIRCUS, San Diego. (619) 235-9756 / www.fernstreetcircus.org, Presidents Way and Park Blvd. in Balboa Park. Beginning with an interactive parade, this down home, yet professional circus aims to please and hits its mark. Aerial routines, jugglers, clowns, trampoline athletes, stilt walkers, music, theatrical lighting, acrobats, trapeze artists, and more send oohs and aaahs racing through the crowds. Ask about Fern Street's after-school program where they teach circus skills to youngsters. The circus runs for about a week with both day time and evening performances. Tickets are $10 for adults; $4 for ages 11 and under.

FRONTIER DAYS RODEO, Temecula. (909) 676-4718 / www.frontierdaysrodeo.com, near Winchester on Diaz Rd. at Northwest Sports Complex. The rodeo's in town and that's no bull. Main events include bull riding, calf roping, steer wrestling, barrel races, trick roping, rodeo clowns, team penning, and more. A carnival is usually going on at the same time, at the other end of Diaz. Rodeos are held Sat. at 2pm and 7pm; Sun. at 2pm. Admission to the matinee rodeos is $8 per person; $10 per person to the one on Sat. night. Children 3 and under are free.

FRONTIER RENDEZVOUS, Oak Glen. (909) 797-7534 / www.rileysfarm.com and (909) 790-2364 / www.rileysbarn.com, 12261 S. Oak Glen Blvd. Two

Riley's farms host a four-day living history encampment include Revolutionary War soldiers, fur traders, Indians, colonials, buckskinners, and vendors that sell period clothing, toys, lanterns, tomahawks, and more. Open Fri. - Memorial Day Mon., 10am - 4:30pm. Admission is $5 per car.

FULLERTON RAILROAD Days, Fullerton. (714) 278-0648 / www.trainweb.com/frpa, 124 E. Santa Fe Ave at the Fullerton Santa Fe Railroad Depot at the Fullerton Transportation Center. Usually held the first weekend in May, kids and adults go loco over going through a large steam locomotive, Amtrak passenger cars, vintage private rail cars, and newer train cars. More activities and events include model trains running in the huge and beautifully landscaped garden layout; more operating train layouts inside a circus tents; mini train rides; vendors selling train-related paraphernalia; a food court; and an antique fire truck and modern police car are on the grounds for show and tell. Open Sat. - Sun., 9am - 5pm. Admission is $3 for adults; ages 12 and under are free.

GEM SHOW, Costa Mesa. See March entry for details.

GREEN MEADOWS FARM, Los Angeles. (800) 393-3276 / www.greenmeadowsproductions.com, 4235 Monterey Rd. at Ernest Debs Regional Park. The Farm is open May through June. See the March entry for details.

GRUBSTAKE DAYS, Yucca Valley. (760) 365-6323 / www.yuccavalley.org, on Grand and Twenty-nine Palms Hwy. at Grubstake Grounds. This celebration commemorates the early mining background of the Morongo Basin. Favorite events include panning for gold, carnival rides and games, a street parade, motor sports, and demolition derbies ($10 for adults, $7 for children), and some equestrian events. Open Thurs. - Fri., 5pm - midnight; Sat. - Sun., noon - midnight. General admission is free.

IMAGINATION CELEBRATION, Orange County. See April entry for details.

INSECT FAIR, Los Angeles. (213) 763-3466 / www.nhm.org, 900 Exposition Blvd. at the Natural History Museum of Los Angeles. See the museum entry in the main section of the book for a description of the museum. This weekend fair really *bugs* me! Come and gawk at and even touch a wide variety of live insects, such as Madagascar hissing cockroaches, millipedes, and more. Every kind of insect product is available to look at and/or purchase. Items include jewelry, t-shirts, toys, silkworms, live critters, a butterfly house, chocolate-covered crickets (poor Jimminy!), mounted insects, and lots more. The fair includes educational presentations and hands-on activities. Tour the museum's Insect Zoo while here. Creep, crawl, or fly here on the second weekend of May between 10am - 5pm. Admission to the fair includes admission to the museum: $8 for adults; $5.50 for srs. and students; $2 for ages 5 - 12; children 4 and under are free.

653

...AL SPEEDWAY, Costa Mesa. See April entry for details.

L... ...OUNTAIN RENDEZVOUS, Julian area. See October entry for detail.

LAKE CASITAS INTERTRIBAL POW WOW, Ojai. (805) 496-6036 / www.goldcoastfestivals.com, 11311 Santa Ana Rd. Enjoy this three-day weekend as more than forty American Indian tribes gather together to perform and compete (for cash prizes) in dance and music. Women's dances include traditional, shawl, jingle, and buckskin. Men compete in fancy, grass, traditional, and more. Special ceremonies plus arts and crafts booths (with beadwork, jewelry, and pottery), food (try a buffalo burger!), and even camping, fishing, and boating at the lake complete the festivities. Seating for the shows is limited, so bring your own chair. A living history program is available to students and teachers on Fri., 10am - 3pm for $3 per person. It's open to the public on Fri., 10am - 5pm; Sat. - Sun., 10am - 7pm. Admission is $7 for adults; $5 for ages 5 - 11; children 4 and under are free. Parking is $3.

MEDIEVAL EVENT, Valley Center. (760) 789-2299 / www.historicenterprises.com/redco or (760) 749-3333 / www.batesfarm.com, 15954 Woods Valley Rd. at Bates Nut Farm. Knights on horseback, archers, dancing, period crafts, storytelling, music, and all the other sights and sounds of a working medieval camp, circa 1471, are yours to enjoy. Note: There is no jousting show, just people going about their daily tasks. School tours are given on Fri. by reservation only. The camp is open Sat., 10am - 4pm. Admission is $5 for adults; $3 ages 5 - 10; children 4 and under are free.

MOTA DAY, Pasadena. (213) 740-8687 / www.gamblehouse.usc.edu. or www.socalhistory.org. The five organizations that comprise MOTA - Museums Of The Arroyo - open their doors for free one Sunday a year and include fun family activities. The museums include Heritage Square Museum at 3800 Homer St., Los Angeles; the Lummis Home and Garden at 200 E. Ave. 43; Southwest Museum at 234 Museum Dr.; Gamble House at 4 Westmoreland Pl.; and Pasadena Historical Museum at 470 W. Walnut St. Look up most of the entries in the main section of the book. The museums are open 11am - 5pm. There is a free shuttle service between the museums.

NATURE'S CHILD OPEN HOUSE, San Dimas. (909) 599-7512, 1628 N. Sycamore Canyon Rd. at the San Dimas Nature Center. Over Memorial Day weekend enjoy Indian dances, nature hikes, face painting, pottery, weaving, beading, games, crafts, and Indian fry bread and sweet corn. The proceeds from the activities provide food and medical care for the animals in the center's sanctuary. Open Sat. - Sun., 10am - 4pm. General admission is free.

OLD PASADENA SUMMER FEST, Pasadena. (626) 797-6803 / www.oldpasadenasummerfest.com, Central Park at Fair Oaks Ave. Memorialize the three-day Memorial Day weekend by participating in the Family Fest, which offers pony and train rides, a petting zoo, face painting, a moonbounce, a giant slide, swing chairs, a Ferris wheel, and hands-on cultural workshops. Also enjoy live entertainment and indulge in Taste of Pasadena, in which local restaurants offer their tempting treats ($1.25 - $7 per person). Festival hours are 10am - 8pm. Admission is free, although certain activities cost.

OPEN HOUSE AT JET PROPULSION LABORATORY, Pasadena. (818) 354-4321 / www.jpl.nasa.gov, 4800 Oak Grove Dr. This annual open house is out of this world! The space research center offers a glimpse into outer space with over 30 exhibits including planetary imaging, spacecraft tracking, presentations, commercial technology booths that display state-of-the-art instruments and products, robotic demonstrations, thinking games for kids, and spacecraft models. This is a "don't miss" event. Open Sat. - Sun., 9am - 5pm. Admission is free. Note: The Open House is sometimes held in June.

POW WOW, Thousand Oaks. (805) 492-8076 / www.designplace.com/chumash, 3290 Lang Ranch Pkwy. at the Chumash Interpretive Center. On Memorial Day weekend this intertribal pow wow showcases fine Native American dancing, drumming, crafts, and face painting, as well as good food such as fry bread and tri-top sandwiches. The Grand Entrance is at noon. Open Sat., 10am - 10pm; Sun., 10am - 6pm. Admission is $5 for adults; $3 for srs. and ages 6 - 16 years; children 5 and under are free.

RAMONA PAGEANT, Hemet. See April entry for details.

RAMONA RODEO, Ramona. (760) 789-1311 / www.ramonarodeo.org or (760) 789-1484 / www.ramonamall.com, 5th St. and Aqua Ln. Kick up your heels 'cause the rodeo's in town the second weekend in May! Rodeo shows include all the favorite featured events, plus a chili cook off, rodeo parade, and numerous vendors. Admission is $8 for adults; $5 for ages 12 and under. Reserved seating is $2 more, but worth it since shows can sell out. Rodeo hours are Fri., 7pm; Sat., at 1pm and 7pm; Sun., 2pm. Arrive early. Parking is $2.

RANCHO SANTA MARGARITA FIESTA RODEO, Rancho Santa Margarita. (949) 589-4272, corner of Santa Margarita Pkwy. and Los Flores St., next to Target. Yippee-aye-ay! This five-day fiesta begins on Thursday night with family activities. Friday starts with a cattle drive from Casper Wilderness Park ending at the rodeo grounds. Friday night is team-roping competition. Professional rodeos are held on the weekend. The two-hour shows (which seat 5,000) include bull riding, calf roping, women's barrel racing, kids' rodeos, bronco riding, bareback riding, and rodeo clowns. There are also carnival rides for kids, game booths, pony rides, and lots of arts and crafts booths. The nights bring country western dancing and more fun. Rodeo grounds are open Fri., 3pm - 11pm; Sat., 10am - midnight; Sun., 10am - 6pm. General admission to the grounds is $2 for adults; $1 for kids. Rodeo tickets in advance are $12 for adults; $10 for ages 3 - 12. Tickets are $2 per person at the gate. Parking is $3.

RENAISSANCE PLEASURE FAIRE, San Bernardino. See April entry for details.

REPTILE SHOW, Long Beach. (562) 570-1745 / www.ci.long-beach.ca.us, 7550 E. Spring St. at El Dorado Nature Center. Members of the Herpetology (new word for the day) Society exhibit hundreds of snakes, lizards, and amphibians to look at and touch. Open Sat., 10am - 3pm. Admission is free. Parking is $5.

SAN BERNARDINO COUNTY FAIR, Victorville. (760) 951-2200 / www.sbcfair.com, 14800 7th St. For nine days, the desert really heats up with excitement when the county fair comes to town. 86 acres of carnival rides, attractions, farm animals, clowns, Destruction Derby, a rodeo, entertainment, and lots more fun. Open Mon. - Fri., 4pm - 11pm; Sat. - Sun., noon - 11pm. General admission is $6 for adults; $4 for srs.; $3 for ages 6 - 12; children 5 and under are free. Activities cost extra. Parking is $3.

SAN DIEGO WILD ANIMAL PARK, Escondido. (619) 234-6541 / www.sandiegozoo.org, 15500 San Pasqual Valley Rd. Get a little wild in the beginning of May as the Wild Animal Park celebrates founder's day and admission is free! Call for the exact date.

SCOTTISH FESTIVAL AND HIGHLAND GATHERING, Costa Mesa. (714) 708-3247 / www.ocfair.com, 88 Fair Dr. at the Orange County Fairgrounds. This Memorial weekend festival features everything Scottish - caber tossing, hammer throws, shot put, sheepdog herding, good food, opening and closing ceremonies, parades, and a lot of tartan. Bagpipes and Highland Fling dancers and country dancing also entertain you and the kids throughout the day. Open Sat. - Sun., 9am - 5pm. One-day admission is $14 for adults; $2 for ages 12 and under.

SPRING VILLAGE FAIRE, Carlsbad. (760) 931-8400 / www.carlsbad.org, at Carlsbad Village Dr. The first Sunday in May is the largest one-day fair held in California, with over 900 exhibitors, international food, and a variety of live entertainment. This type of fair is especially fun for shoppers of all ages as you never know what kind of unique items you might find (and *have* to purchase). It runs from 8am - 5pm. Admission is free, but bring spending money!

STRAWBERRY FESTIVAL, Garden Grove. (714) 638 - 0981 / www.strawberryfestival.org or (714) 638-7950 / www.gardengrovechamber.org, 12862 Euclid Ave. and Stanford. This four-day event, usually held over Memorial Day weekend, features carnival rides, games, a parade (Saturday at 10am), arts and crafts booths, continuous entertainment at the amphitheater, dance recitals, a Berry Beautiful Baby Pageant, the annual redhead round-up, and lots and lots of strawberries! Open Fri., 1pm - 10pm ($15 for an all rides pass); Sat. - Sun., 10am - 10pm; Mon., 10am - 8:30pm. Free general admission; certain activities cost.

STRAWBERRY PICKING, Carlsbad. Exit the 5 Fwy. E. on Cannon Rd. Pick your own sweet fruit from these strawberry fields mid-May through mid-August. The best bet is purchasing a $7 bucket, which holds about 5 ½ of the usual plastic green containers. Pre-picked strawberries are also available to purchase.

SUNSET'S CELEBRATION WEEKEND, Menlo Park. (800) 786-7375 / www.sunset.com., 80 Willow Road, Menlo Park. The celebration, held at Sunset headquarters, is like Sunset magazine in 3-D! Stroll through Sunset's gardens, tour the test kitchen, and watch numerous demonstrations that feature gardening, home-building, and celebrity chef's cooking tips. The Kid's Area has hands-on activities to keep the younger crowd entertained and educated, such as a juggling workshop, craft projects, planting an herb, and more. An Adventure Area offers bronc riding (not on a real horse), rock climbing, trick roping, and more. On-going entertainment can include live bands, dancers, etc. Open Sat. - Sun., 10am - 5pm. Admission is $8 for adults; $6 for srs.; ages 12 and under are free. Park at 1601 Willow Rd.

TEMECULA FRONTIER DAYS RODEO, Temecula. (909) 676-4718 / www.temeculacalifornia.com, Winchester and Diaz Rd. at Northwest Sports Park. This P.R.C.A. rodeo is two days of rootin' tootin' cowboy fun. See all the main rodeo events in an Old West atmosphere. The free Friday show is reserved just for school kids. Not only do they see a mini rodeo, but they can talk with the cowboys and see the horses and bulls. Rodeos are open to the public Sat. at 2pm and 7:30pm; Sun., 2pm. Admission is $10 for the nighttime show; $8 for the daytime ones.

TURTLE AND TORTOISE SHOW, Long Beach. (562) 570-1745 / www.ci.long-beach.ca.us, 7550 E. Spring St. at the El Dorado Nature Center. Do you know the difference between a turtle or a tortoise? Find out here as members of the California Turtle and Tortoise Society bring their favorites, from the smallest turtle to the large Galapagos Island tortoise. All questions are welcome! This Sat. event is open 10am - 3pm. Admission is free. Parking is $5.

VISIT WITH MONTEZUMA, Hollywood Hills. (800) 204-3131 / www.forestlawn.com, 6300 Forest Lawn Dr. at Forest Lawn Memorial Park. A costumed Montezuma talks at the Plaza of Mexican Heritage to an audience of up to 350 people for about thirty minutes about "his" life and achievements - history comes alive! A short, guided explanation of some of the artifacts from the Mexican museum follows the talk. This program takes place on weekdays at 9:30am, 10:30am, and 11:30am. Reservations are necessary. This event repeats in October. Admission is free.

WINGS OVER GILLESPIE, El Cajon. (888) 215-7000 or (619) 448-4505 / www.cafairgroup1.org, 1850 Joe Crosson Dr. at the Gillespie Field Airport. Several fly bys, aerial demonstrations, and parachute teams, plus displays of more than seventy warbirds and vintage aircraft decorate the air and airfield the first Thursday through Saturday in May. Visitors may also tour through a grounded B-17, view antique cars and motorcycles, purchase memorabilia, and talk with aviation celebrities such as WWII Aces, original Flying Tigers, and Tuskegee Airmen. Students are particularly welcome on Friday when kids are given educational tours regarding the aircraft. The air show is open 8am - 5:30pm. Admission is $7 for adults; ages 12 and under are free.

JUNE:

ADVENTURE PLAYGROUND, Huntington Beach. (714) 842-7442 - playground; (714) 374-1626 - recorded info; (714) 536-5486 / www.ci.huntington-beach.ca.us - surrounding park, 7111 Talbot at Huntington Beach Central Park. Open mid-June through mid-August, young Huck Finns can use a raft (push poles are provided) in the shallow waters of a man-made lake. Kids will also love the slide (i.e. tarp-covered hill) which ends in a little mud pool; a rope bridge leading to a tire swing and mini zip line; sand box; and a work-in-progress kid-built "city" of shacks and clubhouses (only for ages 7 years and up). Lumber, hammers, and nails are provided. All guest must wear tennis shoes; no sandals or water shoes allowed. Note: Day campers usually invade during the morning hours. Open Mon. - Sat., 10am - 5pm. Admission is $1 for kids who are Huntington Beach residents; $2 for non-residents; free for adults.

CHALK STREET PAINTING FESTIVAL, Pasadena. (626) 449-3689. Centennial Square. Chalk it all up to having a good time! Hundreds of artists draw marvelous, if temporary, masterpieces out of chalk on the sidewalks of Pasadena at this one-day festival. A children's chalk area is also set up. Live music and food complete the ambiance. Admission is free.

CHERRY FESTIVAL and CHERRY PICKING, Beaumont and Cherry Valley. (909) 845-9541 / www.beaumontcachamber.com - Beaumont Chamber of Commerce; (909) 845-3628 - Cherry Growers Association. I tell you no lie - June is a month ripe for cherry picking, but the season could start in mid-May and go as long as July, depending on the weather. Call first. The three-week, or so, season starts with a three-day festival ($1 admission) that includes a parade, carnival-type rides, game booths, amateur and professional live musical entertainment, and lots of family fun. One of our favorite places to pick cherries, and the place with the most acreage, is Wohlgemuth's Orchard, (909) 845-1548, 1106 E. 11th St. in Beaumont. Admission to the orchards at Wohlgemuth's is $2 for adults; children 11 and under are free. Use the provided cans with ropes and hang them around your neck so cherries can be picked (and sampled) with both hands, working from the ground. Ladders aren't allowed or necessary. The per pound cost of cherries varies according to market value. There are also picnic tables under shade trees here, too, and a bakery. You may also purchase pre-picked cherries. Look for roadside signs along Live Oak Avenida, Brookside, and Cherry Ave. announcing other U-Pics. Note: Dowling Orchard, (909) 845-1217, is not a U-Pic, but it does offer just-picked cherries and a year-round produce market.

CHERRY PICKING, Leona Valley. (661) 266-7116 - Leona Valley Cherry Growers hotline / www.cherriesupic; (661) 270-0615 - Rancher's Market at 9001 Elizabeth Lake Rd. for a free map of the two dozen U-pick orchards. The orchards here don't produce enough of the delicious crop for commercial sale, so the public wins by getting to harvest the cherries themselves! Put a bucket around your neck and start picking, although many orchards also sell pre-picked cherries. The weather-dependent, short season can start as early as May and can last through July. Different types of cherries, such as Bing, Ranier, Cashmere, Montmorency, Tartarians, etc., ripen at various times throughout the season. Call first! We especially enjoyed Bright Ranch, (661) 270-1569, at 10600 Leona Ave., which is a large orchard with prices of $1.25 per pound for Bings, in the summer of 2000. The ranch also has picnic tables on site and refreshments for sale (weekends only). Tip: If you pick a lot of cherries, purchase a cherry pitter!

CIVIL WAR REENACTMENT, Oak Glen. (909) 790-2364 - Riley's Farm and Orchard and (909) 797-4061 - at Riley's Log Cabin at 12201 S. Oak Glen Blvd. These adjacent peaceful farms erupt with a deluge of artillery during this weekend reenactment. Authentic encampments from the Civil War era feature men and women in period dress, pioneer cooking, bullet-making, blacksmithing demonstrations, and more. Along with battles, represented by "soldiers" with various units - the cavalry, dragoons, infantry, and more - are politicians, laundresses, nurses, and temperance workers. What a great way to combine education and fun! The camps are open Sat. - Sun., 10am - 4pm. Admission is $5 per vehicle.

CIVIL WAR REENACTMENT AND ENCAMPMENT, Oak Glen. (909) 797-7534 or (909) 797-5145 /www.rileysfarm.com, 12261 S. Oak Glen Blvd. at Riley's Farm. (This is an adjacent farm to the ones mentioned above.) It's a warm weekend in 1864, give or take 137 + years and the army is on the move. 250 reenactors converge on Riley's Farm to show what life was like during the Civil War time period. Visit soldiers at their encampment; see battle skirmishes with infantry, calvary and artillery units; attend a Ladies Tea and period fashion show; and be immersed in this pivotal time, if only for a day or two. Farm Stays are offered for people who *really* want to live history - they may stay on the farm in rustic cabins for two nights, share in five meals, and be a participant (as part of the civilian attachment) in the reenactments, and maybe churn butter, knead bread, and help plow a field. Overnight farm stays are $250 for adults; $185 for children 3 - 12 years. Encampment hours are Sat. - Sun., 10am - 4:30pm. Admission is $5 for adults; $3 for ages 3 - 12.

COIN & COLLECTIBLES EXPO, Long Beach. See February entry for details.

COLORADO LAGOON MODEL BOAT SHOP, Long Beach. (562) 570-1719, E. Colorado St. and E. Appian Way at Colorado Lagoon. Pre-packaged craft kits have their place in our instant-gratification society, but they have nothing on actually hand crafting a one-of-a-kind, wooden, 12" to 40"-long sailboat, which is balanced by a lead keel. Participants, who must be at least 7 years old, glue, sand, file, lacquer, and paint before the final rigging is done and they learn sailing lingo along the way. All materials, including hand tools, are provided. Boats take between five to seven days to complete, consecutively or in whatever increments you choose. Parents can drop kids off (or stay) anytime Mon. - Thurs., 10am - 3:30pm; Fri. 10am - 1:30pm. The small building "shop", staffed mostly by older kids, is a fenced in area just off the beach by the COLORADO LAGOON. (Look up this entry under the Beaches section.) Bring a picnic lunch and suntan lotion. All participants can sail their finished products in the weekly regattas held on Fri. at 2pm. Help your kids chart their course to a great summer! Boats range from $15 for a 12", up to $30 for a 40".

CRITTER EXPO, Pasadena. (626) 449-9144 /www.kidspacemuseum.org, 360 South El Molino Ave. at Kidspace Children's Museum. All "critters" great and small, the Lord God made them all. Snakes (including a 14-foot Burmese Python), giant lizards, frogs, millipedes, llamas, lambs, goats, and ponies are some of the critters that visit the museum on this special day. Learn about the animals and about rescue efforts for endangered wildlife. The expo runs 11am - 4pm. Admission is $5 per person and includes admission to the museum.

DAIRY FESTIVAL AND TOUR, Chino. (909) 627-6177 / www.chinovalleychamber.com, at the corner of Central and Edison at the Chino Fair Grounds. Milk this festival for all it's worth! Contests here include cheese carving and milk drinking. Entertainment includes a petting zoo, kiddie ride, and best of all, a tour of Van Vliet Dairy. Hop on the provided bus to head over to the dairy for a one-hour tour. Watch cows being milked, learn how a dairy farm operates on a daily basis, and taste fresh cheese, yogurt and ice cream. The festival runs the first Sat. in June, 10am - 4pm. Admission is free.

DEL MAR FAIR, Del Mar. (858) 793-5555 - recording; (858) 755-1161 - fairgrounds / www.delmarfair.com, 2260 Jimmy Durante Blvd. at the Del Mar Fairgrounds. This major, three-week event features everything wonderful in a county fair - carnival rides, flower and garden shows, gem and minerals exhibits, farm animals, livestock judging, food, craft booths, and a festive atmosphere. Call for a schedule of events. Gates open daily at 10am. General admission is $9 for adults; $6 for srs.; $4.50 for ages 6 - 12 years; children 5 and under are free. Parking is $6. Certain activities cost extra.

FAMILY ARTS FESTIVAL, Cerritos. (562) 916-8510 or (562) 916-1296 / www.cerritoscenter.com/friends, 12700 Center Court Dr. at the Cerritos Center for the Performing Arts. This one-day, free festival offers five stages of continuous entertainment which can include Taiko Drummers, country/western, salsa, ballet, jazz, storytelling, and lots more. Other family activities include face-painting, mask-making, and mural-making. Bring your own picnic food or purchase food from on-site vendors. The festival runs Sun., 11am - 4pm.

HUCK FINN'S JUBILEE, Victorville. (909) 780-8810 / www.huckfinn.com, Ridgecrest Ave. in Mojave Narrows Regional Park. The huge, three-day jubilee always falls on Father's Day weekend. It kicks off with a fishing derby at 8am on Fri., followed by a weekend of river raft building contests, egg-tossing contests, a big-top circus, arm wrestling championships, a mountain man encampment, arts and crafts, a Huck Finn look-alike contest, country music, and lots more down home fun. Put on a straw hat and join the throngs of people. Note: Camping is available here, too. Open Fri. - Sat., 7am - 11pm; Sun., 7:30am - 8pm. Admission Fri. - Sat., $10 per day for adults; $15 on Sun.; $5 each day for ages 6 - 11; children 5 and under are free. Parking is free.

HO'OLAULE'A HAWAIIAN FESTIVAL OF THE VALLEY, Northridge. (818) 756-8616 / www.lacity.org/RAP, 10058 Reseda Blvd. at Northridge Park. Aloha! Concurrent festivals run the first weekend in June. The Hawaiian Festival features Pacific Island music, dance, and entertainment from Samoa, Mori, Tahiti, and more; traditional games, crafts, and Polynesian-type food. The community festival, a few booths away, features kiddie rides and games and more vendor booth. Both festivals run Sat. - Sun., 10am - 6pm. General admission is free.

INDIAN FAIR, San Diego. (619) 239-2001 / www.museumofman.org, 1350 El Prado at Museum of Man in Balboa Park. This weekend fair, attended by 1,000 artists and performers representing dozens of tribes, provides one of the largest forums for Native American artistry in the West Coast. It features costumed tribal dancers, traditional storytellers, and a market with arts, crafts, beadwork, pottery, and authentic cuisine. Open 10am - 4:30pm. Admission is $6 for adults; $3 for ages 6 - 17; children 5 and under are free.

INTERNATIONAL SPEEDWAY, Costa Mesa. See April entry for details.

INTERTRIBAL POW WOW, Oceanside. (760) 724-8505, 4050 Mission Ave. at Mission San Luis Rey de Franca. Join a weekend of tribal dancing, arts and crafts, and American Indian games and food. Admission is free.

IRISH FAIR AND MUSIC FESTIVAL, Encino. (818) 503-2511 / www.irishfair.org, Festival Fields at Woodley Park at Burbank and Woodley Ave. Top o' the mornin' to ye. This weekend Irish fair features top-name entertainment, such as Clancy, and Hal Roach; parades; traditional contests, such as fiddle playing and dancing; sheep-herding demonstrations; a dog show featuring Irish breeds; bagpipe music; vendors of Irish wares; and Leprechaun Kingdom for kids. The kingdom features storytelling, jugglers, pony rides, and carnival rides. Another favorite at the festival is a recreation of a medieval Irish village, Tara, where sword-yielding performers recount the village's legends and history. The festival runs Sat. - Sun., 10am - 6pm. Admission is $16 for adults; $13 for students and srs.; children 12 and under are free.

KIDS NATURE FESTIVAL, Pacific Palisades. (310) 364-3591 / www.childrensnatureinstitute.org, near Sunset Blvd. in Temescal Gateway Park. Geared mostly for ages 2 to 10, this outdoor festival has a wonderful variety of things to do and see. Well-known children's bands perform periodically; craft booths are available; and live animals such as snakes, iguanas, millipedes, and tidepool creatures can be touched while some exotic animals such as a lynx, armadillo, and raccoon are shown and spoken of during wildlife presentations. Favorite activities include crawling through hoop tunnels, creating spider webs out of yarn, exploring a cave (made of disguised tents), getting faces painted, and making giant bubbles. On-site nature-themed booths and food vendors complete the festivities. Note: You are welcome to bring a picnic lunch. Open Sat., 10am - 4pm. Admission is $8 for adults; $7 for srs. and children 12 months - 12 years.

KIDSTRAVAGANZA, Riverside. (909) 351-3110 / www.galleriatyler.com, Tyler St. at the Galleria at Tyler. Bring your elementary-school aged children to enjoy half-hour, or so, performances given every Tuesday during the summer at Macy's Court. Shows usually feature song and dance, marionettes, magic, or kids comedy acts. Each Thursday, near the food court, a new craft project is introduced and all the materials are provided for your little artists. Ask about the Galleria's occasional special exhibits, too. Shows are Tues. at 11am. Crafts are Thurs., 1pm - 4pm. Both activities are free.

MARIACHI USA FESTIVAL, Hollywood. (800) MARIACHI (627-4224) or (323) 848-7717 /www.mariachiusa.com or (323) 850-2000 / www.hollywoodbowl.org, 2301 N. Highland Ave. at the Hollywood Bowl. This event celebrates family, culture, and tradition. Bring a picnic dinner and enjoy Mariachi music, Ballet Folkloric, and a fireworks finale. The 4 ½ hour performances are given Sat. at 6pm and Sun. at 5pm. Tip: Purchase tickets early as the concert is usually sold out. Admission is $10 - $127, depending on seating. Parking is $5 - $6.

OPEN HOUSE AT THE HOLLYWOOD BOWL, Hollywood. (323) 850-2000 / www.hollywoodbowl.org, 2301 N. Highland. For six musically hot weeks, forty-five-minute, somewhat interactive, multi-cultural performances are given at the Bowl on the outside stage in the front Plaza entrance. Bring sunscreen. The performances, which are geared for young children, could incorporate dance, music, storytelling, etc. Past shows include Salsa, Call of Africa, Fiery Flamenco, and A Touch of Brass. A craft workshop for ages 3 to 10 that pertains to the theme, follows each performance under a shade awning in the parking lot. Each week brings a different show that is performed twice daily. Shows are Mon. - Fri. at 10am and 11:15am. Workshops are at 11am and 12:15pm. Open House visitors are invited to bring a picnic lunch and watch orchestra rehearsals inside the Bowl area at no additional cost. Rehearsals take place from 9:30am - 12:30pm on most days, except some Mon. and Wed. Tickets for Open House are $3 per person, although non-paying guests outside the roped-off seating area can see and hear the show, too. The workshop is an additional $1. Parking is free.

OUTDOOR FAMILY FILM FESTIVALS. Many parks offer free, nighttime, out-door family entertainment such as concerts and G, or PG, movies. Bring a blanket, picnic dinner, and enjoy a show together! Call your local park for information.

PEARSON PARK AMPHITHEATER, Anaheim. (714) 765-4422 or (714) 765-5274, Lemon and Sycamore Sts. The terrific programs put on through the "Just For Kids" series throughout the summer are geared for kids 4 years old through 6th graders. The shows run approximately two hours. Past programs have included Make-a-Circus, magic shows, puppet shows, a wild west show, the mad scientist, and audience participation shows with songs or storytellers. Fri. shows start at 7pm; call for hours for Sat. shows. Tickets usually cost $2 for adults; $1 for srs. and children 12 and under. Call for specific show information.

QUEEN MARY FIREWORKS, Long Beach. (562) 435-3511 / www.queenmary.com, 1126 Queens Highway at the Queen Mary. Fireworks go off nightly at 9pm for a few days or so before July 4th and then every Sat. night through the beginning of September. As a treat, enjoy a dinner or snack on board the ship before the extravaganza. Tip: The ten-minute or so show can be viewed for free anywhere within sight of the Queen Mary.

REDLANDS BOWL SUMMER MUSIC FESTIVAL, Redlands. (909) 793-7316 / www.relandsbowl.org or www.redlandsweb.com, Brookside Ave. and Eureka St. Two nights a week, from late June through August, the bowl offers symphony music, jazz, and opera as well as musicals, ballet, and dance ensembles. These are great programs for the family! Programs are offered Tues. and Fri. evening at 8:15pm and are free - donations are appreciated. Free, forty-five music appreciation workshops are given for elementary-aged kids on Tues. at 3pm and Sat. at 10am.

RENAISSANCE PLEASURE FAIRE, San Bernardino. See April entry for details.

SAN DIEGO SCOTTISH HIGHLAND GAMES AND GATHERING OF CLANS, Vista. (619) 645-8080 / www.sdhighlandgames.org, Brengle Terrace Park. For almost thirty years, fifty or so clans have come to participate and enjoy first class entertainment at this gathering. The last weekend in June is the one for Scottish merrymaking, which includes highland dancing, Celtic harping, bagpipe competitions, sheep dog herding trials, athletic competitions (such as caber tossing), and lots of good food. Open Sat. - Sun., 9am - 5pm. Admission is $10 for adults (per day); $8 for srs.; $3 for ages 3 - 12. Ask about two-day passes. Parking is $3.

SAWDUST FESTIVAL, Laguna Beach. See July entry for details.

SHAKESPEARE FESTIVAL/L.A., Los Angeles. (213) 481-2273 / www.shakespearefestivalla.org, in the greater Los Angeles area. The bard is back! Each year's program features one play for a month's run at various outdoor locations throughout L.A. County. The actors and actresses are often name-recognizable performers. Call for hours and locations. Admission is a canned food donation. Inquire about the "Simply Shakespeare" readings by noted actors and the one-hour adaptations of the play specifically for students.

STARGAZING, Julian. (619) 594-6182 / www.julianfun.com, Morris Ranch Rd., off Sunrise Hwy. at the Mt. Laguna Observatory. Harken back to the days of Galileo, only with a more powerful, 21" telescope with which to gaze at the heavenlies. Student guides help staff the facility for free public tours Fri. and Sat. evenings through Labor Day.

SUMMER NIGHTS AT THE FORD, Hollywood. (323) 461-3673 or (323) 871-5904 / www.lacountyarts.org, 2580 Cahuenga Blvd. E. at the John Anson Ford Amphitheater. This outdoor amphitheater presents wonderful, one-hour family performances almost every Saturday in July and August, along with a few Sunday afternoon shows. Check the schedule for a complete listing, as family-friendly shows are also given sometimes during the week, too. Bring a picnic lunch and enjoy an intimate setting with shows that feature top-name entertainment in magic, puppetry, storytelling, music, dance, or plays designed for children. Shows on Sat. start at 10am; Sun. shows at 4:30pm. Seats cost $7 per person; five admissions (on the same day) is $25. Ask about Family Day admission. Parking on site costs $5. Shuttle services from 1718 Cherokee in Hollywood are 25¢.

TEMECULA VALLEY BALLOON AND WINE FESTIVAL, Temecula. (909) 676-4713 / www.balloonandwinefestival.com, Warren Rd. at Lake Skinner Recreation Area. Rise and shine for this colorful three-day festival. On the weekends the balloons are filled with hot air starting at 6:30am, an event fascinating to watch. Lift-off is around 7am, with numerous balloons filling the sky in a kaleidoscope of color. Other, less lofty, activities include live entertainment, arts and craft, and a kid's fair with kiddie rides, pony rides, a petting zoo, free tethered balloon rides, and more. The Friday and Saturday night "glows" (i.e. inflated, lighted balloons that glow in the evening sky) occur after sunset. Open Fri., 5pm - 10pm; Sat., 6am - 10:30pm; Sun., 6apm - 6pm. General admission is Fri. $5 for adults; ages 12 and under are free; Sat. - Sun., $15 for adults; $5 for ages 7 - 12; children 6 and under are free. Parking is $3. Certain activities cost extra. Balloon rides are $135 per person and advance reservations are recommended - (800) 965-2122 / www.agrapeescape.com.

THRESHING BEE AND ANTIQUE ENGINE SHOW, Vista. (800) 587-2286 or (760) 941-1791 / www.agsem.com, 2040 N. Santa Fe Ave. at the Antique Gas & Steam Engine Museum. (See this listing in the Museums section of the book.) This show is held on two consecutive weekends in June, and again in October. Watch demonstrations of American crafts, farming, log sawing, and blacksmithing, plus see many of the restored tractors in a parade each day at 1pm; a very unusual-looking parade! Join in some of the activities such as hayrides and square dancing and taste the good, home-cooked food available for purchase. Open Sat. - Sun., 9am - 4:30pm. Admission is $6 for adults; $3 for ages 6 - 12; children 5 and under are free. Camping, with reservations, is $30 for the weekend and includes admission to the show.

WILL GEER THEATRICUM BOTANICUM, Topanga. (310) 455-3723 / www.theatricum.com, 1419 N. Topanga Blvd. This outdoor theater (dress warmly) produces summertime "edutainment." June through September the Kid's Koncerts feature young kid's name brand groups, such as the Parachute Express. Older audiences enjoy plays such as *The Merry Wives of Winsor* and *St. Joan.* Show times vary. Ticket prices also vary depending on the show, although Kid's Koncerts are usually $7 per person. More mature productions are $13 - $20 for adults; $11 - $!4 for srs.; $7 for ages 6 - 12.

VALLEY FAIR (AND RODEO), Burbank (818) 557-1600 / www.sfvalleyfair.org, 11127 Orcas Ave. in Lake View Terrace at Hansen Dam Equestrian Center. The fair is an annual event and most years it also includes a rodeo. Highlights include carnival rides, a livestock auction (on Sat.), a petting zoo, live bands, exhibits of science and agricultural projects, booths with fun family activities, and more. Fair hours are Thurs., 4pm - 10:30pm; Fri. - Sat., 10am - midnight; Sun., 10am - 8:30pm. General admission, which includes the rodeo when it is on, is $6 for adults; $3 for ages 6 - 11; children 5 and under are free. Certain attractions and activities cost extra.

VAN NUYS AIRPORT AVIATION EXPO, Van Nuys. (818) 909-3529 / www.lawa.org, 8030 Balboa Blvd. Look - it's a bird, it's Superman, no - it's a plane! Actually this tremendous weekend expo features over 60 vintage and current military planes. Stunt pilots perform aerobatics, military jets fly overhead, and parachutists make a grand entrance. Besides the exciting air show, tour through several grounded planes (C-141, B-52, and others), and ride a simulator plane. Wear sun block! Open Sat. - Sun., 9am - 5pm. Admission is free.

JULY:

ADVENTURE PLAYGROUND, Huntington Beach. See June entry for details.

ALL NATIONS POW WOW, Big Bear City. (909) 584-7115; (909) 790-1390; (909) 866-4607 - chamber of commerce; at the Los Vaqueros Rodeo arena, off Hwy. 38. This wonderful three-day gathering of the nations involves traditional tribal dances (the hoop dance is our favorite) in full regalia, usually accompanied by drums. Other music, plus arts and crafts and food booths are also on the grounds. Bring your own tribe! (i.e. family) Open Fri., 6pm - 10pm; Sat., 10am - 11pm, Sun., 10am - 6pm. Admission is $4 for adults; $3 for srs.; children 9 and under are free.

CAPISTRANO PAGEANT, San Juan Capistrano. (949) 222-2366 / www.thecapistranopageant.com, Camino Capistrano and Acjachema, next to San Juan Capistrano. This musical production retells the history of early life in this region including the founding of the mission, the legend of Magdalena, Battle of San Pasqual, and life before the Europeans. It runs for one week and is sometimes held on the mission grounds, sometimes elsewhere in the city. Admission is $25 for adults; $20 for srs.; $14 for ages 12 and under.

COLORADO LAGOON MODEL BOAT SHOP, Long Beach. See June entry for details.

FESTIVAL OF ARTS AND PAGEANT OF THE MASTERS, Laguna Beach. (949) 494-1145 / www.foapom.com, 650 Laguna Canyon Rd. at Irvine Bowl Park. This event runs from July through the beginning of September, drawing thousands of visitors. More than 150 artisans and craftsmen display their work here - jewelry, wood crafts, paintings, and more - and at the nearby Sawdust Festival. (See this entry in this section.) Kids are particularly drawn to the ongoing demonstrations, such as glass blowing, print making, water color, and Japanese pottery making. Young aspiring artists should visit the Art Workshop, open daily 11am to 5pm. It supplies free materials for paintings, instruments, paper hat making, and more. The Jr. Art Gallery is juried art work of over 150 school children from Orange County. Kids love looking at other kids' work. Bands play continuously. Call for a schedule of special events. Pageant of the Masters is people in full makeup and costumes who pose and re-create live "pictures" of well-known art works, both classic and contemporary. Each ninety-second picture is accompanied by a narration and full orchestral music. Note that some of the live art works contain nudity (i.e. real, semi-naked bodies). This one-and-a-half-hour production (with over 250 participants) is staged nightly at 8:30pm. Tickets range between $10 - $50 per person. Festival admission is included in the pageant tickets. The festival is open daily 10am - 11:30pm. Admission to the festival is $5 for adults, for an unlimited number of visits during the run of the festival; $3 for srs. and children 12 and under. Metered parking is available on the streets, or take a shuttle for $1 from Lot 5. Certain activities cost extra.

FESTIVAL OF THE KITE, Redondo Beach. See March entry for details. (This one takes place the last Sunday in July.)

FIRE EXPO, San Diego. (858) 541-2277 / www.burninstitute.org, Qualcomm Stadium. Did the title of this event spark your interest? Join firefighters in the largest fire expo in Southern California. For one-day, see live demonstrations, a canine dog demonstration, a Burn Run where 75 engines (one from each of the area's stations) converge, and a helicopter land, plus ride on fire trucks, look at firefighting displays, enjoy the kiddie carnival, and community service group booths. Open 1pm - 7pm. General admission is free. Certain activities cost.

FIREWORKS and 4TH OF JULY SHOWS - Call the recreation departments at your local parks, or City Hall for information. Note: The Hollywood Bowl, (213) 850-2000 / www.hollywoodbowl.org, features a fireworks spectacular, along with outstanding lively music.

FORD FAMILY FUN SUMMER NIGHTS, Hollywood. See June entry for details.

HOLY SPIRIT FESTIVAL, Artesia. (562) 865-4693, 11903 Ashworth Ave. in the Artesia DES. Held the last Thursday through Monday in July, this four-day event celebrates several elements of the Portugese culture. On Sunday, a grand religious procession is followed by marching bands, food booths (including a free lunch or dinner for every visitor), and entertainment. Monday night is the three-hour culmination of the festival with bloodless bullfights put on by professional matadors. The festival hours are Fri., 6pm - midnight; Sat., 5pm - midnight; Sun., 10am - midnight; Mon., 4pm - 9pm. Admission is free.

INDEPENDENCE DAY CELEBRATION, Vista. (760) 724- 4082 / www.co.sandiego.ca.us/parks, 2210 N. Santa Fe Ave. at Rancho Guajome Adobe. Join Civil War reenactors and celebrate Independence Day with special demonstrations, skirmishes with infantry and horsemen (two shows a day), the reading of the Declaration of Independence, kid's crafts, and tours of the historic adobe. Open Sat. - Sun. near 4th of July, 11am - 5pm. Admission is $5 for adults; $3 for ages 5 - 12; children 4 and under are free.

INTERNATIONAL SPEEDWAY, Costa Mesa. See April entry for details.

KIDS ON STAGE AT THE STARLIGHT BOWL, Burbank. (818) 525-3721 or (818) 238-5300 / www.ci.burbank.ca.us, 1249 Lockheed View Dr. at the Starlight Bowl. For three weeks children 5 to 12 years old participate in several different activities at the bowl, led by various artists. Each week features storytelling, crafts, dancing, painting, acting, and/or performing sound effects for an on-stage. Offered Tues. - Thurs., 10am - noon. Tickets are $4 per person.

KIDSWORLD, Santa Monica. (310) 394-1049 or (310) 394-5451 / www.santamonicaplace.com, 3rd St. and Broadway at Santa Monica Place mall. From July through August, the mall has teamed up with L.A. Children's Museum, the Natural History Museum, and other organizations to present musical, theatrical, or educational shows every Friday at 11am and again at 1pm, and craft activities every Saturday, noon to 4pm. Past shows have featured puppetry, music, song, dance, and storytelling. Both days' activities are geared for ages 7 years and under. Enjoy shopping or eating at the 140 shops and restaurants in the mall. Admission to the shows and crafts is free.

KINGSMEN SHAKESPEARE FESTIVAL, Thousand Oaks. (805) 493-3455 / www.kingsmenshakespeare.org, 60 Olsen Rd., California Lutheran University, Kingsmen Park. Two of Shakespeare's plays are featured, such as *Henry V* or *Twelfth Night,* during the six-weekend festival, as well as Elizabethan vendors, crafts, foods, and more. The festival usually runs Fri. - Sun., 5:30pm - 10:30pm each evening. Admission is free.

LA BREA TAR PITS EXCAVATION, Los Angeles. (323) 934-PAGE (7243) /

www.tarpits.org, 5801 Wilshire Blvd. at the George C. Page Museum in Hancock Park. Can you dig it? Well, actually, you can't, but July through mid-September paleontologists can excavate Tar Pit 91 and recover fossils of Ice Age creatures, such as saber-tooth cats, dire wolves, and more. Peek into the pit from the observation area for a look into the past. Excavations take place Wed. - Sun., 10am - 4pm. Admission is free. Admission to the adjacent George C. Page Museum, where recovered fossils are on display along with lots of other exhibits, is $6 for adults; $3.50 for srs. and students; $2 for ages 5 - 12; children 4 and under are free.

LONG BEACH SHAKESPEARE FESTIVAL, Long Beach. (562) 597-1301, www.bardintheyard.com, corner of Argonne and 23rd St. at Stearns Park. Fill your July weekends with culture. This particular group performs a variety of Shakespeare's plays outdoors each year with a pre-show (musicians and dancing) Sat. - Sun. at 4pm; the play at 5pm. Admission is free.

LOTUS FESTIVAL, Los Angeles. (213) 485-8745 or (213) 485-13010 / www.lacity.org, Park Ave. and Glendale Blvd. at Echo Park. A blend of Asian and Pacific Island cultures celebrate the symbolism of the lotus flower, which represents divine creative power and purity, at this old-LA. neighborhood park that contains a lake filled with an abundance of these flowers in bloom. What a beautiful sight! The lotus stay in bloom until late summer. The two-day festival also incorporates music, traditional food, martial arts exhibitions, origami demonstrations, fireworks, dragon-boat races, and children's arts and crafts. Paddle boat rentals are available at the boathouse for $5 for half an hour. The festival is open Sat. - Sun., noon - 8pm. Admission is free, although some activities cost.

OLD FORT MACARTHUR DAYS, San Pedro. (310) 548-2631 / www.ftmac.org, 3601 S. Gaffey St. at Angels Gate Park and Fort MacArthur Military Museum. (See the main entry under Museums for more details.) Military encampments, set up chronologically, and reenactments, representing the time periods from 1776 through present day, are here on the weekend following the 4th of July. Observers can mingle with the soldiers and ask questions about their lives. Reenactments of historic military skirmishes can include the Indian wars, the Calvary, both World Wars, and/or the Korean War. There are also marching drills, rifle-loading drills, and firing demonstrations. On Sunday, some cannons are shot, too. Military vehicles are also on the grounds. Bring a sack lunch or purchase food from the vendors. Booths sell military paraphernalia. Open 9am - 5pm, with skirmishes throughout the day. Admission per day is $5 for adults; $3 for ages 5 - 11; children 4 and under are free. This includes admission to the museum, too.

OJAI SHAKESPEARE FESTIVAL, Ojai. (805) 646-WILL (9455)/ www.ojaishakespeare.org, Ojai Ave. at Libbey Park To see or not to see, that is the question. Shakespearean plays, running from the end of July through the middle of August, are performed in the outdoor Libbey Bowl and are worthy to be seen. Sr. high students perform on weekends at 4pm. Tickets are $8. Professional actors and musicians perform Thurs. - Sun. at 7:30pm. Admission for adults is $15 Thurs., Fri., and Sun.; $18 on Sat. Admission for srs. and students is $12 Thurs., Fri., and Sun.; $15 on Sat.

OLD MINERS DAYS, Big Bear. (909) 866-4607 or (909) 866-5352 - children's events in Meadow Park / www.bigbearchamber.com, on Big Bear Blvd. This three-weekend event features a logger's jubilee, complete with tree cutting and log rolling contests; arts and crafts booths; children's games; cowboy poetry and music festival; pony rides; a Doo Dah parade featuring marchers in crazy costumes; and a grand finale parade. Parade entries range from elegant equestrian units, to floats, to old wagons (old flatbed wagons and the red Radio Flyer types, too), and clowns. There is no general admission fee. The Old Miners Day Trail Ride is 3 days on the trail in wagons. Call (760) 240-4449 for more information.

OPEN HOUSE, Hollywood. See June entry for details.

ORANGE COUNTY FAIR, Costa Mesa. (714) 751-3247 / www.ocfair.com, 88 Fair Dr. at the Orange County Fairgrounds. This huge, seventeen-day event is great fun for the whole family. There are lots of carnival rides and games; rodeos (that last a few hours); acrobats; headline concerts, which are usually included in the price of admission; speedway racing; farm animals, featured in shows and races, and to pet; craft booths; exhibits; demonstrations, such as the firefighters combat challenge; and, of course great food.. Each day brings new attractions and events. There is so much to see and do that one day might just not be enough! Call for information on discount days offered during the fair and for the calendar of special events. General admission is $6 for adults; $5 for srs.; $2 for ages 6 - 12; children 5 and under are free. Discount tickets are available before the fair opens. Parking is $5; a carpool of 4 or more is $3.

PACIFIC ISLANDER FESTIVAL, Chula Vista. (619) 699-8797 / www.pacificislanders.com, 900 Otay Lakes Rd. at Southwestern College. Note: The festival is an annual event, but the location does change. This event invites the thousands of Melanesian, Micronesian, and Polynesian residents of Southern California to celebrate their heritage. Each community sets up their own village where singing and chanting, cultural dances, storytelling, crafts, foods, and even artifacts keep visitors entertained. Open Sat. - Sun., 9am - 5pm. General admission is free.

PEARSON PARK AMPHITHEATER, Anaheim. See June entry for details.

RASPBERRY PICKING, Oak Glen and Moorpark. The tastiest fruits are ones that have just been harvested. Raspberries are usually ripe from mid-July to mid-October. Here are a few places to call in the Oak Glen area: Los Rios Rancho - (909) 797-1005; Riley's Log Cabin Farm and Orchard - (909) 797-4061; Riley's Farm and Orchard - (909) 790-2364; Riley's Farm - (909) 797-5145; and Snow

Line Orchard - (909) 797-3415. In Ventura County in Moorpark, call Tierra Rejada Family Farms at (805) 523-8552. This above entries are also listed in the main section of the book.

REDLANDS BOWL, Redlands. See June entry for details.

REVOLUTIONARY ENCAMPMENT, Buena Park. (714) 220-5200 / www.knotts.com, 8039 Beach Blvd. at Knott's Berry Farm's Independence Hall. The encampment, which takes place around the 4th of July, features historical speeches, battle reenactments (always a highlight), cooking demonstrations, and crafts pertaining to that time period. Call for hours. Admission is free.

REVOLUTIONARY WAR LIVING HISTORY ENCAMPMENT, Yorba Linda. (714) 993-3393 / www.nixonfoundation.org, 18001 Yorba Linda Blvd. at the Richard Nixon Presidential Library and Birthplace. The British are coming . . . on a weekend near the 4th of July. See how townspeople and soldiers lived over 200 years ago as you visit with reenactors dressed in authentic period clothing and watch them cook, barter, work with wood, and even fight in mock skirmishes. Hear a reading of the Declaration of Independence and sign a giant copy of one. Spend some time inside the museum, too. Open 10am - 4:30pm. Admission is museum admission - $5.95 for adults; $2 for ages 8 - 11; children 7 and under are free.

RINGLING BROS. & BARNUM AND BAILEY CIRCUS, Anaheim, Long Beach, Los Angeles, and San Diego. Call Arrowhead Pond for the Anaheim location - (714) 704-2500 / arrowheadpond.com; the Long Beach Convention Center - (562) 436-3636 / www.longbeachcc.com; and Los Angeles Memorial Coliseum and Sports Arena - (213) 748-6136 / www.lacoliseum.com. This is a traditional month for "The Greatest Show on Earth" to come to town. Catch some of the most amazing animal and acrobatic acts ever performed!! Call ahead of time to find out when the parade of circus animals comes through the town. At some locations, come an hour early to participate in free pre-circus activities in the arenas, where visitors can try out a trapeze swing, ride a unicycle (with help), and be a part of a clown act. Tickets range from $11.50 - $32.50, depending on performance date and time, and your seat location.

SAWDUST FESTIVAL, Laguna Beach. (949) 494-3030 / www.sawdustartfestival.org, 935 Laguna Canyon Rd. This three-acre, outdoor arts and crafts festival, with over 200 artisans, goes from the end of June through the beginning of September (almost simultaneous with the Festival of Arts - look up this entry). On-going demonstrations include ceramics such as throwing pots (so to speak), etching, glass blowing, and more. The Children's Art booth allows kids to create art projects - for free! Family-oriented daytime entertainment includes storytelling and juggling. Nighttime entertainment includes listening and dancing to bands. Tram service is available for a nominal fee. The festival is open daily 10am - 10pm. Admission is $6.50 for adults; $5.50 for srs.; $2 for ages 6 - 12; children 5 and under are free. A season pass is $10 per person.

SEA FESTIVAL, Long Beach. (562) 570-1728 / www.cityoflongbeach.com or www.ci.longbeach.com, mostly along Ocean Blvd. and Appian Way. This month-long festival takes place in several areas near the shores of Long Beach. Participant and spectators, landlubbers and seafarers are welcome. Some of the events include a free fishing day for youths 15 years and under (with prizes!); a Chinese Dragon Boat Race and oriental cultural craft exhibition; swimming competitions; beach volleyball; a sand sculpture contest (build with your family 9am - 1:30pm, or just come to see finished masterpieces, 2pm - 4pm); day camps for people with disabilities; and boat races. Call for a schedule of events. Participant fees range according to event; spectators are usually admitted for free.

SHAKESPEARE FESTIVAL/L.A., Los Angeles. See June entry for details.

SOUTHERN CALIFORNIA INDIAN CENTER'S ANNUAL POW WOW, Costa Mesa. (714) 962-6673 / www.indiancenter.org, 88 Fair Dr. at the Orange County Fairgrounds at the Arlington Theater. Come see spectacular, traditional American Indian dancing with more than 1,000 dancers from 300+ tribes and nations. (The hoop dance is our favorite.) Also enjoy handcrafted arts and crafts, storytelling, and a variety of food. Grand Entrances (with the members in tribal regalia) are Fri., 6pm and 8pm; Sat., noon and 7pm; Sun., noon. The pow wow is open Fri., 2pm - 10pm; Sat., 9am - 10pm; Sun., 9am - 6pm. Admission is $6 for adults; $3 for srs. and ages 12 - 17; $1 for ages 6 - 11; children 5 and under are free.

STARGAZING, Julian. See June entry for details.

U.S. OPEN SANDCASTLE COMPETITION, Imperial Beach. (619) 424-6663 / www.ci.imperial-beach.ca.us/sandhm/htm, Imperial Beach Pier. Sign up as a competitor in this sandcastle competition, as there are various categories - age, amateur, masters, etc. - or just to watch other creative people at work. We are amazed at the fantastic designs the sculpturers dream up! A parade is held Sat. at 10am. Other activities include browsing around a street fair, a children's sand-creation contest held Sat. afternoon, and fireworks at night. The adult contests begins around 7:30am Sun. Monetary prizes are awarded. Free admission to watch.

AUGUST:

ADVENTURE PLAYGROUND, Huntington Beach. See June entry for details.

CAMARILLO AIR SHOW, Camarillo. (805) 383-0686 / www.eaa723.org, Pleasant Valley at Camarillo Airport. Fly bys and demonstration flights, usually in the afternoon, are highlights of this air show. Other exhibits and activities include WWII warbirds, vintage aircraft, antique farm equipment, over a hundred home built airplanes, food vendors, and a kids area with a bounce, a maze, and more. Note: Check out the Confederate Air Force World War II

Aviation Museum (see the Museums section) which is on the airfield. Open Sat. - Sun., 8am - 5pm. Admission is $5 for adults; children 11 and under are free.

CAPISTRANO PAGEANT, San Juan Capistrano. See July entry for details.

CASA DE TORTUGA, Fountain Valley. (714) 962-0612, Circulo de Zapata. One weekend a year, this "House of Turtles" hosts an open-house. You'll learn about and see over 800 turtles and tortoises. The pens are staffed by knowledgeable docents. Casa is normally booked 6 months in advance for their tours, so this is a great opportunity to bring your 3-year-old (and up) child! No strollers permitted. Open noon - 4pm. Free admission.

COLORADO LAGOON MODEL BOAT SHOP, Long Beach. See June entry for details.

FESTIVAL OF ARTS AND PAGEANT OF THE MASTERS, Laguna Beach. See July entry for details.

FORD FAMILY FUN SUMMER NIGHTS, Hollywood. See June entry for details.

INTERNATIONAL SPEEDWAY, Costa Mesa. See April entry for details.

KIDSWORLD, Santa Monica. See July entry for details.

MUD MANIA, Long Beach. (562) 570-1755 / www.ci.long-beach.ca.us/park/ranchlc.htm, 4600 Virginia Rd. at Rancho Los Cerritos. Get down and dirty at this one-day event. Stomp around in an adobe mud pit, make real adobe bricks, play Tug O' War over a mud pit, and help whitewash the adobe oven. Tip: Bring a change of clothing. Cleaner activities include making bars of soap and crafting an adobe model out of cardstock. Refreshments and live musical entertainment round out the day. Open Sun., 12:30pm - 4:30pm. Admission is $4 per person; children 2 and under are free.

NISEI WEEK JAPANESE FESTIVAL, Los Angeles. (213) 687-7193 or (213) 625-0414 / www.niseiweek.org, 369 E. First St. in Little Tokyo. This week-long festival, the biggest Japanese festival of the year, takes place at several locations throughout Little Tokyo. A sampling of events and exhibits include martial arts demonstrations, traditional Japanese dancing, games, arts and crafts, Yabusame archery on horseback, Taiko drumming (on huge drums), tofu tasting, calligraphy, bonsai arrangements, and a grand parade with floats. Most of the activities and programs occur on the weekends, Sat.,10am - 6pm; Sun., 10am - 4pm. Call for a schedule of events. Admission is free, although some activities cost.

OLD TOWN TEMECULA WESTERN DAYS CELEBRATION, Temecula. (909) 694-6412 / www.ci.temecula.ca.us, down Main Street. Kick up your heels in this wonderful old western-style town any day of the week, but particularly this weekend. A parade starts off the festivities with equestrian groups, marching bands, fire trucks, police officers, gun fighters, and more. This is followed by stagecoach, trolley and hay wagon rides; historians and reenactors to talk with; a petting zoo; pony rides; vendor and craftsmen booths; street entertainment; contests; Old Town tours; and more. Come dressed in your best western duds. Open Sat. - Sun., noon - 5pm. General admission is free.

OJAI SHAKESPEARE FESTIVAL, Ojai. See July entry for details.

OPEN HOUSE AT THE HOLLYWOOD BOWL, Hollywood. See July entry for details.

PEAR PICKING, Leona Valley. (661) 270-1569, 10600 Leona Ave. at Bright Ranch. Delicious Asian pears ripen in late August, early September. The ranch has acres of U-pic trees, although pre-picked pears are available also. Prices are usually lower than market prices and the fruit is much more flavorful than store-bought. Open daily 8am - 4pm until sold out.

PEAR PICKING, Oak Glen. (909) 797-5145 / www.rileysfarm.com, 12261 S. Oak Glen Blvd. at Riley's Farm. Barlett pears are ready for picking here mid-August to mid-September.

PEARSON PARK AMPHITHEATER, Anaheim. See June entry for details.

RASPBERRY PICKING. See July entry for details.

RENAISSANCE ART FESTIVAL, Long Beach. (562) 438-9903 / www.lbrenaissanceartsfest.com, Queens Highway at Queen Mary Special Events Park by the Queen Mary. Heralding all Lords and Ladies who wish to participate in two days of festivities that harken back to days of old! Renaissance period events and entertainers include jugglers, magicians, English royal court, children's games, hands-on exhibits, fencing instructions, Celtic reenactors, and musical entertainment. Hours are Sat. - Sun., 10am - 6pm. Admission per day is $10 for adults; $7 for srs.; $5 for ages 5 - 12; children 4 and under are free. Tickets bought in advance are less expensive.

RINGLING BROS. & BARNUM AND BAILEY CIRCUS, Anaheim, Long Beach, Los Angeles, and San Diego. See July entry for details.

SAWDUST FESTIVAL, Laguna Beach. See July entry for details.

SEA FESTIVAL, Long Beach. See July entry for details.

STARGAZING, Julian. See June entry for details.

VENTURA COUNTY FAIR, Ventura. (805) 648-3376 / www.seasidepark.org,

10 W. Harbor Blvd. at Seaside Park. This major event is a week and a half long.
The fair offers lots of carnival rides, plus rodeos, pig races, a petting zoo, pony
rides, on-going entertainment, and several buildings that have arts and crafts for
sale as well as vendor demonstrations. Whew! The fair is open daily 11am -
11pm. A fireworks show is put on nightly at 9:30pm. Admission is $7 for adults;
$4 for srs. and ages 6 - 12; children 5 and under are free. Rides and certain
activities cost extra. Parking is $5.

WESTERN DAYS, Yucaipa. (909) 797-1753 - Parrish Ranch; (909) 797-4020 -
Oak Tree Village; (909) 790-2364 - Rileys, Oak Glen Rd. Yee-ha! The Old West
comes to life with gunfights, country music, Indian dancing and drumming,
country crafts, and Western-style barbecue all along Oak Glen Road, at the
above mentioned ranches. Join in the fun Sat. - Sun., 9am - 6pm. Admission is
free.

WOMEN'S TENNIS ASSOCIATION ESTYLE.COM CLASSIC, Manhattan
Beach. (310) 545-3200, 1330 Park View Ave., Manhattan Beach County Club.
For one smashing week, top-seeded women tennis players come to tune-up at the
beach for the U.S. Open. Past participants include the Williams sisters, Lindsay
Davenport, Mary Pierce, and lots more. Bring your sunscreen!

WORLD BODYSURFING CHAMPIONSHIP, Oceanside. (760) 435-4014 /
www.worldbodysurfing.com. Oceanside Beach, near the pier. This three-day
event has been an annual event for over two decades! Over 300 participants,
including several from foreign countries, equipped with swim fins are judged on
length of ride and style, such as barrel rolls and somersaults. Contestants must be
at least 12 years old to enter. The championship is held Fri., 7am - noon; Sat.,
7am - 1pm; Sun., 7am - 3pm. The semi-finals and finals are held on Sun.
Admission to watch is free; $25 to participate.

SEPTEMBER:

APPLE PICKING, Oak Glen. See main section of the book under Oak Glen in
the Edible Adventures section. The season runs from mid-September through
mid-November.

BARSTOW RODEO STAMPEDE, Barstow. (760) 252-3093 /
www.barstowrodeo.com. Yee-ha! The last full weekend in this month brings a
rodeo, complete with bareback, saddle bronc, barrel racing, calf roping, team
roping, steer wrestling, and championship bull riding. Watch the women's barrel
race and mutton bustin' for kids 10 years and under. The crowds go wild over
this! Open Fri. for barbecue and dance around 5pm - 11pm; Sat. show is at
7:30pm; Sun., 5pm. Admission for the rodeo is $10 for adults; children 6 and
under are free.

CABRILLO FESTIVAL, Point Loma. (619) 557-5450 / www.nps.gov/cabr,
Cabrillo Memorial Dr. at Cabrillo National Monument. Journey back in time to

commemorate the life and times of Juan Cabrillo, one of the first explorers of California. The weekend is filled with events and activities - listening to authentically-dressed Spanish soldiers give history talks; observing Native American basket making; sampling food from Mexico, Portugal, Spain, and Native America; enjoying the cultural music and dancing; and watching reenactment of Cabrillo's landing. Open Sat., 10am - 5pm. Admission is free. Parking is $5.

CALIFORNIA INDIAN DAYS, San Diego. (619) 281-5964 / www.balboapark.org, Park Blvd. and President's Way in Balboa Park. Usually held on the third weekend of the month, the celebration showcases American Indian singers and fantastic dancers, as well as tribal arts and crafts to purchase or try making yourself. Open 8am - 6pm. Admission is free.

CIVIL WAR REENACTMENT, Huntington Beach. (714) 962-5771 or (714) 536-5486 / www.hbvisit.com/year.htm, Golden West Ave. in Huntington Beach Central Park. Live through the Civil War time period, if only for a day. Heralded as one of the best reenactments, come visit with soldiers from the North and South who are authentically dressed in uniform and stay in character throughout the duration. Watch mock battles and wander through the encampments. Open Sat. - Sun., 10am - 5pm. Battles are Sat., 1pm and 4pm; Sun., at 11am and 2pm. Admission is free.

COIN & COLLECTIBLES EXPO, Long Beach. See February entry for details.

CORNELIUS JENSEN BIRTHDAY CELEBRATION, Riverside. (909) 369-6055, 4307 Briggs St. at the Jensen-Alvarado Ranch Historic Park. (See the MUSEUMS section for details.) The park celebrates Cornelius's birthday on the last Saturday in September with a lot of hoopla. (If you don't know who he is, come and celebrate anyhow!) Activities include panning for gold and making your own soap, making ice cream, watching tortillas being made, and adobe bricks, among other things. Watch sheep shearing, branding, and spinning and weaving demonstrations. Kick up your heels and keep time with the country music. The party goes from 10am - 4pm. Admission is $4 for adults; $2 for ages 3 -12.

FREE FISHING DAY, all over. The last weekend in September usually includes a free fishing day, meaning that no license is required. Call a park or your favorite fishing hole to see if they are participating in this "reel" deal.

GREEK FESTIVAL, Cardiff-by-the-Sea. (760) 942-0920 / www.greek-fest.com/west/cardif/cardif.html, 3459 Manchester Ave. Live Greek music and dancing, Greek cuisine (i.e. stuffed grape leaves, cheese pita, Greek caviar dip, Baklava, etc.), games, a bazaar, a live auction, and craft booths are a few of the goings-on at this weekend festival. Church tours of Saints Constantine and Helen Greek Orthodox Church are given at 1pm and 4pm each day. The festival is Sat., 10:30am - 10pm; Sun., 11am - 9pm. General admission is $2 for adults; free for children 11 and under. Park at the adjoining Mira Costa College.

GREEN MEADOWS FARM, Los Angeles. (800) 393-3276 /
www.gmpdetails.com, 4235 Monterey Rd. at Ernest Debs Regional Park. The
Farm is here from the end of September through October. See March entry for
details.

"HART" OF THE WEST, Newhall. (661) 259-0855 or (661) 222-7657 /
www.hartmuseum.org, 24151 San Fernando Rd. at the William S. Hart Park and
Museum. (See the Museums section in the main section.) This celebration of
"California is a nation" encompasses many facets of the Old West and usually
takes place the last full weekend of the month. A pow wow, held at the large
picnic area, begins around noon with the all tribes and nations procession,
followed by the Blessing, and on-going dancing (with narration and
interpretation) from each of the Indian nations. Native American wares are for
sale at booths. Mountain men, set up in encampments next to the pow wow,
show how people lived in the mid 1800's, by using period tools, campfire
cooking, and display booths. Some years Civil War reenactments and skirmishes
take place near the adjacent train depot. Sometimes President Lincoln shows up
and recites the Gettysburg Address. A street fair is located just across the street.
Parking is tight. The celebration hours are Sat., 9am - 7pm; Sun., 9am - 6pm.
General admission is free.

HARVEST FESTIVAL, Del Mar. (800) 321-1213 / www.harvestfestival.com, at
the Del Mar Fairgrounds. See October entry for details.

HARVEST FESTIVAL, Long Beach. (800) 321-1213 /
www.harvestfestival.com, 300 E. Ocean Blvd. at the Long Beach Convention
Center. See October entry for details. Hours here are Sat. - Sun., 10am - 7pm;
Mon., 10am - 5pm.

INDIAN MUSEUM CELEBRATION, Lancaster. (661) 942-0662 - museum or
(661) 946-3055 - museum / www.calparksmojave.com, Avenue M at the
Antelope Valley Indian Museum. (Fro details about the museum, look in the
main section of the book.) Over 2,000 attendees enjoy two days of Native
American dances, crafts, storytelling, displays and food booths, plus tours
through the unique museum and nature hikes. Open Sat. - Sun., 10am - 5pm.
Admission is $5 for adults; $1.50 for ages 6 - 12; children 5 and under are free.

INTERNATIONAL SPEEDWAY, Costa Mesa. See April entry for details.

IRISH FAIR AND CELTIC MARKETPLACE, Costa Mesa. (818) 501-3781 or
(714) 284-9558 / www.irishfair.org or www.ocfair.com, 88 Fair Dr. at the
Orange County Fair Grounds. Kiss the Blarney Stone or come to this weekend
festival to receive the same benefits! Enjoy music, song, dance, and lots of
opportunities to shop for something Celtic. Open Sat. - Sun., 10am - 6pm.
Admission is $12 for adults; $10 for srs.; ages 12 and under are free.

JULIAN GRAPE STOMP FESTA, Julian. (760) 765-2072 or (760) 765-1857 / www.julianfun.com, 1150 Julian Orchards at the Menghini Winery. For one juicy weekend enjoy a bunch of fun and stomp around in a ton (literally) of grapes - and yes, this means you. Your feet are first sterilized in a vat of vodka and then you can squish the grapes between your toes. (This wine is not sold commercially!) Other activities include listening to Italian bands, dancing, playing Bocce ball (an Italian lawn game), participating in arts and crafts, and sampling wine (this last part is not for children, obviously). Open 11am - 7pm. Admission is $5 for adults; bambinos 4 and under are gratsi (free).

LOMBARDI'S RANCH, Saugus. See October entry for details.

LONDON BRASS RUBBING CENTER, Long Beach. (562) 436-4047, 525 E. 7th Street at St. Luke's Episcopal Church. Cheerio! Your child will thoroughly enjoy making a medieval brass rubbing, offered from the end of September through November. (This has become one of our favorite fall activities.) On black background paper, use a wax rubbing crayon of gold, silver, or bronze to capture the intricate designs. The facsimiles of over sixty tombstones from England vary in size, and depict knights, Lords, ladies in fancy dress, griffons, Shakespeare, etc. Groups of at least ten people can incorporate a half-hour talk, given by a docent in period dress, to learn more medieval times and the stories of some of the engravings. A complete English tea can be added on to your time here, too, with advanced reservations and a group of at least ten people. The center is open to the public Thurs. - Sun., 10am - 4pm. It is open to groups during this time, too, as well as Tues. and Wed., 10am - 4pm. Teas are served upon request. The price to rub cost between $3 - $12, depending on the size of the brass plate. Groups between ten to twenty people pay $4.75 for a piece worth up to $7.50. Teas are $16.50 for adults; $9.50 for ages 17 and under. This price includes a rubbing and a half-hour lesson/talk, too.

LOS ANGELES COUNTY FAIR, Pomona. (909) 623-3111 / www.fairplex.com, 1101 W. McKinley Ave. at Fairplex. Billed as the world's largest county fair, this three-week event is wonderful (and exhausting). It has lots of carnival rides and games, workshops, country contests, livestock shows, horse-racing, flower and garden shows, music, dancing, booths, and several long buildings filled with exhibits and truly unique items and products for sale. Come early and plan to spend the whole day - there is a lot to see and do (and buy!). Teachers - ask about the free Fairkids field trips. These field trips comes with curriculum that focus on particular aspects of the fair - animals and history, and allow students to enjoy a day at the fair. Call (909) 865-4075 for more information. Fair hours are Mon. - Thurs., 11am - 10pm; Fri., 11am - 11pm; Sat., 10am - 11pm; Sun., 10am - 10pm. General admission is $10 for adults; $7 for srs.; $5 for ages 6 to 12 on Sat. and Sun. (Mon. - Fri. this age group is free); children 5 and under are free. Call to find out about discount admission days. Certain activities cost extra. Parking is $5.

MEXICAN INDEPENDENCE DAY FIESTA, San Diego. (619) 293-0117,

Twiggs and Juan Sts. at Old Town State Historic Park. San Diegans know how to fiesta as they celebrate this one-day event at the Plaza with games, contests, historic reenactments, and more. Fiesta hours are Sat., 11am - 4pm. Admission is free.

MOUNTAIN MAN DAYS (RENDEZVOUS), Banning. (909) 922-9200, 16th and Wilson at Gilman Historic Ranch and Wagon Museum. From Wednesday through Sunday "meet" the trappers, mountain men, and cowboys of the Old West. Visit an 1700 to 1800's-era living history encampment and see clothing, tools, and equipment from this time period. Bring your gold dust ($) to use at the trading posts. Food and drink is available. School tours are by reservation during the week and admission is $2 per person for ages 3 years and up. General public admission on the weekends is $2 for adults; $1 for ages 3 - 12. Public parking is $4.

PIRATE FAIR, Lake Casitas. (805) 496-6036 / www.goldcoastfestivals.com, 11311 Santa Ana Rd. Ahoy mateys! Walk the plank or bring your own motley crew to enjoy treasure hunts and two stages of entertainment featuring jugglers, sword fighters, fire eaters, battle reenactments, and merchants selling plunder. Dress up as a buccaneer, too, for the costume contests. Open Sat. - Sun., 10am - 6pm. Admission is $10 for adults; $5 for ages 5 - 11; children 4 and under are free. Parking is $3.

PORTUGUESE BEND NATIONAL HORSE SHOW, Rolling Hills Estates. (310) 544-1047 or (310) 544-0032 / www.showjump.com/portuguesebend.html, 25851 Hawthorne Blvd. at Ernie Howlett Park. For over forty years, this classy three-day show has featured equestrian events in both grass and sand rings. Past shows have also included a children's carnival, demonstrations by the Long Beach Mounted Police, puppet shows, pony rides, food booths, and more. Feel free to bring a picnic lunch. Gates open Sat. - Mon. at 8am and close at about 4pm. General admission is $4 for adults; $2 for ages 4 - 12; children 3 and under are free. Fri. festival seating is $5 per person; Sat. - Sun., $10. Parking and shuttle service to the site is free.

POWAY DAYS RODEO, Poway. (760) 736-0594 or (858) 748-0016 / www.powayrodeo.com, on Tierra Bonita Rd. at the P.R.C.A. Arena. This "Brand Above the Rest" rodeo is yet another reason to come to Poway! The P.R.C.A. rodeos (i.e. Professional Rodeo Cowboys Association) are one of the best in the nation with cowboys competing in several categories. Favorites events include kid's mutton bustin', rodeo clown acts, and Jr. barrel races. A parade and petting zoo will have your kids hootin' and hollerin' for more. Behind-the-scenes tours are offered an hour-and-a-half before the show. Rodeos are Fri and Sat. at 7:30pm, gates open at 5pm; Sun. at 2:30 pm. Admission is $10 for adults; $7 for srs., military and ages 12 - 14; $5 for ages 5 - 11; children 4 and under are free. Tickets purchased at the gate are an additional $2.

RASPBERRY PICKING. See July entry for details.

REVOLUTIONARY WEEKEND, Simi Valley. (800) 410-8354 / www.lbjlib.utexas.edu/reagan, 40 Presidential Dr. at the Ronald Reagan Presidential Library and Museum. The Brigade of the American Revolution camps at the museum and presents battle reenactments, dance, and demonstrations of on the battle field and at home during the 1770's. Open Sat. - Sun., 10am - 5pm. Admission is $5 for adults; $3 for srs.; ages 15 and under are free. Price includes admission to the museum.

SEAFEST, Corona del Mar. (714) 729-4400 / newportbeach.com, www.tasteofnewport.com This two-weekend fest has two major events; a sand castle and sand sculpting contest, and Taste of Newport, which is a sampling of the many restaurants in the area, plus live entertainment. Call about participating in the sandy events or just come to "sea" the most imaginative things created with sand. Admission to watch is free; Taste of Newport is $12 - $15 for adults; ages 12 and under are free.

TALLSHIPS FESTIVAL, Dana Point. (949) 496-2274 / www.ocean_institute.org or www.tallshipsfestival.com, 24200 Dana Point Harbor Dr. at the Ocean Institute. This festival, held the weekend after Labor Day, begins as majestic tall ships sail into port, entering through a gauntlet of "enemy" cannon blasts. Tour the ships and enjoy demonstrations and exhibits of the sailing arts, such as knot tying, scrimshaw, and wood carvings. Pirate encampment activities include sea chantey concerts, storytelling, and mock trials and weddings. Don't forget to explore the touch tank in the Institute. Sunset cruises on board a tallship and mock cannon battle cruises are also available. All this, plus music, crafts, and food make this festival worth *sea*ing. The ships enter the harbor around 11:30am on Sat. Festival hours are Sat., noon - 5pm; Sun., 10am - 5pm. Free admission to the festival. Cruises are $35 for adults; $20 for ages 4 - 12.

VISIT WITH MONTEZUMA, Los Angeles. See May entry for details.

OCTOBER:

AIR SHOW, Chino. (909) 597-3722 / www.planesoffame.org, 7000 Merrill Ave. at the Air Museum Planes of Fame at Chino airport. Besides the in-air displays of classic and antique aircraft, trainer, liaison, fighter and bomber warbirds, flybys, and jet aircraft at this weekend event, a crowd favorite of aerobatic acts in the sky (e.g. wingwalking, etc.) are featured. Several static (i.e. ground) displays include military aircraft, helicopters, fighter jets, and even a WWII bomber to tour through. Antique cars and vintage race cars will also be on display. Bring a picnic or purchase lunch from food vendors. Gates open at 8am; flying begins around 10am. Admission is $10 for adults; $2 for ages 5 - 11; children 4 and under are free. Tickets include entrance to the museum. Advance discount tickets are available, too.

ARBORFEST, Fullerton. (714) 278-3579 / arboretum.fullerton.edu, 1900

Associated Rd. at Fullerton Arboretum. Pumpkins and bales of hay add to the atmosphere of celebrating harvest time for two days here in early October. There's an apple press to make cider, opportunities to make butter, "wash" clothes the old-fashioned way, watch lace being made, explore the Children's Garden, take a hay wagon ride; and look at bugs at the Ugly Bug Fair. The Heritage House is also open. The fest runs Sat. - Sun., 10am - 4pm. Admission is $5 for adults; ages 17 and under are free.

BATES NUT FARM PUMPKIN PATCH, Valley Center. (760) 749-3333 / www.batesfarm.com, 15954 Woods Valley Rd. This great farm (see the main entry for more details) has an eight-acre (pre-cut) pumpkin patch, along with a corn stalk maze, petting farm (pet animals through the fence), and large picnic area. Weekday educational programs are available for school groups. Weekend events include hayrides, a scarecrow contest, a moon bounce, arts and crafts, and more. Open daily during the month of October 9am - 5pm. Admission is free. Price per pumpkin is based on weight.

CALABASAS PUMPKIN FESTIVAL, Agoura. (818) 225-2227 / www.pumpkin-festival.com, 2813 Cornell Rd. at Paramount Ranch. Kick up your heels for a weekend of autumn country fun in a Wild West setting. On-going live entertainment includes country bands, kids dancing troupes, cloggers, and more. Join in a contest of pumpkin pie eating, pumpkin seed spitting, pumpkin carving, pumpkin bowling, and mechanical bull riding. Visit the Native American Indian Village and watch authentic dancers. Go through the corn maze. Shop at the numerous arts and crafts vendor booths. And don't forget to pick up a pumpkin or two. Open Sat. - Sun., 9am - 5pm. Admission is $8 for adults; $6 for srs. and ages 13 - 17; $4 for ages 4 - 12; children 3 and under are free. On-site parking is $10; off-site parking is $5 and includes free shuttle service.

CALICO DAYS, Yermo. (800) TO-CALICO (862-2542) / www.calicotown.com, 36600 Ghost Town Rd. at Calico Ghost Town. (See this entry in the Potpourri section of the book.) On the three-day Columbus Day weekend relive Calico's glory days with a wild west parade, National Gunfight Stunt Championships, old prospectors burro run, games from the 1880's, and crafts. Walk around the town itself and enjoy its many attractions. Open 9am - 5pm. Admission is $7 for adults; $4 for ages 6- 15 years; children 5 and under are free. On-site camping is also available.

CELEBRATION IN THE PARK, La Mirada. (562) 943-7277 / www.cityoflamirada.org. San Cristobal and San Esteban Drs. at the Neff House. For one day return to turn-of-the-century California at the historic Neff House. Learn to tan a hide (I don't mean spankings) and how to quilt; look at antique toys; try your hand (or face) at an authentic barbershop; enjoy a Victorian tea party; participate in traditional games; picnic on the grounds; and listen to live music. Open Sat., 10:30am- 4pm. Free admission.

COIN & COLLECTIBLES EXPO, Long Beach. See February entry for details.

EDWARDS AIR FORCE BASE AIR SHOW, Kern County. (661) 277-3510 or (661) 277-3517 / www.edwards.af.mil., Rosamond Blvd. at Edwards Air Force Base. Come see an outstanding, one-day air show, complete with acrobatic teams, biplanes, wing-walking, military air-ground task force demonstrations, and much more. (Be prepared for crowds!) Bring folding chairs, water bottles, sunscreen, and hearing protection because some of the planes are loud. Gates open Sat. at 8am; the show begins at 10am; events end at 4pm. Admission is free.

FALL FESTIVAL, Los Angeles. (213) 933-9211 or (213) 549-2140 / www.farmersmarketla.com/index.shtml, 3rd St. and Fairfax at Farmers Market. Enjoy this two-day, old-fashioned festival in the heart of historic L.A. Past activities and events have included a petting zoo; pumpkin patch; live country music; cooking, spinning, gardening, and pottery demonstrations; bobbing for apples; pie-eating contests; and more. Open Sat. - Sun., 10am - 6pm. General admission is free. Some activities may cost.

FALL FESTIVAL, Pomona. (909) 869-2215 or 2224, 3801 W. Temple Ave. at Cal Poly University. This one-day pumpkin patch is very popular local event. Pick your own (pre-cut) pumpkin off the vine; enjoy a horse show featuring the beautiful on-campus Arabian horses (2pm on Sat., $2 per person); pig out at a pancake breakfast ($3 per person); listen to live music; visit the Insect Fair in the campus' University Union that has over 200,000 preserved bugs on display ($4 for adults, $3 ages 12 and under); participate in games; and munch on food. Open 8am - 5pm. General admission is free.

FALL HARVEST FESTIVAL, Moorpark. (805) 529-3690 / www.tierrarejadafamilyfarms.com, 3370 Moorpark Rd. at Tierra Rejada Family Farms. See the main entry for more details on this great farm. Take a wagon ride along the dirt trail through the pumpkin patch. Enjoy Clydesdale-drawn hayrides ($3 for adults; $2 for ages 11 and under), pony rides, a large petting farm, a monster maze ($7 for adults; $5 for ages 11 and under), and country games. School tours vary in price from $2.50 - $6.50 per student. Farm fresh produce is available for purchase as well as gourds, squash, corn stalks, Indian corn, food, drinks, and more. Open daily 9am - 6pm.

FARMERS FAIR AND EXPOSITION, Perris. (909) 657-4221 / www.farmersfair.com, Lake Perris Dr. For almost two weeks, enjoy top-name entertainment, P.R.C.A. rodeos, livestock shows, monster trucks, demolition derby, petting zoo, fishing demonstrations, carnival rides and games, and horticulture and fine art exhibits. Open daily 11am - 11pm. Admission is $7 for adults; $6 for srs., $3 for ages 6 - 11; children 5 and under are free. Auto Club members are offered discounts Mon. - Fri. Rides and some activities cost extra. Parking is $4.

FAULKNER FARM, Santa Paula. (805) 525-3975 or (805) 525-2226 / www.faulknerfarm.com, 14292 W. Telegraph Rd., off Briggs Rd. This seven-acre pumpkin farm, part of a larger working farm, offers a month of family fun in the country. One of the farm's major attractions is pumpkins ranging in size from mini up to 200 pounds. Afternoon weekday hayrides are $1 ($2 on weekends). Weekends also offer a petting zoo (50¢ admission), face painting, western dancing, craft booths, live country and bluegrass entertainment, special farm demonstrations (i.e. milking cows, shearing sheep, etc.), entertainment by local school children, and a variety of fresh foods to purchase, such as jams and squash. Bring your own little punkins here, and have a picnic, too! Call to reserve special school-group "tours," which include educational information about pumpkins, a hayride, a pumpkin, and other goodies for $3 per person. The farm is open from the first Sat. in October through October 30 daily 10am - 5:30pm. Admission is free.

FLEET WEEK, San Diego. (619) 236-1212 / www.sdfleetweek.org/schedules.html. This tribute to the military includes over a week of activity including a parade of ships, fireworks, jeep races, submarine tours, and Naval ship tours, plus it coincides with the Miramar Air show. Check the website for details on specific events and times.

GEM-O-RAMA, Trona. (760) 372-5356 / www1.iwvisp.com/tronagemclub, 3 ½ hours north of L.A. in the small city of Trona, near Ridgecrest. This two-day event, which occurs the second weekend in the month, is worth the trek! It's explanation deserves a full page, however space in this section is limited. A gem and mineral show and a bus trip around the chemical plant are the clean activities. Messy highlights include mineral collecting in gooey black mud for hanksite and borax crystals; trudging / wading knee to hip high in the salt lake, which crunches like new-fallen snow, for halite; and an opportunity to collect flourescent rocks. Bring a short-wave black light for the latter "tour." Also bring sacrificial clothes and shoes, water (to use to wash off), gloves, a heavy hammer, a crowbar (for prying out the specimens), and large boxes lined with trash bags to bring home your treasures. What a unique opportunity to collect saline minerals! Activities begin at 8am on both days and end at 5pm Sat., 4pm Sun. Admission is $5 per vehicle - such a deal!

GEM SHOW, Costa Mesa. See March entry for details.

GRAND MILITARY ENCAMPMENT, San Diego. (619) 239-0512 or (619) 421-6192 / www.balboapark.org, President's Way and Park Blvd. in Balboa Park. This two-day event celebrates the U.S. Armed Forces as is showcases over 200 years of military history. Band concerts, period costumes, Civil War battle reenactments, booths, and more make this weekend memorable. Open 8am - 6pm. Admission is free.

GREAT GREEK CATHEDRAL FEST, Los Angeles. (323) 737-2424, 1324 S. Normandie Ave. at Saint Sophia Greek Orthodox Cathedral. This fest features authentic Greek food (sample souvlaki and baklva), music, traditional folk dances, and a tour of the cathedral. Open Sun., 11am - 10pm. Admission is $3 for adults; free for srs. and ages 11 and under.

GREEN MEADOWS, Los Angeles. See September entry for details.

HALLOWEEN ALTERNATIVES - For alternatives to door-to-door trick or treating, check your local park or church as many of them offer carnival-type of fun, a safer atmosphere, and still plenty of candy!

HARVEST FESTIVAL, Anaheim. (800) 321-1213 / www.harvestfestival.com, 800 W. Katella Ave. at the Anaheim Convention Center. See below entry for details.

HARVEST FESTIVAL, San Diego. (800) 321-1213 / www.harvestfestival.com. See below entry for details.

HARVEST FESTIVAL, Ventura. (800) 321-1213 / www.harvestfestival.com, 10 W. Harbor at Seaside Park. This three-day event is the place to go for all your shopping needs and desires. Life in the nineteenth-century is the theme here, so an old-fashioned ambiance is prevalent through the festival. Over 1,400 craftsman and artisans sell unique items, from hand-carved train whistles to elegant jewelry, and everything in between. There is on-going entertainment of craft demonstrations (which keeps kids intrigued) and live bands. Good food is on the premises, too. Open Fri., 11am - 8pm; Sat., 10am - 7pm; Sun., 10am - 5pm. Admission is $7.50 for adults; $6.50 for srs.; $4 for ages 6 - 12; children 5 and under are free. $1 off admission if you bring a can of food. Parking is $7.

INDUSTRY HILLS CHARITY PRO RODEO, City of Industry. (626) 961-6892, 16200 Temple Ave. at the Industry Hills Equestrian Center. Everyone benefits from this rodeo - several charities receive needed funds, top performers compete in the rodeo for a large purse, and guests have a great time! Besides the main event of the rodeo, visitors enjoy petting zoo, crafts, clowns, Western theme booths, a visit by Smokey the Bear, entertainment, and food. A free complete rodeo show, is given on Friday for school kids in the community from 9:30am - noon. Come before the weekend shows start to enjoy the pre-show fun. The rodeo commences Sat. at 6pm; Sun. at 2pm. Admission is $12 for adults; $10 for srs.; $6 for ages 3 - 11. Prices include parking. A dance, $8 per person, is given after the rodeo on Sat. evening.

INTERNATIONAL FESTIVAL OF MASKS, Los Angeles. (323) 937-4230, 5814 Wilshire Blvd. at Hancock Park. Folkloric dance from all over the world, ethnic music, theater, storytelling, mask makers, and mask vendors contribute to this unusual weekend festival. Sunday's mask parade is an absolute hit with kids. The festival runs 11am - 5pm on both days. Admission is free.

KTLA KIDS DAY L.A., Los Angeles. (323) 913-7390, Crystal Springs or Zoo

Dr. in Griffith Park by the merry-go-round. This one-day "fair" features over 100 service providers offering information on education, safety, arts, health, social services, etc. Participants include KTLA (but you knew that), Mervyns, Target, the sherif's department, the L.A. Zoo, and lots more. Kids and their caregivers take home bags of materials, plus free giveaways. Other events and activities include celebrity appearances, iive entertainment (middle-school bands, singers, and dancers), face painting, crafts, marine touch tanks, and appearances by Warner Brothers cartoon characters, as well as free pony, train, and merry-go-round rides. Discounts are given for the adjacent L.A. Zoo and the Autry Museum, too. Open Sat., 10am - 4pm. Admission is free.

LAGUNA MOUNTAIN RENDEZVOUS, Julian area. (619) 390-0614 or (800) 488-1250. Call for exact location. Experience an authentic 1700's to 1840's Rocky Mountain fur traders encampment in a rustic mountain setting. Demonstrations of primitive survival skills such as cooking, tool making, tomahawk throwing, and black powder target shooting are given over a period of several days. Primitive and modern camping is available on site. This event is geared for fellow buckskinners and traders; the public welcome to visit, but not participate. Open 8am - 5pm. Admission is $3 per person.

LIVE OAK CANYON CHRISTMAS TREE FARM, Redlands. (909) 795-TREE (8733) / www.liveoakcanyon.com, 32335 Live Oak Canyon Rd. This huge (at least in my city eyes) family-operated farm yields bushels of fun in the fall. A free petting zoo is on the grounds, with goats, sheep, pigs, donkeys, ponies, chickens, and ducks. Bring 25¢ to purchase feed. Tractor-drawn hayrides are usually available and are free. A giant hay "castle" is created from hundreds of bales of hay spread out as well as staggered on top of each other. Kids are welcome to climb up the castle "walls" for free and run through the maze burrowed through the bottom layers. Bring a sack lunch, or purchase food from a refreshment stand (usually open on weekends only), and eat at the numerous picnic tables scattered under shade trees. Special weekend events can include craft fairs, live music, pony rides, and other entertainment. Walk along the rows of the pumpkin patch, which feature twelve acres of vine-cut pumpkins. There are also huge piles of pre-picked pumpkins that range from giant pumpkins (make pies for everyone in the neighborhood!), to sweet-tasting white pumpkins, to mini pumpkins. Wagons are available to help tote your load. An on-site store sells decorative fall items such as Indian corn (in all colors), corn stalks, scarecrows, pumpkin carving supplies, and numerous gourds, including the kind used by artists for making instruments, baskets, and other creative endeavors. Elementary-aged school tours are offered for students to learn about pumpkins and to make a gourd birdhouse. Tours starts at $4.50 per student (adults are free) and include a pumpkin and/or gourd to take home. Note: See this entry for December, too. Open end of September through October daily 9am - 6pm. General admission is free.

LOCH PRADO SCOTTISH CLAN GATHERING AND HIGHLAND GAMES, Chino. (909) 597-4260 / www.co.san-bernardino.ca..us/parks/prado.htm, 16700

S. Euclid Ave. at Prado Regional Park. Enjoy the normal great regional park amenities with a Scottish twist. Enjoy Highland dancing, Scottish country dancing, fiddling, living history "experiences", pipes and drums, sheep dogs, a Scottish Marketplace, athletic games (such as tossing the caber), and Sunday Kirkin.(I think this means church.) Overnight camping is available. Sat. - Sun., 9am - 5pm. Admission to the park is $5. Call for admission to the games.

LOMBARDI'S RANCH, Saugus. (805) 296-8697 / www.lombardiranch.com, 29527 Bouquet Canyon Rd. This family-owned and operated working farm opens its gates at the end of September and through the month of October. It offers forty-five-minute school tours during the week that include seeing and learning how pumpkins are grown, harvested, etc., and walking around the farm to see farm animals. The tours, which are $20 per group, are designed for ages 4 years and up and need a minimum of twelve people. Attractions here include a few vehicles to climb in (e.g. a paddy wagon and a real firetruck); a large fiberglass pumpkin slide; a walk through scarecrow alley (with over eighty scarecrows); bales of hay to sit on while munching on a hot dog (sold at the snack bar here); and hundreds of pumpkins (up to 150 lb.), squash, gourds, and Indian corn to purchase. Weekend activities include a petting zoo with goats, sheep, llama, etc. ($1 per person); wagon rides ($3); and face painting ($1 to $3). Ask about entering the scarecrow contest as it offers hundreds of dollars in cash prizes! Open daily 9am - 6pm. The farm is also open June through September, and in November until Thanksgiving to sell fresh fruits and vegetables. Admission is free.

LONDON BRASS RUBBING CENTER, Long Beach. See September entry for details. Ask about the Medieval Feast put on this month. Enjoy a theater presentation and great, traditional food - English bangers, Cornish game hens, ale, pumpkin bread, and more. The cost is $35 per person.

LOS ANGELES COUNTY-WIDE ARTS OPEN HOUSE, Los Angeles. (213) 972-3099 / www.lacountyarts.org. Held the first Saturday in October, this event has over 150+ free events for the whole family that take place all over L.A. County - Santa Monica, Northridge, Pasadena, Long Beach, downtown Los Angeles, Torrance, etc. The wide array of things to see and do include, respectively, museums, libraries, theater shows, dances (i.e. flamenco, hula, ballet, and others), music, classic cars, workshops on drawing comics or African drumming, and lots more. Call the above 24-hour hotline for more info.

LOS ANGELES INTERTRIBAL FESTIVAL, Los Angeles. (805) 496-6036 / www.goldcoastfestivals.com, 4700 Western Heritage Way at Autry Museum of Western Heritage. Representatives from over fifty tribes gather to honor American Indians in the entertainment field with contests, dancing (top dancers complete for prizes), and plenty of music. This is a true showcase of Indian talent in the arts and entertainment fields. Open Sat. - Sun., 10am - 6pm. Admission is $8 for adults; $5 for ages 5 - 11; children 4 and under are free.

MCGRATH STREET PUMPKIN PATCH, Ventura. (805) 658-9972, corner of Knoll Dr. and McGrath St. During the month of October, walk the eight-acre field and choose a vine-cut pumpkin from the patch. Multi-colored Indian corn, squash (heirloom variety), and gourds (the hard-shell kind used by artists and musicians), are for sale here year round. Free, tractor-drawn hayrides are given on the weekends. Llamas, ducks, and rabbits are on site to look at and gently pet. One weekend, a local school puts on a fair geared for younger children. Groups of ten or more can take a field trip during the week to learn all about pumpkins, Indians, and more. Call to make a reservation. Open daily 9am - dusk. Admission is free.

MIRAMAR AIR SHOW, Miramar. (858) 577-1000 or (858) 577-1011; (858) 577-1016 for reserved seats / www.miramarairshow.com or www.mccs.miramar.com, Marine Corps Air Station. This two-day air show features the Blue Angels and military and civilian pilots performing thrilling aviation stunts and maneuvers. On the ground are over 100 displays of airplanes, helicopters, and military equipment, and some simulator rides. Gates open at 7am, the show runs Sat. - Sun., 9am - 4pm. A twilight show is given Sat., 5:30pm - 9pm, featuring aerial stunts and maneuvers, as well as a pyrotechnic display by the flying aircraft. Parking, admission, and blanket seating are free for all shows. Reserved seating ranges from $6 for adults, $3 for ages 3 - 11 for grandstand seats; to $50 for adults, $30 per child for tented patio seats, plus two meals and a program.

NATIONAL FIRE PREVENTION WEEK, all over. Call your local fire station to see if they are doing something special this week. Many offer tours of the fire engines and station houses, and sometimes kids can even dress up like firemen. The safety tips are lifesavers.

OKTOBERFEST, Torrance. (310) 327-4384 / www.alpinevillage.net, 833 W. Torrance Blvd. at Alpine Village. Bratwurst (yum!), live bands from Germany, craft booths, watching a cow being milked, wood-sawing demonstrations, authentic German costumes, and beer - what more could a good German want? (Except maybe sauerkraut, pretzels, and sausages, which I'm sure are also on hand.) This festival is open every Fri. - Sun. for a month, but only Sunday is really appropriate for children. Hours on Sun. are noon - 8pm. Admission is $5 for adults; ages 11 and under are free.

OLD TIME MELODRAMA AND OLIO, Julian. (760) 765-1857 / www.julianfun.com, 2129 Main St. at Julian Town Hall. Each weekend during the month of October, participate in a two-hour, old-time melodrama by booing the villain, cheering the hero, and sighing with the heroine. The shows feature local actors and incorporate a community sing-a-long. Shows are Fri. - Sat., 7:15pm; Sat. - Sun., 1:15pm. Admission is $5 for adults; $2 for ages 2 - 12.

ONCE UPON A STORY, San Juan Capistrano. (949) 768-1916 / hometown.aol.com/sdavis7326/index.htm, at various locations in San Juan.

Enjoy a weekend of tall tales and some great storytelling from some of the best storytellers in the country. Learn fundamentals of storytelling from masters, or come to just be entertained. Your kids might even get their fill of stories, for a day or two at least. Hours are Fri., 7:30pm; Sat., 10am - 10pm. Individually priced story sessions range from $3 to $10 per person. Ask for package deal pricing.

PACIFIC BEACHFEST, Pacific Beach. (858) 273-3303 / www.pacificbeach.org, between Garnet and Thomas Aves. on and near the boardwalk. This one-day, non-alcohol, event signifies the official end of summer in Southern California. Festival activities include lifeguard games, kite flying, sand castle building, dancing to live bands, outrigger canoe exhibitions, and dory boats, kayak, and paddle board races. Purchase food from twenty Pacific Beach restaurants here, such as Asian chicken salads, jambalaya, feta cheese ravioli, and chocolate mousse cake - each item is only $1! Kids can be kept busy with face painting, clowns, cookie decorating, and clay painting. Nearby museums participate by having booths for children here. A fire truck is also on hand to explore. A fireworks show from the Crystal Pier caps the day. Open 11am - 7:30pm. Admission is free. Some activities cost. Beach parking is limited. 8-hour parking on Hornblend St. is $3.

PELTZER FARMS OLD FASHIONED PUMPKIN PATCH, Orange. (714) 289-1129 or (714) 289-0137 / www.peltzerfarms.com, 8415 E. Chapman Ave. This 20-acre patch features pumpkins, naturally, plus a tractor-pulled hayride ($2), pony rides ($3), train rides ($2), a petting zoo ($3 per family of 4), and a cornfield maze. School tours are offered during the week for $5 - $6 per student. The patch is open daily during the month of October, 9m - 8pm. General admission is free.

PINERY PUMPKIN PATCH, Bonita at 5437 Bonita Rd., and Rancho Bernardo at 13421 Highland Valley Rd. (858) 566-7466. Patches are open to the public during the month of October and also offer pre-booked group and family tours (for 8 or more people) during the week. The tour, which is $6 per child (adults are free), includes a pumpkin ($4 value), tractor pulled hayride (50¢), coloring book on growing pumpkins, walk through 8-foot tall corn maze (50¢), and farm animals for viewing, not for petting. Open Mon. - Thurs., 9am - 6pm; Fri. - Sun., 9am - 8pm.

PUMPKIN CITY'S PUMPKIN FARM, Laguna Hills. (949) 768-1103 / www.pumpkincity.com - pumpkin city; (949) 586-8282 - mall, 24203 Avenue De La Carlota at Laguna Hills Mall. This one-acre, fenced-in "farm" takes over part of the mall parking lot for the month of October. The ground is covered with hay, while tractors, cornstalks and bales of hay all around help enhance the autumn mood. There are Indian tepees to go in, a petting zoo to visit, and kids can take a ride on a pony ($3.75), a scale train ($1.75), an elephant (weekends only), and/or a few kiddie rides. Weekend entertainment is provided by costumed characters, country bands, and puppeteers. Group reservations are offered that include special rates on pumpkins and pony rides. And oh yes, there are thousands of pumpkins here of all shapes and sizes - mini pumpkins to ones that weigh up to 200 pounds! The farm is open daily 9:30am - 9pm. Free general admission.

PUMPKIN STATION, Mission Valley. (858) 566-7466, off Mission Center Rd. in the Mission Valley Shopping Center parking lot. Hundreds of pumpkins, plus a few kiddie rides (i.e. trains, Bumble Bee, Swing, cars, and boats), carnival-type games, pony rides, and a petting zoo make this an attractive place to shop for a pumpkin and for fun. Open daily during the month of October 10am - 8pm. Admission is free, but each activity costs.

RASPBERRY PICKING. See July entry for details.

RIDGECREST - INYOKERN AIR SHOW AND BALLOON FESTIVAL, Ridgecrest/Inyokern. (760) 375-UP-UP (8787) / www.rcballoonfest.com, Hwy. 178 at Inyokern Airport. Up, up and away to this three-day weekend festival that's full of hot air. Activities and events include balloon races (at 7am and 4pm); parachutists; gliders, vintage warbirds, and modern military planes both in the air and on the ground; tethered balloon rides (weather permitting); a children's area with rides, clowns, face painting, and arts and crafts; a bus tour to Randsburg from 1pm - 3pm ($5 per person) featuring the Opera House Cafe, bed races, shoot-outs, and skits; hot air balloon glows (7pm); and continuous entertainment. Festival hours are Fri., 2pm - 8pm; Sat. 5:30am - 10pm; Sun., 5:30am - 10pm. General admission, which includes free shuttle service from the parking lot to the airport, is $8 on Fri., $10 on Sat. and Sun. for adults; $5 on Fri. and Sun., $8 on Sun. for ages 5 - 12; children 4 and under are free. 3-day passes for adults are $18 at the gate; $10 for kids. Parking is free.

ROSEBUD PARADE, Pasadena. (626) 449-9144 / www.kidspacemuseum.org, 390 S. El Molino Ave. at Kidspace Children's Museum. (Check out this entry in the main section of the book.) At this Saturday parade, which is a mini version of the Tournament of Roses Parade, children are invited to bring their bikes, trikes, and wagons to create and decorate their "floats" with provided flowers, greenery, and other ornaments. Other activities include face painting, entertainment, and the crowning of the Rosebud King and Queen. Participate or come by to watch the parade which includes local bands and drill teams, and other mini-floats by South Lake businesses. The float decorating starts at 8:30am. The half-hour parade begins at 10:30am along South Lake Ave. The cost of participation is $5 per child.

SAN DIEGO ZOO, San Diego. (619) 234-3153 / www.sandiegozoo.org, Park Blvd. in Balboa Park. The world-famous zoo is free for all ages on the first Monday of October in celebration of Founder's Day. Kids, ages 11 and under, are free for the entire month! What a way to celebrate!

SCANDINAVIAN FESTIVAL, Santa Monica. (323) 661-4273. 2425 Colorado

Ave. at the MGM Plaza. Quick - name all five Scandinavian countries. Even if you can't, enjoy a smorgasbord of folk dancing, colorful national costumes, food, music, storytelling, crafts, and a parade - everything except the fjords. Open 10am - 6pm. Admission is $4 for adults; children 11 and under are free.

STAGECOACH DAYS, Banning. (909) 849-9626 / www.stagecoachdays.com, 22nd and Victory Sts. in A.C. Dysart Park. Commemorating the city as one of the major stops on the transcontinental stagecoach route, this four-day festival pulls out all the stops and features a carnival all four days, a P.R.C.A. rodeo on the weekends with all the major events, a parade on Saturday at 10am, plus shootouts, dances, and Old West themed contests throughout. General admission is a minimal cost. Open Thurs. - Fri., 5:30pm - 10pm; Sat. - Sun., 11am - 11pm. Call for rodeo hours, times, and prices.

ST. KATHERINE GREEK FESTIVAL, Redondo Beach. (310) 540-2434, 72 Knob Hill. Held the first weekend of the month, this thirty-five-year old annual ethnic and religious festival recreates the atmosphere of a Greek village with costumed participants, live Greek music, fresh-baked pastries, cultural arts and crafts, and food booths. A small, kiddie area is on the premises, too. Tours of the church are also offered. I don't know - it's all Greek to me! Open Fri., 6pm - 10pm; Sat., noon - 10pm; Sun., noon - 9pm. General admission is free.

TANAKA FARMS PUMPKIN PATCH, Irvine. (949) 653-2100 or (949) 380-0379, 5380 3/4 University Dr. This five-acre, U-pic pumpkin patch is located on a larger, working farm. Walk the farm to see the rest of the fruits and vegetables currently growing. Half-hour field trips, geared for pre-schoolers through first graders for groups of 10 or more, can be made with advanced reservations. The cost is $5 per child and participants pick their own vegetables and pumpkins. There is also a small corn maze and a wagon ride for children. The U-pic is open daily during the month of October, 10am - 5pm. Pre-picked pumpkins (and other produce) is available daily, 10am - 8pm.

TEMECULA TRACTOR RACE, Temecula. (909) 676-4718 / www.temeculacalifornia.com, at Winchester and Diaz Rd. at Northwest Sports Park. This three-day event, which has been an annual event for over a quarter of a century, consists of getting down and dirty. Tractors, in all classes and categories (i.e. horsepower, pre-1940, diesel-powered, etc.), are raced around an oval track that has a 50' wide by 25" deep mud hole. Volleyball competitors (who play for cash prizes) play the sport here in the mud. Kids are not left out of the fun! An obstacle course with tires and ramps are set up to slosh through. Cleaner activities involve a rock climbing area, games booths, food booths, and a chili cook off. Open Fri., 1pm - dark - free admission. Open Sat. - Sun., 7:30am - 5pm for $10 for adults; $5 for ages 12 and under.

THRESHING BEE AND ANTIQUE ENGINE SHOW, Vista. See June entry for details.

VISIT WITH MICHELANGELO AND LEONARDO DA VINCI, Glendale.
See March entry for details.

WESTERN DAYS AND RODEO, San Dimas. (909) 592-3818 /
www.sandimasrodeo.com. Yee ha! This weekend P.R.C.A. rodeo also features a
parade on Saturday; a Western Village with tents and authentic costumed
participants; American Indians who make a ceremonial Grand Entrance at noon,
plus do storytelling and tribal dances and have tepees set up to go through; a
western street dance; 100 vendors; a carnival; a business expo; and a crafts fair.
Open Sat., 10am - 6pm; Sun., 10am - 5pm. Call for specific rodeo times. General
admission is free. Activities cost. The rodeo is $16 for adults; $8 for children.

WIDE SCREEN FILM FESTIVAL, Long Beach. 6200 Atherton St. at the
Carpenter Performing Arts Center. (562) 985-7000 / www.csulb.edu/~cpac.
Classic motion pictures are shown in the original wide screen format for two
weekends. Most screenings are preceded by a brief introduction by the film's
director or a member of the cast. Many of the films are appropriate for children
such as *Lady and the Tramp, 20,000 Leagues Under the Sea*, etc. There are
matinee and evening shows. Call for a schedule of times and prices.

NOVEMBER:

CIVIL WAR REENACTMENT, Oak Glen. See June entry for details. (This
event takes place at two other "Riley's" farms than the one mentioned below.)

CIVIL WAR REENACTMENT AND ENCAMPMENT, Oak Glen. See June
entry for details.

DOO DAH PARADE, Pasadena. (626) 795-3355 / www.ci.pasadena.ca.us or
www.pasanda.cal.com, near the heart of Old Town in downtown Pasadena. This
spoof of parades is held the Sunday before Thanksgiving. There are no actual
rules regarding the parade or the participants, but the wackier the groups or
presentation, the better. Kids laugh it up as they see some of the funkiest outfits
and most unique dance routines ever performed. Everyone may act up and act
out! The parade goes from 11am - 1pm. Admission is free.

ESCONDIDO RENAISSANCE FAIRE AND SHAKESPEARE IN THE PARK,
(805) 496-6036 / www.goldcoastfestivals.com, 742 Clarence Ln. at Felictia
Park. The age of chivalry is recreated in a natural setting. Experience the glories
of the reign of Queen Elizabeth, battle pageants, jugglers, music in the streets,
games, activities, a kid's play area, and entertainment from days of yore,
including Shakespeare's plays. Open Sat. - Sun., 10am - 5pm. Admission is $10
for adults; $5 for ages 5 - 11; children 4 and under are free. Parking is $2.50.

FALL VILLAGE FAIRE, Carlsbad. See May entry for details.

FESTIVAL OF CULTURES, Orange. (800) 493-3276 /

www.greenmeadowsproductions.com, 701 S. Glassell St. at William Hart Park.
See below entry for details.

FESTIVAL OF CULTURES, Pasadena. (800) 493-3276 /
www.greenmeadowsproductions.com, 360 N. Arroyo Blvd. at Brookside Park,
Rose Bowl. See below entry for details.

FESTIVAL OF CULTURES, Riverside. (800) 493-3276 /
www.greenmeadowsproductions.com, 4600 Crestmore Rd. at Rancho Jurupa
Regional Park. Hola, Jambo, Konichiwa - hello! Experience cultures from
around the word - West Africa, Asia, Native American, and Mexican - through a
series of twenty-minute interactive shows and hands-on programs. Shows
include Wildlife of the World - see and touch different native species such as
goats, sheep, iguanas, and snakes; Africa - native costumes and barefoot dancers,
accompanied by drummers tell the story of their heritage through song and
dance; Mexico - fancy feathered headdresses, as well as fancy footwork, are part
of Mexican dancers' ancient traditions, and are part of the way they tell stories;
Asia - gongs, flutes, drums, and masks are part of the Asian presentations, along
with stories of their past; Native American - dances, chants, and storytelling are
part of seeing and hearing about life in a village. Bring a picnic lunch to enjoy at
the surrounding park. Open various days, 9:30am - 2pm. Admission is $8 per
person; children 2 and under are free. Extra activities ($1 per) are archery, face
painting, and feeding the animals.

FRONTIER RENDEZVOUS, Oak Glen. See May entry for details. This
rendezvous usually takes place over Thanksgiving weekend.

GLORY OF CHRISTMAS, Garden Grove. See December entry for details.

GRIFFITH PARK LIGHT FESTIVAL, Los Angeles. (323) 913-4688, Riverside
Dr (from Los Feliz Blvd. off the I-5) and follow the signs for the drive through;
park at the L.A. Zoo to walk through. Here's a bright idea - make this light
festival an annual drive-through tradition! Turn off the headlights and gaze upon
thousands of lights, from animated scenes depicting attractions around Southern
California, reindeer, the Old West, and lots more, and go through decorated
tunnels. Two tips: Weekend nights are less crowded and if possible, get in the
left hand lane. Open Nov. 24 - Dec. 26, 5pm - 10pm. Admission is free.

HARVEST FAIR, San Bernardino. (909) 384-5426 / www.harvestfair.net, 8088
Palm Ln. Take a trip to the Old West for two weekends in November. There is
so much to see and do - you might just need both weekends to do it all! Set up
like an Old West Boom town, come to enjoy on-going cowboy stunt shows,
square dancing, cloggers, bluegrass music, country music, an antique car show,
carnival rides (the more modern kind), carnival game booths, pony rides,
blacksmith demonstrations, Native American crafts, rope-making
demonstrations, and lots more. Open Sat. - Sun., 10am - 5pm. General admission
is $3 for adults; children 6 and under are free. Activities cost extra.

HARVEST FESTIVAL, Pomona. (800) 321-1213 / www.harvestfestival.com, 1101 McKinley Ave. at Fairplex at the Pomona County Fairgrounds. See October entry for details.

HOLIDAY OF LIGHTS, Del Mar. (858) 793-5555 / www.delmarfair.com, 2260 Jimmy Durante Blvd. (use the Solana Gate entrance) at the Del Mar Fairgrounds. This dazzling drive-through light show extravaganza has more than 300 holiday displays that line the Del Mar Fairgrounds racetrack. Favorite displays include a waving snowman, an animated jumping horse, downhill skiers, a tail-wagging dragon in the lake, a Top Gun Santa, and the 125-foot tunnel of lights. Open Nov. 23 - Jan. 1, Sun. - Thurs., 5:30pm - 10pm; Fri. - Sat., 5:30pm - 11pm. Admission is $9 per vehicle for up to 5 people; $14 per van or car with 6 or more people.

HOLLYWOOD CHRISTMAS PARADE, Hollywood. (323) 469-2337 / www.hollywoodchristmas.com, starting at Gower St. and Sunset Blvd. All the stars come out at night - I mean the stars of Hollywood - for this celebrity-packed parade that is put on the Sunday after Thanksgiving. There are fantastic floats, live bands, equestrian units, and of course, Santa Claus. The two-hour parade goes along a three-mile course through the streets of Hollywood. The parade goes from 6pm to 8pm. Reserved grandstand seating is $30 - $40 per person. Standing room is free, but it does get crowded, so get here early. All-day parking in nearby lots runs from $5 - $15.

HOW THE GRINCH STOLE CHRISTMAS, San Diego. (619) 239-2255 / www.oldglobe.org, Balboa Park at the Old Globe Theater. This Dr. Seuss-inspired production stars a fuzzy green villain who learns how to have a heart in the magical, musical world of Who-ville. Call for show times. Show times are Tues. - Sun., 7:30pm; Wed. - Thurs., 11am; Sat. - Sun., 2pm. Admission is $37 - $42 for adults; $18.50 - $21 for ages 17 and under.

INDIO POW WOW, Indio. See March entry for details.

INTERTRIBAL MARKETPLACE, Highland Park. (323) 221-2164 / www.southwestmuseum.org, 234 Museum Dr. More than 150 nationally-known American Indian artists, traditional dancers, and storytellers, plus ethnic food and craft demonstrations add up to a wonderful weekend marketplace. Explore the Southwest Museum (look up information under the Museums section) while you're here. Open Sat., 10am - 7pm; Sun., 10am - 6pm. Call for admission prices.

LIVE OAK CANYON CHRISTMAS TREE FARM, Redlands. (909) 795-TREE (8733) / www.liveoakcanyon.com, 32335 Live Oak Canyon Rd. Come join in the festivities celebrated here around Christmas time. Warm yourself by a large fire pit, visit with Santa Claus (on certain weekends), listen to carolers (usually on the weekends), and enjoy the hay bale maze, hay rides, and petting zoo. (See the October entry for more details on these attractions.) Walk among a twenty-five acre forest of home-grown Monterey Pines, Sierra Redwoods, and Aleppo Pines. Choose your own Christmas tree here (and have a worker cut it down), or purchase a fir tree shipped fresh from Oregon. A tented gift shop sells fresh wreaths, garland, and other decorations and gift items. Elementary-aged school tours are offered to learn about Christmas trees. Tours are $4.50 per student (adults are free) and include a tree seedling to take home. Open mid-November through to a few days before Christmas daily 9am - 6pm. General admission is free.

LOGANS CANDY, Ontario. (909) 984-5410, 125 W. "B" St. This small retail candy store makes candy canes starting in November. A limited number of tours are offered to visitors to watch the fascinating process of striped candy become a sweet reality. During the half-hour tour, first stand outside and listen to a description of the procedure as you peer in through the storefront window. Flavoring is added and kneaded through a huge amber blob which is then stretched and pulled (think taffy pull) to form the white part of the cane. A smaller blob is dyed red. Next, go inside the store to see the two colors twisted together and shaped into variously-sized candy canes. This is one of our favorite seasonal excursions! Tours are given Mon. - Fri. at 5:30pm, 7pm, and 8:30pm. The cost is $2.25 per child and includes a small bag of candy.

LONDON BRASS RUBBING CENTER, Long Beach. See September entry for details.

MOTHER GOOSE PARADE, El Cajon. (619) 444-8712 / www.sandiego.org, Main, Chambers, 2nd, and Madison Sts. This two-hour parade has been going strong and gaining momentum since 1946. It features over 5,000 participants - bands, equestrian units, clown acts, and the best part of all - lots of floats depicting Mother Goose rhymes and fairy tales. The parade takes place the Sun. before Thanksgiving beginning at about 12:30pm. Admission is free.

PASADENA MODEL RAILROAD CLUB'S OPEN HOUSE, Pasadena. See April entry for details.

PILGRIM PLACE FESTIVAL, Claremont. (909) 621-9581 / www.pilgrimplace.org, 660 Avery Rd. This timely festival takes place on the second Friday and Saturday in November. Thanksgiving is a time to be thankful (and to eat), but do your kids know how this holiday began? Find out by watching the educational highlight here - an hour-long, live reenactment called, *The Pilgrim Story*. This play, which accurately and biblically retells an important story of our heritage, is performed at the outside theater at 1:45pm each day by the retired church professionals who live at this center. Call for special school performances, geared for 5th graders or so, given on the prior Wednesday at 9am and 10:30am. Bring a picnic lunch to enjoy at nearby parks. A favorite activity at the festival is called the Glue In. Tables full of recycled items are available for kids to glue onto a piece of cardboard to create a masterpiece (50¢). Other activities include riding the (motorized) Mayflower (50¢), taking a mini-train ride (50¢), visiting the on-site cultural museum, and going to the Wampanoag Indian Village (50¢) for story time, and games. The festival runs from 10am - 4pm. Free admission and free, but hard-to-come-by, parking.

POW WOW, Indio. See March entry for details.

POW WOW, Santa Fe Springs. (562) 946-6476, 12100 Mora Dr. at Heritage Park. Share in two days of celebrating Native American cultures and intertribal gathering with traditional dancing, drumming, and singing, plus artifacts on display, Native American arts and crafts for sale, Indian fry bread, storytelling, and more. Open Sat., 11am - 10pm; Sun., 11am - 6pm. Admission is free.

SAN DIEGO GRAND PRIX, San Diego. (619) 233-3278 / www.sandiegograndprix.com, at the San Diego Naval Training Center. This three-day street race features top professional motor sport drivers. Along with time trials all during the day, there are kid's activities, car shows, and more. Tip: Arrive early to go through the pits and see the cars and drivers. Watch qualifying races on Fri. and Sat., 8am - 5pm and the finals on Sun., 9am - 4pm. General admission, which means grab a grandstand seat if you can, on Fri. and Sat. is $20 for adults; $15 for military and children 11 and under. Sun. admission (standing room only) is $25 for adults; $15 for military and ages children 11 and under. A reserved seating three-day pass for adults ranges from $75 (the upper row) to $50 (lower row); children's tickets are $50 - $30. Sunday reserved seating is $60 - $40 for adults; $35 - $25 for children. Please call as location and date might change.

SAWDUST WINTER FANTASY, Laguna Beach. (949) 494-3030 / www.sawdustartfestival.org, 935 Laguna Canyon Rd. Three acres of fun in the snow and other cool activities are offered for several consecutive weekends, beginning the one before Thanksgiving. (It is open the Friday after Thanksgiving, too.) Real snow is brought in daily so you can teach your little angels how to make snow angels. Family entertainment includes jugglers, balloon artists, storytellers, and carolers. Children's art activities, like mask making, are different each day and are free! Over 150 artists have booths here, with on-going crafting demonstration. Get your holiday shopping done and keep the kids happy - all at the same time! To complete the fantasy, Santa Claus makes his rounds. Open from 11am - 7pm. Admission is $4 for adults; $2 for ages 6 - 12; children 5 and under are free. A season pass is $5 per person. Parking fees vary depending on which lot you choose.

VETERANS DAY CELEBRATION, Chiriaco Summit. (760) 227-3483, 62-510 Chiriaco Rd. at the General Patton Memorial Museum. Veterans are remembered and celebrated during this one-day event. Entertainment includes a U.S.O. Show, an Army chorus, pipes and drums, military reenactments, fly overs, an appearance by General Patton "himself", and a walk through the museum. Open 9:30am - 4:30pm. The U.S.O. Show starts at 11am. Admission is $3 for adults; free for veterans in uniform ages and ages 11 and under.

DECEMBER:

ANNUAL BAY PARADE OF LIGHTS, San Diego. (619) 234-8791 or (619) 685-7818 / www.sdparadeoflights.org, San Diego Bay. Over 100 boats get decked out with lights and participate in a parade from Shelter Island, past the Embarcadero, Seaport Village, and then on to Coronado ending at the Navy carrier basin. The parade offers prizes to the "best of" in several categories. It runs on two consecutive Sun., 5:30pm - 9pm. Free viewing from the shore.

ARCTIC SNOW HILL / FESTIVAL OF LIGHTS AT SAN DIEGO WILD ANIMAL PARK, Escondido. (619) 234-6541 / www.sandiegozoo.org, 15500 San Pasqual Valley Rd. For a few weeks this month, see the Wild Animal Park in a whole new light! Animated figures move and light up the sky (and some enclosures) to celebrate the holiday season. Children 16 years and under can slip and slide down a 100-yard hill covered in freshly made snow. Both the snow play area and lights festival are open daily 4pm - 8pm. Admission to these attractions is included with the price of admission to the zoo. Admission after 4pm is reduced to $7.95 for adults; $3.95 for ages 3 - 11.

BELMONT SHORE CHRISTMAS PARADE, Belmont Shore. (562) 434-3066 / www.belmontshore.org, on 2nd St. between Bayshore and Quincy. This two-hour street parade starts at 5:30pm on a Sat. and has over 100 entries, including bands, homemade floats, and Santa Claus. Call for exact date. Admission is free.

CHRISTMAS BOAT PARADE OF LIGHTS, Newport Beach. (949) 729-4400, Newport Beach Harbor. The largest and oldest boat parade, with more than 200 participants, usually sets sail nightly, December 17 through December 23. Consider taking the kids on a cruise for a closer look at the beautiful boats. The ideal location for viewing is Balboa Island, but you should arrive before 5:30pm as parking is limited. If you are going to have dinner in this area, be sure to make reservations. The parade hours are from 6:30pm - 8:45pm.

CHRISTMAS BOAT PARADE OF LIGHTS, Oceanside. (760) 722-5751. Call to find out when and where, specifically, the boat parade will be held this year.

CHRISTMAS ON THE PRADO, San Diego. (619) 239-0512, Park Blvd. and President's Way at Balboa Park. This festival marks the opening of the holiday season in San Diego as thousands of people join the celebration. The activities and events include looking at buildings glowing with Christmas lights, tasting holiday fare from around the world, listening to strolling carolers, participating in kid's crafts, enjoying free admission to the many museums here, watching the Santa Lucia procession, delighting in the Singing Christmas Story Tree at the organ pavilion, and applauding the holiday favorites performed at the Casa Del Prado Theatre. Usually open the first weekend of December, 5pm - 9pm. Admission is free.

CHRISTMAS OPEN HOUSE AND PARADE, Coronado. (619) 437-8788 /

www.coronado.ca.us, at First Street at the Ferry Landing Marketplace. Start off your holiday season with a bang as this one-day event, usually held on the first Friday in December, concludes with a fireworks display. During the day, kids will enjoy a parade along Orange Avenue, entertainment, holiday music, pony rides, snow play, and Santa's arrival by ferry (the reindeer are taking a rest). Call for specific hours. Admission is free.

CHRISTMAS PARADE, Fallbrook. (760) 728-5845 / www.fallbrook.ca. This one-day Christmas parade includes 120 groups, including bands and decorated floats. Admission is free.

CHRISTMAS STAR, Los Angeles. (213) 664-1191 / www.griffithobservatory.org, Hillhurst Ave. on the slope of Mt. Hollywood in Griffith Park. From early December through New Year's Day, the observatory projector is programmed for 2,000 years ago, or so. The origin of the Star of Bethlehem is theorized upon through astronomical detective work and incorporating the Bible. Offering up possibilities of exploding stars, aligning planets, meteorites, and other space phenomena, the astronomer/narrator offers a few conclusions. The show ends with information tying modern day Christmas customs with the Roman empire and the winter solstice. Shows are given Tues. - Fri., 3pm and 7:30pm; Sat. - Sun., 1:30pm, 3pm, 4:30pm, and 7:30pm. Tickets are $4 for adults; $3 for srs., $2 for ages 5 - 12.

CRUISE OF LIGHTS, Huntington Beach. (714) 840-7542 / www.philharmonicsociety.org, Peter's Landing. The Huntington Harbor Philharmonic Committee sponsors this event, raising money to donate to the youth music programs in Orange County. From December 13 through December 21 or so, forty-five-minute boat tours are given around the decorated homes of the harbor area. These homes have entered a competition, so you will see the creme de la creme, like the Sweepstakes winner, the Most Beautiful, the Most Traditional, etc. You'll also hear interesting commentary. Some boats along the way are also decked out in their Christmas best. Tours are offered every hour on the half hour from 5:30pm - 8:30pm. Tickets Mon. - Thurs. are $9 for adults, $5 for ages 2 to 12; Fri. - Sun., $10 for adults, $5 for ages 2 to 12.

DISNEY ON ICE. (714) 704-2400 / www.disneyonice.com or www.arrowheadpond.com - Arrowhead Pond in Anaheim; (213) 748-6136/www.lacoliseum.com - L.A. Memorial Coliseum and Sports Arena; (562) 436-3636/ www.longbeachcc.com - Long Beach arena. This ninety-minute, beautiful (and sometimes comical) show on ice usually features characters from Disney's newest film release. Tickets range from $11.50 - $18.50. Opening night tickets are only $10!

DRIVE THROUGH NATIVITY, Chino Hills. (909) 517-1190, the corner of Chino Hills Pkwy. and Eucalyptus at Gordon Ranch Marketplace. Revisit Bethlehem, kind of. Slowly drive past (no walking allowed) nine scenes featuring live performers in still life poses, animals (i.e. camels, sheep, donkeys, etc.), and angels as they "reenact" the scenes of Jesus' birth. Open Fri. - Sun., 5pm - 10pm. Admission is free.

FAMILY CHRISTMAS TREE FARM, El Cajon. (619) 448-5331, 300 Pepper Dr. Select your own Monterey pine, or choose an already cut Noble, Douglas Fir or Grand Fir tree. A petting zoo, hayrides, and a small store with fresh winter greens are also on the premises. Open throughout most of December daily 9am - 5pm.

FANFEST, Pasadena. (626) 793-9911 - 24-hr. hotline; (626) 440-ROSE (7073); or (626) 449-4100 / www.tournamentofroses.com, 1001 Rose Bowl Dr. at the Rose Bowl. Four days before the big parade and football game, fans can participate in numerous activities inside and outside the bowl. A Fanfest pass, which is $10 per person and good for all four days, allows entrance to the following events: the Tournament of Roses Museum, which is a 10,000 square-foot tent that houses historic photographs, artifacts, and interactive exhibits; a stadium tour; the Sports Village, where visitors take part in interactive contests such as kicking a field goal, running obstacle courses, cheerleading and coaching clinics, and visits by former Rose Bowl players; Expo Village, which has free displays and activities for the family (past participants have included Legoland and the Sheriff's Department, among others); a food court; and seeing the floats being decorated. See Rose Parade Float Viewing in this section. Bandfest is $5 per person for two days, from 1pm to 4pm, of high school marching bands from around the world practicing and performing. Or just come for Equesfest, outside the bowl, where admission is free. Here some of the parade's precision equestrian units are showcased, as well as exhibits, such as horse-drawn fire wagons; the unique camel and ostrich races; roping and riding demonstrations; country music; and a Civil War encampment. Ultimate fans can attend the Rose Bowl Kickoff Luncheon ($45 per person) and dine with everybody who's anybody in the Rose Parade or game, including the Rose Queen and her court, athletes, coaches, officials, and the grand marshal. Tickets are available through Ticketmaster at (213) 480-3232 or (714) 740-2000.

FESTIVAL OF CULTURES, Ventura. (800) 493-3276 / www.greenmeadowsproductions.com, Foothill Blvd. and Day Rd. at Arroyo Verde Park. See November entry for details.

FESTIVAL OF LIGHTS, Riverside. (909) 788-9556, Mission Inn Ave and Main St. The Main Street (therefore outdoor) mall is decked out with thousands of lights, including the historic Mission Inn. View Victorian Christmas animated scenes and characters and take a tour of the Inn. (The tour is $8 per person and advanced reservations are needed.) Add to the festivities by taking a horse-drawn carriage ride - call Carriages by Margaret at (909) 789-1620.

FESTIVAL OF LIGHTS PARADE, Palm Springs. (760) 778-8415, on Palm Canyon Rd. near Ramon. The one-day holiday parade includes floats, bands, people, vehicles, and even animals festooned in white lights. Admission is free.

FIRST NIGHT, Escondido. (760) 739-0101. See below description.

FIRST NIGHT, Fullerton. (714) 738-6575 or (714) 738-6545 /
www.firstnight.com, bordered by Lemon, Malden, Chapman, and
Commonwealth Sts. Bring in the New Year all night long! Activities include
entrance to the Fullerton Museum Center, music and dancing in the streets, and a
fun zone for kids that includes kid's karaoke, face painting, a petting zoo, and
rides. Fireworks light up your life at midnight! First Night fun happens between
7pm - midnight. Tickets are $12 for adults; $8 for ages 11 and under.

FIRST NIGHT, San Diego. www.firstnight.com. See above description.

FIRST NIGHT, Santa Fe Springs. (562) 863-4896 or (562) 868-0511. See above
description.

FIRST NIGHT, Whittier. firstnightwhittier.com. See above description. The
bordering streets are Walnut, Philadelphia, Washington, and Pointer. This First
Night starts at about 3pm with kids crafts, a snow play area and so much more,
with the 17 entertainment venues beginning around 6pm. Admission is $10 for
adults; ages 10 and under are free.

FLOATING PARADE OF 1,000 LIGHTS, Long Beach Harbor. (562) 435-4093.
Come enjoy the boats on parade that are adorned with Christmas lights and
decorations. Prizes are awarded in several categories. The best views are from
Shoreline Village, particularly Parkers Lighthouse, although parking is at a
premium.

GARDEN GROVE WINTERFEST CARNIVAL, Garden Grove. (714) 741-
5000, 9301 Westminster at Garden Grove Park. A lot of holiday fun is packed
into the first Saturday of this month! There is a snow play area, pictures with
Santa, games, and a crafts area where kids can make a variety of projects such as
ornaments, wrapping paper, Christmas cards, and more. The carnival runs from
10am - 3pm. General admission is free. Each activity takes one to two tickets,
and tickets are only 25¢ each!

GLORY OF CHRISTMAS, Garden Grove. (714) 54-GLORY (544-5679) /
www.crystalcathedral.org, 12141 Lewis St. at the Crystal Cathedral. Come see
this one-hour, absolutely spectacular, musical production that is a reenactment of
the miraculous birth of Jesus Christ. It's complete with live animals and angels
soaring overhead. (Arrive a little early and see the animals in a farm enclosure
towards the back of the parking lot.) Although show times vary they are usually
at 6:30pm and 8:30pm nightly (no shows on Mon.), with additional shows at
4:30pm on selected Sat. and Sun. Tickets are $20 - $30 for adults; $2 less for srs.
and ages 12 and under. Ask about family discount days, when tickets are $15 per
person.

GRIFFITH PARK LIGHT FESTIVAL, Los Angeles. See November entry for details.

HOLIDAY BOWL PARADE, San Diego. (619) 283-5808 /
www.holidaybowl.com, Harbor Drive. Although football is the focal point of
this one-day event, the colorful parade is also a highlight. Floats, inflatable
balloons, numerous bands, and other entertainment await sports fans of all ages.
The two-hour parade begins at 10am. Admission is free.

HOLIDAY CHRISTMAS PARADE, Oxnard. (800) 269-6273 /
www.oxnardtourism.com. The one-day hometown parade includes floats, bands,
entertainment, and awards ceremony. Admission is free.

HOLIDAY OF LIGHTS, Del Mar. See November entry for details.

ICE SKATING, Los Angeles. (213) 847-4970 or (213) 622-4083, between Olive
and Hill Sts. and 5th and 6th Sts. at Pershing Square. Ice skate outside in sunny
Southern California for the month of December through mid January. As the rink
is sponsored by the L.A. Kings, free hockey clinics are given on certain
weekends. Open Mon. - Thurs., noon - 9pm; Fri. - Sat., 11am - 10pm; Sun.,
11am - 9pm. Admission is $6 an hour; $2 for skate rentals.

LIGHTED STREETS. Is there a street or two in your neighborhood that the
owners have gone all out to decorate every year? One of our family traditions is
to choose one special night during the Christmas season, go out to a restaurant,
and walk up and down the festive streets to enjoy the lights and displays.

LIVE OAK CANYON CHRISTMAS TREE FARM, Redlands. See November
entry for details. Don't miss this one!

LIVING CHRISTMAS CAROL, Rancho Cucamonga. (909) 980-6450, 9240
Archibald Ave. Ba humbug! In cahoots with Capers Production, the huge
Victorian-style Christmas House bed and breakfast puts on an interactive play
based on Dickens' *A Christmas Carol*. A storyteller (i.e. narrator/guide) greets
participants at the door, explaining the premise of the play. Each group of fifteen
people walk through eight rooms of the house (all of which have fireplaces),
watching and even taking part in the different scenes playing in each one. Over
thirty-five actors and actresses, whom visitors view close up, are involved in
portraying Scrooge, his Christmas ghosts, the Cratchits, and townspeople. At the
end, enjoy cider and warm cookies from Mrs. Cratchit in her kitchen and dance
with Scrooge's nephews at the Christmas party. God bless us, every one! Groups
of 15 people depart every 15 minutes for the hour-long play which runs Dec. 23
from 4pm - 8pm; Dec. 24, 1pm - 6pm. Advanced reservations are a must (and
tickets sell out early.) Admission is $20 for adults; $10 for ages 3 - 12; children
2 and under are free. (No strollers allowed.)

LONG BEACH CHRISTMAS WATER PARADE, Long Beach. (562) 436-
3645, Naples Canals. Boat-owners cover their boats with Christmas lights, and

parade past decorated homes along the Naples canals. If you miss the boat parade, just seeing the homes along here is a special treat. Call for dates and hours. Admission is free.

LOS ANGELES HARBOR CHRISTMAS BOAT PARADE, San Pedro. (310) 519-1159, Ports O' Call. Owners go all out to decorate their boats and compete for the best in a wonderful parade that is put on the second Sat. of December.

LAS POSADAS, Los Angeles. (213) 628-7833, Olvera Street. Guests join in a candlelight procession led by actors portraying Mary and Joseph as the couple searches for shelter. The Christmas pageant ends with a more modern celebration of breaking open a pinata. The procession starts at about 7pm. Admission is free.

LAS POSADAS, San Diego. (619) 296-3161 / www.bazaardelmundo.com, Juan St. at Heritage Park. Same description as above. Procession begins at 7pm. Admission is free.

MARINA DEL REY CHRISTMAS BOAT PARADE, Marina del Rey. (310) 823-5411. On the second Saturday of December over eighty boats, decorated to the hilt with Christmas lights and decorations, sail around the marina's main channel. The parade is exciting with winners chosen for Best Theme, Best Humor, Best Music, etc. The best views are from Burton Chase Park or Fisherman's Village.

MISSION BAY CHRISTMAS BOAT PARADE OF LIGHTS, Mission Bay. (858) 488-0501. The lighted boat parade (the title of the event is self-explanatory) begins at Quivira Basin at 7pm and ends with lighting of the Sea World Sky Tower Tree of Lights at 9pm. The best viewing is along Crown Point, the east side of Vacation Island, or the west side of Fiesta Island. There is no admission.

MONARCH BUTTERFLIES, Ventura. (805) 658-4726 - the Office of Cultural Affairs for tour info / www.ci.ventura.ca.us, at Camino Real Park. Thousands of Monarch butterflies arrive in the park during this month. Call for tour times and costs.

MUSEUMS, all over. Many of your favorite museums get all decked out for the holidays, particularly the historical homes. Many also offer holiday programs with special family activities.

OLD FASHIONED CHRISTMAS VILLAGE, La Mesa. (619) 462-3000, La Mesa Blvd. between Acacia Ave. and 4th St. Two Fri. and Sat. evenings in a row this winter wonderland boasts twinkling lights, holiday foods, Christmas music, and a children's carnival with hayrides, holiday crafts, puppet shows, and a visit from Santa. Open 5pm - 9pm. Free admission.

PARADE OF LIGHTS, Ventura. (805) 642-7753 or (805) 985-4852, Spinnaker Way at Ventura Village. This festive boat parade is usually held the first or second weekend in December. Call for specific dates. Take the Bay Queen for an hour-and-a-half cruise, as it goes around the harbor to see homes that are decorated for the holidays. Also, call for the dates when a white Christmas is celebrated at the Village with snow brought in specially for kids.

POINSETTIA FLOWER TOURS, Encinitas. (760) 753-6041, at Paul Ecke Ranch. For one weekend, usually the first one in December, take a "tour" of poinsettias. See the original bright red colored ones and new varieties as you walk through the greenhouses. Call for hours. Reservations are required. Admission is $10 per person.

RANCHO CHRISTMAS, Vista. (760) 724-4082, 2210 N. Santa Fe Ave. at Rancho Guajome Adobe. Celebrate Christmas in an atmosphere of yesteryear. (Look up the adobe under the Museums section of the book.) Kids crafts, such as candlemaking, dipping candy apples, and making corn husk angels, plus pony rides, and other fun activities culminate in the lighting of the luminaries and a caroling program. Open Sat., 10am - 6pm. Admission is $5 for adults; $2 for ages 5 - 12; children 4 and under are free.

ROSE PARADE DECORATING. (626) 440-ROSE (7073) / www.tournamentofroses.com. Call to ask where your assistance might be needed in helping to decorate the Rose Parade floats. Children at least 13 years old and whose parents are Auto Club members can help decorate the AAA float. Call (714) 424-8190 for more information.

ROSE PARADE FLOAT VIEWING, Pasadena. (626) 440-ROSE (7073) / www.tournamentofroses.com, Rosemont Pavilion - 700 Seco St.; Rose Palace - 835 S. Raymond Ave.; Brookside Pavilion - 1001 Rose Bowl Dr. at the Rose Bowl, which has access to those will physical disabilities, on the west side of the Rose Bowl Stadium; and Buena Vista Pavilion - 2144 Buena Vista in Duarte. Come see the famous floats as they are being made, from December 28 through December 31. Workers spend weeks meticulously decorating them using plants, seeds, tree bark, flowers, and single petals. Viewing times are from 9am - 9pm. Admission is $3.

SAN PASQUAL BATTLE REENACTMENT, San Pasqual. (760) 737-2201, 15808 San Pasqual Valley Rd. See the San Pasqual Battlefield State Historic Park in the main section of the book under Museums. On the first Sunday reenactors dress up in 1840's garb; pitch tents; provide music, crafts (i.e. adobe brick making, candle making, etc.), and dance of the era; and best of all, reenact battle (even fire cannons!) a few times throughout the day. Open 10am - 5pm. Admission is free.

SANTA'S ELECTRIC LIGHT PARADE, Temecula. (909) 694-6412 / www.ci.temecula.ca.us. Spectacular evening parade features floats, marching bands, and equestrian groups. The shows begins at 7pm. Admission is free.

STAR OF BETHLEHEM, Santa Ana. (714) 564-6356, W. 17th St. and North Bristol at Tessman Planetarium at Santa Ana College campus. For four nighttime shows and seven daytime shows, starting the end of November through the middle of December, the planetarium sky is reset to around the time of Jesus' birth. After an introduction of astronomy, the astronomer/narrator - via a slide show, Bible passages, and using the planetarium "skies"- discusses how (and when) this miraculous phenomena called the Star of Bethlehem came about, including possible origins of a nova, comet, star, meteorite, or aligning planets. I won't give away the ending. The one-hour presentation is educational, as well as a wonderful blend of science and faith. Nighttime shows start at 7:30pm; daytimes shows at 9:30am. Tickets are $3 per person. Reserve your space early as shows sell out. Note: Check out other planetariums under the Shows and Theaters section in the main section as most of them have this type of show at Christmastime.

TREE LIGHTING CEREMONY, Long Beach. (562) 435-3511 / www.queenmary.com, 1126 Queens Highway at the Queen Mary. "Deck the hull" with the tree lighting ceremony which includes a holiday sing-a-long. The ceremony goes from 6pm - 7:30pm, but the public may board at 4:30pm and take a look around the ship. Admission is free after 4:30pm and parking is reduced to $6.

UPTOWN HOLIDAY PARADE, Whittier. (562) 696-2662 / www.whittieruptown.org. This one-day uptown parade, for us downtown folks, features more than 120 entries including highschool bands, equestrian and marching units, floats, and Santa Claus. Admission is free.

VICTORIAN CHRISTMAS, El Toro. (714) 855-2028, 25151 Serrano Rd. at Heritage Hill Historical Park. On the first Saturday in December, experience Christmas as it was during the turn-of-the century. Walk through these four historic buildings, which are festooned with old-fashioned decorations. Over fifty exhibits display and demonstrate homemade handicrafts like wooden carvings and lace making. A popular display is the antique engines which include a milking machine, a corn husker, and a corn grinder. A free children's crafts area is available for kids to make their own special creations. Genteel entertainment is provided, and Saint Nicholas also pays a visit. Open 10am - 4pm. Admission is $3 for adults; $2 for kids.

VICTORIAN CHRISTMAS, Wilmington. (310) 548-7777 /www.banning.org, 401 E. M St. at the General Phineas Banning Residence Museum. Kick off the Yuletide season by immersing yourself in the 19th century on the first weekend in December at the Banning Museum. Docents greet you dressed in period costumes and show you around the beautifully ecorated house/museum. The lavish Victorian adornments are quite lovely and the costumed carolers, bell ringers, and musicians complete the ambiance. Open Sat. - Sun., 11am - 4pm.

Admission is free. The decorated house is also open to tour through most of December at regular admission prices.

WILDLIGHTS, Palm Desert. (760) 346-5694 / www.livingdesert.org, 47900 Portola Ave. at the Living Desert Wildlife and Botanical Park. A special display, up for only six-weeks, features nearly a dozen, larger-than-life animal and other sculptures illuminated in lights. This can include a gigantic teddy bear, a thirty-foot snowman, assorted desert critters, and a golfing Santa. Live entertainment, good food, a huge model train exhibit, and a visit from Santa Claus (bring your own camera) add to the holiday festivities. The park is open 6pm - 9pm for these wild nights. (The animals are put to bed - it's a people-only party.) Admission is $4 for adults; $2.50 for children 11 and under.

WINTER SNOW FROLIC, Temecula. (909) 694-6410 / www.ci.temecula.ca.us, 30875 Rancho Vista Rd. at the Temecula Community Rec Center. I'm dreaming of a white Christmas and frolicking in tons of fresh snow helps the dream come true. Bring mittens and dress warmly. Start the day by having breakfast with Santa, then enjoy the snow, craft fair and rest of the fun. Breakfast seating is at 8am, 9am, 10am, and 11am. The snow fun goes from 9am - 1pm. Breakfast is $3.50 per person; admission to the snow and craft fair is free.

WINTER WONDERLAND, Beverly Hills. (310) 550-4796 or (310) 550-4765 / www.ci.beverly/hills.ca.us, 471 S. Roxbury Dr. at Roxbury Park. Over a hundred tons of snow turns the park into a winter wonderland for a day. Go down several sled runs, build a snowman in the snowplay area, and enjoy a horse-drawn carriage sleigh ride, a petting zoo, moon bounce, game booths, an ice sculpturer, and children's craft center. Dress warmly! Pre-registration is required for either of the two, two-and-a-half-hour sessions. General admission is $7 for ages 4 and up; children 3 and under are free. Other activities cost extra.

WINTER WONDERLAND, Corona del Mar. (949) 644-3151, between Iris and 5th Ave. at Grant Howald Park. If you don't feel like driving a few hours to the snow, just drive to Corona del Mar for this one-day event. Bring your mittens and have a great time building a snowman or ~~starting~~ having a snow ball fight with your kids. Food and beverages are available for purchase. Open 10am - 1pm. Admission is free.

IDEAS / RESOURCES

(General ideas of where else to go and what to do, plus where to find specific resource information.)

AIRPLANE or HELICOPTER RIDES -
Look in the phone book; call small, local airports for flight information; and/or check the Transportation section for specific flying venues.

ANIMALS (and fertilized chick eggs) -
AA Laboratories in Westminster, (714) 893-5675 / www.egglab.com, sells fertilized eggs - $12.50 for a dozen chick eggs. They also have duck and quail eggs. Incubators rent for $10 a week - home births without the labor pains! Be forewarned, however, that very little instruction comes with your eggs and incubator. Tips: Go to the library to research the process by checking out picture books of developing chicks and ducks. Pick up an information sheet and feed at Blacksmith's Corner, (562) 531-0386 in Bellflower, or at a similar pet store near you. And yes, if you do not want to raise the birds, AA Labs will (usually) take them back and donate them to farms, zoos, etc.

Insect Lore, (800) LIVE BUG (548-3284) / www.insectlore.com. This catalog offers living science kits, giving families the opportunity to observe insects and other critters growing and transforming. Our favorite kits are the butterfly, earthworms and compost, praying mantis, silkworm, ladybird beetles (i.e. ladybugs, to lay people), and frog hatchery. Each kit comes with instructions, information, and eggs or embryos. The catalog also offers owl pellets to dissect, plus other science experiments, books, and visual aids.

Wagon Train Feed & Pet in Orange, (714) 639-7932 / www.wagontrain.net, is a small pet store that also sells chick, duck, and quail eggs, as well as incubators. (See the Pet Store entry in this section for more detail.)

ARCHERY -
Get on target and call the National Archery Association, (719) 578-4576 / www.usarchery.org, who refers callers to local clubs and places to practice. Look under the Great Outdoors section for local parks that offer archery ranges.

ARTS AND CRAFTS -
Many places, including libraries and bookstores, offer free or minimal fee classes / workshops for kids. Also check out: craft stores, such as Michaels, (800) MICHAEL (642-4235) / www.michaels.com - ask about Kids Club Saturdays; Home Depot, www.homedepot.com - most offer free Sat. workshops; Create Your Own Craft Emporium, (310) 453-2005 / www.create-your-own.com - for rubber stamping, scrap booking, sticker art, and weaving classes; Lakeshore Learning Materials stores, (800) 421-5354 / www.lakeshorelearning.com; Piecemakers Country Store, (714) 641-3112 / www.piecemakers.com; and Zany Brainy, (877) WOW-KIDS (969-5437) / www.zanybrainy.com. Look under the Arts and Crafts section in the main part

of the book, too.

AUDIO TAPES -
The following are our favorite, non-singing, tapes / cds:

Adventures in Odyssey, (800) A-FAMILY (232-6459) / www.family.org - Six tapes for about $25. Focus on the Family puts out this series consisting of twelve, half-hour-long, Biblically-based, radio dramas. The stories are centered around a fictional soda shop/Bible room/imagination station/kid's hang-out called Whit's End, and the people that live in the small (made-up) town of Odyssey. Each episode involves kids, families, dilemmas, solutions, morals, wit, and wisdom. I can't recommend these adventures highly enough!

Classical Kids Series - about $10.95 per tape. The tapes can be found in most larger retail record stores or ordered through catalogs such as Rainbow Re-Source Center, (888) 841-3456 / www.rainbowresource.com. Each hour-long tape in this wonderful series tells the story, told in play format, of a famous composer while the composer's music plays in the background. Titles include *Beethoven Lives Upstairs*, *Mozart's Magical Fantasy*, and *Tchaikovsky Discovers America*.

Greathall Productions, (800) 477-6234 / www.greathall.com - about $9.95 per tape. Be enthralled by award-winning storyteller, Jim Weiss. Kids (and adults) of all ages will enjoy the masterful retelling of (mostly) classic stories. Tape titles include *Arabian Nights*, *Sherlock Holmes for Children*, *Three Musketeers*, *Giants!*, *Greek Myths*, *Shakespeare for Children*, and *Animal Tales*. Look up JIM WEISS under the Educational Presentations section in the main part of the book.

BASEBALL -
Call for a game schedule and ask about special days, such as fan appreciation day:

Angels at Edison International Field in Anaheim, (888) 796-HALO (4256) / www.angelsbaseball.com

Dodgers at Dodger Stadium in Los Angeles, (323) 224-1-HIT (448) / www.dodgers.com

Padres at Qualcomm Stadium in San Diego, (888) - MYPADRES (697-2373) / www.padres.com

Minor league games can be major league fun. Check out teams such as Bakersfield Blaze, (661) 322-1363 / www.bakersfieldblaze.com; High Desert Mavericks, (760) 246-6287 / www.hdmavs.com; Lake Elsinore Storm, (909) 245-4487 / www.stormbaseball.com; Lancaster Jethawks, (661) 726-5400 / www.jethawks.com; Long Beach Breakers, (562) 987-4487 / www.breakersbaseball.com; Rancho Cucamonga Quakes, (909) 481-5000 / www.rcquakes.com; and San Bernardino Stampede, (909) 888-9922 / www.stampedebaseball.com

High school and college games are exciting, too.

BASKETBALL -
Clippers at Staples Center in Los Angeles, (213) 742-7555 /

www.clippers.com
Lakers at Staples Center in Los Angeles, (310) 426-6000 / www.lakers.com
Sparks (a women's pro team) at Staples Center in Los Angeles, (310) 426-
    6031 / www.wnba.com/sparks
Also check out high school and college games.

BATTING CAGES -
"Hey batter batter." Cages are great for hitting practice, in season or out.

BILLIARDS -
Many billiard parlors have a family-friendly atmosphere.

BOOKS -
Numerous book stores offer story times and/or craft times. Some of the bigger
book stores, such as Barnes & Noble and Borders, have a huge children's
selection, as well as a children's reading area. Many smaller bookstores cater
specifically to kids and are delightful to browse through. Also look up
Educational Toys, Books, and Games in this section.
Used book stores are a terrific bargain. To name just a few, try:
    Acres of Books in Long Beach, (562) 437-6980 / www.acresofbooks.com -
    one of the largest used book stores in the world.
    Book Baron in Anaheim, (714) 527-7022 / www.bookbaron.com - vintage
    and used books.
    Book City in Hollywood, (213) 466-2525 / www.hollywoodbookcity.com
    and in Burbank, (818) 848-4417 / www.burbbookcity.com - new and used
    books.
    Brindles in Tustin, (714) 731-5773 - new and used books.
Thrift stores and garage sales are another great resource for used books.

BOWLING -
Many alleys offer bumper bowling for kids, where the gutters are covered so
kids almost always knock down a pin or two. (This sounds like something
right up my alley, also.) Cosmic Bowling, sometimes known as Rock 'n Roll
Bowl, is great fun, too. Usually played at nighttime, ordinary lights are turned
out and neon lights take over. The pins, balls, and lanes glow in the dark and
rock music and/or videos play. All this while trying to bowl! Call your local
bowling alley.

CAMPING -
Campgrounds mentioned in this book are usually listed under the Great
Outdoors section. Call Parknet, (800) 444-7275 / www.reserveamerica.com, to
make camping reservations at any California State Park. Check your library or
local book store for books written just on camping. A starting point are several
books put out by Peterson (not me!) and the Guide to ACA-Accredited Camps
in Southern California. Check out the American Camping Association at (800)
428-CAMP (2267) / www.acacamps.org or the National Camping Association
at (800) 966-2267 / www.summercamp.org.

CELEBRITIES -

Call the Walk of Fame at Hollywood Chamber of Commerce, (213) 469-8311 / www.hollywoodchamber.net, to find out when the next celebrity will be honored with a ceremony dedicating his/her star along this famous "walk." Ceremonies occur almost monthly.

CIRCUS -

Check newspapers and sports arenas, or try the following numbers to see when the circus is coming to town:

Big Apple Circus, www.bigapplecircus.org - similar to Cirque Du Solei (see below), this top-notch circus features acrobats and a storyline.

Carson & Barnes, (580) 326-3173 / www.carsonbarnescircus.com - features five rings of continual action, with hundreds of animals, international performers, and lots of razzle dazzle.

Circus Flora, (314) 531-6273 / www.circusflora.org - named for its African elephant, this circus specializes in new circus-style ensemble acts. An intimate show performed in a 1,500-seat Big Top.

Circus Vargas, www.circusvargas.com - this one-ring circus has a small-town feel.

Cirque Du Solei, www.cirquedusoleil.com - artsy and eccentric productions change their theme often and focus on "impossible" body movements. Very unique! Note: No animals are used in this circus.

Fern Street Circus, (619) 235-9756 / www.fernstreetcircus.org - San Diego-based troupe with aerialists, clowns, and acrobats for whimsical entertainment; from a single clown to a three-ring circus. Ask about programs that teach children circus skills in San Diego.

Make A Circus, (415) 242-1414 / www.makeacircus.org - three-to-five-person circus troupe from Northern California presents two-hour workshops to very large groups, for free, at parks throughout Southern California. Kids are invited to first watch a short show; next learn how to tumble, juggle, and act like a circus animal; and finally put on a short show for the audience of parents.

New Pickle Circus / San Francisco School of Circus Arts, (415) 759-8123 / www.sfcircus.org - American and Russian circus acts are presented along with Chinese acrobats, dance, and original music.

Ringling Bros. & Barnum and Bailey Circus, (703) 448-4000 / www.ringling.com - "the greatest show on earth", this multi-ring circus is one of the best known in the Western world. It involves daring animal acts, clowns, and feats of skill presented with theatrical flare and state-of-the-art lighting. Arrive an hour before show time to get into the arena with the clowns and participate in some of the tricks - swinging on a trapeze swing, riding a unicycle (with lots of help), and more.

UniverSoul, (800) 316-7439 / www.universoulcircus.com - black-owned and operated touring circus performs traditional circus acts incorporating clowns and animals against a backdrop of rhythm and blues, urban, hip-hop, and gospel music.

CONSTRUCTION SITES -
If you're "toolin'" around, these sites can give your youngster constructive ideas to build on.

CONVENTION CENTERS -
They host a multitude of activities, many of them geared for children, such as Kid's Stuff Expos, toy shows, circuses, and more. Call them intermittently to see what's going on:
Anaheim, (714) 765-8950 / www.anaheimoc.org
Long Beach, (562) 436-3661 or (562) 436-3636 / www.longbeachcc.com
Los Angeles, (213) 741-1151 / www.lacclink.com
Ontario, (909) 937-3000 / www.ontariocc.com
San Diego, (619) 525-5000 / www.sdccc.org

COOKING -
Kid's cooking classes are offered throughout the year through local parks and recreation departments. A few other suggestions are listed below:
Bristol Farms in Manhattan Beach, (310) 726-1350 / www.bristolfarms.com - three-hour classes offer a variety of subjects for kids 7-12 or teens 13-17. Call for other locations.
Let's Get Cooking in Westlake Village, (818) 991-3940 / www.letsgetcookin.com - once-a-month parent/child classes are held on Sat., as well as workshops for pre-teen/teen, and even classes for children ages 6 years and up. Cook up something new and wonderful if you have a birthday party here, too.

COUNTY FAIR GROUNDS -
Numerous events are held at the following locations throughout the year, such as gem shows, reptiles expos, fairs, cat shows, circuses, Scottish games, horse shows, and lots more. Call for a schedule:
Los Angeles, (909) 623-3111 / www.fairplex.com
Orange, (714) 708-FAIR (3247) / www.ocfair.com
Riverside, (760) 863-8247 / www.datefest.org
San Bernardino, (760) 951-2200 / www.sbcfair.com
San Diego, (858) 755-1161 / www.delmarfair.com
Ventura, (805) 648-3376 / www.seasidepark.org

COUPONS -
Call the visitors center (or Chamber of Commerce) of the city you are planning to visit as they often offer discount coupons towards attractions. For instance, "The Family Values Coupon Book" for Orange County, features savings at over fifty area attractions, hotels, restaurants, and shops. Call (714) 765-8950 / www.anaheim.org for information. The San Diego Visitors Center, (619) 236-1212 / www.sandiego.org, offers a free "value coupon" booklet that saves on main attractions, harbor cruises, restaurants, and more.

CPR/FIRST AID CLASSES -
Call your local Red Cross or hospital for class information. This is a great idea

for babysitters, as well as yourself and your own kids!

EDUCATIONAL TOYS, BOOKS, and GAMES -

There are numerous stores and catalogs that offer good quality, educational products. Some of our favorite stores include Bright Ideas for Learning (in Camarillo), F.A.O. Schwartz, Imaginarium, Lakeshore Learning, Learning Express, Parent Teacher Aids (in Simi Valley), and Zany Brainy, an immediate favorite, (877) WOW KIDS (969-5437) / www.zanybrainy.com. Look in your telephone directory for these listings, and for two other great resources - teacher supply stores and children's bookstores. Many museum gift shops offer a terrific line of educational (and fun) supplies. Also check out the following companies that offer catalogs and/or home workshops for their products:

Discovery Toys, (800) 426-4777 / www.discoverytoysinc.com - carries a fantastic line of toys, books, games, and computer software.

Dorling Kindersley Books, (212) 213-4800 / www.dk.com - offers outstanding books.

Usborne Books, (800) 442-2812 / www.usborne-usa.com - top-notch books.

EQUESTRIAN SHOWS -

English and Western riding, jumping, and prancing are all part of seeing a horse show. Call your local equestrian center for dates and times and/or check the Calendar section for special event shows.

FARMER'S MARKETS -

See Edible Adventures in the main section of the book for details.

FILMING -

Interested in seeing actual filming? The L.A. Film Office, (323) 957-1000 / www.eidc.com, provides a free "shoot sheet" that lists expected location shots for any given day. The Hollywood Visitor Information Center, (213) 689-8822 / www.lscvb.com, can help with directions.

FISHING -

Here's the hook - you have to look under the Great Outdoors section for places to go fish. Contact the Department of Fish and Game, (562) 590-4835 / www.dfg.ca.gov, for free information on fishing, including maps to local lakes, fishing events, stocking guides, fishing clinics, and regulations.

FOOTBALL -

Chargers at Qualcomm Stadium in San Diego, 877-CHARGERS (242-7437) / www.chargers.com

Los Angeles Avengers at Staples Center in Los Angeles, (888) AVENGERS (283-6437) / www.laavengers.com

High school and college games are fun, too.

GYM CLASSES FOR KIDS -
Some suggestions are:

Creative Kids in Los Angeles, (310) 473-6090; Encino, (818) 380-0373 / www.happyallday.com - classes in gymnastics, music, art, fairytale theater, cooking, and more.

Gymboree, www.gymboree.com - check your local phone book for listings. Classes are offered for parents and their children - newborns through 4 years old - that include easy exercise, songs, bubbles, and visits from Gymbo, the clown.

My Gym, (800) 4-My-Gyms (469-4967) / www.my-gym.com - classes in tumbling, songs, games, and gymnastics are offered for the younger set. The franchises are everywhere in Southern California.

Y.M.C.A. - Fun fitness programs are available just for kids.

HOBBIES AND MODELS -
Kids like to collect - anything! For example - bottlecaps, dolls, miniatures (dollhouses), postcards, rocks, sports cards, and stamps. Other hobby ideas include model-making (i.e. cars, planes, rockets, and trains), creating jewelry, and sewing.

HOCKEY -
Ice Dogs at Long Beach Arena in Long Beach, (562) 423-3647/ www.icedogshockey.com

Kings at Staples Center in Los Angeles, (888) KINGSLA (546-4752) / www.lakings.com

Mighty Ducks at Arrowhead Pond in Anaheim, (714) 940-2101 / www.mightyducks.com

San Diego Gulls at the Sports Arena in San Diego, (619) 224-4625 / www.wchl.com/sandiego

HORSEBACK RIDING -
Neigh doubt about it, this is a terrific family outing! Call your local equestrian center.

HOT AIR BALLOON RIDES -
Up, up and away! Hot air balloon rides are recommended for ages 8 and up, as younger children might get scared of the flames shooting out (i.e. the "hot air"); they might get bored; and they can't see very well over the basket. All ages, however, are enthralled by watching the balloon being inflated, either in the morning or at sunset! For a real colorful outing, look in the Calendar section or call the below numbers for Hot Air Balloon Festivals. Most of the companies listed fly over Del Mar, Palm Springs, and/or Temecula. Flights are about an hour and some include a champagne breakfast. Prices are per person. These are just a few names and numbers to get you started:

California Dreamin' in Encinitas, (800) 373-3359 / www.californiadreamin.com - between $120 - $150.

Fantasy Balloon Flights in Palm Springs, (800) GO ABOVE (462-2683) / www.gtesupersite.com/balloonride - adults $135, kids 12 and under $85.

Skysurfer Balloon Company, (800) 660-6809 / www.skysurferballoon.com - about $135.

Sunrise Balloons, (800) 548-9912 / www.sunriseballoons.com - between $125 - $140.

ICE SKATING -
Go figure! Call, for instance, the arenas listed below:

Glacial Garden Skating Arena in Lakewood, (562) 429-1805 / www.glacialgarden.com - three rinks; two for the ice, and one for in-line skating. They also offer broomball which is *fun*tastic!

Disney Ice in Anaheim, (714) 535-7465 / www.disneyice.com - offers public sessions, plus figure skating and hockey classes. It's also the rink where the Mighty Ducks practice!

JUNKYARDS -
One man's trash is another child's treasure. For kids who like to take things apart and make new creations, junkyards are inspiring places to investigate.

KITE FLYING -
Go fly a kite! Check the Calendar section for Kite Festivals.

LIBRARIES -
Your local library has a lot to offer. Besides book, video, and cassette lending, many offer free storytelling on a regular basis and/or finger plays, puppet shows, and crafts. Some libraries also encourage your bookworms by offering summer reading programs. Get a group together and ask for a tour. *A Treasure Hunt in My Library*, by Candace Jackson, is an outstanding book, with curriculum, that takes kids on a tour of the library and teaches them how to use it. Order it through a bookstore or by calling (888) 707-4289 / www.museummania.com. Her website has some on-line treasure hunts. She has also written several great books for kids on specific museums in Southern California.

MAGAZINES -
If you only receive one magazine, make it *Family Fun*. Put out by Disney, each edition is packed with do-able crafts, snacks, party ideas, games, activities, and family-friendly places to travel. Pick it up at the newsstand or call (800) 289-4849 / www.familyfun.com for subscription information. (Currently, $14.95 for 10 issues.)

MALLS -
Going to the mall can be a fun excursion with kids (honest!), especially if the mall has "extra" features, such as a merry-go-round or fountains, or, if it's spectacular in design, has unique shops and restaurants, etc. See the Malls section in the main part of the book for some of our top picks.

MONEY -
Collect money from foreign countries without the expense of traveling there.

Call (800) CURRENCY (287-7362) / www.us.thomascook.com to find the nearest Thomas Cook Foreign Exchange Currency. You may exchange any sum of money for currency from an unlimited number of countries, for only one transaction fee. The fee is usually a $4.95 service fee or 1% of the U.S. amount, whichever amount is greater.

MOVIE THEATERS -

An obvious choice, but movies, and especially matinees, can be a relatively inexpensive and fun treat. For instance:

Super Saver Cinema in Seal Beach, (562) 594-9411 - each show costs $2.

Super Saver in Norwalk, (562) 868-9694 - showings on certain days of the week are only $2.50.

Super Saver in Pomona, (909) 620-1036. Same as above.

AMC Theaters in Long Beach, (562) 435-4262 / www.amctheaters.com - sometimes offer a book of 10 movies for $7.50 during the summer.

The El Capitan Theater - see this in the main entry of the book.

Drive In Theaters include: Azusa Foothill in Azusa, (626) 334-0263; Pacific Vineland Theater in Pico Rivera, (562) 948-3671; South Bay Triple Drive-In/Swapmeet in San Diego, (619) 423-2727; Van Buren Arlington in Riverside (909) 688-2360; Vineland Drive-In in City of Industry, (626) 961-9262 or (626) 369-7224.

See the Shows and Theaters section in the main part of the book for IMAX Theaters.

MUSEUMS -

You can $ee L.A., or ¢.E.E. L.A. The Cultural Entertainment Events card (C.E.E.) offers entrance to nineteen top museums for only $44 a year for the family! These museums include Autry Museum, George C. Page, Kidseum, Natural History, Petersen, and Richard Nixon. Call (818) 957-9400 / www.cee-la.com for more information. The card will also save you money on sporting and theater events.

PARKS -

Almost every local park offers classes or sports programs for free, or at a minimal cost. Ask about kid's cooking classes, sidewalk chalk art day, etc. For a comprehensive listing of California state parks, call (800) 777-0369; (916) 653-6995 / www.parks.ca.gov.

PET STORES -

This is a fun, mini-outing. Ask about tours. Cuddly puppies and adorable rabbits are great, but so are unusual and exotic animals found at some of the stores listed below. Look in your phone book for fish and bird stores, too.

Blacksmith's Corner in Bellflower, (562) 531-0386 - like visiting a mini farm, with its chickens, ducks, pheasants, etc.

La Habra Pets in La Habra, (310) 697-7110 - many exotic reptiles, such as ten-foot long snakes, a six-foot monitor lizard, and several others.

Last Straw Feed Store in Fallbrook, (760) 728-6482 - animals are mostly

s. See a llama, camel, goats, turkeys, chickens, a gigantic Burmese
..., and more.

oric Pets in Fountain Valley, (714) 964-3525 /
w.prehistoricpets.com - Incredible! See exotic snakes (some twenty-
feet long) and monitor lizards from all over the world, plus a small fish
pond in the middle of the store, and more.

Reptropolis in San Clemente, (949) 495-6598 - a variety of snakes, geckos,
iguanas, tarantulas, turtles, and tortoises.

Wagon Train Feed & Pet, (714) 639-7932 / www.wagontrain.net - When we
visited this small pet store it had chicks, ducks, a lamb, a pot-bellied pig,
turtles, chinchillas, and even a hedgehog. The stop here was worth a peek
and pet. Note: They also sell fertilized chick eggs and incubators.

PHOTO ALBUMS -

Tapped dry on how to put together a creative and memorable photo album?
Many stores, such as Aaron Brothers and Michaels, offer acid-free products.
Or, contact the magazines and multi-level company listed below for innovative
ideas and other acid-free products:

Creative Keepsakes magazine, (888) 247-5282 /
www.creatingkeepsakes.com - Browse through and implement the many
ideas given here. Current subscription price is $19.95 for 6 issues.

Creative Memories (company), (800) 468-9335 /
www.creative-memories.com - Call for information on purchasing craft
scissors, and acid-free pages, stickers, cut outs, etc. Or, learn artistic
techniques to organize and crop your photos by hosting or attending a
workshop for you and your friends.

Memory Maker magazine, (303) 452-0048 /
www.memorymakersmagazine.com - Pick up a copy of this beautifully
laid out and inspirational magazine. Current subscription price is $24.95
for 6 issues.

PLAYGROUPS -

Check local parks, newspapers, and "Parenting" magazine for information on
hooking up with a playgroup. This is a great way to share the joys and trials of
raising children. Other resources include:

MOMS, e-mail:momsclub@aol.com - an international, non-profit support
group specifically for stay-at-home moms. Weekly meetings consist of
talking and eating together, listening to a speaker, and going on various
outings. All age children are welcome at all meetings and activities. For
information on a club near you, write to: MOMS Club, 25371 Rye
Canyon, Valencia, CA 91355.

MOPS (Mothers Of Preschooler), (303) 733-5353 / www.mops.org - an
international, Christian-based organization that has local meetings in
almost every city. Moms usually meet at a church and talk, eat, listen to a
speaker, and make a craft while their preschoolers are being cared for by a
Moppet helper. Great organization! Call the headquarters to find a MOPS
near you.

Tot Lot is a playgroup designed for preschoolers (and their parents) to meet and play together at community parks on a regular basis during the week, building those all-important socialization skills. Registration fees go towards crafts, snacks, and even field trips. Call, for example, Lakewood Recreation and Community Services, (562) 866-9771 for information on Tot Lot at Biscailuz, Bolivar, Boyar, Del Valle, and Mayfair parks.

RESTAURANTS -
See the Edible Adventures section in the main part of the book. Try eating at some unusual locations, such as at airports, on boats (such as the Queen Mary), etc. Take your kids out for ethnic foods, too.

ROCKETRY -
Southern California Rocket Association, (714) 529-1598 / home.earthlink.net/~mebowitz, can get you in touch with model rocketry classes (for ages 10 and older).

ROLLER SKATING -
Roll on the sidewalks, around parks, and at rinks. Try:
Surf City Skate Zone in Huntington Beach, (714) 842-9143 - offers roller skating and ice skating under one roof!

SAN DIEGO THEATRE -
The San Diego Performing Arts League, (619) 238-0700 / www.sandiegoperforms.com, puts out a bimonthly booklet called *What's Playing?* It has a complete listing of the music, dance, and theater groups, plus specific show, dates, and prices in the San Diego area. $10 for a year's subscription.

SOCCER -
Los Angeles Galaxy at the Rosebowl in Pasadena, (877) - 3GALAXY (342-5299) / www.lagalaxy.com
San Diego Flash at Douglas Stadium at Mesa College in San Diego, (858) 581-2120 / www.sdflash.com

SPORTS ARENAS -
Many special events are held at sports arenas including sporting events, concerts, Walt Disney's World on Ice, circuses, etc:
Anaheim at Arrowhead Pond, (714) 704-2400 / www.arrowheadpond.com
Inglewood at Great Western Forum, (310) 419-3100 / www.gwforum.com
Long Beach at Long Beach Arena, (562) 436-3636 / www.longbeachcc.com
Los Angeles at L.A. Memorial Coliseum and Sports Arena, (213) 748-6136 / www.lacoliseum.com
Los Angeles at Staples Center, (213) 742-7340 / www.staplescenter.com
San Diego at Qualcomm Stadium, (619) 641-3131 / www.sandiegocity.org/qualcomm
San Diego at Sports Arena, (619) 225-9813 / www.sandiegoarena.com

SPORTING EVENTS -
Check out high school and college events. These local games are a fun, inexpensive introduction to sports.

SUN CLOTHING -
SunGrubbies, (888) 970-1600 / www.sungrubbies.com, makes clothing especially designed to block out harmful rays from the sun.

SWAP MEETS / FLEA MARKETS -
Give your kids a dollar or two to call their own, as there are a lot of inexpensive toys or jewelry items for them to choose from at swap meets. Everyone goes home happy with their treasures! Here's a list of just a few good swap meets / flea markets:

Alpine Village Swapmeet (outdoor) in Torrance, (323) 770-1961 / www.alpinevillage.net - open Tues. - Sun., 8am - 2pm. Admission is free on Thurs.; 50¢ per person other days.

Anaheim Marketplace (indoor) in Anaheim, (714) 999-0888 / www.anaheimindoormarketplace.com - over 250 variety shops and a food court. They also have adjacent batting cages and arcade games. Open Wed. - Mon., 10am - 7pm. Free admission.

Kobey's Swap Meet (outdoor) at the sports arena parking lot in San Diego, (619) 226-0650 / www.kobeyswap.com - the equivalent of twelve footballs fields, this swap meet offers bargains on everything under the sun. Open Thurs. - Sun., 7am - 3pm. Admission is 50¢ on Thurs. and Fri.; $1 on Sat. and Sun. No charge for children 11 years and under.

Orange County Marketplace (outdoor) in Costa Mesa, (949) 723-6616 / www.ocmarketplace.com - one of the best, with over 1,200 vendors, plus a food court. Open weekends, 8am - 3pm. Admission is $2 for adults; children 11 years and under are free.

Pasadena City College Flea Market (outdoor), (626) 585-7906 / www.paccd.cc.ca.us/stulrnsv/flea - a mishmash mixture of merchandise - some great deals, some garage sale items. Open the first Sun. of every month. Admission is free.

Roadium (outdoor) in Torrance, (213) 321-3902 / www.roadium.com - 500 merchants sell new items, some collectibles, bargains, garage-sale stuff, and food daily 7am - 4pm. Admission on Mon., Tues., Thurs., and Fri., is 50¢ per person; Wed., $1.25 for adults; 75¢ for seniors and children; Sat. and Sun., $1.50 per car, plus 50¢ per person.

Rosebowl Flea Mart (outdoor) in Pasadena, (626) 577-3100 or (323) 560-7469 / www.rgcshows.com - more than 2,200 vendors offer everything you've ever seen and many things you've never heard of. Held the second Sun. of each month. Admission is $15 from 6am - 7:30am; $10 from 7:30am - 9am; $6 from 9am until it closes. Parking is $2.

Saugus Speedway Swapmeet (outdoor) in Saugus, (661) 259-3886 / www.saugusspeedway.com - over 700 vendors, this huge swap meet is held every Tues. and Sun., 8am - 3pm. Swapmeets are held on Fri. only in the summer. Admission on Tues. is free; Sun., $1.50 for adults; children

11 years and under are free.

Street Fair by College of the Desert (outdoor) in Palm Desert, (760) 568-9921 / www.codstreetfair.com - new and used items, antiques, a Farmer's market, arts and crafts courtyard, jewelry, and more make this more of a street fair than swap meet ambiance. Held Sat. - Sun., 7am - 2pm; summer hours are 7am - noon. Admission is free.

Tip: Also check out 99¢ Stores which are along the same lines, sans the atmosphere, as swap meets.

SWIMMING and WADING POOLS -

Community pools are open seasonally. Call your local park for information.

THRIFT STORES -

Teach your children the gift of thrift! Give them a few dollars to buy a "new" article of clothing, a toy, or a book. Tip: Main Street, in the city of Ventura, has at least ten thrift stores in a row.

TICKETS -

Audiences Unlimited, (818) 506-0067 or (818) 753-3470 / www.tvtickets.com, offers free tickets to watch filming of almost all of the network television shows and many of their specials. For some shows, the minimum age for kids is 12 years old; for most, it's 18 years old. Call for a schedule or ask them to send you a monthly show schedule.

Times Tix in W. Hollywood, (213) 688-2787 / www.theatrela.org, allows cash-only, day-of-show tickets to be purchased Thurs. - Sun., noon to 6pm for 50% off the regular price. Call (310) 659-3678 for a list of today's shows and availability.

Times Arts Tix in San Diego next to Horton Plaza, (619) 497-5000 / www.sandiegoperforms.com/ARTSTIX.html, has half-price, day-of-performance, theater tickets available on a first-come, first-served, cash-only basis. Call for a listing of the day's shows.

TOURS -

See Tours in the main section of the book. The following are general ideas of where you can go for group tours:

Animal Shelter	Dentist	Newspaper Office
Airport	Factory	Nurseries (plant)
Bakery	Fire Station	Pet Store
Bank	Florist	Police Station
Chiropractor	Grocery Store	Post Office
College/University	Hospital	Printer
Dairy	Hotel	Restaurant

TOYS -

Look in this part of the book under Educational Toys, Books, and Games. Two other listings worth mentioning are:

U.S. Toy Constructive Playthings in Garden Grove, (714) 636-7831 /

www.ustoy.com - Call for a catalog or visit their store. They offer top-of-the-line toys, books, games, puzzles, etc., as well as lower priced, carnival-type "prizes."

Oriental Trading Company, (800) 875-8480 / www.oriental.com - This catalog company offers bulk and individual novelty items, usually priced at the lower end of the scale.

VOLUNTEERING -

Volunteering is a terrific way to spend time with your children while teaching them the real values of life - giving and serving. Check with local missions, churches, and temples, as many have regular times when they go to help feed the homeless. Here are just a few other volunteer agencies:

Adopt-a-Park and Adopt-a-Beach in Orange County, (714) 771-6731 / www.ocparks.com -Ongoing park and beach cleanups at more than 22 local sites for all age participants.

Children's Hunger Fund in Pacoima, (818) 899-5122 / www.chf2serve.org - Volunteers of all ages assemble care packages for disadvantaged children Wed. and Sat., 9am - noon.

Create-a-Smile in Santa Monica, (310) 392-6257 / www.create-a-smile.org - Families (children ages 11 and older) and their pets visit disabled, abused or ill children and adults in nursing homes and hospitals.

Doingsomething, (310) 391-3907 / www.doingsomethingla.org - Introduces volunteers to service organizations via a monthly newsletter ($15 per year) that includes many one-time projects for ages 8 and older including taking dogs for walks at a no-kill shelter, assembling holiday baskets, stocking food pantries, and more.

Florence Crittenton Services in Yorba Linda, (714) 680-9000 / www.flocrit.org - Abused children living here can benefit from volunteers in numerous ways: Christmas gifts; coordinating on a holiday craft project to do with the kids; making holiday decorations; hosting a birthday party; etc.

Food Finders in Orange County, (562) 598-3003 - Families can donate, sort and deliver canned goods, toys, and food year-round.

Fullerton Arboretum in Fullerton, (714) 278-3404 / www.arboretum.fullerton.edu - Family participation is encouraged in nursery projects, such as propagation, transplanting, weeding, etc.

Green Networking for Orange County, www.greennetworking.org - If you're concerned about the environment and don't know how to help or where to find information, this group provides names and numbers of more than 200 environmental groups, businesses, and agencies in Orange County.

Habitat For Humanity, (229) 924-6935 x2551 / www.habitat.org - This non-profit organization is committed to providing low-income, owner-occupied housing by utilizing volunteer labor and donated materials. (Former President Jimmy Carter is one of the more prominent members.) Volunteers are needed to build homes and serve on committees such as finance, construction, and public relations. Kids must be at least 16 years old to work on construction sites, but younger children can help with off-site activities such as registration, making lunches, etc. Check web site for local affiliates or call information.

Heal the Bay, (310) 581-4188; (714) 536-5614 / www.healthebay.org - There's nothing like a day at the beach, especially if you're there to help make it cleaner. Clean up pollution in the Santa Monica Bay, San Pedro Bay, Orange County, and adjacent coastal waters. Call (800) COAST-4U (262-7848) / ceres.ca.gov/coastalcomm for the annual coastal clean up day.

Hugs for Health, (714) 832-HUGS (4847) / www.hugs4health.org - Hugs for the elderly are dispensed liberally through this program that operates mostly in senior-care facilities. All age huggers are welcome.

I Love a Clean San Diego, (858) 467-0103 / www.ilacsd.org - An educational and environmental group sponsoring beach clean-ups, storm drain stenciling, and graffiti removal.

Kids Giving to Kids, (949) 476-9474; (310) 788-9474 / www.wishla.org - Started by the Make-A-Wish Foundation, families can come up with creative fund-raising ideas to sponsor a wish for a child facing a life-threatening illness.

Kids Korps USA, (858) 259-3602 - North San Diego coastal; (858) 538-1386 - North San Diego inland / www.kidskorps.org. Young people ages 4 - 18 can participate in programs from preserving the environment to befriending those in need to helping animals and more.

Kids Who Care, (949) 459-9233 / www.kids-who-care.org - Ages 2 - 12 can serve in monthly activities, such as Salvation Army food distribution, Angel Tree toy collection and distribution, etc.

Los Angeles Regional Foodbank in Los Angeles, (323) 234-3030 - Ages 7 and up can help maintain 300 garden plots in a low income area, as well as participate in local food drive and food collection.

Move a Child Higher in La Canada / Flintridge, (626) 798-1222 - The Riding Club offers therapeutic horseback riding activities to children with disabilities. Volunteers, ages 10 and up, can exercise and groom the horses, and lead and walk alongside the riders.

Orange County Harvest in Orange County, (714) 708-1597 - Kindergartners and up are asked to actually harvest and glean food from fields in Orange County. The food is delivered to Second Harvest Food Bank, (714) 771-1343 / www.2ndharvestoc.org, which in turn donates the produce to local food banks. Gleaning is done usually every Wed., 8am - 10am and Sat., 1pm - 3pm. Pre registration is required.

Points of Light Foundation, (800) 879-5400 / www.pointsoflight.org - The foundation points people to volunteer organizations in their area.

Ronald McDonald House in Orange County, (714) 639-3600 / www.rmhc.com - This house provides a home-away-from-home for up to 20 families who have children receiving treatment for cancer and other serious illnesses at local medical facilities. Opportunities include making or sponsoring a meal, Note: There are other facilities throughout So. Cal.

Second Harvest. See the above Orange County Harvest info.

St. Vincent de Paul in San Diego, (619) 233-8500 www.svdpv.org - Look
up Tours in the main section of the book for details.

Tierra Del Sol Foundation, (818) 352-1419 / www.tierradelsol.org - Serves
adults with developmental and often physical disabilities.

Trails4all, (714) 834-3136 / www.trails4all.org - Coordinates volunteers,
who are at least 8 years old, to help with coastal cleanups, trail
maintenance, and other activities.

Volunteer Agencies, (800) 865-8683 for general information. Call (818)
908-5066 for volunteer opportunities in L.A. and San Fernando Valley. In
Pasadena, call (626) 792-6819.

Volunteer Center of Greater Orange County, (714) 953-5757 /
www.volunteercenter.org - A clearinghouse for a wide variety of age-
appropriate opportunities, including feeding the homeless, visiting the
elderly, planting trees, cleaning up parks, and removing graffiti. The
center even has a guide book on family volunteer activities.

Volunteer Center of San Diego County, (858) 636-4131 or (800)
VOLUNTEER (865-8683) / www.volunteersandiego.org - Includes a
volunteer segment called SAVY (Students Actively Volunteering for
You).

VolunteerMatch, www.volunteermatch.org - On-line website that matches
volunteers with organizations that need them.

Youth Service America, 202-296-2992, www.ysa.org; www.servenet.org -
A national organization "committed to making service the common
experience and expectation of all young Americans."

WILDFLOWER HOTLINES -

Anza Borrego Desert State Park in Anza Borrego, (760) 767-4684 /
www.anzaborrego.statepark.org

Joshua Tree National Park in Joshua Tree / Twentynine Palms, (760) 367-
5500 / www.nps.gov/jotr

Mojave Desert Information Center, (760) 733-4040 /
www.calparksmojave.com

Poppy Reserve in Lancaster, (661) 724-1180 or (661) 942-0662 /
www.calparksmojave.com

Southern California Hotline, Theodore Payne Foundation, (818) 768-3533 /
www.theodorepayne.org

ALPHABETICAL INDEX

INDEX BY CITY

INDEX BY PRICE

Free Occasionally - The following attractions have special days when no admission is charged:

Los Angeles County

Arboretum of Los Angeles County - third Tues. of each month, pg. 137

Fowler Museum - every Thurs. (located under U.C.L.A.), however parking is still $5, pg. 431

George C. Page Museum - first Tues. of each month, pg. 275

Huntington Library, Art Collections and Botanical Gardens - first Thurs. of each month, pg. 289

Kidspace Children's Museum - last Mon. of each month (except Oct.) from 5pm - 8pm, pg. 293

Los Angeles County Museum of Art - second Tues. of each month, pg. 295

Museum of Contemporary Art / Geffen - each Thurs. from 5pm - 8pm, pg. 299

Museum of Neon Art - second Thurs. of each month from 5pm - 8pm, pg. 301

Natural History Museum of L. A. County - first Tues. of each month, pg. 304

Raymond M. Alf Museum - every Wed., pg. 313

South Coast Botanical Garden - third Tues. of each month, pg. 174

San Diego County

Balboa Park Museums - see BALBOA PARK (San Diego), as the museums vary in their "free day", pg. 360

Firehouse Museum - first Thurs. of each month, pg. 368

Museum of Contemporary Art (La Jolla) - first Sun. and third Tues. of each month, pg. 377

San Diego Wild Animal Park - one day in early May, call for date, pg. 578

San Diego Zoo - first Mon. in Oct., pg. 579

Ventura County

Carnegie Art Museum - every Fri. from 3pm - 6pm, pg. 400

Palm Springs

Palm Springs Desert Museum - first Fri. of each month, pg. 618

- Free (!) -

INDEX BY THEME

Notes:

ABOUT THE AUTHOR:

Fun and education are key words in our home. I enjoy home schooling my children; speaking to various groups; reading; hiking; traveling; writing; and whatever else God brings my family's way!

I would appreciate your ideas about this book. Do you have a wonderful place to go with kids that wasn't included in this edition? Please let me know and I'll share it in the next one. You can write to me at:

FUN PLACES TO GO WITH KIDS
P.O. Box 376
Lakewood, CA 90714 - 0376
(562) 867-5223
email: susan@funplaces.com

Notes:

Fün Places to go With Kids
and educational *and adults*
in Southern California

$20.95
($18.95 includes tax, plus $2.00 shipping)

Please send copy(s) of this wonderful, innovative, well-written, absolutely
fantastic, fun book to . . .

NAME _____

ADDRESS _____ CITY _____

STATE _____ ZIP _____ PHONE _____

ENCLOSED IS MY CHECK FOR $ _____ ($20.95 per book, which
includes tax and shipping.)

Make check payable to: **Fun Places**.   Send to:
Fun Places Publishing
P.O. Box 376
Lakewood, CA 90714-0376

--------✂--

Fün Places to go With Kids
and educational *and adults*
in Southern California

$20.95
($18.95 includes tax, plus $2.00 shipping)

Please send copy(s) of this wonderful, innovative, well-written, absolutely
fantastic, fun book to . . .

NAME _____

ADDRESS _____ CITY _____

STATE _____ ZIP _____ PHONE _____

ENCLOSED IS MY CHECK FOR $ _____ ($20.95 per book, which
includes tax and shipping.)

Make check payable to: **Fun Places**.   Send to:
Fun Places Publishing
P.O. Box 376
Lakewood, CA 90714-0376

Notes:

FUN PLACES SCRAPBOOK / JOURNAL

Ever ask your child, "What do you remember most about the place we visited?" and he answers, "It was fun." Good. That's a good start. Ever try to probe a little deeper and still get the same response? If you have invested the time, energy, and money going on an outing with your child, you want to make sure he remembers where you've gone and what you've done, right? That's one of the many reasons we go on outings, field trips, or vacations with our kids - so they remember the wonderful new things we are exposing them to. Aid your child in making memories by encouraging him to scrapbook / journal.

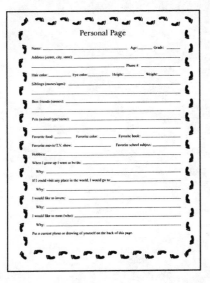

These sample pages are part of the thirty pages found in the FUN PLACES SCRAPBOOK / JOURNAL. The scrapbook / journal gives your kids specific questions to answer, on paper bordered by colorful and fun figures. The one page questions are for younger children or a short excursion. The three pages of questions, pertaining to one outing, are for older children or a more in depth field trip or vacation. There are

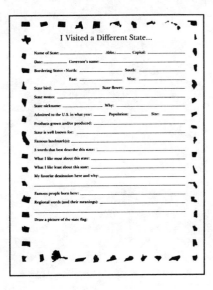

plenty of pages for saving (or drawing) pictures, postcards, and even ticket stubs and brochures. All the pages are bound in a three-ring notebook so pages can be easily added or rearranged. All the prep work is done for you! The scrapbook / journal, which is a perfect supplement to this book, also comes with a host of practical ideas on how to incorporate education with fun.

See next page for more samples and an order coupon.

Notes:

Today I Visited ...
(Short Version)

My Name:_____

Name of Place: _____
Address - city, state: _____
Date: _____ Admission Cost: _____
This place is known for / because of: _____
_____
The first thing I noticed was: _____
_____
I learned about / how to: _____
_____
My favorite thing I saw / did: _____
_____
It was my favorite thing because: _____
_____
I didn't like: _____
_____
I went with: _____
My souvenirs from here include: _____
_____
I got here by (car/train/boat/plane/etc.): _____
On a scale of 1 to 5, I would rate this place a: _____
(1=a total bomb; 2=barely acceptable; 3=OK; 4=pretty good; 5=excellent!)
Additional comments: _____

Picture This!

(For photos, postcards, and/or drawings)

✂ -

FUN PLACES SCRAPBOOK / JOURNAL
$14.95
($12.95 includes tax, plus shipping)

Please send copy(s) of this fun and educational aid to . . .

NAME _____

ADDRESS _____ CITY _____

STATE _____ ZIP _____ PHONE _____

ENCLOSED IS MY CHECK FOR $ _____ ($14.95 per journal,
includes tax and shipping.)

Make check payable to: **Fun Places**.

Send to:
**Fun Places Publishing
P.O. Box 376
Lakewood, CA 90714-0376**

Notes: